C++

HOW TO PROGRAM

Introducing
the New C++14
Standard

TENTH EDITION

Deitel® Series Page

How To Program Series

Android™ How to Program, 3/E
C++ How to Program, 10/E
C How to Program, 8/E
Java™ How to Program, Early Objects Version, 10/E
Java™ How to Program, Late Objects Version, 10/E
Internet & World Wide Web How to Program, 5/E
Visual Basic® 2015 How to Program, 7/E
Visual C#® 2015 How to Program, 6/E

Deitel® Developer Series

Android™ 6 for Programmers: An App-Driven
  Approach, 3/E
C for Programmers with an Introduction to C11
C++11 for Programmers
C# 2015 for Programmers
iOS® 8 for Programmers: An App-Driven Approach
  with Swift™
Java™ for Programmers, 3/E
JavaScript for Programmers
Swift™ for Programmers

Simply Series

Simply Visual Basic® 2010: An App-Driven
  Approach, 4/E
Simply C++: An App-Driven Tutorial Approach

VitalSource Web Books

http://bit.ly/DeitelOnVitalSource

Android™ How to Program, 2/E and 3/E
C++ How to Program, 8/E and 9/E
Simply C++: An App-Driven Tutorial Approach
Java™ How to Program, 9/E and 10/E
Simply Visual Basic® 2010: An App-Driven
  Approach, 4/E
Visual Basic® 2012 How to Program, 6/E
Visual Basic® 2015 How to Program, 7/E
Visual C#® 2012 How to Program, 5/E
Visual C#® 2015 How to Program, 6/E

LiveLessons Video Learning Products

http://deitel.com/books/LiveLessons/

Android™ 6 App Development Fundamentals, 3/e
C++ Fundamentals
Java™ Fundamentals, 2/e
C# 2012 Fundamentals
iOS® 8 App Development Fundamentals with
  Swift™, 3/e
JavaScript Fundamentals
Swift™ Fundamentals

To receive updates on Deitel publications, Resource Centers, training courses, partner offers and more, please join the Deitel communities on

- Facebook®—http://facebook.com/DeitelFan
- Twitter®—http://twitter.com/deitel
- Google+™—http://google.com/+DeitelFan
- YouTube™—http://youtube.com/DeitelTV
- LinkedIn®—http://linkedin.com/company/deitel-&-associates

and register for the free *Deitel® Buzz Online* e-mail newsletter at:

  http://www.deitel.com/newsletter/subscribe.html

To communicate with the authors, send e-mail to:

  deitel@deitel.com

For information on programming-languages corporate training seminars offered by Deitel & Associates, Inc. worldwide, write to deitel@deitel.com or visit:

  http://www.deitel.com/training/

For continuing updates on Pearson/Deitel publications visit:

  http://www.deitel.com
  http://www.pearsonhighered.com/deitel/

Visit the Deitel Resource Centers, which will help you master programming languages, software development, Android™ and iOS® app development, and Internet- and web-related topics:

  http://www.deitel.com/ResourceCenters.html

C++

HOW TO PROGRAM

Introducing
the New C++14
Standard

TENTH EDITION

Paul Deitel
Deitel & Associates, Inc.

Harvey Deitel
Deitel & Associates, Inc.

PEARSON

Boston   Columbus   Hoboken   Indianapolis   New York   San Francisco
Amsterdam   Cape Town   Dubai   London   Madrid   Milan   Munich   Paris   Montreal
Toronto   Delhi   Mexico City   São Paulo   Sydney   Hong Kong   Seoul   Singapore   Taipei   Tokyo

Vice President, Editorial Director: *Marcia Horton*
Acquisitions Editor: *Tracy Johnson*
Editorial Assistant: *Kristy Alaura*
VP of Marketing: *Christy Lesko*
Director of Field Marketing: *Tim Galligan*
Product Marketing Manager: *Bram Van Kempen*
Field Marketing Manager: *Demetrius Hall*
Marketing Assistant: *Jon Bryant*
Director of Product Management: *Erin Gregg*
Team Lead, Program and Project Management: *Scott Disanno*
Program Manager: *Carole Snyder*
Project Manager: *Robert Engelhardt*
Senior Specialist, Program Planning and Support: *Maura Zaldivar-Garcia*
Cover Art: *Finevector / Shutterstock*
Cover Design: *Paul Deitel, Harvey Deitel, Chuti Prasertsith*
R&P Manager: *Rachel Youdelman*
R&P Project Manager: *Timothy Nicholls*
Inventory Manager: *Meredith Maresca*

Credits and acknowledgments borrowed from other sources and reproduced, with permission, in this textbook appear on page vi.

The authors and publisher of this book have used their best efforts in preparing this book. These efforts include the development, research, and testing of the theories and programs to determine their effectiveness. The authors and publisher make no warranty of any kind, expressed or implied, with regard to these programs or to the documentation contained in this book. The authors and publisher shall not be liable in any event for incidental or consequential damages in connection with, or arising out of, the furnishing, performance, or use of these programs.

Library of Congress Cataloging-in-Publication Data on file.

18 2022

PEARSON   ISBN-10: 0-13-444823-5
ISBN-13: 978-0-13-444823-7

In memory of Marvin Minsky,
a founding father of the
field of artificial intelligence.

It was a privilege to be your student in two graduate
courses at M.I.T. Every lecture you gave inspired
your students to think beyond limits.

Harvey Deitel

Trademarks

DEITEL and the double-thumbs-up bug are registered trademarks of Deitel and Associates, Inc.

Carnegie Mellon Software Engineering Institute™ is a trademark of Carnegie Mellon University.

CERT® is registered in the U.S. Patent and Trademark Office by Carnegie Mellon University.

UNIX is a registered trademark of The Open Group.

Microsoft and/or its respective suppliers make no representations about the suitability of the information contained in the documents and related graphics published as part of the services for any purpose. All such documents and related graphics are provided "as is" without warranty of any kind. Microsoft and/ or its respective suppliers hereby disclaim all warranties and conditions with regard to this information, including all warranties and conditions of merchantability, whether express, implied or statutory, fitness for a particular purpose, title and non-infringement. In no event shall Microsoft and/or its respective suppliers be liable for any special, indirect or consequential damages or any damages whatsoever resulting from loss of use, data or profits, whether in an action of contract, negligence or other tortious action, arising out of or in connection with the use or performance of information available from the services.

The documents and related graphics contained herein could include technical inaccuracies or typographical errors. Changes are periodically added to the information herein. Microsoft and/or its respective suppliers may make improvements and/or changes in the product(s) and/or the program(s) described herein at any time. Partial screen shots may be viewed in full within the software version specified.

Microsoft® and Windows® are registered trademarks of the Microsoft Corporation in the U.S.A. and other countries. Screen shots and icons reprinted with permission from the Microsoft Corporation. This book is not sponsored or endorsed by or affiliated with the Microsoft Corporation.

Throughout this book, trademarks are used. Rather than put a trademark symbol in every occurrence of a trademarked name, we state that we are using the names in an editorial fashion only and to the benefit of the trademark owner, with no intention of infringement of the trademark.

Contents

Chapters 23–26 and Appendices F–J are PDF documents posted online at the book's Companion Website, which is accessible from

`http://www.pearsonhighered.com/deitel`

See the inside front cover for more information.

14 File Processing   615

Chapters 23–26 and Appendices F–J are PDF documents posted online at the book's Companion Website, which is accessible from

    http://www.pearsonhighered.com/deitel

See the inside front cover for more information.

23 Other Topics

24 C++11 and C++14: Additional Features

25 ATM Case Study, Part 1: Object-Oriented Design with the UM

26 ATM Case Study, Part 2: Implementing an Object-Oriented Design

Welcome to the C++ computer programming language and *C++ How to Program, Tenth Edition*. We believe that this book and its support materials will give you an informative, challenging and entertaining introduction to C++. The book presents leading-edge computing technologies in a friendly manner appropriate for introductory college course sequences, based on the curriculum recommendations of two key professional organizations—the ACM and the IEEE.[1]

If you haven't already done so, please read the back cover and check out the additional reviewer comments on the inside back cover and the facing page—these capture the essence of the book concisely. In this Preface we provide more detail for students, instructors and professionals.

At the heart of the book is the Deitel signature *live-code approach*—we present most concepts in the context of complete working programs followed by sample executions, rather than in code snippets. Read the **Before You Begin** section to learn how to set up your Linux-based, Windows-based or Apple OS X-based computer to run the hundreds of code examples. All the source code is available at

    http://www.deitel.com/books/cpphtp10

and

    http://www.pearsonhighered.com/deitel

Use the source code we provide to run each program as you study it.

Contacting the Authors

As you read the book, if you have questions, we're easy to reach at

    deitel@deitel.com

We'll respond promptly. For book updates, visit

    http://www.deitel.com/books/cpphtp10

Join the Deitel & Associates, Inc. Social Media Communities

Join the Deitel social media communities on

- Facebook®—http://facebook.com/DeitelFan
- LinkedIn®—http://bit.ly/DeitelLinkedIn

---

1. *Computer Science Curricula 2013 Curriculum Guidelines for Undergraduate Degree Programs in Computer Science*, December 20, 2013, The Joint Task Force on Computing Curricula, Association for Computing Machinery (ACM), IEEE Computer Society.

- Twitter®—http://twitter.com/deitel
- Google+™—http://google.com/+DeitelFan
- YouTube®—http://youtube.com/DeitelTV

and subscribe to the *Deitel® Buzz Online* newsletter

http://www.deitel.com/newsletter/subscribe.html

The C++11 and C++14 Standards

These are exciting times in the programming languages community with each of the major languages striving to keep pace with compelling new programming technologies. In the three decades of C++'s development prior to 2011, only a few new versions of the language were released. Now the ISO C++ Standards Committee is committed to releasing a new standard every three years and the compiler vendors are building in the new features promptly. *C++ How to Program, 10/e* is based on the **C++11** and **C++14** standards published in 2011 and 2014, respectively. C++17 is already under active development. Throughout the book, C++11 and C++14 features are marked with the "11" and "14" icons, respectively, that you see here in the margin. Fig. 1 lists the book's first references to the 77 C++11 and C++14 features we discuss.

C++11 and C++14 features in C++ *How to Program, 10/e*		
Chapter 3 In-class initializers	**Chapter 8** begin/end functions nullptr	**Chapter 13** operator bool for streams
Chapter 4 Keywords new in C++11	**Chapter 9** Delegating constructors	**Chapter 14** quoted stream manipulator (C++14) string objects for file names
Chapter 5 long long int type	**Chapter 10** deleted member functions	**Chapter 15** cbegin/cend container
Chapter 6 Non-deterministic random number generation Scoped enums Specifying the type of an enum's constants Unsigned long long int Using ' to separate groups of digits in a numeric literals (C++14)	explicit conversion operators List initializing a dynamically allocated array List initializers in constructor calls string object literals (C++14) **Chapter 11** final classes final member functions Inheriting base-class constructors	member functions Compiler fix for >> in template types crbegin/crend container member functions forward_list container Global functions cbegin/ cend, rbegin/rend and crbegin/crend (C++14) Heterogeneous lookup in associative containers (C++14)
Chapter 7 array container auto for type inference List initializing a vector Range-based for statement	**Chapter 12** defaulted member functions override keyword	Immutable keys in associative containers

Fig. 1 | First references to C++11 and C++14 features in C++ *How to Program, 10/e*. (Part 1 of 2.)

C++11 and C++14 features in C++ *How to Program, 10/e*

Chapter 15 (cont.)

insert container member functions return iterators

List initialization of key–value pairs

List initialization of pairs

Return value list initialization

shrink_to_fit vector/deque member function

Chapter 16

all_of algorithm

any_of algorithm

copy_if algorithm

copy_n algorithm

equal algorithm that accepts two ranges (**C++14**)

find_if_not algorithm

Generic lambdas (**C++14**)

Lambda expressions

min and max algorithms with initializer_list parameters

minmax algorithm

Chapter 16 (cont.)

minmax_element algorithm

mismatch algorithm that accepts two ranges (**C++14**)

none_of algorithm

random_shuffle is deprecated (**C++14**)—replaced with shuffle and C++11 random-number generation

swap non-member function

Chapter 17

make_unique to create a unique_ptr (**C++14**)

noexcept

unique_ptr smart pointer

Chapter 18

Default type arguments in function templates

Chapter 21

Numeric conversion functions

Chapter 22

Binary literals (**C++14**)

Chapter 24

Aggregate member initialization (**C++14**)

auto and decltype(auto) on return types(**C++14**)

constexpr updated(**C++14**)

decltype

move algorithm

Move assignment operators

move_backward algorithm

Move constructors

Regular expressions

Rvalue references

shared_ptr smart pointer

static_assert objects for file names

Trailing return types for functions

tuple variadic template

tuple addressing via type (**C++14**)

weak_ptr smart pointer

Fig. 1 | First references to C++11 and C++14 features in C++ *How to Program, 10/e*. (Part 2 of 2.)

Key Features of C++ How to Program, 10/e

- *Conforms to the C++11 standard and the new C++14 standard.*

- *Code thoroughly tested on three popular industrial-strength C++14 compilers.* We tested the code examples on GNU™ C++ 5.2.1, Microsoft® Visual Studio® 2015 Community edition and Apple® Clang/LLVM in Xcode® 7.

- *Smart pointers.* Smart pointers help you avoid dynamic memory management errors by providing additional functionality beyond that of built-in pointers. We discuss unique_ptr in Chapter 17, and shared_ptr and weak_ptr in Chapter 24.

- *Early coverage of Standard Library containers, iterators and algorithms, enhanced with C++11 and C++14 capabilities.* The treatment of Standard Library containers, iterators and algorithms in Chapters 15 and 16 has been enhanced with additional C++11 and C++14 features. The vast majority of your data structure needs can be fulfilled by *reusing* these Standard Library capabilities. We'll show you how to build your own *custom* data structures in Chapter 19.

- *Online Chapter 24, C++11 and C++14 Additional Topics.* This chapter includes discussions of regular expressions, shared_ptr and weak_ptr smart pointers, move semantics, multithreading, tuples, decltype, constexpr and more (see Fig. 1).

- *Random-number generation, simulation and game playing.* To help make programs more secure, we include a treatment of C++11's non-deterministic random-number generation capabilities.

- *Pointers.* We provide thorough coverage of the built-in pointer capabilities and the intimate relationship among built-in pointers, C strings and built-in arrays.

- *Visual presentation of searching and sorting, with a simple explanation of Big O.*

- *Printed book contains core content; additional content is online.* Several online chapters and appendices are included. These are available in searchable PDF format on the book's password-protected Companion Website—see the access card information on the inside front cover.

- *Getting Started Videos.* At http://www.deitel.com/books/cpphtp10, we provide links to our getting-started videos that help readers begin using Microsoft Visual Studio 2015 Community edition on Windows, Apple Xcode on OS X and GNU C++ on Linux.

- *Debugger appendices.* On the book's Companion Website we provide Appendix H, Using the Visual Studio Debugger, Appendix I, Using the GNU C++ Debugger and Appendix J, Using the Xcode Debugger.

New in This Edition

- Discussions of the new C++14 capabilities.

- Further integration of C++11 capabilities into the code examples, because the latest compilers are now supporting these features.

- Uniform initialization with list initializer syntax.

- Always using braces in control statements, even for single-statement bodies:

```
if (condition) {
    single-statement or multi-statement body
}
```

- Replaced the Gradebook class with Account, Student and DollarAmount class case studies in Chapters 3, 4 and 5, respectively. DollarAmount processes monetary amounts precisely for business applications.

- C++14 digit separators in large numeric literals.

- *Type* &x is now *Type*& x in accordance with industry idiom.

- *Type* *x is now *Type** x in accordance with industry idiom.

- Using C++11 scoped enums rather than traditional C enums.

- We brought our terminology in line with the C++ standard.

- Key terms in summaries now appear in bold for easy reference.

- Removed extra spaces inside [], (), <> and {} delimiters.

- Replaced most print member functions with toString member functions to make classes more flexible—for example, returning a string gives the client code the option of displaying it on the screen, writing it to a file, concatenating it with other strings, etc.

- Now using ostringstream to create formatted strings for items like the string representations of a Time, rather than outputting formatted data directly to the standard output.

- For simplicity, we deferred using the three-file architecture from Chapter 3 to Chapter 9, so all early class examples define the entire class in a header.

- We reimplement Chapter 10's Array class operator-overloading example with unique_ptrs in Chapter 24. Using raw pointers and dynamic-memory allocation with new and delete is a source of subtle programming errors, especially "memory leaks"—unique_ptr and the other smart pointer types help prevent such errors.

- Using lambdas rather than function pointers in Chapter 16, Standard Library Algorithms. This will get readers comfortable with lambdas, which can be combined with various Standard Library algorithms to perform functional programming in C++. We're planning a more in-depth treatment of functional programming for *C++ How to Program, 11/e.*

- Enhanced Chapter 24 with additional C++14 features.

Object-Oriented Programming

- *Early-objects approach.* The book introduces the basic concepts and terminology of object technology in Chapter 1. You'll develop your first customized classes and objects in Chapter 3. We worked hard to make this chapter especially accessible to novices. Presenting objects and classes early gets you "thinking about objects" immediately and mastering these concepts more thoroughly.[2]

- *C++ Standard Library* **string.** C++ offers *two* types of strings—string class objects (which we begin using in Chapter 3) and C-style pointer-based strings. We've replaced most occurrences of C strings with instances of C++ class string to make programs more robust and eliminate many of the security problems of C strings. We continue to discuss C strings later in the book to prepare you for working with the legacy code in industry. In new development, you should favor string objects.

- *C++ Standard Library* **array.** C++ offers *three* types of arrays—arrays and vectors (which we start using in Chapter 7) and C-style, pointer-based arrays which we discuss in Chapter 8. Our primary treatment of arrays uses the Standard Library's array and vector class templates instead of built-in, C-style, pointer-based arrays. We still cover built-in arrays because they remain useful in C++ and so that you'll be able to read legacy code. In new development, you should favor class template array and vector objects.

- *Crafting valuable classes.* A key goal of this book is to prepare you to build valuable reusable classes. Chapter 10 begins with a test-drive of class template string so you can see an elegant use of operator overloading before you implement your own customized class with overloaded operators. In the Chapter 10 case study,

---

2. For courses that require a late-objects approach, consider our pre-C++11 book *C++ How to Program, Late Objects Version,* which begins with six chapters on programming fundamentals (including two on control statements) and continues with seven chapters that gradually introduce object-oriented programming concepts.

you'll build your own custom `Array` class, then in the Chapter 18 exercises you'll convert it to a class template. You will have truly crafted valuable classes.

- *Case studies in object-oriented programming.* We provide several well-engineered real-world case studies, including the `Account` class in Chapter 3, `Student` class in Chapter 4, `DollarAmount` class in Chapter 5, `GradeBook` class in Chapter 7, the `Time` class in Chapter 9, the `Employee` class in Chapters 11–12 and more.

- *Optional case study: Using the UML to develop an object-oriented design and C++ implementation of an ATM.* The UML™ (Unified Modeling Language™) is the industry-standard graphical language for modeling object-oriented systems. We introduce the UML in the early chapters. Online Chapters 25 and 26 include an *optional* object-oriented design case study using the UML. We design and fully implement the software for a simple automated teller machine (ATM). We analyze a typical requirements document that specifies the system to be built. We determine the classes needed to implement that system, the attributes the classes need to have, the behaviors the classes need to exhibit and we specify how objects of the classes must interact with one another to meet the system requirements. From the design we produce a complete C++ implementation. Students often report that the case study helps them "tie it all together" and truly understand object orientation.

- *Understanding how polymorphism works.* Chapter 12 contains a detailed diagram and explanation of how C++ typically implements polymorphism, `virtual` functions and dynamic binding "under the hood."

- *Object-oriented exception handling.* We integrate basic exception handling early in the book (Chapter 7). Instructors can easily pull more detailed material forward from Chapter 17, Exception Handling: A Deeper Look.

- *Custom template-based data structures.* We provide a rich multi-chapter treatment of data structures—see the Data Structures module in the chapter dependency chart (Fig. 5).

- *Three programming paradigms.* We discuss *structured programming, object-oriented programming* and *generic programming.*

Hundreds of Code Examples

We include a broad range of example programs selected from computer science, information technology, business, simulation, game playing and other topics. The examples are accessible to students in novice-level and intermediate-level C++ courses (Fig. 2).

Examples	
Account class	BasePlusCommissionEmployee class
Array class case study	Binary tree creation and traversal
Author class	BinarySearch test program
Bank account program	Card shuffling and dealing
Bar chart printing program	ClientData class

Fig. 2 | A sampling of the book's examples. (Part 1 of 2.)

Examples

CommissionEmployee class	Poll analysis program
Comparing strings	Polymorphism demonstration
Compilation and linking process	Preincrementing and postincrementing
Compound interest calculations with for	priority_queue adapter class
Converting string objects to C strings	queue adapter class
Counter-controlled repetition	Random-access files
Dice game simulation	Random number generation
DollarAmount class	Recursive function factorial
Credit inquiry program	Rolling a six-sided die 60,000,000 times
Date class	SalariedEmployee class
Downcasting and runtime type information	SalesPerson class
Employee class	Searching and sorting algorithms of the Standard Library
explicit constructor	
fibonacci function	Sequential files
fill algorithms	set class template
Specializations of function template printArray	shared_ptr program
generate algorithms	stack adapter class
GradeBook Class	Stack class
Initializing an array in a declaration	Stack unwinding
Input from an istringstream object	Standard Library string class program
Iterative factorial solution	Stream manipulator showbase
Lambda expressions	string assignment and concatenation
Linked list manipulation	string member function substr
map class template	Student class
Mathematical algorithms of the Standard Library	Summing integers with the for statement
maximum function template	Time class
Merge sort program	unique_ptr object managing dynamically allocated memory
multiset class template	
new throwing bad_alloc on failure	Validating user input with regular expressions
PhoneNumber class	vector class template

Fig. 2 | A sampling of the book's examples. (Part 2 of 2.)

Exercises

- *Self-Review Exercises and Answers.* Extensive self-review exercises *and* answers are included for self-study.

- *Interesting, entertaining and challenging exercises.* Each chapter concludes with a substantial set of exercises, including simple recall of important terminology and concepts, identifying the errors in code samples, writing individual program statements, writing small portions of C++ classes and member and non-member functions, writing complete programs and implementing major projects. Figure 3 lists a sampling of the book's exercises, including our *Making a Difference* exercises, which encourage you to use computers and the Internet to research and work on significant social problems. We hope you'll approach these exercises with your own values, politics and beliefs.

Airline Reservations System	Credit Limits	Phishing Scanner
Advanced String-Manipulation	Crossword Puzzle Generator	Pig Latin
Bubble Sort	Cryptograms	Polymorphic Banking Program
Building Your Own Compiler	De Morgan's Laws	Using Account Hierarchy
Building Your Own Computer	Dice Rolling	Pythagorean Triples
Calculating Salaries	Eight Queens	Salary Calculator
CarbonFootprint Abstract	Emergency Response	Sieve of Eratosthenes
Class: Polymorphism	Enforcing Privacy with Cryp-	Simple Decryption
Card Shuffling and Dealing	tography	Simple Encryption
Computer-Assisted Instruction	Facebook User Base Growth	SMS Language
Computer-Assisted Instruc-	Fibonacci Series	Spam Scanner
tion: Difficulty Levels	Gas Mileage	Spelling Checker
Computer-Assisted Instruc-	Global Warming Facts Quiz	Target-Heart-Rate Calculator
tion: Monitoring Student	Guess the Number Game	Tax Plan Alternatives; The
Performance	Hangman Game	"Fair Tax"
Computer-Assisted Instruction:	Health Records	Telephone number word
Reducing Student Fatigue	Knight's Tour	generator
Computer-Assisted Instruc-	Limericks	"The Twelve Days of Christ-
tion: Varying the Types of	Maze Traversal: Generating	mas" Song
Problems	Mazes Randomly	Tortoise and the Hare
Cooking with Healthier Ingre-	Morse Code	Simulation
dients	Payroll System Modification	Towers of Hanoi
Craps Game Modification	Peter Minuit Problem	World Population Growth

Fig. 3 | A sampling of the book's exercises.

Illustrations and Figures

Abundant tables, line drawings, UML diagrams, programs and program outputs are included. A sampling of the book's drawings and diagrams is shown in (Fig. 4).

Main text drawings and diagrams

Account class diagrams	while repetition statement	Pass-by-value and pass-by-
Data hierarchy	UML activity diagram	reference analysis
Multiple-source-file	for repetition statement UML	Inheritance hierarchy diagrams
compilation and linking	activity diagram	Function-call stack and
Order in which a second-degree	do...while repetition statement	activation records
polynomial is evaluated	UML activity diagram	Recursive calls to function
if single-selection statement	switch multiple-selection	fibonacci
activity diagram	statement activity diagram	Pointer arithmetic diagrams
if...else double-selection	C++'s single-entry/single-exit	CommunityMember Inheritance
statement activity diagram	control statements	hierarchy

Fig. 4 | A sampling of the book's drawings and diagrams. (Part 1 of 2.)

Drawings and diagrams

Main text drawings and diagrams (cont.)

Shape inheritance hierarchy	Graphical representation of a list	Operation `removeFromBack` represented graphically
`public`, `protected` and `private` inheritance	Operation `insertAtFront` represented graphically	Circular, singly linked list
`Employee` hierarchy UML class diagram	Operation `insertAtBack` represented graphically	Doubly linked list
How `virtual` function calls work	Operation `removeFromFront` represented graphically	Circular, doubly linked list
Two self-referential class objects linked together		Graphical representation of a binary tree

(Optional) ATM Case Study drawings and diagrams

Use case diagram for the ATM system from the User's perspective	Classes in the ATM system with attributes and operations	Class diagram showing composition relationships of a class `Car`
Class diagram showing an association among classes	Communication diagram of the ATM executing a balance inquiry	Class diagram for the ATM system model including class `Deposit`
Class diagram showing composition relationships	Communication diagram for executing a balance inquiry	Activity diagram for a `Deposit` transaction
Class diagram for the ATM system model	Sequence diagram that models a `Withdrawal` executing	Sequence diagram that models a `Deposit` executing
Classes with attributes	Use case diagram for a modified version of our ATM system that also allows users to transfer money between accounts	
State diagram for the ATM		
Activity diagram for a `BalanceInquiry` transaction		
Activity diagram for a `Withdrawal` transaction		

Fig. 4 | A sampling of the book's drawings and diagrams. (Part 2 of 2.)

Dependency Chart

C++ How to Program, 10/e is appropriate for most introductory one-and-two-course programming sequences, often called CS1 and CS2. The chart in Fig. 5 shows the dependencies among the chapters to help instructors plan their syllabi. The chart shows the book's modular organization.

Teaching Approach

C++ How to Program, 10/e, contains a rich collection of examples. We stress program clarity and concentrate on building well-engineered software.

Live-code approach. The book is loaded with "live-code" examples—most new concepts are presented in *complete working C++ applications*, followed by one or more executions showing program inputs and outputs.

Rich early coverage of C++ fundamentals. Chapter 2 provides a friendly introduction to C++ programming. We include in Chapters 4 and 5 a clear treatment of control statements and algorithm development.

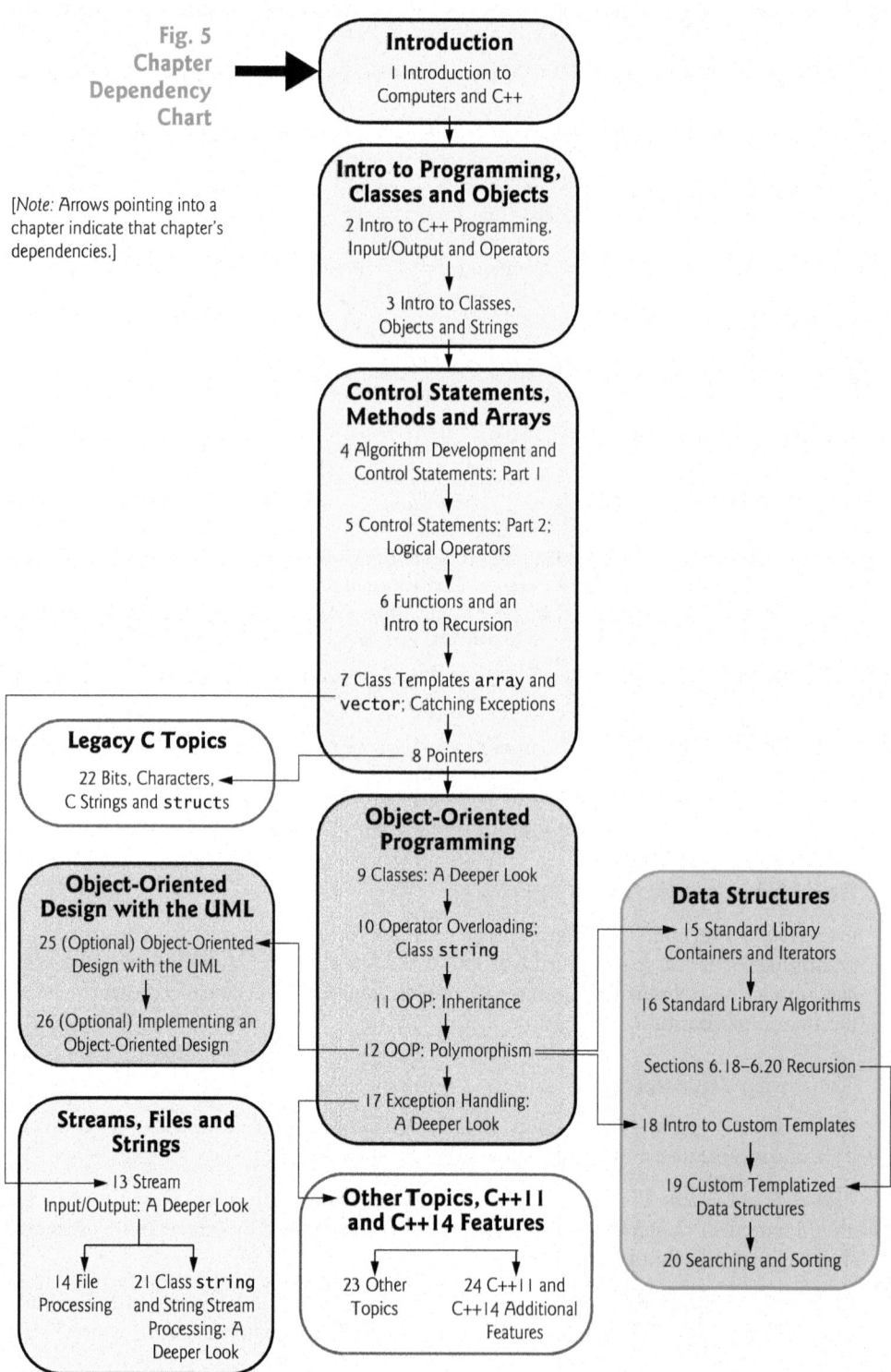

Fig. 5
Chapter
Dependency
Chart

[*Note:* Arrows pointing into a chapter indicate that chapter's dependencies.]

Introduction

1 Introduction to Computers and C++

Intro to Programming, Classes and Objects

2 Intro to C++ Programming, Input/Output and Operators

3 Intro to Classes, Objects and Strings

Control Statements, Methods and Arrays

4 Algorithm Development and Control Statements: Part 1

5 Control Statements: Part 2; Logical Operators

6 Functions and an Intro to Recursion

7 Class Templates array and vector; Catching Exceptions

8 Pointers

Legacy C Topics

22 Bits, Characters, C Strings and structs

Object-Oriented Programming

9 Classes: A Deeper Look

10 Operator Overloading; Class string

11 OOP: Inheritance

12 OOP: Polymorphism

17 Exception Handling: A Deeper Look

Object-Oriented Design with the UML

25 (Optional) Object-Oriented Design with the UML

26 (Optional) Implementing an Object-Oriented Design

Streams, Files and Strings

13 Stream Input/Output: A Deeper Look

14 File Processing

21 Class string and String Stream Processing: A Deeper Look

Other Topics, C++11 and C++14 Features

23 Other Topics

24 C++11 and C++14 Additional Features

Data Structures

15 Standard Library Containers and Iterators

16 Standard Library Algorithms

Sections 6.18–6.20 Recursion

18 Intro to Custom Templates

19 Custom Templatized Data Structures

20 Searching and Sorting

Syntax coloring. For readability, we syntax color all the C++ code, similar to the way most C++ integrated-development environments and code editors syntax color code. Our coloring conventions are as follows:

```
comments appear like this
keywords appear like this
constants and literal values appear like this
all other code appears in black
```

Code highlighting. We place shaded rectangles around the new features in each program.

Using fonts for emphasis. We color the defining occurrence of each key term in bold colored text for easy reference. We emphasize on-screen components in the **bold Helvetica** font (e.g., the **File** menu) and C++ program text in the Lucida font (for example, int x = 5;).

Objectives. We clearly state the chapter objectives.

Programming tips. We include programming tips to help you focus on key aspects of program development. These tips and practices represent the best we've gleaned from a combined eight decades of teaching and industry experience.

Good Programming Practices

The Good Programming Practices *call attention to techniques that will help you produce programs that are clearer, more understandable and more maintainable.*

Common Programming Errors

Pointing out these Common Programming Errors *reduces the likelihood that you'll make them.*

Error-Prevention Tips

These tips contain suggestions for exposing and removing bugs from your programs; many describe aspects of C++ that prevent bugs from getting into programs in the first place.

Performance Tips

These tips highlight opportunities for making your programs run faster or minimizing the amount of memory that they occupy.

Portability Tips

These tips help you write code that will run on a variety of platforms.

Software Engineering Observations

These tips highlight architectural and design issues that affect the construction of software systems, especially large-scale systems.

Summary Bullets. We present a section-by-section, bullet-list summary of each chapter. Each key term is in **bold** followed by the page number of the term's defining occurrence.

Index. For convenient reference, we've included an extensive index, with defining occurrences of key terms highlighted with a bold page number.

Secure C++ Programming

It's difficult to build industrial-strength systems that stand up to attacks from viruses, worms, and other forms of "malware." Today, via the Internet, such attacks can be instantaneous and global in scope. Building security into software from the beginning of the development cycle can greatly reduce vulnerabilities.

The CERT® Coordination Center (www.cert.org) was created to analyze and respond promptly to attacks. CERT—the Computer Emergency Response Team—is a government-funded organization within the Carnegie Mellon University Software Engineering Institute™. CERT publishes and promotes secure coding standards for various popular programming languages to help software developers implement industrial-strength systems which avoid the programming practices that leave systems open to attacks.

We'd like to thank Robert C. Seacord, an adjunct professor in the Carnegie Mellon University School of Computer Science and former Secure Coding Manager at CERT. Mr. Seacord was a technical reviewer for our book, *C How to Program, 7/e*, where he scrutinized our C programs from a security standpoint, recommending that we adhere to key guidelines of the *CERT C Secure Coding Standard*.

We've done the same for *C++ How to Program, 10/e*, adhering to key guidelines of the *CERT C++ Secure Coding Standard*, which you can find at:

```
http://www.securecoding.cert.org
```

We were pleased to discover that we've already been recommending many of these coding practices in our books since the early 1990s. We upgraded our code and discussions to conform to these practices, as appropriate for an introductory/intermediate-level textbook. If you'll be building industrial-strength C++ systems, consider reading *Secure Coding in C and C++, Second Edition* (Robert Seacord, Addison-Wesley Professional, 2013).

Online Chapters, Appendices and Other Content

The book's Companion Website, which is accessible at

```
http://www.pearsonhighered.com/deitel
```

(see the inside front cover for your access key) contains the following videos as well as chapters and appendices in searchable PDF format:

- *VideoNotes*—The Companion Website (see the inside front cover for your access key) also includes extensive videos. Watch and listen as co-author Paul Deitel discusses in-depth the key code examples from the book's core programming-fundamentals and object-oriented-programming chapters.
- Chapter 23, Other Topics
- Chapter 24, C++11 and C++14 Additional Topics
- Chapter 25, ATM Case Study, Part 1: Object-Oriented Design with the UML
- Chapter 26, ATM Case Study, Part 2: Implementing an Object-Oriented Design
- Appendix F, C Legacy Code Topics
- Appendix G, UML 2: Additional Diagram Types

- Appendix H, Using the Visual Studio Debugger
- Appendix I, Using the GNU C++ Debugger
- Appendix J, Using the Xcode Debugger
- Building Your Own Compiler exercise descriptions from Chapter 19 (posted at the Companion Website and at `http://www.deitel.com/books/cpphtp10`).

Obtaining the Software Used in *C++ How to Program, 10/e*

We wrote the code examples in *C++ How to Program, 10/e* using the following free C++ development tools:

- Microsoft's free Visual Studio Community 2015 edition, which includes Visual C++ and other Microsoft development tools. This runs on Windows and is available for download at

    `https://www.visualstudio.com/products/visual-studio-community-vs`

- GNU's free GNU C++ 5.2.1. GNU C++ is already installed on most Linux systems and can also be installed on Mac OS X and Windows systems. There are many versions of Linux—known as Linux distributions—that use different techniques for performing software upgrades. Check your distribution's online documentation for information on how to upgrade GNU C++ to the latest version. GNU C++ is available at

    `http://gcc.gnu.org/install/binaries.html`

- Apple's free Xcode, which OS X users can download from the Mac App Store— click the app's icon in the dock at the bottom of your screen, then search for Xcode in the app store.

Instructor Supplements

The following supplements are available to *qualified instructors only* through Pearson Education's Instructor Resource Center (`http://www.pearsonhighered.com/irc`):

- *Solutions Manual* contains solutions to most of the end-of-chapter exercises. We include *Making a Difference* exercises, many with solutions. **Please do not write to us requesting access to the Pearson Instructor's Resource Center. Access is restricted to college instructors teaching from the book.** Instructors may obtain access only through their Pearson representatives. If you're not a registered faculty member, contact your Pearson representative or visit

    `http://www.pearsonhighered.com/educator/replocator/`

    Solutions are *not* provided for "project" exercises. Check out our Programming Projects Resource Center for lots of additional exercise and project possibilities.

    `http://www.deitel.com/ProgrammingProjects`

- *Test Item File* of multiple-choice questions.
- *Customizable PowerPoint® slides* containing all the code and figures in the text, plus bulleted items that summarize key points in the text.

Online Practice and Assessment with MyProgrammingLab™

MyProgrammingLab™ helps students fully grasp the logic, semantics, and syntax of programming. Through practice exercises and immediate, personalized feedback, MyProgrammingLab improves the programming competence of beginning students who often struggle with the basic concepts and paradigms of popular high-level programming languages.

An optional self-study and homework tool, a MyProgrammingLab course consists of hundreds of small practice problems organized around the structure of this textbook. For students, the system automatically detects errors in the logic and syntax of their code submissions and offers targeted hints that enable students to figure out what went wrong—and why. For instructors, a comprehensive gradebook tracks correct and incorrect answers and stores the code inputted by students for review.

For a full demonstration, to see feedback from instructors and students or to get started using MyProgrammingLab in your course, visit

```
http://www.myprogramminglab.com
```

Acknowledgments

We'd like to thank Barbara Deitel of Deitel & Associates, Inc. for long hours devoted to this project. She painstakingly researched the new capabilities of C++11 and C++14.

We're fortunate to have worked with the dedicated team of publishing professionals at Pearson Higher Education. We appreciate the guidance, wisdom and energy of Tracy Johnson, Executive Editor, Computer Science. Kristy Alaura did an extraordinary job recruiting the book's reviewers and managing the review process. Bob Engelhardt did a wonderful job bringing the book to publication.

Finally, thanks to Abbey Deitel, former President of Deitel & Associates, Inc., and a graduate of Carnegie Mellon University's Tepper School of Management where she received a B.S. in Industrial Management. Abbey managed the business operations of Deitel & Associates, Inc. for 17 years, along the way co-authoring a number of our publications, including the previous *C++ How to Program* editions' versions of Chapter 1.

Reviewers

We wish to acknowledge the efforts of our reviewers. Over its ten editions, the book has been scrutinized by academics teaching C++ courses, current and former members of the C++ standards committee and industry experts using C++ to build industrial-strength, high-performance systems. They provided countless suggestions for improving the presentation. Any remaining flaws in the book are our own.

Tenth Edition reviewers: Chris Aburime, Minnesota State Colleges and Universities System; Gašper Ažman, A9.com Search Technologies and Co-Author of *C++ Today: The Beast is Back*; Danny Kalev, Intel and Former Member of the C++ Standards Committee; Renato Golin, LLVM Tech Lead at Linaro and Co-Owner for the ARM Target in LLVM; Gordon Hogenson, Microsoft, Author of *Foundations of C++/CLI: The Visual C++ Language for .NET 3*; Jonathan Wakely, Redhat, ISO C++ Committee Secretary; José Antonio González Seco, Parliament of Andalusia; Dean Michael Berris, Google, Maintainer of cpp-netlib and Former ISO C++ Committee Member.

Ninth Edition post-publication academic reviewers: Stefano Basagni, Northeastern University; Amr Elkady, Diablo Valley College; Chris Aburime, Minnesota State Colleges and Universities System.

Other recent edition reviewers: Virginia Bailey (Jackson State University), Ed James-Beckham (Borland), Thomas J. Borrelli (Rochester Institute of Technology), Ed Brey (Kohler Co.), Chris Cox (Adobe Systems), Gregory Dai (eBay), Peter J. DePasquale (The College of New Jersey), John Dibling (SpryWare), Susan Gauch (University of Arkansas), Doug Gregor (Apple, Inc.), Jack Hagemeister (Washington State University), Williams M. Higdon (University of Indiana), Anne B. Horton (Lockheed Martin), Terrell Hull (Logicalis Integration Solutions), Linda M. Krause (Elmhurst College), Wing-Ning Li (University of Arkansas), Dean Mathias (Utah State University), Robert A. McLain (Tidewater Community College), James P. McNellis (Microsoft Corporation), Robert Myers (Florida State University), Gavin Osborne (Saskatchewan Institute of Applied Science and Technology), Amar Raheja (California State Polytechnic University, Pomona), April Reagan (Microsoft), Robert C. Seacord (Secure Coding Manager at SEI/CERT, author of *Secure Coding in C and C++*), Raymond Stephenson (Microsoft), Dave Topham (Ohlone College), Anthony Williams (author and C++ Standards Committee member) and Chad Willwerth (University Washington, Tacoma).

As you read the book, we'd sincerely appreciate your comments, criticisms and suggestions for improving the text. Please address all correspondence to:

```
deitel@deitel.com
```

We'll respond promptly. We enjoyed writing *C++ How to Program, Tenth Edition*. We hope you enjoy reading it!

Paul Deitel
Harvey Deitel

About the Authors

Paul Deitel, CEO and Chief Technical Officer of Deitel & Associates, Inc., has over 30 years of experience in computing. He is a graduate of MIT, where he studied Information Technology. He holds the Java Certified Programmer and Java Certified Developer designations and is an Oracle Java Champion. Paul was also named as a Microsoft® Most Valuable Professional (MVP) for C# in 2012–2014. Through Deitel & Associates, Inc., he has delivered hundreds of programming courses worldwide to clients, including Cisco, IBM, Siemens, Sun Microsystems, Dell, Fidelity, NASA at the Kennedy Space Center, the National Severe Storm Laboratory, White Sands Missile Range, Rogue Wave Software, Boeing, SunGard, Nortel Networks, Puma, iRobot, Invensys and many more. He and his co-author, Dr. Harvey Deitel, are the world's best-selling programming-language textbook/professional book/video authors.

Dr. Harvey Deitel, Chairman and Chief Strategy Officer of Deitel & Associates, Inc., has over 50 years of experience in the computer field. Dr. Deitel earned B.S. and M.S. degrees in Electrical Engineering from MIT and a Ph.D. in Mathematics from Boston University—he studied computing in each of these programs before they spun off Computer Science programs. He has extensive college teaching experience, including earning tenure and serving as the Chairman of the Computer Science Department at Boston College before founding Deitel & Associates, Inc., in 1991 with his son, Paul. The Deitels' publications have earned international recognition, with translations published in Japanese, German, Russian, Spanish, French, Polish, Italian, Simplified Chinese, Traditional Chinese, Korean, Portuguese, Greek, Urdu and Turkish. Dr. Deitel has delivered hundreds of programming courses to academic, corporate, government and military clients.

About Deitel & Associates, Inc.

Deitel & Associates, Inc., founded by Paul Deitel and Harvey Deitel, is an internationally recognized authoring and corporate training organization, specializing in computer programming languages, object technology, Internet and web software technology, and Android and iOS app development. The company's clients include academic institutions, many of the world's largest corporations, government agencies and branches of the military. The company offers instructor-led training courses delivered at client sites worldwide on major programming languages and platforms, including C++, C, Java™, Android app development, iOS app development, Swift™, Visual C#®, Visual Basic®, Internet and web programming and a growing list of additional programming and software-development courses.

Through its 40-year publishing partnership with Prentice Hall/Pearson, Deitel & Associates, Inc., publishes leading-edge programming college textbooks, professional books and *LiveLessons* video courses. Deitel & Associates, Inc. and the authors can be reached at:

```
deitel@deitel.com
```

To learn more about Deitel's corporate training curriculum, visit

```
http://www.deitel.com/training
```

To request a proposal for worldwide on-site, instructor-led training at your organization, send an e-mail to deitel@deitel.com.

Individuals wishing to purchase Deitel books can do so via

```
http://bit.ly/DeitelOnAmazon
```

Individuals wishing to purchase Deitel *LiveLessons* video training can do so at:

```
http://bit.ly/DeitelOnInformit
```

All Deitel books and *LiveLessons* videos are also available electronically to Safari Books Online subscribers at:

```
http://SafariBooksOnline.com
```

You can get a free 10-day Safari Books Online trial at:

```
https://www.safaribooksonline.com/register/
```

Bulk orders by corporations, the government, the military and academic institutions should be placed directly with Pearson. For more information, visit

```
http://www.informit.com/store/sales.aspx
```

Before You Begin

This section contains information you should review before using this book and instructions to ensure that your computer is set up properly to compile the example programs.

Font and Naming Conventions

We use fonts to distinguish between features, such as menu names, menu items, and other elements that appear in your IDE (Integrated Development Environment), such as Microsoft's Visual Studio. Our convention is to emphasize IDE features in a sans-serif bold Helvetica font (for example, **File** menu) and to emphasize program text in a sans-serif Lucida font (for example, bool x = true;).

Obtaining the Software Used in *C++ How to Program, 10/e*

Before reading this book, you should download and install a C++ compiler. We wrote *C++ How to Program, 10/e*'s code examples using the following free C++ development tools:

- Microsoft's free Visual Studio Community 2015 edition, which includes the Visual C++ compiler and other Microsoft development tools. This runs on Windows and is available for download at

  https://www.visualstudio.com/products/visual-studio-community-vs

- GNU's free GNU C++ 5.2.1 compiler. GNU C++ is already installed on most Linux systems and also can be installed on Mac OS X and Windows systems. There are many versions of Linux, known as Linux distributions, that use different techniques for performing software upgrades. Check your distribution's online documentation for information on how to upgrade GNU C++ to the latest version. GNU C++ is available at

  http://gcc.gnu.org/install/binaries.html

- Apple's free Xcode, which OS X users can download from the Mac App Store—click the app's icon in the dock at the bottom of your Mac screen, then search for Xcode in the app store.

We also provide links to our getting-started videos for each of these C++ tools at:

  http://www.deitel.com/books/cpphtp10

Obtaining the Code Examples

The examples for *C++ How to Program, 10/e* are available for download at

  http://www.deitel.com/books/cpphtp10

Click the **Download Code Examples** link to download the ZIP archive file to your computer. Write down the location where you saved the file—most browsers will save the file into your user account's Downloads folder.

Throughout the book, steps that require you to access our example code on your computer assume that you've extracted the examples from the ZIP file and placed them in C:\examples on Windows or in your user account's Documents directory on other platforms. You can extract them anywhere you like, but if you choose a different location, you'll need to update our steps accordingly.

Creating Projects

In Section 1.10, we demonstrate how to compile and run programs with

- Microsoft Visual Studio Community 2015 edition on Windows (Section 1.10.1)
- GNU C++ 5.2.1 on Linux (Section 1.10.2)
- Apple Xcode on OS X (Section 1.10.3)

For GNU C++ and Xcode, you must compile your programs with C++14. To do so in GNU C++, include the option -std=c++14 when you compile your code, as in:

```
g++ -std=c++14 YourFileName.cpp
```

For Xcode, after following Section 1.10.3's steps to create a project:

1. Select the root node at the top of the Xcode **Project** navigator.
2. Click the **Build Settings** tab in the **Editors** area.
3. Scroll down to the **Apple LLVM 7.0 - Language - C++** section.
4. For the **C++ Language Dialect** option, select **C++14 [–std=c++14]**.

Getting Your C++ Questions Answered

As you read the book, if you have questions, we're easy to reach at

```
deitel@deitel.com
```

We'll respond promptly.

In addition, the web is loaded with programming information. An invaluable resource for nonprogrammers and programmers alike is the website

```
http://stackoverflow.com
```

on which you can:

- Search for answers to most common programming questions
- Search for error messages to see what causes them
- Ask programming questions to get answers from programmers worldwide
- Gain valuable insights about programming in general

Online C++ Documentation

For documentation on the C++ Standard Library, visit

```
http://cppreference.com
```

and be sure to check out the C++ FAQ at

```
https://isocpp.org/faq
```

Introduction to Computers and C++

1

Objectives

In this chapter you'll learn:

- Exciting recent developments in the computer field.

- Computer hardware, software and networking basics.

- The data hierarchy.

- The different types of programming languages.

- Basic object-technology concepts.

- Some basics of the Internet and the World Wide Web.

- A typical C++ program development environment.

- To test-drive a C++ application.

- Some key recent software technologies.

- How computers can help you make a difference.

Outline

1.1 Introduction

Welcome to C++—a powerful computer programming language that's appropriate for technically oriented people with little or no programming experience, and for experienced programmers to use in building substantial information systems. You're already familiar with the powerful tasks computers perform. Using this textbook, you'll write instructions commanding computers to perform those kinds of tasks. *Software* (i.e., the instructions you write) controls *hardware* (i.e., computers).

You'll learn *object-oriented programming*—today's key programming methodology. You'll create many *software objects* that model *things* in the real world.

C++ is one of today's most popular software development languages. This text provides an introduction to programming in C++11 and C++14—the latest versions standardized through the International Organization for Standardization (ISO) and the International Electrotechnical Commission (IEC).

As of 2008 there were more than a billion general-purpose computers in use. Today, various websites say that number is approximately two billion, and according to the real-time tracker at gsmaintelligence.com, there are now more mobile devices than there are people in the world. According to the International Data Corporation (IDC), the number of mobile Internet users will top two billion in 2016.[1] Smartphone sales surpassed personal computer sales in 2011.[2] Tablet sales were expected to overtake personal-computer sales

---

1. https://www.idc.com/getdoc.jsp?containerId=prUS40855515.
2. http://www.mashable.com/2012/02/03/smartphone-sales-overtake-pcs/.

by 2015.[3] By 2017, the smartphone/tablet app market is expected to exceed $77 billion.[4] This explosive growth is creating significant opportunities for programming mobile applications.

1.2 Computers and the Internet in Industry and Research

These are exciting times in the computer field. Many of the most influential and successful businesses of the last two decades are technology companies, including Apple, IBM, Hewlett Packard, Dell, Intel, Motorola, Cisco, Microsoft, Google, Amazon, Facebook, Twitter, eBay and many more. These companies are major employers of people who study computer science, computer engineering, information systems or related disciplines. At the time of this writing, Apple was the most valuable company in the world. Figure 1.1 provides a few examples of the ways in which computers are improving people's lives in research, industry and society.

Name	Description
Electronic health records	These might include a patient's medical history, prescriptions, immunizations, lab results, allergies, insurance information and more. Making this information available to health care providers across a secure network improves patient care, reduces the probability of error and increases overall efficiency of the health-care system, helping control costs.
Human Genome Project	The Human Genome Project was founded to identify and analyze the 20,000+ genes in human DNA. The project used computer programs to analyze complex genetic data, determine the sequences of the billions of chemical base pairs that make up human DNA and store the information in databases which have been made available over the Internet to researchers in many fields.
AMBER™ Alert	The AMBER (America's Missing: Broadcast Emergency Response) Alert System is used to find abducted children. Law enforcement notifies TV and radio broadcasters and state transportation officials, who then broadcast alerts on TV, radio, computerized highway signs, the Internet and wireless devices. AMBER Alert recently partnered with Facebook, whose users can "Like" AMBER Alert pages by location to receive alerts in their news feeds.
World Community Grid	People worldwide can donate their unused computer processing power by installing a free secure software program that allows the World Community Grid (http://www.worldcommunitygrid.org) to harness unused capacity. This computing power, accessed over the Internet, is used in place of expensive supercomputers to conduct scientific research projects that are making a difference—providing clean water to third-world countries, fighting cancer, growing more nutritious rice for regions fighting hunger and more.

Fig. 1.1 | A few uses for computers. (Part 1 of 3.)

---

3. http://www.forbes.com/sites/louiscolumbus/2014/07/18/gartner-forecasts-tablet-shipments-will-overtake-pcs-in-2015/.
4. http://www.entrepreneur.com/article/236832.

Name	Description
Cloud computing	Cloud computing allows you to use software, hardware and information stored in the "cloud"—i.e., accessed on remote computers via the Internet and available on demand—rather than having it stored on your personal computer. These services allow you to increase or decrease resources to meet your needs at any given time, so they can be more cost effective than purchasing expensive hardware to ensure that you have enough storage and processing power to meet your needs at their peak levels. Using cloud-computing services shifts the burden of managing these applications from the business to the service provider, saving businesses money.
Medical imaging	X-ray computed tomography (CT) scans, also called CAT (computerized axial tomography) scans, take X-rays of the body from hundreds of different angles. Computers are used to adjust the intensity of the X-rays, optimizing the scan for each type of tissue, then to combine all of the information to create a 3D image. MRI scanners use a technique called magnetic resonance imaging, also to produce internal images noninvasively.
GPS	Global Positioning System (GPS) devices use a network of satellites to retrieve location-based information. Multiple satellites send time-stamped signals to the GPS device, which calculates the distance to each satellite, based on the time the signal left the satellite and the time the signal arrived. This information helps determine the device's exact location. GPS devices can provide step-by-step directions and help you locate nearby businesses (restaurants, gas stations, etc.) and points of interest. GPS is used in numerous location-based Internet services such as check-in apps to help you find your friends (e.g., Foursquare and Facebook), exercise apps such as RunKeeper that track the time, distance and average speed of your outdoor jog, dating apps that help you find a match nearby and apps that dynamically update changing traffic conditions.
Robots	Robots can be used for day-to-day tasks (e.g., iRobot's Roomba vacuuming robot), entertainment (e.g., robotic pets), military combat, deep sea and space exploration (e.g., NASA's Mars rover Curiosity) and more. RoboEarth (www.roboearth.org) is "a World Wide Web for robots." It allows robots to learn from each other by sharing information and thus improving their abilities to perform tasks, navigate, recognize objects and more.
E-mail, Instant Messaging, Video Chat and FTP	Internet-based servers support all of your online messaging. E-mail messages go through a mail server that also stores the messages. Instant Messaging (IM) and Video Chat apps, such as Facebook Messenger, AIM, Skype, Yahoo! Messenger, Google Hangouts, Trillian and others allow you to communicate with others in real time by sending your messages and live video through servers. FTP (file transfer protocol) allows you to exchange files between multiple computers (for example, a client computer such as your desktop and a file server) over the Internet.
Internet TV	Internet TV set-top boxes (such as Apple TV, Android TV, Roku and TiVo) allow you to access an enormous amount of content on demand, such as games, news, movies, television shows and more, and they help ensure that the content is streamed to your TV smoothly.

Fig. 1.1 | A few uses for computers. (Part 2 of 3.)

Name	Description
Streaming music services	Streaming music services (such as Apple Music, Pandora, Spotify, Last.fm and more) allow you listen to large catalogues of music over the web, create customized "radio stations" and discover new music based on your feedback.
Game programming	Global video-game revenues are expected to reach $107 billion by 2017 (http://www.polygon.com/2015/4/22/8471789/worldwide-video-games-market-value-2015). The most sophisticated games can cost over $100 million to develop, with the most expensive costing half a billion dollars (http://www.gamespot.com/gallery/20-of-the-most-expensive-games-ever-made/2900-104/). Bethesda's *Fallout 4* earned $750 million in its first day of sales (http://fortune.com/2015/11/16/fallout4-is-quiet-best-seller/)!

Fig. 1.1 | A few uses for computers. (Part 3 of 3.)

1.3 Hardware and Software

Computers can perform calculations and make logical decisions phenomenally faster than human beings can. Many of today's personal computers can perform billions of calculations in one second—more than a human can perform in a lifetime. *Supercomputers* are already performing *thousands of trillions (quadrillions)* of instructions per second! China's National University of Defense Technology's Tianhe-2 supercomputer can perform over 33 quadrillion calculations per second (33.86 *petaflops*)![5] To put that in perspective, *the Tianhe-2 supercomputer can perform in one second about 3 million calculations for every person on the planet!* And supercomputing "upper limits" are growing quickly.

Computers process data under the control of sequences of instructions called computer programs. These programs guide the computer through ordered actions specified by people called computer programmers. The programs that run on a computer are referred to as software. In this book, you'll learn a key programming methodology that's enhancing programmer productivity, thereby reducing software development costs—*object-oriented programming*.

A computer consists of various devices referred to as hardware (e.g., the keyboard, screen, mouse, hard disks, memory, DVD drives and processing units). Computing costs are *dropping dramatically*, owing to rapid developments in hardware and software technologies. Computers that might have filled large rooms and cost millions of dollars decades ago are now inscribed on silicon chips smaller than a fingernail, costing perhaps a few dollars each. Ironically, silicon is one of the most abundant materials on Earth—it's an ingredient in common sand. Silicon-chip technology has made computing so economical that computers have become a commodity.

1.3.1 Moore's Law

Every year, you probably expect to pay at least a little more for most products and services. The opposite has been the case in the computer and communications fields, especially with regard to the hardware supporting these technologies. For many decades, hardware costs have fallen rapidly.

---

5. http://www.top500.org.

Every year or two, the capacities of computers have approximately *doubled* inexpensively. This remarkable trend often is called Moore's Law, named for the person who identified it in the 1960s, Gordon Moore, co-founder of Intel—a leading manufacturer of the processors in today's computers and embedded systems. Moore's Law and related observations apply especially to the amount of memory that computers have for programs, the amount of secondary storage (such as disk storage) they have to hold programs and data over longer periods of time, and their processor speeds—the speeds at which they *execute* their programs (i.e., do their work). These increases make computers more capable, which puts greater demands on programming-language designers to innovate.

Similar growth has occurred in the communications field—costs have plummeted as enormous demand for communications *bandwidth* (i.e., information-carrying capacity) has attracted intense competition. We know of no other fields in which technology improves so quickly and costs fall so rapidly. Such phenomenal improvement is truly fostering the *Information Revolution*.

1.3.2 Computer Organization

Regardless of differences in *physical* appearance, computers can be envisioned as divided into various logical units or sections (Fig. 1.2).

Logical unit	Description
Input unit	This "receiving" section obtains information (data and computer programs) from input devices and places it at the disposal of the other units for processing. Most user input is entered into computers through keyboards, touch screens and mouse devices. Other forms of input include receiving voice commands, scanning images and barcodes, reading from secondary storage devices (such as hard drives, DVD drives, Blu-ray Disc™ drives and USB flash drives—also called "thumb drives" or "memory sticks"), receiving video from a webcam and having your computer receive information from the Internet (such as when you stream videos from YouTube® or download e-books from Amazon). Newer forms of input include position data from a GPS device, and motion and orientation information from an *accelerometer* (a device that responds to up/down, left/right and forward/backward acceleration) in a smartphone or game controller (such as Microsoft® Kinect® for Xbox®, Wii™ Remote and Sony® PlayStation® Move).
Output unit	This "shipping" section takes information the computer has processed and places it on various output devices to make it available for use outside the computer. Most information that's output from computers today is displayed on screens (including touch screens), printed on paper ("going green" discourages this), played as audio or video on PCs and media players (such as Apple's iPods) and giant screens in sports stadiums, transmitted over the Internet or used to control other devices, such as robots and "intelligent" appliances. Information is also commonly output to secondary storage devices, such as hard drives, DVD drives and USB flash drives. Popular recent forms of output are smartphone and game controller vibration, and virtual reality devices like Oculus Rift.

Fig. 1.2 | Logical units of a computer. (Part 1 of 2.)

Logical unit	Description
Memory unit	This rapid-access, relatively low-capacity "warehouse" section retains information that has been entered through the input unit, making it immediately available for processing when needed. The memory unit also retains processed information until it can be placed on output devices by the output unit. Information in the memory unit is *volatile*—it's typically lost when the computer's power is turned off. The memory unit is often called either memory, primary memory or RAM (Random Access Memory). Main memories on desktop and notebook computers contain as much as 128 GB of RAM, though 2 to 16 GB is most common. GB stands for gigabytes; a gigabyte is approximately one billion bytes. A byte is eight bits. A bit is either a 0 or a 1.
Arithmetic and logic unit (ALU)	This "manufacturing" section performs *calculations*, such as addition, subtraction, multiplication and division. It also contains the *decision* mechanisms that allow the computer, for example, to compare two items from the memory unit to determine whether they're equal. In today's systems, the ALU is implemented as part of the next logical unit, the CPU.
Central processing unit (CPU)	This "administrative" section coordinates and supervises the operation of the other sections. The CPU tells the input unit when information should be read into the memory unit, tells the ALU when information from the memory unit should be used in calculations and tells the output unit when to send information from the memory unit to certain output devices. Many of today's computers have multiple CPUs and, hence, can perform many operations simultaneously. A multi-core processor implements multiple processors on a single integrated-circuit chip—a *dual-core processor* has two CPUs, a *quad-core processor* has four and an *octa-core processor* has eight. Today's desktop computers have processors that can execute billions of instructions per second. To take full advantage of multi-core architecture you need to write multithreaded applications, which we introduce in Section 24.3.
Secondary storage unit	This is the long-term, high-capacity "warehousing" section. Programs or data not actively being used by the other units normally are placed on secondary storage devices (e.g., your *hard drive*) until they're again needed, possibly hours, days, months or even years later. Information on secondary storage devices is *persistent*—it's preserved even when the computer's power is turned off. Secondary storage information takes much longer to access than information in primary memory, but its cost per unit is much less. Examples of secondary storage devices include hard drives, DVD drives and USB flash drives, some of which can hold over 2 TB (TB stands for terabytes; a terabyte is approximately one trillion bytes). Typical hard drives on desktop and notebook computers hold up to 2 TB, and some desktop hard drives can hold up to 6 TB.

Fig. 1.2 | Logical units of a computer. (Part 2 of 2.)

1.4 Data Hierarchy

Data items processed by computers form a data hierarchy that becomes larger and more complex in structure as we progress from the simplest data items (called "bits") to richer ones, such as characters and fields. Figure 1.3 illustrates a portion of the data hierarchy.

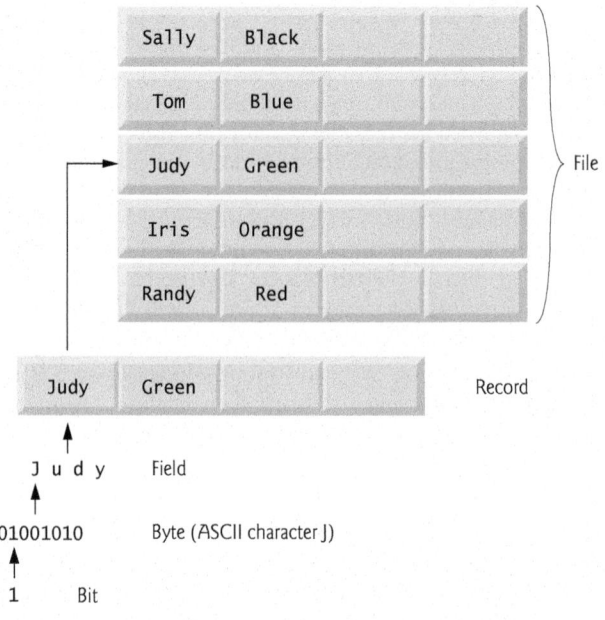

Fig. 1.3 | Data hierarchy.

Bits
The smallest data item in a computer can assume the value 0 or the value 1. It's called a bit (short for "binary digit"—a digit that can assume one of *two* values). Remarkably, the impressive functions performed by computers involve only the simplest manipulations of 0s and 1s—*examining a bit's value, setting a bit's value* and *reversing a bit's value* (from 1 to 0 or from 0 to 1).

Characters
It's tedious for people to work with data in the low-level form of bits. Instead, they prefer to work with *decimal digits* (0–9), *letters* (A–Z and a–z), and *special symbols* (e.g., $, @, %, &, *, (,), –, +, ", :, ? and /). Digits, letters and special symbols are known as characters. The computer's character set is the set of all the characters used to write programs and represent data items. Computers process only 1s and 0s, so a computer's character set represents every character as a pattern of 1s and 0s. C++ supports various character sets (including Unicode®), with some requiring more than one byte per character. Unicode supports many of the world's languages. See Appendix B for more information on the ASCII (American Standard Code for Information Interchange) character set—the popular subset of Unicode that represents uppercase and lowercase letters, digits and some common special characters.

Fields
Just as characters are composed of bits, fields are composed of characters or bytes. A field is a group of characters or bytes that conveys meaning. For example, a field consisting of uppercase and lowercase letters can be used to represent a person's name, and a field consisting of decimal digits could represent a person's age.

Records

Several related fields can be used to compose a record. In a payroll system, for example, the record for an employee might consist of the following fields (possible types for these fields are shown in parentheses):

- Employee identification number (a whole number)
- Name (a string of characters)
- Address (a string of characters)
- Hourly pay rate (a number with a decimal point)
- Year-to-date earnings (a number with a decimal point)
- Amount of taxes withheld (a number with a decimal point).

Thus, a record is a group of related fields. In the preceding example, all the fields belong to the *same* employee. A company might have many employees and a payroll record for each.

Files

A file is a group of related records. [*Note:* More generally, a file contains arbitrary data in arbitrary formats. In some operating systems, a file is viewed simply as a *sequence of bytes*—any organization of the bytes in a file, such as organizing the data into records, is a view created by the application programmer.] It's not unusual for an organization to have many files, some containing billions, or even trillions, of characters of information.

Database

A database is a collection of data organized for easy access and manipulation. The most popular model is the *relational database*, in which data is stored in simple *tables*. A table includes *records* and *fields*. For example, a table of students might include first name, last name, major, year, student ID number and grade-point-average fields. The data for each student is a record, and the individual pieces of information in each record are the fields. You can *search*, *sort* and otherwise manipulate the data based on its relationship to multiple tables or databases. For example, a university might use data from the student database in combination with data from databases of courses, on-campus housing, meal plans, etc.

Big Data

The amount of data being produced worldwide is enormous and growing quickly. According to IBM, approximately 2.5 quintillion bytes (2.5 *exabytes*) of data are created daily[6] and according to Salesforce.com, 90% of the world's data was created in just the past 12 months![7] According to an IDC study, the global data supply will reach 40 *zettabytes* (equal to 40 trillion gigabytes) annually by 2020.[8] Figure 1.4 shows some common byte measurements. Big data applications deal with massive amounts of data and this field is growing quickly, creating lots of opportunity for software developers. According to a study by Gartner Group, over 4 million IT jobs globally were expected to support big data in 2015.[9]

---

6. http://www-01.ibm.com/software/data/bigdata/what-is-big-data.html.
7. https://www.salesforce.com/blog/2015/10/salesforce-channel-ifttt.html.
8. http://recode.net/2014/01/10/stuffed-why-data-storage-is-hot-again-really/.
9. http://tech.fortune.cnn.com/2013/09/04/big-data-employment-boom/.

Unit	Bytes	Which is approximately
1 kilobyte (KB)	1024 bytes	10^3 (1024) bytes exactly
1 megabyte (MB)	1024 kilobytes	10^6 (1,000,000)bytes
1 gigabyte (GB)	1024 megabytes	10^9 (1,000,000,000) bytes
1 terabyte (TB)	1024 gigabytes	10^{12} (1,000,000,000,000) bytes
1 petabyte (PB)	1024 terabytes	10^{15} (1,000,000,000,000,000) bytes
1 exabyte (EB)	1024 petabytes	10^{18} (1,000,000,000,000,000,000) bytes
1 zettabyte (ZB)	1024 exabytes	10^{21} (1,000,000,000,000,000,000,000) bytes

Fig. 1.4 | Byte measurements.

1.5 Machine Languages, Assembly Languages and High-Level Languages

Programmers write instructions in various programming languages, some directly understandable by computers and others requiring intermediate *translation* steps.

Machine Languages

Any computer can directly understand only its own machine language (also called *machine code*), defined by its hardware architecture. Machine languages generally consist of numbers (ultimately reduced to 1s and 0s). Such languages are cumbersome for humans.

Assembly Languages

Programming in machine language was simply too slow and tedious for most programmers. Instead, they began using English-like *abbreviations* to represent elementary operations. These abbreviations formed the basis of assembly languages. *Translator programs* called assemblers were developed to convert assembly-language programs to machine language. Although assembly-language code is clearer to humans, it's incomprehensible to computers until translated to machine language.

High-Level Languages

To speed up the programming process further, high-level languages were developed in which single statements could be written to accomplish substantial tasks. High-level languages, such as C, C++, Java, C#, Swift and Visual Basic, allow you to write instructions that look more like everyday English and contain commonly used mathematical notations. Translator programs called compilers convert high-level language programs into machine language.

The process of compiling a large high-level language program into machine language can take a considerable amount of computer time. Interpreter programs were developed to execute high-level language programs directly (without the need for compilation), although more slowly than compiled programs. Scripting languages such as the popular web languages JavaScript and PHP are processed by interpreters.

Performance Tip 1.1

Interpreters have an advantage over compilers in Internet scripting. An interpreted program can begin executing as soon as it's downloaded to the client's machine, without needing to be compiled before it can execute. On the downside, interpreted scripts generally run slower and consume more memory than compiled code.

1.6 C and C++

C was implemented in 1972 by Dennis Ritchie at Bell Laboratories. It initially became widely known as the UNIX operating system's development language. Today, most of the code for general-purpose operating systems is written in C or C++.

C++ evolved from C, which is available for most computers and is hardware independent. With careful design, it's possible to write C programs that are portable to most computers.

The widespread use of C with various kinds of computers (sometimes called hardware platforms) unfortunately led to many variations. A standard version of C was needed. The American National Standards Institute (ANSI) cooperated with the International Organization for Standardization (ISO) to standardize C worldwide; the joint standard document was published in 1990.

C11 is the latest ANSI standard for the C programming language. It was developed to evolve the C language to keep pace with increasingly powerful hardware and ever more demanding user requirements. C11 also makes C more consistent with C++. For more information on C and C11, see our book *C How to Program, 8/e* and our C Resource Center (located at http://www.deitel.com/C).

C++, an extension of C, was developed by Bjarne Stroustrup in 1979 at Bell Laboratories. Originally called "C with Classes," it was renamed to C++ in the early 1980s. C++ provides a number of features that "spruce up" the C language, but more importantly, it provides capabilities for object-oriented programming that were inspired by the Simula simulation programming language. We say more about C++ and its current version in Section 1.14.

You'll begin developing customized, reusable classes and objects in Chapter 3. The book is object oriented, where appropriate, from the start and throughout the text.

We also provide an *optional* automated teller machine (ATM) case study in Chapters 25–26, which contains a complete C++ implementation. The case study presents a carefully paced introduction to object-oriented design using the UML—an industry standard graphical modeling language for developing object-oriented systems. We guide you through a friendly design and implementation experience intended for the novice.

C++ Standard Library

C++ programs consist of pieces called classes and functions. You can program each piece yourself, but most C++ programmers take advantage of the rich collections of classes and functions in the C++ Standard Library. Thus, there are really two parts to learning the C++ "world." The first is learning the C++ language itself (often referred to as the "core language"); the second is learning how to use the classes and functions in the C++ Standard Library. We discuss many of these classes and functions. P. J. Plauger's book, *The Standard C Library* (Upper Saddle River, NJ: Prentice Hall PTR, 1992), is a must-read for programmers who need a deep understanding of the ANSI C library functions included in C++. Many special-purpose class libraries are supplied by independent software vendors.

Software Engineering Observation 1.1

Use a "building-block" approach to create programs. Avoid reinventing the wheel. Use existing pieces wherever possible. Called software reuse, this practice is central to effective object-oriented programming.

Software Engineering Observation 1.2

When programming in C++, you typically will use the following building blocks: classes and functions from the C++ Standard Library, classes and functions you and your colleagues create, and classes and functions from various popular third-party libraries.

The advantage of creating your own functions and classes is that you'll know exactly how they work. You'll be able to examine the C++ code. The disadvantage is the time-consuming and complex effort that goes into designing, developing and maintaining new functions and classes that are correct and operate efficiently.

Performance Tip 1.2

Using C++ Standard Library functions and classes instead of writing your own versions can improve program performance, because they're written carefully to perform efficiently. This technique also shortens program development time.

Portability Tip 1.1

Using C++ Standard Library functions and classes instead of writing your own improves program portability, because they're included in every C++ implementation.

1.7 Programming Languages

In this section, we provide brief comments on several popular programming languages (Fig. 1.5).

Programming language	Description
Fortran	Fortran (FORmula TRANslator) was developed by IBM Corporation in the mid-1950s to be used for scientific and engineering applications that require complex mathematical computations. It's still widely used and its latest versions support object-oriented programming.
COBOL	COBOL (COmmon Business Oriented Language) was developed in the late 1950s by computer manufacturers, the U.S. government and industrial computer users, based on a language developed by Grace Hopper, a career U.S. Navy officer and computer scientist. COBOL is still widely used for commercial applications that require precise and efficient manipulation of large amounts of data. Its latest version supports object-oriented programming.

Fig. 1.5 | Some other programming languages. (Part 1 of 3.)

Programming language	Description
Pascal	Research in the 1960s resulted in *structured programming*—a disciplined approach to writing programs that are clearer, easier to test and debug and easier to modify than programs produced with previous techniques. The Pascal language developed by Professor Niklaus Wirth in 1971 grew out of this research. It was popular for teaching structured programming for several decades.
Ada	Ada, based on Pascal, was developed under the sponsorship of the U.S. Department of Defense (DOD) during the 1970s and early 1980s. The DOD wanted a single language that would fill most of its needs. The Pascal-based language was named after Lady Ada Lovelace, daughter of the poet Lord Byron. She's credited with writing the world's first computer program in the early 1800s (for the Analytical Engine mechanical computing device designed by Charles Babbage). Ada also supports object-oriented programming.
Basic	Basic was developed in the 1960s at Dartmouth College to familiarize novices with programming techniques. Many of its latest versions are object oriented.
Objective-C	Objective-C is an object-oriented language based on C. It was developed in the early 1980s and later acquired by NeXT, which in turn was acquired by Apple. It became the key programming language for the OS X operating system and all iOS-powered devices (such as iPods, iPhones and iPads).
Swift	Swift, which was introduced in 2014, is Apple's programming language of the future for developing iOS and OS X applications (apps). Swift is a contemporary language that includes popular programming-language features from languages such as Objective-C, Java, C#, Ruby, Python and others. In 2015, Apple released Swift 2 with new and updated features. According to the Tiobe Index, Swift has already become one of the most popular programming languages. Swift is now *open source* (Section 1.11.2), so it can be used on non-Apple platforms as well.
Java	Sun Microsystems in 1991 funded an internal corporate research project led by James Gosling, which resulted in the C++-based object-oriented programming language called Java. A key goal of Java is to enable developers to write programs that will run on a great variety of computer systems and computer-controlled devices. This is sometimes called "write once, run anywhere." Java is used to develop large-scale enterprise applications, to enhance the functionality of web servers (the computers that provide the content we see in our web browsers), to provide applications for consumer devices (e.g., smartphones, tablets, television set-top boxes, appliances, automobiles and more) and for many other purposes. Java is also the key language for developing Android smartphone and tablet apps.
Visual Basic	Microsoft's Visual Basic language was introduced in the early 1990s to simplify the development of Microsoft Windows applications. Its latest versions support object-oriented programming.
C#	Microsoft's three primary object-oriented programming languages are C# (based on C++ and Java), Visual C++ (based on C++) and Visual Basic (based on the original Basic). C# was developed to integrate the web into computer applications, and is now widely used to develop enterprise applications and for mobile application development.

Fig. 1.5 | Some other programming languages. (Part 2 of 3.)

Programming language	Description
PHP	PHP is an object-oriented, *open-source* (see Section 1.11.2) "scripting" language supported by a community of developers and used by numerous websites. PHP is platform independent—implementations exist for all major UNIX, Linux, Mac and Windows operating systems.
Python	Python, another object-oriented scripting language, was released publicly in 1991. Developed by Guido van Rossum of the National Research Institute for Mathematics and Computer Science in Amsterdam (CWI), Python draws heavily from Modula-3—a systems programming language. Python is "extensible"—it can be extended through classes and programming interfaces.
JavaScript	JavaScript is the most widely used scripting language. It's primarily used to add programmability to web pages—for example, animations and interactivity with the user. It's provided with all major web browsers.
Ruby on Rails	Ruby—created in the mid-1990s by Yukihiro Matsumoto—is an open-source, object-oriented programming language with a simple syntax that's similar to Python. Ruby on Rails combines the scripting language Ruby with the Rails web application framework developed by the company 37Signals. Their book, *Getting Real* (http://gettingreal.37signals.com/toc.php), is a must read for web developers. Many Ruby on Rails developers have reported productivity gains over other languages when developing database-intensive web applications.
Scala	Scala (www.scala-lang.org/node/273)—short for "scalable language"—was designed by Martin Odersky, a professor at École Polytechnique Fédérale de Lausanne (EPFL) in Switzerland. Released in 2003, Scala uses both the object-oriented programming and functional programming paradigms and is designed to integrate with Java. Programming in Scala can reduce the amount of code in your applications significantly.

Fig. 1.5 | Some other programming languages. (Part 3 of 3.)

1.8 Introduction to Object Technology

Building software quickly, correctly and economically remains an elusive goal at a time when demands for new and more powerful software are soaring. *Objects*, or more precisely—as we'll see in Chapter 3—the *classes* objects come from, are essentially *reusable* software components. There are date objects, time objects, audio objects, video objects, automobile objects, people objects, etc. Almost any *noun* can be reasonably represented as a software object in terms of *attributes* (e.g., name, color and size) and *behaviors* (e.g., calculating, moving and communicating). Software developers have discovered that using a modular, object-oriented design-and-implementation approach can make software development groups much more productive than was possible with earlier techniques—object-oriented programs are often easier to understand, correct and modify.

The Automobile as an Object

Let's begin with a simple analogy. Suppose you want to *drive a car and make it go faster by pressing its accelerator pedal.* What must happen before you can do this? Well, before you can drive a car, someone has to *design* it. A car typically begins as engineering drawings, similar to the *blueprints* that describe the design of a house. These drawings include the design for an accelerator pedal. The pedal *hides* from the driver the complex mechanisms that actually make the car go faster, just as the brake pedal hides the mechanisms that slow the car, and the steering wheel *hides* the mechanisms that turn the car. This enables people with little or no knowledge of how engines, braking and steering mechanisms work to drive a car easily.

Before you can drive a car, it must be *built* from the engineering drawings that describe it. A completed car has an *actual* accelerator pedal to make the car go faster, but even that's not enough—the car won't accelerate on its own (hopefully!), so the driver must *press* the pedal to accelerate the car.

Functions, Member Functions and Classes

Let's use our car example to introduce some key object-oriented programming concepts. Performing a task in a program requires a function. The function houses the program statements that actually perform its task. It *hides* these statements from its user, just as the accelerator pedal of a car hides from the driver the mechanisms of making the car go faster. In C++, we often create a program unit called a class to house the set of functions that perform the class's tasks—these are known as the class's member functions. For example, a class that represents a bank account might contain a member function to *deposit* money to an account, another to *withdraw* money from an account and a third to *query* what the account's current balance is. A class is similar to a car's engineering drawings, which house the design of an accelerator pedal, brake pedal, steering wheel, and so on.

Instantiation

Just as someone has to *build a car* from its engineering drawings before you can actually drive a car, you must *build an object* from a class before a program can perform the tasks that the class's member functions define. The process of doing this is called *instantiation*. An object is then referred to as an instance of its class.

Reuse

Just as a car's engineering drawings can be *reused* many times to build many cars, you can *reuse* a class many times to build many objects. Reuse of existing classes when building new classes and programs saves time and effort. Reuse also helps you build more reliable and effective systems, because existing classes and components often have gone through extensive *testing, debugging* and *performance tuning*. Just as the notion of *interchangeable parts* was crucial to the Industrial Revolution, reusable classes are crucial to the software revolution that has been spurred by object technology.

Messages and Member-Function Calls

When you drive a car, pressing its gas pedal sends a *message* to the car to perform a task— that is, to go faster. Similarly, you *send messages to an object*. Each message is implemented as a member-function call that tells a member function of the object to perform its task. For example, a program might call a particular bank-account object's *deposit* member function to increase the account's balance.

Attributes and Data Members

A car, besides having capabilities to accomplish tasks, also has *attributes*, such as its color, its number of doors, the amount of gas in its tank, its current speed and its record of total miles driven (i.e., its odometer reading). Like its capabilities, the car's attributes are represented as part of its design in its engineering diagrams (which, for example, include an odometer and a fuel gauge). As you drive an actual car, these attributes are carried along with the car. Every car maintains its *own* attributes. For example, each car knows how much gas is in its own gas tank, but not how much is in the tanks of *other* cars.

An object, similarly, has attributes that it carries along as it's used in a program. These attributes are specified as part of the object's class. For example, a bank-account object has a *balance attribute* that represents the amount of money in the account. Each bank-account object knows the balance in the account it represents, but *not* the balances of the *other* accounts in the bank. Attributes are specified by the class's data members.

Encapsulation

Classes encapsulate (i.e., wrap) attributes and member functions into objects created from those classes—an object's attributes and member functions are intimately related. Objects may communicate with one another, but they're normally not allowed to know how other objects are implemented—implementation details are *hidden* within the objects themselves. This information hiding, as we'll see, is crucial to good software engineering.

Inheritance

A new class of objects can be created quickly and conveniently by inheritance—the new class absorbs the characteristics of an existing class, possibly customizing them and adding unique characteristics of its own. In our car analogy, an object of class "convertible" certainly *is an* object of the more *general* class "automobile," but more *specifically*, the roof can be raised or lowered.

Object-Oriented Analysis and Design (OOAD)

Soon you'll be writing programs in C++. How will you create the code (i.e., the program instructions) for your programs? Perhaps, like many programmers, you'll simply turn on your computer and start typing. This approach may work for small programs (like the ones we present in the early chapters of the book), but what if you were asked to create a software system to control thousands of automated teller machines for a major bank? Or suppose you were asked to work on a team of thousands of software developers building the next generation of the U.S. air traffic control system? For projects so large and complex, you should not simply sit down and start writing programs.

To create the best solutions, you should follow a detailed analysis process for determining your project's requirements (i.e., defining *what* the system is supposed to do) and developing a design that satisfies them (i.e., deciding *how* the system should do it). Ideally, you'd go through this process and carefully review the design (and have your design reviewed by other software professionals) before writing any code. If this process involves analyzing and designing your system from an object-oriented point of view, it's called an object-oriented analysis and design (OOAD) process. Languages like C++ are object oriented. Programming in such a language, called object-oriented programming (OOP), allows you to implement an object-oriented design as a working system.

The UML (Unified Modeling Language)

Although many different OOAD processes exist, a single graphical language for communicating the results of *any* OOAD process has come into wide use. This language, known as the Unified Modeling Language (UML), is now the most widely used graphical scheme for modeling object-oriented systems. We present our first UML diagrams in Chapters 3 and 4, then use them in our deeper treatment of object-oriented programming through Chapter 12. In our *optional* ATM Software Engineering Case Study in Chapters 25–26 we present a simple subset of the UML's features as we guide you through an object-oriented design and implementation experience.

1.9 Typical C++ Development Environment

C++ systems generally consist of three parts: a program development environment, the language and the C++ Standard Library. C++ programs typically go through six phases: edit, preprocess, compile, link, load and execute. The following discussion explains a typical C++ program development environment.

Phase 1: Editing a Program
Phase 1 consists of editing a file with an *editor program*, normally known simply as an *editor* (Fig. 1.6). You type a C++ program (typically referred to as source code) using the editor, make any necessary corrections and save the program on your computer's disk. C++ source code filenames often end with the .cpp, .cxx, .cc or .C (uppercase) extensions which indicate that a file contains C++ source code. See the documentation for your C++ compiler for more information on filename extensions. Two editors widely used on Linux systems are vim and emacs. You can also use a simple text editor, such as Notepad in Windows, to write your C++ code.

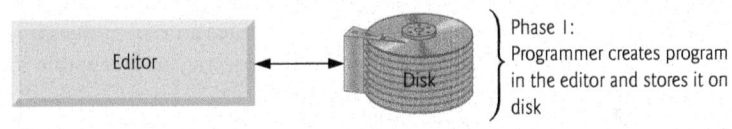

Phase 1:
Programmer creates program in the editor and stores it on disk

Fig. 1.6 | Typical C++ development environment—editing phase.

Integrated development environments (IDEs) are available from many major software suppliers. IDEs provide tools that support the software development process, including editors for writing and editing programs and debuggers for locating logic errors—errors that cause programs to execute incorrectly. Popular IDEs include Microsoft® Visual Studio 2015 Community Edition, NetBeans, Eclipse, Apple's Xcode®, CodeLite and Clion.

Phase 2: Preprocessing a C++ Program
In Phase 2, you give the command to compile the program (Fig. 1.7). In a C++ system, a preprocessor program executes automatically before the compiler's translation phase begins (so we call preprocessing Phase 2 and compiling Phase 3). The C++ preprocessor obeys commands called preprocessing directives, which indicate that certain manipulations are to be performed on the program before compilation. These manipulations usually include (i.e., copy into the program file) other text files to be compiled, and perform various text replacements. The most common preprocessing directives are discussed in the early chapters; a detailed discussion of preprocessor features appears in Appendix E, Preprocessor.

Fig. 1.7 | Typical C++ development environment—preprocessor phase.

Phase 3: Compiling a C++ Program

In Phase 3, the compiler translates the C++ program into machine-language code—also referred to as object code (Fig. 1.8).

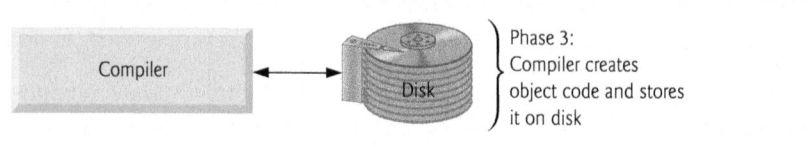

Fig. 1.8 | Typical C++ development environment—compilation phase.

Phase 4: Linking

Phase 4 is called linking. C++ programs typically contain references to functions and data defined elsewhere, such as in the standard libraries or in the private libraries of groups of programmers working on a particular project (Fig. 1.9). The object code produced by the C++ compiler typically contains "holes" due to these missing parts. A linker links the object code with the code for the missing functions to produce an executable program (with no missing pieces). If the program compiles and links correctly, an executable image is produced.

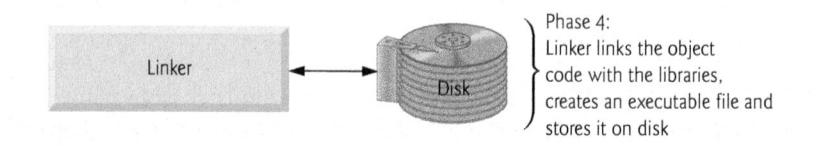

Fig. 1.9 | Typical C++ development environment—linking phase.

Phase 5: Loading

Phase 5 is called loading. Before a program can be executed, it must first be placed in memory (Fig. 1.10). This is done by the loader, which takes the executable image from disk and transfers it to memory. Additional components from shared libraries that support the program are also loaded.

Phase 6: Execution

Finally, the computer, under the control of its CPU, executes the program one instruction at a time (Fig. 1.11). Some modern computer architectures often execute several instructions in parallel.

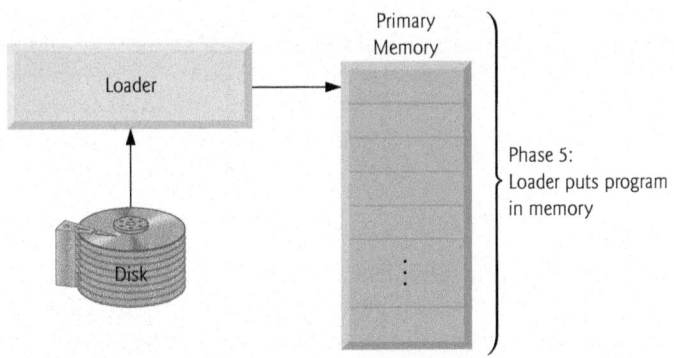

Fig. 1.10 | Typical C++ development environment—loading phase.

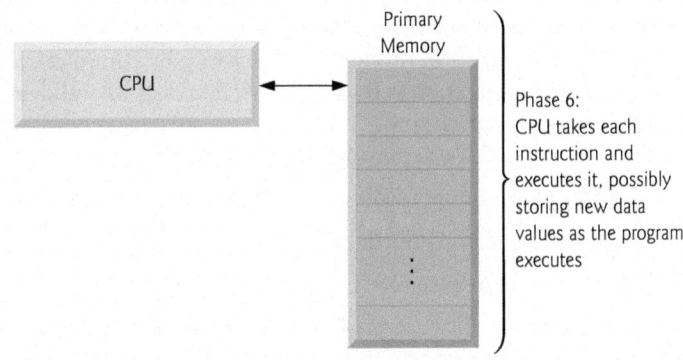

Fig. 1.11 | Typical C++ development environment—execution phase.

Problems That May Occur at Execution Time

Programs might not work on the first try. Each of the preceding phases can fail because of various errors that we'll discuss throughout this book. For example, an executing program might try to divide by zero (an illegal operation for integer arithmetic in C++). This would cause the C++ program to display an error message. If this occurred, you'd have to return to the edit phase, make the necessary corrections and proceed through the remaining phases again to determine that the corrections fixed the problem(s). [*Note:* Most programs in C++ input or output data.] Certain C++ functions take their input from cin (the standard input stream; pronounced "see-in"), which is normally the keyboard, but cin can be redirected to another device. Data is often output to cout (the standard output stream; pronounced "see-out"), which is normally the computer screen, but cout can be redirected to another device. When we say that a program prints a result, we normally mean that the result is displayed on a screen. Data may be output to other devices, such as disks, hard-copy printers or even transmitted over the Internet. There is also a standard error stream referred to as cerr. The cerr stream (normally connected to the screen) is used for displaying error messages.

Common Programming Error 1.1
Errors such as division by zero occur as a program runs, so they're called runtime errors *or* execution-time errors. *Fatal* runtime errors *cause programs to terminate immediately without having successfully performed their jobs.* Nonfatal runtime errors *allow programs to run to completion, often producing incorrect results.*

1.10 Test-Driving a C++ Application

In this section, you'll compile, run and interact with your first C++ application—an entertaining guess-the-number game, which picks a number from 1 to 1000 and prompts you to guess it. If your guess is correct, the game ends. If your guess is not correct, the application indicates whether your guess is higher or lower than the correct number. There is no limit on the number of guesses you can make. [*Note:* For this test drive only, we've modified this application from the exercise you'll be asked to create in Chapter 6, Functions and an Introduction to Recursion. Normally this application randomly selects the correct answer as you execute the program. The modified application uses the same correct answer every time the program executes (though this may vary by compiler), so you can use the *same* guesses we use in this section and see the *same* results as we walk you through interacting with your first C++ application.]

We'll demonstrate running a C++ application using

- Visual Studio 2015 Community Edition for Windows (Section 1.10.1)
- GNU C++ in a shell on Linux (Section 1.10.2)
- Clang/LLVM in Xcode on Mac OS X (Section 1.10.3).

The application runs similarly on all three platforms. You need to read only the section that corresponds to your operating system and compiler. Many development environments are available in which you can compile, build and run C++ applications—CodeLite, Clion, NetBeans and Eclipse are just a few. Consult your instructor or the online documentation for information on your specific development environment.

In the following steps, you'll run the application and enter various numbers to guess the correct number. The elements and functionality that you see in this application are typical of those you'll learn to program in this book. We use fonts to distinguish between features you see on the screen and elements that are not directly related to the screen. We emphasize screen features like titles and menus (e.g., the **File** menu) in a semibold **sans-serif bold** font and emphasize filenames, text displayed by an application and values you should enter into an application (e.g., GuessNumber or 500) in a sans-serif font.

1.10.1 Compiling and Running an Application in Visual Studio 2015 for Windows

In this section, you'll run a C++ program on Windows using Microsoft Visual Studio 2015 Community Edition. We assume that you've already read the Before You Begin section for instructions on installing the IDE and downloading the book's code examples.

There are several versions of Visual Studio available—on some versions, the options, menus and instructions we present might differ slightly. From this point forward, we'll refer to Visual Studio 2015 Community Edition simply as "Visual Studio" or "the IDE."

Step 1: Checking Your Setup

It's important to read this book's Before You Begin section to make sure that you've installed Visual Studio and copied the book's examples to your hard drive correctly.

Step 2: Launching Visual Studio

Open Visual Studio from the **Start** menu. The IDE displays the **Start Page** (Fig. 1.12), which provides links for creating new programs, opening existing programs and learning about the IDE and various programming topics. Close this window for now by clicking the **X** in its tab—you can access this window any time by selecting **View > Start Page**. We use the **>** character to indicate selecting a menu item from a menu. For example, the notation **File > Open** indicates that you should select the **Open** menu item from the **File** menu.

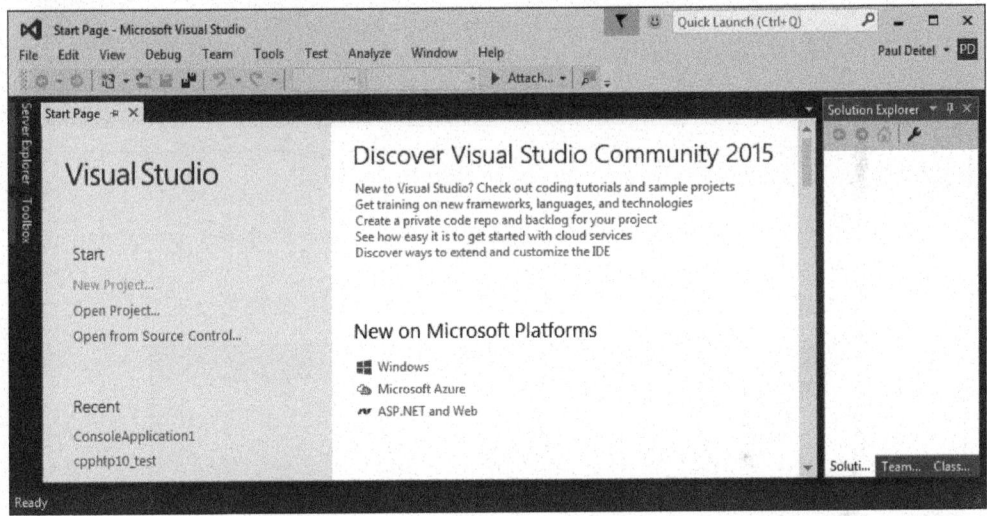

Fig. 1.12 | Visual Studio 2015 Community Edition window showing the **Start Page**.

Step 3: Creating a Project

A project is a group of related files, such as the C++ source-code files that compose an application. Visual Studio organizes applications into projects and solutions, which contain one or more projects. Multiple-project solutions are used to create large-scale applications. Each application in this book will be a solution containing a single project.

The Visual Studio projects we created for this book's examples are **Win32 Console Application** projects that you'll execute from the IDE. To create a project:

1. Select **File > New > Project…**.

2. At the **New Project** dialog's left side, select the category **Installed > Templates > Visual C++ > Win32** (Fig. 1.13).

3. In the **New Project** dialog's middle section, select **Win32 Console Application**.

4. Provide a name for your project in the **Name** field—we specified Guess Number—then click **OK** to display the **Win32 Application Wizard** window, then click **Next >** to display the **Application Settings** step.

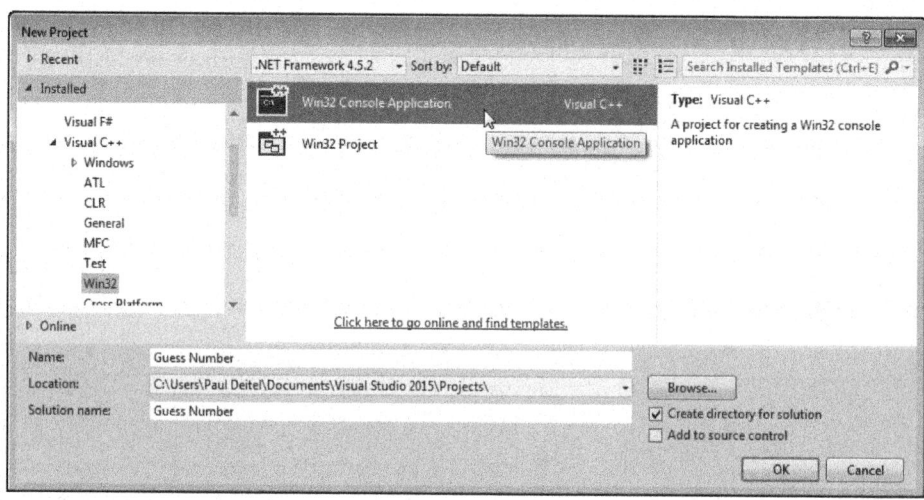

Fig. 1.13 | Visual Studio 2015 Community Edition **New Project** dialog.

5. Configure the settings as shown in Fig. 1.14 to create a solution containing an empty project, then click **Finish**.

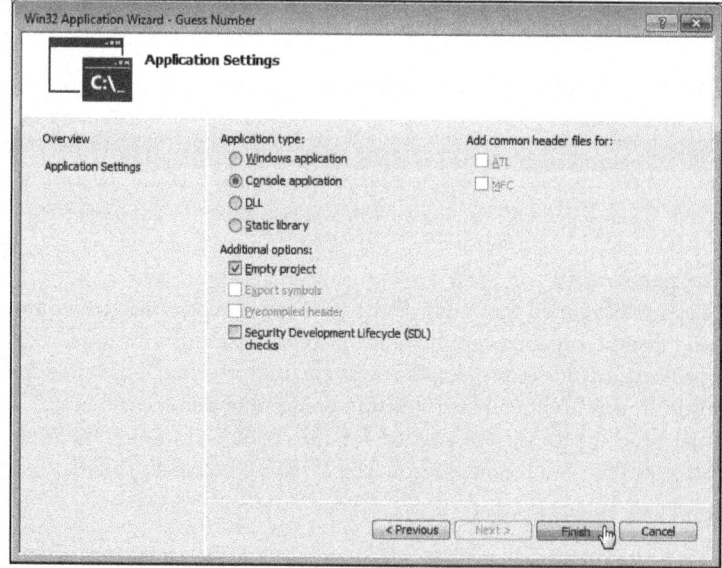

Fig. 1.14 | **Win32 Application Wizard** window's **Application Settings** step.

At this point, the IDE creates your project and places its folder in

```
C:\Users\YourUserAccount\Documents\Visual Studio 2015\Projects
```

then opens the window in Fig. 1.15. This window displays editors as tabbed windows (one for each file) when you're editing code. Also displayed is the **Solution Explorer** in which you can view and manage your application's files. In this book's examples, you'll typically place each program's code files in the **Source Files** folder. If the **Solution Explorer** is not displayed, you can display it by selecting **View > Solution Explorer**.

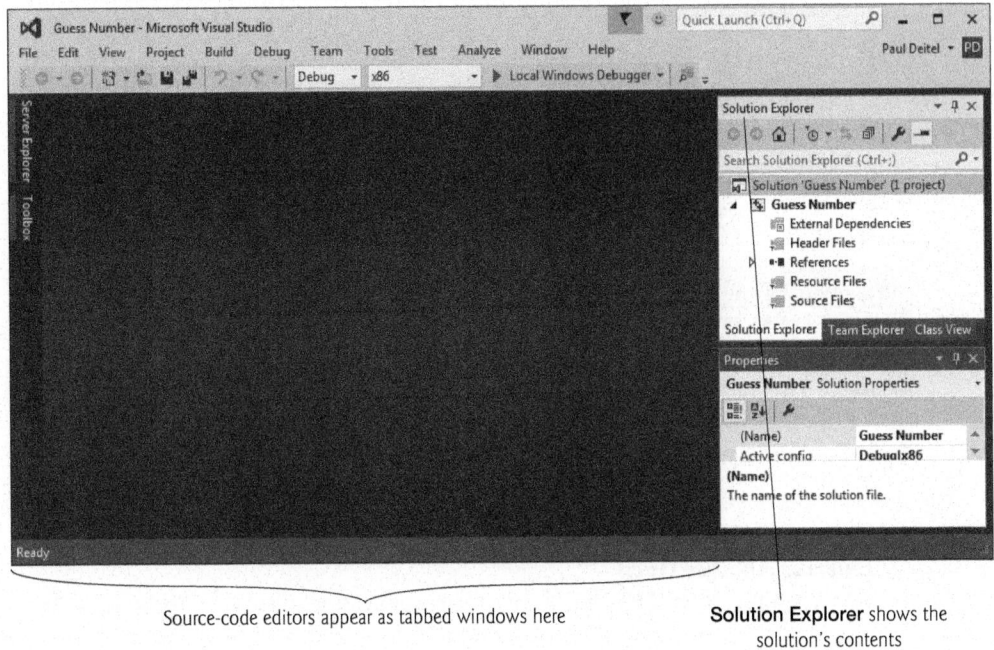

Source-code editors appear as tabbed windows here   **Solution Explorer** shows the
                                                          solution's contents

Fig. 1.15 | Visual Studio window after creating the Guess Number project.

Step 4: Adding the GuessNumber.cpp File into the Project

Next, you'll add GuessNumber.cpp to the project you created in *Step 3*. In Windows Explorer (Windows 7) or File Explorer (Windows 8 and 10), open the ch01 folder in the book's examples folder, then drag GuessNumber.cpp onto the **Source Files** folder in the **Solution Explorer**.[10]

Step 5: Compiling and Running the Project

To compile and run the project so you can test-drive the application, select **Debug > Start without debugging** or simply type *Ctrl + F5*. If the program compiles correctly, the IDE opens a Command Prompt window and executes the program (Fig. 1.16)—we changed the Command Prompt's color scheme to make the screen captures more readable. The application displays "Please type your first guess.", then displays a question mark (?) as a prompt on the next line.

---

10. For the multiple source-code-file programs that you'll see beginning in Chapter 3, drag all the files for a given program to the **Source Files** folder. When you begin creating multiple source-code-file programs yourself, you can right click the **Source Files** folder and select **Add > New Item...** to display a dialog for adding a new file.

Fig. 1.16 | Command Prompt showing the running program.

Step 6: Entering Your First Guess

Type **500** and press *Enter*. The application displays "Too high. Try again." (Fig. 1.17), meaning that the value you entered is greater than the number the application chose as the correct guess.

Fig. 1.17 | Entering an initial guess and receiving feedback.

Step 7: Entering Another Guess

At the next prompt, enter **250** (Fig. 1.18). The application displays "Too high. Try again.", because the value you entered once again is greater than the correct guess.

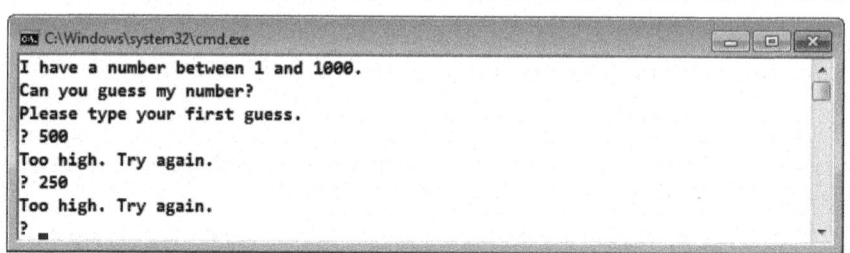

Fig. 1.18 | Entering a second guess and receiving feedback.

Step 8: Entering Additional Guesses

Continue to play the game (Fig. 1.19) by entering values until you guess the correct number. When you guess correctly, the application displays "Excellent! You guessed the number."

Step 9: Playing the Game Again or Exiting the Application

After you guess the correct number, the application asks if you'd like to play another game. At the "Would you like to play again (y or n)?" prompt, entering the one character **y**

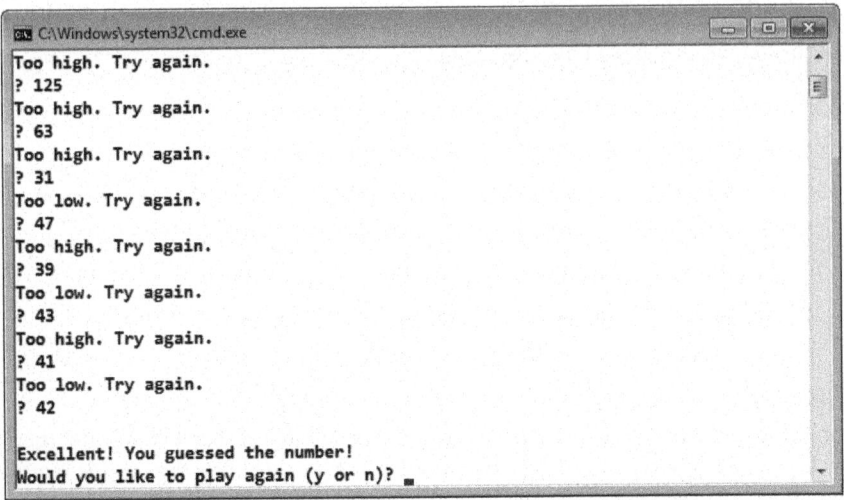

Fig. 1.19 | Entering additional guesses and guessing the correct number.

causes the application to choose a new number and displays the message "Please type your first guess." followed by a question-mark prompt so you can make your first guess in the new game. Entering the character **n** terminates the application. Each time you execute this application from the beginning (*Step 5*), it will choose the same numbers for you to guess.

1.10.2 Compiling and Running Using GNU C++ on Linux

For this test drive, we assume that you read the Before You Begin section and that you placed the downloaded examples in your home directory on your Linux system. Please see your instructor if you have any questions regarding copying the files to your home directory. In this section's figures, we use **bold** text to highlight the text that you type. The prompt in the shell on our system uses the tilde (~) character to represent the home directory, and each prompt ends with the dollar sign ($) character. The prompt will vary among Linux systems.

Step 1: Locating the Completed Application
From a Linux shell, use the command cd to change to the completed application directory (Fig. 1.20) by typing

```
cd examples/ch01
```

then pressing *Enter*.

```
~$ cd examples/ch01
~/examples/ch01$
```

Fig. 1.20 | Changing to the GuessNumber application's directory.

Step 2: Compiling the Application

Before running the application, you must first compile it (Fig. 1.21) by typing

```
g++ -std=c++14 GuessNumber.cpp -o GuessNumber
```

This command compiles the application for C++14 (the current C++ version) and produces an executable file called GuessNumber.

```
~/examples/ch01$ g++ -std=c++14 GuessNumber.cpp -o GuessNumber
~/examples/ch01$
```

Fig. 1.21 | Compiling the GuessNumber application using the g++ command.

Step 3: Running the Application

To run the executable file GuessNumber, type ./GuessNumber at the next prompt, then press *Enter* (Fig. 1.22). The ./ tells Linux to run from the current directory and is required to indicate that GuessNumber is an executable file.

```
~/examples/ch01$ ./GuessNumber
I have a number between 1 and 1000.
Can you guess my number?
Please type your first guess.
?
```

Fig. 1.22 | Running the GuessNumber application.

Step 4: Entering Your First Guess

The application displays "Please type your first guess.", then displays a question mark (?) as a prompt on the next line (Fig. 1.22). At the prompt, enter **500** (Fig. 1.23). [Note that the outputs may vary based on the compiler you're using.]

```
~/examples/ch01$ ./GuessNumber
I have a number between 1 and 1000.
Can you guess my number?
Please type your first guess.
? 500
Too high. Try again.
?
```

Fig. 1.23 | Entering an initial guess.

Step 5: Entering Another Guess

The application displays "Too high. Try again.", meaning that the value you entered is greater than the number the application chose as the correct guess (Fig. 1.23). At the next prompt, enter **250** (Fig. 1.24). This time the application displays "Too low. Try again.", because the value you entered is less than the correct guess.

```
~/examples/ch01$ ./GuessNumber
I have a number between 1 and 1000.
Can you guess my number?
Please type your first guess.
? 500
Too high. Try again.
? 250
Too low. Try again.
?
```

Fig. 1.24 | Entering a second guess and receiving feedback.

Step 6: Entering Additional Guesses

Continue to play the game (Fig. 1.25) by entering values until you guess the correct number. When you guess correctly, the application displays "Excellent! You guessed the number."

```
Too low. Try again.
? 375
Too low. Try again.
? 437
Too high. Try again.
? 406
Too high. Try again.
? 391
Too high. Try again.
? 383
Too low. Try again.
? 387
Too high. Try again.
? 385
Too high. Try again.
? 384
Excellent! You guessed the number.
Would you like to play again (y or n)?
```

Fig. 1.25 | Entering additional guesses and guessing the correct number.

Step 7: Playing the Game Again or Exiting the Application

After you guess the correct number, the application asks if you'd like to play another game. At the "Would you like to play again (y or n)?" prompt, entering the one character **y** causes the application to choose a new number and displays the message "Please type your first guess." followed by a question-mark prompt so you can make your first guess in the new game. Entering the character **n** ends the application, returns you to the shell and awaits your next command. Each time you execute this application from the beginning (i.e., *Step 3*), it will choose the same numbers for you to guess.

1.10.3 Compiling and Running with Xcode on Mac OS X

In this section, we present how to run a C++ program on a Mac OS X using Apple's Xcode IDE.

Step 1: Checking Your Setup

It's important to read this book's Before You Begin section to make sure that you've installed Apple's Xcode IDE and copied the book's examples to your hard drive correctly.

Step 2: Launching Xcode

Open a Finder window, select **Applications** and double click the Xcode icon (■). If this is your first time running Xcode, the **Welcome to Xcode** window will appear (Fig. 1.26). Close this window for now—you can access it any time by selecting **Window > Welcome to Xcode**. We use the **>** character to indicate selecting a menu item from a menu. For example, the notation **File > Open...** indicates that you should select the **Open...** menu item from the **File** menu.

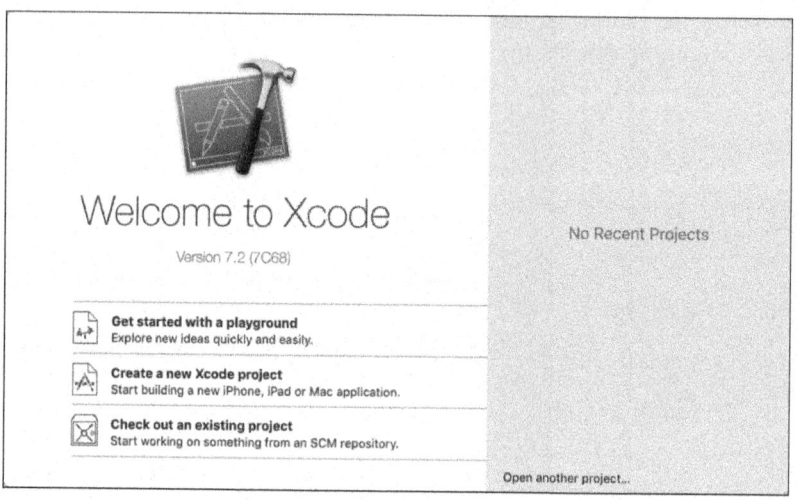

Fig. 1.26 | Welcome to Xcode window.

Step 3: Creating a Project

A project is a group of related files, such as the C++ source-code files that compose an application. The Xcode projects we created for this book's examples are **OS X Command Line Tool** projects that you'll execute directly in the IDE. To create a project:

1. Select **File > New > Project....**

2. In the **OS X** subcategory **Application**, select **Command Line Tool** and click **Next**.

3. Provide a name for your project in the **Product Name** field—we specified **Guess Number**.

4. Ensure that the selected **Language** is **C++** and click **Next**.

5. Specify where you want to store your project, then click **Create**. (See the Before You Begin section for information on configuring a project to use C++14.)

Figure 1.27 shows the workspace window that appears after you create the project. By default, Xcode creates a main.cpp source-code file containing a simple program that displays "Hello, World!". The window is divided into four main areas below the toolbar: the

Navigator area, **Editor** area and **Utilities** area are displayed initially. We'll explain momentarily how to display the **Debug** area in which you'll run and interact with the program.

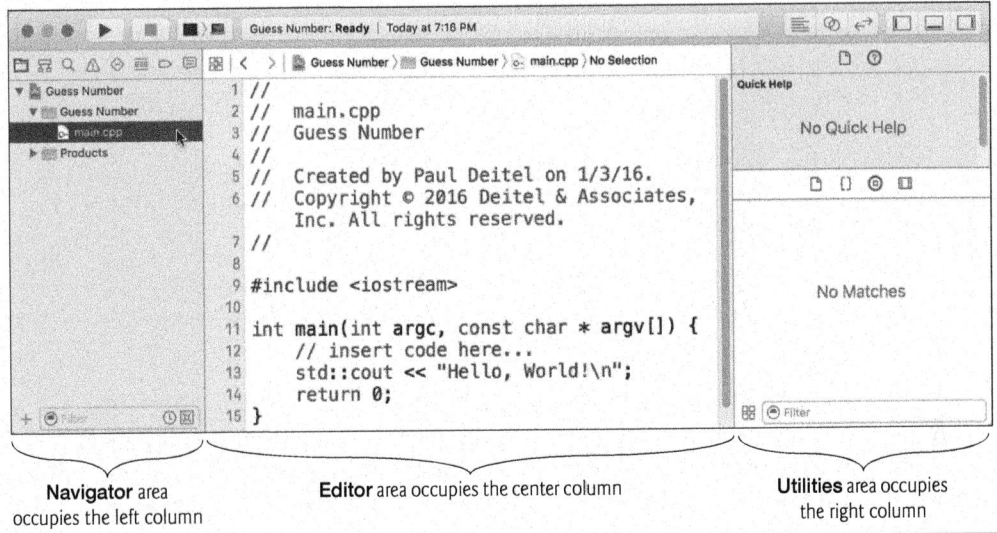

Fig. 1.27 | Sample Xcode C++ project with main.cpp selected.

At the left of the workspace window is the **Navigator** area, which has icons at its top for the *navigators* that can be displayed there. For this book, you'll primarily work with

- **Project** (▣)—Shows all the files and folders in your project.
- **Issue** (⚠)—Shows you warnings and errors generated by the compiler.

You choose which navigator to display by clicking the corresponding button above the **Navigator** area of the window.

To the right of the **Navigator** area is the **Editor** area for editing source code. This area is always displayed in your workspace window. When you select a file in the **Project** navigator, the file's contents are displayed in the **Editor** area. At the right side of the workspace window is the **Utilities** area, which you will not use in this book. The **Debug** area, when displayed, appears below the **Editor** area.

The toolbar contains options for executing a program (Fig. 1.28(a)), a display area (Fig. 1.28(b)) to shows the progress of tasks executing in Xcode (such as the compilation status) and buttons (Fig. 1.28(c)) for hiding and showing areas in the workspace window.

a) The left side of the toolbar

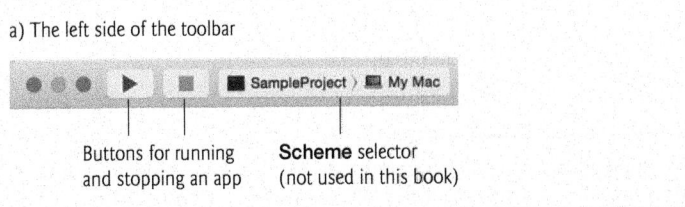

Buttons for running   **Scheme** selector
and stopping an app   (not used in this book)

Fig. 1.28 | Xcode 7 toolbar. (Part 1 of 2.)

b) The middle of the toolbar

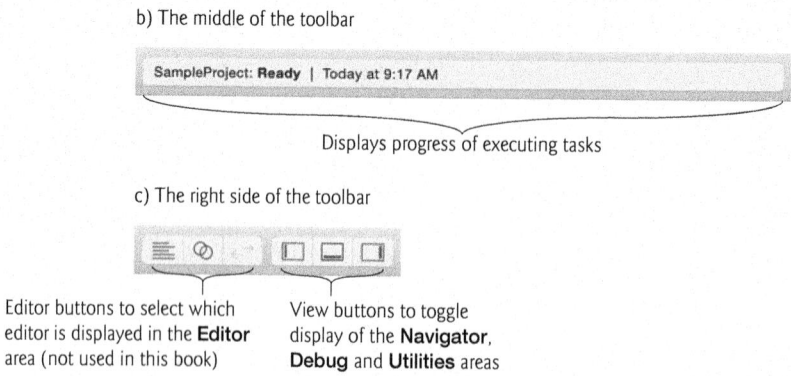

Displays progress of executing tasks

c) The right side of the toolbar

Editor buttons to select which
editor is displayed in the **Editor**
area (not used in this book)

View buttons to toggle
display of the **Navigator**,
Debug and **Utilities** areas

Fig. 1.28 | Xcode 7 toolbar. (Part 2 of 2.)

Step 4: Deleting the main.cpp File from the Project

You won't use main.cpp in this test-drive, so you should delete the file. In the **Project** navigator, right click the main.cpp file and select **Delete**. In the dialog that appears, select **Move to Trash** to delete the file from your system—the file will not be removed completely until you empty your trash.

Step 5: Adding the GuessNumber.cpp File into the Project

Next, you'll add GuessNumber.cpp to the project you created in *Step 3*. In a Finder window, open the ch01 folder in the book's examples folder, then drag GuessNumber.cpp onto the **Guess Number** folder in the **Project** navigator. In the dialog that appears, ensure that **Copy items if needed** is checked, then click **Finish.**[11]

Step 6: Compiling and Running the Project

To compile and run the project so you can test-drive the application, simply click the run (▶) button at the left side of Xcode's toolbar. If the program compiles correctly, Xcode opens the **Debug** area (at the bottom of the **Editor** area) and executes the program in the right half of the **Debug** area (Fig. 1.29). The application displays "Please type your first guess.", then displays a question mark (?) as a prompt on the next line.

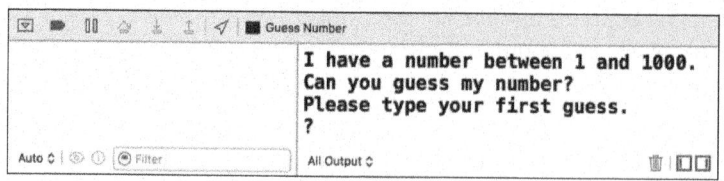

Fig. 1.29 | Debug area showing the running program.

---

11. For the multiple source-code-file programs that you'll see beginning in Chapter 3, drag all the files for a given program to the project's folder. When you begin creating programs with multiple source-code files, you can right click the project's folder and select **New File...** to display a dialog for adding a new file.

Step 7: Entering Your First Guess

Click in the **Debug** area, then type **500** and press *Return*. The application displays "Too low. Try again." (Fig. 1.30), meaning that the value you entered is less than the number the application chose as the correct guess.

```
I have a number between 1 and 1000.
Can you guess my number?
Please type your first guess.
? 500
Too low. Try again.
?
```

Fig. 1.30 | Entering an initial guess and receiving feedback.

Step 8: Entering Another Guess

At the next prompt, enter **750** (Fig. 1.31). The application displays "Too low. Try again.", because the value you entered once again is less than the correct guess.

```
I have a number between 1 and 1000.
Can you guess my number?
Please type your first guess.
? 500
Too low. Try again.
? 750
Too low. Try again.
?
```

Fig. 1.31 | Entering a second guess and receiving feedback.

Step 9: Entering Additional Guesses

Continue to play the game (Fig. 1.32) by entering values until you guess the correct number. When you guess correctly, the application displays "Excellent! You guessed the number."

```
Too low. Try again.
? 875
Too high. Try again.
? 812
Too high. Try again.
? 781
Too low. Try again.
? 797
Too low. Try again.
? 805
Too low. Try again.
? 808

Excellent! You guessed the number!
Would you like to play again (y or n)?
```

Fig. 1.32 | Entering additional guesses and guessing the correct number.

Playing the Game Again or Exiting the Application

After you guess the correct number, the application asks if you'd like to play another game. At the "Would you like to play again (y or n)?" prompt, entering the character **y** causes the application to choose a new number and displays the message "Please type your first guess." followed by a question-mark prompt so you can make your first guess in the new game. Entering the character **n** terminates the application. Each time you execute this application from the beginning (*Step 6*), it will choose the same numbers for you to guess.

1.11 Operating Systems

Operating systems are software systems that make using computers more convenient for users, application developers and system administrators. They provide services that allow each application to execute safely, efficiently and *concurrently* (i.e., in parallel) with other applications. The software that contains the core components of the operating system is called the kernel. Popular desktop operating systems include Linux, Windows and OS X (formerly called Mac OS X)—we used all three in developing this book. Popular mobile operating systems used in smartphones and tablets include Google's Android, Apple's iOS (for iPhone, iPad and iPod Touch devices) and Windows 10 Mobile. You can develop applications in C++ for all of these operating systems.

1.11.1 Windows—A Proprietary Operating System

In the mid-1980s, Microsoft developed the Windows operating system, consisting of a graphical user interface built on top of DOS (Disk Operating System)—an enormously popular personal-computer operating system that users interacted with by typing commands. Windows borrowed from many concepts (such as icons, menus and windows) developed by Xerox PARC and popularized by early Apple Macintosh operating systems. Windows 10 is Microsoft's latest operating system—its features include enhancements to the **Start** menu and user interface, Cortana personal assistant for voice interactions, Action Center for receiving notifications, Microsoft's new Edge web browser, and more. Windows is a *proprietary* operating system—it's controlled by Microsoft exclusively. Windows is by far the world's most widely used desktop operating system.

1.11.2 Linux—An Open-Source Operating System

The Linux operating system is perhaps the greatest success of the *open-source* movement. Open-source software departs from the *proprietary* software development style that dominated software's early years. With open-source development, individuals and companies *contribute* their efforts in developing, maintaining and evolving software in exchange for the right to use that software for their own purposes, typically at *no charge*. Open-source code is often scrutinized by a much larger audience than proprietary software, so errors often get removed faster. Open source also encourages innovation. Enterprise systems companies, such as IBM, Oracle and many others, have made significant investments in Linux open-source development.

Some key organizations in the open-source community are

- the Eclipse Foundation (the Eclipse Integrated Development Environment helps programmers conveniently develop software)

- the Mozilla Foundation (creators of the Firefox web browser)

- the Apache Software Foundation (creators of the Apache web server used to develop web-based applications)
- GitHub (which provides tools for managing open-source projects—it has millions of them under development).

Rapid improvements to computing and communications, decreasing costs and open-source software have made it much easier and more economical to create a software-based business now than just a decade ago. A great example is Facebook, which was launched from a college dorm room and built with open-source software.

The Linux kernel is the core of the most popular open-source, freely distributed, full-featured operating system. It's developed by a loosely organized team of volunteers and is popular in servers, personal computers and embedded systems (such as the computer systems at the heart of smartphones, smart TVs and automobile systems). Unlike that of proprietary operating systems like Microsoft's Windows and Apple's OS X, Linux source code (the program code) is available to the public for examination and modification and is free to download and install. As a result, Linux users benefit from a huge community of developers actively debugging and improving the kernel, and the ability to customize the operating system to meet specific needs.

A variety of issues—such as Microsoft's market power, the small number of user-friendly Linux applications and the diversity of Linux distributions, such as Red Hat Linux, Ubuntu Linux and many others—have prevented widespread Linux use on desktop computers. Linux has become extremely popular on servers and in embedded systems, such as Google's Android-based smartphones.

1.11.3 Apple's OS X; Apple's iOS for iPhone®, iPad® and iPod Touch® Devices

Apple, founded in 1976 by Steve Jobs and Steve Wozniak, quickly became a leader in personal computing. In 1979, Jobs and several Apple employees visited Xerox PARC (Palo Alto Research Center) to learn about Xerox's desktop computer that featured a graphical user interface (GUI). That GUI served as the inspiration for the Apple Macintosh, launched with much fanfare in a memorable Super Bowl ad in 1984.

The Objective-C programming language, created by Brad Cox and Tom Love at Stepstone in the early 1980s, added capabilities for object-oriented programming (OOP) to the C programming language. Steve Jobs left Apple in 1985 and founded NeXT Inc. In 1988, NeXT licensed Objective-C from StepStone and developed an Objective-C compiler and libraries which were used as the platform for the NeXTSTEP operating system's user interface, and Interface Builder—used to construct graphical user interfaces.

Jobs returned to Apple in 1996 when Apple bought NeXT. Apple's OS X operating system is a descendant of NeXTSTEP. Apple's proprietary operating system, iOS, is derived from Apple's OS X and is used in the iPhone, iPad and iPod Touch devices. In 2014, Apple introduced its new Swift programming language, which became open source in 2015. The iOS app-development community is gradually shifting from Objective-C to Swift.

1.11.4 Google's Android

Android—the fastest growing mobile and smartphone operating system—is based on the Linux kernel and Java. Android apps can also be developed in C++ and C. One benefit of developing Android apps is the openness of the platform. The operating system is open source and free.

The Android operating system was developed by Android, Inc., which was acquired by Google in 2005. In 2007, the Open Handset Alliance™

```
http://www.openhandsetalliance.com/oha_members.html
```

was formed to develop, maintain and evolve Android, driving innovation in mobile technology and improving the user experience while reducing costs. According to IDC, after the first six months of 2015, Android had 82.8% of the global smartphone market share, compared to 13.9% for Apple, 2.6% for Microsoft and 0.3% for Blackberry.[12] The Android operating system is used in numerous smartphones, e-reader devices, tablets, in-store touch-screen kiosks, cars, robots, multimedia players and more. There are now more than 1.4 billion Android users.[13]

1.12 The Internet and the World Wide Web

In the late 1960s, ARPA—the Advanced Research Projects Agency of the United States Department of Defense—rolled out plans for networking the main computer systems of approximately a dozen ARPA-funded universities and research institutions. The computers were to be connected with communications lines operating at speeds on the order of 50,000 bits per second, a stunning rate at a time when most people (of the few who even had networking access) were connecting over telephone lines to computers at a rate of 110 bits per second. Academic research was about to take a giant leap forward. ARPA proceeded to implement what quickly became known as the ARPANET, the precursor to today's Internet. Today's fastest Internet speeds are on the order of billions of bits per second with trillion-bits-per-second speeds on the horizon!

Things worked out differently from the original plan. Although the ARPANET enabled researchers to network their computers, its main benefit proved to be the capability for quick and easy communication via what came to be known as electronic mail (e-mail). This is true even on today's Internet, with e-mail, instant messaging, file transfer and social media such as Facebook and Twitter enabling billions of people worldwide to communicate quickly and easily.

The protocol (set of rules) for communicating over the ARPANET became known as the Transmission Control Protocol (TCP). TCP ensured that messages, consisting of sequentially numbered pieces called *packets*, were properly routed from sender to receiver, arrived intact and were assembled in the correct order.

The Internet: A Network of Networks

In parallel with the early evolution of the Internet, organizations worldwide were implementing their own networks for both intraorganization (that is, within an organization) and interorganization (that is, between organizations) communication. A huge variety of networking hardware and software appeared. One challenge was to enable these different

---

12. http://www.idc.com/prodserv/smartphone-os-market-share.jsp.
13. http://www.techtimes.com/articles/90028/20151002/google-says-android-has-more-than-1-4-billion-active-users-worldwide-with-300-million-on-lollipop.htm.

networks to communicate with each other. ARPA accomplished this by developing the Internet Protocol (IP), which created a true "network of networks," the current architecture of the Internet. The combined set of protocols is now called TCP/IP.

Businesses rapidly realized that by using the Internet, they could improve their operations and offer new and better services to their clients. Companies started spending large amounts of money to develop and enhance their Internet presence. This generated fierce competition among communications carriers and hardware and software suppliers to meet the increased infrastructure demand. As a result, bandwidth—the information-carrying capacity of communications lines—on the Internet has increased tremendously, while hardware costs have plummeted.

The World Wide Web: Making the Internet User-Friendly

The World Wide Web (simply called "the web") is a collection of hardware and software associated with the Internet that allows computer users to locate and view multimedia-based documents (documents with various combinations of text, graphics, animations, audios and videos) on almost any subject. The introduction of the web was a relatively recent event. In 1989, Tim Berners-Lee of CERN (the European Organization for Nuclear Research) began to develop a technology for sharing information via "hyperlinked" text documents. Berners-Lee called his invention the HyperText Markup Language (HTML). He also wrote communication protocols such as HyperText Transfer Protocol (HTTP) to form the backbone of his new hypertext information system, which he referred to as the World Wide Web.

In 1994, Berners-Lee founded the World Wide Web Consortium (W3C, http://www.w3.org), devoted to developing web technologies. One of the W3C's primary goals is to make the web universally accessible to everyone regardless of disabilities, language or culture.

Web Services

Web services are software components stored on one computer that can be accessed by an app (or other software component) on another computer over the Internet. With web services, you can create *mashups*, which enable you to rapidly develop apps by combining complementary web services, often from multiple organizations and possibly other forms of information feeds. For example, 100 Destinations (http://www.100destinations.co.uk) combines the photos and tweets from Twitter with the mapping capabilities of Google Maps to allow you to explore countries around the world through the photos of others.

Programmableweb (http://www.programmableweb.com/) provides a directory of over 11,150 APIs and 7,300 mashups, plus how-to guides and sample code for creating your own mashups. According to Programmableweb, the three most widely used APIs for mashups are Google Maps, Twitter and YouTube.

Ajax

Ajax technology helps Internet-based applications perform like desktop applications—a difficult task, given that such applications suffer transmission delays as data is shuttled back and forth between your computer and server computers on the Internet. Using Ajax, applications like Google Maps have achieved excellent performance and approach the look-and-feel of desktop applications.

The Internet of Things
The Internet is no longer just a network of computers—it's an Internet of Things. A *thing* is any object with an IP address and the ability to send data automatically over the Internet—e.g., a car with a transponder for paying tolls, a heart monitor implanted in a human, a smart meter that reports energy usage, mobile apps that can track your movement and location, and smart thermostats that adjust room temperatures based on weather forecasts and activity in the home.

1.13 Some Key Software Development Terminology

Figure 1.33 lists a number of buzzwords that you'll hear in the software development community.

Technology	Description
Agile software development	Agile software development is a set of methodologies that try to get software implemented faster and using fewer resources. Check out the Agile Alliance (www.agilealliance.org) and the Agile Manifesto (www.agilemanifesto.org).
Refactoring	Refactoring involves reworking programs to make them clearer and easier to maintain while preserving their correctness and functionality. It's widely employed with agile development methodologies. Many IDEs contain built-in *refactoring tools* to do major portions of the reworking automatically.
Design patterns	Design patterns are proven architectures for constructing flexible and maintainable object-oriented software. The field of design patterns tries to enumerate those recurring patterns, encouraging software designers to *reuse* them to develop better-quality software using less time, money and effort.
LAMP	LAMP is an acronym for the open-source technologies that many developers use to build web applications inexpensively—it stands for *Linux, Apache, MySQL* and *PHP* (or *Perl* or *Python*—two other popular scripting languages). MySQL is an open-source database-management system. PHP is a popular open-source server-side "scripting" language for developing web applications. Apache is the most popular web server software. The equivalent for Windows development is WAMP—*Windows, Apache, MySQL* and *PHP*.

Fig. 1.33 | Software technologies. (Part 1 of 2.)

Technology	Description
Software as a Service (SaaS)	Software has generally been viewed as a product; most software still is offered this way. If you want to run an application, you buy a software package from a software vendor—often a CD, DVD or web download. You then install that software on your computer and run it as needed. As new versions appear, you upgrade your software, often at considerable cost in time and money. This process can become cumbersome for organizations that must maintain tens of thousands of systems on a diverse array of computer equipment. With Software as a Service (SaaS), the software runs on servers elsewhere on the Internet. When that server is updated, all clients worldwide see the new capabilities—no local installation is needed. You access the service through a browser. Browsers are quite portable, so you can run the same applications on a wide variety of computers from anywhere in the world. Salesforce.com, Google, Microsoft and many other companies offer SaaS.
Platform as a Service (PaaS)	Platform as a Service (PaaS) provides a computing platform for developing and running applications as a service over the web, rather than installing the tools on your computer. Some PaaS providers are Google App Engine, Amazon EC2 and Windows Azure™.
Cloud computing	SaaS and PaaS are examples of cloud computing. You can use software and data stored in the "cloud"—i.e., accessed on remote computers (or servers) via the Internet and available on demand—rather than having it stored locally on your desktop, notebook computer or mobile device. This allows you to increase or decrease computing resources to meet your needs at any given time, which is more cost effective than purchasing hardware to provide enough storage and processing power to meet occasional peak demands. Cloud computing also saves money by shifting to the service provider the burden of managing these apps (such as installing and upgrading the software, security, backups and disaster recovery).
Software Development Kit (SDK)	Software Development Kits (SDKs) include the tools and documentation developers use to program applications.

Fig. 1.33 | Software technologies. (Part 2 of 2.)

Software is complex. Large, real-world software applications can take many months or even years to design and implement. When large software products are under development, they typically are made available to the user communities as a series of releases, each more complete and polished than the last (Fig. 1.34).

Version	Description
Alpha	*Alpha* software is the earliest release of a software product that's still under active development. Alpha versions are often buggy, incomplete and unstable and are released to a relatively small number of developers for testing new features, getting early feedback, etc.
Beta	*Beta* versions are released to a larger number of developers later in the development process after most major bugs have been fixed and new features are nearly complete. Beta software is more stable, but still subject to change.
Release candidates	*Release candidates* are generally *feature complete*, (mostly) bug free and ready for use by the community, which provides a diverse testing environment—the software is used on different systems, with varying constraints and for a variety of purposes.
Final release	Any bugs that appear in the release candidate are corrected, and eventually the final product is released to the general public. Software companies often distribute incremental updates over the Internet.
Continuous beta	Software that's developed using this approach (for example, Google search or Gmail) generally does not have version numbers. It's hosted in the *cloud* (not installed on your computer) and is constantly evolving so that users always have the latest version.

Fig. 1.34 | Software product-release terminology.

1.14 C++11 and C++14: The Latest C++ Versions

C++11 was published by ISO/IEC in 2011. Bjarne Stroustrup, the creator of C++, expressed his vision for the future of the language—the main goals were to make C++ easier to learn, improve library-building capabilities and increase compatibility with the C programming language. C++11 extended the C++ Standard Library and added several features and enhancements to improve performance and security. The three compilers we use in this book

- Visual Studio 2015 Community Edition (Microsoft Windows)
- GNU C++ (Linux)
- Clang/LLVM in Xcode (Mac OS X)

have implemented most C++11 features.

The current C++ standard, C++14, was published by ISO/IEC in 2014. It added several language features and C++ Standard Library enhancements, and fixed bugs from C++11. Throughout this book, we cover features of C++11 and C++14 as appropriate for a book at this level. For a list of C++11 and C++14 features and the compilers that support them, visit

```
http://en.cppreference.com/w/cpp/compiler_support
```

The next version of the C++ standard, C++17, is currently under development. For a list of proposed features, see

```
https://en.wikipedia.org/wiki/C%2B%2B17
```

17

1.15 Boost C++ Libraries

The Boost C++ Libraries (www.boost.org) are free, open-source libraries created by members of the C++ community. They are peer reviewed and portable across many compilers and platforms. Boost has grown to over 130 libraries, with more being added regularly. Today there are thousands of programmers in the Boost open-source community. The Boost libraries work well with the existing C++ Standard Library and often act as a proving ground for capabilities that are eventually absorbed into the C++ Standard Library. For example, the C++11 "regular expression" and "smart pointer" libraries, among others, are based on work done by the Boost community.

Regular expressions are used to match specific character patterns in text. They can be used to validate data to ensure that it's in a particular format, to replace parts of one string with another, or to split a string.

Many common bugs in C and C++ code are related to pointers, a powerful programming capability that C++ absorbed from C. As you'll see, smart pointers help you avoid some key errors associated with traditional pointers.

1.16 Keeping Up to Date with Information Technologies

Figure 1.35 lists key technical and business publications that will help you stay up-to-date with the latest news, trends and technology. You can also find a growing list of Internet- and web-related Resource Centers at www.deitel.com/ResourceCenters.html.

Publication	URL
AllThingsD	allthingsd.com
Bloomberg BusinessWeek	www.businessweek.com
CNET	news.cnet.com
Communications of the ACM	cacm.acm.org
Computerworld	www.computerworld.com
Engadget	www.engadget.com
eWeek	www.eweek.com
Fast Company	www.fastcompany.com
Fortune	fortune.com
GigaOM	gigaom.com

Fig. 1.35 | Technical and business publications. (Part 1 of 2.)

Publication	URL
Hacker News	news.ycombinator.com
IEEE Computer Magazine	www.computer.org/portal/web/computingnow/computer
InfoWorld	www.infoworld.com
Mashable	mashable.com
PCWorld	www.pcworld.com
SD Times	www.sdtimes.com
Slashdot	slashdot.org
Stack Overflow	stackoverflow.com
Technology Review	technologyreview.com
Techcrunch	techcrunch.com
The Next Web	thenextweb.com
The Verge	www.theverge.com
Wired	www.wired.com

Fig. 1.35 | Technical and business publications. (Part 2 of 2.)

Self-Review Exercises

1.1   Fill in the blanks in each of the following statements:
   a) Computers process data under the control of sets of instructions called _____.
   b) The key logical units of the computer are the _____, _____, _____, _____, _____ and _____.
   c) The three types of languages discussed in the chapter are _____, _____ and _____.
   d) The programs that translate high-level language programs into machine language are called _____.
   e) _____ is an operating system for mobile devices based on the Linux kernel and Java.
   f) _____ software is generally feature complete and (supposedly) bug free and ready for use by the community.
   g) The Wii Remote, as well as many smartphones, uses a(n) _____ which allows the device to respond to motion.

1.2   Fill in the blanks in each of the following sentences about the C++ environment.
   a) C++ programs are normally typed into a computer using a(n) _____ program.
   b) In a C++ system, a(n) _____ program executes before the compiler's translation phase begins.
   c) The _____ program combines the output of the compiler with various library functions to produce an executable program.
   d) The _____ program transfers the executable program from disk to memory.

1.3   Fill in the blanks in each of the following statements (based on Section 1.8):
   a) Objects have the property of _____—although objects may know how to communicate with one another across well-defined interfaces, they normally are not allowed to know how other objects are implemented.

b) C++ programmers concentrate on creating _____, which contain data members and the member functions that manipulate those data members and provide services to clients.

c) The process of analyzing and designing a system from an object-oriented point of view is called _____.

d) With _____, new classes of objects are derived by absorbing characteristics of existing classes, then adding unique characteristics of their own.

e) _____ is a graphical language that allows people who design software systems to use an industry-standard notation to represent them.

f) The size, shape, color and weight of an object are considered _____ of the object's class.

Answers to Self-Review Exercises

1.1   a) programs. b) input unit, output unit, memory unit, central processing unit, arithmetic and logic unit, secondary storage unit. c) machine languages, assembly languages, high-level languages. d) compilers. e) Android. f) Release candidate. g) accelerometer.

1.2   a) editor. b) preprocessor. c) linker. d) loader.

1.3   a) information hiding. b) classes. c) object-oriented analysis and design (OOAD). d) inheritance. e) The Unified Modeling Language (UML). f) attributes.

Exercises

1.4   Fill in the blanks in each of the following statements:

a) The logical unit of the computer that receives information from outside the computer for use by the computer is the _____.

b) The process of instructing the computer to solve a problem is called _____.

c) _____ is a type of computer language that uses English-like abbreviations for machine-language instructions.

d) _____ is a logical unit of the computer that sends information which has already been processed by the computer to various devices so that it may be used outside the computer.

e) _____ and _____ are logical units of the computer that retain information.

f) _____ is a logical unit of the computer that performs calculations.

g) _____ is a logical unit of the computer that makes logical decisions.

h) _____ languages are most convenient to the programmer for writing programs quickly and easily.

i) The only language a computer can directly understand is that computer's _____.

j) _____ is a logical unit of the computer that coordinates the activities of all the other logical units.

1.5   Fill in the blanks in each of the following statements:

a) _____ initially became widely known as the development language of the UNIX operating system.

b) The _____ programming language was developed by Bjarne Stroustrup in the early 1980s at Bell Laboratories.

1.6   Fill in the blanks in each of the following statements:

a) C++ programs normally go through six phases—_____, _____, _____, _____, _____ and _____.

b) A(n) _____ provides many tools that support the software development process, such as editors for writing and editing programs, debuggers for locating logic errors in programs, and many other features.

I.7   You're probably wearing on your wrist one of the world's most common types of objects—a watch. Discuss how each of the following terms and concepts applies to the notion of a watch: object, attributes, behaviors, class, inheritance (consider, for example, an alarm clock), modeling, messages, encapsulation, interface and information hiding.

Making a Difference

Throughout the book we've included Making a Difference exercises in which you'll be asked to work on problems that really matter to individuals, communities, countries and the world.

I.8   *(Test Drive: Carbon Footprint Calculator)* Some scientists believe that carbon emissions, especially from the burning of fossil fuels, contribute significantly to global warming and that this can be combatted if individuals take steps to limit their use of carbon-based fuels. Various organizations and individuals are increasingly concerned about their "carbon footprints." Websites such as TerraPass

    http://www.terrapass.com/carbon-footprint-calculator-2/

and Carbon Footprint

    http://www.carbonfootprint.com/calculator.aspx

provide carbon footprint calculators. Test drive these calculators to determine your carbon footprint. Exercises in later chapters will ask you to program your own carbon footprint calculator. To prepare for this, research the formulas for calculating carbon footprints.

I.9   *(Test Drive: Body Mass Index Calculator)* By recent estimates, two-thirds of the people in the United States are overweight and about half of those are obese. This causes significant increases in illnesses such as diabetes and heart disease. To determine whether a person is overweight or obese, you can use a measure called the body mass index (BMI). The United States Department of Health and Human Services provides a BMI calculator at http://www.nhlbi.nih.gov/guidelines/obesity/BMI/bmicalc.htm. Use it to calculate your own BMI. An exercise in Chapter 2 will ask you to program your own BMI calculator. To prepare for this, research the formulas for calculating BMI.

I.10   *(Attributes of Hybrid Vehicles)* In this chapter you learned the basics of classes. Now you'll begin "fleshing out" aspects of a class called "Hybrid Vehicle." Hybrid vehicles are becoming increasingly popular, because they often get much better mileage than purely gasoline-powered vehicles. Browse the web and study the features of four or five of today's popular hybrid cars, then list as many of their hybrid-related attributes as you can. For example, common attributes include city-miles-per-gallon and highway-miles-per-gallon. Also list the attributes of the batteries (type, weight, etc.).

I.11   *(Gender Neutrality)* Some people want to eliminate sexism in all forms of communication. You've been asked to create a program that can process a paragraph of text and replace gender-specific words with gender-neutral ones. Assuming that you've been given a list of gender-specific words and their gender-neutral replacements (e.g., replace "wife" with "spouse," "man" with "person," "daughter" with "child" and so on), explain the procedure you'd use to read through a paragraph of text and manually perform these replacements. How might your procedure generate a strange term like "woperchild," which is actually listed in the Urban Dictionary (www.urbandictionary.com)? In Chapter 4, you'll learn that a more formal term for "procedure" is "algorithm," and that an algorithm specifies the steps to be performed and the order in which to perform them.

I.12   *(Privacy)* Some online e-mail services save all e-mail correspondence for some period of time. Suppose a disgruntled employee of one of these online e-mail services were to post all of the e-mail correspondences for millions of people, including yours, on the Internet. Discuss the issues.

I.13   *(Programmer Responsibility and Liability)* As a programmer in industry, you may develop software that could affect people's health or even their lives. Suppose a software bug in one of your programs were to cause a cancer patient to receive an excessive dose during radiation therapy and that the person either was severely injured or died. Discuss the issues.

1.14   *(2010 "Flash Crash")* An example of the consequences of our dependency on computers was the so-called "flash crash" which occurred on May 6, 2010, when the U.S. stock market fell precipitously in a matter of minutes, wiping out trillions of dollars of investments, and then recovered within minutes. Use the Internet to investigate the causes of this crash and discuss the issues it raises.

Making a Difference Resources

The *Microsoft Imagine Cup* is a global competition in which students use technology to try to solve some of the world's most difficult problems, such as environmental sustainability, ending hunger, emergency response, literacy and more. For more information about the competition and to learn about previous winners' projects, visit `https://www.imaginecup.com/Custom/Index/About`. You can also find several project ideas submitted by worldwide charitable organizations. For additional ideas for programming projects that can make a difference, search the web for "making a difference" and visit the following websites:

`http://www.un.org/millenniumgoals`
The United Nations Millennium Project seeks solutions to major worldwide issues such as environmental sustainability, gender equality, child and maternal health, universal education and more.

`http://www.ibm.com/smarterplanet`
The IBM® Smarter Planet website discusses how IBM is using technology to solve issues related to business, cloud computing, education, sustainability and more.

`http://www.gatesfoundation.org`
The Bill and Melinda Gates Foundation provides grants to organizations that work to alleviate hunger, poverty and disease in developing countries.

`http://nethope.org`
NetHope is a collaboration of humanitarian organizations worldwide working to solve technology problems such as connectivity, emergency response and more.

`http://www.rainforestfoundation.org`
The Rainforest Foundation works to preserve rainforests and to protect the rights of the indigenous people who call the rainforests home. The site includes a list of things you can do to help.

`http://www.undp.org`
The United Nations Development Programme (UNDP) seeks solutions to global challenges such as crisis prevention and recovery, energy and the environment, democratic governance and more.

`http://www.unido.org`
The United Nations Industrial Development Organization (UNIDO) seeks to reduce poverty, give developing countries the opportunity to participate in global trade, and promote energy efficiency and sustainability.

`http://www.usaid.gov/`
USAID promotes global democracy, health, economic growth, conflict prevention, humanitarian aid and more.

2

Introduction to C++ Programming, Input/Output and Operators

Objectives

In this chapter you'll:

- Write basic computer programs in C++.

- Write input and output statements.

- Use fundamental types.

- Learn computer memory concepts.

- Use arithmetic operators.

- Understand the precedence of arithmetic operators.

- Write decision-making statements.

2.1 Introduction

We now introduce C++ programming, which facilitates a disciplined approach to program development. Most of the C++ programs you'll study in this book process data and display results. In this chapter, we present five examples that demonstrate how your programs can display messages and obtain data from the user for processing. The first three examples display messages on the screen. The next obtains two numbers from a user at the keyboard, calculates their sum and displays the result. The accompanying discussion shows you how to perform *arithmetic calculations* and save their results for later use. The fifth example demonstrates *decision making* by showing you how to *compare* two numbers, then display messages based on the comparison results. We analyze each program one line at a time to help you ease into C++ programming.

Compiling and Running Programs

We've posted videos that demonstrate compiling and running programs in Microsoft Visual C++, GNU C++ and Xcode Clang/LLVM at

http://www.deitel.com/books/cpphtp10

2.2 First Program in C++: Printing a Line of Text

Consider a simple program that prints a line of text (Fig. 2.1). This program illustrates several important features of the C++ language. The text in lines 1–10 is the program's *source code* (or *code*). The line numbers are not part of the source code.

```cpp
1  // Fig. 2.1: fig02_01.cpp
2  // Text-printing program.
3  #include <iostream> // enables program to output data to the screen
4
5  // function main begins program execution
6  int main() {
7     std::cout << "Welcome to C++!\n"; // display message
8
9     return 0; // indicate that program ended successfully
10 } // end function main
```

```
Welcome to C++!
```

Fig. 2.1 | Text-printing program.

Comments
Lines 1 and 2

```
// Fig. 2.1: fig02_01.cpp
// Text-printing program.
```

each begin with //, indicating that the remainder of each line is a comment. You insert comments to *document* your programs and to help other people read and understand them. Comments do not cause the computer to perform any action when the program is run—they're *ignored* by the C++ compiler and do *not* cause any machine-language object code to be generated. The comment Text-printing program describes the purpose of the program. A comment beginning with // is called a single-line comment because it terminates at the end of the current line. You also may use comments containing one or more lines enclosed in /* and */, as in

```
/* Fig. 2.1: fig02_01.cpp
   Text-printing program. */
```

 Good Programming Practice 2.1
Every program should begin with a comment that describes the purpose of the program.

#include *Preprocessing Directive*
Line 3

```
#include <iostream> // enables program to output data to the screen
```

is a preprocessing directive, which is a message to the C++ preprocessor (introduced in Section 1.9). Lines that begin with # are processed by the preprocessor *before* the program is compiled. This line notifies the preprocessor to include in the program the contents of the input/output stream header <iostream>. This header is a file containing information the compiler uses when compiling any program that outputs data to the screen or inputs data from the keyboard using C++'s stream input/output. The program in Fig. 2.1 outputs data to the screen, as we'll soon see. We discuss headers in more detail in Chapter 6 and explain the contents of <iostream> in Chapter 13.

 Common Programming Error 2.1
Forgetting to include the <iostream> header in a program that inputs data from the keyboard or outputs data to the screen causes the compiler to issue an error message.

Blank Lines and White Space
Line 4 is simply a *blank line*. You use blank lines, *space characters* and *tab characters* (i.e., "tabs") to make programs easier to read. Together, these characters are known as white space. White-space characters are normally *ignored* by the compiler.

The main *Function*
Line 5

```
// function main begins program execution
```

is a single-line comment indicating that program execution begins at the next line.

Line 6

```
int main() {
```

is a part of every C++ program. The parentheses after main indicate that main is a program building block called a function. C++ programs typically consist of one or more functions and classes (as you'll learn in Chapter 3). Exactly *one* function in every program *must* be named main. Figure 2.1 contains only one function. C++ programs begin executing at function main, even if main is not the first function defined in the program. The keyword int to the left of main indicates that main "returns" an integer (whole number) value. A keyword is a word in code that is reserved by C++ for a specific use. The complete list of C++ keywords can be found in Fig. 4.3. We'll explain what it means for a function to "return a value" when we demonstrate how to create your own functions in Section 3.3. For now, simply include the keyword int to the left of main in each of your programs.

The left brace, {, (end of line 6) must *begin* the body of every function. A corresponding right brace, }, (line 10) must *end* each function's body.

An Output Statement
Line 7

```
std::cout << "Welcome to C++!\n"; // display message
```

instructs the computer to perform an action—namely, to print the characters contained between the double quotation marks. Together, the quotation marks and the characters between them are called a string, a character string or a string literal. In this book, we refer to characters between double quotation marks simply as strings. White-space characters in strings are *not* ignored by the compiler.

The entire line 7, including std::cout, the << operator, the string "Welcome to C++!\n" and the semicolon (;), is called a statement. Most C++ statements end with a semicolon, also known as the statement terminator (we'll see some exceptions to this soon). Preprocessing directives (such as #include) do not end with a semicolon. Typically, output and input in C++ are accomplished with streams of data. Thus, when the preceding statement is executed, it sends the stream of characters Welcome to C++!\n to the standard output stream object—std::cout—which is normally "connected" to the screen.

Common Programming Error 2.2

Omitting the semicolon at the end of a C++ statement is a syntax error. The syntax of a programming language specifies the rules for creating proper programs in that language. A syntax error occurs when the compiler encounters code that violates C++'s language rules (i.e., its syntax). The compiler normally issues an error message to help you locate and fix the incorrect code. Syntax errors are also called compiler errors, compile-time errors or compilation errors, because the compiler detects them during the compilation phase. You cannot execute your program until you correct all the syntax errors in it. As you'll see, some compilation errors are not syntax errors.

Good Programming Practice 2.2

Indent the body of each function one level within the braces that delimit the function's body. This makes a program's functional structure stand out, making the program easier to read.

Good Programming Practice 2.3

Set a convention for the size of indent you prefer, then apply it uniformly. The tab key may be used to create indents, but tab stops may vary. We prefer three spaces per level of indent.

The std Namespace

The std:: before cout is required when we use names that we've brought into the program by the preprocessing directive #include <iostream>. The notation std::cout specifies that we are using a name, in this case cout, that belongs to namespace std. The names cin (the standard input stream) and cerr (the standard error stream)—introduced in Chapter 1—also belong to namespace std. Namespaces are an advanced C++ feature that we discuss in depth in Chapter 23, Other Topics. For now, you should simply remember to include std:: before each mention of cout, cin and cerr in a program. This can be cumbersome—we'll soon introduce using declarations and the using directive, which will enable you to omit std:: before each use of a name in the std namespace.

The Stream Insertion Operator and Escape Sequences

In the context of an output statement, the << operator is referred to as the stream insertion operator. When this program executes, the value to the operator's right, the right operand, is inserted in the output stream. Notice that the << operator points toward where the data goes. A string literal's characters *normally* print exactly as they appear between the double quotes. However, the characters \n are *not* printed on the screen (Fig. 2.1). The backslash (\) is called an escape character. It indicates that a "special" character is to be output. When a backslash is encountered in a string of characters, the next character is combined with the backslash to form an escape sequence. The escape sequence \n means newline. It causes the cursor (i.e., the current screen-position indicator) to move to the beginning of the next line on the screen. Some common escape sequences are listed in Fig. 2.2.

Escape sequence	Description
\n	Newline. Position the screen cursor to the beginning of the next line.
\t	Horizontal tab. Move the screen cursor to the next tab stop.
\r	Carriage return. Position the screen cursor to the beginning of the current line; do not advance to the next line.
\a	Alert. Sound the system bell.
\\	Backslash. Used to print a backslash character.
\'	Single quote. Used to print a single-quote character.
\"	Double quote. Used to print a double-quote character.

Fig. 2.2 | Escape sequences.

The return Statement

Line 9

```
return 0; // indicate that program ended successfully
```

is one of several means we'll use to exit a function. When the return statement is used at the end of main, as shown here, the value 0 indicates that the program has *terminated successfully*. The right brace, }, (line 10) indicates the end of function main. According to the C++ standard, if program execution reaches the end of main without encountering a return statement, it's assumed that the program terminated successfully—exactly as when the last statement in main is a return statement with the value 0. For that reason, we *omit* the return statement at the end of main in subsequent programs.

A Note About Comments

As you write a new program or modify an existing one, you should *keep your comments up-to-date* with the program's code. You'll *often* need to make changes to existing programs—for example, to fix errors (commonly called *bugs*) that prevent a program from working correctly or to enhance a program. Updating your comments as you make code changes helps ensure that the comments accurately reflect what the code does. This will make your programs easier for you and others to understand and modify in the future.

2.3 Modifying Our First C++ Program

We now present two examples that modify the program of Fig. 2.1 to print text on one line by using multiple statements and to print text on several lines by using a single statement.

Printing a Single Line of Text with Multiple Statements

Welcome to C++! can be printed several ways. For example, Fig. 2.3 performs stream insertion in multiple statements (lines 7–8), yet produces the same output as the program of Fig. 2.1. [*Note:* From this point forward, we use a *colored background* to highlight the key features each program introduces.] Each stream insertion resumes printing where the previous one stopped. The first stream insertion (line 7) prints Welcome followed by a space, and because this string did not end with \n, the second stream insertion (line 8) begins printing on the *same* line immediately following the space.

```
1   // Fig. 2.3: fig02_03.cpp
2   // Printing a line of text with multiple statements.
3   #include <iostream> // enables program to output data to the screen
4
5   // function main begins program execution
6   int main() {
7      std::cout << "Welcome ";
8      std::cout << "to C++!\n";
9   } // end function main
```

```
Welcome to C++!
```

Fig. 2.3 | Printing a line of text with multiple statements.

Printing Multiple Lines of Text with a Single Statement

A single statement can print multiple lines by using newline characters, as in line 7 of Fig. 2.4. Each time the \n (newline) escape sequence is encountered in the output stream, the screen cursor is positioned to the beginning of the next line. To get a blank line in your output, place two newline characters back to back, as in line 7.

```
 1    // Fig. 2.4: fig02_04.cpp
 2    // Printing multiple lines of text with a single statement.
 3    #include <iostream> // enables program to output data to the screen
 4
 5    // function main begins program execution
 6    int main() {
 7       std::cout << "Welcome\nto\n\nC++!\n";
 8    } // end function main
```

```
Welcome
to

C++!
```

Fig. 2.4 | Printing multiple lines of text with a single statement.

2.4 Another C++ Program: Adding Integers

Our next program obtains two integers typed by a user at the keyboard, computes their sum and outputs the result using std::cout. Figure 2.5 shows the program and sample inputs and outputs. In the sample execution, we highlight the user's input in bold. The program begins execution with function main (line 6). The left brace (line 6) begins main's body and the corresponding right brace (line 21) ends it.

```
 1    // Fig. 2.5: fig02_05.cpp
 2    // Addition program that displays the sum of two integers.
 3    #include <iostream> // enables program to perform input and output
 4
 5    // function main begins program execution
 6    int main() {
 7       // declaring and initializing variables
 8       int number1{0}; // first integer to add (initialized to 0)
 9       int number2{0}; // second integer to add (initialized to 0)
10       int sum{0}; // sum of number1 and number2 (initialized to 0)
11
12       std::cout << "Enter first integer: "; // prompt user for data
13       std::cin >> number1; // read first integer from user into number1
14
15       std::cout << "Enter second integer: "; // prompt user for data
16       std::cin >> number2; // read second integer from user into number2
17
18       sum = number1 + number2; // add the numbers; store result in sum
19
20       std::cout << "Sum is " << sum << std::endl; // display sum; end line
21    } // end function main
```

```
Enter first integer: 45
Enter second integer: 72
Sum is 117
```

Fig. 2.5 | Addition program that displays the sum of two integers.

Variable Declarations and List Initialization
Lines 8–10

```
int number1{0}; // first integer to add (initialized to 0)
int number2{0}; // second integer to add (initialized to 0)
int sum{0}; // sum of number1 and number2 (initialized to 0)
```

are declarations. The identifiers number1, number2 and sum are the names of variables. A variable is a location in the computer's memory where a value can be stored for use by a program. These declarations specify that the variables number1, number2 and sum are data of type int, meaning that these variables will hold integer (whole number) values, such as 7, –11, 0 and 31914.

Lines 8–10 also *initialize* each variable to 0 by placing a value in braces ({ and }) immediately following the variable's name—this is known as list initialization,[1] which was introduced in C++11. Previously, these declarations would have been written as:

11

```
int number1 = 0; // first integer to add (initialized to 0)
int number2 = 0; // second integer to add (initialized to 0)
int sum = 0; // sum of number1 and number2 (initialized to 0)
```

Error-Prevention Tip 2.1
Although it's not always necessary to initialize every variable explicitly, doing so will help you avoid many kinds of problems.

All variables *must* be declared with a name and a data type *before* they can be used in a program. Several variables of the same type may be declared in one declaration—for example, we could have declared and initialized all three variables in one declaration by using a comma-separated list as follows:

```
int number1{0}, number2{0}, sum{0};
```

This makes the program less readable and prevents us from providing comments that describe each variable's purpose.

Good Programming Practice 2.4
Declare only one variable in each declaration and provide a comment that explains the variable's purpose in the program.

Fundamental Types
We'll soon discuss the type double for specifying *real numbers* and the type char for specifying *character data*. Real numbers are numbers with decimal points, such as 3.4, 0.0 and –11.19. A char variable may hold only a single lowercase letter, uppercase letter, digit or special character (e.g., $ or *). Types such as int, double and char are called fundamental types. Fundamental-type names consist of one or more *keywords* and therefore *must* appear in all lowercase letters. Appendix C contains the complete list of fundamental types.

Identifiers
A variable name (such as number1) is any valid identifier that is *not* a keyword. An identifier is a series of characters consisting of letters, digits and underscores (_) that does *not*

---

1. List initialization is also known as uniform initialization.

begin with a digit. C++ is case sensitive—uppercase and lowercase letters are *different*, so a1 and A1 are *different* identifiers.

Portability Tip 2.1

C++ allows identifiers of any length, but your C++ implementation may restrict identifier lengths. Use identifiers of 31 characters or fewer to ensure portability (and readability).

Good Programming Practice 2.5

Choosing meaningful identifiers helps make a program self-documenting—a person can understand the program simply by reading it rather than having to refer to program comments or documentation.

Good Programming Practice 2.6

Avoid using abbreviations in identifiers. This improves program readability.

Good Programming Practice 2.7

Do not use identifiers that begin with underscores and double underscores, because C++ compilers use names like that for their own purposes internally.

Placement of Variable Declarations

Declarations of variables can be placed almost anywhere in a program, but they *must* appear *before* their corresponding variables are used in the program. For example, in the program of Fig. 2.5, the declaration in line 8

```
int number1{0}; // first integer to add (initialized to 0)
```

could have been placed immediately before line 13

```
std::cin >> number1; // read first integer from user into number1
```

the declaration in line 9

```
int number2{0}; // second integer to add (initialized to 0)
```

could have been placed immediately before line 16

```
std::cin >> number2; // read second integer from user into number2
```

and the declaration in line 10

```
int sum{0}; // sum of number1 and number2 (initialized to 0)
```

could have been placed immediately before line 18

```
sum = number1 + number2; // add the numbers; store result in sum
```

Obtaining the First Value from the User

Line 12

```
std::cout << "Enter first integer: "; // prompt user for data
```

displays Enter first integer: followed by a space. This message is called a prompt because it directs the user to take a specific action. We like to pronounce the preceding statement as "std::cout *gets* the string "Enter first integer: "." Line 13

```
    std::cin >> number1; // read first integer from user into number1
```

uses the standard input stream object cin (of namespace std) and the stream extraction operator, >>, to obtain a value from the keyboard. Using the stream extraction operator with std::cin takes character input from the standard input stream, which is usually the keyboard. We like to pronounce the preceding statement as, "std::cin *gives* a value to number1" or simply "std::cin *gives* number1."

When the computer executes the preceding statement, it waits for the user to enter a value for variable number1. The user responds by typing an integer (as characters), then pressing the *Enter* key (sometimes called the *Return* key) to send the characters to the computer. The computer converts the character representation of the number to an integer and assigns (i.e., copies) this number (or value) to the variable number1. Any subsequent references to number1 in this program will use this same value. Pressing *Enter* also causes the cursor to move to the beginning of the next line on the screen.

Users can, of course, enter *invalid* data from the keyboard. For example, when your program is expecting the user to enter an integer, the user could enter alphabetic characters, special symbols (like # or @) or a number with a decimal point (like 73.5), among others. In these early programs, we assume that the user enters *valid* data. As you progress through the book, you'll learn how to deal with data-entry problems.

Obtaining the Second Value from the User
Line 15

```
    std::cout << "Enter second integer: "; // prompt user for data
```

prints Enter second integer: on the screen, prompting the user to take action. Line 16

```
    std::cin >> number2; // read second integer from user into number2
```

obtains a value for variable number2 from the user.

Calculating the Sum of the Values Input by the User
The assignment statement in line 18

```
    sum = number1 + number2; // add the numbers; store result in sum
```

adds the values of variables number1 and number2 and assigns the result to variable sum using the assignment operator =. We like to read this statement as, "sum *gets* the value of number1 + number2." Most calculations are performed in assignment statements. The = operator and the + operator are called binary operators because each has *two* operands. In the case of the + operator, the two operands are number1 and number2. In the case of the preceding = operator, the two operands are sum and the value of the expression number1 + number2.

 Good Programming Practice 2.8
Place spaces on either side of a binary operator. This makes the operator stand out and makes the program more readable.

Displaying the Result
Line 20

```
    std::cout << "Sum is " << sum << std::endl; // display sum; end line
```

displays the character string Sum is followed by the numerical value of variable sum followed by std::endl—a so-called stream manipulator. The name endl is an abbreviation for "end line" and belongs to namespace std. The std::endl stream manipulator outputs a newline, then "flushes the output buffer." This simply means that, on some systems where outputs accumulate in the machine until there are enough to "make it worthwhile" to display them on the screen, std::endl forces any accumulated outputs to be displayed at that moment. This can be important when the outputs are prompting the user for an action, such as entering data.

The preceding statement outputs multiple values of different types. The stream insertion operator "knows" how to output each type of data. Using multiple stream insertion operators (<<) in a single statement is referred to as concatenating, chaining or cascading stream insertion operations.

Calculations can also be performed in output statements. We could have combined the statements in lines 18 and 20 into the statement

```
std::cout << "Sum is " << number1 + number2 << std::endl;
```

thus eliminating the need for the variable sum.

A powerful feature of C++ is that you can create your own data types called classes (we discuss this capability in Chapter 3 and explore it in depth in Chapter 9). You can then "teach" C++ how to input and output values of these new data types using the >> and << operators (this is called operator overloading—a topic we explore in Chapter 10).

2.5 Memory Concepts

Variable names such as number1, number2 and sum actually correspond to locations in the computer's memory. Every variable has a *name*, a *type*, a *size* and a *value*.

In the addition program of Fig. 2.5, when the statement in line 13

```
std::cin >> number1; // read first integer from user into number1
```

is executed, the integer typed by the user is placed into a memory location to which the name number1 has been assigned by the compiler. Suppose the user enters 45 for number1. The computer will place 45 into the location number1, as shown in Fig. 2.6. When a value is placed in a memory location, the value *overwrites* the previous value in that location; thus, placing a new value into a memory location is said to be a destructive operation.

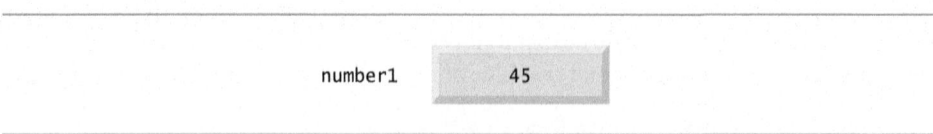

Fig. 2.6 | Memory location showing the name and value of variable number1.

Returning to our addition program, suppose the user enters 72 when the statement

```
std::cin >> number2; // read second integer from user into number2
```

is executed. This value is placed into the location number2, and memory appears as in Fig. 2.7. The variables' locations are not necessarily adjacent in memory.

number1	45
number2	72

Fig. 2.7 | Memory locations after storing values in the variables for number1 and number2.

Once the program has obtained values for number1 and number2, it adds these values and places the total into the variable sum. The statement

```
sum = number1 + number2; // add the numbers; store result in sum
```

replaces whatever value was stored in sum. The calculated sum of number1 and number2 is placed into variable sum without regard to what value may already be in sum—that value is *lost*. After sum is calculated, memory appears as in Fig. 2.8. The values of number1 and number2 appear exactly as they did before the calculation. These values were used, but *not* destroyed, as the computer performed the calculation. Thus, when a value is read *out* of a memory location, the operation is nondestructive.

number1	45
number2	72
sum	117

Fig. 2.8 | Memory locations after calculating and storing the sum of number1 and number2.

2.6 Arithmetic

Most programs perform arithmetic calculations. Figure 2.9 summarizes the arithmetic operators. Note the use of various special symbols not used in algebra. The asterisk (*) indicates *multiplication* and the percent sign (%) is the remainder operator, which we'll discuss shortly. The arithmetic operators in Fig. 2.9 are all *binary* operators—they each take two operands. For example, the expression number1 + number2 contains the binary operator + and the two operands number1 and number2.

Operation	Arithmetic operator	Algebraic expression	C++ expression
Addition	+	$f + 7$	f + 7
Subtraction	-	$p - c$	p - c
Multiplication	*	bm or $b \cdot m$	b * m
Division	/	x/y or $\frac{x}{y}$ or $x \div y$	x / y
Remainder	%	$r \bmod s$	r % s

Fig. 2.9 | Arithmetic operators.

Integer division (i.e., where both the numerator and the denominator are integers) yields an integer quotient; for example, the expression 7 / 4 evaluates to 1 and the expression 17 / 5 evaluates to 3. *Any fractional part in integer division is truncated (i.e., discarded)—no rounding occurs.*

The remainder operator, %, yields the *remainder after integer division* and can be used *only* with integer operands. The expression x % y yields the remainder after x is divided by y. Thus, 7 % 4 yields 3 and 17 % 5 yields 2. In later chapters, we discuss interesting applications of the remainder operator, such as determining whether one number is a *multiple* of another (a special case of this is determining whether a number is *odd* or *even*).

Arithmetic Expressions in Straight-Line Form

Arithmetic expressions in C++ must be entered into the computer in straight-line form. Thus, expressions such as "a divided by b" must be written as a / b, so that all constants, variables and operators appear in a straight line. The algebraic notation

$$\frac{a}{b}$$

is generally *not* acceptable to compilers, although some special-purpose software packages do support more natural notation for complex mathematical expressions.

Parentheses for Grouping Subexpressions

Parentheses are used in C++ expressions in the same manner as in algebraic expressions. For example, to multiply a times the quantity b + c we write a * (b + c).

Rules of Operator Precedence

C++ applies the operators in arithmetic expressions in a precise order determined by the following rules of operator precedence, which are generally the same as those in algebra:

1. Operators in expressions contained within pairs of *parentheses* are evaluated first. Parentheses are said to be at the "highest level of precedence." In cases of nested, or embedded, parentheses, such as

    ```
    (a * (b + c))
    ```

    the operators in the *innermost* pair of parentheses are applied first.

2. Multiplication, division and remainder operations are evaluated next. If an expression contains several multiplication, division and remainder operations, operators are applied from *left to right*. These three operators are said to be on the *same* level of precedence.

3. Addition and subtraction operations are applied last. If an expression contains several addition and subtraction operations, operators are applied from *left to right*. Addition and subtraction also have the *same* level of precedence.

The rules of operator precedence define the order in which C++ applies operators. When we say that certain operators are applied from left to right, we are referring to the associativity of the operators. For example, the addition operators (+) in the expression

```
a + b + c
```

associate from left to right, so a + b is calculated first, then c is added to that sum to determine the whole expression's value. We'll see that some operators associate from *right to left*.

Figure 2.10 summarizes these rules of operator precedence. We expand this table as we introduce additional C++ operators. Appendix A contains the complete precedence chart.

Operator(s)	Operation(s)	Order of evaluation (precedence)
( )	Parentheses	Evaluated first. For *nested* parentheses, such as in the expression a * (b + c / (d + e)), the expression in the *innermost* pair evaluates first. [*Caution:* If you have an expression such as (a + b) * (c - d) in which two sets of parentheses are not nested, but appear "on the same level," the C++ Standard does *not* specify the order in which these parenthesized subexpressions will evaluate.]
* / %	Multiplication Division Remainder	Evaluated second. If there are several, they're evaluated left to right.
+ -	Addition Subtraction	Evaluated last. If there are several, they're evaluated left to right.

Fig. 2.10 | Precedence of arithmetic operators.

Sample Algebraic and C++ Expressions

Now consider several expressions in light of the rules of operator precedence. Each example lists an algebraic expression and its C++ equivalent. The following is an example of an arithmetic mean (average) of five terms:

Algebra: $m = \dfrac{a + b + c + d + e}{5}$

C++: `m = (a + b + c + d + e) / 5;`

The parentheses are required because division has *higher* precedence than addition. The *entire* quantity (a + b + c + d + e) is to be divided by 5. If the parentheses are erroneously omitted, we obtain a + b + c + d + e / 5, which evaluates incorrectly as

$$a + b + c + d + \frac{e}{5}$$

The following is an example of the equation of a straight line:

Algebra: $y = mx + b$

C++: `y = m * x + b;`

No parentheses are required. The multiplication is applied first because multiplication has a *higher* precedence than addition.

The following example contains remainder (%), multiplication, division, addition, subtraction and assignment operations:

Algebra: $z = pr \% q + w/x - y$

C++: `z = p * r % q + w / x - y;`
     6   1   2   4   3   5

The circled numbers under the statement indicate the order in which C++ applies the operators. The multiplication, remainder and division operations are evaluated *first* in left-to-right order (i.e., they associate from left to right) because they have *higher precedence* than addition and subtraction. The addition and subtraction are applied next. These are also applied left to right. The assignment operator is applied *last* because its precedence is *lower* than that of any of the arithmetic operators.

Evaluation of a Second-Degree Polynomial

To develop a better understanding of the rules of operator precedence, consider the evaluation of a second-degree polynomial $y = ax^2 + bx + c$:

```
y  =  a  *  x  *  x  +  b  *  x  +  c;
      6     1     2     4     3     5
```

*There is no arithmetic operator for exponentiation in C++, so we've represented x^2 as x * x.* The circled numbers under the statement indicate the order in which C++ applies the operators. In Chapter 5, we'll discuss the standard library function pow ("power") that performs exponentiation.

Suppose variables a, b, c and x in the preceding second-degree polynomial are initialized as follows: a = 2, b = 3, c = 7 and x = 5. Figure 2.11 illustrates the order in which the operators are applied and the final value of the expression.

Step 1.	y = 2 * 5 * 5 + 3 * 5 + 7;	*(Leftmost multiplication)*
	2 * 5 is 10	
Step 2.	y = 10 * 5 + 3 * 5 + 7;	*(Leftmost multiplication)*
	10 * 5 is 50	
Step 3.	y = 50 + 3 * 5 + 7;	*(Multiplication before addition)*
	3 * 5 is 15	
Step 4.	y = 50 + 15 + 7;	*(Leftmost addition)*
	50 + 15 is 65	
Step 5.	y = 65 + 7;	*(Last addition)*
	65 + 7 is 72	
Step 6.	y = 72	*(Low-precedence assignment—place 72 in y)*

Fig. 2.11 | Order in which a second-degree polynomial is evaluated.

Redundant Parentheses

As in algebra, it's acceptable to place *unnecessary* parentheses in an expression to make it clearer. These are called redundant parentheses. For example, the second-degree polynomial could be parenthesized as follows:

```
y = (a * x * x) + (b * x) + c;
```

2.7 Decision Making: Equality and Relational Operators

We now introduce C++'s if statement, which allows a program to take alternative action based on whether a condition is true or false. Conditions in if statements can be formed by using the relational operators and equality operators summarized in Fig. 2.12. The relational operators all have the same level of precedence and associate left to right. The equality operators both have the same level of precedence, which is *lower* than that of the relational operators, and associate left to right.

Algebraic relational or equality operator	C++ relational or equality operator	Sample C++ condition	Meaning of C++ condition
Relational operators			
>	>	x > y	x is greater than y
<	<	x < y	x is less than y
≥	>=	x >= y	x is greater than or equal to y
≤	<=	x <= y	x is less than or equal to y
Equality operators			
=	==	x == y	x is equal to y
≠	!=	x != y	x is not equal to y

Fig. 2.12 | Relational and equality operators.

Common Programming Error 2.3

Reversing the order of the pair of symbols in the operators !=, >= and <= (by writing them as =!, => and =<, respectively) is normally a syntax error. In some cases, writing != as =! will not be a syntax error, but almost certainly will be a logic error that has an effect at execution time. You'll understand why when you learn about logical operators in Chapter 5. A fatal logic error causes a program to fail and terminate prematurely. A nonfatal logic error allows a program to continue executing, but usually produces incorrect results.

Common Programming Error 2.4

Confusing the equality operator == with the assignment operator = results in logic errors. We like to read the equality operator as "is equal to" or "double equals," and the assignment operator as "gets" or "gets the value of" or "is assigned the value of." As you'll see in Section 5.12, confusing these operators may not necessarily cause an easy-to-recognize syntax error, but may cause subtle logic errors.

Using the *if* Statement

The following example (Fig. 2.13) uses six if statements to compare two numbers input by the user. If a given if statement's condition is *true*, the output statement in the body of that if statement *executes*. If the condition is *false*, the output statement in the body *does not* execute.

```cpp
// Fig. 2.13: fig02_13.cpp
// Comparing integers using if statements, relational operators
// and equality operators.
#include <iostream> // enables program to perform input and output

using std::cout; // program uses cout
using std::cin; // program uses cin
using std::endl; // program uses endl

// function main begins program execution
int main() {
   int number1{0}; // first integer to compare (initialized to 0)
   int number2{0}; // second integer to compare (initialized to 0)

   cout << "Enter two integers to compare: "; // prompt user for data
   cin >> number1 >> number2; // read two integers from user

   if (number1 == number2) {
      cout << number1 << " == " << number2 << endl;
   }

   if (number1 != number2) {
      cout << number1 << " != " << number2 << endl;
   }

   if (number1 < number2) {
      cout << number1 << " < " << number2 << endl;
   }

   if (number1 > number2) {
      cout << number1 << " > " << number2 << endl;
   }

   if (number1 <= number2) {
      cout << number1 << " <= " << number2 << endl;
   }

   if (number1 >= number2) {
      cout << number1 << " >= " << number2 << endl;
   }
} // end function main
```

Fig. 2.13 | Comparing integers using if statements, relational operators and equality operators. (Part 1 of 2.)

```
Enter two integers to compare: 3 7
3 != 7
3 < 7
3 <= 7
```

```
Enter two integers to compare: 22 12
22 != 12
22 > 12
22 >= 12
```

```
Enter two integers to compare: 7 7
7 == 7
7 <= 7
7 >= 7
```

Fig. 2.13 | Comparing integers using if statements, relational operators and equality operators. (Part 2 of 2.)

using Declarations
Lines 6–8

```
using std::cout; // program uses cout
using std::cin; // program uses cin
using std::endl; // program uses endl
```

are using declarations that eliminate the need to repeat the std:: prefix as we did in earlier programs. We can now write cout instead of std::cout, cin instead of std::cin and endl instead of std::endl, respectively, in the remainder of the program.

In place of lines 6–8, many programmers prefer to provide the using directive

```
using namespace std;
```

which enables a program to use *all* the names in any standard C++ header (such as <iostream>) that a program might include. From this point forward in the book, we'll use the preceding directive in our programs.[2]

Variable Declarations and Reading the Inputs from the User
Lines 12–13

```
int number1{0}; // first integer to compare (initialized to 0)
int number2{0}; // second integer to compare (initialized to 0)
```

declare the variables used in the program and initialize them to 0.
Line 16

```
cin >> number1 >> number2; // read two integers from user
```

---

2. In Chapter 23, Other Topics, we'll discuss some issues with using directives in large-scale systems.

uses *cascaded* stream extraction operations to input two integers. Recall that we're allowed to write cin (instead of std::cin) because of line 7. First a value is read into variable number1, then a value is read into variable number2.

Comparing Numbers
The if statement in lines 18–20

```
if (number1 == number2) {
    cout << number1 << " == " << number2 << endl;
}
```

compares the values of variables number1 and number2 to test for equality. If the values are equal, the statement in line 19 displays a line of text indicating that the numbers are equal. If the conditions are true in one or more of the if statements starting in lines 22, 26, 30, 34 and 38, the corresponding body statement displays an appropriate line of text.

Each if statement in Fig. 2.13 contains a single body statement that's indented. Also notice that we've enclosed each body statement in a pair of braces, { }, creating what's called a compound statement or a block.

Good Programming Practice 2.9
Indent the statement(s) in the body of an if statement to enhance readability.

Error-Prevention Tip 2.2
You don't need to use braces, { }, around single-statement bodies, but you must include the braces around multiple-statement bodies. You'll see later that forgetting to enclose multiple-statement bodies in braces leads to errors. To avoid errors, as a rule, always enclose an if statement's body statement(s) in braces.

Common Programming Error 2.5
Placing a semicolon immediately after the right parenthesis after the condition in an if statement is often a logic error (although not a syntax error). The semicolon causes the body of the if statement to be empty, so the if statement performs no action, regardless of whether or not its condition is true. Worse yet, the original body statement of the if statement now becomes a statement in sequence with the if statement and always executes, often causing the program to produce incorrect results.

White Space
Note our use of blank lines in Fig. 2.13. We inserted these for readability. Recall that white-space characters, such as tabs, newlines and spaces, are normally ignored by the compiler. So, statements may be split over several lines and may be spaced according to your preferences. It's a syntax error to split identifiers, strings (such as "hello") and constants (such as the number 1000) over several lines.

Good Programming Practice 2.10
A lengthy statement may be spread over several lines. If a statement must be split across lines, choose meaningful breaking points, such as after a comma in a comma-separated list, or after an operator in a lengthy expression. If a statement is split across two or more lines, indent all subsequent lines and left-align the group of indented lines.

Operator Precedence

Figure 2.14 shows the precedence and associativity of the operators introduced in this chapter. The operators are shown top to bottom in decreasing order of precedence. All these operators, with the exception of the assignment operator =, associate from left to right. Addition is left-associative, so an expression like x + y + z is evaluated as if it had been written (x + y) + z. The assignment operator = associates from *right to left,* so an expression such as x = y = 0 is evaluated as if it had been written x = (y = 0), which, as we'll soon see, first assigns 0 to y, then assigns the *result* of that assignment—0—to x.

Operators	Associativity	Type
( )	*[See caution in Fig. 2.10]*	grouping parentheses
* / %	left to right	multiplicative
+ -	left to right	additive
<< >>	left to right	stream insertion/extraction
< <= > >=	left to right	relational
== !=	left to right	equality
=	right to left	assignment

Fig. 2.14 | Precedence and associativity of the operators discussed so far.

Good Programming Practice 2.11

Refer to the operator precedence and associativity chart (Appendix A) when writing expressions containing many operators. Confirm that the operators in the expression are performed in the order you expect. If you're uncertain about the order of evaluation in a complex expression, break the expression into smaller statements or use parentheses to force the order of evaluation, exactly as you'd do in an algebraic expression. Be sure to observe that some operators such as assignment (=) associate right to left rather than left to right.

2.8 Wrap-Up

You learned many important basic features of C++ in this chapter, including displaying data on the screen, inputting data from the keyboard and declaring variables of fundamental types. In particular, you learned to use the output stream object cout and the input stream object cin to build simple interactive programs. We explained how variables are stored in and retrieved from memory. You also learned how to use arithmetic operators to perform calculations. We discussed the order in which C++ applies operators (i.e., the rules of operator precedence), as well as the associativity of the operators. You also learned how C++'s if statement allows a program to make decisions. Finally, we introduced the equality and relational operators, which we used to form conditions in if statements.

The non-object-oriented applications presented here introduced you to basic programming concepts. As you'll see in Chapter 3, C++ applications typically contain just a few lines of code in function main—these statements normally create the objects that perform the work of the application, then the objects "take over from there." In Chapter 3, you'll learn how to implement your own classes and use objects of those classes in applications.

Summary

Section 2.2 First Program in C++: Printing a Line of Text

- **Single-line comments** (p. 46) begin with //. You insert comments to document your programs and improve their readability.

- **Comments** do not cause the computer to perform any **action** (p. 47) when the program is run—they're ignored by the compiler.

- A **preprocessing directive** (p. 46) begins with # and is a message to the C++ preprocessor. Preprocessing directives are processed before the program is compiled.

- The line **#include <iostream>** (p. 46) tells the C++ preprocessor to include the contents of the input/output stream header, which contains information necessary to compile programs that output data to the screen or input data from the keyboard.

- **White space** (i.e., blank lines, space characters and tab characters; p. 46) makes programs easier to read. White-space characters outside of string literals are ignored by the compiler.

- C++ programs begin executing at **main** (p. 47), even if main does not appear first in the program.

- The keyword int to the left of main indicates that main "returns" an integer value.

- The **body** (p. 47) of every function must be contained in braces ({ and }).

- A **string** (p. 47) in double quotes is sometimes referred to as a **character string, message** or **string literal**. White-space characters in strings are *not* ignored by the compiler.

- Most C++ **statements** (p. 47) end with a semicolon, also known as the statement terminator (we'll see some exceptions to this soon).

- Output and input in C++ are accomplished with **streams** (p. 47) of data.

- The output stream object **std::cout** (p. 47)—normally connected to the screen—is used to output data. Multiple data items can be output by concatenating **stream insertion** (<<; p. 48) operators.

- The input stream object std::cin—normally connected to the keyboard—is used to input data. Multiple data items can be input by concatenating stream extraction (>>) operators.

- The notation std::cout specifies that we are using cout from "namespace" std.

- When a backslash (i.e., an escape character) is encountered in a string of characters, the next character is combined with the backslash to form an **escape sequence** (p. 48).

- The **newline escape sequence \n** (p. 48) moves the cursor to the beginning of the next line on the screen.

- C++ keyword **return** (p. 49) is one of several means to exit a function.

Section 2.4 Another C++ Program: Adding Integers

- All **variables** (p. 51) in a C++ program must be declared before they can be used.

- Variables of type **int** (p. 51) hold integer values, i.e., whole numbers such as 7, –11, 0, 31914.

- A variable can be initialized in its declaration using **list initialization** (p. 51; introduced in C++11)—the variable's initial value is placed in braces ({ and }) immediately following the variable's name.

- A variable name is any valid **identifier** (p. 51) that is not a keyword. An identifier is a series of characters consisting of letters, digits and underscores (_). Identifiers cannot start with a digit. Identifiers can be any length, but some systems or C++ implementations may impose length restrictions.

- A message that directs the user to take a specific action is known as a **prompt** (p. 52).

- C++ is **case sensitive** (p. 52).
- A program reads the user's input with the **std::cin** (p. 53) object and the **stream extraction** (>>; p. 53) operator.
- Most calculations are performed in **assignment statements** (p. 53).

Section 2.5 Memory Concepts
- A variable is a location in **memory** (p. 54) where a value can be stored for use by a program.
- Every variable stored in the computer's memory has a name, a value, a type and a size.
- Whenever a new value is placed in a memory location, the process is **destructive** (p. 54); i.e., the new value replaces the previous value in that location. The previous value is lost.
- When a value is read from memory, the process is **nondestructive** (p. 55); i.e., a copy of the value is read, leaving the original value undisturbed in the memory location.
- The **std::endl stream manipulator** (p. 54) outputs a newline, then "flushes the output buffer."

Section 2.6 Arithmetic
- C++ evaluates **arithmetic expressions** (p. 55) in a precise sequence determined by the **rules of operator precedence** (p. 56) and **associativity** (p. 56).
- Parentheses may be used to group expressions.
- **Integer division** (p. 56) yields an integer quotient. Any fractional part in integer division is truncated.
- The **remainder operator, %** (p. 56), yields the remainder after integer division.

Section 2.7 Decision Making: Equality and Relational Operators
- The **if statement** (p. 59) allows a program to take alternative action based on whether a condition is met. The format for an if statement is

      if (condition) {
          statement;
      }

  If the condition is true, the statement in the body of the if is executed. If the condition is not met, i.e., the condition is false, the body statement is skipped.
- Conditions in if statements are commonly formed by using **equality and relational operators** (p. 59). The result of using these operators is always the value *true* or *false*.
- The **using declaration** (p. 61)

      using std::cout;

  informs the compiler where to find cout (namespace std) and eliminates the need to repeat the std:: prefix. The **using directive** (p. 61)

      using namespace std;

  enables the program to use all the names in any included C++ standard library header.

Self-Review Exercises

2.1 Fill in the blanks in each of the following.
  a) Every C++ program begins execution at the function _____.
  b) A(n) _____ begins the body of every function and a(n) _____ ends the body.
  c) Most C++ statements end with a(n) _____.

d) The escape sequence \n represents the _____ character, which causes the cursor to position to the beginning of the next line on the screen.

e) The _____ statement is used to make decisions.

2.2   State whether each of the following is *true* or *false*. If *false*, explain why. Assume the statement using std::cout; is used.

a) Comments cause the computer to print the text after the // on the screen when the program is executed.

b) The escape sequence \n, when output with cout and the stream insertion operator, causes the cursor to position to the beginning of the next line on the screen.

c) All variables must be declared before they're used.

d) All variables must be given a type when they're declared.

e) C++ considers the variables number and NuMbEr to be identical.

f) Declarations can appear almost anywhere in the body of a C++ function.

g) The remainder operator (%) can be used only with integer operands.

h) The arithmetic operators *, /, %, + and – all have the same level of precedence.

i) A C++ program that prints three lines of output must contain three statements using cout and the stream insertion operator.

2.3   Write a single C++ statement to accomplish each of the following (assume that neither using declarations nor a using directive have been used):

a) Declare the variables c, thisIsAVariable, q76354 and number to be of type int (in one statement) and initialize each to 0.

b) Prompt the user to enter an integer. End your prompting message with a colon (:) followed by a space and leave the cursor positioned after the space.

c) Read an integer from the user at the keyboard and store it in integer variable age.

d) If the variable number is not equal to 7, print "The variable number is not equal to 7".

e) Print the message "This is a C++ program" on one line.

f) Print the message "This is a C++ program" on two lines. End the first line with C++.

g) Print the message "This is a C++ program" with each word on a separate line.

h) Print the message "This is a C++ program". Separate each word from the next by a tab.

2.4   Write a statement (or comment) to accomplish each of the following (assume that using declarations have been used for cin, cout and endl):

a) Document that a program calculates the product of three integers.

b) Declare the variables x, y, z and result to be of type int (in separate statements) and initialize each to 0.

c) Prompt the user to enter three integers.

d) Read three integers from the keyboard and store them in the variables x, y and z.

e) Compute the product of the three integers contained in variables x, y and z, and assign the result to the variable result.

f) Print "The product is " followed by the value of the variable result.

g) Return a value from main indicating that the program terminated successfully.

2.5   Using the statements you wrote in Exercise 2.4, write a complete program that calculates and displays the product of three integers. Add comments to the code where appropriate. [*Note:* You'll need to write the necessary using declarations or directive.]

2.6   Identify and correct the errors in each of the following statements (assume that the statement using std::cout; is used):

a)
```cpp
if (c < 7); {
    cout << "c is less than 7\n";
}
```

b) `if (c => 7) {`

     `cout << "c is equal to or greater than 7\n";`

  `}`

Answers to Self-Review Exercises

2.1   a) `main`. b) left brace (`{`), right brace (`}`). c) semicolon. d) newline. e) `if`.

2.2   a) *False.* Comments do not cause any action to be performed when the program is executed. They're used to document programs and improve their readability.
     b) *True.*
     c) *True.*
     d) *True.*
     e) *False.* C++ is case sensitive, so these variables are different.
     f) *True.*
     g) *True.*
     h) *False.* The operators `*`, `/` and `%` have the same precedence, and the operators `+` and `-` have a lower precedence.
     i) *False.* One statement with `cout` and multiple `\n` escape sequences can print several lines.

2.3   a) `int c{0}, thisIsAVariable{0}, q76354{0}, number{0};`
     b) `std::cout << "Enter an integer: ";`
     c) `std::cin >> age;`
     d) `if (number != 7) {`

       `std::cout << "The variable number is not equal to 7\n";`

     `}`
     e) `std::cout << "This is a C++ program\n";`
     f) `std::cout << "This is a C++\nprogram\n";`
     g) `std::cout << "This\nis\na\nC++\nprogram\n";`
     h) `std::cout << "This\tis\ta\tC++\tprogram\n";`

2.4   a) `// Calculate the product of three integers`
     b) `int x{0};`
        `int y{0};`
        `int z{0};`
        `int result{0};`
     c) `cout << "Enter three integers: ";`
     d) `cin >> x >> y >> z;`
     e) `result = x * y * z;`
     f) `cout << "The product is " << result << endl;`
     g) `return 0;`

2.5   (See program below.)

```
 1   // Calculate the product of three integers
 2   #include <iostream> // enables program to perform input and output
 3   using namespace std; // program uses names from the std namespace
 4
 5   // function main begins program execution
 6   int main() {
 7      int x{0}; // first integer to multiply
 8      int y{0}; // second integer to multiply
 9      int z{0}; // third integer to multiply
10      int result{0}; // the product of the three integers
11
```

```
12        cout << "Enter three integers: "; // prompt user for data
13        cin >> x >> y >> z; // read three integers from user
14        result = x * y * z; // multiply the three integers; store result
15        cout << "The product is " << result << endl; // print result; end line
16    } // end function main
```

2.6   a) *Error:* Semicolon after the right parenthesis of the condition in the if statement.
            Correction: Remove the semicolon after the right parenthesis. [*Note:* The result of this
            error is that the output statement executes whether or not the condition in the if state-
            ment is true.] The semicolon after the right parenthesis is an empty statement that does
            nothing. We'll say more about the empty statement in Chapter 4.
        b) *Error:* The incorrect relational operator =>.
            Correction: Change => to >=, and you may want to change "equal to or greater than" to
            "greater than or equal to" as well.

Exercises

2.7   Discuss the meaning of each of the following objects:
        a) `std::cin`
        b) `std::cout`

2.8   Fill in the blanks in each of the following:
        a) _____ are used to document a program and improve its readability.
        b) The object used to print information on the screen is _____.
        c) A C++ statement that makes a decision is _____.
        d) Most calculations are normally performed by _____ statements.
        e) The _____ object inputs values from the keyboard.

2.9   Write a single C++ statement or line that accomplishes each of the following:
        a) Print the message "Enter two numbers".
        b) Assign the product of variables b and c to variable a.
        c) State that a program performs a payroll calculation (i.e., use text that helps to document
            a program).
        d) Input three integer values from the keyboard into integer variables a, b and c.

2.10   State which of the following are *true* and which are *false*. If *false*, explain your answers.
        a) All operators are evaluated from left to right.
        b) The following are all valid variable names: _under_bar_, m928134, t5, j7, her_sales,
            his_account_total, a, b, c, z, z2.
        c) The statement cout << "a = 5;"; is a typical example of an assignment statement.
        d) A valid arithmetic expression with no parentheses is evaluated from left to right.
        e) The following are all invalid variable names: 3g, 87, 67h2, h22, 2h.

2.11   Fill in the blanks in each of the following:
        a) What arithmetic operations are on the same level of precedence as multiplication?
            _____.
        b) When parentheses are nested, which set of parentheses is evaluated first in an arithmetic
            expression? _____.
        c) A location in the computer's memory that may contain different values at various times
            throughout the execution of a program is called a(n) _____.

2.12   What, if anything, prints when each of the following statements is performed? If nothing
        prints, then answer "nothing." Assume x = 2 and y = 3.
        a) cout << x;

b) cout << x + x;
c) cout << "x=";
d) cout << "x = " << x;
e) cout << x + y << " = " << y + x;
f) z = x + y;
g) cin >> x >> y;
h) // cout << "x + y = " << x + y;
i) cout << "\n";

2.13 Which of the following statements contain variables whose values are replaced?
a) cin >> b >> c >> d >> e >> f;
b) p = i + j + k + 7;
c) cout << "variables whose values are replaced";
d) cout << "a = 5";

2.14 Given the algebraic equation $y = ax^3 + 7$, which of the following, if any, are correct C++ statements for this equation?
a) y = a * x * x * x + 7;
b) y = a * x * x * (x + 7);
c) y = (a * x) * x * (x + 7);
d) y = (a * x) * x * x + 7;
e) y = a * (x * x * x) + 7;
f) y = a * x * (x * x + 7);

2.15 *(Order of Evaluation)* State the order of evaluation of the operators in each of the following C++ statements and show the value of x after each statement is performed.
a) x = 7 + 3 * 6 / 2 - 1;
b) x = 2 % 2 + 2 * 2 - 2 / 2;
c) x = (3 * 9 * (3 + (9 * 3 / (3))));

2.16 *(Arithmetic)* Write a program that asks the user to enter two numbers, obtains the two numbers from the user and prints the sum, product, difference, and quotient of the two numbers.

2.17 *(Printing)* Write a program that prints the numbers 1 to 4 on the same line with each pair of adjacent numbers separated by one space. Do this several ways:
a) Using one statement with one stream insertion operator.
b) Using one statement with four stream insertion operators.
c) Using four statements.

2.18 *(Comparing Integers)* Write a program that asks the user to enter two integers, obtains the numbers from the user, then prints the larger number followed by the words "is larger." If the numbers are equal, print the message "These numbers are equal."

2.19 *(Arithmetic, Smallest and Largest)* Write a program that inputs three integers from the keyboard and prints the sum, average, product, smallest and largest of these numbers. The screen dialog should appear as follows:

```
Input three different integers: 13 27 14
Sum is 54
Average is 18
Product is 4914
Smallest is 13
Largest is 27
```

2.20   *(Diameter, Circumference and Area of a Circle)* Write a program that reads in the radius of a circle as an integer and prints the circle's diameter, circumference and area. Use the constant value 3.14159 for π. Do all calculations in output statements. [*Note:* In this chapter, we've discussed only integer constants and variables. In Chapter 4 we discuss floating-point numbers, i.e., values that have decimal points.]

2.21   *(Displaying Shapes with Asterisks)* Write a program that prints a box, an oval, an arrow and a diamond as follows:

2.22   What does the following code print?

```
cout << "*\n**\n***\n****\n*****" << endl;
```

2.23   *(Largest and Smallest Integers)* Write a program that reads in five integers and determines and prints the largest and the smallest integers in the group. Use only the programming techniques you learned in this chapter.

2.24   *(Odd or Even)* Write a program that reads an integer and determines and prints whether it's odd or even. [*Hint:* Use the remainder operator (%). An even number is a multiple of two. Any multiple of 2 leaves a remainder of zero when divided by 2.]

2.25   *(Multiples)* Write a program that reads in two integers and determines and prints if the first is a multiple of the second. [*Hint:* Use the remainder operator (%).]

2.26   *(Checkerboard Pattern)* Display the following checkerboard pattern with eight output statements, then display the same pattern using as few statements as possible.

```
* * * * * * * *
 * * * * * * * *
* * * * * * * *
 * * * * * * * *
* * * * * * * *
 * * * * * * * *
* * * * * * * *
 * * * * * * * *
```

2.27   *(Integer Equivalent of a Character)* Here is a peek ahead. In this chapter you learned about integers and the type int. C++ can also represent uppercase letters, lowercase letters and a considerable variety of special symbols. C++ uses small integers internally to represent each different character. The set of characters a computer uses and the corresponding integer representations for those characters are called that computer's character set. You can print a character by enclosing that character in single quotes, as with

```
cout << 'A'; // print an uppercase A
```

You can print the integer equivalent of a character using static_cast as follows:

```
cout << static_cast<int>('A'); // print 'A' as an integer
```

This is called a cast operation (we formally introduce casts in Chapter 4). When the preceding statement executes, it prints the value 65 (on systems that use the ASCII character set). Write a program that prints the integer equivalent of a character typed at the keyboard. Store the input in a variable of type char. Test your program several times using uppercase letters, lowercase letters, digits and special characters (such as $).

2.28 *(Digits of an Integer)* Write a program that inputs a five-digit integer, separates the integer into its digits and prints them separated by three spaces each. [*Hint:* Use the integer division and remainder operators.] For example, if the user types in 42339, the program should print:

```
4   2   3   3   9
```

2.29 *(Table)* Using the techniques of this chapter, write a program that calculates the squares and cubes of the integers from 0 to 10. Use tabs to print the following neatly formatted table of values:

```
integer square  cube
0       0       0
1       1       1
2       4       8
3       9       27
4       16      64
5       25      125
6       36      216
7       49      343
8       64      512
9       81      729
10      100     1000
```

Making a Difference

2.30 *(Body Mass Index Calculator)* We introduced the body mass index (BMI) calculator in Exercise 1.9. The formulas for calculating BMI are

$$BMI = \frac{weightInPounds \times 703}{heightInInches \times heightInInches}$$

or

$$BMI = \frac{weightInKilograms}{heightInMeters \times heightInMeters}$$

Create a BMI calculator application that reads the user's weight in pounds and height in inches (or, if you prefer, the user's weight in kilograms and height in meters), then calculates and displays the user's body mass index. Also, the application should display the following information from the Department of Health and Human Services/National Institutes of Health so the user can evaluate his/her BMI:

```
BMI VALUES
Underweight: less than 18.5
Normal:      between 18.5 and 24.9
Overweight:  between 25 and 29.9
Obese:       30 or greater
```

[*Note:* In this chapter, you learned to use the int type to represent whole numbers. The BMI calculations when done with int values will both produce whole-number results. In Chapter 4 you'll learn to use the double type to represent numbers with decimal points. When the BMI calculations are performed with doubles, they'll each produce numbers with decimal points—these are called "floating-point" numbers.]

2.31 *(Car-Pool Savings Calculator)* Research several car-pooling websites. Create an application that calculates your daily driving cost, so that you can estimate how much money could be saved by car pooling, which also has other advantages such as reducing carbon emissions and reducing traffic congestion. The application should input the following information and display the user's cost per day of driving to work:

a) Total miles driven per day.
b) Cost per gallon of gasoline.
c) Average miles per gallon.
d) Parking fees per day.
e) Tolls per day.

Introduction to Classes, Objects, Member Functions and Strings

3

3.1 Introduction[1]

Section 1.8 presented a friendly introduction to object orientation, discussing classes, objects, data members (attributes) and member functions (behaviors).[2] In this chapter's examples, we make those concepts real by building a simple bank-account class. The class maintains as *data members* the attributes name and balance, and provides *member functions* for behaviors including

- querying the balance (getBalance),
- making a deposit that increases the balance (deposit) and
- making a withdrawal that decreases the balance (withdraw).

We'll build the getBalance and deposit member functions into the chapter's examples. You'll add the withdraw member function in Exercise 3.9.

As you'll see, each *class* you create becomes a *new type* you can use to create objects, so C++ is an extensible programming language. If you become part of a development team in industry, you might work on applications that contain hundreds, or even thousands, of custom classes.

---

1. This chapter depends on the terminology and concepts introduced in Section 1.8, Introduction to Object Technology.

2. Unlike classes, fundamental types (like int) do not have member functions.

3.2 Test-Driving an Account Object

Classes *cannot* execute by themselves. A Person object can drive a Car object by telling it what to do (go faster, go slower, turn left, turn right, etc.)—without knowing how the car's internal mechanisms work. Similarly, the main function can "drive" an Account object by calling its member functions—without knowing how the class is implemented. In this sense, main is referred to as a driver program. We show the main program and its output first, so you can see an Account object in action. To help you prepare for the larger programs you'll encounter later in this book and in industry, we define main in its own file (file Account-Test.cpp, Fig. 3.1). We define class Account in its own file as well (file Account.h, Fig. 3.2).

```cpp
1   // Fig. 3.1: AccountTest.cpp
2   // Creating and manipulating an Account object.
3   #include <iostream>
4   #include <string>
5   #include "Account.h"
6
7   using namespace std;
8
9   int main() {
10     Account myAccount; // create Account object myAccount
11
12     // show that the initial value of myAccount's name is the empty string
13     cout << "Initial account name is: " << myAccount.getName();
14
15     // prompt for and read name
16     cout << "\nPlease enter the account name: ";
17     string theName;
18     getline(cin, theName); // read a line of text
19     myAccount.setName(theName); // put theName in myAccount
20
21     // display the name stored in object myAccount
22     cout << "Name in object myAccount is: "
23       << myAccount.getName() << endl;
24   }
```

```
Initial account name is:
Please enter the account name: Jane Green
Name in object myAccount is: Jane Green
```

Fig. 3.1 | Creating and manipulating an Account object.

3.2.1 Instantiating an Object

Typically, you cannot call a member function of a class until you *create an object* of that class.[3] Line 10

```cpp
      Account myAccount; // create Account object myAccount
```

creates an object of class Account called myAccount. The variable's type is Account—the class we define in Fig. 3.2.

---

3. You'll see in Section 9.15 that static member functions are an exception.

3.2.2 Headers and Source-Code Files

When we declare variables of type int, as we did in Chapter 2, the compiler knows what int is—it's a *fundamental type* that's "built into" C++. In line 10, however, the compiler does *not* know in advance what type Account is—it's a user-defined type.

When packaged properly, new classes can be *reused* by other programmers. It's customary to place a reusable class definition in a file known as a header with a .h filename extension.[4] You include (via #include) that header wherever you need to use the class. For example, you can *reuse* the C++ Standard Library's classes in any program by including the appropriate headers.

Class Account is defined in the header Account.h (Fig. 3.2). We tell the compiler what an Account is by including its header, as in line 5 (Fig. 3.1):

```
#include "Account.h"
```

If we omit this, the compiler issues error messages wherever we use class Account and any of its capabilities. In an #include directive, a header that *you* define in *your program* is placed in double quotes (""), rather than the angle brackets (<>) used for C++ Standard Library headers like <iostream>. The double quotes in this example tell the compiler that header is in the same folder as Fig. 3.1, rather than with the C++ Standard Library headers.

Files ending with the .cpp filename extension are source-code files. These define a program's main function, other functions and more, as you'll see in later chapters. You include headers into source-code files (as in Fig. 3.1), though you also may include them in other headers.

3.2.3 Calling Class Account's getName Member Function

The Account class's getName member function returns the account name stored in a particular Account object. Line 13

```
cout << "Initial name is: " << myAccount.getName();
```

displays myAccount's *initial* name by calling the object's getName member function with the expression myAccount.getName(). To call this member function for a specific object, you specify the object's name (myAccount), followed by the dot operator (.), then the member function name (getName) and a set of parentheses. The *empty* parentheses indicate that getName does not require any additional information to perform its task. Soon, you'll see that the setName function requires additional information to perform its task.

From main's view, when the getName member function is called:

1. The program transfers execution from the call (line 13 in main) to member function getName. Because getName was called via the myAccount object, getName "knows" which object's data to manipulate.

2. Next, member function getName performs its task—that is, it *returns* (i.e., gives back) myAccount's name to line 13 where the function was called. The main function does not know the details of how getName performs its task.

3. The cout object displays the name returned by member function getName, then the program continues executing at line 16 in main.

---

4.   C++ Standard Library headers, like <iostream> do not use the .h filename extension.

In this case, line 13 does not display a name, because we have not yet stored a name in the myAccount object.

3.2.4 Inputting a `string` with `getline`

Line 17

```
string theName;
```

creates a `string` variable called `theName` that's used to store the account name entered by the user. `string` variables can hold character string values such as `"Jane Green"`. A `string` is actually an *object* of the C++ Standard Library class `string`, which is defined in the header `<string>`.[5] The class name `string`, like the name `cout`, belongs to namespace `std`. To enable line 17 to compile, line 4 includes the `<string>` header. The using directive in line 7 allows us to write `string` in line 17 rather than `std::string`.

`getline` *Function Receiving a Line of Text from the User*

Sometimes functions are *not* members of a class. Such functions are called global functions. Line 18

```
getline(cin, theName); // read a line of text
```

reads the name from the user and places it in the variable `theName`, using the C++ Standard Library global function `getline` to perform the input. Like class `string`, function `getline` requires the `<string>` header and belongs to namespace `std`.

Consider why we cannot simply write

```
cin >> theName;
```

to obtain the account name. In our sample program execution, we entered the name "Jane Green," which contains multiple words *separated by a space*. (Recall that we highlight user inputs in bold in our sample program executions.) When reading a `string`, `cin` stops at the first *white-space character* (such as a space, tab or newline). Thus, the preceding statement would read only `"Jane"`. The information after `"Jane"` is *not lost*—it can be read by subsequent input statements later in the program.

In this example, we'd like the user to type the complete name (including the space) and press *Enter* to submit it to the program. Then, we'd like to store the *entire* name in the `string` variable `theName`. When you press *Enter* (or *Return*) after typing data, the system inserts a newline in the input stream. Function `getline` reads from the standard input stream object `cin` the characters the user enters, up to, but *not* including, the newline, which is *discarded*; `getline` places the characters in the `string` variable `theName`.

3.2.5 Calling Class Account's `setName` Member Function

The Account class's `setName` member function stores an account name in a particular Account object. Line 19

```
myAccount.setName(theName); // put theName in myAccount
```

---

5. You'll learn additional `string` capabilities in subsequent chapters. Chapter 21 discusses class `string` in detail, presenting many of its member functions.

calls myAccounts's setName member function. A member-function call can supply *arguments* that help the function perform its task. You place the arguments in the function call's parentheses. Here, theName's value (input by line 18) is the *argument* that's passed to setName, which stores theName's value in the object myAccount.

From main's view, when setName is called:

1. The program transfers execution from line 19 in main to setName member function's definition. The call passes to the function the *argument value* in the call's parentheses—that is, theName object's value. Because setName was called via the myAccount object, setName "knows" the exact object to manipulate.

2. Next, member function setName stores the argument's value in the myAccount object.

3. When setName completes execution, program execution returns to where setName was called (line 19), then continues at line 22.

Displaying the Name That Was Entered by the User

To demonstrate that myAccount now contains the name the user entered, lines 22–23

```
cout << "Name in object myAccount is: "
   << myAccount.getName() << endl;
```

call member function getName again. As you can see in the last line of the program's output, the name entered by the user in line 18 is displayed. When the preceding statement completes execution, the end of main is reached, so the program terminates.

3.3 Account Class with a Data Member and *Set* and *Get* Member Functions

Now that we've seen class Account in action (Fig. 3.1), we present class Account's details. Then, we present a UML diagram that summarizes class Account's *attributes* and *operations* in a concise graphical representation.

3.3.1 Account Class Definition

Class Account (Fig. 3.2) contains a name *data member* that stores the account holder's name. A class's data members maintain data for each object of the class. Later in the chapter, we'll add a balance data member to keep track of the money in each Account. Class Account also contains member function setName that a program can call to store a name in an Account object, and member function getName that a program can call to obtain a name from an Account object.

```
1   // Fig. 3.2: Account.h
2   // Account class that contains a name data member
3   // and member functions to set and get its value.
4   #include <string> // enable program to use C++ string data type
5
```

Fig. 3.2 | Account class that contains a name data member and member functions to *set* and *get* its value. (Part 1 of 2.)

```
6   class Account {
7   public:
8      // member function that sets the account name in the object
9      void setName(std::string accountName) {
10         name = accountName; // store the account name
11     }
12
13     // member function that retrieves the account name from the object
14     std::string getName() const {
15         return name; // return name's value to this function's caller
16     }
17  private:
18     std::string name; // data member containing account holder's name
19  }; // end class Account
```

Fig. 3.2 | Account class that contains a name data member and member functions to *set* and *get* its value. (Part 2 of 2.)

3.3.2 Keyword class and the Class Body

The *class definition* begins in line 6:

```
class Account {
```

Every class definition contains the keyword `class` followed immediately by the class's name—in this case, `Account`. Every class's body is enclosed in an opening *left brace* (end of line 6) and a closing *right brace* (line 19). The class definition terminates with a *required* semicolon (line 19). For reusability, place each class definition in a separate header with the `.h` filename extension (`Account.h` in this example).

 Common Programming Error 3.1
Forgetting the semicolon at the end of a class definition is a syntax error.

Identifiers and Camel-Case Naming
Class names, member-function names and data-member names are all *identifiers*. By convention, variable-name identifiers begin with a lowercase letter, and every word in the name after the first word begins with a capital letter—e.g., `firstNumber` starts its second word, `Number`, with a capital `N`. This naming convention is known as camel case, because the uppercase letters stand out like a camel's humps. Also by convention, class names begin with an initial uppercase letter, and member-function and data member-names begin with an initial lowercase letter.

3.3.3 Data Member name of Type string

Recall from Section 1.8 that an object has attributes, implemented as data members. The object carries these with it throughout its lifetime. Each object has its own copy of the class's data members. Normally, a class also contains one or more member functions. These manipulate the data members belonging to particular objects of the class. The data members exist

- *before* a program calls member functions on an object,

- *while* the member functions are executing and
- *after* the member functions complete execution.

Data members are declared *inside* a class definition but *outside* the bodies of the class's member functions. Line 18

```
std::string name; // data member containing account holder's name
```

declares data member name of type string. If there are many Account objects, each has its own name. Because name is a data member, it can be manipulated by each of the class's member functions. The default value for a string is the empty string (i.e., "")—this is why line 13 in main (Fig. 3.1) did not display a name the first time we called myAccount's getName member function. Section 3.4 explains how a string receives its default value.

Good Programming Practice 3.1

By convention, place a class's data members last in the class's body. You can list the class's data members anywhere in the class outside its member-function definitions, but scattering the data members can lead to hard-to-read code.

Use std::with Standard Library Components in Headers

Throughout the Account.h header (Fig. 3.2), we use std:: when referring to string (lines 9, 14 and 18). For subtle reasons that we explain in Section 23.4, headers should *not* contain using directives or using declarations.

3.3.4 setName Member Function

Let's walk through the code of member function setName's definition (lines 9–11):

```
void setName(std::string accountName) {
    name = accountName; // store the name
}
```

We refer to the first line of each function definition (line 9) as the *function header*. The member function's return type (which appears to the left of the function's name) specifies the type of data the member function returns to its *caller* after performing its task. The return type void (line 9) indicates that when setName completes its task, it does *not* return (i.e., give back) any information to its calling function—in this example, line 19 of the main function (Fig. 3.1). As you'll soon see, Account member function getName does return a value.

setName *Parameter*

Our car analogy from Section 1.8 mentioned that pressing a car's gas pedal sends a *message* to the car to perform a task—make the car go faster. But *how fast* should the car accelerate? The farther down you press the pedal, the faster the car accelerates. So the message to the car includes *both* the *task to perform* and *information that helps the car perform that task*. This information is known as a parameter—the parameter's *value* helps the car determine how fast to accelerate. Similarly, a member function can require one or more parameters that represent the data it needs to perform its task.

Member function setName declares the string *parameter* accountName—which receives the name that's passed to setName as an *argument*. When line 19 in Fig. 3.1

```
myAccount.setName(theName); // put theName in myAccount
```

executes, the *argument value* in the call's parentheses (i.e., the value stored in theName) is copied into the corresponding *parameter* (accountName) in the member function's header (line 9 of Fig. 3.2). In Fig. 3.1's sample execution, we entered "Jane Green" for theName, so "Jane Green" was copied into the accountName parameter.

setName *Parameter List*
Parameters like accountName are declared in a parameter list located in the *required* parentheses following the member function's name. Each parameter *must* specify a type (e.g., string) followed by a parameter name (e.g., accountName). When there are multiple parameters, each is separated from the next by a comma, as in

```
(type1 name1, type2 name2, ...)
```

The number and order of *arguments* in a function call *must match* the number and order of *parameters* in the function definition's parameter list.

setName *Member Function Body*
Every *member function body* is delimited by an opening *left brace* (end of line 9 of Fig. 3.2) and a closing *right brace* (line 11). Within the braces are one or more statements that perform the member function's task(s). In this case, the member function body contains a single statement (line 10)

```
name = accountName; // store the account name
```

that assigns the accountName *parameter's* value (a string) to the class's name *data member*, thus storing the account name in the object for which setName was called—myAccount in this example's main program.[6] After line 10 executes, program execution reaches the member function's closing brace (line 11), so the function returns to its *caller*.

Parameters Are Local Variables
In Chapter 2, we declared all of a program's variables in the main function. Variables declared in a particular function's body are local variables which can be used *only* in that function. When a function terminates, the values of its local variables are *lost*. A function's parameters also are local variables of that function.

Argument and Parameter Types Must Be Consistent
The argument types in the member function call must be *consistent* with the types of the corresponding parameters in the member function's definition. (As you'll see in Chapter 6, Functions and an Introduction to Recursion, an argument's type and its corresponding parameter's type are *not* required to be identical.) In our example, the member function call passes one argument of type string (theName)—and the member function definition specifies one parameter of type string (accountName). So in this example, the type of the argument in the member function call happens to exactly match the type of the parameter in the member function header.

---

6. We used different names for the setName member function's parameter (accountName) and the data member (name). It's common idiom in industry to use the same name for both. We'll show you how to do this without ambiguity in Chapter 9.

3.3.5 getName Member Function

Member function getName (lines 14–16)

```
std::string getName() const {
    return name; // return name's value to this function's caller
}
```

returns a particular Account object's name to the caller—a string, as specified by the function's return type. The member function has an empty parameter list, so it does not require additional information to perform its task. When a member function with a return type other than void is called and completes its task, it *must* return a result to its caller. A statement that calls member function getName on an Account object expects to receive the Account's name.

The return statement in line 15

```
return name; // return name's value to this function's caller
```

passes the string value of data member name back to the caller, which then can use the returned value. For example, the statement in lines 22–23 of Fig. 3.1

```
cout << "Name in object myAccount is: "
    << myAccount.getName() << endl;
```

uses the value returned by getName to output the name stored in the myAccount object.

const *Member Functions*

We declared member function getName as const in line 14 of Fig. 3.2

```
std::string getName() const {
```

because in the process of returning the name the function *does not*, and *should not*, modify the Account object on which it's called.

Error-Prevention Tip 3.1

Declaring a member function with const to the right of the parameter list tells the compiler, "this function should not modify the object on which it's called—if it does, please issue a compilation error." This can help you locate errors if you accidentally insert in the member function code that would modify the object.

3.3.6 Access Specifiers private and public

The keyword private (line 17)

```
private:
```

is an access specifier. Access specifiers are always followed by a colon (:). Data member name's declaration (line 18) appears *after* access specifier private: to indicate that name is accessible *only* to class Account's member functions.[7] This is known as data hiding—the data member name is *encapsulated* (hidden) and can be used *only* in class Account's setName and getName member functions. Most data-member declarations appear after the private: access specifier. For the remainder of the text, when we refer to the access specifiers private and public in the text, we'll often omit the colon as we did in this sentence.

---

7.   Or to "friends" of the class as you'll see in Section 9.13.

This class also contains the `public` access specifier (line 7)

```
public:
```

Data members or member functions listed after access specifier `public` (and *before* the next access specifier if there is one) are "available to the public." They can be used by other functions in the program (such as `main`), and by member functions of other classes (if there are any). In Chapter 11, we'll introduce the `protected` access specifier.

Default Access for Class Members

By default, everything in a class is `private`, unless you specify otherwise. Once you list an access specifier, everything from that point has that access until you list another access specifier. We prefer to list `public` only once, grouping everything that's `public`, and we prefer to list `private` only once, grouping everything that's `private`. The access specifiers `public` and `private` may be repeated, but this is unnecessary and can be confusing.

Error-Prevention Tip 3.2
Making a class's data members `private` and member functions `public` facilitates debugging because problems with data manipulations are localized to the member functions.

Common Programming Error 3.2
An attempt by a function that's not a member of a particular class to access a `private` member of that class is a compilation error.

3.3.7 Account UML Class Diagram

We'll often use UML class diagrams to summarize a class's *attributes* and *operations*. In industry, UML diagrams help systems designers specify systems in a concise, graphical, programming-language-independent manner, before programmers implement the systems in specific programming languages. Figure 3.3 presents a UML class diagram for class Account of Fig. 3.2.

Top Compartment

In the UML, each class is modeled in a class diagram as a rectangle with three compartments. In this diagram the top compartment contains the *class name* Account centered horizontally in boldface type.

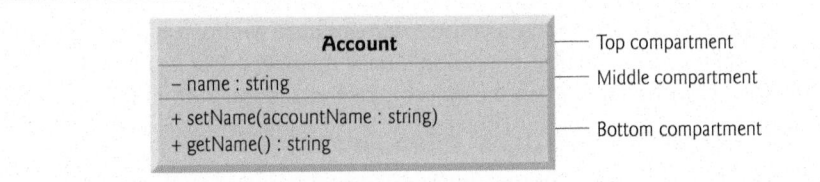

Fig. 3.3 | UML class diagram for class Account of Fig. 3.2.

Middle Compartment

The middle compartment contains the class's attribute name, which corresponds to the data member of the same name in C++. Data member name is `private` in C++, so the

UML class diagram lists a *minus sign (–) access modifier* before the attribute name. Following the attribute name are a *colon* and the *attribute type*, in this case string.

Bottom Compartment
The bottom compartment contains the class's operations, setName and getName, which correspond to the member functions of the same names in C++. The UML models operations by listing the operation name preceded by an *access modifier*, in this case + setName. This plus sign (+) indicates that setName is a public operation in the UML (because it's a public member function in C++). Operation getName is also a public operation.

Return Types
The UML indicates the return type of an operation by placing a colon and the return type after the parentheses following the operation name. Account member function setName does not return a value (because it returns void in C++), so the UML class diagram does not specify a return type after the parentheses of this operation. Member function getName has a string return type.

Parameters
The UML models a parameter by listing the parameter name, followed by a colon and the parameter type in the parentheses after the operation name. The UML has its own data types similar to those of C++—for simplicity, we use the C++ types. Account member function setName has a string parameter called accountName, so the class diagram lists accountName : string between the parentheses following the member function name. Operation getName does not have any parameters, so the parentheses following the operation name in the class diagram are empty, just as they are in the member function's definition in line 14 of Fig. 3.2.

3.4 Account Class: Initializing Objects with Constructors
As mentioned in Section 3.3, when an Account object is created, its string data member name is initialized to the empty string by *default*—we'll discuss how that occurs shortly. But what if you want to provide a name when you first *create* an Account object? Each class can define a constructor that specifies *custom initialization* for objects of that class. A constructor is a special member function that *must* have the *same name* as the class. C++ *requires* a constructor call when *each* object is created, so this is the ideal point to initialize an object's data members.[8]

Like member functions, a constructor can have parameters—the corresponding argument values help initialize the object's data members. For example, you can specify an Account object's name when the object is created, as you'll do in line 11 of Fig. 3.5:

```
Account account1{"Jane Green"};
```

In this case, the string argument "Jane Green" is passed to the Account class's constructor and used to initialize the name data member of the account1 object. The preceding statement assumes that the Account class has a constructor that takes only a string parameter.

---

8.   In Section 9.6, you'll learn that classes can have multiple constructors.

3.4.1 Defining an Account Constructor for Custom Object Initialization

Figure 3.4 shows class `Account` with a constructor that receives an `accountName` parameter and uses it to initialize data member name when an `Account` object is created.

```cpp
 1   // Fig. 3.4: Account.h
 2   // Account class with a constructor that initializes the account name.
 3   #include <string>
 4
 5   class Account {
 6   public:
 7      // constructor initializes data member name with parameter accountName
 8      explicit Account(std::string accountName)
 9         : name{accountName} { // member initializer
10        // empty body
11      }
12
13      // function to set the account name
14      void setName(std::string accountName) {
15         name = accountName;
16      }
17
18      // function to retrieve the account name
19      std::string getName() const {
20         return name;
21      }
22   private:
23      std::string name; // account name data member
24   }; // end class Account
```

Fig. 3.4 | Account class with a constructor that initializes the account name.

Account Class's Constructor Definition
Lines 8–11 of Fig. 3.4

```cpp
explicit Account(std::string accountName)
   : name{accountName} { // member initializer
   // empty body
}
```

define `Account`'s constructor. Normally, constructors are `public`.[9]

A constructor's *parameter list* specifies pieces of data required to initialize an object. Line 8

```cpp
explicit Account(std::string accountName)
```

indicates that the constructor has one `string` parameter called `accountName`. When you create a new `Account` object, you *must* pass a person's name to the constructor, which will receive that name in the *parameter* `accountName`. The constructor will then use account-Name to initialize the *data member* name.

---

9. Section 10.10.2 discusses why you might use a `private` constructor.

The constructor uses a member-initializer list (line 9)

```
: name{accountName}
```

to initialize the name data member with the value of the parameter accountName. *Member initializers* appear between a constructor's parameter list and the left brace that begins the constructor's body. The member initializer list is separated from the parameter list with a colon (:). Each member initializer consists of a data member's *variable name* followed by parentheses containing the member's *initial value*. In this example, name is initialized with the parameter accountName's value. If a class contains more than one data member, each member initializer is separated from the next by a comma. The member initializer list executes *before* the constructor's body executes.

Performance Tip 3.1

You can perform initialization in the constructor's body, but you'll learn in Chapter 9 that it's more efficient to do it with member initializers, and some types of data members must be initialized this way.

explicit *Keyword*

We declared this constructor explicit, because it takes a *single* parameter—this is important for subtle reasons that you'll learn in Section 10.13. For now, just declare *all* single-parameter constructors explicit. Line 8 of Fig. 3.4 does *not* specify a return type, because constructors *cannot* return values—not even void. Also, constructors cannot be declared const (because initializing an object modifies it).

Using the Same Parameter Name in the Constructor and Member Function setName

Recall from Section 3.3.4 that member function parameters are local variables. In Fig. 3.4, the constructor and member function setName both have a parameter called accountName. Though their identifiers are identical, the parameter in line 8 is a local variable of the constructor that's *not* visible to member function setName. Similarly, the parameter in line 14 is a local variable of setName that's *not* visible to the constructor. Such visibility is called *scope*, which is discussed in Section 6.10.

3.4.2 Initializing Account Objects When They're Created

The AccountTest program (Fig. 3.5) initializes two different Account objects using the constructor. Line 11

```
Account account1{"Jane Green"};
```

creates the Account object account1. When you create an object, C++ implicitly calls the class's constructor to *initialize* that object. If the constructor has parameters, you place the corresponding arguments in braces, { and }, to the right of the object's variable name. In line 11, the *argument* "Jane Green" initializes the new object's name data member. Line 12

```
Account account2{"John Blue"};
```

repeats this process, passing the argument "John Blue" to initialize name for account2. Lines 15–16 use each object's getName member function to obtain the names and show that they were indeed initialized when the objects were created. The output shows *different* names, confirming that each Account maintains its *own copy* of data member name.

```
 1   // Fig. 3.5: AccountTest.cpp
 2   // Using the Account constructor to initialize the name data
 3   // member at the time each Account object is created.
 4   #include <iostream>
 5   #include "Account.h"
 6
 7   using namespace std;
 8
 9   int main() {
10      // create two Account objects
11      Account account1{"Jane Green"};
12      Account account2{"John Blue"};
13
14      // display initial value of name for each Account
15      cout << "account1 name is: " << account1.getName() << endl;
16      cout << "account2 name is: " << account2.getName() << endl;
17   }
```

```
account1 name is: Jane Green
account2 name is: John Blue
```

Fig. 3.5 | Using the Account constructor to initialize the name data member at the time each Account object is created.

Default Constructor
Recall that line 10 of Fig. 3.1

```
Account myAccount;
```

creates an Account object *without* placing braces to the right of the object's variable name. In this case, C++ implicitly calls the class's default constructor. In any class that does *not* explicitly define a constructor, the compiler provides a default constructor with no parameters. The default constructor does *not* initialize the class's fundamental-type data members, but *does* call the default constructor for each data member that's an object of another class. For example, in the Account class of Fig. 3.2, the class's default constructor calls class string's default constructor to initialize the data member name to the empty string. An uninitialized fundamental-type variable contains an undefined ("garbage") value.[10]

There's No Default Constructor in a Class That Defines a Constructor
If you define a custom constructor for a class, the compiler will *not* create a default constructor for that class. In that case, you will not be able to create an Account object using

```
Account myAccount;
```

as we did in Fig. 3.1, unless the custom constructor you define has an empty parameter list. We'll show later that C++11 allows you to force the compiler to create the default constructor even if you've defined non-default constructors.

11

---

10. We'll see an exception to this in Section 6.10.

Software Engineering Observation 3.1

Unless default initialization of your class's data members is acceptable, you should generally provide a custom constructor to ensure that your data members are properly initialized with meaningful values when each new object of your class is created.

3.4.3 Account UML Class Diagram with a Constructor

The UML class diagram of Fig. 3.6 models class `Account` of Fig. 3.4, which has a constructor with a `string accountName` parameter. Like operations (Fig. 3.3), the UML models constructors in the *third* compartment of a class diagram. To distinguish a constructor from the class's operations, the UML requires that the word "constructor" be enclosed in guillemets (« and ») and placed before the constructor's name. It's customary to list constructors *before* other operations in the third compartment.

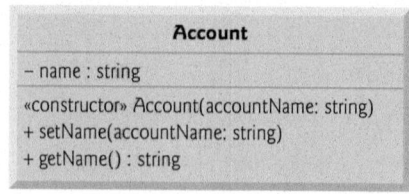

Fig. 3.6 | UML class diagram for the Account class of Fig. 3.4.

3.5 Software Engineering with *Set* and *Get* Member Functions

As you'll see in the next section, *set* and *get* member functions can *validate* attempts to modify `private` data and control how that data is presented to the caller, respectively. These are compelling software engineering benefits.

If a data member were `public`, any client of the class—that is, any other code that calls the class's member functions—could see the data and do whatever it wanted with it, including setting it to an *invalid* value.

You might think that even though a client of the class cannot directly access a `private` data member, the client can nevertheless do whatever it wants with the variable through `public` *set* and *get* functions. You'd think that you could peek at the `private` data (and see exactly how it's stored in the object) any time with the `public` *get* function and that you could modify the `private` data at will through the `public` *set* function.

Actually, *set* functions can be programmed to *validate* their arguments and reject any attempts to *set* the data to bad values, such as

- a negative body temperature
- a day in March outside the range 1 through 31
- a product code not in the company's product catalog, etc.

And a *get* function can present the data in a different form, while the actual data representation remains hidden from the user. For example, a `Grade` class might store a `grade` data member as an `int` between 0 and 100, but a `getGrade` member function might return a letter grade as a `string`, such as "A" for grades between 90 and 100, "B" for grades between 80 and 89, etc. Tightly controlling the *access* to and *presentation* of `private` data can greatly reduce errors, while increasing the robustness, security and usability of your programs.

Conceptual View of an *Account* Object with Encapsulated Data

You can think of an `Account` object as shown in Fig. 3.7. The `private` data member name is *hidden inside* the object (represented by the inner circle containing name) and *protected by an outer layer* of `public` member functions (represented by the outer circle containing `getName` and `setName`). Any client code that needs to interact with the `Account` object can do so *only* by calling the `public` member functions of the protective outer layer.

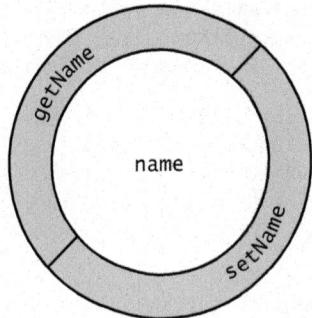

Fig. 3.7 | Conceptual view of an Account object with its encapsulated `private` data member name and protective layer of `public` member functions.

 Software Engineering Observation 3.2

Generally, data members should be `private` *and member functions* `public`. *In Chapter 9, we'll discuss why you might use a* `public` *data member or a* `private` *member function.*

 Software Engineering Observation 3.3

Using `public` *set and get functions to control access to* `private` *data makes programs clearer and easier to maintain. Change is the rule rather than the exception. You should anticipate that your code will be modified, and possibly often.*

3.6 Account Class with a Balance; Data Validation

We now define an `Account` class that maintains a bank account's `balance` in addition to the name. In Chapter 2 we used the data type `int` to represent integers. For simplicity, we'll use data type `int` to represent the account balance. In Chapter 4, you'll see how to represent numbers with *decimal points*.

3.6.1 Data Member `balance`

A typical bank services many accounts, each with its own balance. In this updated `Account` class (Fig. 3.8), line 42

```
int balance{0}; // data member with default initial value
```

declares a data member balance of type int and initializes its value to 0. This is known as
an in-class initializer and was introduced in C++11. Every object of class Account contains
its *own* copies of *both* the name and the balance.

11

```
1   // Fig. 3.8: Account.h
2   // Account class with name and balance data members, and a
3   // constructor and deposit function that each perform validation.
4   #include <string>
5
6   class Account {
7   public:
8      // Account constructor with two parameters
9      Account(std::string accountName, int initialBalance)
10        : name{accountName} { // assign accountName to data member name
11
12        // validate that the initialBalance is greater than 0; if not,
13        // data member balance keeps its default initial value of 0
14        if (initialBalance > 0) { // if the initialBalance is valid
15           balance = initialBalance; // assign it to data member balance
16        }
17     }
18
19     // function that deposits (adds) only a valid amount to the balance
20     void deposit(int depositAmount) {
21        if (depositAmount > 0) { // if the depositAmount is valid
22           balance = balance + depositAmount; // add it to the balance
23        }
24     }
25
26     // function returns the account balance
27     int getBalance() const {
28        return balance;
29     }
30
31     // function that sets the name
32     void setName(std::string accountName) {
33        name = accountName;
34     }
35
36     // function that returns the name
37     std::string getName() const {
38        return name;
39     }
40  private:
41     std::string name; // account name data member
42     int balance{0}; // data member with default initial value
43  }; // end class Account
```

Fig. 3.8 | Account class with name and balance data members, and a constructor and
deposit function that each perform validation.

Account's Member Functions Can All Use *balance*

The statements in lines 15, 22 and 28 use the variable balance even though it was *not* declared in *any* of the member functions. We can use balance in these member functions because it's a *data member* in the same class definition.

3.6.2 Two-Parameter Constructor with Validation

The class has a *constructor* and four *member functions*. It's common for someone opening an account to deposit money immediately, so the constructor (lines 9–17) now receives a second parameter—initialBalance of type int that represents the *starting balance*. We did not declare this constructor explicit (as in Fig. 3.4), because this constructor has more than one parameter.

Lines 14–16 of Fig. 3.8

```
if (initialBalance > 0) { // if the initialBalance is valid
    balance = initialBalance; // assign it to data member balance
}
```

ensure that data member balance is assigned parameter initialBalance's value *only* if that value is greater than 0—this is known as validation or validity checking. If so, line 15 assigns initialBalance's value to data member balance. Otherwise, balance remains at 0—its *default initial value* that was set at line 42 in class Account's definition.

3.6.3 deposit Member Function with Validation

Member function deposit (lines 20–24) does *not* return any data when it completes its task, so its return type is void. The member function receives one int parameter named depositAmount. Lines 21–23

```
if (depositAmount > 0) { // if the depositAmount is valid
    balance = balance + depositAmount; // add it to the balance
}
```

ensure that parameter depositAmount's value is added to the balance only if the parameter value is valid (i.e., greater than zero)—another example of validity checking. Line 22 first adds the current balance and depositAmount, forming a *temporary* sum which is then assigned to balance, *replacing* its prior value (recall that addition has a higher precedence than assignment). It's important to understand that the calculation

```
balance + depositAmount
```

on the right side of the assignment operator in line 22 does *not* modify the balance—that's why the assignment is necessary. Section 4.12 shows a more concise way to write line 22.

3.6.4 getBalance Member Function

Member function getBalance (lines 27–29) allows the class's *clients* to obtain the value of a particular Account object's balance. The member function specifies return type int and an *empty* parameter list. Like member function getName, getBalance is declared const, because in the process of returning the balance the function does not, and should not, modify the Account object on which it's called.

3.6.5 Manipulating Account Objects with Balances

The main function in Fig. 3.9 creates two Account objects (lines 10–11) and attempts to initialize them with a *valid* balance of 50 and an *invalid* balance of -7, respectively—for the purpose of our examples, we assume that balances must be greater than or equal to zero. Lines 14–17 output the account names and balances, which are obtained by calling each Account's getName and getBalance member functions.

```cpp
 1   // Fig. 3.9: AccountTest.cpp
 2   // Displaying and updating Account balances.
 3   #include <iostream>
 4   #include "Account.h"
 5
 6   using namespace std;
 7
 8   int main()
 9   {
10      Account account1{"Jane Green", 50};
11      Account account2{"John Blue", -7};
12
13      // display initial balance of each object
14      cout << "account1: " << account1.getName() << " balance is $"
15         << account1.getBalance();
16      cout << "\naccount2: " << account2.getName() << " balance is $"
17         << account2.getBalance();
18
19      cout << "\n\nEnter deposit amount for account1: "; // prompt
20      int depositAmount;
21      cin >> depositAmount; // obtain user input
22      cout << "adding " << depositAmount << " to account1 balance";
23      account1.deposit(depositAmount); // add to account1's balance
24
25      // display balances
26      cout << "\n\naccount1: " << account1.getName() << " balance is $"
27         << account1.getBalance();
28      cout << "\naccount2: " << account2.getName() << " balance is $"
29         << account2.getBalance();
30
31      cout << "\n\nEnter deposit amount for account2: "; // prompt
32      cin >> depositAmount; // obtain user input
33      cout << "adding " << depositAmount << " to account2 balance";
34      account2.deposit(depositAmount); // add to account2 balance
35
36      // display balances
37      cout << "\n\naccount1: " << account1.getName() << " balance is $"
38         << account1.getBalance();
39      cout << "\naccount2: " << account2.getName() << " balance is $"
40         << account2.getBalance() << endl;
41   }
```

Fig. 3.9 | Displaying and updating Account balances. (Part 1 of 2.)

```
account1: Jane Green balance is $50
account2: John Blue balance is $0

Enter deposit amount for account1: 25
adding 25 to account1 balance

account1: Jane Green balance is $75
account2: John Blue balance is $0

Enter deposit amount for account2: 123
adding 123 to account2 balance

account1: Jane Green balance is $75
account2: John Blue balance is $123
```

Fig. 3.9 | Displaying and updating Account balances. (Part 2 of 2.)

Displaying the Account Objects' Initial Balances

When member function getBalance is called for account1 from line 15, the value of account1's balance is returned from line 28 of Fig. 3.8 and displayed by the output statement in lines 14–15 (Fig. 3.9). Similarly, when member function getBalance is called for account2 from line 17, the value of the account2's balance is returned from line 28 of Fig. 3.8 and displayed by the output statement (Fig. 3.9, lines 16–17). The balance of account2 is initially 0, because the constructor rejected the attempt to start account2 with a negative balance, so the data member balance retains its default initial value.

Reading a Deposit Amount from the User and Making a Deposit

Line 19 prompts the user to enter a deposit amount for account1. Line 20 declares local variable depositAmount to store each deposit amount entered by the user. We did not initialize depositAmount, because as you'll learn momentarily, variable depositAmount's value will be input by the user's input.

Error-Prevention Tip 3.3

Most C++ compilers issue a warning if you attempt to use the value of an uninitialized variable. This helps you avoid dangerous execution-time logic errors. It's always better to get the warnings and errors out of your programs at compilation time rather than execution time.

Line 21 reads the deposit amount from the user and places the value into local variable depositAmount. Line 22 displays the deposit amount. Line 23 calls object account1's deposit member function with the depositAmount as the member function's *argument*. When the member function is called, the argument's value is assigned to the parameter depositAmount of member function deposit (line 20 of Fig. 3.8); then member function deposit adds that value to the balance. Lines 26–29 (Fig. 3.9) output the names and balances of both Accounts again to show that *only* account1's balance has changed.

Line 31 prompts the user to enter a deposit amount for account2. Line 32 obtains the input from the user. Line 33 displays the depositAmount. Line 34 calls object account2's deposit member function with depositAmount as the member function's *argument*; then member function deposit adds that value to the balance. Finally, lines 37–40 output the names and balances of both Accounts again to show that *only* account2's balance has changed.

Duplicated Code in the main Function

The six statements at lines 14–15, 16–17, 26–27, 28–29, 37–38 and 39–40 are almost identical. Each outputs an Account's name and balance, and differs only in the Account object's name—account1 or account2. Duplicate code like this can create *code maintenance problems* when that code needs to be updated. For example, if *six* copies of the same code all have the same error to fix or the same update to be made, you must make that change six times, without making errors. Exercise 3.13 asks you to modify Fig. 3.9 to include function displayAccount that takes as a parameter an Account object and outputs the object's name and balance. You'll then replace main's duplicated statements with six calls to displayAccount.

 Software Engineering Observation 3.4
Replacing duplicated code with calls to a function that contains only one copy of that code can reduce the size of your program and improve its maintainability.

3.6.6 Account UML Class Diagram with a Balance and Member Functions deposit and getBalance

The UML class diagram in Fig. 3.10 concisely models class Account of Fig. 3.8. The diagram models in its second compartment the private attributes name of type string and balance of type int.

Account
– name : string
– balance : int
«constructor» Account(accountName : string, initialBalance : int) + deposit(depositAmount : int) + getBalance() : int + setName(accountName : string) + getName() : string

Fig. 3.10 | UML class diagram for the Account class of Fig. 3.8.

Class Account's constructor is modeled in the third compartment with parameters accountName of type string and initialBalance of type int. The class's four public member functions also are modeled in the third compartment—operation deposit with a depositAmount parameter of type int, operation getBalance with a return type of int, operation setName with an accountName parameter of type string and operation getName with a return type of string.

3.7 Wrap-Up

In this chapter, you created your own classes and member functions, created objects of those classes and called member functions of those objects to perform useful actions. You declared data members of a class to maintain data for each object of the class, and you defined your own member functions to operate on that data. You passed information to a member function as arguments whose values are assigned to the member function's parameters. You learned the difference between a local variable of a member function and a data member of a class, and that only data members that are objects are initialized automatically with calls to their default constructors. You also learned how to use a class's constructor to specify the initial values for an object's data members. You saw how to create UML class diagrams that model the member functions, attributes and constructors of classes.

In the next chapter we begin our introduction to control statements, which specify the order in which a program's actions are performed. You'll use these in your member functions to specify how they should order their tasks.

Summary

Section 3.1 Introduction
- Each class you create becomes a new type you can use to declare variables and create objects.
- C++ is an **extensible programming language** (p. 74)—you can define new class types as needed.

Section 3.2 Test-Driving an **Account** Object
- Classes cannot execute by themselves.
- A main function can "drive" an object by calling its member functions—without knowing how the class is implemented. In this sense, main is referred to as a **driver program** (p. 75).

Section 3.2.1 Instantiating an Object
- Typically, you cannot call a member function of a class until you create an object of that class.

Section 3.2.2 Headers and Source-Code Files
- The compiler knows about fundamental types that are "built into" C++.
- A new type that you create is known as a **user-defined type** (p. 76).
- New classes, when packaged properly, can be reused by other programmers.
- Reusable code (such as a class definition) is placed in a file known as a **header** (p. 76) that you include (via #include) wherever you need to use the code.
- By convention, a header for a user-defined type has a .h filename extension.
- In an #include directive, a user-defined header is placed in double quotes (""), indicating that the header is located with your program, rather than with the C++ Standard Library headers.
- Files ending in .cpp are known as **source-code files** (p. 76).

Section 3.2.3 Calling Class **Account**'s **getName** Member Function
- To call a member function for a specific object, you specify the object's name, followed by a **dot operator** (.; p. 76), then the member function name and a set of parentheses. *Empty* parentheses indicate that the function does not require any additional information to perform its task.
- A member function can return a value from the object on which the function is called.

Section 3.2.4 Inputting a **getline** string with
- Functions that are not members of a class are called **global functions** (p. 77).
- An object of C++ Standard Library class **string** (p. 77) stores character string values. Class string is defined in the **<string>** header (p. 77) and belongs to namespace std.

- C++ Standard Library function **getline** (p. 77), from the <string> header, reads characters up to, but not including, a newline, which is discarded, then places the characters in a string.

Section 3.2.5 Calling Class **Account**'s **setName** Member Function

- A member-function call can supply **arguments** (p. 78) that help the function perform its task.

Section 3.3.1 **Account** Class Definition

- A class's data members maintain data for each object of the class, and its member functions manipulate the class's data members.

Section 3.3.2 Keyword **class** and the Class Body

- A class definition begins with keyword **class** (p. 79) followed immediately by the class's name.
- A class's body is enclosed in an opening left brace and a closing right brace.
- A class definition terminates with a required semicolon.
- Typically, each class definition is placed in a separate header with the .h filename extension.
- Class names, member function names and data member names are all identifiers. By convention, variable-name identifiers begin with a lowercase letter, and every word in the name after the first word begins with a capital letter. This naming convention is known as camel case, because the uppercase letters stand out like a camel's humps. Also by convention, class names begin with an initial uppercase letter, and member function and data member names begin with an initial lowercase letter.

Section 3.3.3 Data Member **name** of Type **string**

- Each object of a class has its own copy of the class's data members.
- An object's data members exist before a program calls member functions on an object, while they are executing and after the member functions complete execution.
- Data members are declared inside a class definition but outside its member functions' bodies.
- The default value for a string is the **empty string** (i.e., ""; p. 80).
- Headers should never contain using directives or using declarations.

Section 3.3.4 **setName** Member Function

- A function's **return type** (p. 79; which appears to the left of the function's name) specifies the type of data the function returns to its caller after performing its task.
- The return type **void** (p. 80) indicates that when a function completes its task, it does not return (i.e., give back) any information to its **calling function** (p. 80).
- **Parameters** (p. 80) specify additional information the function needs to perform its task.
- When you call a function, each argument value in the call's parentheses is copied into the corresponding parameter in the member function definition.
- Parameters are declared in a **parameter list** (p. 81) located in required parentheses following a function's name. Each parameter must specify a type followed by a parameter name.
- Multiple parameters in a function definition are separated by commas.
- The number and order of arguments in a function call must match the number and order of parameters in the function definition's parameter list.
- Every function body is delimited by an opening left brace and a closing right brace. Within the braces are one or more statements that perform the function's task(s).
- When program execution reaches a function's closing brace, the function returns to its caller.

- Variables declared in a particular function's body are **local variables** (p. 81), which can be used only in that function. When a function terminates, the values of its local variables are lost.
- A function's parameters also are local variables of that function.
- The argument types in the member function call must be consistent with the types of the corresponding parameters in the member function's definition.

Section 3.3.5 `getName` Member Function
- When a member function that specifies a return type other than `void` is called and completes its task, it must return a result to its caller.
- The `return` statement (p. 82) passes a value back to a function's caller.
- A member function that does not, and should not, modify the object on which it's called is declared with `const` (p. 82) to the right of its parameter list.

Section 3.3.6 Access Specifiers `private` and `public`
- The keyword `private` (p. 82) is an **access specifier** (p. 82).
- Access specifiers are always followed by a colon (:).
- A `private` data member is accessible only to its class's member functions.
- Most data-member declarations appear after the `private` access specifier.
- Variables or functions listed after the `public` (p. 83) access specifier (and before the next access specifier, if there is one) are "available to the public." They can be used by other functions in the program, and by member functions of other classes.
- By default, everything in a class is `private`, unless you specify otherwise.
- Once you list an access specifier, everything from that point has that access until you list another access specifier.
- Declaring data members `private` is known as **data hiding** (p. 82). `private` data members are encapsulated (hidden) in an object and can be accessed only by member functions of the object's class.

Section 3.3.7 Account UML Class Diagram
- **UML class diagrams** (p. 83) can be used to summarize a class's attributes and operations.
- In the UML, each class is modeled in a class diagram as a rectangle with three compartments.
- The top compartment contains the class name centered horizontally in boldface type.
- The middle compartment contains the class's attribute names, which correspond to the data members of a class.
- A private attribute lists a minus sign (–) access modifier before the attribute name.
- Following the attribute name are a colon and the attribute type.
- The bottom compartment contains the class's **operations** (p. 84), which correspond to the member functions in a class.
- The UML models operations by listing the operation name preceded by an access modifier. A plus sign (+) indicates a public operation in the UML.
- An operation that does not have any parameters specifies empty parentheses following the operation name.
- The UML indicates the return type of an operation by placing a colon and the return type after the parentheses following the operation name.
- For a `void` return type a UML class diagram does not specify anything after the parentheses of the operation.

- The UML models a parameter by listing the parameter name, followed by a colon and the parameter type in the parentheses after the operation name.

Section 3.4 **Account** *Class: Initializing Objects with Constructors*
- Each class can define a **constructor** (p. 84) for custom object initialization.
- A constructor is a special member function that must have the same name as the class.
- C++ requires a constructor call for every object that's created.
- Like member functions, a constructor can specify parameters—the corresponding argument values help initialize the object's data members.

Section 3.4.1 *Declaring an* **Account** *Constructor for Custom Object Initialization*
- Normally, constructors are `public`.
- A constructor's parameter list specifies pieces of data required to initialize an object.
- A constructor uses a **member-initializer list** (p. 86) to initialize its data members with the values of the corresponding parameters.
- Member initializers appear between a constructor's parameter list and the left brace that begins the constructor's body.
- The member-initializer list is separated from the parameter list with a colon (:).
- Each member initializer consists of a data member's variable name followed by parentheses containing the member's initial value.
- Each member initializer in a constructor is separated from the next by a comma.
- The member initializer list executes before the constructor's body executes.
- A constructor that specifies a single parameter should be declared `explicit` (p. 86).
- A constructor does not specify a return type, because constructors cannot return values.
- Constructors cannot be declared `const` (because initializing an object modifies it).

Section 3.4.2 *Initializing* **Account** *Objects When They're Created*
- When you create an object, C++ calls the class's constructor to initialize that object. If a constructor has parameters, the corresponding arguments are placed in braces, { and }, to the right of the object's variable name.
- When you create an object without placing braces to the right of the object's variable name, C++ implicitly calls the class's **default constructor** (p. 87).
- In any class that does not explicitly define a constructor, the compiler provides a default constructor (which always has no parameters).
- The default constructor does not initialize the class's fundamental-type data members, but does call the default constructor for each data member that's an object of another class.
- A `string`'s default constructor initializes the object to the empty `string`.
- An uninitialized fundamental-type variable contains an undefined ("garbage") value.
- If a class defines a constructor, the compiler will not create a default constructor for that class.

Section 3.4.3 **Account** *UML Class Diagram with a Constructor*
- Like operations, the UML models constructors in the third compartment of a class diagram.
- To distinguish a constructor from the class's operations, the UML requires that the word "constructor" be enclosed in **guillemets** (« **and** »; p. 88) and placed before the constructor's name.
- It's customary to list constructors before other operations in the third compartment.

Section 3.5 Software Engineering with Set and Get Member Functions

- Through the use of *set* and *get* member functions, you can validate attempted modifications to private data and control how that data is presented to the caller.
- A **client** (p. 88) of a class is any other code that calls the class's member functions.
- Any client code can see a public data member and do whatever it wanted with it, including setting it to an invalid value.
- *Set* functions can be programmed to validate their arguments and reject any attempts to *set* the data to bad values.
- A *get* function can present the data to a client in a different form.
- Tightly controlling the access to and presentation of private data can greatly reduce errors, while increasing the usability, robustness and security of your programs.

Section 3.6.1 Data Member **balance**

- You can initialize fundamental-type data members in their declarations. This is known as an **in-class initializer** (p. 90) and was introduced in C++11.

Section 3.6.2 Two-Parameter Constructor with Validation

- A constructor can perform **validation** (p. 91) or **validity checking** (p. 91) before modifying a data member.

Section 3.6.3 **deposit** Member Function with Validation

- A *set* function can perform validity checking before modifying a data member.

Self-Review Exercises

3.1　Fill in the blanks in each of the following:

    a) Every class definition contains the keyword _____ followed immediately by the class's name.

    b) A class definition is typically stored in a file with the _____ filename extension.

    c) Each parameter in a function header specifies both a(n) _____ and a(n) _____.

    d) When each object of a class maintains its own version of an attribute, the variable that represents the attribute is also known as a(n) _____.

    e) Keyword public is a(n) _____.

    f) Return type _____ indicates that a function will perform a task but will not return any information when it completes its task.

    g) Function _____ from the <string> library reads characters until a newline character is encountered, then copies those characters into the specified string.

    h) Any file that uses a class can include the class's header via a(n) _____ preprocessing directive.

3.2　State whether each of the following is *true* or *false*. If *false*, explain why.

    a) By convention, function names begin with a capital letter and all subsequent words in the name begin with a capital letter.

    b) Empty parentheses following a function name in a function definition indicate that the function does not require any parameters to perform its task.

    c) Data members or member functions declared with access specifier private are accessible to member functions of the class in which they're declared.

    d) Variables declared in the body of a particular member function are known as data members and can be used in all member functions of the class.

    e) Every function's body is delimited by left and right braces ({ and }).

f) The types of arguments in a function call must be consistent with the types of the corresponding parameters in the function's parameter list.

3.3   What is the difference between a local variable and a data member?

3.4   Explain the purpose of a function parameter. What's the difference between a parameter and an argument?

Answers to Self-Review Exercises

3.1   a) `class`. b) `.h`. c) type, name. d) data member. e) access specifier. f) `void`. g) `getline`. h) `#include`.

3.2   a) False. Function names begin with a lowercase letter and all subsequent words in the name begin with a capital letter. b) True. c) True. d) False. Such variables are local variables and can be used only in the member function in which they're declared. e) True. f) True.

3.3   A local variable is declared in the body of a function and can be used only from its declaration to the closing brace of the block in which it's declared. A data member is declared in a class, but not in the body of any of the class's member functions. Every object of a class has each of the class's data members. Data members are accessible to all member functions of the class.

3.4   A parameter represents additional information that a function requires to perform its task. Each parameter required by a function is specified in the function header. An argument is the value supplied in the function call. When the function is called, the argument value is passed into the function parameter so that the function can perform its task.

Exercises

3.5   *(Default Constructor)* What's a default constructor? How are an object's data members initialized if a class has only a default constructor defined by the compiler?

3.6   *(Data Members)* Explain the purpose of a data member.

3.7   *(Using a Class Without a using Directive)* Explain how a program could use class `string` without inserting a `using` directive.

3.8   *(Set and Get Functions)* Explain why a class might provide a *set* function and a *get* function for a data member.

3.9   *(Modified Account Class)* Modify class `Account` (Fig. 3.8) to provide a member function called `withdraw` that withdraws money from an `Account`. Ensure that the withdrawal amount does not exceed the `Account`'s balance. If it does, the balance should be left unchanged and the member function should display a message indicating `"Withdrawal amount exceeded account balance."` Modify class `AccountTest` (Fig. 3.9) to test member function `withdraw`.

3.10   *(Invoice Class)* Create a class called `Invoice` that a hardware store might use to represent an invoice for an item sold at the store. An `Invoice` should include four data members—a part number (type `string`), a part description (type `string`), a quantity of the item being purchased (type `int`) and a price per item (type `int`). Your class should have a constructor that initializes the four data members. Provide a *set* and a *get* function for each data member. In addition, provide a member function named `getInvoiceAmount` that calculates the invoice amount (i.e., multiplies the quantity by the price per item), then returns the amount as an `int` value. If the quantity is not positive, it should be set to 0. If the price per item is not positive, it should be set to 0. Write a test program that demonstrates class `Invoice`'s capabilities.

3.11   *(Employee Class)* Create a class called `Employee` that includes three pieces of information as data members—a first name (type `string`), a last name (type `string`) and a monthly salary (type int). Your class should have a constructor that initializes the three data members. Provide a *set* and a *get* function for each data member. If the monthly salary is not positive, set it to 0. Write a test program that demonstrates class Employee's capabilities. Create two Employee objects and display each object's *yearly* salary. Then give each Employee a 10 percent raise and display each Employee's yearly salary again.

3.12   *(Date Class)* Create a class called Date that includes three pieces of information as data members—a month (type int), a day (type int) and a year (type int). Your class should have a constructor with three parameters that uses the parameters to initialize the three data members. For the purpose of this exercise, assume that the values provided for the year and day are correct, but ensure that the month value is in the range 1–12; if it isn't, set the month to 1. Provide a *set* and a *get* function for each data member. Provide a member function displayDate that displays the month, day and year separated by forward slashes (/). Write a test program that demonstrates class Date's capabilities.

3.13   *(Removing Duplicated Code in the main Function)* In Fig. 3.9, the main function contains six statements (lines 14–15, 16–17, 26–27, 28–29, 37–38 and 39–40) that each display an Account object's name and balance. Study these statements and you'll notice that they differ only in the Account object being manipulated—account1 or account2. In this exercise, you'll define a new displayAccount function that contains *one* copy of that output statement. The member function's parameter will be an Account object and the member function will output the object's name and balance. You'll then replace the six duplicated statements in main with calls to displayAccount, passing as an argument the specific Account object to output.

Modify Fig. 3.9 to define the following displayAccount function *after* the using directive and *before* main:

```
void displayAccount(Account accountToDisplay) {
    // place the statement that displays
    // accountToDisplay's name and balance here
}
```

Replace the comment in the member function's body with a statement that displays accountToDisplay's name and balance.

Once you've completed displayAccount's declaration, modify main to replace the statements that display each Account's name and balance with calls to displayAccount of the form:

```
displayAccount(nameOfAccountObject);
```

In each call, the argument should be the account1 or account2 object, as appropriate. Then, test the updated program to ensure that it produces the same output as shown in Fig. 3.9.

3.14   *(C++11 List Initializers)* Write a statement that uses list initialization to initialize an object of class Account which provides a constructor that receives an unsigned int, two strings and a double to initialize the accountNumber, firstName, lastName and balance data members of a new object of the class.

Making a Difference

3.15   *(Target-Heart-Rate Calculator)* While exercising, you can use a heart-rate monitor to see that your heart rate stays within a safe range suggested by your trainers and doctors. According to the American Heart Association (AHA) (http://bit.ly/AHATargetHeartRates), the formula for calculating your *maximum heart rate* in beats per minute is 220 minus your age in years. Your *target heart rate* is a range that's 50–85% of your maximum heart rate. [*Note:* These formulas are estimates provided by the AHA. Maximum and target heart rates may vary based on the health, fitness and gender of the individual. **Always consult a physician or qualified health-care professional before beginning or modifying an exercise program.**] Create a class called HeartRates. The class attributes should include the person's first name, last name and date of birth (consisting of separate attributes for the month, day and year of birth). Your class should have a constructor that receives this data as parameters. For each attribute provide *set* and *get* functions. The class also should include a member function that calculates and returns the person's age (in years), a member function that calculates and returns the person's maximum heart rate and a member function that calculates and returns the person's target heart rate. Write a program that prompts for the person's information, instantiates an object of class `HeartRates` and prints the information from that object—including the person's first name, last name and date of birth—then calculates and prints the person's age in (years), maximum heart rate and target-heart-rate range.

3.16   *(Computerization of Health Records)* A health-care issue that has been in the news lately is the computerization of health records. This possibility is being approached cautiously because of sensitive privacy and security concerns, among others. [We address such concerns in later exercises.] Computerizing health records could make it easier for patients to share their health profiles and histories among their various health-care professionals. This could improve the quality of health care, help avoid drug conflicts and erroneous drug prescriptions, reduce costs and, in emergencies, could save lives. In this exercise, you'll design a "starter" `HealthProfile` class for a person. The class attributes should include the person's first name, last name, gender, date of birth (consisting of separate attributes for the month, day and year of birth), height (in inches) and weight (in pounds). Your class should have a constructor that receives this data. For each attribute, provide *set* and *get* functions. The class also should include member functions that calculate and return the user's age in years, maximum heart rate and target-heart-rate range (see Exercise 3.15), and body mass index (BMI; see Exercise 2.30). Write a program that prompts for the person's information, instantiates an object of class `HealthProfile` for that person and prints the information from that object—including the person's first name, last name, gender, date of birth, height and weight—then calculates and prints the person's age in years, BMI, maximum heart rate and target-heart-rate range. It should also display the BMI values chart from Exercise 2.30.

Algorithm Development and Control Statements: Part I

Objectives

In this chapter you'll:

- Learn basic problem-solving techniques.

- Develop algorithms through the process of top-down, stepwise refinement.

- Use the `if` and `if...else` selection statements to choose between alternative actions.

- Use the `while` iteration statement to execute statements in a program repeatedly.

- Use counter-controlled iteration and sentinel-controlled iteration.

- Use nested control statements.

- Use the compound assignment operator and the increment and decrement operators.

- Learn about the portability of fundamental data types.

4.1 Introduction

Before writing a program to solve a problem, you should have a thorough understanding of the problem and a carefully planned approach to solving it. When writing a program, you also should understand the available building blocks and employ proven program-construction techniques. In this chapter and the next, we discuss these issues in presenting the theory and principles of structured programming. The concepts presented here are crucial in building classes and manipulating objects. We discuss C++'s if statement in additional detail and introduce the if...else and while statements—all of these building blocks allow you to specify the logic required for functions to perform their tasks. We also introduce the compound assignment operator and the increment and decrement operators. Finally, we consider the portability of C++'s fundamental types.

4.2 Algorithms

Any computing problem can be solved by executing a series of actions in a specific order. A *procedure* for solving a problem in terms of

1. the actions to execute and
2. the order in which these actions execute

is called an algorithm. The following example demonstrates that correctly specifying the order in which the actions execute is important.

Consider the "rise-and-shine algorithm" one executive follows for getting out of bed and going to work: (1) Get out of bed; (2) take off pajamas; (3) take a shower; (4) get dressed; (5) eat breakfast; (6) carpool to work. This routine gets the executive to work well prepared to make critical decisions. Suppose that the same steps are performed in a slightly different order: (1) Get out of bed; (2) take off pajamas; (3) get dressed; (4) take a shower; (5) eat breakfast; (6) carpool to work. In this case, our executive shows up for work soaking wet. Specifying the order in which statements (actions) execute in a program is called program control. This chapter investigates program control using C++'s control statements.

4.3 Pseudocode

Pseudocode is an informal language that helps you develop algorithms without having to worry about the strict details of C++ language syntax. The pseudocode we present is particularly useful for developing algorithms that will be converted to structured portions of C++ programs. Pseudocode is similar to everyday English—it's convenient and user friendly, but it's not an actual computer programming language. You'll see an algorithm written in pseudocode in Fig. 4.1. You may, of course, use your own native language(s) to develop your own pseudocode style.

Pseudocode does not execute on computers. Rather, it helps you "think out" a program before attempting to write it in a programming language, such as C++. This chapter provides several examples of using pseudocode to develop C++ programs.

The style of pseudocode we present consists purely of characters, so you can type pseudocode conveniently, using any text-editor program. A carefully prepared pseudocode program can easily be converted to a corresponding C++ program.

Pseudocode normally describes only statements representing the *actions* that occur after you convert a program from pseudocode to C++ and the program is run on a computer. Such actions might include *input, output, assignments* or *calculations*. In our pseudocode, we typically do not include variable declarations, but some programmers choose to list variables and mention their purposes.

Addition Program Pseudocode
Let's look at an example of pseudocode that may be written to help a programmer create the addition program of Fig. 2.5. This pseudocode (Fig. 4.1) corresponds to the algorithm that inputs two integers from the user, adds these integers and displays their sum. We show the complete pseudocode listing here—we'll show how to *create pseudocode from a problem statement* later in the chapter.

Notice that the pseudocode statements are simply English statements that convey what task is to be performed in C++. Lines 1–2 correspond to the C++ statements in lines

1	*Prompt the user to enter the first integer*
2	*Input the first integer*
3	
4	*Prompt the user to enter the second integer*
5	*Input the second integer*
6	
7	*Add first integer and second integer, store result*
8	*Display result*

Fig. 4.1 | Pseudocode for the addition program of Fig. 2.5.

13–14 of Fig. 2.5. Lines 4–5 correspond to the statements in lines 16–17 and lines 7–8 correspond to the statements in lines 19 and 21.

4.4 Control Structures

Normally, statements in a program are executed one after the other in the order in which they're written. This process is called sequential execution. Various C++ statements, which we'll soon discuss, enable you to specify that the next statement to execute is *not* necessarily the *next* one in sequence. This is called transfer of control.

During the 1960s, it became clear that the indiscriminate use of transfers of control was the root of much difficulty experienced by software development groups. The blame was pointed at the goto statement (used in most programming languages of the time), which allows you to specify a transfer of control to one of a wide range of destinations in a program.

The research of Bohm and Jacopini[1] had demonstrated that programs could be written *without* any goto statements. The challenge for programmers of the era was to shift their styles to "goto-less programming." The term structured programming became almost synonymous with "goto elimination." Not until the 1970s did most programmers start taking structured programming seriously. The results were impressive. Software development groups reported shorter development times, more frequent on-time delivery of systems and more frequent within-budget completion of software projects. The key to these successes was that structured programs were clearer, easier to debug and modify, and more likely to be bug free in the first place.

Bohm and Jacopini's work demonstrated that all programs could be written in terms of only three control structures—the sequence structure, the selection structure and the iteration structure. We'll discuss how each of these is implemented in C++.

4.4.1 Sequence Structure

The sequence structure is built into C++. Unless directed otherwise, the computer executes C++ statements one after the other in the order in which they're written—that is, in sequence. The UML activity diagram in Fig. 4.2 illustrates a typical sequence structure in

---

1. C. Bohm and G. Jacopini, "Flow Diagrams, Turing Machines, and Languages with Only Two Formation Rules," *Communications of the ACM*, Vol. 9, No. 5, May 1966, pp. 336–371.

which two calculations are performed in order. C++ lets you have as many actions as you want in a sequence structure. As we'll soon see, anywhere a single action may be placed, we may place several actions in sequence.

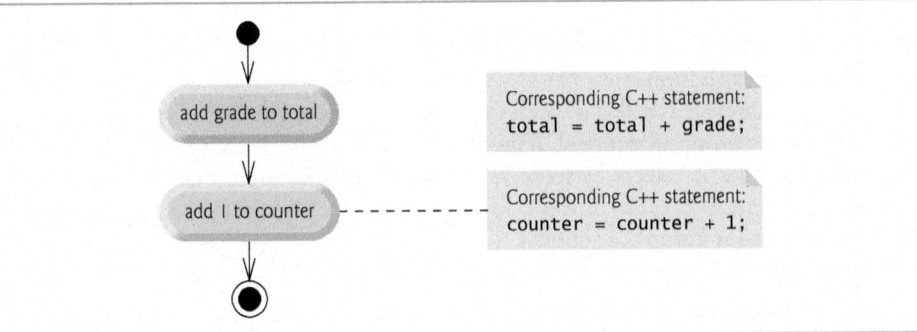

Fig. 4.2 | Sequence-structure activity diagram.

An activity diagram models the workflow (also called the activity) of a portion of a software system. Such workflows may include a portion of an algorithm, like the sequence structure in Fig. 4.2. Activity diagrams are composed of symbols, such as action-state symbols (rectangles with their left and right sides replaced with outward arcs), diamonds and small circles. These symbols are connected by transition arrows, which represent the *flow of the activity*—that is, the *order* in which the actions should occur.

Like pseudocode, activity diagrams help you develop and represent algorithms. Activity diagrams clearly show how control structures operate. We use the UML in this chapter and Chapter 5 to show the flow of control in control statements. Online Chapters 25–26 use the UML in a real-world ATM (automated-teller-machine) case study.

Consider the sequence-structure activity diagram in Fig. 4.2. It contains two action states, each containing an action expression—for example, "add grade to total" or "add 1 to counter"—that specifies a particular action to perform. The arrows in the activity diagram represent transitions, which indicate the *order* in which the actions represented by the action states occur. The program that implements the activities illustrated in Fig. 4.2 first adds `grade` to `total`, then adds 1 to `counter`.

The solid circle at the top of the activity diagram represents the initial state—the *beginning* of the workflow *before* the program performs the modeled actions. The solid circle surrounded by a hollow circle at the bottom of the diagram represents the final state—the *end* of the workflow *after* the program performs its actions.

Figure 4.2 also includes rectangles with the upper-right corners folded over. These are UML notes (like comments in C++)—explanatory remarks that describe the purpose of symbols in the diagram. Figure 4.2 uses UML notes to show the C++ code associated with each action state. A dotted line connects each note with the element it describes. Activity diagrams normally do not show the C++ code that implements the activity. We do this here to illustrate how the diagram relates to C++ code. For more information on the UML, see our optional online object-oriented design case study (Chapters 25–26) or visit www.uml.org.

4.4.2 Selection Statements

C++ has three types of selection statements. The *if statement* performs (selects) an action (or group of actions), if a condition is *true*, or skips it, if the condition is *false*. The *if...else statement* performs an action (or group of actions) if a condition is *true* and performs a different action (or group of actions) if the condition is *false*. The *switch statement* (Chapter 5) performs one of *many* different actions (or group of actions), depending on the value of an expression.

The if statement is called a single-selection statement because it selects or ignores a *single* action (or group of actions). The if...else statement is called a double-selection statement because it selects between *two different* actions (or groups of actions). The switch statement is called a multiple-selection statement because it selects among *many different* actions (or groups of actions).

4.4.3 Iteration Statements

C++ provides four iteration statements (sometimes called repetition statements or looping statements) that enable programs to perform statements repeatedly as long as a condition (called the loop-continuation condition) remains *true*. The iteration statements are the while, do...while, for and range-based for statements. (Chapter 5 presents the do...while and for statements and Chapter 7 presents the range-based for statement.) The while and for statements perform the action (or group of actions) in their bodies *zero or more times*—if the loop-continuation condition is initially *false*, the action (or group of actions) will *not* execute. The do...while statement performs the action (or group of actions) in its body *one or more* times.

Each of the words if, else, switch, while, do and for are C++ keywords. Keywords cannot be used as identifiers, such as variable names, and must be spelled with only lowercase letters. Figure 4.3 provides a complete list of C++ keywords.

C++ Keywords				
Keywords common to the C and C++ programming languages				
asm	auto	break	case	char
const	continue	default	do	double
else	enum	extern	float	for
goto	if	inline	int	long
register	return	short	signed	sizeof
static	struct	switch	typedef	union
unsigned	void	volatile	while	
C++-only keywords				
and	and_eq	bitand	bitor	bool
catch	class	compl	const_cast	delete
dynamic_cast	explicit	export	false	friend
mutable	namespace	new	not	not_eq
operator	or	or_eq	private	protected
public	reinterpret_cast	static_cast	template	this

Fig. 4.3 | C++ keywords. (Part I of 2.)

C++ Keywords				
throw	true	try	typeid	typename
using	virtual	wchar_t	xor	xor_eq
C++11 keywords				
alignas	alignof	char16_t	char32_t	constexpr
decltype	noexcept	nullptr	static_assert	thread_local

Fig. 4.3 | C++ keywords. (Part 2 of 2.)

11

4.4.4 Summary of Control Statements

C++ has only three kinds of control structures, which from this point forward we refer to as *control statements*: the *sequence statement, selection statements* (three types) and *iteration statements* (four types). Every program is formed by combining as many of these statements as is appropriate for the algorithm the program implements. We can model each control statement as an activity diagram. Like Fig. 4.2, each diagram contains an initial state and a final state that represent a control statement's entry point and exit point, respectively. Single-entry/single-exit control statements make it easy to build programs—we simply connect the exit point of one to the entry point of the next. We call this control-statement stacking. We'll learn that there's only one other way in which control statements may be connected—control-statement nesting—in which one control statement appears *inside* another. Thus, algorithms in C++ programs are constructed from only three kinds of control statements, combined in only two ways. This is the essence of simplicity.

4.5 if Single-Selection Statement

We introduced the if single-selection statement briefly in Section 2.7. Programs use selection statements to choose among alternative courses of action. For example, suppose that the passing grade on an exam is 60. The *pseudocode* statement

> *If student's grade is greater than or equal to 60*
> *Print "Passed"*

represents an if statement that determines whether the *condition* "student's grade is greater than or equal to 60" is *true*. If so, "Passed" is printed, and the next pseudocode statement in order is "performed." (Remember, pseudocode is not a real programming language.) If the condition is *false*, the *Print* statement is ignored, and the next pseudocode statement in order is performed. The indentation of the second line of this selection statement is optional, but recommended, because it emphasizes the inherent structure of structured programs.

The preceding pseudocode *If* statement may be written in C++ as

```cpp
if (studentGrade >= 60) {
    cout << "Passed";
}
```

The C++ code corresponds closely to the pseudocode. This is a property of pseudocode that makes it such a useful program development tool.

bool Data Type

You saw in Chapter 2 that decisions can be based on conditions containing relational or equality operators. Actually, in C++, a decision can be based on *any* expression that evaluates to zero or nonzero—if the expression evaluates to *zero*, it's treated as *false*; if the expression evaluates to *nonzero*, it's treated as *true*. C++ also provides the data type `bool` for Boolean variables that can hold only the values `true` and `false`—each of these is a C++ keyword.

Portability Tip 4.1

For compatibility with earlier versions of C, which used integers for Boolean values, the `bool` *value* true *also can be represented by any* nonzero *value (compilers typically use 1) and the* `bool` *value* false *also can be represented as the value* zero.

UML Activity Diagram for an **if** *Statement*

Figure 4.4 illustrates the single-selection `if` statement. This figure contains the most important symbol in an activity diagram—the *diamond*, or decision symbol, which indicates that a *decision* is to be made. The workflow continues along a path determined by the symbol's associated guard conditions, which can be *true* or *false*. Each transition arrow emerging from a decision symbol has a guard condition (specified in *square brackets* next to the arrow). If a guard condition is *true*, the workflow enters the action state to which the transition arrow points. In Fig. 4.4, if the grade is greater than or equal to 60 (i.e., the condition is *true*), the program prints "Passed," then transitions to the activity's final state. If the grade is less than 60 (i.e., the condition is *false*), the program immediately transitions to the final state without displaying a message.

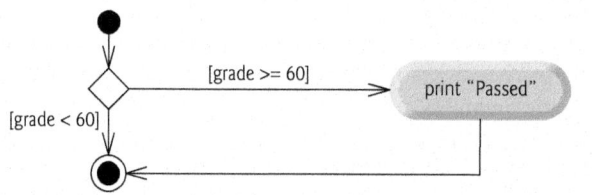

Fig. 4.4 | `if` single-selection statement UML activity diagram.

The `if` statement is a single-entry/single-exit control statement. We'll see that the activity diagrams for the remaining control statements also contain initial states, transition arrows, action states that indicate actions to perform, decision symbols (with associated guard conditions) that indicate decisions to be made, and final states.

4.6 `if...else` Double-Selection Statement

The `if` single-selection statement performs an indicated action only when the condition is *true*; otherwise, the action is skipped. The `if...else` double-selection statement allows you to specify an action to perform when the condition is *true* and another action when the condition is *false*. For example, the pseudocode statement

> *If student's grade is greater than or equal to 60*
> *Print "Passed"*
> *Else*
> *Print "Failed"*

represents an if...else statement that prints "Passed" if the student's grade is greater than or equal to 60, but prints "Failed" if it's less than 60. In either case, after printing occurs, the next pseudocode statement in sequence is "performed."

The preceding *If...Else* pseudocode statement can be written in C++ as

```cpp
if (grade >= 60) {
   cout << "Passed";
}
else {
   cout << "Failed";
}
```

The body of the else is also indented. Whatever indentation convention you choose should be applied consistently throughout your programs.

Good Programming Practice 4.1
Indent both body statements (or groups of statements) of an if...else statement. Many IDEs do this for you.

Good Programming Practice 4.2
If there are several levels of indentation, each level should be indented the same additional amount of space. We prefer three-space indents.

UML Activity Diagram for an if...else Statement
Figure 4.5 illustrates the flow of control in the preceding if...else statement. Once again, the symbols in the UML activity diagram (besides the initial state, transition arrows and final state) represent action states and decisions.

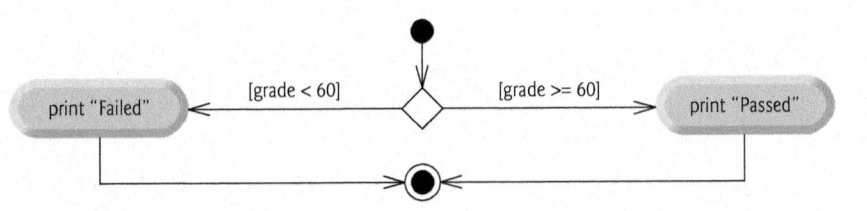

Fig. 4.5 | if...else double-selection statement UML activity diagram.

4.6.1 Nested if...else Statements
A program can test multiple cases by placing if...else statements inside other if...else statements to create nested if...else statements. For example, the following pseudocode

represents a nested if...else that prints A for exam grades greater than or equal to 90, B for grades 80 to 89, C for grades 70 to 79, D for grades 60 to 69 and F for all other grades:

If student's grade is greater than or equal to 90
    Print "A"
else
    If student's grade is greater than or equal to 80
        Print "B"
    else
        If student's grade is greater than or equal to 70
            Print "C"
        else
            If student's grade is greater than or equal to 60
                Print "D"
            else
                Print "F"

We use shading to highlight the nesting. This pseudocode may be written in C++ as

```cpp
if (studentGrade >= 90) {
    cout << "A";
}
else {
    if (studentGrade >= 80) {
        cout << "B";
    }
    else {
        if (studentGrade >= 70) {
            cout << "C";
        }
        else {
            if (studentGrade >= 60) {
                cout << "D";
            }
            else {
                cout << "F";
            }
        }
    }
}
```

If variable studentGrade is greater than or equal to 90, the first four conditions in the nested if...else statement will be *true*, but only the statement in the if part of the first if...else statement will execute. After that statement executes, the else part of the "outermost" if...else statement is skipped. Many programmers prefer to write the preceding nested if...else statement in the following form, which is identical except for the spacing and intentation that the compiler ignores:

```
if (studentGrade >= 90) {
   cout << "A";
}
else if (studentGrade >= 80) {
   cout << "B";
}
else if (studentGrade >= 70) {
   cout << "C";
}
else if (studentGrade >= 60) {
   cout << "D";
}
else {
   cout << "F";
}
```

The latter form avoids deep indentation of the code to the right. Such indentation often leaves little room on a line of code, forcing lines to wrap.

Error-Prevention Tip 4.1
In a nested if...else statement, ensure that you test for all possible cases.

4.6.2 Dangling-else Problem

Throughout the text, we always enclose control statement bodies in braces ({ and }). This avoids a logic error called the "dangling-else" problem. We investigate this problem in Exercises 4.23—4.25.

4.6.3 Blocks

The if statement normally expects only *one* statement in its body. To include *several* statements in the body of an if (or the body of an else for an if...else statement), enclose the statements in braces. As we've done throughout the text, it's good practice to always use the braces. Statements contained in a pair of braces (such as the body of a control statement or function) form a block. A block can be placed anywhere in a function that a single statement can be placed.

The following example includes a block of *multiple* statements in the else part of an if...else statement:

```
if (grade >= 60) {
   cout << "Passed";
}
else
{
   cout << "Failed\n";
   cout << "You must take this course again.";
}
```

In this case, if grade is less than 60, the program executes *both* statements in the body of the else and prints

```
Failed
You must take this course again.
```

Without the braces surrounding the two statements in the else clause, the statement

```
cout << "You must take this course again.";
```

would be outside the body of the else part of the if...else statement and would execute *regardless* of whether the grade was less than 60.

Syntax and Logic Errors

Syntax errors (such as when one brace in a block is left out of the program) are caught by the compiler. A logic error (such as an incorrect calculation) has its effect at execution time. A fatal logic error causes a program to fail and terminate prematurely. A nonfatal logic error allows a program to continue executing but causes it to produce incorrect results.

Empty Statement

Just as a block can be placed anywhere a single statement can be placed, it's also possible to have an empty statement, which is represented by placing a semicolon (;) where a statement would normally be.

Common Programming Error 4.1

Placing a semicolon after the parenthesized condition in an if or if...else statement leads to a logic error in single-selection if statements and a syntax error in double-selection if...else statements (when the if-part contains a body statement).

4.6.4 Conditional Operator (?:)

C++ provides the conditional operator (?:) that can be used in place of an if...else statement. This can make your code shorter and clearer. The conditional operator is C++'s only ternary operator (i.e., an operator that takes *three* operands). Together, the operands and the ?: symbol form a conditional expression. For example, the statement

```
cout << (studentGrade >= 60 ? "Passed" : "Failed");
```

prints the value of the conditional expression. The first operand (to the left of the ?) is a condition, the second operand (between the ? and :) is the value of the conditional expression if the condition is *true* and the third operand (to the right of the :) is the value of the conditional expression if the condition is *false*. The conditional expression in this statement evaluates to the string "Passed" if the condition

```
studentGrade >= 60
```

is *true* and to the string "Failed" if it's *false*. Thus, this statement with the conditional operator performs essentially the same function as the first if...else statement in Section 4.6. The precedence of the conditional operator is low, so the entire conditional expression is normally placed in parentheses. We'll see that conditional expressions can be used in some situations where if...else statements cannot.

The values in a conditional expression also can be actions to execute. For example, the following conditional expression also prints "Passed" or "Failed":

```
grade >= 60 ? cout << "Passed" : cout << "Failed";
```

The preceding is read, "If grade is greater than or equal to 60, then cout << "Passed"; otherwise, cout << "Failed"." This is comparable to an if...else statement. Conditional expressions can appear in some program locations where if...else statements cannot.

4.7 Student Class: Nested if...else Statements

The example of Figs. 4.6–4.7 demonstrates a nested if...else statement that determines a student's letter grade based on the student's average in a course.

Class **Student**

Class Student (Fig. 4.6) stores a student's name and average and provides member functions for manipulating these values. The class contains:

- Data member name of type string (line 65) to store a Student's name.

- Data member average of type int (line 66) to store a Student's average in a course.

- A constructor (lines 8–13) that initializes the name and average.

- Member functions setName and getName (lines 16–23) to *set* and *get* the Student's name.

- Member functions setAverage and getAverage (lines 26–39) to *set* and *get* the Student's average—in Section 5.11, you'll learn how to express lines 29–30 more concisely with logical operators that can test multiple conditions.

- Member function getLetterGrade (lines 42–63), which uses *nested if...else statements* to determine the Student's letter grade based on the Student's average.

After the constructor initializes name in the member-initializer list, the constructor calls member function setAverage, which uses *nested if statements* (lines 29–33) to validate the value used to set the average. These statements ensure that the value is greater than 0 *and* less than or equal to 100; otherwise, average's value is left unchanged. Each if statement contains a *simple condition*—i.e., one that makes only a single test. In Section 5.11, you'll see how to use logical operators to write compound conditions that conveniently combine several simple conditions. If the condition in line 29 is *true*, only then will the condition in line 30 be tested, and *only* if the conditions in both lines 29 *and* 30 are *true* will the statement in line 31 execute.

```
1   // Fig. 4.6: Student.h
2   // Student class that stores a student name and average.
3   #include <string>
4
5   class Student {
6   public:
7      // constructor initializes data members
8      Student(std::string studentName, int studentAverage)
9         : name(studentName) {
10
```

Fig. 4.6 | Student class that stores a student name and average. (Part 1 of 3.)

```
11          // sets average data member if studentAverage is valid
12          setAverage(studentAverage);
13       }
14
15       // sets the Student's name
16       void setName(std::string studentName) {
17          name = studentName;
18       }
19
20       // retrieves the Student's name
21       std::string getName() const {
22          return name;
23       }
24
25       // sets the Student's average
26       void setAverage(int studentAverage) {
27          // validate that studentAverage is > 0 and <= 100; otherwise,
28          // keep data member average's current value
29          if (studentAverage > 0) {
30             if (studentAverage <= 100) {
31                average = studentAverage; // assign to data member
32             }
33          }
34       }
35
36       // retrieves the Student's average
37       int getAverage() const {
38          return average;
39       }
40
41       // determines and returns the Student's letter grade
42       std::string getLetterGrade() const {
43          // initialized to empty string by class string's constructor
44          std::string letterGrade;
45
46          if (average >= 90) {
47             letterGrade = "A";
48          }
49          else if (average >= 80) {
50             letterGrade = "B";
51          }
52          else if (average >= 70) {
53             letterGrade = "C";
54          }
55          else if (average >= 60) {
56             letterGrade = "D";
57          }
58          else {
59             letterGrade = "F";
60          }
61
62          return letterGrade;
63       }
```

Fig. 4.6 | Student class that stores a student name and average. (Part 2 of 3.)

```
64    private:
65        std::string name;
66        int average{0}; // initialize average to 0
67    } // end class Student
```

Fig. 4.6 | Student class that stores a student name and average. (Part 3 of 3.)

Class StudentTest

To demonstrate the nested if...else statements in class Student's getLetterGrade member function, the main function (Fig. 4.7) creates two Student objects (lines 8–9). Next, lines 11–16 display each Student's name, average and letter grade by calling the objects' getName, getAverage and getLetterGrade member functions, respectively.

```
 1    // Fig. 4.7: StudentTest.cpp
 2    // Create and test Student objects.
 3    #include <iostream>
 4    #include "Student.h"
 5    using namespace std;
 6
 7    int main() {
 8        Student account1{"Jane Green", 93};
 9        Student account2{"John Blue", 72};
10
11        cout << account1.getName() << "'s letter grade equivalent of "
12            << account1.getAverage() << " is: "
13            << account1.getLetterGrade() << "\n";
14        cout << account2.getName() << "'s letter grade equivalent of "
15            << account2.getAverage() << " is: "
16            << account2.getLetterGrade() << endl;
17    }
```

```
Jane Green's letter grade equivalent of 93 is: A
John Blue's letter grade equivalent of 72 is: C
```

Fig. 4.7 | Create and test Student objects.

4.8 while Iteration Statement

An iteration statement allows you to specify that a program should repeat an action while some condition remains *true*. The pseudocode statement

> *While there are more items on my shopping list*
> *Purchase next item and cross it off my list*

describes the iteration during a shopping trip. The condition "there are more items on my shopping list" may be *true* or *false*. If it's *true*, then the action "Purchase next item and cross it off my list" is performed. This action will be performed *repeatedly* while the condition remains *true*. The statement(s) contained in the *While* iteration statement constitute its body, which may be a single statement or a block. Eventually, the condition will become *false* (when the shopping list's last item has been purchased and crossed off). At this point, the iteration terminates, and the first statement after the iteration statement executes.

As an example of C++'s while iteration statement, consider a program segment that finds the first power of 3 larger than 100. After the following while statement executes, the variable product contains the result:

```
int product{3};

while (product <= 100) {
    product = 3 * product;
}
```

Each iteration of the while statement multiplies product by 3, so product takes on the values 9, 27, 81 and 243 successively. When product becomes 243, product <= 100 becomes *false*. This terminates the iteration, so the final value of product is 243. At this point, program execution continues with the next statement after the while statement.

 Common Programming Error 4.2

Not providing in the body of a while statement an action that eventually causes the condition in the while to become false results in a logic error called an infinite loop (the loop never terminates).

UML Activity Diagram for a **while** Statement

The UML activity diagram in Fig. 4.8 illustrates the flow of control in the preceding while statement. Once again, the symbols in the diagram (besides the initial state, transition arrows, a final state and three notes) represent an action state and a decision. This diagram introduces the UML's merge symbol. The UML represents ***both*** the merge symbol and the decision symbol as diamonds. The merge symbol joins two flows of activity into one. In this diagram, the merge symbol joins the transitions from the initial state and from the action state, so they both flow into the decision that determines whether the loop should begin (or continue) executing.

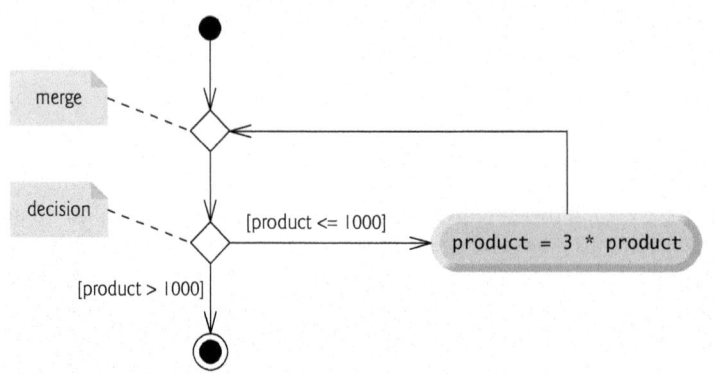

Fig. 4.8 | while iteration statement UML activity diagram.

The decision and merge symbols can be distinguished by the number of "incoming" and "outgoing" transition arrows. A decision symbol has *one* transition arrow pointing *to* the diamond and *two or more* pointing out *from* it to indicate possible transitions from that point. In addition, each transition arrow pointing out of a decision symbol has a guard condition next to it. A merge symbol has two or more transition arrows pointing to the diamond and only one pointing from the diamond, to indicate multiple activity flows merging to continue the activity. None of the transition arrows associated with a merge symbol has a guard condition.

Figure 4.8 clearly shows the iteration of the while statement discussed earlier in this section. The transition arrow emerging from the action state points back to the merge, from which program flow transitions back to the decision that's tested at the beginning of each iteration of the loop. The loop continues executing until the guard condition product > 100 becomes *true*. Then the while statement exits (reaches its final state), and control passes to the next statement in sequence in the program.

4.9 Formulating Algorithms: Counter-Controlled Iteration

To illustrate how algorithms are developed, we solve two variations of a problem that averages student grades. Consider the following problem statement:

> *A class of ten students took a quiz. The grades (integers in the range 0–100) for this quiz are available to you. Determine the class average on the quiz.*

The class average is equal to the sum of the grades divided by the number of students. The algorithm for solving this problem on a computer must input each grade, keep track of the total of all grades entered, perform the averaging calculation and print the result.

4.9.1 Pseudocode Algorithm with Counter-Controlled Iteration

Let's use pseudocode to list the actions to execute and specify the order in which they should execute. We use counter-controlled iteration to input the grades one at a time. This technique uses a variable called a counter (or control variable) to control the number of times a set of statements will execute. Counter-controlled iteration is often called definite iteration, because the number of iterations is known *before* the loop begins executing. In this example, iteration terminates when the counter exceeds 10. This section presents a fully developed pseudocode algorithm (Fig. 4.9) and a corresponding C++ program (Fig. 4.10) that implements the algorithm. In Section 4.10, we demonstrate how to develop pseudocode algorithms from scratch.

1	*Set total to zero*
2	*Set grade counter to one*
3	
4	*While grade counter is less than or equal to ten*
5	*Prompt the user to enter the next grade*
6	*Input the next grade*
7	*Add the grade into the total*
8	*Add one to the grade counter*

Fig. 4.9 | Pseudocode algorithm that uses counter-controlled iteration to solve the class-average problem. (Part 1 of 2.)

9	
10	*Set the class average to the total divided by ten*
11	*Print the class average*

Fig. 4.9 | Pseudocode algorithm that uses counter-controlled iteration to solve the class-average problem. (Part 2 of 2.)

Note the references in the algorithm of Fig. 4.9 to a total and a counter. A total is a variable used to accumulate the sum of several values. A counter is a variable used to count—in this case, the grade counter indicates which of the 10 grades is about to be entered by the user. Variables used to store totals normally are initialized to zero before being used in a program. In pseudocode, we do *not* use braces around the statements that form the body of the pseudocode *While* structure, but you could.

Software Engineering Observation 4.1

Experience has shown that the most difficult part of solving a problem on a computer is developing the algorithm for the solution. Once a correct algorithm has been specified, producing a working C++ program from it is usually straightforward.

4.9.2 Implementing Counter-Controlled Iteration

In Fig. 4.10, the main function implements the class-averaging algorithm described by the pseudocode in Fig. 4.9—it allows the user to enter 10 grades, then calculates and displays the average.

```cpp
1   // Fig. 4.10: ClassAverage.cpp
2   // Solving the class-average problem using counter-controlled iteration.
3   #include <iostream>
4   using namespace std;
5
6   int main() {
7      // initialization phase
8      int total{0}; // initialize sum of grades entered by the user
9      unsigned int gradeCounter{1}; // initialize grade # to be entered next
10
11     // processing phase uses counter-controlled iteration
12     while (gradeCounter <= 10) { // loop 10 times
13        cout << "Enter grade: "; // prompt
14        int grade;
15        cin >> grade; // input next grade
16        total = total + grade; // add grade to total
17        gradeCounter = gradeCounter + 1; // increment counter by 1
18     }
19
20     // termination phase
21     int average{total / 10}; // int division yields int result
22
```

Fig. 4.10 | Solving the class-average problem using counter-controlled iteration. (Part 1 of 2.)

```
23      // display total and average of grades
24      cout << "\nTotal of all 10 grades is " << total;
25      cout << "\nClass average is " << average << endl;
26   }
```

```
Enter grade: 67
Enter grade: 78
Enter grade: 89
Enter grade: 67
Enter grade: 87
Enter grade: 98
Enter grade: 93
Enter grade: 85
Enter grade: 82
Enter grade: 100

Total of all 10 grades is 846
Class average is 84
```

Fig. 4.10 | Solving the class-average problem using counter-controlled iteration. (Part 2 of 2.)

Local Variables in `main`

Lines 8, 9, 14 and 21 declare local variables `total`, `gradeCounter`, `grade` and `average`, respectively. Variable `gradeCounter` is of type `unsigned int`, because it can assume only the values from 1 through 11 (11 terminates the loop), which are all positive values. In general, counters that should store only nonnegative values should be declared with `unsigned` types. Variables of `unsigned` integer types can represent values from 0 to approximately *twice the positive range* of the corresponding signed integer types. You can determine your platform's maximum `unsigned int` value with the constant `UINT_MAX` from `<climits>`. The program's other variables are of type `int`. Variable `grade` stores the user input.

A variable declared in a function body is a local variable and can be used only from the line of its declaration to the closing right brace of the block in which the variable is declared. A local variable's declaration must appear *before* the variable is used; otherwise, a compilation error occurs. Variable `grade`—declared in the body of the `while` loop—can be used only in that block.

Initialization Phase: Initializing Variables `total` and **`gradeCounter`**

Lines 8–9 declare and initialize `total` to 0 and `gradeCounter` to 1. These initializations occur *before* the variables are used in calculations.

Error-Prevention Tip 4.2
Initialize each total and counter, either in its declaration or in an assignment statement. Totals are normally initialized to 0. Counters are normally initialized to 0 or 1, depending on how they're used (we'll show examples of when to use 0 and when to use 1).

Processing Phase: Reading 10 Grades from the User

Line 12 indicates that the `while` statement should continue looping (also called iterating) as long as `gradeCounter`'s value is less than or equal to 10. While this condition remains *true*, the while statement repeatedly executes the statements between the braces that delimit its body (lines 12–18).

Line 13 displays the prompt "Enter grade: ". Line 15 inputs the grade entered by the user and assigns it to variable grade. Then line 16 adds the new grade entered by the user to the total and assigns the result to total, replacing its previous value.

Line 17 adds 1 to gradeCounter to indicate that the program has processed a grade and is ready to input the next grade from the user. Incrementing gradeCounter eventually causes it to exceed 10. Then the loop terminates, because its condition (line 12) becomes *false*.

Termination Phase: Calculating and Displaying the Class Average

When the loop terminates, line 21 performs the averaging calculation in the average variable's initializer. Line 24 displays the text "Total of all 10 grades is " followed by variable total's value. Then, line 25 displays the text "Class average is " followed by variable average's value. When execution reaches line 26, the program terminates.

Notice that this example contains only a main function that performs all the work. In this chapter and in Chapter 3, you've seen examples consisting of a class and a main program that creates an object of the class and calls its member functions. When it does not make sense to try to create a reusable class to demonstrate a concept, we'll place the program's statements entirely within main.

4.9.3 Notes on Integer Division and Truncation

This example's averaging calculation produces an integer result. The program's output indicates that the sum of the grade values in the sample execution is 846, which, when divided by 10, should yield the floating-point number 84.6. However, the result of the calculation total / 10 (line 21 of Fig. 4.10) is the integer 84, because total and 10 are both integers. Dividing two integers results in integer division—any fractional part of the calculation is truncated (i.e., *lost*). In the next section we'll see how to obtain a floating-point result from the averaging calculation.

Common Programming Error 4.3

Assuming that integer division rounds (rather than truncates) can lead to incorrect results. For example, 7 ÷ 4, which yields 1.75 in conventional arithmetic, truncates to 1 in integer arithmetic, rather than rounding to 2.

4.9.4 Arithmetic Overflow

In Fig. 4.10, line 16

```
total = total + grade; // add grade to total
```

adds each grade entered by the user to the total. Even this simple statement has a *potential* problem—adding the integers could result in a value that's *too large* to store in an int variable. This is known as arithmetic overflow and causes *undefined behavior*, which can lead to unintended results and security problems. See, for example,

```
http://en.wikipedia.org/wiki/Integer_overflow#Security_ramifications
```

Figure 2.5 had the same issue in line 19, which calculated the sum of two int values entered by the user:

```
sum = number1 + number2; // add the numbers; store result in sum
```

The maximum and minimum values that can be stored in an int variable are represented by the constants INT_MAX and INT_MIN, respectively, which are defined in the header <climits>. There are similar constants for the other integral types and for floating-point types (header <cfloat>). To see these constants' values on your platform, include the appropriate header in a program that outputs the values with cout, as in

```
cout << "INT_MAX = " << INT_MAX << "\n";
```

For arithmetic calculations like those in line 16 of Fig. 4.10 and line 19 of Fig. 2.5, it's considered a good practice to ensure *before* you perform them that they will *not* overflow. The code for doing this is shown at www.securecoding.cert.org—just search for guideline "INT32-CPP." The code uses the && (logical AND) and || (logical OR) operators, which are introduced in Chapter 5.

4.9.5 Input Validation

Any time a program receives input from the user, various problems might occur. For example, in line 15 of Fig. 4.10

```
cin >> grade; // input next grade
```

we assume that the user will enter an integer grade in the range 0 to 100. However, the user could enter an integer less than 0, an integer greater than 100, an integer outside the range of values that can be stored in an int variable, a number containing a decimal point or a value containing letters or special symbols that's not even an integer.

To ensure that inputs are valid, industrial-strength programs must test for all possible erroneous cases. A program that inputs grades should validate the grades by using range checking to ensure that they're values from 0 to 100. You can then ask the user to reenter any value that's out of range. If a program requires inputs from a specific set of values (e.g., nonsequential product codes), you can ensure that each input matches a value in the set.

4.10 Formulating Algorithms: Sentinel-Controlled Iteration

Let's generalize Section 4.9's class-average problem. Consider the following problem:

> *Develop a class-averaging program that processes grades for an arbitrary number of students each time it's run.*

In the previous class-average example, the problem statement specified the number of students, so the number of grades (10) was known in advance. In this example, no indication is given of how many grades the user will enter during the program's execution. The program must process an *arbitrary* number of grades. How can it determine when to stop the input of grades? How will it know when to calculate and print the class average?

One way to solve this problem is to use a special value called a sentinel value (also called a signal value, a dummy value or a flag value) to indicate "end of data entry." The user enters grades until all legitimate grades have been entered. The user then types the sentinel value to indicate that no more grades will be entered. Sentinel-controlled iteration is often called indefinite iteration because the number of iterations is *not* known before the loop begins executing.

Clearly, a sentinel value must be chosen that cannot be confused with an acceptable input value. Grades on a quiz are nonnegative integers, so –1 is an acceptable sentinel value for this problem. Thus, a run of the class-averaging program might process a stream of inputs such as 95, 96, 75, 74, 89 and –1. The program would then compute and print the class average for the grades 95, 96, 75, 74 and 89; since –1 is the sentinel value, it should *not* enter into the averaging calculation.

4.10.1 Top-Down, Stepwise Refinement: The Top and First Refinement

We approach this class-averaging program with a technique called top-down, stepwise refinement, which is essential to the development of well-structured programs. We begin with a pseudocode representation of the top—a single statement that conveys the overall function of the program:

> *Determine the class average for the quiz*

The top is, in effect, a *complete* representation of a program. Unfortunately, the top rarely conveys sufficient detail from which to write a C++ program. So we now begin the refinement process. We divide the top into a series of smaller tasks and list these in the order in which they'll be performed. This results in the following first refinement:

> *Initialize variables*
> *Input, sum and count the quiz grades*
> *Calculate and print the class average*

This refinement uses only the *sequence structure*—the steps listed should execute in order, one after the other.

 Software Engineering Observation 4.2

Each refinement, as well as the top itself, is a complete specification of the algorithm— only the level of detail varies.

4.10.2 Proceeding to the Second Refinement

The preceding Software Engineering Observation is often all you need for the first refinement in the top-down process. To proceed to the next level of refinement—that is, the second refinement—we commit to specific variables. In this example, we need a running total of the numbers, a count of how many numbers have been processed, a variable to receive the value of each grade as it's entered by the user and a variable to hold the calculated average. The pseudocode statement

> *Initialize variables*

can be refined as follows:

> *Initialize total to zero*
> *Initialize counter to zero*

Only the variables *total* and *counter* need to be initialized before they're used. The variables *average* and *grade* (for the calculated average and the user input, respectively) need not be initialized, because their values will be replaced as they're calculated or input.

The pseudocode statement

> *Input, sum and count the quiz grades*

requires *iteration* to successively input each grade. We do not know in advance how many grades will be entered, so we'll use sentinel-controlled iteration. The user enters grades one at a time. After entering the last grade, the user enters the sentinel value. The program tests for the sentinel value after each grade is input and terminates the loop when the user enters the sentinel value. The second refinement of the preceding pseudocode statement is then

> *Prompt the user to enter the first grade*
> *Input the first grade (possibly the sentinel)*
>
> *While the user has not yet entered the sentinel*
>   *Add this grade into the running total*
>   *Add one to the grade counter*
>   *Prompt the user to enter the next grade*
>   *Input the next grade (possibly the sentinel)*

We simply indent the statements under the *While* to show that they belong to the *While*. Again, pseudocode is only an informal program development aid.

The pseudocode statement

> *Calculate and print the class average*

can be refined as follows:

> *If the counter is not equal to zero*
>   *Set the average to the total divided by the counter*
>   *Print the average*
> *else*
>   *Print "No grades were entered"*

We're careful here to test for the possibility of *division by zero*—a *logic error* that, if undetected, would cause the program to fail or produce invalid output. The complete second refinement of the pseudocode for the class-average problem is shown in Fig. 4.11.

Error-Prevention Tip 4.3
According to the C++ standard, the result of division by zero in floating-point arithmetic is undefined. When performing division (/) or remainder (%) calculations in which the right operand could be zero, test for this and handle it (e.g., display an error message) rather than allowing the calculation to proceed.

---

1   *Initialize total to zero*
2   *Initialize counter to zero*
3

Fig. 4.11 | Class-averaging pseudocode algorithm with sentinel-controlled iteration. (Part 1 of 2.)

4	*Prompt the user to enter the first grade*
5	*Input the first grade (possibly the sentinel)*
6	
7	*While the user has not yet entered the sentinel*
8	*Add this grade into the running total*
9	*Add one to the grade counter*
10	*Prompt the user to enter the next grade*
11	*Input the next grade (possibly the sentinel)*
12	
13	*If the counter is not equal to zero*
14	*Set the average to the total divided by the counter*
15	*Print the average*
16	*else*
17	*Print "No grades were entered"*

Fig. 4.11 | Class-averaging pseudocode algorithm with sentinel-controlled iteration. (Part 2 of 2.)

In Fig. 4.9 and Fig. 4.11, we included blank lines and indentation in the pseudocode to make it more readable. The blank lines separate the algorithms into their phases and set off control statements; the indentation emphasizes the bodies of the control statements.

The pseudocode algorithm in Fig. 4.11 solves the more general class-average problem. This algorithm was developed after two refinements. Sometimes more are needed.

Software Engineering Observation 4.3
Terminate the top-down, stepwise refinement process when you've specified the pseudocode algorithm in sufficient detail for you to convert the pseudocode to C++.

Software Engineering Observation 4.4
Some programmers do not use program development tools like pseudocode. They feel that their ultimate goal is to solve the problem on a computer and that writing pseudocode merely delays the production of final outputs. Although this may work for simple and familiar problems, it can lead to serious errors and delays in large, complex projects.

4.10.3 Implementing Sentinel-Controlled Iteration

In Fig. 4.12, the `main` function implements the pseudocode algorithm of Fig. 4.11. Although each grade entered by the user is an integer, the averaging calculation is likely to produce a number with a decimal point—in other words, a real number or floating-point number (e.g., 7.33, 0.0975 or 1000.12345). The type `int` cannot represent such a number, so this example must use another type to do so. C++ provides data types `float` and `double` to store floating-point numbers in memory. The primary difference between these types is that `double` variables can typically store numbers with larger magnitude and finer detail (i.e., more digits to the right of the decimal point—also known as the number's precision). C++ also supports type `long double` for floating-point values with larger magnitude and more precision than `double`. We say more about floating-point types in Chapter 5.

```cpp
1   // Fig. 4.12: ClassAverage.cpp
2   // Solving the class-average problem using sentinel-controlled iteration.
3   #include <iostream>
4   #include <iomanip> // parameterized stream manipulators
5   using namespace std;
6
7   int main() {
8      // initialization phase
9      int total{0}; // initialize sum of grades
10     unsigned int gradeCounter{0}; // initialize # of grades entered so far
11
12     // processing phase
13     // prompt for input and read grade from user
14     cout << "Enter grade or -1 to quit: ";
15     int grade;
16     cin >> grade;
17
18     // loop until sentinel value read from user
19     while (grade != -1)  {
20        total = total + grade; // add grade to total
21        gradeCounter = gradeCounter + 1; // increment counter
22
23        // prompt for input and read next grade from user
24        cout << "Enter grade or -1 to quit: ";
25        cin >> grade;
26     }
27
28     // termination phase
29     // if user entered at least one grade...
30     if (gradeCounter != 0) {
31        // use number with decimal point to calculate average of grades
32        double average{static_cast<double>(total) / gradeCounter};
33
34        // display total and average (with two digits of precision)
35        cout << "\nTotal of the " << gradeCounter
36           << " grades entered is " << total;
37        cout << setprecision(2) << fixed;
38        cout << "\nClass average is " << average << endl;
39     }
40     else { // no grades were entered, so output appropriate message
41        cout << "No grades were entered" << endl;
42     }
43  }
```

```
Enter grade or -1 to quit: 97
Enter grade or -1 to quit: 88
Enter grade or -1 to quit: 72
Enter grade or -1 to quit: -1

Total of the 3 grades entered is 257
Class average is 85.67
```

Fig. 4.12 | Solving the class-average problem using sentinel-controlled iteration.

Recall that integer division produces an integer result. This program introduces a special operator called a cast operator to *force* the averaging calculation to produce a floating-point numeric result. This program also *stacks* control statements on top of one another (in sequence)—the while statement (lines 19–26) is followed in sequence by an if...else statement (lines 30–42). Much of the code in this program is identical to that in Fig. 4.10, so we concentrate on the new concepts.

Program Logic for Sentinel-Controlled Iteration vs. Counter-Controlled Iteration

Line 10 initializes gradeCounter to 0, because no grades have been entered yet. Remember that this program uses *sentinel-controlled iteration* to input the grades. The program increments gradeCounter only when the user enters a valid grade. Line 32 declares double variable average, which stores the class average as a floating-point number.

Compare the program logic for sentinel-controlled iteration in this program with that for counter-controlled iteration in Fig. 4.10. In counter-controlled iteration, each iteration of the while statement (lines 12–18 of Fig. 4.10) reads a value from the user, for the specified number of iterations. In sentinel-controlled iteration, the program prompts for and reads the first value (lines 14 and 16 of Fig. 4.12) before reaching the while. This value determines whether the program's flow of control should enter the body of the while. If the condition of the while is *false*, the user entered the sentinel value, so the body of the while does not execute (i.e., no grades were entered). If, on the other hand, the condition is *true*, the body begins execution, and the loop adds the grade value to the total and increments the gradeCounter (lines 20–21). Then lines 24–25 in the loop body input the next value from the user. Next, program control reaches the closing right brace of the loop body at line 26, so execution continues with the test of the while's condition (line 19). The condition uses the most recent grade entered by the user to determine whether the loop body should execute again.

The value of variable grade is always input from the user immediately *before* the program tests the while condition. This allows the program to determine whether the value just input is the sentinel value *before* the program processes that value (i.e., adds it to the total). If the sentinel value is input, the loop terminates, and the program does not add –1 to the total.

Good Programming Practice 4.3
In a sentinel-controlled loop, prompts should remind the user of the sentinel.

After the loop terminates, the if...else statement at lines 30–42 executes. The condition at line 30 determines whether any grades were input. If none were input, the if...else statement's else part executes and displays the message "No grades were entered".

Braces in a while Statement

Notice the while statement's *block* in Fig. 4.12 (lines 19–26). Without the braces, the loop would consider its body to be only the first statement, which adds the grade to the total. The last three statements in the block would fall outside the loop body, causing the computer to interpret the code incorrectly as follows:

```
while (grade != -1)
    total = total + grade; // add grade to total
gradeCounter = gradeCounter + 1; // increment counter

// prompt for input and read next grade from user
cout << "Enter grade or -1 to quit: ";
cin >> grade;
```

The preceding code would cause an *infinite loop* in the program if the user did not input the sentinel -1 at line 16 (before the `while` statement).

4.10.4 Converting Between Fundamental Types Explicitly and Implicitly

If at least one grade was entered, line 32 of Fig. 4.12

```
double average{static_cast<double>(total) / gradeCounter};
```

calculates the average. Recall from Fig. 4.10 that integer division yields an integer result. Even though variable `average` is declared as a `double`, if we had written line 32 as

```
double average{total / gradeCounter};
```

it would lose the fractional part of the quotient *before* the result of the division was used to initialize `average`.

static_cast *Operator*

To perform a floating-point calculation with integers in this example, you first create *temporary* floating-point values using the `static_cast operator`. Line 32 converts a temporary *copy* of its operand in parentheses (`total`) to the type in angle brackets (`double`). The value stored in `total` is still an integer. Using a cast operator in this manner is called explicit conversion.

Promotions

After the cast operation, the calculation consists of the temporary `double` copy of `total` divided by the integer `gradeCounter`. For arithmetic, the compiler knows how to evaluate only expressions in which the operand types are *identical*. To ensure this, the compiler performs an operation called promotion (also called implicit conversion) on selected operands. In an expression containing values of data types `int` and `double`, C++ promotes `int` operands to `double` values. So in line 32, C++ promotes a temporary copy of `grade-Counter`'s value to type `double`, then performs the division. Finally, `average` is initialized with the floating-point result. Section 6.5 discusses the allowed fundamental-type promotions.

Cast Operators for Any Type

Cast operators are available for use with every fundamental type and with class types as well. The operator is formed by following keyword `static_cast` with a type name in angle brackets (`<` and `>`). It's a unary operator—that is, it has only one operand. C++ also supports unary versions of the plus (+) and minus (-) operators, so that you can write such expressions as -7 or +5. Cast operators have the second highest precedence (Appendix A).

4.10.5 Formatting Floating-Point Numbers

The formatting capabilities in Fig. 4.12 are discussed here briefly and explained in depth in Chapter 13, Stream Input/Output: A Deeper Look.

setprecision *Parameterized Stream Manipulator*

The call to setprecision (with the argument 2) in line 37

```
cout << setprecision(2) << fixed;
```

indicates that floating-point values should be output with *two* digits of precision to the right of the decimal point (e.g., 92.37). setprecision is a parameterized stream manipulator, because it requires an argument to perform its task. Programs that use these calls must include the header <iomanip> (line 4). The manipulator endl (from the header <iostream>) is a nonparameterized stream manipulator, because it does not require an argument. By default, floating-point values are output with *six* digits of precision.

fixed *Nonparameterized Stream Manipulator*

The stream manipulator fixed (line 37) indicates that floating-point values should be output in fixed-point format, as opposed to scientific notation. Scientific notation is a way of displaying a number as a floating-point number between the values of 1.0 and 10.0, multiplied by a power of 10. For instance, the value 3,100.0 would be displayed in scientific notation as 3.1×10^3. Scientific notation is useful when displaying very large or very small values. Formatting using scientific notation is discussed further in Chapter 13.

Fixed-point formatting forces a floating-point number to display a specific number of digits. Fixed-point formatting also forces the decimal point and trailing zeros to print, even if the value is a whole-number amount, such as 88.00. Without the fixed-point formatting option, 88.00 prints as 88 *without* the trailing zeros and decimal point.

Rounding Floating-Point Numbers

When the stream manipulators fixed and setprecision are used, the *printed* value is rounded to the number of decimal positions indicated by setprecision's argument (2 in this example), although the value in memory remains unaltered. For example, the values 87.946 and 67.543 are output as 87.95 and 67.54, respectively. It's also possible to *force* a decimal point to appear by using stream manipulator showpoint. If showpoint is specified without fixed, then trailing zeros will not print. Like endl, the nonparameterized stream manipulators fixed and showpoint require the header <iostream>.

Together, lines 37 and 38 of Fig. 4.12 output the class average *rounded* to the nearest hundredth and with *exactly* two digits to the right of the decimal point. The three grades entered during the execution of the program in Fig. 4.12 total 257, which yields the average 85.666... and prints with rounding as 85.67.

4.10.6 Unsigned Integers and User Input

In Fig. 4.10, line 10 declared gradeCounter as an unsigned int, because it stores only non-negative values. Figure 4.10 could have also declared as unsigned int the variables grade, total and average. Grades are normally values from 0 to 100, so the total and average *should* each be greater than or equal to 0. We declared those variables as ints, however, because we can't control what the user actually enters—the user could enter *negative* values. Worse yet, the user could enter a value that's not even a number. (We'll show string-processing capabilities later in the book that can be used to check for erroneous inputs.)

Sometimes sentinel-controlled loops use *intentionally* invalid values to terminate a loop. For example, in line 19 of Fig. 4.12, we terminate the loop when the user enters the sentinel -1 (an invalid grade), so it would be improper to declare variable grade as an unsigned int. As you'll see, the end-of-file (EOF) indicator—which is often used to terminate sentinel-controlled loops—is also normally implemented internally in the compiler as a negative number.

4.11 Formulating Algorithms: Nested Control Statements

For the next example, we once again formulate an algorithm by using pseudocode and top-down, stepwise refinement, and write a corresponding C++ program. We've seen that control statements can be stacked on top of one another (in sequence). In this case study, we examine the only other structured way control statements can be connected—namely, by nesting one control statement within another.

4.11.1 Problem Statement

Consider the following problem statement:

> *A college offers a course that prepares students for the state licensing exam for real-estate brokers. Last year, ten of the students who completed this course took the exam. The college wants to know how well its students did on the exam. You've been asked to write a program to summarize the results. You've been given a list of these 10 students. Next to each name is written a 1 if the student passed the exam or a 2 if the student failed.*

> *Your program should analyze the results of the exam as follows:*

> *1. Input each test result (i.e., a 1 or a 2). Display the message "Enter result" on the screen each time the program requests another test result.*

> *2. Count the number of test results of each type.*

> *3. Display a summary of the test results, indicating the number of students who passed and the number who failed.*

> *4. If more than eight students passed the exam, print "Bonus to instructor!"*

Problem Statement Observations

After reading the problem statement carefully, we make the following observations:

1. The program must process test results for 10 students. A counter-controlled loop can be used, because the number of test results is known in advance.

2. Each test result has a numeric value—either a 1 or a 2. Each time it reads a test result, the program must determine whether it's a 1 or a 2. We test for a 1 in our algorithm. If the number is not a 1, we assume that it's a 2. (Exercise 4.20 considers the consequences of this assumption.)

3. Two counters are used to keep track of the exam results—one to count the number of students who passed the exam and one to count the number who failed.

4. After the program has processed all the results, it must decide whether more than eight students passed the exam.

4.11.2 Top-Down, Stepwise Refinement: Pseudocode Representation of the Top

Let's proceed with top-down, stepwise refinement. We begin with a pseudocode representation of the top:

> *Analyze exam results and decide whether a bonus should be paid*

Once again, the top is a *complete* representation of the program, but several refinements are likely to be needed before the pseudocode can evolve naturally into a C++ program.

4.11.3 Top-Down, Stepwise Refinement: First Refinement

Our first refinement is

> *Initialize variables*
> *Input the 10 exam results, and count passes and failures*
> *Print a summary of the exam results and decide whether a bonus should be paid*

Here, too, even though we have a *complete* representation of the entire program, further refinement is necessary. We now commit to specific variables. Counters are needed to record the passes and failures, a counter will be used to control the looping process and a variable is needed to store the user input. The variable in which the user input will be stored is *not* initialized at the start of the algorithm, because its value is read from the user during each iteration of the loop.

4.11.4 Top-Down, Stepwise Refinement: Second Refinement

The pseudocode statement

> *Initialize variables*

can be refined as follows:

> *Initialize passes to zero*
> *Initialize failures to zero*
> *Initialize student counter to one*

Notice that only the counters are initialized at the start of the algorithm.
　　The pseudocode statement

> *Input the 10 exam results, and count passes and failures*

requires a loop that successively inputs the result of each exam. We know in advance that there are precisely 10 exam results, so counter-controlled looping is appropriate. Inside the loop (i.e., *nested* within the loop), a double-selection structure will determine whether each exam result is a pass or a failure and will increment the appropriate counter. The refinement of the preceding pseudocode statement is then

> *While student counter is less than or equal to 10*
>   *Prompt the user to enter the next exam result*
>   *Input the next exam result*
>
>   *If the student passed*
>   *Add one to passes*
>   *Else*
>   *Add one to failures*
>
>   *Add one to student counter*

We use blank lines to isolate the *If...Else* control structure, which improves readability. The pseudocode statement

> *Print a summary of the exam results and decide whether a bonus should be paid*

can be refined as follows:

> *Print the number of passes*
> *Print the number of failures*
>
> *If more than eight students passed*
>   *Print "Bonus to instructor!"*

4.11.5 Complete Second Refinement of the Pseudocode

The complete second refinement appears in Fig. 4.13. Notice that blank lines are also used to set off the *While* structure for program readability. This pseudocode is now sufficiently refined for conversion to C++.

1	*Initialize passes to zero*
2	*Initialize failures to zero*
3	*Initialize student counter to one*
4	
5	*While student counter is less than or equal to 10*
6	*Prompt the user to enter the next exam result*
7	*Input the next exam result*
8	
9	*If the student passed*
10	*Add one to passes*
11	*Else*
12	*Add one to failures*
13	
14	*Add one to student counter*
15	
16	*Print the number of passes*
17	*Print the number of failures*
18	
19	*If more than eight students passed*
20	*Print "Bonus to instructor!"*

Fig. 4.13 | Pseudocode for examination-results problem.

4.11.6 Program That Implements the Pseudocode Algorithm

The program that implements the pseudocode algorithm and two sample executions are shown in Fig. 4.14. Lines 8–10 and 16 of main declare the variables that are used to process the examination results.

Error-Prevention Tip 4.4

Initializing local variables when they're declared helps you avoid any compilation warnings that might arise from attempts to use uninitialized variables and helps you avoid logic errors from using uninitialized variables.

```cpp
1   // Fig. 4.14: Analysis.cpp
2   // Analysis of examination results using nested control statements.
3   #include <iostream>
4   using namespace std;
5
6   int main() {
7      // initializing variables in declarations
8      unsigned int passes{0};
9      unsigned int failures{0};
10     unsigned int studentCounter{1};
11
12     // process 10 students using counter-controlled loop
13     while (studentCounter <= 10) {
14        // prompt user for input and obtain value from user
15        cout << "Enter result (1 = pass, 2 = fail): ";
16        int result;
17        cin >> result;
18
19        // if...else is nested in the while statement
20        if (result == 1) {
21           passes = passes + 1;
22        }
23        else {
24           failures = failures + 1;
25        }
26
27        // increment studentCounter so loop eventually terminates
28        studentCounter = studentCounter + 1;
29     }
30
31     // termination phase; prepare and display results
32     cout << "Passed: " << passes << "\nFailed: " << failures << endl;
33
34     // determine whether more than 8 students passed
35     if (passes > 8) {
36        cout << "Bonus to instructor!" << endl;
37     }
38  }
```

Fig. 4.14 | Analysis of examination results using nested control statements. (Part I of 2.)

```
Enter result (1 = pass, 2 = fail): 1
Enter result (1 = pass, 2 = fail): 2
Enter result (1 = pass, 2 = fail): 1
Enter result (1 = pass, 2 = fail): 1
Enter result (1 = pass, 2 = fail): 1
Enter result (1 = pass, 2 = fail): 1
Enter result (1 = pass, 2 = fail): 1
Enter result (1 = pass, 2 = fail): 1
Enter result (1 = pass, 2 = fail): 1
Enter result (1 = pass, 2 = fail): 1
Passed: 9
Failed: 1
Bonus to instructor!
```

```
Enter result (1 = pass, 2 = fail): 1
Enter result (1 = pass, 2 = fail): 2
Enter result (1 = pass, 2 = fail): 1
Enter result (1 = pass, 2 = fail): 2
Enter result (1 = pass, 2 = fail): 1
Enter result (1 = pass, 2 = fail): 2
Enter result (1 = pass, 2 = fail): 2
Enter result (1 = pass, 2 = fail): 1
Enter result (1 = pass, 2 = fail): 1
Enter result (1 = pass, 2 = fail): 1
Passed: 6
Failed: 4
```

Fig. 4.14 | Analysis of examination results using nested control statements. (Part 2 of 2.)

The while statement (lines 13–29) loops 10 times. During each iteration, the loop inputs and processes one exam result. Notice that the if...else statement (lines 20–25) for processing each result is *nested* in the while statement. If the result is 1, the if...else statement increments passes; otherwise, it assumes the result is 2 and increments failures. Line 28 increments studentCounter before the loop condition is tested again at line 13. After 10 values have been input, the loop terminates and line 32 displays the number of passes and failures. The if statement at lines 35–37 determines whether more than eight students passed the exam and, if so, outputs the message "Bonus to instructor!"

Figure 4.14 shows the input and output from two sample program executions. During the first, the condition at line 35 is *true*—more than eight students passed the exam, so the program outputs a message to bonus the instructor.

4.11.7 Preventing Narrowing Conversions with List Initialization

As you learned in Chapter 2, C++11 introduced list initialization so that you can use one syntax to initialize a variable of *any* type. Consider line 10 of Fig. 4.14:

```
unsigned int studentCounter{1};
```

You also can write this as

```
unsigned int studentCounter = {1};
```

11

though the form without = is preferred. Prior to C++11, you would have written this as

```
unsigned int studentCounter = 1;
```

For fundamental-type variables, list-initialization syntax *prevents* narrowing conversions that could result in *data loss*. For example, previously you could write

```
int x = 12.7;
```

which attempts to assign the double value 12.7 to the int variable x. In this case, C++ converts the double value to an int, by *truncating* the floating-point part (.7), a *narrowing conversion* that loses data. The actual value assigned to x is 12. Many compilers warn you of this, but still allow the statement to compile. However, using list initialization, as in

```
int x{12.7};
```

or

```
int x = {12.7};
```

yields a *compilation error*, thus helping you avoid a potentially subtle logic error. For example, Apple's Xcode LLVM compiler gives the error

```
Type 'double' cannot be narrowed to 'int' in initializer list
```

We'll discuss additional list-initializer features in later chapters.

A Look Back at Fig. 4.10
You might think that the following statement from Fig. 4.10

```
int average{total / 10}; // int division yields int result
```

contains a narrowing conversion, but total and 10 are both int values, so the initializer value is an int. If in the preceding statement total were a double variable or if we used the double literal value 10.0, then the initializer value would have type double. In this case the compiler would issue an errror message due to an attempted narrowing conversion.

4.12 Compound Assignment Operators

The compound assignment operators abbreviate assignment expressions. Statements like

```
variable = variable operator expression;
```

where *operator* is one of the binary operators +, -, *, / or % (or others we discuss later in the text) can be written in the form

```
variable operator= expression;
```

For example, you can abbreviate the statement

```
c = c + 3;
```

with the addition compound assignment operator, +=, as

```
c += 3;
```

The += operator adds the value of the expression on its right to the value of the variable on its left and stores the result in the variable on the left of the operator. Thus, the assignment expression c += 3 adds 3 to c. Figure 4.15 shows the arithmetic compound assignment operators, sample expressions using the operators and explanations of what the operators do.

Assignment operator	Sample expression	Explanation	Assigns
Assume: `int c = 3, d = 5, e = 4, f = 6, g = 12;`			
`+=`	`c += 7`	`c = c + 7`	10 to c
`-=`	`d -= 4`	`d = d - 4`	1 to d
`*=`	`e *= 5`	`e = e * 5`	20 to e
`/=`	`f /= 3`	`f = f / 3`	2 to f
`%=`	`g %= 9`	`g = g % 9`	3 to g

Fig. 4.15 | Arithmetic compound assignment operators.

4.13 Increment and Decrement Operators

C++ provides two unary operators (summarized in Fig. 4.16) for adding 1 to or subtracting 1 from the value of a numeric variable. These are the unary increment operator, ++, and the unary decrement operator, --. A program can increment by 1 the value of a variable called c using the increment operator, ++, rather than the expression c = c + 1 or c += 1. An increment or decrement operator that's prefixed to (placed before) a variable is referred to as the prefix increment or prefix decrement operator, respectively. An increment or decrement operator that's postfixed to (placed after) a variable is referred to as the postfix increment or postfix decrement operator, respectively.

Operator	Operator name	Sample expression	Explanation
`++`	prefix increment	`++a`	Increment a by 1, then use the new value of a in the expression in which a resides.
`++`	postfix increment	`a++`	Use the current value of a in the expression in which a resides, then increment a by 1.
`--`	prefix decrement	`--b`	Decrement b by 1, then use the new value of b in the expression in which b resides.
`--`	postfix decrement	`b--`	Use the current value of b in the expression in which b resides, then decrement b by 1.

Fig. 4.16 | Increment and decrement operators.

Using the prefix increment (or decrement) operator to add 1 to (or subtract 1 from) a variable is known as preincrementing (or predecrementing). This causes the variable to be incremented (decremented) by 1; then the new value of the variable is used in the expression in which it appears.

Using the postfix increment (or decrement) operator to add 1 to (or subtract 1 from) a variable is known as postincrementing (or postdecrementing). This causes the current

value of the variable to be used in the expression in which it appears; then the variable's
value is incremented (decremented) by 1.

Good Programming Practice 4.4

*Unlike binary operators, the unary increment and decrement operators as a matter of style
should be placed next to their operands, with no intervening spaces.*

Difference Between Prefix Increment and Postfix Increment Operators

Figure 4.17 demonstrates the difference between the prefix increment and postfix increment versions of the ++ increment operator. The decrement operator (--) works similarly.

```cpp
1    // Fig. 4.17: Increment.cpp
2    // Prefix increment and postfix increment operators.
3    #include <iostream>
4    using namespace std;
5
6    int main() {
7       // demonstrate postfix increment operator
8       unsigned int c{5}; // initializes c with the value 5
9       cout << "c before postincrement: " << c << endl; // prints 5
10      cout << "    postincrementing c: " << c++ << endl; // prints 5
11      cout << " c after postincrement: " << c << endl; // prints 6
12
13      cout << endl; // skip a line
14
15      // demonstrate prefix increment operator
16      c = 5; // assigns 5 to c
17      cout << " c before preincrement: " << c << endl; // prints 5
18      cout << "    preincrementing c: " << ++c << endl; // prints 6
19      cout << " c after preincrement: " << c << endl; // prints 6
20   }
```

```
c before postincrement: 5
    postincrementing c: 5
 c after postincrement: 6

c before preincrement: 5
    preincrementing c: 6
 c after preincrement: 6
```

Fig. 4.17 | Prefix increment and postfix increment operators.

Line 8 initializes the variable c to 5, and line 9 outputs c's initial value. Line 10 outputs the value of the expression c++. This expression postincrements the variable c, so c's
original value (5) is output, then c's value is incremented (to 6). Thus, line 10 outputs c's
initial value (5) again. Line 11 outputs c's new value (6) to prove that the variable's value
was indeed incremented in line 10.

Line 16 resets c's value to 5, and line 17 outputs c's value. Line 18 outputs the value
of the expression ++c. This expression preincrements c, so its value is incremented; then

the *new* value (6) is output. Line 19 outputs c's value again to show that the value of c is still 6 after line 18 executes.

Simplifying Statements with the Arithmetic Compound Assignment, Increment and Decrement Operators

The arithmetic compound assignment operators and the increment and decrement operators can be used to simplify program statements. For example, the three assignment statements in Fig. 4.14 (lines 21, 24 and 28)

```
passes = passes + 1;
failures = failures + 1;
studentCounter = studentCounter + 1;
```

can be written more concisely with compound assignment operators as

```
passes += 1;
failures += 1;
studentCounter += 1;
```

with prefix increment operators as

```
++passes;
++failures;
++studentCounter;
```

or with postfix increment operators as

```
passes++;
failures++;
studentCounter++;
```

When incrementing or decrementing a variable in a statement by itself, the prefix increment and postfix increment forms have the *same* effect, and the prefix decrement and postfix decrement forms have the *same* effect. It's only when a variable appears in the context of a larger expression that preincrementing and postincrementing the variable have different effects (and similarly for predecrementing and postdecrementing).

Common Programming Error 4.4

Attempting to use the increment or decrement operator on an expression other than one to which a value can be assigned is a syntax error. For example, writing ++(x + 1) is a syntax error, because (x + 1) is not a variable.

Operator Precedence and Associativity

Figure 4.18 shows the precedence and associativity of the operators introduced to this point. The operators are shown top-to-bottom in decreasing order of precedence. The second column indicates the associativity of the operators at each level of precedence. Notice that the conditional operator (?:), the unary operators preincrement (++), predecrement (--), plus (+) and minus (-), and the assignment operators =, +=, -=, *=, /= and %= associate from *right to left*. All other operators in Fig. 4.18 associate from *left to right*. The third column names the various groups of operators.

Good Programming Practice 4.5

Refer to the operator precedence and associativity chart (Appendix A) when writing expressions containing many operators. Confirm that the operators in the expression are performed in the order you expect. If you're uncertain about the order of evaluation in a complex expression, break the expression into smaller statements or use parentheses to force the order of evaluation, exactly as you'd do in an algebraic expression. Be sure to observe that some operators such as assignment (=) associate right to left rather than left to right.

Operators	Associativity	Type
::　()	left to right *[See Fig. 2.10's caution regarding grouping parentheses.]*	primary
++　--　static_cast<*type*>()	left to right	postfix
++　--　+　-	right to left	unary (prefix)
*　/　%	left to right	multiplicative
+　-	left to right	additive
<<　>>	left to right	insertion/extraction
<　<=　>　>=	left to right	relational
==　!=	left to right	equality
?:	right to left	conditional
=　+=　-=　*=　/=　%=	right to left	assignment

Fig. 4.18 | Operator precedence for the operators encountered so far in the text.

4.14 Fundamental Types Are Not Portable

The table in Appendix C lists C++'s fundamental types. Like its predecessor language C, C++ requires all variables to have a type. In C and C++, programmers frequently have to write separate versions of programs to support different computer platforms, because the fundamental types are not guaranteed to be identical from computer to computer. For example, an int on one machine might be represented by 16 bits (2 bytes) of memory, on a second machine by 32 bits (4 bytes), and on another machine by 64 bits (8 bytes).

Portability Tip 4.2

C++'s fundamental types are not portable across all computer platforms that support C++.

4.15 Wrap-Up

In this chapter, we demonstrated how to develop algorithms using top-down, stepwise refinement. Only three types of control statements—sequence, selection and iteration—are needed to develop any algorithm. Specifically, we demonstrated the if single-selection statement, the if...else double-selection statement and the while iteration statement. We used control-statement stacking to total and compute the average of a set of student grades with counter- and sentinel-controlled iteration, and we used control-statement nesting to analyze and make decisions based on a set of exam results. We introduced C++'s compound assignment operators and its increment and decrement operators. Finally, we discussed why C++'s fundamental types are not portable. In Chapter 5, we continue our discussion of control statements, introducing the for, do...while and switch statements.

Summary

Section 4.1 Introduction
- Before writing a program to solve a problem, you should have a thorough understanding of the problem and a carefully planned approach to solving it.

Section 4.2 Algorithms
- A procedure for solving a problem in terms of the **actions** (p. 105) to execute and the **order** (p. 105) in which these actions execute is called an **algorithm** (p. 105).
- Specifying the order in which statements (actions) execute in a program is called **program control** (p. 105). This chapter investigates program control using C++'s **control statements** (p. 105).

Section 4.3 Pseudocode
- **Pseudocode** (p. 105) is an informal language similar to everyday English that helps you develop algorithms without having to worry about the strict details of C++ language syntax.
- Pseudocode helps you "think out" a program before attempting to write it.
- Pseudocode normally describes only statements representing the actions that occur after you convert a program from pseudocode to C++ and the program is run on a computer.

Section 4.4 Control Structures
- Normally, statements in a program are executed one after the other in the order in which they're written—this is called **sequential execution** (p. 106).
- Various C++ statements enable you to specify that the next statement to execute is not necessarily the next one in sequence. This is called **transfer of control** (p. 106).
- Bohm and Jacopini's work demonstrated that all programs could be written in terms of only **sequence** (p. 106), **selection** (p. 106) and **iteration** (p. 106).

Section 4.4.1 Sequence Structure
- The **sequence** (p. 106) structure is built into C++. Unless directed otherwise, the computer executes C++ statements one after the other in the order in which they're written.
- A UML **activity diagram** (p. 106) models the **workflow** (p. 107; also called the **activity**) of a portion of a software system. Such workflows may include a portion of an algorithm.
- Activity diagrams are composed of symbols, such as **action-state symbols** (p. 107), **diamonds** (p. 107) and **small circles** (p. 107). These are connected by **transition arrows** (p. 107), which represent the flow of the activity—that is, the order in which the actions should occur.
- Like pseudocode, activity diagrams help you develop and represent algorithms.
- An **action state** (p. 107) contains an **action expression** (p. 107) that specifies a particular action to perform.

- Transition arrows in the activity diagram represent **transitions** (p. 107), specifying the order in which the actions represented by the action states occur.
- A **solid circle** (p. 107) at the top of the activity diagram represents the **initial state** (p. 107)—the beginning of the workflow before the program performs the modeled actions.
- A **solid circle surrounded by a hollow circle** (p. 107) at the bottom of the diagram represents the **final state**—the end of the workflow after the program performs its actions.
- UML **notes** (p. 107; like comments in C++) are explanatory remarks that describe the purpose of symbols in the diagram. A **dotted line** (p. 107) connects each note with the element it describes.

Section 4.4.2 Selection Statements
- C++ has three types of **selection statements** (p. 108).
- The if **single-selection statement** (p. 108) performs (selects) an action (or group of actions), if a condition is *true*, or skips it, if the condition is *false*.
- The if...else **double-selection statement** (p. 108) performs an action (or group of actions) if a condition is *true* and performs a different action (or group of actions) if the condition is *false*.
- The switch **multiple-selection statement** (p. 108) performs one of many different actions (or group of actions), depending on the value of an expression.

Section 4.4.3 Iteration Statements
- C++ provides four **iteration statements** (p. 108; sometimes called **repetition statements** or **looping statements**) that enable programs to perform statements repeatedly as long as a **loop-continuation condition** (p. 108) remains *true*.
- The iteration statements are the while, do...while, for and range-based for statements.
- The while and for statements perform the action (or group of actions) in their bodies zero or more times—if the loop-continuation condition is initially *false*, the action (or group of actions) will not execute.
- The do...while statement performs its body action(s) one or more times.
- Each of the words if, else, switch, while, do and for is a C++ keyword. Keywords cannot be used as identifiers, such as variable names, and must be spelled with only lowercase letters.

Section 4.4.4 Summary of Control Statements
- Every program is formed by combining as many control statements as is appropriate for the algorithm the program implements.
- **Single-entry/single-exit control statements** (p. 109) make it easy to build programs by connecting the exit point of one to the entry point of the next. We call this **control-statement stacking** (p. 109).
- In **control-statement nesting** (p. 109), one control statement appears inside another.

Section 4.5 if Single-Selection Statement
- In C++, a decision can be based on any expression that can be evaluated as zero or nonzero—if the expression evaluates to zero, it's treated as *false*; if the expression evaluates to nonzero, it's treated as *true*.
- C++ provides the data type **bool** (p. 110) for Boolean variables that can hold only the values **true** (p. 110) and false (p. 110)—each of these is a C++ keyword.
- The UML **decision symbol** (p. 110; a diamond) indicates that a decision is to be made. The workflow continues along a path determined by the symbol's associated **guard conditions**

(p. 110), which can be *true* or *false*. Each transition arrow emerging from a decision symbol has a guard condition (specified in square brackets next to the arrow). If a guard condition is *true*, the workflow enters the action state to which the transition arrow points.

Section 4.6 if...else *Double-Selection Statement*
* The if...else **double-selection statement** (p. 110) allows you to specify an action (or group of actions) to perform when the condition is *true* and another action (or group of actions) when the condition is *false*.

Section 4.6.1 Nested if...else *Statements*
* A program can test multiple cases by placing if...else statements inside other if...else statements to create **nested** if...else **statements** (p. 111).

*Section 4.6.2 Dangling-*else *Problem*
* Enclosing control-statement bodies in braces ({ and }) avoids a logic error called the "dangling-else" problem (Exercises 4.23—4.25).

Section 4.6.3 Blocks
* Statements contained in a pair of braces (such as the body of a control statement or function) form a **block** (p. 113). A block can be placed anywhere in a function that a single statement can be placed.
* Syntax errors are caught by the compiler.
* A **logic error** (p. 113) has its effect at execution time.
* A **fatal logic error** (p. 114) causes a program to fail and terminate prematurely.
* A **nonfatal logic error** (p. 114) allows a program to continue executing but causes it to produce incorrect results.
* Just as a block can be placed anywhere a single statement can be placed, it's also possible to have an **empty statement**, ; (p. 114), where a statement would normally be.

Section 4.6.4 Conditional Operator (?:)
* The **conditional operator** , ?: (p. 114) is C++'s only **ternary operator** (p. 114). Together, the operands and the ?: symbol form a **conditional expression** (p. 114).
* The first operand (to the left of the ?) is a condition, the second operand (between the ? and :) is the value of the conditional expression if the condition is *true* and the third operand (to the right of the :) is the value of the conditional expression if the condition is *false*.

Section 4.8 while *Iteration Statement*
* A while **iteration statement** (p. 118) allows you to specify that a program should repeat an action (or group of actions) while some condition remains *true*.
* UML's **merge symbol** (p. 118; a diamond) joins two flows of activity into one.
* A decision symbol has one transition arrow pointing to the diamond and two or more pointing out from it to indicate possible transitions from that point. In addition, each transition arrow pointing out of a decision symbol has a guard condition next to it.
* A merge symbol has two or more transition arrows pointing to the diamond and only one pointing from the diamond, to indicate multiple activity flows merging to continue the activity. None of the transition arrows associated with a merge symbol has a guard condition.

Section 4.9.1 Pseudocode Algorithm with Counter-Controlled Iteration
- **Counter-controlled iteration** (p. 119) uses a variable called a **counter** (p. 119; or **control variable**) to control the number of times a set of statements will execute. This is often called **definite iteration** (p. 119), because the number of iterations is known before the loop begins executing.

Section 4.9.2 Implementing Counter-Controlled Iteration
- An unsigned int variable can assume only nonnegative values. Variables of unsigned integer types can represent values from 0 to approximately twice the positive range of the corresponding signed integer types.
- You can determine your platform's maximum unsigned int value with the constant UINT_MAX from <climits>.
- A variable declared in a function body is a local variable and can be used only from the line of its declaration to the closing right brace of the block in which the variable is declared.
- A local variable's declaration must appear before the variable is used; otherwise, a compilation error occurs.

Section 4.9.3 Notes on Integer Division and Truncation
- Integer division yields an integer result—any fractional part of the calculation is truncated.

Section 4.9.4 Arithmetic Overflow
- Adding two integers could result in a value that's too large to store in an int variable. This is known as **arithmetic overflow** (p. 122) and causes undefined behavior, which can lead to unintended results and security problems.
- The maximum and minimum values that can be stored in an int variable are represented by the constants INT_MAX and INT_MIN, respectively, which are defined in the header <climits>. There are similar constants for the other integral types and for floating-point types.
- To see these constants' values on your platform, open the headers <climits> and <cfloat> in a text editor (you can search your file system for these files).

Section 4.9.5 Input Validation
- A program uses **range checking** (p. 123) to ensure that values are within a specific range.

Section 4.10 Formulating Algorithms: Sentinel-Controlled Iteration
- In **sentinel-controlled iteration** (p. 124), a special value called a **sentinel value** (p. 123; also called a **signal value**, a **dummy value** or a **flag value**) is used to indicate "end of data entry."
- Sentinel-controlled iteration is often called **indefinite iteration** (p. 124) because the number of iterations is not known before the loop begins executing.

Section 4.10.1 Top-Down, Stepwise Refinement: The Top and First Refinement
- **Top-down, stepwise refinement** (p. 124) is essential to the development of well-structured programs.
- Begin with a pseudocode representation of the **top** (p. 124)—a single statement that, in effect, is a complete representation of a program.
- The top rarely conveys sufficient detail from which to write a C++ program. So in the **first refinement** (p. 124), we refine the top into a series of smaller tasks and list these in the order in which they'll be performed. This refinement uses only tasks in sequence.

Section 4.10.2 Proceeding to the Second Refinement
- In the **second refinement** (p. 124), we commit to specific variables and logic.

Section 4.10.3 Implementing Sentinel-Controlled Iteration
- A number with a decimal point is called a real number or **floating-point number** (p. 126; e.g., 7.33, 0.0975 or 1000.12345).
- C++ provides types **float** (p. 126) and **double** (p. 126) to store floating-point numbers in memory.
- **double** variables can typically store numbers with larger magnitude and finer detail (i.e., more **precision**; p. 126).
- C++ also supports type **long double** (p. 126) for floating-point values with larger magnitude and more precision than **double**.

Section 4.10.4 Converting Between Fundamental Types Explicitly and Implicitly
- The **static_cast operator** (p. 129) converts a temporary copy of its operand in parentheses to the type in angle brackets (**double**). Using a cast operator in this manner is called **explicit conversion** (p. 129).
- For arithmeitc, the compiler knows how to evaluate only expressions in which the operand types are identical. To ensure this, the compiler performs an operation called **promotion** (p. 129; also called **implicit conversion**) on selected operands.
- In an expression containing values of data types **int** and **double**, C++ **promotes** (p. 129) **int** operands to **double** values.
- **static_cast** is a **unary operator** (p. 129)—it has only one operand.
- C++ also supports unary versions of the plus (+) and minus (-) operators, so that you can write such expressions as -7 or +5.

Section 4.10.5 Formatting Floating-Point Numbers
- **setprecision** (p. 130) is a **parameterized stream manipulator** (p. 130) that specifies the number of digits of **precision** to the right of the decimal point when a floating-point number is output.
- Programs that use parameterized stream manipulators must include the header **<iomanip>** (p. 130).
- The manipulator **endl** (from the header **<iostream>**) is a **nonparameterized stream manipulator** (p. 130), because it does not require an argument.
- By default, floating-point values are output with six digits of precision.
- The stream manipulator **fixed** (p. 130) indicates that floating-point values should be output in **fixed-point format** (p. 130), as opposed to **scientific notation** (p. 130).
- Scientific notation displays a floating-point number between 1.0 and 10.0, multiplied by a power of 10. Scientific notation is useful when displaying very large or very small values.
- Fixed-point formatting forces the decimal point and trailing zeros to print, even if the value is a whole number amount.
- When the stream manipulators **fixed** and **setprecision** are used in a program, the printed value is **rounded** (p. 130) to the number of decimal positions indicated by **setprecision**'s argument, although the value in memory remains unaltered.
- It's also possible to force a decimal point to appear by using stream manipulator **showpoint** (p. 130). If **showpoint** is specified without **fixed**, then trailing zeros will not print.
- Nonparameterized stream manipulators **fixed** and **showpoint** require the header **<iostream>**.

Section 4.11.7 Preventing Narrowing Conversions with List Initialization
- For fundamental-type variables, list-initialization syntax prevents **narrowing conversions** (p. 136) that could result in data loss.

Section 4.12 Compound Assignment Operators
- The **compound assignment operators** +=, -=, *=, /= and %= (p. 136) abbreviate assignment expressions.

Section 4.13 Increment and Decrement Operators
- The **increment** (p. 137; ++) and **decrement** (p. 137; --) operators increment or decrement a variable by 1, respectively. If the operator is prefixed to the variable, the variable is incremented or decremented by 1 first, then its new value is used in the expression in which it appears. If the operator is postfixed to the variable, the variable is first used in the expression in which it appears, then the variable's value is incremented or decremented by 1.

Section 4.14 Fundamental Types Are Not Portable
- All variables must have a type.
- The fundamental types are not guaranteed to be identical from computer to computer. An int on one machine might be represented by 16 bits (2 bytes) of memory, on a second machine by 32 bits (4 bytes), and on another machine by 64 bits (8 bytes).

Self-Review Exercises

4.1 Answer each of the following questions.
- a) All programs can be written in terms of three types of control statements: _____, _____ and _____.
- b) The _____ selection statement is used to execute one action when a condition is *true* or a different action when that condition is *false*.
- c) Repeating a set of instructions a specific number of times is called _____ iteration.
- d) When it isn't known in advance how many times a set of statements will be repeated, a(n) _____ value can be used to terminate the iteration.

4.2 Write four different C++ statements that each add 1 to integer variable x.

4.3 Write C++ statements to accomplish each of the following:
- a) In one statement, assign the sum of the current value of x and y to z and postincrement the value of x.
- b) Determine whether the value of the variable count is greater than 10. If it is, print "Count is greater than 10".
- c) Predecrement the variable x by 1, then subtract it from the variable total.
- d) Calculate the remainder after q is divided by divisor and assign the result to q. Write this statement two different ways.

4.4 Write C++ statements to accomplish each of the following tasks.
- a) Declare variable sum to be of type unsigned int and initialize it to 0.
- b) Declare variable x to be of type unsigned int and initialize it to 1.
- c) Add variable x to variable sum and assign the result to variable sum.
- d) Print "The sum is: " followed by the value of variable sum.

4.5 Combine the statements that you wrote in Exercise 4.4 into a program that calculates and prints the sum of the integers from 1 to 10. Use the while statement to loop through the calculation and increment statements. The loop should terminate when the value of x becomes 11.

4.6   State the values of *each* of these unsigned int variables after the calculation is performed. Assume that, when each statement begins executing, all variables have the integer value 5.

 a) product *= x++;
 b) quotient /= ++x;

4.7   Write single C++ statements or portions of statements that do the following:

 a) Input unsigned int variable x with cin and >>.
 b) Input unsigned int variable y with cin and >>.
 c) Declare unsigned int variable i and initialize it to 1.
 d) Declare unsigned int variable power and initialize it to 1.
 e) Multiply variable power by x and assign the result to power.
 f) Preincrement variable i by 1.
 g) Determine whether i is less than or equal to y.
 h) Output integer variable power with cout and <<.

4.8   Write a C++ program that uses the statements in Exercise 4.7 to calculate x raised to the y power. The program should have a while iteration statement.

4.9   Identify and correct the errors in each of the following:

 a) ```
     while (c <= 5) {
         product *= c;
         ++c;
     ```
 b)  ```
     cin << value;
     ```
 c) ```
     if (gender == 1) {
         cout << "Woman" << endl;
     else; {
         cout << "Man" << endl;
     }
     ```

4.10   What's wrong with the following while iteration statement?

```
while (z >= 0) {
    sum += z;
}
```

Answers to Self-Review Exercises

4.1   a) Sequence, selection and iteration. b) if...else. c) Counter-controlled or definite. d) Sentinel, signal, flag or dummy.

4.2   ```
       x = x + 1;
       x += 1;
       ++x;
       x++;
       ```

4.3   a) ```
           z = x++ + y;
           ```
       b)  ```
           if (count > 10) {
               cout << "Count is greater than 10" << endl;
           }
           ```
       c) ```
           total -= --x;
           ```
       d)  ```
           q %= divisor;
           q = q % divisor;
           ```

4.4   a) unsigned int sum{0};
       b) unsigned int x{1};

    c) `sum += x;`
      or
      `sum = sum + x;`
    d) `cout << "The sum is: " << sum << endl;`

4.5   See the following code:

```cpp
// Exercise 4.5: Calculate.cpp
// Calculate the sum of the integers from 1 to 10
#include <iostream>
using namespace std;

int main() {
   unsigned int sum{0};
   unsigned int x{1};

   while (x <= 10) { // while x is less than or equal to 10
      sum += x; // add x to sum
      ++x; // increment x
   }

   cout << "The sum is: " << sum << endl;
}
```

```
The sum is: 55
```

4.6   a) `product = 25, x = 6;`
       b) `quotient = 0, x = 6;`

4.7   a) `cin >> x;`
       b) `cin >> y;`
       c) `unsigned int i{1};`
       d) `unsigned int power{1};`
       e) `power *= x;`
          or
          `power = power * x;`
       f) `++i;`
       g) `if (i <= y)`
       h) `cout << power << endl;`

4.8   See the following code:

```cpp
// Exercise 4.8 Solution: power.cpp
// Raise x to the y power.
#include <iostream>
using namespace std;

int main() {
   unsigned int i{1}; // initialize i to begin counting from 1
   unsigned int power{1}; // initialize power

   cout << "Enter base as an integer: ";  // prompt for base
   unsigned int x; // base
   cin >> x; // input base

```

```
14      cout << "Enter exponent as an integer: "; // prompt for exponent
15      unsigned int y; // exponent
16      cin >> y; // input exponent
17
18      // count from 1 to y and multiply power by x each time
19      while (i <= y) {
20         power *= x;
21         ++i;
22      } // end while
23
24      cout << power << endl; // display result
25   } // end main
```

```
Enter base as an integer: 2
Enter exponent as an integer: 3
8
```

4.9 a) *Error:* Missing the closing right brace of the while body.
   Correction: Add closing right brace after the statement ++c;.
b) *Error:* Used stream insertion instead of stream extraction.
   Correction: Change << to >>.
c) *Error:* Semicolon after else is a logic error. The second output statement always executes.
   Correction: Remove the semicolon after else.

4.10 The value of the variable z is never changed in the while statement. Therefore, if the loop-continuation condition (z >= 0) is initially *true*, an infinite loop is created. To prevent the infinite loop, z must be decremented so that it eventually becomes less than 0.

Exercises

4.11 *(Correct the Code Errors)* Identify and correct the error(s) in each of the following:

a)
```
if (age >= 65); {
   cout << "Age is greater than or equal to 65" << endl;
}
else {
   cout << "Age is less than 65 << endl";
}
```

b)
```
if (age >= 65) {
   cout << "Age is greater than or equal to 65" << endl;
else; {
   cout << "Age is less than 65 << endl";
}
```

c)
```
unsigned int x{1};
unsigned int total;

while (x <= 10) {
   total += x;
   ++x;
}
```

d)
```
While (x <= 100)
   total += x;
   ++x;
```

e) while (y > 0) {
        cout << y << endl;
        ++y;
    }

4.12   *(What Does this Program Do?)* What does the following program print?

```
1    // Exercise 4.12: Mystery.cpp
2    #include <iostream>
3    using namespace std;
4
5    int main() {
6        unsigned int x{1};
7        unsigned int total{0};
8
9        while (x <= 10) {
10            int y = x * x;
11            cout << y << endl;
12            total += y;
13            ++x;
14        }
15
16        cout << "Total is " << total << endl;
17    }
```

For Exercises 4.13—4.16, perform each of these steps:

    a) Read the problem statement.
    b) Formulate the algorithm using pseudocode and top-down, stepwise refinement.
    c) Write a C++ program.
    d) Test, debug and execute the C++ program.

4.13   *(Gas Mileage)* Drivers are concerned with the mileage obtained by their automobiles. One driver has kept track of several trips by recording miles driven and gallons used for each trip. Develop a C++ program that uses a while statement to input the miles driven and gallons used for each trip. The program should calculate and display the miles per gallon obtained for each trip and print the combined miles per gallon obtained for all tankfuls up to this point.

```
Enter miles driven (-1 to quit): 287
Enter gallons used: 13
MPG this trip: 22.076923
Total MPG: 22.076923

Enter miles driven (-1 to quit): 200
Enter gallons used: 10
MPG this trip: 20.000000
Total MPG: 21.173913

Enter the miles driven (-1 to quit): 120
Enter gallons used: 5
MPG this trip: 24.000000
Total MPG: 21.678571

Enter the miles used (-1 to quit): -1
```

4.14   *(Credit Limits)* Develop a C++ program that will determine whether a department-store customer has exceeded the credit limit on a charge account. For each customer, the following facts are available:

a) Account number (an integer)
b) Balance at the beginning of the month
c) Total of all items charged by this customer this month
d) Total of all credits applied to this customer's account this month
e) Allowed credit limit

The program should use a `while` statement to input each of these facts, calculate the new balance (= beginning balance + charges − credits) and determine whether the new balance exceeds the customer's credit limit. For those customers whose credit limit is exceeded, the program should display the customer's account number, credit limit, new balance and the message "Credit Limit Exceeded."

```
Enter account number (or -1 to quit): 100
Enter beginning balance: 5394.78
Enter total charges: 1000.00
Enter total credits: 500.00
Enter credit limit: 5500.00
New balance is 5894.78
Account:      100
Credit limit: 5500.00
Balance:      5894.78
Credit Limit Exceeded.

Enter Account Number (or -1 to quit): 200
Enter beginning balance: 1000.00
Enter total charges: 123.45
Enter total credits: 321.00
Enter credit limit: 1500.00
New balance is 802.45

Enter Account Number (or -1 to quit): -1
```

4.15   *(Sales-Commission Calculator)* A large company pays its salespeople on a commission basis. The salespeople each receive $200 per week plus 9% of their gross sales for that week. For example, a salesperson who sells $5000 worth of chemicals in a week receives $200 plus 9% of $5000, or a total of $650. Develop a C++ program that uses a `while` statement to input each salesperson's gross sales for last week and calculates and displays that salesperson's earnings. Process one salesperson's figures at a time.

```
Enter sales in dollars (-1 to end): 5000.00
Salary is: $650.00

Enter sales in dollars (-1 to end): 6000.00
Salary is: $740.00

Enter sales in dollars (-1 to end): 7000.00
Salary is: $830.00

Enter sales in dollars (-1 to end): -1
```

4.16   *(Salary Calculator)* Develop a C++ program that uses a `while` statement to determine the gross pay for each of several employees. The company pays "straight time" for the first 40 hours worked by each employee and pays "time-and-a-half" for all hours worked in excess of 40 hours. You are given a list of the employees of the company, the number of hours each employee worked last week and the hourly rate of each employee. Your program should input this information for each employee and should determine and display the employee's gross pay.

```
Enter hours worked (-1 to end): 39
Enter hourly rate of the employee ($00.00): 10.00
Salary is $390.00

Enter hours worked (-1 to end): 40
Enter hourly rate of the employee ($00.00): 10.00
Salary is $400.00

Enter hours worked (-1 to end): 41
Enter hourly rate of the employee ($00.00): 10.00
Salary is $415.00

Enter hours worked (-1 to end): -1
```

4.17   *(Find the Largest)* The process of finding the largest number (i.e., the maximum of a group of numbers) is used frequently in computer applications. For example, a program that determines the winner of a sales contest inputs the number of units sold by each salesperson. The salesperson who sells the most units wins the contest. Write a C++ program that uses a while statement to determine and print the largest of 10 numbers input by the user. Your program should use three variables, as follows:

  a) counter—A counter to count to 10 (i.e., to keep track of how many numbers have been input and to determine when all 10 numbers have been processed).
  b) number—The current number input to the program.
  c) largest—The largest number found so far.

4.18   *(Tabular Output)* Write a C++ program that uses a while statement and the tab escape sequence \t to print the following table of values:

N	10*N	100*N	1000*N
1	10	100	1000
2	20	200	2000
3	30	300	3000
4	40	400	4000
5	50	500	5000

4.19   *(Find the Two Largest Numbers)* Using an approach similar to that in Exercise 4.17, find the *two* largest values among the 10 numbers. [*Note:* You must input each number only once.]

4.20   *(Validating User Input)* The examination-results program of Fig. 4.14 assumes that any value input by the user that's not a 1 must be a 2. Modify the application to validate its inputs. On any input, if the value entered is other than 1 or 2, keep looping until the user enters a correct value.

4.21   *(What Does this Program Do?)* What does the following program print?

```cpp
1   // Exercise 4.21: Mystery2.cpp
2   #include <iostream>
3   using namespace std;
4
5   int main() {
6      unsigned int count{1};
7
8      while (count <= 10) {
9         cout << (count % 2 == 1 ? "****" : "++++++++") << endl;
10        ++count;
11     }
12  }
```

4.22   *(What Does this Program Do?)* What does the following program print?

```
 1   // Exercise 4.22: Mystery3.cpp
 2   #include <iostream>
 3   using namespace std;
 4
 5   int main() {
 6      unsigned int row{10};
 7
 8      while (row >= 1) {
 9         unsigned int column{1};
10
11         while (column <= 10) {
12            cout << (row % 2 == 1 ? "<" : ">");
13            ++column;
14         }
15
16         --row;
17         cout << endl;
18      }
19   }
```

4.23   *(Dangling-else Problem)* C++ compilers always associate an else with the immediately preceding if unless told to do otherwise by the placement of braces ({ and }). This behavior can lead to what is referred to as the dangling-else problem. The indentation of the nested statement

```
if (x > 5)
   if (y > 5)
      cout << "x and y are > 5";
else
   cout << "x is <= 5";
```

appears to indicate that if x is greater than 5, the nested if statement determines whether y is also greater than 5. If so, the statement outputs the string "x and y are > 5". Otherwise, it appears that if x is not greater than 5, the else part of the if...else outputs the string "x is <= 5". Beware! This nested if...else statement does *not* execute as it appears. The compiler actually interprets the statement as

```
if (x > 5)
   if (y > 5)
      cout << "x and y are > 5";
   else
      cout << "x is <= 5";
```

in which the body of the first if is a *nested* if...else. The outer if statement tests whether x is greater than 5. If so, execution continues by testing whether y is also greater than 5. If the second condition is *true*, the proper string—"x and y are > 5"—is displayed. However, if the second condition is *false*, the string "x is <= 5" is displayed, even though we know that x is greater than 5. Equally bad, if the outer if statement's condition is *false*, the inner if...else is skipped and nothing is displayed. For this exercise, add braces to the preceding code snippet to force the nested if...else statement to execute as it was originally intended.

4.24   *(Another Dangling-else Problem)* Based on the dangling-else discussion in Exercise 4.23, state the output for each of the following code snippets when x is 9 and y is 11 and when x is 11 and y is 9. We eliminated the indentation from the following code to make the problem more challenging. [*Hint:* Apply indentation conventions you've learned.]

```
a)  if (x < 10)
    if (y > 10)
    cout << "*****" << endl;
    else
    cout << "#####" << endl;
    cout << "$$$$$" << endl;
b)  if (x < 10)
    {
    if (y > 10)
    cout << "*****" << endl;
    }
    else
    {
    cout << "#####" << endl;
    cout << "$$$$$" << endl;
    }
```

4.25   *(Another Dangling-else Problem)* Based on the dangling-else discussion in Exercise 4.23, modify the following code to produce the output shown. Use proper indentation techniques. You must not make any additional changes other than inserting braces. We eliminated the indentation from the following code to make the problem more challenging. [*Note:* It's possible that no modification is necessary.]

```
if ( y == 8 )
if ( x == 5 )
cout << "@@@@@" << endl;
else
cout << "#####" << endl;
cout << "$$$$$" << endl;
cout << "&&&&&" << endl;
```

a) Assuming x = 5 and y = 8, the following output is produced.

```
@@@@@
$$$$$
&&&&&
```

b) Assuming x = 5 and y = 8, the following output is produced.

```
@@@@@
```

c) Assuming x = 5 and y = 8, the following output is produced.

```
@@@@@
&&&&&
```

d) Assuming x = 5 and y = 7, the following output is produced. [*Note:* The last three output statements after the else are all part of a block.]

```
#####
$$$$$
&&&&&
```

4.26   *(Square of Asterisks)* Write a program that reads in the size of the side of a square, then prints a hollow square of that size out of asterisks and blanks. Your program should work for squares of all side sizes between 1 and 20. For example, if your program reads a size of 5, it should print

```
*****
*   *
*   *
*   *
*****
```

4.27   *(Palindromes)* A palindrome is a number or a text phrase that reads the same backward as forward. For example, each of the following five-digit integers is a palindrome: 12321, 55555, 45554 and 11611. Write a program that reads in a five-digit integer and determines whether it's a palindrome. [*Hint:* Use the division and remainder operators to separate the number into its individual digits.]

4.28   *(Printing the Decimal Equivalent of a Binary Number)* Input an integer containing only 0s and 1s (i.e., a "binary" integer) and print its decimal equivalent. Use the remainder and division operators to pick off the "binary" number's digits one at a time from right to left. Much as in the decimal number system, where the rightmost digit has a positional value of 1, the next digit left has a positional value of 10, then 100, then 1000, and so on, in the binary number system the rightmost digit has a positional value of 1, the next digit left has a positional value of 2, then 4, then 8, and so on. Thus the decimal number 234 can be interpreted as 2 * 100 + 3 * 10 + 4 * 1. The decimal equivalent of binary 1101 is 1 * 1 + 0 * 2 + 1 * 4 + 1 * 8 or 1 + 0 + 4 + 8, or 13. [*Note:* To learn more about binary numbers, refer to Appendix D.]

4.29   *(Checkerboard Pattern of Asterisks)* Write a program that displays the following checkerboard pattern. Your program must use only three output statements, one of each of the following forms:

```
cout << "* ";
cout << ' ';
cout << endl;
```

```
* * * * * * * *
 * * * * * * * *
* * * * * * * *
 * * * * * * * *
* * * * * * * *
 * * * * * * * *
* * * * * * * *
 * * * * * * * *
```

4.30   *(Multiples of 2 with an Infinite Loop)* Write a program that prints the powers of the integer 2, namely 2, 4, 8, 16, 32, 64, etc. Your while loop should not terminate (i.e., you should create an infinite loop). To do this, simply use the keyword *true* as the expression for the while statement. What happens when you run this program?

4.31   *(Calculating a Circle's Diameter, Circumference and Area)* Write a program that reads the radius of a circle (as a double value) and computes and prints the diameter, the circumference and the area. Use the value 3.14159 for π.

4.32   What's wrong with the following statement? Provide the correct statement to accomplish what the programmer was probably trying to do.

```
cout << ++( x + y );
```

4.33   *(Sides of a Triangle)* Write a program that reads three nonzero double values and determines and prints whether they could represent the sides of a triangle.

4.34 *(Sides of a Right Triangle)* Write a program that reads three nonzero integers and determines and prints whether they're the sides of a right triangle.

4.35 *(Factorial)* The factorial of a nonnegative integer n is written $n!$ (pronounced "n factorial") and is defined as follows:

$n! = n \cdot (n-1) \cdot (n-2) \cdot \ldots \cdot 1$ (for values of n greater than 1)

and

$n! = 1$ (for $n = 0$ or $n = 1$).

For example, $5! = 5 \cdot 4 \cdot 3 \cdot 2 \cdot 1$, which is 120. Use `while` statements in each of the following:

a) Write a program that reads a nonnegative integer and computes and prints its factorial.

b) Write a program that estimates the value of the mathematical constant e by using the formula:

$$e = 1 + \frac{1}{1!} + \frac{1}{2!} + \frac{1}{3!} + \cdots$$

Prompt the user for the desired accuracy of e (i.e., the number of terms in the summation).

c) Write a program that computes the value of e^x by using the formula

$$e^x = 1 + \frac{x}{1!} + \frac{x^2}{2!} + \frac{x^3}{3!} + \cdots$$

Prompt the user for the desired accuracy of e (i.e., the number of terms in the summation).

4.36 *(Modified Account Class)* Modify class `Account` (Exercise 3.9) to represent the `balance` data member as type `double`. Also, display all `double` amounts with two digits to the right of the decimal point.

Making a Difference

4.37 *(Enforcing Privacy with Cryptography)* The explosive growth of Internet communications and data storage on Internet-connected computers has greatly increased privacy concerns. The field of cryptography is concerned with coding data to make it difficult (and hopefully—with the most advanced schemes—impossible) for unauthorized users to read. In this exercise you'll investigate a simple scheme for encrypting and decrypting data. A company that wants to send data over the Internet has asked you to write a program that will encrypt the data so that it may be transmitted more securely. All the data is transmitted as four-digit integers. Your application should read a four-digit integer entered by the user and encrypt it as follows: Replace each digit with the result of adding 7 to the digit and getting the remainder after dividing the new value by 10. Then swap the first digit with the third, and swap the second digit with the fourth. Then print the encrypted integer. Write a separate application that inputs an encrypted four-digit integer and decrypts it (by reversing the encryption scheme) to form the original number. [*Optional reading project:* Research "public key cryptography" in general and the PGP (Pretty Good Privacy) specific public-key scheme. You may also want to investigate the RSA scheme, which is widely used in industrial-strength applications.]

4.38 *(World Population Growth)* World population has grown considerably over the centuries. Continued growth could eventually challenge the limits of breathable air, drinkable water, arable cropland and other precious resources. There is evidence that growth has been slowing in recent years and that world population could peak some time this century, then start to decline.

For this exercise, research world population growth issues online. *Be sure to investigate various viewpoints.* Get estimates for the current world population and its growth rate (the percentage by which it is likely to increase this year). Write a program that calculates world population growth each year for the next 75 years, *using the simplifying assumption that the current growth rate will stay constant*. Print the results in a table. The first column should display the year from year 1 to year

75. The second column should display the anticipated world population at the end of that year. The third column should display the numerical increase in the world population that would occur that year. Using your results, determine the year in which the population would be double what it is today, if this year's growth rate were to persist.

Control Statements: Part 2;
Logical Operators

5

Objectives

In this chapter you'll:

- Learn the essentials of counter-controlled iteration.

- Use the **for** and do...**while** iteration statements to execute statements in a program repeatedly.

- Understand multiple selection using the **switch** selection statement.

- Use the **break** and **continue** program-control statements to alter the flow of control.

- Use the logical operators to form compound conditions in control statements.

- Understand the representational errors associated with using floating-point data types to hold monetary values.

- Understand some of the challenges of processing monetary amounts as we begin building a **DollarAmount** class, which uses integers and integer arithmetic to represent and manipulate monetary amounts.

5.1 Introduction

This chapter continues our presentation of structured-programming theory and principles by introducing all but one of C++'s remaining control statements. We demonstrate C++'s for, do...while and switch statements. Through examples using while and for, we explore the essentials of counter-controlled iteration. We also use compound-interest calculations to begin investigating the issues of processing monetary amounts. First, we discuss the representational errors associated with floating-point types. Then, we develop a new DollarAmount class that uses very large integers to precisely represent monetary amounts. As you'll see, the class uses only precise integer arithmetic, thus eliminating the kind of representational errors associated with floating-point types. We use a switch statement to count the number of A, B, C, D and F grade equivalents in a set of numeric grades entered by the user. We introduce the break and continue program-control statements. We discuss C++'s logical operators, which enable you to combine simple conditions in control statements. Finally, we summarize C++'s control statements and the proven problem-solving techniques presented in this chapter and Chapter 4.

5.2 Essentials of Counter-Controlled Iteration

This section uses the while iteration statement introduced in Chapter 4 to formalize the elements of counter-controlled iteration:

1. a control variable (or loop counter)

2. the control variable's initial value

3. the control variable's increment that's applied during each iteration of the loop

4. the loop-continuation condition that determines if looping should continue.

Consider the application of Fig. 5.1, which uses a loop to display the numbers from 1 through 10.

```
 1   // Fig. 5.1: WhileCounter.cpp
 2   // Counter-controlled iteration with the while iteration statement.
 3   #include <iostream>
 4   using namespace std;
 5
 6   int main() {
 7      unsigned int counter{1}; // declare and initialize control variable
 8
 9      while (counter <= 10) { // loop-continuation condition
10         cout << counter << " ";
11         ++counter; // increment control variable
12      }
13
14      cout << endl;
15   }
```

```
1  2  3  4  5  6  7  8  9  10
```

Fig. 5.1 | Counter-controlled iteration with the while iteration statement.

In Fig. 5.1, the elements of counter-controlled iteration are defined in lines 7, 9 and 11. Line 7 declares the control variable (counter) as an unsigned int, *reserves space* for it in memory and sets its *initial value* to 1. Declarations that require initialization are *executable* statements. In C++, it's more precise to call a variable declaration that also reserves memory a definition. Because definitions are declarations, too, we'll use the term "declaration" except when the distinction is important.

Line 10 displays control variable counter's value once per iteration of the loop. Line 11 *increments* the control variable by 1 for each iteration of the loop. The while's loop-continuation condition (line 9) tests whether the value of the control variable is less than or equal to 10 (the final value for which the condition is *true*). The program performs the while's body even when the control variable is 10. The loop terminates when the control variable exceeds 10 (that is, when counter becomes 11).

Error-Prevention Tip 5.1

Floating-point values are approximate, so controlling counting loops with floating-point variables can result in imprecise counter values and inaccurate tests for termination. Control counting loops with integer values.

5.3 for Iteration Statement

Section 5.2 presented the essentials of counter-controlled iteration. The while statement can be used to implement any counter-controlled loop. C++ also provides the for iteration statement, which specifies the counter-controlled-iteration details in a single line of code. Figure 5.2 reimplements the application of Fig. 5.1 using for.

When the for statement (lines 9–11) begins executing, the control variable counter is *declared* and *initialized* to 1. (Recall from Section 5.2 that the first two elements of counter-controlled iteration are the *control variable* and its *initial value*.) Next, the program checks the *loop-continuation condition*, counter <= 10, which is between the two

```
1   // Fig. 5.2: ForCounter.cpp
2   // Counter-controlled iteration with the for iteration statement.
3   #include <iostream>
4   using namespace std;
5
6   int main() {
7      // for statement header includes initialization,
8      // loop-continuation condition and increment
9      for (unsigned int counter{1}; counter <= 10; ++counter) {
10        cout << counter << "  ";
11     }
12
13     cout << endl;
14  }
```

```
1  2  3  4  5  6  7  8  9  10
```

Fig. 5.2 | Counter-controlled iteration with the for iteration statement.

required semicolons. Because counter's initial value is 1, the condition is *true*. So, the body statement (line 10) displays control variable counter's value (1). After executing the loop's body, the program increments counter in the expression ++counter, which appears to the right of the second semicolon. Then the program performs the loop-continuation test again to determine whether the program should continue with the loop's next iteration. At this point, counter's value is 2, so the condition is still *true* (the *final value* of 10 is not exceeded)—thus, the program executes the body statement again. This process continues until the numbers 1–10 have been displayed and the counter's value becomes 11. At this point, the loop-continuation test fails, iteration terminates and the program continues executing at the first statement after the for (line 13).

Figure 5.2 uses (in line 9) the loop-continuation condition counter <= 10. If you incorrectly specified counter < 10 as the condition, the loop would iterate only nine times. This is a common *logic error* called an off-by-one error.

Common Programming Error 5.1
Using an incorrect relational operator or an incorrect final value of a loop counter in the loop-continuation condition of an iteration statement can cause an off-by-one error.

Error-Prevention Tip 5.2
Using the final value and operator <= in a loop's condition helps avoid off-by-one errors. For a loop that outputs 1 to 10, the loop-continuation condition should be counter <= 10 rather than counter < 10 (which causes an off-by-one error) or counter < 11 (which is correct). Many programmers prefer so-called zero-based counting, in which to count 10 times, counter would be initialized to zero and the loop-continuation test would be counter < 10.

Error-Prevention Tip 5.3
Write loop conditions carefully to prevent loop counters from overflowing.

*A Closer Look at the **for** Statement's Header*

Figure 5.3 takes a closer look at the for statement in Fig. 5.2. The first line—including the keyword for and everything in parentheses after for (line 9 in Fig. 5.2)—is sometimes called the for statement header. The for header "does it all"—it specifies each item needed for counter-controlled iteration with a control variable.

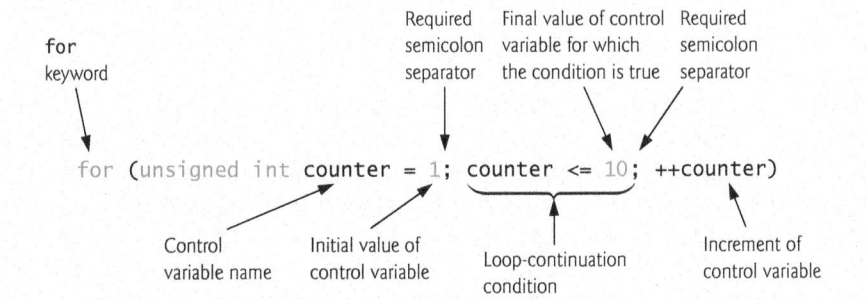

Fig. 5.3 | for statement header components.

*General Format of a **for** Statement*

The general format of the for statement is

```
for (initialization; loopContinuationCondition; increment) {
    statement
}
```

where the *initialization* expression optionally names the loop's control variable and provides its initial value, *loopContinuationCondition* determines whether the loop should continue executing and *increment* modifies the control variable's value, so that the loop-continuation condition eventually becomes *false*. The two semicolons in the for header are required. If the loop-continuation condition is initially *false*, the program does *not* execute the for statement's body. Instead, execution proceeds with the statement following the for.

*Representing a **for** Statement with an Equivalent **while** Statement*

The for statement often can be represented with an equivalent while statement as follows:

```
initialization;

while (loopContinuationCondition) {
    statement
    increment;
}
```

In Section 5.10, we show a case in which a for statement cannot be represented with an equivalent while statement. Typically, for statements are used for counter-controlled iteration and while statements for sentinel-controlled iteration. However, while and for can each be used for either iteration type.

*Scope of a **for** Statement's Control Variable*

If the *initialization* expression in the for header declares the control variable, it can be used *only* in that for statement—not beyond it. This restricted use is known as the variable's scope, which defines where it can be used in a program. For example, a *local variable* can be used *only* in the function that declares it and *only* from its declaration point to the right brace which closes that block. Scope is discussed in detail in Chapter 6, Functions and an Introduction to Recursion.

Common Programming Error 5.2
When a for statement's control variable is declared in the initialization section of the for's header, using the control variable after the for's body is a compilation error.

Expressions in a **for** Statement's Header Are Optional

All three expressions in a for header are optional. If the *loopContinuationCondition* is omitted, C++ assumes that the loop-continuation condition is *always true*, thus creating an *infinite loop*. You might omit the *initialization* expression if the program initializes the control variable *before* the loop. You might omit the *increment* expression if the program calculates the increment in the loop's body or if no increment is needed. The increment expression in a for acts as if it were a standalone statement at the end of the for's body. Therefore, the increment expressions

```
counter = counter + 1
counter += 1
++counter
counter++
```

are equivalent in a for statement. Many programmers prefer counter++ because it's concise and because a for loop evaluates its increment expression *after* its body executes, so the postfix increment form seems more natural. In this case, the variable being incremented does not appear in a larger expression, so preincrementing and postincrementing have the *same* effect. We prefer preincrement.

Common Programming Error 5.3
Placing a semicolon immediately to the right of the right parenthesis of a for header makes that for's body an empty statement. This is normally a logic error.

Error-Prevention Tip 5.4
Infinite loops occur when the loop-continuation condition in an iteration statement never becomes false. To prevent this situation in a counter-controlled loop, ensure that the control variable is modified during each iteration of the loop so that the loop-continuation condition will eventually become false. In a sentinel-controlled loop, ensure that the sentinel value is able to be input.

Placing Arithmetic Expressions in a **for** Statement's Header

The initialization, loop-continuation condition and increment portions of a for statement can contain arithmetic expressions. For example, assume that x = 2 and y = 10. If x and y are not modified in the body of the loop, the statement

```
for (unsigned int j = x; j <= 4 * x * y; j += y / x)
```

is equivalent to the statement

```
for (unsigned int j = 2; j <= 80; j += 5)
```

The increment of a for statement may also be *negative*, in which case it's a decrement, and the loop counts *downward*.

Using a **for** Statement's Control Variable in the Statement's Body

Programs frequently display the control-variable value or use it in calculations in the loop body, but this use is not required. The control variable is commonly used to control iteration *without* being mentioned in the body of the for.

> **Error-Prevention Tip 5.5**
>
> *Although the value of the control variable can be changed in the body of a for loop, avoid doing so, because this practice can lead to subtle errors. If a program must modify the control variable's value in the loop's body, use* while *rather than* for.

UML Activity Diagram for the **for** Statement

The for statement's UML activity diagram is similar to that of the while statement (Fig. 4.8). Figure 5.4 shows the activity diagram of the for statement in Fig. 5.2. The diagram makes it clear that initialization occurs only once—*before* the loop-continuation test is evaluated the first time—and that incrementing occurs *each* time through the loop *after* the body statement executes.

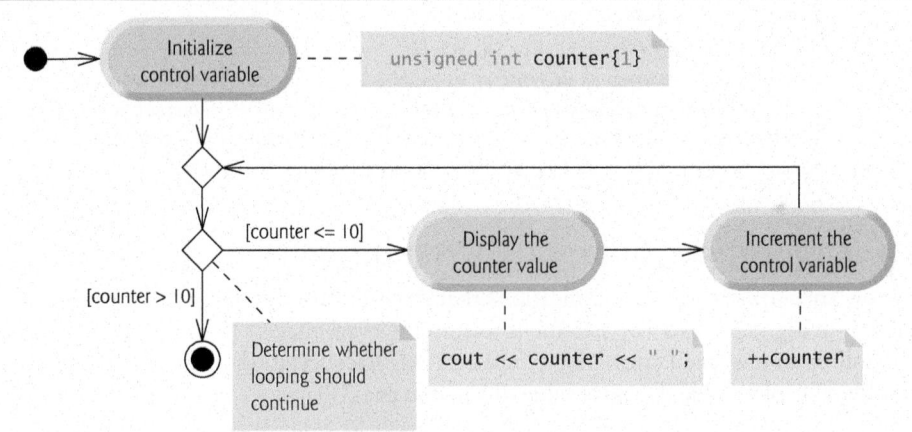

Fig. 5.4 | UML activity diagram for the for statement in Fig. 5.2.

5.4 Examples Using the for Statement

The following examples show techniques for varying the control variable in a for statement. In each case, we write *only* the appropriate for header. Note the change in the relational operator for the loops that *decrement* the control variable.

a) Vary the control variable from 1 to 100 in increments of 1.

```
for (unsigned int i{1}; i <= 100; i++)
```

b) Vary the control variable from 100 *down* to 1 in *decrements* of 1.

```
for (unsigned int i{100}; i >= 1; i--)
```

c) Vary the control variable from 7 to 77 in increments of 7.

```
for (unsigned int i{7}; i <= 77; i += 7)
```

d) Vary the control variable from 20 *down* to 2 in *decrements* of 2.

```
for (unsigned int i{20}; i >= 2; i -= 2)
```

e) Vary the control variable over the values 2, 5, 8, 11, 14, 17, 20.

```
for (unsigned int i{2}; i <= 20; i += 3)
```

f) Vary the control variable over the values 99, 88, 77, 66, 55, 44, 33, 22, 11, 0. We use int rather than unsigned int here because the condition does not become false until i's value is -11, so the control variable must be able to represent both positive and negative values.

```
for (int i{99}; i >= 0; i -= 11)
```

Common Programming Error 5.4

Using an incorrect relational operator in the loop-continuation condition of a loop that counts downward (e.g., using i <= 1 instead of i >= 1 in a loop counting down to 1) is usually a logic error.

Common Programming Error 5.5

Do not use equality operators (!= or ==) in a loop-continuation condition if the loop's control variable increments or decrements by more than 1. For example, consider the for statement header for (unsigned int counter{1}; counter != 10; counter += 2). The loop-continuation test counter != 10 never becomes false (resulting in an infinite loop) because counter increments by 2 after each iteration (and never becomes 10).

5.5 Application: Summing Even Integers

We now consider two sample applications that demonstrate simple uses of for. The application in Fig. 5.5 uses a for statement to sum the even integers from 2 to 20 and store the result in an unsigned int variable called total. Each iteration of the loop (lines 10–12) adds control variable number's value to variable total.

```
1   // Fig. 5.5: Sum.cpp
2   // Summing integers with the for statement.
3   #include <iostream>
4   using namespace std;
5
6   int main() {
7      unsigned int total{0};
8
9      // total even integers from 2 through 20
10     for (unsigned int number{2}; number <= 20; number += 2) {
11        total += number;
12     }
13
```

Fig. 5.5 | Summing integers with the for statement. (Part 1 of 2.)

```
14      cout << "Sum is " << total << endl;
15   }
```

```
Sum is 110
```

Fig. 5.5 | Summing integers with the for statement. (Part 2 of 2.)

The *initialization* and *increment* expressions can be comma-separated lists that enable you to use multiple initialization expressions or multiple increment expressions. For example, although this is discouraged, you could merge the for statement's body (line 11) into the increment portion of the for header by using a comma as in

```
total += number, number += 2
```

The comma between the expressions total += number and number += 2 is the comma operator, which guarantees that a list of expressions evaluates from left to right. The comma operator has the lowest precedence of all C++ operators. The value and type of a comma-separated list of expressions is the value and type of the *rightmost* expression. The comma operator is often used in for statements that require *multiple initialization expressions* and/or *multiple increment expressions*.

Good Programming Practice 5.1
Place only expressions involving the control variables in the initialization and increment sections of a for statement.

Good Programming Practice 5.2
For readability limit the size of control-statement headers to a single line if possible.

5.6 Application: Compound-Interest Calculations

Let's use the for statement to compute compound interest. Consider the following problem:

> *A person invests $1,000 in a savings account yielding 5% interest. Assuming that all the interest is left on deposit, calculate and print the amount of money in the account at the end of each year for 10 years. Use the following formula to determine the amounts:*
>
> $$a = p(1 + r)^n$$
>
> *where*
>
> p is the original amount invested (i.e., the principal)
> r is the annual interest rate (e.g., use 0.05 for 5%)
> n is the number of years
> a is the amount on deposit at the end of the nth year.

The solution to this problem (Fig. 5.6) involves a loop that performs the indicated calculation for each of the 10 years the money remains on deposit. For this solution, we use double values for the monetary calculations, then we discuss the problems with using floating-point types to represent monetary amounts. In the next section, we'll develop a new

DollarAmount class that uses very large integers to precisely represent monetary amounts. As you'll see, the class performs monetary calculations using only integer arithmetic.

```cpp
1   // Fig. 5.6: Interest.cpp
2   // Compound-interest calculations with for.
3   #include <iostream>
4   #include <iomanip>
5   #include <cmath> // for pow function
6   using namespace std;
7
8   int main() {
9      // set floating-point number format
10     cout << fixed << setprecision(2);
11
12     double principal{1000.00}; // initial amount before interest
13     double rate{0.05}; // interest rate
14
15     cout << "Initial principal: " << principal << endl;
16     cout << "   Interest rate:   " << rate << endl;
17
18     // display headers
19     cout << "\nYear" << setw(20) << "Amount on deposit" << endl;
20
21     // calculate amount on deposit for each of ten years
22     for (unsigned int year{1}; year <= 10; year++) {
23        // calculate amount on deposit at the end of the specified year
24        double amount = principal * pow(1.0 + rate, year);
25
26        // display the year and the amount
27        cout << setw(4) << year << setw(20) << amount << endl;
28     }
29  }
```

```
Initial principal: 1000.00
   Interest rate:    0.05

Year    Amount on deposit
   1            1050.00
   2            1102.50
   3            1157.63
   4            1215.51
   5            1276.28
   6            1340.10
   7            1407.10
   8            1477.46
   9            1551.33
  10            1628.89
```

Fig. 5.6 | Compound-interest calculations with for.

Lines 12–13 in main declare double variables principal and rate, and initialize principal to 1000.00 and rate to 0.05. C++ treats floating-point literals like 1000.00 and 0.05 as type double. Similarly, C++ treats whole-number literals like 7 and -22 as type int. Lines 15–16 display the initial principal and the interest rate.

Formatting with Field Widths and Justification

The output statement in line 10 before the for loop and the output statement in line 27 in the for loop combine to print the values of the variables year and amount with the formatting specified by the *parameterized* stream manipulators setprecision and setw and the *nonparameterized* stream manipulator fixed. The stream manipulator setw(4) specifies that the next value output should appear in a field width of 4—i.e., cout << prints the value with *at least* four character positions. If the value to be output is *less* than four character positions wide, the value is right justified in the field by default. If the value to be output is *more* than four character positions wide, the field width is extended with additional character positions to the right to accommodate the entire value. To indicate that values should be output left justified, simply output nonparameterized stream manipulator left (found in header <iostream>). Right justification can be restored by outputting nonparameterized stream manipulator right.

The other formatting in the output statements indicates that variable amount is printed as a fixed-point value with a decimal point (specified in line 10 with the stream manipulator fixed) right justified in a field of 20 character positions (specified in line 27 with setw(20)) and two digits of precision to the right of the decimal point (specified in line 10 with manipulator setprecision(2)). We applied the stream manipulators fixed and setprecision to the output stream cout before the for loop because these format settings remain in effect until they're changed—such settings are called sticky settings and they do *not* need to be applied during each iteration of the loop. However, the field width specified with setw applies *only* to the *next* value output. We discuss C++'s powerful input/output formatting capabilities in Chapter 13, Stream Input/Output: A Deeper Look.

Performing the Interest Calculations with Standard Library Function pow

The for statement (lines 22–28) executes its body 10 times, varying the unsigned int control variable year from 1 to 10 in increments of 1. This loop terminates when year becomes 11. Variable year represents n in the problem statement.

C++ does *not* include an exponentiation operator, so we use the standard library function pow (line 24) from the header <cmath>. The call pow(x, y) calculates the value of x raised to the yth power. The function receives two double arguments and returns a double value. Line 24 performs the calculation $a = p(1 + r)^n$, where a is amount, p is principal, r is rate and n is year.

The body of the for statement contains the calculation 1.0 + rate as pow's first argument. This calculation produces the *same* result each time through the loop, so repeating it in every iteration of the loop is wasteful.

Performance Tip 5.1

In loops, avoid calculations for which the result never changes—such calculations should typically be placed before the loop. Many of today's sophisticated optimizing compilers will place such calculations before loops in the compiled code.

Floating-Point Number Precision and Memory Requirements

Variables of type float represent single-precision floating-point numbers and have approximately seven significant digits on most of today's systems. Variables of type double represent double-precision floating-point numbers. These require twice as much memory as float variables and provide approximately 15 significant digits on most of today's systems—approximately double the precision of `float` variables. Most programmers represent floating-point numbers with type `double`. In fact, C++ treats all floating-point numbers you type in a program's source code (such as 7.33 and 0.0975) as `double` values by default. Such values in the source code are known as floating-point literals. See Appendix C for the fundamental types' value ranges.

Floating-Point Numbers Are Approximations

In conventional arithmetic, floating-point numbers often arise as a result of division—when we divide 10 by 3, the result is 3.3333333..., with the sequence of 3s repeating infinitely. The computer allocates only a *fixed* amount of space to hold such a value, so clearly the stored floating-point value can be only an *approximation*. As you can see, `double` suffers from what we call representational error.

Common Programming Error 5.6

Using floating-point numbers in a manner that assumes they're represented exactly (e.g., using them in comparisons for equality) can lead to incorrect results. Floating-point numbers are represented only approximately.

Floating-point numbers have numerous applications, especially for measured values. For example, when we speak of a "normal" body temperature of 98.6 degrees Fahrenheit, we do not need to be precise to a large number of digits. When we read the temperature on a thermometer as 98.6, it may actually be 98.5999473210643. Calling this number simply 98.6 is fine for most applications involving body temperatures. Due to the imprecise nature of floating-point numbers, type `double` is preferred over type `float`, because `double` variables can represent floating-point numbers more precisely. For this reason, we use type `double` throughout the book.

A Warning about Displaying Rounded Values

We declared variables `amount`, `principal` and `rate` to be of type `double` in this example. We're dealing with fractional parts of dollars and thus need a type that allows decimal points in its values. Unfortunately, floating-point numbers can cause trouble. Here's a simple explanation of what can go wrong when using `double` (or `float`) to represent dollar amounts (assuming that dollar amounts are displayed with two digits to the right of the decimal point): Two calculated `double` dollar amounts stored in the machine could be 14.234 (which would normally be rounded to 14.23 for display purposes) and 18.673 (which would normally be rounded to 18.67 for display purposes). When these amounts are added, they produce the internal sum 32.907, which would normally be rounded to 32.91 for display purposes. Thus, your output could appear as

```
  14.23
+ 18.67
  32.91
```

but a person adding the individual numbers as displayed would expect the sum to be 32.90. You've been warned!

Error-Prevention Tip 5.6

Do not use variables of type double (or float) to perform precise monetary calculations. The imprecision of floating-point numbers can lead to errors.

Even Common Dollar Amounts Can Have Representational Error in Floating Point
Even simple dollar amounts, such as those you might see on a grocery or restaurant bill, can have representational errors when they're stored as doubles. To see this, we created a simple program with the declaration

```
double d = 123.02;
```

then displayed variable d's value with many digits of precision to the right of the decimal point—we ask you to do this in Exercise 5.36. The resulting output showed 123.02 as 123.0199999..., which is another example of a representational error. Though some dollar amounts can be represented precisely as double, many cannot. In the next section, we'll build a class that represents and processes dollar amounts using only integer arithmetic. This eliminates the representational errors associated with double values, because integers are represented exactly.

5.7 Case Study: Integer-Based Monetary Calculations with Class DollarAmount

In Chapter 3, we developed an Account class. A typical dollar Account balance—such as $437.19—has a whole number of dollars (e.g., 437) to the left of the decimal point and a whole number of cents (e.g., 19) to the right. For simplicity, class Account represented its balance with type int, which of course limited balances to whole dollar amounts.

Representing Dollar Amounts as Floating-Point Numbers
Rather than int, we need a type that allows us to represent a dollar amount as a number with a decimal point. In Fig. 5.6's compound-interest example, we processed dollar amounts as type double. This introduced representational error and rounding issues:

1. There were representational errors, because we stored precise decimal dollar amounts and interest rates as doubles. As you'll see in this section, you can avoid these by performing all calculations using integer arithmetic—even interest calculations.

2. There was rounding of the floating-point values. We cannot avoid rounding on interest calculations, because they result in fractional pennies when working with dollar amounts. Those fractional pennies must be rounded to the hundredths place. With integer arithmetic we can exercise precise control over rounding without suffering the representational errors associated with floating-point calculations.

In addition, there are many points in monetary calculations in which rounding may occur. For example, on a restaurant bill, the tax could be calculated on each individual item, resulting in many separate rounding operations, or it could be calculated only once on the total bill amount—these alternate approaches could yield different results.

Performing monetary calculations with doubles can cause problems for organizations that require precise dollar amounts—such as banks, insurances companies and businesses in general. A bank, for example, must keep precise track of all its customers' balances. Imagine the problems that a large financial institution with millions of accounts would have if its customer balances didn't "add up," preventing the organization from tying out its books. For this reason, it's crucial to perform monetary calculations using integer arithmetic rather than floating-point arithmetic. As you'll see in our next example, even interest calculations can be done with integer arithmetic.

Integer-Based Monetary Calculations

Throughout this book, we focus on *crafting valuable classes*. In this section, we begin developing a DollarAmount class for precise control over monetary amounts. The class represents dollar amounts in whole numbers of pennies—for example, $1,000 is stored as 100000. A key benefit of this approach is that integer values are represented *exactly* in memory.

First, we'll assume that class DollarAmount already exists, with capabilities including

- a constructor to initialize a DollarAmount object to a whole number of pennies

- an add member function that adds a DollarAmount object into the DollarAmount object on which this function is called

- a subtract member function that subtracts a DollarAmount object from the DollarAmount object on which this function is called

- an addInterest member function that calculates annual interest on the amount in the DollarAmount object on which the function is called and adds the interest to the amount in that object, and

- a toString member function that returns a DollarAmount's string representation.

The class performs *all* calculations using integer arithmetic—no floating-point calculations are used, so DollarAmounts always represent their values precisely. We'll use these capabilities in Fig. 5.7 to demonstrate adding and subtracting DollarAmounts, and to reimplement Fig. 5.6's compound-interest example using DollarAmounts. Then we'll present the class and walk through the code. As you'll see, the interest calculations still require rounding, but class DollarAmount will control precisely how that rounding occurs using integer arithmetic.

This version of class DollarAmount will feel a bit clunky, requiring you to call member functions such as add, subtract, addInterest and toString. In Chapter 10, Operator Overloading, we'll do better. There, you'll see how to manipulate your DollarAmount objects conveniently with operators like +, -, >> and << that you've used with fundamental types. You'll be able to make other refinements to the class as you work through the later chapters. Crafting a valuable class like DollarAmount—which helps you solve a practical, real-world problem—is one of the key "light-bulb moments" in learning C++. We'll point out others in the forthcoming chapters.

Representing Monetary Amounts Is a Complex Issue

Dealing with monetary amounts is more complex than what we show here. There are many currencies worldwide, with different conventions for thousands separators, decimal separators, currency symbols, and more. In addition, rounding rules can vary by currency, government, company, etc. Some programming languages have types that make it easier to work with monetary values. Various C++ libraries have classes for this purpose, but they tend to be complex and beyond our scope. Boost's C++ multiprecision library is one such example.

5.7.1 Demonstrating Class DollarAmount

Figure 5.7 adds DollarAmounts, subtracts DollarAmounts and calculates compound interest with DollarAmounts. Lines 10–11 create DollarAmount objects d1 and d2 and initializes them to 12345 pennies (i.e., $123.45) and 1576 pennies (i.e., $15.76), respectively. Lines 13–14 display the DollarAmount objects' values by calling each object's toString member function to get a string representation of the object. Next, line 15 calls d1's add member function, passing d2 as an argument. This statement adds both objects' values and stores the result in the object d1. Finally, line 16 displays d1's modified value. Lines 18–21 and 23–26 demonstrate DollarAmount's subtract member function. Line 20 subtracts d2 from d1, which modifies d1 again. Line 25 subtracts d1 from d2 to demonstrate a negative DollarAmount as the result of a calculation. The first three lines of the output show the results of these addition and subtraction operations.

```cpp
1   // Fig. 5.7: Interest.cpp
2   // Compound-interest calculations with class DollarAmount and integers.
3   #include <iostream>
4   #include <iomanip>
5   #include <string>
6   #include "DollarAmount.h"
7   using namespace std;
8
9   int main() {
10     DollarAmount d1{12345}; // $123.45
11     DollarAmount d2{1576}; // $15.76
12
13     cout << "After adding d2 (" << d2.toString() << ") into d1 ("
14        << d1.toString() << "), d1 = ";
15     d1.add(d2); // modifies object d1
16     cout << d1.toString() << "\n";
17
18     cout << "After subtracting d2 (" << d2.toString() << ") from d1 ("
19        << d1.toString() << "), d1 = ";
20     d1.subtract(d2); // modifies object d1
21     cout << d1.toString() << "\n";
22
23     cout << "After subtracting d1 (" << d1.toString() << ") from d2 ("
24        << d2.toString() << "), d2 = ";
25     d2.subtract(d1); // modifies object d2
26     cout << d2.toString() << "\n\n";
27
28     cout << "Enter integer interest rate and divisor. For example:\n"
29        << "for     2%, enter:     2 100\n"
30        << "for   2.3%, enter:    23 1000\n"
31        << "for  2.37%, enter:   237 10000\n"
32        << "for 2.375%, enter: 2375 100000\n> ";
33     int rate; // whole-number interest rate
34     int divisor; // divisor for rate
35     cin >> rate >> divisor;
36
37     DollarAmount balance{100000}; // initial principal amount in pennies
38     cout << "\nInitial balance: " << balance.toString() << endl;
39
40     // display headers
41     cout << "\nYear" << setw(20) << "Amount on deposit" << endl;
```

Fig. 5.7 | Compound-interest calculations with class DollarAmount and integers. (Part 1 of 3.)

```
42
43      // calculate amount on deposit for each of ten years
44      for (unsigned int year{1}; year <= 10; year++) {
45          // increase balance by rate % (i.e., rate / divisor)
46          balance.addInterest(rate, divisor);
47
48          // display the year and the amount
49          cout << setw(4) << year << setw(20) << balance.toString() << endl;
50      }
51  }
```

```
After adding d2 (15.76) into d1 (123.45), d1 = 139.21
After subtracting d2 (15.76) from d1 (139.21), d1 = 123.45
After subtracting d1 (123.45) from d2 (15.76), d2 = -107.69

Enter integer interest rate and divisor. For example:
for      2%, enter:     2 100
for    2.3%, enter:    23 1000
for   2.37%, enter:   237 10000
for  2.375%, enter: 2375 100000
> 5 100

Initial balance: 1000.00

Year    Amount on deposit
   1            1050.00
   2            1102.50
   3            1157.63
   4            1215.51
   5            1276.29
   6            1340.10
   7            1407.11
   8            1477.47
   9            1551.34
  10            1628.91
```

```
After adding d2 (15.76) into d1 (123.45), d1 = 139.21
After subtracting d2 (15.76) from d1 (139.21), d1 = 123.45
After subtracting d1 (123.45) from d2 (15.76), d2 = -107.69

Enter integer interest rate and divisor. For example:
for      2%, enter:     2 100
for    2.3%, enter:    23 1000
for   2.37%, enter:   237 10000
for  2.375%, enter: 2375 100000
> 525 10000

Initial balance: 1000.00

Year    Amount on deposit
   1            1052.50
   2            1107.76
```

Fig. 5.7 | Compound-interest calculations with class DollarAmount and integers. (Part 2 of 3.)

3	1165.92
4	1227.13
5	1291.55
6	1359.36
7	1430.73
8	1505.84
9	1584.90
10	1668.11

Fig. 5.7 | Compound-interest calculations with class DollarAmount and integers. (Part 3 of 3.)

Calculating Compound Interest with DollarAmount

Class DollarAmount's addInterest member function calculates an interest amount and adds it to the DollarAmount object on which the function is called. The function receives two arguments:

- an integer representation of the interest rate and
- an integer divisor (a power of 10)

To determine the interest amount, addInterest multiplies the DollarAmount object's number of pennies by the integer representation of the interest rate, then divides the result by the integer divisor. For example:

- To calculate 5% interest, enter the integers 5 and 100. In integer arithmetic, multiplying a DollarAmount by 5, then dividing the result by 100 calculates 5% of the DollarAmount's value.

- To calculate 5.25% interest, enter the integers 525 and 10000. In integer arithmetic, multiplying a DollarAmount by 525, then dividing the result by 10000 calculates 5.25% of the DollarAmount's value.

Lines 28–35 prompt for and input the rate and divisor. Line 37 creates the DollarAmount object balance and initializes it to 100000 pennies (i.e., $1,000)—the initial principal, which we display at line 38. Lines 44–50 perform the interest calculations. Line 46 calls the addInterest member function to perform the interest calculation for the current year. Then, line 49 displays the current year and a string representation of the balance. You can confirm that you entered the interest rate properly by looking at the new balance for year 1 in the output. For example, when calculating 5% interest, the first year's end-of-year balance will be 1050.00, and when calculating 5.25% interest, the first year's balance will be 1052.50.

5.7.2 Class DollarAmount

Figure 5.8 defines class DollarAmount with data member amount (line 41) representing an integer number of pennies.

```
1   // Fig. 5.8: DollarAmount.h
2   // DollarAmount class stores dollar amounts as a whole numbers of pennies
3   #include <string>
```

Fig. 5.8 | DollarAmount class stores dollar amounts as whole numbers of pennies. (Part 1 of 2.)

```
 4  #include <cmath>
 5
 6  class DollarAmount {
 7  public:
 8      // initialize amount from an int64_t value
 9      explicit DollarAmount(int64_t value) : amount{value} { }
10
11      // add right's amount to this object's amount
12      void add(DollarAmount right) {
13          // can access private data of other objects of the same class
14          amount += right.amount;
15      }
16
17      // subtract right's amount from this object's amount
18      void subtract(DollarAmount right) {
19          // can access private data of other objects of the same class
20          amount -= right.amount;
21      }
22
23      // uses integer arithmetic to calculate interest amount,
24      // then calls add with the interest amount
25      void addInterest(int rate, int divisor) {
26          // create DollarAmount representing the interest
27          DollarAmount interest{
28              (amount * rate + divisor / 2) / divisor
29          };
30
31          add(interest); // add interest to this object's amount
32      }
33
34      // return a string representation of a DollarAmount object
35      std::string toString() const {
36          std::string dollars{std::to_string(amount / 100)};
37          std::string cents{std::to_string(std::abs(amount % 100))};
38          return dollars + "." + (cents.size() == 1 ? "0" : "") + cents;
39      }
40  private:
41      int64_t amount{0}; // dollar amount in pennies
42  };
```

Fig. 5.8 | DollarAmount class stores dollar amounts as whole numbers of pennies. (Part 2 of 2.)

C++11 Type int64_t

11 We'd like data member amount to be able to store from small numbers of cents to large dollar values so that our DollarAmounts can be used for all likely monetary applications. On most computers, an int is a value from −2,147,483,647 to 2,147,483,647. For amounts stored in pennies, this would limit a DollarAmount to approximately ±$21 million—way too small for many monetary applications, so we need a much larger range. C++11's long long type supports values in the range −9,223,372,036,854,775,808 to 11 9,223,372,036,854,775,807 as a *minimum*. This would enable a DollarAmount's value to be ±$92 quadrillion, likely more than enough for every known monetary application.

The range of long long (and C++'s other integer types) can vary across platforms. For portability, we'd prefer to use a type that's *identical* on all platforms. To help with this, C++11 introduced new integer-type names so you can choose the appropriate range of values for your program. For class DollarAmount, we chose int64_t, which supports the *exact* range −9,223,372,036,854,775,808 to 9,223,372,036,854,775,807. For a list of C++11's other new integer-type names, see the header <cstdint>.

11

DollarAmount *Constructor*
For simplicity, class DollarAmount's constructor (Fig. 5.8, line 9) receives a whole number of pennies and uses this value to initialize the data member amount. In Exercise 5.30, you'll define a DollarAmount constructor that receives two parameters representing the whole number of dollars and whole number of cents, then uses those values to calculate and store the appropriate number of pennies. (Exercises 5.30—5.34 are related to enhancing and using class DollarAmount.)

DollarAmount *Member Functions* add *and* subtract
The add member function (line 12–15) receives another DollarAmount object as an argument and adds its value to the DollarAmount object on which add is called. Line 14 uses the += operator to add right.amount (that is, the amount in the argument object) to the current object's amount, thus modifying the object. The expression right.amount accesses the private amount data member in the object right. This is a special relationship among objects of the same class—a member function of a class can access both the private data of the object on which that function is called and the private data of other objects of the same class that are passed to the function. The subtract member function (lines 18–21) works similarly to add, but uses the -= operator to subtract right.amount from the current object's amount.

DollarAmount *Member Function* addInterest
The addInterest member function (line 25–32) performs the interest calculation using its rate and divisor parameters, then adds the interest to the amount. Interest calculations normally yield fractional results that require rounding. We perform only integer arithmetic calculations with integer results here, so we completely avoid the representational error of double, but as you'll see, rounding is still required.

For this example, we use *half-up rounding*. First, consider rounding the floating-point values 0.75 and 0.25 to the nearest integer. Using half-up rounding, values .5 and higher should round up and everything else should round down, so 0.75 rounds up to 1 and 0.25 rounds down to 0.

Now, let's consider rounding the results of an integer interest calculation. Assume that we're calculating 5% interest on $10.75. In integer arithmetic, we treat 10.75 as 1075, and to calculate 5% interest, we multiply by 5, then divide by 100. In the interest calculation, we first multiply 1075 by 5, yielding the integer value 5375, which represents 53 whole pennies and 75 hundredths of a penny. In this case, the 75 hundredths of a penny should round up to a whole penny, resulting in 54 whole pennies. More generally:

- 50 to 99 hundredths should round up to the next higher whole penny
- 1 to 49 hundredths should round down to the next lower whole penny.

If we divide 5375 by 100 to complete the interest calculation, the result is 53, which is incorrect—remember that integer arithmetic truncates the fractional part of the calculation. To fix this, we must add an amount to 5375 so that dividing by 100 yields 54 whole pennies. Adding 50 enables us to ensure that 50 to 99 hundredths round up. For example:

- 5350 + 50 yields 5400—dividing that by 100 yields 54
- 5375 + 50 yields 5425—dividing that by 100 yields 54
- 5399 + 50 yields 5449—dividing that by 100 yields 54

Similarly:

- 5301 + 50 yields 5351—dividing that by 100 yields 53
- 5325 + 50 yields 5375—dividing that by 100 yields 53
- 5349 + 50 yields 5399—dividing that by 100 yields 53

Lines 27–29 in addInterest initialize the DollarAmount interest with the result of the following calculation, which performs the half-up rounding described above:

```
(amount * rate + divisor / 2) / divisor
```

Here, rather than adding 50 to the result of amount * rate, we add divisor / 2. Adding 50 is correct when the divisor is 100, but for other divisors, this would not round to the correct digit position. Consider 5.25% interest on $10.75. In integer arithmetic, we treat 10.75 as 1075, and to calculate 5.25% interest, we multiply by 525, then divide by 10000. We first multiply 1075 by 525, yielding the integer value 564375, which represents 56 whole pennies and 4375 *ten-thousandths* of a penny. This should round down to 56 whole pennies. To round correctly, in this case, we need to add 5000—that is, half of the divisor 10000.

After the interest is calculated, line 31 calls member function add, passing the new DollarAmount object interest as an argument—this updates the amount in the DollarAmount object on which addInterest was called. Note that any member function of a class can call any other directly to perform operations on the same object of the class.

Member Function *toString*

The toString member function (line 35–39) returns a string representation of the DollarAmount object's dollar amount. First, lines 36 and 37 use the division and remainder operators to get the amount's dollars and cents portions, respectively. We pass each integer to the C++ Standard Library function to_string (from header <string>), which converts a numeric value to a string object. Line 37 also uses the C++ Standard Library function abs (from header <cmath>) to get the absolute value of the cents. This ensures that the cents are always represented as a positive number so that a minus sign does not appear to the right of the decimal point.

Line 38 produces the string to return by "adding" string literals and string objects using the + operator—this is known as string concatenation. The resulting string contains the number of dollars, a decimal point and the number of cents. To ensure that there are always two digits to the right of the decimal point, we call string member function size on the string cents—this function returns the number of characters in the string cents. If the result is 1, we concatenate a leading 0 before the number of cents.

Banker's Rounding

Half-up rounding is a biased technique—fractional amounts of .1, .2, .3 and .4 round down, and .5, .6, .7, .8 and .9 round up. In this technique, four values round down and five round up. Because more values round up than down, this can lead to discrepancies in monetary calculations. Banker's rounding fixes this problem by rounding .5 to the nearest *even* integer—e.g., 0.5 rounds to 0, 1.5 and 2.5 round to 2, 3.5 and 4.5 round to 4, etc. In Exercise 5.32, you'll modify addInterest to use banker's rounding, then retest the compound-interest program.

Even int64_t Is Limited

Though class DollarAmount can represent extremely large monetary values, the range of values supported by int64_t is still limited. Through C++'s class mechanism, you'll see that you can define a class that you might call BigInteger or HugeInteger (as you'll do in Exercise 10.9), which could store and manipulate integers of *any* size. By doing so, you will have truly crafted another valuable class.

A Note About Arithmetic Operators and Modifying Operands

Lines 14 and 20 modify the DollarAmount object when performing arithmetic calculations. This is different from how the arithmetic operators work with fundamental types. For example, the expression value1 + value2 adds two values and produces a temporary result, but the + operator does not modify its left or right operands. In Chapter 10, we'll demonstrate C++'s operator overloading capabilities that enable you to define operators for use with your own types.

5.8 do...while Iteration Statement

The do...while iteration statement is similar to the while statement. In the while, the program tests the loop-continuation condition at the *beginning* of the loop, *before* executing the loop's body; if the condition is *false*, the body *never* executes. The do...while statement tests the loop-continuation condition *after* executing the loop's body; therefore, *the body always executes at least once*. When a do...while statement terminates, execution continues with the next statement in sequence. Figure 5.9 uses a do...while to output the numbers 1–10.

```
1   // Fig. 5.9: DoWhileTest.cpp
2   // do...while iteration statement.
3   #include <iostream>
4   using namespace std;
5
6   int main() {
7      unsigned int counter{1};
8
9      do {
10        cout << counter << " ";
11        ++counter;
12     } while (counter <= 10); // end do...while
```

Fig. 5.9 | do...while iteration statement. (Part 1 of 2.)

```
13
14      cout << endl;
15    }
```

```
1  2  3  4  5  6  7  8  9  10
```

Fig. 5.9 | do...while iteration statement. (Part 2 of 2.)

Line 7 declares and initializes control variable counter. Upon entering the do...while statement, line 10 outputs counter's value and line 11 increments counter. Then the program evaluates the loop-continuation test at the *bottom* of the loop (line 12). If the condition is *true*, the loop continues at the first body statement (line 10). If the condition is *false*, the loop terminates and the program continues at the next statement after the loop.

UML Activity Diagram for the *do...while Iteration Statement*

Figure 5.10 contains the UML activity diagram for the do...while statement. This diagram makes it clear that the loop-continuation condition is not evaluated until *after* the loop performs the action state *at least once*. Compare this activity diagram with that of the while statement (Fig. 4.8).

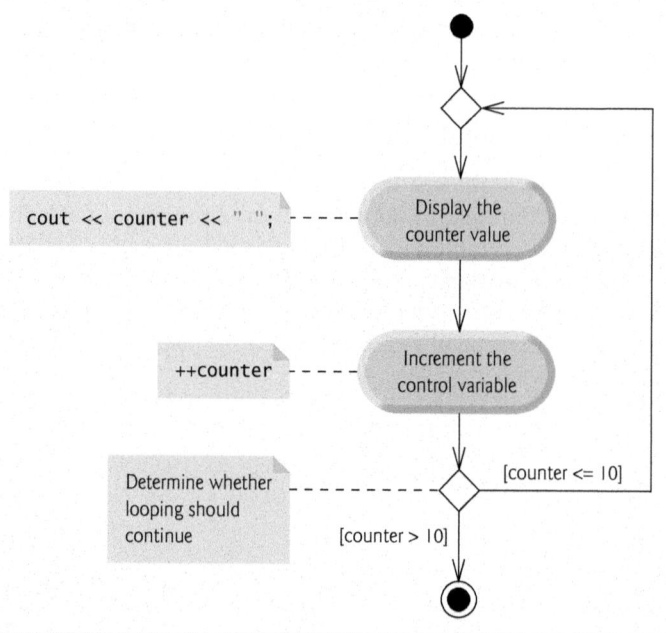

Fig. 5.10 | do...while iteration statement UML activity diagram.

5.9 switch Multiple-Selection Statement

C++ provides the switch multiple-selection statement to choose among many different actions based on the possible values of a variable or expression. Each action is associated with the value of an integral constant expression (i.e., any combination of character and integer constants that evaluates to a constant integer value).

Using a switch Statement to Count A, B, C, D and F Grades

Figure 5.11 calculates the class average of a set of numeric grades entered by the user, and uses a switch statement to determine whether each grade is the equivalent of an A, B, C, D or F and to increment the appropriate grade counter. The program also displays a summary of the number of students who received each grade.

```cpp
 1   // Fig. 5.11: LetterGrades.cpp
 2   // Using a switch statement to count letter grades.
 3   #include <iostream>
 4   #include <iomanip>
 5   using namespace std;
 6
 7   int main() {
 8      int total{0}; // sum of grades
 9      unsigned int gradeCounter{0}; // number of grades entered
10      unsigned int aCount{0}; // count of A grades
11      unsigned int bCount{0}; // count of B grades
12      unsigned int cCount{0}; // count of C grades
13      unsigned int dCount{0}; // count of D grades
14      unsigned int fCount{0}; // count of F grades
15
16      cout << "Enter the integer grades in the range 0-100.\n"
17         << "Type the end-of-file indicator to terminate input:\n"
18         << "   On UNIX/Linux/Mac OS X type <Ctrl> d then press Enter\n"
19         << "   On Windows type <Ctrl> z then press Enter\n";
20
21      int grade;
22
23      // loop until user enters the end-of-file indicator
24      while (cin >> grade) {
25         total += grade; // add grade to total
26         ++gradeCounter; // increment number of grades
27
28         //  increment appropriate letter-grade counter
29         switch (grade / 10) {
30            case 9:  // grade was between 90
31            case 10: // and 100, inclusive
32               ++aCount;
33               break; // exits switch
34
35            case 8: // grade was between 80 and 89
36               ++bCount;
37               break; // exits switch
38
39            case 7: // grade was between 70 and 79
40               ++cCount;
41               break; // exits switch
42
```

Fig. 5.11 | Using a switch statement to count letter grades. (Part 1 of 3.)

```
43              case 6: // grade was between 60 and 69
44                  ++dCount;
45                  break; // exits switch
46
47              default: // grade was less than 60
48                  ++fCount;
49                  break; // optional; exits switch anyway
50          } // end switch
51      } // end while
52
53      // set floating-point number format
54      cout << fixed << setprecision(2);
55
56      // display grade report
57      cout << "\nGrade Report:\n";
58
59      // if user entered at least one grade...
60      if (gradeCounter != 0) {
61          // calculate average of all grades entered
62          double average = static_cast<double>(total) / gradeCounter;
63
64          // output summary of results
65          cout << "Total of the " << gradeCounter << " grades entered is "
66              << total << "\nClass average is " << average
67              << "\nNumber of students who received each grade:"
68              << "\nA: " << aCount << "\nB: " << bCount << "\nC: " << cCount
69              << "\nD: " << dCount << "\nF: " << fCount << endl;
70      }
71      else { // no grades were entered, so output appropriate message
72          cout << "No grades were entered" << endl;
73      }
74  }
```

```
Enter the integer grades in the range 0-100.
Type the end-of-file indicator to terminate input:
   On UNIX/Linux/Mac OS X type <Ctrl> d then press Enter
   On Windows type <Ctrl> z then press Enter
99
92
45
57
63
71
76
85
90
100
^Z

Grade Report:
Total of the 10 grades entered is 778
Class average is 77.80
```

Fig. 5.11 | Using a switch statement to count letter grades. (Part 2 of 3.)

```
Number of students who received each grade:
A: 4
B: 1
C: 2
D: 1
F: 2
```

Fig. 5.11 | Using a switch statement to count letter grades. (Part 3 of 3.)

The main function (Fig. 5.11) declares local variables total (line 8) and grade-Counter (line 9) to keep track of the sum of the grades entered by the user and the number of grades entered, respectively. Lines 10–14 declare and initialize to 0 counter variables for each grade category. The main function has two key parts. Lines 24–51 read an arbitrary number of integer grades from the user using sentinel-controlled iteration, update variables total and gradeCounter, and increment an appropriate letter-grade counter for each grade entered. Lines 54–73 output a report containing the total of all grades entered, the average grade and the number of students who received each letter grade.

Reading Grades from the User

Lines 16–19 prompt the user to enter integer grades or type the end-of-file indicator to terminate the input. The end-of-file indicator is a system-dependent keystroke combination used to indicate that there's *no more data to input*. In Chapter 14, File Processing, you'll see how the end-of-file indicator is used when a program reads its input from a file.

On UNIX/Linux/Mac OS X systems, end-of-file is entered by typing the sequence

```
<Ctrl> d
```

on a line by itself. This notation means to simultaneously press both the *Ctrl* key and the *d* key. On Windows systems, end-of-file can be entered by typing

```
<Ctrl> z
```

[*Note:* On some systems, you must press *Enter* after typing the end-of-file key sequence. Also, Windows typically displays the characters ^Z on the screen when the end-of-file indicator is typed, as shown in the output of Fig. 5.11.]

Portability Tip 5.1
The keystroke combinations for entering end-of-file are system dependent.

The while statement (lines 24–51) obtains the user input. Line 24

```
while (cin >> grade) {
```

performs the input in the while statement's condition. In this case, the loop-continuation condition evaluates to *true* if cin successfully reads an int value. If the user enters the end-of-file indicator, the condition evaluates to *false*.

If the condition evaluates to *true*, line 25 adds grade to total and line 26 increments gradeCounter. These variables are used to compute the average of the grades. Next, lines 29–50 use a switch statement to increment the appropriate letter-grade counter based on the numeric grade entered.

Processing the Grades

The switch statement (lines 29–50) determines which counter to increment. We assume that the user enters a valid grade in the range 0–100. A grade in the range 90–100 represents A, 80–89 represents B, 70–79 represents C, 60–69 represents D and 0–59 represents F. The switch statement consists of a block that contains a sequence of case labels and an optional default case. These are used in this example to determine which counter to increment based on the grade.

When the flow of control reaches the switch, the program evaluates the expression in the parentheses (grade / 10) following keyword switch. This is the switch's controlling expression. The program compares this expression's value with each case label. The expression must have a signed or unsigned integral type—bool, char, char16_t, char32_t, wchar_t, int, long or long long. The expression can also use the C++11 signer or unsigned integral types, such as int64_t and uint64_t—see the <cstdint> header for a complete list of these type names.

The controlling expression in line 29 performs integer division, which *truncates the fractional part* of the result. When we divide a value from 0 to 100 by 10, the result is always a value from 0 to 10. We use several of these values in our case labels. If the user enters the integer 85, the controlling expression evaluates to 8. The switch compares 8 with each case label. If a match occurs (case 8: at line 35), that case's statements execute. For 8, line 36 increments bCount, because a grade in the 80s is a B. The break statement (line 37) causes program control to proceed with the first statement after the switch—in this program, we reach the end of the while loop, so control returns to the loop-continuation condition in line 24 to determine whether the loop should continue executing.

The cases in our switch explicitly test for the values 10, 9, 8, 7 and 6. Note the cases at lines 30–31 that test for the values 9 and 10 (both of which represent the grade A). Listing cases consecutively in this manner with no statements between them enables the cases to perform the same set of statements—when the controlling expression evaluates to 9 or 10, the statements in lines 32–33 will execute. The switch statement does *not* provide a mechanism for testing *ranges* of values, so *every* value you need to test must be listed in a separate case label. Each case can have multiple statements. The switch statement differs from other control statements in that it does *not* require braces around multiple statements in a case.

case *without a* **break** *Statement*

Without break statements, each time a match occurs in the switch, the statements for that case and subsequent cases execute until a break statement or the end of the switch is encountered. This is often referred to as "falling through" to the statements in subsequent cases. (This feature is perfect for writing a concise program that displays the iterative song "The Twelve Days of Christmas" in Exercise 5.28.)

 Common Programming Error 5.7

Forgetting a break statement when one is needed in a switch *is a logic error.*

The **default** *Case*

If no match occurs between the controlling expression's value and a case label, the default case (lines 47–49) executes. We use the default case in this example to process all controlling-expression values that are less than 6—that is, all failing grades. If no match occurs and the switch does not contain a default case, program control simply continues with the first statement after the switch.

Error-Prevention Tip 5.7
In a switch, ensure that you test for all possible values of the controlling expression.

Displaying the Grade Report
Lines 54–73 output a report based on the grades entered (as shown in the input/output window in Fig. 5.11). Line 60 determines whether the user entered at least one grade—this helps us avoid dividing by zero. If so, line 62 calculates the average of the grades. Lines 65–69 then output the total of all the grades, the class average and the number of students who received each letter grade. If no grades were entered, line 72 outputs an appropriate message. The output in Fig. 5.11 shows a sample grade report based on 10 grades.

switch Statement UML Activity Diagram
Figure 5.12 shows the UML activity diagram for the general switch statement. Most switch statements use a break in each case to terminate the switch statement after processing the case. Figure 5.12 emphasizes this by including break statements in the activity diagram. The diagram makes it clear that the break statement at the end of a case causes control to exit the switch statement immediately.

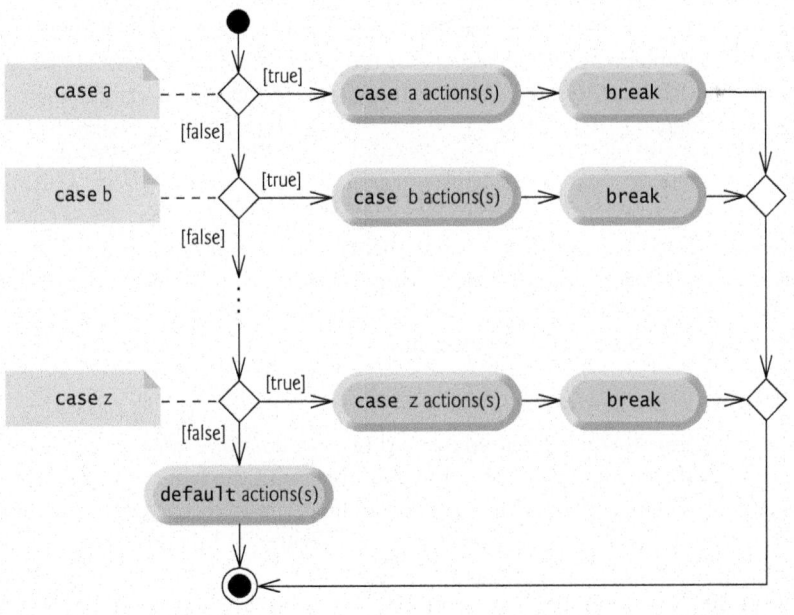

Fig. 5.12 | switch multiple-selection statement UML activity diagram with break statements.

The break statement is *not* required for the switch's last case (or the optional default case, when it appears last), because execution continues with the next statement after the switch.

Error-Prevention Tip 5.8

Provide a default case in switch statements. This focuses you on the need to process exceptional conditions.

Good Programming Practice 5.3

Although each case and the default case in a switch can occur in any order, place the default case last. When the default case is listed last, the break for that case is not required.

Notes on the Expression in Each case of a switch

When using the switch statement, remember that each case must contain a constant integral expression—that is, any combination of integer constants that evaluates to a constant integer value (e.g., –7, 0 or 221). An integer constant is simply an integer value. In addition, you can use character constants—specific characters in single quotes, such as 'A', '7' or '$'—which represent the integer values of characters and enum constants (introduced in Section 6.8). (Appendix B shows the integer values of the characters in the ASCII character set, which is a subset of the Unicode® character set.)

The expression in each case also can be a constant variable—a variable containing a value which does not change for the entire program. Such a variable is declared with keyword const (discussed in Chapter 6).

In Chapter 12, Object-Oriented Programming: Polymorphism, we present a more elegant way to implement switch logic—we use a technique called *polymorphism* to create programs that are often clearer, easier to maintain and easier to extend than programs using switch logic.

5.10 break and continue Statements

In addition to selection and iteration statements, C++ provides statements break (which we discussed in the context of the switch statement) and continue to alter the flow of control. The preceding section showed how break can be used to terminate a switch statement's execution. This section discusses how to use break in iteration statements.

5.10.1 break Statement

The break statement, when executed in a while, for, do...while or switch, causes *immediate* exit from that statement—execution continues with the first statement after the control statement. Common uses of the break statement are to escape early from a loop or to skip the remainder of a switch (as in Fig. 5.11). Figure 5.13 demonstrates a break statement exiting a for.

When the if statement nested at lines 10–12 in the for statement (lines 9–15) detects that count is 5, the break statement at line 11 executes. This terminates the for statement, and the program proceeds to line 17 (immediately after the for statement), which displays a message indicating the value of the control variable when the loop terminated. The loop fully executes its body only four times instead of 10.

```
1   // Fig. 5.13: BreakTest.cpp
2   // break statement exiting a for statement.
3   #include <iostream>
4   using namespace std;
5
6   int main() {
7      unsigned int count; // control variable also used after loop
8
9      for (count = 1; count <= 10; count++) { // loop 10 times
10         if (count == 5) {
11            break; // terminates loop if count is 5
12         }
13
14         cout << count << " ";
15      }
16
17      cout << "\nBroke out of loop at count = " << count << endl;
18   }
```

```
1 2 3 4
Broke out of loop at count = 5
```

Fig. 5.13 | break statement exiting a for statement.

5.10.2 continue Statement

The continue statement, when executed in a while, for or do…while, skips the remaining statements in the loop body and proceeds with the *next iteration* of the loop. In while and do…while statements, the program evaluates the loop-continuation test immediately after the continue statement executes. In a for statement, the increment expression executes, then the program evaluates the loop-continuation test.

```
1   // Fig. 5.14: ContinueTest.cpp
2   // continue statement terminating an iteration of a for statement.
3   #include <iostream>
4   using namespace std;
5
6   int main() {
7      for (unsigned int count{1}; count <= 10; count++) { // loop 10 times
8         if (count == 5) {
9            continue; // skip remaining code in loop body if count is 5
10         }
11
12         cout << count << " ";
13      }
14
15      cout << "\nUsed continue to skip printing 5" << endl;
16   }
```

Fig. 5.14 | continue statement terminating an iteration of a for statement. (Part 1 of 2.)

```
1 2 3 4 6 7 8 9 10
Used continue to skip printing 5
```

Fig. 5.14 | continue statement terminating an iteration of a for statement. (Part 2 of 2.)

Figure 5.14 uses continue (line 9) to skip the statement at line 12 when the nested if determines that count's value is 5. When the continue statement executes, program control continues with the increment of the control variable in the for statement (line 7).

In Section 5.3, we stated that while could be used in most cases in place of for. This is *not* true when the increment expression in the while follows a continue statement. In this case, the increment does *not* execute before the program evaluates the iteration-continuation condition, so the while does not execute in the same manner as the for.

Software Engineering Observation 5.1

Some programmers feel that break *and* continue *violate structured programming. Since the same effects are achievable with structured-programming techniques, these programmers do not use* break *or* continue.

Software Engineering Observation 5.2

There's a tension between achieving quality software engineering and achieving the best-performing software. Sometimes one of these goals is achieved at the expense of the other. For all but the most performance-intensive situations, apply the following rule of thumb: First, make your code simple and correct; then make it fast and small, but only if necessary.

5.11 Logical Operators

The if, if...else, while, do...while and for statements each require a *condition* to determine how to continue a program's flow of control. So far, we've studied only simple conditions, such as count <= 10, number != sentinelValue and total > 1000. Simple conditions are expressed in terms of the relational operators >, <, >= and <= and the equality operators == and !=, and each expression tests only one condition. To test *multiple* conditions in the process of making a decision, we performed these tests in separate statements or in nested if or if...else statements. Sometimes control statements require more complex conditions to determine a program's flow of control.

C++'s logical operators enable you to form more complex conditions by *combining* simple conditions. The logical operators are && (logical AND), || (logical OR) and ! (logical negation).

5.11.1 Logical AND (&&) Operator

Suppose we wish to ensure at some point in a program that two conditions are *both true* before we choose a certain path of execution. In this case, we can use the && (logical AND) operator, as follows:

```
if (gender == FEMALE && age >= 65) {
    ++seniorFemales;
}
```

This if statement contains two simple conditions. The condition gender == FEMALE compares variable gender to the constant FEMALE to determine whether a person is female. The condition age >= 65 might be evaluated to determine whether a person is a senior citizen. The if statement considers the combined condition

```
gender == FEMALE && age >= 65
```

which is *true* if and only if *both* simple conditions are *true*. In this case, the if statement's body increments seniorFemales by 1. If either or both of the simple conditions are *false*, the program skips the increment. Some programmers find that the preceding combined condition is more readable when *redundant* parentheses are added, as in

```
(gender == FEMALE) && (age >= 65)
```

The table in Fig. 5.15 summarizes the && operator. The table shows all four possible combinations of the bool values false and true values for *expression1* and *expression2*. Such tables are called truth tables. C++ evaluates to zero (*false*) or nonzero (*true*) all expressions that include relational operators, equality operators or logical operators.

expression1	expression2	expression1 && expression2
false	false	false
false	true	false
true	false	false
true	true	true

Fig. 5.15 | && (logical AND) operator truth table.

5.11.2 Logical OR (||) Operator

Now suppose we wish to ensure that *either or both* of two conditions are *true* before we choose a certain path of execution. In this case, we use the || (logical OR) operator, as in the following program segment:

```
if ((semesterAverage >= 90) || (finalExam >= 90)) {
    cout << "Student grade is A\n";
}
```

This statement also contains two simple conditions. The condition semesterAverage >= 90 evaluates to determine whether the student deserves an A in the course because of a solid performance throughout the semester. The condition finalExam >= 90 evaluates to determine whether the student deserves an A in the course because of an outstanding performance on the final exam. The if statement then considers the combined condition

```
(semesterAverage >= 90) || (finalExam >= 90)
```

and awards the student an A if *either or both* of the simple conditions are *true*. The only time the message "Student grade is A" is *not* printed is when *both* of the simple conditions are *false*. Figure 5.16 is a truth table for the operator logical OR (||). Operator && has a higher precedence than operator ||. Both operators associate from left to right.

expression1	expression2	expression1 || expression2
false	false	false
false	true	true
true	false	true
true	true	true

Fig. 5.16 | \|\| (logical OR) operator truth table.

5.11.3 Short-Circuit Evaluation

The parts of an expression containing && or \|\| operators are evaluated *only* until it's known whether the condition is *true* or *false*. Thus, evaluation of the expression

```
(gender == FEMALE) && (age >= 65)
```

stops immediately if gender *is not* equal to FEMALE (i.e., the entire expression is *false*) and continues if gender *is* equal to FEMALE (i.e., the entire expression could still be *true* if the condition age >= 65 is *true*). This feature of logical AND and logical OR expressions is called short-circuit evaluation.

Common Programming Error 5.8

In expressions using operator &&, a condition—we'll call this the dependent condition*— may require another condition to be true for the evaluation of the dependent condition to be meaningful. In this case, the dependent condition should be placed after the && operator to prevent errors. Consider the expression (i != 0) && (10 / i == 2). The dependent condition (10 / i == 2) must appear after the && operator to prevent the possibility of division by zero.*

5.11.4 Logical Negation (!) Operator

The ! (logical negation, also called logical NOT or logical complement) operator "reverses" the meaning of a condition. Unlike the logical operators && and \|\|, which are **binary** operators that combine two conditions, the logical negation operator is a *unary* operator that has only one condition as an operand. To execute code only when a condition is *false*, place the logical negation operator *before* the original condition, as in the program segment

```
if (!(grade == sentinelValue)) {
   cout << "The next grade is " << grade << "\n";
}
```

which executes the body statement only if grade is *not* equal to sentinelValue. The parentheses around the condition grade == sentinelValue are needed because the logical negation operator has a *higher* precedence than the equality operator.

In most cases, you can avoid using logical negation by expressing the condition differently with an appropriate relational or equality operator. For example, the previous statement may also be written as follows:

```
if (grade != sentinelValue) {
   cout << "The next grade is " << grade << "\n";
}
```

This flexibility can help you express a condition in a more convenient manner. Figure 5.17 is a truth table for the logical negation operator.

expression	!expression
false	true
true	false

Fig. 5.17 | ! (logical negation) operator truth table.

5.11.5 Logical Operators Example

Figure 5.18 uses logical operators to produce the truth tables discussed in this section. The output shows each expression that's evaluated and its bool result. By default, bool values true and false are displayed by cout and the stream insertion operator as 1 and 0, respectively. We use stream manipulator boolalpha (a *sticky* manipulator) in line 8 to specify that the value of each bool expression should be displayed as either the word "true" or the word "false." Lines 8–12 produce the truth table for &&. Lines 15–19 produce the truth table for ||. Lines 22–24 produce the truth table for !.

```cpp
1   // Fig. 5.18: LogicalOperators.cpp
2   // Logical operators.
3   #include <iostream>
4   using namespace std;
5
6   int main() {
7      // create truth table for && (logical AND) operator
8      cout << boolalpha << "Logical AND (&&)"
9         << "\nfalse && false: " << (false && false)
10        << "\nfalse && true: " << (false && true)
11        << "\ntrue && false: " << (true && false)
12        << "\ntrue && true: " << (true && true) << "\n\n";
13
14     // create truth table for || (logical OR) operator
15     cout << "Logical OR (||)"
16        << "\nfalse || false: " << (false || false)
17        << "\nfalse || true: " << (false || true)
18        << "\ntrue || false: " << (true || false)
19        << "\ntrue || true: " << (true || true) << "\n\n";
20
21     // create truth table for ! (logical negation) operator
22     cout << "Logical negation (!)"
23        << "\n!false: " << (!false)
24        << "\n!true: " << (!true) << endl;
25  }
```

Fig. 5.18 | Logical operators. (Part 1 of 2.)

```
Logical AND (&&)
false && false: false
false && true: false
true && false: false
true && true: true

Logical OR (||)
false || false: false
false || true: true
true || false: true
true || true: true

Logical negation (!)
!false: true
!true: false
```

Fig. 5.18 | Logical operators. (Part 2 of 2.)

Precedence and Associativity of the Operators Presented So Far
Figure 5.19 shows the precedence and associativity of the C++ operators introduced so far. The operators are shown from top to bottom in decreasing order of precedence.

Operators	Associativity	Type
:: ()	left to right *[See caution in Fig. 2.10 regarding grouping parentheses.]*	primary
++ -- static_cast<*type*>()	left to right	postfix
++ -- + - !	right to left	unary (prefix)
* / %	left to right	multiplicative
+ -	left to right	additive
<< >>	left to right	insertion/extraction
< <= > >=	left to right	relational
== !=	left to right	equality
&&	left to right	logical AND
||	left to right	logical OR
?:	right to left	conditional
= += -= *= /= %=	right to left	assignment
,	left to right	comma

Fig. 5.19 | Operator precedence and associativity.

5.12 Confusing the Equality (==) and Assignment (=) Operators

There's one error that C++ programmers, no matter how experienced, tend to make so frequently that we feel it requires a separate section. That error is accidentally swapping the operators == (equality) and = (assignment). What makes this so damaging is that it ordinarily does *not* cause *syntax errors*—statements with these errors tend to compile correctly and the programs run to completion, often generating incorrect results through *runtime logic errors*. Some compilers issue a *warning* when = is used in a context where == is expected.

Two aspects of C++ contribute to these problems. One is that *any expression that produces a value can be used in the decision portion of any control statement*. If the value of the expression is zero, it's treated as the value false, and if the value is nonzero, it's treated as the value true. The second is that assignments produce a value—namely, the value assigned to the variable on the left side of the assignment operator. For example, suppose we intend to write

```
if (payCode == 4) { // good
    cout << "You get a bonus!" << endl;
}
```

but we accidentally write

```
if (payCode = 4) { // bad
    cout << "You get a bonus!" << endl;
}
```

The first if statement properly awards a bonus to the person whose payCode is equal to 4. The second one—which contains the error—evaluates the assignment expression in the if condition to the constant 4. *Any nonzero value is interpreted as* true, so this condition *always* evaluates as true and the person *always* receives a bonus regardless of what the actual paycode is! Even worse, the paycode has been *modified* when it was only supposed to be *examined!*

lvalues *and* rvalues

You can prevent the preceding problem with a simple trick, but first it's helpful to know what's allowed to the left of an assignment operator. Variable names are said to be *lvalues* (for "left values") because they can be used on an assignment operator's *left* side. Literals are said to be *rvalues* (for "right values") because they can be used on only an assignment operator's *right* side. *Lvalues* can also be used as *rvalues* on the right side of an assignment, but not vice versa.

 Error-Prevention Tip 5.9

Programmers normally write conditions such as x == 7 with the variable name (an lvalue) on the left and the literal (an rvalue) on the right. Placing the literal on the left, as in 7 == x, enables the compiler to issue an error if you accidentally replace the == operator with =. The compiler treats this as a compilation error, because you can't change a literal's value.

Using == in Place of =

There's another equally unpleasant situation. Suppose you want to assign a value to a variable with a simple statement like

```
x = 1;
```

but instead write

```
    x == 1;
```

Here, too, this is *not* a syntax error. Rather, the compiler simply evaluates the expression. If x is equal to 1, the condition is *true* and the expression evaluates to a nonzero (*true*) value. If x is not equal to 1, the condition is *false* and the expression evaluates to 0. Regardless of the expression's value, there's no assignment operator, so the value simply is lost. The value of x remains unaltered, probably causing an execution-time logic error. Error-Prevention Tip 5.10 below will help you spot these.

Common Programming Error 5.9

Using operator == for assignment and using operator = for equality are logic errors.

Error-Prevention Tip 5.10

Use your text editor to search for all occurrences of = in your program and check that you have the correct assignment. relational or equality operator in each place.

5.13 Structured-Programming Summary

Just as architects design buildings by employing the collective wisdom of their profession, so should programmers design programs. Our field is much younger than architecture, and our collective wisdom is considerably sparser. We've learned that structured programming produces programs that are easier than unstructured programs to understand, test, debug, modify and even prove correct in a mathematical sense.

C++ Control Statements Are Single-Entry/Single-Exit

Figure 5.20 uses UML activity diagrams to summarize C++'s control statements. The initial and final states indicate the *single entry point* and the *single exit point* of each control statement. Arbitrarily connecting individual symbols in an activity diagram can lead to unstructured programs. Therefore, the programming profession has chosen a limited set of control statements that can be combined in only two simple ways to build structured programs.

For simplicity, C++ includes only *single-entry/single-exit* control statements—there's only one way to enter and only one way to exit each control statement. Connecting control statements in sequence to form structured programs is simple. The *final state* of one control statement is connected to the *initial state* of the next—that is, the control statements are placed one after another in a program in sequence. We call this *control-statement stacking*. The rules for forming structured programs also allow for control statements to be *nested*.

Rules for Forming Structured Programs

Figure 5.21 shows the rules for forming structured programs. The rules assume that action states may be used to indicate *any* action. The rules also assume that we begin with the simplest activity diagram (Fig. 5.22) consisting of only an initial state, an action state, a final state and transition arrows.

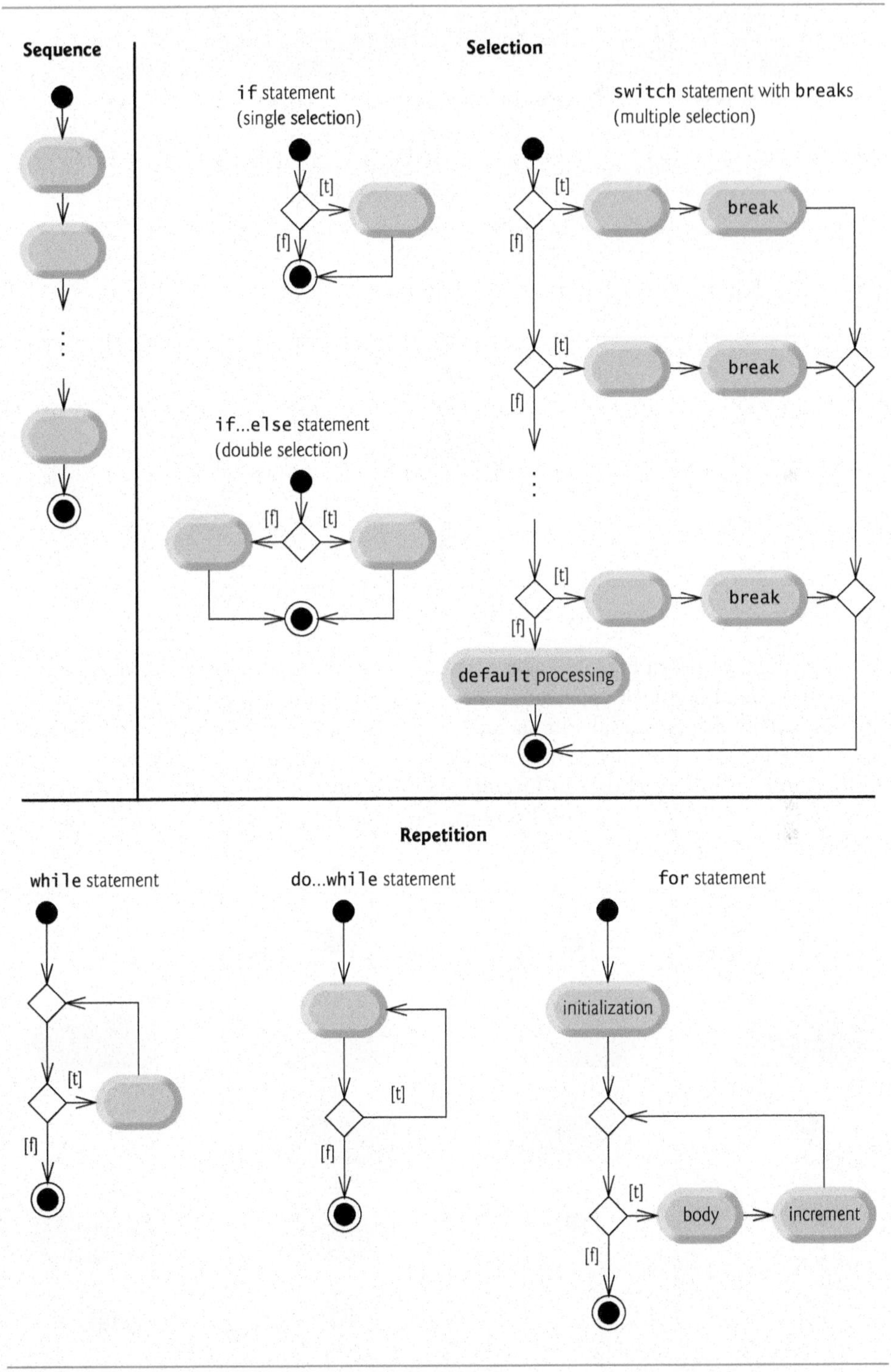

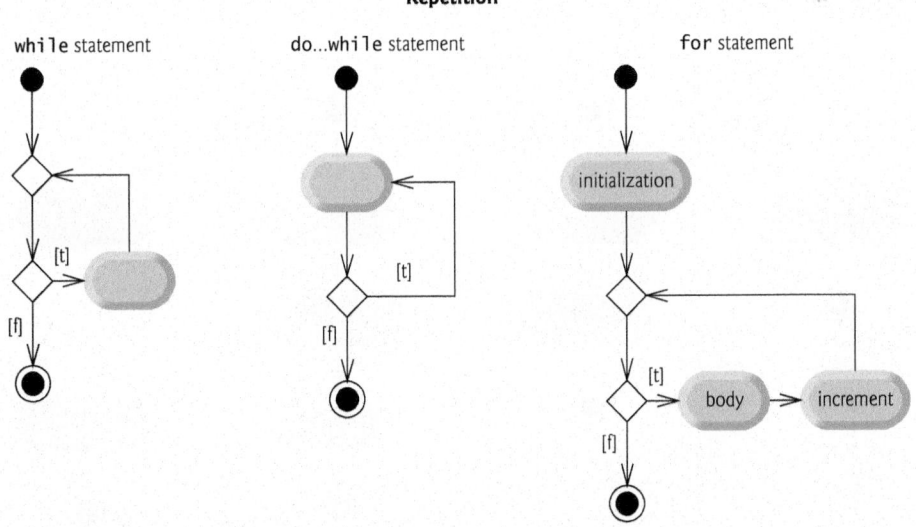

Fig. 5.20 | C++'s single-entry/single-exit sequence, selection and iteration statements.

Rules for forming structured programs
1.   Begin with the simplest activity diagram (Fig. 5.22).
2.   Any action state can be replaced by two action states in sequence.
3.   Any action state can be replaced by any control statement (sequence of action states, if, if...else, switch, while, do...while or for).
4.   Rules 2 and 3 can be applied as often as you like and in any order.

Fig. 5.21 | Rules for forming structured programs.

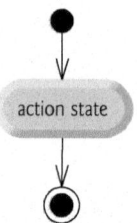

Fig. 5.22 | Simplest activity diagram.

Applying the rules in Fig. 5.21 always results in a properly structured activity diagram with a neat, building-block appearance. For example, repeatedly applying rule 2 to the simplest activity diagram results in an activity diagram containing many action states in sequence (Fig. 5.23). Rule 2 generates a *stack* of control statements, so let's call rule 2 the stacking rule. The vertical dashed lines in Fig. 5.23 are not part of the UML—we use them to separate the four activity diagrams that demonstrate rule 2 of Fig. 5.21 being applied.

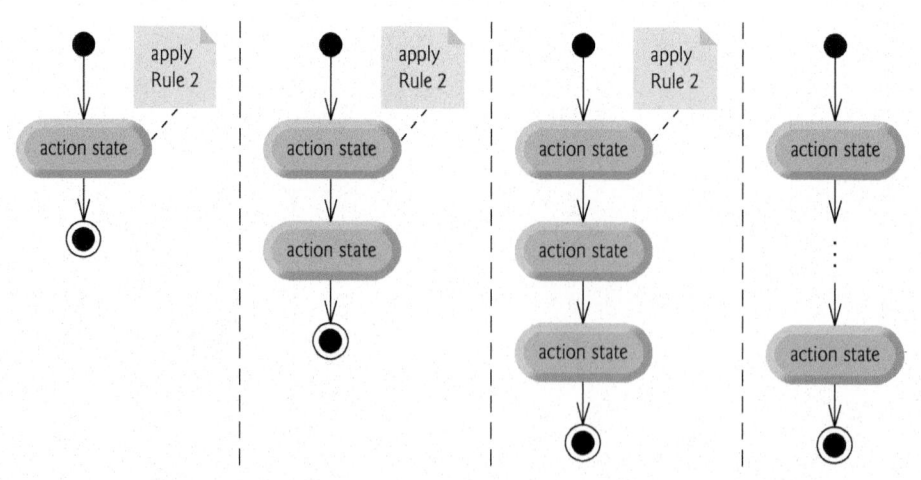

Fig. 5.23 | Repeatedly applying rule 2 of Fig. 5.21 to the simplest activity diagram.

Rule 3 is called the nesting rule. Repeatedly applying rule 3 to the simplest activity diagram results in one with neatly *nested* control statements. For example, in Fig. 5.24, the action state in the simplest activity diagram is replaced with a double-selection (if...else) statement. Then rule 3 is applied again to the action states in the double-selection statement, replacing each with a double-selection statement. The dashed action-state symbol around each double-selection statement represents the action state that was replaced. [*Note:* The dashed arrows and dashed action-state symbols shown in Fig. 5.24 are not part of the UML. They're used here to illustrate that *any* action state can be replaced with a control statement.]

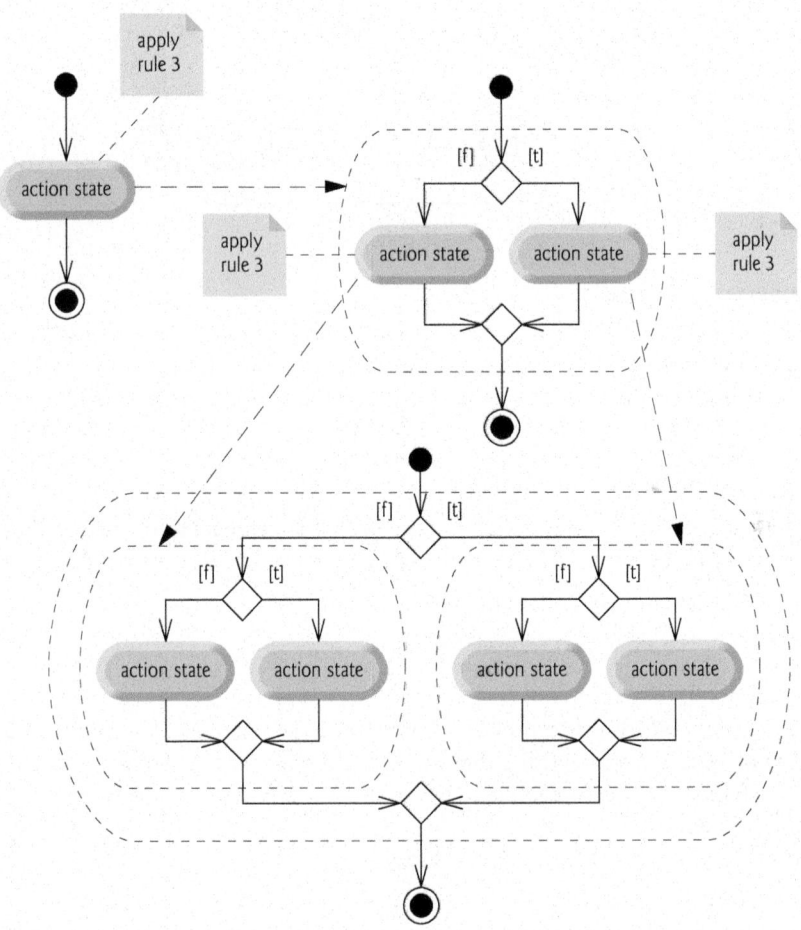

Fig. 5.24 | Repeatedly applying rule 3 of Fig. 5.21 to the simplest activity diagram.

Rule 4 generates larger, more involved and more deeply nested statements. The diagrams that emerge from applying the rules in Fig. 5.21 constitute the set of all possible structured activity diagrams and hence the set of all possible structured programs. The beauty of the structured approach is that we use *only seven* simple single-entry/single-exit control statements and assemble them in *only two* simple ways.

If the rules in Fig. 5.21 are followed, an "unstructured' activity diagram (like the one in Fig. 5.25) cannot be created. If you're uncertain about whether a particular diagram is structured, apply the rules of Fig. 5.21 in reverse to reduce it to the simplest activity diagram. If you can reduce it, the original diagram is structured; otherwise, it's not.

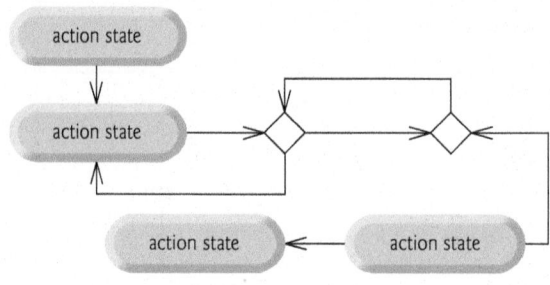

Fig. 5.25 | "Unstructured" activity diagram.

Three Forms of Control

Structured programming promotes simplicity. Only three forms of control are needed to implement an algorithm:

- sequence
- selection
- iteration

The sequence structure is trivial. Simply list the statements to execute in the order in which they should execute. Selection is implemented in one of three ways:

- `if` statement (single selection)
- `if...else` statement (double selection)
- `switch` statement (multiple selection)

In fact, it's straightforward to prove that the simple `if` statement is sufficient to provide *any* form of selection—everything that can be done with the `if...else` statement and the `switch` statement can be implemented by combining `if` statements (although perhaps not as clearly and efficiently).

Iteration is implemented in one of three ways:

- `while` statement
- `do...while` statement
- `for` statement

[*Note:* There's a fourth iteration statement—the *range-based* `for` *statement*—that we discuss in Section 7.5.] It's straightforward to prove that the `while` statement is sufficient to provide *any* form of iteration. Everything that can be done with `do...while` and `for` can be done with the `while` statement (although perhaps not as conveniently).

Combining these results illustrates that *any* form of control ever needed in a C++ program can be expressed in terms of

- sequence
- `if` statement (selection)
- `while` statement (iteration)

and that these can be combined in only two ways—*stacking* and *nesting*.

5.14 Wrap-Up

In this chapter, we completed our introduction to control statements, which enable you to control the flow of execution in member functions. Chapter 4 discussed `if`, `if...else` and `while`. This chapter demonstrated `for`, `do...while` and `switch`. We discussed the representational errors associated with floating-point types, then developed a `DollarAmount` class that used very large integers to precisely represent monetary amounts. We used only precise integer arithmetic when manipulating `DollarAmount`s. We showed that any algorithm can be developed using combinations of the sequence structure, the three types of selection statements—`if`, `if...else` and `switch`—and the three types of iteration statements—`while`, `do...while` and `for`. In this chapter and Chapter 4, we discussed how you can combine these building blocks to utilize proven program-construction and problem-solving techniques. You used the `break` statement to exit a `switch` statement and to immediately terminate a loop, and used a `continue` statement to terminate a loop's current iteration and proceed with the loop's next iteration. This chapter also introduced C++'s logical operators, which enable you to use more complex conditional expressions in control statements. In Chapter 6, we examine functions in greater depth.

Summary

Section 5.2 Essentials of Counter-Controlled Iteration

- **Counter-controlled iteration** (p. 160) requires a control variable, the initial value of the control variable, the increment by which the control variable is modified each time through the loop (also known as each iteration of the loop) and the loop-continuation condition that determines whether looping should continue.
- In C++, a variable declaration that also reserves memory is a **definition** (p. 161).

Section 5.3 `for` Iteration Statement

- The `while` statement can be used to implement any counter-controlled loop.
- The **for statement** (p. 161) specifies all the details of counter-controlled iteration in its header
- When the `for` statement begins executing, its control variable is optionally declared and initialized. If the loop-continuation condition is initially *true*, the body executes. After executing the loop's body, the increment expression executes. Then the loop-continuation test is performed again to determine whether the program should continue with the next iteration of the loop.
- The general format of the `for` statement is

```
for (initialization; loopContinuationCondition; increment) {
    statement
}
```

where the *initialization* expression names the loop's control variable and provides its initial value, *loopContinuationCondition* determines whether the loop should continue executing and *increment* modifies the control variable's value, so that the loop-continuation condition eventually becomes *false*. The two semicolons in the for header are required.

- Most for statements can be represented with equivalent while statements as follows:

    initialization;

    ```
    while (loopContinuationCondition) {
        statement
        increment;
    }
    ```

- Typically, for statements are used for counter-controlled iteration and while statements for sentinel-controlled iteration.

- If the *initialization* expression in the for header declares the control variable, the control variable can be used only in that for statement—it will not exist outside the for statement.

- The expressions in a for header are optional. If the *loopContinuationCondition* is omitted, C++ assumes that it's always *true*, thus creating an infinite loop. You might omit the *initialization* expression if the control variable is initialized before the loop. You might omit the *increment* expression if the increment is calculated with statements in the loop's body or if no increment is needed.

- The increment expression in a for acts as if it's a standalone statement at the end of the for's body.

- A for statement can count downward by using a negative increment—i.e., a **decrement** (p. 165).

- If the loop-continuation condition is initially *false*, the for statement's body does not execute.

Section 5.5 Application: Summing Even Integers

- The initialization and increment expressions can be comma-separated lists that enable you to use multiple initialization expressions or multiple increment expressions.

- The comma between the expressions is a comma operator, which guarantees that a list of expressions evaluates from left to right.

- The comma operator has the lowest precedence of all C++ operators.

- The value and type of a comma-separated list of expressions is the value and type of the rightmost expression.

Section 5.6 Application: Compound-Interest Calculations

- C++ treats floating-point literals like 1000.0 and 0.05 as type double. Similarly, C++ treats whole-number literals like 7 and -22 as type int.

- Standard library function **pow(x, y)** (p. 169) calculates the value of x raised to the yth power. Function pow takes two arguments of type double and returns a double value.

- Parameterized stream manipulator **setw** (p. 169) specifies the field width in which the next value output should appear, right justified by default. If the value is larger than the field width, the field width is extended to accommodate the entire value. Stream manipulator **left** (p. 169) causes a value to be left justified and **right** (p. 169) can be used to restore right justification.

- **Sticky output-formatting settings** (p. 169) remain in effect until they're changed.

- Type double suffers from what we call **representational error** (p. 170), because double cannot precisely represent all decimal values.

Section 5.7 Case Study: Integer-Based Monetary Calculations with Class DollarAmount

- You cannot avoid rounding on interest calculations, because they result in fractional pennies when working with dollar amounts.

- With integer arithmetic you can exercise precise control over rounding without suffering the representational errors associated with floating-point calculations.

Section 5.7.2 Class DollarAmount

- On most computers, an int is a value from –2,147,483,647 to 2,147,483,647—way too small for many monetary applications.

- C++11's **long long** (p. 176) type supports values in the range –9,223,372,036,854,775,808 to 9,223,372,036,854,775,807 as a minimum.

- The range of long long (and C++'s other integer types) can vary across platforms. For portability, C++11 introduced new integer-type names so you can choose the appropriate range of values for your program. An **int64_t** (p. 177) supports the exact range –9,223,372,036,854,775,808 to 9,223,372,036,854,775,807.

- For a list of C++11's integer-type names, see the header <cstdint> (p. 177).

- A member function can access both the private data of the object on which that function is called and the private data of other objects of the same class that are passed to the function.

- In half-up rounding, values .5 and higher round up and everything else rounds down.

- C++ Standard Library function **to_string** (p. 178; from header <string>) converts a numeric value to a string object.

- C++ Standard Library function **abs** (p. 178; from header <cmath>) returns the absolute value of its argument.

- "Adding" string literals and string objects using the + operator is known as **string concatenation** (p. 178).

- string member function **size** (p. 178) returns the number of characters in the string.

- Half-up rounding is a biased technique, because fewer values round down than up—fractional amounts of .1, .2, .3 and .4 round down, and .5, .6, .7, .8 and .9 round up. **Banker's rounding** (p. 179) fixes this problem by rounding .5 to the nearest *even* integer.

Section 5.8 do...while Iteration Statement

- The **do...while statement** (p. 179) is similar to the while statement. In the while, the program tests the loop-continuation condition at the beginning of the loop, before executing its body; if the condition is *false*, the body never executes. The do...while statement tests the loop-continuation condition *after* executing the loop's body; therefore, the body always executes at least once.

Section 5.9 switch Multiple-Selection Statement

- The **switch multiple-selection statement** (p. 180) performs different actions based on its controlling expression's value.

- The end-of-file indicator is a system-dependent keystroke combination that terminates user input. On UNIX/Linux/Mac OS X systems, end-of-file is entered by typing the sequence *<Ctrl> d* on a line by itself. This notation means to simultaneously press both the *Ctrl* key and the *d* key. On Windows systems, enter end-of-file by typing *<Ctrl> z*.

- When you perform input with cin in a condition, the condition evaluates to *true* if the input is successful or evaluates to *false* if the user enters the end-of-file indicator.

- The switch statement consists of a block that contains a sequence of **case labels** (p. 184) and an optional **default case** (p. 184).

- In a switch, the program evaluates the controlling expression and compares its value with each case label. If a match occurs, the program executes the statements for that case.

- Listing cases consecutively with no statements between them enables the cases to perform the same set of statements.

- Every value you wish to test in a switch must be listed in a separate case label.

- Each case can have multiple statements, and these need not be placed in braces.

- A case's statements typically end with a **break statement** (p. 184) that terminates the switch's execution.

- Without break statements, each time a match occurs in the switch, the statements for that case and subsequent cases execute until a break statement or the end of the switch is encountered.

- If no match occurs between the controlling expression's value and a case label, the optional default case executes. If no match occurs and the switch does not contain a default case, program control simply continues with the first statement after the switch.

Section 5.10 **break** and **continue** Statements

- The break statement, when executed in a while, for, do...while or switch, causes immediate exit from that statement.

- The **continue statement** (p. 186), when executed in a while, for or do...while, skips the loop's remaining body statements and proceeds with its next iteration. In while and do...while statements, the program evaluates the loop-continuation test immediately. In a for statement, the increment expression executes, then the program evaluates the loop-continuation test.

Section 5.11 Logical Operators

- Simple conditions are expressed in terms of the relational operators >, <, >= and <= and the equality operators == and !=, and each expression tests only one condition.

- **Logical operators** (p. 188) enable you to form more complex conditions by combining simple conditions. The logical operators are && (logical AND), || (logical OR) and ! (logical negation).

- To ensure that two conditions are *both true*, use the && (logical AND) operator. If either or both of the simple conditions are *false*, the entire expression is *false*.

- To ensure that either *or* both of two conditions are *true*, use the || (logical OR) operator, which evaluates to *true* if either or both of its simple conditions are *true*.

- A condition using && or || operators uses **short-circuit evaluation** (p. 190)—they're evaluated only until it's known whether the condition is *true* or *false*.

- The unary ! (**logical negation**; p. 190) operator "reverses" the value of a condition.

- By default, bool values true and false are displayed by cout as 1 and 0, respectively. Stream manipulator **boolalpha** (p. 191) specifies that the value of each bool expression should be displayed as either the word "true" or the word "false."

Section 5.12 Confusing the Equality (==) and Assignment (=) Operators

- Any expression that produces a value can be used in the decision portion of any control statement. If the value of the expression is zero, it's treated as false, and if the value is nonzero, it's treated as true.

- An assignment produces a value—namely, the value assigned to the variable on the left side of the assignment operator.
- Programmers normally write conditions such as x == 7 with the variable name (an *lvalue*) on the left and the literal (an *rvalue*) on the right. Placing the literal on the left, as in 7 == x, enables the compiler to issue an error if you accidentally replace the == operator with = . The compiler treats this as a compilation error, because you can't change a literal's value.

Self-Review Exercises

5.1 Fill in the blanks in each of the following statements:
   a) Typically, _____ statements are used for counter-controlled iteration and _____ statements for sentinel-controlled iteration.
   b) The do...while statement tests the loop-continuation condition _____ executing the loop's body; therefore, the body always executes at least once.
   c) The _____ statement selects among multiple actions based on the possible values of an integer variable or expression.
   d) The _____ statement, when executed in an iteration statement, skips the remaining statements in the loop body and proceeds with the next iteration of the loop.
   e) The _____ operator can be used to ensure that two conditions are *both* true before choosing a certain path of execution.
   f) If the loop-continuation condition in a for header is initially _____, the program does not execute the for statement's body.

5.2 State whether each of the following is *true* or *false*. If the answer is *false*, explain why.
   a) The default case is required in the switch selection statement.
   b) The break statement is required in the default case of a switch selection statement to exit the switch properly.
   c) The expression (x > y && a < b) is true if either the expression x > y is true or the expression a < b is true.
   d) An expression containing the || operator is true if either or both of its operands are true.

5.3 Write a C++ statement or a set of C++ statements to accomplish each of the following:
   a) Sum the odd integers between 1 and 99 using a for statement. Use the unsigned int variables sum and count.
   b) Print the value 333.546372 in a 15-character field with precisions of 1, 2 and 3. Print each number on the same line. Left-justify each number in its field. What three values print?
   c) Calculate the value of 2.5 raised to the power 3 using function pow. Print the result with a precision of 2 in a field width of 10 positions. What prints?
   d) Print the integers from 1 to 20 using a while loop and the unsigned int counter variable x. Print only 5 integers per line. [*Hint:* When x % 5 is 0, print a newline character; otherwise, print a tab character.]
   e) Repeat Exercise 5.3(d) using a for statement.

5.4 Find the errors in each of the following code segments and explain how to correct them.
   a)
```
unsigned int x{1};
while (x <= 10); {
    ++x;
}
```
   b)
```
for (double y{0.1}; y != 1.0; y += .1) {
    cout << y << endl;
}
```

c) ```cpp
switch (n) {
    case 1:
        cout << "The number is 1" << endl;
    case 2:
        cout << "The number is 2" << endl;
        break;
    default:
        cout << "The number is not 1 or 2" << endl;
}
```
d) The following code should print the values 1 to 10.
```cpp
unsigned int n{1};
while (n < 10) {
    cout << n++ << endl;
}
```

Answers to Self-Review Exercises

5.1   a) for, while. b) after. c) switch. d) continue. e) && (conditional AND). f) false.

5.2   a) False. The default case is optional. Nevertheless, it's considered good software engineering to always provide a default case.
     b) False. The break statement is used to exit the switch statement. The break statement is not required when the default case is the last case. Nor will the break statement be required if having control proceed with the next case makes sense.
     c) False. When using the && operator, both of the relational expressions must be true for the entire expression to be true.
     d) True.

5.3   a)
```cpp
unsigned int sum{0};
for (unsigned int count{1}; count <= 99; count += 2) {
    sum += count;
}
```
     b)
```cpp
cout << fixed << left
    << setprecision(1) << setw(15) << 333.546372
    << setprecision(2) << setw(15) << 333.546372
    << setprecision(3) << setw(15) << 333.546372 << endl;
```
Output is:
```
333.5          333.55         333.546
```
     c)
```cpp
cout << fixed << setprecision(2) << setw(10) << pow(2.5, 3) << endl;
```
Output is:
```
    15.63
```
     d)
```cpp
unsigned int x{1};
while (x <= 20) {
    if (x % 5 == 0) {
        cout << x << endl;
    }
    else {
        cout << x << '\t';
    }

    ++x;
}
```
```

```
e) for (unsigned int x = 1; x <= 20; ++x) {
      if (x % 5 == 0) {
         cout << x << endl;
      }
      else {
         cout << x << '\t';
      }
   }
```

5.4 a) *Error:* The semicolon after the while header causes an infinite loop.
        Correction: Delete the semicolon after the while header.
     b) *Error:* Using a floating-point number to control a for iteration statement.
        Correction: Use an unsigned int and perform the proper calculation to get the values.

```
for (unsigned int y = 1; y != 10; ++y) {
   cout << (static_cast< double >(y) / 10) << endl;
}
```

     c) *Error:* Missing break statement in the first case.
        Correction: Add a break statement at the end of the first case. This is not an error if you
        want the statement of case 2: to execute every time the case 1: statement executes.
     d) *Error:* Improper relational operator used in the loop-continuation condition.
        Correction: Use <= rather than <, or change 10 to 11.

Exercises

5.5 Describe the four basic elements of counter-controlled iteration.

5.6 Compare and contrast the while and for iteration statements.

5.7 Discuss a situation in which it would be more appropriate to use a do...while statement
than a while statement. Explain why.

5.8 Compare and contrast the break and continue statements.

5.9 *(Find the Code Errors)* Find the error(s), if any, in each of the following:
     a)
```
For (unsigned int x{100}, x >= 1, ++x) {
   cout << x << endl;
}
```
     b) The following code should print whether integer value is odd or even:
```
switch (value % 2) {
   case 0:
      cout << "Even integer" << endl;
   case 1:
      cout << "Odd integer" << endl;
}
```
     c) The following code should output the odd integers from 19 to 1:
```
for (unsigned int x{19}; x >= 1; x += 2) {
   cout << x << endl;
}
```
     d) The following code should output the even integers from 2 to 100:
```
unsigned int counter{2};

do {
   cout << counter << endl;
   counter += 2;
} While ( counter < 100 );
```

5.10 What does the following program do?

```cpp
// Exercise 5.10: Printing.cpp
#include <iostream>
using namespace std;

int main() {
   for (int i{1}; i <= 10; i++) {
      for (int j{1}; j <= 5; j++) {
         cout << '@';
      }

      cout << endl;
   }
}
```

5.11 *(Find the Smallest Value)* Write an application that finds the smallest of several integers. Assume that the first value read specifies the number of values to input from the user.

5.12 *(Calculating the Product of Odd Integers)* Write an application that calculates the product of the odd integers from 1 to 15.

5.13 *(Factorials)* *Factorials* are used frequently in probability problems. The factorial of a positive integer *n* (written *n*! and pronounced "*n* factorial") is equal to the product of the positive integers from 1 to *n*. Write an application that calculates the factorials of 1 through 20. Use type long. Display the results in tabular format. What difficulty might prevent you from calculating the factorial of 100?

5.14 *(Modified Compound-Interest Program)* Modify the compound-interest application of Fig. 5.6 to repeat its steps for interest rates of 5%, 6%, 7%, 8%, 9% and 10%. Use a for loop to vary the interest rate.

5.15 *(Triangle-Printing Program)* Write an application that displays the following patterns separately, one below the other. Use for loops to generate the patterns. All asterisks (*) should be printed by a single statement of the form cout << '*'; which causes the asterisks to print side by side. A statement of the form cout << '\n'; can be used to move to the next line. A statement of the form cout << ' '; can be used to display a space for the last two patterns. There should be no other output statements in the program. [*Hint:* The last two patterns require that each line begin with an appropriate number of blank spaces.]

```
(a)            (b)             (c)             (d)
*              **********      **********               *
**             *********        *********              **
***            ********          ********             ***
****           *******            *******            ****
*****          ******              ******           *****
******         *****                *****          ******
*******        ****                  ****         *******
********       ***                    ***        ********
*********      **                      **       *********
**********     *                        *      **********
```

5.16 *(Bar-Chart Printing Program)* One interesting application of computers is to display graphs and bar charts. Write an application that reads five numbers between 1 and 30. For each number that's read, your program should display the same number of adjacent asterisks. For example, if your program reads the number 7, it should display *******. Display the bars of asterisks *after* you read all five numbers.

5.17   *(Calculating Sales)* An online retailer sells five products whose retail prices are as follows: Product 1, $2.98; product 2, $4.50; product 3, $9.98; product 4, $4.49 and product 5, $6.87. Write an application that reads a series of pairs of numbers as follows:

a) product number

b) quantity sold

Your program should use a `switch` statement to determine the retail price for each product. It should calculate and display the total retail value of all products sold. Use a sentinel-controlled loop to determine when the program should stop looping and display the final results.

5.18   Assume that i = 1, j = 2, k = 3 and m = 2. What does each of the following statements print?

a) `cout << (i == 1) << endl;`

b) `cout << (j == 3) << endl;`

c) `cout << (i >= 1 && j < 4) << endl;`

d) `cout << (m <= 99 && k < m) << endl;`

e) `cout << (j >= i || k == m) << endl;`

f) `cout << (k + m < j || 3 - j >= k) << endl;`

g) `cout << (!m ) << endl;`

h) `cout << (!( j - m)) << endl;`

i) `cout << (!(k > m)) << endl;`

5.19   *(Calculating the Value of π)* Calculate the value of π from the infinite series

$$\pi = 4 - \frac{4}{3} + \frac{4}{5} - \frac{4}{7} + \frac{4}{9} - \frac{4}{11} + \cdots$$

Print a table that shows the value of π approximated by computing the first 200,000 terms of this series. How many terms do you have to use before you first get a value that begins with 3.14159?

5.20   *(Pythagorean Triples)* A right triangle can have sides whose lengths are all integers. The set of three integer values for the lengths of the sides of a right triangle is called a Pythagorean triple. The lengths of the three sides must satisfy the relationship that the sum of the squares of two of the sides is equal to the square of the hypotenuse. Write an application that displays a table of the Pythagorean triples for side1, side2 and the hypotenuse, all no larger than 500. Use a triple-nested for loop that tries all possibilities. This is an example of "brute-force" computing. You'll learn in more advanced computer-science courses that for many interesting problems there's no known algorithmic approach other than using sheer brute force.

5.21   *(Modified Triangle-Printing Program)* Modify Exercise 5.15 to combine your code from the four separate triangles of asterisks such that all four patterns print side by side. [*Hint:* Make clever use of nested for loops.]

5.22   *(De Morgan's Laws)* In this chapter, we discussed the logical operators &&, || and !. De Morgan's laws can sometimes make it more convenient for us to express a logical expression. These laws state that the expression !(*condition1* && *condition2*) is logically equivalent to the expression (!*condition1* || !*condition2*). Also, the expression !(*condition1* || *condition2*) is logically equivalent to the expression (!*condition1* && !*condition2*). Use De Morgan's laws to write equivalent expressions for each of the following, then write an application to show that both the original expression and the new expression in each case produce the same value:

a) `!(x < 5) && !(y >= 7)`

b) `!(a == b) || !(g != 5)`

c) `!((x <= 8) && (y > 4))`

d) `!((i > 4) || (j <= 6))`

5.23   *(Diamond-Printing Program)* Write an application that prints the following diamond shape. You may use output statements that print a single asterisk (*), a single space or a single newline character. Maximize your use of iteration (with nested for statements), and minimize the number of output statements.

```
    *
   ***
  *****
 *******
*********
 *******
  *****
   ***
    *
```

5.24   *(Modified Diamond-Printing Program)* Modify the application you wrote in Exercise 5.23 to read an odd number in the range 1 to 19 to specify the number of rows in the diamond. Your program should then display a diamond of the appropriate size.

5.25   *(Removing break and continue)* A criticism of the break statement and the continue statement is that each is *unstructured*. Actually, these statements can *always* be replaced by structured statements, although doing so can be awkward. Describe in general how you'd remove any break statement from a loop in a program and replace it with some structured equivalent. [*Hint:* The break statement exits a loop from the body of the loop. The other way to exit is by failing the loop-continuation test. Consider using in the loop-continuation test a second test that indicates "early exit because of a 'break' condition."] Use the technique you develop here to remove the break statement from the application in Fig. 5.13.

5.26   What does the following program segment do?

```
for (unsigned int i{1}; i <= 5; i++) {
    for (unsigned int j{1}; j <= 3; j++) {
        for (unsigned int k{1}; k <= 4; k++) {
            cout << '*';
        }
        cout << endl;
    }
    cout << endl;
}
```

5.27   *(Replacing continue with a Structured Equivalent)* Describe in general how you'd remove any continue statement from a loop in a program and replace it with some structured equivalent. Use the technique you develop here to remove the continue statement from the program in Fig. 5.14.

5.28   *("The Twelve Days of Christmas" Song)* Write an application that uses iteration and switch statements to print the song "The Twelve Days of Christmas." One switch statement should be used to print the day ("first," "second," and so on). A separate switch statement should be used to print the remainder of each verse. Visit the website en.wikipedia.org/wiki/The_Twelve_Days_of_Christmas_(song) for the lyrics of the song.

5.29   *(Peter Minuit Problem)* Legend has it that, in 1626, Peter Minuit purchased Manhattan Island for $24.00 in barter. Did he make a good investment? To answer this question, modify the compound-interest program of Fig. 5.6 to begin with a principal of $24.00 and to calculate the amount of interest on deposit if that money had been kept on deposit until this year (e.g., 390 years through 2016). Place the for loop that performs the compound-interest calculation in an outer for loop that varies the interest rate from 5% to 10% to observe the wonders of compound interest.

5.30 *(DollarAmount Constructor with Two Parameters)* Enhance class DollarAmount (Fig. 5.8) with a constructor that receives two parameters representing the whole number of dollars and the whole number of cents. Use these to calculate and store in the data member amount the total number of pennies. Test the class with your new constructor.

5.31 *(DollarAmount Arithmetic)* Enhance class DollarAmount from Exercise 5.30 with a divide member function that receives an int parameter, divides the data member amount by that value and stores the result in the data member. Use rounding techniques similar to the addInterest member function. Test your new divide member function.

5.32 *(DollarAmount with Banker's Rounding)* The DollarAmount class's addInterest member function uses the *biased* half-up rounding technique in which fractional amounts of .1, .2, .3 and .4 round down, and .5, .6, .7, .8 and .9 round up. In this technique, four values round down and five round up. Banker's rounding fixes this problem by rounding .5 to the nearest *even* integer—e.g., 0.5 rounds to 0, 1.5 and 2.5 round to 2, 3.5 and 4.5 round to 4, etc. Enhance class DollarAmount from Exercise 5.31 by reimplementing addInterest to use banker's rounding, then retest the compound-interest program.

5.33 *(DollarAmount with dollars and cents Data Members)* Reimplement class DollarAmount from Exercise 5.32 to store data members dollars and cents, rather than amount. Modify the body of each constructor and member function appropriately to manipulate the dollars and cents data members.

5.34 *(Account Class That Stores a DollarAmount)* Upgrade the Account class from Exercise 3.9 to define its balance data member as an object of class DollarAmount from Exercise 5.33. Reimplement the bodies of class Account's constructor and member functions accordingly.

5.35 *(Displaying the Interest Rate in the DollarAmount Example)* Enhance the main program in Fig. 5.7 to display the interest rate based on the two integers entered by the user. For example, if the user enters 2 and 100, display 2.0%, and if the user enters 2015 and 100000, display 2.015%.

5.36 *(Showing That double Values Are Approximate)* Create a program that assigns 123.02 to a double variable, then displays the variable's value with many digits of precision to the right of the decimal point. Which precision first shows you the representational error of storing 123.02 in a double variable?

Making a Difference

5.37 *(Global Warming Facts Quiz)* The controversial issue of global warming has been widely publicized by the film "An Inconvenient Truth," featuring former Vice President Al Gore. Mr. Gore and a U.N. network of scientists, the Intergovernmental Panel on Climate Change, shared the 2007 Nobel Peace Prize in recognition of "their efforts to build up and disseminate greater knowledge about man-made climate change." Research *both* sides of the global warming issue online (you might want to search for phrases like "global warming skeptics"). Create a five-question multiple-choice quiz on global warming, each question having four possible answers (numbered 1–4). Be objective and try to fairly represent both sides of the issue. Next, write an application that administers the quiz, calculates the number of correct answers (zero through five) and returns a message to the user. If the user correctly answers five questions, print "Excellent"; if four, print "Very good"; if three or fewer, print "Time to brush up on your knowledge of global warming," and include a list of some of the websites where you found your facts.

5.38   *(Tax Plan Alternatives; The "FairTax")* There are many (often controversial) proposals to make taxation *"fairer."* Check out the FairTax initiative in the United States at www.fairtax.org. Research how the proposed FairTax works. One suggestion is to eliminate income taxes and most other taxes in favor of a 23% consumption tax on all products and services that you buy. Some Fair-Tax opponents question the 23% figure and say that because of the way the tax is calculated, it would be more accurate to say the rate is 30%—check this carefully. Write a program that prompts the user to enter expenses in various expense categories they have (e.g., housing, food, clothing, transportation, education, health care, vacations), then prints the estimated FairTax that person would pay.

6 Functions and an Introduction to Recursion

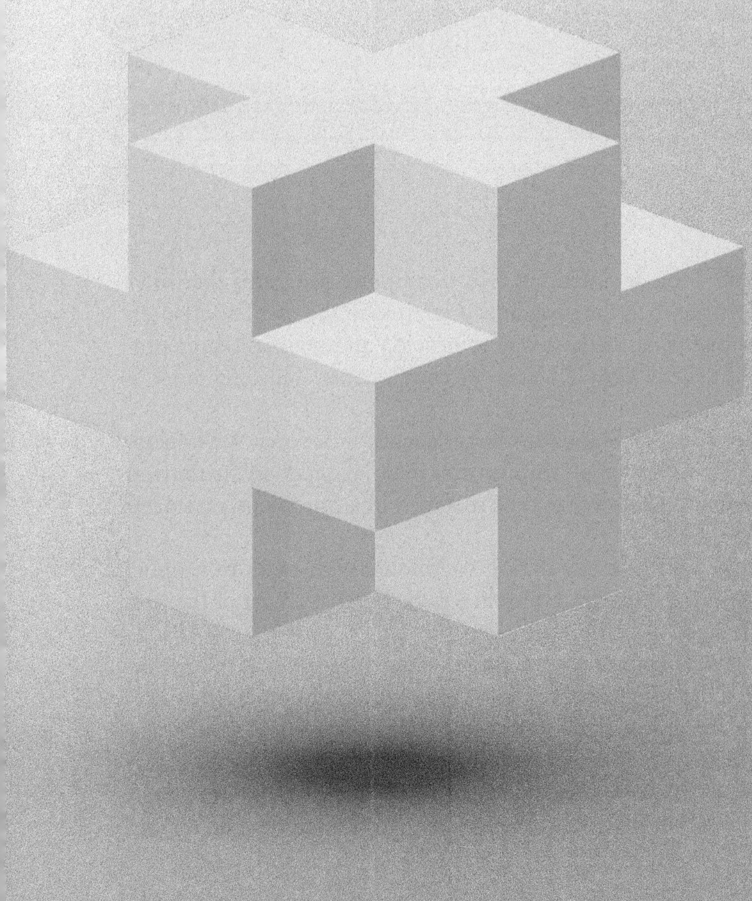

Objectives

In this chapter you'll:

- Construct programs modularly from functions.
- Use common math library functions.
- Use function prototypes to declare a function.
- Use random-number generation to implement game-playing applications.
- Use C++14 digit separators to make numeric literals more readable
- Understand how the visibility of identifiers is limited to specific regions of programs.
- Understand how the function call/return mechanism is supported by the function-call stack and activation records.
- Understand the mechanisms for passing data to functions and returning results.
- Use inline functions, references and default arguments.
- Define with the same name overloaded functions that perform different tasks based on the number and types of their arguments.
- Define function templates that can generate families of overloaded functions.
- Write and use recursive functions.

6.1 Introduction

In this chapter, we take a deeper look at functions. Most computer programs that solve real-world problems are much larger than the programs presented in the first few chapters of this book. Experience has shown that the best way to develop and maintain large programs is to construct them from small, simple pieces, or components. This technique is called divide and conquer.

We'll overview a portion of the C++ Standard Library's math functions. We'll introduce function prototypes and discuss how the compiler uses them, if necessary, to convert the type of an argument in a function call to the type specified in a function's parameter list.

Next, we'll take a brief diversion into simulation techniques with random number generation and develop a version of a popular casino dice game that uses most of the programming techniques you've learned.

We then present C++'s scope rules, which determine where identifiers can be referenced in a program. You'll learn how C++ keeps track of which function is currently executing, how parameters and other local variables of functions are maintained in memory and how a function knows where to return after it completes execution. We discuss topics that help improve program performance—inline functions that can eliminate the overhead of a function call and reference parameters that can be used to pass large data items to functions efficiently.

Many of the applications you develop will have more than one function of the same name. This technique, called function overloading, is used to implement functions that perform similar tasks for arguments of different types or different numbers of arguments. We consider function templates—a mechanism for concisely defining a family of overloaded functions. The chapter concludes with a discussion of functions that call themselves, either directly, or indirectly (through another function)—a topic called recursion.

6.2 Program Components in C++

C++ programs are typically written by combining "prepackaged" functions and classes available in the C++ Standard Library with new functions and classes you write. The C++ Standard Library provides a rich collection of functions for common mathematical calculations, string manipulations, character manipulations, input/output, error checking and many other useful operations.

Functions allow you to modularize a program by separating its tasks into self-contained units. You've used a combination of library functions and your own functions in almost every program you've written.

There are several motivations for modularizing a program with functions:

- Software reuse. For example, in earlier programs, we did not have to define how to read a line of text from the keyboard—C++ provides this capability via the `getline` function of the `<string>` header.

- Avoiding code repetition.

- Dividing a program into meaningful functions makes the program easier to test, debug and maintain.

Software Engineering Observation 6.1

To promote software reusability, every function should be limited to performing a single, well-defined task, and the name of the function should express that task effectively.

As you know, a function is invoked by a function call, and when the called function completes its task, it either returns a *result* or simply returns *control* to the caller. An analogy to this program structure is the hierarchical form of management (Figure 6.1).

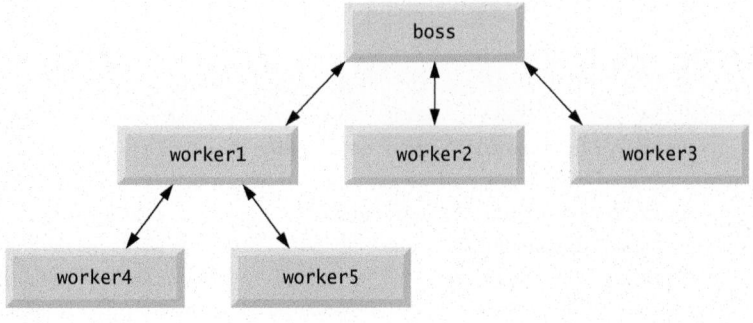

Fig. 6.1 | Hierarchical boss-function/worker-function relationship.

A boss (similar to the calling function) asks a worker (similar to a called function) to perform a task and report back (i.e., return) the results after completing the task. The boss function does *not* know how the worker function performs its designated tasks. The worker may also call other worker functions, unbeknownst to the boss. This *hiding of implementation details* promotes good software engineering. Figure 6.1 shows the boss function communicating with several worker functions. The boss function divides the responsibilities among the worker functions, and worker1 acts as a "boss function" to worker4 and worker5. The relationship does not need to be hierarchical, but often it is, which makes it easier to test, debug, update and maintain programs.

6.3 Math Library Functions

Some functions, such as main, are *not* members of a class. These functions are called global functions. We introduce various functions from the <cmath> header here to present the concept of global functions that do not belong to a particular class.

The <cmath> header provides a collection of functions that perform common mathematical calculations. For example, you can calculate the square root of 900.0 with the function call

```
sqrt(900.0)
```

This expression evaluates to 30.0. Function sqrt takes an argument of type double and returns a double result. There's no need to create any objects before calling function sqrt. Also, *all* functions in the <cmath> header are *global* functions—therefore, each is called simply by specifying the name of the function followed by parentheses containing the function's arguments.

Error-Prevention Tip 6.1
Do not call sqrt with a negative argument. For industrial-strength code, always check that the arguments you pass to math functions are valid.

Function arguments may be constants, variables or more complex expressions. If c = 13.0, d = 3.0 and f = 4.0, then the statement

```
cout << sqrt(c + d * f) << endl;
```

displays the square root of 13.0 + 3.0 * 4.0 = 25.0—namely, 5.0. Some math library functions are summarized in Fig. 6.2. In the figure, the variables x and y are of type double.

Function	Description	Example
ceil(x)	rounds x to the smallest integer not less than x	ceil(9.2) is 10.0 ceil(-9.8) is -9.0
cos(x)	trigonometric cosine of x (x in radians)	cos(0.0) is 1.0
exp(x)	exponential function e^x	exp(1.0) is 2.718282 exp(2.0) is 7.389056

Fig. 6.2 | Math library functions. (Part 1 of 2.)

Function	Description	Example
fabs(x)	absolute value of x	fabs(5.1) is 5.1 fabs(0.0) is 0.0 fabs(-8.76) is 8.76
floor(x)	rounds x to the largest integer not greater than x	floor(9.2) is 9.0 floor(-9.8) is -10.0
fmod(x, y)	remainder of x/y as a floating-point number	fmod(2.6, 1.2) is 0.2
log(x)	natural logarithm of x (base e)	log(2.718282) is 1.0 log(7.389056) is 2.0
log10(x)	logarithm of x (base 10)	log10(10.0) is 1.0 log10(100.0) is 2.0
pow(x, y)	x raised to power y (x^y)	pow(2, 7) is 128 pow(9, .5) is 3
sin(x)	trigonometric sine of x (x in radians)	sin(0.0) is 0
sqrt(x)	square root of x (where x is a nonnegative value)	sqrt(9.0) is 3.0
tan(x)	trigonometric tangent of x (x in radians)	tan(0.0) is 0

Fig. 6.2 | Math library functions. (Part 2 of 2.)

6.4 Function Prototypes

In this section, we create a user-defined function called maximum that returns the largest of its three int arguments. When the application executes, the main function (lines 9–17 of Fig. 6.3) reads three integers from the user. Then, the output statement (lines 15–16) calls maximum, which in this example is defined *after* main (lines 20–34)—we'll discuss the order of this example's function definitions momentarily. Function maximum returns the largest value to line 16, which displays the result. The sample outputs show that maximum determines the largest value regardless of whether it's the first, second or third argument.

```
1   // Fig. 6.3: fig06_03.cpp
2   // maximum function with a function prototype.
3   #include <iostream>
4   #include <iomanip>
5   using namespace std;
6
7   int maximum(int x, int y, int z); // function prototype
8
9   int main() {
10     cout << "Enter three integer values: ";
11     int int1, int2, int3;
12     cin >> int1 >> int2 >> int3;
13
```

Fig. 6.3 | maximum function with a function prototype. (Part 1 of 2.)

```
14      // invoke maximum
15      cout << "The maximum integer value is: "
16          << maximum(int1, int2, int3) << endl;
17   }
18
19   // returns the largest of three integers
20   int maximum(int x, int y, int z) {
21       int maximumValue{x}; // assume x is the largest to start
22
23       // determine whether y is greater than maximumValue
24       if (y > maximumValue) {
25           maximumValue = y; // make y the new maximumValue
26       }
27
28       // determine whether z is greater than maximumValue
29       if (z > maximumValue) {
30           maximumValue = z; // make z the new maximumValue
31       }
32
33       return maximumValue;
34   }
```

```
Enter three integer grades: 86 67 75
The maximum integer value is: 86
```

```
Enter three integer grades: 67 86 75
The maximum integer value is: 86
```

```
Enter three integer grades: 67 75 86
The maximum integer value is: 86
```

Fig. 6.3 | maximum function with a function prototype. (Part 2 of 2.)

Logic of Function maximum

Function maximum first assumes that parameter x has the largest value, so line 21 declares local variable maximumValue and initializes it to parameter x's value. Of course, it's possible that parameter y or z contains the actual largest value, so we must compare each of these with maximumValue. The if statement in lines 24–26 determines whether y is greater than maximumValue and, if so, assigns y to maximumValue. The if statement in lines 29–31 determines whether z is greater and, if so, assigns z to maximumValue. At this point the largest value is in maximumValue, so line 33 returns that value to the call in line 16.

Function Prototype for maximum

In preceding chapters, we created classes Account, Student and DollarAmount, each with various member functions. We defined each class in a header (.h) and included it before main in a program's source-code file. Doing this ensures that the class (and thus its member functions) is defined before main creates and manipulates objects of that class. The compiler then can ensure that we call each class's constructors and member functions correcly—for example, passing each the correct number and types of arguments.

For a function that's not defined in a class, you must either define the function before using it or you must *declare* that the function exists, as we do in line 7 of Fig. 6.3:

```
int maximum(int x, int y, int z); // function prototype
```

This is a function prototype, which *describes the* maximum *function without revealing its implementation*. A function prototype is a *declaration* of a function that tells the compiler the function's name, its return type and the types of its parameters. This function prototype indicates that the function returns an int, has the name maximum and requires three int parameters to perform its task. Notice that the function prototype is the *same* as the first line of the corresponding function definition (line 20), but ends with a *required* semicolon.

Good Programming Practice 6.1

Parameter names in function prototypes are optional (they're ignored by the compiler), but many programmers use these names for documentation purposes. We used parameter names in Fig. 6.3's function prototype for demonstration purposes, but generally we do not use them in this book's subsequent examples.

When compiling the program, the compiler uses the prototype to

- Ensure that maximum's first line (line 20) matches its prototype (line 7).
- Check that the call to maximum (line 16) contains the correct number and types of arguments, and that the types of the arguments are in the correct order (in this case, all the arguments are of the same type).
- Ensure that the value returned by the function can be used correctly in the expression that called the function—for example, for a function that returns void you *cannot* call the function on right side of an assignment.
- Ensure that each argument is *consistent* with the type of the corresponding parameter—for example, a parameter of type double can receive values like 7.35, 22 or –0.03456, but not a string like "hello". If the arguments passed to a function do *not* match the types specified in the function's prototype, the compiler attempts to convert the arguments to those types. Section 6.5 discusses this conversion and what happens if the conversion is not allowed.

Common Programming Error 6.1

Declaring function parameters of the same type as int x, y instead of int x, int y is a syntax error—a type is required for each parameter in the parameter list.

Common Programming Error 6.2

Compilation errors occur if the function prototype, header and calls do not all agree in the number, type and order of arguments and parameters, and in the return type.

Software Engineering Observation 6.2

A function that has many parameters may be performing too many tasks. Consider dividing the function into smaller functions that perform the separate tasks. Limit the function header to one line if possible.

Commas in Function Calls Are Not Comma Operators

Multiple parameters are specified in both the function prototype and the function header as a comma-separated list, as are multiple arguments in a function call.

Portability Tip 6.1

The commas used in line 16 of Fig. 6.3 to separate the arguments to function maximum *are not comma operators as discussed in Section 5.5. The comma operator guarantees that its operands are evaluated left to right. The order of evaluation of a function's arguments, however, is not specified by the C++ standard. Thus, different compilers can evaluate function arguments in different orders.*

Portability Tip 6.2

Sometimes when a function's arguments are expressions, such as those with calls to other functions, the order in which the compiler evaluates the arguments could affect the values of one or more of the arguments. If the evaluation order changes between compilers, the argument values passed to the function could vary, causing subtle logic errors.

Error-Prevention Tip 6.2

If you have doubts about the order of evaluation of a function's arguments and whether the order would affect the values passed to the function, evaluate the arguments in separate assignment statements before the function call, assign the result of each expression to a local variable, then pass those variables as arguments to the function.

Returning Control from a Function to Its Caller

Previously, you've seen that when a program calls a function, the function performs its task, then returns control (and possibly a value) to the point where the function was called. In a function that does *not* return a result (i.e., it has a void return type), we showed that control returns when the program reaches the function-ending right brace. You also can explicitly return control to the caller by executing the statement

```
return;
```

6.5 Function-Prototype and Argument-Coercion Notes

A function prototype is required unless the function is defined before it's used. When you use a standard library function like sqrt, you do not have access to the function's definition, therefore it cannot be defined in your code before you call the function. Instead, you must include its corresponding header (<cmath>), which contains the function's prototype.

Common Programming Error 6.3

If a function is defined before it's called, then its definition also serves as the function's prototype, so a separate prototype is unnecessary. If a function is called before it's defined, and that function does not have a function prototype, a compilation error occurs.

Software Engineering Observation 6.3

Always provide function prototypes, even though it's possible to omit them when functions are defined before they're used. Providing the prototypes avoids tying the code to the order in which functions are defined (which can easily change as a program evolves).

6.5.1 Function Signatures and Function Prototypes

The portion of a function prototype that includes the *name of the function* and the *types of its arguments* is called the function signature or simply the signature. The function's return type is not part of the function signature. The scope of a function is the region of a program in which the function is known and accessible. *Functions in the same scope must have unique signatures.* We'll say more about scope in Section 6.10.

In Fig. 6.3, if the function prototype in line 7 had been written

```
void maximum(int, int, int);
```

the compiler would report an error, because the void return type in the function prototype would differ from the int return type in the function header. Similarly, such a prototype would cause the statement

```
cout << maximum(6, 7, 0);
```

to generate a compilation error, because that statement depends on maximum to return a value to be displayed.

Error-Prevention Tip 6.3

Function prototypes help you find many types of errors at compile time. It's always better to eliminate errors at compile time rather than at run time.

6.5.2 Argument Coercion

An important feature of function prototypes is argument coercion—i.e., forcing arguments to the appropriate types specified by the parameter declarations. For example, a program can call a function with an integer argument, even though the function prototype specifies a double parameter—the function will still work correctly, provided this is not a narrowing conversion (discussed in Section 4.11.7).

6.5.3 Argument-Promotion Rules and Implicit Conversions[1]

Sometimes, argument values that do not correspond precisely to the parameter types in the function prototype can be converted by the compiler to the proper type before the function is called. These conversions occur as specified by C++'s promotion rules, which indicate the *implicit conversions* allowed between fundamental types. An int can be converted to a double. A double can also be converted to an int, but this narrowing conversion *truncates* the double's fractional part—recall from Section 4.11.7 that list initializers do not allow narrowing conversions. Keep in mind that double variables can hold numbers of much greater magnitude than int variables, so the loss of data in a narrowing conversion may be considerable. Values may also be modified when converting large integer types to small integer types (e.g., long to short), signed to unsigned or unsigned to signed. Unsigned integers range from 0 to approximately twice the positive range of the corresponding signed type.

The promotion rules also apply to expressions containing values of two or more data types; such expressions are referred to as mixed-type expressions. The type of each value in a mixed-type expression is promoted to the "highest" type in the expression (actually a *temporary* version of each value is created and used for the expression—the original values

---

1.   Promotions and conversions are complex topics discussed in Section 4 and the beginning of Section 5 of the C++ standard.

remain unchanged). Figure 6.4 lists the arithmetic data types in order from "highest type" to "lowest type."

Data types	
long double	
double	
float	
unsigned long long int	(synonymous with unsigned long long)
long long int	(synonymous with long long)
unsigned long int	(synonymous with unsigned long)
long int	(synonymous with long)
unsigned int	(synonymous with unsigned)
int	
unsigned short int	(synonymous with unsigned short)
short int	(synonymous with short)
unsigned char	
char and signed char	
bool	

Fig. 6.4 | Promotion hierarchy for arithmetic data types; the "highest" types are at the top.

Conversions Can Result in Incorrect Values

Converting values to *lower* fundamental types can cause errors due to narrowing conversions. Therefore, a value can be converted to a lower fundamental type only by *explicitly* assigning the value to a variable of lower type (some compilers will issue a warning in this case) or by using a *cast operator* (see Section 4.10). Function argument values are converted to the parameter types in a function prototype as if they were being assigned directly to variables of those types. If a `square` function that uses an integer parameter is called with a floating-point argument, the argument is converted to `int` (a lower type and thus a narrowing conversion), and `square` could return an incorrect value. For example, `square(4.5)` would return 16, not 20.25. Some compilers warn you about the narrowing conversion. For example, Microsoft Visual C++ issues the warning,

```
'argument': conversion from 'double' to 'int', possible loss of data
```

Common Programming Error 6.4

A compilation error occurs if the arguments in a function call cannot be implicitly converted to the expected types specified in the function's prototype.

6.6 C++ Standard Library Headers

The C++ Standard Library is divided into many portions, each with its own header. The headers contain the function prototypes for the related functions that form each portion of the library. The headers also contain definitions of various class types and functions, as well as constants needed by those functions. A header "instructs" the compiler on how to interface with library and user-written components.

Figure 6.5 lists some common C++ Standard Library headers, most of which are discussed later in this book. The term "macro" that's used several times in Fig. 6.5 is discussed in detail in Appendix E, Preprocessor.

Standard Library header	Explanation
`<iostream>`	Contains function prototypes for the C++ standard input and output functions, introduced in Chapter 2, and is covered in more detail in Chapter 13, Stream Input/Output: A Deeper Look.
`<iomanip>`	Contains function prototypes for stream manipulators that format streams of data. This header is first used in Section 4.10 and is discussed in more detail in Chapter 13, Stream Input/Output: A Deeper Look.
`<cmath>`	Contains function prototypes for math library functions (Section 6.3).
`<cstdlib>`	Contains function prototypes for conversions of numbers to text, text to numbers, memory allocation, random numbers and various other utility functions. Portions of the header are covered in Section 6.7; Chapter 11, Operator Overloading; Class string; Chapter 17, Exception Handling: A Deeper Look; Chapter 22, Bits, Characters, C Strings and structs; and Appendix F, C Legacy Code Topics.
`<ctime>`	Contains function prototypes and types for manipulating the time and date. This header is used in Section 6.7.
`<array>`, `<vector>`, `<list>`, `<forward_list>`, `<deque>`, `<queue>`, `<stack>`, `<map>`, `<unordered_map>`, `<unordered_set>`, `<set>`, `<bitset>`	These headers contain classes that implement the C++ Standard Library containers. Containers store data during a program's execution. The `<vector>` header is first introduced in Chapter 7, Class Templates array and vector; Catching Exceptions. We discuss all these headers in Chapter 15, Standard Library Containers and Iterators. `<array>`, `<forward_list>`, `<unordered_map>` and `<unordered_set>` were all introduced in C++11.
`<cctype>`	Contains function prototypes for functions that test characters for certain properties (such as whether the character is a digit or a punctuation), and function prototypes for functions that can be used to convert lowercase letters to uppercase letters and vice versa. These topics are discussed in Chapter 22, Bits, Characters, C Strings and structs.
`<cstring>`	Contains function prototypes for C-style string-processing functions. This header is used in Chapter 10, Operator Overloading; Class string.
`<typeinfo>`	Contains classes for runtime type identification (determining data types at execution time). This header is discussed in Section 12.9.
`<exception>`, `<stdexcept>`	These headers contain classes that are used for exception handling (discussed in Chapter 17, Exception Handling: A Deeper Look).

Fig. 6.5 | C++ Standard Library headers. (Part 1 of 2.)

11

Standard Library header	Explanation
<memory>	Contains classes and functions used by the C++ Standard Library to allocate memory to the C++ Standard Library containers. This header is used in Chapter 17, Exception Handling: A Deeper Look.
<fstream>	Contains function prototypes for functions that perform input from and output to files on disk (discussed in Chapter 14, File Processing).
<string>	Contains the definition of class string from the C++ Standard Library (discussed in Chapter 21, Class string and String Stream Processing).
<sstream>	Contains function prototypes for functions that perform input from strings in memory and output to strings in memory (discussed in Chapter 21, Class string and String Stream Processing).
<functional>	Contains classes and functions used by C++ Standard Library algorithms. This header is used in Chapter 15.
<iterator>	Contains classes for accessing data in the C++ Standard Library containers. This header is used in Chapter 15.
<algorithm>	Contains functions for manipulating data in C++ Standard Library containers. This header is used in Chapter 15.
<cassert>	Contains macros for adding diagnostics that aid program debugging. This header is used in Appendix E, Preprocessor.
<cfloat>	Contains the floating-point size limits of the system.
<climits>	Contains the integral size limits of the system.
<cstdio>	Contains function prototypes for the C-style standard input/output library functions.
<locale>	Contains classes and functions normally used by stream processing to process data in the natural form for different languages (e.g., monetary formats, sorting strings, character presentation, etc.).
<limits>	Contains classes for defining the numerical data type limits on each computer platform—this is C++'s version of <climits> and <cfloat>.
<utility>	Contains classes and functions that are used by many C++ Standard Library headers.

Fig. 6.5 | C++ Standard Library headers. (Part 2 of 2.)

6.7 Case Study: Random-Number Generation[2]

We now take a brief and hopefully entertaining diversion into a popular programming application, namely simulation and game playing. In this and the next section, we develop a game-playing program that includes multiple functions.

The element of chance can be introduced into computer applications by using the C++ Standard Library function **rand**. Consider the following statement:

```
i = rand();
```

---

2. In Section 6.9, we'll present C++11's random-number capabilities for building more secure applications.

The function rand generates an unsigned integer between 0 and RAND_MAX (a symbolic constant defined in the <cstdlib> header). You can determine the value of RAND_MAX for your system simply by displaying the constant. If rand truly produces integers at random, every number between 0 and RAND_MAX has an equal *chance* (or probability) of being chosen each time rand is called.

The range of values produced directly by the function rand often is different than what a specific application requires. For example, a program that simulates coin tossing might require only 0 for "heads" and 1 for "tails." A program that simulates rolling a six-sided die would require random integers in the range 1 to 6. A program that randomly predicts the next type of spaceship (out of four possibilities) that will fly across the horizon in a video game might require random integers in the range 1 through 4.

6.7.1 Rolling a Six-Sided Die

To demonstrate rand, Fig. 6.6 simulates 20 rolls of a six-sided die and displays the value of each roll. The function prototype for the rand function is in <cstdlib>. To produce integers in the range 0 to 5, we use the remainder operator (%) with rand as follows:

```
rand() % 6
```

This is called scaling. The number 6 is called the scaling factor. We then shift the range of numbers produced by adding 1 to our previous result. Figure 6.6 confirms that the results are in the range 1 to 6. If you execute this program more than once, you'll see that it produces the same "random" values each time. We'll show how to fix this in Figure 6.8.

```cpp
1   // Fig. 6.6: fig06_06.cpp
2   // Shifted, scaled integers produced by 1 + rand() % 6.
3   #include <iostream>
4   #include <iomanip>
5   #include <cstdlib> // contains function prototype for rand
6   using namespace std;
7
8   int main() {
9      // loop 20 times
10     for (unsigned int counter{1}; counter <= 20; ++counter) {
11        // pick random number from 1 to 6 and output it
12        cout << setw(10) << (1 + rand() % 6);
13
14        // if counter is divisible by 5, start a new line of output
15        if (counter % 5 == 0) {
16           cout << endl;
17        }
18     }
19  }
```

6	6	5	5	6
5	1	1	5	3
6	6	2	4	2
6	2	3	4	1

Fig. 6.6 | Shifted, scaled integers produced by 1 + rand() % 6.

6.7.2 Rolling a Six-Sided Die 60,000,000 Times

To show that values produced by rand occur with approximately equal likelihood, Fig. 6.7 simulates 60,000,000 rolls of a die. Each integer in the range 1 to 6 should appear approximately 10,000,000 times (one-sixth of the rolls). This is confirmed by the program's output.

```cpp
 1   // Fig. 6.7: fig06_07.cpp
 2   // Rolling a six-sided die 60,000,000 times.
 3   #include <iostream>
 4   #include <iomanip>
 5   #include <cstdlib> // contains function prototype for rand
 6   using namespace std;
 7
 8   int main() {
 9      unsigned int frequency1{0}; // count of 1s rolled
10      unsigned int frequency2{0}; // count of 2s rolled
11      unsigned int frequency3{0}; // count of 3s rolled
12      unsigned int frequency4{0}; // count of 4s rolled
13      unsigned int frequency5{0}; // count of 5s rolled
14      unsigned int frequency6{0}; // count of 6s rolled
15      int face; // stores each roll of the die
16
17      // summarize results of 60,000,000 rolls of a die
18      for (unsigned int roll{1}; roll <= 60'000'000; ++roll) {
19         face = 1 + rand() % 6; // random number from 1 to 6
20
21         // determine roll value 1-6 and increment appropriate counter
22         switch (face) {
23            case 1:
24               ++frequency1; // increment the 1s counter
25               break;
26            case 2:
27               ++frequency2; // increment the 2s counter
28               break;
29            case 3:
30               ++frequency3; // increment the 3s counter
31               break;
32            case 4:
33               ++frequency4; // increment the 4s counter
34               break;
35            case 5:
36               ++frequency5; // increment the 5s counter
37               break;
38            case 6:
39               ++frequency6; // increment the 6s counter
40               break;
41            default: // invalid value
42               cout << "Program should never get here!";
43         }
44      }
45
46      cout << "Face" << setw(13) << "Frequency" << endl; // output headers
```

Fig. 6.7 | Rolling a six-sided die 60,000,000 times. (Part 1 of 2.)

```
47        cout << "   1" << setw(13) << frequency1
48            << "\n   2" << setw(13) << frequency2
49            << "\n   3" << setw(13) << frequency3
50            << "\n   4" << setw(13) << frequency4
51            << "\n   5" << setw(13) << frequency5
52            << "\n   6" << setw(13) << frequency6 << endl;
53   }
```

```
Face    Frequency
 1       9999294
 2      10002929
 3       9995360
 4      10000409
 5      10005206
 6       9996802
```

Fig. 6.7 | Rolling a six-sided die 60,000,000 times. (Part 2 of 2.)

As the output shows, we can simulate rolling a six-sided die by scaling and shifting the values rand produces. The default case (lines 41–42) in the switch should *never* execute, because the switch's controlling expression (face) *always* has values in the range 1–6. We provide the default case as a matter of good practice. After we study arrays in Chapter 7, we show how to replace the entire switch in Fig. 6.7 elegantly with a single-line statement. This will be another of those "light-bulb" moments.

 Error-Prevention Tip 6.4
Provide a default case in a switch to catch errors even if you are absolutely, positively certain that you have no bugs!

C++14 Digit Separators for Numeric Literals

Prior to C++14, you'd represent the integer value 60,000,000 as 60000000 in a program. Typing numeric literals with many digits can be error prone. To make numeric literals more readable, C++14 allows you to insert between groups of digits in numeric literals the digit separator ' (a single-quote character)—for example, 60'000'000 (line 18) represents the integer value 60,000,000. You might wonder why single-quote characters are used rather than commas. If we use 60,000,000 in line 18, C++ treats the commas as *comma operators* and the value of 60,000,000 would be the *rightmost* expression (000). The loop-continuation condition would immediately be *false*—a logic error in this program.

14

6.7.3 Randomizing the Random-Number Generator with srand

Executing the program of Fig. 6.6 again produces

```
6        6        5        5        6
5        1        1        5        3
6        6        2        4        2
6        2        3        4        1
```

This is the *same* sequence of values shown in Fig. 6.6. How can these be random numbers?

Error-Prevention Tip 6.5
When debugging a simulation program, random-number repeatability is essential for proving that corrections to the program work properly.

Function rand actually generates pseudorandom numbers. Repeatedly calling rand produces a sequence of numbers that appears to be random. However, the sequence *repeats* itself each time the program executes. Once a program has been thoroughly debugged, it can be conditioned to produce a *different* sequence of random numbers for each execution. This is called randomizing and is accomplished with the C++ Standard Library function srand from the header <cstdlib>. Function srand takes an unsigned integer argument and seeds the rand function to produce a different sequence of random numbers for each execution.

Demonstrating **srand**

Figure 6.8 demonstrates function srand. The program produces a *different* sequence of random numbers each time it executes, provided that the user enters a *different* seed. We used the *same* seed in the first and third sample outputs, so the *same* series of 10 numbers is displayed in each of those outputs.

Software Engineering Observation 6.4
Ensure that your program seeds the random-number generator differently (and only once) each time the program executes; otherwise, an attacker would easily be able to determine the sequence of pseudorandom numbers that would be produced.

```
1   // Fig. 6.8: fig06_08.cpp
2   // Randomizing the die-rolling program.
3   #include <iostream>
4   #include <iomanip>
5   #include <cstdlib> // contains prototypes for functions srand and rand
6   using namespace std;
7
8   int main() {
9      unsigned int seed{0}; // stores the seed entered by the user
10
11     cout << "Enter seed: ";
12     cin >> seed;
13     srand(seed); // seed random number generator
14
15     // loop 10 times
16     for (unsigned int counter{1}; counter <= 10; ++counter) {
17        // pick random number from 1 to 6 and output it
18        cout << setw(10) << (1 + rand() % 6);
19
20        // if counter is divisible by 5, start a new line of output
21        if (counter % 5 == 0) {
22           cout << endl;
23        }
24     }
25  }
```

Fig. 6.8 | Randomizing the die-rolling program. (Part 1 of 2.)

```
Enter seed: 67
          6           1           4           6           2
          1           6           1           6           4
```

```
Enter seed: 432
          4           6           3           1           6
          3           1           5           4           2
```

```
Enter seed: 67
          6           1           4           6           2
          1           6           1           6           4
```

Fig. 6.8 | Randomizing the die-rolling program. (Part 2 of 2.)

6.7.4 Seeding the Random-Number Generator with the Current Time

To randomize *without* having to enter a seed each time, we can use a statement like

```
srand(static_cast<unsigned int>(time(0)));
```

This causes the computer to read its *clock* to obtain the value for the seed. Function `time` (with the argument 0 as written in the preceding statement) typically returns the current time as the number of seconds since January 1, 1970, at midnight Greenwich Mean Time (GMT). This value (which is of type `time_t`) is converted to an `unsigned int` and used as the seed to the random-number generator—the `static_cast` in the preceding statement eliminates a compiler warning that's issued if you pass a `time_t` value to a function that expects an `unsigned int`. The function prototype for `time` is in <ctime>.

6.7.5 Scaling and Shifting Random Numbers

Previously, we simulated the rolling of a six-sided die with the statement

```
unsigned int face{1 + rand() % 6};
```

which always assigns an integer (at random) to variable `face` in the range $1 \le \text{face} \le 6$. The width of this range (i.e., the number of consecutive integers in the range) is 6 and the starting number in the range is 1. Referring to the preceding statement, we see that the width of the range is determined by the number used to scale `rand` with the remainder operator (i.e., 6), and the starting number of the range is equal to the number (i.e., 1) that is added to the expression `rand % 6`. We can generalize this result as

```
type variableName{shiftingValue + rand() % scalingFactor};
```

where the *shiftingValue* is equal to the *first number* in the desired range of consecutive integers and the *scalingFactor* is equal to the *width* of the desired range of consecutive integers.

6.8 Case Study: Game of Chance; Introducing Scoped enums

One of the most popular games of chance is a dice game known as "craps," which is played in casinos and back alleys worldwide. The rules of the game are straightforward:

> *A player rolls two dice. Each die has six faces. These faces contain 1, 2, 3, 4, 5 and 6 spots. After the dice have come to rest, the sum of the spots on the two upward faces is calculated. If the sum is 7 or 11 on the first roll, the player wins. If the sum is 2, 3 or 12 on the first roll (called "craps"), the player loses (i.e., the "house" wins). If the sum is 4, 5, 6, 8, 9 or 10 on the first roll, then that sum becomes the player's "point." To win, you must continue rolling the dice until you "make your point." The player loses by rolling a 7 before making the point.*

The program in Fig. 6.9 simulates the game. In the rules, notice that the player must roll two dice on the first roll and on all subsequent rolls. We define function rollDice (lines 64–73) to roll the dice and compute and print their sum. The function is defined once, but called from lines 19 and 41. The function takes no arguments and returns the sum of the two dice, so empty parentheses and the return type unsigned int are indicated in the function prototype (line 8) and function header (line 64).

```
1   // Fig. 6.9: fig06_09.cpp
2   // Craps simulation.
3   #include <iostream>
4   #include <cstdlib> // contains prototypes for functions srand and rand
5   #include <ctime> // contains prototype for function time
6   using namespace std;
7
8   unsigned int rollDice(); // rolls dice, calculates and displays sum
9
10  int main() {
11     // scoped enumeration with constants that represent the game status
12     enum class Status {CONTINUE, WON, LOST}; // all caps in constants
13
14     // randomize random number generator using current time
15     srand(static_cast<unsigned int>(time(0)));
16
17     unsigned int myPoint{0}; // point if no win or loss on first roll
18     Status gameStatus; // can be CONTINUE, WON or LOST
19     unsigned int sumOfDice{rollDice()}; // first roll of the dice
20
21     // determine game status and point (if needed) based on first roll
22     switch (sumOfDice) {
23        case 7: // win with 7 on first roll
24        case 11: // win with 11 on first roll
25           gameStatus = Status::WON;
26           break;
27        case 2: // lose with 2 on first roll
28        case 3: // lose with 3 on first roll
29        case 12: // lose with 12 on first roll
30           gameStatus = Status::LOST;
31           break;
```

Fig. 6.9 | Craps simulation. (Part 1 of 3.)

```
32          default: // did not win or lose, so remember point
33              gameStatus = Status::CONTINUE; // game is not over
34              myPoint = sumOfDice; // remember the point
35              cout << "Point is " << myPoint << endl;
36              break; // optional at end of switch
37      }
38
39      // while game is not complete
40      while (Status::CONTINUE == gameStatus) { // not WON or LOST
41          sumOfDice = rollDice(); // roll dice again
42
43          // determine game status
44          if (sumOfDice == myPoint) { // win by making point
45              gameStatus = Status::WON;
46          }
47          else {
48              if (sumOfDice == 7) { // lose by rolling 7 before point
49                  gameStatus = Status::LOST;
50              }
51          }
52      }
53
54      // display won or lost message
55      if (Status::WON == gameStatus) {
56          cout << "Player wins" << endl;
57      }
58      else {
59          cout << "Player loses" << endl;
60      }
61  }
62
63  // roll dice, calculate sum and display results
64  unsigned int rollDice() {
65      int die1{1 + rand() % 6}; // first die roll
66      int die2{1 + rand() % 6}; // second die roll
67      int sum{die1 + die2}; // compute sum of die values
68
69      // display results of this roll
70      cout << "Player rolled " << die1 << " + " << die2
71          << " = " << sum << endl;
72      return sum;
73  }
```

```
Player rolled 2 + 5 = 7
Player wins
```

```
Player rolled 6 + 6 = 12
Player loses
```

Fig. 6.9 | Craps simulation. (Part 2 of 3.)

```
Player rolled 1 + 3 = 4
Point is 4
Player rolled 4 + 6 = 10
Player rolled 2 + 4 = 6
Player rolled 6 + 4 = 10
Player rolled 2 + 3 = 5
Player rolled 2 + 4 = 6
Player rolled 1 + 1 = 2
Player rolled 4 + 4 = 8
Player rolled 4 + 3 = 7
Player loses
```

```
Player rolled 3 + 3 = 6
Point is 6
Player rolled 5 + 3 = 8
Player rolled 4 + 5 = 9
Player rolled 2 + 1 = 3
Player rolled 1 + 5 = 6
Player wins
```

Fig. 6.9 | Craps simulation. (Part 3 of 3.)

C++11: Scoped enums

The player may win or lose on the first roll or on any subsequent roll. The program tracks this with variable gameStatus, which is declared to be of the new type Status (line 18). Line 12 declares a user-defined type called a scoped enumeration (C++11) which is introduced by the keywords enum class, followed by a type name (Status) and a set of identifiers representing integer constants. The values of these enumeration constants are of type int, start at 0 (unless specified otherwise) and increment by 1. In the preceding enumeration, the constant CONTINUE has the value 0, WON has the value 1 and LOST has the value 2. The identifiers in an enum class must be *unique*, but separate enumeration constants *can* have the same integer value. Variables of user-defined type Status can be assigned only one of the three values declared in the enumeration.

Good Programming Practice 6.2

By convention, you should capitalize the first letter of an enum class's name.

Good Programming Practice 6.3

Use only uppercase letters in enumeration constant names. This makes these constants stand out in a program and reminds you that enumeration constants are not variables.

To reference a scoped enum constant, you *must* qualify the constant with the scoped enum's type name (Status) and the scope-resolution operator (::), as in Status::CONTINUE. When the game is won, the program sets variable gameStatus to Status::WON (lines 25 and 45). When the game is lost, the program sets variable gameStatus to Status::LOST (lines 30 and 49). Otherwise, the program sets variable gameStatus to Status::CONTINUE (line 33) to indicate that the dice must be rolled again.

Error-Prevention Tip 6.6
Qualifying an enum class*'s constant with its typename and* :: *explicitly identifies the constant as being in the scope of the specified* enum class*. If another* enum class *contains the same identifier for one of its constants, it's always clear which version of the constant is being used, because the typename and* :: *are required.*

Another popular scoped enumeration is

```
enum class Months {JAN = 1, FEB, MAR, APR, MAY, JUN, JUL, AUG,
   SEP, OCT, NOV, DEC};
```

which creates user-defined type Months with enumeration constants representing the months of the year. The first value in the preceding enumeration is explicitly set to 1, so the remaining values increment from 1, resulting in the values 1 through 12. Any enumeration constant can be assigned an integer value in the enumeration definition, and subsequent enumeration constants each have a value 1 higher than the preceding constant in the list until the next explicit setting.

Error-Prevention Tip 6.7
Use unique values for an enum*'s constants to help prevent hard-to-find logic errors.*

Winning or Losing on the First Roll
After the first roll, if the game is won or lost, the program skips the body of the while statement (lines 40–52) because gameStatus is not equal to Status::CONTINUE. The program proceeds to the if...else statement in lines 55–60, which prints "Player wins" if gameStatus is equal to WON and "Player loses" if gameStatus is equal to Status::LOST.

Continuing to Roll
After the first roll, if the game is not over, the program saves the sum in myPoint (line 34). Execution proceeds with the while statement, because gameStatus is Status::CONTINUE. During each iteration of the while, the program calls rollDice to produce a new sum. If sum matches myPoint, the program sets gameStatus to Status::WON (line 45), the while-test fails, the if...else statement prints "Player wins" and execution terminates. If sum is equal to 7, the program sets gameStatus to Status::LOST (line 49), the while-test fails, the if...else statement prints "Player loses" and execution terminates.

The craps program uses two functions—main and rollDice—and the switch, while, if...else, nested if...else and nested if statements. We further investigate the game of craps in the exercises.

Enumeration Types Prior to C++11
Prior to C++11, enumerations were defined with the keyword enum followed by a type name and a set of integer constants represented by identifiers, as in

```
enum Status {CONTINUE, WON, LOST};
```

The constants were *unscoped*—you'd refer to them simply as CONTINUE, WON and LOST. If two or more unscoped enums contain constants with the same names, this can lead to naming conflicts and compilation errors.

Error-Prevention Tip 6.8t

Use scoped enums to avoid the potential naming conflicts that can occur with unscoped enum constants.

11

C++11—Specifying the Type of an **enum**'s Constants (Optional)

An enumeration's constants have integer values. An *unscoped* enum's underlying type depends on its constants' values and is guaranteed to be large enough to store its constants' values. A *scoped* enum's underlying integral type is int, but you can specify a different type by following the type name with a colon (:) and the integral type. For example, we can specify that the constants in the enum class Status should have type unsigned int, as in

```
enum class Status : unsigned int {CONTINUE, WON, LOST};
```

Common Programming Error 6.5

A compilation error occurs if an enum constant's value is outside the range that can be represented by the enum's underlying type.

11

6.9 C++11 Random Numbers

According to CERT, function rand does not have "good statistical properties" and can be predictable, which makes programs that use rand less secure (CERT guideline MSC50-CPP). C++11 provides a *more secure* library of random-number capabilities that can produce nondeterministic random numbers—a set of random numbers that can't be predicted. Such random-number generators are used in simulations and security scenarios where predictability is undesirable. These new capabilities are located in the C++ Standard Library's <random> header.

Random-number generation is a mathematically sophisticated topic for which mathematicians have developed many random-number generation algorithms with different statistical properties. For flexibility based on how random numbers are used in programs, C++11 provides many classes that represent various random-number generation *engines* and *distributions*. An engine implements a random-number generation algorithm that produces pseudorandom numbers. A distribution controls the range of values produced by an engine, the types of those values (e.g., int, double, etc.) and the statistical properties of the values. In this section, we'll use the default random-number generation engine—default_random_engine—and a uniform_int_distribution, which *evenly* distributes pseudorandom integers over a specified range of values. The default range is from 0 to the maximum value of an int on your platform.

Rolling a Six-Sided Die

Figure 6.10 uses the default_random_engine and the uniform_int_distribution to roll a six-sided die. Line 13 creates a default_random_engine object named engine. Its constructor argument *seeds* the random-number generation engine with the current time. If you don't pass a value to the constructor, the default seed will be used and the program will produce the *same* sequence of numbers each time it executes—this is useful for testing purposes. Line 14 creates randomInt—a uniform_int_distribution object that produces unsigned int values (as specified by <unsigned int>) in the range 1 to 6 (as specified by the constructor arguments). The expression `randomInt(engine)` (line 19) returns one unsigned int value in the range 1 to 6.

```cpp
1   // Fig. 6.10: fig06_10.cpp
2   // Using a C++11 random-number generation engine and distribution
3   // to roll a six-sided die.
4   #include <iostream>
5   #include <iomanip>
6   #include <random> // contains C++11 random number generation features
7   #include <ctime>
8   using namespace std;
9
10  int main() {
11     // use the default random-number generation engine to
12     // produce uniformly distributed pseudorandom int values from 1 to 6
13     default_random_engine engine{static_cast<unsigned int>(time(0))};
14     uniform_int_distribution<unsigned int> randomInt{1, 6};
15
16     // loop 10 times
17     for (unsigned int counter{1}; counter <= 10; ++counter) {
18        // pick random number from 1 to 6 and output it
19        cout << setw(10) << randomInt(engine);
20
21        // if counter is divisible by 5, start a new line of output
22        if (counter % 5 == 0) {
23           cout << endl;
24        }
25     }
26  }
```

```
         2         1         2         3         5
         6         1         5         6         4
```

Fig. 6.10 | Using a C++11 random-number generation engine and distribution to roll a six-sided die.

The notation `<unsigned int>` in line 14 indicates that `uniform_int_distribution` is a *class template*. In this case, any integer type can be specified in the angle brackets (< and >). In Chapter 18, we discuss how to create class templates and various other chapters show how to use existing class templates from the C++ Standard Library. For now, you should feel comfortable using class template `uniform_int_distribution` by mimicking the syntax shown in the example.

6.10 Scope Rules

The portion of a program where an identifier can be used is known as its *scope*. For example, when we declare a local variable in a block, it can be referenced only in that block and in blocks nested within that block. This section discusses block scope and global namespace scope. Later we'll see other scopes, including class scope in Chapter 9, and function scope, function-prototype scope and namespace scope in Chapter 23.

Block Scope

Identifiers declared *inside* a block have block scope, which begins at the identifier's declaration and ends at the terminating right brace (}) of the enclosing block. Local variables have block scope, as do function parameters (even though they're declared outside the block's braces). Any block can contain variable declarations. When blocks are nested and an identifier in an outer block has the same name as an identifier in an inner block, the one in the outer block is "hidden" until the inner block terminates—the inner block "sees" its own local variable's value and not that of the enclosing block's identically named variable.

Common Programming Error 6.6

Accidentally using the same name for an identifier in an inner block that's used for an identifier in an outer block, when in fact you want the identifier in the outer block to be active for the duration of the inner block, is typically a logic error.

Error-Prevention Tip 6.9

Avoid variable names in inner scopes that hide names in outer scopes. Most compilers will warn you about this issue.

Local variables also may be declared `static`. Such variables also have block scope, but unlike other local variables, a `static` *local variable retains its value when the function returns to its caller.* The next time the function is called, the `static` local variable contains the value it had when the function last completed execution. The following statement declares `static` local variable `count` and initializes to 1:

```
static unsigned int count{1};
```

All `static` local variables of numeric types are initialized to zero by default. The following statement declares `static` local variable `count` and initializes it to 0:

```
static unsigned int count;
```

Global Namespace Scope

An identifier declared *outside* any function or class has *global namespace scope.* Such an identifier is "known" in all functions from the point at which it's declared until the end of the file. Function definitions, function prototypes placed outside a function, class definitions and global variables all have global namespace scope. Global variables are created by placing variable declarations *outside* any class or function definition. Such variables retain their values throughout a program's execution.

Software Engineering Observation 6.5

Declaring a variable as global rather than local allows unintended side effects to occur when a function that does not need access to the variable accidentally or maliciously modifies it. This is another example of the principle of least privilege—except for truly global resources such as cin and cout, global variables should be avoided. In general, variables should be declared in the narrowest scope in which they need to be accessed.

Software Engineering Observation 6.6

Variables used only in a particular function should be declared as local variables in that function rather than as global variables.

Scope Demonstration

Figure 6.11 demonstrates scoping issues with global variables, local variables and static local variables. Line 10 declares and initializes global variable x to 1. This global variable is hidden in any block (or function) that declares a variable named x. In main, line 13 displays the value of global variable x. Line 15 declares a local variable x and initializes it to 5. Line 17 outputs this variable to show that the global x is hidden in main. Next, lines 19–23 define a new block in main in which another local variable x is initialized to 7 (line 20). Line 22 outputs this variable to show that it *hides* x in the outer block of main as well as the global x. When the block exits, the variable x with value 7 is destroyed automatically. Next, line 25 outputs the local variable x in the outer block of main to show that it's *no longer hidden*.

```cpp
1   // Fig. 6.11: fig06_11.cpp
2   // Scoping example.
3   #include <iostream>
4   using namespace std;
5
6   void useLocal(); // function prototype
7   void useStaticLocal(); // function prototype
8   void useGlobal(); // function prototype
9
10  int x{1}; // global variable
11
12  int main() {
13     cout << "global x in main is " << x << endl;
14
15     int x{5}; // local variable to main
16
17     cout << "local x in main's outer scope is " << x << endl;
18
19     { // block starts a new scope
20        int x{7}; // hides both x in outer scope and global x
21
22        cout << "local x in main's inner scope is " << x << endl;
23     }
24
25     cout << "local x in main's outer scope is " << x << endl;
26
27     useLocal(); // useLocal has local x
28     useStaticLocal(); // useStaticLocal has static local x
29     useGlobal(); // useGlobal uses global x
30     useLocal(); // useLocal reinitializes its local x
31     useStaticLocal(); // static local x retains its prior value
32     useGlobal(); // global x also retains its prior value
33
34     cout << "\nlocal x in main is " << x << endl;
35  }
36
37  // useLocal reinitializes local variable x during each call
38  void useLocal() {
39     int x{25}; // initialized each time useLocal is called
```

Fig. 6.11 | Scoping example. (Part 1 of 2.)

```
40
41      cout << "\nlocal x is " << x << " on entering useLocal" << endl;
42      ++x;
43      cout << "local x is " << x << " on exiting useLocal" << endl;
44   }
45
46   // useStaticLocal initializes static local variable x only the
47   // first time the function is called; value of x is saved
48   // between calls to this function
49   void useStaticLocal() {
50      static int x{50}; // initialized first time useStaticLocal is called
51
52      cout << "\nlocal static x is " << x << " on entering useStaticLocal"
53         << endl;
54      ++x;
55      cout << "local static x is " << x << " on exiting useStaticLocal"
56         << endl;
57   }
58
59   // useGlobal modifies global variable x during each call
60   void useGlobal() {
61      cout << "\nglobal x is " << x << " on entering useGlobal" << endl;
62      x *= 10;
63      cout << "global x is " << x << " on exiting useGlobal" << endl;
64   }
```

```
global x in main is 1
local x in main's outer scope is 5
local x in main's inner scope is 7
local x in main's outer scope is 5

local x is 25 on entering useLocal
local x is 26 on exiting useLocal

local static x is 50 on entering useStaticLocal
local static x is 51 on exiting useStaticLocal

global x is 1 on entering useGlobal
global x is 10 on exiting useGlobal

local x is 25 on entering useLocal
local x is 26 on exiting useLocal

local static x is 51 on entering useStaticLocal
local static x is 52 on exiting useStaticLocal

global x is 10 on entering useGlobal
global x is 100 on exiting useGlobal

local x in main is 5
```

Fig. 6.11 | Scoping example. (Part 2 of 2.)

To demonstrate other scopes, the program defines three functions, each of which takes no arguments and returns nothing. Function useLocal (lines 38–44) declares local variable x (line 39) and initializes it to 25. When the program calls useLocal, the function prints the variable, increments it and prints it again before the function returns program control to its caller. Each time the program calls this function, the function *recreates* local variable x and *reinitializes* it to 25.

Function useStaticLocal (lines 49–57) declares static variable x and initializes it to 50. Local variables declared as static retain their values even when they're out of scope (i.e., the function in which they're declared is not executing). When the program calls useStaticLocal, the function prints x, increments it and prints it again before the function returns program control to its caller. In the next call to this function, static local variable x contains the value 51. The *initialization* in line 50 *occurs only once*—the first time useStaticLocal is called.

Function useGlobal (lines 60–64) does not declare any variables. Therefore, when it refers to variable x, the global x (line 10, preceding main) is used. When the program calls useGlobal, the function prints the global variable x, multiplies it by 10 and prints it again before the function returns to its caller. The next time the program calls useGlobal, the global variable has its modified value, 10. After executing functions useLocal, useStaticLocal and useGlobal twice each, the program prints the local variable x in main again to show that none of the function calls modified the value of x in main, because the functions all referred to variables in other scopes.

6.11 Function-Call Stack and Activation Records

To understand how C++ performs function calls, we first need to consider a data structure (i.e., collection of related data items) known as a stack. Think of a stack as analogous to a pile of dishes. When a dish is placed on the pile, it's normally placed at the *top*—referred to as pushing the dish onto the stack. Similarly, when a dish is removed from the pile, it's normally removed from the top—referred to as popping the dish off the stack. Stacks are known as last-in, first-out (LIFO) data structures—the last item pushed (inserted) on the stack is the first item popped (removed) from the stack.

Function-Call Stack
One of the most important mechanisms for computer science students to understand is the function-call stack (sometimes referred to as the program-execution stack). This data structure—working "behind the scenes"—supports the function call/return mechanism. It also supports the creation, maintenance and destruction of each called function's local variables. As we'll see in Figs. 6.13–6.15, last-in, first-out (LIFO) behavior is *exactly* what a function needs in order to return to the function that called it.

Stack Frames
As each function is called, it may, in turn, call other functions, which may, in turn, call other functions—all *before* any of the functions return. Each function eventually must return control to the function that called it. So, somehow, the system must keep track of the *return addresses* that each function needs to return control to the function that called it. The function-call stack is the perfect data structure for handling this information. Each time a function calls another function, an entry is *pushed* onto the stack. This entry, called a stack frame or an activation record, contains the *return address* that the called function needs in order to return to the calling function. It also contains some additional informa-

tion we'll soon discuss. If the called function returns instead of calling another function before returning, the stack frame for the function call is *popped*, and control transfers to the return address in the popped stack frame.

The beauty of the call stack is that each called function *always* finds the information it needs to return to its caller at the *top* of the call stack. And, if a function makes a call to another function, a stack frame for the new function call is simply *pushed* onto the call stack. Thus, the return address required by the newly called function to return to its caller is now located at the *top* of the stack.

Local Variables and Stack Frames

The stack frames have another important responsibility. Most functions have local variables—parameters and any local variables the function declares. Non-static local variables need to exist while a function is executing. They need to remain active if the function makes calls to other functions. But when a called function returns to its caller, the called function's non-static local variables need to "go away." The called function's stack frame is a perfect place to reserve the memory for the called function's non-static local variables. That stack frame exists as long as the called function is active. When that function returns—and no longer needs its non-static local variables—its stack frame is *popped* from the stack, and those non-static local variables no longer exist.

Stack Overflow

Of course, the amount of memory in a computer is finite, so only a certain amount of memory can be used to store activation records on the function-call stack. If more function calls occur than can have their activation records stored on the function-call stack, a fatal error known as stack overflow occurs.[3]

Function-Call Stack in Action

Now let's consider how the call stack supports the operation of a square function called by main (lines 9–13 of Fig. 6.12).

```cpp
1   // Fig. 6.12: fig06_12.cpp
2   // square function used to demonstrate the function
3   // call stack and activation records.
4   #include <iostream>
5   using namespace std;
6
7   int square(int); // prototype for function square
8
9   int main() {
10     int a{10}; // value to square (local variable in main)
11
12     cout << a << " squared: " << square(a) << endl; // display a squared
13  }
```

Fig. 6.12 | square function used to demonstrate the function-call stack and activation records. (Part 1 of 2.)

---

3. This is how the website stackoverflow.com got its name. This is a great website for getting answers to your programming questions.

```
14
15   // returns the square of an integer
16   int square(int x) { // x is a local variable
17       return x * x; // calculate square and return result
18   }
```

```
10 squared: 100
```

Fig. 6.12 | square function used to demonstrate the function-call stack and activation records. (Part 2 of 2.)

First, the operating system calls main—this *pushes* an activation record onto the stack (shown in Fig. 6.13). The activation record tells main how to return to the operating system (i.e., transfer to return address R1) and contains the space for main's local variable (i.e., a, which is initialized to 10).

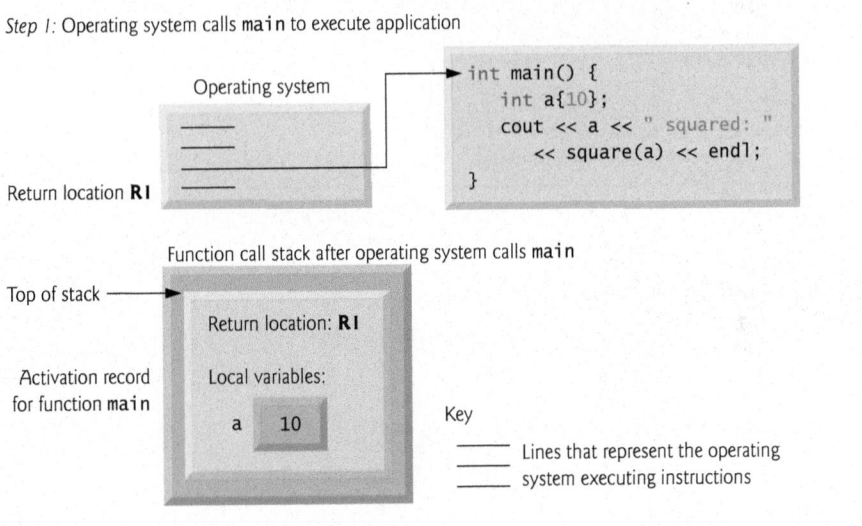

Fig. 6.13 | Function-call stack after the operating system calls main to execute the program.

Function main—before returning to the operating system—now calls function square in line 12 of Fig. 6.12. This causes a stack frame for square (lines 16–18) to be pushed onto the function-call stack (Fig. 6.14). This stack frame contains the return address that square needs to return to main (i.e., R2) and the memory for square's local variable (i.e., x).

After square calculates the square of its argument, it needs to return to main—and no longer needs the memory for its variable x. So square's stack frame is *popped* from the stack—giving square the return location in main (i.e., R2) and losing square's local variable (*Step 3*). Figure 6.15 shows the function-call stack *after* square's activation record has been *popped*.

Step 2: **main** calls function **square** to perform calculation

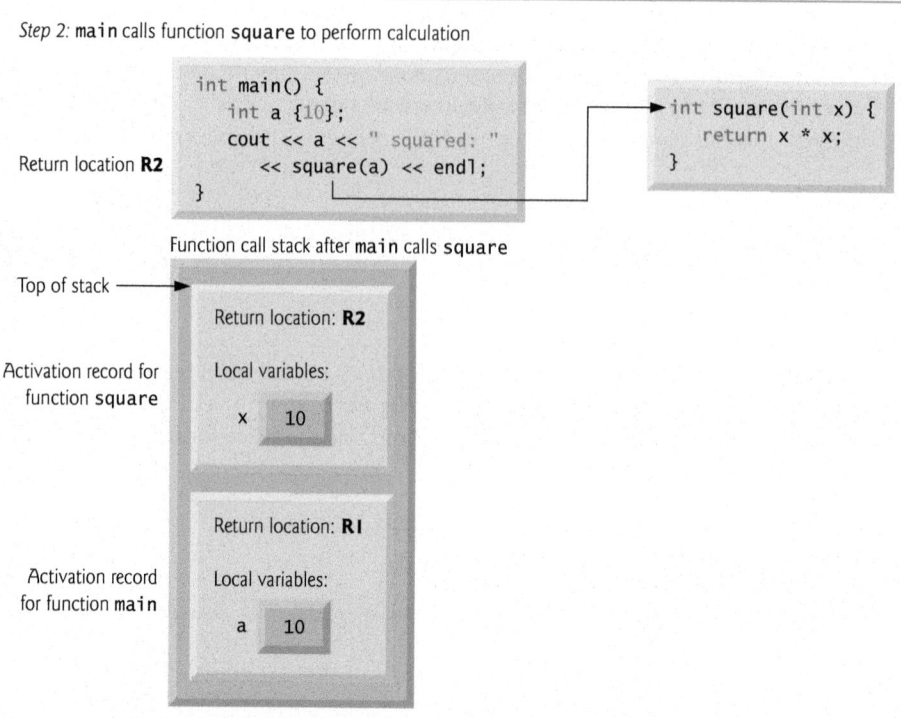

Fig. 6.14 | Function-call stack after **main** calls **square** to perform the calculation.

Step 3: **square** returns its result to **main**

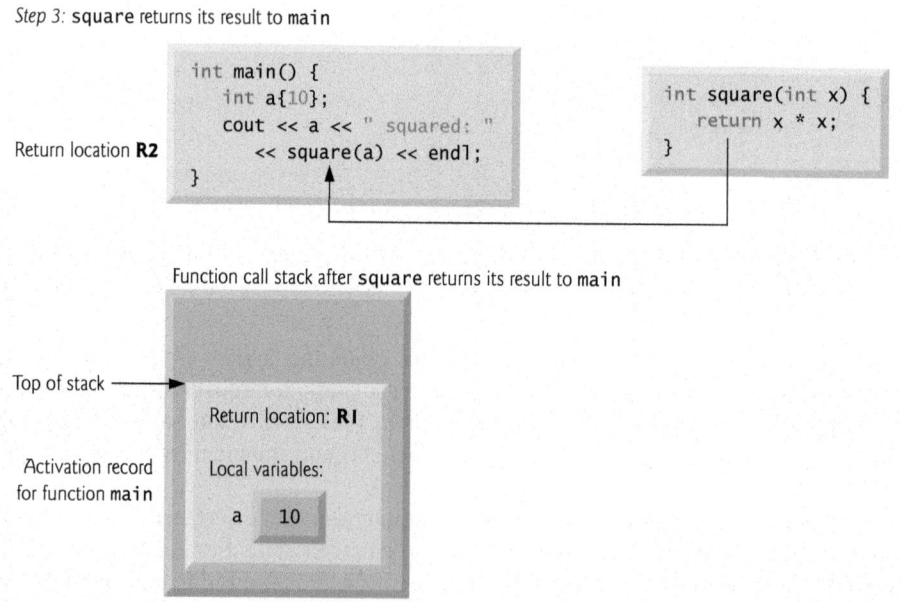

Fig. 6.15 | Function-call stack after function **square** returns to **main**.

Function main now displays the result of calling square (Fig. 6.12, line 12). Reaching the closing right brace of main causes its stack frame to be *popped* from the stack, giving main the address it needs to return to the operating system (i.e., R1 in Fig. 6.13)—at this point, main's local variable (i.e., a) no longer exists.

You've now seen how valuable the stack data structure is in implementing a key mechanism that supports program execution. Data structures have many important applications in computer science. We discuss stacks, queues, lists, trees and other data structures in Chapter 15, Standard Library Containers and Iterators, and Chapter 19, Custom Templatized Data Structures.

6.12 Inline Functions

Implementing a program as a set of functions is good from a software engineering standpoint, but function calls involve execution-time overhead. C++ provides inline functions to help reduce function-call overhead. Placing the qualifier inline before a function's return type in the function definition *advises* the compiler to generate a copy of the function's body code in *every* place where the function is called (when appropriate) to avoid a function call. This often makes the program larger. The compiler can ignore the inline qualifier and generally does so for all but the *smallest* functions. Reusable inline functions are typically placed in headers, so that their definitions can be included in each source file that uses them.

Software Engineering Observation 6.7
If you change the definition of an inline function, you must recompile all of that function's clients.

Performance Tip 6.1
Compilers can inline code for which you have not explicitly used the inline keyword. Today's optimizing compilers are so sophisticated that it's best to leave inlining decisions to the compiler.

Figure 6.16 uses inline function cube (lines 9–11) to calculate the volume of a cube. Keyword const in function cube's parameter list (line 9) tells the compiler that the function does *not* modify variable side. This ensures that side's value is *not* changed by the function during the calculation. (Keyword const is discussed in additional detail in Chapters 7–9.)

Software Engineering Observation 6.8
The const qualifier should be used to enforce the principle of least privilege. Using this principle to properly design software can greatly reduce debugging time and improper side effects and can make a program easier to modify and maintain.

```
1   // Fig. 6.16: fig06_16.cpp
2   // inline function that calculates the volume of a cube.
3   #include <iostream>
4   using namespace std;
```

Fig. 6.16 | inline function that calculates the volume of a cube. (Part 1 of 2.)

```
 5
 6    // Definition of inline function cube. Definition of function appears
 7    // before function is called, so a function prototype is not required.
 8    // First line of function definition acts as the prototype.
 9    inline double cube(const double side) {
10        return side * side * side; // calculate cube
11    }
12
13    int main() {
14        double sideValue; // stores value entered by user
15        cout << "Enter the side length of your cube: ";
16        cin >> sideValue; // read value from user
17
18        // calculate cube of sideValue and display result
19        cout << "Volume of cube with side "
20            << sideValue << " is " << cube(sideValue) << endl;
21    }
```

```
Enter the side length of your cube: 3.5
Volume of cube with side 3.5 is 42.875
```

Fig. 6.16 | inline function that calculates the volume of a cube. (Part 2 of 2.)

6.13 References and Reference Parameters

Two ways to pass arguments to functions in many programming languages are pass-by-value and pass-by-reference. When an argument is passed by value, a *copy* of the argument's value is made and passed (on the function-call stack) to the called function. Changes to the copy do *not* affect the original variable's value in the caller. This prevents the *accidental side effects* that so greatly hinder the development of correct and reliable software systems. So far, each argument in the book has been passed by value.

Performance Tip 6.2
One disadvantage of pass-by-value is that, if a large data item is being passed, copying that data can take a considerable amount of execution time and memory space.

Reference Parameters

This section introduces reference parameters—the first of the two means C++ provides for performing pass-by-reference. With *pass-by-reference*, the caller gives the called function the ability to *access the caller's data directly*, and to *modify* that data.

Performance Tip 6.3
Pass-by-reference is good for performance reasons, because it can eliminate the pass-by-value overhead of copying large amounts of data.

Software Engineering Observation 6.9
Pass-by-reference can weaken security; the called function can corrupt the caller's data.

After this section's example, we'll show how to achieve the performance advantage of pass-by-reference while *simultaneously* achieving the software engineering advantage of protecting the caller's data from corruption.

A reference parameter is an *alias* for its corresponding argument in a function call. To indicate that a function parameter is passed by reference, simply follow the parameter's type in the function prototype by an *ampersand (&)*; use the same convention when listing the parameter's type in the function header. For example, the parameter declaration

```
int& number
```

when read from *right to left* is pronounced "number is a reference to an int." In the function call, simply mention the variable by name (e.g., number) to pass it by reference. In the called function's body, the reference parameter actually refers to the *original variable* in the calling function, and the original variable can be *modified* directly by the called function. As always, the function prototype and header must agree. Note the placement of & in the preceding declaration—some C++ programmers prefer to write the equivalent form int &number.[4]

Passing Arguments by Value and by Reference

Figure 6.17 compares pass-by-value and pass-by-reference with reference parameters. The "styles" of the arguments in the calls to function squareByValue and function squareByReference are identical—both variables are simply mentioned by name in the function calls. *Without checking the function prototypes or function definitions, it isn't possible to tell from the calls alone whether either function can modify its arguments.* Because function prototypes are *mandatory*, the compiler has no trouble resolving the ambiguity. Chapter 8 discusses *pointers*, which enable an alternate form of pass-by-reference in which the style of the function call clearly indicates pass-by-reference (and the potential for modifying the caller's arguments).

Common Programming Error 6.7

Because reference parameters are mentioned only by name in the body of the called function, you might inadvertently treat reference parameters as pass-by-value parameters. This can cause unexpected side effects if the original variables are changed by the function.

```
 1   // Fig. 6.17: fig06_17cpp
 2   // Passing arguments by value and by reference.
 3   #include <iostream>
 4   using namespace std;
 5
 6   int squareByValue(int); // function prototype (value pass)
 7   void squareByReference(int&); // function prototype (reference pass)
 8
 9   int main() {
10      int x{2}; // value to square using squareByValue
11      int z{4}; // value to square using squareByReference
```

Fig. 6.17 | Passing arguments by value and by reference. (Part 1 of 2.)

---

4. We used this placement in our prior editions. We now attach the & to the type name to normalize our book with the C++ standard.

```
12
13    // demonstrate squareByValue
14    cout << "x = " << x << " before squareByValue\n";
15    cout << "Value returned by squareByValue: "
16       << squareByValue(x) << endl;
17    cout << "x = " << x << " after squareByValue\n" << endl;
18
19    // demonstrate squareByReference
20    cout << "z = " << z << " before squareByReference" << endl;
21    squareByReference(z);
22    cout << "z = " << z << " after squareByReference" << endl;
23 }
24
25 // squareByValue multiplies number by itself, stores the
26 // result in number and returns the new value of number
27 int squareByValue(int number) {
28    return number *= number; // caller's argument not modified
29 }
30
31 // squareByReference multiplies numberRef by itself and stores the result
32 // in the variable to which numberRef refers in function main
33 void squareByReference(int& numberRef) {
34    numberRef *= numberRef; // caller's argument modified
35 }
```

```
x = 2 before squareByValue
Value returned by squareByValue: 4
x = 2 after squareByValue

z = 4 before squareByReference
z = 16 after squareByReference
```

Fig. 6.17 | Passing arguments by value and by reference. (Part 2 of 2.)

References as Aliases within a Function

References can also be used as aliases for other variables *within* a function (although they typically are used with functions as shown in Fig. 6.17). For example, the code

```
int count{1}; // declare integer variable count
int& cRef{count}; // create cRef as an alias for count
++cRef; // increment count (using its alias cRef)
```

increments variable count by using its alias cRef. Reference variables *must* be initialized in their declarations and *cannot* be reassigned as aliases to other variables. In this sense, references are *constant*. All operations supposedly performed on the *alias* (i.e., the reference) are actually performed on the *original* variable. The alias is simply another name for the original variable. Unless it's a reference to a constant (discussed below), a reference's initializer must be an *lvalue* (e.g., a variable name), not a constant or *rvalue* expression (e.g., the result of a calculation).

const References

To specify that a reference parameter should not be allowed to modify the corresponding argument, place the const qualifier *before* the type name in the parameter's declaration.

For example, consider class `Account` (Fig. 3.2). For simplicity in that early example, we used pass-by-value in the `setName` member function, which was defined with the header

```
void setName(std::string accountName)
```

When this member function was called, it received a copy of its `string` argument. `string` objects can be large, so this copy operation degrades an application's performance.

For this reason, `string` objects (and objects in general) should be passed to functions by reference. Class `Account`'s `setName` member function does not need to modify its argument, so following the principle of least privilege, we'd declare the parameter as

```
const std::string& accountName
```

Read from right to left, the `accountName` parameter is a reference to a *string constant*. We get the performance of passing the `string` by reference, but `setName` treats the argument as a constant, so it cannot modify the value in the caller—just like with pass-by-value. Code that calls `setName` would still pass the `string` argument exactly as we did in Fig. 3.1.

Performance Tip 6.4

For passing large objects, use a `const` reference parameter to simulate the appearance and security of pass-by-value and avoid the overhead of passing a copy of the large object.

Similarly, class `Account`'s `getName` member function was defined with the header

```
std::string getName() const
```

which indicates that a `string` is returned by value. Changing this to

```
const std::string& getName() const
```

indicates that the `string` should be returned by reference (eliminating the overhead of copying a `string`) and that the caller cannot modify the returned `string`.

Returning a Reference to a Local Variable

Functions can return references to local variables, but this can be dangerous. When returning a reference to a local variable—unless that variable is declared `static`—the reference refers to a variable that's *discarded* when the function terminates. An attempt to access such a variable yields *undefined behavior*. References to undefined variables are called dangling references.

Common Programming Error 6.8

Returning a reference to a local variable in a called function is a logic error for which compilers typically issue a warning. Compilation warnings indicate potential problems, so most software-engineering teams have policies requiring code to compile without warnings.

6.14 Default Arguments

It's common for a program to invoke a function repeatedly with the *same* argument value for a particular parameter. In such cases, you can specify that such a parameter has a default argument, i.e., a default value to be passed to that parameter. When a program *omits* an argument for a parameter with a default argument in a function call, the compiler rewrites the function call and inserts the default value of that argument.

boxVolume *Function with Default Arguments*

Figure 6.18 demonstrates using default arguments to calculate a box's volume. The function prototype for boxVolume (lines 7–8) specifies that all three parameters have default values of 1 by placing = 1 to the right of each parameter. We provided variable names in the function prototype as documentation, so a programmer using this function understands the purpose of each parameter—recall that parameter names are *not* required in function prototypes.

```cpp
 1   // Fig. 6.18: fig06_18.cpp
 2   // Using default arguments.
 3   #include <iostream>
 4   using namespace std;
 5
 6   // function prototype that specifies default arguments
 7   unsigned int boxVolume(unsigned int length = 1, unsigned int width = 1,
 8      unsigned int height = 1);
 9
10   int main() {
11      // no arguments--use default values for all dimensions
12      cout << "The default box volume is: " << boxVolume();
13
14      // specify length; default width and height
15      cout << "\n\nThe volume of a box with length 10,\n"
16         << "width 1 and height 1 is: " << boxVolume(10);
17
18      // specify length and width; default height
19      cout << "\n\nThe volume of a box with length 10,\n"
20         << "width 5 and height 1 is: " << boxVolume(10, 5);
21
22      // specify all arguments
23      cout << "\n\nThe volume of a box with length 10,\n"
24         << "width 5 and height 2 is: " << boxVolume(10, 5, 2)
25         << endl;
26   }
27
28   // function boxVolume calculates the volume of a box
29   unsigned int boxVolume(unsigned int length, unsigned int width,
30      unsigned int height) {
31      return length * width * height;
32   }
```

```
The default box volume is: 1

The volume of a box with length 10,
width 1 and height 1 is: 10

The volume of a box with length 10,
width 5 and height 1 is: 50

The volume of a box with length 10,
width 5 and height 2 is: 100
```

Fig. 6.18 | Using default arguments.

The first call to boxVolume (line 12) specifies no arguments, thus using all three default values of 1. The second call (line 16) passes only a length argument, thus using default values of 1 for the width and height arguments. The third call (line 20) passes arguments for only length and width, thus using a default value of 1 for the height argument. The last call (line 24) passes arguments for length, width and height, thus using no default values. Any arguments passed to the function explicitly are assigned to the function's parameters from left to right. Therefore, when boxVolume receives one argument, the function assigns the value of that argument to its length parameter (i.e., the leftmost parameter in the parameter list). When boxVolume receives two arguments, the function assigns the values of those arguments to its length and width parameters in that order. Finally, when boxVolume receives all three arguments, the function assigns the values of those arguments to its length, width and height parameters, respectively.

Notes Regarding Default Arguments

Default arguments *must* be the rightmost (trailing) arguments in a function's parameter list. When calling a function with two or more default arguments, if an omitted argument is *not* the rightmost argument, then all arguments to the right of that argument also *must* be omitted. Default arguments must be specified with the *first* occurrence of the function name—typically, in the function prototype. If the function prototype is omitted because the function definition also serves as the prototype, then the default arguments should be specified in the function header. Default values can be any expression, including constants, global variables or function calls. Default arguments also can be used with inline functions.

Good Programming Practice 6.4
Using default arguments can simplify writing function calls. However, some programmers feel that explicitly specifying all arguments is clearer.

6.15 Unary Scope Resolution Operator

C++ provides the unary scope resolution operator (::) to access a global variable when a local variable of the same name is in scope.[5] The unary scope resolution operator cannot be used to access a *local* variable of the same name in an outer block. A global variable can be accessed directly without the unary scope resolution operator if the name of the global variable is not the same as that of a local variable in scope.

Figure 6.19 shows the unary scope resolution operator with local and global variables of the same name (lines 6 and 9). To emphasize that the local and global versions of variable number are distinct, the program declares one variable int and the other double.

```
1   // Fig. 6.19: fig06_19.cpp
2   // Unary scope resolution operator.
3   #include <iostream>
4   using namespace std;
```

Fig. 6.19 | Unary scope resolution operator. (Part 1 of 2.)

---

5.   The C++ standard also refers to the scope resolution operator (::) as the scope operator.

```
 5
 6   int number{7}; // global variable named number
 7
 8   int main() {
 9      double number{10.5}; // local variable named number
10
11      // display values of local and global variables
12      cout << "Local double value of number = " << number
13         << "\nGlobal int value of number = " << ::number << endl;
14   }
```

```
Local double value of number = 10.5
Global int value of number = 7
```

Fig. 6.19 | Unary scope resolution operator. (Part 2 of 2.)

Good Programming Practice 6.5

Always using the unary scope resolution operator (::) to refer to global variables (even if there is no collision with a local-variable name) makes it clear that you're intending to access a global variable rather than a local variable.

Software Engineering Observation 6.10

Always using the unary scope resolution operator (::) to refer to global variables makes programs easier to modify by reducing the risk of name collisions with nonglobal variables.

Error-Prevention Tip 6.10

Always using the unary scope resolution operator (::) to refer to a global variable eliminates logic errors that might occur if a nonglobal variable hides the global variable.

Error-Prevention Tip 6.11

Avoid using variables of the same name for different purposes in a program. Although this is allowed in various circumstances, it can lead to errors.

6.16 Function Overloading

C++ enables several functions of the same name to be defined, as long as they have different signatures. This is called function overloading. The C++ compiler selects the proper function to call by examining the number, types and order of the arguments in the call. Function overloading is used to create several functions of the *same* name that perform similar tasks, but on *different* data types. For example, many functions in the math library are overloaded for different numeric types—the C++ standard requires float, double and long double overloaded versions of the math library functions discussed in Section 6.3.

Good Programming Practice 6.6

Overloading functions that perform closely related tasks can make programs more readable and understandable.

*Overloaded **square** Functions*

Figure 6.20 uses overloaded `square` functions to calculate the square of an `int` (lines 7–10) and the square of a `double` (lines 13–16). Line 19 invokes the `int` version of function `square` by passing the literal value 7. C++ treats whole-number literal values as type `int`. Similarly, line 21 invokes the `double` version of function `square` by passing the literal value 7.5, which C++ treats as a `double`. In each case the compiler chooses the proper function to call, based on the type of the argument. The last two lines of the output window confirm that the proper function was called in each case.

```cpp
1   // Fig. 6.20: fig06_20.cpp
2   // Overloaded square functions.
3   #include <iostream>
4   using namespace std;
5
6   // function square for int values
7   int square(int x) {
8      cout << "square of integer " << x << " is ";
9      return x * x;
10  }
11
12  // function square for double values
13  double square(double y) {
14     cout << "square of double " << y << " is ";
15     return y * y;
16  }
17
18  int main() {
19     cout << square(7); // calls int version
20     cout << endl;
21     cout << square(7.5); // calls double version
22     cout << endl;
23  }
```

```
square of integer 7 is 49
square of double 7.5 is 56.25
```

Fig. 6.20 | Overloaded square functions.

How the Compiler Differentiates Among Overloaded Functions

Overloaded functions are distinguished by their *signatures*. A signature is a combination of a function's name and its parameter types (in order). The compiler encodes each function identifier with the types of its parameters (sometimes referred to as name mangling or name decoration) to enable type-safe linkage. Type-safe linkage ensures that the proper overloaded function is called and that the types of the arguments conform to the types of the parameters. Figure 6.21 was compiled with GNU C++. Rather than showing the execution output of the program (as we normally would), we show the mangled function names produced in assembly language by GNU C++.

For GNU C++, each mangled name (other than `main`) begins with two underscores (__) followed by the letter Z, a number and the function name. The number that follows Z specifies how many characters are in the function's name. For example, function `square`

```
 1    // Fig. 6.21: fig06_21.cpp
 2    // Name mangling to enable type-safe linkage.
 3
 4    // function square for int values
 5    int square(int x) {
 6        return x * x;
 7    }
 8
 9    // function square for double values
10    double square(double y) {
11        return y * y;
12    }
13
14    // function that receives arguments of types
15    // int, float, char and int&
16    void nothing1(int a, float b, char c, int& d) { }
17
18    // function that receives arguments of types
19    // char, int, float& and double&
20    int nothing2(char a, int b, float& c, double& d) {
21        return 0;
22    }
23
24    int main() { }
```

```
__Z6squarei
__Z6squared
__Z8nothing1ifcRi
__Z8nothing2ciRfRd
main
```

Fig. 6.21 | Name mangling to enable type-safe linkage.

has 6 characters in its name, so its mangled name is prefixed with __Z6. Following the function name is an encoding of its parameter list:

- For function square that receives an int (line 5), i represents int, as shown in the output's first line.

- For function square that receives a double (line 10), d represents double, as shown in the output's second line.

- For function nothing1 (line 16), i represents an int, f represents a float, c represents a char and Ri represents an int& (i.e., a reference to an int), as shown in the output's third line.

- For function nothing2 (line 20), c represents a char, i represents an int, Rf represents a float& and Rd represents a double&.

The compiler distinguishes the two square functions by their parameter lists—one specifies i for int and the other d for double. The return types of the functions are *not* specified in the mangled names. *Overloaded functions can have different return types, but if they do, they must also have different parameter lists.* Function-name mangling is compiler specific. For example, Visual C++ produces the name square@@YAHH@Z for the square function at line 5. The GNU C++ compiler did not mangle main's name; however, some compilers do. For example, Visual C++ uses _main.

Common Programming Error 6.9
Creating overloaded functions with identical parameter lists and different return types is a compilation error.

The compiler uses only the parameter lists to distinguish between overloaded functions. Such functions need *not* have the same number of parameters. Use caution when overloading functions with default parameters, because this may cause ambiguity.

Common Programming Error 6.10
A function with default arguments omitted might be called identically to another overloaded function; this is a compilation error. For example, having a program that contains both a function that explicitly takes no arguments and a function of the same name that contains all default arguments results in a compilation error when an attempt is made to use that function name in a call passing no arguments. The compiler cannot determine which version of the function to choose.

Overloaded Operators

In Chapter 10, we discuss how to overload *operators* to define how they should operate on objects of user-defined data types. (In fact, we've been using many overloaded operators to this point, including the stream insertion << and the stream extraction >> operators, which are overloaded for *all* the fundamental types. We say more about overloading << and >> to be able to handle objects of user-defined types in Chapter 10.)

6.17 Function Templates

Overloaded functions are normally used to perform *similar* operations that involve *different* program logic on different data types. If the program logic and operations are *identical* for each data type, overloading may be performed more compactly and conveniently by using function templates. You write a single function template definition. Given the argument types provided in calls to this function, C++ automatically generates separate function template specializations to handle each type of call appropriately. Thus, defining a single function template essentially defines a whole family of overloaded functions.

maximum *Function Template*

Figure 6.22 defines a maximum function template (lines 3–18) that determines the largest of three values. All function template definitions begin with the template keyword (line 3) followed by a template parameter list enclosed in angle brackets (< and >). Every parameter in the template parameter list is preceded by keyword typename or keyword class (they are synonyms in this context). The type parameters are placeholders for fundamental types or user-defined types. These placeholders, in this case, T, are used to specify the types of the function's parameters (line 4), to specify the function's return type (line 4) and to declare variables within the body of the function definition (line 5). A function template is defined like any other function, but uses the type parameters as *placeholders* for actual data types.

```
 1   // Fig. 6.22: maximum.h
 2   // Function template maximum header.
 3   template <typename T>  // or template<class T>
 4   T maximum(T value1, T value2, T value3) {
 5      T maximumValue{value1}; // assume value1 is maximum
 6
 7      // determine whether value2 is greater than maximumValue
 8      if (value2 > maximumValue) {
 9         maximumValue = value2;
10      }
11
12      // determine whether value3 is greater than maximumValue
13      if (value3 > maximumValue) {
14         maximumValue = value3;
15      }
16
17      return maximumValue;
18   }
```

Fig. 6.22 | Function template maximum header.

The function template declares a single type parameter T (line 3) as a placeholder for the type of the data to be tested by function maximum. The name of a type parameter must be *unique* in the template parameter list for a particular template definition. When the compiler detects a maximum invocation in the program source code, the *type* of the arguments in the maximum call is substituted for T throughout the template definition, and C++ creates a complete function for determining the maximum of three values of the specified type—all three must have the same type, since we use only one type parameter in this example. Then the newly created function is compiled—templates are a means of *code generation*. (We'll use C++ Standard Library templates that require multiple type parameters in Chapter 15.)

Using Function Template maximum
Figure 6.23 uses the maximum function template to determine the largest of three int values, three double values and three char values, respectively (lines 15, 24 and 33). Because each call uses arguments of a different type, the compiler creates a separate function definition for each—one expecting three int values, one expecting three double values and one expecting three char values, respectively.

```
 1   // Fig. 6.23: fig06_23.cpp
 2   // Function template maximum test program.
 3   #include <iostream>
 4   #include "maximum.h" // include definition of function template maximum
 5   using namespace std;
 6
 7   int main() {
 8      // demonstrate maximum with int values
 9      cout << "Input three integer values: ";
10      int int1, int2, int3;
11      cin >> int1 >> int2 >> int3;
```

Fig. 6.23 | Function template maximum test program. (Part 1 of 2.)

```
12
13      // invoke int version of maximum
14      cout << "The maximum integer value is: "
15         << maximum(int1, int2, int3);
16
17      // demonstrate maximum with double values
18      cout << "\n\nInput three double values: ";
19      double double1, double2, double3;
20      cin >> double1 >> double2 >> double3;
21
22      // invoke double version of maximum
23      cout << "The maximum double value is: "
24         << maximum(double1, double2, double3);
25
26      // demonstrate maximum with char values
27      cout << "\n\nInput three characters: ";
28      char char1, char2, char3;
29      cin >> char1 >> char2 >> char3;
30
31      // invoke char version of maximum
32      cout << "The maximum character value is: "
33         << maximum(char1, char2, char3) << endl;
34   }
```

```
Input three integer values: 1 2 3
The maximum integer value is: 3

Input three double values: 3.3 2.2 1.1
The maximum double value is: 3.3

Input three characters: A C B
The maximum character value is: C
```

Fig. 6.23 | Function template maximum test program. (Part 2 of 2.)

maximum *Function Template Specialization for Type* int

The *function template specialization* created for type int replaces each occurrence of T with int as follows:

```
int maximum(int value1, int value2, int value3) {
   int maximumValue{value1}; // assume value1 is maximum

   // determine whether value2 is greater than maximumValue
   if (value2 > maximumValue) {
      maximumValue = value2;
   }

   // determine whether value3 is greater than maximumValue
   if (value3 > maximumValue) {
      maximumValue = value3;
   }

   return maximumValue;
}
```

6.18 Recursion

For some problems, it's useful to have functions *call themselves*. A recursive function is a function that calls itself, either directly, or indirectly (through another function). [*Note:* The C++ standard document indicates that main should not be called within a program or recursively. Its sole purpose is to be the starting point for program execution.] This section and the next present simple examples of recursion. Recursion is discussed at length in upper-level computer science courses. Figure 6.29 (at the end of Section 6.20) summarizes the extensive recursion examples and exercises in the book.

Recursion Concepts

We first consider recursion conceptually, then examine programs containing recursive functions. Recursive problem-solving approaches have a number of elements in common. A recursive function is called to solve a problem. The function knows how to solve only the *simplest case(s)*, or so-called base case(s). If the function is called with a base case, the function simply returns a result. If the function is called with a more complex problem, it typically divides the problem into two conceptual pieces—a piece that the function knows how to do and a piece that it does not know how to do. To make recursion feasible, the latter piece *must* resemble the original problem, but be a slightly simpler or smaller version. This new problem looks like the original, so the function calls a copy of itself to work on the smaller problem—this is referred to as a recursive call and is also called the recursion step. The recursion step often includes the keyword return, because its result will be combined with the portion of the problem the function knew how to solve to form the result passed back to the original caller, possibly main.

Common Programming Error 6.11

Omitting the base case or writing the recursion step incorrectly so that it does not converge on the base case causes an infinite recursion error, typically causing a stack overflow. This is analogous to the problem of an infinite loop in an iterative (nonrecursive) solution.

The recursion step executes while the original call to the function is still "open," i.e., it has not yet finished executing. The recursion step can result in many more such recursive calls, as the function keeps dividing each new subproblem with which the function is called into two conceptual pieces. In order for the recursion to eventually terminate, each time the function calls itself with a slightly simpler version of the original problem, this sequence of smaller and smaller problems must eventually *converge* on the base case. At that point, the function recognizes the base case and returns a result to the previous copy of the function, and a sequence of returns ensues up the line until the original call eventually returns the final result to main. This sounds quite exotic compared to the kind of problem solving we've been using to this point. As an example of these concepts at work, let's write a recursive program to perform a popular mathematical calculation.

Factorial

The factorial of a nonnegative integer n, written $n!$ (pronounced "n factorial"), is the product

$$n \cdot (n-1) \cdot (n-2) \cdot \ldots \cdot 1$$

with 1! equal to 1, and 0! defined to be 1. For example, 5! is the product $5 \cdot 4 \cdot 3 \cdot 2 \cdot 1$, which is equal to 120.

Iterative Factorial

The factorial of an integer, number, greater than or equal to 0, can be calculated iteratively (nonrecursively) by using a for statement as follows:

```
factorial = 1;
for (unsigned int counter{number}; counter >= 1; --counter) {
    factorial *= counter;
}
```

Recursive Factorial

A *recursive* definition of the factorial function is arrived at by observing the following algebraic relationship:

$$n! = n \cdot (n-1)!$$

For example, 5! is clearly equal to 5 * 4! as is shown by the following:

$$5! = 5 \cdot 4 \cdot 3 \cdot 2 \cdot 1$$
$$5! = 5 \cdot (4 \cdot 3 \cdot 2 \cdot 1)$$
$$5! = 5 \cdot (4!)$$

Evaluating 5!

The evaluation of 5! would proceed as shown in Fig. 6.24, which illustrates how the succession of recursive calls proceeds until 1! is evaluated to be 1, terminating the recursion. Figure 6.24(b) shows the values returned from each recursive call to its caller until the final value is calculated and returned.

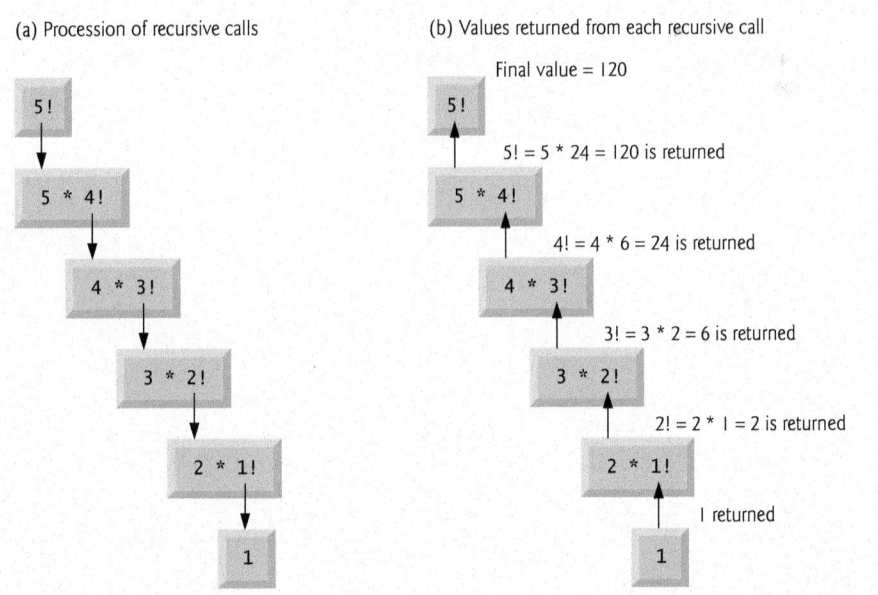

(a) Procession of recursive calls

(b) Values returned from each recursive call

Final value = 120

5! = 5 * 24 = 120 is returned

4! = 4 * 6 = 24 is returned

3! = 3 * 2 = 6 is returned

2! = 2 * 1 = 2 is returned

1 returned

Fig. 6.24 | Recursive evaluation of 5!.

Using a Recursive *factorial* Function to Calculate Factorials

Figure 6.25 uses recursion to calculate and print the factorials of the integers 0–10. (The choice of the data type unsigned long is explained momentarily.) The recursive function factorial (lines 18–25) first determines whether the *terminating condition* number <= 1 (i.e., the base case; line 19) is *true*. If number is less than or equal to 1, the factorial function returns 1 (line 20), no further recursion is necessary and the function terminates. If number is greater than 1, line 23 expresses the problem as the product of number and a *recursive call* to factorial evaluating the factorial of number - 1, which is a slightly *simpler* problem than the original calculation factorial(number).

```cpp
1   // Fig. 6.25: fig06_25.cpp
2   // Recursive function factorial.
3   #include <iostream>
4   #include <iomanip>
5   using namespace std;
6
7   unsigned long factorial(unsigned long); // function prototype
8
9   int main() {
10     // calculate the factorials of 0 through 10
11     for (unsigned int counter{0}; counter <= 10; ++counter) {
12        cout << setw(2) << counter << "! = " << factorial(counter)
13           << endl;
14     }
15  }
16
17  // recursive definition of function factorial
18  unsigned long factorial(unsigned long number) {
19     if (number <= 1) { // test for base case
20        return 1; // base cases: 0! = 1 and 1! = 1
21     }
22     else { // recursion step
23        return number * factorial(number - 1);
24     }
25  }
```

```
 0! = 1
 1! = 1
 2! = 2
 3! = 6
 4! = 24
 5! = 120
 6! = 720
 7! = 5040
 8! = 40320
 9! = 362880
10! = 3628800
```

Fig. 6.25 | Recursive function factorial.

Why We Chose Type *unsigned long* in This Example

Function factorial has been declared to receive a parameter of type unsigned long and return a result of type unsigned long. This is shorthand notation for unsigned long int.

The C++ standard requires that a variable of type unsigned long int be *at least as big as* an int. Typically, an unsigned long int is stored in at least four bytes (32 bits); such a variable can hold a value in the range 0 to at least 4,294,967,295. (A long int is also typically stored in at least four bytes and can hold a value at least in the range –2,147,483,647 to 2,147,483,647.) As can be seen in Fig. 6.25, factorial values become large quickly. We chose the data type unsigned long so that the program can calculate factorials greater than 7! on computers with small (such as two-byte) integers. Unfortunately, the function factorial produces large values so quickly that even unsigned long does not help us compute many factorial values before even the size of an unsigned long variable is exceeded.

C++11 Type unsigned long long int

C++11's unsigned long long int type (which can be abbreviated as unsigned long long) enables you to store values in at least 8 bytes (64 bits), which can hold numbers as large as 18,446,744,073,709,551,615.

11

Representing Even Larger Numbers

Variables of type double could be used to calculate factorials of larger numbers, but as you know, doubles cannot represent all values precisely. As we'll see when we discuss object-oriented programming in more depth, C++ allows us to create classes that can represent arbitrarily large integers. Such classes already are available in popular class libraries, and we work on similar classes of our own in Exercise 9.14 and Exercise 10.9.

6.19 Example Using Recursion: Fibonacci Series

The Fibonacci series

> 0, 1, 1, 2, 3, 5, 8, 13, 21, …

begins with 0 and 1 and has the property that each subsequent Fibonacci number is the sum of the previous two Fibonacci numbers.

The series occurs in nature and, in particular, describes a form of spiral. The ratio of successive Fibonacci numbers converges on a constant value of 1.618…. This number frequently occurs in nature and has been called the golden ratio or the golden mean. Humans tend to find the golden mean aesthetically pleasing. Architects often design windows, rooms and buildings whose length and width are in the ratio of the golden mean. Postcards are often designed with a golden mean length/width ratio. A web search for "Fibonacci in nature" reveals many interesting examples, including flower petals, shells, spiral galaxies, hurricanes and more.

Recursive Fibonacci Definition

The Fibonacci series can be defined recursively as follows:

> fibonacci(0) = 0
> fibonacci(1) = 1
> fibonacci(n) = fibonacci(n – 1) + fibonacci(n – 2)

The program of Fig. 6.26 calculates the nth Fibonacci number recursively by using function fibonacci. Fibonacci numbers tend to become large quickly, although slower than factorials do. Therefore, we chose the data type unsigned long for the parameter type and the return type in function `fibonacci`. Figure 6.26 shows the execution of the program, which displays the Fibonacci values for several numbers.

```cpp
1   // Fig. 6.26: fig06_26.cpp
2   // Recursive function fibonacci.
3   #include <iostream>
4   using namespace std;
5
6   unsigned long fibonacci(unsigned long); // function prototype
7
8   int main() {
9      // calculate the fibonacci values of 0 through 10
10     for (unsigned int counter{0}; counter <= 10; ++counter)
11        cout << "fibonacci(" << counter << ") = "
12           << fibonacci(counter) << endl;
13
14     // display higher fibonacci values
15     cout << "\nfibonacci(20) = " << fibonacci(20) << endl;
16     cout << "fibonacci(30) = " << fibonacci(30) << endl;
17     cout << "fibonacci(35) = " << fibonacci(35) << endl;
18  }
19
20  // recursive function fibonacci
21  unsigned long fibonacci(unsigned long number) {
22     if ((0 == number) || (1 == number)) { // base cases
23        return number;
24     }
25     else { // recursion step
26        return fibonacci(number - 1) + fibonacci(number - 2);
27     }
28  }
```

```
fibonacci(0) = 0
fibonacci(1) = 1
fibonacci(2) = 1
fibonacci(3) = 2
fibonacci(4) = 3
fibonacci(5) = 5
fibonacci(6) = 8
fibonacci(7) = 13
fibonacci(8) = 21
fibonacci(9) = 34
fibonacci(10) = 55

fibonacci(20) = 6765
fibonacci(30) = 832040
fibonacci(35) = 9227465
```

Fig. 6.26 | Recursive function `fibonacci`.

The application begins with a `for` statement that calculates and displays the Fibonacci values for the integers 0–10 and is followed by three calls to calculate the Fibonacci values of the integers 20, 30 and 35 (lines 15–17). The calls to `fibonacci` in `main` (lines 12 and

15–17) are *not* recursive calls, but the calls from line 26 of fibonacci are recursive. Each time the program invokes fibonacci (lines 21–28), the function immediately tests the base case to determine whether number is equal to 0 or 1 (line 22). If this is *true*, line 23 returns number. Interestingly, if number is greater than 1, the recursion step (line 26) generates *two* recursive calls, each for a slightly smaller problem than the original call to fibonacci.

Evaluating fibonacci(3)

Figure 6.27 shows how function fibonacci would evaluate fibonacci(3). This figure raises some interesting issues about the *order* in which C++ compilers evaluate the operands of operators. This is a *separate* issue from the order in which operators are applied to their operands, namely, the order dictated by the rules of operator precedence and associativity. Figure 6.27 shows that evaluating fibonacci(3) causes two recursive calls, namely, fibonacci(2) and fibonacci(1). In what order are these calls made?

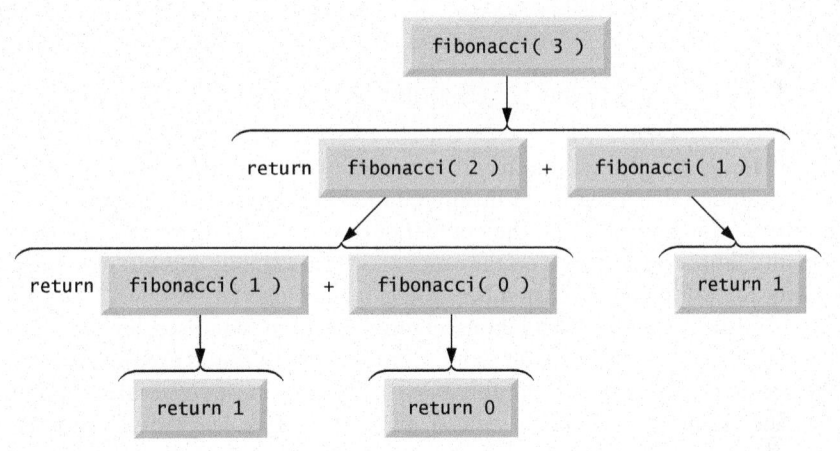

Fig. 6.27 | Set of recursive calls to function fibonacci.

Order of Evaluation of Operands

Most programmers simply assume that the operands are evaluated left to right. C++ does *not* specify the order in which the operands of most operators (including +) are to be evaluated. Therefore, you must make no assumption about the order in which these calls execute. The calls could in fact execute fibonacci(2) first, then fibonacci(1), or they could execute in the reverse order: fibonacci(1), then fibonacci(2). In this program and in most others, it turns out that the final result would be the same. However, in some programs the evaluation of an operand can have side effects (changes to data values) that could affect the final result of the expression.

C++ specifies the order of evaluation of the operands of only *four* operators—&&, ||, comma (,) and ?:. The first three are binary operators whose two operands are guaranteed to be evaluated left to right. The last operator is C++'s only *ternary* operator—its leftmost operand is always evaluated first; if it evaluates to *true*, the middle operand evaluates next and the last operand is ignored; if the leftmost operand evaluates to *false*, the third operand evaluates next and the middle operand is ignored.

Portability Tip 6.3

Programs that depend on the order of evaluation of the operands of operators other than && *,* || *,* ?: *and the comma (,) operator can function differently with different compilers and can lead to logic errors.*

Common Programming Error 6.12

Writing programs that depend on the order of evaluation of the operands of operators other than && *,* || *,* ?: *and the comma (,) operator can lead to logic errors.*

Error-Prevention Tip 6.12

Do not depend on the order in which operands are evaluated. To ensure that side effects are applied in the correct order, break complex expressions into separate statements.

Common Programming Error 6.13

Recall that the && *and* || *operators use short-circuit evaluation. Placing an expression with a side effect on the right side of a* && *or* || *operator is a logic error if that expression should always be evaluated.*

Exponential Complexity

A word of caution is in order about recursive programs like the one we use here to generate Fibonacci numbers. Each level of recursion in function fibonacci has a *doubling* effect on the number of function calls; i.e., the number of recursive calls that are required to calculate the *n*th Fibonacci number is on the order of 2^n. This rapidly gets out of hand. Calculating only the 20th Fibonacci number would require on the order of 2^{20} or about a million calls, calculating the 30th Fibonacci number would require on the order of 2^{30} or about a billion calls, and so on. Computer scientists refer to this as exponential complexity. Problems of this nature can humble even the world's most powerful computers as *n* becomes large! Complexity issues in general, and exponential complexity in particular, are discussed in detail in the upper-level computer science course typically called Algorithms.

Performance Tip 6.5

Avoid Fibonacci-style recursive programs that result in an exponential "explosion" of calls.

6.20 Recursion vs. Iteration

In the two prior sections, we studied two recursive functions that can also be implemented with simple iterative programs. This section compares the two approaches and discusses why you might choose one approach over the other in a particular situation.

- Both iteration and recursion are *based on a control statement*: Iteration uses a *iteration statement*; recursion uses a *selection statement*.

- Both iteration and recursion involve *iteration*: Iteration explicitly uses an *iteration statement*; recursion achieves iteration through *repeated function calls*.

- Iteration and recursion each involve a *termination test*: Iteration terminates when the *loop-continuation condition fails*; recursion terminates when a *base case is recognized*.

- Counter-controlled iteration and recursion each *gradually approach termination*: Iteration *modifies a counter* until the counter assumes a value that makes the loop-continuation condition fail; recursion produces *simpler versions of the original problem* until the base case is reached.

- Both iteration and recursion *can occur infinitely*: An *infinite loop* occurs with iteration if the loop-continuation test never becomes *false*; *infinite recursion* occurs if the recursion step does not reduce the problem during each recursive call in a manner that converges on the base case.

Iterative Factorial Implementation

To illustrate the differences between iteration and recursion, let's examine an iterative solution to the factorial problem (Fig. 6.28). An iteration statement is used (lines 22–24 of Fig. 6.28) rather than the selection statement of the recursive solution (lines 19–24 of Fig. 6.25). Both solutions use a termination test. In the recursive solution, line 19 (Fig. 6.25) tests for the base case. In the iterative solution, line 22 (Fig. 6.28) tests the loop-continuation condition—if the test fails, the loop terminates. Finally, instead of producing simpler versions of the original problem, the iterative solution uses a counter that is modified until the loop-continuation condition becomes *false*.

```cpp
1   // Fig. 6.28: fig06_28.cpp
2   // Iterative function factorial.
3   #include <iostream>
4   #include <iomanip>
5   using namespace std;
6
7   unsigned long factorial(unsigned int); // function prototype
8
9   int main() {
10     // calculate the factorials of 0 through 10
11     for (unsigned int counter{0}; counter <= 10; ++counter) {
12        cout << setw(2) << counter << "! = " << factorial(counter)
13           << endl;
14     }
15  }
16
17  // iterative function factorial
18  unsigned long factorial(unsigned int number) {
19     unsigned long result{1};
20
21     // iterative factorial calculation
22     for (unsigned int i{number}; i >= 1; --i) {
23        result *= i;
24     }
25
26     return result;
27  }
```

Fig. 6.28 | Iterative function factorial. (Part 1 of 2.)

```
 0! = 1
 1! = 1
 2! = 2
 3! = 6
 4! = 24
 5! = 120
 6! = 720
 7! = 5040
 8! = 40320
 9! = 362880
10! = 3628800
```

Fig. 6.28 | Iterative function `factorial`. (Part 2 of 2.)

Negatives of Recursion

Recursion has negatives. It repeatedly invokes the mechanism, and consequently the *overhead, of function calls*. This can be expensive in both processor time and memory space. Each recursive call causes *another copy of the function variables* to be created; this can consume considerable memory. Iteration normally occurs within a function, so the overhead of repeated function calls and extra memory assignment is omitted. So why choose recursion? Software Engineering Observation 6.11 disusses two reasons.

Software Engineering Observation 6.11

Any problem that can be solved recursively can also be solved iteratively (nonrecursively). A recursive approach is normally chosen when the recursive approach more naturally mirrors the problem and results in a program that's easier to understand and debug. Another reason to choose a recursive solution is that an iterative solution may not be apparent when a recursive solution is.

Performance Tip 6.6

Avoid using recursion in performance situations. Recursive calls take time and consume additional memory.

Common Programming Error 6.14

Accidentally having a nonrecursive function call itself, either directly or indirectly (through another function), is a logic error.

Summary of Recursion Examples and Exercises in This Book

Figure 6.29 summarizes the recursion examples and exercises in the text.

Location in text	Recursion examples and exercises
Chapter 6	
Section 6.18, Fig. 6.25	Factorial function
Section 6.19, Fig. 6.26	Fibonacci function

Fig. 6.29 | Summary of recursion examples and exercises in the text. (Part 1 of 2.)

Location in text	Recursion examples and exercises
Exercise 6.36	Recursive exponentiation
Exercise 6.38	Towers of Hanoi
Exercise 6.40	Visualizing recursion
Exercise 6.41	Greatest common divisor
Exercise 6.43, Exercise 6.44	"What does this program do?" exercise
Chapter 7	
Exercise 7.17	"What does this program do?" exercise
Exercise 7.20	"What does this program do?" exercise
Exercise 7.28	Determine whether a string is a palindrome
Exercise 7.29	Eight Queens
Exercise 7.30	Print an array
Exercise 7.31	Print a string backward
Exercise 7.32	Minimum value in an array
Exercise 7.33	Maze traversal
Exercise 7.34	Generating mazes randomly
Chapter 19	
Section 19.6, Figs. 19.20–19.22	Binary tree insert
Section 19.6, Figs. 19.20–19.22	Preorder traversal of a binary tree
Section 19.6, Figs. 19.20–19.22	Inorder traversal of a binary tree
Section 19.6, Figs. 19.20–19.22	Postorder traversal of a binary tree
Exercise 19.20	Print a linked list backward
Exercise 19.21	Search a linked list
Exercise 19.22	Binary tree search
Exercise 19.23	Level order traversal of a binary tree
Exercise 19.24	Printing tree
Chapter 20	
Section 20.3.3, Fig. 20.6	Mergesort
Exercise 20.8	Linear search
Exercise 20.9	Binary search
Exercise 20.10	Quicksort

Fig. 6.29 | Summary of recursion examples and exercises in the text. (Part 2 of 2.)

6.21 Wrap-Up

In this chapter, you learned more about functions, including function prototypes, function signatures, function headers and function bodies. We overviewed the math library functions. You learned about argument coercion, or the forcing of arguments to the appropriate types specified by the parameter declarations of a function. We demonstrated how to use functions rand and srand to generate sets of random numbers that can be used for simulations, then presented C++11's nondeterministic capabilities for producing more secure random numbers. We introduced C++14's digit separators for more readable numeric literals. We showed how to define sets of constants with scoped enums. You learned about the scope of variables. Two different ways to pass arguments to functions were covered—pass-by-value and pass-by-reference. For pass-by-reference, a reference is used as an alias to a variable. We showed how to implement inline functions and functions that receive default arguments. You learned that multiple functions in one class can be overloaded by providing functions with the same name and different signatures. Such functions can be used to perform the same or similar tasks, using different types or different numbers of parameters. We demonstrated a simpler way of overloading functions using function templates, where a function is defined once but can be used for several different types. You then studied recursion, where a function calls itself to solve a problem.

In Chapter 7, you'll learn how to maintain lists and tables of data in arrays and object-oriented vectors. You'll see a more elegant array-based implementation of the dice-rolling application.

Summary

Section 6.1 Introduction
- Experience has shown that the best way to develop and maintain a large program is to construct it from small, simple pieces, or components. This technique is called **divide and conquer** (p. 212).

Section 6.2 Program Components in C++
- C++ programs are typically written by combining new functions and classes you write with "prepackaged" functions and classes available in the C++ Standard Library.
- Functions allow you to modularize a program by separating its tasks into self-contained units.
- The statements in the function bodies are written only once, are reused from perhaps several locations in a program and are hidden from other functions.

Section 6.3 Math Library Functions
- Sometimes functions are not members of a class. These are called **global functions** (p. 214).
- The prototypes for global functions are often placed in headers, so that they can be reused in any program that includes the header and that can link to the function's object code.

Section 6.4 Function Prototypes
- For a function that's not defined in a class, you must either define the function before using it or you must declare that the function exists by using a function prototype.
- A **function prototype** (p. 217) is a declaration of a function that tells the compiler the function's name, its return type and the types of its parameters
- A function prototype ends with a required semicolon.
- Parameter names in function prototypes are optional (they're ignored by the compiler), but many programmers use these names for documentation purposes.
- The compiler uses the prototype to ensure that the function header matches the function prototype; to check that each function call contains the correct number and types of arguments and

that the types of the arguments are in the correct order; to ensure that the value returned by the function can be used correctly in the calling expression; and to ensure that each argument is consistent with the type of the corresponding parameter.

- In a function with a void return type, control returns to the caller when the program reaches the function-ending right brace or by executing the statement

```
return;
```

Section 6.5 Function-Prototype and Argument-Coercion Notes
- The portion of a function prototype that includes the name of the function and the types of its arguments is called the **function signature** (p. 219) or simply the **signature**.
- An important feature of function prototypes is **argument coercion** (p. 219)—i.e., forcing arguments to the appropriate types specified by the parameter declarations.
- Arguments can be converted by the compiler to the parameter types as specified by C++'s **promotion rules** (p. 219). The promotion rules indicate the implicit conversions that the compiler can perform between fundamental types.

Section 6.6 C++ Standard Library Headers
- The C++ Standard Library is divided into many portions, each with its own header. The headers also contain definitions of various class types, functions and constants.
- A header "instructs" the compiler on how to interface with library components.

Section 6.7 Case Study: Random-Number Generation
- Calling **rand** (p. 222) repeatedly produces a sequence of **pseudorandom numbers** (p. 226). The sequence repeats itself each time the program executes.
- To make numeric literals more readable, C++14 allows you to insert between groups of digits in numeric literals the **digit separator '** (p. 225; a single-quote character).
- To randomize the numbers produced by rand, pass an unsigned integer argument (typically from function **time**; p. 227) to function **srand** (p. 226), which seeds the rand function.
- Random numbers in a range can be generated with

    type variableName{shiftingValue + rand() % *scalingFactor}*;

where *shiftingValue* (p. 227) is equal to the first number in the desired range of consecutive integers and *scalingFactor* (p. 227) is equal to the width of the desired range of consecutive integers.

Section 6.8 Case Study: Game of Chance; Introducing Scoperd **enums**
- A **scoped enumeration** (p. 230)—introduced by the keywords **enum class** followed by a type name—is a set of named integer constants that start at 0, unless specified otherwise, and increment by 1.
- To reference a scoped enum constant, you must qualify the constant with the scoped enum's type name and the scope resolution operator (::). If another scoped enum contains the same identifier for one of its constants, it's always clear which version of the constant is being used.
- A scoped enum's underlying integral type is int by default.
- C++11 allows you to specify an enum's underlying integral type by following the enum's type name with a colon (:) and the integral type.
- A compilation error occurs if an enum constant's value is outside the range that can be represented by the enum's underlying type.
- Unscoped enums can lead to naming collisions and logic errors.

- An unscoped enum's underlying integral type depends on its constants' values—the type is guaranteed to be large enough to store the constant values specified.

Section 6.9 C++11 Random Numbers

- According to CERT, function rand does not have "good statistical properties" and can be predictable, which makes programs that use rand less secure.

- C++11 provides a new, more secure library of random-number capabilities that can produce nondeterministic random numbers for simulations and security scenarios where predictability is undesirable. These new capabilities are located in the C++ Standard Library's <random> header.

- For flexibility based on how random numbers are used in programs, C++11 provides many classes that represent various random-number generation engines and distributions. An engine implements a random-number generation algorithm that produces pseudorandom numbers. A distribution controls the range of values produced by an engine, the types of those values and the statistical properties of the values.

- A `default_random_engine` (p. 232) represents the default random-number generation engine.

- The `uniform_int_distribution` (p. 232) evenly distributes pseudorandom integers over a specified range of values. The default range is from 0 to the maximum value of an int on your platform.

Section 6.10 Scope Rules

- An identifier declared outside any function or class has **global namespace scope** (p. 233).

- **Global variable** (p. 234) declarations are placed outside any class or function definition. Global variables retain their values throughout the program's execution. Global variables and functions can be referenced by any function that follows their declarations or definitions.

- Identifiers declared inside a block have **block scope** (p. 233), which begins at the identifier's declaration and ends at the terminating right brace (}) of the block in which the identifier is declared.

- `static` (p. 234) local variables also have block scope, but retain their values when the function in which they're declared returns to its caller.

- An identifier declared outside any function or class has global namespace scope. Such an identifier is "known" in all functions from the point at which it's declared until the end of the file.

Section 6.11 Function-Call Stack and Activation Records

- **Stacks** (p. 237) are known as last-in, first-out (LIFO) data structures—the last item **pushed** (inserted; p. 237) on the stack is the first item **popped** (removed; p. 237) from the stack.

- The **function-call stack** (p. 237) supports the function call/return mechanism and the creation, maintenance and destruction of each called function's non-`static` local variables.

- Each time a function calls another function, a **stack frame** or an **activation record** (p. 237) is pushed onto the stack containing the return address that the called function needs to return to the calling function, and the function call's non-`static` local variables and parameters.

- The stack frame exists as long as the called function is active. When the called function returns, its stack frame is popped from the stack, and its non-`static` local variables no longer exist.

Section 6.12 Inline Functions

- C++ provides **inline functions** (p. 241) to help reduce function-call overhead—especially for small functions. Placing the qualifier `inline` (p. 241) before a function's return type in the function definition advises the compiler to generate a copy of the function's code in every place that the function is called to avoid a function call.

- Compilers can inline code for which you have not explicitly used the `inline` keyword. Today's optimizing compilers are so sophisticated that it's best to leave inlining decisions to the compiler.

Section 6.13 References and Reference Parameters
- With **pass-by-value** (p. 242), a *copy* of the argument's value is made and passed to the called function. Changes to the copy do not affect the original variable's value in the caller.
- With **pass-by-reference** (p. 242), the caller gives the called function the ability to access the caller's data directly and to modify it if the called function chooses to do so.
- A **reference parameter** (p. 243) is an alias for its corresponding argument in a function call.
- To indicate that a function parameter is passed by reference, follow the parameter's type in the function prototype and header by an ampersand (&).
- All operations performed on a reference are actually performed on the original variable.

Section 6.14 Default Arguments
- When a function is called repeatedly with the same argument for a particular parameter, you can specify that such a parameter has a **default argument** (p. 245).
- When a program omits an argument for a parameter with a default argument, the compiler inserts the default value of that argument to be passed to the function call.
- Default arguments must be the rightmost (trailing) arguments in a function's parameter list.
- Default arguments are specified in the function prototype.

Section 6.15 Unary Scope Resolution Operator
- C++ provides the **unary scope resolution operator** (p. 247; ::) to access a global variable when a local variable of the same name is in scope.

Section 6.16 Function Overloading
- C++ enables several functions of the same name to be defined, as long as these functions have different sets of parameters. This capability is called **function overloading** (p. 248).
- When an overloaded function is called, the C++ compiler selects the proper function by examining the number, types and order of the arguments in the call.
- Overloaded functions are distinguished by their signatures.
- The compiler encodes each function identifier with the types of its parameters to enable **type-safe linkage** (p. 249). Type-safe linkage ensures that the proper overloaded function is called and that the types of the arguments conform to the types of the parameters.

Section 6.17 Function Templates
- Overloaded functions typically perform similar operations that involve different program logic on different data types. If the program logic and operations are identical for each data type, overloading may be performed more compactly and conveniently using **function templates** (p. 251).
- Given the argument types provided in calls to a function template, C++ automatically generates separate **function template specializations** (p. 251) to handle each type of call appropriately.
- All function template definitions begin with the `template` keyword (p. 251) followed by a **template parameter list** (p. 251) enclosed in angle brackets (< and >).
- The **type parameters** (p. 252) are preceded by keyword `typename` (or `class`) and are placeholders for fundamental types or user-defined types. These placeholders are used to specify the types of the function's parameters, to specify the function's return type and to declare variables within the body of the function definition.

Section 6.18 Recursion
- A **recursive function** (p. 254) calls itself, either directly or indirectly.

- A recursive function knows how to solve only the simplest case(s), or so-called base case(s). If the function is called with a **base case** (p. 254), the function simply returns a result.

- If the function is called with a more complex problem, the function typically divides the problem into two conceptual pieces—a piece that the function knows how to do and a piece that it does not know how to do. To make recursion feasible, the latter piece must resemble the original problem, but be a slightly simpler or slightly smaller version of it.

- For recursion to terminate, the sequence of **recursive calls** (p. 254) must converge on the base case.

- C++11's unsigned long long int type (which can be abbreviated as unsigned long long) on some systems enables you to store values in at least 8 bytes (64 bits) which can hold numbers as large as 18,446,744,073,709,551,615.

Section 6.19 Example Using Recursion: Fibonacci Series
- The ratio of successive Fibonacci numbers converges on a constant value of 1.618.... This number frequently occurs in nature and has been called the **golden ratio** or the **golden mean** (p. 257).

Section 6.20 Recursion vs. Iteration
- Iteration and recursion are similar: both are based on a control statement, involve iteration, involve a termination test, gradually approach termination and can occur infinitely.

- Recursion repeatedly invokes the mechanism, and overhead, of function calls. This can be expensive in both processor time and memory space. Each **recursive call** (p. 254) causes another copy of the function's variables to be created; this can consume considerable memory.

Self-Review Exercises

6.1 Answer each of the following:
   a) Program components in C++ are called _____ and_____.
   b) A function is invoked with a(n) _____.
   c) A variable known only within the function in which it's defined is called a(n) _____.
   d) The _____ statement in a called function passes the value of an expression back to the calling function.
   e) The keyword _____ is used in a function header to indicate that a function does not return a value or to indicate that a function contains no parameters.
   f) An identifier's _____ is the portion of the program in which the identifier can be used.
   g) The three ways to return control from a called function to a caller are _____, _____ and _____.
   h) A(n) _____ allows the compiler to check the number, types and order of the arguments passed to a function.
   i) Function _____ is used to produce random numbers.
   j) Function _____ is used to set the random-number seed to randomize the number sequence generated by function rand.
   k) A variable declared outside any block or function is a(n) _____ variable.
   l) For a local variable in a function to retain its value between calls to the function, it must be declared _____.
   m) A function that calls itself either directly or indirectly (i.e., through another function) is a(n) _____ function.
   n) A recursive function typically has two components—one that provides a means for the recursion to terminate by testing for a(n) _____ case and one that expresses the problem as a recursive call for a slightly simpler problem than the original call.
   o) It's possible to have various functions with the same name that operate on different types or numbers of arguments. This is called function _____.

p) The _____ enables access to a global variable with the same name as a variable in the current scope.

q) The _____ qualifier is used to declare read-only variables.

r) A function _____ enables a single function to be defined to perform a task on many different data types.

6.2 For the program in Fig. 6.30, state the scope (global namespace scope or block scope) of each of the following elements:

a) The variable x in main.

b) The variable y in function cube's definition.

c) The function cube.

d) The function main.

e) The function prototype for cube.

```
1   // Exercise 6.2: ex06_02.cpp
2   #include <iostream>
3   using namespace std;
4
5   int cube(int y); // function prototype
6
7   int main() {
8      int x{0};
9
10     for (x = 1; x <= 10; x++) { // loop 10 times
11        cout << cube(x) << endl; // calculate cube of x and output results
12     }
13  }
14
15  // definition of function cube
16  int cube(int y) {
17     return y * y * y;
18  }
```

Fig. 6.30 | Program for Exercise 6.2.

6.3 Write a program that tests whether the examples of the math library function calls shown in Fig. 6.2 actually produce the indicated results.

6.4 Give the function header for each of the following functions:

a) Function hypotenuse that takes two double-precision, floating-point arguments, side1 and side2, and returns a double-precision, floating-point result.

b) Function smallest that takes three integers, x, y and z, and returns an integer.

c) Function instructions that does not receive any arguments and does not return a value. [*Note:* Such functions are commonly used to display instructions to a user.]

d) Function intToDouble that takes an integer argument, number, and returns a double-precision, floating-point result.

6.5 Give the function prototype (without parameter names) for each of the following:

a) The function described in Exercise 6.4(a).

b) The function described in Exercise 6.4(b).

c) The function described in Exercise 6.4(c).

d) The function described in Exercise 6.4(d).

6.6 Write a declaration for double-precision, floating-point variable lastVal that should retain its value between calls to the function in which it's defined.

6.7 Find the error(s) in each of the following program segments, and explain how the error(s) can be corrected (see also Exercise 6.46):

a)
```cpp
void g() {
    cout << "Inside function g" << endl;
    void h() {
        cout << "Inside function h" << endl;
    }
}
```

b)
```cpp
int sum(int x, int y) {
    int result{0};

    result = x + y;
}
```

c)
```cpp
int sum(int n) { // assume n is nonnegative
    if (0 == n)
        return 0;
    else
        n + sum(n - 1);
}
```

d)
```cpp
void f(double a); {
    float a;
    cout << a << endl;
}
```

e)
```cpp
void product() {
    int a{0};
    int b{0};
    int c{0};
    cout << "Enter three integers: ";
    cin >> a >> b >> c;
    int result{a * b * c};
    cout << "Result is " << result;
    return result;
}
```

6.8 Why would a function prototype contain a parameter type declaration such as `double&`?

6.9 *(True/False)* All arguments to function calls in C++ are passed by value.

6.10 Write a complete program that prompts the user for the radius of a sphere, and calculates and prints the volume of that sphere. Use an `inline` function `sphereVolume` that returns the result of the following expression: `(4.0 / 3.0 * 3.14159 * pow(radius, 3))`.

Answers to Self-Review Exercises

6.1 a) functions, classes. b) function call. c) local variable. d) return. e) void. f) scope. g) return;, return *expression*; or encounter the closing right brace of a function. h) function prototype. i) rand. j) srand. k) global. l) static. m) recursive. n) base. o) overloading. p) unary scope resolution operator (::). q) const. r) template.

6.2 a) block scope. b) block scope. c) global namespace scope. d) global namespace scope. e) global namespace scope.

6.3   See the following program:

```cpp
// Exercise 6.3: ex06_03.cpp
// Testing the math library functions.
#include <iostream>
#include <iomanip>
#include <cmath>
using namespace std;

int main() {
   cout << fixed << setprecision(1);

   cout << "sqrt(" << 9.0 << ") = " << sqrt(9.0);
   cout << "\nexp(" << 1.0 << ") = " << setprecision(6)
      << exp(1.0) << "\nexp(" << setprecision(1) << 2.0
      << ") = " << setprecision(6) << exp(2.0);
   cout << "\nlog(" << 2.718282 << ") = " << setprecision(1)
      << log(2.718282)
      << "\nlog(" << setprecision(6) << 7.389056 << ") = "
      << setprecision(1) << log(7.389056);
   cout << "\nlog10(" << 10.0 << ") = " << log10(10.0)
      << "\nlog10(" << 100.0 << ") = " << log10(100.0) ;
   cout << "\nfabs(" << 5.1 << ") = " << fabs(5.1)
      << "\nfabs(" << 0.0 << ") = " << fabs(0.0)
      << "\nfabs(" << -8.76 << ") = " << fabs(-8.76);
   cout << "\nceil(" << 9.2 << ") = " << ceil(9.2)
      << "\nceil(" << -9.8 << ") = " << ceil(-9.8);
   cout << "\nfloor(" << 9.2 << ") = " << floor(9.2)
      << "\nfloor(" << -9.8 << ") = " << floor(-9.8);
   cout << "\npow(" << 2.0 << ", " << 7.0 << ") = "
      << pow(2.0, 7.0) << "\npow(" << 9.0 << ", "
      << 0.5 << ") = " << pow(9.0, 0.5);
   cout << setprecision(3) << "\nfmod("
      << 2.6 << ", " << 1.2 << ") = "
      << fmod(2.6, 1.2) << setprecision(1);
   cout << "\nsin(" << 0.0 << ") = " << sin(0.0);
   cout << "\ncos(" << 0.0 << ") = " << cos(0.0);
   cout << "\ntan(" << 0.0 << ") = " << tan(0.0) << endl;
}
```

```
sqrt(9.0) = 3.0
exp(1.0) = 2.718282
exp(2.0) = 7.389056
log(2.718282) = 1.0
log(7.389056) = 2.0
log10(10.0) = 1.0
log10(100.0) = 2.0
fabs(5.1) = 5.1
fabs(0.0) = 0.0
fabs(-8.8) = 8.8
ceil(9.2) = 10.0
ceil(-9.8) = -9.0
floor(9.2) = 9.0
floor(-9.8) = -10.0
pow(2.0, 7.0) = 128.0
pow(9.0, 0.5) = 3.0
fmod(2.600, 1.200) = 0.200
sin(0.0) = 0.0
cos(0.0) = 1.0
tan(0.0) = 0.0
```

6.4   a)   `double hypotenuse(double side1, double side2)`
          b)   `int smallest(int x, int y, int z)`
          c)   `void instructions()`
          d)   `double intToDouble(int number)`

6.5   a)   `double hypotenuse(double, double);`
          b)   `int smallest(int, int, int);`
          c)   `void instructions();`
          d)   `double intToDouble(int);`

6.6   `static double lastVal;`

6.7   a)   *Error:* Function h is defined in function g.
            Correction: Move the definition of h out of the definition of g.
          b)   *Error:* The function is supposed to return an integer, but does not.
            Correction: Place a `return result;` statement at the end of the function's body or delete variable `result` and place the following statement in the function:

               `return x + y;`

          c)   *Error:* The result of `n + sum(n - 1)` is not returned; `sum` returns an improper result.
            Correction: Rewrite the statement in the `else` clause as

               `return n + sum(n - 1);`

          d)   *Errors:* Semicolon after the right parenthesis that encloses the parameter list, and redefining the parameter a in the function definition.
            Corrections: Delete the semicolon after the right parenthesis of the parameter list, and delete the declaration `float a;`.
          e)   *Error:* The function returns a value when it isn't supposed to.
            Correction: Eliminate the `return` statement or change the return type.

6.8   This creates a reference parameter of type "reference to `double`" that enables the function to modify the original variable in the calling function.

6.9   *False.* C++ enables pass-by-reference using reference parameters (and pointers, as we discuss in Chapter 8).

6.10   See the following program:

```
1   // Exercise 6.10 Solution: ex06_10.cpp
2   // Inline function that calculates the volume of a sphere.
3   #include <iostream>
4   #include <cmath>
5   using namespace std;
6
7   const double PI{3.14159}; // define global constant PI
8
9   // calculates volume of a sphere
10  inline double sphereVolume(const double radius) {
11     return 4.0 / 3.0 * PI * pow(radius, 3);
12  }
13
14  int main() {
15     // prompt user for radius
16     cout << "Enter the length of the radius of your sphere: ";
17     double radiusValue;
18     cin >> radiusValue; // input radius
19
```

```
20      // use radiusValue to calculate volume of sphere and display result
21      cout << "Volume of sphere with radius " << radiusValue
22          << " is " << sphereVolume(radiusValue) << endl;
23   }
```

Exercises

6.11   Show the value of x after each of the following statements is performed:

   a) `x = fabs(7.5);`
   b) `x = floor(7.5);`
   c) `x = fabs(0.0);`
   d) `x = ceil(0.0);`
   e) `x = fabs(-6.4);`
   f) `x = ceil(-6.4);`
   g) `x = ceil(-fabs(-8 + floor(-5.5)));`

6.12   *(Parking Charges)* A parking garage charges a $20.00 minimum fee to park for up to three hours. The garage charges an additional $5.00 per hour for each hour *or part thereof* in excess of three hours. The maximum charge for any given 24-hour period is $50.00. Assume that no car parks for longer than 24 hours at a time. Write a program that calculates and prints the parking charges for each of three customers who parked their cars in this garage yesterday. You should enter the hours parked for each customer. Your program should print the results in a neat tabular format and should calculate and print the total of yesterday's receipts. The program should use the function `calculateCharges` to determine the charge for each customer. Your outputs should appear in the following format:

```
Car     Hours      Charge
1        1.5       20.00
2        4.0       25.00
3       24.0       50.00
TOTAL   29.5       95.50
```

6.13   *(Rounding Numbers)* An application of function `floor` is rounding a value to the nearest integer. The statement

```
y = floor(x + 0.5);
```

rounds the number x to the nearest integer and assigns the result to y. Write a program that reads several numbers and uses the preceding statement to round each of these numbers to the nearest integer. For each number processed, print both the original number and the rounded number.

6.14   *(Rounding Numbers)* Function `floor` can be used to round a number to a specific decimal place. The statement

```
y = floor(x * 10 + 0.5) / 10;
```

rounds x to the tenths position (the first position to the right of the decimal point). The statement

```
y = floor(x * 100 + 0.5) / 100;
```

rounds x to the hundredths position (the second position to the right of the decimal point). Write a program that defines four functions to round a number x in various ways:

   a) `roundToInteger(number)`
   b) `roundToTenths(number)`
   c) `roundToHundredths(number)`
   d) `roundToThousandths(number)`

For each value read, your program should print the original value, the number rounded to the nearest integer, the number rounded to the nearest tenth, the number rounded to the nearest hundredth and the number rounded to the nearest thousandth.

6.15   *(Short-Answer Questions)* Answer each of the following questions:
a)   What does it mean to choose numbers "at random?"
b)   Why is the rand function useful for simulating games of chance?
c)   Why would you randomize a program by using srand? Under what circumstances is it desirable not to randomize?
d)   Why is it often necessary to scale or shift the values produced by rand?
e)   Why is computerized simulation of real-world situations a useful technique?

6.16   *(Random Numbers)* Write statements that assign random integers to the variable *n* in the following ranges:
a) $1 \leq n \leq 2$
b) $1 \leq n \leq 100$
c) $0 \leq n \leq 9$
d) $1000 \leq n \leq 1112$
e) $-1 \leq n \leq 1$
f) $-3 \leq n \leq 11$

6.17   *(Random Numbers)* Write a single statement that prints a number at random from each of the following sets:
a)   2, 4, 6, 8, 10.
b)   3, 5, 7, 9, 11.
c)   6, 10, 14, 18, 22.

6.18   *(Exponentiation)* Write a function integerPower(*base*, *exponent*) that returns the value of
$base^{exponent}$

For example, integerPower(3, 4) = 3 * 3 * 3 * 3. Assume that *exponent* is a positive, nonzero integer and that *base* is an integer. Do not use any math library functions.

6.19   *(Hypotenuse Calculations)* Define a function hypotenuse that calculates the hypotenuse of a right triangle when the other two sides are given. The function should take two double arguments and return the hypotenuse as a double. Use this function in a program to determine the hypotenuse for each of the triangles shown below.

Triangle	Side 1	Side 2
1	3.0	4.0
2	5.0	12.0
3	8.0	15.0

6.20   *(Multiples)* Write a function isMultiple that determines for a pair of integers whether the second is a multiple of the first. The function should take two integer arguments and return true if the second is a multiple of the first, false otherwise. Use this function in a program that inputs a series of pairs of integers.

6.21   *(Even Numbers)* Write a program that inputs a series of integers and passes them one at a time to function isEven, which uses the remainder operator to determine whether an integer is even. The function should take an integer argument and return true if the integer is even and false otherwise.

6.22   *(Square of Asterisks)* Write a function that displays at the left margin of the screen a solid square of asterisks whose side is specified in integer parameter side. For example, if side is 4, the function displays the following:

```
****
****
****
****
```

6.23   *(Square of Any Character)* Modify the function created in Exercise 6.22 to form the square out of whatever character is contained in character parameter fillCharacter. Thus, if side is 5 and fillCharacter is #, then this function should print the following:

```
#####
#####
#####
#####
#####
```

6.24   *(Separating Digits)* Write program segments that accomplish each of the following:
   a)   Calculate the integer part of the quotient when integer a is divided by integer b.
   b)   Calculate the integer remainder when integer a is divided by integer b.
   c)   Use the program pieces developed in (a) and (b) to write a function that inputs an integer between 1 and 32767 and prints it as a series of digits, each pair of which is separated by two spaces. For example, the integer 4562 should print as follows:

```
4   5   6   2
```

6.25   *(Calculating Number of Seconds)* Write a function that takes the time as three integer arguments (hours, minutes and seconds) and returns the number of seconds since the last time the clock "struck 12." Use this function to calculate the amount of time in seconds between two times, both of which are within one 12-hour cycle of the clock.

6.26   *(Celsius and Fahrenheit Temperatures)* Implement the following integer functions:
   a)   Function celsius returns the Celsius equivalent of a Fahrenheit temperature.
   b)   Function fahrenheit returns the Fahrenheit equivalent of a Celsius temperature.
   c)   Use these functions to write a program that prints charts showing the Fahrenheit equivalents of all Celsius temperatures from 0 to 100 degrees, and the Celsius equivalents of all Fahrenheit temperatures from 32 to 212 degrees. Print the outputs in a neat tabular format that minimizes the number of lines of output while remaining readable.

6.27   *(Find the Minimum)* Write a program that inputs three double-precision, floating-point numbers and passes them to a function that returns the smallest number.

6.28   *(Perfect Numbers)* An integer is said to be a *perfect number* if the sum of its divisors, including 1 (but not the number itself), is equal to the number. For example, 6 is a perfect number, because 6 = 1 + 2 + 3. Write a function isPerfect that determines whether parameter number is a perfect number. Use this function in a program that determines and prints all the perfect numbers between 1 and 1000. Print the divisors of each perfect number to confirm that the number is indeed perfect. Challenge the power of your computer by testing numbers much larger than 1000.

6.29   *(Prime Numbers)* An integer is said to be *prime* if it's divisible by only 1 and itself. For example, 2, 3, 5 and 7 are prime, but 4, 6, 8 and 9 are not.

    a)   Write a function that determines whether a number is prime.

    b)   Use this function in a program that determines and prints all the prime numbers between 2 and 10,000. How many of these numbers do you really have to test before being sure that you've found all the primes?

    c)   Initially, you might think that $n/2$ is the upper limit for which you must test to see whether a number is prime, but you need only go as high as the square root of n. Why? Rewrite the program, and run it both ways. Estimate the performance improvement.

6.30   *(Reverse Digits)* Write a function that takes an integer value and returns the number with its digits reversed. For example, given the number 7631, the function should return 1367.

6.31   *(Greatest Common Divisor)* The *greatest common divisor (GCD)* of two integers is the largest integer that evenly divides each of the numbers. Write a function gcd that returns the greatest common divisor of two integers.

6.32   *(Quality Points for Numeric Grades)* Write a function qualityPoints that inputs a student's average and returns 4 if a student's average is 90–100, 3 if the average is 80–89, 2 if the average is 70–79, 1 if the average is 60–69 and 0 if the average is lower than 60.

6.33   *(Coin Tossing)* Write a program that simulates coin tossing. For each toss of the coin, the program should print Heads or Tails. Let the program toss the coin 100 times and count the number of times each side of the coin appears. Print the results. The program should call a separate function flip that takes no arguments and returns 0 for tails and 1 for heads. [*Note:* If the program realistically simulates the coin tossing, then each side of the coin should appear approximately half the time.]

6.34   *(Guess-the-Number Game)* Write a program that plays the game of "guess the number" as follows: Your program chooses the number to be guessed by selecting an integer at random in the range 1 to 1000. The program then displays the following:

```
I have a number between 1 and 1000.
Can you guess my number?
Please type your first guess.
```

The player then types a first guess. The program responds with one of the following:

```
1. Excellent! You guessed the number!
   Would you like to play again (y or n)?
2. Too low. Try again.
3. Too high. Try again.
```

If the player's guess is incorrect, your program should loop until the player finally gets the number right. Your program should keep telling the player Too high or Too low to help the player "zero in" on the correct answer.

6.35   *(Guess-the-Number Game Modification)* Modify the program of Exercise 6.34 to count the number of guesses the player makes. If the number is 10 or fewer, print "Either you know the secret or you got lucky!" If the player guesses the number in 10 tries, then print "Ahah! You know the secret!" If the player makes more than 10 guesses, then print "You should be able to do better!" Why should it take no more than 10 guesses? Well, with each "good guess" the player should be able to eliminate half of the numbers. Now show why any number from 1 to 1000 can be guessed in 10 or fewer tries.

6.36   *(Recursive Exponentiation)* Write a recursive function power(base, exponent) that, when invoked, returns

   $base^{exponent}$

For example, power(3, 4) = 3 * 3 * 3 * 3. Assume that exponent is an integer greater than or equal to 1. *Hint:* The recursion step would use the relationship

   $base^{exponent} = base \cdot base^{exponent-1}$

and the terminating condition occurs when exponent is equal to 1, because

   $base^1 = base$

6.37   *(Fibonacci Series: Iterative Solution)* Write a *nonrecursive* version of the function fibonacci from Fig. 6.26.

6.38   *(Towers of Hanoi)* In this chapter, you studied functions that can be easily implemented both recursively and iteratively. In this exercise, we present a problem whose recursive solution demonstrates the elegance of recursion, and whose iterative solution may not be as apparent.

The Towers of Hanoi is one of the most famous classic problems every budding computer scientist must grapple with. Legend has it that in a temple in the Far East, priests are attempting to move a stack of golden disks from one diamond peg to another (Fig. 6.31). The initial stack has 64 disks threaded onto one peg and arranged from bottom to top by decreasing size. The priests are attempting to move the stack from one peg to another under the constraints that exactly one disk is moved at a time and at no time may a larger disk be placed above a smaller disk. Three pegs are provided, one being used for temporarily holding disks. Supposedly, the world will end when the priests complete their task, so there is little incentive for us to facilitate their efforts.

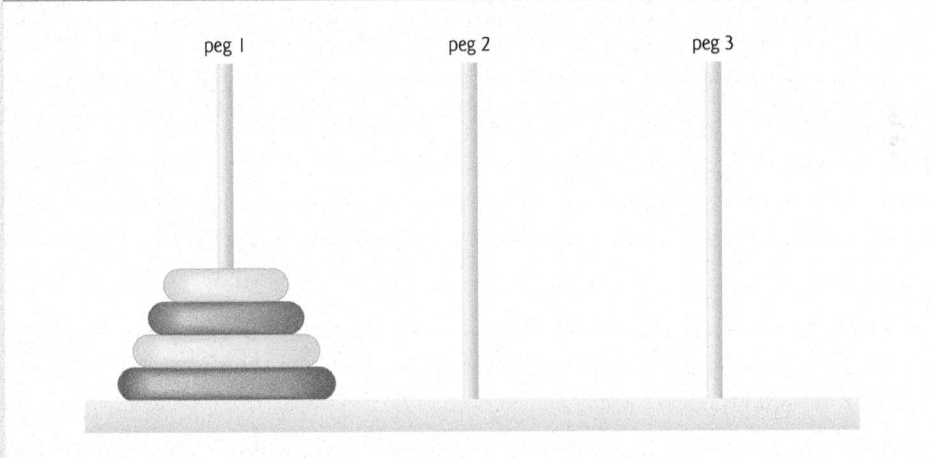

Fig. 6.31 | Towers of Hanoi for the case with four disks.

Let's assume that the priests are attempting to move the disks from peg 1 to peg 3. We wish to develop an algorithm that prints the precise sequence of peg-to-peg disk transfers.

If we were to approach this problem with conventional methods, we would rapidly find ourselves hopelessly knotted up in managing the disks. Instead, attacking this problem with recursion in mind allows the steps to be simple. Moving *n* disks can be viewed in terms of moving only *n* – 1 disks (hence, the recursion), as follows:

    a) Move $n - 1$ disks from peg 1 to peg 2, using peg 3 as a temporary holding area.

    b) Move the last disk (the largest) from peg 1 to peg 3.

    c) Move the $n - 1$ disks from peg 2 to peg 3, using peg 1 as a temporary holding area.

The process ends when the last task involves moving $n = 1$ disk (i.e., the base case). This task is accomplished by simply moving the disk, without the need for a temporary holding area. Write a program to solve the Towers of Hanoi problem. Use a recursive function with four parameters:

    a) The number of disks to be moved

    b) The peg on which these disks are initially threaded

    c) The peg to which this stack of disks is to be moved

    d) The peg to be used as a temporary holding area

Display the precise instructions for moving the disks from the starting peg to the destination peg. To move a stack of three disks from peg 1 to peg 3, the program displays the following moves:

$$1 \rightarrow 3 \text{ (This means move one disk from peg 1 to peg 3.)}$$
$$1 \rightarrow 2$$
$$3 \rightarrow 2$$
$$1 \rightarrow 3$$
$$2 \rightarrow 1$$
$$2 \rightarrow 3$$
$$1 \rightarrow 3$$

6.39 *(Towers of Hanoi: Iterative Version)* Any program that can be implemented recursively can be implemented iteratively, although sometimes with more difficulty and less clarity. Try writing an iterative version of the Towers of Hanoi. If you succeed, compare your iterative version with the recursive version developed in Exercise 6.38. Investigate issues of performance, clarity and your ability to demonstrate the correctness of the programs.

6.40 *(Visualizing Recursion)* It's interesting to watch recursion "in action." Modify the factorial function of Fig. 6.25 to print its local variable and recursive call parameter. For each recursive call, display the outputs on a separate line and add a level of indentation. Do your utmost to make the outputs clear, interesting and meaningful. Your goal here is to design and implement an output format that helps a person understand recursion better. You may want to add such display capabilities to the many other recursion examples and exercises throughout the text.

6.41 *(Recursive Greatest Common Divisor)* The greatest common divisor of integers x and y is the largest integer that evenly divides both x and y. Write a recursive function gcd that returns the greatest common divisor of x and y, defined recursively as follows: If y is equal to 0, then gcd(x, y) is x; otherwise, gcd(x, y) is gcd(y, x % y), where % is the remainder operator. [*Note:* For this algorithm, x must be larger than y.]

6.42 *(Distance Between Points)* Write function distance that calculates the distance between two points *(x1, y1)* and *(x2, y2)*. All numbers and return values should be of type double.

6.43 What does the following program do?

```
1    // Exercise 6.44: ex06_44.cpp
2    // What does this program do?
3    #include <iostream>
4    using namespace std;
5
6    int mystery(int, int); // function prototype
7
8    int main() {
9       cout << "Enter two integers: ";
10      int x{0};
11      int y{0};
```

```
12      cin >> x >> y;
13      cout << "The result is " << mystery(x, y) << endl;
14   }
15
16   // Parameter b must be a positive integer to prevent infinite recursion
17   int mystery(int a, int b) {
18      if (1 == b) { // base case
19         return a;
20      }
21      else { // recursion step
22         return a + mystery(a, b - 1);
23      }
24   }
```

6.44   After you determine what the program of Exercise 6.43 does, modify the program to function properly after removing the restriction that the second argument be nonnegative.

6.45   *(Math Library Functions)* Write a program that tests as many of the math library functions in Fig. 6.2 as you can. Exercise each of these functions by having your program print out tables of return values for a diversity of argument values.

6.46   *(Find the Error)* Find the error in each of the following program segments and explain how to correct it:

a) `float cube(float); // function prototype`

   ```
   cube(float number) { // function definition
      return number * number * number;
   }
   ```
b) `int randomNumber{srand()};`
c) `float y{123.45678};`
   ```
   int x;
   x = y;
   cout << static_cast<float>(x) << endl;
   ```
d) `double square(double number) {`
   ```
      double number{0};
      return number * number;
   }
   ```
e) `int sum(int n) {`
   ```
      if (0 == n) {
         return 0;
      }
      else {
         return n + sum(n);
      }
   }
   ```

6.47   *(Craps Game Modification)* Modify the craps program of Fig. 6.9 to allow wagering. Package as a function the portion of the program that runs one game of craps. Initialize variable bankBalance to 1000 dollars. Prompt the player to enter a wager. Use a while loop to check that wager is less than or equal to bankBalance and, if not, prompt the user to reenter wager until a valid wager is entered. After a correct wager is entered, run one game of craps. If the player wins, increase bankBalance by wager and print the new bankBalance. If the player loses, decrease bankBalance by wager, print the new bankBalance, check on whether bankBalance has become zero and, if so, print the message "Sorry. You busted!" As the game progresses, print various messages to create some "chatter" such as "Oh, you're going for broke, huh?", "Aw cmon, take a chance!" or "You're up big. Now's the time to cash in your chips!".

6.48   *(Circle Area)* Write a C++ program that prompts the user for the radius of a circle, then calls inline function circleArea to calculate the area of that circle.

6.49   *(Pass-by-Value vs. Pass-by-Reference)* Write a complete C++ program with the two alternate functions specified below, each of which simply triples the variable count defined in main. Then compare and contrast the two approaches. These two functions are
   a) function tripleByValue that passes a copy of count by value, triples the copy and returns the new value and
   b) function tripleByReference that passes count by reference via a reference parameter and triples the original value of count through its alias (i.e., the reference parameter).

6.50   *(Unary Scope Resolution Operator)* What's the purpose of the unary scope resolution operator?

6.51   *(Function Template minimum)* Write a program that uses a function template called minimum to determine the smaller of two arguments. Test the program using integer, character and floating-point number arguments.

6.52   *(Function Template maximum)* Write a program that uses a function template called maximum to determine the larger of two arguments. Test the program using integer, character and floating-point number arguments.

6.53   *(Find the Error)* Determine whether the following program segments contain errors. For each error, explain how it can be corrected. [*Note:* For a particular program segment, it's possible that no errors are present.]

   a)
```
template <typename A>
int sum(int num1, int num2, int num3) {
    return num1 + num2 + num3;
}
```
   b)
```
void printResults(int x, int y) {
    cout << "The sum is " << x + y << '\n';
    return x + y;
}
```
   c)
```
template <A>
A product(A num1, A num2, A num3) {
    return num1 * num2 * num3;
}
```
   d)
```
double cube(int);
int cube(int);
```

6.54   *(C++11 Random Numbers: Modified Craps Game)* Modify the program of Fig. 6.9 to use the new C++11 random-number generation features shown in Section 6.9.

6.55   *(C++11 Scoped enum)* Create a scoped enum named AccountType containing constants named SAVINGS, CHECKING and INVESTMENT.

6.56   *(Function Prototypes and Definitions)* Explain the difference between a function prototype and a function definition.

Making a Difference

As computer costs decline, it becomes feasible for every student, regardless of economic circumstance, to have a computer and use it in school. This creates exciting possibilities for improving the educational experience of all students worldwide, as suggested by the next five exercises. [*Note:* Check out initiatives such as the One Laptop Per Child Project (www.laptop.org). Also, research "green" laptops—and note the key "going green" characteristics of these devices. Look into the Electronic Product Environmental Assessment Tool (www.epeat.net), which can help you assess the "greenness" of desktops, notebooks and monitors to help you decide which products to purchase.]

6.57   *(Computer-Assisted Instruction)* The use of computers in education is referred to as *computer-assisted instruction (CAI)*. Write a program that will help an elementary-school student learn multiplication. Use the rand function to produce two positive one-digit integers. The program should then prompt the user with a question, such as

```
How much is 6 times 7?
```

The student then inputs the answer. Next, the program checks the student's answer. If it's correct, display the message "Very good!" and ask another multiplication question. If the answer is wrong, display the message "No. Please try again." and let the student try the same question repeatedly until the student finally gets it right. A separate function should be used to generate each new question. This function should be called once when the application begins execution and each time the user answers the question correctly.

6.58   *(Computer-Assisted Instruction: Reducing Student Fatigue)* One problem in CAI environments is student fatigue. This can be reduced by varying the computer's responses to hold the student's attention. Modify the program of Exercise 6.57 so that various comments are displayed for each answer as follows:

Possible responses to a correct answer:

```
Very good!
Excellent!
Nice work!
Keep up the good work!
```

Possible responses to an incorrect answer:

```
No. Please try again.
Wrong. Try once more.
Don't give up!
No. Keep trying.
```

Use random-number generation to choose a number from 1 to 4 that will be used to select one of the four appropriate responses to each correct or incorrect answer. Use a switch statement to issue the responses.

6.59   *(Computer-Assisted Instruction: Monitoring Student Performance)* More sophisticated computer-assisted instruction systems monitor the student's performance over a period of time. The decision to begin a new topic is often based on the student's success with previous topics. Modify the program of Exercise 6.58 to count the number of correct and incorrect responses typed by the student. After the student types 10 answers, your program should calculate the percentage that are correct. If the percentage is lower than 75%, display "Please ask your teacher for extra help.", then reset the program so another student can try it. If the percentage is 75% or higher, display "Congratulations, you are ready to go to the next level!", then reset the program so another student can try it.

6.60   *(Computer-Assisted Instruction: Difficulty Levels)* Exercises 6.57–6.59 developed a computer-assisted instruction program to help teach an elementary-school student multiplication. Modify the program to allow the user to enter a difficulty level. At a difficulty level of 1, the program should use only single-digit numbers in the problems; at a difficulty level of 2, numbers as large as two digits, and so on.

6.61 *(Computer-Assisted Instruction: Varying the Types of Problems)* Modify the program of Exercise 6.60 to allow the user to pick a type of arithmetic problem to study. An option of 1 means addition problems only, 2 means subtraction problems only, 3 means multiplication problems only, 4 means division problems only and 5 means a random mixture of all these types.

Class Templates **array** and **vector**; Catching Exceptions

Objectives

In this chapter you'll:

- Use C++ Standard Library class template **array**—a fixed-size collection of related data items.

- Declare **arrays**, initialize **arrays** and refer to the elements of **arrays**.

- Use **arrays** to store, sort and search lists and tables of values.

- Use the range-based **for** statement.

- Pass **arrays** to functions.

- Use C++ Standard Library function **sort** to arrange **array** elements in ascending order.

- Use C++ Standard Library function **binary_search** to locate an element in a sorted **array**.

- Declare and manipulate multidimensional **arrays**.

- Use one- and two-dimensional **arrays** to build a real-world **GradeBook** class.

- Use C++ Standard Library class template **vector**—a variable-size collection of related data items.

7.1 Introduction

This chapter introduces the topic of data structures—*collections* of related data items. We discuss arrays, which are *fixed-size* collections consisting of data items of the *same* type, and vectors, which are collections (also of data items of the *same* type) that can grow and shrink *dynamically* at execution time. Both array and vector are C++ standard library *class templates*. To use them, you must include the <array> and <vector> headers, respectively.

After discussing how arrays are declared, created and initialized, we present examples that demonstrate several common array manipulations. We show how to *search* arrays to find particular elements and *sort* arrays to put their data in *order*.

We build two versions of an instructor GradeBook case study that use arrays to maintain sets of student grades *in memory* and analyze student grades. We introduce the *exception-handling* mechanism and use it to allow a program to continue executing when it attempts to access an array or vector element that does not exist.

7.2 `arrays`

An array is a *contiguous* group of memory locations that all have the *same* type. To refer to a particular location or element in the array, we specify the name of the array and the position number of the particular element in the array.

Figure 7.1 shows an integer array called c that contains 12 elements. You refer to any one of these elements by giving the array name followed by the particular element's *position number* in square brackets ([]). The position number is more formally called a subscript or index (this number specifies the number of elements from the beginning of the array). The first element has subscript 0 (zero) and is sometimes called the zeroth element. Thus, the elements of array c are c[0] (pronounced "c sub zero"), c[1], c[2] and so on. The highest subscript in array c is 11, which is 1 less than the number of elements in the array (12). array names follow the same conventions as other variable names.

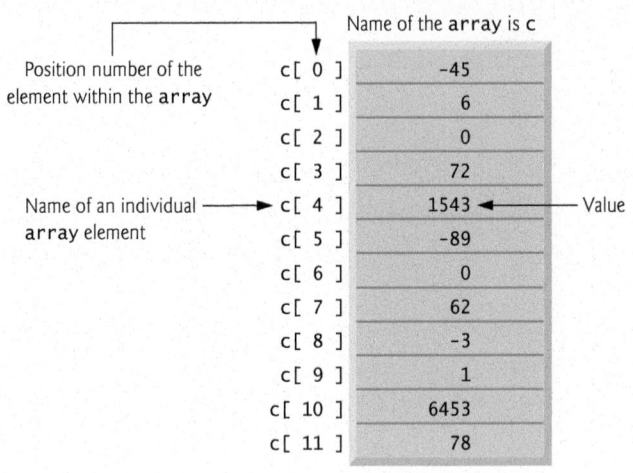

Fig. 7.1 | array of 12 elements.

A subscript must be an integer or integer expression (using any integral type). If a program uses an expression as a subscript, then the program evaluates the expression to determine the subscript. For example, if we assume that variable a is equal to 5 and that variable b is equal to 6, then the statement

```
c[a + b] += 2;
```

adds 2 to array element c[11]. A subscripted array name is an *lvalue*—it can be used on the left side of an assignment, just as non-array variable names can.

Let's examine array c in Fig. 7.1 more closely. The name of the entire array is c. Each array *knows its own size*, which can be determined by calling its size member function as in c.size(). Its 12 elements are referred to as c[0] to c[11]. The value of c[0] is -45, the value of c[7] is 62 and the value of c[11] is 78. To print the sum of the values contained in the first three elements of array c, we'd write

```
cout << c[0] + c[1] + c[2] << endl;
```

To divide the value of c[6] by 2 and assign the result to the variable x, we'd write

```
x = c[6] / 2;
```

Common Programming Error 7.1

Note the difference between the "seventh element of the array" and "array element 7." Subscripts begin at 0, so the "seventh element of the array" has the subscript 6, while "array element 7" has the subscript 7 and is actually the eighth element of the array. This distinction is a frequent source of off-by-one errors. To avoid such errors, we refer to specific array elements explicitly by their array name and subscript number (e.g., c[6] or c[7]).

The brackets that enclose a subscript are actually an *operator* that has the same precedence as parentheses used to call a function. Figure 7.2 shows the precedence and associativity of the operators introduced so far. The operators are shown top to bottom in decreasing order of precedence with their associativity and type.

Operators	Associativity	Type
`::` `()`	left to right *[See caution in Fig. 2.10 regarding grouping parentheses.]*	primary
`()` `[]` `++` `--` `static_cast<type>(operand)`	left to right	postfix
`++` `--` `+` `-` `!`	right to left	unary (prefix)
`*` `/` `%`	left to right	multiplicative
`+` `-`	left to right	additive
`<<` `>>`	left to right	insertion/extraction
`<` `<=` `>` `>=`	left to right	relational
`==` `!=`	left to right	equality
`&&`	left to right	logical AND
`||`	left to right	logical OR
`?:`	right to left	conditional
`=` `+=` `-=` `*=` `/=` `%=`	right to left	assignment
`,`	left to right	comma

Fig. 7.2 | Precedence and associativity of the operators introduced to this point.

7.3 Declaring arrays

arrays occupy space in memory. To specify the type of the elements and the number of elements required by an array use a declaration of the form

```
array<type, arraySize> arrayName;
```

The notation *<type, arraySize>* indicates that array is a *class template*. The compiler reserves the appropriate amount of memory based on the *type* of the elements and the *arraySize*. (Recall that a declaration which reserves memory is more specifically known as a *definition*.) The *arraySize* must be an unsigned integer. To tell the compiler to reserve 12 elements for integer array c, use the declaration

```
array<int, 12> c; // c is an array of 12 int values
```

arrays can be declared to contain values of most data types. For example, an array of type string can be used to store character strings.

7.4 Examples Using arrays

The following examples demonstrate how to declare, initialize and manipulate arrays.

7.4.1 Declaring an array and Using a Loop to Initialize the array's Elements

The program in Fig. 7.3 declares five-element integer array n (line 9). Line 5 includes the <array> header, which contains the definition of class template array. Lines 12–14 use a for statement to initialize the array elements to zeros. Like other non-static local variables, arrays are *not* implicitly initialized to zero (static arrays are). The first output statement (line 16) displays the column headings for the columns printed in the subsequent for statement (lines 19–21), which prints the array in tabular format. Remember that setw specifies the field width in which only the *next* value is to be output.

```cpp
1   // Fig. 7.3: fig07_03.cpp
2   // Initializing an array's elements to zeros and printing the array.
3   #include <iostream>
4   #include <iomanip>
5   #include <array>
6   using namespace std;
7
8   int main() {
9      array<int, 5> n; // n is an array of 5 int values
10
11     // initialize elements of array n to 0
12     for (size_t i{0}; i < n.size(); ++i) {
13        n[i] = 0; // set element at location i to 0
14     }
15
16     cout << "Element" << setw(10) << "Value" << endl;
17
18     // output each array element's value
19     for (size_t j{0}; j < n.size(); ++j) {
20        cout << setw(7) << j << setw(10) << n[j] << endl;
21     }
22  }
```

```
Element    Value
      0        0
      1        0
      2        0
      3        0
      4        0
```

Fig. 7.3 | Initializing an array's elements to zeros and printing the array.

In this program, the control variables i (line 12) and j (line 19) that specify array subscripts are declared to be of type size_t. According to the C++ standard size_t represents an unsigned integral type. This type is recommended for any variable that represents an array's size or an array's subscripts. Type size_t is defined in the std namespace and is in header <cstddef>, which is included by various other headers. If you attempt to compile a program that uses type size_t and receive errors indicating that it's not defined, simply add #include <cstddef> to your program.

7.4.2 Initializing an array in a Declaration with an Initializer List

The elements of an array also can be initialized in the array declaration by following the array name with a brace-delimited comma-separated list of initializers. The program in Fig. 7.4 uses an initializer list to initialize an integer array with five values (line 9) and prints the array in tabular format (lines 11–16).

```cpp
1   // Fig. 7.4: fig07_04.cpp
2   // Initializing an array in a declaration.
3   #include <iostream>
4   #include <iomanip>
5   #include <array>
6   using namespace std;
7
8   int main() {
9      array<int, 5> n{32, 27, 64, 18, 95}; // list initializer
10
11     cout << "Element" << setw(10) << "Value" << endl;
12
13     // output each array element's value
14     for (size_t i{0}; i < n.size(); ++i) {
15        cout << setw(7) << i << setw(10) << n[i] << endl;
16     }
17  }
```

```
Element     Value
      0        32
      1        27
      2        64
      3        18
      4        95
```

Fig. 7.4 | Initializing an array in a declaration.

Fewer Initializers Than **array** Elements

If there are *fewer* initializers than array elements, the remaining array elements are initialized to zero. For example, the elements of array n in Fig. 7.3 could have been initialized to zero with the declaration

```cpp
array<int, 5> n{}; // initialize elements of array n to 0
```

which initializes the elements to zero, because there are fewer initializers (none in this case) than array elements. This technique can be used only in the array's declaration, whereas the initialization technique shown in Fig. 7.3 can be used repeatedly during program execution to "reinitialize" an array's elements.

More Initializers Than **array** Elements

If an initializer list is specified in an array declaration, the number of initializers must be less than or equal to the array size. The array declaration

```cpp
array<int, 5> n{32, 27, 64, 18, 95, 14};
```

causes a compilation error, because there are six initializers and only five array elements.

7.4.3 Specifying an array's Size with a Constant Variable and Setting array Elements with Calculations

Figure 7.5 sets the elements of a 5-element array named values to the even integers 2, 4, 6, 8 and 10 (lines 14–16) and prints the array in tabular format (lines 18–23). These numbers are generated (line 15) by multiplying each successive value of the loop counter, i, by 2 and adding 2.

```cpp
 1   // Fig. 7.5: fig07_05.cpp
 2   // Set array s to the even integers from 2 to 10.
 3   #include <iostream>
 4   #include <iomanip>
 5   #include <array>
 6   using namespace std;
 7
 8   int main() {
 9      // constant variable can be used to specify array size
10      const size_t arraySize{5}; // must initialize in declaration
11
12      array<int, arraySize> values; // array values has 5 elements
13
14      for (size_t i{0}; i < values.size(); ++i) { // set the values
15         values[i] = 2 + 2 * i;
16      }
17
18      cout << "Element" << setw(10) << "Value" << endl;
19
20      // output contents of array s in tabular format
21      for (size_t j{0}; j < values.size(); ++j) {
22         cout << setw(7) << j << setw(10) << values[j] << endl;
23      }
24   }
```

```
Element    Value
      0        2
      1        4
      2        6
      3        8
      4       10
```

Fig. 7.5 | Set array s to the even integers from 2 to 10.

Constant Variables

Line 10 uses the const qualifier to declare a constant variable arraySize with the value 5. Constant variables are also called named constants or read-only variables. A constant variable *must* be initialized when it's declared and *cannot* be modified thereafter. Attempting to modify arraySize after it's initialized, as in

```cpp
arraySize = 7;
```

results in the following errors[1] from Visual C++, GNU C++ and LLVM, respectively:

- Visual C++: `'arraySize': you cannot assign to a variable that is const`
- GNU C++: `error: assignment of read-only variable 'x'`
- LLVM: `Read-only variable is not assignable`

Common Programming Error 7.2
Not initializing a constant variable when it's declared is a compilation error.

Common Programming Error 7.3
Assigning a value to a constant variable in a separate statement from its declaration is a compilation error.

Good Programming Practice 7.1
Defining the size of an `array` as a constant variable instead of a literal constant makes programs clearer and easier to update. This technique eliminates so-called magic numbers— *numeric values that are not explained. Using a constant variable allows you to provide a name for a literal constant and can help explain the purpose of the value in the program.*

7.4.4 Summing the Elements of an `array`

Often, the elements of an `array` represent a series of values to be used in a calculation. For example, if the elements of an `array` represent exam grades, a professor may wish to total the elements of the `array` and use that sum to calculate the class average for the exam.

The program in Fig. 7.6 sums the values contained in the four-element integer `array` a. The program declares, creates and initializes the `array` in line 9. The `for` statement (lines 13–15) performs the calculations. The values being supplied as initializers for `array` a also could be read into the program—for example, from the user at the keyboard or from a file on disk (see Chapter 14, File Processing). For example, the `for` statement

```
for (size_t j{0}; j < a.size(); ++j) {
   cin >> a[j];
}
```

reads one value at a time from the keyboard and stores the value in element a[j].

```
1   // Fig. 7.6: fig07_06.cpp
2   // Compute the sum of the elements of an array.
3   #include <iostream>
4   #include <array>
5   using namespace std;
6
7   int main() {
8      const size_t arraySize{4}; // specifies size of array
```

Fig. 7.6 | Compute the sum of the elements of an `array`. (Part 1 of 2.)

---

1. In error messages, some compilers refer to a const fundamental-type variable as a "const object." The C++ standard defines an "object" as any "region of storage." Like class objects, fundamental-type variables also occupy space in memory, so they're often referred to as "objects" as well.

```
 9      array<int, arraySize> a{10, 20, 30, 40};
10      int total{0};
11
12      // sum contents of array a
13      for (size_t i{0}; i < a.size(); ++i) {
14         total += a[i];
15      }
16
17      cout << "Total of array elements: " << total << endl;
18   }
```

```
Total of array elements: 100
```

Fig. 7.6 | Compute the sum of the elements of an array. (Part 2 of 2.)

7.4.5 Using a Bar Chart to Display array Data Graphically

Many programs present data to users graphically. For example, numeric values are often displayed as bars in a bar chart, with longer bars representing proportionally larger numeric values. One simple way to display numeric data graphically is with a bar chart that shows each numeric value as a bar of asterisks (*).

Professors often like to examine grade distributions on an exam. A professor might graph the number of grades in each of several categories to visualize the grade distribution. Suppose the grades were 87, 68, 94, 100, 83, 78, 85, 91, 76 and 87. There was one grade of 100, two grades in the 90s, four grades in the 80s, two grades in the 70s, one grade in the 60s and no grades below 60. Our next program (Fig. 7.7) stores this data in an array of 11 elements, each corresponding to a grade range. For example, n[0] indicates the number of grades in the range 0–9, n[7] indicates the number of grades in the range 70–79 and n[10] indicates the number of grades of 100. The GradeBook classes that you'll see in Figs. 7.13 and 7.19 contain code that calculates grade frequencies based on a set of grades. In this example, we initialize the array n with frequency values.

The program (Fig. 7.7) reads the numbers from the array and graphs the information as a bar chart, displaying each grade range followed by a bar of asterisks indicating the number of grades in that range. To label each bar, lines 17–25 output a grade range (e.g., "70-79: ") based on the current value of counter variable i. The *nested* for statement (lines 28–30) outputs the current bar as the appropriate number of asterisks. Note the loop-continuation condition in line 28 (stars < n[i]). Each time the program reaches the *inner* for, the loop counts from 0 up to n[i], thus using a value in array n to determine the number of asterisks to display. In this example, n[0]–n[5] contain zeros because no students received a grade below 60. Thus, the program displays no asterisks next to the first six grade ranges.

```
1   // Fig. 7.7: fig07_07.cpp
2   // Bar chart printing program.
3   #include <iostream>
4   #include <iomanip>
5   #include <array>
6   using namespace std;
```

Fig. 7.7 | Bar chart printing program. (Part 1 of 2.)

```
7
8   int main() {
9      const size_t arraySize{11};
10     array<unsigned int, arraySize> n{0, 0, 0, 0, 0, 0, 1, 2, 4, 2, 1};
11
12     cout << "Grade distribution:" << endl;
13
14     // for each element of array n, output a bar of the chart
15     for (size_t i{0}; i < n.size(); ++i) {
16        // output bar labels ("0-9:", ..., "90-99:", "100:")
17        if (0 == i) {
18           cout << "  0-9: ";
19        }
20        else if (10 == i) {
21           cout << "  100: ";
22        }
23        else {
24           cout << i * 10 << "-" << (i * 10) + 9 << ": ";
25        }
26
27        // print bar of asterisks
28        for (unsigned int stars{0}; stars < n[i]; ++stars) {
29           cout << '*';
30        }
31
32        cout << endl; // start a new line of output
33     }
34  }
```

```
Grade distribution:
  0-9:
 10-19:
 20-29:
 30-39:
 40-49:
 50-59:
 60-69: *
 70-79: **
 80-89: ****
 90-99: **
  100: *
```

Fig. 7.7 | Bar chart printing program. (Part 2 of 2.)

7.4.6 Using the Elements of an array as Counters

Sometimes, programs use counter variables to summarize data, such as the results of a survey. In Fig. 6.7, we used separate counters in our die-rolling program to track the number of occurrences of each side of a die as the program rolled the die 60,000,000 times. An array version of this program is shown in Fig. 7.8. This version also uses the new C++11 random-number generation capabilities that were introduced in Section 6.9.

Figure 7.8 uses the array frequency (line 17) to count the occurrences of die value. *The single statement in line 21 of this program replaces the entire switch statement in lines 22–43 of Fig. 6.7.* Line 21 uses a random value to determine which frequency element to

```
 1   // Fig. 7.8: fig07_08.cpp
 2   // Die-rolling program using an array instead of switch.
 3   #include <iostream>
 4   #include <iomanip>
 5   #include <array>
 6   #include <random>
 7   #include <ctime>
 8   using namespace std;
 9
10   int main() {
11      // use the default random-number generation engine to
12      // produce uniformly distributed pseudorandom int values from 1 to 6
13      default_random_engine engine(static_cast<unsigned int>(time(0)));
14      uniform_int_distribution<unsigned int> randomInt(1, 6);
15
16      const size_t arraySize{7}; // ignore element zero
17      array<unsigned int, arraySize> frequency{}; // initialize to 0s
18
19      // roll die 60,000,000 times; use die value as frequency index
20      for (unsigned int roll{1}; roll <= 60'000'000; ++roll) {
21         ++frequency[randomInt(engine)];
22      }
23
24      cout << "Face" << setw(13) << "Frequency" << endl;
25
26      // output each array element's value
27      for (size_t face{1}; face < frequency.size(); ++face) {
28         cout << setw(4) << face << setw(13) << frequency[face] << endl;
29      }
30   }
```

```
Face    Frequency
   1     9997901
   2     9999110
   3    10001172
   4    10003619
   5     9997606
   6    10000592
```

Fig. 7.8 | Die-rolling program using an array instead of switch.

increment during each iteration of the loop. The calculation in line 21 produces a random subscript from 1 to 6, so array frequency must be large enough to store six counters. We use a seven-element array in which we ignore frequency[0]—it's clearer to have the die face value 1 increment frequency[1] than frequency[0]. Thus, each face value is used *directly* as a subscript for array frequency. We also replace lines 46–51 of Fig. 6.7 by looping through array frequency to output the results (Fig. 7.8, lines 27–29).

7.4.7 Using arrays to Summarize Survey Results

Our next example uses arrays to summarize the results of data collected in a survey. Consider the following problem statement:

> *Twenty students were asked to rate on a scale of 1 to 5 the quality of the food in the*
> *student cafeteria, with 1 being "awful" and 5 being "excellent." Place the 20 responses*
> *in an integer array and determine the frequency of each rating.*

This is a popular type of array-processing application (Fig. 7.9). We wish to summarize the number of responses of each rating (that is, 1–5). The array responses (lines 14–15) is a 20-element integer array of the students' responses to the survey. The array responses is declared const, as its values do not (and should not) change. We use a six-element array frequency (line 18) to count the number of occurrences of each response. Each element of the array is used as a counter for one of the survey responses and is initialized to zero. As in Fig. 7.8, we ignore frequency[0].

```cpp
 1    // Fig. 7.9: fig07_09.cpp
 2    // Poll analysis program.
 3    #include <iostream>
 4    #include <iomanip>
 5    #include <array>
 6    using namespace std;
 7
 8    int main() {
 9       // define array sizes
10       const size_t responseSize{20}; // size of array responses
11       const size_t frequencySize{6}; // size of array frequency
12
13       // place survey responses in array responses
14       const array<unsigned int, responseSize> responses{
15          1, 2, 5, 4, 3, 5, 2, 1, 3, 1, 4, 3, 3, 3, 2, 3, 3, 2, 2, 5};
16
17       // initialize frequency counters to 0
18       array<unsigned int, frequencySize> frequency{};
19
20       // for each answer, select responses element and use that value
21       // as frequency subscript to determine element to increment
22       for (size_t answer{0}; answer < responses.size(); ++answer) {
23          ++frequency[responses[answer]];
24       }
25
26       cout << "Rating" << setw(12) << "Frequency" << endl;
27
28       // output each array element's value
29       for (size_t rating{1}; rating < frequency.size(); ++rating) {
30          cout << setw(6) << rating << setw(12) << frequency[rating] << endl;
31       }
32    }
```

```
Rating   Frequency
     1           3
     2           5
     3           7
     4           2
     5           3
```

Fig. 7.9 | Poll analysis program.

The first for statement (lines 22–24) takes the responses one at a time from the array responses and increments one of the five counters in the frequency array (frequency[1] to frequency[5]). The key statement in the loop is line 23, which increments the appropriate frequency counter, depending on the value of responses[answer].

Let's consider several iterations of the for loop. When control variable answer is 0, the value of responses[answer] is the value of responses[0] (i.e., 1 in line 15), so the program interprets ++frequency[responses[answer]] as

```
++frequency[1]
```

which increments the value in array element 1. To evaluate the expression in line 23, start with the value in the *innermost* set of square brackets (answer). Once you know answer's value (which is the value of the control variable in line 22), plug it into the expression and evaluate the expression in the next outer set of square brackets (i.e., responses[answer], which is a value selected from the responses array in lines 14–15). Then use the resulting value as the subscript for the frequency array to specify which counter to increment.

When answer is 1, responses[answer] is the value of responses[1], which is 2, so the program interprets ++frequency[responses[answer]] as

```
++frequency[2]
```

which increments array element 2.

When answer is 2, responses[answer] is the value of responses[2], which is 5, so the program interprets ++frequency[responses[answer]] as

```
++frequency[5]
```

which increments array element 5, and so on. Regardless of the number of responses processed in the survey, the program requires *only* a six-element array (ignoring element zero) to summarize the results, because all the response values are between 1 and 5 and the subscript values for a six-element array are 0 through 5.

Bounds Checking for **array** Subscripts

If the data in responses contained an invalid value, such as 13, the program would have attempted to add 1 to frequency[13], which is *outside* the bounds of the array. *When you use the [] operator to access an array element, C++ provides no automatic array bounds checking to prevent you from referring to an element that does not exist.* Thus, an executing program can "walk off" either end of an array without warning. In Section 7.10, we demonstrate the class template vector's at member function, which performs bounds checking for you. Class template array also has an at member function.

It's important to ensure that every subscript you use to access an array element is within the array's bounds—that is, greater than or equal to 0 and less than the number of array elements.

Allowing programs to read from or write to array elements outside the bounds of arrays are common *security flaws*. Reading from out-of-bounds array elements can cause a program to crash or even appear to execute correctly while using bad data. Writing to an out-of-bounds element (known as a *buffer overflow*) can corrupt a program's data in memory, crash a program and allow attackers to exploit the system and execute their own code. For more information on buffer overflows, see http://en.wikipedia.org/wiki/Buffer_overflow.

Common Programming Error 7.4

Referring to an element outside the array bounds is an execution-time *logic error, not a syntax error.*

Error-Prevention Tip 7.1

When looping through an array, *the index should never go below 0 and should always be less than the total number of array elements (one less than the size of the* array). *Make sure that the loop-termination condition prevents accessing elements outside this range. In Section 7.5, you'll learn about the range-based* for *statement, which can help prevent accessing elements outside an array's (or other container's) bounds.*

7.4.8 Static Local arrays and Automatic Local arrays

Chapter 6 discussed the storage-class specifier static. A static local variable in a function definition exists for the program's duration but is visible *only* in the function's body.

Performance Tip 7.1

We can apply static *to a local* array *declaration so that it's* not *created and initialized each time the program calls the function and is* not *destroyed each time the function terminates. This can improve performance, especially when using large* arrays.

A program initializes static local arrays when their declarations are first encountered. If a static array is not initialized explicitly by you, each element of that array is initialized to *zero* by the compiler when the array is created. Recall that C++ does *not* perform such default initialization for other local variables.

Figure 7.10 demonstrates functions staticArrayInit (lines 23–40) with a static local array (line 25) and automaticArrayInit (lines 43–60) with an automatic local array (line 45)—local variables are sometimes called automatic variables because they're automatically destroyed when the function finishes executing.

Function staticArrayInit is called twice (lines 13 and 17). The static local array1 is *initialized to zero* by the compiler the first time the function is called. The function prints the array's elements, then adds 5 to and prints each element again. The second time the function is called, the static array contains the *modified* values stored during the first function call. Function automaticArrayInit also is called twice (lines 14 and 18). Automatic local array2's elements are initialized (line 45) with the values 1, 2 and 3. The function prints the array, adds 5 to each element and prints the array again. The second time the function is called, the array elements are *reinitialized* to 1, 2 and 3. The array is recreated and reinitialized during each call to automaticArrayInit.

```
1   // Fig. 7.10: fig07_10.cpp
2   // static array initialization and automatic array initialization.
3   #include <iostream>
4   #include <array>
5   using namespace std;
6
7   void staticArrayInit(); // function prototype
```

Fig. 7.10 | static array initialization and automatic array initialization. (Part 1 of 3.)

```
 8   void automaticArrayInit(); // function prototype
 9   const size_t arraySize{3};
10
11   int main() {
12      cout << "First call to each function:\n";
13      staticArrayInit();
14      automaticArrayInit();
15
16      cout << "\n\nSecond call to each function:\n";
17      staticArrayInit();
18      automaticArrayInit();
19      cout << endl;
20   }
21
22   // function to demonstrate a static local array
23   void staticArrayInit(void) {
24      // initializes elements to 0 first time function is called
25      static array<int, arraySize> array1; // static local array
26
27      cout << "\nValues on entering staticArrayInit:\n";
28
29      // output contents of array1
30      for (size_t i{0}; i < array1.size(); ++i) {
31         cout << "array1[" << i << "] = " << array1[i] << "   ";
32      }
33
34      cout << "\nValues on exiting staticArrayInit:\n";
35
36      // modify and output contents of array1
37      for (size_t j{0}; j < array1.size(); ++j) {
38         cout << "array1[" << j << "] = " << (array1[j] += 5) << "   ";
39      }
40   }
41
42   // function to demonstrate an automatic local array
43   void automaticArrayInit(void) {
44      // initializes elements each time function is called
45      array<int, arraySize> array2{1, 2, 3}; // automatic local array
46
47      cout << "\n\nValues on entering automaticArrayInit:\n";
48
49      // output contents of array2
50      for (size_t i{0}; i < array2.size(); ++i) {
51         cout << "array2[" << i << "] = " << array2[i] << "   ";
52      }
53
54      cout << "\nValues on exiting automaticArrayInit:\n";
55
56      // modify and output contents of array2
57      for (size_t j{0}; j < array2.size(); ++j) {
58         cout << "array2[" << j << "] = " << (array2[j] += 5) << "   ";
59      }
60   }
```

Fig. 7.10 | static array initialization and automatic array initialization. (Part 2 of 3.)

```
First call to each function:

Values on entering staticArrayInit:
array1[0] = 0   array1[1] = 0   array1[2] = 0
Values on exiting staticArrayInit:
array1[0] = 5   array1[1] = 5   array1[2] = 5

Values on entering automaticArrayInit:
array2[0] = 1   array2[1] = 2   array2[2] = 3
Values on exiting automaticArrayInit:
array2[0] = 6   array2[1] = 7   array2[2] = 8

Second call to each function:

Values on entering staticArrayInit:
array1[0] = 5   array1[1] = 5   array1[2] = 5
Values on exiting staticArrayInit:
array1[0] = 10   array1[1] = 10   array1[2] = 10

Values on entering automaticArrayInit:
array2[0] = 1   array2[1] = 2   array2[2] = 3
Values on exiting automaticArrayInit:
array2[0] = 6   array2[1] = 7   array2[2] = 8
```

Fig. 7.10 | static array initialization and automatic array initialization. (Part 3 of 3.)

7.5 Range-Based for Statement

As we've shown, it's common to process *all* the elements of an array. The C++11 range-based for statement allows you to do this *without using a counter*, thus avoiding the possibility of "stepping outside" the array and eliminating the need for you to implement your own bounds checking. Figure 7.11 uses the range-based for to display an array's contents (lines 12–14 and 23–25) and to multiply each of the array's element values by 2 (lines 17–19).

> **Error-Prevention Tip 7.2**
> *When processing all elements of an array, if you don't need access to an array element's subscript, use the range-based for statement.*

```cpp
 1  // Fig. 7.11: fig07_11.cpp
 2  // Using range-based for to multiply an array's elements by 2.
 3  #include <iostream>
 4  #include <array>
 5  using namespace std;
 6
 7  int main() {
 8     array<int, 5> items{1, 2, 3, 4, 5};
 9
10     // display items before modification
11     cout << "items before modification: ";
```

Fig. 7.11 | Using range-based for to multiply an array's elements by 2. (Part 1 of 2.)

```
12      for (int item : items) {
13          cout << item << " ";
14      }
15
16      // multiply the elements of items by 2
17      for (int& itemRef : items) {
18          itemRef *= 2;
19      }
20
21      // display items after modification
22      cout << "\nitems after modification: ";
23      for (int item : items) {
24          cout << item << " ";
25      }
26
27      cout << endl;
28  }
```

```
items before modification: 1 2 3 4 5
items after modification: 2 4 6 8 10
```

Fig. 7.11 | Using range-based for to multiply an array's elements by 2. (Part 2 of 2.)

Using the Range-Based **for** to Display an **array's** Contents

The range-based for statement simplifies the code for iterating through an array. Line 12 can be read as "for each iteration, assign the next element of items to int variable item, then execute the loop's body." Thus, for each iteration, item represents one element *value* (but *not* a subscript) in items. In the range-based for's header, you declare a so-called range variable to the left of the colon (:) and specify the name of an array to the right. You can use the range-based for statement with most of the C++ Standard Library's prebuilt data structures (commonly called *containers*). Lines 12–14 are equivalent to the following counter-controlled iteration:

```
for (int counter{0}; counter < items.size(); ++counter) {
    cout << items[counter] << " ";
}
```

Using the Range-Based **for** to Modify an **array's** Contents

Lines 17–19 use a range-based for statement to multiply each element of items by 2. In line 17, the range variable's declaration indicates that itemRef is an int&—that is, a *reference*. Recall that a reference is an *alias* for another variable in memory—in this case, one of the array's elements. We use an int reference because items contains int values and we want to *modify* each element's value—because itemRef is declared as a *reference*, any change you make to itemRef *changes* the corresponding element value in the array.

Using an Element's Subscript

The range-based for statement can be used in place of the counter-controlled for statement whenever code looping through an array does *not* require access to the element's subscript. For example, totaling the integers in an array (as in Fig. 7.6) requires access only to the element *values*—the elements' subscripts are irrelevant. However, if a program must use subscripts for some reason other than simply to loop through an array (e.g., to print a subscript number next to each array element value, as in the examples earlier in this chapter), you should use the counter-controlled for statement.

7.6 Case Study: Class GradeBook Using an array to Store Grades

We now present the first part of our case study on developing a GradeBook class that instructors can use to maintain students' grades on an exam and display a grade report that includes the grades, class average, lowest grade, highest grade and a grade distribution bar chart. The version of class GradeBook presented in this section stores the grades for one exam in a one-dimensional array. In Section 7.9, we present a version of class GradeBook that uses a two-dimensional array to store students' grades for *several* exams.

Storing Student Grades in an **array** in Class **GradeBook**
Figure 7.12 shows the output that summarizes the 10 grades we store in an object of class GradeBook (Fig. 7.13), which uses an array of integers to store the grades of 10 students for a single exam. The array grades is declared as a data member in line 142 of Fig. 7.13—therefore, each GradeBook object maintains its own set of grades.

```
Welcome to the grade book for
CS101 Introduction to C++ Programming!

The grades are:

Student  1:  87
Student  2:  68
Student  3:  94
Student  4: 100
Student  5:  83
Student  6:  78
Student  7:  85
Student  8:  91
Student  9:  76
Student 10:  87

Class average is 84.90
Lowest grade is 68
Highest grade is 100

Grade distribution:
  0-9:
 10-19:
 20-29:
 30-39:
 40-49:
 50-59:
 60-69: *
 70-79: **
 80-89: ****
 90-99: **
   100: *
```

Fig. 7.12 | Output of the GradeBook example that stores grades in an array.

```cpp
 1  // Fig. 7.13: GradeBook.h
 2  // Definition of class GradeBook that uses an array to store test grades.
 3  #include <string>
 4  #include <array>
 5  #include <iostream>
 6  #include <iomanip> // parameterized stream manipulators
 7
 8  // GradeBook class definition
 9  class GradeBook {
10  public:
11     // constant number of students who took the test
12     static const size_t students{10}; // note public data
13
14     // constructor initializes courseName and grades array
15     GradeBook(const std::string& name,
16        const std::array<int, students>& gradesArray)
17        : courseName{name}, grades{gradesArray} {
18     }
19
20     // function to set the course name
21     void setCourseName(const std::string& name) {
22        courseName = name; // store the course name
23     }
24
25     // function to retrieve the course name
26     const std::string& getCourseName() const {
27        return courseName;
28     }
29
30     // display a welcome message to the GradeBook user
31     void displayMessage() const {
32        // call getCourseName to get the name of this GradeBook's course
33        std::cout << "Welcome to the grade book for\n" << getCourseName()
34           << "!" << std::endl;
35     }
36
37     // perform various operations on the data (none modify the data)
38     void processGrades() const {
39        outputGrades(); // output grades array
40
41        // call function getAverage to calculate the average grade
42        std::cout << std::setprecision(2) << std::fixed;
43        std::cout << "\nClass average is " << getAverage() << std::endl;
44
45        // call functions getMinimum and getMaximum
46        std::cout << "Lowest grade is " << getMinimum()
47           << "\nHighest grade is " << getMaximum() << std::endl;
48
49        outputBarChart(); // display grade distribution chart
50     }
51
```

Fig. 7.13 | Definition of class GradeBook that uses an array to store test grades. (Part 1 of 3.)

```
52      // find minimum grade
53      int getMinimum() const {
54         int lowGrade{100}; // assume lowest grade is 100
55
56         // loop through grades array
57         for (int grade : grades) {
58            // if current grade lower than lowGrade, assign it to lowGrade
59            if (grade < lowGrade) {
60               lowGrade = grade; // new lowest grade
61            }
62         }
63
64         return lowGrade; // return lowest grade
65      }
66
67      // find maximum grade
68      int getMaximum() const {
69         int highGrade{0}; // assume highest grade is 0
70
71         // loop through grades array
72         for (int grade : grades) {
73            // if current grade higher than highGrade, assign it to highGrade
74            if (grade > highGrade) {
75               highGrade = grade; // new highest grade
76            }
77         }
78
79         return highGrade; // return highest grade
80      }
81
82      // determine average grade for test
83      double getAverage() const {
84         int total{0}; // initialize total
85
86         // sum grades in array
87         for (int grade : grades) {
88            total += grade;
89         }
90
91         // return average of grades
92         return static_cast<double>(total) / grades.size();
93      }
94
95      // output bar chart displaying grade distribution
96      void outputBarChart() const {
97         std::cout << "\nGrade distribution:" << std::endl;
98
99         // stores frequency of grades in each range of 10 grades
100        const size_t frequencySize{11};
101        std::array<unsigned int, frequencySize> frequency{}; // init to 0s
102
```

Fig. 7.13 | Definition of class GradeBook that uses an array to store test grades. (Part 2 of 3.)

```
103            // for each grade, increment the appropriate frequency
104            for (int grade : grades) {
105                ++frequency[grade / 10];
106            }
107
108            // for each grade frequency, print bar in chart
109            for (size_t count{0}; count < frequencySize; ++count) {
110                // output bar labels ("0-9:", ..., "90-99:", "100:")
111                if (0 == count) {
112                    std::cout << "  0-9: ";
113                }
114                else if (10 == count) {
115                    std::cout << "  100: ";
116                }
117                else {
118                    std::cout << count * 10 << "-" << (count * 10) + 9 << ": ";
119                }
120
121                // print bar of asterisks
122                for (unsigned int stars{0}; stars < frequency[count]; ++stars) {
123                    std::cout << '*';
124                }
125
126                std::cout << std::endl; // start a new line of output
127            }
128        }
129
130        // output the contents of the grades array
131        void outputGrades() const {
132            std::cout << "\nThe grades are:\n\n";
133
134            // output each student's grade
135            for (size_t student{0}; student < grades.size(); ++student) {
136                std::cout << "Student " << std::setw(2) << student + 1 << ": "
137                    << std::setw(3) << grades[student] << std::endl;
138            }
139        }
140    private:
141        std::string courseName; // course name for this grade book
142        std::array<int, students> grades; // array of student grades
143    };
```

Fig. 7.13 | Definition of class GradeBook that uses an array to store test grades. (Part 3 of 3.)

The size of the array in line 142 of Fig. 7.13 is specified by public static const data member students (declared in line 12), which is public so that it's accessible to the class's clients. We'll soon see an example of a client program using this constant. Declaring students with the const qualifier indicates that this data member is *constant*—its value cannot be changed after being initialized. Keyword static in this variable declaration indicates that the data member is *shared by all objects of the class*—so in this particular implementation of class GradeBook, all GradeBook objects store grades for the same number of students. Recall from Section 3.3 that when each object of a class maintains its own copy of an attribute, the variable that represents the attribute is known as a data member—each object of the class has a *separate* copy of the variable in memory. There are variables for which each object of a class does *not* have a separate copy. That's the case with static data members, which are also known as class variables. When objects of a class containing static data members are created, all the objects share one copy of the class's static data members. A static data member can be accessed within the class definition and the member-function definitions like any other data member. As you'll soon see, a public static data member can also be accessed outside of the class, *even when no objects of the class exist*, using the class name followed by the scope resolution operator (::) and the name of the data member. You'll learn more about static data members in Chapter 9.

Constructor

The class's constructor (lines 15–18) has two parameters—the course name and a reference to an array of grades. When a program creates a GradeBook object (e.g., line 13 of Fig. 7.14), the program passes an existing int array to the constructor, which copies the array's values into the data member grades (line 17 of Fig. 7.13). The grade values in the passed array could have been input from a user or read from a file on disk (as we discuss in Chapter 14, File Processing). In our test program, we simply initialize an array with a set of grade values (Fig. 7.14, lines 9–10). Once the grades are stored in data member grades of class GradeBook, all the class's member functions can access the grades array as needed to perform various calculations. Note that the constructor receives both the string and the array by reference—this is more efficient than receiving copies of the original string and array. The constructor does not need to modify either the original string or array, so we also declared each parameter as const to ensure that the constructor does not accidentally modify the original data in the caller. We also declared function setCourseName to receives its string argument by reference.

Member Function processGrades

Member function processGrades (lines 38–50 of Fig. 7.13) contains a series of member function calls that output a report summarizing the grades. Line 39 calls member function outputGrades to print the contents of the array grades. Lines 135–138 in member function outputGrades use a for statement to output each student's grade. Although array indices start at 0, a professor would typically number students starting at 1. Thus, lines 136–137 output student + 1 as the student number to produce grade labels "Student 1: ", "Student 2: ", and so on.

Member Function getAverage

Member function processGrades next calls member function getAverage (line 43) to obtain the average of the grades. Member function getAverage (lines 83–93) totals the values in array grades before calculating the average. The averaging calculation in line 92 uses grades.size() to determine the number of grades being averaged.

Member Functions getMinimum and getMaximum

Lines 46–47 in processGrades call member functions getMinimum and getMaximum to determine the lowest and highest grades of any student on the exam, respectively. Let's examine how member function getMinimum finds the *lowest* grade. Because the highest grade allowed is 100, we begin by assuming that 100 is the lowest grade (line 54). Then, we compare each of the elements in the array to the lowest grade, looking for smaller values. Lines

57–62 in member function getMinimum loop through the array, and line 59 compares each grade to lowGrade. If a grade is less than lowGrade, lowGrade is set to that grade. When line 64 executes, lowGrade contains the lowest grade in the array. Member function getMaximum (lines 68–80) works similarly to member function getMinimum.

Member Function outputBarChart
Finally, line 49 in member function processGrades calls member function outputBarChart to print a distribution chart of the grade data using a technique similar to that in Fig. 7.7. In that example, we manually calculated the number of grades in each category (i.e., 0–9, 10–19, …, 90–99 and 100) by simply looking at a set of grades. In Fig. 7.13, lines 104–106 use a technique similar to that in Fig. 7.8 and Fig. 7.9 to calculate the frequency of grades in each category. Line 100 declares and creates array frequency of 11 unsigned ints to store the frequency of grades in each grade category. For each grade in array grades, lines 104–106 increment the appropriate element of the frequency array. To determine which element to increment, line 105 divides the current grade by 10 using integer division. For example, if grade is 85, line 105 increments frequency[8] to update the count of grades in the range 80–89. Lines 109–127 next print the bar chart (see Fig. 7.12) based on the values in array frequency. Like lines 28–30 of Fig. 7.7, lines 122–124 of Fig. 7.13 use a value in array frequency to determine the number of asterisks to display in each bar.

Testing Class GradeBook
The program of Fig. 7.14 creates an object of class GradeBook using the int array grades (declared and initialized in lines 9–10). The scope resolution operator (::) is used in the expression GradeBook::students (line 9) to access class GradeBook's static constant students. We use this constant here to create an array that's the same size as the array stored as a data member in class GradeBook. Line 11 declares a string representing the course name. Line 13 passes the course name and the array of grades to the GradeBook constructor. Line 14 displays a welcome message, and line 15 invokes the GradeBook object's processGrades member function.

```cpp
1   // Fig. 7.14: fig07_14.cpp
2   // Creates GradeBook object using an array of grades.
3   #include <array>
4   #include "GradeBook.h" // GradeBook class definition
5   using namespace std;
6
7   int main() {
8      // array of student grades
9      const array<int, GradeBook::students> grades{
10         87, 68, 94, 100, 83, 78, 85, 91, 76, 87};
11     string courseName{"CS101 Introduction to C++ Programming"};
12
13     GradeBook myGradeBook(courseName, grades);
14     myGradeBook.displayMessage();
15     myGradeBook.processGrades();
16  }
```

Fig. 7.14 | Creates a GradeBook object' using an array of grades, then invokes member function processGrades to analyze them.

7.7 Sorting and Searching arrays

In this section, we use the built-in C++ Standard Library sort function to arrange the elements in an array into ascending order and the built-in binary_search function to determine whether a value is in the array.

7.7.1 Sorting

Sorting data—placing it into ascending or descending order—is one of the most important computing applications. A bank sorts all checks by account number so that it can prepare individual bank statements at the end of each month. Telephone companies sort their phone directories by last name—and within all entries with the *same* last name, sort those by first name—to make it easy to find phone numbers. Virtually every organization must sort some data and, in many cases, massive amounts of it. Sorting data is an intriguing problem that has attracted some of the most intense research efforts in the field of computer science. In Chapter 20, we investigate and implement several sorting schemes, discuss their performance and introduce Big O (pronounced "Big Oh") notation for characterizing how hard each scheme works to accomplish its task.

7.7.2 Searching

Often it may be necessary to determine whether an array contains a value that matches a certain key value. The process of finding a particular element of an array is called searching. In Chapter 20, we investigate and implement two search algorithms—the simple but slow *linear search* for searching an *unordered* array and the more complex but much faster *binary search* for searching an *ordered* array.

7.7.3 Demonstrating Functions sort and binary_search

Figure 7.15 begins by creating an unsorted array of strings (lines 12–13) and displaying the contents of the array (lines 17–19). Next, line 21 uses C++ Standard Library function sort to sort the elements of the array colors into ascending order. The sort function's arguments specify the range of elements that should be sorted—in this case, the entire array. The arguments colors.begin() and colors.end() represent the array's beginning and end, respectively—we'll discuss the complete details of begin and end in Chapter 15. As you'll see, function sort can be used to sort the elements of several different types of data structures. Lines 25–27 display the contents of the sorted array.

```
1   // Fig. 7.15: fig07_15.cpp
2   // Sorting and searching arrays.
3   #include <iostream>
4   #include <iomanip>
5   #include <array>
6   #include <string>
7   #include <algorithm> // contains sort and binary_search
8   using namespace std;
9
10  int main() {
```

Fig. 7.15 | Sorting and searching arrays. (Part 1 of 2.)

```
11        const size_t arraySize{7}; // size of array colors
12        array<string, arraySize> colors{"red", "orange", "yellow",
13           "green", "blue", "indigo", "violet"};
14
15        // output original array
16        cout << "Unsorted array:\n";
17        for (string color : colors) {
18           cout << color << " ";
19        }
20
21        sort(colors.begin(), colors.end()); // sort contents of colors
22
23        // output sorted array
24        cout << "\nSorted array:\n";
25        for (string item : colors) {
26           cout << item << " ";
27        }
28
29        // search for "indigo" in colors
30        bool found{binary_search(colors.begin(), colors.end(), "indigo")};
31        cout << "\n\n\"indigo\" " << (found ? "was" : "was not")
32           << " found in colors" << endl;
33
34        // search for "cyan" in colors
35        found = binary_search(colors.begin(), colors.end(), "cyan");
36        cout << "\"cyan\" " << (found ? "was" : "was not")
37           << " found in colors" << endl;
38     }
```

```
Unsorted array:
red orange yellow green blue indigo violet
Sorted array:
blue green indigo orange red violet yellow

"indigo" was found in colors
"cyan" was not found in colors
```

Fig. 7.15 | Sorting and searching arrays. (Part 2 of 2.)

Lines 30 and 35 use `binary_search` to determine whether a value is in the array. The sequence of values first must be sorted in ascending order—`binary_search` does *not* verify this for you. The function's first two arguments represent the range of elements to search and the third is the *search key*—the value to locate in the array. The function returns a `bool` indicating whether the value was found. In Chapter 16, we'll use the C++ Standard function `find` to obtain the location of a search key in an array.

7.8 Multidimensional arrays

You can use arrays with two dimensions (i.e., subscripts) to represent tables of values consisting of information arranged in rows and columns. To identify a particular table element, we must specify two subscripts—by convention, the first identifies the element's *row* and the second identifies the element's *column*. arrays that require two subscripts to identify a particular element are called two-dimensional arrays or 2-D arrays. arrays with two or more dimensions are known as multidimensional arrays. Figure 7.16 illustrates a two-dimensional array, a. The array contains three rows and four columns, so it's said to be a 3-by-4 array. In general, an array with *m* rows and *n* columns is called an *m*-by-*n* array.

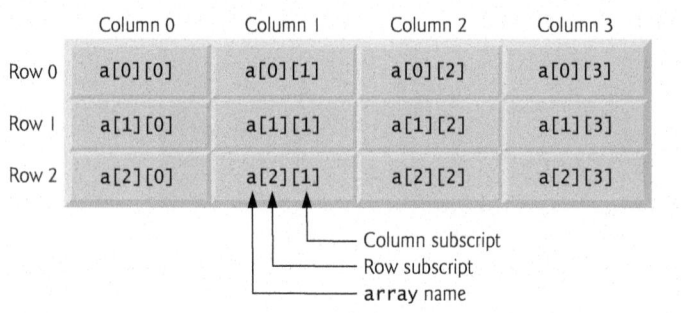

Fig. 7.16 | Two-dimensional array with three rows and four columns.

Every element in array a is identified in Fig. 7.16 by an element name of the form a[i][j], where a is the name of the array, and i and j are the subscripts that uniquely identify each element in a. Notice that the names of the elements in row 0 all have a *first* subscript of 0; the names of the elements in column 3 all have a *second* subscript of 3.

 Common Programming Error 7.5

Referencing a two-dimensional array element a[x][y] incorrectly as a[x, y] is an error. Actually, a[x, y] is treated as a[y], because C++ evaluates the expression x, y (containing a comma operator) simply as y (the last of the comma-separated expressions).

Figure 7.17 demonstrates initializing two-dimensional arrays in declarations. Lines 12–13 each declare an array of arrays with two rows and three columns. Notice the nested array type declaration. In each array, the type of its elements is specified as

        array<int, columns>

indicating that each array contains as its elements three-element arrays of int values—the constant columns has the value 3.

```
1   // Fig. 7.17: fig07_17.cpp
2   // Initializing multidimensional arrays.
3   #include <iostream>
4   #include <array>
5   using namespace std;
6
7   const size_t rows{2};
8   const size_t columns{3};
9   void printArray(const array<array<int, columns>, rows>&);
10
```

Fig. 7.17 | Initializing multidimensional arrays. (Part 1 of 2.)

```
11    int main() {
12        array<array<int, columns>, rows> array1{1, 2, 3, 4, 5, 6};
13        array<array<int, columns>, rows> array2{1, 2, 3, 4, 5};
14
15        cout << "Values in array1 by row are:" << endl;
16        printArray(array1);
17
18        cout << "\nValues in array2 by row are:" << endl;
19        printArray(array2);
20    }
21
22    // output array with two rows and three columns
23    void printArray(const array<array<int, columns>, rows>& a) {
24        // loop through array's rows
25        for (auto const& row : a) {
26            // loop through columns of current row
27            for (auto const& element : row) {
28                cout << element << ' ';
29            }
30
31            cout << endl; // start new line of output
32        }
33    }
```

```
Values in array1 by row are:
1 2 3
4 5 6

Values in array2 by row are:
1 2 3
4 5 0
```

Fig. 7.17 | Initializing multidimensional arrays. (Part 2 of 2.)

The declaration of `array1` (line 12) provides six initializers. The compiler initializes the elements of row 0 followed by the elements of row 1. So, the first three values initialize row 0's elements to 1, 2 and 3, and the last three initialize row 1's elements to 4, 5 and 6. The declaration of `array2` (line 13) provides only five initializers. The initializers are assigned to row 0, then row 1. Any elements that do not have an explicit initializer are initialized to *zero*, so `array2[1][2]` is 0.

The program calls function `printArray` to output each `array`'s elements. Notice that the function prototype (line 9) and definition (lines 23–33) specify that the function receives a two-row and three-column array. The parameter receives the `array` by reference and is declared `const` because the function does not modify the `array`'s elements.

*Nested Range-Based **for** Statements*

To process the elements of a two-dimensional array, we use a nested loop in which the *outer* loop iterates through the *rows* and the *inner* loop iterates through the *columns* of a given row. Function `printArray`'s nested loop is implemented with range-based for statements. Lines 25 and 27 introduce the C++11 `auto` keyword, which tells the compiler to infer (determine) a variable's data type based on the variable's initializer value. The outer

11

loop's range variable row is initialized with an element from the parameter a. Looking at the array's declaration, you can see that the array contains elements of type

```
array<int, columns>
```

so the compiler infers that row refers to a three-element array of int values (again, columns is 3). The const& in row's declaration indicates that the reference *cannot* be used to modify the rows and prevents each row from being *copied* into the range variable. The inner loop's range variable element is initialized with one element of the array represented by row, so the compiler infers that element refers to an int because each row contains three int values. In an IDE, you can typically hover your mouse over a variable declared with auto and the IDE will display the variable's inferred type. Line 28 displays the value from a given row and column.

Nested Counter-Controlled **for** *Statements*
We could have implemented the nested loop with counter-controlled iteration as follows:

```
for (size_t row{0}; row < a.size(); ++row) {
   for (size_t column{0}; column < a[row].size(); ++column) {
      cout << a[row][column] << ' ';
   }

   cout << endl;
}
```

Other Common Two-Dimensional **array** *Manipulations*
The following for statement sets all the elements in row 2 of array a in Fig. 7.16 to zero:

```
for (size_t column{0}; column < 4; ++column) {
   a[2][column] = 0;
}
```

The for statement varies only the second subscript (i.e., the column subscript). The preceding for statement is equivalent to the following assignment statements:

```
a[2][0] = 0;
a[2][1] = 0;
a[2][2] = 0;
a[2][3] = 0;
```

The following nested counter-controlled for statement determines the total of *all* the elements in array a in Fig. 7.16:

```
total = 0;
for (size_t row{0}; row < a.size(); ++row) {
   for (size_t column{0}; column < a[row].size(); ++column) {
      total += a[row][column];
   }
}
```

The for statement totals the elements of the array one row at a time. The outer for statement begins by setting row (i.e., the row subscript) to 0, so the elements of row 0 may be totaled by the inner for statement. The outer for statement then increments row to 1, so the elements of row 1 can be totaled. Then, the outer for statement increments row to 2, so the elements of row 2 can be totaled. When the nested for statement terminates, total contains the sum of all the array elements. This nested loop can be implemented with range-based for statements as:

```
total = 0;

for (auto row : a) { // for each row
    for (auto column : row) { // for each column in row
        total += column;
    }
}
```

7.9 Case Study: Class GradeBook Using a Two-Dimensional array

In Section 7.6, we presented class GradeBook (Fig. 7.13), which used a one-dimensional array to store student grades on a single exam. In most semesters, students take several exams. Professors are likely to want to analyze grades across the entire semester, both for a single student and for the class as a whole.

Storing Student Grades in a Two-Dimensional array in Class GradeBook

Figure 7.18 shows the output that summarizes 10 students' grades on three exams. We store the grades as a two-dimensional array in an object of the next version of class Grade-Book (Fig. 7.19). Each row of the array represents a single student's grades for the entire course, and each column represents all the grades the students earned for one particular exam. A client program, such as Fig. 7.20, passes the array as an argument to the Grade-Book constructor. Since there are 10 students and three exams, we use a ten-by-three array to store the grades.

```
Welcome to the grade book for
CS101 Introduction to C++ Programming!

The grades are:
             Test 1  Test 2  Test 3  Average
Student  1      87      96      70    84.33
Student  2      68      87      90    81.67
Student  3      94     100      90    94.67
Student  4     100      81      82    87.67
Student  5      83      65      85    77.67
Student  6      78      87      65    76.67
Student  7      85      75      83    81.00
Student  8      91      94     100    95.00
Student  9      76      72      84    77.33
Student 10      87      93      73    84.33

Lowest grade in the grade book is 65
Highest grade in the grade book is 100

Overall grade distribution:
  0-9:
 10-19:
```

Fig. 7.18 | Output of GradeBook that uses two-dimensional arrays. (Part 1 of 2.)

```
20-29:
30-39:
40-49:
50-59:
60-69: ***
70-79: ******
80-89: ***********
90-99: *******
  100: ***
```

Fig. 7.18 | Output of GradeBook that uses two-dimensional arrays. (Part 2 of 2.)

```
 1  // Fig. 7.19: GradeBook.h
 2  // Definition of class GradeBook that uses a
 3  // two-dimensional array to store test grades.
 4  #include <array>
 5  #include <string>
 6  #include <iostream>
 7  #include <iomanip> // parameterized stream manipulators
 8
 9  // GradeBook class definition
10  class GradeBook {
11  public:
12     // constants
13     static const size_t students{10}; // number of students
14     static const size_t tests{3}; // number of tests
15
16     // two-argument constructor initializes courseName and grades array
17     GradeBook(const std::string& name,
18        std::array<std::array<int, tests>, students>& gradesArray)
19        : courseName(name), grades(gradesArray) {
20     }
21
22     // function to set the course name
23     void setCourseName(const std::string& name) {
24        courseName = name; // store the course name
25     }
26
27     // function to retrieve the course name
28     const std::string& getCourseName() const {
29        return courseName;
30     }
31
32     // display a welcome message to the GradeBook user
33     void displayMessage() const {
34        // call getCourseName to get this GradeBook's course name
35        std::cout << "Welcome to the grade book for\n" << getCourseName()
36           << "!" << std::endl;
37     }
38
```

Fig. 7.19 | Definition of class GradeBook that uses a two-dimensional array to store test grades. (Part 1 of 4.)

```cpp
39      // perform various operations on the data
40      void processGrades() const {
41         outputGrades(); // output grades array
42
43         // call functions getMinimum and getMaximum
44         std::cout << "\nLowest grade in the grade book is " << getMinimum()
45            << "\nHighest grade in the grade book is " << getMaximum()
46            << std::endl;
47
48         outputBarChart(); // display grade distribution chart
49      }
50
51      // find minimum grade in the entire gradebook
52      int getMinimum() const {
53         int lowGrade{100}; // assume lowest grade is 100
54
55         // loop through rows of grades array
56         for (auto const& student : grades) {
57            // loop through columns of current row
58            for (auto const& grade : student) {
59               if (grade < lowGrade) { // if grade is lower than lowGrade
60                  lowGrade = grade; // grade is new lowest grade
61               }
62            }
63         }
64
65         return lowGrade; // return lowest grade
66      }
67
68      // find maximum grade in the entire gradebook
69      int getMaximum() const {
70         int highGrade{0}; // assume highest grade is 0
71
72         // loop through rows of grades array
73         for (auto const& student : grades) {
74            // loop through columns of current row
75            for (auto const& grade : student) {
76               if (grade > highGrade) { // if grade is higher than highGrade
77                  highGrade = grade; // grade is new highest grade
78               }
79            }
80         }
81
82         return highGrade; // return highest grade
83      }
84
85      // determine average grade for particular set of grades
86      double getAverage(const std::array<int, tests>& setOfGrades) const {
87         int total{0}; // initialize total
88
```

Fig. 7.19 | Definition of class GradeBook that uses a two-dimensional array to store test grades. (Part 2 of 4.)

```
89            // sum grades in array
90            for (int grade : setOfGrades) {
91               total += grade;
92            }
93
94            // return average of grades
95            return static_cast<double>(total) / setOfGrades.size();
96         }
97
98         // output bar chart displaying grade distribution
99         void outputBarChart() const {
100           std::cout << "\nOverall grade distribution:" << std::endl;
101
102           // stores frequency of grades in each range of 10 grades
103           const size_t frequencySize{11};
104           std::array<unsigned int, frequencySize> frequency{}; // init to 0s
105
106           // for each grade, increment the appropriate frequency
107           for (auto const& student : grades) {
108              for (auto const& test : student) {
109                 ++frequency[test / 10];
110              }
111           }
112
113           // for each grade frequency, print bar in chart
114           for (size_t count{0}; count < frequencySize; ++count) {
115              // output bar label ("0-9:", ..., "90-99:", "100:")
116              if (0 == count) {
117                 std::cout << "    0-9: ";
118              }
119              else if (10 == count) {
120                 std::cout << "    100: ";
121              }
122              else {
123                 std::cout << count * 10 << "-" << (count * 10) + 9 << ": ";
124              }
125
126              // print bar of asterisks
127              for (unsigned int stars{0}; stars < frequency[count]; ++stars)
128                 std::cout << '*';
129
130              std::cout << std::endl; // start a new line of output
131           }
132        }
133
134        // output the contents of the grades array
135        void outputGrades() const {
136           std::cout << "\nThe grades are:\n\n";
137           std::cout << "               "; // align column heads
138
```

```
139            // create a column heading for each of the tests
140            for (size_t test{0}; test < tests; ++test) {
141                std::cout << "Test " << test + 1 << "   ";
142            }
143
144            std::cout << "Average" << std::endl;
145
146            // create rows/columns of text representing array grades
147            for (size_t student{0}; student < grades.size(); ++student) {
148                std::cout << "Student " << std::setw(2) << student + 1;
149
150                // output student's grades
151                for (size_t test{0}; test < grades[student].size(); ++test) {
152                    std::cout << std::setw(8) << grades[student][test];
153                }
154
155                // call member function getAverage to calculate student's
156                // average; pass one row of grades as the argument
157                double average{getAverage(grades[student])};
158                std::cout << std::setw(9) << std::setprecision(2) << std::fixed
159                    << average << std::endl;
160            }
161        }
162    private:
163        std::string courseName; // course name for this grade book
164        std::array<std::array<int, tests>, students> grades; // 2D array
165    };
```

Fig. 7.19 | Definition of class GradeBook that uses a two-dimensional array to store test grades. (Part 4 of 4.)

Overview of Class *GradeBook's Functions*

Each of class GradeBook's member functions is similar to its counterpart in the earlier one-dimensional array version of class GradeBook (Fig. 7.13). Member function getMinimum (lines 52–66 of Fig. 7.19) determines the lowest grade of all students for the semester. Member function getMaximum (lines 69–83) determines the highest grade of all students for the semester. Member function getAverage (lines 86–96) determines a particular student's semester average. Member function outputBarChart (lines 99–132) outputs a bar chart of the distribution of all student grades for the semester. Member function output-Grades (lines 135–161) outputs the two-dimensional array in a tabular format, along with each student's semester average.

Functions *getMinimum and getMaximum*

Member functions getMinimum, getMaximum, outputBarChart and outputGrades each loop through array grades by using nested range-based for or counter-controlled for statements. For example, consider the nested for statement (lines 56–63) in member function getMinimum. The outer for statement loops through the rows that represent each student and the inner for loops through the grades of a given student. Each grade is compared with variable lowGrade in the body of the inner for statement. If a grade is less than lowGrade, lowGrade is set to that grade. This repeats until all rows and columns of grades have been traversed. When execution of the nested statement is complete, lowGrade contains the smallest grade in the two-dimensional array. Member function getMaximum works similarly to member function getMinimum.

Function outputBarChart

Member function outputBarChart in Fig. 7.19 is nearly identical to the one in Fig. 7.13. However, to output the overall grade distribution for a whole semester, the function uses a nested for statement (lines 107–111 in Fig. 7.19) to increment the elements of the one-dimensional array frequency, based on all the grades in the two-dimensional array. The rest of the code in the two outputBarChart member functions is identical.

Function outputGrades

Member function outputGrades (lines 135–161) uses nested counter-controlled for statements to output values of the array grades, in addition to each student's semester average. The output in Fig. 7.18 shows the result, which resembles the tabular format of a professor's physical grade book. Lines 140–142 print the column headings for each test. We use a counter-controlled for statement so that we can identify each test with a number. Similarly, the for statement in lines 147–160 first outputs a row label using a counter variable to identify each student (line 148). Although array indices start at 0, lines 141 and 148 output test + 1 and student + 1, respectively, to produce test and student numbers starting at 1 (see Fig. 7.18). The inner for statement in lines 151–153 of Fig. 7.19 uses the outer for statement's counter variable student to loop through a specific row of array grades and output each student's test grade. Finally, line 157 obtains each student's semester average by passing the current row of grades (i.e., grades[student]) to member function getAverage.

Function getAverage

Member function getAverage (lines 86–96) takes as an argument a one-dimensional array of test results for a particular student. When line 157 calls getAverage, the first argument is grades[student], which specifies that a particular row of the two-dimensional array grades should be passed to getAverage. For example, based on the array created in Fig. 7.20, the argument grades[1] represents the three values (a one-dimensional array of grades) stored in row 1 of the two-dimensional array grades. A two-dimensional array's rows are one-dimensional arrays. Member function getAverage calculates the sum of the array elements, divides the total by the number of test results and returns the floating-point result as a double value (Fig. 7.19, line 95).

Testing Class GradeBook

The program in Fig. 7.20 creates an object of class GradeBook (Fig. 7.19) using the two-dimensional array of ints named grades (declared and initialized in lines 9–19 of Fig. 7.20). Line 9 accesses class GradeBook's static constants students and tests to indicate the size of each dimension of array grades. Line 21 passes a course name and grades to the GradeBook constructor. Lines 22–23 then invoke myGradeBook's displayMessage and processGrades member functions to display a welcome message and obtain a report summarizing the students' grades for the semester, respectively.

```
 1    // Fig. 7.20: fig07_20.cpp
 2    // Creates GradeBook object using a two-dimensional array of grades.
 3    #include <array>
 4    #include "GradeBook.h" // GradeBook class definition
 5    using namespace std;
 6
 7    int main() {
 8       // two-dimensional array of student grades
 9       array<array<int, GradeBook::tests>, GradeBook::students> grades{
10          {87, 96, 70},
11          {68, 87, 90},
12          {94, 100, 90},
13          {100, 81, 82},
14          {83, 65, 85},
15          {78, 87, 65},
16          {85, 75, 83},
17          {91, 94, 100},
18          {76, 72, 84},
19          {87, 93, 73}};
20
21       GradeBook myGradeBook("CS101 Introduction to C++ Programming", grades);
22       myGradeBook.displayMessage();
23       myGradeBook.processGrades();
24    }
```

Fig. 7.20 | Creates a GradeBook object using a two-dimensional array of grades, then invokes member function processGrades to analyze them.

7.10 Introduction to C++ Standard Library Class Template vector

We now introduce C++ Standard Library class template vector, which is similar to class template array, but also supports *dynamic resizing*. Except for the features that modify a vector, the other features shown in Fig. 7.21 also work for arrays. Standard class template vector is defined in header <vector> (line 5) and belongs to namespace std. Chapter 15 discusses the full functionality of vector. At the end of this section, we'll demonstrate class vector's *bounds checking* capabilities and introduce C++'s *exception-handling* mechanism, which can be used to detect and handle an out-of-bounds vector index.

```
 1    // Fig. 7.21: fig07_21.cpp
 2    // Demonstrating C++ Standard Library class template vector.
 3    #include <iostream>
 4    #include <iomanip>
 5    #include <vector>
 6    #include <stdexcept>
 7    using namespace std;
 8
 9    void outputVector(const vector<int>&); // display the vector
10    void inputVector(vector<int>&); // input values into the vector
```

Fig. 7.21 | Demonstrating C++ Standard Library class template vector. (Part 1 of 4.)

```
11
12   int main() {
13      vector<int> integers1(7); // 7-element vector<int>
14      vector<int> integers2(10); // 10-element vector<int>
15
16      // print integers1 size and contents
17      cout << "Size of vector integers1 is " << integers1.size()
18         << "\nvector after initialization:";
19      outputVector(integers1);
20
21      // print integers2 size and contents
22      cout << "\nSize of vector integers2 is " << integers2.size()
23         << "\nvector after initialization:";
24      outputVector(integers2);
25
26      // input and print integers1 and integers2
27      cout << "\nEnter 17 integers:" << endl;
28      inputVector(integers1);
29      inputVector(integers2);
30
31      cout << "\nAfter input, the vectors contain:\n"
32         << "integers1:";
33      outputVector(integers1);
34      cout << "integers2:";
35      outputVector(integers2);
36
37      // use inequality (!=) operator with vector objects
38      cout << "\nEvaluating: integers1 != integers2" << endl;
39
40      if (integers1 != integers2) {
41         cout << "integers1 and integers2 are not equal" << endl;
42      }
43
44      // create vector integers3 using integers1 as an
45      // initializer; print size and contents
46      vector<int> integers3{integers1}; // copy constructor
47
48      cout << "\nSize of vector integers3 is " << integers3.size()
49         << "\nvector after initialization: ";
50      outputVector(integers3);
51
52      // use overloaded assignment (=) operator
53      cout << "\nAssigning integers2 to integers1:" << endl;
54      integers1 = integers2; // assign integers2 to integers1
55
56      cout << "integers1: ";
57      outputVector(integers1);
58      cout << "integers2: ";
59      outputVector(integers2);
60
61      // use equality (==) operator with vector objects
62      cout << "\nEvaluating: integers1 == integers2" << endl;
63
```

Fig. 7.21 | Demonstrating C++ Standard Library class template vector. (Part 2 of 4.)

```
64        if (integers1 == integers2) {
65            cout << "integers1 and integers2 are equal" << endl;
66        }
67
68        // use square brackets to use the value at location 5 as an rvalue
69        cout << "\nintegers1[5] is " << integers1[5];
70
71        // use square brackets to create lvalue
72        cout << "\n\nAssigning 1000 to integers1[5]" << endl;
73        integers1[5] = 1000;
74        cout << "integers1: ";
75        outputVector(integers1);
76
77        // attempt to use out-of-range subscript
78        try {
79            cout << "\nAttempt to display integers1.at(15)" << endl;
80            cout << integers1.at(15) << endl; // ERROR: out of range
81        }
82        catch (out_of_range& ex) {
83            cerr << "An exception occurred: " << ex.what() << endl;
84        }
85
86        // changing the size of a vector
87        cout << "\nCurrent integers3 size is: " << integers3.size() << endl;
88        integers3.push_back(1000); // add 1000 to the end of the vector
89        cout << "New integers3 size is: " << integers3.size() << endl;
90        cout << "integers3 now contains: ";
91        outputVector(integers3);
92    }
93
94    // output vector contents
95    void outputVector(const vector<int>& items) {
96        for (int item : items) {
97            cout << item << " ";
98        }
99
100       cout << endl;
101   }
102
103   // input vector contents
104   void inputVector(vector<int>& items) {
105       for (int& item : items) {
106           cin >> item;
107       }
108   }
```

```
Size of vector integers1 is 7
vector after initialization: 0 0 0 0 0 0 0

Size of vector integers2 is 10
vector after initialization: 0 0 0 0 0 0 0 0 0 0
```

Fig. 7.21 | Demonstrating C++ Standard Library class template vector. (Part 3 of 4.)

```
Enter 17 integers:
1 2 3 4 5 6 7 8 9 10 11 12 13 14 15 16 17

After input, the vectors contain:
integers1: 1 2 3 4 5 6 7
integers2: 8 9 10 11 12 13 14 15 16 17

Evaluating: integers1 != integers2
integers1 and integers2 are not equal

Size of vector integers3 is 7
vector after initialization: 1 2 3 4 5 6 7

Assigning integers2 to integers1:
integers1: 8 9 10 11 12 13 14 15 16 17
integers2: 8 9 10 11 12 13 14 15 16 17

Evaluating: integers1 == integers2
integers1 and integers2 are equal

integers1[5] is 13

Assigning 1000 to integers1[5]
integers1: 8 9 10 11 12 1000 14 15 16 17

Attempt to display integers1.at(15)
An exception occurred: invalid vector<T> subscript

Current integers3 size is: 7
New integers3 size is: 8
integers3 now contains: 1 2 3 4 5 6 7 1000
```

Fig. 7.21 | Demonstrating C++ Standard Library class template vector. (Part 4 of 4.)

Creating *vector Objects*

Lines 13–14 create two vector objects that store values of type int—integers1 contains seven elements, and integers2 contains 10 elements. By default, all the elements of each vector object are set to 0. Like arrays, vectors can be defined to store most data types, by replacing int in vector<int> with the appropriate type.

Notice that we used parentheses rather than braces to pass the size argument to each vector object's constructor. When creating a vector, if the braces contain one value of the vector's element type, the braces are treated as a *one-element initializer list*, rather than a call to the constructor that sets the vector's size. So the following declaration

```
vector<int> integers1{7};
```

actually creates a one-element vector<int> containing the int value 7, not a 7-element vector.

vector Member Function size; Function outputVector

Line 17 uses vector member function size to obtain the size (i.e., the number of elements) of integers1. Line 19 passes integers1 to function outputVector (lines 95–101), which uses a range-based for statement to obtain the value in each element of the vector for output. As with class template array, you can also do this using a counter-controlled loop and the subscript ([]) operator. Lines 22 and 24 perform the same tasks for integers2.

Function inputVector

Lines 28–29 pass integers1 and integers2 to function inputVector (lines 104–108) to read values for each vector's elements from the user. The function uses a range-based for statement with a range variable that's a reference to an int. Because the range variable is a reference to a vector element, the reference can be used t store a input value in the corresponding element.

Comparing vector Objects for Inequality

Line 40 demonstrates that vector objects can be compared with one another using the != operator. If the contents of two vectors are not equal, the operator returns true; otherwise, it returns false.

Initializing One vector with the Contents of Another

The C++ Standard Library class template vector allows you to create a new vector object that's initialized with the contents of an existing vector. Line 46 creates a vector object integers3 and initializes it with a copy of integers1. This invokes vector's so-called *copy constructor* to perform the copy operation. You'll learn about copy constructors in detail in Chapter 10. Lines 48–50 output the size and contents of integers3 to demonstrate that it was initialized correctly.

Assigning vectors and Comparing vectors for Equality

Line 54 assigns integers2 to integers1, demonstrating that the assignment (=) operator can be used with vector objects. Lines 56–59 output the contents of both objects to show that they now contain identical values. Line 64 then compares integers1 to integers2 with the equality (==) operator to determine whether the contents of the two objects are equal (which they are) after the assignment in line 54.

Using the [] Operator to Access and Modify vector Elements

Lines 69 and 73 use square brackets ([]) to obtain a vector element and use it as an *rvalue* and as an *lvalue*, respectively. Recall from Section 5.12 that an *rvalue* cannot be modified, but an *lvalue* can. As is the case with arrays, *C++ is not required to perform bounds checking when vector elements are accessed with square brackets.*[2] Therefore, you must ensure that operations using [] do not accidentally attempt to manipulate elements outside the bounds of the vector. Standard class template vector does, however, provide bounds checking in its member function at (as does class template array), which we use at line 80 and discuss shortly.

Exception Handling: Processing an Out-of-Range Subscript

An exception indicates a problem that occurs while a program executes. The name "exception" suggests that the problem occurs infrequently. Exception handling enables you to create fault-tolerant programs that can process (or *handle*) exceptions. In many cases, this allows a program to continue executing as if no problems were encountered. For example, Fig. 7.21 still runs to completion, even though an attempt was made to access an out-of-range subscript. More severe problems might prevent a program from continuing normal execution, instead requiring the program to notify the user of the problem, then terminate.

---

2. Some compilers have options for bounds checking to help prevent buffer overflows.

When a function detects a problem, such as an invalid array subscript or an invalid argument, it throws an exception—that is, an exception occurs. Here we introduce exception handling briefly. We'll discuss it in detail in Chapter 17.

The **try** *Statement*

To handle an exception, place any code that might throw an exception in a try statement (lines 78–84). The try block (lines 78–81) contains the code that might *throw* an exception, and the catch block (lines 82–84) contains the code that *handles* the exception if one occurs. As you'll see in Chapter 17, you can have many catch blocks to handle different types of exceptions that might be thrown in the corresponding try block. If the code in the try block executes successfully, lines 82–84 are ignored. The braces that delimit try and catch blocks' bodies are required.

The vector member function at provides bounds checking and throws an exception if its argument is an invalid subscript. By default, this causes a C++ program to terminate. If the subscript is valid, function at returns either

- a reference to the element at that location—this is a modifiable *lvalue* that can be used to change the value of the corresponding vector element, or

- a const reference to the element at that location—this is a nonmodifiable *lvalue* that *cannot* be used to change the value of the corresponding vector element.

A nonmodifiable *lvalue* is treated as a const object. If at is called on a const array or via a reference that's declared const, the function returns a const reference.

Executing the **catch** *Block*

When the program calls vector member function at with the argument 15 (line 80), the function attempts to access the element at location 15, which is *outside* the vector's bounds—integers1 has only 10 elements at this point. Because bounds checking is performed at execution time, vector member function at generates an exception—specifically line 80 throws an out_of_range exception (from header <stdexcept>) to notify the program of this problem. At this point, the try block terminates immediately and the catch block begins executing—if you declared any variables in the try block, they're now out of scope and are not accessible in the catch block.

The catch block declares a type (out_of_range) and an exception parameter (ex) that it receives as a *reference*. The catch block can handle exceptions of the specified type. Inside the block, you can use the parameter's identifier to interact with a caught exception object.

Performance Tip 7.2

Catching an exception by reference increases performance by preventing the exception object from being copied when it's caught. You'll see in later chapters that catching by reference is also important when defining catch blocks that process related exception types.

what *Member Function of the Exception Parameter*

When lines 82–84 *catch* the exception, the program displays a message indicating the problem that occurred. Line 83 calls the exception object's what member function to get the error message that's stored in the exception object and display it. Once the message is displayed in this example, the exception is considered handled and the program continues with the next statement after the catch block's closing brace. In this example, lines 87–91 execute next. We use exception handling again in Chapters 9–12 and Chapter 17 presents a deeper look.

Changing the Size of a *vector*

One of the key differences between a vector and an array is that a vector can *dynamically grow* and *shrink* as the number of elements it needs to accommodate varies. To demonstrate this, line 87 shows the current size of integers3, line 88 calls the vector's `push_back` member function to add a new element containing 1000 to the end of the vector and line 89 shows the new size of integers3. Line 91 then displays integers3's new contents.

C++11: List Initializing a *vector*

Many of the array examples in this chapter used list initializers to specify the initial array element values. C++11 also allows this for vectors (and other C++ Standard Library data structures).

11

7.11 Wrap-Up

This chapter began our introduction to data structures, exploring the use of C++ Standard Library class templates array and vector to store data in and retrieve data from lists and tables of values. The chapter examples demonstrated how to declare an array, initialize an array and refer to individual elements of an array. We passed arrays to functions by reference and used the const qualifier to prevent the called function from modifying the array's elements, thus enforcing the principle of least privilege. You learned how to use C++11's range-based for statement to manipulate all the elements of an array. We also showed how to use C++ Standard Library functions sort and binary_search to sort and search an array, respectively. You learned how to declare and manipulate multidimensional arrays of arrays. We used nested counter-controlled and nested range-based for statements to iterate through all the rows and columns of a two-dimensional array. We also showed how to use auto to infer a variable's type based on its initializer value. Finally, we demonstrated the capabilities of C++ Standard Library class template vector. In that example, we discussed how to access array and vector elements with bounds checking and demonstrated basic exception-handling concepts. In later chapters, we'll continue our coverage of data structures.

We've now introduced the basic concepts of classes, objects, control statements, functions, array objects and vector objects. In Chapter 8, we present one of C++'s most powerful features—the pointer. Pointers keep track of where data and functions are stored in memory, which allows us to manipulate those items in interesting ways. As you'll see, C++ also provides a language element called an array (different from the class template array) that's closely related to pointers. In contemporary C++ code, its considered better practice to use C++11's array class template rather than traditional arrays.

Summary

Section 7.1 Introduction

- Data structures (p. 284) are collections of related data items. arrays (p. 284) are data structures consisting of related data items of the same type. arrays are "static" entities in that they remain the same size throughout their lifetimes.

Section 7.2 arrays

- An array is a consecutive group of memory locations that share the same type.
- Each array knows its own size, which can be determined by calling its **size member function** (p. 285).
- To refer to a particular location or element in an array, we specify the **name of the array** (p. 285) and the position number of the particular element in the array.
- A program refers to any one of an array's elements by giving the name of the array followed by the **index** (p. 284) of the particular element in **square brackets** (`[]`).
- The first element in every array has index **zero** (p. 285) and is sometimes called the zeroth element.
- An index must be an integer or integer expression (using any integral type).
- The brackets used to enclose the index are an operator with the same precedence as parentheses.

Section 7.3 Declaring arrays

- arrays occupy space in memory. You specify the type of each element and the number of elements required by an array as follows:

      array<*type*, *arraySize*> *arrayName*;

  and the compiler reserves the appropriate amount of memory.
- arrays can be declared to contain almost any data type. For example, an array of type char can be used to store a character string.

Section 7.4 Examples Using arrays

- The elements of an array can be initialized in the array declaration by following the array name with an **initializer list** (p. 288)—a **comma-separated list (enclosed in braces) of initializers** (p. 288).
- When initializing an array with an initializer list, if there are fewer initializers than elements in the array, the remaining elements are initialized to zero. The number of initializers must be less than or equal to the array size.
- A constant variable that's used to specify an array's size must be initialized when it's declared and cannot be modified thereafter.
- C++ has no array **bounds checking** (p. 295) by default. You should ensure that all array references remain within the bounds of the array.
- A static local variable in a function definition exists for the duration of the program but is visible only in the function body.
- A program initializes static local arrays when their declarations are first encountered. If a static array is not initialized explicitly by you, each element of that array is initialized to zero by the compiler when the array is created.

Section 7.5 Range-Based for Statement

- The new C++11 **range-based for statement** (p. 298) allows to manipulate all the elements of an array without using a counter, thus avoiding the possibility of "stepping outside" the array and eliminating the need for you to implement your own bounds checking.
- A range-based for statement's header contains a range variable declaration to the left of the colon and the name of a container to the right, as in

      for (*rangeVariableDeclaration* : *container*)

- The range variable represents successive elements on successive iterations of the loop.

- You can use the range-based for statement with most of the C++ Standard Library's prebuilt data structures (commonly called containers).

- You can use a range-based for statement to modify each element by making the range variable a reference.

- The range-based for statement can be used in place of the counter-controlled for statement whenever code looping through an array does not require access to the element's subscript.

Section 7.6 Case Study: Class GradeBook Using an array to Store Grades

- **Class variables** (**static data members**; p. 304) are shared by all objects of the class in which the variables are declared.

- A static data member can be accessed within the class definition and the member-function definitions like any other data member.

- A public static data member can also be accessed outside of the class, even when no objects of the class exist, using the class name followed by the scope resolution operator (::) and the name of the data member.

Section 7.7 Sorting and Searching arrays

- Sorting data—placing it into ascending or descending order—is one of the most important computing applications.

- The process of finding a particular element of an array is called searching.

- C++ Standard Library function sort sorts an array's elements into ascending order. The function's arguments specify the range of elements that should be sorted. You'll see that function sort can be used on other types of containers too.

- C++ Standard Library function binary_search determines whether a value is in an array. The sequence of values must be sorted in ascending order first. The function's first two arguments represent the range of elements to search and the third is the search key—the value to locate. The function returns a bool indicating whether the value was found.

Section 7.8 Multidimensional arrays

- **Multidimensional arrays** (p. 308) with two dimensions are often used to represent tables of values (p. 307) consisting of information arranged in rows and columns.

- arrays that require two subscripts to identify a particular element are called two-dimensional arrays (p. 308). An array with m rows and n columns is called an m-by-n array (p. 308).

Section 7.9 Case Study: Class GradeBook Using a Two-Dimensional array

- In a variable declaration, the **keyword auto** (p. 309) can be used in place of a type name to infer the variable's type based on the variable's initializer value.

Section 7.10 Introduction to C++ Standard Library Class Template vector

- C++ Standard Library **class template vector** (p. 317) is similar to array but also supports resizing.

- By default, all the elements of an integer vector object are set to 0.

- A vector can be defined to store any data type using a declaration of the form

    vector<*type*> *name*(*size*);

- **Member function size** (p. 320) of class template vector returns the number of elements in the vector on which it's invoked.

- The value of an element of a vector can be accessed or modified using square brackets ([]).

- Objects of standard class template vector can be compared directly with the equality (==) and inequality (!=) operators. The assignment (=) operator can also be used with vector objects.

- A nonmodifiable *lvalue* (a const reference) is an expression that identifies an object in memory (such as an element in a vector), but cannot be used to modify that object. A modifiable *lvalue* (a non-const reference) also identifies an object in memory, but can be used to modify the object.

- An **exception** (p. 321) indicates a problem that occurs while a program executes. The name "exception" suggests that the problem occurs infrequently—if the "rule" is that a statement normally executes correctly, then the problem represents the "exception to the rule."

- **Exception handling** (p. 321) enables you to create **fault-tolerant programs** (p. 321) that can resolve exceptions.

- To handle an exception, place the code that might **throw an exception** (p. 322) in a try statement.

- The **try block** (p. 322) contains the code that might throw an exception, and the **catch block** (p. 322) contains the code that handles the exception if one occurs.

- When a try block terminates, any variables declared in the try block go out of scope.

- A catch block declares a type and an exception parameter. Inside the catch block, you can use the parameter's identifier to interact with a caught exception object.

- An exception object's **what member function** (p. 322) returns the exception's error message.

Self-Review Exercises

7.1 *(Fill in the Blanks)* Answer each of the following:
  a) Lists and tables of values can be stored in _____ or _____.
  b) An array's elements are related by the fact that they have the same _____ and _____.
  c) The number used to refer to a particular element of an array is called its _____.
  d) A(n) _____ should be used to declare the size of an array, because it eliminates magic numbers.
  e) The process of placing the elements of an array in order is called _____ the array.
  f) The process of determining if an array contains a particular key value is called _____ the array.
  g) An array that uses two subscripts is referred to as a(n) _____ array.

7.2 *(True or False)* State whether the following are *true* or *false*. If the answer is *false*, explain why.
  a) A given array can store many different types of values.
  b) An array subscript should normally be of data type float.
  c) If there are fewer initializers in an initializer list than the number of elements in the array, the remaining elements are initialized to the last value in the initializer list.
  d) It's an error if an initializer list has more initializers than there are elements in the array.

7.3 *(Write C++ Statements)* Write one or more statements that perform the following tasks for an array called fractions:
  a) Define a constant variable arraySize to represent the size of an array and initialize it to 10.
  b) Declare an array with arraySize elements of type double, and initialize the elements to 0.
  c) Name the fourth element of the array.
  d) Refer to array element 4.
  e) Assign the value 1.667 to array element 9.
  f) Assign the value 3.333 to the seventh element of the array.

g) Display array elements 6 and 9 with two digits of precision to the right of the decimal point, and show the output that's actually displayed on the screen.

h) Display all the array elements using a counter-controlled for statement. Define the integer variable i as a control variable for the loop. Show the output.

i) Display all the array elements separated by spaces using a range-based for statement.

7.4 *(Two-Dimensional array Questions)* Answer the following questions regarding a two-dimensional array called table:

a) Declare the array to store int values and to have 3 rows and 3 columns. Assume that the constant variable arraySize has been defined to be 3.

b) How many elements does the array contain?

c) Use a counter-controlled for statement to initialize each element of the array to the sum of its subscripts.

d) Write a nested for statement that displays the values of each element of array table in tabular format with 3 rows and 3 columns. Each row and column should be labeled with the row or column number. Assume that the array was initialized with an initializer list containing the values from 1 through 9 in order. Show the output.

7.5 *(Find the Error)* Find and correct the error in each of the following program segments:

a) `#include <iostream>;`

b) `arraySize = 10; // arraySize was declared const`

c) Assume that `array<int, 10> b{};`
```
for (size_t i{0}; i <= b.size(); ++i) {
    b[i] = 1;
}
```

d) Assume that a is a two-dimensional array of int values with two rows and two columns:
`a[1, 1] = 5;`

Answers to Self-Review Exercises

7.1 a) arrays, vectors. b) array name, type. c) subscript or index. d) constant variable. e) sorting. f) searching. g) two-dimensional.

7.2 a) False. An array can store only values of the same type.

b) False. An array subscript should be an integer or an integer expression.

c) False. The remaining elements are initialized to zero.

d) True.

7.3 a) `const size_t arraySize{10};`

b) `array<double, arraySize> fractions{0.0};`

c) `fractions[3]`

d) `fractions[4]`

e) `fractions[9] = 1.667;`

f) `fractions[6] = 3.333;`

g) `cout << fixed << setprecision(2);`
`cout << fractions[6] << ' ' << fractions[9] << endl;`
Output: 3.33 1.67

h) `for (size_t i{0}; i < fractions.size(); ++i) {`
    `cout << "fractions[" << i << "] = " << fractions[i] << endl;`
`}`
Output:
`fractions[0] = 0.0`
`fractions[1] = 0.0`
`fractions[2] = 0.0`

```
      fractions[3] = 0.0
      fractions[4] = 0.0
      fractions[5] = 0.0
      fractions[6] = 3.333
      fractions[7] = 0.0
      fractions[8] = 0.0
      fractions[9] = 1.667
```

i) ```
    for (double element : fractions)
       cout << element << ' ';
    ```

7.4  a)  `array<array<int, arraySize>, arraySize> table;`
     b)  Nine.
     c)  ```
         for (size_t row{0}; row < table.size(); ++row) {
            for (size_t column{0}; column < table[row].size(); ++column) {
               table[row][column] = row + column;
            }
         }
         ```
     d) ```
         cout << "   [0] [1] [2]" << endl;
         for (size_t i{0}; i < arraySize; ++i) {
            cout << '[' << i << "] ";
            for (size_t j{0}; j < arraySize; ++j) {
               cout << setw(3) << table[i][j] << "   ";
            }
            cout << endl;
         }
         ```
         *Output:*
         ```
               [0] [1] [2]
         [0]   1   2   3
         [1]   4   5   6
         [2]   7   8   9
         ```

7.5  a)  *Error:* Semicolon at end of #include preprocessing directive.
         *Correction:* Eliminate semicolon.
     b)  *Error:* Assigning a value to a constant variable using an assignment statement.
         *Correction:* Initialize the constant variable in a const size_t arraySize declaration.
     c)  *Error:* Referencing an array element outside the bounds of the array (b[10]).
         *Correction:* Change the loop-continuation condition to use < rather than <=.
     d)  *Error:* array subscripting done incorrectly.
         *Correction:* Change the statement to a[1][1] = 5;

## Exercises

7.6  **(Fill in the Blanks)** Fill in the blanks in each of the following:
     a)  The names of the four elements of array p are _____, _____, _____ and
         _____.
     b)  Naming an array, stating its type and specifying the number of elements in the array
         is called _____ the array.
     c)  When accessing an array element, by convention, the first subscript in a two-dimensional array identifies an element's _____ and the second subscript identifies an element's _____.
     d)  An *m*-by-*n* array contains _____ rows, _____ columns and _____ elements.
     e)  The name of the element in row 3 and column 5 of array d is _____.
         ```

7.7 *(True or False)* Determine whether each of the following is *true* or *false*. If *false*, explain why.
a) To refer to a particular location or element within an array, we specify the name of the array and the value of the particular element.
b) An array definition reserves space for an array.
c) To reserve 100 locations for integer array p, you write

   p[100];

d) A for statement must be used to initialize the elements of a 15-element array to zero.
e) Nested for statements must be used to total the elements of a two-dimensional array.

7.8 *(Write C++ Statements)* Write C++ statements to accomplish each of the following:
a) Display the value of element 6 of character array alphabet.
b) Input a value into element 4 of one-dimensional floating-point array grades.
c) Initialize each of the 5 elements of one-dimensional integer array values to 8.
d) Total and display the elements of floating-point array temperatures of 100 elements.
e) Copy array a into the first portion of array b. Assume that both arrays contain doubles and that arrays a and b have 11 and 34 elements, respectively.
f) Determine and display the smallest and largest values contained in 99-element floating-point array w.

7.9 *(Two-Dimensional array Questions)* Consider a 2-by-3 integer array t.
a) Write a declaration for t.
b) How many rows does t have?
c) How many columns does t have?
d) How many elements does t have?
e) Write the names of all the elements in row 1 of t.
f) Write the names of all the elements in column 2 of t.
g) Write a statement that sets the element of t in the first row and second column to zero.
h) Write a series of statements that initialize each element of t to zero. Do not use a loop.
i) Write a nested counter-controlled for statement that initializes each element of t to zero.
j) Write a nested range-based for statement that initializes each element of t to zero.
k) Write a statement that inputs the values for the elements of t from the keyboard.
l) Write a series of statements that determine and display the smallest value in array t.
m) Write a statement that displays the elements in row 0 of t.
n) Write a statement that totals the elements in column 2 of t.
o) Write a series of statements that prints the array t in neat, tabular format. List the column subscripts as headings across the top and list the row subscripts at the left of each row.

7.10 *(Salesperson Salary Ranges)* Use a one-dimensional array to solve the following problem. A company pays its salespeople on a commission basis. The salespeople each receive $200 per week plus 9 percent of their gross sales for that week. For example, a salesperson who grosses $5000 in sales in a week receives $200 plus 9 percent of $5000, or a total of $650. Write a program (using an array of counters) that determines how many of the salespeople earned salaries in each of the following ranges (assume that each salesperson's salary is truncated to an integer amount):
a) $200–299
b) $300–399
c) $400–499
d) $500–599
e) $600–699
f) $700–799
g) $800–899
h) $900–999
i) $1000 and over

7.11   *(One-Dimensional* **array** *Questions)* Write statements that perform the following one-dimensional array operations:
   a) Initialize the 10 elements of integer array counts to zero.
   b) Add 1 to each of the 15 elements of integer array bonus.
   c) Read 12 values for the array of doubles named monthlyTemperatures from the keyboard.
   d) Print the 5 values of integer array bestScores in column format.

7.12   *(Find the Errors)* Find the error(s) in each of the following statements:
   a) Assume that a is an array of three ints.

```
cout << a[1] << " " << a[2] << " " << a[3] << endl;
```

   b) `array<double, 3> f{1.1, 10.01, 100.001, 1000.0001};`
   c) Assume that d is an array of doubles with two rows and 10 columns.

```
d[1, 9] = 2.345;
```

7.13   *(Duplicate Elimination with* **array***)* Use a one-dimensional array to solve the following problem. Read in 20 numbers, each of which is between 10 and 100, inclusive. As each number is read, validate it and store it in the array only if it isn't a duplicate of a number already read. After reading all the values, display only the unique values that the user entered. Provide for the "worst case" in which all 20 numbers are different. Use the smallest possible array to solve this problem.

7.14   *(Duplicate Elimination with* **vector***)* Reimplement Exercise 7.13 using a vector. Begin with an empty vector and use its push_back function to add each unique value to the vector.

7.15   *(Two-Dimensional* **array** *Initialization)* Label the elements of a 3-by-5 two-dimensional array sales to indicate the order in which they're set to zero by the following program segment:

```
for (size_t row{0}; row < sales.size(); ++row) {
   for (size_t column{0}; column < sales[row].size(); ++column) {
      sales[row][column] = 0;
   }
}
```

7.16   *(Dice Rolling)* Write a program that simulates the rolling of two dice. The sum of the two values should then be calculated. [*Note:* Each die can show an integer value from 1 to 6, so the sum of the two values will vary from 2 to 12, with 7 being the most frequent sum and 2 and 12 being the least frequent sums.] Figure 7.22 shows the 36 possible combinations of the two dice. Your program should roll the two dice 36,000,000 times. Use a one-dimensional array to tally the numbers of times each possible sum appears. Print the results in a tabular format. Also, determine if the totals are reasonable (i.e., there are six ways to roll a 7, so approximately one-sixth of all the rolls should be 7).

	1	2	3	4	5	6
1	2	3	4	5	6	7
2	3	4	5	6	7	8
3	4	5	6	7	8	9
4	5	6	7	8	9	10
5	6	7	8	9	10	11
6	7	8	9	10	11	12

Fig. 7.22 | The 36 possible outcomes of rolling two dice.

7.17   *(What Does This Code Do?)* What does the following program do?

```
1   // Ex. 7.17: Ex07_17.cpp
2   // What does this program do?
3   #include <iostream>
4   #include <array>
5   using namespace std;
6
7   const size_t arraySize{10};
8   int whatIsThis(const array<int, arraySize>&, size_t); // prototype
9
10  int main() {
11     array<int, arraySize> a{1, 2, 3, 4, 5, 6, 7, 8, 9, 10};
12
13     int result{whatIsThis(a, arraySize)};
14
15     cout << "Result is " << result << endl;
16  }
17
18  // What does this function do?
19  int whatIsThis(const array<int, arraySize>& b, size_t size) {
20     if (size == 1) { // base case
21        return b[0];
22     }
23     else { // recursive step
24        return b[size - 1] + whatIsThis(b, size - 1);
25     }
26  }
```

Fig. 7.23 | What does this program do?

7.18   *(Craps Game Modification)* Modify the program of Fig. 6.9 to play 1000 games of craps. The program should keep track of the statistics and answer the following questions:
   a)   How many games are won on the 1st roll, 2nd roll, …, 20th roll, and after the 20th roll?
   b)   How many games are lost on the 1st roll, 2nd roll, …, 20th roll, and after the 20th roll?
   c)   What are the chances of winning at craps? [*Note:* You should discover that craps is one of the fairest casino games. What do you suppose this means?]
   d)   What's the average length of a game of craps?
   e)   Do the chances of winning improve with the length of the game?

7.19   *(Converting vector Example of Section 7.10 to array)* Convert the vector example of Fig. 7.21 to use arrays. Eliminate any vector-only features.

7.20   *(What Does This Code Do?)* What does the following program do?

```
1   // Ex. 7.20: Ex07_20.cpp
2   // What does this program do?
3   #include <iostream>
4   #include <array>
5   using namespace std;
6
7   const size_t arraySize{10};
8   void someFunction(const array<int, arraySize>&, size_t); // prototype
9
```

Fig. 7.24 | What does this program do? (Part 1 of 2.)

```
10   int main() {
11      array<int, arraySize> a{1, 2, 3, 4, 5, 6, 7, 8, 9, 10};
12
13      cout << "The values in the array are:" << endl;
14      someFunction(a, 0);
15      cout << endl;
16   }
17
18   // What does this function do?
19   void someFunction(const array<int, arraySize>& b, size_t current) {
20      if (current < b.size()) {
21         someFunction(b, current + 1);
22         cout << b[current] << "  ";
23      }
24   }
```

Fig. 7.24 | What does this program do? (Part 2 of 2.)

7.21   *(Sales Summary)* Use a two-dimensional `array` to solve the following problem. A company has four salespeople (1 to 4) who sell five different products (1 to 5). Once a day, each salesperson passes in a slip for each different type of product sold. Each slip contains the following:

   a) The salesperson number

   b) The product number

   c) The total dollar value of that product sold that day

Thus, each salesperson passes in between 0 and 5 sales slips per day. Assume that the information from all of the slips for last month is available. Write a program that will read all this information for last month's sales (one salesperson's data at a time) and summarize the total sales by salesperson by product. All totals should be stored in the two-dimensional `array` `sales`. After processing all the information for last month, print the results in tabular format with each of the columns representing a particular salesperson and each of the rows representing a particular product. Cross total each row to get the total sales of each product for last month; cross total each column to get the total sales by salesperson for last month. Your tabular printout should include these cross totals to the right of the totaled rows and to the bottom of the totaled columns.

7.22   *(Knight's Tour)* One of the more interesting puzzlers for chess buffs is the Knight's Tour problem. The question is this: Can the chess piece called the knight move around an empty chessboard and touch each of the 64 squares once and only once? We study this intriguing problem in depth in this exercise.

     The knight makes L-shaped moves (over two in one direction then over one in a perpendicular direction). Thus, from a square in the middle of an empty chessboard, the knight can make eight different moves (numbered 0 through 7) as shown in Fig. 7.25.

   a) Draw an 8-by-8 chessboard on a sheet of paper and attempt a Knight's Tour by hand. Put a 1 in the first square you move to, a 2 in the second square, a 3 in the third, etc. Before starting the tour, estimate how far you think you'll get, remembering that a full tour consists of 64 moves. How far did you get? Was this close to your estimate?

   b) Now let's develop a program that will move the knight around a chessboard. The board is represented by an 8-by-8 two-dimensional `array` `board`. Each of the squares is initialized to zero. We describe each of the eight possible moves in terms of both their horizontal and vertical components. For example, a move of type 0, as shown in Fig. 7.25, consists of moving two squares horizontally to the right and one square vertically upward. Move 2 consists of moving one square horizontally to the left and two squares

Fig. 7.25 | The eight possible moves of the knight.

vertically upward. Horizontal moves to the left and vertical moves upward are indicated with negative numbers. The eight moves may be described by two one-dimensional arrays, horizontal and vertical, as follows:

```
horizontal[0] = 2      vertical[0] = -1
horizontal[1] = 1      vertical[1] = -2
horizontal[2] = -1     vertical[2] = -2
horizontal[3] = -2     vertical[3] = -1
horizontal[4] = -2     vertical[4] = 1
horizontal[5] = -1     vertical[5] = 2
horizontal[6] = 1      vertical[6] = 2
horizontal[7] = 2      vertical[7] = 1
```

Let the variables currentRow and currentColumn indicate the row and column of the knight's current position. To make a move of type moveNumber, where moveNumber is between 0 and 7, your program uses the statements

```
currentRow += vertical[moveNumber];
currentColumn += horizontal[moveNumber];
```

Keep a counter that varies from 1 to 64. Record the latest count in each square the knight moves to. Remember to test each potential move to see if the knight has already visited that square, and, of course, test every potential move to make sure that the knight does not land off the chessboard. Now write a program to move the knight around the chessboard. Run the program. How many moves did the knight make?

c) After attempting to write and run a Knight's Tour program, you've probably developed some valuable insights. We'll use these to develop a heuristic (or strategy) for moving the knight. Heuristics do not guarantee success, but a carefully developed heuristic greatly improves the chance of success. You may have observed that the outer squares are more troublesome than the squares nearer the center of the board. In fact, the most troublesome, or inaccessible, squares are the four corners.

Intuition may suggest that you should attempt to move the knight to the most troublesome squares first and leave open those that are easiest to get to, so when the board gets congested near the end of the tour, there will be a greater chance of success.

We may develop an "accessibility heuristic" by classifying each square according to how accessible it's then always moving the knight to the square (within the knight's L-shaped moves, of course) that's least accessible. We label a two-dimensional array accessibility with numbers indicating from how many squares each particular square is accessible. On a blank chessboard, each center square is rated as 8, each corner square is rated as 2 and the other squares have accessibility numbers of 3, 4 or 6 as follows:

```
2  3  4  4  4  4  3  2
3  4  6  6  6  6  4  3
4  6  8  8  8  8  6  4
4  6  8  8  8  8  6  4
4  6  8  8  8  8  6  4
4  6  8  8  8  8  6  4
3  4  6  6  6  6  4  3
2  3  4  4  4  4  3  2
```

Now write a version of the Knight's Tour program using the accessibility heuristic. At any time, the knight should move to the square with the lowest accessibility number. In case of a tie, the knight may move to any of the tied squares. Therefore, the tour may begin in any of the four corners. [*Note:* As the knight moves around the chessboard, your program should reduce the accessibility numbers as more and more squares become occupied. In this way, at any given time during the tour, each available square's accessibility number will remain equal to precisely the number of squares from which that square may be reached.] Run this version of your program. Did you get a full tour? Now modify the program to run 64 tours, one starting from each square of the chessboard. How many full tours did you get?

d) Write a version of the Knight's Tour program which, when encountering a tie between two or more squares, decides what square to choose by looking ahead to those squares reachable from the "tied" squares. Your program should move to the square for which the next move would arrive at a square with the lowest accessibility number.

7.23 (*Knight's Tour: Brute Force Approaches*) In Exercise 7.22, we developed a solution to the Knight's Tour problem. The approach used, called the "accessibility heuristic," generates many solutions and executes efficiently.

As computers continue increasing in power, we'll be able to solve more problems with sheer computer power and relatively unsophisticated algorithms. This is the "brute force" approach to problem solving.

a) Use random number generation to enable the knight to walk around the chessboard (in its legitimate L-shaped moves, of course) at random. Your program should run one tour and print the final chessboard. How far did the knight get?

b) Most likely, the preceding program produced a relatively short tour. Now modify your program to attempt 1000 tours. Use a one-dimensional `array` to keep track of the number of tours of each length. When your program finishes attempting the 1000 tours, it should print this information in neat tabular format. What was the best result?

c) Most likely, the preceding program gave you some "respectable" tours, but no full tours. Now "pull all the stops out" and simply let your program run until it produces a full tour. [*Caution:* This version of the program could run for hours on a powerful computer.] Once again, keep a table of the number of tours of each length, and print this table when the first full tour is found. How many tours did your program attempt before producing a full tour? How much time did it take?

d) Compare the brute force version of the Knight's Tour with the accessibility heuristic version. Which required a more careful study of the problem? Which algorithm was more difficult to develop? Which required more computer power? Could we be certain (in advance) of obtaining a full tour with the accessibility heuristic approach? Could we be certain (in advance) of obtaining a full tour with the brute force approach? Argue the pros and cons of brute-force problem-solving in general.

7.24 (*Eight Queens*) Another puzzler for chess buffs is the Eight Queens problem. Simply stated: Is it possible to place eight queens on an empty chessboard so that no queen is "attacking" any other, i.e., no two queens are in the same row, the same column, or along the same diagonal? Use the thinking developed in Exercise 7.22 to formulate a heuristic for solving the Eight Queens problem. Run your program. [*Hint:* It's possible to assign a value to each square of the chessboard indicating how many squares of an empty chessboard are "eliminated" if a queen is placed in that square. Each of the corners would be assigned the value 22, as in Fig. 7.26. Once these "elimination numbers" are placed in all 64 squares, an appropriate heuristic might be: Place the next queen in the square with the smallest elimination number. Why is this strategy intuitively appealing?]

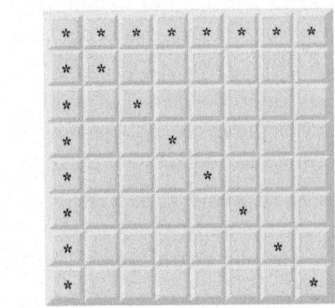

Fig. 7.26 | The 22 squares eliminated by placing a queen in the upper-left corner.

7.25 (*Eight Queens: Brute Force Approaches*) In this exercise, you'll develop several brute-force approaches to solving the Eight Queens problem introduced in Exercise 7.24.
    a) Solve the Eight Queens exercise, using the random brute force technique developed in Exercise 7.23.
    b) Use an exhaustive technique, i.e., try all possible combinations of eight queens.
    c) Why do you suppose the exhaustive brute force approach may not be appropriate for solving the Knight's Tour problem?
    d) Compare and contrast the random and exhaustive brute force approaches in general.

7.26 (*Knight's Tour: Closed-Tour Test*) In the Knight's Tour, a full tour occurs when the knight makes 64 moves, touching each square of the board once and only once. A closed tour occurs when the 64th move is one move away from the location in which the knight started the tour. Modify the Knight's Tour program you wrote in Exercise 7.22 to test for a closed tour if a full tour has occurred.

7.27 (*The Sieve of Eratosthenes*) A prime integer is any integer that's evenly divisible only by itself and 1. The Sieve of Eratosthenes is a method of finding prime numbers. It operates as follows:
    a) Create an array with all elements initialized to 1 (true). array elements with prime subscripts will remain 1. All other array elements will eventually be set to zero. You'll ignore elements 0 and 1 in this exercise.
    b) Starting with array subscript 2, every time an array element is found whose value is 1, loop through the remainder of the array and set to zero every element whose subscript is a multiple of the subscript for the element with value 1. For array subscript 2, all elements beyond 2 in the array that are multiples of 2 will be set to zero (subscripts 4, 6, 8, 10, etc.); for array subscript 3, all elements beyond 3 in the array that are multiples of 3 will be set to zero (subscripts 6, 9, 12, 15, etc.); and so on.

When this process is complete, the array elements that are still set to one indicate that the subscript is a prime number. These can then be printed. Write a program that uses an array of 1000 elements to determine and print the prime numbers between 2 and 999.

Recursion Exercises

7.28 (*Palindromes*) A palindrome is a string that's spelled the same way forward and backward. Examples of palindromes include "radar" and "able was i ere i saw elba." Write a recursive function testPalindrome that returns true if a string is a palindrome, and false otherwise. Note that like an array, the square brackets ([]) operator can be used to iterate through the characters in a string.

7.29 (*Eight Queens*) Modify the Eight Queens program you created in Exercise 7.24 to solve the problem recursively.

7.30 (*Print an array*) Write a recursive function printArray that takes an array, a starting subscript and an ending subscript as arguments, returns nothing and prints the array. The function should stop processing and return when the starting subscript equals the ending subscript.

7.31 (*Print a String Backward*) Write a recursive function stringReverse that takes a string and a starting subscript as arguments, prints the string backward and returns nothing. The function should stop processing and return when the end of the string is encountered. Note that like an array the square brackets ([]) operator can be used to iterate through the characters in a string.

7.32 (*Find the Minimum Value in an array*) Write a recursive function recursiveMinimum that takes an integer array, a starting subscript and an ending subscript as arguments, and returns the smallest element of the array. The function should stop processing and return when the starting subscript equals the ending subscript.

7.33 (*Maze Traversal*) The grid of hashes (#) and dots (.) in Fig. 7.27 is a two-dimensional built-in array representation of a maze. In the two-dimensional built-in array, the hashes represent the walls of the maze and the dots represent squares in the possible paths through the maze. Moves can be made only to a location in the built-in array that contains a dot.

There is a simple algorithm for walking through a maze that guarantees finding the exit (assuming that there is an exit). If there is not an exit, you'll arrive at the starting location again. Place your right hand on the wall to your right and begin walking forward. Never remove your hand from the wall. If the maze turns to the right, you follow the wall to the right. As long as you do not remove your hand from the wall, eventually you'll arrive at the exit of the maze. There may be a shorter path than the one you've taken, but you are guaranteed to get out of the maze if you follow the algorithm.

Fig. 7.27 | Two-dimensional built-in array representation of a maze.

Write recursive function mazeTraverse to walk through the maze. The function should receive arguments that include a 12-by-12 built-in array of chars representing the maze and the starting location of the maze. As mazeTraverse attempts to locate the exit from the maze, it should place the character X in each square in the path. The function should display the maze after each move, so the user can watch as the maze is solved.

7.34 (*Generating Mazes Randomly*) Write a function mazeGenerator that randomly produces a maze. The function should take as arguments a two-dimensional 12-by-12 built-in array of chars and references to the int variables that represent the row and column of the maze's entry point. Try your function mazeTraverse from Exercise 7.33, using several randomly generated mazes.

Making a Difference

7.35   *(Polling)* The Internet and the web enable people to network, join a cause, and so on. The presidential candidates use the Internet to get out their messages and raise money. In this exercise, you'll write a polling program that allows users to rate five social-consciousness issues from 1 to 10 (most important). Pick five causes (e.g., political issues, global environmental issues). Use a one-dimensional string array topics to store the causes. To summarize the survey responses, use a 5-row, 10-column two-dimensional array responses (of type int), each row corresponding to an element in the topics array. When the program runs, it should ask the user to rate each issue. Have your friends and family respond to the survey. Then have the program display a summary of the results, including:

  a) A tabular report with the five topics down the left side and the 10 ratings across the top, listing in each column the number of ratings received for each topic.
  b) To the right of each row, show the average of the ratings for that issue.
  c) Which issue received the highest point total? Display both the issue and the point total.
  d) Which issue received the lowest point total? Display both the issue and the point total.

Pointers

8

Objectives

In this chapter you'll:

- Learn what pointers are.

- Declare and initialize pointers.

- Use the address (&) and indirection (*) pointer operators.

- Learn the similarities and differences between pointers and references.

- Use pointers to pass arguments to functions by reference.

- Use built-in arrays.

- Use **const** with pointers.

- Use operator **sizeof** to determine the number of bytes that store a value of a particular type.

- Understand pointer expressions and pointer arithmetic.

- Understand the close relationships between pointers and built-in arrays.

- Use pointer-based strings.

- Use C++11 capabilities, including **nullptr** and Standard Library functions **begin** and **end**.

8.1 Introduction

This chapter discusses *pointers*—one of C++'s most powerful, yet challenging to use, capabilities. Our goals here are to help you determine when it's appropriate to use pointers, and show how to use them *correctly* and *responsibly*.

In Chapter 6, we saw that references can be used to perform pass-by-reference. Pointers also enable pass-by-reference and can be used to create and manipulate dynamic data structures that can grow and shrink, such as linked lists, queues, stacks and trees. This chapter explains basic pointer concepts. Chapter 19 presents examples of creating and using pointer-based dynamic data structures.

We also show the intimate relationship among *built-in arrays* and pointers. C++ inherited built-in arrays from the C programming language. As we saw in Chapter 7, the C++ Standard Library classes array and vector provide more robust implementations of arrays as full-fledged objects.

Similarly, C++ actually offers two types of strings—string class objects (which we've been using since Chapter 3) and *C-style, pointer-based strings (C strings)*. This chapter briefly introduces C strings to deepen your knowledge of pointers and built-in arrays. C strings were widely used in older C and C++ software. We discuss C strings in depth in Appendix F.

Software Engineering Observation 8.1

In new software development projects, you should favor array *and* vector *objects to built-in arrays, and* string *objects to C strings.*

We'll examine the use of pointers with class objects in Chapter 12, where we'll see that the "polymorphic processing" associated with object-oriented programming is performed with references and pointers.

8.2 Pointer Variable Declarations and Initialization

Pointer variables contain *memory addresses* as their values. Normally, a variable *directly* contains a specific value. A pointer contains the *memory address* of a variable that, in turn, contains a specific value. In this sense, a variable name directly references a value, and a pointer indirectly references a value (Fig. 8.1). Referencing a value through a pointer is called indirection. Diagrams typically represent a pointer as an *arrow* from the *variable that contains an address* to the *variable located at that address* in memory.

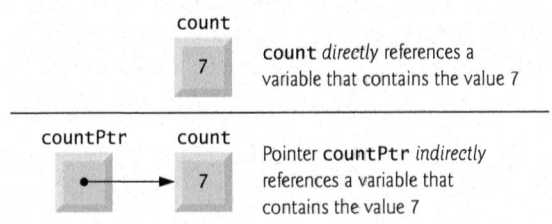

Fig. 8.1 | Directly and indirectly referencing a variable.

8.2.1 Declaring Pointers

Pointers, like any other variables, must be declared *before* they can be used. For example, for the pointer countPtr in Fig. 8.1, the declaration

```
int* countPtr, count;
```

declares the variable countPtr to be of type int* (i.e., a pointer to an int value) and is read (*right to left*), "countPtr is a pointer to int." Variable count in the preceding declaration is declared to be an int, but *not* a pointer to an int. The * in the declaration applies *only* to the first variable. Each variable being declared as a pointer *must* be preceded by an asterisk (*). When * appears in a declaration, it's *not* an operator; rather, it indicates that the variable being declared is a pointer. Pointers can be declared to point to objects of *any* data type.

Common Programming Error 8.1

*Assuming that the * used to declare a pointer distributes to all names in a declaration's comma-separated list of variables can lead to errors. Each pointer must be declared with the * prefixed to the name (with or without spaces in between). Declaring only one variable per declaration helps avoid these types of errors and improves program readability.*

Good Programming Practice 8.1

Although it's not a requirement, we like to include the letters Ptr *in each pointer variable name to make it clear that the variable is a pointer and must be handled accordingly.*

8.2.2 Initializing Pointers

Pointers should be initialized to `nullptr` (added in C++11) or to a memory address either when they're declared or in an assignment. A pointer with the value `nullptr` "points to nothing" and is known as a null pointer. From this point forward, when we refer to a "null pointer" we mean a pointer with the value `nullptr`.

Error-Prevention Tip 8.1

Initialize all pointers to prevent pointing to unknown or uninitialized areas of memory.

8.2.3 Null Pointers Prior to C++11

In earlier versions of C++, the value specified for a null pointer was 0 or NULL. NULL is defined in several standard library headers to represent the value 0. Initializing a pointer to NULL is equivalent to initializing a pointer to 0, but prior to C++11, 0 was used by convention. The value 0 is the *only* integer value that can be assigned directly to a pointer variable without first *casting* the integer to a pointer type (normally via a `reinterpret_cast`; Section 14.8).

8.3 Pointer Operators

The unary operators & and * are used to create pointer values and "dereference" pointers, respectively.

8.3.1 Address (&) Operator

The address operator (&) is a unary operator that *obtains the memory address of its operand.* For example, assuming the declarations

```
int y{5}; // declare variable y
int* yPtr{nullptr}; // declare pointer variable yPtr
```

the statement

```
yPtr = &y; // assign address of y to yPtr
```

assigns the address of the variable y to pointer variable yPtr. Then variable yPtr is said to "point to" y. Now, yPtr *indirectly* references variable y's value (5). The use of the & in the preceding statement is *not* the same as its use in a *reference variable declaration*, where it's always preceded by a data-type name. When declaring a reference, the & is part of the *type*. In an expression like &y, the & is the *address operator*.

Figure 8.2 shows a representation of memory after the preceding assignment. The "pointing relationship" is indicated by drawing an arrow from the box that represents the pointer yPtr in memory to the box that represents the variable y in memory.

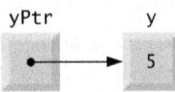

Fig. 8.2 | Graphical representation of a pointer pointing to a variable in memory.

Figure 8.3 shows another pointer representation in memory with integer variable y stored at memory location 600000 and pointer variable yPtr stored at location 500000. The operand of the address operator must be an *lvalue*—the address operator *cannot* be applied to literals or to expressions that result in temporary values (like the results of calculations).

yPtr		y	
location 500000	600000	location 600000	5

Fig. 8.3 | Representation of y and yPtr in memory.

8.3.2 Indirection (*) Operator

The unary * operator—commonly referred to as the indirection operator or dereferencing operator—*returns an* lvalue *representing the object to which its pointer operand points.* For example (referring again to Fig. 8.2), the statement

```
cout << *yPtr << endl;
```

displays the value of variable y, namely, 5, just as the statement

```
cout << y << endl;
```

would. Using * in this manner is called dereferencing a pointer. A *dereferenced pointer* may also be used as an *lvalue* on the *left* side of an assignment statement, as in

```
*yPtr = 9;
```

which would assign 9 to y in Fig. 8.3—in the preceding statement, *yPtr is an *alias* for y. The *dereferenced pointer* may also be used to receive an input value as in

```
cin >> *yPtr;
```

which places the input value in y.

Common Programming Error 8.2
Dereferencing an uninitialized pointer results in undefined behavior that could cause a fatal execution-time error. This could also lead to accidentally modifying important data, allowing the program to run to completion, possibly with incorrect results.

Error-Prevention Tip 8.2
Dereferencing a null pointer results in undefined behavior and typically causes a fatal execution-time error. Ensure that a pointer is not null before dereferencing it.

8.3.3 Using the Address (&) and Indirection (*) Operators

The program in Fig. 8.4 demonstrates the & and * pointer operators. Memory locations are output by << in this example as *hexadecimal* (i.e., base-16) integers. (See Appendix D, Number Systems, for more information on hexadecimal integers.) The address of a (line 10) and the value of aPtr (line 11) are identical in the output, confirming that the address of a is indeed assigned to the pointer variable aPtr. The outputs from lines 12–13 confirm that *aPtr has the same value as a.

Portability Tip 8.1

The memory addresses output by this program with cout and << are platform dependent, so you may get different results when you run the program.

```
1   // Fig. 8.4: fig08_04.cpp
2   // Pointer operators & and *.
3   #include <iostream>
4   using namespace std;
5
6   int main() {
7      int a{7}; // initialize a with 7
8      int* aPtr = &a; // initialize aPtr with the address of int variable a
9
10     cout << "The address of a is " << &a
11        << "\nThe value of aPtr is " << aPtr;
12     cout << "\n\nThe value of a is " << a
13        << "\nThe value of *aPtr is " << *aPtr << endl;
14  }
```

```
The address of a is 002DFD80
The value of aPtr is 002DFD80

The value of a is 7
The value of *aPtr is 7
```

Fig. 8.4 | Pointer operators & and *.

Precedence and Associativity of the Operators Discussed So Far
Figure 8.5 lists the precedence and associativity of the operators introduced to this point. The address (&) and dereferencing operator (*) are *unary operators* on the third level.

Operators	Associativity	Type
:: ()	left to right *[See caution in Fig. 2.10 regarding grouping parentheses.]*	primary
() [] ++ -- static_cast<*type*> (*operand*)	left to right	postfix

Fig. 8.5 | Operator precedence and associativity of the operators discussed so far. (Part 1 of 2.)

Operators	Associativity	Type
++ -- + - ! & *	right to left	unary (prefix)
* / %	left to right	multiplicative
+ -	left to right	additive
<< >>	left to right	stream insertion/ extraction
< <= > >=	left to right	relational
== !=	left to right	equality
&&	left to right	logical AND
||	left to right	logical OR
?:	right to left	conditional
= += -= *= /= %=	right to left	assignment
,	left to right	comma

Fig. 8.5 | Operator precedence and associativity of the operators discussed so far. (Part 2 of 2.)

8.4 Pass-by-Reference with Pointers

There are three ways in C++ to pass arguments to a function:

- pass-by-value
- pass-by-reference with a reference argument
- pass-by-reference with a pointer argument.

Chapter 6 compared and contrasted the first two. Here, we explain pass-by-reference with a pointer argument.

Chapter 6 showed that return can return one value from a called function or simply return control. You also learned that arguments can be passed to a function using reference parameters, which enable the called function to modify the original values of the arguments in the caller. Reference parameters also enable programs to pass large data objects to a function without the overhead of pass-by-value which, of course, copies the object. Pointers, like references, also can be used to modify variables in the caller or to pass large data objects by reference to avoid the overhead of copying the objects.

You can use pointers and the indirection operator (*) to accomplish pass-by-reference (exactly as pass-by-reference is done in C programs—C does not have references). When calling a function with a variable that should be modified, the *address* of the variable is passed. This is normally accomplished by applying the address operator (&) to the name of the variable whose value will be modified.

An Example of Pass-By-Value

Figures 8.6 and 8.7 present two versions of a function that cubes an integer. Figure 8.6 passes variable number *by value* (line 12) to function cubeByValue (lines 17–19), which cubes its argument and passes the result back to main using a return statement (line 18). The new value is assigned to number (line 12) in main. The calling function has the opportunity to examine the function call's result *before* modifying variable number's value. For example, we could have stored the result of cubeByValue in another variable, examined its value and assigned the result to number only after determining that the returned value was reasonable.

```
1   // Fig. 8.6: fig08_06.cpp
2   // Pass-by-value used to cube a variable's value.
3   #include <iostream>
4   using namespace std;
5
6   int cubeByValue(int); // prototype
7
8   int main() {
9      int number{5};
10
11     cout << "The original value of number is " << number;
12     number = cubeByValue(number); // pass number by value to cubeByValue
13     cout << "\nThe new value of number is " << number << endl;
14  }
15
16  // calculate and return cube of integer argument
17  int cubeByValue(int n) {
18     return n * n * n; // cube local variable n and return result
19  }
```

```
The original value of number is 5
The new value of number is 125
```

Fig. 8.6 | Pass-by-value used to cube a variable's value.

An Example of Pass-By-Reference with Pointers

Figure 8.7 passes the variable number to function cubeByReference using *pass-by-reference with a pointer argument* (line 13)—the *address* of number is passed to the function. Function cubeByReference (lines 18–20) specifies parameter nPtr (a pointer to int) to receive its argument. The function *uses the dereferenced pointer*—*nPtr, an alias for number in main—to cube the value to which nPtr points (line 19). This *directly* changes the value of number in main (line 10). Line 19 can be made clearer with redundant parentheses:

```
*nPtr = (*nPtr) * (*nPtr) * (*nPtr); // cube *nPtr
```

```
1   // Fig. 8.7: fig08_07.cpp
2   // Pass-by-reference with a pointer argument used to cube a
3   // variable's value.
4   #include <iostream>
5   using namespace std;
6
7   void cubeByReference(int*); // prototype
8
9   int main() {
10     int number{5};
11
```

Fig. 8.7 | Pass-by-reference with a pointer argument used to cube a variable's value. (Part 1 of 2.)

```
12       cout << "The original value of number is " << number;
13       cubeByReference(&number); // pass number address to cubeByReference
14       cout << "\nThe new value of number is " << number << endl;
15    }
16
17    // calculate cube of *nPtr; modifies variable number in main
18    void cubeByReference(int* nPtr) {
19       *nPtr = *nPtr * *nPtr * *nPtr; // cube *nPtr
20    }
```

```
The original value of number is 5
The new value of number is 125
```

Fig. 8.7 | Pass-by-reference with a pointer argument used to cube a variable's value. (Part 2 of 2.)

A function receiving an *address* as an argument must define a pointer parameter to receive the address. For example, the header for function cubeByReference (line 18) specifies that cubeByReference receives the address of an int variable (i.e., a pointer to an int) as an argument, stores the address in nPtr and does *not* return a value.

Function cubeByReference's prototype (line 7) contains int* in parentheses. As with other types, it isn't necessary to include the names of pointer parameters in prototypes—parameter names included for documentation purposes are ignored by the compiler.

Insight: Pass-By-Reference with a Pointer Actually Passes the Pointer By Value

Passing a variable by reference with a pointer *does not actually pass anything by reference*—a pointer to that variable is *passed by value* and is *copied* into the function's corresponding pointer parameter. The called function can then access that variable in the caller simply by dereferencing the pointer, thus accomplishing *pass-by-reference*.

Graphical Analysis of Pass-By-Value and Pass-By-Reference

Figures 8.8–8.9 analyze graphically the execution of Fig. 8.6 and Fig. 8.7, respectively. In the diagrams, the values in rectangles above a given expression or variable represent the value of that expression or variable. Each diagram's right column shows functions cubeByValue (Fig. 8.6) and cubeByReference (Fig. 8.7) *only* when they're executing.

Step 1: Before main calls cubeByValue:

```
int main() {                          number

   int number{5};                        5

   number = cubeByValue(number);
}
```

Fig. 8.8 | Pass-by-value analysis of the program of Fig. 8.6. (Part 1 of 2.)

Step 2: After **cubeByValue** receives the call:

```
int main() {                          number
    int number{5};                     5
    number = cubeByValue(number);
}
```
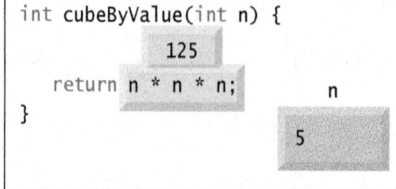

```
int cubeByValue( int n ) {
    return n * n * n;              n
}
                                   5
```

Step 3: After **cubeByValue** cubes parameter n and before **cubeByValue** returns to **main**:

```
int main() {                          number
    int number{5};                     5
    number = cubeByValue(number);
}
```

```
int cubeByValue(int n) {
                        125
    return n * n * n;             n
}
                                  5
```

Step 4: After **cubeByValue** returns to **main** and before assigning the result to **number**:

```
int main() {                          number
    int number{5};                     5
                     125
    number = cubeByValue(number);
}
```

Step 5: After **main** completes the assignment to **number**:

```
int main() {                          number
    int number{5};                    125
        125
    number = cubeByValue(number);
}
```

Fig. 8.8 | Pass-by-value analysis of the program of Fig. 8.6. (Part 2 of 2.)

Step 1: Before **main** calls **cubeByReference**:

```
int main() {                          number
    int number{5};                     5
    cubeByReference(&number);
}
```

Fig. 8.9 | Pass-by-reference analysis of the program of Fig. 8.7. (Part 1 of 2.)

Step 2: After `cubeByReference` receives the call and before `*nPtr` is cubed:

```
int main() {                                    number

    int number{5};                                 5

    cubeByReference(&number);
}
```
```
void cubeByReference( int* nPtr ) {

    *nPtr = *nPtr * *nPtr * *nPtr;
}
                                                nPtr
call establishes this pointer
```

Step 3: Before `*nPtr` is assigned the result of the calculation 5 * 5 * 5:

```
int main() {                                    number

    int number{5};                                 5

    cubeByReference(&number);
}
```
```
void cubeByReference(int* nPtr) {
                             125
    *nPtr = *nPtr * *nPtr * *nPtr;
}
                                                nPtr
```

Step 4: After `*nPtr` is assigned 125 and before program control returns to `main`:

```
int main() {                                    number

    int number{5};                                125

    cubeByReference(&number);
}
```
```
void cubeByReference(int* nPtr) {
         125
    *nPtr = *nPtr * *nPtr * *nPtr;
}
called function modifies caller's    nPtr
variable
```

Step 5: After `cubeByReference` returns to `main`:

```
int main() {                                    number

    int number{5};                                125

    cubeByReference(&number);
}
```

Fig. 8.9 | Pass-by-reference analysis of the program of Fig. 8.7. (Part 2 of 2.)

8.5 Built-In Arrays

In Chapter 7, we used the `array` class template to represent *fixed-size* lists and tables of values. Here we present *built-in arrays*, which are also *fixed-size* data structures.

8.5.1 Declaring and Accessing a Built-In Array

To specify the type of the elements and the number of elements required by a built-in array, use a declaration of the form:

> *type arrayName[arraySize]* ;

The compiler reserves the appropriate amount of memory. The *arraySize* must be an integer constant greater than zero. For example, to tell the compiler to reserve 12 elements for built-in array of ints named c, use the declaration

```
int c[12]; // c is a built-in array of 12 integers
```

As with array objects, you use the subscript ([]) operator to access the individual elements of a built-in array. Recall from Chapter 7 that the subscript ([]) operator does *not* provide bounds checking for array objects—this is also true for built-in arrays.

8.5.2 Initializing Built-In Arrays

You can initialize the elements of a built-in array using an *initializer list*. For example,

```
int n[5]{50, 20, 30, 10, 40};
```

creates a built-in array of five ints and initializes them to the values in the initializer list. If you provide fewer initializers than the number of elements, the remaining elements are *value initialized*—fundamental numeric types are set to 0, bools are set to false, pointers are set to nullptr and class objects are initialized by their default constructors. If you provide too many initializers a compilation error occurs.

If a built-in array's size is *omitted* from a declaration with an initializer list, the compiler sizes the built-in array to the number of elements in the initializer list. For example,

```
int n[]{50, 20, 30, 10, 40};
```

creates a five-element array.

Error-Prevention Tip 8.3

Always specify a built-in array's size, even when providing an initializer list. This enables the compiler to generate an error message if there are more initializers than array elements.

8.5.3 Passing Built-In Arrays to Functions

The value of a built-in array's name is implicitly convertible to the address of the built-in array's first element. So arrayName is implicitly convertible to &arrayName[0]. For this reason, you don't need to take the address (&) of a built-in array to pass it to a function—you simply pass the built-in array's name. As you saw in Section 8.4, a function that receives a pointer to a variable in the caller can *modify* that variable in the caller. For built-in arrays, this means that the called function can modify *all* the elements of a built-in array in the caller—unless the function precedes the corresponding built-in array parameter with const to indicate that the elements should *not* be modified.

Software Engineering Observation 8.2

Applying the const type qualifier to a built-in array parameter in a function definition to prevent the original built-in array from being modified in the function body is another example of the principle of least privilege. Functions should not be given the capability to modify a built-in array unless it's absolutely necessary.

8.5.4 Declaring Built-In Array Parameters

You can declare a built-in array parameter in a function header, as follows:

```
int sumElements(const int values[], const size_t numberOfElements)
```

which indicates that the function's first argument should be a one-dimensional built-in array of `int`s that should *not* be modified by the function. Unlike `array` objects, built-in arrays don't know their own size, so a function that processes a built-in array should have parameters to receive both the built-in array *and* its size.

The preceding header can also be written as:

```
int sumElements(const int* values, const size_t numberOfElements)
```

The compiler does not differentiate between a function that receives a pointer and a function that receives a built-in array. This, of course, means that the function must "know" when it's receiving a built-in array or simply a single variable that's being passed by reference. When the compiler encounters a function parameter for a one-dimensional built-in array of the form `const int values[]`, the compiler converts the parameter to the pointer notation `const int* values` (that is, "values is a pointer to an integer constant"). These forms of declaring a one-dimensional built-in array parameter are interchangeable.

Good Programming Practice 8.2
When declaring a built-in array parameter, for clarity use the [] notation rather than pointer notation.

8.5.5 C++11: Standard Library Functions begin and end

In Section 7.7, we showed how to sort an `array` object with the C++ Standard Library function `sort`. We sorted an `array` of `string`s called `colors` as follows:

```
sort(colors.begin(), colors.end()); // sort contents of colors
```

The `array` class's `begin` and `end` functions specified that the entire `array` should be sorted. Function `sort` (and many other C++ Standard Library functions) can also be applied to built-in arrays. For example, to sort the built-in array `n` (Section 8.5.2), you can write:

```
sort(begin(n), end(n)); // sort contents of built-in array n
```

C++11's new `begin` and `end` functions (from header `<iterator>`) each receive a built-in array as an argument and return a pointer that can be used to represent ranges of elements to process in C++ Standard Library functions like `sort`.

8.5.6 Built-In Array Limitations

Built-in arrays have several limitations:

- They *cannot be compared* using the relational and equality operators—you must use a loop to compare two built-in arrays element by element.
- They *cannot be assigned* to one another—an array name is effectively a pointer that is `const`.
- They *don't know their own size*—a function that processes a built-in array typically receives *both* the built-in array's name and its size as arguments.

- They *don't provide automatic bounds checking*—you must ensure that array-access expressions use subscripts that are within the built-in array's bounds.

8.5.7 Built-In Arrays Sometimes Are Required

In contemporary C++ code, you should use the more robust array (or vector) objects to represent lists and tables of values. However, there are cases in which built-in arrays *must* be used, such as processing a program's command-line arguments. You supply these to a program by placing them after the program's name when executing it from the command line. Such arguments typically pass options to a program. For example, on a Windows system, the command

```
dir /p
```

uses the /p argument to list the contents of the current directory, pausing after each screen of information. Similarly, on Linux or OS X, the following command uses the -la argument to list the contents of the current directory with details about each file and directory:

```
ls -la
```

Command-line arguments are passed to main as a built-in array of pointer-based strings (Section 8.10)—C++ inherited these capabilities from C. Appendix F shows how to process command-line arguments.

8.6 Using const with Pointers

Recall that const enables you to inform the compiler that the value of a particular variable should *not* be modified. Many possibilities exist for using (or *not* using) const with function parameters, so how do you choose the most appropriate? Let the principle of least privilege be your guide. Always give a function *enough* access to the data in its parameters to accomplish its specified task, *but no more*. This section discusses how to combine const with pointer declarations to enforce the principle of least privilege.

Chapter 6 explained that when an argument is passed by value, a *copy* of the argument is passed to the function. If the copy is *modified* in the *called* function, the original value in the caller does *not* change. In some instances, even the copy of the argument's value should *not* be altered in the called function.

Consider a function that takes a pointer to the initial element of a built-in array and the array's size as arguments and subsequently displays the built-in array's elements. Such a function should loop through the elements and output each individually. The built-in array's size is used in the function's body to determine the highest subscript so the loop can terminate when the displaying completes. The size does not need to change in the function body, so it should be declared const to *ensure* that it will not change. Because the built-in array is only being displayed, it, too, should be declared const. This is especially important because built-in arrays are *always* passed by reference and could easily be changed in the called function. An attempt to modify a const value is a *compilation* error.

Software Engineering Observation 8.3

If a value does not (or should not) change in the body of a function to which it's passed, the parameter should be declared const.

Error-Prevention Tip 8.4

Before using a function, check its function prototype to determine the parameters that it can and cannot modify.

There are four ways to pass a pointer to a function:

- a *nonconstant pointer to nonconstant data*,
- a *nonconstant pointer to constant data* (Fig. 8.10),
- a *constant pointer to nonconstant data* (Fig. 8.11) and
- a *constant pointer to constant data* (Fig. 8.12).

Each combination provides a different level of access privilege.

8.6.1 Nonconstant Pointer to Nonconstant Data

The highest access is granted by a nonconstant pointer to nonconstant data:

- the *data can be modified* through the dereferenced pointer, and
- the *pointer can be modified* to point to other data.

Such a pointer's declaration (e.g., int* countPtr) does *not* include const.

8.6.2 Nonconstant Pointer to Constant Data

A nonconstant pointer to constant data is:

- a pointer that can be modified to point to *any* data of the appropriate type, but
- the data to which it points *cannot* be modified through that pointer.

Such a pointer might be used to *receive* a built-in array argument to a function that should be allowed to read the elements, but *not* modify them. Any attempt to modify the data in the function results in a compilation error. The declaration for such a pointer places const to the *left* of the pointer's type, as in[1]

```
const int* countPtr;
```

The declaration is read from *right to left* as "countPtr is a pointer to an integer *constant*" or more precisely, "countPtr is a *non-constant* pointer to an integer *constant*."

Figure 8.10 demonstrates GNU C++'s compilation error message produced when attempting to compile a function that receives a *nonconstant pointer* to *constant data*, then tries to use that pointer to modify the data.

```
1   // Fig. 8.10: fig08_10.cpp
2   // Attempting to modify data through a
3   // nonconstant pointer to constant data.
4
5   void f(const int*); // prototype
```

Fig. 8.10 | Attempting to modify data through a nonconstant pointer to const data. (Part 1 of 2.)

---

1.   Some programmers prefer to write this as int const* countPtr; to make it obvious that const applies to the int, not the pointer. They'd read this declaration from right to left as "countPtr is a pointer to a constant integer."

```
6
7   int main() {
8       int y{0};
9
10      f(&y); // f will attempt an illegal modification
11  }
12
13  // constant variable cannot be modified through xPtr
14  void f(const int* xPtr) {
15      *xPtr = 100; // error: cannot modify a const object
16  }
```

GNU C++ compiler error message:

```
fig08_10.cpp: In function 'void f(const int*)':
fig08_10.cpp:17:12: error: assignment of read-only location '* xPtr'
```

Fig. 8.10 | Attempting to modify data through a nonconstant pointer to `const` data. (Part 2 of 2.)

When a function is called with a built-in array as an argument, its contents are effectively passed by reference because the built-in array's name is implicitly convertible to the address of the built-in array's first element. However, *by default, objects such as arrays and vectors are passed by value—a copy of the entire object is passed.* This requires the execution-time overhead of making a *copy* of each data item in the object and storing it on the function call stack. When a *pointer* to an object is passed, only a copy of the *address* of the object must be made—the *object itself is not copied.*

Performance Tip 8.1
If they do not need to be modified by the called function, pass large objects using pointers to constant data or references to constant data, to obtain the performance benefits of pass-by-reference and avoid the copy overhead of pass-by-value.

Software Engineering Observation 8.4
Passing large objects using pointers to constant data, or references to constant data offers the security of pass-by-value.

Software Engineering Observation 8.5
Use pass-by-value to pass fundamental-type arguments (e.g., `ints`, `doubles`, etc.) to a function unless the caller explicitly requires that the called function be able to directly modify the value in the caller. This is another example of the principle of least privilege.

8.6.3 Constant Pointer to Nonconstant Data

A constant pointer to nonconstant data is a pointer that:

- always points to the same memory location, and
- the data at that location *can* be modified through the pointer.

Pointers that are declared `const` *must be initialized when they're declared,* but if the pointer is a function parameter, it's *initialized with the pointer that's passed to the function.*

Figure 8.11 attempts to modify a constant pointer. Line 9 declares pointer ptr to be of type int* const. The declaration is read from *right to left* as "ptr is a constant pointer to a nonconstant integer." The pointer is *initialized* with the address of integer variable x. Line 12 attempts to *assign* the address of y to ptr, but the compiler generates an error message. No error occurs when line 11 assigns the value 7 to *ptr—the nonconstant value to which ptr points *can* be modified using the dereferenced ptr, even though ptr itself has been declared const.

```
1   // Fig. 8.11: fig08_11.cpp
2   // Attempting to modify a constant pointer to nonconstant data.
3
4   int main() {
5      int x, y;
6
7      // ptr is a constant pointer to an integer that can be modified
8      // through ptr, but ptr always points to the same memory location.
9      int* const ptr{&x}; // const pointer must be initialized
10
11     *ptr = 7; // allowed: *ptr is not const
12     ptr = &y; // error: ptr is const; cannot assign to it a new address
13   }
```

Microsoft Visual C++ compiler error message:

```
'ptr': you cannot assign to a variable that is const
```

Fig. 8.11 | Attempting to modify a constant pointer to nonconstant data.

8.6.4 Constant Pointer to Constant Data

The *minimum* access privilege is granted by a constant pointer to constant data:

- such a pointer *always* points to the *same* memory location, and
- the data at that location *cannot* be modified via the pointer.

This is how a built-in array should be passed to a function that *only reads* from the array, using array subscript notation, and *does not modify* it. The program of Fig. 8.12 declares pointer variable ptr to be of type const int* const (line 12). This declaration is read from *right to left* as "ptr is a *constant pointer to an integer constant*." The figure shows the Xcode LLVM compiler's error messages that are generated when an attempt is made to modify the data to which ptr points (line 16) and when an attempt is made to modify the address stored in the pointer variable (line 17)—these show up on the lines of code with the errors in the Xcode text editor. In line 14, no errors occur when the program attempts to dereference ptr, or when the program attempts to output the value to which ptr points, because *neither* the pointer *nor* the data it points to is being modified in this statement.

```
1   // Fig. 8.12: fig08_12.cpp
2   // Attempting to modify a constant pointer to constant data.
3   #include <iostream>
```

Fig. 8.12 | Attempting to modify a constant pointer to constant data. (Part 1 of 2.)

```
4   using namespace std;
5
6   int main() {
7       int x{5}, y;
8
9       // ptr is a constant pointer to a constant integer.
10      // ptr always points to the same location; the integer
11      // at that location cannot be modified.
12      const int* const ptr{&x};
13
14      cout << *ptr << endl;
15
16      *ptr = 7; // error: *ptr is const; cannot assign new value
17      ptr = &y; // error: ptr is const; cannot assign new address
18  }
```

Xcode LLVM compiler error message:

```
Read-only variable is not assignable
Read-only variable is not assignable
```

Fig. 8.12 | Attempting to modify a constant pointer to constant data. (Part 2 of 2.)

8.7 sizeof Operator

The *compile time* unary operator `sizeof` determines the size in bytes of a built-in array or of any other data type, variable or constant *during program compilation*. When applied to a built-in array's *name*, as in Fig. 8.13 (line 12), `sizeof` returns the *total number of bytes in the built-in array* as a value of type `size_t`. The computer we used to compile this program stores variables of type `double` in 8 bytes of memory, and `numbers` is declared to have 20 elements (line 10), so it uses 160 bytes in memory. When applied to a *pointer parameter* (line 20) in a function that *receives a built-in array as an argument*, the `sizeof` operator returns the size of the *pointer* in bytes (4 on the system we used)—*not* the built-in array's size.

Common Programming Error 8.3

Using the sizeof operator in a function to find the size in bytes of a built-in array parameter results in the size in bytes of a pointer, not the size in bytes of the built-in array.

```
1   // Fig. 8.13: fig08_13.cpp
2   // Sizeof operator when used on a built-in array's name
3   // returns the number of bytes in the built-in array.
4   #include <iostream>
5   using namespace std;
6
7   size_t getSize(double*); // prototype
8
9   int main() {
10      double numbers[20]; // 20 doubles; occupies 160 bytes on our system
```

Fig. 8.13 | sizeof operator when applied to a built-in array's name returns the number of bytes in the built-in array. (Part 1 of 2.)

```
11
12       cout << "The number of bytes in the array is " << sizeof(numbers);
13
14       cout << "\nThe number of bytes returned by getSize is "
15           << getSize(numbers) << endl;
16   }
17
18   // return size of ptr
19   size_t getSize(double* ptr) {
20       return sizeof(ptr);
21   }
```

```
The number of bytes in the array is 160
The number of bytes returned by getSize is 4
```

Fig. 8.13 | sizeof operator when applied to a built-in array's name returns the number of bytes in the built-in array. (Part 2 of 2.)

The number of *elements* in a built-in array can be determined using the results of two sizeof operations. For example, to determine the number of elements in the built-in array numbers, use the following expression (which is evaluated at *compile time*):

```
sizeof numbers / sizeof(numbers[0])
```

The expression divides the number of bytes in numbers (160, assuming 8-byte doubles) by the number of bytes in the built-in array's zeroth element (8)—resulting in the number of elements in numbers (20).

Determining the Sizes of the Fundamental Types, a Built-In Array and a Pointer

Figure 8.14 uses sizeof to calculate the number of bytes used to store many of the standard data types. The output was produced using the default settings in Xcode 7.2 on Mac OS X. Type sizes are *platform dependent*. When we run this program on Windows, for example, long is 4 bytes and and long long is 8 bytes, whereas on our Mac, they're both 8 bytes.

```
 1   // Fig. 8.14: fig08_14.cpp
 2   // sizeof operator used to determine standard data type sizes.
 3   #include <iostream>
 4   using namespace std;
 5
 6   int main() {
 7       char c; // variable of type char
 8       short s; // variable of type short
 9       int i; // variable of type int
10       long l; // variable of type long
11       long long ll; // variable of type long long
12       float f; // variable of type float
13       double d; // variable of type double
14       long double ld; // variable of type long double
15       int array[20]; // built-in array of int
16       int* ptr{array}; // variable of type int *
```

Fig. 8.14 | sizeof operator used to determine standard data type sizes. (Part 1 of 2.)

```
17
18      cout << "sizeof c = " << sizeof c
19         << "\tsizeof(char) = " << sizeof(char)
20         << "\nsizeof s = " << sizeof s
21         << "\tsizeof(short) = " << sizeof(short)
22         << "\nsizeof i = " << sizeof i
23         << "\tsizeof(int) = " << sizeof(int)
24         << "\nsizeof l = " << sizeof l
25         << "\tsizeof(long) = " << sizeof(long)
26         << "\nsizeof ll = " << sizeof ll
27         << "\tsizeof(long long) = " << sizeof(long long)
28         << "\nsizeof f = " << sizeof f
29         << "\tsizeof(float) = " << sizeof(float)
30         << "\nsizeof d = " << sizeof d
31         << "\tsizeof(double) = " << sizeof(double)
32         << "\nsizeof ld = " << sizeof ld
33         << "\tsizeof(long double) = " << sizeof(long double)
34         << "\nsizeof array = " << sizeof array
35         << "\nsizeof ptr = " << sizeof ptr << endl;
36   }
```

```
sizeof c = 1      sizeof(char) = 1
sizeof s = 2      sizeof(short) = 2
sizeof i = 4      sizeof(int) = 4
sizeof l = 8      sizeof(long) = 8
sizeof ll = 8     sizeof(long long) = 8
sizeof f = 4      sizeof(float) = 4
sizeof d = 8      sizeof(double) = 8
sizeof ld = 16    sizeof(long double) = 16
sizeof array = 80
sizeof ptr = 8
```

Fig. 8.14 | sizeof operator used to determine standard data type sizes. (Part 2 of 2.)

Portability Tip 8.2

The number of bytes used to store a particular data type may vary among systems. When writing programs that depend on data type sizes, always use sizeof to determine the number of bytes used to store the data types.

Operator sizeof can be applied to any expression or type name. When sizeof is applied to a variable name (which is not a built-in array's name) or other expression, the number of bytes used to store the specific type of the expression is returned. The parentheses used with sizeof are required *only* if a type name (e.g., int) is supplied as its operand. The parentheses used with sizeof are *not* required when sizeof's operand is an expression. Remember that sizeof is a *compile-time* operator, so its operand is not evaluated at runtime.

8.8 Pointer Expressions and Pointer Arithmetic

This section describes the operators that can have pointers as operands and how these operators are used with pointers. C++ enables pointer arithmetic—a few arithmetic operations may be performed on pointers. *Pointer arithmetic is appropriate only for pointers that point to built-in array elements.*

A pointer may be incremented (++) or decremented (--), an integer may be added to a pointer (+ or +=) or subtracted from a pointer (- or -=), or one pointer may be subtracted from another of the same type—this particular operation is appropriate only for two pointers that point to elements of the *same* built-in array.

> **Portability Tip 8.3**
> *Most computers today have four-byte or eight-byte integers. Because the results of pointer arithmetic depend on the size of the memory objects a pointer points to, pointer arithmetic is machine dependent.*

Assume that int v[5] has been declared and that its first element is at memory location 3000. Assume that pointer vPtr has been initialized to point to v[0] (i.e., the value of vPtr is 3000). Figure 8.15 illustrates this situation for a machine with four-byte integers. Variable vPtr can be initialized to point to v with either of the following statements (because a built-in array's name implicitly converts to the address of its zeroth element):

```
int* vPtr{v};
int* vPtr{&v[0]};
```

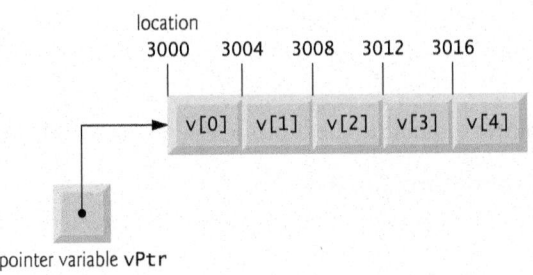

Fig. 8.15 | Built-in array v and a pointer variable int* vPtr that points to v.

8.8.1 Adding Integers to and Subtracting Integers from Pointers

In conventional arithmetic, the addition 3000 + 2 yields the value 3002. This is normally *not* the case with pointer arithmetic. When an integer is added to, or subtracted from, a pointer, the pointer is *not* simply incremented or decremented by that integer, but by that integer *times the size of the memory object to which the pointer refers.* The number of bytes depends on the memory object's data type. For example, the statement

```
vPtr += 2;
```

would produce 3008 (from the calculation 3000 + 2 * 4), assuming that an int is stored in four bytes of memory. In the built-in array v, vPtr would now point to v[2] (Fig. 8.16). If an integer is stored in eight bytes of memory, then the preceding calculation would result in memory location 3016 (3000 + 2 * 8).

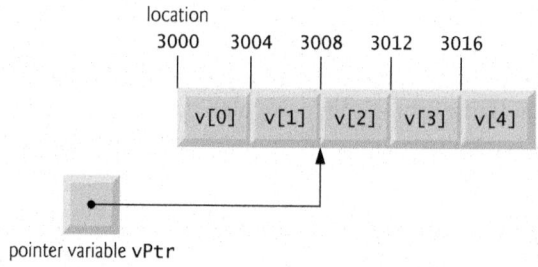

location

Fig. 8.16 | Pointer vPtr after pointer arithmetic.

If vPtr had been incremented to 3016, which points to v[4], the statement

```
vPtr -= 4;
```

would set vPtr back to 3000—the beginning of the built-in array. If a pointer is being incremented or decremented by one, the increment (++) and decrement (--) operators can be used. Each of the statements

```
++vPtr;
vPtr++;
```

increments the pointer to point to the built-in array's *next* element. Each of the statements

```
--vPtr;
vPtr--;
```

decrements the pointer to point to the built-in array's *previous* element.

 Error-Prevention Tip 8.5

There's no bounds checking on pointer arithmetic. You must ensure that every pointer arithmetic operation that adds an integer to or subtracts an integer from a pointer results in a pointer that references an element within the built-in array's bounds.

8.8.2 Subtracting Pointers

Pointer variables pointing to the *same* built-in array may be subtracted from one another. For example, if vPtr contains the address 3000 and v2Ptr contains the address 3008, the statement

```
x = v2Ptr - vPtr;
```

would assign to x the *number of built-in array elements* from vPtr to v2Ptr—in this case, 2. *Pointer arithmetic is meaningful only on a pointer that points to a built-in array.* We cannot assume that two variables of the same type are stored contiguously in memory unless they're adjacent elements of a built-in array.

 Common Programming Error 8.4

Subtracting or comparing two pointers that do not refer to elements of the same built-in array is a logic error.

8.8.3 Pointer Assignment

A pointer can be assigned to another pointer if both pointers are of the *same* type. Otherwise, a cast operator (normally a `reinterpret_cast`; discussed in Section 14.8) must be used to convert the value of the pointer on the right of the assignment to the pointer type on the left of the assignment. The exception to this rule is the pointer to void (i.e., `void*`), which is a generic pointer capable of representing *any* pointer type. Any pointer to a fundamental type or class type can be assigned to a pointer of type `void*` without casting. However, a pointer of type `void*` *cannot* be assigned directly to a pointer of another type—the pointer of type `void*` must first be *cast* to the proper pointer type.

Common Programming Error 8.5

Assigning a pointer of one type to a pointer of another (other than `void*`) *without using a cast is a compilation error.*

8.8.4 Cannot Dereference a `void*`

A `void*` pointer *cannot* be dereferenced. For example, the compiler "knows" that an `int*` points to four bytes of memory on a machine with four-byte integers. Dereferencing an `int*` creates an *lvalue* that is an alias for the `int`'s four bytes in memory. A `void*`, however, simply contains a memory address for an *unknown* data type. You cannot dereference a `void*` because the compiler does *not* know the type of the data to which the pointer refers and thus not the number of bytes.

Common Programming Error 8.6

The allowed operations on `void*` *pointers are: comparing* `void*` *pointers with other pointers, casting* `void*` *pointers to other pointer types and assigning addresses to* `void*` *pointers. All other operations on* `void*` *pointers are compilation errors.*

8.8.5 Comparing Pointers

Pointers can be compared using equality and relational operators. Comparisons using relational operators are meaningless unless the pointers point to elements of the *same* built-in array. Pointer comparisons compare the *addresses* stored in the pointers. A comparison of two pointers pointing to the same built-in array could show, for example, that one pointer points to a higher-numbered element of the built-in array than the other pointer does. A common use of pointer comparison is determining whether a pointer has the value `nullptr`, 0 or `NULL` (i.e., the pointer does not point to anything).

8.9 Relationship Between Pointers and Built-In Arrays

Built-in arrays and pointers are intimately related in C++ and may be used *almost* interchangeably. Pointers can be used to do any operation involving array subscripting.

Assume the following declarations

```
int b[ 5 ]; // create 5-element int array b; b is a const pointer
int* bPtr; // create int pointer bPtr, which isn't a const pointer
```

We can set `bPtr` to the address of the first element in the built-in array `b` with the statement

```
bPtr = b; // assign address of built-in array b to bPtr
```

This is equivalent to assigning the address of the first element as follows:

```
bPtr = &b[0]; // also assigns address of built-in array b to bPtr
```

The expression

```
b += 3
```

causes a compilation error, because it attempts to *modify* the value of the built-in array's name with pointer arithmetic.

8.9.1 Pointer/Offset Notation

Built-in array element b[3] can alternatively be referenced with the pointer expression

```
*(bPtr + 3)
```

The 3 in the preceding expression is the offset to the pointer. When the pointer points to the beginning of a built-in array, the offset indicates which built-in array element should be referenced, and the offset value is identical to the subscript. This notation is referred to as pointer/offset notation. The parentheses are necessary, because the precedence of * is higher than that of +. Without the parentheses, the preceding expression would add 3 to a copy of *bPtr's value (i.e., 3 would be added to b[0], assuming that bPtr points to the beginning of the built-in array).

Just as the built-in array element can be referenced with a pointer expression, the *address*

```
&b[3]
```

can be written with the pointer expression

```
bPtr + 3
```

8.9.2 Pointer/Offset Notation with the Built-In Array's Name as the Pointer

The built-in array name can be treated as a pointer and used in pointer arithmetic. For example, the expression

```
*(b + 3)
```

also refers to the element b[3]. In general, all subscripted built-in array expressions can be written with a pointer and an offset. In this case, pointer/offset notation was used with the built-in array's name as a pointer. The preceding expression does *not* modify the built-in array's name; b still points to the built-in array's first element.

8.9.3 Pointer/Subscript Notation

Pointers can be subscripted exactly as built-in arrays can. For example, the expression

```
bPtr[1]
```

refers to b[1]; this expression uses pointer/subscript notation.

Good Programming Practice 8.3

For clarity, use built-in array notation instead of pointer notation when manipulating built-in arrays.

8.9.4 Demonstrating the Relationship Between Pointers and Built-In Arrays

Figure 8.17 demonstrates the four notations we just discussed:

- *array subscript notation*
- *pointer/offset notation with the built-in array's name as a pointer*
- *pointer subscript notation*
- *pointer/offset notation with a pointer*

to accomplish the same task, namely displaying the four elements of the built-in array of ints named b.

```cpp
1   // Fig. 8.17: fig08_17.cpp
2   // Using subscripting and pointer notations with built-in arrays.
3   #include <iostream>
4   using namespace std;
5
6   int main() {
7      int b[]{10, 20, 30, 40}; // create 4-element built-in array b
8      int* bPtr{b}; // set bPtr to point to built-in array b
9
10     // output built-in array b using array subscript notation
11     cout << "Array b displayed with:\n\nArray subscript notation\n";
12
13     for (size_t i{0}; i < 4; ++i) {
14        cout << "b[" << i << "] = " << b[i]    << '\n';
15     }
16
17     // output built-in array b using array name and pointer/offset notation
18     cout << "\nPointer/offset notation where "
19        << "the pointer is the array name\n";
20
21     for (size_t offset1{0}; offset1 < 4; ++offset1) {
22        cout << "*(b + " << offset1 << ") = " << *(b + offset1)    << '\n';
23     }
24
25     // output built-in array b using bPtr and array subscript notation
26     cout << "\nPointer subscript notation\n";
27
28     for (size_t j{0}; j < 4; ++j) {
29        cout << "bPtr[" << j << "] = " << bPtr[j]    << '\n';
30     }
31
32     cout << "\nPointer/offset notation\n";
33
34     // output built-in array b using bPtr and pointer/offset notation
35     for (size_t offset2{0}; offset2 < 4; ++offset2) {
36        cout << "*(bPtr + " << offset2 << ") = "
37           << *(bPtr + offset2)    << '\n';
38     }
39  }
```

Fig. 8.17 | Using subscripting and pointer notations with built-in arrays. (Part 1 of 2.)

```
Array b displayed with:

Array subscript notation
b[0] = 10
b[1] = 20
b[2] = 30
b[3] = 40

Pointer/offset notation where the pointer is the array name
*(b + 0) = 10
*(b + 1) = 20
*(b + 2) = 30
*(b + 3) = 40

Pointer subscript notation
bPtr[0] = 10
bPtr[1] = 20
bPtr[2] = 30
bPtr[3] = 40

Pointer/offset notation
*(bPtr + 0) = 10
*(bPtr + 1) = 20
*(bPtr + 2) = 30
*(bPtr + 3) = 40
```

Fig. 8.17 | Using subscripting and pointer notations with built-in arrays. (Part 2 of 2.)

8.10 Pointer-Based Strings (Optional)

We've already used the C++ Standard Library string class to represent strings as full-fledged objects. Chapter 21 presents class string in detail. This section introduces C-style, pointer-based strings (as defined by the C programming language), which we'll simply call C strings. *C++'s string class is preferred for use in new programs, because it eliminates many of the security problems and bugs that can be caused by manipulating C strings.* We cover C strings here for a deeper understanding of pointers and built-in arrays, and because there are some cases (such as command-line arguments) in which C string processing is required. Also, if you work with legacy C and C++ programs, you're likely to encounter pointer-based strings. We cover C strings in detail in Appendix F.

Characters and Character Constants

Characters are the fundamental building blocks of C++ source programs. Every program is composed of a sequence of characters that—when grouped together meaningfully—is interpreted by the compiler as instructions and data used to accomplish a task. A program may contain character constants. A character constant is an integer value represented as a character in single quotes. The *value* of a character constant is the integer value of the character in the machine's character set. For example, 'z' represents the integer value of z (122 in the ASCII character set; see Appendix B), and '\n' represents the integer value of newline (10 in the ASCII character set).

Strings

A string is a series of characters treated as a single unit. A string may include letters, digits and various special characters such as +, -, *, /and $. String literals, or string constants, in C++ are written in double quotation marks as follows:

```
"John Q. Doe"           (a name)
"9999 Main Street"      (a street address)
"Maynard, Massachusetts" (a city and state)
"(201) 555-1212"        (a telephone number)
```

Pointer-Based Strings

A pointer-based string is a built-in array of characters ending with a null character ('\0'), which marks where the string terminates in memory. A string is accessed via a pointer to its first character. The result of sizeof for a string literal is the length of the string *including* the terminating null character.

String Literals as Initializers

A string literal may be used as an initializer in the declaration of either a built-in array of chars or a variable of type const char*. The declarations

```
char color[]{"blue"};
const char* colorPtr{"blue"};
```

each initialize a variable to the string "blue". The first declaration creates a *five-element* built-in array color containing the characters 'b', 'l', 'u', 'e' *and* '\0'. The second declaration creates pointer variable colorPtr that points to the letter b in the string "blue" (which ends in '\0') somewhere in memory. String literals exist for the duration of the program and may be *shared* if the same string literal is referenced from multiple locations in a program. String literals cannot be modified.

Character Constants as Initializers

The declaration char color[] = "blue"; could also be written

```
char color[]{'b', 'l', 'u', 'e', '\0'};
```

which uses character constants in single quotes (') as initializers for each element of the built-in array. When declaring a built-in array of chars to contain a string, the built-in array must be large enough to store the string *and* its terminating null character. The compiler determines the size of the built-in array in the preceding declaration, based on the number of initializers in the initializer list.

Common Programming Error 8.7

Not allocating sufficient space in a built-in array of chars to store the null character that terminates a string is a logic error.

Common Programming Error 8.8

Creating or using a C string that does not contain a terminating null character can lead to logic errors.

Error-Prevention Tip 8.6

When storing a string of characters in a built-in array of chars, be sure that the built-in array is large enough to hold the largest string that will be stored. C++ allows strings of any length. If a string is longer than the built-in array of chars in which it's to be stored, characters beyond the end of the built-in array will overwrite data in memory following the built-in array, leading to logic errors and potential security breaches.

Accessing Characters in a C String

Because a C string is a built-in array of characters, we can access individual characters in a string directly with array subscript notation. For example, in the preceding declaration, `color[0]` is the character `'b'`, `color[2]` is `'u'` and `color[4]` is the null character.

Reading Strings into Built-In Arrays of **char** *with* **cin**

A string can be read into a built-in array of chars using `cin`. For example, the following statement reads a string into the built-in 20-element array of chars named `word`:

```
cin >> word;
```

The string entered by the user is stored in `word`. The preceding statement reads characters until a white-space character or end-of-file indicator is encountered. The string should be no longer than 19 characters to leave room for the terminating null character. The `setw` stream manipulator can be used to ensure that the string read into `word` does not exceed the size of the built-in array. For example, the statement

```
cin >> setw(20) >> word;
```

specifies that `cin` should read a maximum of 19 characters into `word` and save the 20th location to store the terminating null character for the string. The `setw` stream manipulator is not a sticky setting—it applies *only* to the next value being input. If more than 19 characters are entered, the remaining characters are not saved in `word`, but they will be in the input stream and can be read by the next input operation. Of course, any input operation can also fail. We show how to detect input failures in Section 13.8.

Reading Lines of Text into Built-In Arrays of **char** *with* **cin.getline**

In some cases, it's desirable to input an *entire line of text* into a built-in array of chars. For this purpose, the `cin` object provides the member function `getline`, which takes three arguments—a *built-in array of chars* in which the line of text will be stored, a *length* and a *delimiter character*. For example, the statements

```
char sentence[80];
cin.getline(sentence, 80, '\n');
```

declare `sentence` as a built-in array of 80 characters and read a line of text from the keyboard into the built-in array. The function stops reading characters when the delimiter character `'\n'` is encountered, when the *end-of-file indicator* is entered or when the number of characters read so far is one less than the length specified in the second argument. The last character in the built-in array is reserved for the terminating null character. If the delimiter character is encountered, it's read and *discarded*. The third argument to `cin.getline` has `'\n'` as a default value, so the preceding function call could have been written as:

```
cin.getline(sentence, 80);
```

Chapter 13, Stream Input/Output: A Deeper Look, provides a detailed discussion of `cin.getline` and other input/output functions.

Displaying C Strings
A built-in array of chars representing a null-terminated string can be output with cout and <<. The statement

```
cout << sentence;
```

displays the built-in array sentence. Like cin, cout does not care how large the built-in array of chars is. The characters are output until a *terminating null character* is encountered; the null character is *not* displayed. [*Note:* cin and cout assume that built-in arrays of chars should be processed as strings terminated by null characters; cin and cout do not provide similar input and output processing capabilities for other built-in array types.]

8.11 Note About Smart Pointers

Later in the book, we introduce dynamic memory management with pointers, which allows you at execution time to create and destroy objects as needed. Improperly managing this process is a source of subtle errors. We'll discuss "smart pointers," which help you avoid dynamic memory management errors by providing additional functionality beyond that of built-in pointers.

8.12 Wrap-Up

In this chapter we provided a detailed introduction to pointers—variables that contain memory addresses as their values. We began by demonstrating how to declare and initialize pointers. You saw how to use the address operator (&) to assign the address of a variable to a pointer and the indirection operator (*) to access the data stored in the variable indirectly referenced by a pointer. We discussed passing arguments by reference using pointer arguments.

We discussed how to declare and use built-in arrays, which C++ inherited from the C programming language. You learned how to use const with pointers to enforce the principle of least privilege. We demonstrated using nonconstant pointers to nonconstant data, nonconstant pointers to constant data, constant pointers to nonconstant data, and constant pointers to constant data. We discussed the compile-time sizeof operator, which can be used to determine the sizes of data types and variables in bytes at compile time.

We discussed how to use pointers in arithmetic and comparison expressions. You saw that pointer arithmetic can be used to move from one element of a built-in array to another. We briefly introduced pointer-based strings.

In the next chapter, we begin our deeper treatment of classes. You'll learn about the scope of a class's members and how to keep objects in a consistent state. You'll also learn about using special member functions called constructors and destructors, which execute when an object is created and destroyed, respectively. In addition, we'll demonstrate using default arguments with constructors and using default memberwise assignment to assign one object of a class to another object of the same class. We'll also discuss the danger of returning a reference to a private data member of a class.

Summary

Section 8.2 Pointer Variable Declarations and Initialization

- Pointers are variables that contain as their values memory addresses of other variables.
- The declaration

      int* ptr;

  declares ptr to be a pointer to a variable of type int and is read, "ptr is a pointer to int." The * as used here in a declaration indicates that the variable is a pointer.
- You can initialize a pointer with an address of an object of the same type or with **nullptr** (p. 342).
- The only integer that can be assigned to a pointer without casting is 0.

Section 8.3 Pointer Operators

- The **& (address) operator** (p. 342) obtains the memory address of its operand.
- The operand of the address operator must be a variable name (or another *lvalue*); the address operator cannot be applied to literals or to expressions that result in temporary values (like the results of calculations).
- The * **indirection** (or **dereferencing) operator** (p. 343) returns a synonym for the name of the object that its operand points to in memory. This is called **dereferencing the pointer** (p. 343).

Section 8.4 Pass-by-Reference with Pointers

- When calling a function with a variable that the caller wants the called function to modify, the address of the variable may be passed. The called function then uses the indirection operator (*) to dereference the pointer and modify the value of the variable in the calling function.
- A function receiving an address as an argument must have a pointer as its corresponding parameter.

Section 8.5 Built-In Arrays

- Built-in arrays—like array objects—are fixed-size data structures.
- To specify the type of the elements and the number of elements required by a built-in array, use a declaration of the form:

      type arrayName[arraySize];

  The compiler reserves the appropriate amount of memory. The *arraySize* must be an integer constant greater than zero.
- As with array objects, you use the subscript ([]) operator to access the individual elements of a built-in array.
- The subscript ([]) operator does not provide bounds checking for array objects or built-in arrays.
- You can initialize the elements of a built-in array using an initializer list. If you provide fewer initializers than the number of built-in array elements, the remaining elements are initialized to 0. If you provide too many initializers a compilation error occurs.
- If the built-in array's size is omitted from a declaration with an initializer list, the compiler sizes the built-in array to the number of elements in the initializer list.
- The value of a built-in array's name is implicitly convertible to the address in memory of the built-in array's first element.
- To pass a built-in array to a function simply pass the built-in array's name. The called function can modify all the elements of a built-in array in the caller—unless the function precedes the corresponding built-in array parameter with const to indicate that the built-in array's elements should not be modified.

- Built-in arrays don't know their own size, so a function that processes a built-in array should have parameters to receive both the built-in array and its size.

- The compiler does not differentiate between a function that receives a pointer and a function that receives a one-dimensional built-in array. A function must "know" when it's receiving a built-in array or simply a single variable that's being passed by reference.

- The compiler converts a function parameter for a one-dimensional built-in array like const int values[] to the pointer notation const int* values. These forms are interchangeable—for clarity you should use the [] when the function expects a built-in array argument.

- Function sort (and many other library functions) can also be applied to built-in arrays.

- C++11's begin and end functions (from header <iterator>) each receive a built-in array as an argument and return a pointer that can be used with C++ Standard Library functions like sort to represent the range of built-in array elements to process.

- Built-in arrays cannot be compared to one another using the relational and equality operators.

- Built-in arrays cannot be assigned to one another.

- Built-in arrays don't provide automatic bounds checking.

- In contemporary C++ code, you should use objects of the more robust array and vector class templates to represent lists and tables of values.

Section 8.6 Using *const* with Pointers
- The const qualifier enables you to inform the compiler that the value of a particular variable cannot be modified through the specified identifier.

- There are four ways to pass a pointer to a function—a **nonconstant pointer to nonconstant data** (p. 353), a **nonconstant pointer to constant data** (p. 353), a **constant pointer to nonconstant data** (p. 354), and a **constant pointer to constant data** (p. 355).

- To pass a single built-in array element by reference using pointers, pass the element's address.

Section 8.7 *sizeof* Operator
- sizeof (p. 356) determines the size in bytes of a type, variable or constant at compile time.

- When applied to a built-in array name, sizeof returns the total number of bytes in the built-in array. When applied to a built-in array parameter, sizeof returns the size of a pointer.

Section 8.8 Pointer Expressions and Pointer Arithmetic
- C++ enables pointer arithmetic (p. 358)—arithmetic operations that may be performed on pointers.

- Pointer arithmetic is appropriate only for pointers that point to built-in array elements.

- The arithmetic operations that may be performed on pointers are incrementing (++) a pointer, decrementing (--) a pointer, adding (+ or +=) an integer to a pointer, subtracting (- or -=) an integer from a pointer and subtracting one pointer from another—this particular operation is appropriate only for two pointers that point to elements of the same built-in array.

- When an integer is added or subtracted from a pointer, the pointer is incremented or decremented by that integer times the size of the object to which the pointer refers.

- Pointers of the same type can be assigned to one another. A void* pointer is a generic pointer type that can hold pointer values of any type.

- The only valid operations on a void* pointer are comparing void* pointers with other pointers, assigning addresses to void* pointers and casting void* pointers to valid pointer types.

- Pointers can be compared using the equality and relational operators. Comparisons using relational operators are meaningful only if the pointers point to members of the same array.

Section 8.9 Relationship Between Pointers and Built-In Arrays

- Pointers that point to built-in arrays can be subscripted exactly as built-in array names can.

- In **pointer/offset notation** (p. 362), if the pointer points to the first element of a built-in array, the offset is the same as an array subscript.

- All subscripted array expressions can be written with a pointer and an offset, using either the built-in array's name as a pointer or using a separate pointer that points to the built-in array.

Section 8.10 Pointer-Based Strings (Optional)

- A **character constant** (p. 364) is an integer value represented as a character in single quotes. The value of a character constant is the integer value of the character in the machine's character set.

- A string is a series of characters treated as a single unit. A string may include letters, digits and various special characters such as +, -, *, /and $.

- **String literals** or **string constants** (p. 365) are written in double quotation marks.

- A pointer-based string is a built-in array of chars ending with a **null character** (`'\0'`; p. 365), which marks where the string terminates in memory. A string is accessed via a pointer to its first character.

- The result of `sizeof` for a string literal is the length of the string including the terminating null character.

- A string literal may be used as an initializer for a built-in array of chars or a variable of type `const char*`.

- You should always declare a pointer to a string literal as `const char*`.

- When declaring a built-in array of chars to contain a C string, the built-in array must be large enough to store the C string and its terminating null character.

- If a string is longer than the built-in array of chars in which it's to be stored, characters beyond the end of the built-in array will overwrite data in memory following the built-in array, leading to logic errors.

- You can access individual characters in a string directly with array subscript notation.

- A string can be read into a built-in array of chars using stream extraction with `cin`. Characters are read until a whitespace character or end-of-file indicator is encountered. The `setw` stream manipulator should be used to ensure that the string read into a built-in array of chars does not exceed the size of the built-in array.

- The `cin` object provides the member function `getline` (p. 366) to input an entire line of text into a built-in array of chars. The function takes three arguments—a built-in array of chars in which the line of text will be stored, a length and a delimiter character. The third argument has `'\n'` as a default value.

- A built-in array of chars representing a null-terminated string can be output with `cout` and `<<`. The characters of the string are output until a terminating null character is encountered.

Self-Review Exercises

8.1 Answer each of the following:
   a) A pointer is a variable that contains as its value the _____ of another variable.
   b) A pointer should be initialized to _____ or _____.
   c) The only integer that can be assigned directly to a pointer is _____.

8.2 State whether each of the following is *true* or *false*. If the answer is *false*, explain why.
   a) The address operator & can be applied only to constants and to expressions.

b) A pointer that is declared to be of type void* can be dereferenced.

c) A pointer of one type can't be assigned to one of another type without a cast operation.

8.3   For each of the following, write C++ statements that perform the specified task. Assume that double-precision, floating-point numbers are stored in eight bytes and that the starting address of the built-in array is at location 1002500 in memory. Each part of the exercise should use the results of previous parts where appropriate.

a) Declare a built-in array of type double called numbers with 10 elements, and initialize the elements to the values 0.0, 1.1, 2.2, ..., 9.9. Assume that the constant size has been defined as 10.

b) Declare a pointer nPtr that points to a variable of type double.

c) Use a for statement to display the elements of built-in array numbers using array subscript notation. Display each number with one digit to the right of the decimal point.

d) Write two separate statements that each assign the starting address of built-in array numbers to the pointer variable nPtr.

e) Use a for statement to display the elements of built-in array numbers using pointer/offset notation with pointer nPtr.

f) Use a for statement to display the elements of built-in array numbers using pointer/offset notation with the built-in array's name as the pointer.

g) Use a for statement to display the elements of built-in array numbers using pointer/subscript notation with pointer nPtr.

h) Refer to the fourth element of built-in array numbers using array subscript notation, pointer/offset notation with the built-in array's name as the pointer, pointer subscript notation with nPtr and pointer/offset notation with nPtr.

i) Assuming that nPtr points to the beginning of built-in array numbers, what address is referenced by nPtr + 8? What value is stored at that location?

j) Assuming that nPtr points to numbers[5], what address is referenced by nPtr after nPtr -= 4 is executed? What's the value stored at that location?

8.4   For each of the following, write a statement that performs the specified task. Assume that double variables number1 and number2 have been declared and that number1 has been initialized to 7.3.

a) Declare the variable doublePtr to be a pointer to an object of type double and initialize the pointer to nullptr.

b) Assign the address of variable number1 to pointer variable doublePtr.

c) Display the value of the object pointed to by doublePtr.

d) Assign the value of the object pointed to by doublePtr to variable number2.

e) Display the value of number2.

f) Display the address of number1.

g) Display the address stored in doublePtr. Is the address the same as that of number1?

8.5   Perform the task specified by each of the following statements:

a) Write the function header for a function called exchange that takes two pointers to double-precision, floating-point numbers x and y as parameters and does not return a value.

b) Write the function prototype without parameter names for the function in part (a).

c) Write two statements that each initialize the built-in array of chars named vowel with the string of vowels, "AEIOU".

8.6   Find the error in each of the following program segments. Assume the following declarations and statements:

```
int* zPtr; // zPtr will reference built-in array z
int number;
int z[5]{1, 2, 3, 4, 5};
```

a) ++zPtr;

b) `// use pointer to get first value of a built-in array`
   `number = zPtr;`
c) `// assign built-in array element 2 (the value 3) to number`
   `number = *zPtr[2];`
d) `// display entire built-in array z`
   ```
   for (size_t i{0}; i <= 5; ++i) {
       cout << zPtr[i] << endl;
   }
   ```
e) `++z;`

Answers to Self-Review Exercises

8.1 a) address. b) `nullptr`, an address. c) 0.

8.2 a) False. The operand of the address operator must be an *lvalue*; the address operator cannot be applied to literals or to expressions that result in temporary values.
   b) False. A pointer to void cannot be dereferenced. Such a pointer does not have a type that enables the compiler to determine the type of the data and the number of bytes of memory to which the pointer points.
   c) False. Pointers of any type can be assigned to void pointers. Pointers of type void can be assigned to pointers of other types only with an explicit type cast.

8.3 a) `double numbers[size]{0.0, 1.1, 2.2, 3.3, 4.4, 5.5, 6.6, 7.7, 8.8, 9.9};`
   b) `double* nPtr;`
   c) ```
      cout << fixed << showpoint << setprecision(1);
      for (size_t i{0}; i < size; ++i) {
          cout << numbers[i] << ' ';
      }
      ```
   d) `nPtr = numbers;`
      `nPtr = &numbers[0];`
   e) ```
      cout << fixed << showpoint << setprecision(1);
      for (size_t j{0}; j < size; ++j) {
          cout << *(nPtr + j) << ' ';
      }
      ```
   f) ```
      cout << fixed << showpoint << setprecision(1);
      for (size_t k{0}; k < size; ++k) {
          cout << *(numbers + k) << ' ';
      }
      ```
   g) ```
      cout << fixed << showpoint << setprecision(1);
      for (size_t m{0}; m < size; ++m) {
          cout << nPtr[m] << ' ';
      }
      ```
   h) `numbers[3]`
      `*(numbers + 3)`
      `nPtr[3]`
      `*(nPtr + 3)`
   i) The address is 1002500 + 8 * 8 = 1002564. The value is 8.8.
   j) The address of `numbers[5]` is 1002500 + 5 * 8 = 1002540.
      The address of `nPtr -= 4` is 1002540 - 4 * 8 = 1002508.
      The value at that location is 1.1.

8.4 a) `double* doublePtr{nullptr};`
   b) `doublePtr = &number1;`

c) `cout <<` "The value of *fPtr is " `<< *doublePtr << endl;`

d) `number2 = *doublePtr;`

e) `cout <<` "The value of number2 is " `<< number2 << endl;`

f) `cout <<` "The address of number1 is " `<< &number1 << endl;`

g) `cout <<` "The address stored in fPtr is " `<< doublePtr << endl;`
   Yes, the value is the same.

8.5   a) `void` `exchange(double* x, double* y)`

b) `void` `exchange(double*, double*);`

c) `char vowel[]{`"AEIOU"`};`
   `char vowel[]{`'A', 'E', 'I', 'O', 'U', '\0'`};`

8.6   a) *Error:* zPtr has not been initialized.
   Correction: Initialize zPtr with zPtr = z; (Parts *b–e* depend on this correction.)

b) *Error:* The pointer is not dereferenced.
   Correction: Change the statement to number = *zPtr;

c) *Error:* zPtr[2] is not a pointer and should not be dereferenced.
   Correction: Change *zPtr[2] to zPtr[2].

d) *Error:* Referring to an out-of-bounds built-in array element with pointer subscripting.
   Correction: To prevent this, change the relational operator in the for statement to < or change the 5 to a 4.

e) *Error:* Trying to modify a built-in array's name with pointer arithmetic.
   Correction: Use a pointer variable instead of the built-in array's name to accomplish pointer arithmetic, or subscript the built-in array's name to refer to a specific element.

Exercises

8.7   *(True or False)* State whether the following are *true* or *false*. If *false*, explain why.

a) Two pointers that point to different built-in arrays cannot be compared meaningfully.

b) Because the name of a built-in array is implicitly convertible to a pointer to the first element of the built-in array, built-in array names can be manipulated in the same manner as pointers.

8.8   *(Write C++ Statements)* For each of the following, write C++ statements that perform the specified task. Assume that unsigned integers are stored in four bytes and that the starting address of the built-in array is at location 1002500 in memory.

a) Declare an unsigned int built-in array values with five elements initialized to the even integers from 2 to 10. Assume that the constant size has been defined as 5.

b) Declare a pointer vPtr that points to an object of type unsigned int.

c) Use a for statement to display the elements of built-in array values using array subscript notation.

d) Write two separate statements that assign the starting address of built-in array values to pointer variable vPtr.

e) Use a for statement to display the elements of built-in array values using pointer/offset notation.

f) Use a for statement to display the elements of built-in array values using pointer/offset notation with the built-in array's name as the pointer.

g) Use a for statement to display the elements of built-in array values by subscripting the pointer to the built-in array.

h) Refer to the fifth element of values using array subscript notation, pointer/offset notation with the built-in array name's as the pointer, pointer subscript notation and pointer/offset notation.

i) What address is referenced by vPtr + 3? What value is stored at that location?

j) Assuming that vPtr points to values[4], what address is referenced by vPtr -= 4? What value is stored at that location?

8.9 *(Write C++ Statements)* For each of the following, write a single statement that performs the specified task. Assume that long variables value1 and value2 have been declared and value1 has been initialized to 200000.

a) Declare the variable longPtr to be a pointer to an object of type long.
b) Assign the address of variable value1 to pointer variable longPtr.
c) Display the value of the object pointed to by longPtr.
d) Assign the value of the object pointed to by longPtr to variable value2.
e) Display the value of value2.
f) Display the address of value1.
g) Display the address stored in longPtr. Is the address displayed the same as value1's?

8.10 *(Function Headers and Prototypes)* Perform the task in each of the following:

a) Write the function header for function zero that takes a long integer built-in array parameter bigIntegers and a second parameter representing the array's size and does not return a value.
b) Write the function prototype for the function in part (a).
c) Write the function header for function add1AndSum that takes an integer built-in array parameter oneTooSmall and a second parameter representing the array's size and returns an integer.
d) Write the function prototype for the function described in part (c).

8.11 *(Find the Code Errors)* Find the error in each of the following segments. If the error can be corrected, explain how.

a) ```
   int* number;
   cout << number << endl;
   ```
b) ```
   double* realPtr;
   long* integerPtr;
   integerPtr = realPtr;
   ```
c) ```
   int* x, y;
   x = y;
   ```
d) ```
   char s[]{"this is a character array"};
   for (; *s != '\0'; ++s) {
      cout << *s << ' ';
   }
   ```
e) ```
   short* numPtr, result;
   void* genericPtr{numPtr};
   result = *genericPtr + 7;
   ```
f) ```
   double x = 19.34;
   double xPtr{&x};
   cout << xPtr << endl;
   ```

8.12 *(Simulation: The Tortoise and the Hare)* In this exercise, you'll re-create the classic race of the tortoise and the hare. You'll use random number generation to develop a simulation of this memorable event.

Our contenders begin the race at "square 1" of 70 squares. Each square represents a possible position along the race course. The finish line is at square 70. The first contender to reach or pass square 70 is rewarded with a pail of fresh carrots and lettuce. The course weaves its way up the side of a slippery mountain, so occasionally the contenders lose ground.

There is a clock that ticks once per second. With each tick of the clock, your program should use function moveTortoise and moveHare to adjust the position of the animals according to the rules in Fig. 8.18. These functions should use pointer-based pass-by-reference to modify the position of the tortoise and the hare.

Animal	Move type	Percentage of the time	Actual move
Tortoise	Fast plod	50%	3 squares to the right
	Slip	20%	6 squares to the left
	Slow plod	30%	1 square to the right
Hare	Sleep	20%	No move at all
	Big hop	20%	9 squares to the right
	Big slip	10%	12 squares to the left
	Small hop	30%	1 square to the right
	Small slip	20%	2 squares to the left

Fig. 8.18 | Rules for moving the tortoise and the hare.

Use variables to keep track of the positions of the animals (i.e., position numbers are 1–70). Start each animal at position 1 (i.e., the "starting gate"). If an animal slips left before square 1, move the animal back to square 1.

Generate the percentages in Fig. 8.18 by producing a random integer i in the range $1 \le i \le 10$. For the tortoise, perform a "fast plod" when $1 \le i \le 5$, a "slip" when $6 \le i \le 7$ or a "slow plod" when $8 \le i \le 10$. Use a similar technique to move the hare.

Begin the race by displaying

```
BANG !!!!!
AND THEY'RE OFF !!!!!
```

For each tick of the clock (i.e., each iteration of a loop), display a 70-position line showing the letter T in the tortoise's position and the letter H in the hare's position. Occasionally, the contenders land on the same square. In this case, the tortoise bites the hare and your program should display OUCH!!! beginning at that position. All positions other than the T, the H or the OUCH!!! (in case of a tie) should be blank.

After displaying each line, test whether either animal has reached or passed square 70. If so, display the winner and terminate the simulation. If the tortoise wins, display TORTOISE WINS!!! YAY!!! If the hare wins, display Hare wins. Yuch. If both animals win on the same clock tick, you may want to favor the tortoise (the "underdog"), or you may want to display It's a tie. If neither animal wins, perform the loop again to simulate the next tick of the clock.

8.13 *(What Does This Code Do?)* What does this program do?

```cpp
1   // Ex. 8.13: ex08_13.cpp
2   // What does this program do?
3   #include <iostream>
4   using namespace std;
5
6   void mystery1(char*, const char*); // prototype
7
```

Fig. 8.19 | What does this program do? (Part 1 of 2.)

```
 8    int main() {
 9       char string1[80];
10       char string2[80];
11
12       cout << "Enter two strings: ";
13       cin >> string1 >> string2;
14       mystery1(string1, string2);
15       cout << string1 << endl;
16    }
17
18    // What does this function do?
19    void mystery1(char* s1, const char* s2) {
20       while (*s1 != '\0') {
21          ++s1;
22       }
23
24       for (; (*s1 = *s2); ++s1, ++s2) {
25          ; // empty statement
26       }
27    }
```

Fig. 8.19 | What does this program do? (Part 2 of 2.)

8.14 *(What Does This Code Do?)* What does this program do?

```
 1    // Ex. 8.14: ex08_14.cpp
 2    // What does this program do?
 3    #include <iostream>
 4    using namespace std;
 5
 6    int mystery2(const char*); // prototype
 7
 8    int main() {
 9       char string1[80];
10
11       cout << "Enter a string: ";
12       cin >> string1;
13       cout << mystery2(string1) << endl;
14    }
15
16    // What does this function do?
17    int mystery2(const char* s) {
18       unsigned int x;
19
20       for (x = 0; *s != '\0'; ++s) {
21          ++x;
22       }
23
24       return x;
25    }
```

Fig. 8.20 | What does this program do?

Special Section: Building Your Own Computer

In the next several problems, we take a temporary diversion away from the world of high-level-language programming. We "peel open" a simply hypothetical computer and look at its internal structure. We introduce machine-language programming and write several machine-language programs. To make this an especially valuable experience, we then build a computer (using software-based *simulation*) on which you can execute your machine-language programs![2]

8.15   (*Machine-Language Programming*) Let's create a computer we'll call the Simpletron. As its name implies, it's a simple machine, but, as we'll soon see, it's a powerful one as well. The Simpletron runs programs written in the only language it directly understands, that is, Simpletron Machine Language, or SML for short.

The Simpletron contains an *accumulator*—a "special register" in which information is put before the Simpletron uses that information in calculations or examines it in various ways. All information in the Simpletron is handled in terms of *words*. A word is a signed four-digit decimal number, such as +3364, -1293, +0007, -0001, etc. The Simpletron is equipped with a 100-word memory, and these words are referenced by their location numbers 00, 01, …, 99.

Before running an SML program, we must *load,* or place, the program into memory. The first instruction (or statement) of every SML program is always placed in location 00. The simulator will start executing at this location.

Each instruction written in SML occupies one word of the Simpletron's memory; thus, instructions are signed four-digit decimal numbers. Assume that the sign of an SML instruction is always plus, but the sign of a data word may be either plus or minus. Each location in the Simpletron's memory may contain an instruction, a data value used by a program or an unused (and hence undefined) area of memory. The first two digits of each SML instruction are the *operation code* that specifies the operation to be performed. SML operation codes are shown in Fig. 8.21.

Operation code	Meaning
Input/output operations	
`const int read{10};`	Read a word from the keyboard into a specific location in memory.
`const int write{11};`	Write a word from a specific location in memory to the screen.
Load and store operations	
`const int load{20};`	Load a word from a specific location in memory into the accumulator.
`const int store{21};`	Store a word from the accumulator into a specific location in memory.
Arithmetic operations	
`const int add{30};`	Add a word from a specific location in memory to the word in the accumulator (leave result in accumulator).
`const int subtract{31};`	Subtract a word from a specific location in memory from the word in the accumulator (leave result in accumulator).

Fig. 8.21 | Simpletron Machine Language (SML) operation codes. (Part 1 of 2.)

---

2.   In Exercises 19.30–19.34, we'll "peel open" a simple hypothetical compiler that will translate statements in a simple high-level language to the machine language you use here. You'll write programs in that high-level language, compile them into machine language and run that machine language on your computer simulator.

Operation code	Meaning
const int divide{32};	Divide a word from a specific location in memory into the word in the accumulator (leave result in accumulator).
const int multiply{33};	Multiply a word from a specific location in memory by the word in the accumulator (leave result in accumulator).
Transfer-of-control operations	
const int branch{40};	Branch to a specific location in memory.
const int branchneg{41};	Branch to a specific location in memory if the accumulator is negative.
const int branchzero{42};	Branch to a specific location in memory if the accumulator is zero.
const int halt{43};	Halt—the program has completed its task.

Fig. 8.21 | Simpletron Machine Language (SML) operation codes. (Part 2 of 2.)

The last two digits of an SML instruction are the *operand*—the address of the memory location containing the word to which the operation applies.

Now let's consider two simple SML programs. The first (Fig. 8.22) reads two numbers from the keyboard and computes and displays their sum. The instruction +1007 reads the first number from the keyboard and places it into location 07 (which has been initialized to zero). Instruction +1008 reads the next number into location 08. The *load* instruction, +2007, places (copies) the first number into the accumulator, and the *add* instruction, +3008, adds the second number to the number in the accumulator. *All SML arithmetic instructions leave their results in the accumulator.* The *store* instruction, +2109, places (copies) the result back into memory location 09. Then the *write* instruction, +1109, takes the number and displays it (as a signed four-digit decimal number). The *halt* instruction, +4300, terminates execution.

Location	Number	Instruction
00	+1007	(Read A)
01	+1008	(Read B)
02	+2007	(Load A)
03	+3008	(Add B)
04	+2109	(Store C)
05	+1109	(Write C)
06	+4300	(Halt)
07	+0000	(Variable A)
08	+0000	(Variable B)
09	+0000	(Result C)

Fig. 8.22 | SML Example 1.

The SML program in Fig. 8.23 reads two numbers from the keyboard, then determines and displays the larger value. Note the use of the instruction +4107 as a conditional transfer of control, much the same as C++'s if statement.

Location	Number	Instruction
00	+1009	(Read A)
01	+1010	(Read B)
02	+2009	(Load A)
03	+3110	(Subtract B)
04	+4107	(Branch negative to 07)
05	+1109	(Write A)
06	+4300	(Halt)
07	+1110	(Write B)
08	+4300	(Halt)
09	+0000	(Variable A)
10	+0000	(Variable B)

Fig. 8.23 | SML Example 2.

Now write SML programs to accomplish each of the following tasks:

a) Use a sentinel-controlled loop to read positive numbers and compute and display their sum. Terminate input when a negative number is entered.

b) Use a counter-controlled loop to read seven numbers, some positive and some negative, and compute and display their average.

c) Read a series of numbers, and determine and display the largest number. The first number read indicates how many numbers should be processed.

8.16 (*Computer Simulator*) It may at first seem outrageous, but in this problem you are going to build your own computer. No, you won't be soldering components together. Rather, you'll use the powerful technique of *software-based simulation* to create a *software model* of the Simpletron. Your Simpletron simulator will turn the computer you are using into a Simpletron, and you actually will be able to run, test and debug the SML programs you wrote in Exercise 8.15.

When you run your Simpletron simulator, it should begin by displaying

```
*** Welcome to Simpletron! ***

*** Please enter your program one instruction ***
*** (or data word) at a time. I will type the ***
*** location number and a question mark (?).  ***
*** You then type the word for that location.  ***
*** Type the sentinel -99999 to stop entering ***
*** your program. ***
```

Your program should simulate the Simpletron's memory with a single-subscripted, 100-element built-in array memory. Now assume that the simulator is running, and let's examine the dialog as we enter the program of the second example of Exercise 8.15:

```
00 ? +1009
01 ? +1010
02 ? +2009
03 ? +3110
```

```
04 ?  +4107
05 ?  +1109
06 ?  +4300
07 ?  +1110
08 ?  +4300
09 ?  +0000
10 ?  +0000
11 ?  -99999

*** Program loading completed ***
*** Program execution begins  ***
```

The numbers to the right of each ? in the preceding dialog represent the SML program instructions input by the user.

The SML program has now been placed (or loaded) into built-in array memory. Now the Simpletron executes your SML program. Execution begins with the instruction in location 00 and, like C++, continues sequentially, unless directed to another part of the program by a transfer of control.

Use variable accumulator to represent the accumulator register. Use variable instruction-Counter to keep track of the location in memory that contains the instruction being performed. Use variable operationCode to indicate the operation currently being performed (i.e., the left two digits of the instruction word). Use variable operand to indicate the memory location on which the current instruction operates. Thus, operand is the rightmost two digits of the instruction currently being performed. Do not execute instructions directly from memory. Rather, transfer the next instruction to be performed from memory to a variable called instructionRegister. Then "pick off" the left two digits and place them in operationCode, and "pick off" the right two digits and place them in operand. When Simpletron begins execution, the special registers are all initialized to zero.

Now let's "walk through" the execution of the first SML instruction, +1009 in memory location 00. This is called an *instruction execution cycle.*

The instructionCounter tells us the location of the next instruction to be performed. We *fetch* the contents of that location from memory by using the C++ statement

```
instructionRegister = memory[instructionCounter];
```

The operation code and operand are extracted from the instruction register by the statements

```
operationCode = instructionRegister / 100;
operand = instructionRegister % 100;
```

Now, the Simpletron must determine that the operation code is actually a *read* (versus a *write*, a *load*, etc.). A switch differentiates among the 12 operations of SML. In the switch statement, the behavior of various SML instructions is simulated as shown in Fig. 8.24 (we leave the others to you).

SML instruction	Behavior
read	`cin >> memory[operand];`
load	`accumulator = memory[operand];`
add	`accumulator += memory[operand];`
branch	We'll discuss the branch instructions shortly.
halt	This instruction displays the message `*** Simpletron execution terminated ***`

Fig. 8.24 | Behavior of SML instructions.

The *halt* instruction also causes the Simpletron to display the name and contents of each register, as well as the complete contents of memory. Such a printout is often called a *register and memory dump*. To help you program your dump function, a sample dump format is shown in Fig. 8.25. Note that a dump after executing a Simpletron program would show the actual values of instructions and data values at the moment execution terminated. To format numbers with their sign as shown in the dump, use stream manipulator showpos. To disable the display of the sign, use stream manipulator noshowpos. For numbers that have fewer than four digits, you can format numbers with leading zeros between the sign and the value by using the following statement before outputting the value:

```
cout << setfill('0') << internal;
```

```
REGISTERS:
accumulator           +0000
instructionCounter       00
instructionRegister   +0000
operationCode            00
operand                  00

MEMORY:
        0     1     2     3     4     5     6     7     8     9
 0  +0000 +0000 +0000 +0000 +0000 +0000 +0000 +0000 +0000 +0000
10  +0000 +0000 +0000 +0000 +0000 +0000 +0000 +0000 +0000 +0000
20  +0000 +0000 +0000 +0000 +0000 +0000 +0000 +0000 +0000 +0000
30  +0000 +0000 +0000 +0000 +0000 +0000 +0000 +0000 +0000 +0000
40  +0000 +0000 +0000 +0000 +0000 +0000 +0000 +0000 +0000 +0000
50  +0000 +0000 +0000 +0000 +0000 +0000 +0000 +0000 +0000 +0000
60  +0000 +0000 +0000 +0000 +0000 +0000 +0000 +0000 +0000 +0000
70  +0000 +0000 +0000 +0000 +0000 +0000 +0000 +0000 +0000 +0000
80  +0000 +0000 +0000 +0000 +0000 +0000 +0000 +0000 +0000 +0000
90  +0000 +0000 +0000 +0000 +0000 +0000 +0000 +0000 +0000 +0000
```

Fig. 8.25 | A sample register and memory dump.

Parameterized stream manipulator setfill (from header <iomanip>) specifies the fill character that will appear between the sign and the value when a number is displayed with a field width of five characters but does not have four digits. (One position in the field width is reserved for the sign.) Stream manipulator internal indicates that the fill characters should appear between the sign and the numeric value .

Let's proceed with the execution of our program's first instruction—+1009 in location 00. As we've indicated, the switch statement simulates this by performing the C++ statement

```
cin >> memory[operand];
```

A question mark (?) should be displayed on the screen before the cin statement executes to prompt the user for input. The Simpletron waits for the user to type a value and press the *Enter* key. The value is then read into location 09.

At this point, simulation of the first instruction is complete. All that remains is to prepare the Simpletron to execute the next instruction. The instruction just performed was not a transfer of control, so we need merely increment the instruction counter register as follows:

```
++instructionCounter;
```

This completes the simulated execution of the first instruction. The entire process (i.e., the instruction execution cycle) begins anew with the fetch of the next instruction to execute.

Now let's consider how to simulate the branching instructions (i.e., the transfers of control). All we need to do is adjust the value in the instructionCounter appropriately. Therefore, the unconditional branch instruction (40) is simulated in the switch as

```
instructionCounter = operand;
```

The conditional "branch if accumulator is zero" instruction is simulated as

```
if (0 == accumulator) {
    instructionCounter = operand;
}
```

At this point, you should implement your Simpletron simulator and run each of the SML programs you wrote in Exercise 8.15. The variables that represent the Simpletron simulator's memory and registers should be defined in main and passed to other functions by value or by reference as appropriate.

Your simulator should check for various types of errors. During the program loading phase, for example, each number the user types into the Simpletron's memory must be in the range -9999 to +9999. Your simulator should use a while loop to test that each number entered is in this range and, if not, keep prompting the user to reenter the number until the user enters a correct number.

During the execution phase, your simulator should check for various serious errors, such as attempts to divide by zero, attempts to execute invalid operation codes, accumulator overflows (i.e., arithmetic operations resulting in values larger than +9999 or smaller than -9999) and the like. Such serious errors are called fatal errors. When a fatal error is detected, your simulator should display an error message such as

```
*** Attempt to divide by zero ***
*** Simpletron execution abnormally terminated ***
```

and should display a full register and memory dump in the format we've discussed previously. This will help the user locate the error in the program.

8.17 (*Project: Modifications to the Simpletron Simulator*) In Exercise 8.16, you wrote a software simulation of a computer that executes programs written in Simpletron Machine Language (SML). In this exercise, we propose several modifications and enhancements to the Simpletron Simulator. In Exercises 19.30–19.34, we propose building a compiler that converts programs written in a high-level programming language (a variation of BASIC) to SML. Some of the following modifications and enhancements may be required to execute the programs produced by the compiler. [*Note:* Some modifications may conflict with others and therefore must be done separately.]

a) Extend the Simpletron Simulator's memory to contain 1000 memory locations to enable the Simpletron to handle larger programs.

b) Allow the simulator to perform remainder calculations. This requires an additional Simpletron Machine Language instruction.

c) Allow the simulator to perform exponentiation calculations. This requires an additional Simpletron Machine Language instruction.

d) Modify the simulator to use hexadecimal values (see Appendix D, Number Systems) rather than integer values to represent Simpletron Machine Language instructions.

e) Modify the simulator to allow output of a newline. This requires an additional Simpletron Machine Language instruction.

f) Modify the simulator to process floating-point values in addition to integer values.

g) Modify the simulator to handle string input. [*Hint:* Each Simpletron word can be divided into two groups, each holding a two-digit integer. Each two-digit integer represents the ASCII decimal equivalent of a character. Add a machine-language instruction that inputs a string and store the string beginning at a specific Simpletron memory location. The first half of the word at that location will be a count of the number of characters in the string (i.e., the length of the string). Each succeeding half-word contains one ASCII character expressed as two decimal digits. The machine-language instruction converts each character into its ASCII equivalent and assigns it to a half-word.]

h) Modify the simulator to handle output of strings stored in the format of part (g). [*Hint:* Add a machine-language instruction that will display a string beginning at a certain Simpletron memory location. The first half of the word at that location is a count of the number of characters in the string (i.e., the length of the string). Each succeeding half-word contains one ASCII character expressed as two decimal digits. The machine-language instruction checks the length and displays the string by translating each two-digit number into its equivalent character.]

i) Modify the simulator to include instruction SML_DEBUG that displays a memory dump after each instruction executes. Give SML_DEBUG an operation code of 44. The word +4401 turns on debug mode, and +4400 turns off debug mode.

Classes: A Deeper Look

9

9.1 Introduction

This chapter takes a deeper look at classes. We use Time, Date and Employee class case studies, and other examples, to demonstrate several class construction capabilities. We begin with a Time class engineered to separate its *interface* from its *implementation* for reuse. The example also demonstrates using an *include guard* in a header to prevent header code from being included in the same source code file more than once, which typically results in compilation errors. In addition, class Time uses an ostringstream to create string representations of the time in standard and universal time formats. We also explain the compilation and linking process from the standpoint of the class-implementation programmer, the client-code programmer and the application user.

We demonstrate how client code can access a class's `public` members via

- the name of an object and the dot operator (`.`)
- a reference to an object and the dot operator (`.`)
- a pointer to an object and the arrow operator (`->`)

We discuss access functions that can read or write an object's data members. A common use of access functions is to test the truth or falsity of conditions—such functions are known as *predicate functions*. We also demonstrate the notion of a *utility function* (also called a *helper function*)—a `private` member function that supports the operation of the class's `public` member functions, but is *not* intended for use by clients of the class.

We show how default arguments can be used in constructors to enable client code to initialize objects using a variety of arguments. Next, we discuss a special member function called a destructor that's part of every class and is used to perform "termination housekeeping" on an object before it's destroyed. We demonstrate the order in which constructors and destructors are called.

We show that returning a reference or pointer to `private` data breaks the encapsulation of a class, allowing client code to directly access an object's data. We use default memberwise assignment to assign an object of a class to another object of the same class.

We use `const` objects and `const` member functions to prevent modifications of objects and enforce the principle of least privilege. We discuss *composition*—a form of reuse in which a class can have objects of other classes as members. Next, we use *friendship* to specify that a nonmember function can also access a class's non-`public` members—a technique that's often used in operator overloading (Chapter 10) for performance and structural reasons. We discuss the `this` pointer, which is an implicit argument in all calls to a class's non-`static` member functions, allowing them to access the correct object's data members and non-`static` member functions. We motivate the need for `static` class members and show how to use them in your own classes.

9.2 Time Class Case Study: Separating Interface from Implementation

Each of our prior class-definition examples placed a class in a header for *reuse*, then included the header into a source-code file containing `main`, so we could create and manipulate objects of the class. Unfortunately, placing a complete class definition in a header *reveals the entire implementation of the class to the class's clients*—a header is simply a text file that anyone can open and read.

Conventional software engineering wisdom says that to use an object of a class, the client code (e.g., `main`) needs to know *only*

- what member functions to call
- what arguments to provide to each member function, and
- what return type to expect from each member function.

The client code does not need to know how those functions are implemented.

If client code *does* know how a class is implemented, the programmer might write client code based on the class's implementation details. Ideally, if that implementation changes, the class's clients should not have to change. *Hiding the class's implementation details makes it easier to change the class's implementation while minimizing, and hopefully eliminating, changes to client code.*

Our first example in this chapter creates and manipulates an object of class Time. We demonstrate two important C++ software engineering concepts:

- Separating interface from implementation.

- Using an *include guard* in a header to prevent the header code from being included into the same source code file more than once. Since a class can be defined only once, using such preprocessing directives prevents multiple-definition errors.

9.2.1 Interface of a Class

Interfaces define and standardize the ways in which things such as people and systems interact with one another. For example, a radio's controls serve as an interface between the radio's users and its internal components. The controls allow users to perform a limited set of operations (such as changing the station, adjusting the volume, and choosing between AM and FM stations). Various radios may implement these operations differently—some provide push buttons, some provide dials and some support voice commands. The interface specifies *what* operations a radio permits users to perform but does not specify *how* the operations are implemented inside the radio.

Similarly, the interface of a class describes *what* services a class's clients can use and how to *request* those services, but not *how* the class carries out the services. A class's public interface consists of the class's public member functions (also known as the class's public services). As you'll soon see, you can specify a class's interface by writing a class definition that lists *only* the class's member-function prototypes and the class's data members.

9.2.2 Separating the Interface from the Implementation

To separate the class's interface from its implementation, we break up class Time into two files—the header Time.h (Fig. 9.1) in which class Time is defined, and the source-code file Time.cpp (Fig. 9.2) in which Time's member functions are defined—so that

1. the class is *reusable*,

2. the clients of the class know what member functions the class provides, how to call them and what return types to expect, and

3. the clients do *not* know how the class's member functions are implemented.

By convention, member-function definitions are placed in a source-code file of the same base name (e.g., Time) as the class's header but with a .cpp filename extension (some compilers support other filename extensions as well). The source-code file in Fig. 9.3 defines function main (the client code). Section 9.3 shows a diagram and explains how this three-file program is compiled from the perspectives of the Time class programmer and the client-code programmer—and what the Time application user sees.

9.2.3 Time Class Definition

The header Time.h (Fig. 9.1) contains Time's class definition (lines 11–20). Instead of function definitions, the class contains function prototypes (lines 13–15) that *describe the class's public interface without revealing the member-function implementations.* The function prototype in line 13 indicates that setTime requires three int parameters and returns void. The prototypes for member functions toUniversalString and toStandardString (lines 14–15) each specify that the function takes no arguments and returns a string. This particular class does not define a constructor, but classes with constructors would also declare those constructors in the header (as we will do in subsequent examples).

```cpp
1    // Fig. 9.1: Time.h
2    // Time class definition.
3    // Member functions are defined in Time.cpp
4    #include <string>
5
6    // prevent multiple inclusions of header
7    #ifndef TIME_H
8    #define TIME_H
9
10   // Time class definition
11   class Time {
12   public:
13      void setTime(int, int, int); // set hour, minute and second
14      std::string toUniversalString() const; // 24-hour time format string
15      std::string toStandardString() const; // 12-hour time format string
16   private:
17      unsigned int hour{0}; // 0 - 23 (24-hour clock format)
18      unsigned int minute{0}; // 0 - 59
19      unsigned int second{0}; // 0 - 59
20   };
21
22   #endif
```

Fig. 9.1 | Time class definition.

The header still specifies the class's private data members (lines 17–19) as well—in this case, each uses a C++11 in-class list initializer to set the data member to 0. Again, the compiler *must* know the data members of the class to determine how much memory to reserve for each object of the class. Including the header Time.h in the client code (line 6 of Fig. 9.3) provides the compiler with the information it needs to ensure that the client code calls the member functions of class Time correctly.

11

Include Guard[1]
In Fig. 9.1, the class definition is enclosed in the following include guard (lines 7, 8 and 22):

```cpp
#ifndef TIME_H
#define TIME_H
   ...
#endif
```

When we build larger programs, other definitions and declarations will also be placed in headers. The preceding include guard prevents the code between #ifndef (which means "if not defined") and #endif from being #included if the name TIME_H has been *defined*.

---

1. The nonstandard—but widely supported—preprocessor directive #pragma once can be used with many C++ compilers as an alternate way to implement an include guard.

When Time.h is #included the first time, the identifier TIME_H is not yet defined. In this case, the #define directive defines TIME_H and the preprocessor includes the Time.h header's contents in the .cpp file. If the header is #included again, TIME_H *is defined* already and the code between #ifndef and #endif is ignored by the preprocessor. Attempts to include a header multiple times (inadvertently) typically occur in large programs with many headers that may themselves include other headers.

Error-Prevention Tip 9.1

Use #ifndef, #define and #endif preprocessing directives to form an include guard that prevents headers from being included more than once in a source-code file.

Good Programming Practice 9.1

By convention, use the name of the header in uppercase with the period replaced by an underscore in the #ifndef and #define preprocessing directives of a header.

9.2.4 Time Class Member Functions

The source-code file Time.cpp (Fig. 9.2) *defines* class Time's member functions, which were *declared* in lines 13–15 of Fig. 9.1. Note that for the const member functions toUniversalString and toStandardString, the const keyword *must* appear in *both* the function prototypes (Fig. 9.1, lines 14–15) and the function definitions (Fig. 9.2, lines 26 and 34).

```
 1   // Fig. 9.2: Time.cpp
 2   // Time class member-function definitions.
 3   #include <iomanip> // for setw and setfill stream manipulators
 4   #include <stdexcept> // for invalid_argument exception class
 5   #include <sstream> // for ostringstream class
 6   #include <string>
 7   #include "Time.h" // include definition of class Time from Time.h
 8
 9   using namespace std;
10
11   // set new Time value using universal time
12   void Time::setTime(int h, int m, int s) {
13      // validate hour, minute and second
14      if ((h >= 0 && h < 24) && (m >= 0 && m < 60) && (s >= 0 && s < 60)) {
15         hour = h;
16         minute = m;
17         second = s;
18      }
19      else {
20         throw invalid_argument(
21            "hour, minute and/or second was out of range");
22      }
23   }
24
25   // return Time as a string in universal-time format (HH:MM:SS)
26   string Time::toUniversalString() const {
27      ostringstream output;
```

Fig. 9.2 | Time class member-function definitions. (Part 1 of 2.)

```
28        output << setfill('0') << setw(2) << hour << ":"
29           << setw(2) << minute << ":" << setw(2) << second;
30        return output.str(); // returns the formatted string
31     }
32
33     // return Time as string in standard-time format (HH:MM:SS AM or PM)
34     string Time::toStandardString() const {
35        ostringstream output;
36        output << ((hour == 0 || hour == 12) ? 12 : hour % 12) << ":"
37           << setfill('0') << setw(2) << minute << ":" << setw(2)
38           << second << (hour < 12 ? " AM" : " PM");
39        return output.str(); // returns the formatted string
40     }
```

Fig. 9.2 | Time class member-function definitions. (Part 2 of 2.)

9.2.5 Scope Resolution Operator (: :)

Each member function's name (lines 12, 26 and 34) is preceded by the class name and the scope resolution operator (::). This "ties" them to the (now separate) Time class definition (Fig. 9.1), which declares the class's members. The Time:: tells the compiler that each member function is within that class's scope and its name is known to other class members.

Without "Time::" preceding each function name, these functions would *not* be recognized by the compiler as Time member functions. Instead, the compiler would consider them "free" or "loose" functions, like main—these are also called *global functions*. Such functions cannot access Time's private data or call the class's member functions, without specifying an object. So, the compiler would *not* be able to compile these functions. For example, lines 28–29 and 36–38 in Fig. 9.2 that access data members hour, minute and second would cause compilation errors because these variables are not declared as local variables in each function—the compiler would not know that hour, minute and second are already declared in class Time.

 Common Programming Error 9.1
When defining a class's member functions outside that class, omitting the class name and scope resolution operator (::) that should precede the function names causes compilation errors.

9.2.6 Including the Class Header in the Source-Code File

To indicate that the member functions in Time.cpp are part of class Time, we must first include the Time.h header (Fig. 9.2, line 7). This allows us to use the class name Time in the Time.cpp file (lines 12, 26 and 34). When compiling Time.cpp, the compiler uses the information in Time.h to ensure that

- the first line of each member function (lines 12, 26 and 34) matches its prototype in the Time.h file—for example, the compiler ensures that setTime accepts three int parameters and returns nothing, and

- each member function knows about the class's data members and other member functions—e.g., lines 28–29 and 36–38 can access data members hour, minute and second because they're declared in Time.h as data members of class Time.

9.2.7 Time Class Member Function setTime and Throwing Exceptions

Function setTime (lines 12–23) is a public function that declares three int parameters and uses them to set the time. Line 14 tests each argument to determine whether the value is in range, and, if so, lines 15–17 assign the values to the hour, minute and second data members, respectively. The hour value must be greater than or equal to 0 and less than 24, because universal-time format represents hours as integers from 0 to 23 (e.g., 11 AM is hour 11, 1 PM is hour 13 and 11 PM is hour 23; midnight is hour 0 and noon is hour 12). Similarly, both minute and second must be greater than or equal to 0 and less than 60.

If any of the values is outside its range, setTime throws an exception (lines 20–21) of type invalid_argument (from header <stdexcept>), which notifies the client code that an invalid argument was received. As you saw in Section 7.10, you can use try...catch to catch exceptions and attempt to recover from them, which we'll do in Fig. 9.3. The throw statement creates a new object of type invalid_argument. The parentheses following the class name indicate a call to the invalid_argument constructor that allows us to specify a custom error-message string. After the exception object is created, the throw statement immediately terminates function setTime and the exception is returned to the code that attempted to set the time.

Invalid values cannot be stored in the data members of a Time object, because

- when a Time object is created, its default constructor is called and each data member is initialized to 0, as specified in lines 17–19 of Fig. 9.1—setting hour, minute and second to 0 is the universal-time equivalent of 12 AM (midnight)—and

- all subsequent attempts by a client to modify the data members are scrutinized by function setTime.

9.2.8 Time Class Member Function toUniversalString and String Stream Processing

Member function toUniversalString (lines 26–31 of Fig. 9.2) takes no arguments and returns a string containing the time formatted as universal time with three colon-separated pairs of digits. For example, if the time were 1:30:07 PM, toUniversalString would return 13:30:07.

As you know, cout is the standard output stream. Objects of class ostringstream (from the header <sstream>) provide the same functionality, but write their output to string objects in memory. You use class ostringstream's str member function to get the formatted string.

Member function toUniversalString creates an ostringstream object named output (line 27), then uses it like cout in lines 28–29 to create the formatted string. Line 28 uses parameterized stream manipulator setfill to specify the fill character that's displayed when an integer is output in a field *wider* than the number of digits in the value. The fill characters appear to the *left* of the digits in the number, because the number is *right aligned* by default—for *left-aligned* values (specified with the left stream manipulator) the fill characters would appear to the right. In this example, if the minute value is 2, it will be displayed as 02, because the fill character is set to zero ('0'). If the number being output fills the specified field, the fill character will not be displayed. Once the fill character is specified with setfill, it applies for *all* subsequent values that are displayed in fields wider than the value being displayed—setfill is a *sticky* setting. This is in contrast to setw, which applies *only* to the next value displayed—setw is a *nonsticky* setting. Line 30 calls ostringstream's str member function to get the formatted string, which is returned to the client.

Error-Prevention Tip 9.2

Each sticky setting (such as a fill character or precision) should be restored to its previous setting when it's no longer needed. Failure to do so may result in incorrectly formatted output later in a program. Section 13.7.8 discusses how to reset the formatting for an output stream.

9.2.9 Time Class Member Function toStandardString

Function toStandardString (lines 34–40) takes no arguments and returns a string containing the time formatted as standard time with the hour, minute and second values separated by colons and followed by an AM or PM indicator (e.g., 10:54:27 AM and 1:27:06 PM). Like function toUniversalString, function toStandardString uses setfill('0') to format the minute and second as two-digit values with leading zeros if necessary. Line 36 uses the conditional operator (?:) to determine the value of hour to be displayed—if the hour is 0 or 12 (AM or PM, respectively), it appears as 12; otherwise, we use the remainder operator (%) to have the hour appear as a value from 1 to 11. The conditional operator in line 38 determines whether AM or PM will be displayed. Line 39 calls ostringstream's str member function to return the formatted string.

9.2.10 Implicitly Inlining Member Functions

If a member function is defined in a class's body, the member function is implicitly declared *inline*. Remember that the compiler reserves the right not to inline any function.

Performance Tip 9.1

Defining a member function inside the class definition inlines the member function (if the compiler chooses to do so). This can improve performance.

Software Engineering Observation 9.1

Only the simplest and most stable member functions (i.e., whose implementations are unlikely to change) should be defined in the class header, because every change to the header requires you to recompile every source-code file that's dependent on that header (a time-consuming task in large systems).

9.2.11 Member Functions vs. Global Functions

The toUniversalString and toStandardString member functions take no arguments, because these member functions implicitly know that they're to create string representations of the data for the ***particular Time object on which they're invoked***. This can make member-function calls more concise than conventional function calls in procedural programming.

Software Engineering Observation 9.2

Using an object-oriented programming approach often requires fewer arguments when calling functions. This benefit derives from the fact that encapsulating data members and member functions within a class gives the member functions the right to access the data members.

Software Engineering Observation 9.3

Member functions are usually shorter than functions in non-object-oriented programs, because the data stored in data members have ideally been validated by a constructor or by member functions that store new data. Because the data is already in the object, the member-function calls often have no arguments or fewer arguments than function calls in non-object-oriented languages. Thus, the calls, the function definitions and the function prototypes are shorter. This improves many aspects of program development.

Error-Prevention Tip 9.3

The fact that member-function calls generally take either no arguments or fewer arguments than conventional function calls in non-object-oriented languages reduces the likelihood of passing the wrong arguments, the wrong types of arguments or the wrong number of arguments.

9.2.12 Using Class Time

As you know, once a class like Time is defined, it can be used as a type in declarations, such as:

```
Time sunset; // object of type Time
array<Time, 5> arrayOfTimes; // array of 5 Time objects
Time& dinnerTimeRef{sunset}; // reference to a Time object
Time* timePtr{&sunset}; // pointer to a Time object
```

Figure 9.3 creates and manipulates a Time object. Separating Time's interface from the implementation of its member functions does *not* affect the way that this client code uses the class. It affects only how the program is compiled and linked, which we discuss in Section 9.3. Line 6 of Fig. 9.3 includes the Time.h header so the compiler knows how much space to reserve for the Time object t (line 16) and can ensure that Time objects are created and manipulated correctly in the client code.

```
1   // Fig. 9.3: fig09_03.cpp
2   // Program to test class Time.
3   // NOTE: This file must be compiled with Time.cpp.
4   #include <iostream>
5   #include <stdexcept> // invalid_argument exception class
6   #include "Time.h" // definition of class Time from Time.h
7   using namespace std;
8
9   // displays a Time in 24-hour and 12-hour formats
10  void displayTime(const string& message, const Time& time) {
11     cout << message << "\nUniversal time: " << time.toUniversalString()
12        << "\nStandard time: " << time.toStandardString() << "\n\n";
13  }
14
15  int main() {
16     Time t; // instantiate object t of class Time
17
18     displayTime("Initial time:", t); // display t's initial value
```

Fig. 9.3 | Program to test class Time. (Part 1 of 2.)

```
19      t.setTime(13, 27, 6); // change time
20      displayTime("After setTime:", t); // display t's new value
21
22      // attempt to set the time with invalid values
23      try {
24         t.setTime(99, 99, 99); // all values out of range
25      }
26      catch (invalid_argument& e) {
27         cout << "Exception: " << e.what() << "\n\n";
28      }
29
30      // display t's value after attempting to set an invalid time
31      displayTime("After attempting to set an invalid time:", t);
32   }
```

```
Initial time:
Universal time: 00:00:00
Standard time: 12:00:00 AM

After setTime:
Universal time: 13:27:06
Standard time: 1:27:06 PM

Exception: hour, minute and/or second was out of range

After attempting to set an invalid time:
Universal time: 13:27:06
Standard time: 1:27:06 PM
```

Fig. 9.3 | Program to test class Time. (Part 2 of 2.)

Throughout the program, we display 24-hour and 12-hour string representations of a Time object using function displayTime (lines 10–13), which calls Time member functions toUniversalString and toStandardString. Line 16 creates the Time object t. Recall that class Time does not define a constructor, so line 16 invokes the compiler-generated default constructor, and t's hour, minute and second are set to 0 via their initializers in class Time's definition. Then, line 18 displays the time in universal and standard formats, respectively, to confirm that the members were initialized properly. Line 19 sets a new valid time by calling member function setTime, and line 20 again displays the time in both formats.

Calling *setTime* with Invalid Values

To illustrate that the setTime member function validates its arguments, line 24 calls set-Time with *invalid* arguments of 99 for the hour, minute and second. This statement is placed in a try block (lines 23–25) in case setTime throws an invalid_argument exception, which it will do. When this occurs, the exception is caught at lines 26–28, and line 27 displays the exception's error message by calling its what member function. Line 31 displays the time again to confirm that setTime did *not* change the time when invalid arguments were supplied.

9.2.13 Object Size

People new to object-oriented programming often suppose that objects must be quite large because they contain data members and member functions. *Logically*, this is true—you may think of objects as containing data and functions (and our discussion has certainly encouraged this view); *physically*, however, this is *not* the case.

Performance Tip 9.2

Objects contain only *data, so objects are much smaller than if they also contained member functions. The compiler creates one copy (only) of the member functions separate from all objects of the class. All objects of the class* share *this one copy. Each object, of course, needs its own copy of the class's data, because the data can vary among the objects. The function code is the same for all objects of the class and, hence, can be shared among them.*

9.3 Compilation and Linking Process

The diagram in Fig. 9.4 shows the compilation and linking process that results in an executable Time application that can be used by instructors. Often a class's interface and implementation will be created and compiled by one programmer and used by a separate programmer who implements the client code that uses the class. So, the diagram shows what's required by both the *class-implementation programmer* and the *client-code programmer*. The dashed lines in the diagram show the pieces required by the class-implementation programmer, the client-code programmer and the Time *application user*, respectively. [*Note:* Figure 9.4 is *not* a UML diagram.]

A *class-implementation programmer* responsible for creating a reusable Time class creates the header Time.h and the source-code file Time.cpp that #includes the header, then compiles the source-code file to create Time's object code. To hide the class's member-function implementation details, the *class-implementation programmer* would provide the *client-code programmer* with the header Time.h (which specifies the class's interface and data members) and the Time object code (i.e., the machine-code instructions that represent Time's member functions). The *client-code programmer* is *not* given Time.cpp, so the client remains unaware of how Time's member functions are implemented.

The *client-code programmer* needs to know only Time's interface to use the class and must be able to link its object code. Since the interface of the class is part of the class definition in the Time.h header, the *client-code programmer* must have access to this file and must #include it in the client's source-code file. When the client code is compiled, the compiler uses the class definition in Time.h to ensure that the main function creates and manipulates objects of class Time correctly.

To create the executable Time application, the last step is to link

1. the object code for the main function (i.e., the client code),

2. the object code for class Time's member-function implementations, and

3. the C++ Standard Library object code for the C++ classes (e.g., string) used by the *class-implementation programmer* and the *client-code programmer*.

The linker's output is the *executable* Time application that users can execute to create and manipulate a Time object. Compilers and IDEs typically invoke the linker for you after compiling your code.

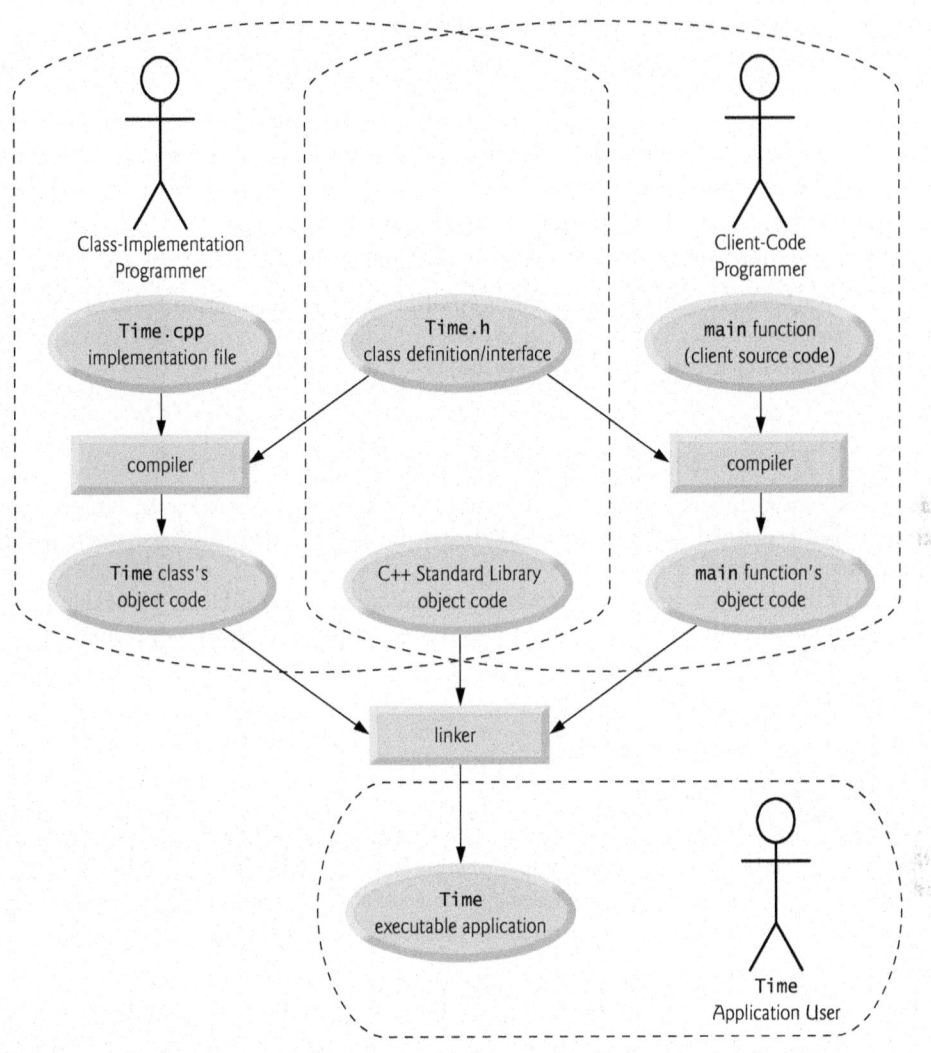

Fig. 9.4 | Compilation and linking process that produces an executable application.

Compiling Programs Containing Two or More Source-Code Files

In Section 1.10, we demonstrated how to compile and run C++ applications that contained one source-code (.cpp) file. To perform the compilation and linking processes for *multiple* source-code files:

- In Microsoft Visual Studio, add to your project (as shown in Section 1.10.1) all the headers and source-code files that make up a program, then build and run the project. You can place the headers in the project's **Header Files** folder and the source-code files in the project's **Source Files** folder, but these are mainly for organizing files in large projects. We tested the book's programs by placing all the files for each program in the project's **Source Files** folder.

- For GNU C++, open a shell and change to the directory containing all the files for a given program, then execute the following command:

```
g++ -std=c++14 *.cpp -o ExecutableName
```

The `*.cpp` specifies that you wish to compile and link *all* of the source-code files in the current directory—the preprocessor automatically locates the program-specific headers in that directory.

- For Apple Xcode, add to your project (as shown in Section 1.10.3) all the headers and source-code files that make up a program, then build and run the project.

For further information on compiling multiple-source-file programs with other compilers, see the compiler's documentation. We provide links to various C++ compilers in our C++ Resource Center at `http://www.deitel.com/cplusplus/`.

9.4 Class Scope and Accessing Class Members

A class's data members and member functions belong to that class's scope. Nonmember functions are defined at *global namespace scope*, by default. (We discuss namespaces in more detail in Section 23.4.)

Within a class's scope, class members are immediately accessible by all of that class's member functions and can be referenced by name. Outside a class's scope, `public` class members are referenced through

- an *object name*,
- a *reference* to an object, or
- a *pointer* to an object

We refer to these as handles on an object. The handle's type enables the compiler to determine the interface (e.g., the member functions) accessible to the client via that handle. [We'll see in Section 9.14 that an *implicit handle* (called the `this` pointer) is inserted by the compiler on every reference to a data member or member function from within an object.]

Dot (.) and Arrow (->) Member-Selection Operators

As you know, you can use an object's name—or a reference to an object—followed by the dot member-selection operator (`.`) to access an object's members. To reference an object's members via a pointer to an object, follow the pointer name by the arrow member-selection operator (`->`) and the member name, as in *pointerName->memberName*.

Accessing `public` Class Members Through Objects, References and Pointers

Consider an `Account` class that has a `public` `setBalance` member function. Given the following declarations:

```
Account account; // an Account object

// accountRef refers to an Account object
Account& accountRef{account};

// accountPtr points to an Account object
Account* accountPtr{&account};
```

You can invoke member function `setBalance` using the dot (.) and arrow (->) member selection operators as follows:

```
// call setBalance via the Account object
account.setBalance(123.45);

// call setBalance via a reference to the Account object
accountRef.setBalance(123.45);

// call setBalance via a pointer to the Account object
accountPtr->setBalance(123.45);
```

9.5 Access Functions and Utility Functions

Access Functions

Access functions can read or display data, not modify it. Another common use of access functions is to test the truth or falsity of conditions—such functions are often called predicate functions. An example would be an `empty` function for any container class—a class capable of holding many objects, such as an `array` or a `vector`. A program might test empty before attempting to read another item from the container object.[2]

Utility Functions

A utility function (also called a helper function) is a `private` member function that supports the operation of a class's other member functions. Utility functions are declared `private` because they're not intended for use by the class's clients. A popular use of a utility function would be to place in a function some common code that would otherwise be duplicated in several other member functions.

9.6 Time Class Case Study: Constructors with Default Arguments

The program of Figs. 9.5–9.7 enhances class `Time` to demonstrate how arguments can be passed to a constructor implicitly.

9.6.1 Constructors with Default Arguments

Like other functions, constructors can specify *default arguments*. Line 13 of Fig. 9.5 declares a `Time` constructor with default arguments, specifying a default value of zero for each argument passed to the constructor. The constructor is declared `explicit` because it can be called with one argument. We discuss `explicit` constructors in detail in Section 10.13.

```
1   // Fig. 9.5: Time.h
2   // Time class containing a constructor with default arguments.
3   // Member functions defined in Time.cpp.
4   #include <string>
5
```

Fig. 9.5 | Time class containing a constructor with default arguments. (Part 1 of 2.)

2. Many programmers prefer to begin the names of predicate functions with the word "is." For example, useful predicate functions for our `Time` class might be `isAM` and `isPM`.

```
6    // prevent multiple inclusions of header
7    #ifndef TIME_H
8    #define TIME_H
9
10   // Time class definition
11   class Time {
12   public:
13      explicit Time(int = 0, int = 0, int = 0); // default constructor
14
15      // set functions
16      void setTime(int, int, int); // set hour, minute, second
17      void setHour(int); // set hour (after validation)
18      void setMinute(int); // set minute (after validation)
19      void setSecond(int); // set second (after validation)
20
21      // get functions
22      unsigned int getHour() const; // return hour
23      unsigned int getMinute() const; // return minute
24      unsigned int getSecond() const; // return second
25
26      std::string toUniversalString() const; // 24-hour time format string
27      std::string toStandardString() const; // 12-hour time format string
28   private:
29      unsigned int hour{0}; // 0 - 23 (24-hour clock format)
30      unsigned int minute{0}; // 0 - 59
31      unsigned int second{0}; // 0 - 59
32   };
33
34   #endif
```

Fig. 9.5 | Time class containing a constructor with default arguments. (Part 2 of 2.)

In Fig. 9.6, lines 11–13 define the Time constructor that receives values for parameters hour, minute and second that will be used to initialize private data members hour, minute and second, respectively. *A constructor that defaults all its arguments is also a default constructor—that is, a constructor that can be invoked with no arguments. There can be at most one default constructor per class.* The version of class Time in this example provides *set* and *get* functions for each data member. The Time constructor now calls setTime, which calls the set-Hour, setMinute and setSecond functions to validate and assign values to the data members.

Software Engineering Observation 9.4

Any change to the default argument values of a function requires the client code to be recompiled (to ensure that the program still functions correctly).

```
1    // Fig. 9.6: Time.cpp
2    // Member-function definitions for class Time.
3    #include <iomanip>
4    #include <stdexcept>
5    #include <sstream>
```

Fig. 9.6 | Member-function definitions for class Time. (Part 1 of 3.)

```cpp
 6   #include <string>
 7   #include "Time.h" // include definition of class Time from Time.h
 8   using namespace std;
 9
10   // Time constructor initializes each data member
11   Time::Time(int hour, int minute, int second) {
12      setTime(hour, minute, second); // validate and set time
13   }
14
15   // set new Time value using universal time
16   void Time::setTime(int h, int m, int s) {
17      setHour(h); // set private field hour
18      setMinute(m); // set private field minute
19      setSecond(s); // set private field second
20   }
21
22   // set hour value
23   void Time::setHour(int h) {
24      if (h >= 0 && h < 24) {
25         hour = h;
26      }
27      else {
28         throw invalid_argument("hour must be 0-23");
29      }
30   }
31
32   // set minute value
33   void Time::setMinute(int m) {
34      if (m >= 0 && m < 60) {
35         minute = m;
36      }
37      else {
38         throw invalid_argument("minute must be 0-59");
39      }
40   }
41
42   // set second value
43   void Time::setSecond(int s) {
44      if (s >= 0 && s < 60) {
45         second = s;
46      }
47      else {
48         throw invalid_argument("second must be 0-59");
49      }
50   }
51
52   // return hour value
53   unsigned int Time::getHour() const {return hour;}
54
55   // return minute value
56   unsigned Time::getMinute() const {return minute;}
57
```

Fig. 9.6 | Member-function definitions for class Time. (Part 2 of 3.)

```
58   // return second value
59   unsigned Time::getSecond() const {return second;}
60
61   // return Time as a string in universal-time format (HH:MM:SS)
62   string Time::toUniversalString() const {
63      ostringstream output;
64      output << setfill('0') << setw(2) << getHour() << ":"
65         << setw(2) << getMinute() << ":" << setw(2) << getSecond();
66      return output.str();
67   }
68
69   // return Time as string in standard-time format (HH:MM:SS AM or PM)
70   string Time::toStandardString() const {
71      ostringstream output;
72      output << ((getHour() == 0 || getHour() == 12) ? 12 : getHour() % 12)
73         << ":" << setfill('0') << setw(2) << getMinute() << ":" << setw(2)
74         << getSecond() << (hour < 12 ? " AM" : " PM");
75      return output.str();
76   }
```

Fig. 9.6 | Member-function definitions for class Time. (Part 3 of 3.)

In Fig. 9.6, line 12 of the constructor calls member function setTime with the values passed to the constructor (or the default values). Function setTime calls setHour to ensure that the value supplied for hour is in the range 0–23, then calls setMinute and setSecond to ensure that the values for minute and second are each in the range 0–59. Functions setHour (lines 23–30), setMinute (lines 33–40) and setSecond (lines 43–50) each throw an exception if an out-of-range argument is received.

Function main in Fig. 9.7 initializes five Time objects—one with all three arguments defaulted in the implicit constructor call (line 15), one with one argument specified (line 16), one with two arguments specified (line 17), one with three arguments specified (line 18) and one with three invalid arguments specified (line 28). Each explicit constructor call (lines 16–18 and 28) uses C++11 list-initializer syntax. The program displays each object in universal-time and standard-time formats. For Time object t5 (line 28), the program displays an error message because the constructor arguments are out of range.

```
1    // Fig. 9.7: fig09_07.cpp
2    // Constructor with default arguments.
3    #include <iostream>
4    #include <stdexcept>
5    #include "Time.h" // include definition of class Time from Time.h
6    using namespace std;
7
8    // displays a Time in 24-hour and 12-hour formats
9    void displayTime(const string& message, const Time& time) {
10      cout << message << "\nUniversal time: " << time.toUniversalString()
11         << "\nStandard time: " << time.toStandardString() << "\n\n";
12   }
13
```

Fig. 9.7 | Constructor with default arguments. (Part 1 of 2.)

```
14    int main() {
15        Time t1; // all arguments defaulted
16        Time t2{2}; // hour specified; minute and second defaulted
17        Time t3{21, 34}; // hour and minute specified; second defaulted
18        Time t4{12, 25, 42}; // hour, minute and second specified
19
20        cout << "Constructed with:\n\n";
21        displayTime("t1: all arguments defaulted", t1);
22        displayTime("t2: hour specified; minute and second defaulted", t2);
23        displayTime("t3: hour and minute specified; second defaulted", t3);
24        displayTime("t4: hour, minute and second specified", t4);
25
26        // attempt to initialize t5 with invalid values
27        try {
28            Time t5{27, 74, 99}; // all bad values specified
29        }
30        catch (invalid_argument& e) {
31            cerr << "Exception while initializing t5: " << e.what() << endl;
32        }
33    }
```

```
Constructed with:

t1: all arguments defaulted
Universal time: 00:00:00
Standard time: 12:00:00 AM

t2: hour specified; minute and second defaulted
Universal time: 02:00:00
Standard time: 2:00:00 AM

t3: hour and minute specified; second defaulted
Universal time: 21:34:00
Standard time: 9:34:00 PM

t4: hour, minute and second specified
Universal time: 12:25:42
Standard time: 12:25:42 PM

Exception while initializing t5: hour must be 0-23
```

Fig. 9.7 | Constructor with default arguments. (Part 2 of 2.)

Notes Regarding Class *Time's* Set *and* Get *Functions and Constructor*

Time's *set* and *get* functions are called throughout the class's body. In particular, function setTime (lines 16–20 of Fig. 9.6) calls functions setHour, setMinute and setSecond, and functions toUniversalString and toStandardString call functions getHour, getMinute and getSecond in lines 64–65 and lines 72–74.

In each case, these functions could have accessed the class's private data directly. However, consider changing the representation of the time from three int values (requiring 12 bytes of memory on systems with four-byte ints) to a single int value representing the total number of seconds that have elapsed since midnight (requiring only four bytes of memory). If we made such a change, only the bodies of the functions that access the private data directly would need to change—in particular, the individual *set* and *get* functions for the hour, minute and second. There would be no need to modify the bodies of functions setTime, toUniversalString or toStandardString, because they do *not* access the data directly.

Similarly, the Time constructor could be written to include a copy of the appropriate statements from function setTime. Doing so may be slightly more efficient, because the extra call to setTime is eliminated. However, duplicating statements in multiple functions or constructors makes changing the class's internal data representation more difficult. Having the Time constructor call setTime and having setTime call setHour, setMinute and setSecond enables us to limit the changes to code that validates the hour, minute or second to the corresponding *set* function. This reduces the likelihood of errors when altering the class's implementation.

Software Engineering Observation 9.5

If a member function of a class already provides all or part of the functionality required by a constructor or other member functions of the class, call that member function from the constructor or other member functions. This simplifies the maintenance of the code and reduces the likelihood of an error if the code implementation is modified. As a general rule: Avoid repeating code.

Common Programming Error 9.2

A constructor can call other member functions of the class, such as set or get functions, but because the constructor is initializing the object, the data members may not yet be initialized. Using data members before they have been properly initialized can cause logic errors.

Software Engineering Observation 9.6

Making data members private and controlling access, especially write access, to those data members through public member functions helps ensure data integrity.

Error-Prevention Tip 9.4

The benefits of data integrity are not automatic simply because data members are made private—you must provide appropriate validity checking.

9.6.2 Overloaded Constructors and C++11 Delegating Constructors

Section 6.16 showed how to overload functions. A class's constructors and member functions can also be overloaded. Overloaded constructors typically allow objects to be initialized with different types and/or numbers of arguments. To overload a constructor, provide in the class definition a prototype for each version of the constructor, and provide a separate constructor definition for each overloaded version. This also applies to the class's member functions.

In Figs. 9.5–9.7, the Time constructor with three parameters had a default argument for each parameter. We could have defined that constructor instead as four overloaded constructors with the following prototypes:

```
Time(); // default hour, minute and second to 0
explicit Time(int); // init hour; default minute and second to 0
Time(int, int); // initialize hour and minute; default second to 0
Time(int, int, int); // initialize hour, minute and second
```

Just as a constructor can call a class's other member functions to perform tasks, C++11 allows constructors to call other constructors in the same class. The calling constructor is known as a delegating constructor—it *delegates* its work to another constructor. This is useful when overloaded constructors have common code that previously would have been defined in a private utility function and called by all the constructors.

The first three of the four Time constructors declared above can delegate work to one with three int arguments, passing 0 as the default value for the extra parameters. To do so, you use a member initializer with the name of the class as follows:

```
Time::Time() : Time{0, 0, 0} {} // delegate to Time(int, int, int)

// delegate to Time(int, int, int)
Time::Time(int hour) : Time{hour, 0, 0} {}

// delegate to Time(int, int, int)
Time::Time(int hour, int minute) : Time{hour, minute, 0} {}
```

9.7 Destructors

A destructor is another type of special member function. The name of the destructor for a class is the tilde character (~) followed by the class name. This naming convention has intuitive appeal, because as we'll see in a later chapter, the tilde operator is the bitwise complement operator, and, in a sense, the destructor is the complement of the constructor. A destructor may not specify parameters or a return type.

A class's destructor is called *implicitly* when an object is destroyed. This occurs, for example, as an object is destroyed when program execution leaves the scope in which that object was instantiated. *The destructor itself does not actually release the object's memory*—it performs termination housekeeping[3] *before* the object's memory is reclaimed, so the memory may be reused to hold new objects.

Even though destructors have not been defined for the classes presented so far, *every class has exactly one destructor*. If you do not *explicitly* define a destructor, the compiler defines an "empty" destructor.[4] In Chapter 10, we'll build destructors appropriate for classes whose objects contain dynamically allocated memory (e.g., for arrays and strings) or use other system resources (e.g., files on disk, which we study in Chapter 14). We discuss how to dynamically allocate and deallocate memory in Chapter 10. In Chapter 17, we'll explain why exceptions should not be thrown from destructors.

9.8 When Constructors and Destructors Are Called

Constructors and destructors are called *implicitly* when object are created and when they're about to be removed from memory, respectively. The order in which these function calls occur depends on the order in which execution enters and leaves the scopes where the objects are instantiated. Generally, destructor calls are made in the *reverse order* of the corresponding constructor calls, but as we'll see in Figs. 9.8–9.10, the global and static objects can alter the order in which destructors are called.

---

3. For example, we'll show in Section 14.3.6 that a file stream object's destructor closes the file.
4. We'll see that such an *implicitly* created destructor does, in fact, perform important operations on class-type objects that are created through composition (Section 9.12) and inheritance (Chapter 11).

9.8.1 Constructors and Destructors for Objects in Global Scope

Constructors are called for objects defined in global scope (also called global namespace scope) *before* any other function (including `main`) in that program begins execution (although the order of execution of global object constructors between files is *not* guaranteed). The corresponding destructors are called when `main` terminates. Function `exit` forces a program to terminate immediately and does *not* execute the destructors of local objects. The `exit` function often is used to terminate a program when a fatal unrecoverable error occurs. Function `abort` performs similarly to function `exit` but forces the program to terminate *immediately*, without allowing programmer-defined cleanup code of any kind to be called. Function `abort` is usually used to indicate an *abnormal termination* of the program. (See Appendix F for more information on functions `exit` and `abort`.)

9.8.2 Constructors and Destructors for Non-static Local Objects

The constructor for a non-`static` local object is called when execution reaches the point where that object is defined—the corresponding destructor is called when execution leaves the object's scope (i.e., the block in which that object is defined has finished executing). Constructors and destructors for non-`static` local objects are called each time execution enters and leaves the scope of the object. Destructors are not called for local objects if the program terminates with a call to function `exit` or function `abort`.

9.8.3 Constructors and Destructors for static Local Objects

The constructor for a `static` local object is called only *once*, when execution first reaches the point where the object is defined—the corresponding destructor is called when `main` terminates or the program calls function `exit`. Global and `static` objects are destroyed in the *reverse* order of their creation. Destructors are *not* called for `static` objects if the program terminates with a call to function `abort`.

9.8.4 Demonstrating When Constructors and Destructors Are Called

The program of Figs. 9.8–9.10 demonstrates the order in which constructors and destructors are called for global, local and local `static` objects of class `CreateAndDestroy` (Fig. 9.8 and Fig. 9.9). Each object of class `CreateAndDestroy` contains an integer (objectID) and a `string` (message) that are used in the program's output to identify the object (Fig. 9.8, lines 14–15). This mechanical example is purely for pedagogic purposes. For this reason, line 17 of the destructor in Fig. 9.9 determines whether the object being destroyed has an `objectID` value 1 or 6 and, if so, outputs a newline character. This line makes the program's output easier to follow.

```
1   // Fig. 9.8: CreateAndDestroy.h
2   // CreateAndDestroy class definition.
3   // Member functions defined in CreateAndDestroy.cpp.
4   #include <string>
5
6   #ifndef CREATE_H
7   #define CREATE_H
```

Fig. 9.8 | CreateAndDestroy class definition. (Part 1 of 2.)

```
8
9    class CreateAndDestroy {
10   public:
11      CreateAndDestroy(int, std::string); // constructor
12      ~CreateAndDestroy(); // destructor
13   private:
14      int objectID; // ID number for object
15      sdt::string message; // message describing object
16   };
17
18   #endif
```

Fig. 9.8 | CreateAndDestroy class definition. (Part 2 of 2.)

```
1    // Fig. 9.9: CreateAndDestroy.cpp
2    // CreateAndDestroy class member-function definitions.
3    #include <iostream>
4    #include "CreateAndDestroy.h"// include CreateAndDestroy class definition
5    using namespace std;
6
7    // constructor sets object's ID number and descriptive message
8    CreateAndDestroy::CreateAndDestroy(int ID, string messageString)
9       : objectID{ID}, message{messageString} {
10      cout << "Object " << objectID << "   constructor runs   "
11         << message << endl;
12   }
13
14   // destructor
15   CreateAndDestroy::~CreateAndDestroy() {
16      // output newline for certain objects; helps readability
17      cout << (objectID == 1 || objectID == 6 ? "\n" : "");
18
19      cout << "Object " << objectID << "   destructor runs   "
20         << message << endl;
21   }
```

Fig. 9.9 | CreateAndDestroy class member-function definitions.

Figure 9.10 defines object first (line 10) in global scope. Its constructor is actually called *before* any statements in main execute and its destructor is called at program termination *after* the destructors for all objects with automatic storage duration have run.

```
1    // Fig. 9.10: fig09_10.cpp
2    // Order in which constructors and
3    // destructors are called.
4    #include <iostream>
5    #include "CreateAndDestroy.h" // include CreateAndDestroy class definition
6    using namespace std;
7
8    void create(); // prototype
```

Fig. 9.10 | Order in which constructors and destructors are called. (Part 1 of 2.)

```
 9
10   CreateAndDestroy first{1, "(global before main)"}; // global object
11
12   int main() {
13      cout << "\nMAIN FUNCTION: EXECUTION BEGINS" << endl;
14      CreateAndDestroy second{2, "(local in main)"};
15      static CreateAndDestroy third{3, "(local static in main)"};
16
17      create(); // call function to create objects
18
19      cout << "\nMAIN FUNCTION: EXECUTION RESUMES" << endl;
20      CreateAndDestroy fourth{4, "(local in main)"};
21      cout << "\nMAIN FUNCTION: EXECUTION ENDS" << endl;
22   }
23
24   // function to create objects
25   void create() {
26      cout << "\nCREATE FUNCTION: EXECUTION BEGINS" << endl;
27      CreateAndDestroy fifth{5, "(local in create)"};
28      static CreateAndDestroy sixth{6, "(local static in create)"};
29      CreateAndDestroy seventh{7, "(local in create)"};
30      cout << "\nCREATE FUNCTION: EXECUTION ENDS" << endl;
31   }
```

```
Object 1   constructor runs   (global before main)

MAIN FUNCTION: EXECUTION BEGINS
Object 2   constructor runs   (local in main)
Object 3   constructor runs   (local static in main)

CREATE FUNCTION: EXECUTION BEGINS
Object 5   constructor runs   (local in create)
Object 6   constructor runs   (local static in create)
Object 7   constructor runs   (local in create)

CREATE FUNCTION: EXECUTION ENDS
Object 7   destructor runs    (local in create)
Object 5   destructor runs    (local in create)

MAIN FUNCTION: EXECUTION RESUMES
Object 4   constructor runs   (local in main)

MAIN FUNCTION: EXECUTION ENDS
Object 4   destructor runs    (local in main)
Object 2   destructor runs    (local in main)

Object 6   destructor runs    (local static in create)
Object 3   destructor runs    (local static in main)

Object 1   destructor runs    (global before main)
```

Fig. 9.10 | Order in which constructors and destructors are called. (Part 2 of 2.)

Function main (lines 12–22) declares three objects. Objects second (line 14) and fourth (line 20) are local objects, and object third (line 15) is a static local object. The constructor for each of these objects is called when execution reaches the point where that object is declared. The destructors for objects fourth then second are called—in the *reverse* of the order in which their constructors were called—when execution reaches the end of main. Because object third is static, it exists until program termination. The destructor for object third is called *before* the destructor for global object first, but *after* all other objects are destroyed.

Function create (lines 25–31) declares three objects—fifth (line 27) and seventh (line 29) as local automatic objects, and sixth (line 28) as a static local object. The destructors for objects seventh then fifth are called—the *reverse* of the order in which their constructors were called—when create terminates. Because sixth is static, it exists until program termination. The destructor for sixth is called *before* the destructors for third and first, but *after* all other objects are destroyed.

9.9 Time Class Case Study: A Subtle Trap — Returning a Reference or a Pointer to a private Data Member

A reference to an object is an alias for the name of the object and, hence, may be used on the left side of an assignment statement. In this context, the reference makes a perfectly acceptable *lvalue* that can receive a value.

A member function can return a reference to a private data member of that class. If the reference return type is declared const, the reference is a nonmodifiable *lvalue* and cannot be used to modify the data. However, if the reference return type is not declared const, subtle errors can occur.

The program of Figs. 9.11–9.13 uses a simplified Time class (Fig. 9.11 and Fig. 9.12) to demonstrate returning a reference to a private data member with member function badSetHour (declared in Fig. 9.11 in line 13 and defined in Fig. 9.12 in lines 25–34). Such a reference return actually makes a call to member function badSetHour an alias for private data member hour! The function call can be used in any way that the private data member can be used, including as an *lvalue* in an assignment statement, thus *enabling clients of the class to clobber the class's private data at will!* A similar problem would occur if a pointer to the private data were to be returned by the function.

```
 1   // Fig. 9.11: Time.h
 2   // Time class declaration.
 3   // Member functions defined in Time.cpp
 4
 5   // prevent multiple inclusions of header
 6   #ifndef TIME_H
 7   #define TIME_H
 8
 9   class Time {
10   public:
11      void setTime(int, int, int);
12      unsigned int getHour() const;
13      unsigned int& badSetHour(int); // dangerous reference return
14   private:
15      unsigned int hour{0};
```

Fig. 9.11 | Time class declaration. (Part 1 of 2.)

```
16        unsigned int minute{0};
17        unsigned int second{0};
18     };
19
20     #endif
```

Fig. 9.11 | Time class declaration. (Part 2 of 2.)

```
1     // Fig. 9.12: Time.cpp
2     // Time class member-function definitions.
3     #include <stdexcept>
4     #include "Time.h" // include definition of class Time
5     using namespace std;
6
7     // set values of hour, minute and second
8     void Time::setTime(int h, int m, int s) {
9        // validate hour, minute and second
10       if ((h >= 0 && h < 24) && (m >= 0 && m < 60) && (s >= 0 && s < 60)) {
11          hour = h;
12          minute = m;
13          second = s;
14       }
15       else {
16          throw invalid_argument(
17             "hour, minute and/or second was out of range");
18       }
19    }
20
21    // return hour value
22    unsigned int Time::getHour() const {return hour;}
23
24    // poor practice: returning a reference to a private data member.
25    unsigned int& Time::badSetHour(int hh) {
26       if (hh >= 0 && hh < 24) {
27          hour = hh;
28       }
29       else {
30          throw invalid_argument("hour must be 0-23");
31       }
32
33       return hour; // dangerous reference return
34    }
```

Fig. 9.12 | Time class member-function definitions.

Figure 9.13 declares Time object t (line 9) and reference hourRef (line 12), which is initialized with the reference returned by the call t.badSetHour(20). Line 14 displays the value of the alias hourRef. This shows how hourRef *breaks the encapsulation of the class*—statements in main should not have access to the private data in an object of the class. Next, line 15 uses the alias to set the value of hour to 30 (an invalid value) and line 16 displays the value returned by function getHour to show that assigning a value to hourRef actually modifies the private data in the Time object t. Finally, line 20 uses the badSetHour function call itself as an *lvalue* and assigns 74 (another invalid value) to the reference returned by the function. Line 25 again displays the value returned by function getHour to show that assigning a value to the result of the function call in line 20 modifies the private data in the Time object t.

> **Software Engineering Observation 9.7**
>
> *Returning a reference or a pointer to a private data member breaks the encapsulation of the class and makes the client code dependent on the representation of the class's data. There are cases where doing this is appropriate—we'll show an example of this when we build our custom Array class in Section 10.10.*

```cpp
1   // Fig. 9.13: fig09_13.cpp
2   // Demonstrating a public member function that
3   // returns a reference to a private data member.
4   #include <iostream>
5   #include "Time.h" // include definition of class Time
6   using namespace std;
7
8   int main() {
9      Time t; // create Time object
10
11     // initialize hourRef with the reference returned by badSetHour
12     unsigned int& hourRef{t.badSetHour(20)}; // 20 is a valid hour
13
14     cout << "Valid hour before modification: " << hourRef;
15     hourRef = 30; // use hourRef to set invalid value in Time object t
16     cout << "\nInvalid hour after modification: " << t.getHour();
17
18     // Dangerous: Function call that returns
19     // a reference can be used as an lvalue!
20     t.badSetHour(12) = 74; // assign another invalid value to hour
21
22     cout << "\n\n*******************************************************\n"
23        << "POOR PROGRAMMING PRACTICE!!!!!!!!\n"
24        << "t.badSetHour(12) as an lvalue, invalid hour: "
25        << t.getHour()
26        << "\n*******************************************************" << endl;
27  }
```

```
Valid hour before modification: 20
Invalid hour after modification: 30

*******************************************************
POOR PROGRAMMING PRACTICE!!!!!!!!
t.badSetHour(12) as an lvalue, invalid hour: 74
*******************************************************
```

Fig. 9.13 | public member function that returns a reference to a private data member.

9.10 Default Memberwise Assignment

The assignment operator (=) can be used to assign an object to another object of the same class. By default, such assignment is performed by memberwise assignment (also called copy assignment)—each data member of the object on the *right* of the assignment operator is assigned individually to the *same* data member in the object on the *left* of the assignment operator. Figures 9.14–9.15 define a Date class. Line 15 of Fig. 9.16 uses default memberwise assignment to assign the data members of Date object date1 to the corresponding data members of Date object date2. In this case, the month member of date1 is assigned to the month member of date2, the day member of date1 is assigned to the day member of date2 and the year member of date1 is assigned to the year member of date2. [*Caution:* Memberwise assignment can cause serious problems when used with a class whose data members contain pointers to dynamically allocated memory; we discuss these problems in Chapter 10 and show how to deal with them.]

```cpp
1   // Fig. 9.14: Date.h
2   // Date class declaration.  Member functions are defined in Date.cpp.
3   #include <string>
4
5   // prevent multiple inclusions of header
6   #ifndef DATE_H
7   #define DATE_H
8
9   // class Date definition
10  class Date {
11  public:
12     explicit Date(unsigned int = 1, unsigned int = 1, unsigned int = 2000);
13     std::string toString() const;
14  private:
15     unsigned int month;
16     unsigned int day;
17     unsigned int year;
18  };
19
20  #endif
```

Fig. 9.14 | Date class declaration.

```cpp
1   // Fig. 9.15: Date.cpp
2   // Date class member-function definitions.
3   #include <sstream>
4   #include <string>
5   #include "Date.h" // include definition of class Date from Date.h
6   using namespace std;
7
8   // Date constructor (should do range checking)
9   Date::Date(unsigned int m, unsigned int d, unsigned int y)
10     : month{m}, day{d}, year{y} {}
11
12  // print Date in the format mm/dd/yyyy
13  string Date::toString() const {
14     ostringstream output;
15     output << month << '/' << day << '/' << year;
16     return output.str();
17  }
```

Fig. 9.15 | Date class member-function definitions.

```
 1   // Fig. 9.16: fig09_16.cpp
 2   // Demonstrating that class objects can be assigned
 3   // to each other using default memberwise assignment.
 4   #include <iostream>
 5   #include "Date.h" // include definition of class Date from Date.h
 6   using namespace std;
 7
 8   int main() {
 9      Date date1{7, 4, 2004};
10      Date date2; // date2 defaults to 1/1/2000
11
12      cout << "date1 = " << date1.toString()
13         << "\ndate2 = " << date2.toString() << "\n\n";
14
15      date2 = date1; // default memberwise assignment
16
17      cout << "After default memberwise assignment, date2 = "
18         << date2.toString() << endl;
19   }
```

```
date1 = 7/4/2004
date2 = 1/1/2000

After default memberwise assignment, date2 = 7/4/2004
```

Fig. 9.16 | Class objects can be assigned to each other using default memberwise assignment.

Objects may be passed as function arguments and may be returned from functions. Such passing and returning is performed using pass-by-value by default—a *copy* of the object is passed or returned. In such cases, C++ creates a new object and uses a copy constructor to copy the original object's values into the new object. For each class, the compiler provides a default copy constructor that copies each member of the original object into the corresponding member of the new object. Like memberwise assignment, copy constructors can cause serious problems when used with a class whose data members contain pointers to dynamically allocated memory. Chapter 10 discusses how to define customized copy constructors that properly copy such objects.

9.11 const Objects and const Member Functions

Let's see how the principle of least privilege applies to objects. Some objects need to be modifiable and some do not. You may use const to specify that an object *is not* modifiable and that any attempt to modify the object should result in a compilation error. The statement

```
const Time noon{12, 0, 0};
```

declares a const object noon of class Time and initializes it to 12 noon. It's possible to instantiate const and non-const objects of the same class.

Error-Prevention Tip 9.5
Attempts to modify a const object are caught at compile time rather than causing execution-time errors.

Performance Tip 9.3

Declaring variables and objects const *when appropriate can improve performance—compilers can perform optimizations on constants that cannot be performed on non-const variables.*

C++ disallows member-function calls for const *objects unless the member functions themselves are also declared* const. This is true even for *get* member functions that do *not* modify the object. *This is also a key reason that we've declared as* const *all member functions that do not modify the objects on which they're called.*

Common Programming Error 9.3

Defining as const *a member function that calls a non-const member function of the class on the same object is a compilation error.*

Common Programming Error 9.4

Invoking a non-const member function on a const *object is a compilation error.*

An interesting problem arises for constructors and destructors, each of which typically modifies objects. A constructor *must* be allowed to modify an object so that the object can be initialized. A destructor must be able to perform its termination housekeeping before an object's memory is reclaimed by the system. Attempting to declare a constructor or destructor const is a compilation error. The "constness" of a const object is enforced from the time the constructor *completes* initialization of the object until that object's destructor is called.

Using const *and Non-*const *Member Functions*

The program of Fig. 9.17 uses class Time from Figs. 9.5–9.6, but removes const from function toStandardString's prototype and definition so that we can show a compilation error. We create two Time objects—non-const object wakeUp (line 6) and const object noon (line 7). The program attempts to invoke non-const member functions setHour (line 11) and toStandardString (line 15) on the const object noon. In each case, the compiler generates an error message. The program also illustrates the three other member-function-call combinations on objects—a non-const member function on a non-const object (line 10), a const member function on a non-const object (line 12) and a const member function on a const object (lines 13–14). The error messages generated for non-const member functions called on a const object are shown in the output window.

```
1   // Fig. 9.17: fig09_17.cpp
2   // const objects and const member functions.
3   #include "Time.h" // include Time class definition
4
5   int main() {
6      Time wakeUp{6, 45, 0}; // non-constant object
7      const Time noon{12, 0, 0}; // constant object
8
```

Fig. 9.17 | const objects and const member functions. (Part 1 of 2.)

```
 9                                    // OBJECT      MEMBER FUNCTION
10      wakeUp.setHour(18);           // non-const   non-const
11      noon.setHour(12);             // const       non-const
12      wakeUp.getHour();             // non-const   const
13      noon.getMinute();             // const       const
14      noon.toUniversalString();     // const       const
15      noon.toStandardString();      // const       non-const
16   }
```

Microsoft Visual C++ compiler error messages:

```
C:\examples\ch09\fig09_17\fig09_17.cpp(11): error C2662:
   'void Time::setHour(int)': cannot convert 'this' pointer from 'const Time'
   to 'Time &'
C:\examples\ch09\fig09_17\fig09_17.cpp(11): note: Conversion loses qualifiers
C:\examples\ch09\fig09_17\fig09_17.cpp(15): error C2662:
   'std::string Time::toStandardString(void)': cannot convert 'this' pointer
   from 'const Time' to 'Time &'
C:\examples\ch09\fig09_17\fig09_17.cpp(15): note: Conversion loses qualifiers
```

Fig. 9.17 | const objects and const member functions. (Part 2 of 2.)

A constructor must be a non-const member function, but it can still be used to initialize a const object (Fig. 9.17, line 7). Recall from Fig. 9.6 that the Time constructor's definition calls another non-const member function—setTime—to perform the initialization of a Time object. Invoking a non-const member function from the constructor call as part of the initialization of a const object is allowed.

Line 15 in Fig. 9.17 generates a compilation error even though member function toStandardString of class Time *does not* modify the object on which it's called. The fact that a member function does not modify an object is *not* sufficient—the function must *explicitly* be declared const.

9.12 Composition: Objects as Members of Classes

An AlarmClock object needs to know when it's supposed to sound its alarm, so why not include a Time object as a member of the AlarmClock class? Such a software-reuse capability is called composition (or aggregation) and is sometimes referred to as a *has-a* relationship—*a class can have objects of other classes as members.*[5]

You've actually been using composition since Chapter 3. In that chapter's examples, class Account contained a string object as a data member.

Previously, we saw how to pass arguments to the constructor of an object we created in main. Now we show how a class's constructor can pass arguments to member-object constructors via member initializer*s*.

---

5. As you'll see in Chapter 11, classes also may be derived from other classes that provide attributes and behaviors the new classes can use—this is called inheritance.

Software Engineering Observation 9.8

Data members are constructed in the order in which they're declared in the class definition (not in the order they're listed in the constructor's member-initializer list) and before their enclosing class objects are constructed.

The next program uses classes Date (Figs. 9.18–9.19) and Employee (Figs. 9.20–9.21) to demonstrate composition. Class Employee's definition (Fig. 9.20) contains private data members firstName, lastName, birthDate and hireDate. Members birthDate and hireDate are const objects of class Date, which contains private data members month, day and year. The Employee constructor's prototype (Fig. 9.20, lines 14–15) specifies that the constructor has four parameters (first, last, dateOfBirth and dateOfHire). The first two parameters are passed via member initializers to the string class constructor for the firstName and lastName data members. The last two are passed via member initializers to the Date class constructor for the birthDate and hireDate data members.

```
1    // Fig. 9.18: Date.h
2    // Date class definition; Member functions defined in Date.cpp
3    #include <string>
4
5    #ifndef DATE_H
6    #define DATE_H
7
8    class Date {
9    public:
10       static const unsigned int monthsPerYear{12}; // months in a year
11       explicit Date(unsigned int = 1, unsigned int = 1, unsigned int = 1900);
12       std::string toString() const; // date string in month/day/year format
13       ~Date(); // provided to confirm destruction order
14    private:
15       unsigned int month; // 1-12 (January-December)
16       unsigned int day; // 1-31 based on month
17       unsigned int year; // any year
18
19       // utility function to check if day is proper for month and year
20       unsigned int checkDay(int) const;
21    };
22
23    #endif
```

Fig. 9.18 | Date class definition.

```
1    // Fig. 9.19: Date.cpp
2    // Date class member-function definitions.
3    #include <array>
4    #include <iostream>
5    #include <sstream>
6    #include <stdexcept>
7    #include "Date.h" // include Date class definition
8    using namespace std;
```

Fig. 9.19 | Date class member-function definitions. (Part 1 of 2.)

```
9
10   // constructor confirms proper value for month; calls
11   // utility function checkDay to confirm proper value for day
12   Date::Date(unsigned int mn, unsigned int dy, unsigned int yr)
13      : month{mn}, day{checkDay(dy)}, year{yr} {
14      if (mn < 1 || mn > monthsPerYear) { // validate the month
15         throw invalid_argument("month must be 1-12");
16      }
17
18      // output Date object to show when its constructor is called
19      cout << "Date object constructor for date " << toString() << endl;
20   }
21
22   // print Date object in form month/day/year
23   string Date::toString() const {
24      ostringstream output;
25      output << month << '/' << day << '/' << year;
26      return output.str();
27   }
28
29   // output Date object to show when its destructor is called
30   Date::~Date() {
31      cout << "Date object destructor for date " << toString() << endl;
32   }
33
34   // utility function to confirm proper day value based on
35   // month and year; handles leap years, too
36   unsigned int Date::checkDay(int testDay) const {
37      static const array<int, monthsPerYear + 1> daysPerMonth{
38         0, 31, 28, 31, 30, 31, 30, 31, 31, 30, 31, 30, 31};
39
40      // determine whether testDay is valid for specified month
41      if (testDay > 0 && testDay <= daysPerMonth[month]) {
42         return testDay;
43      }
44
45      // February 29 check for leap year
46      if (month == 2 && testDay == 29 && (year % 400 == 0 ||
47         (year % 4 == 0 && year % 100 != 0))) {
48         return testDay;
49      }
50
51      throw invalid_argument("Invalid day for current month and year");
52   }
```

Fig. 9.19 | Date class member-function definitions. (Part 2 of 2.)

```
1   // Fig. 9.20: Employee.h
2   // Employee class definition showing composition.
3   // Member functions defined in Employee.cpp.
4   #include <string>
```

Fig. 9.20 | Employee class definition showing composition. (Part 1 of 2.)

```
5
6    #ifndef EMPLOYEE_H
7    #define EMPLOYEE_H
8
9    #include <string>
10   #include "Date.h" // include Date class definition
11
12   class Employee {
13   public:
14      Employee(const std::string&, const std::string&,
15         const Date&, const Date&);
16      std::string toString() const;
17      ~Employee(); // provided to confirm destruction order
18   private:
19      std::string firstName; // composition: member object
20      std::string lastName; // composition: member object
21      const Date birthDate; // composition: member object
22      const Date hireDate; // composition: member object
23   };
24
25   #endif
```

Fig. 9.20 | Employee class definition showing composition. (Part 2 of 2.)

```
1    // Fig. 9.21: Employee.cpp
2    // Employee class member-function definitions.
3    #include <iostream>
4    #include <sstream>
5    #include "Employee.h" // Employee class definition
6    #include "Date.h" // Date class definition
7    using namespace std;
8
9    // constructor uses member initializer list to pass initializer
10   // values to constructors of member objects
11   Employee::Employee(const string& first, const string& last,
12      const Date &dateOfBirth, const Date &dateOfHire)
13      : firstName{first}, // initialize firstName
14        lastName{last}, // initialize lastName
15        birthDate{dateOfBirth}, // initialize birthDate
16        hireDate{dateOfHire} { // initialize hireDate
17      // output Employee object to show when constructor is called
18      cout << "Employee object constructor: "
19         << firstName << ' ' << lastName << endl;
20   }
21
22   // print Employee object
23   string Employee::toString() const {
24      ostringstream output;
25      output << lastName << ", " << firstName << " Hired: "
26         << hireDate.toString() << " Birthday: " << birthDate.toString();
27      return output.str();
28   }
```

Fig. 9.21 | Employee class member-function definitions. (Part 1 of 2.)

```
29
30   // output Employee object to show when its destructor is called
31   Employee::~Employee() {
32      cout << "Employee object destructor: "
33         << lastName << ", " << firstName << endl;
34   }
```

Fig. 9.21 | Employee class member-function definitions. (Part 2 of 2.)

Employee *Constructor's Member-Initializer List*

The colon (:) following the constructor's header (Fig. 9.21, line 13) begins the member-initializer list. The member initializers specify the Employee constructor parameters being passed to the constructors of the string and Date data members. Parameters first, last, dateOfBirth and dateOfHire are passed to the constructors for objects firstName, last-Name, birthDate and hireDate, respectively. The order of the member initializers does not matter. They're executed in the order that the member objects are declared in class Employee.

> **Good Programming Practice 9.2**
>
> *For clarity, list the member initializers in the order that the class's data members are declared.*

Date *Class's Default Copy Constructor*

As you study class Date (Fig. 9.18), notice that the class does *not* provide a constructor that receives a parameter of type Date. So, why can the Employee constructor's member-initializer list initialize the birthDate and hireDate objects by passing Date objects to their Date constructors? As we mentioned in Section 9.10, the compiler provides each class with a *default copy constructor* that copies each data member of the constructor's argument object into the corresponding member of the object being initialized. Chapter 10 discusses how you can define *customized* copy constructors.

Testing Classes Date *and* Employee

Figure 9.22 creates two Date objects (lines 9–10) and passes them as arguments to the constructor of the Employee object created in line 11. There are actually *five* constructor calls when an Employee is constructed:

- two calls to the string class's constructor (lines 13–14 of Fig. 9.21),
- two calls to the Date class's default copy constructor (lines 15–16 of Fig. 9.21),
- and the call to the Employee class's constructor.

Line 13 outputs the Employee object's data. When each Date object is created in lines 9–10, the Date constructor defined in lines 12–20 of Fig. 9.19 displays a line of output to show that the constructor was called (see the first two lines of the sample output). Note that line 11 of Fig. 9.22 causes two Date constructor calls that do not appear in this program's output. When each of the Employee's Date member objects is initialized in the Employee constructor's member-initializer list (Fig. 9.21, lines 15–16), the default copy constructor for class Date is called. Since this constructor is defined implicitly by the compiler, it does not contain any output statements to demonstrate when it's called.] ⋅

```
1   // Fig. 9.22: fig09_22.cpp
2   // Demonstrating composition--an object with member objects.
3   #include <iostream>
4   #include "Date.h" // Date class definition
5   #include "Employee.h" // Employee class definition
6   using namespace std;
7
8   int main() {
9      Date birth{7, 24, 1949};
10     Date hire{3, 12, 1988};
11     Employee manager{"Bob", "Blue", birth, hire};
12
13     cout << "\n" << manager.toString() << endl;
14  }
```

```
Date object constructor for date 7/24/1949
Date object constructor for date 3/12/1988
Employee object constructor: Bob Blue

Blue, Bob  Hired: 3/12/1988  Birthday: 7/24/1949
Employee object destructor: Blue, Bob
Date object destructor for date 3/12/1988
Date object destructor for date 7/24/1949
Date object destructor for date 3/12/1988
Date object destructor for date 7/24/1949
```

Fig. 9.22 | Demonstrating composition—an object with member objects.

Class Date and class Employee each include a destructor (lines 30–32 of Fig. 9.19 and lines 31–34 of Fig. 9.21, respectively) that prints a message when an object of its class is destructed. This enables us to confirm in the program output that objects are constructed from the *inside out* and destructed in the *reverse* order, from the *outside in* (i.e., the Date *member* objects are destructed after the Employee object that *contains* them).

Notice the last four lines in the output of Fig. 9.22. The last two lines are the outputs of the Date destructor running on Date objects hire (Fig. 9.22, line 10) and birth (line 9), respectively. The outputs confirm that the three objects created in main are destructed in the *reverse* of the order in which they were constructed. The Employee destructor output is five lines from the bottom. The fourth and third lines from the bottom of the output window show the destructors running for the Employee's member objects hireDate (Fig. 9.20, line 22) and birthDate (line 21). The last two lines of the output correspond to the Date objects created in lines 10 and 9 of Fig. 9.22.

These outputs confirm that the Employee object is destructed from the *outside in*— i.e., the Employee destructor runs first (output shown five lines from the bottom of the output window), then the member objects are destructed in the *reverse order* from which they were constructed. Class string's destructor does not contain output statements, so we do *not* see the firstName and lastName objects being destructed. Again, Fig. 9.22's output did not show the constructors running for member objects birthDate and hireDate, because these objects were initialized with the *default* Date class copy constructors provided by the compiler.

What Happens When You Do Not Use the Member-Initializer List?

If a member object is *not* initialized through a member initializer, the member object's *default constructor* will be called *implicitly*. Values, if any, established by the default constructor can be overridden by *set* functions. However, for complex initialization, this approach may require significant additional work and time.

Performance Tip 9.4

Initialize member objects explicitly through member initializers. This eliminates the overhead of "doubly initializing" member objects—once when the member object's default constructor is called and again when set functions are called in the constructor body (or later) to initialize the member object.

Common Programming Error 9.5

A compilation error occurs if a member object is not initialized with a member initializer and the member object's class does not provide a default constructor (i.e., the member object's class defines one or more constructors, but none is a default constructor).

Software Engineering Observation 9.9

If a data member is an object of another class, making that member object public *does not violate the encapsulation and hiding of that member object's* private *members. But, it does violate the encapsulation and hiding of the enclosing class's implementation, so member objects of class types should still be* private.

9.13 friend Functions and friend Classes

A friend function of a class is a non-member function that has the right to access the public *and* non-public class members. Standalone functions, entire classes or member functions of other classes may be declared to be *friends* of another class.

This section presents a mechanical example of how a friend function works. In Chapter 10 we'll show friend functions that overload operators for use with class objects—as you'll see, sometimes a member function cannot be used for certain overloaded operators.

Declaring a friend

To declare a non-member function as a friend of a class, place the function prototype in the class definition and precede it with the keyword friend. To declare all member functions of class ClassTwo as friends of class ClassOne, place a declaration of the form

```
friend class ClassTwo;
```

in the definition of class ClassOne. The friend declaration(s) can appear *anywhere* in a class and are not affected by access specifiers public or private (or protected, which we discuss in Chapter 11).

Friendship is *granted, not taken*—for class B to be a friend of class A, class A must *explicitly* declare that class B is its friend. Friendship is not *symmetric*—if class A is a friend of class B, you cannot infer that class B is a friend of class A. Friendship is not *transitive*—if class A is a friend of class B and class B is a friend of class C, you cannot infer that class A is a friend of class C.

Modifying a Class's *private* Data with a *friend* Function

Figure 9.23 defines friend function setX to set the private data member x of class Count. As a convention, we place the friend declaration (line 8) *first* in the class definition, even before public member functions are declared—again, this friend declaration can appear *anywhere* in the class.

```cpp
 1   // Fig. 9.23: fig09_23.cpp
 2   // Friends can access private members of a class.
 3   #include <iostream>
 4   using namespace std;
 5
 6   // Count class definition
 7   class Count {
 8      friend void setX(Count&, int); // friend declaration
 9   public:
10      int getX() const {return x;}
11   private:
12      int x{0};
13   };
14
15   // function setX can modify private data of Count
16   // because setX is declared as a friend of Count (line 8)
17   void setX(Count& c, int val) {
18      c.x = val; // allowed because setX is a friend of Count
19   }
20
21   int main() {
22      Count counter; // create Count object
23
24      cout << "counter.x after instantiation: " << counter.getX() << endl;
25      setX(counter, 8); // set x using a friend function
26      cout << "counter.x after call to setX friend function: "
27         << counter.getX() << endl;
28   }
```

```
counter.x after instantiation: 0
counter.x after call to setX friend function: 8
```

Fig. 9.23 | Friends can access private members of a class.

Function setX (lines 17–19) is a standalone (global) function—it isn't a member function of class Count. For this reason, when setX is called for object counter, line 25 passes counter as an argument to setX rather than using a handle (such as the name of the object) to call the function, as in

```cpp
counter.setX(8); // error: setX not a member function
```

Function setX is allowed to access class Count's private data member x (line 18) only because setX was declared as a friend of the class (line 8). If you remove the friend declaration in line 8, you'll receive error messages indicating that function setX cannot modify class Count's private data member x.

Overloaded *friend* Functions

It's possible to specify overloaded functions as friends of a class. Each function intended to be a friend must be explicitly declared in the class definition as a friend of the class.

Software Engineering Observation 9.10

Even though the prototypes for friend functions appear in the class definition, friends are not member functions.

Software Engineering Observation 9.11

Member access notions of private, protected and public are not relevant to friend declarations, so friend declarations can be placed anywhere in a class definition.

Good Programming Practice 9.3

Place all friendship declarations first inside the class definition's body and do not precede them with any access specifier.

9.14 Using the this Pointer

There's only one copy of each class's functionality, but there can be *many* objects of a class, so how do member functions know *which* object's data members to manipulate? Every object has access to its own address through a pointer called this (a C++ keyword). The this pointer is *not* part of the object itself—i.e., the memory occupied by the this pointer is not reflected in the result of a sizeof operation on the object. Rather, the this pointer is passed (by the compiler) as an *implicit* argument to each of the object's non-static member functions. Section 9.15 introduces static class members and explains why the this pointer is *not* implicitly passed to static member functions.

Using the *this* Pointer to Avoid Naming Collisions

Member functions use the this pointer *implicitly* (as we've done so far) or *explicitly* to reference an object's data members and other member functions. A common *explicit* use of the this pointer is to avoid *naming conflicts* between a class's data members and member-function parameters (or other local variables). If a member function contains a local variable and data member with the *same* name, as in the following setHour function:

```
// set hour value
void Time::setHour(int hour) {
    if (hour >= 0 && hour < 24) {
        this->hour = hour; // use this-> to access data member
    }
    else {
        throw invalid_argument("hour must be 0-23");
    }
}
```

the local variable is said to *hide* or *shadow* the data member—using just the variable name in the member function's body refers to the *local variable* rather than the data member. However, you can access the data member hour by qualifying its name with this->. So the following statement assigns the hour *parameter's* value to the *data member* hour

```
this->hour = hour; // use this-> to access data member
```

Good Programming Practice 9.4
A widely accepted practice to minimize the proliferation of identifier names is to use the same name for a set function's parameter and the data member it sets, and to reference the data member in the set function's body via this->.

Type of the **this** *Pointer*

The type of the this pointer depends on the type of the object and whether the member function in which this is used is declared const:

- In a non-const member function of class Employee, the this pointer has the type Employee* const—a constant pointer to a *nonconstant* Employee.

- In a const member function, this has the type const Employee* const—a constant pointer to a *constant* Employee.

9.14.1 Implicitly and Explicitly Using the this Pointer to Access an Object's Data Members

Figure 9.24 demonstrates the implicit and explicit use of the this pointer to enable a member function of class Test to print the private data x of a Test object. In the next example and in Chapter 10, we show some substantial and subtle examples of using this.

```
 1   // Fig. 9.24: fig09_24.cpp
 2   // Using the this pointer to refer to object members.
 3   #include <iostream>
 4   using namespace std;
 5
 6   class Test {
 7   public:
 8      explicit Test(int);
 9      void print() const;
10   private:
11      int x{0};
12   };
13
14   // constructor
15   Test::Test(int value) : x{value} {} // initialize x to value
16
17   // print x using implicit then explicit this pointers;
18   // the parentheses around *this are required
19   void Test::print() const {
20      // implicitly use the this pointer to access the member x
21      cout << "        x = " << x;
22
23      // explicitly use the this pointer and the arrow operator
24      // to access the member x
25      cout << "\n  this->x = " << this->x;
26
```

Fig. 9.24 | Using the this pointer to refer to object members. (Part 1 of 2.)

```
27        // explicitly use the dereferenced this pointer and
28        // the dot operator to access the member x
29        cout << "\n(*this).x = " << (*this).x << endl;
30   }
31
32   int main() {
33        Test testObject{12}; // instantiate and initialize testObject
34        testObject.print();
35   }
```

```
        x = 12
   this->x = 12
(*this).x = 12
```

Fig. 9.24 | Using the this pointer to refer to object members. (Part 2 of 2.)

For illustration purposes, member function print (lines 19–30) first prints x by using the this pointer *implicitly* (line 21)—only the name of the data member is specified. Then print uses two different notations to access x through the this pointer—the arrow operator (->) off the this pointer (line 25) and the dot operator (.) off the *dereferenced* this pointer (line 29). Note the parentheses around *this (line 29) when used with the dot member-selection operator (.). The parentheses are required because the dot operator has higher precedence than the * operator. Without the parentheses, the expression *this.x would be evaluated as if it were parenthesized as *(this.x), which is a *compilation error*, because the dot operator cannot be used with a pointer.

One interesting use of the this pointer is to prevent an object from being assigned to itself. As we'll see in Chapter 10, *self-assignment* can cause serious errors when the object contains pointers to dynamically allocated storage.

9.14.2 Using the this Pointer to Enable Cascaded Function Calls

Another use of the this pointer is to enable cascaded member-function calls—that is, invoking multiple functions sequentially in the same statement (as in line 10 of Fig. 9.27). The program of Figs. 9.25–9.27 modifies class Time's *set* functions setTime, setHour, setMinute and setSecond such that each returns a reference to the Time object on which it's called to enable cascaded member-function calls. Notice in Fig. 9.26 that the last statement in the body of each of these member functions returns *this (lines 21, 33, 45 and 57) into a return type of Time&.

```
1   // Fig. 9.25: Time.h
2   // Time class modified to enable cascaded member-function calls.
3   #include <string>
4
5   // Time class definition.
6   // Member functions defined in Time.cpp.
7   #ifndef TIME_H
8   #define TIME_H
9
```

Fig. 9.25 | Time class modified to enable cascaded member-function calls. (Part 1 of 2.)

```
10   class Time {
11   public:
12      explicit Time(int = 0, int = 0, int = 0); // default constructor
13
14      // set functions (the Time& return types enable cascading)
15      Time& setTime(int, int, int); // set hour, minute, second
16      Time& setHour(int); // set hour
17      Time& setMinute(int); // set minute
18      Time& setSecond(int); // set second
19
20      unsigned int getHour() const; // return hour
21      unsigned int getMinute() const; // return minute
22      unsigned int getSecond() const; // return second
23      std::string toUniversalString() const; // 24-hour time format string
24      std::string toStandardString() const; // 12-hour time format string
25   private:
26      unsigned int hour{0}; // 0 - 23 (24-hour clock format)
27      unsigned int minute{0}; // 0 - 59
28      unsigned int second{0}; // 0 - 59
29   };
30
31   #endif
```

Fig. 9.25 | Time class modified to enable cascaded member-function calls. (Part 2 of 2.)

```
1    // Fig. 9.26: Time.cpp
2    // Time class member-function definitions.
3    #include <iomanip>
4    #include <sstream>
5    #include <stdexcept>
6    #include "Time.h" // Time class definition
7    using namespace std;
8
9    // constructor function to initialize private data;
10   // calls member function setTime to set variables;
11   // default values are 0 (see class definition)
12   Time::Time(int hr, int min, int sec) {
13      setTime(hr, min, sec);
14   }
15
16   // set values of hour, minute, and second
17   Time& Time::setTime(int h, int m, int s) { // note Time& return
18      setHour(h);
19      setMinute(m);
20      setSecond(s);
21      return *this; // enables cascading
22   }
23
24   // set hour value
25   Time& Time::setHour(int h) { // note Time& return
```

Fig. 9.26 | Time class member-function definitions modified to enable cascaded member-function calls. (Part 1 of 3.)

```
26        if (h >= 0 && h < 24) {
27            hour = h;
28        }
29        else {
30            throw invalid_argument("hour must be 0-23");
31        }
32
33        return *this; // enables cascading
34    }
35
36    // set minute value
37    Time& Time::setMinute(int m) { // note Time& return
38        if (m >= 0 && m < 60) {
39            minute = m;
40        }
41        else {
42            throw invalid_argument("minute must be 0-59");
43        }
44
45        return *this; // enables cascading
46    }
47
48    // set second value
49    Time& Time::setSecond(int s) { // note Time& return
50        if (s >= 0 && s < 60) {
51            second = s;
52        }
53        else {
54            throw invalid_argument("second must be 0-59");
55        }
56
57        return *this; // enables cascading
58    }
59
60    // get hour value
61    unsigned int Time::getHour() const {return hour;}
62
63    // get minute value
64    unsigned int Time::getMinute() const {return minute;}
65
66    // get second value
67    unsigned int Time::getSecond() const {return second;}
68
69    // return Time as a string in universal-time format (HH:MM:SS)
70    string Time::toUniversalString() const {
71        ostringstream output;
72        output << setfill('0') << setw(2) << getHour() << ":"
73            << setw(2) << getMinute() << ":" << setw(2) << getSecond();
74        return output.str();
75    }
76
```

Fig. 9.26 | Time class member-function definitions modified to enable cascaded member-function calls. (Part 2 of 3.)

```
77   // return Time as string in standard-time format (HH:MM:SS AM or PM)
78   string Time::toStandardString() const {
79      ostringstream output;
80      output << ((getHour() == 0 || getHour() == 12) ? 12 : getHour() % 12)
81         << ":" << setfill('0') << setw(2) << getMinute() << ":" << setw(2)
82         << getSecond() << (hour < 12 ? " AM" : " PM");
83      return output.str();
84   }
```

Fig. 9.26 | Time class member-function definitions modified to enable cascaded member-function calls. (Part 3 of 3.)

The program of Fig. 9.27 creates Time object t (line 8), then uses it in *cascaded member-function calls* (lines 10 and 18). Why does the technique of returning *this as a reference work? The dot operator (.) associates from left to right, so line 10

```
        t.setHour(18).setMinute(30).setSecond(22);
```

first evaluates t.setHour(18), then returns a reference to (the updated) object t as the value of this function call. The remaining expression is then interpreted as

```
        t.setMinute(30).setSecond(22);
```

The t.setMinute(30) call executes and returns a reference to the (further updated) object t. The remaining expression is interpreted as

```
        t.setSecond(22);
```

```
1    // Fig. 9.27: fig09_27.cpp
2    // Cascading member-function calls with the this pointer.
3    #include <iostream>
4    #include "Time.h" // Time class definition
5    using namespace std;
6
7    int main() {
8       Time t; // create Time object
9
10      t.setHour(18).setMinute(30).setSecond(22); // cascaded function calls
11
12      // output time in universal and standard formats
13      cout << "Universal time: " << t.toUniversalString()
14         << "\nStandard time: " << t.toStandardString();
15
16      // cascaded function calls
17      cout << "\n\nNew standard time: "
18         << t.setTime(20, 20, 20).toStandardString() << endl;
19   }
```

```
Universal time: 18:30:22
Standard time: 6:30:22 PM

New standard time: 8:20:20 PM
```

Fig. 9.27 | Cascading member-function calls with the this pointer.

Line 18 (Fig. 9.27) also uses cascading. Note that we cannot chain another Time member-function call after toStandardString here, because it does *not* return a reference to t—we could, however, place a call to a string member function, because toStandardString returns a string. Placing the call to toStandardString before the call to setTime in line 18 results in a compilation error, because the string returned by toStandardString does not have a setTime function. Chapter 10 presents several practical examples of using cascaded function calls. One such example uses multiple << operators with cout to output multiple values in a single statement.

9.15 static Class Members

There is an important exception to the rule that each object of a class has its own copy of all the data members of the class. In certain cases, only *one* copy of a variable should be *shared* by *all* objects of a class. A static data member is used for these and other reasons. Such a variable represents "classwide" information, i.e., data that is shared by *all* instances and is *not* specific to any one object of the class. Recall, for example, that the GradeBook classes in Chapter 7 use static data members to store constants representing the number of grades that all GradeBook objects can hold.

9.15.1 Motivating Classwide Data

Let's further motivate the need for static classwide data with an example. Suppose that we have a video game with Martians and other space creatures. Each Martian tends to be brave and willing to attack other space creatures when the Martian is aware that at least five Martians are present. If fewer than five are present, each Martian becomes cowardly. So each Martian needs to know the martianCount. We could endow each object of class Martian with martianCount as a data member. If we do, every Martian will have a *separate* copy of the data member. Every time we create a new Martian, we'll have to update the data member martianCount in all Martian objects. Doing this would require every Martian object to have, or have access to, handles to all other Martian objects in memory. This wastes space with the redundant copies of the martianCount and wastes time in updating the separate copies. Instead, we declare martianCount to be static. This makes martianCount classwide data. Every Martian can access martianCount as if it were a data member of the Martian, but only *one* copy of the static variable martianCount is maintained in the program. This saves space. We save time by having the Martian constructor increment static variable martianCount and having the Martian destructor decrement martianCount. Because there's only one copy, we do not have to increment or decrement separate copies of martianCount for each Martian object.

Performance Tip 9.5

Use static data members to save storage when a single copy of the data for all objects of a class will suffice—such as a constant that can be shared by all objects of the class.

9.15.2 Scope and Initialization of static Data Members

A class's static data members have *class scope*. A static data member *must* be initialized *exactly* once. Fundamental-type static data members are initialized by default to 0. Prior to C++11, a static const data member of int or enum type could be initialized in its declaration in the class definition—all other static const data members had to be defined and intialized *at global namespace scope* (i.e., outside the body of the class definition). In C++11, all static const data members can have in-class initializers. If a static data member is an object of a class that provides a default constructor, the static data member need not be initialized because its default constructor will be called.

9.15.3 Accessing static Data Members

A class's private (and protected; Chapter 11) static members are normally accessed through the class's public member functions or friends. *A class's static members exist even when no objects of that class exist.* To access a public static class member when no objects of the class exist, simply prefix the class name and the scope resolution operator (::) to the name of the data member. For example, if our preceding variable martianCount is public, it can be accessed with the expression Martian::martianCount, even when there are no Martian objects. (Of course, using public data is discouraged.)

To access a private or protected static class member when *no* objects of the class exist, provide a public static member function and call the function by prefixing its name with the class name and scope resolution operator. A static member function is a service of the *class*, *not* of a specific *object* of the class.

> **Software Engineering Observation 9.12**
>
> *A class's static data members and static member functions exist and can be used even if no objects of that class have been instantiated.*

9.15.4 Demonstrating static Data Members

The program of Figs. 9.28–9.30 demonstrates a private static data member called count (Fig. 9.28, line 23) and a public static member function called getCount (Fig. 9.28, line 17). In Fig. 9.29, line 8 defines and initializes the data member count to zero *at global namespace scope* and line 12 defines static member function getCount. Notice that neither line 8 nor line 12 includes keyword static, yet both lines define static class members. The static keyword cannot be applied to a member definition that appears outside the class definition. Data member count maintains a count of the number of objects of class Employee that have been instantiated. When objects of class Employee exist, member count can be referenced through *any* member function of an Employee object—in Fig. 9.29, count is referenced by both line 18 in the constructor and line 27 in the destructor.

```
1   // Fig. 9.28: Employee.h
2   // Employee class definition with a static data member to
3   // track the number of Employee objects in memory
4   #ifndef EMPLOYEE_H
5   #define EMPLOYEE_H
6
7   #include <string>
8
```

Fig. 9.28 | Employee class definition with a static data member to track the number of Employee objects in memory. (Part 1 of 2.)

```
 9   class Employee {
10   public:
11      Employee(const std::string&, const std::string&); // constructor
12      ~Employee(); // destructor
13      std::string getFirstName() const; // return first name
14      std::string getLastName() const; // return last name
15
16      // static member function
17      static unsigned int getCount(); // return # of objects instantiated
18   private:
19      std::string firstName;
20      std::string lastName;
21
22      // static data
23      static unsigned int count; // number of objects instantiated
24   };
25
26   #endif
```

Fig. 9.28 | Employee class definition with a static data member to track the number of Employee objects in memory. (Part 2 of 2.)

```
 1   // Fig. 9.29: Employee.cpp
 2   // Employee class member-function definitions.
 3   #include <iostream>
 4   #include "Employee.h" // Employee class definition
 5   using namespace std;
 6
 7   // define and initialize static data member at global namespace scope
 8   unsigned int Employee::count{0}; // cannot include keyword static
 9
10   // define static member function that returns number of
11   // Employee objects instantiated (declared static in Employee.h)
12   unsigned int Employee::getCount() {return count;}
13
14   // constructor initializes non-static data members and
15   // increments static data member count
16   Employee::Employee(const string& first, const string& last)
17      : firstName(first), lastName(last) {
18      ++count; // increment static count of employees
19      cout << "Employee constructor for " << firstName
20         << ' ' << lastName << " called." << endl;
21   }
22
23   // destructor decrements the count
24   Employee::~Employee() {
25      cout << "~Employee() called for " << firstName
26         << ' ' << lastName << endl;
27      --count; // decrement static count of employees
28   }
29
```

Fig. 9.29 | Employee class member-function definitions. (Part 1 of 2.)

```
30   // return first name of employee
31   string Employee::getFirstName() const {return firstName;}
32
33   // return last name of employee
34   string Employee::getLastName() const {return lastName;}
```

Fig. 9.29 | Employee class member-function definitions. (Part 2 of 2.)

Figure 9.30 uses static member function getCount to determine the number of Employee objects in memory at various points in the program. The program calls Employee::getCount() before any Employee objects have been created (line 11), after two Employee objects have been created (line 22) and after those Employee objects have been destroyed (line 33). Lines 15–28 in main define a *nested scope*. Recall that local variables exist until the scope in which they're defined terminates. In this example, we create two Employee objects in the nested scope (lines 16–17). As each constructor executes, it increments class Employee's static data member count. These Employee objects are destroyed when the program reaches line 28. At that point, each object's destructor executes and decrements class Employee's static data member count.

```
 1   // Fig. 9.30: fig09_30.cpp
 2   // static data member tracking the number of objects of a class.
 3   #include <iostream>
 4   #include "Employee.h" // Employee class definition
 5   using namespace std;
 6
 7   int main() {
 8      // no objects exist; use class name and binary scope resolution
 9      // operator to access static member function getCount
10      cout << "Number of employees before instantiation of any objects is "
11         << Employee::getCount() << endl; // use class name
12
13      // the following scope creates and destroys
14      // Employee objects before main terminates
15      {
16         Employee e1{"Susan", "Baker"};
17         Employee e2{"Robert", "Jones"};
18
19         // two objects exist; call static member function getCount again
20         // using the class name and the scope resolution operator
21         cout << "Number of employees after objects are instantiated is "
22            << Employee::getCount();
23
24         cout << "\n\nEmployee 1: "
25            << e1.getFirstName() << " " << e1.getLastName()
26            << "\nEmployee 2: "
27            << e2.getFirstName() << " " << e2.getLastName() << "\n\n";
28      }
29
```

Fig. 9.30 | static data member tracking the number of objects of a class. (Part 1 of 2.)

```
30       // no objects exist, so call static member function getCount again
31       // using the class name and the scope resolution operator
32       cout << "\nNumber of employees after objects are deleted is "
33          << Employee::getCount() << endl;
34    }
```

```
Number of employees before instantiation of any objects is 0
Employee constructor for Susan Baker called.
Employee constructor for Robert Jones called.
Number of employees after objects are instantiated is 2

Employee 1: Susan Baker
Employee 2: Robert Jones

~Employee() called for Robert Jones
~Employee() called for Susan Baker

Number of employees after objects are deleted is 0
```

Fig. 9.30 | static data member tracking the number of objects of a class. (Part 2 of 2.)

A member function should be declared static if it does *not* access non-static data members or non-static member functions of the class. Unlike non-static member functions, a static member function does *not* have a this pointer, because static data members and static member functions exist independently of any objects of a class. The this pointer *must* refer to a specific *object* of the class, and when a static member function is called, there might *not* be any objects of its class in memory.

Common Programming Error 9.6

Using the this pointer in a static member function is a compilation error.

Common Programming Error 9.7

Declaring a static member function const is a compilation error. The const qualifier indicates that a function cannot modify the contents of the object on which it operates, but static member functions exist and operate independently of any objects of the class.

9.16 Wrap-Up

This chapter deepened our coverage of classes, using a Time class case study to introduce several new features. We showed how to engineer a class to separate its interface from its implementation. We used an include guard to prevent the code in a header (.h) file from being included multiple times in the same source code (.cpp) file.

You created formatted strings using ostringstream objects. You learned how to use the arrow operator to access an object's members via a pointer of the object's class type. You learned that member functions have class scope—the member function's name is known only to the class's other members unless referred to by a client of the class via an object name, a reference to an object of the class, a pointer to an object of the class or the scope resolution operator. We also discussed access functions (commonly used to retrieve the values of data members or to test the truth or falsity of conditions), and utility functions (`private` member functions that support the operation of the class's `public` member functions).

You learned that a constructor can specify default arguments that enable it to be called in a variety of ways. You also learned that any constructor that can be called with no arguments is a default constructor and that there can be at most one default constructor per class. We discussed destructors for performing termination housekeeping on an object of a class before that object is destroyed, and demonstrated the order in which an object's constructors and destructors are called.

We demonstrated the problems that can occur when a member function returns a reference or a pointer to a `private` data member, which breaks the encapsulation of the class. We also showed that objects of the same type can be assigned to one another using default memberwise assignment—in Chapter 10, we'll discuss how this can cause problems when an object contains pointer members.

You learned how to specify `const` objects and `const` member functions to prevent modifications to objects, thus enforcing the principle of least privilege. You also learned that, through composition, a class can have objects of other classes as members. We demonstrated how to declare and use `friend` functions.

You learned that the `this` pointer is passed as an implicit argument to each of a class's non-`static` member functions, allowing them to access the correct object's data members and other non-`static` member functions. We used the `this` pointer explicitly to access the class's members and to enable cascaded member-function calls. We motivated the notion of `static` data members and member functions and demonstrated how to declare and use them.

In Chapter 10, we continue our study of classes and objects by showing how to enable C++'s operators to work with class-type objects—a process called operator overloading. For example, you'll see how to overload the `<<` operator so it can be used to output a complete array without explicitly using an iteration statement.

Summary

Section 9.2 Time Class Case Study: Separating Interface from Implementation

- Placing a complete class definition in a header reveals the entire implementation of the class to the class's clients—a header is simply a text file that anyone can open and read.

- Conventional software engineering wisdom says that to use an object of a class, the client code needs to know only: what member functions to call, what arguments to provide to each member function and what return type to expect from each member function. The client code does not need to know how those functions are implemented.

Section 9.2.1 Interface of a Class

- **Interfaces** (p. 388) define and standardize the ways in which things such as people and systems interact with one another.

- The interface of a class describes what services a class's clients can use and how to request those services, but not how the class carries out the services.

- A class's `public` interface consists of the class's `public` member functions (also known as the class's `public` services).

- You can specify a class's interface by writing a class definition that lists only the class's member-function prototypes and the class's data members.

Section 9.2.2 Separating the Interface from the Implementation

- To separate the class's interface from its implementation, we break up the class into two files—a header in which the class is defined and a source-code file in which the class's member functions are defined.
- By convention, member-function definitions are placed in a source-code file of the same base name as the class's header but with a .cpp filename extension (some compilers support other filename extensions as well).

Section 9.2.3 Time Class Definition

- A class definition that contains function prototypes rather than definitions describes the class's public interface without revealing the class's member-function implementations.
- The class's header still specifies the class's private data members as well—the compiler must know the data members of the class to determine how much memory to reserve for each object of the class.
- Including the class's header in the client code provides the compiler with the information it needs to ensure that the client code calls the class's member functions correctly.
- An **include guard** (p. 389)—consisting of #ifndef, #define and #endif—prevents a header from being #included multiple times in the same source-code file.
- Attempts to include a header multiple times (inadvertently) typically occur in large programs with many headers that may themselves include other headers.

Section 9.2.5 Scope Resolution Operator (::)

- When member functions are defined outside a class's definition, each member function's name must be preceded by the class name and the scope resolution operator (::). This "ties" each member function to the class definition, which declares the class's members, telling the compiler that each member function is within that **class's scope** (p. 391).

Section 9.2.6 Including the Class Header in the Source-Code File

- The source-code file containing a class's member-function definitions must include the class's header. This enables the compiler to ensure that the first line of each member function matches its prototype in the class's header and that each member function knows about the class's data members and other member functions.

Section 9.2.7 Time Class Member Function setTime and Throwing Exceptions

- A function can **throw an exception** (p. 392) of type invalid_argument (p. 392) to notify the client code that an invalid argument was received.
- A **throw statement** (p. 392) creates and throws an object of the type specified to the right of the throw keyword.
- After an exception object is created, the throw statement immediately terminates the function and the exception is returned to the calling function.

Section 9.2.8 Time Class Member Function toUniversalString and String Stream Processing

- Objects of class ostringstream (p. 392; from the header <sstream>) provide the same functionality as cout, but write their output to string objects in memory.

- Class ostringstream's **str** (p. 392) member function returns the string created by an ostringstream.

- Parameterized stream manipulator **setfill** (p. 392) specifies the **fill character** (p. 392) that's displayed when an integer is output in a field wider than the number of digits in the value.

- The fill characters appear to the *left* of the digits in the number for a right-aligned value—for left aligned values, the fill characters appear to the right.

- Once the fill character is specified with setfill, it applies for all subsequent values that are displayed in fields wider than the value being displayed—this is a sticky setting.

Section 9.2.10 Implicitly Inlining Member Functions
- A member function defined in a class's body is implicitly declared inline.

Section 9.2.11 Member Functions vs. Global Functions
- Classes often contain member functions that take no arguments, because these member functions implicitly know the data members for the particular object on which they're invoked. This can make member-function calls more concise and less error prone than conventional function calls in procedural programming.

Section 9.2.12 Using Class Time
- Once a class is defined, it can be used as a type in declarations of objects, references and pointers.

Section 9.2.13 Object Size
- People new to object-oriented programming often suppose that objects must be quite large because they contain data members and member functions. Logically, this is true; physically, however, this is not the case—member functions are stored separately from the objects of a class.

Section 9.3 Compilation and Linking Process
- Often a class's interface and implementation will be created and compiled by one programmer and used by a separate programmer who implements the client code that uses the class.

- A class-implementation programmer responsible for creating a reusable class creates the header and the source-code file that #includes the header, then compiles the source-code file to create the class's object code.

- To hide the class's member-function implementation details, the class-implementation programmer would provide the client-code programmer with the class's header (which specifies the class's interface and data members) and the class's object code (i.e., the machine-code instructions that represent the class's member functions).

- The client-code programmer is not given the source-code file with the class's member function definitions, so the client remains unaware of how the class's member functions are implemented.

- The client-code programmer needs to know only the class's interface to use the class and must be able to link its object code. Since the interface of the class is part of the class definition in the class's header, the client-code programmer must have access to this file and must #include it in the client's source-code file.

- To create the executable application, the last step is to link the object code for the client code, the object code for the member-function implementations of the class(es) used by the client code and the C++ Standard Library object code used by the class-implementation programmer and the client-code programmer.

- The linker's output is the executable application. Compilers and IDEs typically invoke the linker for you after compiling your code.

Section 9.4 Class Scope and Accessing Class Members
- A class's data members and member functions belong to that class's scope.
- Nonmember functions are defined at global namespace scope.
- Within a class's scope, class members are immediately accessible by all of that class's member non-static functions and can be referenced by name.
- Outside a class's scope, class members are referenced through one of the handles on an object—an object name, a reference to an object or a pointer to an object.
- Variables declared in a member function have block scope and are known only to that function.
- The dot member selection operator (.) is preceded by an object's name or by a reference to an object to access the object's public members.
- The **arrow member selection operator** (->; p. 398) is preceded by a pointer to an object to access that object's public members.

Section 9.5 Access Functions and Utility Functions
- **Access functions** (p. 399) read or display data. They can also be used to test the truth or falsity of conditions—such functions are often called predicate functions.
- A **utility function** (p. 399) is a private member function that supports the operation of the class's public member functions. Utility functions are not intended to be used by clients of a class.

Section 9.6.1 Constructors with Default Arguments
- Like other functions, constructors can specify default arguments.

Section 9.6.2 Overloaded Constructors and C++11 Delegating Constructors
- To overload a constructor, provide in the class definition a prototype for each version of the constructor, and provide a separate constructor definition for each overloaded version. This also applies to the class's member functions.
- Just as a constructor can call a class's other member functions to perform tasks, C++11 allows constructors to call other constructors in the same class. To do so, you use a member initializer with the name of the class.
- The calling constructor is known as a **delegating constructor** (p. 405)—it delegates its work to another constructor. This is useful when overloaded constructors have common code that previously would have been defined in a private utility function and called by all the constructors.

Section 9.7 Destructors
- A class's **destructor** (p. 387) is called implicitly when an object of the class is destroyed.
- The name of the destructor for a class is the tilde (~) character followed by the class name.
- A destructor does not release an object's storage—it performs **termination housekeeping** (p. 405) before the system reclaims an object's memory, so the memory may be reused to hold new objects.
- A destructor receives no parameters and returns no value. A class may have only one destructor.
- If you do not explicitly provide a destructor, the compiler creates an "empty" destructor, so every class has exactly one destructor.

Section 9.8 When Constructors and Destructors Are Called
- The order in which constructors and destructors are called depends on the order in which execution enters and leaves the scopes where the objects are instantiated.

- Generally, destructor calls are made in the reverse order of the corresponding constructor calls, but the global and local static objects' destructors are called after all non-static local objects are destroyed.

- Function exit forces a program to terminate immediately and does not execute the destructors of local objects. exit often is used to terminate a program when a fatal unrecoverable error occurs.

- Function abort forces the program to terminate immediately, without allowing programmer-defined cleanup code of any kind to be called. abort is usually used to indicate an abnormal termination of the program.

Section 9.9 *Time Class Case Study: A Subtle Trap—Returning a Reference or a Pointer to a* private *Data Member*

- A reference to an object is an alias for the name of the object and, hence, may be used on the left side of an assignment statement. In this context, the reference makes a perfectly acceptable *lvalue* that can receive a value.

- If the function returns a reference to const data, then the reference cannot be used as a modifiable *lvalue*.

Section 9.10 *Default Memberwise Assignment*

- The assignment operator (=) can be used to assign an object to another object of the same type. By default, such assignment is performed by **memberwise assignment** (p. 411).

- Objects may be passed by value to or returned by value from functions. C++ creates a new object and uses a **copy constructor** (p. 413) to copy the original object's values into the new object.

- For each class, the compiler provides a default copy constructor that copies each member of the original object into the corresponding member of the new object.

Section 9.11 const *Objects and* const *Member Functions*

- The keyword const can be used to specify that an object is not modifiable and that any attempt to modify the object should result in a compilation error.

- C++ compilers disallow non-const member function calls on const objects.

- An attempt by a const member function to modify an object of its class is a compilation error.

- A member function is specified as const both in its prototype and in its definition.

- A const object must be initialized.

- Constructors and destructors cannot be declared const.

Section 9.12 *Composition: Objects as Members of Classes*

- A class can have objects of other classes as members—this concept is called composition.

- Member objects are constructed in the order in which they're declared in the class definition and before their enclosing class objects are constructed.

- If a member initializer is not provided for a member object, the member object's **default constructor** (p. 415) will be called implicitly.

Section 9.13 friend *Functions and* friend *Classes*

- A friend function (p. 421) of a class is defined outside that class's scope, yet has the right to access all of the class's members. Standalone functions or entire classes may be declared to be friends.

- A friend declaration can appear anywhere in the class.

- The friendship relation is neither symmetric nor transitive.

Section 9.14 Using the this Pointer

- Every object has access to its own address through the **this pointer** (p. 423).

- An object's this pointer is not part of the object itself—i.e., the size of the memory occupied by the this pointer is not reflected in the result of a sizeof operation on the object.

- The this pointer is passed as an implicit argument to each non-static member function.

- Objects use the this pointer implicitly (as we've done to this point) or explicitly to reference their data members and member functions.

- The this pointer enables **cascaded member-function calls** (p. 425) in which multiple functions are invoked in the same statement.

Section 9.15 static Class Members

- A **static data member** (p. 429) represents "classwide" information (i.e., a property of the class shared by all instances, not a property of a specific object of the class).

- static data members have class scope and can be declared public, private or protected.

- A class's static members exist even when no objects of that class exist.

- To access a public static class member when no objects of the class exist, simply prefix the class name and the scope resolution operator (::) to the name of the data member.

- The static keyword cannot be applied to a member definition that appears outside the class definition.

- A member function should be declared **static** (p. 430) if it does not access non-static data members or non-static member functions of the class. Unlike non-static member functions, a static member function does not have a this pointer, because static data members and static member functions exist independently of any objects of a class.

Self-Review Exercises

9.1   Fill in the blanks in each of the following:

     a) Class members are accessed via the _____ operator in conjunction with the name of an object (or reference to an object) of the class or via the _____ operator in conjunction with a pointer to an object of the class.

     b) Class members specified as _____ are accessible only to member functions of the class and friends of the class.

     c) _____ class members are accessible anywhere an object of the class is in scope.

     d) _____ can be used to assign an object of a class to another object of the same class.

     e) A nonmember function must be declared by the class as a(n) _____ of a class to have access to that class's private data members.

     f) A constant object must be _____; it cannot be modified after it's created.

     g) A(n) _____ data member represents classwide information.

     h) An object's non-static member functions have access to a "self pointer" to the object called the _____ pointer.

     i) Keyword _____ specifies that an object or variable is not modifiable.

     j) If a member initializer is not provided for a member object of a class, the object's _____ is called.

     k) A member function should be static if it does not access _____ class members.

     l) Member objects are constructed _____ their enclosing class object.

     m) When a member function is defined outside the class definition, the function header must include the class name and the _____, followed by the function name to "tie" the member function to the class definition.

9.2 Find the error(s) in each of the following and explain how to correct it (them):

a) Assume the following prototype is declared in class Time:

```
void ~Time(int);
```

b) Assume the following prototype is declared in class Employee:

```
int Employee(string, string);
```

c) The following is a definition of class Example:

```cpp
class Example {
public:
   Example(int y = 10) : data(y) { }

   int getIncrementedData() const {
      return ++data;
   }

   static int getCount() {
      cout << "Data is " << data << endl;
      return count;
   }
private:
   int data;
   static int count;
};
```

Answers to Self-Review Exercises

9.1 a) dot (.), arrow (->). b) private. c) public. d) Default memberwise assignment (performed by the assignment operator). e) friend. f) initialized. g) static. h) this. i) const. j) default constructor. k) non-static. l) before. m) :: scope resolution operator.

9.2 a) *Error:* Destructors are not allowed to return values (or even specify a return type) or take arguments.
Correction: Remove the return type void and the parameter int from the declaration.

b) *Error:* Constructors are not allowed to return values.
Correction: Remove the return type int from the declaration.

c) *Error:* The class definition for Example has two errors. The first occurs in function get-IncrementedData. The function is declared const, but it modifies the object.
Correction: To correct the first error, remove the const keyword from the definition of getIncrementedData. [*Note:* It would also be appropriate to rename this member function, as *get* functions are typically const member functions.]
Error: The second error occurs in function getCount. This function is declared static, so it's not allowed to access any non-static class member (i.e., data).
Correction: To correct the second error, remove the output line from the getCount definition.

Exercises

9.3 *(Scope Resolution Operator)* What's the purpose of the scope resolution operator?

9.4 *(Enhancing Class Time)* Provide a constructor that's capable of using the current time from the time and localtime functions—declared in the C++ Standard Library header <ctime>—to initialize an object of the Time class. For descriptions of C++ Standard Library headers, classes and functions, see http://cppreference.com.

9.5 *(Complex Class)* Create a class called Complex for performing arithmetic with complex numbers. Write a program to test your class. Complex numbers have the form

        realPart + imaginaryPart * *i*

where *i* is

$$\sqrt{-1}$$

Use double variables to represent the private data of the class. Provide a constructor that enables an object of this class to be initialized when it's declared. The constructor should contain default values in case no initializers are provided. Provide public member functions that perform the following tasks:

- a) add—Adds two Complex numbers: The real parts are added together and the imaginary parts are added together.
- b) subtract—Subtracts two Complex numbers: The real part of the right operand is subtracted from the real part of the left operand, and the imaginary part of the right operand is subtracted from the imaginary part of the left operand.
- c) toString—Returns a string representation of a Complex number in the form (a, b), where a is the real part and b is the imaginary part.

In Chapter 10, you'll learn how to overload +, - and << so you can write expressions like a + b and a - b and cout << a to add, subtract and output Complex objects. [*Note:* The C++ Standard Library provides its own class complex for complex-number arithmetic. For information on this class, visit http://en.cppreference.com/w/cpp/numeric/complex.]

9.6 *(Rational Class)* Create a class called Rational for performing arithmetic with fractions. Write a program to test your class. Use integer variables to represent the private data of the class—the numerator and the denominator. Provide a constructor that enables an object of this class to be initialized when it's declared. The constructor should contain default values in case no initializers are provided and should store the fraction in reduced form. For example, the fraction

$$\frac{2}{4}$$

would be stored in the object as 1 in the numerator and 2 in the denominator. Provide public member functions that perform each of the following tasks:

- a) add—Adds two Rational numbers. The result should be stored in reduced form.
- b) subtract—Subtracts two Rational numbers. Store the result in reduced form.
- c) multiply—Multiplies two Rational numbers. Store the result in reduced form.
- d) divide—Divides two Rational numbers. The result should be stored in reduced form.
- e) toRationalString—Returns a string representation of a Rational number in the form a/b, where a is the numerator and b is the denominator.
- f) toDouble—Returns the Rational number as a double.

In Chapter 10, you'll learn how to overload +, -, *, / and << so you can write expressions like a + b, a - b, a * b, a - b and cout << a to add, subtract, multiply, divide and output Complex objects.

9.7 *(Enhancing Class Time)* Modify the Time class of Figs. 9.5–9.6 to include a tick member function that increments the time stored in a Time object by one second. Write a program that tests the tick member function in a loop that prints the time in standard format during each iteration of the loop to illustrate that the tick member function works correctly. Be sure to test the following cases:

- a) Incrementing into the next minute.
- b) Incrementing into the next hour.
- c) Incrementing into the next day (i.e., 11:59:59 PM to 12:00:00 AM).

9.8 *(Enhancing Class Date)* Modify the Date class of Figs. 9.14–9.15 to perform error checking on the initializer values for data members month, day and year. Also, provide a member function nextDay to increment the day by one. Write a program that tests function nextDay in a loop that prints the date during each iteration to illustrate that nextDay works correctly. Be sure to test the following cases:

    a) Incrementing into the next month.

    b) Incrementing into the next year.

9.9   *(Combining Class Time and Class Date)* Combine the modified Time class of Exercise 9.7 and the modified Date class of Exercise 9.8 into one class called DateAndTime. Modify the tick function to call the nextDay function if the time increments into the next day. Modify functions toStandardString and toUniversalString so that each returns a string containing the date and time. Write a program to test the new class DateAndTime. Specifically, test incrementing the time into the next day.

9.10   *(Returning Error Indicators from Class Time's set Functions)* Modify the *set* functions in the Time class of Figs. 9.5–9.6 to return appropriate error values if an attempt is made to *set* a data member of an object of class Time to an invalid value. Write a program that tests your new version of class Time. Display error messages when *set* functions return error values.

9.11   *(Rectangle Class)* Create a class Rectangle with attributes length and width, each of which defaults to 1. Provide member functions that calculate the perimeter and the area of the rectangle. Also, provide *set* and *get* functions for the length and width attributes. The *set* functions should verify that length and width are each floating-point numbers larger than 0.0 and less than 20.0.

9.12   *(Enhancing Class Rectangle)* Create a more sophisticated Rectangle class than the one you created in Exercise 9.11. This class stores only the Cartesian coordinates of the four corners of the rectangle. The constructor calls a *set* function that accepts four sets of coordinates and verifies that each of these is in the first quadrant with no single *x*- or *y*-coordinate larger than 20.0. The *set* function also verifies that the supplied coordinates do, in fact, specify a rectangle. Provide member functions that calculate the length, width, perimeter and area. The length is the larger of the two dimensions. Include a predicate function square that determines whether the rectangle is a square.

9.13   *(Enhancing Class Rectangle)* Modify class Rectangle from Exercise 9.12 to include a draw function that displays the rectangle inside a 25-by-25 box enclosing the portion of the first quadrant in which the rectangle resides. Include a setFillCharacter function to specify the character out of which the body of the rectangle will be drawn. Include a setPerimeterCharacter function to specify the character that will be used to draw the border of the rectangle. If you feel ambitious, you might include functions to scale the size of the rectangle and move it around within the designated portion of the first quadrant.

9.14   *(HugeInteger Class)* Create a class HugeInteger that uses a 40-element array of digits to store integers as large as 40 digits each. Provide member functions input, output, add and subtract. For comparing HugeInteger objects, provide functions isEqualTo, isNotEqualTo, isGreaterThan, isLessThan, isGreaterThanOrEqualTo and isLessThanOrEqualTo—each of these is a "predicate" function that simply returns true if the relationship holds between the two HugeIntegers and returns false if the relationship does not hold. Also, provide a predicate function isZero. If you feel ambitious, provide member functions multiply, divide and remainder. In Chapter 10, you'll learn how to overload input, output, arithmetic, equality and relational operators so that you can write expressions containing HugeInteger objects, rather than explicitly calling member functions.

9.15   *(TicTacToe Class)* Create a class TicTacToe that will enable you to write a complete program to play the game of tic-tac-toe. The class contains as private data a 3-by-3 two-dimensional array of integers. The constructor should initialize the empty board to all zeros. Allow two human players. Wherever the first player moves, place a 1 in the specified square. Place a 2 wherever the second player moves. Each move must be to an empty square. After each move, determine whether the game has been won or is a draw. If you feel ambitious, modify your program so that the computer makes the moves for one of the players. Also, allow the player to specify whether he or she wants to go first or second. If you feel exceptionally ambitious, develop a program that will play three-dimensional tic-tac-toe on a 4-by-4-by-4 board. [*Caution:* This is an extremely challenging project that could take many weeks of effort!]

9.16   *(Friendship)* Explain the notion of friendship. Explain the negative aspects of friendship as described in the text.

9.17   *(Constructor Overloading)* Can a Time class definition that includes *both* of the following constructors:

```
Time(int h = 0, int m = 0, int s = 0);
Time();
```

be used to default construct a Time object? If not, explain why.

9.18   *(Constructors and Destructors)* What happens when a return type, even void, is specified for a constructor or destructor?

9.19   *(Date Class Modification)* Modify class Date in Fig. 9.18 to have the following capabilities:

a) Output the date in multiple formats such as

```
DDD YYYY
MM/DD/YY
June 14, 1992
```

b) Use overloaded constructors to create Date objects initialized with dates of the formats in part (a).

c) Create a Date constructor that reads the system date using the standard library functions of the <ctime> header and sets the Date members. See your compiler's reference documentation or http://en.cppreference.com/w/cpp/chrono/c for information on the functions in header <ctime>. You might also want to check out C++11's chrono library at http://en.cppreference.com/w/cpp/chrono.

In Chapter 10, we'll be able to create operators for testing the equality of two dates and for comparing dates to determine whether one date is prior to, or after, another.

9.20   *(SavingsAccount Class)* Create a SavingsAccount class. Use a static data member annualInterestRate to store the annual interest rate for each of the savers. Each member of the class contains a private data member savingsBalance indicating the amount the saver currently has on deposit. Provide member function calculateMonthlyInterest that calculates the monthly interest by multiplying the savingsBalance by annualInterestRate divided by 12; this interest should be added to savingsBalance. Provide a static member function modifyInterestRate that sets the static annualInterestRate to a new value. Write a driver program to test class SavingsAccount. Instantiate two different objects of class SavingsAccount, saver1 and saver2, with balances of $2000.00 and $3000.00, respectively. Set the annualInterestRate to 3 percent. Then calculate the monthly interest and print the new balances for each of the savers. Then set the annualInterestRate to 4 percent, calculate the next month's interest and print the new balances for each of the savers.

9.21   *(IntegerSet Class)* Create class IntegerSet for which each object can hold integers in the range 0 through 100. Represent the set internally as a vector of bool values. Element a[i] is true if integer *i* is in the set. Element a[j] is false if integer *j* is not in the set. The default constructor initializes a set to the so-called "empty set," i.e., a set for which all elements contain false.

a) Provide member functions for the common set operations. For example, provide a unionOfSets member function that creates a third set that is the set-theoretic union of two existing sets (i.e., an element of the result is set to true if that element is true in either or both of the existing sets, and an element of the result is set to false if that element is false in each of the existing sets).

b) Provide an intersectionOfSets member function which creates a third set which is the set-theoretic intersection of two existing sets (i.e., an element of the result is set to false if that element is false in either or both of the existing sets, and an element of the result is set to true if that element is true in each of the existing sets).

c) Provide an insertElement member function that places a new integer *k* into a set by setting a[k] to true. Provide a deleteElement member function that deletes integer *m* by setting a[m] to false.

d) Provide a toString member function that returns a set as a string containing a list of numbers separated by spaces. Include only those elements that are present in the set (i.e., their position in the vector has a value of true). Return --- for an empty set.

e) Provide an isEqualTo member function that determines whether two sets are equal.

f) Provide an additional constructor that receives an array of integers, and uses the array to initialize a set object.

Now write a driver program to test your IntegerSet class. Instantiate several IntegerSet objects. Test that all your member functions work properly.

9.22 *(Time Class Modification)* It would be perfectly reasonable for the Time class of Figs. 9.5–9.6 to represent the time internally as the number of seconds since midnight rather than the three integer values hour, minute and second. Clients could use the same public member functions and get the same results. Modify the Time class of Fig. 9.5 to implement the time as the number of seconds since midnight and show that there is no visible change in functionality to the clients of the class. [*Note:* This exercise nicely demonstrates the virtues of implementation hiding.]

9.23 *(Card Shuffling and Dealing)* Create a program to shuffle and deal a deck of cards. The program should consist of class Card, class DeckOfCards and a driver program. Class Card should provide:

a) Data members face and suit—use enumerations to represent the faces and suits.

b) A constructor that receives two enumeration constants representing the face and suit and uses them to initialize the data members.

c) Two static arrays of strings representing the faces and suits.

d) A toString function that returns the Card as a string in the form "*face* of *suit*." You can use the + operator to concatenate strings.

Class DeckOfCards should contain:

a) An array of Cards named deck to store the Cards.

b) An integer currentCard representing the next card to deal.

c) A default constructor that initializes the Cards in the deck.

d) A shuffle function that shuffles the Cards in the deck. The shuffle algorithm should iterate through the array of Cards. For each Card, randomly select another Card in the deck and swap the two Cards.

e) A dealCard function that returns the next Card object from the deck.

f) A moreCards function that returns a bool value indicating whether there are more Cards to deal.

The driver program should create a DeckOfCards object, shuffle the cards, then deal the 52 cards—the output should be similar to Fig. 9.31.

9.24 *(Card Shuffling and Dealing)* Modify the program you developed in Exercise 9.23 so that it deals a five-card poker hand. Then write functions to accomplish each of the following:

a) Determine whether the hand contains a pair.

b) Determine whether the hand contains two pairs.

c) Determine whether the hand contains three of a kind (e.g., three jacks).

d) Determine whether the hand contains four of a kind (e.g., four aces).

e) Determine whether the hand contains a flush (i.e., all five cards of the same suit).

Six of Spades	Eight of Spades	Six of Clubs	Nine of Hearts
Queen of Hearts	Seven of Clubs	Nine of Spades	King of Hearts
Three of Diamonds	Deuce of Clubs	Ace of Hearts	Ten of Spades
Four of Spades	Ace of Clubs	Seven of Diamonds	Four of Hearts
Three of Clubs	Deuce of Hearts	Five of Spades	Jack of Diamonds
King of Clubs	Ten of Hearts	Three of Hearts	Six of Diamonds
Queen of Clubs	Eight of Diamonds	Deuce of Diamonds	Ten of Diamonds
Three of Spades	King of Diamonds	Nine of Clubs	Six of Hearts
Ace of Spades	Four of Diamonds	Seven of Hearts	Eight of Clubs
Deuce of Spades	Eight of Hearts	Five of Hearts	Queen of Spades
Jack of Hearts	Seven of Spades	Four of Clubs	Nine of Diamonds
Ace of Diamonds	Queen of Diamonds	Five of Clubs	King of Spades
Five of Diamonds	Ten of Clubs	Jack of Spades	Jack of Clubs

Fig. 9.31 | Sample card-shuffling-and-dealing output.

f) Determine whether the hand contains a straight (i.e., five cards of consecutive face values).

9.25   *(Project: Card Shuffling and Dealing)* Use the functions from Exercise 9.24 to write a program that deals two five-card poker hands, evaluates each hand and determines which is the better hand.

9.26   *(Project: Card Shuffling and Dealing)* Modify the program you developed in Exercise 9.25 so that it can simulate the dealer. The dealer's five-card hand is dealt "face down" so the player cannot see it. The program should then evaluate the dealer's hand, and, based on the quality of the hand, the dealer should draw one, two or three more cards to replace the corresponding number of unneeded cards in the original hand. The program should then reevaluate the dealer's hand.

9.27   *(Project: Card Shuffling and Dealing)* Modify the program you developed in Exercise 9.26 so that it handles the dealer's hand, but the player is allowed to decide which cards of the player's hand to replace. The program should then evaluate both hands and determine who wins. Now use this new program to play 20 games against the computer. Who wins more games, you or the computer? Have one of your friends play 20 games against the computer. Who wins more games? Based on the results of these games, make appropriate modifications to refine your poker-playing program. Play 20 more games. Does your modified program play a better game?

Making a Difference

9.28   *(Project: Emergency Response Class)* The North American emergency response service, *9-1-1*, connects callers to a local Public Service Answering Point (PSAP). Traditionally, the PSAP would ask the caller for identification information—including the caller's address, phone number and the nature of the emergency, then dispatch the appropriate emergency responders (such as the police, an ambulance or the fire department). *Enhanced 9-1-1 (or E9-1-1)* uses computers and databases to determine the caller's physical address, directs the call to the nearest PSAP, and displays the caller's phone number and address to the call taker. *Wireless Enhanced 9-1-1* provides call takers with identification information for wireless calls. Rolled out in two phases, the first phase required carriers to provide the wireless phone number and the location of the cell site or base station transmitting the call. The second phase required carriers to provide the location of the caller (using technologies such as GPS). To learn more about 9-1-1, visit http://www.fcc.gov/pshs/services/911-services/Welcome.html and http://people.howstuffworks.com/9-1-1.htm.

An important part of creating a class is determining the class's attributes (data members). For this class-design exercise, research 9-1-1 services on the Internet. Then, design a class called Emergency that might be used in an object-oriented 9-1-1 emergency response system. List the attributes that an object of this class might use to represent the emergency. For example, the class might include information on who reported the emergency (including their phone number), the location of the emergency, the time of the report, the nature of the emergency, the type of response and the status of the response. The class attributes should completely describe the nature of the problem and what's happening to resolve that problem.

Operator Overloading; Class string

Objectives

In this chapter you'll:

- Learn how operator overloading can help you craft valuable classes.

- Overload unary and binary operators.

- Convert objects from one class to another.

- Use overloaded operators and additional features of class **string**.

- Create **PhoneNumber**, **Date** and **Array** classes that provide overloaded operators.

- Perform dynamic memory allocation with **new** and **delete**.

- Understand how keyword **explicit** prevents a constructor from being used for implicit conversions.

- Experience a "light-bulb moment" when you'll truly appreciate the elegance and beauty of the class concept.

10.1 Introduction

This chapter shows how to enable C++'s operators to work with class objects—a process called operator overloading. One example of an overloaded operator built into C++ is <<, which is used *both* as the stream insertion operator *and* as the bitwise left-shift operator (which is discussed in Chapter 22). Similarly, >> also is overloaded; it's used both as

- the stream extraction operator—defined via operator overloading in the C++ Standard Library—and
- the bitwise right-shift operator—defined as part of the C++ language.

You've been using overloaded operators since early in the book. Various overloads are built into the base C++ language itself. For example, C++ overloads the addition operator (+) and the subtraction operator (-) to perform differently, depending on their context in integer, floating-point and pointer arithmetic with data of fundamental types.

You can overload *most* operators to be used with class objects—the compiler generates the appropriate code based on the *types* of the operands. The jobs performed by overloaded operators also can be performed by explicit function calls, but operator notation is often more natural.

Our examples start by demonstrating the C++ Standard Library's class `string`, which has lots of overloaded operators. This enables you to see overloaded operators in use before implementing your own. Next, we create a `PhoneNumber` class that enables us to use overloaded operators >> and << to conveniently input and output fully formatted, 10-digit phone numbers, such as (555) 555-5555. We then present a `Date` class that overloads the prefix and postfix increment (++) operators to add one day to the value of a `Date`. The class also overloads the += operator to allow a program to increment a `Date` by the number of days specified on the right side of the operator.

Next, we present a capstone case study—an Array class that uses overloaded operators and other capabilities to solve various problems with pointer-based arrays. This is one of the most important case studies in the book. Many of our students have indicated that the Array case study is their "light bulb moment," helping them truly understand what classes and object technology are all about. As part of this class, we'll overload the stream insertion, stream extraction, assignment, equality, relational and subscript operators. Once you master this Array class, you'll indeed understand the essence of object technology— crafting, using and reusing valuable classes.

The chapter concludes with discussions of how you can convert between types (including class types), problems with certain implicit conversions and how to prevent those problems.

10.2 Using the Overloaded Operators of Standard Library Class string

Figure 10.1 demonstrates many of class string's overloaded operators and several other useful member functions, including empty, substr and at. Function empty determines whether a string is empty, function substr (for "substring") returns a string that's a portion of an existing string and function at returns the character at a specific index in a string (after checking that the index is in range). Chapter 21 presents class string in detail.

```cpp
1   // Fig. 10.1: fig10_01.cpp
2   // Standard Library string class test program.
3   #include <iostream>
4   #include <string>
5   using namespace std;
6
7   int main() {
8      string s1{"happy"};
9      string s2{" birthday"};
10     string s3; // creates an empty string
11
12     // test overloaded equality and relational operators
13     cout << "s1 is \"" << s1 << "\"; s2 is \"" << s2
14        << "\"; s3 is \"" << s3 << "\""
15        << "\n\nThe results of comparing s2 and s1:" << boolalpha
16        << "\ns2 == s1 yields " << (s2 == s1)
17        << "\ns2 != s1 yields " << (s2 != s1)
18        << "\ns2 >  s1 yields " << (s2 > s1)
19        << "\ns2 <  s1 yields " << (s2 < s1)
20        << "\ns2 >= s1 yields " << (s2 >= s1)
21        << "\ns2 <= s1 yields " << (s2 <= s1);
22
23     // test string member function empty
24     cout << "\n\nTesting s3.empty():\n";
25
26     if (s3.empty()) {
27        cout << "s3 is empty; assigning s1 to s3;\n";
```

Fig. 10.1 | Standard Library string class test program. (Part 1 of 3.)

```
28          s3 = s1; // assign s1 to s3
29          cout << "s3 is \"" << s3 << "\"";
30       }
31
32       // test overloaded string concatenation assignment operator
33       cout << "\n\ns1 += s2 yields s1 = ";
34       s1 += s2; // test overloaded concatenation
35       cout << s1;
36
37       // test string concatenation with a C string
38       cout << "\n\ns1 += \" to you\" yields\n";
39       s1 += " to you";
40       cout << "s1 = " << s1;
41
42       // test string concatenation with a C++14 string-object literal
43       cout << "\n\ns1 += \", have a great day!\" yields\n";
44       s1 += ", have a great day!"s; // s after " for string-object literal
45       cout << "s1 = " << s1 << "\n\n";
46
47       // test string member function substr
48       cout << "The substring of s1 starting at location 0 for\n"
49          << "14 characters, s1.substr(0, 14), is:\n"
50          << s1.substr(0, 14) << "\n\n";
51
52       // test substr "to-end-of-string" option
53       cout << "The substring of s1 starting at\n"
54          << "location 15, s1.substr(15), is:\n" << s1.substr(15) << "\n";
55
56       // test copy constructor
57       string s4{s1};
58       cout << "\ns4 = " << s4 << "\n\n";
59
60       // test overloaded copy assignment (=) operator with self-assignment
61       cout << "assigning s4 to s4\n";
62       s4 = s4;
63       cout << "s4 = " << s4;
64
65       // test using overloaded subscript operator to create lvalue
66       s1[0] = 'H';
67       s1[6] = 'B';
68       cout << "\n\ns1 after s1[0] = 'H' and s1[6] = 'B' is:\n"
69          << s1 << "\n\n";
70
71       // test subscript out of range with string member function "at"
72       try {
73          cout << "Attempt to assign 'd' to s1.at(100) yields:\n";
74          s1.at(100) = 'd'; // ERROR: subscript out of range
75       }
76       catch (out_of_range& ex) {
77          cout << "An exception occurred: " << ex.what() << endl;
78       }
79    }
```

Fig. 10.1 | Standard Library string class test program. (Part 2 of 3.)

```
s1 is "happy"; s2 is " birthday"; s3 is ""

The results of comparing s2 and s1:
s2 == s1 yields false
s2 != s1 yields true
s2 >  s1 yields false
s2 <  s1 yields true
s2 >= s1 yields false
s2 <= s1 yields true

Testing s3.empty():
s3 is empty; assigning s1 to s3;
s3 is "happy"

s1 += s2 yields s1 = happy birthday

s1 += " to you" yields
s1 = happy birthday to you

s1 += ", have a great day!" yields
s1 = happy birthday to you, have a great day!

The substring of s1 starting at location 0 for
14 characters, s1.substr(0, 14), is:
happy birthday

The substring of s1 starting at
location 15, s1.substr(15), is:
to you, have a great day!

s4 = happy birthday to you, have a great day!

assigning s4 to s4
s4 = happy birthday to you, have a great day!

s1 after s1[0] = 'H' and s1[6] = 'B' is:
Happy Birthday to you, have a great day!

Attempt to assign 'd' to s1.at(100) yields:
An exception occurred: invalid string position
```

Fig. 10.1 | Standard Library string class test program. (Part 3 of 3.)

Creating string Objects and Displaying Them with cout and Operator <<

Lines 8–10 create three string objects:

- s1 is initialized with the literal "happy",

- s2 is initialized with the literal " birthday" and

- s3 uses the default string constructor to create an empty string.

Lines 13–14 output these three objects, using cout and operator <<, which the string class designers overloaded to handle string objects.

Comparing string Objects with the Equality and Relational Operators

Lines 15–21 show the results of comparing s2 to s1 by using class string's overloaded equality and relational operators, which perform lexicographical comparisons (that is, like a dictionary ordering) using the numerical values of the characters in each string (see Appendix B, ASCII Character Set).

Normally, when you output a condition's value 0 is displayed for *false* or 1 for *true*. However, we used the stream manipulator boolalpha (line 15) to set the output stream to display condition values as the strings "false" and "true".

string Member Function empty

Line 26 uses string member function empty, which returns true if the string is empty; otherwise, it returns false. The object s3 was initialized with the default constructor, so it is indeed empty.

string Copy Assignment Operator

Line 28 demonstrates class string's overloaded copy assignment operator by assigning s1 to s3. Line 29 outputs s3 to demonstrate that the assignment worked correctly.

string Concatenation and C++14 string-object Literals

Line 34 demonstrates class string's overloaded += operator for *string concatenation assignment.* In this case, the contents of s2 are appended to s1, thus modifying its value. Then line 35 outputs the resulting string that's stored in s1. Line 39 demonstrates that you also may append a C-string literal to a string object by using operator +=. Line 40 displays the result.

Similarly, line 44 concatenates s1 with a C++14 string-object literal which is indicated by placing the letter s immediately following the closing " of a string literal, as in

```
", have a great day!"s
```

The preceding literal actually results in a call to a C++ Standard Library function that returns a string object containing the literal's characters. Line 45 displays the new value of s1.

string Member Function substr

Class string provides member function substr (lines 50 and 54) to return a string containing a *portion* of the string object on which the function is called. The call in line 50 obtains a 14-character substring (specified by the second argument) of s1 starting at position 0 (specified by the first argument). The call to substr in line 54 obtains a substring starting from position 15 of s1. When the second argument is not specified, substr returns the *remainder* of the string on which it's called.

string Copy Constructor

Line 57 creates string object s4 and initializes it with a copy of s1. This calls class string's copy constructor, which copies the contents of s1 into the new object s4. You'll see how to define a custom copy constructor for your own class in Section 10.10.

Testing Self-Assignment with the string Copy Assignment Operator

Line 62 uses class string's overloaded copy assignment (=) operator to demonstrate that it handles *self-assignment* properly—we'll see when we build class Array later in the chapter that self-assignment can be dangerous for objects that manage their own memory, and we'll show how to deal with the issues. Line 63 confirms that s4 still has the same value after the self-assignment.

string *Class [] Operator*

Lines 66–67 use class string's overloaded [] operator to create *lvalues* that enable new characters to replace existing characters in s1. Lines 68–69 output the new value of s1. *Class* string*'s overloaded* [] *operator does not perform any bounds checking.* Therefore, *you must ensure that operations using class* string*'s overloaded* [] *operator do not accidentally manipulate elements outside the bounds of the* string. Class string *does* provide bounds checking in its member function at, which throws an exception if its argument is an *invalid* subscript. If the subscript is valid, function at returns the character at the specified location as a modifiable *lvalue* or a nonmodifiable *lvalue* (e.g., a const reference), depending on the context in which the call appears. For example:

- If at is called on a non-const string object, the function returns a modifiable *lvalue*, which could be used on the left of an assignment (=) operator to assign a new value to that location in the string.

- If at is called on a const string object, the function returns a nonmodifiable *lvalue* that can be used to obtain, but not modify, the value at that location in the string.

Line 74 demonstrates a call to function at with an invalid subscript; this throws an out_of_range exception.

10.3 Fundamentals of Operator Overloading

As you saw in Fig. 10.1, overloaded operators provide a concise notation for manipulating string objects. You can use operators with your own user-defined types as well. Although C++ does *not* allow *new* operators to be created, it *does* allow most existing operators to be overloaded so that, when they're used with objects, they have meaning appropriate to those objects.

10.3.1 Operator Overloading Is Not Automatic

You must write operator-overloading functions to perform the desired operations. An operator is overloaded by writing a non-static member function definition or non-member function definition as you normally would, except that the function name starts with the keyword operator followed by the symbol for the operator being overloaded. For example, the function name operator+ would be used to overload the addition operator (+) for use with objects of a particular user-defined type. When operators are overloaded as member functions, they must be non-static, because *they must be called on an object of the class* and operate on that object.

10.3.2 Operators That You Do Not Have to Overload

To use an operator on an object of a class, you must define overloaded operator functions for that class—with three exceptions:

- The *assignment operator (=)* may be used with *most* classes to perform *memberwise assignment* of the data members—each data member is assigned from the assignment's "source" object (on the right) to the "target" object (on the left). Memberwise assignment is dangerous for classes with pointer members, so we'll explicitly overload the assignment operator for such classes. [*Note:* This is also true of the C++11 move assignment operator, which we discuss in Chapter 24.]

- The *address (&) operator* returns a pointer to the object; this operator also can be overloaded.

- The *comma operator* evaluates the expression to its left then the expression to its right, and returns the value of the latter expression. This operator also can be overloaded.

10.3.3 Operators That Cannot Be Overloaded

Most of C++'s operators can be overloaded. Figure 10.2 shows the operators that cannot be overloaded.[1]

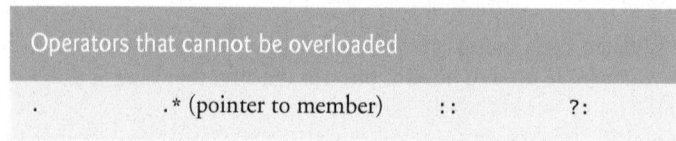

Operators that cannot be overloaded		
. .* (pointer to member) ::		?:

Fig. 10.2 | Operators that cannot be overloaded.

10.3.4 Rules and Restrictions on Operator Overloading

As you prepare to overload operators for your own classes, there are several rules and restrictions you should keep in mind:

- *An operator's precedence cannot be changed by overloading.* Parentheses can be used to *force* the order of evaluation of overloaded operators in an expression.

- *An operator's associativity cannot be changed by overloading*—if an operator normally associates from left to right, then so do all of its overloaded versions.

- *An operator's "arity"* (that is, the number of operands an operator takes) *cannot be changed*—overloaded unary operators remain unary operators; overloaded binary operators remain binary operators. C++'s only ternary operator, ?:, cannot be overloaded. Operators &, *, + and - all have both unary and binary versions that can be separately overloaded.

- *Only existing operators can be overloaded*—you cannot create new ones.

- You *cannot* overload operators to change how an operator works on fundamental-type values. For example, you cannot make the + operator subtract two ints. Operator overloading works only with *objects of user-defined types or with a mixture of an object of a user-defined type and an object of a fundamental type.*

- Related operators, like + and +=, must be overloaded separately.

- When overloading (), [], -> or any of the assignment operators, the operator overloading function *must* be declared as a class member. For all other overload-

---

1. Although it's possible to overload the address (&), comma (,), && and || operators, you should avoid doing so to avoid subtle errors. For insights on this, see CERT guideline DCL10-CPP.

able operators, the operator overloading functions can be member functions or non-member functions.

Software Engineering Observation 10.1
Overload operators for class types so they work as closely as possible to the way built-in operators work on fundamental types.

10.4 Overloading Binary Operators

A binary operator can be overloaded as a non-`static` member function with one parameter or as a non-member function with two parameters (one of those parameters must be either a class object or a reference to a class object). A non-member operator function often is declared as `friend` of a class for performance reasons.

Binary Overloaded Operators as Member Functions

Consider using `<` to compare two objects of a `String` class that you define. When overloading binary operator `<` as a non-`static` member function, if y and z are `String`-class objects, then y `<` z is treated by the compiler as if y.operator<(z) had been written, invoking the operator< member function with one argument declared below:

```
class String {
public:
    bool operator<(const String&) const;
    ...
};
```

Overloaded operator functions for binary operators can be member functions *only* when the *left* operand is an object of the class in which the function is a member.

Binary Overloaded Operators as Non-Member Functions

As a non-member function, binary operator `<` *must* take *two* arguments—*one* of which *must* be an object (or a reference to an object) of the class that the overloaded operator is associated with. If y and z are `String`-class objects or references to `String`-class objects, then y `<` z is treated as if the call operator<(y, z) had been written in the program, invoking function operator<, which is declared as follows:

```
bool operator<(const String&, const String&);
```

10.5 Overloading the Binary Stream Insertion and Stream Extraction Operators

You can input and output fundamental-type data using the stream extraction operator `>>` and the stream insertion operator `<<`, respectively. The C++ class libraries overload these binary operators for each fundamental type, including pointers and char * strings. You can also overload these operators to perform input and output for your own types. The program of Figs. 10.3–10.5 overloads these operators to input `PhoneNumber` objects in the format

```
(555) 555-5555
```

and to output them in the format

```
Area code: 555
Exchange: 555
Line: 5555
(555) 555-5555
```

The program assumes telephone numbers are input correctly.

```cpp
1   // Fig. 10.3: PhoneNumber.h
2   // PhoneNumber class definition
3   #ifndef PHONENUMBER_H
4   #define PHONENUMBER_H
5
6   #include <iostream>
7   #include <string>
8
9   class PhoneNumber {
10     friend std::ostream& operator<<(std::ostream&, const PhoneNumber&);
11     friend std::istream& operator>>(std::istream&, PhoneNumber&);
12  private:
13     std::string areaCode; // 3-digit area code
14     std::string exchange; // 3-digit exchange
15     std::string line; // 4-digit line
16  };
17
18  #endif
```

Fig. 10.3 | PhoneNumber class with overloaded stream insertion and stream extraction operators as `friend` functions.

```cpp
1   // Fig. 10.4: PhoneNumber.cpp
2   // Overloaded stream insertion and stream extraction operators
3   // for class PhoneNumber.
4   #include <iomanip>
5   #include "PhoneNumber.h"
6   using namespace std;
7
8   // overloaded stream insertion operator; cannot be a member function
9   // if we would like to invoke it with cout << somePhoneNumber;
10  ostream& operator<<(ostream& output, const PhoneNumber& number) {
11     output << "Area code: " << number.areaCode << "\nExchange: "
12        << number.exchange << "\nLine: " << number.line << "\n"
13        << "(" << number.areaCode << ") " << number.exchange << "-"
14        << number.line << "\n";
15     return output; // enables cout << a << b << c;
16  }
17
```

Fig. 10.4 | Overloaded stream insertion and stream extraction operators for class PhoneNumber. (Part 1 of 2.)

```
18   // overloaded stream extraction operator; cannot be a member function
19   // if we would like to invoke it with cin >> somePhoneNumber;
20   istream& operator>>(istream& input, PhoneNumber& number) {
21      input.ignore(); // skip (
22      input >> setw(3) >> number.areaCode; // input area code
23      input.ignore(2); // skip ) and space
24      input >> setw(3) >> number.exchange; // input exchange
25      input.ignore(); // skip dash (-)
26      input >> setw(4) >> number.line; // input line
27      return input; // enables cin >> a >> b >> c;
28   }
```

Fig. 10.4 | Overloaded stream insertion and stream extraction operators for class PhoneNumber. (Part 2 of 2.)

```
 1   // Fig. 10.5: fig10_05.cpp
 2   // Demonstrating class PhoneNumber's overloaded stream insertion
 3   // and stream extraction operators.
 4   #include <iostream>
 5   #include "PhoneNumber.h"
 6   using namespace std;
 7
 8   int main() {
 9      PhoneNumber phone; // create object phone
10
11      cout << "Enter phone number in the form (555) 555-5555:" << endl;
12
13      // cin >> phone invokes operator>> by implicitly issuing
14      // the non-member function call operator>>(cin, phone)
15      cin >> phone;
16
17      cout << "\nThe phone number entered was:\n";
18
19      // cout << phone invokes operator<< by implicitly issuing
20      // the non-member function call operator<<(cout, phone)
21      cout << phone << endl;
22   }
```

```
Enter phone number in the form (555) 555-5555:
(800) 555-1212

The phone number entered was:
Area code: 800
Exchange: 555
Line: 1212
(800) 555-1212
```

Fig. 10.5 | Overloaded stream insertion and stream extraction operators.

Overloading the Stream Extraction (>>) Operator

The stream extraction operator function operator>> (Fig. 10.4, lines 20–28) takes the istream reference input and the PhoneNumber reference number as arguments and returns an `istream` reference. The function inputs phone numbers of the form (555) 555-5555 into objects of class `PhoneNumber`. When the compiler sees the expression

```
cin >> phone
```

in line 15 of Fig. 10.5, the compiler generates the *non-member function call*

```
operator>>(cin, phone);
```

When this call executes, reference parameter `input` (Fig. 10.4, line 20) becomes an alias for `cin` and reference parameter `number` becomes an alias for `phone`.

The operator function reads as `string`s the three parts of the telephone number into the `areaCode` (line 22), `exchange` (line 24) and `line` (line 26) data members of the `PhoneNumber` object referenced by parameter `number`—the function is a friend of the class, so it can access a `PhoneNumber`'s `private` members. Stream manipulator `setw` limits the number of characters read into each `string`. *When used with `cin` and `strings`, `setw` restricts the number of characters read to the number of characters specified by its argument* (i.e., `setw(3)` allows three characters to be read). The parentheses, space and dash characters are skipped by calling `istream` member function `ignore` (Fig. 10.4, lines 21, 23 and 25), which discards the specified number of characters in the input stream (one character by default).

Function `operator>>` returns `istream` reference `input` (the alias for `cin`). This enables input operations on `PhoneNumber` objects to be *cascaded* with input operations on other `PhoneNumber` objects or other data types. For example, a program can input two `PhoneNumber` objects in one statement as follows:

```
cin >> phone1 >> phone2;
```

First, the expression `cin >> phone1` executes by making the non-member function call

```
operator>>(cin, phone1);
```

This call then returns a reference to `cin` as the value of `cin >> phone1`, so the remaining portion of the expression is interpreted as `cin >> phone2`. This executes by making the non-member function call

```
operator>>(cin, phone2);
```

Good Programming Practice 10.1

Overloaded operators should mimic the functionality of their built-in counterparts—e.g., the + operator should perform addition, not subtraction. Avoid excessive or inconsistent use of operator overloading, as this can make a program cryptic and difficult to read.

Overloading the Stream Insertion (<<) Operator

The stream insertion operator function (Fig. 10.4, lines 10–16) takes an `ostream` reference (`output`) and a `const PhoneNumber` reference (`number`) as arguments and returns an `ostream` reference. Function `operator<<` displays objects of type `PhoneNumber`. When the compiler sees the expression

```
cout << phone
```

in line 21 of Fig. 10.5, the compiler generates the non-member function call

```
operator<<(cout, phone);
```

Function operator<< displays the parts of the telephone number as strings, because they're stored as string objects. To prove that the stream extraction operator read the individual pieces of a PhoneNumber properly, function operator<< displays each data member separately, then displays a properly formatted phone number.

Overloaded Operators as Non-Member *friend* Functions

The functions operator>> and operator<< are declared in PhoneNumber as *non-member, friend functions* (Fig. 10.3, lines 10–11). They're *non-member functions* because the object of class PhoneNumber must be the operator's *right* operand. If these were to be PhoneNumber *member functions*, the following awkward statements would have to be used to output and input a PhoneNumber, respectively:

```
phone << cout;
phone >> cin;
```

Such statements would be confusing to most C++ programmers, who are familiar with cout and cin appearing as the *left* operands of these operators. Overloaded operator functions for binary operators can be member functions only when the *left* operand is an object of the class in which the function is a member.

Overloaded input and output operators are declared as friends *if they need to access non-*public *class members directly for performance or because the class may not offer appropriate* get *functions.* Also, the PhoneNumber reference in function operator<<'s parameter list (Fig. 10.4, line 10) is const, because the function simply outputs a PhoneNumber, and the PhoneNumber reference in function operator>>'s parameter list (line 20) is non-const, because the function must modify the PhoneNumber object to store the telephone number.

Software Engineering Observation 10.2
New input/output capabilities for user-defined types are added to C++ without modifying standard input/output library classes. This is another example of C++'s extensibility.

The overloaded stream insertion operator (<<) is used in an expression in which the left operand has type ostream&, as in cout << classObject. To use the operator in this manner where the *right* operand is an object of a user-defined class, it must be overloaded as a *non-member function*. To be a member function, operator << would have to be a member of class ostream. This is not possible for user-defined classes, since we are *not allowed to modify C++ Standard Library classes*. Similarly, the overloaded stream extraction operator (>>) is used in an expression in which the *left* operand has the type istream&, as in cin >> classObject, and the *right* operand is an object of a user-defined class, so it, too, must be a *non-member function*. Also, each of these overloaded operator functions may require access to the private data members of the class object being output or input, so these overloaded operator functions can be made friend functions of the class for performance reasons.

10.6 Overloading Unary Operators

A unary operator for a class can be overloaded as a non-static member function with no arguments or as a non-member function with one argument that must be an object (or a reference to an object) of the class. Member functions that implement overloaded operators must be non-`static` so that they can access the non-`static` data in each object of the class.

Unary Overloaded Operators as Member Functions

Consider overloading unary operator ! to test whether an object of your own `String` class is empty. Such a function would return a `bool` result. When a unary operator such as ! is overloaded as a member function with no arguments and the compiler sees the expression !s (in which s is an object of class `String`), the compiler generates the function call s.op-erator!(). The operand s is the `String` object for which the `String` class member function operator! is being invoked. The function is declared as follows:

```
class String {
public:
    bool operator!() const;
    ...
};
```

Unary Overloaded Operators as Non-Member Functions

A unary operator such as ! may be overloaded as a *non-member function* with one parameter. If s is a `String` class object (or a reference to a `String` class object), then !s is treated as if the call operator!(s) had been written, invoking the *non-member* operator! function that's declared as follows:

```
bool operator!(const String&);
```

10.7 Overloading the Increment and Decrement Operators

The prefix and postfix versions of the increment and decrement operators can all be overloaded. We'll see how the compiler distinguishes between the prefix version and the postfix version of an increment or decrement operator.

To overload the prefix and postfix increment operators, each overloaded operator function must have a distinct signature, so that the compiler will be able to determine which version of ++ is intended. The prefix versions are overloaded exactly as any other prefix unary operator would be. Everything stated in this section for overloading prefix and postfix increment operators applies to overloading predecrement and postdecrement operators. In the next section, we examine a `Date` class with overloaded prefix and postfix increment operators.

Overloading the Prefix Increment Operator

Suppose that we want to add 1 to the day in a `Date` object named d1. When the compiler sees the preincrementing expression ++d1, if the overloaded operator is defined as a member function, the compiler generates the *member-function call*

```
d1.operator++()
```

The prototype for this operator member function would be

```
Date& operator++();
```

If the prefix increment operator is implemented as a *non-member function*, then, when the compiler sees the expression ++d1, the compiler generates the function call

```
operator++(d1)
```

The prototype for this non-member operator function would be declared as

```
Date& operator++(Date&);
```

Overloading the Postfix Increment Operator

Overloading the postfix increment operator presents a challenge, because the compiler must be able to distinguish between the signatures of the overloaded prefix and postfix increment operator functions. The convention that has been adopted is that, when the compiler sees the postincrementing expression d1++, it generates the member-function call

```
d1.operator++(0)
```

The prototype for this operator member function is

```
Date operator++(int)
```

The argument 0 is strictly a *dummy value* that enables the compiler to distinguish between the prefix and postfix increment operator functions. The same syntax is used to differentiate between the prefix and postfix decrement operator functions.

If the postfix increment is implemented as a *non-member function*, then, when the compiler sees the expression d1++, the compiler generates the function call

```
operator++(d1, 0)
```

The prototype for this function would be

```
Date operator++(Date&, int);
```

Once again, the 0 argument is used by the compiler to distinguish between the prefix and postfix increment operators implemented as non-member functions. Note that the *postfix increment operator* returns Date objects *by value*, whereas the prefix increment operator returns Date objects *by reference*—the postfix increment operator typically returns a temporary object that contains the original value of the object before the increment occurred. C++ treats such objects as *rvalues*, which *cannot be used on the left side of an assignment*. The prefix increment operator returns the actual incremented object with its new value. Such an object *can* be used as an *lvalue* in a continuing expression.

Performance Tip 10.1
The extra object that's created by the postfix *increment (or decrement) operator can result in a performance problem—especially when the operator is used in a loop. For this reason, you should prefer the overloaded* prefix *increment and decrement operators.*

10.8 Case Study: A Date Class

The program of Figs. 10.6–10.8 demonstrates a Date class, which uses overloaded prefix and postfix increment operators to add 1 to the day in a Date object, while causing appropriate increments to the month and year if necessary. The Date header (Fig. 10.6) specifies that Date's public interface includes an overloaded stream insertion operator (line 10), a default constructor (line 12), a `setDate` function (line 13), an overloaded prefix increment operator (line 14), an overloaded postfix increment operator (line 15), an overloaded += addition assignment operator (line 16), a function to test for leap years (line 17) and a function to determine whether a day is the last day of the month (line 18).

```cpp
1   // Fig. 10.6: Date.h
2   // Date class definition with overloaded increment operators.
3   #ifndef DATE_H
4   #define DATE_H
5
6   #include <array>
7   #include <iostream>
8
9   class Date {
10     friend std::ostream& operator<<(std::ostream&, const Date&);
11  public:
12     Date(int m = 1, int d = 1, int y = 1900); // default constructor
13     void setDate(int, int, int); // set month, day, year
14     Date& operator++(); // prefix increment operator
15     Date operator++(int); // postfix increment operator
16     Date& operator+=(unsigned int); // add days, modify object
17     static bool leapYear(int); // is year a leap year?
18     bool endOfMonth(int) const; // is day at the end of month?
19  private:
20     unsigned int month;
21     unsigned int day;
22     unsigned int year;
23
24     static const std::array<unsigned int, 13> days; // days per month
25     void helpIncrement(); // utility function for incrementing date
26  };
27
28  #endif
```

Fig. 10.6 | Date class definition with overloaded increment operators.

```cpp
1   // Fig. 10.7: Date.cpp
2   // Date class member- and friend-function definitions.
3   #include <iostream>
4   #include <string>
5   #include "Date.h"
6   using namespace std;
7
8   // initialize static member; one classwide copy
9   const array<unsigned int, 13> Date::days{
10     0, 31, 28, 31, 30, 31, 30, 31, 31, 30, 31, 30, 31};
11
12  // Date constructor
13  Date::Date(int month, int day, int year) {
14     setDate(month, day, year);
15  }
```

Fig. 10.7 | Date class member- and friend-function definitions. (Part 1 of 3.)

```
16
17   // set month, day and year
18   void Date::setDate(int mm, int dd, int yy) {
19      if (mm >= 1 && mm <= 12) {
20         month = mm;
21      }
22      else {
23         throw invalid_argument{"Month must be 1-12"};
24      }
25
26      if (yy >= 1900 && yy <= 2100) {
27         year = yy;
28      }
29      else {
30         throw invalid_argument{"Year must be >= 1900 and <= 2100"};
31      }
32
33      // test for a leap year
34      if ((mn == 2 && leapYear(year) && dd >= 1 && dd <= 29) ||
35          (dd >= 1 && dd <= days[mn])) {
36         day = dd;
37      }
38      else {
39         throw invalid_argument{
40            "Day is out of range for current month and year"};
41      }
42   }
43
44   // overloaded prefix increment operator
45   Date& Date::operator++() {
46      helpIncrement(); // increment date
47      return *this; // reference return to create an lvalue
48   }
49
50   // overloaded postfix increment operator; note that the
51   // dummy integer parameter does not have a parameter name
52   Date Date::operator++(int) {
53      Date temp{*this}; // hold current state of object
54      helpIncrement();
55
56      // return unincremented, saved, temporary object
57      return temp; // value return; not a reference return
58   }
59
60   // add specified number of days to date
61   Date& Date::operator+=(unsigned int additionalDays) {
62      for (unsigned int i = 0; i < additionalDays; ++i) {
63         helpIncrement();
64      }
65
66      return *this; // enables cascading
67   }
68
```

Fig. 10.7 | Date class member- and friend-function definitions. (Part 2 of 3.)

```
69   // if the year is a leap year, return true; otherwise, return false
70   bool Date::leapYear(int testYear) {
71      return (testYear % 400 == 0 ||
72         (testYear % 100 != 0 && testYear % 4 == 0));
73   }
74
75   // determine whether the day is the last day of the month
76   bool Date::endOfMonth(int testDay) const {
77      if (month == 2 && leapYear(year)) {
78         return testDay == 29; // last day of Feb. in leap year
79      }
80      else {
81         return testDay == days[month];
82      }
83   }
84
85   // function to help increment the date
86   void Date::helpIncrement() {
87      // day is not end of month
88      if (!endOfMonth(day)) {
89         ++day; // increment day
90      }
91      else {
92         if (month < 12) { // day is end of month and month < 12
93            ++month; // increment month
94            day = 1; // first day of new month
95         }
96         else { // last day of year
97            ++year; // increment year
98            month = 1; // first month of new year
99            day = 1; // first day of new month
100        }
101     }
102  }
103
104  // overloaded output operator
105  ostream& operator<<(ostream& output, const Date& d) {
106     static string monthName[13]{"", "January", "February",
107        "March", "April", "May", "June", "July", "August",
108        "September", "October", "November", "December"};
109     output << monthName[d.month] << ' ' << d.day << ", " << d.year;
110     return output; // enables cascading
111  }
```

Fig. 10.7 | Date class member- and friend-function definitions. (Part 3 of 3.)

```
1   // Fig. 10.8: fig10_08.cpp
2   // Date class test program.
3   #include <iostream>
4   #include "Date.h" // Date class definition
5   using namespace std;
6
```

Fig. 10.8 | Date class test program. (Part 1 of 2.)

```
 7   int main() {
 8      Date d1{12, 27, 2010}; // December 27, 2010
 9      Date d2; // defaults to January 1, 1900
10
11      cout << "d1 is " << d1 << "\nd2 is " << d2;
12      cout << "\n\nd1 += 7 is " << (d1 += 7);
13
14      d2.setDate(2, 28, 2008);
15      cout << "\n\n  d2 is " << d2;
16      cout << "\n++d2 is " << ++d2 << " (leap year allows 29th)";
17
18      Date d3{7, 13, 2010};
19
20      cout << "\n\nTesting the prefix increment operator:\n"
21         << "  d3 is " << d3 << endl;
22      cout << "++d3 is " << ++d3 << endl;
23      cout << "  d3 is " << d3;
24
25      cout << "\n\nTesting the postfix increment operator:\n"
26         << "  d3 is " << d3 << endl;
27      cout << "d3++ is " << d3++ << endl;
28      cout << "  d3 is " << d3 << endl;
29   }
```

```
d1 is December 27, 2010
d2 is January 1, 1900

d1 += 7 is January 3, 2011

  d2 is February 28, 2008
++d2 is February 29, 2008 (leap year allows 29th)

Testing the prefix increment operator:
  d3 is July 13, 2010
++d3 is July 14, 2010
  d3 is July 14, 2010

Testing the postfix increment operator:
  d3 is July 14, 2010
d3++ is July 14, 2010
  d3 is July 15, 2010
```

Fig. 10.8 | Date class test program. (Part 2 of 2.)

Function main (Fig. 10.8) creates two Date objects (lines 8–9)—d1 is initialized to December 27, 2010 and d2 is initialized by default to January 1, 1900. The Date constructor (defined in Fig. 10.7, lines 13–15) calls setDate (defined in Fig. 10.7, lines 18–42) to validate the month, day and year specified. Invalid values for the month, day or year result in invalid_argument exceptions.

Line 11 of main (Fig. 10.8) outputs each Date object, using the overloaded stream insertion operator (defined in Fig. 10.7, lines 105–111). Line 12 of main uses the overloaded operator += (defined in Fig. 10.7, lines 61–67) to add seven days to d1. Line 14 in Fig. 10.8 uses function setDate to set d2 to February 28, 2008, which is a leap year. Then, line 16 preincrements d2 to show that the date increments properly to February 29. Next, line 18 creates a Date object, d3, which is initialized with the date July 13, 2010. Then line 22 increments d3 by 1 with the overloaded prefix increment operator. Lines 20–23 output d3 before and after the preincrement operation to confirm that it worked correctly. Finally, line 27 increments d3 with the overloaded postfix increment operator. Lines 25–28 output d3 before and after the postincrement operation to confirm that it worked correctly.

Date *Class Prefix Increment Operator*

Overloading the prefix increment operator is straightforward. The prefix increment operator (defined in Fig. 10.7, lines 45–48) calls utility function helpIncrement (defined in lines 86–102) to increment the date. This function deals with "wraparounds" or "carries" that occur when we increment past a month's last day, which requires incrementing the month. If the month is already 12, then the year must also be incremented and the month must be set to 1. Function helpIncrement uses function endOfMonth to determine whether the end of a month has been reached and increment the day correctly.

The overloaded prefix increment operator returns a reference to the current Date object (i.e., the one that was just incremented). This occurs because the current object, *this, is returned as a Date&. This enables a preincremented Date object to be used as an *lvalue*, which is how the built-in prefix increment operator works for fundamental types.

Date *Class Postfix Increment Operator*

Overloading the postfix increment operator (defined in Fig. 10.7, lines 52–58) is trickier. To emulate the effect of the postincrement, we must return an *unincremented copy* of the Date object. For example, if int variable x has the value 7, the statement

```
cout << x++ << endl;
```

outputs the *original* value of x. We'd like our postfix increment operator to operate the same way on a Date object. On entry to operator++, we save the current object (*this) in temp (line 53). Next, we call helpIncrement to increment the current Date object. Then, line 57 returns temp—the *unincremented copy* of the original Date object. This function *cannot* return a reference to the local Date object temp, because a local variable is destroyed when the function in which it's declared exits. Thus, declaring the return type to this function as Date& would return a reference to an object that no longer exists.

10.9 Dynamic Memory Management

You can control the *allocation* and *deallocation* of memory in a program for objects and for arrays of any built-in or user-defined type. This is known as dynamic memory management and is performed with the operators new and delete. We'll use these capabilities to implement our Array class in the next section.

You can use the new operator to dynamically allocate (i.e., reserve) the exact amount of memory required to hold an object or built-in array at execution time. The object or built-in array is created in the free store (also called the heap)—a region of memory assigned to each program for storing dynamically allocated objects.[2] Once memory is allo-

---

2. Operator new could fail to obtain the needed memory, in which case a bad_alloc exception would occur. Chapter 17 shows how to deal with new failures.

cated, you can access it via the pointer returned by operator new. When you no longer need the memory, you can *return* it to the free store by using the delete operator to deallocate (i.e., release) the memory, which can then be reused by future new operations.[3]

Obtaining Dynamic Memory with **new**
Consider the following statement:

```
Time* timePtr{new Time};
```

The new operator allocates storage of the proper size for an object of type Time, calls a constructor to initialize the object and returns a pointer to the type specified to the right of the new operator (i.e., a Time *). In the preceding statement, class Time's default constructor is called, because we did not supply arguments to initialize the Time object. If new is unable to find sufficient space in memory for the object, it indicates that an error occurred by throwing an exception.

Releasing Dynamic Memory with **delete**
To destroy a dynamically allocated object and free the space for the object, use the delete operator as follows:

```
delete timePtr;
```

This statement first calls the destructor for the object to which timePtr points, then deallocates the memory associated with the object, returning the memory to the free store.

Common Programming Error 10.1
Not releasing dynamically allocated memory when it's no longer needed can cause the system to run out of memory prematurely. This is sometimes called a "memory leak."

Error-Prevention Tip 10.1
Do not delete memory that was not allocated by new. Doing so results in undefined behavior.

Error-Prevention Tip 10.2
After you delete a block of dynamically allocated memory, be sure not to delete the same block again. One way to guard against this is to immediately set the pointer to nullptr. Deleting a nullptr has no effect.

Initializing Dynamic Memory
You can provide an initializer for a newly created fundamental-type variable, as in

```
double* ptr{new double{3.14159}};
```

which initializes a newly created double to 3.14159 and assigns the resulting pointer to ptr. The same syntax can be used to specify arguments to an object's constructor, as in

```
Time* timePtr{new Time{12, 45, 0}};
```

which initializes a new Time object to 12:45 PM and assigns its pointer to timePtr.

---

3. Operators new and delete *can* be overloaded, but this is beyond the scope of the book. If you do overload new, then you should overload delete in the same scope to avoid subtle dynamic memory management errors.

*Dynamically Allocating Built-In Arrays with **new[]***
You can also use the new operator to allocate built-in arrays dynamically. For example, a 10-element integer array can be allocated and assigned to gradesArray as follows:

```
int* gradesArray{new int[10]{}};
```

which declares int pointer gradesArray and assigns to it a pointer to the first element of a dynamically allocated 10-element array of ints. The list-initializer braces following new int[10]—which are allowed as of C++11—initialize the array's elements, setting fundamental-type elements to 0, bools to false and pointers to nullptr. If the elements are class objects, they're initialized by their default constructors. The list-initializer braces may also contain a comma-separated list of initializers for the array's elements.

The size of a built-in array created at compile time must be specified using an integral constant expression; however, a dynamically allocated array's size can be specified using *any* nonnegative integral expression that can be evaluated at execution time.

*Releasing Dynamically Allocated Built-In Arrays with **delete[]***
To deallocate the memory to which gradesArray points, use the statement

```
delete[] gradesArray;
```

If the pointer points to a built-in array of objects, the statement first calls the destructor for every object in the array, then deallocates the memory. If the preceding statement did *not* include the square brackets ([]) and gradesArray pointed to a built-in array of objects, the result is *undefined*—some compilers call the destructor only for the first object in the array. Using delete or delete[] on a nullptr has no effect.

> **Common Programming Error 10.2**
> *Using delete instead of delete[] for built-in arrays of objects can lead to runtime logic errors. To ensure that every object in the array receives a destructor call, always delete memory allocated as an array with operator delete[]. Similarly, always delete memory allocated as an individual element with operator delete—the result of deleting a single object with operator delete[] is undefined.*

*C++11: Managing Dynamically Allocated Memory with **unique_ptr***
C++11's unique_ptr is a "smart pointer" for managing dynamically allocated memory. When a unique_ptr goes out of scope, its destructor *automatically* returns the managed memory to the free store. In Chapter 17, we introduce unique_ptr and show how to use it to manage dynamically allocated objects or a dynamically allocated built-in arrays.

10.10 Case Study: Array Class

We discussed built-in arrays in Chapter 8. Pointer-based arrays have many problems, including:

- A program can easily "walk off" either end of a built-in array, because *C++ does not check whether subscripts fall outside the range of the array* (though you can still do this explicitly).

- Built-in arrays of size *n* must number their elements 0, ..., *n* – 1; alternate subscript ranges are *not* allowed.

- An entire built-in array cannot be input or output at once; each element must be read or written individually (unless the array is a null-terminated C string).

- Two built-in arrays cannot be meaningfully compared with equality or relational operators (because the array names are simply pointers to where the arrays begin in memory and two arrays will always be at different memory locations).

- When a built-in array is passed to a general-purpose function designed to handle arrays of any size, the array's *size* must be passed as an additional argument.

- One built-in array cannot be assigned to another with the assignment operator(s).

Class development is an interesting, creative and intellectually challenging activity—always with the goal of crafting valuable classes. With C++, you can implement more robust array capabilities via classes and operator overloading as has been done with class templates array and vector in the C++ Standard Library. In this section, we'll develop our own custom array class that's preferable to built-in arrays. When we refer to "arrays" in this case study, we mean built-in arrays.

In this example, we create a powerful Array class that performs range checking to ensure that subscripts remain within the bounds of the Array. The class allows one Array object to be assigned to another with the assignment operator. Array objects know their size, so the size does not need to be passed separately to functions that receive Array parameters. Entire Arrays can be input or output with the stream extraction and stream insertion operators, respectively. You can compare Arrays with the equality operators == and !=.

As a new C++ programmer, you're likely to encounter C++ legacy code that uses older C++ features and techniques. Though current C++ compilers fully support using smart pointers to simplify dynamic memory management, we explicitly manage class Array's dynamic memory using built-in pointers and operators new and delete to help you understand, maintain and modify the code you'll see in industry.

10.10.1 Using the Array Class

The program of Figs. 10.9–10.11 demonstrates class Array and its overloaded operators. First we walk through main (Fig. 10.9) and the program's output, then we consider the class definition (Fig. 10.10) and each of its member-function definitions (Fig. 10.11).

```
 1   // Fig. 10.9: fig10_09.cpp
 2   // Array class test program.
 3   #include <iostream>
 4   #include <stdexcept>
 5   #include "Array.h"
 6   using namespace std;
 7
 8   int main() {
 9      Array integers1{7}; // seven-element Array
10      Array integers2; // 10-element Array by default
11
12      // print integers1 size and contents
13      cout << "Size of Array integers1 is " << integers1.getSize()
14         << "\nArray after initialization: " << integers1;
```

Fig. 10.9 | Array class test program. (Part 1 of 3.)

```
15
16      // print integers2 size and contents
17      cout << "\nSize of Array integers2 is " << integers2.getSize()
18         << "\nArray after initialization: " << integers2;
19
20      // input and print integers1 and integers2
21      cout << "\nEnter 17 integers:" << endl;
22      cin >> integers1 >> integers2;
23
24      cout << "\nAfter input, the Arrays contain:\n"
25         << "integers1: " << integers1
26         << "integers2: " << integers2;
27
28      // use overloaded inequality (!=) operator
29      cout << "\nEvaluating: integers1 != integers2" << endl;
30
31      if (integers1 != integers2) {
32         cout << "integers1 and integers2 are not equal" << endl;
33      }
34
35      // create Array integers3 using integers1 as an
36      // initializer; print size and contents
37      Array integers3{integers1}; // invokes copy constructor
38
39      cout << "\nSize of Array integers3 is " << integers3.getSize()
40         << "\nArray after initialization: " << integers3;
41
42      // use overloaded assignment (=) operator
43      cout << "\nAssigning integers2 to integers1:" << endl;
44      integers1 = integers2; // note target Array is smaller
45
46      cout << "integers1: " << integers1 << "integers2: " << integers2;
47
48      // use overloaded equality (==) operator
49      cout << "\nEvaluating: integers1 == integers2" << endl;
50
51      if (integers1 == integers2) {
52         cout << "integers1 and integers2 are equal" << endl;
53      }
54
55      // use overloaded subscript operator to create rvalue
56      cout << "\nintegers1[5] is " << integers1[5];
57
58      // use overloaded subscript operator to create lvalue
59      cout << "\n\nAssigning 1000 to integers1[5]" << endl;
60      integers1[5] = 1000;
61      cout << "integers1: " << integers1;
62
63      // attempt to use out-of-range subscript
64      try {
65         cout << "\nAttempt to assign 1000 to integers1[15]" << endl;
66         integers1[15] = 1000; // ERROR: subscript out of range
67      }
```

Fig. 10.9 | Array class test program. (Part 2 of 3.)

```
68        catch (out_of_range& ex) {
69            cout << "An exception occurred: " << ex.what() << endl;
70        }
71    }
```

```
Size of Array integers1 is 7
Array after initialization: 0  0  0  0  0  0  0

Size of Array integers2 is 10
Array after initialization: 0  0  0  0  0  0  0  0  0  0

Enter 17 integers:
1 2 3 4 5 6 7 8 9 10 11 12 13 14 15 16 17

After input, the Arrays contain:
integers1: 1  2  3  4  5  6  7
integers2: 8  9  10  11  12  13  14  15  16  17

Evaluating: integers1 != integers2
integers1 and integers2 are not equal

Size of Array integers3 is 7
Array after initialization: 1  2  3  4  5  6  7

Assigning integers2 to integers1:
integers1: 8  9  10  11  12  13  14  15  16  17
integers2: 8  9  10  11  12  13  14  15  16  17

Evaluating: integers1 == integers2
integers1 and integers2 are equal

integers1[5] is 13

Assigning 1000 to integers1[5]
integers1: 8  9  10  11  12  1000  14  15  16  17

Attempt to assign 1000 to integers1[15]
An exception occurred: Subscript out of range
```

Fig. 10.9 | Array class test program. (Part 3 of 3.)

Creating *Arrays, Outputting Their Size and Displaying Their Contents*

The program begins by instantiating two objects of class Array—integers1 (Fig. 10.9, line 9) with seven elements, and integers2 (line 10) with the default Array size—10 elements (specified by the Array default constructor's prototype in Fig. 10.10, line 13). Lines 13–14 in Fig. 10.9 use member function getSize to determine the size of integers1, then output integers1's contents, using the Array overloaded stream insertion operator. The sample output confirms that the Array elements were set correctly to zeros by the constructor. Next, lines 17–18 output the size of Array integers2, then output integers2's contents, using the Array overloaded stream insertion operator.

Using the Overloaded Stream Extraction Operator to Fill an *Array*

Line 21 prompts the user to input 17 integers. Line 22 uses the Array overloaded stream extraction operator to read the first seven values into integers1 and the remaining 10 values into `integers2`. Lines 24–26 output the two arrays with the overloaded `Array` stream insertion operator to confirm that the input was performed correctly.

Using the Overloaded Inequality Operator
Line 31 tests the overloaded inequality operator by evaluating the condition

```
integers1 != integers2
```

The program output shows that the `Array`s are not equal.

Initializing a New Array with a Copy of an Existing Array's Contents
Line 37 instantiates a third `Array` called `integers3` and initializes it with a copy of `Array` `integers1`. This invokes class `Array`'s copy constructor to copy the elements of `integers1` into `integers3`. We discuss the details of the copy constructor shortly. The copy constructor can also be invoked by writing line 37 as follows:

```
Array integers3 = integers1;
```

The equal sign in the preceding statement is *not* the assignment operator. When an equal sign appears in the declaration of an object, it invokes a constructor for that object. This form can be used to pass only a single argument to a constructor—specifically, the value on the right side of the = symbol.

Lines 39–40 output the size of `integers3`, then output `integers3`'s contents, using the `Array` overloaded stream insertion operator to confirm that `integers3`'s elements were set correctly by the copy constructor.

Using the Overloaded Assignment Operator
Line 44 tests the overloaded assignment operator (=) by assigning `integers2` to `integers1`. Line 46 display both `Array` objects' contents to confirm that the assignment was successful. `Array` `integers1` originally held 7 integers, but was resized to hold a copy of the 10 elements in `integers2`. As we'll see, the overloaded assignment operator performs this resizing operation in a manner that's transparent to the client code.

Using the Overloaded Equality Operator
Line 51 uses the overloaded equality operator (==) to confirm that objects `integers1` and `integers2` are indeed *identical* after the assignment in line 44.

Using the Overloaded Subscript Operator
Line 56 uses the overloaded subscript operator to refer to `integers1[5]`—an in-range element of `integers1`. This subscripted name is used as an *rvalue* to print the value stored in `integers1[5]`. Line 60 uses `integers1[5]` as a modifiable *lvalue* on the left side of an assignment statement to assign a new value, 1000, to element 5 of `integers1`. We'll see that `operator[]` returns a reference to use as the modifiable *lvalue* after the operator confirms that 5 is a valid subscript for `integers1`.

Line 66 attempts to assign the value 1000 to `integers1[15]`—an *out-of-range* element. In this example, `operator[]` determines that the subscript is out of range and throws an `out_of_range` exception.

Interestingly, the array subscript operator [] is not restricted for use only with arrays; it also can be used, for example, to select elements from other kinds of *container classes*, such as strings and dictionaries. Also, when overloaded operator[] functions are defined, *subscripts no longer have to be integers*—characters, strings or even objects of user-defined classes also could be used. In Chapter 15, we discuss the Standard Library map class that allows string subscripts.

10.10.2 Array Class Definition

Now that we've seen how this program operates, let's walk through the class header (Fig. 10.10). As we refer to each member function in the header, we discuss that function's implementation in Fig. 10.11. In Fig. 10.10, lines 32–33 represent the private data members of class Array. Each Array object consists of a size member indicating the number of elements in the Array and an int pointer—ptr—that points to the dynamically allocated pointer-based array of integers managed by the Array object.

```cpp
 1  // Fig. 10.10: Array.h
 2  // Array class definition with overloaded operators.
 3  #ifndef ARRAY_H
 4  #define ARRAY_H
 5
 6  #include <iostream>
 7
 8  class Array {
 9     friend std::ostream& operator<<(std::ostream&, const Array&);
10     friend std::istream& operator>>(std::istream&, Array&);
11
12  public:
13     explicit Array(int = 10); // default constructor
14     Array(const Array&); // copy constructor
15     ~Array(); // destructor
16     size_t getSize() const; // return size
17
18     const Array& operator=(const Array&); // assignment operator
19     bool operator==(const Array&) const; // equality operator
20
21     // inequality operator; returns opposite of == operator
22     bool operator!=(const Array& right) const {
23        return ! (*this == right); // invokes Array::operator==
24     }
25
26     // subscript operator for non-const objects returns modifiable lvalue
27     int& operator[](int);
28
29     // subscript operator for const objects returns rvalue
30     int operator[](int) const;
31  private:
32     size_t size; // pointer-based array size
33     int* ptr; // pointer to first element of pointer-based array
34  };
35
36  #endif
```

Fig. 10.10 | Array class definition with overloaded operators.

```
1   // Fig. 10.11: Array.cpp
2   // Array class member- and friend-function definitions.
3   #include <iostream>
4   #include <iomanip>
5   #include <stdexcept>
6
7   #include "Array.h" // Array class definition
8   using namespace std;
9
10  // default constructor for class Array (default size 10)
11  Array::Array(int arraySize)
12     : size{(arraySize > 0 ? static_cast<size_t>(arraySize) :
13         throw invalid_argument{"Array size must be greater than 0"})},
14       ptr{new int[size]{}} { /* empty body */ }
15
16  // copy constructor for class Array;
17  // must receive a reference to an Array
18  Array::Array(const Array& arrayToCopy)
19     : size{arrayToCopy.size}, ptr{new int[size]} {
20     for (size_t i{0}; i < size; ++i) {
21        ptr[i] = arrayToCopy.ptr[i]; // copy into object
22     }
23  }
24
25  // destructor for class Array
26  Array::~Array() {
27     delete[] ptr; // release pointer-based array space
28  }
29
30  // return number of elements of Array
31  size_t Array::getSize() const {
32     return size; // number of elements in Array
33  }
34
35  // overloaded assignment operator;
36  // const return avoids: (a1 = a2) = a3
37  const Array& Array::operator=(const Array& right) {
38     if (&right != this) { // avoid self-assignment
39        // for Arrays of different sizes, deallocate original
40        // left-side Array, then allocate new left-side Array
41        if (size != right.size) {
42           delete[] ptr; // release space
43           size = right.size; // resize this object
44           ptr = new int[size]; // create space for Array copy
45        }
46
47        for (size_t i{0}; i < size; ++i) {
48           ptr[i] = right.ptr[i]; // copy array into object
49        }
50     }
51
52     return *this; // enables x = y = z, for example
53  }
```

Fig. 10.11 | Array class member- and friend-function definitions. (Part 1 of 3.)

```
54
55   // determine if two Arrays are equal and
56   // return true, otherwise return false
57   bool Array::operator==(const Array& right) const {
58      if (size != right.size) {
59         return false; // arrays of different number of elements
60      }
61
62      for (size_t i{0}; i < size; ++i) {
63         if (ptr[i] != right.ptr[i]) {
64            return false; // Array contents are not equal
65         }
66      }
67
68      return true; // Arrays are equal
69   }
70
71   // overloaded subscript operator for non-const Arrays;
72   // reference return creates a modifiable lvalue
73   int& Array::operator[](int subscript) {
74      // check for subscript out-of-range error
75      if (subscript < 0 || subscript >= size) {
76         throw out_of_range{"Subscript out of range"};
77      }
78
79      return ptr[subscript]; // reference return
80   }
81
82   // overloaded subscript operator for const Arrays
83   // const reference return creates an rvalue
84   int Array::operator[](int subscript) const {
85      // check for subscript out-of-range error
86      if (subscript < 0 || subscript >= size) {
87         throw out_of_range{"Subscript out of range"};
88      }
89
90      return ptr[subscript]; // returns copy of this element
91   }
92
93   // overloaded input operator for class Array;
94   // inputs values for entire Array
95   istream& operator>>(istream& input, Array& a) {
96      for (size_t i{0}; i < a.size; ++i) {
97         input >> a.ptr[i];
98      }
99
100     return input; // enables cin >> x >> y;
101  }
102
103  // overloaded output operator for class Array
104  ostream& operator<<(ostream& output, const Array& a) {
105     // output private ptr-based array
106     for (size_t i{0}; i < a.size; ++i) {
```

Fig. 10.11 | Array class member- and friend-function definitions. (Part 2 of 3.)

```
107        output << a.ptr[i] << " ";
108     }
109
110     output << endl;
111     return output; // enables cout << x << y;
112  }
```

Fig. 10.11 | Array class member- and `friend`-function definitions. (Part 3 of 3.)

Overloading the Stream Insertion and Stream Extraction Operators as *friends*

Lines 9–10 of Fig. 10.10 declare the overloaded stream insertion operator and the overloaded stream extraction operator as `friend`s of class `Array`. When the compiler sees an expression like `cout << arrayObject`, it invokes *non-member function* `operator<<` with the call

```
operator<<(cout, arrayObject)
```

When the compiler sees an expression like `cin >> arrayObject`, it invokes *non-member function* `operator>>` with the call

```
operator>>(cin, arrayObject)
```

Again, these stream insertion and stream extraction operator functions *cannot* be members of class `Array`, because the `Array` object is always mentioned on the *right* side of the stream insertion or stream extraction operator.

Function `operator<<` (defined in Fig. 10.11, lines 104–112) prints the number of elements indicated by `size` from the integer array to which `ptr` points. Function `operator>>` (defined in Fig. 10.11, lines 95–101) inputs directly into the array to which `ptr` points. Each of these operator functions returns an appropriate reference to enable *cascaded* output or input statements, respectively. These functions have access to an `Array`'s `private` data because they're declared as `friend`s of class `Array`. We could have used class `Array`'s `getSize` and `operator[]` functions in the bodies of `operator<<` and `operator>>`, in which case these operator functions would not need to be `friend`s of class `Array`.

Range-Based *for* Does Not Work with Dynamically Allocated Built-In Arrays

You might be tempted to replace the counter-controlled `for` statement in lines 96–98 (Fig. 10.11) and many of the other `for` statements in class `Array`'s implementation with the C++11 range-based `for` statement. Unfortunately, range-based `for` does *not* work with dynamically allocated built-in arrays.

Array Default Constructor

Line 13 of Fig. 10.10 declares the class's default constructor and specifies a default size of 10 elements. When the compiler sees a declaration like line 10 in Fig. 10.9, it invokes class `Array`'s default constructor to set the size of the `Array` to 10 elements. The default constructor (defined in Fig. 10.11, lines 11–14) validates and assigns the argument to data member `size`, uses `new` to obtain the memory for the *internal pointer-based representation* of this `Array` and assigns the pointer returned by `new` to data member `ptr`. The initializer for `ptr`

```
new int[size]{}
```

uses an empty initializer list to set all the elements of the dynamically allocated built-in array to 0.

Array Copy Constructor

Line 14 of Fig. 10.10 declares a copy constructor (defined in Fig. 10.11, lines 18–23) that initializes an Array by making a copy of an existing Array object. *Such copying must be done carefully to avoid the pitfall of leaving both Array objects pointing to the same dynamically allocated memory.* This is exactly the problem that would occur with default memberwise copying, if the compiler is allowed to define a default copy constructor for this class. Copy constructors are invoked whenever a copy of an object is needed, such as in

- passing an object by value to a function,
- returning an object by value from a function or
- initializing an object with a copy of another object of the same class.

The copy constructor is called in a declaration when an object of class Array is instantiated and initialized with another object of class Array, as in the declaration in line 37 of Fig. 10.9.

The copy constructor for Array copies the size of the initializer Array into data member size, uses new to obtain the memory for the internal pointer-based representation of this Array and assigns the pointer returned by new to data member ptr. Then the copy constructor uses a for statement to copy all the elements of the initializer Array into the new Array object. An object of a class can look at the private data of any other object of that class (using a handle that indicates which object to access).

Software Engineering Observation 10.3
The argument to a copy constructor should be a const reference to allow a const object to be copied.

Common Programming Error 10.3
If the copy constructor simply copied the pointer in the source object to the target object's pointer, then both would point to the same dynamically allocated memory. The first destructor to execute would delete the dynamically allocated memory, and the other object's ptr would point to memory that's no longer allocated, a situation called a dangling pointer—this would likely result in a serious runtime error (such as early program termination) when the pointer was used.

Array Destructor

Line 15 of Fig. 10.10 declares the class's destructor (defined in Fig. 10.11, lines 26–28). The destructor is invoked when an object of class Array goes out of scope. The destructor uses delete[] to release the memory allocated dynamically by new in the constructor.

Error-Prevention Tip 10.3
If after deleting dynamically allocated memory, the pointer will continue to exist in memory, set the pointer's value to nullptr to indicate that the pointer no longer points to memory in the free store. When the pointer is set to nullptr, the program loses access to that free-store space, which could be reallocated for a different purpose. If you do not set the pointer to nullptr, your code could inadvertently access the reallocated memory, causing subtle, nonrepeatable logic errors. We did not set ptr to nullptr in the destructor, because after the destructor executes, the Array object no longer exists in memory.

getSize *Member Function*
Line 16 of Fig. 10.10 declares function `getSize` (defined in Fig. 10.11, lines 31–33) that returns the number of elements in the `Array`.

Overloaded Assignment Operator
Line 18 of Fig. 10.10 declares the overloaded assignment operator function for the class. When the compiler sees the expression `integers1 = integers2` in line 44 of Fig. 10.9, the compiler invokes member function `operator=` with the call

```
integers1.operator=(integers2)
```

Member function `operator=`'s implementation (Fig. 10.11, lines 37–53) tests for self-assignment (line 38) in which an `Array` object is being assigned to itself. When `this` is equal to the `right` operand's address, a *self-assignment* is being attempted, so the assignment is skipped (i.e., the object already is itself; in a moment we'll see why self-assignment is dangerous). If it isn't a self-assignment, then the function determines whether the sizes of the two `Array`s are identical (line 41); in that case, the original array of integers in the left-side `Array` object is *not* reallocated. Otherwise, `operator=` uses `delete[]` (line 42) to release the memory originally allocated to the target `Array`, copies the `size` of the source `Array` to the `size` of the target `Array` (line 43), uses new to allocate the memory for the target `Array` and places the pointer returned by new into the `Array`'s `ptr` member (line 44). Then the `for` statement in lines 47–49 copies the elements from the source `Array` to the target `Array`. Regardless of whether this is a self-assignment, the member function returns the current object (i.e., `*this` in line 52) as a constant reference; this enables cascaded `Array` assignments such as `x = y = z`, but prevents ones like `(x = y) = z` because z cannot be assigned to the const `Array` reference that's returned by `(x = y)`. If self-assignment occurs, and function `operator=` did not test for this case, `operator=` would unnecessarily copy the elements of the `Array` into itself.

> **Software Engineering Observation 10.4**
> *A copy constructor, a destructor and an overloaded assignment operator are usually provided as a group for any class that uses dynamically allocated memory. With the addition of move semantics in C++11, other functions should also be provided, as you'll see in Chapter 24.*

> **Common Programming Error 10.4**
> *Not providing a copy constructor and overloaded assignment operator for a class when objects of that class contain pointers to dynamically allocated memory is a potential logic error.*

C++11: Move Constructor and Move Assignment Operator
C++11 adds the notions of a *move constructor* and a *move assignment operator*. We defer a discussion of these new functions until Chapter 24, C++11 and C++14 Additional Features. This discussion will affect the two preceding tips.

C++11: Deleting Unwanted Member Functions from Your Class
Prior to C++11, you could prevent class objects from being *copied* or *assigned* by declaring as `private` the class's copy constructor and overloaded assignment operator. As of C++11,

you can simply *delete* these functions from your class. To do so in class `Array`, replace the prototypes in lines 14 and 18 of Fig. 10.10 with

```
Array(const Array&) = delete;
const Array& operator=(const Array&) = delete;
```

Though you can delete *any* member function, it's most commonly used with member functions that the compiler can *auto-generate*—the default constructor, copy constructor, assignment operator, and in C++ 11, the move constructor and move assignment operator.

Overloaded Equality and Inequality Operators

Line 19 of Fig. 10.10 declares the overloaded equality operator (`==`) for the class. When the compiler sees the expression `integers1 == integers2` in line 51 of Fig. 10.9, the compiler invokes member function `operator==` with the call

```
integers1.operator==(integers2)
```

Member function `operator==` (defined in Fig. 10.11, lines 57–69) immediately returns `false` if the `size` members of the `Array`s are not equal. Otherwise, `operator==` compares each pair of elements. If they're all equal, the function returns `true`. The first pair of elements to differ causes the function to return `false` immediately.

Lines 22–24 of Fig. 10.10 define the overloaded inequality operator (`!=`). Member function `operator!=` uses the overloaded `operator==` function to determine whether one `Array` is *equal* to another, then returns the *opposite* of that result. Writing `operator!=` in this manner enables you to *reuse* `operator==`, which reduces the amount of code that must be written in the class. Also, the full function definition for `operator!=` is in the `Array` header. This allows the compiler to *inline* the definition of `operator!=`.

Overloaded Subscript Operators

Lines 27 and 30 of Fig. 10.10 declare two overloaded subscript operators (defined in Fig. 10.11 in lines 73–80 and 84–91, respectively). When the compiler sees the expression `integers1[5]` (Fig. 10.9, line 56), it invokes the appropriate overloaded `operator[]` member function by generating the call

```
integers1.operator[](5)
```

The compiler creates a call to the `const` version of `operator[]` (Fig. 10.11, lines 84–91) when the subscript operator is used on a `const Array` object. For example, if you pass an `Array` to a function that receives the `Array` as a `const Array&` named `z`, then the `const` version of `operator[]` is required to execute a statement such as

```
cout << z[3] << endl;
```

Remember, a program can invoke only the `const` member functions of a `const` object.

Each definition of `operator[]` determines whether the subscript it receives as an argument is *in range*—and if not, each throws an `out_of_range` exception. If the subscript is in range, the non-const version of `operator[]` returns the appropriate `Array` element as a reference so that it may be used as a modifiable *lvalue* (e.g., on the *left* side of an assignment statement). If the subscript is in range, the `const` version of `operator[]` returns a copy of the appropriate element of the `Array`.

11 *C++11: Managing Dynamically Allocated Memory with* `unique_ptr`

In this case study, class `Array`'s destructor used `delete[]` to return the dynamically allocated built-in array to the free store. C++11 enables you to use `unique_ptr` to ensure that this dynamically allocated memory is deleted automatically when the `Array` object goes out of scope. In Chapter 17, we introduce `unique_ptr` and show how to use it to manage dynamically allocated objects or dynamically allocated built-in arrays.

11 *C++11: Passing a List Initializer to a Constructor*

In Fig. 7.4, we showed how to initialize an `array` object with a comma-separated list of initializers in braces, as in

```
array<int, 5> n{32, 27, 64, 18, 95};
```

You can also use list initializers when you declare objects of your own classes. For example, you can provide an `Array` constructor that would enable the following declarations:

```
Array integers{1, 2, 3, 4, 5};
```

or

```
Array integers = {1, 2, 3, 4, 5};
```

each of which creates an `Array` object with five elements containing the integers from 1 to 5.

To support list initialization, you can define a constructor that receives an *object* of the class template `initializer_list`. For class `Array`, you'd include the `<initializer_list>` header. Then, you'd define a constructor with the first line:

```
Array::Array(initializer_list<int> list)
```

You can determine the number of elements in the `list` parameter by calling its `size` member function. To obtain each initializer and copy it into the `Array` object's dynamically allocated built-in array, you can use a range-based `for` as follows:

```
size_t i{0};
for (int item : list) {
   ptr[i++] = item;
}
```

10.11 Operators as Member vs. Non-Member Functions

Whether an operator function is implemented as a *member function* or as a *non-member function*, the operator is still used the same way in expressions. So which is best?

When an operator function is implemented as a *member function*, the *leftmost* (or only) operand must be an object (or a reference to an object) of the operator's class. If the left operand *must* be an object of a different class or a fundamental type, this operator function *must* be implemented as a *non-member function* (as we did in Section 10.5 when overloading `<<` and `>>` as the stream insertion and stream extraction operators, respectively). A *non-member operator function* can be made a `friend` of a class if that function must access `private` or `protected` members of that class directly.

Operator member functions of a specific class are called (implicitly by the compiler) only when the *left* operand of a binary operator is specifically an object of that class, or when the *single operand of a unary operator* is an object of that class.

Commutative Operators

Another reason why you might choose a non-member function to overload an operator is to enable the operator to be *commutative*. For example, suppose we have

- a fundamental type variable, number, of type long int and
- an object bigInteger, of class HugeInteger—a class in which integers may be arbitrarily large rather than being limited by the machine word size of the underlying hardware (class HugeInteger is developed in the chapter exercises).

Both the expressions bigInteger + number (the sum of a HugeInteger and a long int) and number + bigInteger (the sum of a long int and a HugeInteger) can produce a temporary HugeInteger containing the sum of the values. Thus, we require the addition operator to be *commutative* (exactly as it is with two fundamental-type operands).

The problem is that the class object must appear on the left of the addition operator if that operator is to be overloaded as a *member function*. So, we *also* overload the operator as a non-member function to allow the HugeInteger to appear on the right of the addition. The operator+ function that deals with the HugeInteger on the left can still be a member function. The non-member function can simply swap its arguments and call the member function. You also could define both overloads as non-member functions.

10.12 Converting Between Types

Most programs process information of many types. Sometimes all the operations "stay within a type." For example, adding an int to an int produces an int. It's often necessary, however, to convert data of one type to data of another type. This can happen in assignments, in calculations, in passing values to functions and in returning values from functions. The compiler knows how to perform certain conversions among fundamental types. You can use cast operators to force conversions among fundamental types.

But what about user-defined types? The compiler cannot know in advance how to convert among user-defined types, and between user-defined types and fundamental types, so you must specify how to do this. Such conversions can be performed with conversion constructors—constructors that can be called with a single argument (we'll refer to these as *single-argument constructors*). Such constructors can turn objects of other types (including fundamental types) into objects of a particular class.

Conversion Operators

A conversion operator (also called a *cast operator*) also can be used to convert an object of one class to another type. Such a conversion operator must be a *non-static member function*. The function prototype

```
MyClass::operator string() const;
```

declares an overloaded cast operator function for converting an object of class MyClass into a temporary string object. The operator function is declared const because it does *not* modify the original object. The return type of an overloaded cast operator function is implicitly the type to which the object is being converted. If s is a class object, when the compiler sees the expression static_cast<string>(s), the compiler generates the call

```
s.operator string()
```

to convert the operand s to a string.

Overloaded Cast Operator Functions

Overloaded cast operator functions can be defined to convert objects of user-defined types into fundamental types or into objects of other user-defined types. The prototypes

```
MyClass::operator int() const;
MyClass::operator OtherClass() const;
```

declare *overloaded cast operator functions* that can convert an object of user-defined type My-Class into an integer or into an object of user-defined type OtherClass, respectively.

Implicit Calls to Cast Operators and Conversion Constructors

One of the nice features of cast operators and conversion constructors is that, when necessary, the compiler can call these functions *implicitly* to create *temporary* objects. For example, if an object s of a user-defined class appears in a program at a location where a string is expected, such as

```
display(s); // argument expected to be a string object
```

the compiler can call the overloaded cast-operator function operator string to convert the object into a string and use the resulting string in the expression. With this cast operator provided for a class, the function display does *not* have to be overloaded with a version that receives an object of your class as an argument.

Software Engineering Observation 10.5

When a conversion constructor or conversion operator is used to perform an implicit *conversion, C++ can apply* only one *implicit constructor or operator function call (i.e., a single user-defined conversion) to try to match the needs of another overloaded operator. The compiler will not satisfy an overloaded operator's needs by performing a series of implicit, user-defined conversions.*

10.13 explicit Constructors and Conversion Operators

Recall that we've been declaring as explicit every constructor that can be called with one argument, including multiparameter constructors for which we specify default arguments. With the exception of copy constructors, any constructor that can be called with a *single argument* and is *not* declared explicit can be used by the compiler to perform an *implicit conversion*. The constructor's argument is converted to an object of the class in which the constructor is defined. The conversion is automatic—a cast is not required.

In some situations, implicit conversions are undesirable or error-prone. For example, our Array class in Fig. 10.10 defines a constructor that takes a single int argument. The intent of this constructor is to create an Array object containing the number of elements specified by the int argument. However, if this constructor were not declared explicit it could be misused by the compiler to perform an *implicit conversion*.

Common Programming Error 10.5

Unfortunately, the compiler might use implicit conversions in cases that you do not expect, resulting in ambiguous expressions that generate compilation errors or result in execution-time logic errors.

Accidentally Using a Single-Argument Constructor as a Conversion Constructor
The program (Fig. 10.12) uses the Array class of Figs. 10.10–10.11 to demonstrate an improper implicit conversion. To allow this implicit conversion, we removed the explicit keyword from line 13 in Array.h (Fig. 10.10).

```cpp
1   // Fig. 10.12: fig10_12.cpp
2   // Single-argument constructors and implicit conversions.
3   #include <iostream>
4   #include "Array.h"
5   using namespace std;
6
7   void outputArray(const Array&); // prototype
8
9   int main() {
10      Array integers1{7}; // 7-element Array
11      outputArray(integers1); // output Array integers1
12      outputArray(3); // convert 3 to an Array and output Array's contents
13   }
14
15   // print Array contents
16   void outputArray(const Array& arrayToOutput) {
17      cout << "The Array received has " << arrayToOutput.getSize()
18          << " elements. The contents are:\n" << arrayToOutput << endl;
19   }
```

```
The Array received has 7 elements.
The contents are: 0  0  0  0  0  0  0

The Array received has 3 elements.
The contents are: 0  0  0
```

Fig. 10.12 | Single-argument constructors and implicit conversions.

Line 10 in main (Fig. 10.12) instantiates Array object integers1 and calls the *single-argument constructor* with the int value 7 to specify the number of elements in the Array. Recall from Fig. 10.11 that the Array constructor that receives an int argument initializes all the Array elements to 0. Line 11 in Fig. 10.12 calls function outputArray (defined in lines 16–19), which receives as its argument a const Array& to an Array. The function outputs the number of elements in its Array argument and the contents of the Array. In this case, the size of the Array is 7, so seven 0s are output.

Line 12 calls function outputArray with the int value 3 as an argument. However, this program does *not* contain a function called outputArray that takes an int argument. So, the compiler determines whether the argument 3 can be converted to an Array object. Because class Array provides a constructor with one int argument and that constructor is not declared explicit, the compiler assumes the constructor is a *conversion constructor* and uses it to convert the argument 3 into a temporary Array object containing three elements. Then, the compiler passes the temporary Array object to function outputArray to output the Array's contents. Thus, even though we do not *explicitly* provide an outputArray function that receives an int argument, the compiler is able to compile line 12. The output shows the contents of the three-element Array containing 0s.

Preventing Implicit Conversions with Single-Argument Constructors

The reason we've been declaring every single-argument contructor preceded by the keyword `explicit` is to *suppress implicit conversions via conversion constructors when such conversions should not be allowed.* A constructor that's declared `explicit` *cannot* be used in an *implicit* conversion. In the example of Figure 10.13, we use the original version of `Array.h` from Fig. 10.10, which included the keyword `explicit` in the declaration of the *single-argument constructor* in line 13

```
explicit Array(int = 10); // default constructor
```

Figure 10.13 presents a slightly modified version of the program in Fig. 10.12. When this program in Fig. 10.13 is compiled, the compiler produces an error message, such as

```
'void outputArray(const Array &)': cannot convert argument 1
from 'int' to 'const Array &'
```

on Visual C++, indicating that the integer value passed to `outputArray` in line 12 *cannot* be converted to a `const Array&`. Line 13 demonstrates how the `explicit` constructor can be used to create a temporary Array of 3 elements and pass it to function `outputArray`.

Error-Prevention Tip 10.4

Always use the `explicit` *keyword on single-argument constructors unless they're intended to be used as conversion constructors.*

```cpp
 1   // Fig. 10.13: fig10_13.cpp
 2   // Demonstrating an explicit constructor.
 3   #include <iostream>
 4   #include "Array.h"
 5   using namespace std;
 6
 7   void outputArray(const Array&); // prototype
 8
 9   int main() {
10      Array integers1{7}; // 7-element Array
11      outputArray(integers1); // output Array integers1
12      outputArray(3); // convert 3 to an Array and output Array's contents
13      outputArray(Array{3}); // explicit single-argument constructor call
14   }
15
16   // print Array contents
17   void outputArray(const Array& arrayToOutput) {
18      cout << "The Array received has " << arrayToOutput.getSize()
19         << " elements. The contents are:\n" << arrayToOutput << endl;
20   }
```

Fig. 10.13 | Demonstrating an `explicit` constructor.

11 C++11: `explicit` Conversion Operators

Just as you can declare single-argument constructors `explicit`, you can declare conversion operators `explicit` to prevent the compiler from using them to perform implicit conversions. For example, the prototype

```
explicit MyClass::operator string() const;
```

declares MyClass's string cast operator explicit, thus requiring you to invoke it explicitly with static_cast.

10.14 Overloading the Function Call Operator ()

Overloading the function call operator () is powerful, because functions can take an *arbitrary* number of comma-separated parameters. In a *customized* String class, for example, you could overload this operator to select a substring from a String—the operator's two integer parameters could specify the *start location* and the *length of the substring to be selected*. The operator() function could check for such errors as a *start location out of range* or a *negative substring length*.

The overloaded function call operator must be a *non-static* member function and could be defined with the first line:

```
String String::operator()(size_t index, size_t length) const
```

In this case, it should be a const member function because obtaining a substring should *not* modify the original String object.

Suppose string1 is a String object containing the string "AEIOU". When the compiler encounters the expression string1(2, 3), it generates the member-function call

```
string1.operator()(2, 3)
```

which returns a String containing "IOU".

Another possible use of the function call operator is to enable an alternate Array subscripting notation. Instead of using C++'s double-square-bracket notation, such as in chessBoard[row][column], you might prefer to overload the function call operator to enable the notation chessBoard(row, column), where chessBoard is an object of a modified two-dimensional Array class. Exercise 10.7 asks you to build this class. We demonstrate an overloaded function call operator in Chapter 16.

10.15 Wrap-Up

In this chapter, you learned how to overload operators to work with class objects. We demonstrated standard C++ class string, which makes extensive use of overloaded operators to create a robust, reusable class that can replace C strings. Next, we discussed several restrictions that the C++ standard places on overloaded operators. We then presented a PhoneNumber class that overloaded operators << and >> to conveniently output and input phone numbers, respectively. You also saw a Date class that overloaded the prefix and postfix increment (++) operators and we showed a special syntax that's required to differentiate between the prefix and postfix versions of the increment (++) operator.

Next, we introduced the concept of dynamic memory management. You learned that you can create and destroy objects dynamically with the new and delete operators, respectively. Then, we presented a capstone Array class case study that used overloaded operators and other capabilities to solve various problems with pointer-based arrays. This case study helped you truly understand what classes and object technology are all about—crafting, using and reusing valuable classes. As part of this class, you saw overloaded stream insertion, stream extraction, assignment, equality and subscript operators.

You learned reasons for implementing overloaded operators as member functions or as non-member functions. The chapter concluded with discussions of converting between types (including class types), problems with certain implicit conversions defined by single-argument constructors and how to prevent those problems by using explicit constructors.

In the next chapter, we continue our discussion of classes by introducing inheritance. We'll see that when classes share common attributes and behaviors, it's possible to define those attributes and behaviors in a common "base" class and "inherit" those capabilities into new class definitions, enabling you to create the new classes with a minimal amount of code.

Summary

Section 10.1 Introduction
- C++ enables you to overload most operators to be sensitive to the context in which they're used—the compiler generates the appropriate code based on the types of the operands.
- One example of an overloaded operator built into C++ is operator <<, which is used both as the stream insertion operator and as the bitwise left-shift operator. Similarly, >> is also overloaded; it's used both as the stream extraction operator and as the bitwise right-shift operator. Both of these operators are overloaded in the C++ Standard Library.
- C++ overloads + and - to perform differently, depending on their context in integer arithmetic, floating-point arithmetic and pointer arithmetic.
- The jobs performed by overloaded operators can also be performed by explicit function calls, but operator notation is often more natural.

Section 10.2 Using the Overloaded Operators of Standard Library Class string
- Standard class string is defined in header <string> and belongs to namespace std.
- Class string provides many overloaded operators, including equality, relational, assignment, addition assignment (for concatenation) and subscript operators.
- The stream manipulator **boolalpha** (p. 452) sets an output stream to display condition values as the strings "false" and "true", rather than 0 and 1.
- Class string provides member function **empty** (p. 452), which returns true if the string is empty; otherwise, it returns false.
- A C++14 **string-object literal** (p. 452) is indicated by placing the letter s immediately following the closing " of a string literal.
- Standard class string member function **substr** (p. 452) obtains a substring of a length specified by the second argument, starting at the position specified by the first argument. When the second argument is not specified, substr returns the remainder of the string on which it's called.
- Class string's overloaded [] operator does not perform any bounds checking. Therefore, you must ensure that operations using standard class string's overloaded [] operator do not accidentally manipulate elements outside the bounds of the string.

- Standard class string provides bounds checking with member function **at** (p. 453), which "throws an exception" if its argument is an invalid subscript. By default, this causes the program to terminate. If the subscript is valid, function at returns a reference or a const reference to the character at the specified location depending on the context.

Section 10.3 Fundamentals of Operator Overloading

- An operator is overloaded by writing a non-static member-function definition or non-member function definition in which the function name is the keyword operator followed by the symbol for the operator being overloaded.
- When operators are overloaded as member functions, they must be non-static, because they must be called on an object of the class and operate on that object.
- To use an operator on class objects, you must define an overloaded operator function, with three exceptions—the assignment operator (=), the address operator (&) and the comma operator (,).
- You cannot change the precedence and associativity of an operator by overloading.
- You cannot change the "arity" of an operator (i.e., the number of operands an operator takes).
- You cannot create new operators—only existing operators can be overloaded.
- You cannot change the meaning of how an operator works on objects of fundamental types.
- Overloading an assignment operator and an addition operator for a class does not imply that += is also overloaded. You must explicitly overload operator += for that class.
- Overloaded (), [], -> and assignment operators must be declared as class members. For the other operators, the operator overloading functions can be class members or non-member functions.

Section 10.4 Overloading Binary Operators

- A binary operator can be overloaded as a non-static member function with one argument or as a non-member function with two arguments (one of those arguments must be either a class object or a reference to a class object).

Section 10.5 Overloading the Binary Stream Insertion and Stream Extraction Operators

- The overloaded stream insertion operator (<<) is used in an expression in which the left operand has type ostream&. For this reason, it must be overloaded as a non-member function. Similarly, the overloaded stream extraction operator (>>) must be a non-member function.
- When used with cin, setw restricts the number of characters read to the number of characters specified by its argument.
- istream member function ignore discards the specified number of characters in the input stream (one character by default).
- Overloaded input and output operators are declared as friends if they need to access non-public class members directly for performance reasons.

Section 10.6 Overloading Unary Operators

- A unary operator for a class can be overloaded as a non-static member function with no arguments or as a non-member function with one argument; that argument must be either an object of the class or a reference to an object of the class.
- Member functions that implement overloaded operators must be non-static so that they can access the non-static data in each object of the class.

Section 10.7 Overloading the Increment and Decrement Operators

- The prefix and postfix increment and decrement operators can all be overloaded.

- To overload the pre- and post-increment operators, each overloaded operator function must have a distinct signature. The prefix versions are overloaded like any other unary operator. The postfix increment operator's unique signature is accomplished by providing a second argument, which must be of type `int`. This argument is not supplied in the client code. It's used implicitly by the compiler to distinguish between the prefix and postfix versions of the increment operator. The same syntax is used to differentiate between the prefix and postfix decrement operator functions.

Section 10.9 Dynamic Memory Management

- **Dynamic memory management** (p. 466) enables you to control the allocation and deallocation of memory in a program for any built-in or user-defined type.

- The **free store** (sometimes called the **heap**; p. 466) is a region of memory assigned to each program for storing objects dynamically allocated at execution time.

- The **new operator** (p. 466) allocates storage of the proper size for an object, runs the object's constructor and returns a pointer of the correct type. If `new` is unable to find space in memory for the object, it indicates that an error occurred by "throwing" an "exception." This usually causes the program to terminate immediately, unless the exception is handled.

- To destroy a dynamically allocated object and free its space, use the **delete operator** (p. 466).

- A built-in array of objects can be allocated dynamically with `new` as in

    Type `*ptr{new` *Type*`[`*numberOfElements*`]{}};`

  The preceding built-in array is deleted with **delete[]** (p. 468) as in

    `delete[] ptr;`

Section 10.10 Case Study: **Array Class**

- A copy constructor initializes a new object of a class by copying the members of an existing one. Classes that contain dynamically allocated memory typically provide a copy constructor, a destructor and an overloaded assignment operator.

- The implementation of member function `operator=` should test for **self-assignment** (p. 478), in which an object is being assigned to itself.

- The compiler calls the `const` version of `operator[]` when the subscript operator is used on a `const` object and calls the non-`const` version of the operator when it's used on a non-`const` object.

- The subscript operator (`[]`) can be used to select elements from other types of containers. Also, with overloading, the index values no longer need to be integers.

Section 10.11 Operators as Member vs. Non-Member Functions

- Operator functions can be member or non-member functions—non-member functions are often made `friend`s for performance reasons. Member functions use the `this` pointer implicitly to obtain one of their class object arguments (the left operand for binary operators). Arguments for both operands of a binary operator must be explicitly listed in a non-member function call.

- When an operator function is implemented as a member function, the leftmost (or only) operand must be an object (or a reference to an object) of the operator's class.

- If the left operand must be an object of a different class or a fundamental type, this operator function must be implemented as a non-member function.

- A non-member operator function can be made a `friend` of a class if that function must access `private` or `protected` members of that class directly.

- Another reason to choose a non-member function to overload an operator is to enable the operator to be commutative.

Section 10.12 Converting Between Types

- The compiler cannot know in advance how to convert among user-defined types, and between user-defined types and fundamental types, so you must specify how to do this. Such conversions can be performed with **conversion constructors** (p. 481)—single-argument constructors that turn objects of other types (including fundamental types) into objects of a particular class.

- A constructor that can be called with a single argument can be used as a conversion constructor.

- A **conversion operator** (p. 481) must be a non-`static` member function. Overloaded **cast-operator functions** (p. 481) can be defined for converting objects of user-defined types into fundamental types or into objects of other user-defined types.

- An overloaded cast operator function does not specify a return type—the return type is the type to which the object is being converted.

- When necessary, the compiler can call cast operators and conversion constructors implicitly.

Section 10.13 `explicit` Constructors and Conversion Operators

- A constructor that's declared `explicit` (p. 484) cannot be used in an implicit conversion.

Section 10.14 Overloading the Function Call Operator ()

- Overloading the **function call operator** () (p. 485) is powerful, because functions can have an arbitrary number of parameters.

Self-Review Exercises

10.1   Fill in the blanks in each of the following:

  a) Suppose a and b are integer variables and we form the sum a + b. Now suppose c and d are floating-point variables and we form the sum c + d. The two + operators here are clearly being used for different purposes. This is an example of _____.

  b) Keyword _____ introduces an overloaded-operator function definition.

  c) To use operators on class objects, they must be overloaded, with the exception of operators _____, _____ and _____.

  d) The _____, _____ and _____ of an operator cannot be changed by overloading the operator.

  e) The operators that cannot be overloaded are _____, _____, _____ and _____.

  f) The _____ operator reclaims memory previously allocated by new.

  g) The _____ operator dynamically allocates memory for an object of a specified type and returns a(n) _____ to that type.

  h) Append a(n) _____ after the closing quote (") of a string literal to indicate that it's a C++14 string-object literal.

10.2   Explain the multiple meanings of the operators << and >>.

10.3   In what context might the name `operator/` be used?

10.4   (True/False) Only existing operators can be overloaded.

10.5   How does the precedence of an overloaded operator compare with the precedence of the original operator?

Answers to Self-Review Exercises

10.1   a) operator overloading. b) operator. c) assignment (=), address (&), comma (,). d) precedence, associativity, "arity." e) ., ?:, .*, and ::. f) delete. g) new, pointer. h) s.

10.2   Operator >> is both the right-shift operator and the stream extraction operator, depending on its context. Operator << is both the left-shift operator and the stream insertion operator, depending on its context.

10.3   For operator overloading: It would be the name of a function that would provide an overloaded version of the / operator for a specific class.

10.4   True.

10.5   The precedence is identical.

Exercises

10.6   *(Memory Allocation and Deallocation Operators)* Compare and contrast dynamic memory allocation and deallocation operators new, new [], delete and delete[].

10.7   *(Overloading the Parentheses Operator)* One nice example of overloading the function call operator () is to allow another form of double-array subscripting popular in some programming languages. Instead of saying

        chessBoard[row][column]

for an array of objects, overload the function call operator to allow the alternate form

        chessBoard(row, column)

    Create a class DoubleSubscriptedArray that has similar features to class Array in Figs. 10.10–10.11. At construction time, the class should be able to create a DoubleSubscriptedArray of any number of rows and columns. The class should supply operator() to perform double-subscripting operations. For example, in a 3-by-5 DoubleSubscriptedArray called chessBoard, the user could write chessBoard(1, 3) to access the element at row 1 and column 3. Remember that operator() can receive *any* number of arguments. The underlying representation of the DoubleSubscriptedArray could be a single-subscripted array of integers with *rows * columns* number of elements. Function operator() should perform the proper pointer arithmetic to access each element of the underlying array. There should be *two* versions of operator()—one that returns int& (so that an element of a DoubleSubscriptedArray can be used as an *lvalue*) and one that returns int. The class should also provide the following operators: ==, !=, =, << (for outputting the DoubleSubscriptedArray in row and column format) and >> (for inputting the entire DoubleSubscriptedArray contents).

10.8   *(Complex Class)* Consider class Complex shown in Figs. 10.14–10.16. The class enables operations on so-called *complex numbers*. These are numbers of the form realPart + imaginaryPart * *i*, where *i* has the value

    $\sqrt{-1}$

a) Modify the class to enable input and output of complex numbers via overloaded >> and << operators, respectively (you should remove the toString function from the class).
b) Overload the multiplication operator to enable multiplication of two complex numbers as in algebra.
c) Overload the == and != operators to allow comparisons of complex numbers.

After doing this exercise, you might want to read about the Standard Library's complex class (from header <complex>).

```
 1   // Fig. 10.14: Complex.h
 2   // Complex class definition.
 3   #include <string>
 4
 5   #ifndef COMPLEX_H
 6   #define COMPLEX_H
 7
 8   class Complex {
 9   public:
10      explicit Complex(double = 0.0, double = 0.0); // constructor
11      Complex operator+(const Complex&) const; // addition
12      Complex operator-(const Complex&) const; // subtraction
13      std::string toString() const;
14   private:
15      double real; // real part
16      double imaginary; // imaginary part
17   };
18
19   #endif
```

Fig. 10.14 | Complex class definition.

```
 1   // Fig. 10.15: Complex.cpp
 2   // Complex class member-function definitions.
 3   #include <string>
 4   #include "Complex.h" // Complex class definition
 5   using namespace std;
 6
 7   // Constructor
 8   Complex::Complex(double realPart, double imaginaryPart)
 9      : real{realPart}, imaginary{imaginaryPart} { }
10
11   // addition operator
12   Complex Complex::operator+(const Complex& operand2) const {
13      return Complex{real + operand2.real, imaginary + operand2.imaginary};
14   }
15
16   // subtraction operator
17   Complex Complex::operator-(const Complex& operand2) const {
18      return Complex{real - operand2.real, imaginary - operand2.imaginary};
19   }
20
21   // return string representation of a Complex object in the form: (a, b)
22   string Complex::toString() const {
23      return "("s + to_string(real) + ", "s + to_string(imaginary) + ")"s;
24   }
```

Fig. 10.15 | Complex class member-function definitions.

```
25   // Fig. 10.16: fig10_16.cpp
26   // Complex class test program.
27   #include <iostream>
28   #include "Complex.h"
29   using namespace std;
30
```

Fig. 10.16 | Complex class test program. (Part I of 2.)

```
31   int main() {
32      Complex x;
33      Complex y{4.3, 8.2};
34      Complex z{3.3, 1.1};
35
36      cout << "x: " << x.toString() << "\ny: " << y.toString()
37         << "\nz: " << z;
38
39      x = y + z;
40      cout << "\n\nx = y + z:\n" << x.toString() << " = " << y.toString()
41         << " + " << z.toString();
42
43      x = y - z;
44      cout << "\n\nx = y - z:\n" << x.toString() << " = " << y.toString()
45         << " - " << z.toString() << endl;
46   }
```

```
x: (0, 0)
y: (4.3, 8.2)
z: (3.3, 1.1)

x = y + z:
(7.6, 9.3) = (4.3, 8.2) + (3.3, 1.1)

x = y - z:
(1, 7.1) = (4.3, 8.2) - (3.3, 1.1)
```

Fig. 10.16 | Complex class test program. (Part 2 of 2.)

10.9   *(HugeInteger Class)* A machine with 32-bit integers can represent integers in the range of approximately −2 billion to +2 billion. This fixed-size restriction is rarely troublesome, but there are applications in which we would like to be able to use a much wider range of integers. This is what C++ was built to do, namely, create powerful new data types. Consider class `HugeInteger` of Figs. 10.17–10.19, which is similar to the `HugeInteger` class in Exercise 9.14. Study the class carefully, then respond to the following:

a) Describe precisely how it operates.
b) What restrictions does the class have?
c) Overload the * multiplication operator.
d) Overload the / division operator.
e) Overload all the relational and equality operators.

[*Note:* We do not show an assignment operator or copy constructor for class `HugeInteger`, because the assignment operator and copy constructor provided by the compiler are capable of copying the entire array data member properly.]

```
1    // Fig. 10.17: HugeInteger.h
2    // HugeInteger class definition.
3    #ifndef HugeInteger_H
4    #define HugeInteger_H
5
6    #include <array>
7    #include <iostream>
8    #include <string>
9
```

Fig. 10.17 | HugeInteger class definition. (Part 1 of 2.)

```
10    class HugeInteger {
11       friend std::ostream& operator<<(std::ostream&, const HugeInteger&);
12    public:
13       static const int digits{40}; // maximum digits in a HugeInteger
14
15       HugeInteger(long = 0); // conversion/default constructor
16       HugeInteger(const std::string&); // conversion constructor
17
18       // addition operator; HugeInteger + HugeInteger
19       HugeInteger operator+(const HugeInteger&) const;
20
21       // addition operator; HugeInteger + int
22       HugeInteger operator+(int) const;
23
24       // addition operator;
25       // HugeInteger + string that represents large integer value
26       HugeInteger operator+(const std::string&) const;
27    private:
28       std::array<short, digits> integer{}; // default init to 0s
29    };
30
31    #endif
```

Fig. 10.17 | HugeInteger class definition. (Part 2 of 2.)

```
1     // Fig. 10.18: HugeInteger.cpp
2     // HugeInteger member-function and friend-function definitions.
3     #include <cctype> // isdigit function prototype
4     #include "HugeInteger.h" // HugeInteger class definition
5     using namespace std;
6
7     // default constructor; conversion constructor that converts
8     // a long integer into a HugeInteger object
9     HugeInteger::HugeInteger(long value) {
10       // place digits of argument into array
11       for (int j{digits - 1}; value != 0 && j >= 0; j--) {
12          integer[j] = value % 10;
13          value /= 10;
14       }
15    }
16
17    // conversion constructor that converts a character string
18    // representing a large integer into a HugeInteger object
19    HugeInteger::HugeInteger(const string& number) {
20       // place digits of argument into array
21       int length{number.size()};
22
23       for (int j{digits - length}, k{0}; j < digits; ++j, ++k) {
24          if (isdigit(number[k])) { // ensure that character is a digit
25             integer[j] = number[k] - '0';
26          }
27       }
28    }
29
```

Fig. 10.18 | HugeInteger member-function and friend-function definitions. (Part 1 of 2.)

```
30   // addition operator; HugeInteger + HugeInteger
31   HugeInteger HugeInteger::operator+(const HugeInteger& op2) const {
32      HugeInteger temp; // temporary result
33      int carry = 0;
34
35      for (int i{digits - 1}; i >= 0; i--) {
36         temp.integer[i] = integer[i] + op2.integer[i] + carry;
37
38         // determine whether to carry a 1
39         if (temp.integer[i] > 9) {
40            temp.integer[i] %= 10;   // reduce to 0-9
41            carry = 1;
42         }
43         else { // no carry
44            carry = 0;
45         }
46      }
47
48      return temp; // return copy of temporary object
49   }
50
51   // addition operator; HugeInteger + int
52   HugeInteger HugeInteger::operator+(int op2) const {
53      // convert op2 to a HugeInteger, then invoke
54      // operator+ for two HugeInteger objects
55      return *this + HugeInteger(op2);
56   }
57
58   // addition operator;
59   // HugeInteger + string that represents large integer value
60   HugeInteger HugeInteger::operator+(const string& op2) const {
61      // convert op2 to a HugeInteger, then invoke
62      // operator+ for two HugeInteger objects
63      return *this + HugeInteger(op2);
64   }
65
66   // overloaded output operator
67   ostream& operator<<(ostream& output, const HugeInteger& num) {
68      int i;
69
70      // skip leading zeros
71      for (i = 0; (i < HugeInteger::digits) && (0 == num.integer[i]); ++i) { }
72
73      if (i == HugeInteger::digits) {
74         output << 0;
75      }
76      else {
77         for (; i < HugeInteger::digits; ++i) {
78            output << num.integer[i];
79         }
80      }
81
82      return output;
83   }
```

Fig. 10.18 | HugeInteger member-function and friend-function definitions. (Part 2 of 2.)

```
 1   // Fig. 10.19: fig10_19.cpp
 2   // HugeInteger test program.
 3   #include <iostream>
 4   #include "HugeInteger.h"
 5   using namespace std;
 6
 7   int main() {
 8      HugeInteger n1{7654321};
 9      HugeInteger n2{7891234};
10      HugeInteger n3{"99999999999999999999999999999"};
11      HugeInteger n4{"1"};
12      HugeInteger n5;
13
14      cout << "n1 is " << n1 << "\nn2 is " << n2
15         << "\nn3 is " << n3 << "\nn4 is " << n4
16         << "\nn5 is " << n5 << "\n\n";
17
18      n5 = n1 + n2;
19      cout << n1 << " + " << n2 << " = " << n5 << "\n\n";
20
21      cout << n3 << " + " << n4 << "\n= " << (n3 + n4) << "\n\n";
22
23      n5 = n1 + 9;
24      cout << n1 << " + " << 9 << " = " << n5 << "\n\n";
25
26      n5 = n2 + "10000";
27      cout << n2 << " + " << "10000" << " = " << n5 << endl;
28   }
```

```
n1 is 7654321
n2 is 7891234
n3 is 99999999999999999999999999999
n4 is 1
n5 is 0

7654321 + 7891234 = 15545555

99999999999999999999999999999 + 1
= 100000000000000000000000000000

7654321 + 9 = 7654330

7891234 + 10000 = 7901234
```

Fig. 10.19 | HugeInteger test program.

10.10 *(RationalNumber Class)* Create a RationalNumber(fractions) class like the one in Exercise 9.6. Provide the following capabilities:

    a) Create a constructor that prevents a 0 denominator in a fraction, reduces or simplifies fractions that are not in reduced form and avoids negative denominators.

    b) Overload the addition, subtraction, multiplication and division operators for this class.

    c) Overload the relational and equality operators for this class.

10.11 *(Polynomial Class)* Develop class Polynomial. The internal representation of a Polynomial is an array of terms. Each term contains a coefficient and an exponent—e.g., the term

$$2x^4$$

has the coefficient 2 and the exponent 4. Develop a complete class containing proper constructor and destructor functions as well as *set* and *get* functions. The class should also provide the following overloaded operator capabilities:

   a) Overload the addition operator (+) to add two Polynomials.
   b) Overload the subtraction operator (-) to subtract two Polynomials.
   c) Overload the assignment operator to assign one Polynomial to another.
   d) Overload the multiplication operator (*) to multiply two Polynomials.
   e) Overload the addition assignment operator (+=), subtraction assignment operator (-=), and multiplication assignment operator (*=).

10.12 *(DollarAmount Class Enhancement)* Enhance class DollarAmount from Exercise 5.32 with overloaded addition (+), subtraction (-), multiplication (*) and division (/) operators.

10.13 *(DollarAmount Class Enhancement)* Enhance class DollarAmount from Exercise 10.12 to make the overloaded addition, subtraction and multiplication operators commutative.

Object-Oriented Programming: Inheritance

Objectives

In this chapter you'll:

- Learn what inheritance is.

- Understand the notions of base classes and derived classes and the relationships between them.

- Use the **protected** member access specifier.

- Use constructors and destructors in inheritance hierarchies.

- Understand the order in which constructors and destructors are called in inheritance hierarchies.

- Understand the differences between **public**, **protected** and **private** inheritance.

- Use inheritance to customize existing software.

11.1 Introduction

This chapter continues our discussion of object-oriented programming (OOP) by introducing inheritance in which you create a class that absorbs an existing class's capabilities, then *customizes* or enhances them. Inheritance can save time during program development by taking advantage of proven, high-quality software.

When creating a class, instead of writing completely new data members and member functions, you can specify that the new class should inherit the members of an existing class. This existing class is called the base class, and the new class is called the derived class. Other programming languages, such as Java and C#, refer to the base class as the superclass and the derived class as the subclass. A derived class represents a *more specialized* group of objects.

C++ offers public, protected and private inheritance. In this chapter, we concentrate on public inheritance and briefly explain the other two. With public inheritance, every object of a derived class is also an object of that derived class's base class. However, base-class objects are *not* objects of their derived classes. For example, if we have Vehicle as a base class and Car as a derived class, then all Cars are Vehicles, but not all Vehicles are Cars—for example, a Vehicle could also be a Truck or a Boat.

We distinguish between the *is-a* relationship and the *has-a* relationship. The *is-a* relationship represents inheritance. In an *is-a* relationship, an object of a derived class also can be treated as an object of its base class—for example, a Car *is a* Vehicle, so any attributes and behaviors of a Vehicle are also attributes and behaviors of a Car. By contrast, the *has-a* relationship represents *composition*, which was discussed in Chapter 9. In a *has-a* relationship, an object *contains* one or more objects of other classes as members. For example, a Car has many components—it *has a* steering wheel, *has a* brake pedal, *has a* transmission, etc.

11.2 Base Classes and Derived Classes

Figure 11.1 lists several simple examples of base classes and derived classes. Base classes tend to be *more general* and derived classes tend to be *more specific*.

Base class	Derived classes
Student	GraduateStudent, UndergraduateStudent
Shape	Circle, Triangle, Rectangle, Sphere, Cube
Loan	CarLoan, HomeImprovementLoan, MortgageLoan
Employee	Faculty, Staff
Account	CheckingAccount, SavingsAccount

Fig. 11.1 | Inheritance examples.

Because every derived-class object *is an* object of its base class, and one base class can have *many* derived classes, the set of objects represented by a base class typically is *larger* than the set of objects represented by any of its derived classes. For example, the base class Vehicle represents all vehicles, including cars, trucks, boats, airplanes, bicycles and so on. By contrast, derived-class Car represents a *smaller, more specific* subset of all vehicles.

Inheritance relationships form class hierarchies. A base class exists in a hierarchical relationship with its derived classes. Although classes can exist independently, once they're employed in inheritance relationships, they become affiliated with other classes. A class becomes either a base class—supplying members to other classes, a derived class—inheriting its members from other classes, or *both*.

11.2.1 CommunityMember Class Hierarchy

Let's develop a simple inheritance hierarchy with five levels (represented by the UML class diagram in Fig. 11.2). A university community has thousands of CommunityMembers. These CommunityMembers consist of Employees, Students and alumni (each of class Alumnus). Employees are either Faculty or Staff. Faculty are either Administrators or Teachers. Some Administrators, however, are also Teachers. We've used *multiple inheritance* to form class AdministratorTeacher. With single inheritance, a class is derived from *one* base class. With multiple inheritance, a derived class inherits simultaneously from *two or more* (possibly unrelated) base classes. We discuss multiple inheritance in Chapter 23, Other Topics.

Each arrow in the hierarchy (Fig. 11.2) represents an *is-a* relationship. For example, as we follow the arrows in this class hierarchy, we can state "an Employee *is a* CommunityMember" and "a Teacher *is a* Faculty member." CommunityMember is the direct base class of Employee, Student and Alumnus. In addition, CommunityMember is an indirect base class of all the other classes in the diagram. An indirect base class is inherited from two or more levels up the class hierarchy.

Starting from the bottom of the diagram, you can follow the arrows upward and apply the *is-a* relationship to the topmost base class. For example, an AdministratorTeacher *is an* Administrator, *is a* Faculty member, *is an* Employee and *is a* CommunityMember.

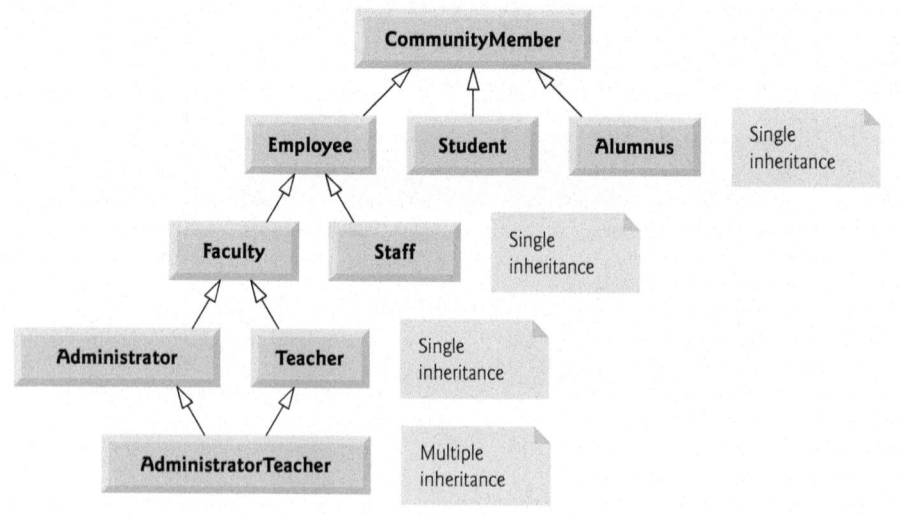

Fig. 11.2 | Inheritance hierarchy for university CommunityMembers.

11.2.2 Shape Class Hierarchy

Now consider the Shape inheritance hierarchy in Fig. 11.3. This hierarchy begins with base-class Shape. Classes TwoDimensionalShape and ThreeDimensionalShape derive from base-class Shape—a TwoDimensionalShape *is a* Shape and a ThreeDimensionalShape *is a* Shape. The third level of this hierarchy contains *more specific* types of TwoDimensional-Shapes and ThreeDimensionalShapes. As in Fig. 11.2, we can follow the arrows from the bottom of the diagram upward to the topmost base class in this hierarchy to identify several *is-a* relationships. For instance, a Triangle *is a* TwoDimensionalShape and *is a* Shape, while a Sphere *is a* ThreeDimensionalShape and *is a* Shape.

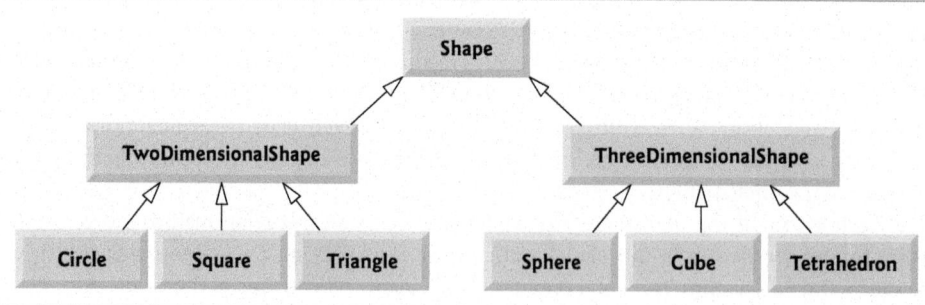

Fig. 11.3 | Inheritance hierarchy for Shapes.

   To specify that class TwoDimensionalShape (Fig. 11.3) is derived from (or inherits from) class Shape, class TwoDimensionalShape's definition could begin as follows:

```
class TwoDimensionalShape : public Shape
```

This is an example of public inheritance, the most commonly used form. We'll also discuss private inheritance and protected inheritance (Section 11.5). With all forms of inheritance, private members of a base class are *not* accessible directly from that class's derived classes, but these private base-class members are still inherited (i.e., they're still considered parts of the derived classes). With public inheritance, all other base-class members retain their original member access when they become members of the derived class (e.g., public members of the base class become public members of the derived class, and, as we'll soon see, protected members of the base class become protected members of the derived class). Through inherited base-class member functions, the derived class can manipulate private members of the base class (if these inherited member functions provide such functionality in the base class).

Inheritance is *not* appropriate for every class relationship. In some cases, the *has-a* relationship (*composition*) is more appropriate. For example, given the classes Employee, BirthDate and TelephoneNumber, it's improper to say that an Employee *is a* BirthDate or that an Employee *is a* TelephoneNumber. However, it is appropriate to say that an Employee *has a* BirthDate and that an Employee *has a* TelephoneNumber.

It's possible to treat base-class objects and derived-class objects similarly; their commonalities are expressed in the members of the base class. In Chapter 12, we consider many examples that take advantage of this relationship.

11.3 Relationship between Base and Derived Classes

In this section, we use an inheritance hierarchy containing types of employees in a company's payroll application to discuss the relationship between a base class and a derived class. Commission employees (who will be represented as objects of a base class) are paid a percentage of their sales, while base-salaried commission employees (who will be represented as objects of a derived class) receive a base salary plus a percentage of their sales. We divide our discussion of the relationship between commission employees and base-salaried commission employees into a carefully paced series of examples.

11.3.1 Creating and Using a CommissionEmployee Class

Let's examine CommissionEmployee's class definition (Figs. 11.4–11.5). The CommissionEmployee header (Fig. 11.4) specifies class CommissionEmployee's public services, which include a constructor (lines 10–11) and member functions earnings (line 28) and toString (line 29). Lines 13–26 declare public *get* and *set* functions that manipulate the class's data members (declared in lines 31–35) firstName, lastName, socialSecurityNumber, grossSales and commissionRate. Member functions setGrossSales (defined in lines 46–52 of Fig. 11.5) and setCommissionRate (defined in lines 58–64 of Fig. 11.5), for example, validate their arguments before assigning the values to data members grossSales and commissionRate, respectively.

```
1   // Fig. 11.4: CommissionEmployee.h
2   // CommissionEmployee class definition represents a commission employee.
3   #ifndef COMMISSION_H
4   #define COMMISSION_H
```

Fig. 11.4 | CommissionEmployee class definition represents a commission employee. (Part 1 of 2.)

```
5
6   #include <string> // C++ standard string class
7
8   class CommissionEmployee {
9   public:
10     CommissionEmployee(const std::string&, const std::string&,
11        const std::string&, double = 0.0, double = 0.0);
12
13     void setFirstName(const std::string&); // set first name
14     std::string getFirstName() const; // return first name
15
16     void setLastName(const std::string&); // set last name
17     std::string getLastName() const; // return last name
18
19     void setSocialSecurityNumber(const std::string&); // set SSN
20     std::string getSocialSecurityNumber() const; // return SSN
21
22     void setGrossSales(double); // set gross sales amount
23     double getGrossSales() const; // return gross sales amount
24
25     void setCommissionRate(double); // set commission rate (percentage)
26     double getCommissionRate() const; // return commission rate
27
28     double earnings() const; // calculate earnings
29     std::string toString() const; // create string representation
30  private:
31     std::string firstName;
32     std::string lastName;
33     std::string socialSecurityNumber;
34     double grossSales; // gross weekly sales
35     double commissionRate; // commission percentage
36  };
37
38  #endif
```

Fig. 11.4 | CommissionEmployee class definition represents a commission employee. (Part 2 of 2.)

```
1   // Fig. 11.5: CommissionEmployee.cpp
2   // Class CommissionEmployee member-function definitions.
3   #include <iomanip>
4   #include <stdexcept>
5   #include <sstream>
6   #include "CommissionEmployee.h" // CommissionEmployee class definition
7   using namespace std;
8
9   // constructor
10  CommissionEmployee::CommissionEmployee(const string& first,
11     const string& last, const string& ssn, double sales, double rate) {
12     firstName = first; // should validate
13     lastName = last; // should validate
```

Fig. 11.5 | Implementation file for CommissionEmployee class that represents an employee who is paid a percentage of gross sales. (Part 1 of 3.)

```
14      socialSecurityNumber = ssn; // should validate
15      setGrossSales(sales); // validate and store gross sales
16      setCommissionRate(rate); // validate and store commission rate
17  }
18
19  // set first name
20  void CommissionEmployee::setFirstName(const string& first) {
21      firstName = first; // should validate
22  }
23
24  // return first name
25  string CommissionEmployee::getFirstName() const {return firstName;}
26
27  // set last name
28  void CommissionEmployee::setLastName(const string& last) {
29      lastName = last; // should validate
30  }
31
32  // return last name
33  string CommissionEmployee::getLastName() const {return lastName;}
34
35  // set social security number
36  void CommissionEmployee::setSocialSecurityNumber(const string& ssn) {
37      socialSecurityNumber = ssn; // should validate
38  }
39
40  // return social security number
41  string CommissionEmployee::getSocialSecurityNumber() const {
42      return socialSecurityNumber;
43  }
44
45  // set gross sales amount
46  void CommissionEmployee::setGrossSales(double sales) {
47      if (sales < 0.0) {
48          throw invalid_argument("Gross sales must be >= 0.0");
49      }
50
51      grossSales = sales;
52  }
53
54  // return gross sales amount
55  double CommissionEmployee::getGrossSales() const {return grossSales;}
56
57  // set commission rate
58  void CommissionEmployee::setCommissionRate(double rate) {
59      if (rate <= 0.0 || rate >= 1.0) {
60          throw invalid_argument("Commission rate must be > 0.0 and < 1.0");
61      }
62
63      commissionRate = rate;
64  }
```

Fig. 11.5 | Implementation file for CommissionEmployee class that represents an employee who is paid a percentage of gross sales. (Part 2 of 3.)

```
65
66   // return commission rate
67   double CommissionEmployee::getCommissionRate() const {
68      return commissionRate;
69   }
70
71   // calculate earnings
72   double CommissionEmployee::earnings() const {
73      return commissionRate * grossSales;
74   }
75
76   // return string representation of CommissionEmployee object
77   string CommissionEmployee::toString() const {
78      ostringstream output;
79      output << fixed << setprecision(2); // two digits of precision
80      output << "commission employee: " << firstName << " " << lastName
81         << "\nsocial security number: " << socialSecurityNumber
82         << "\ngross sales: " << grossSales
83         << "\ncommission rate: " << commissionRate;
84      return output.str();
85   }
```

Fig. 11.5 | Implementation file for CommissionEmployee class that represents an employee who is paid a percentage of gross sales. (Part 3 of 3.)

CommissionEmployee *Constructor*

The CommissionEmployee constructor definition *purposely does not use member-initializer syntax* in the first several examples of this section. This will enable us to demonstrate how private and protected specifiers affect member access in derived classes. As shown in Fig. 11.5, lines 12–14, we assign values to data members firstName, lastName and socialSecurityNumber in the constructor body. Later in this section, we'll return to using member-initializer lists in the constructors.

We do not validate the values of the constructor's arguments first, last and ssn before assigning them to the corresponding data members. We certainly could validate the first and last names—perhaps by ensuring that they're of a reasonable length. Similarly, a social security number could be validated to ensure that it contains nine digits, with or without dashes (e.g., 123-45-6789 or 123456789).

CommissionEmployee *Member Functions* earnings *and* toString

Member function earnings (lines 72–74) calculates a CommissionEmployee's earnings. Line 73 multiplies the commissionRate by the grossSales and returns the result. Member function toString (lines 77–85) displays the values of a CommissionEmployee object's data members.

Testing Class CommissionEmployee

Figure 11.6 tests class CommissionEmployee. Line 10 instantiates CommissionEmployee object employee and invokes the constructor to initialize the object with "Sue" as the first name, "Jones" as the last name, "222-22-2222" as the social security number, 10000 as the gross sales amount and .06 as the commission rate. Lines 14–20 use employee's *get* functions to display the values of its data members. Lines 22–23 invoke the object's member functions setGrossSales and setCommissionRate to change the values of data members grossSales and commissionRate, respectively. Lines 24–25 then call employee's toString member function to get and output the updated CommissionEmployee information. Finally, line 28 displays the CommissionEmployee's earnings, calculated by the object's earnings member function using the updated values of data members grossSales and commissionRate.

```cpp
1   // Fig. 11.6: fig11_06.cpp
2   // CommissionEmployee class test program.
3   #include <iostream>
4   #include <iomanip>
5   #include "CommissionEmployee.h" // CommissionEmployee class definition
6   using namespace std;
7
8   int main() {
9      // instantiate a CommissionEmployee object
10     CommissionEmployee employee{"Sue", "Jones", "222-22-2222", 10000, .06};
11
12     // get commission employee data
13     cout << fixed << setprecision(2); // set floating-point formatting
14     cout << "Employee information obtained by get functions: \n"
15        << "\nFirst name is " << employee.getFirstName()
16        << "\nLast name is " << employee.getLastName()
17        << "\nSocial security number is "
18        << employee.getSocialSecurityNumber()
19        << "\nGross sales is " << employee.getGrossSales()
20        << "\nCommission rate is " << employee.getCommissionRate() << endl;
21
22     employee.setGrossSales(8000); // set gross sales
23     employee.setCommissionRate(.1); // set commission rate
24     cout << "\nUpdated employee information from function toString: \n\n"
25        << employee.toString();
26
27     // display the employee's earnings
28     cout << "\n\nEmployee's earnings: $" << employee.earnings() << endl;
29  }
```

```
Employee information obtained by get functions:

First name is Sue
Last name is Jones
Social security number is 222-22-2222
Gross sales is 10000.00
Commission rate is 0.06

Updated employee information from function toString:

commission employee: Sue Jones
social security number: 222-22-2222
gross sales: 8000.00
commission rate: 0.10

Employee's earnings: $800.00
```

Fig. 11.6 | CommissionEmployee class test program.

11.3.2 Creating a BasePlusCommissionEmployee Class Without Using Inheritance

We now discuss the second part of our introduction to inheritance by creating and testing *a completely new and independent* class BasePlusCommissionEmployee (Figs. 11.7–11.8), which contains a first name, last name, social security number, gross sales amount, commission rate *and* base salary.

```cpp
1   // Fig. 11.7: BasePlusCommissionEmployee.h
2   // BasePlusCommissionEmployee class definition represents an employee
3   // that receives a base salary in addition to commission.
4   #ifndef BASEPLUS_H
5   #define BASEPLUS_H
6
7   #include <string> // C++ standard string class
8
9   class BasePlusCommissionEmployee {
10  public:
11     BasePlusCommissionEmployee(const std::string&, const std::string&,
12        const std::string&, double = 0.0, double = 0.0, double = 0.0);
13
14     void setFirstName(const std::string&); // set first name
15     std::string getFirstName() const; // return first name
16
17     void setLastName(const std::string&); // set last name
18     std::string getLastName() const; // return last name
19
20     void setSocialSecurityNumber(const std::string&); // set SSN
21     std::string getSocialSecurityNumber() const; // return SSN
22
23     void setGrossSales(double); // set gross sales amount
24     double getGrossSales() const; // return gross sales amount
25
26     void setCommissionRate(double); // set commission rate
27     double getCommissionRate() const; // return commission rate
28
29     void setBaseSalary(double); // set base salary
30     double getBaseSalary() const; // return base salary
31
32     double earnings() const; // calculate earnings
33     std::string toString() const; // create string representation
34  private:
35     std::string firstName;
36     std::string lastName;
37     std::string socialSecurityNumber;
38     double grossSales; // gross weekly sales
39     double commissionRate; // commission percentage
40     double baseSalary; // base salary
41  };
42
43  #endif
```

Fig. 11.7 | BasePlusCommissionEmployee class header.

```
1   // Fig. 11.8: BasePlusCommissionEmployee.cpp
2   // Class BasePlusCommissionEmployee member-function definitions.
3   #include <iomanip>
4   #include <stdexcept>
5   #include <sstream>
6   #include "BasePlusCommissionEmployee.h"
7   using namespace std;
8
9   // constructor
10  BasePlusCommissionEmployee::BasePlusCommissionEmployee(
11     const string& first, const string& last, const string& ssn,
12     double sales, double rate, double salary) {
13     firstName = first; // should validate
14     lastName = last; // should validate
15     socialSecurityNumber = ssn; // should validate
16     setGrossSales(sales); // validate and store gross sales
17     setCommissionRate(rate); // validate and store commission rate
18     setBaseSalary(salary); // validate and store base salary
19  }
20
21  // set first name
22  void BasePlusCommissionEmployee::setFirstName(const string& first) {
23     firstName = first; // should validate
24  }
25
26  // return first name
27  string BasePlusCommissionEmployee::getFirstName() const {
28     return firstName;
29  }
30
31  // set last name
32  void BasePlusCommissionEmployee::setLastName(const string& last) {
33     lastName = last; // should validate
34  }
35
36  // return last name
37  string BasePlusCommissionEmployee::getLastName() const {return lastName;}
38
39  // set social security number
40  void BasePlusCommissionEmployee::setSocialSecurityNumber(
41     const string& ssn) {
42     socialSecurityNumber = ssn; // should validate
43  }
44
45  // return social security number
46  string BasePlusCommissionEmployee::getSocialSecurityNumber() const {
47     return socialSecurityNumber;
48  }
49
```

Fig. 11.8 | BasePlusCommissionEmployee class represents an employee who receives a base salary in addition to a commission. (Part 1 of 3.)

```
50   // set gross sales amount
51   void BasePlusCommissionEmployee::setGrossSales(double sales) {
52      if (sales < 0.0) {
53         throw invalid_argument("Gross sales must be >= 0.0");
54      }
55
56      grossSales = sales;
57   }
58
59   // return gross sales amount
60   double BasePlusCommissionEmployee::getGrossSales() const {
61      return grossSales;
62   }
63
64   // set commission rate
65   void BasePlusCommissionEmployee::setCommissionRate(double rate) {
66      if (rate <= 0.0 || rate >= 1.0) {
67         throw invalid_argument("Commission rate must be > 0.0 and < 1.0");
68      }
69
70      commissionRate = rate;
71   }
72
73   // return commission rate
74   double BasePlusCommissionEmployee::getCommissionRate() const {
75      return commissionRate;
76   }
77
78   // set base salary
79   void BasePlusCommissionEmployee::setBaseSalary(double salary) {
80      if (salary < 0.0) {
81         throw invalid_argument("Salary must be >= 0.0");
82      }
83
84      baseSalary = salary;
85   }
86
87   // return base salary
88   double BasePlusCommissionEmployee::getBaseSalary() const {
89      return baseSalary;
90   }
91
92   // calculate earnings
93   double BasePlusCommissionEmployee::earnings() const {
94      return baseSalary + (commissionRate * grossSales);
95   }
96
97   // return string representation of BasePlusCommissionEmployee object
98   string BasePlusCommissionEmployee::toString() const {
99      ostringstream output;
100     output << fixed << setprecision(2); // two digits of precision
```

Fig. 11.8 | BasePlusCommissionEmployee class represents an employee who receives a base salary in addition to a commission. (Part 2 of 3.)

```
101      output << "base-salaried commission employee: " << firstName << ' '
102         << lastName << "\nsocial security number: " << socialSecurityNumber
103         << "\ngross sales: " << grossSales
104         << "\ncommission rate: " << commissionRate
105         << "\nbase salary: " << baseSalary;
106      return output.str();
107   }
```

Fig. 11.8 | BasePlusCommissionEmployee class represents an employee who receives a base salary in addition to a commission. (Part 3 of 3.)

Defining Class BasePlusCommissionEmployee

The BasePlusCommissionEmployee header (Fig. 11.7) specifies class BasePlusCommissionEmployee's public services, which include the BasePlusCommissionEmployee constructor (lines 11–12) and member functions earnings (line 32) and toString (line 33). Lines 14–30 declare public *get* and *set* functions for the class's private data members (declared in lines 35–40) firstName, lastName, socialSecurityNumber, grossSales, commissionRate and baseSalary. These variables and member functions encapsulate all the necessary features of a base-salaried commission employee. Note the similarity between this class and class CommissionEmployee (Figs. 11.4–11.5)—in this example, we do *not* yet exploit that similarity.

Class BasePlusCommissionEmployee's earnings member function (defined in lines 93–95 of Fig. 11.8) computes the earnings of a base-salaried commission employee. Line 94 returns the result of adding the employee's base salary to the product of the commission rate and the employee's gross sales.

Testing Class BasePlusCommissionEmployee

Figure 11.9 tests class BasePlusCommissionEmployee. Lines 10–11 instantiate object employee of class BasePlusCommissionEmployee, passing "Bob", "Lewis", "333-33-3333", 5000, .04 and 300 to the constructor as the first name, last name, social security number, gross sales, commission rate and base salary, respectively. Lines 15–22 use BasePlusCommissionEmployee's *get* functions to retrieve the values of the object's data members for output. Line 23 invokes the object's setBaseSalary member function to change the base salary. Member function setBaseSalary (Fig. 11.8, lines 79–85) ensures that data member baseSalary is not assigned a negative value, because an employee's base salary cannot be negative. Lines 24–25 of Fig. 11.9 invoke the object's toString member function to get the updated BasePlusCommissionEmployee's information, and line 28 calls member function earnings to display the BasePlusCommissionEmployee's earnings.

```
1    // Fig. 11.9: fig11_09.cpp
2    // BasePlusCommissionEmployee class test program.
3    #include <iostream>
4    #include <iomanip>
5    #include "BasePlusCommissionEmployee.h"
6    using namespace std;
7
```

Fig. 11.9 | BasePlusCommissionEmployee class test program. (Part 1 of 2.)

```
8   int main() {
9       // instantiate BasePlusCommissionEmployee object
10      BasePlusCommissionEmployee employee{"Bob", "Lewis", "333-33-3333",
11          5000, .04, 300};
12
13      // get commission employee data
14      cout << fixed << setprecision(2); // set floating-point formatting
15      cout << "Employee information obtained by get functions: \n"
16          << "\nFirst name is " << employee.getFirstName()
17          << "\nLast name is " << employee.getLastName()
18          << "\nSocial security number is "
19          << employee.getSocialSecurityNumber()
20          << "\nGross sales is " << employee.getGrossSales()
21          << "\nCommission rate is " << employee.getCommissionRate()
22          << "\nBase salary is " << employee.getBaseSalary() << endl;
23      employee.setBaseSalary(1000); // set base salary
24      cout << "\nUpdated employee information from function toString: \n\n"
25          << employee.toString();
26
27      // display the employee's earnings
28      cout << "\n\nEmployee's earnings: $" << employee.earnings() << endl;
29  }
```

```
Employee information obtained by get functions:

First name is Bob
Last name is Lewis
Social security number is 333-33-3333
Gross sales is 5000.00
Commission rate is 0.04
Base salary is 300.00

Updated employee information from function toString:

base-salaried commission employee: Bob Lewis
social security number: 333-33-3333
gross sales: 5000.00
commission rate: 0.04
base salary: 1000.00

Employee's earnings: $1200.00
```

Fig. 11.9 | BasePlusCommissionEmployee class test program. (Part 2 of 2.)

Exploring the Similarities Between Class BasePlusCommissionEmployee and Class CommissionEmployee

Most of the code for class BasePlusCommissionEmployee (Figs. 11.7–11.8) is *similar, if not identical*, to the code for class CommissionEmployee (Figs. 11.4–11.5). For example, in class BasePlusCommissionEmployee, private data members firstName and lastName and member functions setFirstName, getFirstName, setLastName and getLastName are identical to those of class CommissionEmployee. Classes CommissionEmployee and Base-PlusCommissionEmployee also both contain private data members socialSecurity-Number, commissionRate and grossSales, as well as *get* and *set* functions to manipulate these members. In addition, the BasePlusCommissionEmployee constructor is *almost* identical to that of class CommissionEmployee, except that BasePlusCommissionEmployee's constructor *also* sets the baseSalary. The other additions to class BasePlusCommission-Employee are private data member baseSalary *and* member functions setBaseSalary and getBaseSalary. Class BasePlusCommissionEmployee's toString member function is *nearly identical* to that of class CommissionEmployee, except that BasePlusCommissionEmployee's toString *also* outputs the value of data member baseSalary.

We literally *copied* code from class CommissionEmployee and *pasted* it into class Base-PlusCommissionEmployee, then modified class BasePlusCommissionEmployee to include a base salary and member functions that manipulate the base salary. This *copy-and-paste approach* is error prone and time consuming.

Software Engineering Observation 11.1

Copying and pasting code from one class to another can spread many physical copies of the same code and can spread errors throughout a system, creating a code-maintenance nightmare. To avoid duplicating code (and possibly errors), use inheritance, rather than the "copy-and-paste" approach, in situations where you want one class to "absorb" the data members and member functions of another class.

Software Engineering Observation 11.2

With inheritance, the common data members and member functions of all the classes in the hierarchy are declared in a base class. When changes are required for these common features, you need to make the changes only in the base class—derived classes then inherit the changes. Without inheritance, changes would need to be made to all the source-code files that contain a copy of the code in question.

11.3.3 Creating a CommissionEmployee-BasePlusCommissionEmployee Inheritance Hierarchy

Now we create and test a new BasePlusCommissionEmployee class (Figs. 11.10–11.11) that *derives from* class CommissionEmployee (Figs. 11.4–11.5). In this example, a Base-PlusCommissionEmployee object *is a* CommissionEmployee (because inheritance passes on the capabilities of class CommissionEmployee), but class BasePlusCommissionEmployee *also* has data member baseSalary (Fig. 11.10, line 21). The *colon (:)* in line 10 of the class definition indicates inheritance. Keyword public indicates the *type of inheritance*. As a derived class (formed with public inheritance), BasePlusCommissionEmployee inherits *all* the members of class CommissionEmployee, *except* for the constructor—each class provides its *own* constructors that are specific to the class. (Destructors, too, are not inherited.) Thus, the public services of BasePlusCommissionEmployee include its constructor (lines 12–13) and the public member functions inherited from class CommissionEmployee— *although we cannot see these inherited member functions* in BasePlusCommissionEmployee's source code, they're nevertheless a part of derived-class BasePlusCommissionEmployee. The derived class's public services also include member functions setBaseSalary, get-BaseSalary, earnings and toString (lines 15–19).

Figure 11.11 shows BasePlusCommissionEmployee's member-function implementations. The constructor (lines 10–16) introduces base-class initializer syntax (line 14), which uses a member initializer to pass arguments to the base-class (CommissionEmployee)

```
1   // Fig. 11.10: BasePlusCommissionEmployee.h
2   // BasePlusCommissionEmployee class derived from class
3   // CommissionEmployee.
4   #ifndef BASEPLUS_H
5   #define BASEPLUS_H
6
7   #include <string> // C++ standard string class
8   #include "CommissionEmployee.h" // CommissionEmployee class declaration
9
10  class BasePlusCommissionEmployee : public CommissionEmployee {
11  public:
12     BasePlusCommissionEmployee(const std::string&, const std::string&,
13        const std::string&, double = 0.0, double = 0.0, double = 0.0);
14
15     void setBaseSalary(double); // set base salary
16     double getBaseSalary() const; // return base salary
17
18     double earnings() const; // calculate earnings
19     std::string toString() const; // create string representation
20  private:
21     double baseSalary; // base salary
22  };
23
24  #endif
```

Fig. 11.10 | BasePlusCommissionEmployee class definition indicating inheritance relationship with class CommissionEmployee.

```
1   // Fig. 11.11: BasePlusCommissionEmployee.cpp
2   // Class BasePlusCommissionEmployee member-function definitions.
3   #include <iomanip>
4   #include <sstream>
5   #include <stdexcept>
6   #include "BasePlusCommissionEmployee.h"
7   using namespace std;
8
9   // constructor
10  BasePlusCommissionEmployee::BasePlusCommissionEmployee(
11     const string& first, const string& last, const string& ssn,
12     double sales, double rate, double salary)
13     // explicitly call base-class constructor
14     : CommissionEmployee(first, last, ssn, sales, rate) {
15     setBaseSalary(salary); // validate and store base salary
16  }
17
18  // set base salary
19  void BasePlusCommissionEmployee::setBaseSalary(double salary) {
20     if (salary < 0.0) {
21        throw invalid_argument("Salary must be >= 0.0");
22     }
```

Fig. 11.11 | BasePlusCommissionEmployee implementation file: private base-class data cannot be accessed from derived class. (Part 1 of 2.)

```
23
24      baseSalary = salary;
25  }
26
27  // return base salary
28  double BasePlusCommissionEmployee::getBaseSalary() const {
29      return baseSalary;
30  }
31
32  // calculate earnings
33  double BasePlusCommissionEmployee::earnings() const {
34      // derived class cannot access the base class's private data
35      return baseSalary + (commissionRate * grossSales);
36  }
37
38  // returns string representation of BasePlusCommissionEmployee object
39  string BasePlusCommissionEmployee::toString() const {
40      ostringstream output;
41      output << fixed << setprecision(2); // two digits of precision
42
43      // derived class cannot access the base class's private data
44      output << "base-salaried commission employee: " << firstName << ' '
45          << lastName << "\nsocial security number: " << socialSecurityNumber
46          << "\ngross sales: " << grossSales
47          << "\ncommission rate: " << commissionRate
48          << "\nbase salary: " << baseSalary;
49      return output.str();
50  }
```

Compilation Errors from the Clang/LLVM Compiler in Xcode 7.2

```
BasePlusCommissionEmployee.cpp:34:25:
   'commissionRate' is a private member of 'CommissionEmployee'
BasePlusCommissionEmployee.cpp:34:42:
   'grossSales' is a private member of 'CommissionEmployee'
BasePlusCommissionEmployee.cpp:42:55:
   'firstName' is a private member of 'CommissionEmployee'
BasePlusCommissionEmployee.cpp:43:10:
   'lastName' is a private member of 'CommissionEmployee'
BasePlusCommissionEmployee.cpp:43:54:
   'socialSecurityNumber' is a private member of 'CommissionEmployee'
BasePlusCommissionEmployee.cpp:44:31:
   'grossSales' is a private member of 'CommissionEmployee'
BasePlusCommissionEmployee.cpp:45:35:
   'commissionRate' is a private member of 'CommissionEmployee'
```

Fig. 11.11 | BasePlusCommissionEmployee implementation file: private base-class data cannot be accessed from derived class. (Part 2 of 2.)

constructor. C++ requires that a derived-class constructor call its base-class constructor to initialize the base-class data members that are inherited into the derived class. Line 14 does this by *explicitly* invoking the CommissionEmployee constructor by name, passing the constructor's parameters first, last, ssn, sales and rate as arguments to initialize the base-class data members firstName, lastName, socialSecurityNumber, grossSales and commissionRate, respectively. The compiler would issue an error if BasePlusCommissionEmployee's constructor did *not* invoke class CommissionEmployee's constructor *explicitly*—in this case, C++ attempts to invoke class CommissionEmployee's default constructor *implicitly*, but the class does *not* have such a constructor. Recall from Chapter 3 that the compiler provides a default constructor with no parameters in any class that does *not* explicitly include a constructor. However, CommissionEmployee *does* explicitly include a constructor, so a default constructor is *not* provided.

Common Programming Error 11.1

When a derived-class constructor calls a base-class constructor, the arguments passed to the base-class constructor must be consistent with the number and types of parameters specified in one of the base-class constructors; otherwise, a compilation error occurs.

Performance Tip 11.1

In a derived-class constructor, invoking base-class constructors and initializing member objects explicitly in the member initializer list prevents duplicate initialization in which a default constructor is called, then data members are modified again in the derived-class constructor's body.

Compilation Errors from Accessing Base-Class private Members
The compiler generates errors for line 35 of Fig. 11.11 because base-class CommissionEmployee's data members commissionRate and grossSales are private—derived-class BasePlusCommissionEmployee's member functions are *not* allowed to access base-class CommissionEmployee's private data. The compiler issues additional errors in lines 44–47 of BasePlusCommissionEmployee's toString member function for the same reason. As you can see, C++ rigidly enforces restrictions on accessing private data members, so that *even a derived class (which is intimately related to its base class) cannot access the base class's private data.*

Preventing the Errors in BasePlusCommissionEmployee
We purposely included the erroneous code in Fig. 11.11 to emphasize that a derived class's member functions *cannot* access its base class's private data. The errors in BasePlusCommissionEmployee could have been prevented by using the *get* member functions inherited from class CommissionEmployee. For example, line 35 could have invoked getCommissionRate and getGrossSales to access CommissionEmployee's private data members commissionRate and grossSales, respectively. Similarly, lines 44–47 could have used appropriate *get* member functions to retrieve the values of the base class's data members. In the next example, we show how using protected data *also* allows us to avoid the errors encountered in this example.

Including the Base-Class Header in the Derived-Class Header with #include
Notice that we #include the base class's header in the derived class's header (line 8 of Fig. 11.10). This is necessary for three reasons. First, for the derived class to use the base class's name in line 10, we must tell the compiler that the base class exists—the class definition in CommissionEmployee.h does exactly that.

The second reason is that the compiler uses a class definition to determine the *size* of an object of that class (as we discussed in Section 9.3). A client program that creates an object of a class #includes the class definition to enable the compiler to reserve the proper amount of memory for the object. When using inheritance, a derived-class object's size depends on the data members declared explicitly in its class definition *and* the data members *inherited* from its direct and indirect base classes. Including the base class's definition in line 8 of Fig. 11.10 allows the compiler to determine the memory requirements for the base class's data members that become part of a derived-class object and thus contribute to its total size.

The last reason for line 8 is to allow the compiler to determine whether the derived class uses the base class's inherited members properly. For example, in the program of Figs. 11.10–11.11, the compiler uses the base-class header to determine that the data members being accessed by the derived class are private in the base class. Since these are *inaccessible* to the derived class, the compiler generates errors. The compiler also uses the base class's *function prototypes* to *validate* function calls made by the derived class to the inherited base-class functions.

Linking Process in an Inheritance Hierarchy

In Section 9.3, we discussed the linking process for creating an executable Time application. In that example, you saw that the client's object code was linked with the object code for class Time, as well as the object code for any C++ Standard Library classes used either in the client code or in class Time.

The linking process is similar for a program that uses classes in an inheritance hierarchy. The process requires the object code for all classes used in the program and the object code for the direct and indirect base classes of any derived classes used by the program. Suppose a client wants to create an application that uses class BasePlusCommission-Employee, which is a derived class of CommissionEmployee (we'll see an example of this in Section 11.3.4). When compiling the client application, the client's object code must be linked with the object code for classes BasePlusCommissionEmployee and Commission-Employee, because BasePlusCommissionEmployee inherits member functions from its base-class CommissionEmployee. The code is also linked with the object code for any C++ Standard Library used in class CommissionEmployee, class BasePlusCommission-Employee or the client code. This provides the program with access to the implementations of all of the functionality that the program may use.

11.3.4 CommissionEmployee–BasePlusCommissionEmployee Inheritance Hierarchy Using protected Data

Chapter 3 introduced access specifiers public and private. A base class's public members are accessible within its body and anywhere that the program has a handle (i.e., a name, reference or pointer) to an object of that class or one of its derived classes, including in derived classes. A base class's private members are accessible only within its body and to the friends of that base class. In this section, we introduce the access specifier protected.

Using protected access offers an intermediate level of protection between public and private access. To enable class BasePlusCommissionEmployee to *directly access* Commis-sionEmployee data members firstName, lastName, socialSecurityNumber, grossSales and `commissionRate`, we can declare those members as `protected` in the base class. A base class's `protected` members *can* be accessed within the body of that base class, by members and `friend`s of that base class, and by members and `friend`s of any classes derived from that base class.

Defining Base-Class `CommissionEmployee` with `protected` Data

Class `CommissionEmployee` (Fig. 11.12) now declares data members `firstName`, `lastName`, `socialSecurityNumber`, `grossSales` and `commissionRate` as protected (lines 30–35) rather than `private`. The member-function implementations are identical to those in Fig. 11.5, so `CommissionEmployee.cpp` is not shown here.

```cpp
1   // Fig. 11.12: CommissionEmployee.h
2   // CommissionEmployee class definition with protected data.
3   #ifndef COMMISSION_H
4   #define COMMISSION_H
5
6   #include <string> // C++ standard string class
7
8   class CommissionEmployee {
9   public:
10     CommissionEmployee(const std::string&, const std::string&,
11       const std::string&, double = 0.0, double = 0.0);
12
13     void setFirstName(const std::string&); // set first name
14     std::string getFirstName() const; // return first name
15
16     void setLastName(const std::string&); // set last name
17     std::string getLastName() const; // return last name
18
19     void setSocialSecurityNumber(const std::string&); // set SSN
20     std::string getSocialSecurityNumber() const; // return SSN
21
22     void setGrossSales(double); // set gross sales amount
23     double getGrossSales() const; // return gross sales amount
24
25     void setCommissionRate(double); // set commission rate
26     double getCommissionRate() const; // return commission rate
27
28     double earnings() const; // calculate earnings
29     std::string toString() const; // return string representation
30   protected:
31     std::string firstName;
32     std::string lastName;
33     std::string socialSecurityNumber;
34     double grossSales; // gross weekly sales
35     double commissionRate; // commission percentage
36   };
37
38   #endif
```

Fig. 11.12 | `CommissionEmployee` class definition that declares protected data to allow access by derived classes.

Class BasePlusCommissionEmployee

The definition of class BasePlusCommissionEmployee from Figs. 11.10–11.11 remains *unchanged*, so we do *not* show it again here. Now that BasePlusCommissionEmployee inherits from the updated class CommissionEmployee (Fig. 11.12), BasePlusCommissionEmployee objects *can* access inherited data members that are declared protected in class CommissionEmployee (i.e., data members firstName, lastName, socialSecurityNumber, grossSales and commissionRate). As a result, the compiler does *not* generate errors when compiling the BasePlusCommissionEmployee earnings and toString member-function definitions in Fig. 11.11 (lines 33–36 and 39–50, respectively). This shows the special privileges that a derived class is granted to access protected base-class data members. Objects of a derived class also can access protected members in *any* of that derived class's *indirect* base classes.

Class BasePlusCommissionEmployee does *not* inherit class CommissionEmployee's constructor. However, class BasePlusCommissionEmployee's constructor (Fig. 11.11, lines 10–16) calls class CommissionEmployee's constructor explicitly with member-initializer syntax (line 14). Recall that BasePlusCommissionEmployee's constructor must *explicitly* call the constructor of class CommissionEmployee, because CommissionEmployee does *not* contain a default constructor that could be invoked implicitly.

Testing the Modified BasePlusCommissionEmployee Class

To test the updated class hierarchy, we reused the test program from Fig. 11.9. As shown in Fig. 11.13, the output is identical to that of Fig. 11.9.

```
Employee information obtained by get functions:

First name is Bob
Last name is Lewis
Social security number is 333-33-3333
Gross sales is 5000.00
Commission rate is 0.04
Base salary is 300.00

Updated employee information from function toString:

base-salaried commission employee: Bob Lewis
social security number: 333-33-3333
gross sales: 5000.00
commission rate: 0.04
base salary: 1000.00

Employee's earnings: $1200.00
```

Fig. 11.13 | protected base-class data can be accessed from derived class.

We created the first class BasePlusCommissionEmployee *without using inheritance* and created this version of BasePlusCommissionEmployee *using inheritance*; however, both classes provide the *same* functionality. The code for derived-class BasePlusCommissionEmployee (i.e., the header and implementation files) is considerably *shorter* than the code for the noninherited version of the class, because the inherited version absorbs much of its functionality from CommissionEmployee, whereas the noninherited version does not absorb any functionality. Also, there is now only *one* copy of the Commission-Employee functionality declared and defined in class CommissionEmployee. This makes the source code easier to maintain, modify and debug, because the source code related to a CommissionEmployee exists only in the files CommissionEmployee.h and Commission-Employee.cpp.

Notes on Using **protected** Data

In this example, we declared base-class data members as protected, so derived classes can modify the data directly. Inheriting protected data members slightly improves performance, because we can directly access the members without incurring the overhead of calls to *set* or *get* member functions.

Software Engineering Observation 11.3

In most cases, it's better to use private *data members to encourage proper software engineering, and leave code optimization issues to the compiler. Your code will be easier to maintain, modify and debug.*

Using protected data members creates two serious problems. First, the derived-class object does *not* have to use a member function to set the value of the base class's protected data member. An *invalid* value can easily be assigned to the protected data member, thus leaving the object in an *inconsistent* state—e.g., with CommissionEmployee's data member grossSales declared as protected, a derived-class object can assign a negative value to grossSales. The second problem with using protected data members is that derived-class member functions are more likely to be written so that they *depend on the base-class implementation*. Derived classes should depend only on the base-class services (i.e., non-private member functions) and *not* on the base-class implementation. With protected data members in the base class, if the base-class implementation changes, we may need to modify *all* derived classes of that base class. For example, if for some reason we were to change the names of data members firstName and lastName to first and last, then we'd have to do so for all occurrences in which a derived class references these base-class data members directly. Such software is said to be fragile or brittle, because a small change in the base class can "break" the derived-class implementation. You should be able to change the base-class implementation while still providing the *same* services to derived classes. Of course, if the base-class services change, we must reimplement our derived classes—good object-oriented design attempts to prevent this.

Software Engineering Observation 11.4

It's appropriate to use the protected *access specifier when a base class should provide a service (i.e., a non-private member function) only to its derived classes and* friends.

Software Engineering Observation 11.5

Declaring base-class data members private *(as opposed to declaring them* protected*) enables you to change the base-class implementation without having to change derived-class implementations.*

11.3.5 CommissionEmployee–BasePlusCommissionEmployee Inheritance Hierarchy Using private Data

We now reexamine our hierarchy once more, this time using *best software engineering practices*. Class CommissionEmployee now declares data members firstName, lastName, socialSecurityNumber, grossSales and commissionRate as private, as shown previously in lines 31–35 of Fig. 11.4.

Changes to Class CommissionEmployee's Member-Function Definitions

In the CommissionEmployee constructor implementation (Fig. 11.14, lines 10–15), we use member initializers (line 12) to set the values of the members firstName, lastName and socialSecurityNumber. Though we do not do so here, the derived-class BasePlusCommissionEmployee (Fig. 11.15) can invoke non-private base-class member functions (setFirstName, getFirstName, setLastName, getLastName, setSocialSecurityNumber and getSocialSecurityNumber) to manipulate these data members, as can any client code of class BasePlusCommissionEmployee (such as main).

```cpp
1  // Fig. 11.14: CommissionEmployee.cpp
2  // Class CommissionEmployee member-function definitions.
3  #include <iomanip>
4  #include <stdexcept>
5  #include <sstream>
6  #include "CommissionEmployee.h" // CommissionEmployee class definition
7  using namespace std;
8
9  // constructor
10 CommissionEmployee::CommissionEmployee(const string &first,
11    const string &last, const string &ssn, double sales, double rate)
12    : firstName(first), lastName(last), socialSecurityNumber(ssn) {
13    setGrossSales(sales); // validate and store gross sales
14    setCommissionRate(rate); // validate and store commission rate
15 }
16
17 // set first name
18 void CommissionEmployee::setFirstName(const string& first) {
19    firstName = first; // should validate
20 }
21
22 // return first name
23 string CommissionEmployee::getFirstName() const {return firstName;}
24
25 // set last name
26 void CommissionEmployee::setLastName(const string& last) {
27    lastName = last; // should validate
28 }
29
30 // return last name
31 string CommissionEmployee::getLastName() const {return lastName;}
32
```

Fig. 11.14 | CommissionEmployee class implementation file: CommissionEmployee class uses member functions to manipulate its private data. (Part 1 of 2.)

```cpp
33   // set social security number
34   void CommissionEmployee::setSocialSecurityNumber(const string& ssn) {
35      socialSecurityNumber = ssn; // should validate
36   }
37
38   // return social security number
39   string CommissionEmployee::getSocialSecurityNumber() const {
40      return socialSecurityNumber;
41   }
42
43   // set gross sales amount
44   void CommissionEmployee::setGrossSales(double sales) {
45      if (sales < 0.0) {
46         throw invalid_argument("Gross sales must be >= 0.0");
47      }
48
49      grossSales = sales;
50   }
51
52   // return gross sales amount
53   double CommissionEmployee::getGrossSales() const {return grossSales;}
54
55   // set commission rate
56   void CommissionEmployee::setCommissionRate(double rate) {
57      if (rate <= 0.0 || rate >= 1.0) {
58         throw invalid_argument("Commission rate must be > 0.0 and < 1.0");
59      }
60
61      commissionRate = rate;
62   }
63
64   // return commission rate
65   double CommissionEmployee::getCommissionRate() const {
66      return commissionRate;
67   }
68
69   // calculate earnings
70   double CommissionEmployee::earnings() const {
71      return getCommissionRate() * getGrossSales();
72   }
73
74   // return string representation of CommissionEmployee object
75   string CommissionEmployee::toString() const {
76      ostringstream output;
77      output << fixed << setprecision(2); // two digits of precision
78      output << "commission employee: "
79         << getFirstName() << ' ' << getLastName()
80         << "\nsocial security number: " << getSocialSecurityNumber()
81         << "\ngross sales: " << getGrossSales()
82         << "\ncommission rate: " << getCommissionRate();
83      return output.str();
84   }
```

Fig. 11.14 | CommissionEmployee class implementation file: CommissionEmployee class uses member functions to manipulate its private data. (Part 2 of 2.)

In the body of the constructor and in the bodies of member functions earnings (Fig. 11.14, lines 70–72) and toString (lines 75–84), we call the class's *set* and *get* member functions to access the class's private data members. If we decide to change the data member names, the earnings and toString definitions will *not* require modification—only the definitions of the *get* and *set* member functions that directly manipulate the data members will need to change. *These changes occur solely within the base class—no changes to the derived class are needed.* Localizing the effects of changes like this is a good software engineering practice.

Performance Tip 11.2

Using a member function to access a data member's value can be slightly slower than accessing the data directly. However, today's optimizing compilers perform many optimizations implicitly (such as inlining set *and* get *member-function calls). You should write code that adheres to proper software engineering principles, and leave optimization to the compiler. A good rule is, "Do not second-guess the compiler."*

Changes to Class *BasePlusCommissionEmployee's Member-Function Definitions*

Class BasePlusCommissionEmployee inherits CommissionEmployee's public member functions and can access the private base-class members via the inherited member functions. The class's header remains unchanged from Fig. 11.10. The class has several changes to its member-function implementations (Fig. 11.15) that distinguish it from the previous version of the class (Figs. 11.10–11.11). Member functions earnings (Fig. 11.15, lines 32–34) and toString (lines 37–42) each invoke member function getBaseSalary to obtain the base salary value, rather than accessing baseSalary directly. This insulates earnings and toString from potential changes to the implementation of data member baseSalary. For example, if we decide to rename data member baseSalary or change its type, only member functions setBaseSalary and getBaseSalary will need to change.

```
1   // Fig. 11.15: BasePlusCommissionEmployee.cpp
2   // Class BasePlusCommissionEmployee member-function definitions.
3   #include <stdexcept>
4   #include <sstream>
5   #include "BasePlusCommissionEmployee.h"
6   using namespace std;
7
8   // constructor
9   BasePlusCommissionEmployee::BasePlusCommissionEmployee(
10     const string& first, const string& last, const string& ssn,
11     double sales, double rate, double salary)
12     // explicitly call base-class constructor
13     : CommissionEmployee(first, last, ssn, sales, rate) {
14     setBaseSalary(salary); // validate and store base salary
15  }
16
```

Fig. 11.15 | BasePlusCommissionEmployee class that inherits from class CommissionEmployee but cannot directly access the class's private data. (Part 1 of 2.)

```
17   // set base salary
18   void BasePlusCommissionEmployee::setBaseSalary(double salary) {
19      if (salary < 0.0) {
20         throw invalid_argument("Salary must be >= 0.0");
21      }
22
23      baseSalary = salary;
24   }
25
26   // return base salary
27   double BasePlusCommissionEmployee::getBaseSalary() const {
28      return baseSalary;
29   }
30
31   // calculate earnings
32   double BasePlusCommissionEmployee::earnings() const {
33      return getBaseSalary() + CommissionEmployee::earnings();
34   }
35
36   // return string representation of BasePlusCommissionEmployee object
37   string BasePlusCommissionEmployee::toString() const {
38      ostringstream output;
39      output << "base-salaried " << CommissionEmployee::toString()
40         << "\nbase salary: " << getBaseSalary();
41      return output.str();
42   }
```

Fig. 11.15 | BasePlusCommissionEmployee class that inherits from class CommissionEmployee but cannot directly access the class's private data. (Part 2 of 2.)

BasePlusCommissionEmployee *Member Function* earnings

Class BasePlusCommissionEmployee's earnings function (Fig. 11.15, lines 32–34) redefines class CommissionEmployee's earnings member function (Fig. 11.14, lines 70–72) to calculate the earnings of a BasePlusCommissionEmployee. Class BasePlusCommissionEmployee's version of earnings obtains the portion of the employee's earnings based on commission alone by calling base-class CommissionEmployee's earnings function with the expression CommissionEmployee::earnings() as shown in line 33 of Fig. 11.15. BasePlusCommissionEmployee's earnings function then adds the base salary to this value to calculate the total earnings of the employee. Note the syntax used to invoke a redefined base-class member function from a derived class—place the base-class name and the scope resolution operator (::) before the base-class member-function name. This member-function invocation is a good software engineering practice: Recall from Chapter 9 that, if an object's member function performs the actions needed by another object, we should call that member function rather than duplicating its code body. By having BasePlusCommissionEmployee's earnings function invoke CommissionEmployee's earnings function to calculate part of a BasePlusCommissionEmployee object's earnings, we avoid duplicating the code and reduce code-maintenance problems.

Common Programming Error 11.2

When a base-class member function is redefined in a derived class, the derived-class version often calls the base-class version to do additional work. Failure to use the :: operator prefixed with the name of the base class when referencing the base class's member function causes in-finite recursion, because the derived-class member function would then call itself.

BasePlusCommissionEmployee *Member Function* toString

Similarly, BasePlusCommissionEmployee's toString function (Fig. 11.15, lines 37–42) re-defines class CommissionEmployee's toString function (Fig. 11.14, lines 75–84) to output the appropriate base-salaried commission employee information. The new version displays "base-salaried" followed by the part of a BasePlusCommissionEmployee object's infor-mation returned by calling CommissionEmployee's toString member function with the qualified name CommissionEmployee::toString() (Fig. 11.15, line 39)—this returns a string containing "commission employee" and the values of class CommissionEmployee's private data members. BasePlusCommissionEmployee's toString function then outputs the remainder of a BasePlusCommissionEmployee object's information (i.e., the value of class BasePlusCommissionEmployee's base salary preceded by "base salary:").

Testing the Modified Class Hierarchy

Once again, this example uses the BasePlusCommissionEmployee test program from Fig. 11.9 and produces the same output. Although each "base-salaried commission em-ployee" class behaves identically, the version in this example is the best engineered. *By us-ing inheritance and by calling member functions that hide the data and ensure consistency, we've efficiently and effectively constructed a well-engineered class.*

Summary of the CommissionEmployee–BasePlusCommissionEmployee *Examples*

In this section, you saw an evolutionary set of examples that was designed to teach key ca-pabilities for good software engineering with inheritance. You learned how to create a de-rived class using inheritance, how to use protected base-class members to enable a derived class to access inherited base-class data members and how to redefine base-class functions to provide versions that are more appropriate for derived-class objects. In addition, you learned how to apply software engineering techniques from Chapter 9 and this chapter to create classes that are easy to maintain, modify and debug.

11.4 Constructors and Destructors in Derived Classes

Instantiating a derived-class object begins a *chain* of constructor calls in which the derived-class constructor, before performing its own tasks, invokes its direct base class's constructor either *explicitly* (via a base-class member initializer) or *implicitly* (calling the base class's de-fault constructor). Similarly, if the base class is derived from another class, the base-class constructor is required to invoke the constructor of the next class up in the hierarchy, and so on. The last constructor called in this chain is the one of the class at the base of the hi-erarchy, whose body actually finishes executing *first*. The most-derived-class constructor's body finishes executing *last*. Each base-class constructor initializes the base-class data members that the derived-class object inherits. In the CommissionEmployee/Base-PlusCommissionEmployee hierarchy that we've been studying, when a program creates a BasePlusCommissionEmployee object, the CommissionEmployee constructor is called. Since class CommissionEmployee is at the base of the hierarchy, its constructor executes, initializing the private CommissionEmployee data members that are part of the BasePlusCommissionEmployee object. When CommissionEmployee's constructor completes execution, it returns control to BasePlusCommissionEmployee's constructor, which initializes the BasePlusCommissionEmployee object's baseSalary.

Software Engineering Observation 11.6

When a program creates a derived-class object, the derived-class constructor immediately calls the base-class constructor, the base-class constructor's body executes, then the derived class's member initializers execute and finally the derived-class constructor's body executes. This process cascades up the hierarchy if it contains more than two levels.

When a derived-class object is destroyed, the program calls that object's destructor. This begins a chain (or cascade) of destructor calls in which the derived-class destructor and the destructors of the direct and indirect base classes and the classes' members execute in *reverse* of the order in which the constructors executed. When a derived-class object's destructor is called, the destructor performs its task, then invokes the destructor of the next base class up the hierarchy. This process repeats until the destructor of the final base class at the top of the hierarchy is called. Then the object is removed from memory.

Software Engineering Observation 11.7

Suppose that we create an object of a derived class where both the base class and the derived class contain (via composition) objects of other classes. When an object of that derived class is created, first the constructors for the base class's member objects execute, then the base-class constructor body executes, then the constructors for the derived class's member objects execute, then the derived class's constructor body executes. Destructors for derived-class objects are called in the reverse of the order in which their corresponding constructors are called.

By default, base-class constructors, destructors and overloaded assignment operators (Chapter 10) are *not* inherited by derived classes. Derived-class constructors, destructors and overloaded assignment operators, however, can call base-class versions.

11   *C++11: Inheriting Base-Class Constructors*

Sometimes a derived class's constructors simply specify the same parameters as the base class's constructors and simply pass the constructor arguments to the base-class's constructors. For such cases, C++11 allows you to specify that a derived class should *inherit* a base class's constructors. To do so, *explicitly* include a using declaration of the form

> using *BaseClass*::*BaseClass*;

anywhere in the derived-class definition. In the preceding declaration, *BaseClass* is the base class's name. With a few exceptions (listed below), for each constructor in the base class, the compiler generates a derived-class constructor that calls the corresponding base-class constructor. Each generated constructor has the same name as the derived class. The generated constructors perform only *default initialization* for the derived class's additional data members.

When you inherit constructors:

- Each generated constructor has the *same* access specifier (public, protected or private) as its corresponding base-class constructor.

- The default, copy and move constructors are *not* inherited.

- If a constructor is *deleted* in the base class by placing = delete in its prototype, the corresponding constructor in the derived class is *also* deleted.

- If the derived class does not explicitly define constructors, the compiler still generates a default constructor in the derived class.

- A given base-class constructor is *not* inherited if a constructor that you explicitly define in the derived class has the *same* parameter list.

- A base-class constructor's default arguments are *not* inherited. Instead, the compiler generates *overloaded constructors* in the derived class. For example, if the base class declares the constructor

```
BaseClass(int = 0, double = 0.0);
```

the compiler generates the following *two* derived-class constructors *without* default arguments

```
DerivedClass();
DerivedClass(int);
DerivedClass(int, double);
```

These each call the *BaseClass* constructor that specifies the default arguments.

11.5 public, protected and private Inheritance

When deriving a class from a base class, the base class may be inherited through public, protected or private inheritance. We normally use public inheritance in this book. Use of protected inheritance is rare. Chapter 19 demonstrates private inheritance as an alternative to composition. Figure 11.16 summarizes for each type of inheritance the accessibility of base-class members in a derived class. The first column contains the base-class member access specifiers.

When deriving a class with public inheritance, public members of the base class become public members of the derived class, and protected members of the base class become protected members of the derived class. A base class's private members are *never* accessible directly from a derived class, but can be accessed through calls to the public and protected member functions of the base class.

When deriving a class from a base class, the base class may be inherited through public, protected or private inheritance. We normally use public inheritance in this book. Use of protected inheritance is rare. Chapter 19 demonstrates private inheritance as an alternative to composition. Figure 11.16 summarizes for each type of inheritance the accessibility of base-class members in a derived class. The first column contains the base-class member access specifiers.

Base-class member-access specifier	Type of inheritance		
	public inheritance	protected inheritance	private inheritance
public	public in derived class. Can be accessed directly by member functions, friend functions and nonmember functions.	protected in derived class. Can be accessed directly by member functions and friend functions.	private in derived class. Can be accessed directly by member functions and friend functions.
protected	protected in derived class. Can be accessed directly by member functions and friend functions.	protected in derived class. Can be accessed directly by member functions and friend functions.	private in derived class. Can be accessed directly by member functions and friend functions.
private	Hidden in derived class. Can be accessed by member functions and friend functions through public or protected member functions of the base class.	Hidden in derived class. Can be accessed by member functions and friend functions through public or protected member functions of the base class.	Hidden in derived class. Can be accessed by member functions and friend functions through public or protected member functions of the base class.

Fig. 11.16 | Summary of base-class member accessibility in a derived class.

11.6 Wrap-Up

This chapter introduced inheritance—the ability to create a class by absorbing an existing class's data members and member functions and embellishing them with new capabilities. Through a series of examples using an employee inheritance hierarchy, you learned the notions of base classes and derived classes and used public inheritance to create a derived class that inherits members from a base class. The chapter introduced the access specifier protected—derived-class member functions can access protected base-class members. You learned how to access redefined base-class members by qualifying their names with the base-class name and scope resolution operator (::). You also saw the order in which constructors and destructors are called for objects of classes that are part of an inheritance hierarchy. Finally, we explained the three types of inheritance—public, protected and private—and the accessibility of base-class members in a derived class when using each type.

In Chapter 12, Object-Oriented Programming: Polymorphism, we build on our discussion of inheritance by introducing polymorphism—an object-oriented concept that enables us to write programs that handle, in a more general manner, objects of a wide variety of classes related by inheritance. After studying Chapter 12, you'll be familiar with classes, objects, encapsulation, inheritance and polymorphism—the essential concepts of object-oriented programming.

Summary

Section 11.1 Introduction

- **Inheritance** (p. 498) enables you to create a class that absorbs an existing class's capabilities, then customizes or enhances them. The existing class is called the **base class** (p. 498), and the new class is referred to as the **derived class** (p. 498).
- Every object of a derived class is also an object of that class's base class. However, a base-class object is not an object of that class's derived classes.
- The *is-a* **relationship** (p. 498) represents inheritance. In an *is-a* relationship, an object of a derived class also can be treated as an object of its base class.

Section 11.2 Base Classes and Derived Classes

- A **direct base class** (p. 499) is the one from which a derived class explicitly inherits. An **indirect base class** (p. 499) is inherited from two or more levels up the **class hierarchy** (p. 499).
- With **single inheritance** (p. 499), a class is derived from one base class. With **multiple inheritance** (p. 499), a class inherits from multiple (possibly unrelated) base classes.
- A derived class represents a more specialized group of objects.
- Inheritance relationships form class hierarchies.
- It's possible to treat base-class objects and derived-class objects similarly; the commonality shared between the object types is expressed in the base class's data members and member functions.

Section 11.4 Constructors and Destructors in Derived Classes

- When an object of a derived class is instantiated, the base class's constructor is called immediately to initialize the base-class data members in the derived-class object, then the derived-class constructor initializes the additional derived-class data members.
- When a derived-class object is destroyed, the destructors are called in the reverse order of the constructors—first the derived-class destructor is called, then the base-class destructor is called.
- A base class's `public` members are accessible anywhere that the program has a handle to an object of that base class or to an object of one of that base class's derived classes.
- A base class's `private` members are accessible only within the base class or from its friends.
- A base class's `protected` members can be accessed by members and `friend`s of that base class and by members and `friend`s of any classes derived from that base class.
- In C++11, a derived class can inherit constructors from its base class by including anywhere in the derived-class definition a `using` declaration of the form

      using *BaseClass*::*BaseClass*;

Section 11.5 `public`, `protected` and `private` Inheritance

- Declaring data members `private`, while providing non-`private` member functions to manipulate and perform validity checking on this data, enforces good software engineering.
- When deriving a class, the base class may be declared as either `public`, `protected` or `private`.
- When deriving a class with **`public` inheritance** (p. 525), `public` members of the base class become `public` members of the derived class, and `protected` members of the base class become `protected` members of the derived class.
- When deriving a class with **`protected` inheritance** (p. 525), `public` and `protected` members of the base class become `protected` members of the derived class.
- When deriving a class with **`private` inheritance** (p. 525), `public` and `protected` members of the base class become `private` members of the derived class.

Self-Review Exercises

11.1 Fill in the blanks in each of the following statements:

a) _____ enables new classes to absorb the data and behaviors of existing classes and embellish these classes with new capabilities.

b) A base class's _____ and _____ members can be accessed in the base-class definition, in derived-class definitions and in `friend`s of the base class and derived classes.

c) In a(n) _____ relationship, an object of a derived class also can be treated as an object of its base class.

d) In a(n) _____ relationship, a class object has one or more objects of other classes as members.

e) In single inheritance, a class exists in a(n) _____ relationship with its derived classes.

f) A base class's _____ members are accessible within that base class and anywhere that the program has a handle to an object of that class or one of its derived classes.

g) A base class's `protected` access members have a level of protection between those of `public` and _____ access.

h) C++ provides for _____, which allows a derived class to inherit from many base classes, even if the base classes are unrelated.

i) When an object of a derived class is instantiated, the base class's _____ is called implicitly or explicitly to do any necessary initialization of the base-class data members in the derived-class object.

j) When deriving a class with `public` inheritance, `public` members of the base class become _____ members of the derived class, and `protected` members of the base class become _____ members of the derived class.

k) When deriving from a class with `protected` inheritance, `public` members of the base class become _____ members of the derived class, and `protected` members of the base class become _____ members of the derived class.

11.2 State whether each of the following is *true* or *false*. If *false*, explain why.

a) Base-class constructors are not automatically inherited by derived classes.

b) A *has-a* relationship is implemented via inheritance.

c) A `Car` class has an *is-a* relationship with the `SteeringWheel` and `Brakes` classes.

d) When a derived-class object is destroyed, the destructors are called in the reverse order of the constructors.

Answers to Self-Review Exercises

11.1 a) Inheritance. b) `public`, `protected`. c) *is-a* or inheritance (for `public` inheritance). d) *has-a* or composition or aggregation. e) hierarchical. f) `public`. g) `private`. h) multiple inheritance. i) constructor. j) `public`, `protected`. k) `protected`, `protected`.

11.2 a) True. b) False. A *has-a* relationship is implemented via composition. An *is-a* relationship is implemented via inheritance. c) False. This is an example of a *has-a* relationship. Class `Car` has an *is-a* relationship with class `Vehicle`. d) True.

Exercises

11.3 *(Composition as an Alternative to Inheritance)* Many programs written with inheritance can be written with composition instead, and vice versa. Rewrite class `BasePlusCommissionEmployee` of the `CommissionEmployee–BasePlusCommissionEmployee` hierarchy to use composition rather than inheritance. After you do this, assess the relative merits of the two approaches for designing classes `CommissionEmployee` and `BasePlusCommissionEmployee`, as well as for object-oriented programs in general. Which approach is more natural? Why?

11.4   *(Inheritance Advantage)* Discuss the ways in which inheritance saves time during program development and helps prevent errors.

11.5   *(Protected vs. Private Base Classes)* Some programmers prefer not to use protected access because they believe it breaks the encapsulation of the base class. Discuss the relative merits of using protected access vs. using private access in base classes.

11.6   *(Student Inheritance Hierarchy)* Draw an inheritance hierarchy for students at a university similar to the hierarchy shown in Fig. 11.2. Use Student as the base class of the hierarchy, then include classes UndergraduateStudent and GraduateStudent that derive from Student. Continue to extend the hierarchy as deep (i.e., as many levels) as possible. For example, Freshman, Sophomore, Junior and Senior might derive from UndergraduateStudent, and DoctoralStudent and Masters-Student might derive from GraduateStudent. After drawing the hierarchy, discuss the relationships that exist between the classes. [*Note:* You do not need to write any code for this exercise.]

11.7   *(Richer Shape Hierarchy)* The world of shapes is much richer than the shapes included in the inheritance hierarchy of Fig. 11.3. Write down all the shapes you can think of—both two-dimensional and three-dimensional—and form them into a more complete Shape hierarchy with as many levels as possible. Your hierarchy should have the base-class Shape from which class TwoDimensionalShape and class ThreeDimensionalShape are derived. [*Note:* You do not need to write any code for this exercise.] We'll use this hierarchy in the exercises of Chapter 12 to process a set of distinct shapes as objects of base-class Shape. (This technique, called polymorphism, is the subject of Chapter 12.)

11.8   *(Quadrilateral Inheritance Hierarchy)* Draw an inheritance hierarchy for classes Quadrilateral, Trapezoid, Parallelogram, Rectangle and Square. Use Quadrilateral as the base class of the hierarchy. Make the hierarchy as deep as possible.

11.9   *(Package Inheritance Hierarchy)* Package-delivery services, such as FedEx®, DHL® and UPS®, offer a number of different shipping options, each with specific costs associated. Create an inheritance hierarchy to represent various types of packages. Use class Package as the base class of the hierarchy, then include classes TwoDayPackage and OvernightPackage that derive from Package.

Base-class Package should include data members representing the name, address, city, state and ZIP code for both the sender and the recipient of the package, in addition to data members that store the weight (in ounces) and cost per ounce to ship the package. Package's constructor should initialize these data members. Ensure that the weight and cost per ounce contain positive values. Package should provide a public member function calculateCost that returns a double indicating the cost associated with shipping the package. Package's calculateCost function should determine the cost by multiplying the weight by the cost per ounce.

Derived-class TwoDayPackage should inherit the functionality of base-class Package, but also include a data member that represents a flat fee that the shipping company charges for two-day-delivery service. TwoDayPackage's constructor should receive a value to initialize this data member. TwoDayPackage should redefine member function calculateCost so that it computes the shipping cost by adding the flat fee to the weight-based cost calculated by base-class Package's calculate-Cost function.

Class OvernightPackage should inherit directly from class Package and contain an additional data member representing an additional fee per ounce charged for overnight-delivery service. OvernightPackage should redefine member function calculateCost so that it adds the additional fee per ounce to the standard cost per ounce before calculating the shipping cost. Write a test program that creates objects of each type of Package and tests member function calculateCost.

11.10   *(Account Inheritance Hierarchy)* Create an inheritance hierarchy that a bank might use to represent customers' bank accounts. All customers at this bank can deposit (i.e., credit) money into their accounts and withdraw (i.e., debit) money from their accounts. More specific types of accounts also exist. Savings accounts, for instance, earn interest on the money they hold. Checking accounts, on the other hand, charge a fee per transaction (i.e., credit or debit).

Create an inheritance hierarchy containing base-class Account and derived classes Savings-Account and CheckingAccount that inherit from class Account. Base-class Account should include one data member of type double to represent the account balance. The class should provide a constructor that receives an initial balance and uses it to initialize the data member. The constructor should validate the initial balance to ensure that it's greater than or equal to 0.0. If not, the balance should be set to 0.0 and the constructor should display an error message, indicating that the initial balance was invalid. The class should provide three member functions. Member function credit should add an amount to the current balance. Member function debit should withdraw money from the Account and ensure that the debit amount does not exceed the Account's balance. If it does, the balance should be left unchanged and the function should print the message "Debit amount exceeded account balance." Member function getBalance should return the current balance.

Derived-class SavingsAccount should inherit the functionality of an Account, but also include a data member of type double indicating the interest rate (percentage) assigned to the Account. SavingsAccount's constructor should receive the initial balance, as well as an initial value for the SavingsAccount's interest rate. SavingsAccount should provide a public member function calculateInterest that returns a double indicating the amount of interest earned by an account. Member function calculateInterest should determine this amount by multiplying the interest rate by the account balance. [Note: SavingsAccount should inherit member functions credit and debit as is without redefining them.]

Derived-class CheckingAccount should inherit from base-class Account and include an additional data member of type double that represents the fee charged per transaction. Checking-Account's constructor should receive the initial balance, as well as a parameter indicating a fee amount. Class CheckingAccount should redefine member functions credit and debit so that they subtract the fee from the account balance whenever either transaction is performed successfully. CheckingAccount's versions of these functions should invoke the base-class Account version to perform the updates to an account balance. CheckingAccount's debit function should charge a fee only if money is actually withdrawn (i.e., the debit amount does not exceed the account balance). [Hint: Define Account's debit function so that it returns a bool indicating whether money was withdrawn. Then use the return value to determine whether a fee should be charged.]

After defining the classes in this hierarchy, write a program that creates objects of each class and tests their member functions. Add interest to the SavingsAccount object by first invoking its calculateInterest function, then passing the returned interest amount to the object's credit function.

Object-Oriented Programming: Polymorphism

Objectives

In this chapter you'll:

- See how polymorphism makes programming more convenient and systems more extensible.

- Understand the relationships among objects in an inheritance hierarchy.

- Use C++11's **overrides** keyword when overriding a base-class virtual function in a derived class.

- Use C++11's **default** keyword to autogenerate a **virtual** destructor.

- Use C++11's **final** keyword to indicate that a base-class virtual function cannot be overridden.

- Create an inheritance hierarchy with both abstract and concrete classes.

- Determine an object's type at runtime using runtime type information (RTTI), **dynamic_cast**, **typeid** and **type_info**.

- Understand how C++ can implement **virtual** functions and dynamic binding.

- Use **virtual** destructors to ensure that all appropriate destructors run on an object.

12.1 Introduction

We now continue our study of OOP by explaining and demonstrating polymorphism with inheritance hierarchies. Polymorphism enables you to "program in the *general*" rather than "program in the *specific*." In particular, you can write programs that process objects of classes that are part of the *same* class hierarchy as if they were all objects of the hierarchy's base class. As we'll soon see, polymorphism works off base-class *pointer handles* and base-class *reference handles*, but *not* off name handles.

Implementing for Extensibility

With polymorphism, you can design and implement systems that are easily *extensible*—new classes can be added with little or no modification to the general portions of the program, as long as the new classes are part of the inheritance hierarchy that the program processes generally. The only parts of a program that must be altered to accommodate new classes are those that require direct knowledge of the new classes that you add to the hierarchy. For example, if we create class Tortoise that inherits from class Animal (which might respond to a move message by crawling one inch), we need to write only the Tortoise class and the part of the simulation that instantiates a Tortoise object. The portions of the simulation that process each Animal generally can remain the same.

Optional Discussion of Polymorphism "Under the Hood"
A key feature of this chapter is its optional detailed discussion of polymorphism, virtual functions and dynamic binding "under the hood," which uses a detailed diagram to explain how polymorphism is typically implemented in C++.

12.2 Introduction to Polymorphism: Polymorphic Video Game

Suppose we have to design a video game that manipulates objects of many *different* types, including objects of classes Martian, Venutian, Plutonian, SpaceShip and LaserBeam. Imagine that each of these classes inherits from the common base class SpaceObject, which contains the member function draw. Each derived class implements this function in a manner appropriate for that class. A screen-manager program maintains a container (e.g., a vector) that holds SpaceObject *pointers* to objects of the various classes. To refresh the screen, the screen manager periodically sends each object the *same* message—namely, draw. Each type of object responds in a unique way. For example, a Martian object might draw itself in red with the appropriate number of antennae, a SpaceShip object might draw itself as a silver flying saucer, and a LaserBeam object might draw itself as a bright red beam across the screen. The *same* message (in this case, draw) sent to a *variety* of objects has *many forms* of results—hence the term polymorphism.

A polymorphic screen manager facilitates adding new classes to a system with minimal modifications to its code. Suppose that we want to add objects of class Mercurian to our video game. To do so, we must build a class Mercurian that inherits from SpaceObject, and provides its *own* definition of member function draw. Then, when *pointers* to objects of class Mercurian appear in the container, you do not need to modify the code for the screen manager. The screen manager simply invokes member function draw in the *same* way on *every* object in the container, *regardless* of the object's type, so the new Mercurian objects just "plug right in." Thus, without modifying the system (other than to include—and create objects of—the new classes), you can use polymorphism to accommodate additional classes, including ones that were *not even envisioned* when the system was created.

Software Engineering Observation 12.1

Polymorphism enables you to deal in generalities *and let the execution-time environment concern itself with the* specifics. *You can direct a variety of objects to behave in manners appropriate to those objects* without even knowing their types—*as long as those objects belong to the same inheritance hierarchy and are being accessed off a common base-class pointer or a common base-class reference.*

Software Engineering Observation 12.2

Polymorphism promotes extensibility: *Software written to invoke polymorphic behavior is written independently of the specific types of the objects to which messages are sent. Thus, new types of objects that can respond to existing messages can be incorporated into such a system without modifying the base system. Only client code that instantiates new objects must be modified to accommodate new types.*

12.3 Relationships Among Objects in an Inheritance Hierarchy

Section 11.3 created an employee class hierarchy, in which class BasePlusCommission-Employee inherited from class CommissionEmployee. The Chapter 11 examples manipulated CommissionEmployee and BasePlusCommissionEmployee objects by using the objects' names to invoke their member functions. We now examine the relationships among classes in a hierarchy more closely. The next several sections present a series of examples that demonstrate how base-class and derived-class *pointers* can be aimed at base-class and derived-class objects, and how those pointers can be used to invoke member functions that manipulate those objects.

- In Section 12.3.1, we assign the address of a derived-class object to a base-class pointer, then show that invoking a function via the base-class pointer invokes the *base-class* functionality in the derived-class object—i.e., the *type of the handle determines which function is called.*

- In Section 12.3.2, we assign the address of a base-class object to a derived-class pointer, which results in a compilation error. We discuss the error message and investigate why the compiler does not allow such an assignment.

- In Section 12.3.3, we assign the address of a derived-class object to a base-class pointer, then examine how the base-class pointer can be used to invoke only the base-class functionality—*when we attempt to invoke derived-class-only member functions through the base-class pointer, compilation errors occur.*

- Finally, in Section 12.4, we demonstrate how to get *polymorphic* behavior from base-class pointers aimed at derived-class objects. We introduce virtual functions and polymorphism by declaring a base-class function as virtual. We then assign the address of a derived-class object to the base-class pointer and use that pointer to invoke derived-class functionality—*precisely the capability we need to achieve polymorphic behavior.*

A key concept in these examples is to demonstrate that with public inheritance *an object of a derived class can be treated as an object of its base class.* This enables various interesting manipulations. For example, a program can create an array of base-class pointers that point to objects of many derived-class types. Despite the fact that the derived-class objects are of *different types*, the compiler allows this because each derived-class object *is an* object of its base class. However, *we cannot treat a base-class object as an object of any of its derived classes.* For example, a CommissionEmployee is not a BasePlusCommissionEmployee in the hierarchy defined in Chapter 11—a CommissionEmployee does *not* have a baseSalary data member and does *not* have member functions setBaseSalary and getBaseSalary. The *is-a* relationship applies only from a *derived class* to its *direct and indirect base classes.*

12.3.1 Invoking Base-Class Functions from Derived-Class Objects

The example in Fig. 12.1 reuses the final versions of classes CommissionEmployee and BasePlusCommissionEmployee from Section 11.3.5. The example demonstrates three ways to aim base- and derived-class pointers at base- and derived-class objects. The first two are natural and straightforward—we aim a base-class pointer at a base-class object and invoke base-class functionality, and we aim a derived-class pointer at a derived-class object and invoke derived-class functionality. Then, we demonstrate the relationship between derived classes and base classes (i.e., the *is-a* relationship of inheritance) by aiming a base-class pointer at a derived-class object and showing that the base-class functionality is indeed available in the derived-class object.

```cpp
 1  // Fig. 12.1: fig12_01.cpp
 2  // Aiming base-class and derived-class pointers at base-class
 3  // and derived-class objects, respectively.
 4  #include <iostream>
 5  #include <iomanip>
 6  #include "CommissionEmployee.h"
 7  #include "BasePlusCommissionEmployee.h"
 8  using namespace std;
 9
10  int main() {
11     // create base-class object
12     CommissionEmployee commissionEmployee{
13        "Sue", "Jones", "222-22-2222", 10000, .06};
14
15     // create derived-class object
16     BasePlusCommissionEmployee basePlusCommissionEmployee{
17        "Bob", "Lewis", "333-33-3333", 5000, .04, 300};
18
19     cout << fixed << setprecision(2); // set floating-point formatting
20
21     // output objects commissionEmployee and basePlusCommissionEmployee
22     cout << "DISPLAY BASE-CLASS AND DERIVED-CLASS OBJECTS:\n"
23        << commissionEmployee.toString() // base-class toString
24        << "\n\n"
25        << basePlusCommissionEmployee.toString(); // derived-class toString
26
27     // natural: aim base-class pointer at base-class object
28     CommissionEmployee* commissionEmployeePtr{&commissionEmployee};
29     cout << "\n\nCALLING TOSTRING WITH BASE-CLASS POINTER TO "
30        << "\nBASE-CLASS OBJECT INVOKES BASE-CLASS TOSTRING FUNCTION:\n"
31        << commissionEmployeePtr->toString(); // base version
32
33     // natural: aim derived-class pointer at derived-class object
34     BasePlusCommissionEmployee* basePlusCommissionEmployeePtr{
35        &basePlusCommissionEmployee}; // natural
36     cout << "\n\nCALLING TOSTRING WITH DERIVED-CLASS POINTER TO "
37        << "\nDERIVED-CLASS OBJECT INVOKES DERIVED-CLASS "
38        << "TOSTRING FUNCTION:\n"
39        << basePlusCommissionEmployeePtr->toString(); // derived version
40
41     // aim base-class pointer at derived-class object
42     commissionEmployeePtr = &basePlusCommissionEmployee;
```

Fig. 12.1 | Assigning addresses of base-class and derived-class objects to base-class and derived-class pointers. (Part 1 of 2.)

```
43      cout << "\n\nCALLING TOSTRING WITH BASE-CLASS POINTER TO "
44          << "DERIVED-CLASS OBJECT\nINVOKES BASE-CLASS TOSTRING "
45          << "FUNCTION ON THAT DERIVED-CLASS OBJECT:\n"
46          << commissionEmployeePtr->toString() // base version
47          << endl;
48   }
```

```
DISPLAY BASE-CLASS AND DERIVED-CLASS OBJECTS:
commission employee: Sue Jones
social security number: 222-22-2222
gross sales: 10000.00
commission rate: 0.06

base-salaried commission employee: Bob Lewis
social security number: 333-33-3333
gross sales: 5000.00
commission rate: 0.04
base salary: 300.00

CALLING TOSTRING WITH BASE-CLASS POINTER TO
BASE-CLASS OBJECT INVOKES BASE-CLASS TOSTRING FUNCTION:
commission employee: Sue Jones
social security number: 222-22-2222
gross sales: 10000.00
commission rate: 0.06

CALLING TOSTRING WITH DERIVED-CLASS POINTER TO
DERIVED-CLASS OBJECT INVOKES DERIVED-CLASS TOSTRING FUNCTION:
base-salaried commission employee: Bob Lewis
social security number: 333-33-3333
gross sales: 5000.00
commission rate: 0.04
base salary: 300.00

CALLING TOSTRING WITH BASE-CLASS POINTER TO DERIVED-CLASS OBJECT
INVOKES BASE-CLASS TOSTRING FUNCTION ON THAT DERIVED-CLASS OBJECT:
commission employee: Bob Lewis
social security number: 333-33-3333
gross sales: 5000.00
commission rate: 0.04
```

Fig. 12.1 | Assigning addresses of base-class and derived-class objects to base-class and derived-class pointers. (Part 2 of 2.)

Recall that each BasePlusCommissionEmployee object *is a* CommissionEmployee that *also* has a base salary. Class BasePlusCommissionEmployee's earnings member function (lines 32–34 of Fig. 11.15) redefines class CommissionEmployee's earnings member function (lines 70–72 of Fig. 11.14) to include the object's base salary. Class BasePlusCommissionEmployee's toString member function (lines 37–42 of Fig. 11.15) redefines class CommissionEmployee's version (lines 75–84 of Fig. 11.14) to display the same information *plus* the employee's base salary.

Creating Objects and Displaying Their Contents

In Fig. 12.1, lines 12–13 create a CommissionEmployee object and lines 16–17 create a BasePlusCommissionEmployee object. Lines 23 and 25 use each object's name to invoke its toString member function.

Aiming a Base-Class Pointer at a Base-Class Object

Line 28 creates commissionEmployeePtr—a pointer to a CommissionEmployee object— and initializes it with the address of base-class object commissionEmployee. Line 31 uses the pointer to invoke member function toString on the CommissionEmployee object. This invokes the version of toString defined in *base class* CommissionEmployee.

Aiming a Derived-Class Pointer at a Derived-Class Object

Similarly, lines 34–35 create basePlusCommissionEmployeePtr—a pointer to a BasePlusCommissionEmployee object—and initialize it with the address of derived-class object basePlusCommissionEmployee. Line 39 uses the pointer to invoke member function toString on the BasePlusCommissionEmployee object. This invokes the version of toString defined in *derived class* BasePlusCommissionEmployee.

Aiming a Base-Class Pointer at a Derived-Class Object

Line 42 then assigns the address of derived-class object basePlusCommissionEmployee to base-class pointer commissionEmployeePtr, which line 46 uses to invoke member function toString. This "crossover" is allowed because an object of a derived class *is an* object of its base class. Despite the fact that the base-class CommissionEmployee pointer points to a *derived-class* BasePlusCommissionEmployee object, the *base-class* CommissionEmployee's toString member function is invoked, rather than BasePlusCommissionEmployee's toString function—notice in this case that neither "base-salaried" nor the BasePlusCommissionEmployee's base salary is displayed.

The output of each toString member-function invocation in this program reveals that the invoked functionality depends on the *type of the pointer* (or *reference*, as you'll soon see) used to invoke the function, *not* the type of the object for which the member function is called. In Section 12.4, when we introduce virtual functions, we demonstrate that it's possible to invoke the object type's functionality, *rather than* invoke the pointer type's (or reference type's) functionality. We'll see that this is crucial to implementing polymorphic behavior—the key topic of this chapter.

12.3.2 Aiming Derived-Class Pointers at Base-Class Objects

In Section 12.3.1, we assigned the address of a derived-class object to a base-class pointer and explained that the C++ compiler allows this assignment, because a derived-class object *is a* base-class object. We take the opposite approach in Fig. 12.2, as we aim a derived-class pointer at a base-class object. [*Note:* This program reuses the final versions of classes CommissionEmployee and BasePlusCommissionEmployee from Section 11.3.5.] Lines 7–8 of Fig. 12.2 create a CommissionEmployee object. Lines 12–13 attempt to create and initialize a BasePlusCommissionEmployee pointer with the address of base-class object commissionEmployee, but the compiler generates an error, because a CommissionEmployee is *not* a BasePlusCommissionEmployee.

```
1   // Fig. 12.2: fig12_02.cpp
2   // Aiming a derived-class pointer at a base-class object.
3   #include "CommissionEmployee.h"
4   #include "BasePlusCommissionEmployee.h"
5
6   int main() {
7      CommissionEmployee commissionEmployee{
8         "Sue", "Jones", "222-22-2222", 10000, .06};
9
10     // aim derived-class pointer at base-class object
11     // Error: a CommissionEmployee is not a BasePlusCommissionEmployee
12     BasePlusCommissionEmployee* basePlusCommissionEmployeePtr{
13        &commissionEmployee};
14  }
```

Microsoft Visual C++ compiler error message:

```
c:\examples\ch12\fig12_02\fig12_02.cpp(13):
   error C2440: 'initializing': cannot convert from 'CommissionEmployee *'
   to 'BasePlusCommissionEmployee *'
```

Fig. 12.2 | Aiming a derived-class pointer at a base-class object.

Consider the consequences if the compiler were to allow this assignment. Through a BasePlusCommissionEmployee pointer, we can invoke *every* BasePlusCommission-Employee member function, including setBaseSalary, for the object to which the pointer points (i.e., the base-class object commissionEmployee). However, the CommissionEmployee object does *not* provide a setBaseSalary member function, *nor* does it provide a baseSalary data member to set. This could lead to problems, because member function setBaseSalary would assume that there's a baseSalary data member to set at its "usual location" in a BasePlusCommissionEmployee object. This memory does not belong to the CommissionEmployee object, so member function setBaseSalary might overwrite other important data in memory, possibly data that belongs to a different object.

12.3.3 Derived-Class Member-Function Calls via Base-Class Pointers

Off a base-class pointer, the compiler allows us to invoke *only* base-class member functions. Thus, if a base-class pointer is aimed at a derived-class object, and an attempt is made to access a *derived-class-only member function*, a compilation error will occur. Figure 12.3 shows the consequences of attempting to invoke a derived-class-only member function off a base-class pointer. [*Note:* We're again reusing the versions of classes CommissionEmployee and BasePlusCommissionEmployee from Section 11.3.5.]

```
1   // Fig. 12.3: fig12_03.cpp
2   // Attempting to invoke derived-class-only member functions
3   // via a base-class pointer.
4   #include <string>
5   #include "CommissionEmployee.h"
```

Fig. 12.3 | Attempting to invoke derived-class-only functions via a base-class pointer. (Part 1 of 2.)

```
6   #include "BasePlusCommissionEmployee.h"
7   using namespace std;
8
9   int main() {
10      BasePlusCommissionEmployee basePlusCommissionEmployee{
11         "Bob", "Lewis", "333-33-3333", 5000, .04, 300};
12
13      // aim base-class pointer at derived-class object (allowed)
14      CommissionEmployee* commissionEmployeePtr{&basePlusCommissionEmployee};
15
16      // invoke base-class member functions on derived-class
17      // object through base-class pointer (allowed)
18      string firstName{commissionEmployeePtr->getFirstName()};
19      string lastName{commissionEmployeePtr->getLastName()};
20      string ssn{commissionEmployeePtr->getSocialSecurityNumber()};
21      double grossSales{commissionEmployeePtr->getGrossSales()};
22      double commissionRate{commissionEmployeePtr->getCommissionRate()};
23
24      // attempt to invoke derived-class-only member functions
25      // on derived-class object through base-class pointer (disallowed)
26      double baseSalary{commissionEmployeePtr->getBaseSalary()};
27      commissionEmployeePtr->setBaseSalary(500);
28   }
```

GNU C++ compiler error messages:

```
fig12_03.cpp:26:45: error: 'class CommissionEmployee' has no member named
'getBaseSalary'
    double baseSalary{commissionEmployeePtr->getBaseSalary()};
                                             ^
fig12_03.cpp:27:27: error: 'class CommissionEmployee' has no member named
'setBaseSalary'
    commissionEmployeePtr->setBaseSalary(500);
```

Fig. 12.3 | Attempting to invoke derived-class-only functions via a base-class pointer. (Part 2 of 2.)

Lines 10–11 create a BasePlusCommissionEmployee object. Line 14 creates commissionEmployeePtr—a pointer to a CommissionEmployee object—and initializes it with the address of the derived-class object basePlusCommissionEmployee. Again, this is allowed, because a BasePlusCommissionEmployee *is a* CommissionEmployee (in the sense that a BasePlusCommissionEmployee object contains all the functionality of a CommissionEmployee object).

Lines 18–22 invoke base-class member functions getFirstName, getLastName, getSocialSecurityNumber, getGrossSales and getCommissionRate off the base-class pointer. All of these calls are allowed, because BasePlusCommissionEmployee *inherits* these member functions from CommissionEmployee.

We know that commissionEmployeePtr is aimed at a BasePlusCommissionEmployee object, so in lines 26–27 we attempt to invoke BasePlusCommissionEmployee member functions getBaseSalary and setBaseSalary. The compiler generates errors on both of these calls, because these functions are *not* member functions of base-class CommissionEmployee. The handle can be used to invoke *only* those functions that are members of that handle's associated class type. (In this case, off a CommissionEmployee*, we can invoke only CommissionEmployee member functions setFirstName, getFirstName, setLastName, getLastName, setSocialSecurityNumber, getSocialSecurityNumber, setGrossSales, getGrossSales, setCommissionRate, getCommissionRate, earnings and toString.)

Downcasting
The compiler will allow access to derived-class-only members from a base-class pointer that's aimed at a derived-class object *if* we explicitly cast the base-class pointer to a derived-class pointer—this is known as downcasting. As you know, it's possible to aim a base-class pointer at a derived-class object. However, as we demonstrated in Fig. 12.3, a base-class pointer can be used to invoke *only* the functions declared in the base class. Downcasting allows a derived-class-specific operation on a derived-class object pointed to by a base-class pointer. Downcasting is a potentially *dangerous* operation. Section 12.9 demonstrates how to *safely* use downcasting.

12.4 Virtual Functions and Virtual Destructors

In Section 12.3.1, we aimed a base-class CommissionEmployee pointer at a derived-class BasePlusCommissionEmployee object, then invoked member function toString through that pointer. Recall that the *type of the handle* determined which class's functionality to invoke. In that case, the CommissionEmployee pointer invoked the CommissionEmployee member function toString on the BasePlusCommissionEmployee object, even though the pointer was aimed at a BasePlusCommissionEmployee object that has its own custom toString function.

12.4.1 Why virtual Functions Are Useful

Suppose that shape classes such as Circle, Triangle, Rectangle and Square are all derived from base class Shape. Each of these classes might be endowed with the ability to *draw itself* via a member function draw, but the function for each shape is quite different. In a program that draws a set of shapes, it would be useful to be able to treat all the shapes *generally* as objects of the base class Shape. Then, to draw any shape, we could simply use a base-class Shape pointer to invoke function draw and let the program determine *dynamically* (i.e., at runtime) which derived-class draw function to use, based on the type of the object to which the base-class Shape pointer points at any given time. This is *polymorphic behavior*.

Software Engineering Observation 12.3

With virtual functions, the type of the object—not the type of the handle used to invoke the object's member function—determines which version of a virtual function to invoke.

12.4.2 Declaring virtual Functions

To enable this behavior, we declare draw in the base class as a virtual function, and we override draw in *each* of the derived classes to draw the appropriate shape. From an implementation perspective, *overriding* a function is no different than *redefining* one (which is the approach we've been using until now). An overridden function in a derived class has the *same signature and return type* (i.e., *prototype*) as the function it overrides in its base class. If we *do not* declare the base-class function as virtual, we can *redefine* that function.

By contrast, if we *do* declare the base-class function as virtual, we can *override* that function to enable *polymorphic behavior*. We declare a virtual function by preceding the function's prototype with the keyword virtual in the base class. For example,

```
virtual void draw() const;
```

would appear in base class Shape. The preceding prototype declares that function draw is a virtual function that takes no arguments and returns nothing. This function is declared const because a draw function typically would not make changes to the Shape object on which it's invoked. Virtual functions do *not* have to be const functions.

Software Engineering Observation 12.4

Once a function is declared virtual, *it remains* virtual *all the way down the inheritance hierarchy from that point, even if that function is not explicitly declared* virtual *when a derived class overrides it.*

Good Programming Practice 12.1

Even though certain functions are implicitly virtual *because of a declaration made higher in the class hierarchy, for clarity explicitly declare these functions* virtual *at every level of the class hierarchy.*

Software Engineering Observation 12.5

When a derived class chooses not to override a virtual *function from its base class, the derived class simply inherits its base class's* virtual *function implementation.*

12.4.3 Invoking a virtual Function Through a Base-Class Pointer or Reference

If a program invokes a virtual function through a base-class pointer to a derived-class object (e.g., shapePtr->draw()) or a base-class reference to a derived-class object (e.g., shapeRef.draw()), the program will choose the correct derived-class function *dynamically* (i.e., at execution time) *based on the object type—not the pointer or reference type*. Choosing the appropriate function to call at execution time (rather than at compile time) is known as dynamic binding.

12.4.4 Invoking a virtual Function Through an Object's Name

When a virtual function is called by referencing a specific object by *name* and using the dot member-selection operator (e.g., squareObject.draw()), the function invocation is *resolved at compile time* (this is called static binding) and the virtual function that's called is the one defined for (or inherited by) the class of that particular object—this is *not* polymorphic behavior. Dynamic binding with virtual functions occurs only off pointers and references.

12.4.5 virtual Functions in the CommissionEmployee Hierarchy

Now let's see how virtual functions can enable polymorphic behavior in our employee hierarchy. Figures 12.4–12.5 are the headers for classes CommissionEmployee and BasePlusCommissionEmployee, respectively. We've modified these to declare each class's earnings and toString member functions as virtual (lines 28–29 of Fig. 12.4 and lines 17–18 of Fig. 12.5). Because functions earnings and toString are virtual in class

CommissionEmployee, class BasePlusCommissionEmployee's earnings and toString functions *override* class CommissionEmployee's. In addition, class BasePlusCommissionEmployee's earnings and toString functions are declared with C++11's override keyword.

11

 Error-Prevention Tip 12.1

To help prevent errors, apply C++11's override keyword to the prototype of every derived-class function that overrides a base-class virtual function. This enables the compiler to check whether the base class has a virtual member function with the same signature. If not, the compiler generates an error. Not only does this ensure that you override the base-class function with the appropriate signature, it also prevents you from accidentally hiding a base-class function that has the same name and a different signature.

Now, if we aim a base-class CommissionEmployee pointer at a derived-class BasePlusCommissionEmployee object, and the program uses that pointer to call either function earnings or toString, the BasePlusCommissionEmployee object's corresponding function will be invoked *polymorphically*. There were *no* changes to the member-function implementations of classes CommissionEmployee and BasePlusCommissionEmployee, so we reuse the versions of Figs. 11.14 and 11.15.

```cpp
1  // Fig. 12.4: CommissionEmployee.h
2  // CommissionEmployee class with virtual earnings and toString functions.
3  #ifndef COMMISSION_H
4  #define COMMISSION_H
5
6  #include <string> // C++ standard string class
7
8  class CommissionEmployee {
9  public:
10    CommissionEmployee(const std::string&, const std::string&,
11       const std::string&, double = 0.0, double = 0.0);
12
13    void setFirstName(const std::string&); // set first name
14    std::string getFirstName() const; // return first name
15
16    void setLastName(const std::string&); // set last name
17    std::string getLastName() const; // return last name
18
19    void setSocialSecurityNumber(const std::string&); // set SSN
20    std::string getSocialSecurityNumber() const; // return SSN
21
22    void setGrossSales(double); // set gross sales amount
23    double getGrossSales() const; // return gross sales amount
24
25    void setCommissionRate(double); // set commission rate (percentage)
26    double getCommissionRate() const; // return commission rate
27
28    virtual double earnings() const; // calculate earnings
29    virtual std::string toString() const; // string representation
30  private:
```

Fig. 12.4 | CommissionEmployee class header declares earnings and toString as virtual. (Part 1 of 2.)

```
31        std::string firstName;
32        std::string lastName;
33        std::string socialSecurityNumber;
34        double grossSales; // gross weekly sales
35        double commissionRate; // commission percentage
36    };
37
38    #endif
```

Fig. 12.4 | CommissionEmployee class header declares earnings and toString as virtual. (Part 2 of 2.)

```
1     // Fig. 12.5: BasePlusCommissionEmployee.h
2     // BasePlusCommissionEmployee class derived from class CommissionEmployee.
3     #ifndef BASEPLUS_H
4     #define BASEPLUS_H
5
6     #include <string> // C++ standard string class
7     #include "CommissionEmployee.h" // CommissionEmployee class declaration
8
9     class BasePlusCommissionEmployee : public CommissionEmployee {
10    public:
11        BasePlusCommissionEmployee(const std::string&, const std::string&,
12            const std::string&, double = 0.0, double = 0.0, double = 0.0);
13
14        void setBaseSalary(double); // set base salary
15        double getBaseSalary() const; // return base salary
16
17        virtual double earnings() const override; // calculate earnings
18        virtual std::string toString() const override; // string representation
19    private:
20        double baseSalary; // base salary
21    };
22
23    #endif
```

Fig. 12.5 | BasePlusCommissionEmployee class header declares earnings and toString functions as virtual and override.

We modified Fig. 12.1 to create the program of Fig. 12.6. Lines 32–44 of Fig. 12.6 demonstrate again that a CommissionEmployee pointer aimed at a CommissionEmployee object can be used to invoke CommissionEmployee functionality, and a BasePlusCommissionEmployee pointer aimed at a BasePlusCommissionEmployee object can be used to invoke BasePlusCommissionEmployee functionality. Line 47 aims the base-class pointer commissionEmployeePtr at derived-class object basePlusCommissionEmployee. When line 54 invokes member function toString off the base-class pointer, the derived-class BasePlusCommissionEmployee's toString member function is invoked, so line 54 outputs different text than line 46 does in Fig. 12.1 (when member function toString was *not* declared virtual). We see that declaring a member function virtual causes the program to *dynamically* determine which function to invoke *based on the type of object to which the handle points, rather than on the type of the handle.* When commissionEmployeePtr points to a CommissionEmployee object, class CommissionEmployee's toString function is invoked (Fig. 12.6, line 36), and when commissionEmployeePtr points to a Base-PlusCommissionEmployee object, class BasePlusCommissionEmployee's toString function is invoked (line 54). Thus, the same toString message—sent off a base-class pointer to a variety of derived-class objects—takes on *many forms*. This is *polymorphic* behavior.

```
1   // Fig. 12.6: fig12_06.cpp
2   // Introducing polymorphism, virtual functions and dynamic binding.
3   #include <iostream>
4   #include <iomanip>
5   #include "CommissionEmployee.h"
6   #include "BasePlusCommissionEmployee.h"
7   using namespace std;
8
9   int main() {
10     // create base-class object
11     CommissionEmployee commissionEmployee{
12        "Sue", "Jones", "222-22-2222", 10000, .06};
13
14     // create derived-class object
15     BasePlusCommissionEmployee basePlusCommissionEmployee{
16        "Bob", "Lewis", "333-33-3333", 5000, .04, 300};
17
18     cout << fixed << setprecision(2); // set floating-point formatting
19
20     // output objects using static binding
21     cout << "INVOKING TOSTRING FUNCTION ON BASE-CLASS AND DERIVED-CLASS "
22        << "\nOBJECTS WITH STATIC BINDING\n"
23        << commissionEmployee.toString() // static binding
24        << "\n\n"
25        << basePlusCommissionEmployee.toString(); // static binding
26
27     // output objects using dynamic binding
28     cout << "\n\nINVOKING TOSTRING FUNCTION ON BASE-CLASS AND "
29        << "\nDERIVED-CLASS OBJECTS WITH DYNAMIC BINDING";
30
31     // natural: aim base-class pointer at base-class object
32     const CommissionEmployee* commissionEmployeePtr{&commissionEmployee};
33     cout << "\n\nCALLING VIRTUAL FUNCTION TOSTRING WITH BASE-CLASS POINTER"
34        << "\nTO BASE-CLASS OBJECT INVOKES BASE-CLASS "
35        << "TOSTRING FUNCTION:\n"
36        << commissionEmployeePtr->toString(); // base version
37
38     // natural: aim derived-class pointer at derived-class object
39     const BasePlusCommissionEmployee* basePlusCommissionEmployeePtr{
40        &basePlusCommissionEmployee}; // natural
41     cout << "\n\nCALLING VIRTUAL FUNCTION TOSTRING WITH DERIVED-CLASS "
42        << "POINTER\nTO DERIVED-CLASS OBJECT INVOKES DERIVED-CLASS "
43        << "TOSTRING FUNCTION:\n"
44        << basePlusCommissionEmployeePtr->toString(); // derived version
```

Fig. 12.6 | Demonstrating polymorphism by invoking a derived-class virtual function via a base-class pointer to a derived-class object. (Part I of 2.)

```
45
46      // aim base-class pointer at derived-class object
47      commissionEmployeePtr = &basePlusCommissionEmployee;
48      cout << "\n\nCALLING VIRTUAL FUNCTION TOSTRING WITH BASE-CLASS POINTER"
49          << "\nTO DERIVED-CLASS OBJECT INVOKES DERIVED-CLASS "
50          << "TOSTRING FUNCTION:\n";
51
52      // polymorphism; invokes BasePlusCommissionEmployee's toString
53      // via base-class pointer to derived-class object
54      cout<< commissionEmployeePtr->toString() << endl;
55  }
```

```
INVOKING TOSTRING FUNCTION ON BASE-CLASS AND DERIVED-CLASS
OBJECTS WITH STATIC BINDING
commission employee: Sue Jones
social security number: 222-22-2222
gross sales: 10000.00
commission rate: 0.06

base-salaried commission employee: Bob Lewis
social security number: 333-33-3333
gross sales: 5000.00
commission rate: 0.04
base salary: 300

INVOKING TOSTRING FUNCTION ON BASE-CLASS AND
DERIVED-CLASS OBJECTS WITH DYNAMIC BINDING

CALLING VIRTUAL FUNCTION TOSTRING WITH BASE-CLASS POINTER
TO BASE-CLASS OBJECT INVOKES BASE-CLASS TOSTRING FUNCTION:
commission employee: Sue Jones
social security number: 222-22-2222
gross sales: 10000.00
commission rate: 0.06

CALLING VIRTUAL FUNCTION TOSTRING WITH DERIVED-CLASS POINTER
TO DERIVED-CLASS OBJECT INVOKES DERIVED-CLASS TOSTRING FUNCTION:
base-salaried commission employee: Bob Lewis
social security number: 333-33-3333
gross sales: 5000.00
commission rate: 0.04
base salary: 300

CALLING VIRTUAL FUNCTION TOSTRING WITH BASE-CLASS POINTER
TO DERIVED-CLASS OBJECT INVOKES DERIVED-CLASS TOSTRING FUNCTION:
base-salaried commission employee: Bob Lewis
social security number: 333-33-3333
gross sales: 5000.00
commission rate: 0.04
base salary: 300
```

Fig. 12.6 | Demonstrating polymorphism by invoking a derived-class virtual function via a base-class pointer to a derived-class object. (Part 2 of 2.)

12.4.6 `virtual` Destructors

A problem can occur when using polymorphism to process dynamically allocated objects of a class hierarchy. So far you've seen destructors that are not declared with keyword `virtual`. If a derived-class object with a non-`virtual` destructor is destroyed by applying the `delete` operator to a *base-class pointer* to the object, the C++ standard specifies that the behavior is *undefined*.

The simple solution to this problem is to create a `public virtual destructor` in the base class. If a base-class destructor is declared `virtual`, the destructors of any derived classes are *also* `virtual`. For example, in class `CommissionEmployee`'s definition (Fig. 12.4), we can define the `virtual` destructor as follows:

```
virtual ~CommissionEmployee() {};
```

Now, if an object in the hierarchy is destroyed explicitly by applying the `delete` operator to a *base-class pointer*, the destructor for the *appropriate class* is called, based on the object to which the base-class pointer points. Remember, when a derived-class object is destroyed, the base-class part of the derived-class object is also destroyed, so it's important for the destructors of *both* the derived and base classes to execute. The base-class destructor automatically executes after the derived-class destructor. From this point forward, we'll include a `virtual` destructor in every class that contains `virtual` functions and requires a destructor.

> **Error-Prevention Tip 12.2**
>
> *If a class has `virtual` functions, always provide a `virtual` destructor, even if one is not required for the class. This ensures that a custom derived-class destructor (if there is one) will be invoked when a derived-class object is deleted via a base-class pointer.*

> **Common Programming Error 12.1**
>
> *Constructors cannot be `virtual`. Declaring a constructor `virtual` is a compilation error.*

The preceding destructor definition also may be written as follows:

```
virtual ~CommissionEmployee() = default;
```

In C++11, you can tell the compiler to explicitly generate the default version of a *default constructor, copy constructor, move constructor, copy assignment operator, move assignment operator* or *destructor* by following the special member function's prototype with `= default`. This is useful, for example, when you explicitly define a constructor for a class and still want the compiler to generate a default constructor as well—in that case, add the following declaration to your class definition:

```
ClassName() = default;
```

12.4.7 C++11: `final` Member Functions and Classes

Prior to C++11, a derived class could override *any* of its base class's `virtual` functions. In C++11, a base-class `virtual` function that's declared `final` in its prototype, as in

```
virtual someFunction(parameters) final;
```

cannot be overridden in any derived class—this guarantees that the base class's `final` member function definition will be used by all base-class objects and by all objects of the base class's direct *and* indirect derived classes. Similarly, prior to C++11, *any* existing class could be used as a base class in a hierarchy. As of C++11, you can declare a class as `final` to prevent it from being used as a base class, as in

```
class MyClass final { // this class cannot be a base class
    // class body
};
```

Attempting to override a `final` member function or inherit from a `final` base class results in a compilation error.

12.5 Type Fields and switch Statements

One way to determine an object's type is to use a `switch` statement to check the value of a field in the object. This allows us to distinguish among object types, then invoke an appropriate action for a particular object, similar to what you can do with polymorphism. For example, in a hierarchy of shapes, if each shape object has a `shapeType` attribute, a `switch` could check the object's `shapeType` to determine which `toString` function to call.

Using `switch` logic exposes programs to a variety of potential problems. For example, you might forget to include a type test when one is warranted, or might forget to test all possible cases in a `switch` statement. When modifying a `switch`-based system by adding new types, you might forget to insert the new cases in *all* relevant `switch` statements. Every addition or deletion of a class requires the modification of every associated `switch` statement in the system; tracking these changes can be time consuming and error prone.

Software Engineering Observation 12.6
Polymorphic programming can eliminate the need for `switch` logic. By using the polymorphism mechanism to perform the equivalent logic, you can avoid the kinds of errors typically associated with `switch` logic.

Software Engineering Observation 12.7
An interesting consequence of using polymorphism is that programs take on a simplified appearance. They contain less branching logic and simpler sequential code.

12.6 Abstract Classes and Pure virtual Functions

When we think of a class as a type, we assume that programs will create objects of that type. However, there are cases in which it's useful to define *classes from which you never intend to instantiate any objects*. Such classes are called abstract classes. Because these classes normally are used as base classes in inheritance hierarchies, we refer to them as abstract base classes. These classes cannot be used to instantiate objects, because, as we'll soon see, abstract classes are *incomplete*—derived classes must define the "missing pieces" before objects of these classes can be instantiated. We build programs with abstract classes in Section 12.7.

An abstract class is a base class from which other classes can inherit. Classes that can be used to instantiate objects are called concrete classes. Such classes define or inherit implementations for *every* member function they declare. A good example of this is the shape hierarchy in Fig. 11.3, which begins with abstract base class `Shape`. We could have an *abstract* base class `TwoDimensionalShape` and derive such *concrete* classes as `Circle`,

Square and Triangle. We could also have an *abstract* base class ThreeDimensionalShape and derive such *concrete* classes as Cube, Sphere and Tetrahedron. Abstract base classes are *too generic* to define real objects; we need to be *more specific* before we can think of instantiating objects. For example, if someone tells you to "draw the two-dimensional shape," what shape would you draw? Concrete classes provide the *specifics* that make it possible to instantiate objects.

12.6.1 Pure virtual Functions

A class is made *abstract* by declaring one or more of its virtual functions to be "pure." A pure virtual function is specified by placing "= 0" in its declaration, as in

```
virtual void draw() const = 0; // pure virtual function
```

The "= 0" is a pure specifier. Pure virtual functions do *not* provide implementations. Each *concrete* derived class *must override all* base-class pure virtual functions with concrete implementations of those functions; otherwise, the derived class is also abstract.

The difference between a virtual function and a pure virtual function is that a virtual function *has* an implementation and gives the derived class the *option* of overriding the function; by contrast, a pure virtual function does *not* have an implementation and *requires* the derived class to override the function for that derived class to be *concrete*; otherwise the derived class remains *abstract*.

Pure virtual functions are used when it does *not* make sense for the base class to have an implementation of a function, but you want to force all concrete derived classes to implement the function. Returning to our earlier example of space objects, it does not make sense for the base class SpaceObject to have an implementation for function draw (as there's no way to draw a generic space object without having specific information about what type of space object is being drawn). An example of a function that would be defined as virtual (and not pure virtual) would be one that returns a name for the object. We can name a generic SpaceObject (for instance, as "space object"), so a default implementation for this function can be provided, and the function does not need to be *pure* virtual. The function is still declared virtual, however, because it's expected that derived classes will override this function to provide *more specific* names for the derived-class objects.

Software Engineering Observation 12.8

An abstract class defines a common public interface for the various classes that derive from it in a class hierarchy. An abstract class contains one or more pure virtual functions that concrete derived classes must *override.*

Common Programming Error 12.2

Failure to override a pure virtual function in a derived class makes that class abstract. Attempting to instantiate an object of an abstract class causes a compilation error.

Software Engineering Observation 12.9

An abstract class has at least one pure virtual function. An abstract class also can have data members and concrete functions (including constructors and destructors), which are subject to the normal rules of inheritance by derived classes.

Although we *cannot* instantiate objects of an abstract base class, we *can* use the abstract base class to declare *pointers* and *references* that can refer to objects of any *concrete* classes derived from the abstract class. Programs typically use such pointers and references to manipulate derived-class objects polymorphically.

12.6.2 Device Drivers: Polymorphism in Operating Systems

Polymorphism is particularly effective for implementing *layered software systems*. In operating systems, for example, each type of physical device could operate quite differently from the others. Even so, commands to *read* or *write* data from and to devices, respectively, may have a certain uniformity. The *write* message sent to a *device-driver* object needs to be interpreted specifically in the context of that device driver and how that device driver manipulates devices of a specific type. However, the *write* call itself really is no different from the *write* to any other device in the system—place some number of *bytes* from memory onto that device. An object-oriented operating system could use an abstract base class to provide an interface appropriate for all device drivers. Then, through inheritance from that abstract base class, derived classes are formed that all operate similarly. The capabilities (i.e., the `public` functions) offered by the device drivers are provided as pure `virtual` functions in the abstract base class. The implementations of these pure `virtual` functions are provided in the derived classes that correspond to the specific types of device drivers. This architecture also allows new devices to be *added* to a system easily. The user can just plug in the device and install its new device driver. The operating system "talks" to this new device through its device driver, which has the same `public` member functions as all other device drivers—those defined in the device driver abstract base class.

12.7 Case Study: Payroll System Using Polymorphism

This section reexamines the `CommissionEmployee`–`BasePlusCommissionEmployee` hierarchy that we explored throughout Section 11.3. In this example, we use an abstract class and polymorphism to perform payroll calculations based on the type of employee. We create an enhanced employee hierarchy to solve the following problem:

> *A company pays its employees weekly. The employees are of three types:* Salaried employees *are paid a fixed weekly salary regardless of the number of hours worked,* commission employees *are paid a percentage of their sales and* base-salary-plus-commission employees *receive a base salary plus a percentage of their sales. For the current pay period, the company has decided to reward base-salary-plus-commission employees by adding 10 percent to their base salaries. The company wants to implement a C++ program that performs its payroll calculations polymorphically.*

We use abstract class `Employee` to represent the general concept of an employee. The classes that derive directly from `Employee` are `SalariedEmployee` and `CommissionEmployee`. Class `BasePlusCommissionEmployee` derives from `CommissionEmployee` and represents the last employee type. The UML class diagram in Fig. 12.7 shows the inheritance hierarchy for our polymorphic employee payroll application. The abstract class name `Employee` is *italicized*, per the convention of the UML.

Abstract base class `Employee` declares the "interface" to the hierarchy—that is, the set of member functions that a program can invoke on *all* `Employee` objects. Each employee, regardless of the way his or her earnings are calculated, has a first name, a last name and a

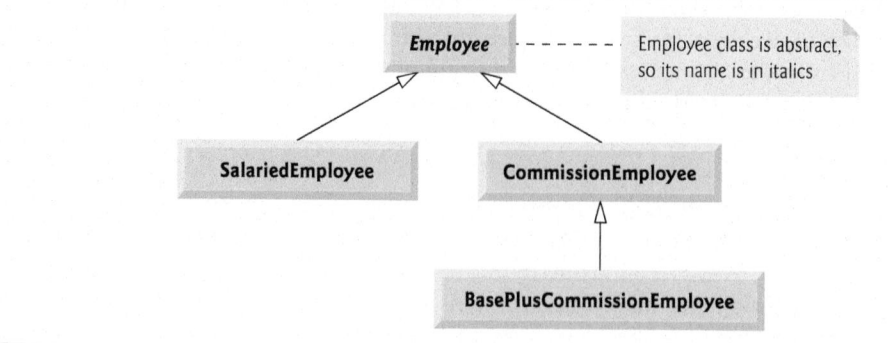

Fig. 12.7 | Employee hierarchy UML class diagram.

social security number, so private data members firstName, lastName and socialSecurityNumber appear in abstract base class Employee.

> **Software Engineering Observation 12.10**
>
> *A derived class can inherit interface and/or implementation from a base class. Hierarchies designed for implementation inheritance tend to have their functionality high in the hierarchy—each derived class inherits one or more member functions from a base class, and the derived class uses the base-class definitions. Hierarchies designed for interface inheritance tend to have their functionality lower in the hierarchy—a base class specifies one or more functions that should be defined by every derived class, but the individual derived classes provide their own implementations of the function(s).*

The following sections implement the Employee class hierarchy. The first four sections each implement one of the abstract or concrete classes. The last section implements a test program that builds objects of the concrete classes and processes the objects polymorphically.

12.7.1 Creating Abstract Base Class Employee

Class Employee (Figs. 12.9–12.10, discussed in further detail shortly) provides functions earnings and toString, in addition to various *get* and *set* functions that manipulate Employee's data members. An earnings function certainly applies generally to all employees, but each earnings calculation depends on the employee's class. So we declare earnings as pure virtual in base class Employee because *a default implementation does not make sense* for that function—there's not enough information to determine what amount earnings should return.

Each derived class *overrides* earnings with an appropriate implementation. To calculate an employee's earnings, the program assigns the address of an employee's object to a base-class Employee *pointer*, then invokes the earnings function on that object.

The test program maintains a vector of Employee pointers, each of which points to an Employee object. *Of course, there cannot be Employee objects, because Employee is an abstract class—with inheritance, however, all objects of all concrete derived classes of Employee may nevertheless be thought of as Employee objects.* The program iterates through the vector and calls function earnings for each Employee object. C++ processes these function calls *polymorphically.* Including earnings as a pure virtual function in Employee *forces* every direct derived class of Employee that wishes to be a *concrete* class to *override* earnings.

Function toString in class Employee returns a string containing the first name, last name and social security number of the employee. As we'll see, each derived class of Employee overrides function toString to output the employee's type (e.g., "salaried employee:") followed by the rest of the employee's information. Each each derived class's toString could also call earnings, even though earnings is a pure-virtual function in base class Employee, because each *concrete* class is guaranteed to have an implementation of earnings. For this reason, even class Employee's toString function can call earnings— at runtime, when you call toString through an Employee pointer or reference, you're always calling it on an object of a *concrete* derived-class.

The diagram in Fig. 12.8 shows each of the four classes in the hierarchy down the left side and functions earnings and toString across the top. For each class, the diagram shows the desired results of each function. Italic text represents where the *values* from a particular object are used in the earnings and toString functions. Class Employee specifies "= 0" for function earnings to indicate that it's a pure virtual function and hence has *no* implementation. Each derived class overrides this function to provide an appropriate implementation. We do not list base class Employee's *get* and *set* functions because they're *not* overridden in any of the derived classes—each of these functions is inherited and used "as is" by each of the derived classes.

	earnings	toString
Employee	= 0	*firstName lastName* social security number: *SSN*
Salaried- Employee	*weeklySalary*	salaried employee: *firstName lastName* social security number: *SSN* weekly salary: *weeklySalary*
Commission- Employee	*commissionRate* * *grossSales*	commission employee: *firstName lastName* social security number: *SSN* gross sales: *grossSales*; commission rate: *commissionRate*
BasePlus- Commission- Employee	(*commissionRate* * *grossSales*) + *baseSalary*	base-salaried commission employee: *firstName lastName* social security number: *SSN* gross sales: *grossSales*; commission rate: *commissionRate*; base salary: *baseSalary*

Fig. 12.8 | Polymorphic interface for the Employee hierarchy classes.

Employee *Class Header*

Let's consider class Employee's header (Fig. 12.9). The public member functions include a constructor that takes the first name, last name and social security number as arguments (line 10); a C++11 default virtual destructor (line 11) that the compiler generates; *set*

11

functions that set the first name, last name and social security number (lines 13, 16 and 19, respectively); *get* functions that return the first name, last name and social security number (lines 14, 17 and 20, respectively); pure virtual function earnings (line 23) and virtual function toString (line 24).

```cpp
1   // Fig. 12.9: Employee.h
2   // Employee abstract base class.
3   #ifndef EMPLOYEE_H
4   #define EMPLOYEE_H
5
6   #include <string> // C++ standard string class
7
8   class Employee {
9   public:
10     Employee(const std::string&, const std::string&, const std::string &);
11     virtual ~Employee() = default; // compiler generates virtual destructor
12
13     void setFirstName(const std::string&); // set first name
14     std::string getFirstName() const; // return first name
15
16     void setLastName(const std::string&); // set last name
17     std::string getLastName() const; // return last name
18
19     void setSocialSecurityNumber(const std::string&); // set SSN
20     std::string getSocialSecurityNumber() const; // return SSN
21
22     // pure virtual function makes Employee an abstract base class
23     virtual double earnings() const = 0; // pure virtual
24     virtual std::string toString() const; // virtual
25   private:
26     std::string firstName;
27     std::string lastName;
28     std::string socialSecurityNumber;
29   };
30
31   #endif // EMPLOYEE_H
```

Fig. 12.9 | Employee abstract base class.

Recall that we declared earnings as a pure virtual function because first we must know the *specific* Employee type to determine the appropriate earnings calculation. Declaring this function as pure virtual indicates that each concrete derived class *must* provide an earnings implementation and that a program can use base-class Employee pointers (or references) to invoke function earnings *polymorphically* for *any* type of Employee.

Employee Class Member-Function Definitions
Figure 12.10 contains the member-function definitions for class Employee. No implementation is provided for virtual function earnings. The Employee constructor (lines 9–11) does not validate the social security number. Normally, such validation should be provided.

```
1   // Fig. 12.10: Employee.cpp
2   // Abstract-base-class Employee member-function definitions.
3   // Note: No definitions are given for pure virtual functions.
4   #include <sstream>
5   #include "Employee.h" // Employee class definition
6   using namespace std;
7
8   // constructor
9   Employee::Employee(const string& first, const string& last,
10      const string& ssn)
11      : firstName(first), lastName(last), socialSecurityNumber(ssn) {}
12
13  // set first name
14  void Employee::setFirstName(const string& first) {firstName = first;}
15
16  // return first name
17  string Employee::getFirstName() const {return firstName;}
18
19  // set last name
20  void Employee::setLastName(const string& last) {lastName = last;}
21
22  // return last name
23  string Employee::getLastName() const {return lastName;}
24
25  // set social security number
26  void Employee::setSocialSecurityNumber(const string& ssn) {
27     socialSecurityNumber = ssn; // should validate
28  }
29
30  // return social security number
31  string Employee::getSocialSecurityNumber() const {
32     return socialSecurityNumber;
33  }
34
35  // toString Employee's information (virtual, but not pure virtual)
36  string Employee::toString() const {
37     return getFirstName() + " "s + getLastName() +
38        "\nsocial security number: "s + getSocialSecurityNumber();
39  }
```

Fig. 12.10 | Employee class implementation file.

The virtual function toString (lines 36–39) provides an implementation that will be *overridden* in *each* of the derived classes. Each of these functions will, however, use the Employee class's version of toString to get a string containing the information *common to all classes* in the Employee hierarchy.

12.7.2 Creating Concrete Derived Class SalariedEmployee

Class SalariedEmployee (Figs. 12.11–12.12) derives from class Employee (line 9 of Fig. 12.11). The public member functions include a constructor that takes a first name, a last name, a social security number and a weekly salary as arguments (lines 11–12); a C++11 default virtual destructor (line 13); a *set* function to assign a new nonnegative

11

value to data member weeklySalary (line 15); a *get* function to return weeklySalary's value (line 16); a virtual function earnings that calculates a SalariedEmployee's earnings (line 19) and a virtual function toString (line 20) that outputs the employee's type, namely, "salaried employee: " followed by employee-specific information produced by base class Employee's toString function and SalariedEmployee's getWeekly-Salary function.

```
1   // Fig. 12.11: SalariedEmployee.h
2   // SalariedEmployee class derived from Employee.
3   #ifndef SALARIED_H
4   #define SALARIED_H
5
6   #include <string> // C++ standard string class
7   #include "Employee.h" // Employee class definition
8
9   class SalariedEmployee : public Employee {
10  public:
11     SalariedEmployee(const std::string&, const std::string&,
12        const std::string&, double = 0.0);
13     virtual ~SalariedEmployee() = default; // virtual destructor
14
15     void setWeeklySalary(double); // set weekly salary
16     double getWeeklySalary() const; // return weekly salary
17
18     // keyword virtual signals intent to override
19     virtual double earnings() const override; // calculate earnings
20     virtual std::string toString() const override; // string representation
21  private:
22     double weeklySalary; // salary per week
23  };
24
25  #endif // SALARIED_H
```

Fig. 12.11 | SalariedEmployee class header.

SalariedEmployee Class Member-Function Definitions

Figure 12.12 contains the member-function definitions for SalariedEmployee. The class's constructor passes the first name, last name and social security number to the Employee constructor (line 12) to initialize the private data members that are inherited from the base class, but not directly accessible in the derived class. Function earnings (line 30) overrides pure virtual function earnings in Employee to provide a *concrete* implementation that returns the SalariedEmployee's weekly salary. If we did not define earnings, class SalariedEmployee would be an *abstract* class, and attempting to instantiate a SalariedEmployee object would cause a compilation error. In class SalariedEmployee's header, we declared member functions earnings and toString as virtual (lines 19–20 of Fig. 12.11)—actually, placing the virtual keyword before these member functions is *redundant*. We defined them as virtual in base class Employee, so they remain virtual functions all the way down the class hierarchy. Explicitly declaring such functions virtual at every level of the hierarchy promotes program clarity. Not declaring earnings as pure virtual signals our intent to provide an implementation in this concrete class.

```
I    // Fig. 12.12: SalariedEmployee.cpp
2    // SalariedEmployee class member-function definitions.
3    #include <iomanip>
4    #include <stdexcept>
5    #include <sstream>
6    #include "SalariedEmployee.h" // SalariedEmployee class definition
7    using namespace std;
8
9    // constructor
10   SalariedEmployee::SalariedEmployee(const string& first,
11      const string& last, const string& ssn, double salary)
12      : Employee(first, last, ssn) {
13      setWeeklySalary(salary);
14   }
15
16   // set salary
17   void SalariedEmployee::setWeeklySalary(double salary) {
18      if (salary < 0.0) {
19         throw invalid_argument("Weekly salary must be >= 0.0");
20      }
21
22      weeklySalary = salary;
23   }
24
25   // return salary
26   double SalariedEmployee::getWeeklySalary() const {return weeklySalary;}
27
28   // calculate earnings;
29   // override pure virtual function earnings in Employee
30   double SalariedEmployee::earnings() const {return getWeeklySalary();}
31
32   // return a string representation of SalariedEmployee's information
33   string SalariedEmployee::toString() const {
34      ostringstream output;
35      output << fixed << setprecision(2);
36      output << "salaried employee: "
37         << Employee::toString() // reuse abstract base-class function
38         << "\nweekly salary: " << getWeeklySalary();
39      return output.str();
40   }
```

Fig. 12.12 | SalariedEmployee class implementation file.

Function toString of class SalariedEmployee (lines 33–40 of Fig. 12.12) overrides Employee function toString. If class SalariedEmployee did not override toString, SalariedEmployee would inherit the Employee version of toString. In that case, SalariedEmployee's toString function would simply return the employee's full name and social security number, which does not adequately represent a SalariedEmployee. To create a string representation of a SalariedEmployee's complete information, the derived class's toString function returns "salaried employee: " followed by the base-class Employee-specific information (i.e., first name, last name and social security number) returned by *invoking the base class's toString function* using the scope resolution operator (line 37). Without Employee::, the toString call would cause *infinite recursion*. The string produced by SalariedEmployee's toString function also contains the employee's weekly salary obtained by invoking the class's getWeeklySalary function.

12.7.3 Creating Concrete Derived Class CommissionEmployee

The CommissionEmployee class (Figs. 12.13–12.14) derives from Employee (Fig. 12.13, line 9). The member-function implementations in Fig. 12.14 include a constructor (lines 10–15) that takes a first name, last name, social security number, sales amount and commission rate; *set* functions (lines 18–24 and 30–36) to assign new values to data members grossSales and commissionRate, respectively; *get* functions (lines 27 and 39–41) that retrieve their values; function earnings (lines 44–46) to calculate a CommissionEmployee's earnings; and function toString (lines 49–56) to output the employee's type, namely, "commission employee: " and employee-specific information. The constructor passes the first name, last name and social security number to the Employee constructor (line 12) to initialize Employee's private data members. Function toString calls base-class function toString (line 52) to get a string representation of the Employee-specific information.

```cpp
1   // Fig. 12.13: CommissionEmployee.h
2   // CommissionEmployee class derived from Employee.
3   #ifndef COMMISSION_H
4   #define COMMISSION_H
5
6   #include <string> // C++ standard string class
7   #include "Employee.h" // Employee class definition
8
9   class CommissionEmployee : public Employee {
10  public:
11     CommissionEmployee(const std::string&, const std::string&,
12        const std::string&, double = 0.0, double = 0.0);
13     virtual ~CommissionEmployee() = default; // virtual destructor
14
15     void setCommissionRate(double); // set commission rate
16     double getCommissionRate() const; // return commission rate
17
18     void setGrossSales(double); // set gross sales amount
19     double getGrossSales() const; // return gross sales amount
20
21     // keyword virtual signals intent to override
22     virtual double earnings() const override; // calculate earnings
23     virtual std::string toString() const override; // string representation
24  private:
25     double grossSales; // gross weekly sales
26     double commissionRate; // commission percentage
27  };
28
29  #endif // COMMISSION_H
```

Fig. 12.13 | CommissionEmployee class header.

```cpp
 1   // Fig. 12.14: CommissionEmployee.cpp
 2   // CommissionEmployee class member-function definitions.
 3   #include <iomanip>
 4   #include <stdexcept>
 5   #include <sstream>
 6   #include "CommissionEmployee.h" // CommissionEmployee class definition
 7   using namespace std;
 8
 9   // constructor
10   CommissionEmployee::CommissionEmployee(const string &first,
11      const string &last, const string &ssn, double sales, double rate)
12      : Employee(first, last, ssn) {
13      setGrossSales(sales);
14      setCommissionRate(rate);
15   }
16
17   // set gross sales amount
18   void CommissionEmployee::setGrossSales(double sales) {
19      if (sales < 0.0) {
20         throw invalid_argument("Gross sales must be >= 0.0");
21      }
22
23      grossSales = sales;
24   }
25
26   // return gross sales amount
27   double CommissionEmployee::getGrossSales() const {return grossSales;}
28
29   // set commission rate
30   void CommissionEmployee::setCommissionRate(double rate) {
31      if (rate <= 0.0 || rate > 1.0) {
32         throw invalid_argument("Commission rate must be > 0.0 and < 1.0");
33      }
34
35      commissionRate = rate;
36   }
37
38   // return commission rate
39   double CommissionEmployee::getCommissionRate() const {
40      return commissionRate;
41   }
42
43   // calculate earnings; override pure virtual function earnings in Employee
44   double CommissionEmployee::earnings() const {
45      return getCommissionRate() * getGrossSales();
46   }
47
48   // return a string representation of CommissionEmployee's information
49   string CommissionEmployee::toString() const {
50      ostringstream output;
51      output << fixed << setprecision(2);
```

Fig. 12.14 | CommissionEmployee class implementation file. (Part 1 of 2.)

```
52        output << "commission employee: " << Employee::toString()
53           << "\ngross sales: " << getGrossSales()
54           << "; commission rate: " << getCommissionRate();
55        return output.str();
56   }
```

Fig. 12.14 | CommissionEmployee class implementation file. (Part 2 of 2.)

12.7.4 Creating Indirect Concrete Derived Class BasePlusCommissionEmployee

Class BasePlusCommissionEmployee (Figs. 12.15–12.16) directly inherits from class CommissionEmployee (line 9 of Fig. 12.15) and therefore is an *indirect* derived class of class Employee. Class BasePlusCommissionEmployee's member-function implementations in Fig. 12.16 include a constructor (lines 10–15) that takes as arguments a first name, a last name, a social security number, a sales amount, a commission rate *and* a base salary. It then passes the first name, last name, social security number, sales amount and commission rate to the CommissionEmployee constructor (line 13) to initialize the inherited members. BasePlusCommissionEmployee also contains a *set* function (lines 18–24) to assign a new value to data member baseSalary and a *get* function (lines 27–29) to return baseSalary's value. Function earnings (lines 33–35) calculates a BasePlusCommissionEmployee's earnings. Line 34 in function earnings calls base class CommissionEmployee's earnings function to calculate the commission-based portion of the employee's earnings. Base-PlusCommissionEmployee's toString function (lines 38–44) returns "base-salaried", followed by the result of base-class CommissionEmployee's toString function, then the base salary. The resulting string begins with "base-salaried commission employee: " followed by the rest of the BasePlusCommissionEmployee's information. Recall that CommissionEmployee's toString gets a string containing the employee's first name, last name and social security number by invoking the toString function of its base class (i.e., Employee). BasePlusCommissionEmployee's toString initiates a chain of functions calls that spans *all three levels* of the Employee hierarchy.

```
1    // Fig. 12.15: BasePlusCommissionEmployee.h
2    // BasePlusCommissionEmployee class derived from CommissionEmployee.
3    #ifndef BASEPLUS_H
4    #define BASEPLUS_H
5
6    #include <string> // C++ standard string class
7    #include "CommissionEmployee.h" // CommissionEmployee class definition
8
9    class BasePlusCommissionEmployee : public CommissionEmployee {
10   public:
11      BasePlusCommissionEmployee(const std::string&, const std::string&,
12         const std::string&, double = 0.0, double = 0.0, double = 0.0);
13      virtual ~BasePlusCommissionEmployee() = default; // virtual destructor
14
15      void setBaseSalary(double); // set base salary
16      double getBaseSalary() const; // return base salary
```

Fig. 12.15 | BasePlusCommissionEmployee class header. (Part 1 of 2.)

```
17
18     // keyword virtual signals intent to override
19     virtual double earnings() const override; // calculate earnings
20     virtual std::string toString() const override; // string representation
21  private:
22     double baseSalary; // base salary per week
23  };
24
25  #endif // BASEPLUS_H
```

Fig. 12.15 | BasePlusCommissionEmployee class header. (Part 2 of 2.)

```
1  // Fig. 12.16: BasePlusCommissionEmployee.cpp
2  // BasePlusCommissionEmployee member-function definitions.
3  #include <iomanip>
4  #include <stdexcept>
5  #include <sstream>
6  #include "BasePlusCommissionEmployee.h"
7  using namespace std;
8
9  // constructor
10 BasePlusCommissionEmployee::BasePlusCommissionEmployee(
11    const string& first, const string& last, const string& ssn,
12    double sales, double rate, double salary)
13    : CommissionEmployee(first, last, ssn, sales, rate) {
14    setBaseSalary(salary); // validate and store base salary
15 }
16
17 // set base salary
18 void BasePlusCommissionEmployee::setBaseSalary(double salary) {
19    if (salary < 0.0) {
20       throw invalid_argument("Salary must be >= 0.0");
21    }
22
23    baseSalary = salary;
24 }
25
26 // return base salary
27 double BasePlusCommissionEmployee::getBaseSalary() const {
28    return baseSalary;
29 }
30
31 // calculate earnings;
32 // override virtual function earnings in CommissionEmployee
33 double BasePlusCommissionEmployee::earnings() const {
34    return getBaseSalary() + CommissionEmployee::earnings();
35 }
36
37 // return a string representation of a BasePlusCommissionEmployee
38 string BasePlusCommissionEmployee::toString() const {
39    ostringstream output;
40    output << fixed << setprecision(2);
```

Fig. 12.16 | BasePlusCommissionEmployee class implementation file. (Part 1 of 2.)

```
41      output << "base-salaried " << CommissionEmployee::toString()
42         << "; base salary: " << getBaseSalary();
43   return output.str();
44 }
```

Fig. 12.16 | BasePlusCommissionEmployee class implementation file. (Part 2 of 2.)

12.7.5 Demonstrating Polymorphic Processing

To test our Employee hierarchy, the program in Fig. 12.17 creates an object of each of the three concrete classes SalariedEmployee, CommissionEmployee and BasePlusCommissionEmployee. The program manipulates these objects, first with *static binding*, then *polymorphically*, using a vector of Employee base-class pointers. Lines 20–25 create objects of each of the three concrete Employee derived classes. Lines 28–34 output each Employee's information and earnings. Each member-function invocation in lines 29–34 is an example of *static binding*—at *compile time*, because we are using *name handles* (not *pointers* or *references* that could be set at *execution time*), the *compiler* can identify each object's type to determine which toString and earnings functions are called.

```
 1   // Fig. 12.17: fig12_17.cpp
 2   // Processing Employee derived-class objects with static binding
 3   // then polymorphically using dynamic binding.
 4   #include <iostream>
 5   #include <iomanip>
 6   #include <vector>
 7   #include "Employee.h"
 8   #include "SalariedEmployee.h"
 9   #include "CommissionEmployee.h"
10   #include "BasePlusCommissionEmployee.h"
11   using namespace std;
12
13   void virtualViaPointer(const Employee* const); // prototype
14   void virtualViaReference(const Employee&); // prototype
15
16   int main() {
17      cout << fixed << setprecision(2); // set floating-point formatting
18
19      // create derived-class objects
20      SalariedEmployee salariedEmployee{
21         "John", "Smith", "111-11-1111", 800};
22      CommissionEmployee commissionEmployee{
23         "Sue", "Jones", "333-33-3333", 10000, .06};
24      BasePlusCommissionEmployee basePlusCommissionEmployee{
25         "Bob", "Lewis", "444-44-4444", 5000, .04, 300};
26
27      // output each Employee's information and earnings using static binding
28      cout << "EMPLOYEES PROCESSED INDIVIDUALLY USING STATIC BINDING\n"
29         << salariedEmployee.toString()
30         << "\nearned $" << salariedEmployee.earnings() << "\n\n"
```

Fig. 12.17 | Processing Employee derived-class objects with static binding then polymorphically using dynamic binding. (Part 1 of 3.)

```
31              << commissionEmployee.toString()
32              << "\nearned $" << commissionEmployee.earnings() << "\n\n"
33              << basePlusCommissionEmployee.toString()
34              << "\nearned $" << basePlusCommissionEmployee.earnings() << "\n\n";
35
36     // create and initialize vector of three base-class pointers
37     vector<Employee *> employees{&salariedEmployee, &commissionEmployee,
38         &basePlusCommissionEmployee};
39
40     cout << "EMPLOYEES PROCESSED POLYMORPHICALLY VIA DYNAMIC BINDING\n\n";
41
42     // call virtualViaPointer to print each Employee's information
43     // and earnings using dynamic binding
44     cout << "VIRTUAL FUNCTION CALLS MADE OFF BASE-CLASS POINTERS\n";
45
46     for (const Employee* employeePtr : employees) {
47         virtualViaPointer(employeePtr);
48     }
49
50     // call virtualViaReference to print each Employee's information
51     // and earnings using dynamic binding
52     cout << "VIRTUAL FUNCTION CALLS MADE OFF BASE-CLASS REFERENCES\n";
53
54     for (const Employee* employeePtr : employees) {
55         virtualViaReference(*employeePtr); // note dereferencing
56     }
57 }
58
59 // call Employee virtual functions toString and earnings off a
60 // base-class pointer using dynamic binding
61 void virtualViaPointer(const Employee* const baseClassPtr) {
62     cout << baseClassPtr->toString()
63         << "\nearned $" << baseClassPtr->earnings() << "\n\n";
64 }
65
66 // call Employee virtual functions toString and earnings off a
67 // base-class reference using dynamic binding
68 void virtualViaReference(const Employee& baseClassRef) {
69     cout << baseClassRef.toString()
70         << "\nearned $" << baseClassRef.earnings() << "\n\n";
71 }
```

```
EMPLOYEES PROCESSED INDIVIDUALLY USING STATIC BINDING
salaried employee: John Smith
social security number: 111-11-1111
weekly salary: 800.00
earned $800.00

commission employee: Sue Jones
social security number: 333-33-3333
gross sales: 10000.00; commission rate: 0.06
earned $600.00
```

Fig. 12.17 | Processing Employee derived-class objects with static binding then polymorphically using dynamic binding. (Part 2 of 3.)

```
base-salaried commission employee: Bob Lewis
social security number: 444-44-4444
gross sales: 5000.00; commission rate: 0.04; base salary: 300.00
earned $500.00

EMPLOYEES PROCESSED POLYMORPHICALLY VIA DYNAMIC BINDING

VIRTUAL FUNCTION CALLS MADE OFF BASE-CLASS POINTERS
salaried employee: John Smith
social security number: 111-11-1111
weekly salary: 800.00
earned $800.00

commission employee: Sue Jones
social security number: 333-33-3333
gross sales: 10000.00; commission rate: 0.06
earned $600.00

base-salaried commission employee: Bob Lewis
social security number: 444-44-4444
gross sales: 5000.00; commission rate: 0.04; base salary: 300.00
earned $500.00

VIRTUAL FUNCTION CALLS MADE OFF BASE-CLASS REFERENCES
salaried employee: John Smith
social security number: 111-11-1111
weekly salary: 800.00
earned $800.00

commission employee: Sue Jones
social security number: 333-33-3333
gross sales: 10000.00; commission rate: 0.06
earned $600.00

base-salaried commission employee: Bob Lewis
social security number: 444-44-4444
gross sales: 5000.00; commission rate: 0.04; base salary: 300.00
earned $500.00
```

Fig. 12.17 | Processing Employee derived-class objects with static binding then polymorphically using dynamic binding. (Part 3 of 3.)

Lines 37–38 create and initialize the vector employees, which contains three Employee pointers that are aimed at the objects salariedEmployee, commissionEmployee and base-PlusCommissionEmployee, respectively. The compiler allows the elements to be initialized with the addresses of these objects, because a SalariedEmployee *is an* Employee, a CommissionEmployee *is an* Employee and a BasePlusCommissionEmployee *is an* Employee. So, we can assign the addresses of SalariedEmployee, CommissionEmployee and BasePlusCommissionEmployee objects to base-class Employee pointers, even though Employee is an *abstract* class.

Lines 46–48 traverse vector employees and invoke function virtualViaPointer (lines 61–64) for each element in employees. Function virtualViaPointer receives in parameter baseClassPtr the address stored in an employees element. Each call to virtualViaPointer uses baseClassPtr to invoke virtual functions toString (line 62) and earnings (line 63). Function virtualViaPointer does *not* contain *any* SalariedEmployee, CommissionEmployee or BasePlusCommissionEmployee type information. The function knows *only* about base-class type Employee. Therefore, the compiler *cannot know* which concrete class's functions to call through baseClassPtr. Yet at execution time, each virtual-function invocation correctly calls the function on the object to which baseClassPtr currently points. The output illustrates that the appropriate functions for each class are indeed invoked and that each object's proper information is displayed. For instance, the weekly salary is displayed for the SalariedEmployee, and the gross sales are displayed for the CommissionEmployee and BasePlusCommissionEmployee. Also, obtaining the earnings of each Employee polymorphically in line 63 produces the same results as obtaining these employees' earnings via *static binding* in lines 30, 32 and 34. All virtual function calls to toString and earnings are resolved at *runtime* with *dynamic binding*.

Lines 54–56 traverse employees and invoke function virtualViaReference (lines 68–71) for each vector element. Function virtualViaReference receives in its parameter baseClassRef (of type const Employee&) a *reference* to the object obtained by *dereferencing the pointer* stored in each employees element (line 55). Each call to virtualViaReference invokes virtual functions toString (line 69) and earnings (line 70) via baseClassRef to demonstrate that *polymorphic processing occurs with base-class references as well*. Each virtual function invocation calls the function on the object to which baseClassRef refers at runtime. This is another example of *dynamic binding*. The output produced using base-class references is identical to the output produced using base-class pointers and via static binding earlier in the program.

12.8 (Optional) Polymorphism, Virtual Functions and Dynamic Binding "Under the Hood"

C++ makes polymorphism easy to program. It's certainly possible to program for polymorphism in non-object-oriented languages such as C, but doing so requires complex and potentially dangerous pointer manipulations. This section discusses how C++ can implement polymorphism, virtual functions and dynamic binding internally. This will give you a solid understanding of how these capabilities really work. More importantly, it will help you appreciate the *overhead* of polymorphism—in terms of additional *memory consumption* and *processor time*. This can help you determine when to use polymorphism and when to avoid it. C++ Standard Library classes like array and vector are implemented *without* polymorphism and virtual functions to avoid the associated execution-time overhead and achieve optimal performance.

First, we'll explain the data structures that the compiler builds at *compile time* to support polymorphism at execution time. You'll see that polymorphism is accomplished through three levels of pointers, i.e., *triple indirection*. Then we'll show how an executing program uses these data structures to execute virtual functions and achieve the *dynamic binding* associated with polymorphism. Our discussion explains a *possible* implementation; this is not a language requirement.

When C++ compiles a class that has one or more virtual functions, it builds a virtual function table (*vtable*) for that class. The *vtable* contains pointers to the class's virtual functions—a pointer to a function contains the starting address in memory of the code that performs the function's task. Just as an array name is implicitly convertible to the address of the array's first element, a function name is implicitly convertible to the starting address of its code. An executing program uses the *vtable* to select the proper function implementation each time a virtual function of that class is called on any object of that class. The leftmost column of Fig. 12.18 illustrates the *vtables* for the classes Employee, SalariedEmployee, CommissionEmployee and BasePlusCommissionEmployee.

Employee *Class* vtable

In the Employee class *vtable*, the first function pointer is set to 0 (i.e., nullptr), because function earnings is a *pure* virtual function and therefore *lacks an implementation*. The second function pointer points to function toString, which returns a string containing the employee's full name and social security number. [*Note:* We've abbreviated the output of each toString function in this figure to conserve space.] Any class that has one or more nullptrs (represented with the value 0) in its *vtable* is an *abstract* class. Classes without any nullptrs in their *vtables* (such as SalariedEmployee, CommissionEmployee and BasePlusCommissionEmployee) are *concrete* classes.

SalariedEmployee *Class* vtable

Class SalariedEmployee overrides function earnings to return the employee's weekly salary, so the function pointer points to the earnings function of class SalariedEmployee. SalariedEmployee also overrides toString, so the corresponding function pointer points to the SalariedEmployee member function that returns "salaried employee: " followed by the employee's name, social security number and weekly salary.

CommissionEmployee *Class* vtable

The earnings function pointer in the *vtable* for class CommissionEmployee points to the CommissionEmployee's earnings function that returns the employee's gross sales multiplied by the commission rate. The toString function pointer points to the CommissionEmployee version of the function, which returns the employee's type, name, social security number, commission rate and gross sales. As in class SalariedEmployee, both functions override the functions in class Employee.

BasePlusCommissionEmployee *Class* vtable

The earnings function pointer in the *vtable* for class BasePlusCommissionEmployee points to the BasePlusCommissionEmployee's earnings function, which returns the employee's base salary plus gross sales multiplied by commission rate. The toString function pointer points to the BasePlusCommissionEmployee version of the function, which returns the employee's base salary plus the type, name, social security number, commission rate and gross sales. Both functions override the functions in class CommissionEmployee.

Inheriting Concrete virtual *Functions*

In our Employee case study, each *concrete* class provides its own implementation for virtual functions earnings and toString. You've learned that each class that inherits *directly* from abstract base class Employee *must implement* earnings in order to be a *concrete* class, because earnings is a pure virtual function. These classes do *not* need to implement function toString, however, to be considered concrete—toString is *not a pure* virtual function and derived classes can inherit class Employee's implementation of toString.

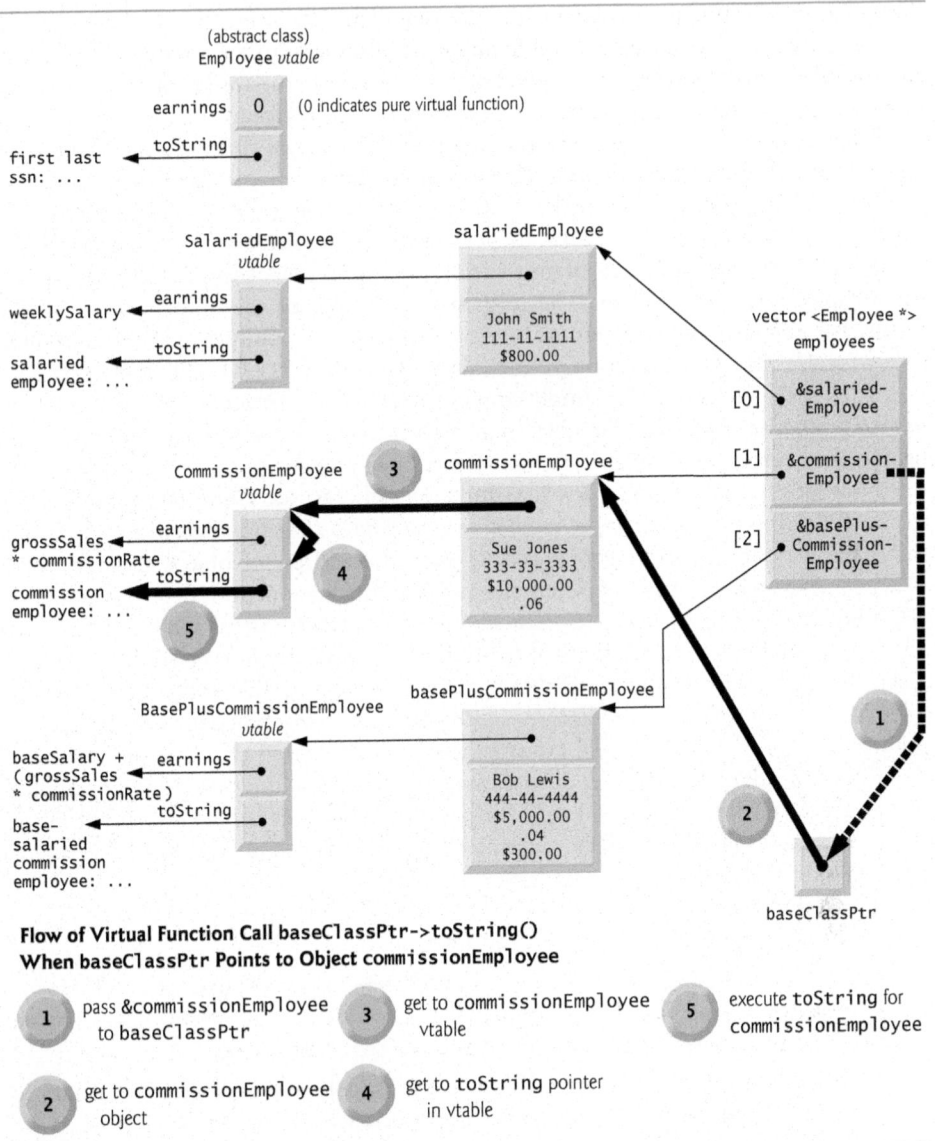

**Flow of Virtual Function Call baseClassPtr->toString()
When baseClassPtr Points to Object commissionEmployee**

1 pass &commissionEmployee to baseClassPtr	**3** get to commissionEmployee vtable	**5** execute toString for commissionEmployee
2 get to commissionEmployee object	**4** get to toString pointer in vtable	

Fig. 12.18 | How virtual function calls work.

Furthermore, class BasePlusCommissionEmployee does *not* have to implement either function toString or earnings—both function implementations can be inherited from concrete class CommissionEmployee. If a class in our hierarchy were to inherit function implementations in this manner, the *vtable* pointers for these functions would simply point to the function implementation that was being inherited. For example, if BasePlusCommissionEmployee did not override earnings, the earnings function pointer in the *vtable* for class BasePlusCommissionEmployee would point to the same earnings function as the *vtable* for class CommissionEmployee.

Three Levels of Pointers to Implement Polymorphism

Polymorphism is accomplished through an elegant data structure involving *three levels of pointers*. We've discussed one level—the function pointers in the *vtable*. These point to the actual functions that execute when a virtual function is invoked.

Now we consider the second level of pointers. *Whenever an object of a class with one or more virtual functions is instantiated, the compiler attaches to the object a pointer to the* vtable *for that class*. This pointer is normally at the front of the object, but it isn't required to be implemented that way. In Fig. 12.18, these pointers are associated with the objects created in Fig. 12.17 (one object for each of the types SalariedEmployee, CommissionEmployee and BasePlusCommissionEmployee). The diagram shows each of the object's data member values. For example, the salariedEmployee object contains a pointer to the SalariedEmployee *vtable*; the object also contains the values John Smith, 111-11-1111 and $800.00.

The third level of pointers simply contains the handles to the objects that receive the virtual function calls. The handles in this level may also be *references*. Figure 12.18 depicts the vector employees that contains Employee *pointers*.

Now let's see how a typical virtual function call executes. Consider in the function virtualViaPointer the call baseClassPtr->toString() (line 62 of Fig. 12.17). Assume that baseClassPtr contains employees[1] (i.e., the address of object commissionEmployee in employees). When the compiler compiles this statement, it determines that the call is indeed being made via a *base-class pointer* and that toString is a virtual function.

The compiler determines that toString is the *second* entry in each of the *vtables*. To locate this entry, the compiler notes that it will need to skip the first entry. Thus, the compiler compiles an offset or displacement into the table of machine-language object-code pointers to find the code that will execute the virtual function call. The size in bytes of the offset depends on the number of bytes used to represent a function pointer on an individual platform. For example, on a 32-bit platform, a pointer is typically stored in four bytes, whereas on a 64-bit platform, a pointer is typically stored in eight bytes. We assume four bytes for this discussion.

The compiler generates code that performs the following operations [*Note:* The numbers in the list correspond to the circled numbers in Fig. 12.18]:

1. Select the *i*th entry of employees (in this case, the address of object commissionEmployee) and pass it as an argument to function virtualViaPointer. This sets parameter baseClassPtr to point to commissionEmployee.

2. *Dereference* that pointer to get to the commissionEmployee object—which, as you recall, begins with a pointer to the CommissionEmployee *vtable*.

3. *Dereference* commissionEmployee's *vtable* pointer to get to the CommissionEmployee *vtable*.

4. Skip the offset of four bytes to select the toString function pointer.

5. *Dereference* the toString function pointer to form the "name" of the actual function to execute, and use the function-call operator () to execute the appropriate toString function, which in this case returns the employee's type, name, social security number, gross sales and commission rate.

Figure 12.18's data structures may appear complex, but this complexity is managed by the compiler and *hidden* from you, making polymorphic programming straightforward. The pointer dereferencing operations and memory accesses that occur on every virtual function call require some additional execution time. The *vtables* and the *vtable* pointers added to the objects require some additional memory.

Performance Tip 12.1

Polymorphism, as typically implemented with virtual functions and dynamic binding in C++, is efficient. For most applications, you can use these capabilities with nominal impact on performance.

Performance Tip 12.2

Virtual functions and dynamic binding enable polymorphic programming as an alternative to switch logic programming. Optimizing compilers normally generate polymorphic code that's nearly as efficient as hand-coded switch-based logic. Polymorphism's overhead is acceptable for most applications. In some situations—such as real-time applications with stringent performance requirements—polymorphism's overhead may be too high.

12.9 Case Study: Payroll System Using Polymorphism and Runtime Type Information with Downcasting, dynamic_cast, typeid and type_info

Recall from the problem statement at the beginning of Section 12.7 that, for the current pay period, our fictitious company has decided to reward BasePlusCommissionEmployees by adding 10 percent to their base salaries. When processing Employee objects polymorphically in Section 12.7.5, we did not need to worry about the "specifics." Now, however, to adjust the base salaries of BasePlusCommissionEmployees, we have to determine the *specific type* of each Employee object *at execution time*, then act appropriately. This section demonstrates the powerful capabilities of runtime type information (RTTI) and dynamic casting, which enable a program to determine an object's type at execution time and act on that object accordingly.[1]

Figure 12.19 uses the Employee hierarchy from Section 12.7 and increases by 10 percent each BasePlusCommissionEmployee's base salary. Lines 20–24 create and initialize the three-element vector named employees that stores pointers to Employee objects. The elements are initialized with the addresses of *dynamically allocated* objects of classes SalariedEmployee (Figs. 12.11–12.12), CommissionEmployee (Figs. 12.13–12.14) and BasePlusCommissionEmployee (Figs. 12.15–12.16). Lines 27–44 of Fig. 12.19 iterate through the employees vector and display each Employee's information by invoking member function toString (line 28). Recall that because toString is declared virtual in *base class* Employee, the system invokes the appropriate *derived-class* object's toString function.

```
1   // Fig. 12.19: fig12_19.cpp
2   // Demonstrating downcasting and runtime type information.
3   // NOTE: You may need to enable RTTI on your compiler
4   // before you can compile this application.
```

Fig. 12.19 | Demonstrating downcasting and runtime type information. (Part 1 of 3.)

1. Some compilers require that RTTI be enabled before it can be used in a program. The compilers we used for testing this book's examples—GNU C++ 5.2.1, Visual C++ 2015 and Xcode 7.2 Clang/ LLVM—each enable RTTI by default.

```
5   #include <iostream>
6   #include <iomanip>
7   #include <vector>
8   #include <typeinfo>
9   #include "Employee.h"
10  #include "SalariedEmployee.h"
11  #include "CommissionEmployee.h"
12  #include "BasePlusCommissionEmployee.h"
13  using namespace std;
14
15  int main() {
16     // set floating-point output formatting
17     cout << fixed << setprecision(2);
18
19     // create and initialize vector of three base-class pointers
20     vector<Employee*> employees{
21        new SalariedEmployee("John", "Smith", "111-11-1111", 800),
22        new CommissionEmployee("Sue", "Jones", "333-33-3333", 10000, .06),
23        new BasePlusCommissionEmployee(
24           "Bob", "Lewis", "444-44-4444", 5000, .04, 300)};
25
26     // polymorphically process each element in vector employees
27     for (Employee* employeePtr : employees) {
28        cout << employeePtr->toString() << endl; // output employee
29
30        // attempt to downcast pointer
31        BasePlusCommissionEmployee* derivedPtr =
32           dynamic_cast<BasePlusCommissionEmployee*>(employeePtr);
33
34        // determine whether element points to a BasePlusCommissionEmployee
35        if (derivedPtr != nullptr) { // true for "is a" relationship
36           double oldBaseSalary = derivedPtr->getBaseSalary();
37           cout << "old base salary: $" << oldBaseSalary << endl;
38           derivedPtr->setBaseSalary(1.10 * oldBaseSalary);
39           cout << "new base salary with 10% increase is: $"
40              << derivedPtr->getBaseSalary() << endl;
41        }
42
43        cout << "earned $" << employeePtr->earnings() << "\n\n";
44     }
45
46     // release objects pointed to by vector's elements
47     for (const Employee* employeePtr : employees) {
48        // output class name
49        cout << "deleting object of "
50           << typeid(*employeePtr).name() << endl;
51
52        delete employeePtr;
53     }
54  }
```

Fig. 12.19 | Demonstrating downcasting and runtime type information. (Part 2 of 3.)

```
salaried employee: John Smith
social security number: 111-11-1111
weekly salary: 800.00
earned $800.00

commission employee: Sue Jones
social security number: 333-33-3333
gross sales: 10000.00; commission rate: 0.06
earned $600.00

base-salaried commission employee: Bob Lewis
social security number: 444-44-4444
gross sales: 5000.00; commission rate: 0.04; base salary: 300.00
old base salary: $300.00
new base salary with 10% increase is: $330.00
earned $530.00

deleting object of class SalariedEmployee
deleting object of class CommissionEmployee
deleting object of class BasePlusCommissionEmployee
```

Fig. 12.19 | Demonstrating downcasting and runtime type information. (Part 3 of 3.)

Determining an Object's Type with dynamic_cast

In this example, as we encounter a BasePlusCommissionEmployee object, we wish to increase its base salary by 10 percent. Since we process the Employees polymorphically, we cannot (with the techniques you've learned so far) be certain as to which type of Employee is being manipulated at any given time. This creates a problem, because BasePlusCommissionEmployee employees *must be identified when we encounter them* so they can receive the 10 percent salary increase. To accomplish this, we use operator dynamic_cast (lines 31–32) to determine whether the current Employee's type is BasePlusCommissionEmployee. This is the *downcast* operation we referred to in Section 12.3.3. Lines 31–32 *dynamically downcast* employeePtr from type Employee* to type BasePlusCommissionEmployee*. If employeePtr points to an object that *is a* BasePlusCommissionEmployee object, then that object's *address* is assigned to derived-class pointer derivedPtr; otherwise, nullptr is assigned to derivedPtr. We *must* use dynamic_cast here, rather than static_cast, to perform type checking on the underlying object—a static_cast would simply cast the Employee* to a BasePlusCommissionEmployee* regardless of the underlying object's type. With a static_cast, the program would attempt to increase *every* Employee's base salary, resulting in undefined behavior for each object that's not a BasePlusCommissionEmployee.

If the value returned by the dynamic_cast operator in lines 31–32 *is not* nullptr, the object *is* the correct type, and the if statement (lines 35–41) performs the special processing required for the BasePlusCommissionEmployee object. Lines 36, 38 and 40 invoke BasePlusCommissionEmployee functions getBaseSalary and setBaseSalary to retrieve and update the employee's salary.

Calculating the Current **Employee**'s Earnings

Line 43 invokes member function earnings on the object to which employeePtr points. Recall that earnings is declared virtual in the base class, so the program invokes the derived-class object's earnings function—another example of *dynamic binding*.

Displaying an **Employee**'s *Type*

Lines 47–53 display each employee's *object type* and use the delete operator to deallocate the dynamic memory to which each vector element points. Operator typeid (line 50) returns a *reference* to an object of class type_info that contains the information about the type of its operand, including the name of that type. When invoked, type_info member function name (line 50) returns a pointer-based string containing the typeid argument's *type name* (e.g., "class BasePlusCommissionEmployee"). To use typeid, the program must include header <typeinfo> (line 8).

 Portability Tip 12.1

The string returned by type_info *member function* name *may vary by compiler.*

Compilation Errors That We Avoided By Using **dynamic_cast**

We avoid several compilation errors in this example by *downcasting* an Employee pointer to a BasePlusCommissionEmployee pointer (lines 31–32). If we remove the dynamic_cast from line 32 and attempt to assign the current Employee pointer directly to BasePlusCommissionEmployee pointer derivedPtr, we'll receive a compilation error. C++ does *not* allow a program to assign a base-class pointer to a derived-class pointer because the *is-a* relationship does *not* apply—a CommissionEmployee is *not* a BasePlusCommissionEmployee. The *is-a* relationship applies only between the derived class and its base classes, not vice versa.

Similarly, if lines 36, 38 and 40 used the base-class pointer from the current element of employees, rather than derived-class pointer derivedPtr, to invoke derived-class-only functions getBaseSalary and setBaseSalary, we'd receive a compilation error at each of these lines. As you learned in Section 12.3.3, attempting to invoke *derived-class-only functions* through a *base-class pointer* is *not* allowed. Although lines 36, 38 and 40 execute only if derivedPtr is not nullptr (i.e., if the cast *can* be performed), we *cannot* attempt to invoke derived-class BasePlusCommissionEmployee functions getBaseSalary and setBaseSalary on the base-class Employee pointer.

12.10 Wrap-Up

In this chapter we discussed polymorphism, which enables us to "program in the general" rather than "program in the specific," and we showed how this makes programs more extensible. We began with an example of how polymorphism would allow a screen manager to display several "space" objects. We then demonstrated how base-class and derived-class pointers can be aimed at base-class and derived-class objects. We said that aiming base-class pointers at base-class objects is natural, as is aiming derived-class pointers at derived-class objects. Aiming base-class pointers at derived-class objects is also natural because a derived-class object *is an* object of its base class. You learned why aiming derived-class pointers at base-class objects is dangerous and why the compiler disallows such assignments.

We introduced virtual functions, which enable the proper functions to be called when objects at various levels of an inheritance hierarchy are referenced (at execution time) via base-class pointers or references. This is known as dynamic binding. We discussed virtual destructors, and how they ensure that all appropriate destructors in an inheritance hierarchy run on a derived-class object when that object is deleted via a base-class pointer or reference.

Next, we discussed pure `virtual` functions and abstract classes (classes with one or more pure `virtual` functions). You learned that abstract classes cannot be used to instantiate objects, while concrete classes can. We demonstrated using abstract classes in an inheritance hierarchy. You learned how polymorphism works "under the hood" with *vtables* created by the compiler.

We used runtime type information (RTTI) and dynamic casting to determine the type of an object at execution time and act on that object accordingly. We used the `typeid` operator to get a `type_info` object containing a given object's type information.

In the next chapter, we discuss many of C++'s I/O capabilities and demonstrate several stream manipulators that perform various formatting tasks.

Summary

Section 12.1 Introduction

- **Polymorphism** (p. 532) enables us to write programs that process objects of classes that are part of the same class hierarchy as if they were all objects of the hierarchy's base class.

- With polymorphism, we can design and implement systems that are easily extensible—new classes can be added with little or no modification to the general portions of the program. The only parts of a program that must be altered to accommodate new classes are those that require direct knowledge of the new classes that you add to the hierarchy.

Section 12.2 Introduction to Polymorphism: Polymorphic Video Game

- With polymorphism, one function call can cause different actions to occur, depending on the type of the object on which the function is invoked.

- This makes it possible to design and implement more extensible systems. Programs can be written to process objects of types that may not exist when the program is under development.

Section 12.3 Relationships Among Objects in an Inheritance Hierarchy

- C++ enables polymorphism—the ability for objects of different classes related by inheritance to respond differently to the same member-function call.

Section 12.4.2 Declaring `virtual` Functions

- Polymorphism is implemented via **virtual functions** (p. 540) and **dynamic binding** (p. 541).

Section 12.4.3 Invoking a `virtual` Function Through a Base-Class Pointer or Reference

- When a base-class pointer or reference is used to call a `virtual` function, C++ chooses the correct overridden function in the appropriate derived class associated with the object.

Section 12.4.4 Invoking a `virtual` Function Through an Object's Name

- If a `virtual` function is called by referencing a specific object by name and using the dot member-selection operator, the reference is resolved at compile time (this is called **static binding**; p. 541); the `virtual` function that's called is the one defined for the class of that particular object.

- Derived classes can override a base-class `virtual` function if necessary, but if they do not, the base class's implementation is used.

Section 12.4.5 virtual Functions in the CommissionEmployee Hierarchy

- To help prevent errors, apply C++11's **override** keyword (p. 542) to the prototype of every derived-class function that overrides a base-class virtual function. This enables the compiler to check whether the base class has a virtual member function with the same signature. If not, the compiler generates an error.

Section 12.4.6 virtual Destructors

- Declare a **virtual base-class destructor** (p. 546) if the class contains virtual functions. This makes all derived-class destructors virtual, even though they do not have the same name as the base-class destructor. If an object in the hierarchy is destroyed explicitly by applying the delete operator to a base-class pointer to a derived-class object, the destructor for the appropriate class is called. After a derived-class destructor runs, the destructors for all of that class's base classes run all the way up the hierarchy.
- In C++11, you can tell the compiler to explicitly generate the default version of a default constructor, copy constructor, move constructor, copy assignment operator, move assignment operator or destructor by following the special member function's prototype with = **default** (p. 546).

Section 12.4.7 C++11: final Member Functions and Classes

- In C++11, a base-class virtual function that's declared **final** (p. 546) in its prototype cannot be overridden in any derived class.
- In C++11, you can **declare a class as final** (p. 547) to prevent it from being used as a base class.
- Attempting to override a final member function or inherit from a final base class results in a compilation error.

Section 12.5 Type Fields and switch Statements

- Polymorphic programming with virtual functions can eliminate the need for switch logic. You can use the virtual function mechanism to perform the equivalent logic automatically, thus avoiding the kinds of errors typically associated with switch logic.

Section 12.6 Abstract Classes and Pure virtual Functions

- **Abstract classes** (p. 547) are typically used as base classes, so we refer to them as **abstract base classes** (p. 547). No objects of an abstract class may be instantiated.
- Classes from which objects can be instantiated are **concrete classes** (p. 547).

Section 12.6.1 Pure Virtual Functions

- You create an abstract class by declaring one or more **pure virtual functions** (p. 548) with pure specifiers (= 0) in their declarations.
- If a class is derived from a class with a pure virtual function and that derived class does not supply a definition for that pure virtual function, then that virtual function remains pure in the derived class. Consequently, the derived class is also an abstract class.
- Although we cannot instantiate objects of abstract base classes, we can declare pointers and references to objects of abstract base classes. Such pointers and references can be used to enable polymorphic manipulations of derived-class objects instantiated from concrete derived classes.

Section 12.8 (Optional) Polymorphism, Virtual Functions and Dynamic Binding "Under the Hood"

- Dynamic binding requires that at runtime, the call to a virtual member function be routed to the virtual function version appropriate for the class. A virtual function table called the *vtable* (p. 563) is implemented as an array containing function pointers. Each class with virtual functions has a *vtable*. For each virtual function in the class, the *vtable* has an entry containing a function pointer to the version of the virtual function to use for an object of that class. The virtual function to use for a particular class could be the function defined in that class, or it could be a function inherited either directly or indirectly from a base class higher in the hierarchy.

- When a base class provides a virtual member function, derived classes can override the virtual function, but they do not have to override it.

- Each object of a class with virtual functions contains a pointer to the *vtable* for that class. When a function call is made from a base-class pointer to a derived-class object, the appropriate function pointer in the *vtable* is obtained and dereferenced to complete the call at execution time.

- Any class that has one or more nullptr pointers in its *vtable* is an abstract class. Classes without any nullptr *vtable* pointers are concrete classes.

- New kinds of classes are regularly added to systems and accommodated by dynamic binding.

Section 12.9 Case Study: Payroll System Using Polymorphism and Runtime Information with Downcasting, dynamic_cast, typeid and type_info

- Operator **dynamic_cast** (p. 567) checks the type of the object to which a pointer points, then determines whether the type has an *is-a* relationship with the type to which the pointer is being converted. If so, dynamic_cast returns the object's address. If not, dynamic_cast returns nullptr.

- Operator **typeid** (p. 570) returns a reference to a **type_info object** (p. 570) that contains information about the operand's type, including the type name. To use typeid, the program must include header **<typeinfo>** (p. 570).

- When invoked, type_info member function **name** (p. 570) returns a pointer-based string that contains the name of the type that the type_info object represents.

- Operators dynamic_cast and typeid are part of C++'s **runtime type information** (**RTTI**; p. 567) feature, which allows a program to determine an object's type at runtime.

Self-Review Exercises

12.1   Fill in the blanks in each of the following statements:
   a) Treating a base-class object as a(n) _____ can cause errors.
   b) Polymorphism helps eliminate _____ logic.
   c) If a class contains at least one pure virtual function, it's a(n) _____ class.
   d) Classes from which objects can be instantiated are called _____ classes.
   e) Operator _____ can be used to downcast base-class pointers safely.
   f) Operator typeid returns a reference to a(n) _____ object.
   g) _____ involves using a base-class pointer or reference to invoke virtual functions on base-class and derived-class objects.
   h) Overridable functions are declared using keyword _____.
   i) Casting a base-class pointer to a derived-class pointer is called _____.

12.2   State whether each of the following is *true* or *false*. If *false*, explain why.
   a) All virtual functions in an abstract base class must be declared as pure virtual functions.
   b) Referring to a derived-class object with a base-class handle is dangerous.
   c) A class is made abstract by declaring that class virtual.
   d) If a base class declares a pure virtual function, a derived class must implement that function to become a concrete class.
   e) Polymorphic programming can eliminate the need for switch logic.

Answers to Self-Review Exercises

12.1   a) derived-class object. b) switch. c) abstract. d) concrete. e) dynamic_cast. f) type_info. g) Polymorphism. h) virtual. i) downcasting.

12.2   a) False. An abstract base class can include virtual functions with implementations. b) False. Referring to a base-class object with a derived-class handle is dangerous. c) False. Classes are never declared virtual. Rather, a class is made abstract by including at least one pure virtual function in the class. d) True. e) True.

Exercises

12.3   *(Programming in the General)* How is it that polymorphism enables you to program "in the general" rather than "in the specific"? Discuss the key advantages of programming "in the general."

12.4   *(Polymorphism vs.* **switch** *logic)* Discuss the problems of programming with switch logic. Explain why polymorphism can be an effective alternative to using switch logic.

12.5   *(Inheriting Interface vs. Implementation)* Distinguish between inheriting interface and inheriting implementation. How do inheritance hierarchies designed for inheriting interface differ from those designed for inheriting implementation?

12.6   *(Virtual Functions)* What are virtual functions? Describe a circumstance in which virtual functions would be appropriate.

12.7   *(Dynamic Binding vs. Static Binding)* Distinguish between static binding and dynamic binding. Explain the use of virtual functions and the *vtable* in dynamic binding.

12.8   *(Virtual Functions vs. Pure Virtual Functions)* Distinguish between virtual functions and pure virtual functions.

12.9   *(Polymorphism and Extensibility)* How does polymorphism promote extensibility?

12.10   *(Polymorphic Application)* You've been asked to develop a flight simulator that will have elaborate graphical outputs. Explain why polymorphic programming could be especially effective for a problem of this nature.

12.11   *(Payroll-System Modification)* Modify the payroll system of Figs. 12.9–12.17 to include private data member birthDate in class Employee. Use class Date from Figs. 10.6–10.7 to represent an employee's birthday. Assume that payroll is processed once per month. Create a vector of Employee pointers to store the various employee objects. In a loop, calculate the payroll for each Employee (polymorphically), and add a $100.00 bonus to the person's payroll amount if the current month is the month in which the Employee's birthday occurs.

12.12   *(Package Inheritance Hierarchy)* Use the Package inheritance hierarchy created in Exercise 11.9 to create a program that displays the address information and calculates the shipping costs for several Packages. The program should contain a vector of Package pointers to objects of classes TwoDayPackage and OvernightPackage. Loop through the vector to process the Packages polymorphically. For each Package, invoke *get* functions to obtain the address information of the sender and the recipient, then print the two addresses as they would appear on mailing labels. Also, call each Package's calculateCost member function and print the result. Keep track of the total shipping cost for all Packages in the vector, and display this total when the loop terminates.

12.13   *(Polymorphic Banking Program Using* **Account** *Hierarchy)* Develop a polymorphic banking program using the Account hierarchy created in Exercise 11.10. Create a vector of Account pointers to SavingsAccount and CheckingAccount objects. For each Account in the vector, allow the user to specify an amount of money to withdraw from the Account using member function debit and an amount of money to deposit into the Account using member function credit. As you process each Account, determine its type. If an Account is a SavingsAccount, calculate the amount of interest owed to the Account using member function calculateInterest, then add the interest to the account balance using member function credit. After processing an Account, print the updated account balance obtained by invoking base-class member function getBalance.

12.14   *(Payroll-System Modification)* Modify the payroll system of Figs. 12.9–12.17 to include additional Employee subclasses PieceWorker and HourlyWorker. A PieceWorker represents an employee whose pay is based on the number of pieces of merchandise produced. An HourlyWorker represents an employee whose pay is based on an hourly wage and the number of hours worked. Hourly workers receive overtime pay (1.5 times the hourly wage) for all hours worked in excess of 40 hours.

Class PieceWorker should contain private data member wage (to store the employee's wage per piece) and pieces (to store the number of pieces produced). Class HourlyWorker should contain private data members wage (to store the employee's wage per hour) and hours (to store the hours worked). In class PieceWorker, provide a concrete implementation of member function earnings that calculates the employee's earnings by multiplying the number of pieces produced by the wage per piece. In class HourlyWorker, provide a concrete implementation of member function earnings that calculates the employee's earnings by multiplying the number of hours worked by the wage per hour. If the number of hours worked is over 40, be sure to pay the HourlyWorker for the overtime hours. Add a pointer to an object of each new class into the vector of Employee pointers in main. For each Employee, display its string representation and earnings.

Making a Difference

12.15   *(CarbonFootprint Abstract Class: Polymorphism)* Using an abstract class with only pure virtual functions, you can specify similar behaviors for possibly disparate classes. Governments and companies worldwide are becoming increasingly concerned with carbon footprints (annual releases of carbon dioxide into the atmosphere) from buildings burning various types of fuels for heat, vehicles burning fuels for power, and the like. Many scientists blame these greenhouse gases for the phenomenon called global warming. Create three small classes unrelated by inheritance—classes Building, Car and Bicycle. Give each class some unique appropriate attributes and behaviors that it does not have in common with other classes. Write an abstract class CarbonFootprint with only a pure virtual getCarbonFootprint member function. Have each of your classes inherit from that abstract class and implement the getCarbonFootprint member function to calculate an appropriate carbon footprint for that class (check out a few websites that explain how to calculate carbon footprints). Write an application that creates objects of each of the three classes, places pointers to those objects in a vector of CarbonFootprint pointers, then iterates through the vector, polymorphically invoking each object's getCarbonFootprint member function. For each object, print some identifying information and the object's carbon footprint.

Stream Input/Output: A Deeper Look

Objectives

In this chapter you'll:

- Use C++ object-oriented stream input/output.

- Perform input and output of individual characters.

- Use unformatted I/O for high performance.

- Use stream manipulators to display integers in octal and hexadecimal formats.

- Specify precision for both input and output.

- Display floating-point values in both scientific and fixed-point notation.

- Set and restore the format state.

- Control justification and padding.

- Determine the success or failure of input/output operations.

- Tie output streams to input streams.

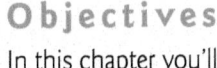

13.1 Introduction

This chapter discusses a range of capabilities sufficient for performing most common input/output operations and overviews the remaining capabilities. We've already demonstrated I/O with string objects in earlier chapters and discuss it in more detail in Chapter 21. The string processing demonstrated in this chapter focuses on char* strings. In earlier chapters, we introduced various I/O features—here we provide a more complete treatment.

C++ uses *type-safe I/O.* Each I/O operation is executed in a manner sensitive to the data type. If an I/O function has been defined to handle a particular data type, then that function is called to handle that data type. If there is no match between the type of the actual data and a function for handling that data type, the compiler generates an error. Thus, improper data cannot "sneak" through the system (as can occur in C, allowing for some subtle and bizarre errors).

As you saw in Chapter 10, you can specify how to perform I/O for objects of user-defined types by overloading the stream insertion operator (<<) and the stream extraction operator (>>).

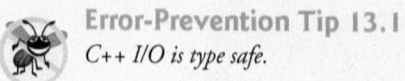

Error-Prevention Tip 13.1
C++ I/O is type safe.

Software Engineering Observation 13.1

C++ enables a common treatment of I/O for predefined types and user-defined types. This commonality facilitates software development and reuse.

Software Engineering Observation 13.2

In C++ programs, prefer C++-style I/O to C-style I/O.

13.2 Streams

C++ I/O occurs in streams, which are sequences of bytes. In input operations, the bytes flow from a device (e.g., a keyboard, a disk drive, a network connection) to main memory. In output operations, bytes flow from main memory to a device (e.g., a display screen, a printer, a disk drive, a network connection).

An application associates meaning with bytes. The bytes could represent characters, raw data, graphics images, digital speech, digital music, digital video or any other information an application may require. The system I/O mechanisms should transfer bytes from devices to memory (and vice versa) reliably. The time these transfers take typically is far greater than the time the processor requires to manipulate data internally. I/O operations require careful planning and tuning to ensure optimal performance.

C++ provides both "low-level" and "high-level" I/O capabilities. Low-level I/O capabilities (i.e., unformatted I/O) specify that some number of bytes should be transferred device-to-memory or memory-to-device. In such transfers, the individual byte is the item of interest. Such low-level capabilities provide high-speed, high-volume transfers but are not particularly convenient.

Programmers generally prefer a higher-level view of I/O (i.e., formatted I/O), in which bytes are grouped into meaningful units, such as integers, floating-point numbers, characters, strings and user-defined types. These type-oriented capabilities are satisfactory for most I/O other than high-volume file processing.

13.2.1 Classic Streams vs. Standard Streams

In the past, the C++ classic stream libraries supported only char-based I/O. Because a char normally occupies *one* byte, it can represent only a limited set of characters (such as those in the ASCII character set used by most readers of this book, or other popular character sets). Many languages use alphabets that contain more characters than a single-byte char can represent. The ASCII character set does not provide these characters, but the Unicode® character set does. Unicode is an extensive international character set that represents the majority of the world's languages, mathematical symbols and much more. C++ provides Unicode support via the types wchar_t (the original C++ type for processing Unicode) and C++11 types char16_t and char32_t. In addition, the standard stream libraries are implemented as class templates—like classes array and vector that you saw in Chapter 7. These class templates can be specialized for the various character types—we use the predefined stream-library specializations for type char in this book. For more information on Unicode, visit http://www.unicode.org.

11

13.2.2 iostream Library Headers

The C++ stream libraries provide hundreds of I/O capabilities. Most of our C++ programs include the <iostream> header, which declares basic services required for all stream-I/O operations. The <iostream> header defines the cin, cout, cerr and clog objects, which correspond to the standard input stream, the standard output stream, the unbuffered standard error stream and the buffered standard error stream, respectively—cerr, clog and buffering are discussed in the next section. Both unformatted- and formatted-I/O services are provided. As you know, the <iomanip> header declares the parameterized stream manipulators—such as setprecision (Section 4.10.5) and setw (Section 5.6)—for formatted I/O.

13.2.3 Stream Input/Output Classes and Objects

The iostream library provides many class templates for performing common I/O operations. This chapter focuses on the following class templates:

- basic_istream for stream input operations
- basic_ostream for stream output operations

Though we do not use it in this chapter, class basic_iostream provides *both* stream input and stream output operations.

In Chapter 7, you *specialized* the class templates array and vector for use with specific types—for example, you used array<int> to create an array class-template specialization for an array that stores int values. For each of the class templates basic_istream, basic_ostream and basic_iostream, the iostream library defines a specialization that performs char-based I/O.[1] The library also defines convenient short names (i.e., aliases) for these specializations:

- istream is a basic_istream<char> that enables char input—this is cin's type.
- ostream is a basic_ostream<char> that enables char output—this is the type of cout, cerr and clog.
- iostream is a basic_iostream<char> that enables both char input and output.

We used the aliases istream and ostream in Chapter 10 when we overloaded the stream extraction and stream insertion operators.

iostream Library Aliases Are Defined with **typedef**
The iostream library defines each alias with the typedef specifier, which you'll sometimes use to create more readable type names. For example, the following statement defines the alias CardPtr as a *synonym* for type Card*:

```
typedef Card* CardPtr;
```

Section 22.3 discusses typedef in detail.

Standard Stream Objects **cin**, **cout**, **cerr** *and* **clog**
Predefined object cin is an istream object and is said to be "connected to" (or attached to) the *standard input device*, which usually is the keyboard. The stream extraction operator (>>) as used in

---

1. This chapter discusses only the iostream library template specializations for char I/O.

```
int grade;
cin >> grade; // data "flows" in the direction of the arrows
```

causes a value for int variable grade to be input from cin to memory. The compiler selects the appropriate overloaded stream extraction operator, based on the type of the variable grade. The >> operator is overloaded to input data items of fundamental types, strings and pointer values.

The predefined object cout is an ostream object and is said to be "connected to" the *standard output device*, which usually is the display screen. The stream insertion operator (<<), as used in the following statement, causes the value of variable grade to be output from memory to the standard output device:

```
cout << grade; // data "flows" in the direction of the arrows
```

The compiler determines the data type of grade (assuming grade has been declared properly) and selects the appropriate stream insertion operator. The << operator is overloaded to output data items of fundamental types, strings and pointer values.

The predefined object cerr is an ostream object and is said to be "connected to" the *standard error device*, normally the screen. Outputs to object cerr are unbuffered, meaning that each stream insertion to cerr causes its output to appear *immediately*—this is appropriate for notifying a user promptly about errors.

The predefined object clog is an object of the ostream class and is said to be "connected to" the *standard error device*. Outputs to clog are buffered. This means that each insertion to clog could cause its output to be held in a buffer (that is, an area in memory) until the buffer is filled or until the buffer is flushed. Buffering is an I/O performance-enhancement technique discussed in operating-systems courses.

13.3 Stream Output

Formatted and unformatted output capabilities are provided by ostream. Capabilities include output of standard data types with the stream insertion operator (<<); output of characters via the put member function; unformatted output via the write member function; output of integers in decimal, octal and hexadecimal formats; output of floating-point values with various precision, with forced decimal points, in scientific notation (e.g., 1.234567e-03) and in fixed notation (e.g., 0.00123457); output of data justified in fields of designated widths; output of data in fields padded with specified characters; and output of uppercase letters in scientific notation and hexadecimal notation. We'll demonstrate all of these capabilities in this chapter.

13.3.1 Output of char* Variables

C++ determines data types automatically—an improvement over C, but this feature sometimes "gets in the way." For example, suppose we want to print the address stored in a char* pointer. The << operator has been overloaded to output a char* as a *null-terminated C-style string*. To output the *address*, you can cast the char* to a void* (this can be done to any pointer variable). Figure 13.1 demonstrates printing a char* variable in both string and address formats. The address prints here as a hexadecimal (base-16) number—in general, the way addresses print is *implementation dependent*. To learn more about hexadecimal numbers, see Appendix D, Number Systems. We say more about controlling the bases of numbers in Section 13.6.1 and Section 13.7.4.

```cpp
1   // Fig. 13.1: Fig13_01.cpp
2   // Printing the address stored in a char* variable.
3   #include <iostream>
4   using namespace std;
5
6   int main() {
7       const char* const word{"again"};
8
9       // display the value of char* variable word, then display
10      // the value of word after a static_cast to void*
11      cout << "Value of word is: " << word
12          << "\nValue of static_cast<const void*>(word) is: "
13          << static_cast<const void*>(word) << endl;
14  }
```

```
Value of word is: again
Value of static_cast<const void*>(word) is: 00DE8B30
```

Fig. 13.1 | Printing the address stored in a char* variable.

13.3.2 Character Output Using Member Function put

The basic_ostream member function put outputs one character at a time. For example, the statement

```cpp
cout.put('A');
```

displays a single character A. Calls to put may be *cascaded*, as in the statement

```cpp
cout.put('A').put('\n');
```

which outputs the letter A followed by a newline character. As with <<, the preceding statement executes in this manner, because the dot operator (.) associates from left to right, and the put member function returns a reference to the ostream object (cout) that received the put call. The put function also may be called with a numeric expression that represents an ASCII value, as in the following statement, which also outputs A:

```cpp
cout.put(65);
```

13.4 Stream Input

Formatted and unformatted input capabilities are provided by istream. The stream extraction operator (>>) normally skips white-space characters (such as blanks, tabs and newlines) in the input stream; later we'll see how to change this behavior.

Using the Result of a Stream Extraction as a Condition

After each input, the stream extraction operator returns a *reference* to the stream object that received the extraction message (e.g., cin in the expression cin >> grade). If that reference is used as a condition (e.g., in a while statement's loop-continuation condition), the stream's overloaded bool cast operator function (added in C++11) is implicitly invoked to convert the reference into true or false value, based on the success or failure, respectively, of the last input operation. When an attempt is made to read past the end of a stream, the stream's overloaded bool cast operator returns false to indicate *end-of-file*. We used this capability in line 24 of Fig. 5.11.

11

13.4.1 get and getline Member Functions

The get member function with *no arguments* inputs *one* character from the designated stream (including white-space characters and other nongraphic characters, such as the key sequence that represents end-of-file) and returns it as the value of the function call. This version of get returns EOF when *end-of-file* is encountered on the stream. EOF normally has the value –1 and is defined in a header that's indirectly included in your code via stream library headers like <iostream>.

Using Member Functions eof, get *and* put
Figure 13.2 demonstrates member functions eof and get on input stream cin and member function put on output stream cout. This program uses get to read characters into the int variable character, so that we can test each character entered to see if it's EOF We use int because on many platforms char can represent only nonnegative values and EOF is typically –1. The program first prints the value of cin.eof()—i.e., false (0 on the output)—to show that *end-of-file* has *not* occurred on cin. The user enters a line of text and presses *Enter* followed by end-of-file (*<Ctrl> z* on Microsoft Windows systems, *<Ctrl> d* on Linux and Mac systems). Line 14 reads each character, which line 15 outputs to cout using member function put. When end-of-file is encountered, the while statement ends, and line 20 displays the value of cin.eof(), which is now true (1 on the output), to show that end-of-file has been set on cin. This program uses the version of istream member function get that takes no arguments and returns the character being input (line 14). Function eof returns true only after the program attempts to read past the last character in the stream.

```
1   // Fig. 13.2: Fig13_02.cpp
2   // get, put and eof member functions.
3   #include <iostream>
4   using namespace std;
5
6   int main() {
7      int character; // use int, because char cannot represent EOF
8
9      // prompt user to enter line of text
10     cout << "Before input, cin.eof() is " << cin.eof()
11        << "\nEnter a sentence followed by Enter and end-of-file:\n";
12
13     // use get to read each character; use put to display it
14     while ((character = cin.get()) != EOF) {
15        cout.put(character);
16     }
```

Fig. 13.2 | get, put and eof member functions. (Part 1 of 2.)

```
17
18     // display end-of-file character
19     cout << "\nEOF in this system is: " << character
20        << "\nAfter input of EOF, cin.eof() is " << cin.eof() << endl;
21  }
```

```
Before input, cin.eof() is 0
Enter a sentence followed by end-of-file:
Testing the get and put member functions
Testing the get and put member functions
^Z

EOF in this system is: -1
After input of EOF, cin.eof() is 1
```

Fig. 13.2 | get, put and eof member functions. (Part 2 of 2.)

The get member function with a character-reference argument inputs the next character from the input stream (even if this is a *white-space character*) and stores it in the character argument. This version of get returns a reference to the istream object for which the get member function is being invoked.

A third version of get takes three arguments—a built-in array of chars, a size limit and a delimiter (with default value '\n'). This version reads characters from the input stream. It either reads *one fewer* than the specified maximum number of characters and terminates or terminates as soon as the *delimiter* is read. A null character is inserted to terminate the input string in the character array used as a buffer by the program. The delimiter is not placed in the character array but *does remain in the input stream* (the delimiter will be the next character read). Thus, the result of a second consecutive get is an empty line, unless the delimiter character is removed from the input stream (possibly with cin.ignore()).

Comparing cin and cin.get
Figure 13.3 compares input using the stream extraction operator with cin (which reads characters until a white-space character is encountered) and input using cin.get. The call to cin.get (line 20) does *not* specify a delimiter, so the *default* '\n' character is used.

```
1   // Fig. 13.3: Fig13_03.cpp
2   // Contrasting input of a string via cin and cin.get.
3   #include <iostream>
4   using namespace std;
5
6   int main() {
7      // create two char arrays, each with 80 elements
8      const int SIZE{80};
9      char buffer1[SIZE];
10     char buffer2[SIZE];
11
```

Fig. 13.3 | Contrasting input of a string via cin and cin.get. (Part 1 of 2.)

```
12        // use cin to input characters into buffer1
13        cout << "Enter a sentence:\n";
14        cin >> buffer1;
15
16        // display buffer1 contents
17        cout << "\nThe string read with cin was:\n" << buffer1 << "\n\n";
18
19        // use cin.get to input characters into buffer2
20        cin.get(buffer2, SIZE);
21
22        // display buffer2 contents
23        cout << "The string read with cin.get was:\n" << buffer2 << endl;
24    }
```

```
Enter a sentence:
Contrasting string input with cin and cin.get

The string read with cin was:
Contrasting

The string read with cin.get was:
 string input with cin and cin.get
```

Fig. 13.3 | Contrasting input of a string via cin and cin.get. (Part 2 of 2.)

Using Member Function getline

Member function getline operates similarly to the third version of the get member function and *inserts a null character* after the line in the built-in array of chars. The getline function removes the delimiter from the stream (i.e., reads the character and discards it), but does *not* store it in the character array. The program of Fig. 13.4 demonstrates the use of the getline member function to input a line of text (line 12).

```
1    // Fig. 13.4: Fig13_04.cpp
2    // Inputting characters using cin member function getline.
3    #include <iostream>
4    using namespace std;
5
6    int main() {
7       const int SIZE{80};
8       char buffer[SIZE]; // create array of 80 characters
9
10       // input characters in buffer via cin function getline
11       cout << "Enter a sentence:\n";
12       cin.getline(buffer, SIZE);
13
14       // display buffer contents
15       cout << "\nThe sentence entered is:\n" << buffer << endl;
16    }
```

Fig. 13.4 | Inputting characters using cin member function getline. (Part 1 of 2.)

```
Enter a sentence:
Using the getline member function

The sentence entered is:
Using the getline member function
```

Fig. 13.4 | Inputting characters using `cin` member function `getline`. (Part 2 of 2.)

13.4.2 `istream` Member Functions peek, putback and ignore

The `istream` member function `ignore` (which you first used in Section 10.5) reads and *discards* characters. It receives two arguments:

- a designated number of characters—the default argument value is 1—and
- a delimiter at which to stop ignoring characters—the default delimiter is `EOF`.

The function discards the specified number of characters, or fewer characters if the delimiter is encountered in the input stream.

The `putback` member function places the previous character obtained by a `get` from an input stream back into that stream. This function is useful for applications that scan an input stream looking for a field beginning with a specific character. When that character is input, the application returns the character to the stream, so the character can be included in the input data.

The `peek` member function returns the next character from an input stream but does not remove the character from the stream.

13.4.3 Type-Safe I/O

C++ offers type-safe I/O. The `<<` and `>>` operators are overloaded to accept data items of specific types. If unexpected data is processed, various error bits are set, which the user may query to determine whether an I/O operation succeeded or failed. If operators `<<` and `>>` have not been overloaded for a user-defined type and you attempt to use those operators to input into or output the contents of an object of that user-defined type, the compiler reports an error. This enables the program to "stay in control." We discuss this more in Section 13.8.

13.5 Unformatted I/O Using read, write and gcount

Unformatted input/output is performed using `istream`'s `read` and `ostream`'s `write` member functions, respectively—`read` inputs *bytes* to a built-in array of `char`s in memory; `write` outputs bytes from a built-in array of `char`s. These bytes are *not formatted* in any way. They're input or output simply as raw bytes. For example, the call

```
char buffer[]{"HAPPY BIRTHDAY"};
cout.write(buffer, 10);
```

outputs the first 10 bytes of `buffer` (including null characters, if any, that would cause output with `cout` and `<<` to terminate). The call

```
cout.write("ABCDEFGHIJKLMNOPQRSTUVWXYZ", 10);
```

displays the first 10 characters of the alphabet.

The read member function inputs a designated number of characters into a built-in array of `char`s. If *fewer* than the designated number of characters are read, `failbit` is set.

Section 13.8 shows how to determine whether `failbit` has been set. Member function `gcount` reports the number of characters read by the last input operation.

Figure 13.5 demonstrates `istream` member functions `read` and `gcount`, and `ostream` member function `write`. The program inputs 20 characters (from a longer input sequence) into the array `buffer` with `read` (line 12), determines the number of characters input with `gcount` (line 16) and outputs the characters in `buffer` with `write` (line 16).

```
1   // Fig. 13.5: Fig13_05.cpp
2   // Unformatted I/O using read, gcount and write.
3   #include <iostream>
4   using namespace std;
5
6   int main() {
7      const int SIZE{80};
8      char buffer[SIZE]; // create array of 80 characters
9
10     // use function read to input characters into buffer
11     cout << "Enter a sentence:\n";
12     cin.read(buffer, 20);
13
14     // use functions write and gcount to display buffer characters
15     cout << "\nThe sentence entered was:\n";
16     cout.write(buffer, cin.gcount());
17     cout << endl;
18  }
```

```
Enter a sentence:
Using the read, write, and gcount member functions
The sentence entered was:
Using the read, writ
```

Fig. 13.5 | Unformatted I/O using `read`, `gcount` and `write`.

13.6 Stream Manipulators: A Deeper Look

As you've seen, C++ provides various stream manipulators that perform formatting tasks. The stream manipulators provide capabilities such as

- setting field widths
- setting precision
- setting and unsetting format state
- setting the fill character in fields
- flushing streams
- inserting a newline into the output stream (and flushing the stream)
- inserting a null character into the output stream
- skipping white space in the input stream

These features are described in the sections that follow.

13.6.1 Integral Stream Base: dec, oct, hex and setbase

Integers are interpreted normally as decimal (base 10) values. To change the base in which integers are interpreted on a stream, insert the hex manipulator to set the base to hexadecimal (base 16) or insert the oct manipulator to set the base to octal (base 8). Insert the dec manipulator to reset the stream base to decimal. These are all *sticky* manipulators.

A stream's base also may be changed by the setbase parameterized stream manipulator (header <iomanip>), which takes an int argument of 10, 8, or 16 to set the base to decimal, octal or hexadecimal, respectively. The stream base value remains the same until changed explicitly; setbase settings are sticky. Figure 13.6 demonstrates stream manipulators hex, oct, dec and setbase. For more information on decimal, octal and hexadecimal numbers, see Appendix D, Number Systems.

```cpp
1   // Fig. 13.6: Fig13_06.cpp
2   // Using stream manipulators hex, oct, dec and setbase.
3   #include <iostream>
4   #include <iomanip>
5   using namespace std;
6
7   int main() {
8      int number;
9
10     cout << "Enter a decimal number: ";
11     cin >> number; // input number
12
13     // use hex stream manipulator to show hexadecimal number
14     cout << number << " in hexadecimal is: " << hex << number << "\n";
15
16     // use oct stream manipulator to show octal number
17     cout << dec << number << " in octal is: " << oct << number << "\n";
18
19     // use setbase stream manipulator to show decimal number
20     cout << setbase(10) << number << " in decimal is: " << number << endl;
21  }
```

```
Enter a decimal number: 20
20 in hexadecimal is: 14
20 in octal is: 24
20 in decimal is: 20
```

Fig. 13.6 | Using stream manipulators hex, oct, dec and setbase.

13.6.2 Floating-Point Precision (precision, setprecision)

We can control the precision of floating-point numbers (i.e., the number of digits to the right of the decimal point) with the setprecision stream manipulator or the precision member function of ostream. A call to either sets the precision for all subsequent output operations until the next precision-setting call. A call to member function precision with no argument returns the current precision setting—you can use this value to *restore the original precision* eventually after a sticky setting is no longer needed. Figure 13.7 uses both member function precision (line 17) and the setprecision manipulator (line 25) to print a table that shows the square root of 2, with precision varying from 0 to 9.

```cpp
 1   // Fig. 13.7: Fig13_07.cpp
 2   // Controlling precision of floating-point values.
 3   #include <iostream>
 4   #include <iomanip>
 5   #include <cmath>
 6   using namespace std;
 7
 8   int main() {
 9      double root2{sqrt(2.0)}; // calculate square root of 2
10
11      cout << "Square root of 2 with precisions 0-9.\n"
12         << "Precision set by ostream member function precision:\n";
13      cout << fixed; // use fixed-point notation
14
15      // display square root using ostream function precision
16      for (int places{0}; places <= 9; ++places) {
17         cout.precision(places);
18         cout << root2 << "\n";
19      }
20
21      cout << "\nPrecision set by stream manipulator setprecision:\n";
22
23      // set precision for each digit, then display square root
24      for (int places{0}; places <= 9; ++places) {
25         cout << setprecision(places) << root2 << "\n";
26      }
27   }
```

```
Square root of 2 with precisions 0-9.
Precision set by ostream member function precision:
1
1.4
1.41
1.414
1.4142
1.41421
1.414214
1.4142136
1.41421356
1.414213562

Precision set by stream manipulator setprecision:
1
1.4
1.41
1.414
1.4142
1.41421
1.414214
1.4142136
1.41421356
1.414213562
```

Fig. 13.7 | Controlling precision of floating-point values.

13.6.3 Field Width (width, setw)

The width member function (of classes istream and ostream) sets the *field width* (i.e., the number of character positions in which a value should be output or the maximum number of characters that should be input) and *returns the previous field width*. If values output are narrower than the field width, fill characters are inserted as padding. A value wider than the designated width will *not* be truncated—the *full number* will be printed. The width function with no argument returns the current setting.

Common Programming Error 13.1

The width setting applies only for the next insertion or extraction (i.e., the width setting is not sticky); afterward, the width is set implicitly to 0 (that is, input and output will be performed with default settings). Assuming that the width setting applies to all subsequent outputs is a logic error.

Common Programming Error 13.2

When a field is not sufficiently wide to handle outputs, the outputs print as wide as necessary, which can yield confusing outputs.

Figure 13.8 demonstrates the width member function for both input and output. On input into a char array, *a maximum of one fewer characters than the width will be read*, because provision is made for the null character to be placed in the input string. Remember that stream extraction *terminates* when *nonleading white space* is encountered. The setw stream manipulator also may be used to set the field width. [*Note:* When prompted for input in Fig. 13.8, enter a line of text and press *Enter* followed by end-of-file (*<Ctrl> z* on Microsoft Windows systems and *<Ctrl> d* on Linux and OS X systems).]

```
1   // Fig. 13.8: Fig13_08.cpp
2   // width member function of classes istream and ostream.
3   #include <iostream>
4   using namespace std;
5
6   int main() {
7      int widthValue{4};
8      char sentence[10];
9
10     cout << "Enter a sentence:\n";
11     cin.width(5); // input only 5 characters from sentence
12
13     // set field width, then display characters based on that width
14     while (cin >> sentence) {
15        cout.width(widthValue++);
16        cout << sentence << "\n";
17        cin.width(5); // input 5 more characters from sentence
18     }
19  }
```

Fig. 13.8 | width member function of class classes istream and ostream. (Part 1 of 2.)

```
Enter a sentence:
This is a test of the width member function
This
   is
      a
   test
      of
      the
      widt
          h
        memb
           er
         func
         tion
```

Fig. 13.8 | width member function of class classes istream and ostream. (Part 2 of 2.)

13.6.4 User-Defined Output Stream Manipulators

You can create your own stream manipulators. Figure 13.9 shows how to create and use *new* nonparameterized stream manipulators bell (lines 8–10), carriageReturn (lines 13–15), tab (lines 18–20) and endLine (lines 24–26). For output stream manipulators, the return type and parameter must be of type ostream&. When line 30 inserts the endLine manipulator in the output stream, function endLine is called and line 25 outputs the escape sequence \n and the flush manipulator (which flushes the output buffer) to the standard output stream cout. Similarly, when lines 31–39 insert the manipulators tab, bell and carriageReturn in the output stream, their corresponding functions—tab, bell and carriageReturn—are called, which in turn output various escape sequences.

```cpp
1   // Fig. 13.9: Fig13_09.cpp
2   // Creating and testing user-defined, nonparameterized
3   // stream manipulators.
4   #include <iostream>
5   using namespace std;
6
7   // bell manipulator (using escape sequence \a)
8   ostream& bell(ostream& output) {
9      return output << '\a'; // issue system beep
10  }
11
12  // carriageReturn manipulator (using escape sequence \r)
13  ostream& carriageReturn(ostream& output) {
14     return output << '\r'; // issue carriage return
15  }
16
17  // tab manipulator (using escape sequence \t)
18  ostream& tab(ostream& output) {
19     return output << '\t'; // issue tab
20  }
21
```

Fig. 13.9 | Creating and testing user-defined, nonparameterized stream manipulators. (Part 1 of 2.)

```
22    // endLine manipulator (using escape sequence \n and flush stream
23    // manipulator to simulate endl)
24    ostream& endLine(ostream& output) {
25       return output << '\n' << flush; // issue endl-like end of line
26    }
27
28    int main() {
29       // use tab and endLine manipulators
30       cout << "Testing the tab manipulator:" << endLine
31          << 'a' << tab << 'b' << tab << 'c' << endLine;
32
33       cout << "Testing the carriageReturn and bell manipulators:"
34          << endLine << "..........";
35
36       cout << bell; // use bell manipulator
37
38       // use carriageReturn and endLine manipulators
39       cout << carriageReturn << "-----" << endLine;
40    }
```

```
Testing the tab manipulator:
a       b       c
Testing the carriageReturn and bell manipulators:
-----.....
```

Fig. 13.9 | Creating and testing user-defined, nonparameterized stream manipulators. (Part 2 of 2.)

13.7 Stream Format States and Stream Manipulators

Various stream manipulators can be used to specify the kinds of formatting to be performed during stream-I/O operations. Stream manipulators control the output's format settings. Figure 13.10 lists each stream manipulator that controls a given stream's format state. We show examples of many of these stream manipulators in the next several sections, and you've already seen examples of several of these manipulators.

Manipulator	Description
skipws	*Skip white-space characters* on an input stream. This setting is reset with stream manipulator noskipws.
left	*Left justify* output in a field. *Padding* characters appear to the *right* if necessary.
right	*Right justify* output in a field. *Padding* characters appear to the *left* if necessary.
internal	Indicate that a number's *sign* should be *left justified* in a field and a number's *magnitude* should be *right justified* in that same field (i.e., *padding* characters appear *between* the sign and the number).
boolalpha	Specify that *bool values* should be displayed as the word true or false. The manipulator noboolalpha sets the stream back to displaying bool values as 1 (true) and 0 (false).

Fig. 13.10 | Format state stream manipulators from `<iostream>`. (Part 1 of 2.)

Manipulator	Description
dec	Specify that integers should be treated as *decimal* (base 10) values.
oct	Specify that integers should be treated as *octal* (base 8) values.
hex	Specify that integers should be treated as *hexadecimal* (base 16) values.
showbase	Specify that the *base* of a number is to be output *ahead* of the number (a leading 0 for octals; a leading 0x or 0X for hexadecimals). This setting is reset with stream manipulator noshowbase.
showpoint	Specify that floating-point numbers should be output with a *decimal point*. This is used normally with fixed to *guarantee* a certain number of digits to the *right* of the decimal point, even if they're zeros. This setting is reset with stream manipulator noshowpoint.
uppercase	Specify that *uppercase letters* (i.e., X and A through F) should be used in a *hexadecimal* integer and that *uppercase* E should be used when representing a floating-point value in *scientific notation*. This setting is reset with stream manipulator nouppercase.
showpos	Specify that *positive* numbers should be preceded by a plus sign (**+**). This setting is reset with stream manipulator noshowpos.
scientific	Specify output of a floating-point value in *scientific notation*.
fixed	Specify output of a floating-point value in *fixed-point notation* with a specific number of digits to the *right* of the decimal point.

Fig. 13.10 | Format state stream manipulators from `<iostream>`. (Part 2 of 2.)

13.7.1 Trailing Zeros and Decimal Points (showpoint)

Stream manipulator showpoint is a sticky setting that forces a floating-point number to be output with its *decimal point* and *trailing zeros*. For example, the floating-point value 79.0 prints as 79 without using showpoint and prints as 79.00000 (or as many trailing zeros as are specified by the current *precision*) using showpoint. To reset the showpoint setting, output the stream manipulator noshowpoint. The program in Fig. 13.11 shows how to use stream manipulator showpoint to control the printing of *trailing zeros* and *decimal points* for floating-point values. Recall that the *default precision* of a floating-point number is 6. When neither the fixed nor the scientific stream manipulator is used, the precision represents the number of significant digits to display (i.e., the total number of digits to display), *not* the number of digits to display after decimal point.

```
1  // Fig. 13.11: Fig13_11.cpp
2  // Controlling the printing of trailing zeros and
3  // decimal points in floating-point values.
4  #include <iostream>
5  using namespace std;
6
7  int main() {
```

Fig. 13.11 | Controlling the printing of trailing zeros and decimal points in floating-point values. (Part 1 of 2.)

```
 8      // display double values with default stream format
 9      cout << "Before using showpoint"
10         << "\n9.9900 prints as: " << 9.9900
11         << "\n9.9000 prints as: " << 9.9000
12         << "\n9.0000 prints as: " << 9.0000;
13
14      // display double value after showpoint
15      cout << showpoint
16         << "\n\nAfter using showpoint"
17         << "\n9.9900 prints as: " << 9.9900
18         << "\n9.9000 prints as: " << 9.9000
19         << "\n9.0000 prints as: " << 9.0000 << endl;
20   }
```

```
Before using showpoint
9.9900 prints as: 9.99
9.9000 prints as: 9.9
9.0000 prints as: 9

After using showpoint
9.9900 prints as: 9.99000
9.9000 prints as: 9.90000
9.0000 prints as: 9.00000
```

Fig. 13.11 | Controlling the printing of trailing zeros and decimal points in floating-point values. (Part 2 of 2.)

13.7.2 Justification (`left`, `right` and `internal`)

Stream manipulators `left` and `right` enable fields to be *left justified* with *padding* characters to the *right* or *right justified* with *padding* characters to the *left*, respectively. The padding character is specified by the `fill` member function or the `setfill` parameterized stream manipulator (which we discuss in Section 13.7.3). Figure 13.12 uses the `setw`, `left` and `right` manipulators to left justify and right justify integer data in a field—we wrap each field in quotes to you can see the leading and trailing space in the field.

```
 1   // Fig. 13.12: Fig13_12.cpp
 2   // Left and right justification with stream manipulators left and right.
 3   #include <iostream>
 4   #include <iomanip>
 5   using namespace std;
 6
 7   int main() {
 8      int x{12345};
 9
10      // display x right justified (default)
11      cout << "Default is right justified:\n\"" << setw(10) << x << "\"";
12
```

Fig. 13.12 | Left and right justification with stream manipulators `left` and `right`. (Part 1 of 2.)

```
13      // use left manipulator to display x left justified
14      cout << "\n\nUse left to left justify x:\n\""
15         << left << setw(10) << x << "\"";
16
17      // use right manipulator to display x right justified
18      cout << "\n\nUse right to right justify x:\n\""
19         << right << setw(10) << x << "\"" << endl;
20   }
```

```
Default is right justified:
"     12345"

Use left to left justify x:
"12345     "

Use right to right justify x:
"     12345"
```

Fig. 13.12 | Left and right justification with stream manipulators left and right. (Part 2 of 2.)

Stream manipulator internal indicates that a number's *sign* (or *base* when using stream manipulator showbase) should be *left justified* within a field, that the number's *magnitude* should be *right justified* and that *intervening spaces* should be *padded* with the *fill character*. Figure 13.13 shows the internal stream manipulator specifying internal spacing (line 9). Note that showpos forces the plus sign to print (line 9). To reset the showpos setting, output the stream manipulator noshowpos.

```
 1   // Fig. 13.13: Fig13_13.cpp
 2   // Printing an integer with internal spacing and plus sign.
 3   #include <iostream>
 4   #include <iomanip>
 5   using namespace std;
 6
 7   int main() {
 8      // display value with internal spacing and plus sign
 9      cout << internal << showpos << setw(10) << 123 << endl;
10   }
```

```
+       123
```

Fig. 13.13 | Printing an integer with internal spacing and plus sign.

13.7.3 Padding (fill, setfill)

The fill member function specifies the *fill character* to be used with justified fields; *spaces* are used for padding by default. The function returns the prior padding character. The setfill manipulator also sets the *padding character*. Figure 13.14 demonstrates function fill (line 29) and stream manipulator setfill (lines 33 and 36) to set the fill character.

```cpp
 1   // Fig. 13.14: Fig13_14.cpp
 2   // Using member function fill and stream manipulator setfill to change
 3   // the padding character for fields larger than the printed value.
 4   #include <iostream>
 5   #include <iomanip>
 6   using namespace std;
 7
 8   int main() {
 9      int x{10000};
10
11      // display x
12      cout << x << " printed as int right and left justified\n"
13         << "and as hex with internal justification.\n"
14         << "Using the default pad character (space):\n";
15
16      // display x
17      cout << setw(10) << x << "\n";
18
19      // display x with left justification
20      cout << left << setw(10) << x << "\n";
21
22      // display x with base as hex with internal justification
23      cout << showbase << internal << setw(10) << hex << x << "\n\n";
24
25      cout << "Using various padding characters:" << endl;
26
27      // display x using padded characters (right justification)
28      cout << right;
29      cout.fill('*');
30      cout << setw(10) << dec << x << "\n";
31
32      // display x using padded characters (left justification)
33      cout << left << setw(10) << setfill('%') << x << "\n";
34
35      // display x using padded characters (internal justification)
36      cout << internal << setw(10) << setfill('^') << hex << x << endl;
37   }
```

```
10000 printed as int right and left justified
and as hex with internal justification.
Using the default pad character (space):
     10000
10000
0x    2710

Using various padding characters:
*****10000
10000%%%%%
0x^^^^2710
```

Fig. 13.14 | Using member function fill and stream manipulator setfill to change the padding character for fields larger than the printed values.

13.7.4 Integral Stream Base (dec, oct, hex, showbase)

C++ provides stream manipulators dec, hex and oct to specify that integers are to be displayed as decimal, hexadecimal and octal values, respectively. Stream insertions *default* to *decimal* if none of these manipulators is used. With stream extraction, integers prefixed with 0 (zero) are treated as *octal* values, integers prefixed with 0x or 0X are treated as *hexadecimal* values, and all other integers are treated as *decimal* values. Once a particular base is specified for a stream, all integers on that stream are processed using that base until a different base is specified or until the program terminates.

Stream manipulator showbase forces the *base* of an integral value to be output. Decimal numbers are output by default, octal numbers are output with a leading 0, and hexadecimal numbers are output with either a leading 0x or a leading 0X (as we discuss in Section 13.7.6, stream manipulator uppercase determines which option is chosen). Figure 13.15 demonstrates the use of stream manipulator showbase to force an integer to print in decimal, octal and hexadecimal formats. To reset the showbase setting, output the stream manipulator noshowbase.

```
1   // Fig. 13.15: Fig13_15.cpp
2   // Stream manipulator showbase.
3   #include <iostream>
4   using namespace std;
5
6   int main() {
7      int x{100};
8
9      // use showbase to show number base
10     cout << "Printing octal and hexadecimal values with showbase:\n"
11        << showbase;
12
13     cout << x << endl; // print decimal value
14     cout << oct << x << endl; // print octal value
15     cout << hex << x << endl; // print hexadecimal value
16  }
```

```
Printing octal and hexadecimal values with showbase:
100
0144
0x64
```

Fig. 13.15 | Stream manipulator showbase.

13.7.5 Floating-Point Numbers; Scientific and Fixed Notation (scientific, fixed)

When a floating-point number is displayed without specifying its format, the value determines the output format—some numbers are displayed in scientific notation and others in fixed-point notation. The sticky stream manipulators scientific and fixed control the output format of floating-point numbers. Stream manipulator scientific forces the output of a floating-point number to display in scientific format. Stream manipulator fixed forces a floating-point number to display in fixed-point notation with a specific number of digits to the right of the decimal point—as specified by member function precision or stream manipulator setprecision.

Figure 13.16 demonstrates displaying floating-point numbers in fixed and scientific formats using stream manipulators scientific (line 16) and fixed (line 20). The exponent format in scientific notation might vary among compilers.

```cpp
1    // Fig. 13.16: Fig13_16.cpp
2    // Floating-point values displayed in system default,
3    // scientific and fixed formats.
4    #include <iostream>
5    using namespace std;
6
7    int main() {
8       double x{0.001234567};
9       double y{1.946e9};
10
11      // display x and y in default format
12      cout << "Displayed in default format:\n" << x << '\t' << y;
13
14      // display x and y in scientific format
15      cout << "\n\nDisplayed in scientific format:\n"
16         << scientific << x << '\t' << y;
17
18      // display x and y in fixed format
19      cout << "\n\nDisplayed in fixed format:\n"
20         << fixed << x << '\t' << y << endl;
21   }
```

```
Displayed in default format:
0.00123457      1.946e+09

Displayed in scientific format:
1.234567e-03    1.946000e+09

Displayed in fixed format:
0.001235        1946000000.000000
```

Fig. 13.16 | Floating-point values displayed in system default, scientific and fixed formats.

13.7.6 Uppercase/Lowercase Control (uppercase)

Stream manipulator uppercase outputs an uppercase X or E with hexadecimal-integer values or with scientific notation floating-point values, respectively (Fig. 13.17). Using stream manipulator uppercase also causes all letters in a hexadecimal value to be uppercase. By default, the letters for hexadecimal values and the exponents in scientific notation floating-point values appear in *lowercase*. To reset the uppercase setting, output the stream manipulator nouppercase.

```
 1   // Fig. 13.17: Fig13_17.cpp
 2   // Stream manipulator uppercase.
 3   #include <iostream>
 4   using namespace std;
 5
 6   int main() {
 7      cout << "Printing uppercase letters in scientific\n"
 8         << "notation exponents and hexadecimal values:\n";
 9
10      // use std::uppercase to display uppercase letters; use std::hex and
11      // std::showbase to display hexadecimal value and its base
12      cout << uppercase << 4.345e10 << "\n"
13         << hex << showbase << 123456789 << endl;
14   }
```

```
Printing uppercase letters in scientific
notation exponents and hexadecimal values:
4.345E+10
0X75BCD15
```

Fig. 13.17 | Stream manipulator uppercase.

13.7.7 Specifying Boolean Format (boolalpha)

C++ provides data type bool, whose values may be false or true, as a preferred alternative to the old style of using 0 to indicate false and any nonzero value to indicate true. A bool variable outputs as 0 or 1 by default. However, we can use stream manipulator boolalpha to set the output stream to display bool values as the strings "true" and "false". Use stream manipulator noboolalpha to set the output stream to display bool values as integers (i.e., the default setting). The program of Fig. 13.18 demonstrates these stream manipulators. Line 10 displays the bool value, which line 7 set to true, as an integer. Line 14 uses manipulator boolalpha to display the bool value as a string. Lines 17–18 then change the bool's value and use manipulator noboolalpha, so line 21 can display the bool value as an integer. Line 25 uses manipulator boolalpha to display the bool value as a string. Both boolalpha and noboolalpha are sticky settings.

Good Programming Practice 13.1
Displaying bool values as true or false, rather than nonzero or 0, respectively, makes program outputs clearer.

```
 1   // Fig. 13.18: Fig13_18.cpp
 2   // Stream manipulators boolalpha and noboolalpha.
 3   #include <iostream>
 4   using namespace std;
 5
 6   int main() {
 7      bool booleanValue{true};
```

Fig. 13.18 | Stream manipulators boolalpha and noboolalpha. (Part I of 2.)

```
 8
 9      // display default true booleanValue
10      cout << "booleanValue is " << booleanValue;
11
12      // display booleanValue after using boolalpha
13      cout << "\nbooleanValue (after using boolalpha) is "
14         << boolalpha << booleanValue;
15
16      cout << "\n\nswitch booleanValue and use noboolalpha\n";
17      booleanValue = false; // change booleanValue
18      cout << noboolalpha; // use noboolalpha
19
20      // display default false booleanValue after using noboolalpha
21      cout << "\nbooleanValue is " << booleanValue;
22
23      // display booleanValue after using boolalpha again
24      cout << "\nbooleanValue (after using boolalpha) is "
25         << boolalpha << booleanValue << endl;
26   }
```

```
booleanValue is 1
booleanValue (after using boolalpha) is true

switch booleanValue and use noboolalpha

booleanValue is 0
booleanValue (after using boolalpha) is false
```

Fig. 13.18 | Stream manipulators boolalpha and noboolalpha. (Part 2 of 2.)

13.7.8 Setting and Resetting the Format State via Member Function flags

Throughout Section 13.7, we've been using stream manipulators to change output format characteristics. We now discuss how to return an output stream's format to its default state after having applied several manipulations. Member function flags without an argument returns the current format settings as an fmtflags data type, which represents the format state. Member function flags with an fmtflags argument sets the format state as specified by the argument and returns the prior state settings. The initial settings of the value that flags returns might vary among compilers. The program of Fig. 13.19 uses member function flags to save the stream's original format state (line 16), then restore the original format settings (line 24).

```
1   // Fig. 13.19: Fig13_19.cpp
2   // flags member function.
3   #include <iostream>
4   using namespace std;
5
6   int main() {
```

Fig. 13.19 | flags member function. (Part 1 of 2.)

```
7       int integerValue{1000};
8       double doubleValue{0.0947628};
9
10      // display flags value, int and double values (original format)
11      cout << "The value of the flags variable is: " << cout.flags()
12         << "\nPrint int and double in original format:\n"
13         << integerValue << '\t' << doubleValue;
14
15      // use cout flags function to save original format
16      ios_base::fmtflags originalFormat{cout.flags()};
17      cout << showbase << oct << scientific; // change format
18
19      // display flags value, int and double values (new format)
20      cout << "\n\nThe value of the flags variable is: " << cout.flags()
21         << "\nPrint int and double in a new format:\n"
22         << integerValue << '\t' << doubleValue;
23
24      cout.flags(originalFormat); // restore format
25
26      // display flags value, int and double values (original format)
27      cout << "\n\nThe restored value of the flags variable is: "
28         << cout.flags() << "\nPrint values in original format again:\n"
29         << integerValue << '\t' << doubleValue << endl;
30   }
```

```
The value of the flags variable is: 513
Print int and double in original format:
1000    0.0947628

The value of the flags variable is: 012011
Print int and double in a new format:
01750   9.476280e-02

The restored value of the flags variable is: 513
Print values in original format again:
1000    0.0947628
```

Fig. 13.19 | flags member function. (Part 2 of 2.)

13.8 Stream Error States

Each stream object contains a set of state bits that represent a stream's state—sticky format settings, error indicators, etc. Earlier in the book, we indicated that you can test, for example, whether an input was successful. You can test this through bits of class ios_base—the base class of the stream classes. Stream extraction sets the stream's failbit to *true* if the wrong type of data is input. Similarly, stream extraction sets the stream's badbit to *true* if the operation fails in an unrecoverable manner—for example, if a disk fails when a program is reading a file from that disk. Figure 13.20 shows how to use bits like failbit and badbit to determine a stream's state.[2] In industrial-strength code, you'll want to perform similar tests on every I/O operation. Chapter 22 discusses bits and bit manipulation in detail.

---

2. The actual values output by this program may vary among compilers.

```cpp
1   // Fig. 13.20: Fig13_20.cpp
2   // Testing error states.
3   #include <iostream>
4   using namespace std;
5
6   int main() {
7      int integerValue;
8
9      // display results of cin functions
10     cout << "Before a bad input operation:"
11        << "\ncin.rdstate(): " << cin.rdstate()
12        << "\n    cin.eof(): " << cin.eof()
13        << "\n   cin.fail(): " << cin.fail()
14        << "\n    cin.bad(): " << cin.bad()
15        << "\n   cin.good(): " << cin.good()
16        << "\n\nExpects an integer, but enter a character: ";
17
18     cin >> integerValue; // enter character value
19
20     // display results of cin functions after bad input
21     cout << "\nAfter a bad input operation:"
22        << "\ncin.rdstate(): " << cin.rdstate()
23        << "\n    cin.eof(): " << cin.eof()
24        << "\n   cin.fail(): " << cin.fail()
25        << "\n    cin.bad(): " << cin.bad()
26        << "\n   cin.good(): " << cin.good();
27
28     cin.clear(); // clear stream
29
30     // display results of cin functions after clearing cin
31     cout << "\n\nAfter cin.clear()" << "\ncin.fail(): " << cin.fail()
32        << "\ncin.good(): " << cin.good() << endl;
33  }
```

```
Before a bad input operation:
cin.rdstate(): 0
    cin.eof(): 0
   cin.fail(): 0
    cin.bad(): 0
   cin.good(): 1

Expects an integer, but enter a character: A

After a bad input operation:
cin.rdstate(): 2
    cin.eof(): 0
   cin.fail(): 1
    cin.bad(): 0
   cin.good(): 0

After cin.clear()
cin.fail(): 0
cin.good(): 1
```

Fig. 13.20 | Testing error states.

Member Function eof
The program begins by displaying the stream's state before receiving any input from the user (lines 10–15). Line 12 uses member function eof to determine whether end-of-file has been encountered on the stream. In this case, the function returns 0 (*false*). The function checks the value of the stream's eofbit data member, which is set to *true* for an input stream after *end-of-file* is encountered after an attempt to extract data *beyond* the end of the stream.

Member Function fail
Line 13 uses the fail member function to determine whether a stream operation has failed. The function checks the value of the stream's failbit data member, which is set to *true*, for example, on an a stream when a *format error* occurs and as a result no characters are input (e.g., when you attempt to read a number and the user enters a string). In this case, the function returns 0 (*false*). When such an error occurs on input, the characters are *not* lost. Usually, recovering from such input errors is possible.

Member Function bad
Line 14 uses the bad member function to determine whether a stream operation failed. The function checks the value of the stream's badbit data member, which is set to *true* for a stream when an error occurs that results in the *loss of data*—such as reading from a file when the disk on which the file is stored fails. In this case, the function returns 0 (*false*). Generally, such serious failures are nonrecoverable.

Member Function good
Line 15 uses the good member function, which returns true if the bad, fail and eof functions would *all* return false. The function checks the stream's goodbit, which is set to *true* for a stream if *none* of the bits eofbit, failbit or badbit is set to *true* for the stream. In this case, the function returns 1 (*true*). I/O operations should be performed only on "good" streams.

Member Function rdstate
The rdstate member function (line 11) returns the stream's overall *error state*. The function's return value could be tested, for example, by a switch statement that examines eofbit, badbit, failbit and goodbit. The *preferred* means of testing the state of a stream is to use member functions eof, bad, fail and good—using these functions does not require you to be familiar with particular status bits.

Causing an Error in the Input Stream and Redisplaying the Stream's State
Line 18 reads a value into an int variable. You should enter a string rather than an int to force an error to occur in the input stream. At this point, the input fails and lines 21–26 once again call the streams's state functions. In this case, fail returns 1 (*true*), because the input failed. Function rdstate also returns a nonzero value (*true*), because at least one of the member functions eof, bad and fail returned true. Once an error occurs in the stream, function good returns 0 (*false*).

Clearing the Error State So You May Continue Using the Stream
After an error occurs, you can no longer use the stream until you reset its error state. The clear member function (line 28) is used to *restore* a stream's state to "good," so that I/O

may proceed on that stream. Lines 31–32 then show that fail returns 0 (*false*) and good returns 1 (*true*), so the input stream can be used again.

The default argument for clear is goodbit, so the statement

```
cin.clear();
```

clears cin and sets goodbit for the stream. The statement

```
cin.clear(ios::failbit)
```

sets the failbit. You might want to do this when performing input on cin with a user-defined type and encountering a problem. The name clear might seem inappropriate in this context, but it's correct.

Overloaded Operators ! and *bool*

Overloaded operators can be used to test a stream's state in conditions. The operator! member function—inherited into the stream classes from class basic_ios—returns true if the badbit, the failbit or *both* are *true*. The operator bool member function (added in C++11) returns false if the badbit is *true*, the failbit is *true* or both are *true*. These functions are useful in I/O processing when a true/false condition is being tested under the control of a selection statement or iteration statement. For example, you could use an if statement of the form

```
if (!cin) {
    // process invalid input stream
}
```

to execute code if cin's stream is invalid due to a failed input. Similarly, you've already seen a while condition of the form

```
while (cin >> variableName) {
    // process valid input
}
```

which enables the loop to execute as long as each input operation is successful and terminates the loop if an input fails or the end-of-file indicator is encountered.

13.9 Tying an Output Stream to an Input Stream

Interactive applications generally involve an istream for input *and* an ostream for output. When a prompting message appears on the screen, the user responds by entering the appropriate data. Obviously, the prompt needs to appear *before* the input operation proceeds. With output buffering, outputs appear only

- when the buffer *fills*
- when outputs are *flushed* explicitly by the program or
- automatically at the end of the program.

C++ provides member function tie to synchronize (i.e., "tie together") the operation of an istream and an ostream to ensure that outputs appear *before* their subsequent inputs. The call

```
cin.tie(&cout);
```

ties cout (an ostream) to cin (an istream). Actually, this particular call is redundant, because C++ performs this operation automatically to create a user's standard input/output environment. However, the user would tie other istream/ostream pairs explicitly. To untie an input stream, inputStream, from an output stream, use the call

```
inputStream.tie(0);
```

13.10 Wrap-Up

This chapter provided a deeper look at how C++ performs input/output using streams. You learned about the stream-I/O classes and objects, as well as the stream I/O template class hierarchy. We discussed ostream's formatted and unformatted output capabilities performed by the put and write functions. You learned about istream's formatted and unformatted input capabilities performed by the eof, get, getline, peek, putback, ignore and read functions. We discussed stream manipulators and member functions that perform formatting tasks:

- dec, oct, hex and setbase for displaying integers
- precision and setprecision for controlling floating-point precision
- and width and setw for setting field width.

You also learned additional formatting with iostream manipulators and member functions:

- showpoint for displaying decimal point and trailing zeros
- left, right and internal for justification
- fill and setfill for padding
- scientific and fixed for displaying floating-point numbers in scientific and fixed notation
- uppercase for uppercase/lowercase control
- boolalpha for specifying Boolean format
- and flags and fmtflags for resetting the format state.

In the next chapter, you'll learn about file processing, including how persistent data is stored and how to manipulate it.

Summary

Section 13.1 Introduction
- I/O operations are performed in a manner sensitive to the type of the data.

Section 13.2 Streams
- C++ I/O occurs in **streams** (p. 579). A stream is a sequence of bytes.
- Low-level I/O-capabilities specify that bytes should be transferred device-to-memory or memory-to-device. High-level I/O is performed with bytes grouped into meaningful units such as integers, strings and user-defined types.

- C++ provides both unformatted-I/O and formatted-I/O operations. **Unformatted-I/O** (p. 579) transfers are fast, but process raw data that is difficult for people to use. Formatted I/O processes data in meaningful units, but requires extra processing time that can degrade the performance.

Section 13.2.2 iostream *Library Headers*

- The <iostream> header declares all stream-I/O operations.
- The <iomanip> header declares the parameterized stream manipulators.

Section 13.2.3 *Stream Input/Output Classes and Objects*

- The **basic_istream template** (p. 580) supports stream input operations.
- The **basic_ostream template** (p. 580) supports stream output operations.
- The basic_iostream template supports both stream input and stream output operations.
- The istream object cin is tied to the standard input device, normally the keyboard.
- The ostream object cout is tied to the standard output device, normally the screen.
- The ostream object cerr is tied to the standard error device, normally the screen. Outputs to cerr are **unbuffered** (p. 581)—each insertion to cerr appears immediately.
- The ostream object clog is tied to the standard error device, normally the screen. Outputs to clog are **buffered** (p. 581).
- The C++ compiler determines data types automatically for input and output.

Section 13.3 *Stream Output*

- Addresses are displayed in hexadecimal format by default.
- To print the address in a pointer variable, cast the pointer to void *.
- Member function put outputs one character. Calls to put may be cascaded.

Section 13.4 *Stream Input*

- Stream input is performed with the stream extraction operator >>, which automatically skips white-space characters in the input stream and returns false after end-of-file is encountered.
- A series of values can be input using the stream extraction operation in a while loop header. The extraction returns 0 when end-of-file is encountered or an error occurs.
- The **get** member function (p. 583) with no arguments inputs one character and returns the character; EOF is returned if end-of-file is encountered on the stream.
- Member function get with a character-reference argument inputs the next character from the input stream and stores it in the character argument. This version of get returns a reference to the istream object for which the get member function is being invoked.
- Member function get with three arguments—a character array, a size *limit* and a delimiter (with default value newline)—reads characters from the input stream up to a maximum of *limit* − 1 characters, or until the delimiter is read. The input string is terminated with a null character. The delimiter is not placed in the character array but remains in the input stream.
- Member function **getline** (p. 585) operates like the three-argument get member function. The getline function removes the delimiter from the input stream but does not store it in the string.
- Member function ignore skips the specified number of characters (the default is 1) in the input stream; it terminates if the specified delimiter is encountered (the default delimiter is EOF).
- The **putback** member function (p. 586) places the previous character obtained by a get on a stream back into that stream.

- The **peek** member function (p. 586) returns the next character from an input stream but does not extract (remove) the character from the stream.
- C++ offers **type-safe I/O** (p. 586). If unexpected data is processed by the << and >> operators, various error bits are set, which can be tested to determine whether an I/O operation succeeded or failed. If operator << has not been overloaded for a user-defined type, a compiler error is reported.

Section 13.5 Unformatted I/O Using read, write and gcount
- Unformatted I/O is performed with member functions **read** and **write** (p. 586). These input or output bytes to or from memory, beginning at a designated memory address.
- The **gcount** member function (p. 587) returns the number of characters input by the previous read operation on that stream.
- Member function read inputs a specified number of characters into a character array. failbit is set if fewer than the specified number of characters are read.

Section 13.6 Stream Manipulators: A Deeper Look
- To change the base in which integers output, use the manipulator **hex** (p. 588) to set the base to hexadecimal (base 16) or **oct** (p. 588) to set the base to octal (base 8). Use manipulator **dec** (p. 588) to reset the base to decimal. The base remains the same until changed explicitly.
- The parameterized stream manipulator **setbase** (p. 588) also sets the base for integer output. setbase takes one integer argument of 10, 8 or 16 to set the base.
- Floating-point precision can be controlled with the setprecision stream manipulator or the **precision** member function (p. 588). Both set the precision for all subsequent output operations until the next precision-setting call. The precision member function with no argument returns the current precision value.
- Parameterized manipulators require the inclusion of the <iomanip> header.
- Member function **width** (p. 590) sets the field width and returns the previous width. Values narrower than the field are padded with fill characters. The field-width setting applies only for the next insertion or extraction, then input is performed using the default settings. Values wider than a field are printed in their entirety. Function width with no argument returns the current width setting. Manipulator setw also sets the width.
- For input, the setw stream manipulator establishes a maximum string size; if a larger string is entered, the larger line is broken into pieces no larger than the designated size.
- You can create your own stream manipulators.

Section 13.7 Stream Format States and Stream Manipulators
- Stream manipulator **showpoint** (p. 593) forces a floating-point number to be output with a decimal point and with the number of significant digits specified by the precision.
- Stream manipulators **left** and **right** (p. 594) cause fields to be left justified with padding characters to the right or right justified with padding characters to the left.
- Stream manipulator **internal** (p. 595) indicates that a number's sign (or base when using stream manipulator **showbase**; p. 597) should be left justified within a field, its magnitude should be right justified and intervening spaces should be padded with the fill character.
- Member function **fill** (p. 595) specifies the fill character to be used with stream manipulators left, right and internal (space is the default); the prior padding character is returned. Stream manipulator setfill also sets the fill character.

- Stream manipulators oct, hex and dec specify that integers are to be treated as octal, hexadecimal or decimal values, respectively. Integer output defaults to decimal if none of these is set; stream extractions process the data in the form the data is supplied.

- Stream manipulator showbase forces the base of an integral value to be output.

- Stream manipulator **scientific** (p. 597) is used to output a floating-point number in scientific format. Stream manipulator fixed is used to output a floating-point number with the precision specified by the precision member function.

- Stream manipulator **uppercase** (p. 598) outputs an uppercase X or E for hexadecimal integers and scientific notation floating-point values, respectively. Hexadecimal values appear in all uppercase.

- Member function **flags** (p. 600) with no argument returns the current format state (p. 600) as a long value. Function flags with a long argument sets the format state specified by the argument.

Section 13.8 Stream Error States

- Stream extraction causes **failbit** (p. 601) to be set for improper input and **badbit** (p. 601) to be set if the operation fails.

- The state of a stream may be tested through bits in class ios_base.

- The **eofbit** (p. 603) is set for an input stream after end-of-file is encountered during an input operation. The **eof** member function reports whether the eofbit has been set.

- A stream's failbit is set when a format error occurs. The **fail** member function (p. 603) reports whether a stream operation has failed; it's normally possible to recover from such errors.

- A stream's badbit is set when an error occurs that results in data loss. Member function bad reports whether a stream operation failed. Such serious failures are normally nonrecoverable.

- The **good** member function (p. 603) returns true if the bad, fail and eof functions would all return false. I/O operations should be performed only on "good" streams.

- The **rdstate** member function (p. 603) returns the error state of the stream.

- Member function **clear** (p. 603) restores a stream's state to "good," so that I/O may proceed.

Section 13.9 Tying an Output Stream to an Input Stream

- C++ provides the **tie** member function (p. 604) to synchronize istream and ostream operations to ensure that outputs appear before subsequent inputs.

Self-Review Exercises

13.1   *(Fill in the Blanks)* Answer each of the following:

a) Input/output in C++ occurs as _____ of bytes.

b) The stream manipulators for justification are _____, _____ and _____.

c) Member function _____ can be used to set and reset format state.

d) Most C++ programs that do I/O should include the _____ header that contains the declarations required for all stream-I/O operations.

e) When using parameterized manipulators, the header _____ must be included.

f) The _____ stream manipulator causes positive numbers to display with a plus sign.

g) The ostream member function _____ is used to perform unformatted output.

h) Input operations are supported by class _____.

i) Standard error stream outputs are directed to the stream objects _____ or _____.

j) Output operations are supported by class _____.

k) The symbol for the stream insertion operator is _____.

l) The four objects that correspond to the standard devices on the system include _____, _____, _____ and _____.

m) The symbol for the stream extraction operator is _____.

n) The stream manipulators _____, _____ and _____ specify that integers should be displayed in octal, hexadecimal and decimal formats, respectively.

13.2 *(True or False)* State whether each of the following is *true* or *false*. If the answer is *false*, explain why.

a) The stream member function flags with a long argument sets the flags state variable to its argument and returns its previous value.

b) The stream insertion operator << and the stream extraction operator >> are overloaded to handle all standard data types—including strings and memory addresses (stream insertion only)—and all user-defined data types.

c) The stream member function flags with no arguments resets the stream's format state.

d) Input with the stream extraction operator >> always skips leading white-space characters in the input stream, by default.

e) The stream member function rdstate returns the current state of the stream.

f) The cout stream normally is connected to the display screen.

g) The stream member function good returns true if the bad, fail and eof member functions all return false.

h) The cin stream normally is connected to the display screen.

i) If a nonrecoverable error occurs during a stream operation, the bad member function will return true.

j) Output to cerr is unbuffered and output to clog is buffered.

k) Stream manipulator showpoint forces floating-point values to print with the default six digits of precision unless the precision value has been changed, in which case floating-point values print with the specified precision.

l) The ostream member function put outputs the specified number of characters.

m) The stream manipulators dec, oct and hex affect only the next integer output operation.

13.3 *(Write a C++ Statement)* For each of the following, write a single statement that performs the indicated task.

a) Output the string "Enter your name: ".

b) Use a stream manipulator that causes the exponent in scientific notation and the letters in hexadecimal values to print in capital letters.

c) Output the address of the variable myString of type char *.

d) Use a stream manipulator to ensure that floating-point values print in scientific notation.

e) Output the address in variable integerPtr of type int *.

f) Use a stream manipulator such that, when integer values are output, the integer base for octal and hexadecimal values is displayed.

g) Output the value pointed to by floatPtr of type float *.

h) Use a stream member function to set the fill character to '*' for printing in field widths larger than the values being output. Repeat this statement with a stream manipulator.

i) Output the characters 'O' and 'K' in one statement with ostream function put.

j) Get the value of the next character to input without extracting it from the stream.

k) Input a single character into variable charValue of type char, using the istream member function get in two different ways.

l) Input and discard the next six characters in the input stream.

m) Use istream member function read to input 50 characters into char array line.

n) Read 10 characters into character array name. Stop reading characters if the '.' delimiter is encountered. Do not remove the delimiter from the input stream. Write another statement that performs this task and removes the delimiter from the input.

o) Use the istream member function gcount to determine the number of characters input into character array line by the last call to istream member function read, and output that number of characters, using ostream member function write.

p) Output 124, 18.376, 'Z', 1000000 and "String", separated by spaces.

q) Display cout's current precision setting.

r) Input an integer value into int variable months and a floating-point value into float variable percentageRate.

s) Print 1.92, 1.925 and 1.9258 separated by tabs and with 3 digits of precision, using a stream manipulator.

t) Print integer 100 in octal, hexadecimal and decimal, using stream manipulators and separated by tabs.

u) Print integer 100 in decimal, octal and hexadecimal separated by tabs, using a stream manipulator to change the base.

v) Print 1234 right justified in a 10-digit field.

w) Read characters into character array line until the character 'z' is encountered, up to a limit of 20 characters (including a terminating null character). Do not extract the delimiter character from the stream.

x) Use integer variables x and y to specify the field width and precision used to display the double value 87.4573, and display the value.

13.4 *(Find and Correct Code Errors)* Identify the error in each of the following statements and explain how to correct it.

a) `cout << "Value of x <= y is: " << x <= y;`
b) The following statement should print the integer value of 'c'.
`cout << 'c';`
c) `cout << ""A string in quotes"";`

13.5 *(Show Outputs)* For each of the following, show the output.

a) `cout << "12345\n";`
`cout.width(5);`
`cout.fill('*');`
`cout << 123 << "\n" << 123;`
b) `cout << setw(10) << setfill('$') << 10000;`
c) `cout << setw(8) << setprecision(3) << 1024.987654;`
d) `cout << showbase << oct << 99 << "\n" << hex << 99;`
e) `cout << 100000 << "\n" << showpos << 100000;`
f) `cout << setw(10) << setprecision(2) << scientific << 444.93738;`

Answers to Self-Review Exercises

13.1 a) streams. b) left, right and internal. c) flags. d) <iostream>. e) <iomanip>. f) showpos. g) write. h) istream. i) cerr or clog. j) ostream. k) <<. l) cin, cout, cerr and clog. m) >>. n) oct, hex and dec.

13.2 a) False. The stream member function flags with a fmtflags argument sets the flags state variable to its argument and returns the prior state settings. b) False. The stream insertion and stream extraction operators are not overloaded for all user-defined types. You must specifically provide the overloaded operator functions to overload the stream operators for use with each user-defined type you create. c) False. The stream member function flags with no arguments returns the current format settings as a fmtflags data type, which represents the format state. d) True. e) True.

f) True. g) True. h) False. The cin stream is connected to the standard input of the computer, which normally is the keyboard. i) True. j) True. k) True. l) False. The ostream member function put outputs its single-character argument. m) False. The stream manipulators dec, oct and hex set the output format state for integers to the specified base until the base is changed again or the program terminates.

13.3   a) `cout << "Enter your name: ";`
     b) `cout << uppercase;`
     c) `cout << static_cast<void*>(myString);`
     d) `cout << scientific;`
     e) `cout << integerPtr;`
     f) `cout << showbase;`
     g) `cout << *floatPtr;`
     h) `cout.fill('*');`
       `cout << setfill('*');`
     i) `cout.put('O').put('K');`
     j) `cin.peek();`
     k) `charValue = cin.get();`
       `cin.get(charValue);`
     l) `cin.ignore(6);`
     m) `cin.read(line, 50);`
     n) `cin.get(name, 10, '.');`
       `cin.getline(name, 10, '.');`
     o) `cout.write(line, cin.gcount());`
     p) `cout << 124 << ' ' << 18.376 << " Z " << 1000000 << " String";`
     q) `cout << cout.precision();`
     r) `cin >> months >> percentageRate;`
     s) `cout << setprecision(3) << 1.92 << '\t' << 1.925 << '\t' << 1.9258;`
     t) `cout << oct << 100 << '\t' << hex << 100 << '\t' << dec << 100;`
     u) `cout << 100 << '\t' << setbase(8) << 100 << '\t' << setbase(16) << 100;`
     v) `cout << setw(10) << 1234;`
     w) `cin.get(line, 20, 'z');`
     x) `cout << setw(x) << setprecision(y) << 87.4573;`

13.4   a) *Error:* The precedence of the << operator is higher than that of <=, which causes the statement to be evaluated improperly and also causes a compiler error.
     Correction: Place parentheses around the expression x <= y.
     b) *Error:* In C++, characters are not treated as small integers, as they are in C.
     Correction: To print the numerical value for a character in the computer's character set, the character must be cast to an integer value, as in the following:
       `cout << static_cast<int>('c');`
     c) *Error:* Quote characters cannot be printed in a string unless an escape sequence is used.
     Correction: Print the string:
       `cout << "\"A string in quotes\"";`

13.5   a) `12345`
       `**123`
       `123`
     b) `$$$$$10000`
     c) `1024.988`
     d) `0143`
       `0x63`

   e) 100000
       +100000
   f)   4.45e+002

Exercises

13.6 *(Write C++ Statements)* Write a statement for each of the following:
   a) Print integer 40000 left justified in a 15-digit field.
   b) Read a string into character array variable state.
   c) Print 200 with and without a sign.
   d) Print the decimal value 100 in hexadecimal form preceded by 0x.
   e) Read characters into array charArray until the character 'p' is encountered, up to a limit of 10 characters (including the terminating null character). Extract the delimiter from the input stream, and discard it.
   f) Print 1.234 in a 9-digit field with preceding zeros.

13.7 *(Inputting Decimal, Octal and Hexadecimal Values)* Write a program to test the inputting of integer values in decimal, octal and hexadecimal formats. Output each integer read by the program in all three formats. Test the program with the following input data: 10, 010, 0x10.

13.8 *(Printing Pointer Values as Integers)* Write a program that prints pointer values, using casts to all the integer data types. Which ones print strange values? Which ones cause errors?

13.9 *(Printing with Field Widths)* Write a program to test the results of printing the integer value 12345 and the floating-point value 1.2345 in various-sized fields. What happens when the values are printed in fields containing fewer digits than the values?

13.10 *(Rounding)* Write a program that prints the value 100.453627 rounded to the nearest digit, tenth, hundredth, thousandth and ten-thousandth.

13.11 *(Length of a String)* Write a program that inputs a string from the keyboard and determines the length of the string. Print the string in a field width that is twice the length of the string.

13.12 *(Converting Fahrenheit to Celsius)* Write a program that converts integer Fahrenheit temperatures from 0 to 212 degrees to floating-point Celsius temperatures with 3 digits of precision. Use the formula

```
celsius = 5.0 / 9.0 * (fahrenheit - 32);
```

to perform the calculation. The output should be printed in two right-justified columns and the Celsius temperatures should be preceded by a sign for both positive and negative values.

13.13 In some programming languages, strings are entered surrounded by either single or double quotation marks. Write a program that reads the three strings suzy, "suzy" and 'suzy'. Are the single and double quotes ignored or read as part of the string?

13.14 *(Reading Phone Numbers with an Overloaded Stream Extraction Operator)* In Fig. 10.5, the stream extraction and stream insertion operators were overloaded for input and output of objects of the PhoneNumber class. Rewrite the stream extraction operator to perform the following error checking on input. The operator>> function will need to be reimplemented.
   a) Input the entire phone number into an array. Test that the proper number of characters has been entered. There should be a total of 14 characters read for a phone number of the form (800) 555-1212. Use istream member-function clear to set failbit for improper input.
   b) The area code and exchange do not begin with 0 or 1. Test the first digit of the area-code and exchange portions of the phone number to be sure that neither begins with 0 or 1. Use istream member-function clear to set failbit for improper input.

c) The middle digit of an area code used to be limited to 0 or 1 (though this has changed). Test the middle digit for a value of 0 or 1. Use the istream member-function clear to set failbit for improper input. If none of the above operations results in failbit being set for improper input, copy the parts of the telephone number into the PhoneNumber object's areaCode, exchange and line members. If failbit has been set on the input, have the program print an error message and end, rather than print the phone number.

13.15 *(Point Class)* Write a program that accomplishes each of the following:

a) Create a user-defined class Point that contains the private integer data members xCoordinate and yCoordinate and declares stream insertion and stream extraction over-loaded operator functions as friends of the class.

b) Define the stream insertion and stream extraction operator functions. The stream ex-traction operator function should determine whether the data entered is valid, and, if not, it should set the failbit to indicate improper input. The stream insertion operator should not be able to display the point after an input error occurred.

c) Write a main function that tests input and output of user-defined class Point, using the overloaded stream extraction and stream insertion operators.

13.16 *(Complex Class)* Write a program that accomplishes each of the following:

a) Create a user-defined class Complex that contains the private integer data members real and imaginary and declares stream insertion and stream extraction overloaded operator functions as friends of the class.

b) Define the stream insertion and stream extraction operator functions. The stream ex-traction operator function should determine whether the data entered is valid, and, if not, it should set failbit to indicate improper input. The input should be of the form

```
3 + 8i
```

c) The values can be negative or positive, and it's possible that one of the two values is not provided, in which case the appropriate data member should be set to 0. The stream insertion operator should not be able to display the point if an input error occurred. For negative imaginary values, a minus sign should be printed rather than a plus sign.

d) Write a main function that tests input and output of user-defined class Complex, using the overloaded stream extraction and stream insertion operators.

13.17 *(Printing a Table of ASCII Values)* Write a program that uses a for statement to print a table of ASCII values for the characters in the ASCII character set from 33 to 126. The program should print the decimal value, octal value, hexadecimal value and character value for each character. Use the stream manipulators dec, oct and hex to print the integer values.

13.18 *(String-Terminating Null Character)* Write a program to show that the getline and three-argument get istream member functions both end the input string with a string-terminating null character. Also, show that get leaves the delimiter character on the input stream, whereas getline extracts the delimiter character and discards it. What happens to the unread characters in the stream?

File Processing

14

Objectives

In this chapter you'll:

- Create, read, write and update files.

- Perform sequential file processing.

- Perform random-access file processing.

- Use high-performance unformatted I/O operations.

- Understand the differences between formatted-data and raw-data file processing.

- Build a transaction-processing program using random-access file processing.

- Understand the concept of object serialization.

14.1 Introduction

Storage of data in memory is *temporary*. Files are used for data persistence—*permanent* retention of data. Computers store files on secondary storage devices, such as hard disks, CDs, DVDs, flash drives and tapes. In this chapter, we explain how to build C++ programs that create, update and process data files. We consider both *sequential files* and *random-access files*. We compare *formatted-data* file processing and *raw-data* file processing. We've already shown how to output data to a string in memory using an ostringstream—Chapter 21 continues that discussion and demonstrates how to read data from strings in memory using an istringstream.

14.2 Files and Streams

C++ views each file simply as *a sequence of bytes* (Fig. 14.1). Each file ends either with an end-of-file marker or at a specific byte number recorded in an operating-system-maintained administrative data structure. When a file is *opened*, an object is created, and a stream is associated with the object. In Chapter 13, we saw that objects cin, cout, cerr and clog are created when <iostream> is included. The streams associated with these objects provide communication channels between a program and a particular file or device. For example, the cin object (standard input stream object) enables a program to input data from the keyboard or from other devices, the cout object (standard output stream object) enables a program to output data to the screen or other devices, and the cerr and clog objects (standard error stream objects) enable a program to output error messages to the screen or other devices.

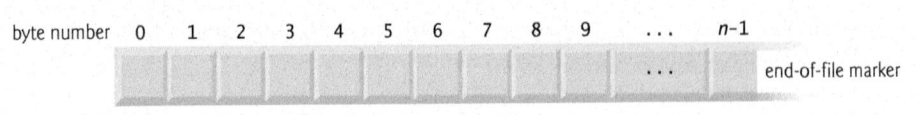

byte number   0   1   2   3   4   5   6   7   8   9   ...   n–1

end-of-file marker

Fig. 14.1 | C++'s simple view of a file of *n* bytes.

File-Processing Class Templates

To perform file processing in C++, headers `<iostream>` and `<fstream>` must be included. Header `<fstream>` includes the definitions for the stream class templates

- `basic_ifstream`—a subclass of `basic_istream` for file input
- `basic_ofstream`—a subclass of `basic_ostream` for file output
- `basic_fstream`—a subclass of `basic_iostream` for file input *and* output.

Each has a predefined specialization for `char` I/O. In addition, the `<fstream>` library provides `typedef` aliases for these template specializations:

- `ifstream` is an alias for `basic_ifstream<char>`
- `ofstream` is an alias for `basic_ofstream<char>`
- `fstream` is an alias for `basic_fstream<char>` .

All the I/O capabilities described in Chapter 13 also can be applied to file streams.

14.3 Creating a Sequential File

C++ imposes no structure on files. Thus, a concept like that of a record (Section 1.4) does not exist in C++. You must structure files to meet the application's requirements. The following example shows how you can impose a simple record structure on a file.

Figure 14.2 creates a sequential file that might be used in an accounts-receivable system to help manage the money owed to a company by its credit clients. For each client, the program obtains the client's account number, name and balance (i.e., the amount the client owes the company for goods and services received in the past). The data obtained for each client constitutes a *record* for that client. The account number serves as the *record key*; that is, the program creates and maintains the records of the file in account-number order. This program assumes the user enters the records in account-number order. In a comprehensive accounts receivable system, a *sorting* capability would be provided for the user to enter records *in any* order—the records then would be sorted and written to the file.

```
1   // Fig. 14.2: Fig14_02.cpp
2   // Creating a sequential file.
3   #include <iostream>
4   #include <string>
5   #include <fstream> // contains file stream processing types
6   #include <cstdlib> // exit function prototype
7   using namespace std;
```

Fig. 14.2 | Creating a sequential file. (Part 1 of 2.)

```
8
9    int main() {
10       // ofstream constructor opens file
11       ofstream outClientFile{"clients.txt", ios::out};
12
13       // exit program if unable to create file
14       if (!outClientFile) { // overloaded ! operator
15          cerr << "File could not be opened" << endl;
16          exit(EXIT_FAILURE);
17       }
18
19       cout << "Enter the account, name, and balance.\n"
20          << "Enter end-of-file to end input.\n? ";
21
22       int account; // the account number
23       string name; // the account owner's name
24       double balance; // the account balance
25
26       // read account, name and balance from cin, then place in file
27       while (cin >> account >> name >> balance) {
28          outClientFile << account << ' ' << name << ' ' << balance << endl;
29          cout << "? ";
30       }
31    }
```

```
Enter the account, name, and balance.
Enter end-of-file to end input.
? 100 Jones 24.98
? 200 Doe 345.67
? 300 White 0.00
? 400 Stone -42.16
? 500 Rich 224.62
? ^Z
```

Fig. 14.2 | Creating a sequential file. (Part 2 of 2.)

14.3.1 Opening a File

Figure 14.2 writes data to a file, so we open the file for output by creating an ofstream object. Two arguments are passed to the object's constructor (line 11)—the filename and the file-open mode. For an ofstream object, the file-open mode can be either ios::out (the default) to *output* data to a file or ios::app to *append* data to the end of a file (without modifying any data already in the file). Line 11 creates an ofstream object named out-ClientFile associated with the file clients.txt that's opened for output—because we did not specify a path to the file (that is, it's location), the file will be in the same directory as the program. The ofstream constructor opens the file—this establishes a "line of communication" with the file. Prior to C++11, the filename was specified as a pointer-based string—as of C++11, it also can be specified as a string object.

Since ios::out is the default, the second constructor argument in line 11 is not required, so we could have used the statement

```
ofstream outClientFile{"clients.txt"};
```

Existing files opened with mode `ios::out` are truncated—all data in the file is *discarded*. If the specified file does *not* yet exist, then the `ofstream` object *creates* the file, using that filename. Figure 14.3 lists the file-open modes. These modes can also be combined, as we discuss in Section 14.9.

Error-Prevention Tip 14.1
Use caution when opening an existing file for output (`ios::out`), especially when you want to preserve the file's contents, which will be discarded without warning.

Mode	Description
`ios::app`	*Append* all output to the end of the file.
`ios::ate`	Open a file for output and move to the end of the file (normally used to append data to a file). Data can be written *anywhere* in the file.
`ios::in`	Open a file for *input*.
`ios::out`	Open a file for *output*.
`ios::trunc`	*Discard* the file's contents (this also is the default action for `ios::out`).
`ios::binary`	Open a file for binary, i.e., *nontext*, input or output.

Fig. 14.3 | File-open modes.

14.3.2 Opening a File via the open Member Function

You can create an `ofstream` object *without* opening a specific file—in this case, a file can be attached to the object later. For example, the statement

```
ofstream outClientFile;
```

creates an `ofstream` object that's not yet associated with a file. The `ofstream` member function open opens a file and attaches it to an *existing* `ofstream` object as follows:

```
outClientFile.open("clients.txt", ios::out);
```

Once again, `ios::out` is the default value for the second argument.

14.3.3 Testing Whether a File Was Opened Successfully

After creating an `ofstream` object and *attempting* to open it, the `if` statement in lines 14–17 (Fig. 14.2) uses the overloaded `ios` member function `operator!` (discussed in Chapter 13) to determine whether the open operation succeeded. Recall that `operator!` returns `true` if either the `failbit` or the `badbit` is set for the stream—in this case, one or both would be set because the open operation failed. Some possible reasons are:

- attempting to open a *nonexistent* file for reading
- attempting to open a file for reading or writing from a directory that you don't have permission to access, and
- opening a file for writing when no disk space is available.

If the condition indicates an unsuccessful attempt to open the file, line 15 outputs an error message, and line 16 invokes function `exit` to terminate the program. The argument to exit is returned to the environment from which the program was invoked. Passing EXIT_SUCCESS (defined in <cstdlib>) to exit indicates that the program terminated *normally*; passing any other value (in this case EXIT_FAILURE) indicates that the program terminated due to an *error*.

14.3.4 Overloaded bool Operator

As we discussed in Chapter 13, a stream's overloaded operator bool (added in C++11) converts the stream to a true or false value, so it can be tested in a condition. If the fail-bit or badbit has been set for the stream, the overloaded operator returns false. The condition in the while statement (lines 27–30) *implicitly* invokes the operator bool member function on cin. The condition remains *true* as long as neither the failbit nor the badbit has been set for cin. Entering the *end-of-file* indicator sets the failbit for cin. Recall from Chapter 13 that you also can call member function eof on the input object.

14.3.5 Processing Data

If line 11 opens the file successfully, the program begins processing data. Lines 19–20 prompt the user to enter either the various fields for each record or the end-of-file indicator when data entry is complete. Figure 14.4 lists the keyboard combinations for entering end-of-file for various computer systems.

Computer system	Keyboard combination
UNIX/Linux/Mac OS X	*<Ctrl-d>* (on a line by itself)
Microsoft Windows	*<Ctrl-z>* (followed by pressing *Enter*)

Fig. 14.4 | End-of-file key combinations.

Line 27 extracts each set of data and determines whether end-of-file has been entered. When end-of-file is encountered or bad data is entered, operator bool returns false and the while statement terminates. The user enters end-of-file to inform the program to process no additional data. The end-of-file indicator is set when the user enters the end-of-file key combination. The while statement loops until the end-of-file indicator is set (or bad data is entered).

Line 28 writes a set of data to the file clients.txt, using the stream insertion operator << and the outClientFile object associated with the file at the beginning of the program. The data may be retrieved by a program designed to read the file (see Section 14.4). The file created in Fig. 14.2 is simply a *text file*, so it can be viewed by any text editor.

14.3.6 Closing a File

Once the user enters the end-of-file indicator, main terminates. This implicitly invokes outClientFile's destructor, which *closes* the clients.txt file. You also can close the ofstream object *explicitly*, using member function close as follows:

```
outClientFile.close();
```

Error-Prevention Tip 14.2
Always close a file as soon as it's no longer needed in a program.

14.3.7 Sample Execution

In the sample execution for the program of Fig. 14.2, the user enters information for five accounts, then signals that data entry is complete by entering end-of-file (^Z is displayed for Microsoft Windows). This dialog window does *not* show how the data records appear in the file. To verify that the program created the file successfully, the next section shows how to create a program that reads this file and prints its contents.

14.4 Reading Data from a Sequential File

Files store data so it may be *retrieved* for processing when needed. The previous section demonstrated how to create a file for sequential access. We now discuss how to *read* data sequentially from a file. Figure 14.5 reads and displays the records from the clients.txt file that we created using the program of Fig. 14.2. Creating an ifstream object opens a file for *input*. The ifstream constructor can receive the filename and the file-open mode as arguments. Line 14 creates an ifstream object called inClientFile and associates it with the clients.txt file. The arguments in parentheses are passed to the ifstream constructor, which opens the file and establishes a "line of communication" with the file.

Good Programming Practice 14.1
If a file's contents should not be modified, use ios::in *to open it only for input. This prevents unintentional modification of the file's contents and is another example of the principle of least privilege.*

```cpp
 1  // Fig. 14.5: Fig14_05.cpp
 2  // Reading and printing a sequential file.
 3  #include <iostream>
 4  #include <fstream> // file stream
 5  #include <iomanip>
 6  #include <string>
 7  #include <cstdlib>
 8  using namespace std;
 9
10  void outputLine(int, const string&, double); // prototype
11
12  int main() {
13     // ifstream constructor opens the file
14     ifstream inClientFile("clients.txt", ios::in);
15
16     // exit program if ifstream could not open file
17     if (!inClientFile) {
18        cerr << "File could not be opened" << endl;
19        exit(EXIT_FAILURE);
20     }
21
```

Fig. 14.5 | Reading and printing a sequential file. (Part 1 of 2.)

```
22       cout << left << setw(10) << "Account" << setw(13)
23          << "Name" << "Balance\n" << fixed << showpoint;
24
25       int account; // the account number
26       string name; // the account owner's name
27       double balance; // the account balance
28
29       // display each record in file
30       while (inClientFile >> account >> name >> balance) {
31          outputLine(account, name, balance);
32       }
33    }
34
35    // display single record from file
36    void outputLine(int account, const string& name, double balance) {
37       cout << left << setw(10) << account << setw(13) << name
38          << setw(7) << setprecision(2) << right << balance << endl;
39    }
```

```
Account   Name         Balance
100       Jones          24.98
200       Doe           345.67
300       White           0.00
400       Stone         -42.16
500       Rich          224.62
```

Fig. 14.5 | Reading and printing a sequential file. (Part 2 of 2.)

14.4.1 Opening a File for Input

Objects of class ifstream are opened for *input* by default, so the statement

```
ifstream inClientFile("clients.txt");
```

opens clients.txt for input. Just as with an ofstream object, an ifstream object can be created without opening a specific file, because a file can be attached to it later. Before attempting to retrieve data from the file, line 17 uses the condition !inClientFile to determine whether the file was opened successfully.

14.4.2 Reading from the File

Line 30 reads a set of data (i.e., a record) from the file. After line 30 executes the first time, account has the value 100, name has the value "Jones" and balance has the value 24.98. Each time line 30 executes, it reads another record into the variables account, name and balance. Line 31 displays the records, using function outputLine (lines 36–39), which uses parameterized stream manipulators to format the data for display. When the end of file is reached, the implicit call to operator bool in the while condition returns false, the ifstream destructor closes the file and the program terminates.

14.4.3 File-Position Pointers

Programs normally read sequentially from the beginning of a file and read all the data consecutively until the desired data is found. It might be necessary to process the file sequentially several times (from the beginning) during the execution of a program. istream and ostream provide member functions—seekg ("seek get") and seekp ("seek put"), respectively—to *reposition the file-position pointer* (the byte number of the next byte in the file to be read or written). Each istream object has a *get pointer*, which indicates the byte number in the file from which the next *input* is to occur, and each ostream object has a *put pointer*, which indicates the byte number in the file at which the next *output* should be placed. The statement

```
inClientFile.seekg(0);
```

repositions the file-position pointer to the *beginning* of the file (location 0) attached to inClientFile. The argument to seekg is an integer. A second argument can be specified to indicate the seek direction, which can be ios::beg (the default) for positioning relative to the *beginning* of a stream, ios::cur for positioning relative to the *current position* in a stream or ios::end for positioning backward relative to the *end* of a stream. The file-position pointer is an integer value that specifies the location in the file as a number of bytes from the file's starting location (this is also referred to as the offset from the beginning of the file). Some examples of positioning the *get* file-position pointer are

```
// position to the nth byte of fileObject (assumes ios::beg)
fileObject.seekg(n);

// position n bytes in fileObject
fileObject.seekg(n, ios::cur);

// position n bytes back from end of fileObject
fileObject.seekg(n, ios::end);

// position at end of fileObject
fileObject.seekg(0, ios::end);
```

The same operations can be performed using ostream member function seekp. Member functions tellg and tellp are provided to return the current locations of the *get* and *put* pointers, respectively. The following statement assigns the *get* file-position pointer value to variable location of type long:

```
location = fileObject.tellg();
```

14.4.4 Case Study: Credit Inquiry Program

Figure 14.6 enables a credit manager to display the account information for those customers with zero balances (i.e., customers who do not owe the company any money), credit (negative) balances (i.e., customers to whom the company owes money), and debit (positive) balances (i.e., customers who owe the company money for goods and services received in the past). The program displays a menu and allows the credit manager to enter one of three options to obtain credit information. Option 1 produces a list of accounts with zero balances. Option 2 produces a list of accounts with credit balances. Option 3 produces a list of accounts with debit balances. Option 4 terminates program execution. Entering an invalid option displays the prompt to enter another choice. Lines 61–62 enable the program to read from the beginning of the file after end-of-file has been read.

```
1   // Fig. 14.6: Fig14_06.cpp
2   // Credit inquiry program.
3   #include <iostream>
```

Fig. 14.6 | Credit inquiry program. (Part 1 of 4.)

```
 4   #include <fstream>
 5   #include <iomanip>
 6   #include <string>
 7   #include <cstdlib>
 8   using namespace std;
 9
10   enum class RequestType {
11       ZERO_BALANCE = 1, CREDIT_BALANCE, DEBIT_BALANCE, END};
12   RequestType getRequest();
13   bool shouldDisplay(RequestType, double);
14   void outputLine(int, const string&, double);
15
16   int main() {
17       // ifstream constructor opens the file
18       ifstream inClientFile{"clients.txt", ios::in};
19
20       // exit program if ifstream could not open file
21       if (!inClientFile) {
22           cerr << "File could not be opened" << endl;
23           exit(EXIT_FAILURE);
24       }
25
26       // get user's request (e.g., zero, credit or debit balance)
27       RequestType request{getRequest()};
28
29       // process user's request
30       while (request != RequestType::END) {
31           switch (request) {
32               case RequestType::ZERO_BALANCE:
33                   cout << "\nAccounts with zero balances:\n";
34                   break;
35               case RequestType::CREDIT_BALANCE:
36                   cout << "\nAccounts with credit balances:\n";
37                   break;
38               case RequestType::DEBIT_BALANCE:
39                   cout << "\nAccounts with debit balances:\n";
40                   break;
41           }
42
43           int account; // the account number
44           string name; // the account owner's name
45           double balance; // the account balance
46
47           // read account, name and balance from file
48           inClientFile >> account >> name >> balance;
49
50           // display file contents (until eof)
51           while (!inClientFile.eof()) {
52               // display record
53               if (shouldDisplay(request, balance)) {
54                   outputLine(account, name, balance);
55               }
```

Fig. 14.6 | Credit inquiry program. (Part 2 of 4.)

```
56
57              // read account, name and balance from file
58              inClientFile >> account >> name >> balance;
59          }
60
61          inClientFile.clear(); // reset eof for next input
62          inClientFile.seekg(0); // reposition to beginning of file
63          request = getRequest(); // get additional request from user
64      }
65
66      cout << "End of run." << endl;
67  }
68
69  // obtain request from user
70  RequestType getRequest() {
71      // display request options
72      cout << "\nEnter request\n"
73          << " 1 - List accounts with zero balances\n"
74          << " 2 - List accounts with credit balances\n"
75          << " 3 - List accounts with debit balances\n"
76          << " 4 - End of run" << fixed << showpoint;
77      int type; // request from user
78
79      do { // input user request
80          cout << "\n? ";
81          cin >> type;
82      } while (type < static_cast<int>(RequestType::ZERO_BALANCE) ||
83          type > static_cast<int>(RequestType::END));
84
85      return static_cast<RequestType>(type);
86  }
87
88  // determine whether to display given record
89  bool shouldDisplay(RequestType type, double balance) {
90      // determine whether to display zero balances
91      if (type == RequestType::ZERO_BALANCE && balance == 0) {
92          return true;
93      }
94
95      // determine whether to display credit balances
96      if (type == RequestType::CREDIT_BALANCE && balance < 0) {
97          return true;
98      }
99
100     // determine whether to display debit balances
101     if (type == RequestType::DEBIT_BALANCE && balance > 0) {
102         return true;
103     }
104
105     return false;
106 }
107
```

Fig. 14.6 | Credit inquiry program. (Part 3 of 4.)

```
108   // display single record from file
109   void outputLine(int account, const string& name, double balance) {
110       cout << left << setw(10) << account << setw(13) << name
111           << setw(7) << setprecision(2) << right << balance << endl;
112   }
```

```
Enter request
 1 - List accounts with zero balances
 2 - List accounts with credit balances
 3 - List accounts with debit balances
 4 - End of run
? 1

Accounts with zero balances:
300       White           0.00

Enter request
 1 - List accounts with zero balances
 2 - List accounts with credit balances
 3 - List accounts with debit balances
 4 - End of run
? 2

Accounts with credit balances:
400       Stone          -42.16

Enter request
 1 - List accounts with zero balances
 2 - List accounts with credit balances
 3 - List accounts with debit balances
 4 - End of run
? 3

Accounts with debit balances:
100       Jones          24.98
200       Doe            345.67
500       Rich           224.62

Enter request
 1 - List accounts with zero balances
 2 - List accounts with credit balances
 3 - List accounts with debit balances
 4 - End of run
? 4
End of run.
```

Fig. 14.6 | Credit inquiry program. (Part 4 of 4.)

14.5 C++14: Reading and Writing Quoted Text

Many text files contain quoted text, such as "C++ How to Program". For example, in files representing HTML5 web pages, attribute values are enclosed in quotes. If you're building a web browser to display the contents of such a web page, you must be able to read those quoted strings and remove the quotes.

Suppose you need to read from a text file, as you did in Fig. 14.5, but with each account's data formatted as follows:

```
100 "Janie Jones" 24.98
```

Recall that the stream extraction operator >> treats white space as a delimiter. So, if we read the preceding data using the expression in line 30 of Fig. 14.5

```
inClientFile >> account >> name >> balance
```

the first stream extraction reads 100 into the int variable account and the second reads only "Janie into the string variable name (the opening double quote would be part of the string in name). The third stream extraction fails while attempting to read a value for the double variable balance, because the next token (i.e., piece of data) in the input stream— Jones"—is not a double.

Reading Quoted Text

C++14's new stream manipulator—quoted (header <iomanip>)—enables a program to read quoted text from a stream, *including* any white space characters in the quoted text, and discards the double quote delimiters. For example, if we read the preceding data using the expression

```
inClientFile >> account >> quoted(name) >> balance
```

the first stream extraction reads 100 into account, the second reads Janie Jones as one string and stores it in name without the double-quote delimiters, and the third stream extraction reads 24.98 into balance. If the quoted data contains \" escape sequences, each is read and stored in the string as the escape sequence \"—not as ".

Writing Quoted Text

Similarly, you can write quoted text to a stream. For example, if name contains Janie Jones, the statement

```
outputStream << quoted(name);
```

writes to the text-based outputStream

```
"Janie Jones"
```

14.6 Updating Sequential Files

Data that is formatted and written to a sequential file as shown in Section 14.3 cannot be modified without the risk of destroying other data in the file. For example, if the name "White" needs to be changed to "Worthington," the old name cannot be overwritten without corrupting the file. The record for White was written to the file as

```
300 White 0.00
```

If this record were rewritten beginning at the same location in the file using the longer name, the record would be

```
300 Worthington 0.00
```

The new record contains six more characters than the original record. Therefore, the characters beyond the "h" in "Worthington" would overwrite the 0.00 and the beginning of the next sequential record in the file. The problem is that, in the formatted input/output model using the stream insertion operator << and the stream extraction operator >>, fields—and hence records—can *vary* in size. For example, values 7, 14, –117, 2074, and 27383 are all ints, which store the same number of "raw data" bytes internally (typically four bytes on 32-bit machines and potentially eight bytes on some 64-bit machines). However, these integers become different-sized fields, depending on their actual values, when output as formatted text (character sequences). Therefore, the formatted input/output model usually is not used to update records *in place*. Sections 14.7–14.11 show how to perform in-place updates with fixed-length records.

Such updating can be done, but awkwardly. For example, to make the preceding name change, the records before 300 White 0.00 in a sequential file could be *copied* to a new file, the updated record then written to the new file, and the records after 300 White 0.00 copied to the new file. Then the old file could be deleted and the new file renamed. This requires processing *every* record in the file to update one record. If many records are being updated in one pass of the file, though, this technique can be acceptable.

14.7 Random-Access Files

So far, we've seen how to create sequential files and search them to locate information. Sequential files are inappropriate for instant-access applications, in which a particular record must be located immediately. Common instant-access applications are airline reservation systems, banking systems, point-of-sale systems, automated teller machines and other kinds of transaction-processing systems that require rapid access to specific data. A bank might have hundreds of thousands (or even millions) of other customers, yet, when a customer uses an automated teller machine, the program checks that customer's almost instantly for sufficient funds. This kind of instant access is made possible with random-access files. Individual records of a random-access file can be accessed directly (and quickly) without having to search other records.

As we've said, C++ does not impose structure on a file. So the application that wants to use random-access files must create them. A variety of techniques can be used. Perhaps the easiest method is to require that all records in a file be of the *same fixed length*. Using same-size, fixed-length records makes it easy for a program to quickly calculate (as a function of the record size and the record key) the exact location of any record relative to the beginning of the file. We'll soon see how this facilitates *immediate access* to specific records, even in enormous files.

Figure 14.7 illustrates C++'s view of a random-access file composed of fixed-length records (each record, in this case, is 100 bytes long). A random-access file is like a railroad train with many same-size cars—some empty and some with contents.

Data can be inserted into a random-access file without destroying other data in the file. Data stored previously also can be updated or deleted without rewriting the entire file. In the following sections, we explain how to create a random-access file, enter data into the file, read the data both sequentially and randomly, update the data and delete data that is no longer needed.

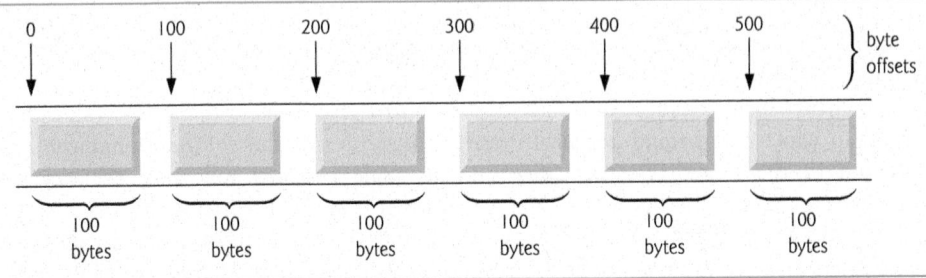

Fig. 14.7 | C++ view of a random-access file.

14.8 Creating a Random-Access File

The ostream member function write outputs to the specified stream a fixed number of bytes, beginning at a specific location in memory. When the stream is associated with a file, function write writes the data *at the location in the file specified by the put file-position pointer*. The istream member function read inputs a fixed number of bytes from the specified stream to an area in memory beginning at a specified address. If the stream is associated with a file, function read inputs bytes at the location in the file specified by the "get" file-position pointer.

14.8.1 Writing Bytes with ostream Member Function write

Writing the integer number to a file using the statement

```
outFile << number;
```

for a four-byte integer could output 1 to 11 bytes—up to 10 digits for a number in the range –2,147,483,647 to 2,147,483,647, plus a sign for a negative number. Instead, we can use the statement

```
outFile.write(
    reinterpret_cast<const char*>(&number), sizeof(number));
```

which always writes in *binary* the *four* bytes used that represent the integer number. Function write treats its first argument as a group of bytes by viewing the object in memory as a const char*, which is a pointer to a byte (recall that a char is 1 byte). Starting from that location, function write outputs the number of bytes specified by its second argument—an integer of type size_t. As we'll see, istream function read can subsequently be used to read the four bytes back into integer variable number.

14.8.2 Converting Between Pointer Types with the reinterpret_cast Operator

Unfortunately, most pointers that we pass to function write as the first argument are *not* of type const char*. To output objects of other types, we must convert the pointers to those objects to type const char*; otherwise, the compiler will not compile calls to function write. C++ provides the reinterpret_cast operator for cases like this to make it clear that you're treating data as an *unrelated* type. Without a reinterpret_cast, the write statement that outputs the integer number will not compile because the compiler does *not* allow a pointer of type int* (the type returned by the expression &number) to be passed to a function that expects an argument of type const char*—as far as the compiler is concerned, these types are *inconsistent* (that is, not compatible).

A reinterpret_cast is performed at *compile time* and does *not* change the value of the object to which its operand points. Instead, it requests that the compiler reinterpret the operand as the target type (specified in the angle brackets following the keyword reinterpret_cast). In Fig. 14.10, we use reinterpret_cast to convert a ClientData pointer to a const char*, which reinterprets a ClientData object as its bytes that should be output to a file. Random-access file-processing programs rarely write a single field to a file. Typically, they write one object of a class at a time, as we show in the following examples.

Error-Prevention Tip 14.3

Unfortunately, it's easy to use reinterpret_cast to perform dangerous manipulations that could lead to serious execution-time errors.

Portability Tip 14.1

reinterpret_cast is compiler dependent and can cause programs to behave differently on different platforms. Use this operator only if it's absolutely necessary.

Portability Tip 14.2

A program that reads unformatted data (written by write) must be compiled and execut-ed on a system compatible with the program that wrote the data, because different systems may represent internal data differently.

14.8.3 Credit-Processing Program

Consider the following problem statement:

> *Using random-access file-processing techniques, create a credit-processing program capable of storing at most 100 fixed-length records for a company that can have up to 100 customers. Each record should consist of an account number that acts as the record key, a last name, a first name and a balance. The program should be able to update an account, insert a new account, delete an account and insert all the account records into a formatted text file for printing.*

The next few sections create this credit-processing program. Figure 14.10 illustrates open-ing a random-access file, defining the record format using an object of class ClientData (Figs. 14.8–14.9) and writing data to the disk in *binary* format. This program initializes all 100 records of the file credit.dat with *empty* objects, using function write. Each emp-ty object contains the account number 0, empty last- and first-name strings and the bal-ance 0.0.

```
1   // Fig. 14.8: ClientData.h
2   // Class ClientData definition used in Fig. 14.10-Fig. 14.13.
3   #ifndef CLIENTDATA_H
4   #define CLIENTDATA_H
5
6   #include <string>
```

Fig. 14.8 | Class ClientData definition used in Fig. 14.10–Fig. 14.13. (Part 1 of 2.)

```
7
8    class ClientData {
9    public:
10       // default ClientData constructor
11       ClientData(int = 0, const std::string& = "",
12          const std::string& = "", double = 0.0);
13
14       // accessor functions for accountNumber
15       void setAccountNumber(int);
16       int getAccountNumber() const;
17
18       // accessor functions for lastName
19       void setLastName(const std::string&);
20       std::string getLastName() const;
21
22       // accessor functions for firstName
23       void setFirstName(const std::string&);
24       std::string getFirstName() const;
25
26       // accessor functions for balance
27       void setBalance(double);
28       double getBalance() const;
29    private:
30       int accountNumber;
31       char lastName[15];
32       char firstName[10];
33       double balance;
34    };
35
36    #endif
```

Fig. 14.8 | Class ClientData definition used in Fig. 14.10–Fig. 14.13. (Part 2 of 2.)

```
1    // Fig. 14.9: ClientData.cpp
2    // Class ClientData stores customer's credit information.
3    #include <string>
4    #include "ClientData.h"
5    using namespace std;
6
7    // default ClientData constructor
8    ClientData::ClientData(int accountNumberValue, const string& lastName,
9       const string& firstName, double balanceValue)
10       : accountNumber(accountNumberValue), balance(balanceValue) {
11       setLastName(lastName);
12       setFirstName(firstName);
13    }
14
15    // get account-number value
16    int ClientData::getAccountNumber() const {return accountNumber;}
17
```

Fig. 14.9 | ClientData class stores a customer's credit information. (Part 1 of 2.)

```
18   // set account-number value
19   void ClientData::setAccountNumber(int accountNumberValue) {
20      accountNumber = accountNumberValue; // should validate
21   }
22
23   // get last-name value
24   string ClientData::getLastName() const {return lastName;}
25
26   // set last-name value
27   void ClientData::setLastName(const string& lastNameString) {
28      // copy at most 15 characters from string to lastName
29      size_t length{lastNameString.size()};
30      length = (length < 15 ? length : 14);
31      lastNameString.copy(lastName, length);
32      lastName[length] = '\0'; // append null character to lastName
33   }
34
35   // get first-name value
36   string ClientData::getFirstName() const {return firstName;}
37
38   // set first-name value
39   void ClientData::setFirstName(const string& firstNameString) {
40      // copy at most 10 characters from string to firstName
41      size_t length{firstNameString.size()};
42      length = (length < 10 ? length : 9);
43      firstNameString.copy(firstName, length);
44      firstName[length] = '\0'; // append null character to firstName
45   }
46
47   // get balance value
48   double ClientData::getBalance() const {return balance;}
49
50   // set balance value
51   void ClientData::setBalance(double balanceValue) {balance = balanceValue;}
```

Fig. 14.9 | ClientData class stores a customer's credit information. (Part 2 of 2.)

Objects of class string *do not have uniform size*, rather they use dynamically allocated memory to accommodate strings of various lengths. We must maintain fixed-length records, so class ClientData stores the client's first and last name in fixed-length char arrays (declared in Fig. 14.8, lines 31–32). Member functions setLastName (Fig. 14.9, lines 27–33) and setFirstName (Fig. 14.9, lines 39–45) each copy the characters of a string object into the corresponding char array. Consider function setLastName. Line 29 invokes the string member function size to get the length of lastNameString. Line 30 ensures that the length is fewer than 15 characters, then line 31 copies length characters from lastNameString into the char array lastName using string member function copy. Line 32 inserts a null character into the char array to terminate the pointer-based string in lastName. Member function setFirstName performs the same steps for the first name.

14.8.4 Opening a File for Output in Binary Mode

In Fig. 14.10, line 10 creates an ofstream object for the file credit.dat. The second argument to the constructor—ios::out | ios::binary—indicates that we are opening the file for output in *binary mode*, which is *required* if we are to write *fixed-length records*. Multiple file-open modes are combined by separating each open mode from the next with the | operator, which is known as the *bitwise inclusive OR operator*. (Chapter 22 discusses this operator in detail.) Lines 22–23 cause the blankClient (which was constructed with default arguments at line 18) to be written to the credit.dat file associated with ofstream object outCredit. Remember that operator sizeof returns the size in bytes of the object contained in parentheses (see Chapter 8). The first argument to function write must be of type const char*. However, the data type of &blankClient is ClientData*. To convert &blankClient to const char*, line 23 uses the reinterpret_cast operator, so the call to write compiles without issuing a compilation error.

```cpp
1   // Fig. 14.10: Fig14_10.cpp
2   // Creating a randomly accessed file.
3   #include <iostream>
4   #include <fstream>
5   #include <cstdlib>
6   #include "ClientData.h" // ClientData class definition
7   using namespace std;
8
9   int main() {
10      ofstream outCredit{"credit.dat", ios::out | ios::binary};
11
12      // exit program if ofstream could not open file
13      if (!outCredit) {
14         cerr << "File could not be opened." << endl;
15         exit(EXIT_FAILURE);
16      }
17
18      ClientData blankClient; // constructor zeros out each data member
19
20      // output 100 blank records to file
21      for (int i{0}; i < 100; ++i) {
22         outCredit.write(
23            reinterpret_cast<const char*>(&blankClient), sizeof(ClientData));
24      }
25   }
```

Fig. 14.10 | Creating a random-access file with 100 blank records sequentially.

14.9 Writing Data Randomly to a Random-Access File

Figure 14.11 writes data to the file credit.dat and uses the combination of fstream functions seekp and write to store data at *exact* locations in the file. Function seekp sets the *put* file-position pointer to a specific position in the file, then function write outputs the data. Line 6 includes the header ClientData.h defined in Fig. 14.8, so the program can use ClientData objects.

```cpp
 1   // Fig. 14.11: Fig14_11.cpp
 2   // Writing to a random-access file.
 3   #include <iostream>
 4   #include <fstream>
 5   #include <cstdlib>
 6   #include "ClientData.h" // ClientData class definition
 7   using namespace std;
 8
 9   int main() {
10      fstream outCredit{"credit.dat", ios::in | ios::out | ios::binary};
11
12      // exit program if fstream cannot open file
13      if (!outCredit) {
14         cerr << "File could not be opened." << endl;
15         exit(EXIT_FAILURE);
16      }
17
18      cout << "Enter account number (1 to 100, 0 to end input)\n? ";
19
20      int accountNumber;
21      string lastName;
22      string firstName;
23      double balance;
24
25      cin >> accountNumber; // read account number
26
27      // user enters information, which is copied into file
28      while (accountNumber > 0 && accountNumber <= 100) {
29         // user enters last name, first name and balance
30         cout << "Enter lastname, firstname and balance\n? ";
31         cin >> lastName;
32         cin >> firstName;
33         cin >> balance;
34
35         // create ClientData object
36         ClientData client{accountNumber, lastName, firstName, balance};
37
38         // seek position in file of user-specified record
39         outCredit.seekp(
40            (client.getAccountNumber() - 1) * sizeof(ClientData));
41
42
43         // write user-specified information in file
44         outCredit.write(
45            reinterpret_cast<const char*>(&client), sizeof(ClientData));
46
47         // enable user to enter another account
48         cout << "Enter account number\n? ";
49         cin >> accountNumber;
50      }
51   }
```

Fig. 14.11 | Writing to a random-access file. (Part 1 of 2.)

```
Enter account number (1 to 100, 0 to end input)
? 37
Enter lastname, firstname and balance
? Barker Doug 0.00
Enter account number
? 29
Enter lastname, firstname and balance
? Brown Nancy -24.54
Enter account number
? 96
Enter lastname, firstname and balance
? Stone Sam 34.98
Enter account number
? 88
Enter lastname, firstname and balance
? Smith Dave 258.34
Enter account number
? 33
Enter lastname, firstname and balance
? Dunn Stacey 314.33
Enter account number
? 0
```

Fig. 14.11 | Writing to a random-access file. (Part 2 of 2.)

14.9.1 Opening a File for Input and Output in Binary Mode

Line 10 uses the fstream object outCredit to open the existing credit.dat file. The file is opened for input and output in *binary mode* by combining the file-open modes ios::in, ios::out and ios::binary. Note that because we include ios::in, if the file does *not* exist, an error will occur and the file will not be opened. Opening the existing credit.dat file in this manner ensures that this program can manipulate the records written to the file by the program of Fig. 14.10, rather than creating the file from scratch.

14.9.2 Positioning the File-Position Pointer

Lines 39–40 position the *put* file-position pointer for object outCredit to the byte location calculated by

```
(client.getAccountNumber() - 1) * sizeof(ClientData)
```

Because the account number is between 1 and 100, we subtract 1 from the account number when calculating the byte location of the record. Thus, for record 1, the file-position pointer is set to byte 0—the beginning of the file. For record 2, the the file-position pointer is set to 1 * sizeof(ClientData), and so on.

14.10 Reading from a Random-Access File Sequentially

In the previous sections, we created a random-access file and wrote data to that file. In this section, we develop a program that reads the file sequentially and prints only those records that contain data. These programs produce an additional benefit. See if you can determine what it is; we'll reveal it at the end of this section.

The istream function read inputs a specified number of bytes from the current position in the stream into an object. For example, line 28 (Fig. 14.12) reads the number of sizeof(ClientData) bytes from the file associated with inCredit and stores the data in client. Function read requires a first argument of type char*. Since &client is of type ClientData*, &client must be cast to char* using the cast operator reinterpret_cast.

```cpp
1   // Fig. 14.12: Fig14_12.cpp
2   // Reading a random-access file sequentially.
3   #include <iostream>
4   #include <iomanip>
5   #include <fstream>
6   #include <cstdlib>
7   #include "ClientData.h" // ClientData class definition
8   using namespace std;
9
10  void outputLine(ostream&, const ClientData&); // prototype
11
12  int main() {
13     ifstream inCredit{"credit.dat", ios::in | ios::binary};
14
15     // exit program if ifstream cannot open file
16     if (!inCredit) {
17        cerr << "File could not be opened." << endl;
18        exit(EXIT_FAILURE);
19     }
20
21     // output column heads
22     cout << left << setw(10) << "Account" << setw(16) << "Last Name"
23        << setw(11) << "First Name" << setw(10) << right << "Balance\n";
24
25     ClientData client; // create record
26
27     // read first record from file
28     inCredit.read(reinterpret_cast<char*>(&client), sizeof(ClientData));
29
30     // read all records from file
31     while (inCredit) {
32        // display record
33        if (client.getAccountNumber() != 0) {
34           outputLine(cout, client);
35        }
36
37        // read next from file
38        inCredit.read(reinterpret_cast<char*>(&client), sizeof(ClientData));
39     }
40  }
41
42  // display single record
43  void outputLine(ostream& output, const ClientData& record) {
44     output << left << setw(10) << record.getAccountNumber()
45        << setw(16) << record.getLastName()
46        << setw(11) << record.getFirstName()
47        << setw(10) << setprecision(2) << right << fixed
48        << showpoint << record.getBalance() << endl;
49  }
```

Fig. 14.12 | Reading a random-access file sequentially. (Part 1 of 2.)

Account	Last Name	First Name	Balance
29	Brown	Nancy	-24.54
33	Dunn	Stacey	314.33
37	Barker	Doug	0.00
88	Smith	Dave	258.34
96	Stone	Sam	34.98

Fig. 14.12 | Reading a random-access file sequentially. (Part 2 of 2.)

Figure 14.12 reads every record in the credit.dat file sequentially, checks each record to determine whether it contains data, and displays formatted outputs for records containing data. The condition in line 31 implicitly uses the stream's operator bool to determine whether the end of file was reached or whether an error occurred when reading from the file—in both cases the while statement terminates. The data input from the file is output by function outputLine (lines 43–49), which takes two arguments—a reference to an ostream object and a clientData structure to be output. The ostream parameter type is interesting, because any ostream object (such as cout) or any object of a derived class of ostream (such as an object of type ofstream) can be supplied as the argument. This means that the *same* function can be used, for example, to perform output to the standard-output stream and to a file stream without writing separate functions.

What about that additional benefit we promised at the beginning of this section? If you examine the output window, you'll notice that the records are listed in *sorted order* (by account number). This is a consequence of how we stored these records in the file, using direct-access techniques. Sorting using direct-access techniques is relatively fast. *The speed is achieved by making the file large enough to hold every possible record that might be created.* This, of course, means that the file could be occupied *sparsely* most of the time, resulting in a waste of storage. This is an example of the *space–time trade-off:* By using *large amounts of space*, we can develop *a much faster sorting algorithm.* Fortunately, the continuous reduction in price of storage units has made this less of an issue.

14.11 Case Study: A Transaction-Processing Program

We now present a substantial transaction-processing program (Fig. 14.13) using a random-access file to achieve instant-access processing. The program maintains a bank's account information. It updates existing accounts, adds new accounts, deletes accounts and stores a formatted listing of all current accounts in a text file. We assume that the program of Fig. 14.10 has been executed to create the file credit.dat and that the program of Fig. 14.11 has been executed to insert the initial data. Line 25 opens the credit.dat file by creating an fstream object for both reading and writing in binary format.

```
1   // Fig. 14.13: Fig14_13.cpp
2   // This program reads a random-access file sequentially, updates
3   // data previously written to the file, creates data to be placed
4   // in the file, and deletes data previously stored in the file.
```

Fig. 14.13 | Bank-account program. (Part 1 of 6.)

```
 5   #include <iostream>
 6   #include <fstream>
 7   #include <iomanip>
 8   #include <cstdlib>
 9   #include "ClientData.h" // ClientData class definition
10   using namespace std;
11
12   enum class Choice {PRINT = 1, UPDATE, NEW, DELETE, END};
13
14   Choice enterChoice();
15   void createTextFile(fstream&);
16   void updateRecord(fstream&);
17   void newRecord(fstream&);
18   void deleteRecord(fstream&);
19   void outputLine(ostream&, const ClientData& );
20   int getAccount(const char* const);
21
22   int main() {
23
24      // open file for reading and writing
25      fstream inOutCredit{"credit.dat", ios::in | ios::out | ios::binary};
26
27      // exit program if fstream cannot open file
28      if (!inOutCredit) {
29         cerr << "File could not be opened." << endl;
30         exit (EXIT_FAILURE);
31      }
32
33      Choice choice; // store user choice
34
35      // enable user to specify action
36      while ((choice = enterChoice()) != Choice::END) {
37         switch (choice) {
38            case Choice::PRINT: // create text file from record file
39               createTextFile(inOutCredit);
40               break;
41            case Choice::UPDATE: // update record
42               updateRecord(inOutCredit);
43               break;
44            case Choice::NEW: // create record
45               newRecord(inOutCredit);
46               break;
47            case Choice::DELETE: // delete existing record
48               deleteRecord(inOutCredit);
49               break;
50            default: // display error if user does not select valid choice
51               cerr << "Incorrect choice" << endl;
52               break;
53         }
54
55         inOutCredit.clear(); // reset end-of-file indicator
56      }
57   }
```

Fig. 14.13 | Bank-account program. (Part 2 of 6.)

```
58
59   // enable user to input menu choice
60   Choice enterChoice() {
61      // display available options
62      cout << "\nEnter your choice\n"
63         << "1 - store a formatted text file of accounts\n"
64         << "    called \"print.txt\" for printing\n"
65         << "2 - update an account\n"
66         << "3 - add a new account\n"
67         << "4 - delete an account\n"
68         << "5 - end program\n? ";
69
70      int menuChoice;
71      cin >> menuChoice; // input menu selection from user
72      return static_cast<Choice>(menuChoice);
73   }
74
75   // create formatted text file for printing
76   void createTextFile(fstream& readFromFile) {
77      ofstream outPrintFile("print.txt", ios::out); // create text file
78
79      // exit program if ofstream cannot create file
80      if (!outPrintFile) {
81         cerr << "File could not be created." << endl;
82         exit(EXIT_FAILURE);
83      }
84
85      // output column heads
86      outPrintFile << left << setw(10) << "Account" << setw(16)
87         << "Last Name" << setw(11) << "First Name" << right
88         << setw(10) << "Balance" << endl;
89
90      // set file-position pointer to beginning of readFromFile
91      readFromFile.seekg(0);
92
93      // read first record from record file
94      ClientData client;
95      readFromFile.read(
96         reinterpret_cast<char*>(&client), sizeof(ClientData));
97
98      // copy all records from record file into text file
99      while (!readFromFile.eof()) {
100        // write single record to text file
101        if (client.getAccountNumber() != 0) { // skip empty records
102           outputLine(outPrintFile, client);
103        }
104
105        // read next record from record file
106        readFromFile.read(
107           reinterpret_cast<char*>(&client), sizeof(ClientData));
108     }
109  }
110
```

Fig. 14.13 | Bank-account program. (Part 3 of 6.)

```
111   // update balance in record
112   void updateRecord(fstream& updateFile) {
113      // obtain number of account to update
114      int accountNumber{getAccount("Enter account to update")};
115
116      // move file-position pointer to correct record in file
117      updateFile.seekg((accountNumber - 1) * sizeof(ClientData));
118
119      // create record object and read first record from file
120      ClientData client;
121      updateFile.read(reinterpret_cast<char*>(&client), sizeof(ClientData));
122
123      // update record
124      if (client.getAccountNumber() != 0) {
125         outputLine(cout, client); // display the record
126
127         // request user to specify transaction
128         cout << "\nEnter charge (+) or payment (-): ";
129         double transaction; // charge or payment
130         cin >> transaction;
131
132         // update record balance
133         double oldBalance = client.getBalance();
134         client.setBalance(oldBalance + transaction);
135         outputLine(cout, client); // display the record
136
137         // move file-position pointer to correct record in file
138         updateFile.seekp((accountNumber - 1) * sizeof(ClientData));
139
140         // write updated record over old record in file
141         updateFile.write(
142            reinterpret_cast<const char*>(&client), sizeof(ClientData));
143      }
144      else { // display error if account does not exist
145         cerr << "Account #" << accountNumber
146            << " has no information." << endl;
147      }
148   }
149
150   // create and insert record
151   void newRecord(fstream& insertInFile) {
152      // obtain number of account to create
153      int accountNumber{getAccount("Enter new account number")};
154
155      // move file-position pointer to correct record in file
156      insertInFile.seekg((accountNumber - 1) * sizeof(ClientData));
157
158      // read record from file
159      ClientData client;
160      insertInFile.read(
161         reinterpret_cast<char*>(&client), sizeof(ClientData));
```

Fig. 14.13 | Bank-account program. (Part 4 of 6.)

```
162
163      // create record, if record does not previously exist
164      if (client.getAccountNumber() == 0) {
165         string lastName;
166         string firstName;
167         double balance;
168
169         // user enters last name, first name and balance
170         cout << "Enter lastname, firstname, balance\n? ";
171         cin >> setw(15) >> lastName;
172         cin >> setw(10) >> firstName;
173         cin >> balance;
174
175         // use values to populate account values
176         client.setLastName(lastName);
177         client.setFirstName(firstName);
178         client.setBalance(balance);
179         client.setAccountNumber(accountNumber);
180
181         // move file-position pointer to correct record in file
182         insertInFile.seekp((accountNumber - 1) * sizeof(ClientData));
183
184         // insert record in file
185         insertInFile.write(
186            reinterpret_cast<const char*>(&client), sizeof(ClientData));
187      }
188      else { // display error if account already exists
189         cerr << "Account #" << accountNumber
190            << " already contains information." << endl;
191      }
192   }
193
194   // delete an existing record
195   void deleteRecord(fstream& deleteFromFile) {
196      // obtain number of account to delete
197      int accountNumber{getAccount("Enter account to delete")};
198
199      // move file-position pointer to correct record in file
200      deleteFromFile.seekg((accountNumber - 1) * sizeof(ClientData));
201
202      // read record from file
203      ClientData client;
204      deleteFromFile.read(
205         reinterpret_cast<char*>(&client), sizeof(ClientData));
206
207      // delete record, if record exists in file
208      if (client.getAccountNumber() != 0) {
209         ClientData blankClient; // create blank record
210
211         // move file-position pointer to correct record in file
212         deleteFromFile.seekp((accountNumber - 1) * sizeof(ClientData));
213
```

Fig. 14.13 | Bank-account program. (Part 5 of 6.)

```
214          // replace existing record with blank record
215          deleteFromFile.write(
216             reinterpret_cast<const char*>(&blankClient), sizeof(ClientData));
217
218          cout << "Account #" << accountNumber << " deleted.\n";
219       }
220       else { // display error if record does not exist
221          cerr << "Account #" << accountNumber << " is empty.\n";
222       }
223    }
224
225    // display single record
226    void outputLine(ostream& output, const ClientData& record) {
227       output << left << setw(10) << record.getAccountNumber()
228          << setw(16) << record.getLastName()
229          << setw(11) << record.getFirstName()
230          << setw(10) << setprecision(2) << right << fixed
231          << showpoint << record.getBalance() << endl;
232    }
233
234    // obtain account-number value from user
235    int getAccount(const char* const prompt) {
236       int accountNumber;
237
238       // obtain account-number value
239       do {
240          cout << prompt << " (1 - 100): ";
241          cin >> accountNumber;
242       } while (accountNumber < 1 || accountNumber > 100);
243
244       return accountNumber;
245    }
```

Fig. 14.13 | Bank-account program. (Part 6 of 6.)

The program has five options (Option 5 is for terminating the program). Option 1 calls function createTextFile to store a formatted list of all the account information in a text file called print.txt that may be printed. Function createTextFile (lines 76–109) takes an fstream object as an argument to be used to input data from the credit.dat file. Function createTextFile invokes istream member function read (lines 95–96) and uses the sequential-file-access techniques of Fig. 14.12 to input data from credit.dat. Function outputLine, discussed in Section 14.10, outputs the data to file print.txt. Note that function createTextFile uses istream member function seekg (line 91) to ensure that the file-position pointer is at the beginning of the file before reading the file's contents. After choosing Option 1, the print.txt file contains

Account	Last Name	First Name	Balance
29	Brown	Nancy	-24.54
33	Dunn	Stacey	314.33
37	Barker	Doug	0.00
88	Smith	Dave	258.34
96	Stone	Sam	34.98

Option 2 calls updateRecord (lines 112–148) to update an account. This function updates only an *existing* record, so the function first determines whether the specified record is *empty*—we use function getAccount (lines 235–245) to read from the user the number of the record to update. Line 121 reads data into object client, using istream member function read. Then line 124 compares the value returned by getAccountNumber of the client object to zero to determine whether the record contains information. If this value is zero, lines 145–146 print an error message indicating that the record is empty. If the record contains information, line 125 displays the record, using function outputLine, line 130 inputs the transaction amount and lines 133–142 calculate the new balance and rewrite the record to the file. A typical execution for Option 2 is

```
Enter account to update (1 - 100): 37
37          Barker          Doug              0.00

Enter charge (+) or payment (-): +87.99
37          Barker          Doug             87.99
```

Option 3 calls function newRecord (lines 151–192) to add a new account to the file. If the user enters an account number for an *existing* account, newRecord displays an error message indicating that the account exists (lines 189–190). This function adds a new account in the same manner as the program of Fig. 14.11. A typical execution for Option 3 is

```
Enter new account number (1 - 100): 22
Enter lastname, firstname, balance
? Johnston Sarah 247.45
```

Option 4 calls function deleteRecord (lines 195–223) to delete a record from the file. Line 197 prompts the user to enter the account number. Only an *existing* record may be deleted, so, if the specified account is empty, line 221 displays an error message. If the account exists, lines 209–216 reinitialize that account by writing an empty record (blank-Client) to the file. Line 218 displays a message to inform the user that the record has been deleted. A typical execution for Option 4 is

```
Enter account to delete (1 - 100): 29
Account #29 deleted.
```

14.12 Object Serialization

This chapter and Chapter 13 introduced the object-oriented style of input/output. In Chapter 10, we showed how to input and output objects using operator overloading. We accomplished object input by overloading the stream extraction operator, >>, for the appropriate istream. We accomplished object output by overloading the stream insertion operator, <<, for the appropriate ostream. In both cases, only an object's data members were input or output, and, in each case, they were in a format meaningful only for objects of that particular type. An object's member functions are *not* input or output with the object's data; rather, *one copy of the class's member functions remains available internally and is shared by all objects of the class.*

When object data members are output to a disk file, we *lose* the object's type information. We store only the values of the object's attributes, not type information, on the disk. If the program that reads this data knows the object type to which the data corresponds, the program can read the data into an object of that type as we did in our random-access file examples. However, our random-access files are not portable, because the size of a ClientData object is platform dependent.

An interesting problem occurs when we store objects of different types in the same file. How can we distinguish them (or their collections of data members) as we read them into a program? The problem is that objects typically do *not* have type fields (we discussed this issue in Chapter 12).

One approach used by several programming languages is called object serialization. A so-called serialized object is an object represented in a *platform-independent* manner as a sequence of bytes that includes the object's *data* as well as information about the object's *type* and the *types of data stored in the object.* After a serialized object has been written to a file, it can be read from the file and deserialized—that is, the type information and bytes that represent the object and its data can be used to *recreate* the object in memory. C++ does *not* provide a built-in serialization mechanism; however, there are third-party and open-source C++ libraries that support object serialization. The open-source Boost C++ Libraries (www.boost.org) provide support for serializing objects in text, binary and extensible markup language (XML) formats (www.boost.org/libs/serialization/doc/index.html).

14.13 Wrap-Up

In this chapter, we presented various file-processing techniques to manipulate persistent data. We discussed both character-based and byte-based streams, and considered various file-processing class templates in header <fstream>. You learned how to use sequential file processing to manipulate records stored in order, by a record-key field. You also learned how to use random-access files to "instantly" retrieve and manipulate fixed-length records. We presented a substantial transaction-processing program using a random-access file to achieve "instant-access" processing. Finally, we discussed the basic concepts of object serialization.

We introduced the Standard Library array and vector classes in Chapter 7. In the next chapter, you'll learn about the Standard Library's other predefined data structures (known as containers) as well as the basics of iterators, which are used to manipulate container elements.

Summary

Section 14.1 Introduction
- Files are used for **data persistence** (p. 616)—permanent retention of data.
- Computers store files on **secondary storage devices** (p. 616), such as hard disks, CDs, DVDs, flash memory and tapes.

Section 14.2 Files and Streams

- C++ views each file simply as a sequence of bytes.

- Each file ends either with an end-of-file marker or at a specific byte number recorded in a system-maintained, administrative data structure.

- When a file is opened, an object is created, and a stream is associated with the object.

- To perform file processing in C++, headers `<iostream>` and `<fstream>` must be included.

- Header `<fstream>` includes the definitions for the stream class templates `basic_ifstream` (for file input), `basic_ofstream` (for file output) and `basic_fstream` (for file input and output).

- Each class template has a predefined template specialization that enables char I/O. The `<fstream>` library provides `typedef` aliases for these template specializations. The `typedef` `ifstream` represents a specialization of `basic_ifstream` that enables char input from a file. The `typedef` `ofstream` represents a specialization of `basic_ofstream` that enables char output to files. The `typedef` `fstream` represents a specialization of `basic_fstream` that enables char input from, and output to, files.

- The file-processing templates derive from class templates `basic_istream`, `basic_ostream` and `basic_iostream`, respectively. Thus, all member functions, operators and manipulators that belong to these templates also can be applied to file streams.

Section 14.3 Creating a Sequential File

- C++ imposes no structure on a file; you must structure files to meet the application's requirements.

- A file can be opened for output when an `ofstream` object is created. Two arguments are passed to the object's constructor—the **filename** (p. 618) and the **file-open mode** (p. 618).

- For an **ofstream** (p. 618) object, the file-open mode can be either `ios::out` (p. 618) to output data to a file or **ios::app** (p. 618) to append data to the end of a file. Existing files opened with mode `ios::out` are **truncated** (p. 619). If the specified file does not exist, the `ofstream` object creates the file using that filename.

- By default, `ofstream` objects are opened for output.

- An `ofstream` object can be created without opening a specific file—a file can be attached to the object later with member function **open** (p. 619).

- The overloaded operator ! for a stream determines whether a stream was opened correctly. This operator can be used in a condition that returns *true* if either the `failbit` or the `badbit` is set for the stream on the open operation.

- The overloaded operator `bool` for a stream converts the stream to `true` or `false`. If the `failbit` or `badbit` has been set for a stream, `false` is returned.

- Entering the end-of-file indicator sets the `failbit` for `cin`.

- The `operator bool` function can be used to test an input object for end-of-file instead of calling the `eof` member function explicitly on the input object.

- When a stream object's destructor is called, the corresponding stream is closed. You also can close the stream object explicitly, using the stream's `close` member function.

Section 14.4 Reading Data from a Sequential File

- Files store data so it may be retrieved for processing when needed.

- Creating an `ifstream` object opens a file for input. The `ifstream` constructor can receive the filename and the file open mode as arguments.

- Open a file for input only if the file's contents should not be modified.

- Objects of class `ifstream` are opened for input by default.

- An ifstream object can be created without opening a specific file; a file can be attached to it later.

- To retrieve data sequentially from a file, programs normally start reading from the beginning of the file and read all the data consecutively until the desired data is found.

- The member functions for repositioning the **file-position pointer** (p. 623) are **seekg** ("seek get"; p. 623) for istream and **seekp** ("seek put"; p. 623) for ostream. Each istream has a "get pointer," which indicates the byte number in the file from which the next input is to occur, and each ostream has a "put pointer," which indicates the byte number in the file at which the next output should be placed.

- The argument to **seekg** (p. 623) is a long integer. A second argument can be specified to indicate the **seek direction** (p. 623), which can be **ios::beg** (the default; p. 623) for positioning relative to the beginning of a stream, **ios::cur** (p. 623) for positioning relative to the current position in a stream or **ios::end** (p. 623) for positioning relative to the end of a stream.

- The **file-position pointer** (p. 623) is an integer value that specifies the location in the file as a number of bytes from the file's starting location (i.e., the **offset** (p. 623) from the beginning of the file).

- Member functions **tellg** (p. 623) and **tellp** (p. 623) are provided to return the current locations of the "get" and "put" pointers, respectively.

Section 14.5 C++14: Reading and Writing Quoted Text

- C++14's stream manipulator **quoted** (p. 627; header <iomanip>) enables a program to read quoted text from a stream, including any white space characters in the quoted text, and discards the double-quote delimiters.

- You also can use quoted to write quoted text to a stream.

Section 14.6 Updating Sequential Files

- Data that is formatted and written to a sequential file cannot be modified without the risk of destroying other data in the file. The problem is that records can vary in size.

Section 14.7 Random-Access Files

- Sequential files are inappropriate for **instant-access applications** (p. 628), in which a particular record must be located immediately.

- Instant access is made possible with **random-access files** (p. 628). Individual records of a random-access file can be accessed directly (and quickly) without having to search other records.

- The easiest method to format files for random access is to require that all records in a file be of the same fixed length. Using same-size, fixed-length records makes it easy for a program to calculate (as a function of the record size and the record key) the exact location of any record relative to the beginning of the file.

- Data can be inserted into a random-access file without destroying other data in the file.

- Data stored previously can be updated or deleted without rewriting the entire file.

Section 14.8 Creating a Random-Access File

- The ostream member function **write** outputs a fixed number of bytes, beginning at a specific location in memory, to the specified stream. Function write writes the data at the location in the file specified by the "put" file-position pointer.

- The istream member function **read** (p. 629) inputs a fixed number of bytes from the specified stream to an area in memory beginning at a specified address. If the stream is associated with a file, function read inputs bytes at the location in the file specified by the "get" file-position pointer.

- Function write treats its first argument as a group of bytes by viewing the object in memory as a const char*, which is a pointer to a byte (remember that a char is one byte). Starting from that location, function write outputs the number of bytes specified by its second argument. The istream function read can subsequently be used to read the bytes back into memory.

- The **reinterpret_cast** operator (p. 629) converts a pointer of one type to a pointer of an unrelated type.

- A reinterpret_cast is performed at compile time and does not change the value of the object to which its operand points.

- A program that reads unformatted data must be compiled and executed on a system compatible with the program that wrote the data—different systems may represent internal data differently.

- Objects of class string do not have uniform size, rather they use dynamically allocated memory to accommodate strings of various lengths.

Section 14.9 Writing Data Randomly to a Random-Access File
- Multiple file-open modes are combined by separating each open mode from the next with the bitwise inclusive-OR operator (|).

- The string member function **size** (p. 632) gets the length of a string.

- The file-open mode **ios::binary** (p. 633) indicates that a file should be opened in binary mode.

Section 14.10 Reading from a Random-Access File Sequentially
- A function that receives an ostream parameter can receive any ostream object (such as cout) or any object of a derived class of ostream (such as an object of type ofstream) as an argument. This means that the same function can be used, for example, to perform output to the standard-output stream and to a file stream without writing separate functions.

Section 14.12 Object Serialization
- When object data members are output to a disk file, we lose the object's type information. We store only the values of the object's attributes, not type information, on the disk. If the program that reads this data knows the object type to which the data corresponds, the program can read the data into an object of that type.

- A so-called **serialized object** (p. 644) is an object represented as a sequence of bytes that includes the object's data as well as information about the object's type and the types of data stored in the object. A serialized object can be read from the file and **deserialized** (p. 644).

- The open-source Boost Libraries provide support for **serializing objects** (p. 644) in text, binary and extensible markup language (XML) formats.

Self-Review Exercises

14.1 *(Fill in the Blanks)* Fill in the blanks in each of the following:
   a) Member function _____ of the file streams fstream, ifstream and ofstream closes a file.
   b) The ostream member function _____ is normally used when writing data to a file in random-access applications.
   c) Member function _____ of the file streams fstream, ifstream and ofstream opens a file.
   d) The istream member function _____ is normally used when reading data from a file in random-access applications.
   e) Member functions _____ and _____ of istream and ostream set the file-position pointer to a specific location in an input or output stream, respectively.

14.2 *(True or False)* State which of the following are *true* and which are *false*. If *false*, explain why.
   a) Member function read cannot be used to read data from the input object cin.

b) You must create the cin, cout, cerr and clog objects explicitly.

c) A program must call function close explicitly to close a file associated with an ifstream, ofstream or fstream object.

d) If the file-position pointer points to a location in a sequential file other than the beginning of the file, the file must be closed and reopened to read from the beginning of the file.

e) The ostream member function write can write to standard-output stream cout.

f) Data in sequential files always is updated without overwriting nearby data.

g) Searching all records in a random-access file to find a specific record is unnecessary.

h) Records in random-access files must be of uniform length.

i) Member functions seekp and seekg must seek relative to the beginning of a file.

14.3 Assume that each of the following statements applies to the same program.

a) Write a statement that opens file oldmast.dat for input; use an ifstream object called inOldMaster.

b) Write a statement that opens file trans.dat for input; use an ifstream object called inTransaction.

c) Write a statement that opens file newmast.dat for output (and creation); use ofstream object outNewMaster.

d) Write a statement that reads a record from the file oldmast.dat. The record consists of integer accountNumber, string name (containing spaces) and floating-point currentBalance. Use ifstream object inOldMaster.

e) Write a statement that reads a record from the file trans.dat. The record consists of integer accountNum and floating-point dollarAmount. Use ifstream object inTransaction.

f) Write a statement that writes a record to the file newmast.dat. The record consists of integer accountNum, string name, and floating-point currentBalance. Use ofstream object outNewMaster.

14.4 Find the error(s) and show how to correct it (them) in each of the following.

a) File payables.dat referred to by ofstream object outPayable has not been opened.

```
outPayable << account << company << amount << endl;
```

b) The following statement should read a record from the file payables.dat. The ifstream object inPayable refers to this file, and ifstream object inReceivable refers to the file receivables.dat.

```
inReceivable >> account >> company >> amount;
```

c) The file tools.dat should be opened to add data to the file without discarding the current data.

```
ofstream outTools("tools.dat", ios::out);
```

Answers to Self-Review Exercises

14.1 a) close. b) write. c) open. d) read. e) seekg, seekp.

14.2 a) False. Function read can read from any input stream object derived from istream.

b) False. These four streams are created automatically for you. The <iostream> header must be included in a file to use them. This header includes declarations for each predefined stream object.

c) False. The files will be closed when destructors for ifstream, ofstream or fstream objects execute when the stream objects go out of scope or before program execution terminates, but it's a good programming practice to close all files explicitly with close once they're no longer needed.

d) False. Member functions seekp and seekg can be used to reposition the "put" or "get" file-position pointers, respectively, to the beginning of the file.

e) True.

f) False. In most cases, sequential file records are not of uniform length. Therefore, it's possible that updating a record will cause other data to be overwritten.

g) True.

h) False. Records in a random-access file normally are of uniform length.

i) False. It's possible to seek from the beginning of the file, from the end of the file and from the current position in the file.

14.3 a) `ifstream inOldMaster{"oldmast.dat", ios::in};`
    b) `ifstream inTransaction{"trans.dat", ios::in};`
    c) `ofstream outNewMaster{"newmast.dat", ios::out};`
    d) `inOldMaster >> accountNumber >> quoted(name) >> currentBalance;`
    e) `inTransaction >> accountNum >> dollarAmount;`
    f) `outNewMaster << accountNum << " " << name << " " << currentBalance;`

14.4 a) *Error:* The file payables.dat has not been opened before the attempt is made to output data to the stream.
    Correction: Use ofstream function open to open payables.dat for output.
    b) *Error:* The incorrect ifstream object is being used to read a record from the file named payables.dat.
    Correction: Use ifstream object inPayable to refer to payables.dat.
    c) *Error:* The file's contents are discarded because the file is opened for output (ios::out).
    Correction: To add data to the file, open the file either for updating (ios::ate) or for appending (ios::app).

Exercises

14.5 *(Fill in the Blanks)* Fill in the blanks in each of the following:
    a) Computers store large amounts of data on secondary storage devices as _____.
    b) The standard stream objects declared by header <iostream> are _____, _____, _____ and _____.
    c) ostream member function _____ repositions the file-position pointer in a file.
    d) _____ is the default file-open mode for an ofstream.
    e) istream member function _____ repositions the file-position pointer in a file.

14.6 *(File Matching)* Exercise 14.3 asked you to write a series of single statements. Actually, these statements form the core of an important type of file-processing program, namely, a file-matching program. In commercial data processing, it's common to have several files in each application system. In an accounts-receivable system, for example, there is generally a master file containing detailed information about each customer, such as the customer's name, address, telephone number, outstanding balance, credit limit, discount terms, contract arrangements and, possibly, a condensed history of recent purchases and cash payments.

As transactions occur (e.g., sales are made and cash payments arrive), they're entered into a file. At the end of each business period (a month for some companies, a week for others and a day in some cases), the file of transactions (called trans.dat in Exercise 14.3) is applied to the master file (called oldmast.dat in Exercise 14.3), thus updating each account's record of purchases and payments. During an updating run, the master file is rewritten as a new file (newmast.dat), which is then used at the end of the next business period to begin the updating process again.

File-matching programs must deal with certain problems that do not exist in single-file programs. For example, a match does not always occur. A customer on the master file might not have made any purchases or cash payments in the current business period, and therefore no record for this customer will appear on the transaction file. Similarly, a customer who did make some pur-chases or cash payments may have just moved to this community, and the company may not have had a chance to create a master record for this customer.

Use the statements from Exercise 14.3 as a basis for writing a complete file-matching accounts-receivable program. Use the account number on each file as the record key for matching purposes. Assume that each file is a sequential file with records stored in increasing order by account number.

When a match occurs (i.e., records with the same account number appear on both the master and transaction files), add the dollar amount on the transaction file to the current balance on the master file, and write the newmast.dat record. (Assume purchases are indicated by positive amounts on the transaction file and payments are indicated by negative amounts.) When there is a master record for a particular account but no corresponding transaction record, merely write the master record to newmast.dat. When there is a transaction record but no corresponding master record, print the error message "Unmatched transaction record for account number ..." (fill in the account number from the transaction record).

14.7   **(File Matching Test Data)** After writing the program of Exercise 14.6, write a simple pro-gram to create some test data for checking out the program. Use the sample account data in Figs. 14.14–14.15.

Master file Account number	Name	Balance
100	Alan Jones	348.17
300	Mary Smith	27.19
500	Sam Sharp	0.00
700	Suzy Green	–14.22

Fig. 14.14 | Master file data.

Transaction file Account number	Transaction amount
100	27.14
300	62.11
400	100.56
900	82.17

Fig. 14.15 | Transaction file data.

14.8   **(File-Matching Test)** Run the program of Exercise 14.6, using the files of test data created in Exercise 14.7. Print the new master file. Check that the accounts have been updated correctly.

14.9   **(File-Matching Enhancement)** It's common to have several transaction records with the same record key, because a particular customer might make several purchases and cash payments during a business period. Rewrite your accounts-receivable file-matching program of Exercise 14.6 to provide for the possibility of handling several transaction records with the same record key. Mod-ify the test data of Exercise 14.7 to include the additional transaction records in Fig. 14.16.

Account number	Dollar amount
300	83.89
700	80.78
700	1.53

Fig. 14.16 | Transaction records to add.

14.10 Write a series of statements that accomplish each of the following. Assume that we've defined class Person that contains the private data members

```
char lastName[15];
char firstName[10];
int age;
int id;
```

and public member functions

```
// accessor functions for id
void setId(int);
int getId() const;

// accessor functions for lastName
void setLastName(const string&);
string getLastName() const;

// accessor functions for firstName
void setFirstName(const string&);
string getFirstName() const;

// accessor functions for age
void setAge(int);
int getAge() const;
```

Also assume that any random-access files have been opened properly.

a) Initialize nameage.dat with 100 records that store values lastName ="unassigned", firstName = "" and age = 0.

b) Input 10 last names, first names and ages, and write them to the file.

c) Update a record that already contains information. If the record does not contain information, inform the user "No info".

d) Delete a record that contains information by reinitializing that particular record.

14.11 *(Hardware Inventory)* You own a hardware store and need to keep an inventory that can tell you what different tools you have, how many of each you have on hand and the cost of each one. Write a program that initializes the random-access file hardware.dat to 100 empty records, lets you input the data concerning each tool, enables you to list all your tools, lets you delete a record for a tool that you no longer have and lets you update *any* information in the file. The tool identification number should be the record number. Use the information in Fig. 14.17 to start your file.

Record #	Tool name	Quantity	Cost
3	Electric sander	7	57.98
17	Hammer	76	11.99

Fig. 14.17 | Hardware inventory records. (Part 1 of 2.)

Record #	Tool name	Quantity	Cost
24	Jig saw	21	11.00
39	Lawn mower	3	79.50
56	Power saw	18	99.99
68	Screwdriver	106	6.99
77	Sledge hammer	11	21.50
83	Wrench	34	7.50

Fig. 14.17 | Hardware inventory records. (Part 2 of 2.)

14.12 (*Telephone-Number Word Generator*) Standard telephone keypads contain the digits 0 through 9. The numbers 2 through 9 each have three letters associated with them, as is indicated by the following table:

Digit	Letter	Digit	Letter
2	A B C	6	M N O
3	D E F	7	P Q R S
4	G H I	8	T U V
5	J K L	9	W X Y Z

Fig. 14.18 | Telephone digit-to-letter mappings.

Many people find it difficult to memorize phone numbers, so they use the correspondence between digits and letters to develop seven-letter words that correspond to their phone numbers. For example, a person whose telephone number is 686-2377 might use the correspondence indicated in the above table to develop the seven-letter word "NUMBERS."

Businesses frequently attempt to get telephone numbers that are easy for their clients to remember. If a business can advertise a simple word for its customers to dial, then no doubt the business will receive a few more calls. Each seven-letter word corresponds to exactly one seven-digit telephone number. The restaurant wishing to increase its take-home business could surely do so with the number 825-3688 (i.e., "TAKEOUT"). Each seven-digit phone number corresponds to many separate seven-letter words. Unfortunately, most of these represent unrecognizable juxtapositions of letters. It's possible, however, that the owner of a barber shop would be pleased to know that the shop's telephone number, 424-7288, corresponds to "HAIRCUT." A veterinarian with the phone number 738-2273 would be happy to know that the number corresponds to "PETCARE."

Write a program that, given a seven-digit number, writes to a file every possible seven-letter word corresponding to that number. There are 2187 (3 to the seventh power) such words. Avoid phone numbers with the digits 0 and 1.

14.13 (*sizeof Operator*) Write a program that uses the sizeof operator to determine the sizes in bytes of the various data types on your computer system. Write the results to the file data-size.dat, so that you may print the results later. The results should be displayed in two-column format with the type name in the left column and the size of the type in the right column, as in Fig. 14.19. [*Note:* The sizes of the built-in data types on your computer might differ from those listed here.]

```
char                     1
unsigned char            1
short int                2
unsigned short int       2
int                      4
unsigned int             4
long int                 4
unsigned long int        4
long long int            8
unsigned long long int   8
float                    4
double                   8
long double             10
```

Fig. 14.19 | Sample output for Exercise 14.13.

Making a Difference

14.14 *(Phishing Scanner)* Phishing is a form of identity theft in which, in an e-mail, a sender posing as a trustworthy source attempts to acquire private information, such as your user names, passwords, credit-card numbers and social security number. Phishing e-mails claiming to be from popular banks, credit-card companies, auction sites, social networks and online payment services may look quite legitimate. These fraudulent messages often provide links to spoofed (fake) websites where you're asked to enter sensitive information.

Visit www.snopes.com and other websites to find lists of the top phishing scams. Also check out the Anti-Phishing Working Group

> www.antiphishing.org/

and the FBI's Cyber Investigations website

> https://www.fbi.gov/about-us/investigate/cyber/cyber

where you'll find information about the latest scams and how to protect yourself.

Create a list of 30 words, phrases and company names commonly found in phishing messages. Assign a point value to each based on your estimate of its likeliness to be in a phishing message (e.g., one point if it's somewhat likely, two points if moderately likely, or three points if highly likely). Write a program that scans a file of text for these terms and phrases. For each occurrence of a keyword or phrase within the text file, add the assigned point value to the total points for that word or phrase. For each keyword or phrase found, output one line with the word or phrase, the number of occurrences and the point total. Then show the point total for the entire message. Does your program assign a high point total to some actual phishing e-mails you've received? Does it assign a high point total to some legitimate e-mails you've received?

Standard Library Containers and Iterators

Objectives

In this chapter you'll:

- Be introduced to the Standard Library containers, iterators and algorithms.

- Use the **vector**, **list** and **deque** sequence containers.

- Use the **set**, **multiset**, **map** and **multimap** associative containers.

- Use the **stack**, **queue** and **priority_queue** container adapters.

- Use iterators to access container elements.

- Use the **copy** algorithm and **ostream_iterators** to output a container.

- Understand how to use the **bitset** "near container" to manipulate a collection of bit flags.

15.1 Introduction

The Standard Library defines powerful, template-based, reusable components that implement many common data structures and algorithms used to process those data structures. We began introducing templates in Chapters 6–7 and use them extensively here and in Chapters 16, 18 and 19. Historically, the features presented in this chapter were often referred to as the *Standard Template Library* or *STL*.[1] We'll occasionally refer to these features as the STL. In the C++ standard document, these features are simply referred to as part of the C++ Standard Library.

Containers, Iterators and Algorithms

This chapter introduces three key components of the Standard Library—containers (*templatized* data structures), iterators and algorithms. Containers are data structures capable of storing objects of *almost* any data type (there are some restrictions). We'll see that there are three styles of container classes—*first-class containers, container adapters* and *near containers*.

Common Member Functions Among Containers

Each container has associated member functions—a subset of these is defined in *all* containers. We illustrate most of this common functionality in our examples of array (which was introduced in Chapter 7), vector (also introduced in Chapter 7 and covered in more depth here), list (Section 15.5.2) and deque (pronounced "deck"; Section 15.5.3).

Iterators

Iterators, which have properties similar to those of *pointers*, are used to manipulate container elements. *Built-in arrays* also can be manipulated by Standard Library algorithms, using pointers as iterators. We'll see that manipulating containers with iterators is convenient and provides tremendous expressive power when combined with Standard Library algorithms—in some cases, reducing many lines of code to a single statement.

---

1. The STL was developed by Alexander Stepanov and Meng Lee at Hewlett Packard and is based on their generic programming research, with significant contributions from David Musser.

Algorithms

Standard Library algorithms are function templates that perform such common data manipulations as *searching*, *sorting* and *comparing elements or entire containers*. The Standard Library provides many algorithms. Most of them use iterators to access container elements. Each algorithm has minimum requirements for the kinds of iterators that can be used with it. We'll see that containers support specific kinds of iterators, some more powerful than others. The iterators a *container* supports determine whether the container can be used with a specific algorithm. Iterators encapsulate the mechanisms used to traverse containers and access their elements. This encapsulation enables many of the algorithms to be applied to various containers *independently* of the underlying container implementation. This also enables you to create new algorithms that can process the elements of *multiple* container types.

Custom Templatized Data Structures

In Chapter 19, we'll build our own *custom* templatized data structures, including linked lists, queues, stacks and trees:

- Linked lists are collections of data items logically "lined up in a row"—insertions and removals are made *anywhere* in a linked list.

- *Stacks* are important in compilers and operating systems: Insertions and removals are made *only* at one end of a stack—its *top*. Section 6.11 discussed the importance of stacks in the function call and return mechanism.

- Queues represent *waiting lines*; insertions are made at the *back* (also referred to as the *tail*) of a queue and removals are made from the *front* (also referred to as the *head*) of a queue.

- Binary trees are nonlinear, hierarchical data structures that facilitate searching and sorting data, *duplicate elimination* and *compiling* expressions into machine code.

Each of these data structures has many other interesting applications. We'll carefully weave linked objects together with pointers. Pointer-based code is complex and can be error prone—the slightest omissions or oversights can lead to serious *memory-access violations* and *memory-leak* errors with no forewarning from the compiler. If many programmers on a large project implement custom containers and algorithms for different tasks, the code becomes difficult to modify, maintain and debug.

Software Engineering Observation 15.1
Avoid reinventing the wheel; when possible, program with the components of the C++ Standard Library.

Error-Prevention Tip 15.1
The prepackaged, templatized Standard Library containers are sufficient for most applications. Using the proven Standard Library containers, iterators and algorithms helps you reduce testing and debugging time.

Performance Tip 15.1
The Standard Library was conceived and designed for performance and flexibility.

15.2 Introduction to Containers[2]

The Standard Library container types are shown in Fig. 15.1. The containers are divided into four major categories—sequence containers, ordered associative containers, unordered associative containers and container adapters.

Container class	Description
Sequence containers	
array	Fixed size. Direct access to any element.
deque	Rapid insertions and deletions at front or back. Direct access to any element.
forward_list	Singly linked list, rapid insertion and deletion anywhere. Added in C++11.
list	Doubly linked list, rapid insertion and deletion anywhere.
vector	Rapid insertions and deletions at back. Direct access to any element.
Ordered associative containers—keys are maintained in sorted order	
set	Rapid lookup, no duplicates allowed.
multiset	Rapid lookup, duplicates allowed.
map	One-to-one mapping, no duplicates allowed, rapid key-based lookup.
multimap	One-to-many mapping, duplicates allowed, rapid key-based lookup.
Unordered associative containers	
unordered_set	Rapid lookup, no duplicates allowed.
unordered_multiset	Rapid lookup, duplicates allowed.
unordered_map	One-to-one mapping, no duplicates allowed, rapid key-based lookup.
unordered_multimap	One-to-many mapping, duplicates allowed, rapid key-based lookup.
Container adapters	
stack	Last-in, first-out (LIFO).
queue	First-in, first-out (FIFO).
priority_queue	Highest-priority element is always the first element out.

Fig. 15.1 | Standard Library container classes and container adapters.

Containers Overview

The *sequence containers* represent *linear* data structures (i.e., all of their elements are conceptually "lined up in a row"), such as arrays, vectors and linked lists. We'll study linked data structures in Chapter 19, Custom Templatized Data Structures. *Associative containers* are *nonlinear* data structures that typically can locate elements stored in the containers quickly. Such containers can store sets of values or key–value pairs in which each key has

---

2. This section is intended as an introduction to a reference-oriented chapter. You may want to read it quickly and refer back to it as necessary when reading the rest of the chapter. Starting in Section 15.3, we present concrete live-code examples.

an associated value—for example, a program might associate employee IDs with Employee objects. As you'll see, some associative containers allow multiple values for each key. The keys in associative containers are *immutable* (they cannot be modified) as of C++11. The sequence containers and associative containers are collectively referred to as the first-class containers. Stacks and queues are typically constrained versions of sequence containers. For this reason, the Standard Library implements class templates stack, queue and priority_queue as container adapters that enable a program to view a sequence container in a constrained manner. Class string supports the same functionality as a sequence container, but stores only character data.

Near Containers

There are other container types that are considered near containers—built-in arrays, bitsets for maintaining sets of flag values and valarrays for performing high-speed *mathematical vector* operations (not to be confused with the vector container). These types are considered *near containers* because they exhibit some, but not all, capabilities of the *first-class containers*.

Common Container Functions

Most containers provide similar functionality. Many operations apply to all containers, and other operations apply to subsets of similar containers. Figure 15.2 describes the many functions that are commonly available in most Standard Library containers. Overloaded operators <, <=, >, >=, == and != perform element-by-element comparisons. Overloaded operators <, <=, >, >=, == and != are *not* provided for priority_queues. Overloaded operators <, <=, > and >= are *not* provided for the *unordered associative containers*. Member functions rbegin, rend, crbegin and crend are *not* available in a forward_list. Before using any container, you should study its capabilities.

Member function	Description
default constructor	A constructor that *initializes an empty container*. Normally, each container has several constructors that provide different ways to initialize the container.
copy constructor	A constructor that initializes the container to be a *copy* of an existing container of the same type.
move constructor	A move constructor (added in C++11 and discussed in Chapter 24) moves the contents of an existing container into a new container of the same type—the old container no longer contains the data. This avoids the overhead of copying each element of the argument container.
destructor	Destructor function for cleanup after a container is no longer needed.
empty	Returns true if there are *no* elements in the container; otherwise, returns false.
insert	Inserts an item in the container.
size	Returns the number of elements currently in the container.

Fig. 15.2 | Common member functions for most Standard Library containers. (Part 1 of 2.)

Member function	Description
copy operator=	Copies the elements of one container into another.
move operator=	The move assignment operator (added in C++11 and discussed in Chapter 24) moves the elements of one container into another container of the same type—the old container no longer contains the data. This *avoids the overhead of copying* each element of the argument container.
operator<	Returns true if the contents of the first container are *less than* the second; otherwise, returns false.
operator<=	Returns true if the contents of the first container are *less than or equal to* the second; otherwise, returns false.
operator>	Returns true if the contents of the first container are *greater than* the second; otherwise, returns false.
operator>=	Returns true if the contents of the first container are *greater than or equal to* the second; otherwise, returns false.
operator==	Returns true if the contents of the first container are *equal to* the contents of the second; otherwise, returns false.
operator!=	Returns true if the contents of the first container are *not equal to* the contents of the second; otherwise, returns false.
swap	Swaps the elements of two containers. As of C++11, there is a non-member-function version of swap that swaps the contents of its two arguments (which must be of the same container type) using *move* operations rather than *copy* operations.
max_size	Returns the *maximum number of elements* for a container.
begin	Overloaded to return either an iterator or a const_iterator that refers to the *first element* of the container.
end	Overloaded to return either an iterator or a const_iterator that refers to the *next position after the end* of the container.
cbegin (C++11)	Returns a const_iterator that refers to the container's *first element*.
cend (C++11)	Returns a const_iterator that refers to the *next position after the end* of the container.
rbegin	The two versions of this function return either a reverse_iterator or a const_reverse_iterator that refers to the *last element* of the container.
rend	The two versions of this function return either a reverse_iterator or a const_reverse_iterator that refers to the *position before the first element* of the container.
crbegin (C++11)	Returns a const_reverse_iterator that refers to the *last element* of the container.
crend (C++11)	Returns a const_reverse_iterator that refers to the *position before the first element* of the container.
erase	Removes *one or more* elements from the container.
clear	Removes *all* elements from the container.

Fig. 15.2 | Common member functions for most Standard Library containers. (Part 2 of 2.)

First-Class Container Common Nested Types

Figure 15.3 shows the common first-class container *nested types* (types defined inside each container class definition). These are used in template-based declarations of variables, parameters to functions and return values from functions (as you'll see in this chapter and Chapter 16). For example, `value_type` in each container always represents the type of elements stored in the container. The types `reverse_iterator` and `const_reverse_iterator` are not provided by class `forward_list`.

typedef	Description
allocator_type	The type of the object used to allocate the container's memory—not included in class template `array`.
value_type	The type of element stored in the container.
reference	A reference for the container's element type.
const_reference	A reference for the container's element type that can be used only to *read* elements in the container and to perform `const` operations.
pointer	A pointer for the container's element type.
const_pointer	A pointer for the container's element type that can be used only to *read* elements and to perform `const` operations.
iterator	An iterator that points to an element of the container's element type.
const_iterator	An iterator that points to an element of the container's element type. Used only to *read* elements and to perform `const` operations.
reverse_iterator	A reverse iterator that points to an element of the container's element type. Iterates through a container back-to-front.
const_reverse_iterator	A reverse iterator that points to an element of the container's element type and can be used only to *read* elements and to perform `const` operations. Used to iterate through a container in reverse.
difference_type	The type of the result of subtracting two iterators that refer to the same container (the overloaded - operator is not defined for iterators of `list`s and associative containers).
size_type	The type used to count items in a container and index through a sequence container (cannot index through a `list`).

Fig. 15.3 | Nested types found in first-class containers.

Requirements for Container Elements

Before using a Standard Library container, it's important to ensure that the type of objects being stored in the container supports a *minimum* set of functionality. When an object is inserted into a container, a *copy* of the object is made. For this reason, the object type should provide a *copy constructor* and *copy assignment operator* (custom or default versions, depending on whether the class uses dynamic memory). Also, the *ordered associative containers* and many algorithms require elements to be *compared*—for this reason, the object type should provide *less-than (<)* and *equality (==) operators*. As of C++11, objects can also be *moved* into container elements, in which case the object type needs a *move constructor* and *move assignment operator*—Chapter 24 discusses *move semantics*.

11

15.3 Introduction to Iterators

Iterators have many similarities to *pointers* and are used to point to *first-class container* elements and for other purposes. Iterators hold *state* information sensitive to the particular containers on which they operate; thus, iterators are implemented for each type of container. Certain iterator operations are uniform across containers. For example, the *dereferencing operator (*)* dereferences an iterator so that you can use the element to which it points. The *++ operation on an iterator* moves it to the container's *next element* (much as incrementing a pointer into a built-in array aims the pointer at the next array element).

First-class containers provide member functions begin and end. Function begin returns an iterator pointing to the *first* element of the container. Function end returns an iterator pointing to the *first element past the end of the container* (one past the end)—a nonexistent element that's frequently used to determine when the end of a container is reached. If iterator i points to a particular element, then ++i points to the "next" element and *i refers to the element pointed to by i. The iterator resulting from end is typically used in an equality or inequality comparison to determine whether the "moving iterator" (i in this case) has reached the end of the container.

An object of a container's iterator type refers to a container element that *can* be modified. An object of a container's const_iterator type refers to a container element that *cannot* be modified.

Using istream_iterator for Input and ostream_iterator for Output

We use iterators with sequences (also called ranges). These can be in containers, or they can be input sequences or output sequences. Figure 15.4 demonstrates input from the standard input (a sequence of data for input into a program), using an istream_iterator, and output to the standard output (a sequence of data for output from a program), using an ostream_iterator. The program inputs two integers from the user and displays their sum. As you'll see later in this chapter, istream_iterators and ostream_iterators can be used with the Standard Library algorithms to create powerful statements. For example, starting in Fig. 15.11, you'll use an ostream_iterator with the copy algorithm to copy a container's *entire* contents to the standard output stream with a single statement.

```
 1   // Fig. 15.4: fig15_04.cpp
 2   // Demonstrating input and output with iterators.
 3   #include <iostream>
 4   #include <iterator> // ostream_iterator and istream_iterator
 5   using namespace std;
 6
 7   int main() {
 8      cout << "Enter two integers: ";
 9
10      // create istream_iterator for reading int values from cin
11      istream_iterator<int> inputInt{cin};
12
13      int number1{*inputInt}; // read int from standard input
14      ++inputInt; // move iterator to next input value
15      int number2{*inputInt}; // read int from standard input
```

Fig. 15.4 | Demonstrating input and output with iterators. (Part 1 of 2.)

```
16
17      // create ostream_iterator for writing int values to cout
18      ostream_iterator<int> outputInt{cout};
19
20      cout << "The sum is: ";
21      *outputInt = number1 + number2; // output result to cout
22      cout << endl;
23  }
```

```
Enter two integers: 12 25
The sum is: 37
```

Fig. 15.4 | Demonstrating input and output with iterators. (Part 2 of 2.)

istream_iterator

Line 11 creates an istream_iterator that's capable of *extracting* (inputting) int values from the standard input object cin. Line 13 *dereferences* iterator inputInt to read the first integer from cin and assigns that integer to number1. The dereferencing operator * applied to iterator inputInt gets the value from the stream associated with inputInt; this is similar to *dereferencing a pointer*. Line 14 positions iterator inputInt to the next value in the input stream. Line 15 inputs the next integer from inputInt and assigns it to number2.

ostream_iterator

Line 18 creates an ostream_iterator that's capable of inserting (outputting) int values in the standard output object cout. Line 21 outputs an integer to cout by assigning to *outputInt the sum of number1 and number2. Notice that we use the dereferenced outputInt iterator as an *lvalue* in the assignment statement. If you want to output another value using outputInt, the iterator must be incremented with ++ first. Either the prefix or postfix increment can be used—we use the prefix form for *performance* reasons because it does not create a temporary object.

Error-Prevention Tip 15.2

*The * (dereferencing) operator when applied to a const iterator returns a reference to const for the container element, disallowing the use of non-const member functions.*

Iterator Categories and Iterator Category Hierarchy

Figure 15.5 describes the iterator categories. Each provides a specific set of functionality.

Category	Description
input	Used to read an element from a container. An input iterator can move only in the *forward* direction (i.e., from the beginning of the container to the end) one element at a time. Input iterators support *only* one-pass algorithms—the same input iterator *cannot* be used to pass through a sequence twice.

Fig. 15.5 | Iterator categories. (Part 1 of 2.)

Category	Description
output	Used to write an element to a container. An output iterator can move only in the *forward* direction one element at a time. Output iterators support *only* one-pass algorithms—the same output iterator *cannot* be used to pass through a sequence twice.
forward	Combines the capabilities of *input and output iterators* and retains their position in the container (as state information). Such iterators can be used to pass through a sequence more than once (for so-called multipass algorithms).
bidirectional	Combines the capabilities of a *forward iterator* with the ability to move in the *backward* direction (i.e., from the end of the container toward the beginning). Bidirectional iterators support multipass algorithms, such as reversing the elements of a container.
random access	Combines the capabilities of a *bidirectional iterator* with the ability to *directly* access *any* element of the container, i.e., to jump forward or backward by an arbitrary number of elements. These can also be compared with relational operators.

Fig. 15.5 | Iterator categories. (Part 2 of 2.)

Figure 15.6 illustrates the hierarchy of iterator categories. As you follow the hierarchy from bottom to top, each iterator category supports all the functionality of the categories *below* it in the figure. Thus the "weakest" iterator types are at the bottom and the most powerful one is at the top. Note that this is *not* an inheritance hierarchy.

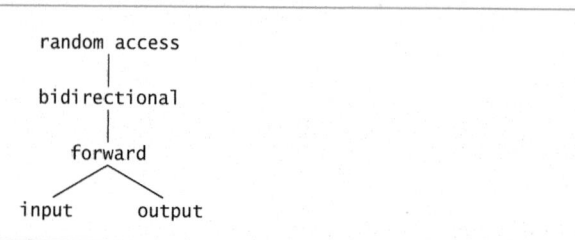

Fig. 15.6 | Iterator category hierarchy.

Container Support for Iterators

The iterator category that each container supports determines whether that container can be used with specific algorithms. *Containers that support random-access iterators can be used with all Standard Library algorithms*—with the exception that if an algorithm requires changes to a container's size, the algorithm can't be used on built-in arrays or array objects. Pointers into *built-in* arrays can be used in place of iterators with most algorithms. Figure 15.7 shows the iterator category of each container. The first-class containers, strings and built-in arrays are all traversable with iterators.

Predefined Iterator typedefs

Figure 15.8 shows the predefined iterator typedefs that are found in the Standard Library container class definitions. Not every typedef is defined for every container. We use const

Container	Iterator type	Container	Iterator type
Sequence containers (first class)		*Unordered associative containers (first class)*	
vector	random access	unordered_set	bidirectional
array	random access	unordered_multiset	bidirectional
deque	random access	unordered_map	bidirectional
list	bidirectional	unordered_multimap	bidirectional
forward_list	forward		
Ordered associative containers (first class)		*Container adapters*	
set	bidirectional	stack	none
multiset	bidirectional	queue	none
map	bidirectional	priority_queue	none
multimap	bidirectional		

Fig. 15.7 | Iterator types supported by each container.

versions of the iterators for traversing const *containers* or non-const containers that should not be modified. We use *reverse iterators* to traverse containers in the *reverse* direction.

Error-Prevention Tip 15.3

Operations performed on a const_iterator *return references to const to prevent modification to elements of the container being manipulated. Using* const_iterators *where appropriate is another example of the principle of least privilege.*

Predefined typedefs for iterator types	Direction of ++	Capability
iterator	forward	read/write
const_iterator	forward	read
reverse_iterator	backward	read/write
const_reverse_iterator	backward	read

Fig. 15.8 | Iterator typedefs.

Iterator Operations
Figure 15.9 shows operations that can be performed on each iterator type. In addition to the operators shown for all iterators, iterators must provide default constructors, copy constructors and copy assignment operators. A *forward* iterator supports ++ and all of the *input* and *output* iterator capabilities. A *bidirectional* iterator supports -- and all the capabilities of *forward* iterators. A *random-access* iterator supports all of the operations shown in the table. For input iterators and output iterators, it's not possible to save the iterator, then use the saved value later.

Iterator operation	Description
All iterators	
++p	Preincrement an iterator.
p++	Postincrement an iterator.
p = p1	Assign one iterator to another.
Input iterators	
*p	Dereference an iterator as an *rvalue*.
p->m	Use the iterator to read the element m.
p == p1	Compare iterators for equality.
p != p1	Compare iterators for inequality.
Output iterators	
*p	Dereference an iterator as an *lvalue*.
p = p1	Assign one iterator to another.
Forward iterators	Forward iterators provide all the functionality of both input iterators and output iterators.
Bidirectional iterators	
--p	Predecrement an iterator.
p--	Postdecrement an iterator.
Random-access iterators	
p += i	Increment the iterator p by i positions.
p -= i	Decrement the iterator p by i positions.
p + i *or* i + p	Expression value is an iterator positioned at p incremented by i positions.
p - i	Expression value is an iterator positioned at p decremented by i positions.
p - p1	Expression value is an integer representing the distance between two elements in the same container.
p[i]	Return a reference to the element offset from p by i positions
p < p1	Return true if iterator p is *less than* iterator p1 (i.e., iterator p is *before* iterator p1 in the container); otherwise, return false.
p <= p1	Return true if iterator p is *less than or equal to* iterator p1 (i.e., iterator p is *before* iterator p1 or *at the same location* as iterator p1 in the container); otherwise, return false.
p > p1	Return true if iterator p is *greater than* iterator p1 (i.e., iterator p is *after* iterator p1 in the container); otherwise, return false.
p >= p1	Return true if iterator p is *greater than or equal to* iterator p1 (i.e., iterator p is *after* iterator p1 or *at the same location* as iterator p1 in the container); otherwise, return false.

Fig. 15.9 | Iterator operations for each type of iterator.

15.4 Introduction to Algorithms

The Standard Library provides scores of *algorithms* you'll use frequently to manipulate a variety of containers. *Inserting, deleting, searching, sorting* and others are appropriate for some or all of the sequence and associative containers. *The algorithms operate on container elements only indirectly through iterators.* Many algorithms operate on sequences of elements defined by iterators pointing to the *first element* of the sequence and to *one element past the last element.* It's also possible to *create your own new algorithms* that operate in a similar fashion so they can be used with the Standard Library containers and iterators. In this chapter, we'll use the copy algorithm in many examples to copy a container's contents to the standard output. We discuss many Standard Library algorithms in Chapter 16.

15.5 Sequence Containers

The C++ Standard Template Library provides five *sequence containers*—array, vector, deque, list and forward_list. Class templates array, vector and deque are typically based on built-in arrays. Class templates list and forward_list implement linked-list data structures, which we discuss in Chapter 19. We've already discussed and used class template array extensively, so we do not cover it again here. We've also already introduced class template vector—we discuss it in more detail here.

Performance and Choosing the Appropriate Container

Figure 15.2 presented the operations common to *most* of the Standard Library containers. Beyond these operations, each container typically provides a variety of other capabilities. Many of these are common to several containers, but they're not always equally efficient for each container.

Software Engineering Observation 15.2

It's usually preferable to reuse Standard Library containers rather than developing custom templatized data structures. vector *is typically satisfactory for most applications.*

Performance Tip 15.2

Insertion at the back of a vector *is efficient. The* vector *simply grows, if necessary, to accommodate the new item. It's expensive to insert (or delete) an element in the middle of a* vector—*the entire portion of the* vector *after the insertion (or deletion) point must be moved, because* vector *elements occupy contiguous cells in memory.*

Performance Tip 15.3

Applications that require frequent insertions and deletions at both ends of a container normally use a deque *rather than a* vector. *Although we can insert and delete elements at the front and back of both a* vector *and a* deque, *class* deque *is more efficient than* vector *for doing insertions and deletions at the front.*

Performance Tip 15.4

Applications with frequent insertions and deletions in the middle and/or at the extremes of a container normally use a list, *due to its efficient implementation of insertion and deletion anywhere in the data structure.*

15.5.1 vector Sequence Container

Class template vector, which we introduced in Section 7.10, provides a dynamic data structure with *contiguous* memory locations. This enables efficient, direct access to any element of a vector via the subscript operator [], exactly as with a built-in array. Classs template vector is most commonly used when the data in the container must be easily accessible via a subscript or will be sorted, and when the number of elements may need to grow. When a vector's memory is exhausted, the vector *allocates* a larger built-in array, *copies* (or *moves*; Chapter 24) the original elements into the new built-in array and *deallocates* the old built-in array.

Performance Tip 15.5
Choose the vector container for the best random-access performance in a container that can grow.

Performance Tip 15.6
Objects of class template vector provide rapid indexed access with the overloaded subscript operator [] because they're stored in contiguous memory like a built-in array or an array object.

Using **vectors** and Iterators
Figure 15.10 illustrates several functions of the vector class template. Many of these functions are available in every *first-class container*. You must include header <vector> to use class template vector.

```
1   // Fig. 15.10: Fig15_10.cpp
2   // Standard Library vector class template.
3   #include <iostream>
4   #include <vector> // vector class-template definition
5   using namespace std;
6
7   // prototype for function template printVector
8   template <typename T> void printVector(const vector<T>& integers2);
9
10  int main() {
11     vector<int> integers; // create vector of ints
12
13     cout << "The initial size of integers is: " << integers.size()
14        << "\nThe initial capacity of integers is: " << integers.capacity();
15
16     // function push_back is in vector, deque and list
17     integers.push_back(2);
18     integers.push_back(3);
19     integers.push_back(4);
20
21     cout << "\nThe size of integers is: " << integers.size()
22        << "\nThe capacity of integers is: " << integers.capacity();
23     cout << "\n\nOutput built-in array using pointer notation: ";
24     const size_t SIZE{6}; // define array size
```

Fig. 15.10 | Standard Library vector class template. (Part 1 of 2.)

```
25        int values[SIZE]{1, 2, 3, 4, 5, 6}; // initialize values
26
27        // display array using pointer notation
28        for (const int* ptr = cbegin(values); ptr != cend(values); ++ptr) {
29           cout << *ptr << ' ';
30        }
31
32        cout << "\nOutput vector using iterator notation: ";
33        printVector(integers);
34        cout << "\nReversed contents of vector integers: ";
35
36        // display vector in reverse order using const_reverse_iterator
37        for (auto reverseIterator = integers.crbegin();
38           reverseIterator != integers.crend(); ++reverseIterator) {
39           cout << *reverseIterator << ' ';
40        }
41
42        cout << endl;
43     }
44
45     // function template for outputting vector elements
46     template <typename T> void printVector(const vector<T>& integers2) {
47        // display vector elements using const_iterator
48        for (auto constIterator = integers2.cbegin();
49           constIterator != integers2.cend(); ++constIterator) {
50           cout << *constIterator << ' ';
51        }
52     }
```

```
The initial size of integers is: 0
The initial capacity of integers is: 0
The size of integers is: 3
The capacity of integers is: 4

Output built-in array using pointer notation: 1 2 3 4 5 6
Output vector using iterator notation: 2 3 4
Reversed contents of vector integers: 4 3 2
```

Fig. 15.10 | Standard Library vector class template. (Part 2 of 2.)

Creating a **vector**

Line 11 defines an object called integers of class template vector that stores int values. vector's default constructor creates an empty vector with no elements (i.e., its size is 0) and no storage for elements (i.e., its capacity is 0, so the vector will have to allocate memory when elements are added to it).

vector *Member Functions* **size** *and* **capacity**

Lines 13–14 demonstrate the size and capacity functions; each initially returns 0 for integers. Function size—available in *every* container except forward_List—returns the number of elements currently stored in the container. Function capacity (specific to vector and deque) returns the number of elements that can be stored in the vector before the vector needs to *dynamically resize itself* to accommodate more elements.

vector Member Function *push_back*

Lines 17–19 use function `push_back`—available in *sequence containers* other than array and forward_list—to append an element to the vector. If the vector's capacity is full (that is, its size equals its capacity), the vector increases its size—some implementations have the vector *double* its capacity. Sequence containers other than array and vector also provide a `push_front` function.

> **Performance Tip 15.7**
>
> *It can be wasteful to double a vector's size when more space is needed. For example, a full vector of 1,000,000 elements resizes to accommodate 2,000,000 elements when one new element is added. This leaves 999,999 unused elements. You can use resize and reserve to control space usage better.*

Updated *size* and *capacity* After Modifying a *vector*

Lines 21–22 call `size` and `capacity` again to show the vector's new size and capacity after the three push_back operations. Function `size` returns 3—the number of elements added to the vector. Function `capacity` returns 4 (which may vary by compiler), indicating that we can add one more element before the vector needs to add more memory:

- When we added the first element, the vector allocated space for one element, and the size became 1 to indicate that the vector contained only one element.

- When we added the second element, the capacity *doubled* to 2 and the size became 2 as well.

- When we added the third element, the capacity doubled again to 4.

When the vector eventually fills its allocated capacity and the program attempts to add one more element to the vector, the vector will double its capacity to eight elements. The doubling behavior described above is implementation dependent.

vector Growth

The manner in which a vector grows to accommodate more elements—a time-consuming operation—is *not* specified by the C++ Standard. C++ library implementers use various schemes to minimize the overhead of *resizing* a vector. Hence, the output of this program may vary, depending on the vector implementation that comes with your compiler. Some library implementers allocate a large initial capacity. If a vector stores a small number of elements, such capacity may be a waste of space. However, it can greatly improve performance if a program adds many elements to a vector and does not have to reallocate memory to accommodate those elements. This is a classic *space–time trade-off*. Library implementors must balance the amount of memory used against the amount of time required to perform various vector operations.

Outputting Built-in Array Contents with Pointers

Lines 28–30 demonstrate how to output the contents of the built-in array `values` (defined at line 25) using pointers and pointer arithmetic. Pointers into a built-in array can be used as iterators. Recall from Section 8.5 that C++11 functions `begin` and `end` from the header `<iterator>` each take a built-in array as an argument. Function `begin` returns an iterator pointing to the built-in array's first element and function `end` returns an iterator representing the position one element *after* the end of the built-in array.

Lines 28–30 use C++14's global cbegin and cend functions, which work the same way as functions begin and end, but return const iterators that cannot be used to modify the data. C++14 also introduces the global rbegin, rend, crbegin and crend functions for iterating through a built-in array or a container from back to front. Functions rbegin and rend return iterators that can be used to modify data, and crbegin and crend return const iterators that cannot be used to modify data. Functions begin and end and their C++14 const and reverse versions may *also* receive container objects as arguments—each function calls the corresponding member function in its container argument.

14

Note that we use the != operator in the loop-continuation condition at line 28. When iterating using iterators, it's common for the loop-continuation condition to test whether the iterator has reached the end of the built-in array or the container. This technique is used by many Standard Library algorithms.

*Outputting **vector** Contents with Iterators*

Line 33 calls function printVector (defined in lines 46–52) to output the contents of a vector using iterators. The function receives a reference to a const vector. The for statement in lines 48–51 initializes control variable constIterator using vector member function cbegin (added in C++11), which returns a const_iterator to the vector's first element. We infer the control variable's type (vector<int>::const_iterator) using the auto keyword.

11

The loop continues as long as constIterator has not reached the end of the vector. This is determined by comparing constIterator to the result of calling the vector's cend member function (also added in C++11), which returns a const_iterator indicating the *location past the last element* of the vector. If constIterator is equal to this value, the end of the vector has been reached. Prior to C++11, you would have used the overloaded end member function to get the const_iterator. Functions cbegin, begin, cend and end are available for all first-class containers.

11

The body of the loop dereferences constIterator to get the current element's value. Remember that the iterator acts like a pointer to the element and that operator * is overloaded to return a reference to the element. The expression ++constIterator (line 49) positions the iterator to the vector's next element. Note that you can replace lines 48–51 with the following range-based for statement, which uses iterators in the same manner shown in printVector:

```
for (auto const& item : integers2) {
   cout << item << ' ';
}
```

Common Programming Error 15.1

Attempting to dereference an iterator positioned outside its container is a runtime logic error—the iterator returned by end or cend should never be dereferenced or incremented.

*Displaying the **vector's** Contents in Reverse with **const_reverse_iterators***

Lines 37–40 use a for statement (similar to the one in printVector) to iterate through the vector in reverse. C++11 added vector member functions crbegin and crend which return const_reverse_iterators that represent the starting and ending points when iterating through a container in reverse. Most first-class containers support this type of iter-

11

ator. Class vector also provides member functions rbegin and rend to obtain non-const reverse_iterators.

C++11: shrink_to_fit

As of C++11, you can ask a vector or deque to return unneeded memory to the system by calling member function shrink_to_fit. This *requests* that the container reduce its capacity to the number of elements in the container. According to the C++ standard, implementations can *ignore* this request so that they can perform implementation-specific optimizations.

vector *Element-Manipulation Functions*

Figure 15.11 illustrates functions for retrieving and manipulating vector elements. Line 13 initializes a vector<int> with the vector constructor that receives a C++11 list initializer. Line 14 uses an overloaded vector constructor that takes two iterators as arguments to initialize integers with a copy of a range of elements from the vector values—in this case, the range from values.cbegin() (the beginning of values) up to, but not including, values.cend() (which points to the element *after* the end of values).

```cpp
 1   // Fig. 15.11: fig15_15.cpp
 2   // Testing Standard Library vector class template
 3   // element-manipulation functions.
 4   #include <iostream>
 5   #include <vector> // vector class-template definition
 6   #include <algorithm> // copy algorithm
 7   #include <iterator> // ostream_iterator iterator
 8   #include <stdexcept> // out_of_range exception
 9   using namespace std;
10
11   int main() {
12
13      vector<int> values{1, 2, 3, 4, 5, 6};
14      vector<int> integers{values.cbegin(), values.cend()};
15      ostream_iterator<int> output{cout, " "};
16
17      cout << "Vector integers contains: ";
18      copy(integers.cbegin(), integers.cend(), output);
19
20      cout << "\nFirst element of integers: " << integers.front()
21         << "\nLast element of integers: " << integers.back();
22
23      integers[0] = 7; // set first element to 7
24      integers.at(2) = 10; // set element at position 2 to 10
25
26      // insert 22 as 2nd element
27      integers.insert(integers.cbegin() + 1, 22);
28
29      cout << "\n\nContents of vector integers after changes: ";
30      copy(integers.cbegin(), integers.cend(), output);
31
```

Fig. 15.11 | vector class template element-manipulation functions. (Part 1 of 2.)

```
32        // access out-of-range element
33        try {
34           integers.at(100) = 777;
35        }
36        catch (out_of_range &outOfRange) { // out_of_range exception
37           cout << "\n\nException: " << outOfRange.what();
38        }
39
40        integers.erase(integers.cbegin()); // erase first element
41        cout << "\n\nVector integers after erasing first element: ";
42        copy(integers.cbegin(), integers.cend(), output);
43
44        // erase remaining elements
45        integers.erase(integers.cbegin(), integers.cend());
46        cout << "\nAfter erasing all elements, vector integers "
47           << (integers.empty() ? "is" : "is not") << " empty";
48
49        // insert elements from the vector values
50        integers.insert(integers.cbegin(), values.cbegin(), values.cend());
51        cout << "\n\nContents of vector integers before clear: ";
52        copy(integers.cbegin(), integers.cend(), output);
53
54        // empty integers; clear calls erase to empty a collection
55        integers.clear();
56        cout << "\nAfter clear, vector integers "
57           << (integers.empty() ? "is" : "is not") << " empty" << endl;
58     }
```

```
Vector integers contains: 1 2 3 4 5 6
First element of integers: 1
Last element of integers: 6

Contents of vector integers after changes: 7 22 2 10 4 5 6

Exception: invalid vector<T> subscript

Vector integers after erasing first element: 22 2 10 4 5 6
After erasing all elements, vector integers is empty

Contents of vector integers before clear: 1 2 3 4 5 6
After clear, vector integers is empty
```

Fig. 15.11 | vector class template element-manipulation functions. (Part 2 of 2.)

ostream_iterator

Line 15 defines an ostream_iterator called output that can be used to output integers separated by single spaces via cout. An ostream_iterator<int> outputs only values of type int or a compatible type. The first argument to the constructor specifies the output stream, and the second argument is a string specifying the separator for the values output—in this case, the string contains a space character. We use the ostream_iterator (defined in header <iterator>) to output the contents of the vector in this example.

copy *Algorithm*

Line 18 uses Standard Library algorithm `copy` (from header `<algorithm>`) to output the entire contents of `integers` to the standard output. The algorithm copies each element in a range from the location specified by the iterator in its first argument and up to, but *not* including, the location specified by the iterator in its second argument. These two arguments must satisfy *input iterator* requirements—they must be iterators through which values can be read from a container, such as `const_iterator`s. They must also represent a range of elements—applying ++ to the first iterator must eventually cause it to reach the second iterator argument in the range. The elements are copied to the location specified by the *output iterator* (i.e., an iterator through which a value can be stored or output) specified as the last argument. In this case, the output iterator is an `ostream_iterator` attached to `cout`, so the elements are copied to the standard output.

vector *Member Functions* front *and* back

Lines 20–21 use functions `front` and `back` (available for most *sequence containers*) to determine the vector's first and last elements, respectively. Notice the difference between functions `front` and `begin`. Function `front` returns a reference to the first element in the vector, while function `begin` returns a *random-access iterator* pointing to the first element in the vector. Also notice the difference between functions `back` and `end`. Function `back` returns a reference to the vector's last element, whereas function `end` returns a *random access iterator* pointing to the location *after* the last element.

> **Common Programming Error 15.2**
> *The results of* front *and* back *are undefined when called on an empty* vector.

Accessing *vector Elements*

Lines 23–24 illustrate two ways to access `vector` elements. These can also be used with `deque` containers. Line 23 uses the subscript operator that's overloaded to return either a reference to the value at the specified location or a reference to that `const` value, depending on whether the container is `const`. Function `at` (line 24) performs the same operation, but with *bounds checking*. Function `at` first checks the value supplied as an argument and determines whether it's in the vector's bounds. If not, function `at` throws an `out_of_range` exception (as demonstrated in lines 33–38). Figure 15.12 shows some of the Standard Library exception types—we discuss others in Chapter 17.

Exception type	Description
`out_of_range`	Indicates when a subscript is out of range—e.g., when an invalid subscript is specified to `vector` member function `at`.
`invalid_argument`	Indicates that an invalid argument was passed to a function.
`length_error`	Indicates an attempt to create too long a container, `string`, etc.
`bad_alloc`	Indicates that an attempt to allocate memory with `new` (or with an allocator) failed because not enough memory was available.

Fig. 15.12 | Some exception types in header `<stdexcept>`.

vector *Member Function* insert

Line 27 of Fig. 15.11 uses one of the several overloaded insert functions provided by each *sequence container* (except array, which has a fixed size, and forward_list, which has the function insert_after instead). Line 27 inserts the value 22 before the element at the location specified by the iterator in the first argument. In this example, the iterator is pointing to the vector's second element, so 22 is inserted as the second element and the original second element becomes the third element. Other versions of insert allow inserting multiple copies of the same value starting at a particular position, or inserting a range of values from another container, starting at a particular position. As of C++11, the version of member function insert in line 27 returns an iterator pointing to the item that was inserted.

vector *Member Function* erase

Lines 40 and 45 use the two erase functions that are available in all *first-class containers* (except array, which has a fixed size, and forward_list, which has the function erase_after instead). Line 40 erases the element at the location specified by the iterator argument (in this example, the first element). Line 45 specifies that all elements in the range specified by the two iterator arguments should be erased. In this example, all the elements are erased. Line 47 uses function empty (available for all containers and adapters) to confirm that the vector is empty.

Common Programming Error 15.3

Normally erase *destroys the objects that are erased from a container. However, erasing an element that is a pointer to a dynamically allocated object does* not delete *the dynamically allocated memory—this can lead to a memory leak. If the element is a* unique_ptr *(Section 17.9), the* unique_ptr *would be destroyed and the dynamically allocated memory would be deleted. If the element is a* shared_ptr *(Chapter 24), the reference count to the dynamically allocated object would be decremented and the memory would be deleted only* if the reference count reached 0.

vector *Member Function* insert *with Three Arguments (Range* insert*)*

Line 50 demonstrates the version of function insert that uses the second and third arguments to specify the starting location and ending location in a sequence of values (in this case, from the vector values) that should be inserted into the vector. Remember that the ending location specifies the position in the sequence *after* the last element to be inserted; copying occurs up to, but *not* including, this location. As of C++11, this version of member function insert returns an iterator pointing to the first item that was inserted—if nothing was inserted, the function returns its first argument.

vector *Member Function* clear

Finally, line 55 uses function clear (found in all *first-class containers* except array) to empty the vector—this does not necessarily return any of the vector's memory to the system. We'll cover many common container member functions in the next few sections. We'll also cover many functions that are specific to each container.

15.5.2 list Sequence Container

The list *sequence container* (from header <list>) allows insertion and deletion operations at *any* location in the container. If most of the insertions and deletions occur at the *ends* of the container, the deque data structure (Section 15.5.3) provides a more efficient implementation. Class template list is implemented as a *doubly linked list*—every node in the list contains a pointer to the previous node in the list and to the next node in the list. This enables class template list to support *bidirectional iterators* that allow the container to be traversed both forward and backward. Any algorithm that requires *input, output, forward* or *bidirectional iterators* can operate on a list. Many list member functions manipulate the elements of the container as an ordered set of elements.

C++11: *forward_list Container*

C++11's forward_list sequence container (header <forward_list>) is implemented as a *singly linked list*—every node in the list contains a pointer to the next node in the list. This enables class template list to support *forward iterators* that allow the container to be traversed in the forward direction. Any algorithm that requires *input, output* or *forward iterators* can operate on a forward_list.

list Member Functions

In addition to the member functions in Fig. 15.2 and the common member functions of all *sequence containers* discussed in Section 15.5, class template list provides other member functions, including splice, push_front, pop_front, remove, remove_if, unique, merge, reverse and sort. Several of these member functions are list-optimized implementations of the Standard Library algorithms presented in Chapter 16. Both push_front and pop_front are also supported by forward_list and deque. Figure 15.13 demonstrates several features of class list. Remember that many of the functions presented in Figs. 15.10–15.11 can be used with class list, so we focus on the new features in this example's discussion.

```cpp
1   // Fig. 15.13: fig15_13.cpp
2   // Standard library list class template.
3   #include <iostream>
4   #include <vector>
5   #include <list> // list class-template definition
6   #include <algorithm> // copy algorithm
7   #include <iterator> // ostream_iterator
8   using namespace std;
9
10  // prototype for function template printList
11  template <typename T> void printList(const list<T>& listRef);
12
13  int main() {
14     list<int> values; // create list of ints
15     list<int> otherValues; // create list of ints
16
17     // insert items in values
18     values.push_front(1);
19     values.push_front(2);
20     values.push_back(4);
21     values.push_back(3);
22
```

Fig. 15.13 | Standard Library list class template. (Part 1 of 3.)

```
23      cout << "values contains: ";
24      printList(values);
25
26      values.sort(); // sort values
27      cout << "\nvalues after sorting contains: ";
28      printList(values);
29
30      // insert elements of ints into otherValues
31      vector<int> ints{2, 6, 4, 8};
32      otherValues.insert(otherValues.cbegin(), ints.cbegin(), ints.cend());
33      cout << "\nAfter insert, otherValues contains: ";
34      printList(otherValues);
35
36      // remove otherValues elements and insert at end of values
37      values.splice(values.cend(), otherValues);
38      cout << "\nAfter splice, values contains: ";
39      printList(values);
40
41      values.sort(); // sort values
42      cout << "\nAfter sort, values contains: ";
43      printList(values);
44
45      // insert elements of ints into otherValues
46      otherValues.insert(otherValues.cbegin(), ints.cbegin(), ints.cend());
47      otherValues.sort(); // sort the list
48      cout << "\nAfter insert and sort, otherValues contains: ";
49      printList(otherValues);
50
51      // remove otherValues elements and insert into values in sorted order
52      values.merge(otherValues);
53      cout << "\nAfter merge:\n   values contains: ";
54      printList(values);
55      cout << "\n   otherValues contains: ";
56      printList(otherValues);
57
58      values.pop_front(); // remove element from front
59      values.pop_back(); // remove element from back
60      cout << "\nAfter pop_front and pop_back:\n   values contains: ";
61      printList(values);
62
63      values.unique(); // remove duplicate elements
64      cout << "\nAfter unique, values contains: ";
65      printList(values);
66
67      values.swap(otherValues); // swap elements of values and otherValues
68      cout << "\nAfter swap:\n   values contains: ";
69      printList(values);
70      cout << "\n   otherValues contains: ";
71      printList(otherValues);
72
73      // replace contents of values with elements of otherValues
74      values.assign(otherValues.cbegin(), otherValues.cend());
```

Fig. 15.13 | Standard Library `list` class template. (Part 2 of 3.)

```
75      cout << "\nAfter assign, values contains: ";
76      printList(values);
77
78      // remove otherValues elements and insert into values in sorted order
79      values.merge(otherValues);
80      cout << "\nAfter merge, values contains: ";
81      printList(values);
82
83      values.remove(4); // remove all 4s
84      cout << "\nAfter remove(4), values contains: ";
85      printList(values);
86      cout << endl;
87   }
88
89   // printList function template definition; uses
90   // ostream_iterator and copy algorithm to output list elements
91   template <typename T> void printList(const list<T>& listRef) {
92      if (listRef.empty()) { // list is empty
93         cout << "List is empty";
94      }
95      else {
96         ostream_iterator<T> output{cout, " "};
97         copy(listRef.cbegin(), listRef.cend(), output);
98      }
99   }
```

```
values contains: 2 1 4 3
values after sorting contains: 1 2 3 4
After insert, otherValues contains: 2 6 4 8
After splice, values contains: 1 2 3 4 2 6 4 8
After sort, values contains: 1 2 2 3 4 4 6 8
After insert and sort, otherValues contains: 2 4 6 8
After merge:
   values contains: 1 2 2 2 3 4 4 4 6 6 8 8
   otherValues contains: List is empty
After pop_front and pop_back:
   values contains: 2 2 2 3 4 4 4 6 6 8
After unique, values contains: 2 3 4 6 8
After swap:
   values contains: List is empty
   otherValues contains: 2 3 4 6 8
After assign, values contains: 2 3 4 6 8
After merge, values contains: 2 2 3 3 4 4 6 6 8 8
After remove(4), values contains: 2 2 3 3 6 6 8 8
```

Fig. 15.13 | Standard Library `list` class template. (Part 3 of 3.)

Creating `list` Objects

Lines 14–15 create two `list` objects capable of storing ints. Lines 18–19 use function
`push_front` to insert integers at the beginning of values. Function push_front is specific
to classes forward_list, list and deque. Lines 20–21 use function push_back to insert
integers at the end of values. *Function push_back is common to all sequence containers*, except array and forward_list.

list *Member Function* sort

Line 26 uses list member function sort to arrange the elements in the list in *ascending order*. A second version of function sort allows you to supply a *binary predicate function* that takes two arguments (values in the list), performs a comparison and returns a bool value indicating whether the first argument should come before the second in the sorted contents. This function determines the order in which the elements of the list are sorted. This version could be particularly useful for a list that stores pointers rather than values. [*Note:* We demonstrate a *unary predicate function* in Fig. 16.4. A unary predicate function takes a single argument, performs a comparison using that argument and returns a bool value indicating the result.]

list *Member Function* splice

Line 37 uses list function splice to remove the elements in otherValues and insert them into values before the iterator position specified as the first argument. There are two other versions of this function. Function splice with three arguments allows one element to be removed from the container specified as the second argument from the location specified by the iterator in the third argument. Function splice with four arguments uses the last two arguments to specify a range of locations that should be removed from the container in the second argument and placed at the location specified in the first argument. Class template forward_list provides a similar member function named splice_after.

list *Member Function* merge

After inserting more elements in otherValues and *sorting* both values and otherValues, line 52 uses list member function merge to remove all elements of otherValues and insert them in sorted order into values. Both lists *must* be *sorted* in the *same* order before this operation is performed. A second version of merge enables you to supply a *binary predicate function* that takes two arguments (values in the list) and returns a bool value. The predicate function specifies the sorting order used by merge.

list *Member Function* pop_front

Line 58 uses list function pop_front to remove the first element in the list. Line 59 uses function pop_back (available for *sequence containers* other than array and forward_list) to remove the last element in the list.

list *Member Function* unique

Line 63 uses list function unique to *remove duplicate elements* in the list. The list should be in *sorted* order (so that all duplicates are side by side) before this operation is performed, to guarantee that all duplicates are eliminated. A second version of unique enables you to supply a *predicate function* that takes two arguments (values in the list) and returns a bool value specifying whether two elements are equal.

list *Member Function* swap

Line 67 uses function swap (available to all *first-class containers*) to exchange the contents of values with the contents of otherValues.

list *Member Functions* assign *and* remove

Line 74 uses list function assign (available to all *sequence containers*) to replace the contents of values with the contents of otherValues in the range specified by the two iterator arguments. A second version of `assign` replaces the original contents with copies of the value specified in the second argument. The first argument of the function specifies the number of copies. Line 83 uses `list` function remove to delete all copies of the value 4 from the `list`.

15.5.3 deque Sequence Container

Class deque provides many of the benefits of a `vector` and a `list` in one container. The term deque is short for "double-ended queue." Class deque is implemented to provide efficient indexed access (using subscripting) for reading and modifying its elements, much like a `vector`. Class deque is also implemented for *efficient insertion and deletion operations at its front and back*, much like a `list` (although a `list` is also capable of efficient insertions and deletions in the *middle* of the `list`). Class deque provides support for random-access iterators, so deques can be used with all Standard Library algorithms. One of the most common uses of a deque is to maintain a *first-in, first-out queue* of elements. In fact, a deque is the default underlying implementation for the queue adaptor (Section 15.7.2).

Additional storage for a deque can be allocated at either end of the deque in blocks of memory that are typically maintained as a built-in array of pointers to those blocks.[3] Due to the *noncontiguous memory layout* of a deque, a deque iterator must be more "intelligent" than the pointers that are used to iterate through `vectors`, `arrays` or built-in arrays.

Performance Tip 15.8
In general, deque has higher overhead than vector.

Performance Tip 15.9
Insertions and deletions in the middle of a deque are optimized to minimize the number of elements copied, so it's more efficient than a vector but less efficient than a list for this kind of modification.

Class deque provides the same basic operations as class `vector`, but like `list` adds member functions push_front and pop_front to allow insertion and deletion at the beginning of the deque, respectively.

Figure 15.14 demonstrates features of class deque. Remember that many of the functions presented in Fig. 15.10, Fig. 15.11 and Fig. 15.13 also can be used with class deque. Header <deque> must be included to use class deque.

```
1   // Fig. 15.14: fig15_14.cpp
2   // Standard Library deque class template.
3   #include <iostream>
4   #include <deque> // deque class-template definition
5   #include <algorithm> // copy algorithm
6   #include <iterator> // ostream_iterator
7   using namespace std;
8
```

Fig. 15.14 | Standard Library deque class template. (Part 1 of 2.)

---

3. This is an implementation-specific detail, not a requirement of the C++ standard.

```
 9   int main() {
10       deque<double> values; // create deque of doubles
11       ostream_iterator<double> output{cout, " "};
12
13       // insert elements in values
14       values.push_front(2.2);
15       values.push_front(3.5);
16       values.push_back(1.1);
17
18       cout << "values contains: ";
19
20       // use subscript operator to obtain elements of values
21       for (size_t i{0}; i < values.size(); ++i) {
22           cout << values[i] << ' ';
23       }
24
25       values.pop_front(); // remove first element
26       cout << "\nAfter pop_front, values contains: ";
27       copy(values.cbegin(), values.cend(), output);
28
29       // use subscript operator to modify element at location 1
30       values[1] = 5.4;
31       cout << "\nAfter values[1] = 5.4, values contains: ";
32       copy(values.cbegin(), values.cend(), output);
33       cout << endl;
34   }
```

```
values contains: 3.5 2.2 1.1
After pop_front, values contains: 2.2 1.1
After values[1] = 5.4, values contains: 2.2 5.4
```

Fig. 15.14 | Standard Library deque class template. (Part 2 of 2.)

Line 10 instantiates a deque that can store double values. Lines 14–16 use functions push_front and push_back to insert elements at the beginning and end of the deque.

The for statement in lines 21–23 uses the subscript operator to retrieve the value in each element of the deque for output. The condition uses function size to ensure that we do not attempt to access an element *outside* the bounds of the deque.

Line 25 uses function pop_front to demonstrate removing the first element of the deque. Line 30 uses the subscript operator to obtain an *lvalue*. This enables values to be assigned directly to any element of the deque.

15.6 Associative Containers

The *associative containers* provide *direct access* to store and retrieve elements via keys (often called search keys). The four *ordered associative containers* are multiset, set, multimap and map. Each of these maintains its keys in *sorted order*. There are also four corresponding *unordered associative containers*—unordered_multiset, unordered_set, unordered_multimap and unordered_map—that offer the most of the same capabilities as their ordered counterparts. The primary difference between the ordered and unordered associative containers is that the unordered ones do *not* maintain their keys in *sorted* order. In this section, we focus on the *ordered associative containers*.

Performance Tip 15.10

The unordered associative containers might offer better performance for cases in which it's not necessary to maintain keys in sorted order.

Iterating through an *ordered associative container* traverses it in the sort order for that container. Classes multiset and set provide operations for manipulating sets of values where the values themselves are the keys. The primary difference between a multiset and a set is that a multiset *allows duplicate keys* and a set does not. Classes multimap and map provide operations for manipulating values associated with keys (these values are sometimes referred to as mapped values). The primary difference between a multimap and a map is that a multimap allows *duplicate keys* with associated values to be stored and a map allows only *unique keys* with associated values. In addition to the common container member functions, *ordered associative containers* also support several member functions that are specific to associative containers. Examples of each of the *ordered associative containers* and their common member functions are presented in the next several subsections.

15.6.1 multiset Associative Container

The multiset *ordered associative container* (from header <set>) provides fast storage and retrieval of keys and allows duplicate keys. The elements' ordering is determined by a so-called comparator function object. For example, in an integer multiset, elements can be sorted in *ascending order* by ordering the keys with comparator function object less<int>. We discuss function objects in detail in Section 16.5. For this chapter, we'll simply show how to use less<int> when declaring ordered associative containers. The data type of the keys in all *ordered associative containers* must support comparison based on the comparator function object—keys sorted with less<T> must support comparison with operator<. If the keys used in the *ordered associative containers* are of user-defined data types, those types must supply the appropriate comparison operators. A multiset supports *bidirectional iterators* (but not *random-access iterators*). If the order of the keys is not important, use unordered_multiset (header <unordered_set>).

Figure 15.15 demonstrates the multiset *ordered associative container* for a multiset of ints with keys that are sorted in *ascending order*. Containers multiset and set (Section 15.6.2) provide the same basic functionality.

```
1   // Fig. 15.15: fig15_15.cpp
2   // Standard Library multiset class template
3   #include <array>
4   #include <iostream>
5   #include <set> // multiset class-template definition
6   #include <algorithm> // copy algorithm
7   #include <iterator> // ostream_iterator
8   using namespace std;
9
10  int main() {
```

Fig. 15.15 | Standard Library multiset class template. (Part 1 of 3.)

```
11      multiset<int, less<int>> intMultiset; // multiset of ints
12
13      cout << "There are currently " << intMultiset.count(15)
14         << " values of 15 in the multiset\n";
15
16      intMultiset.insert(15); // insert 15 in intMultiset
17      intMultiset.insert(15); // insert 15 in intMultiset
18      cout << "After inserts, there are " << intMultiset.count(15)
19         << " values of 15 in the multiset\n\n";
20
21      // find 15 in intMultiset; find returns iterator
22      auto result{intMultiset.find(15)};
23
24      if (result != intMultiset.end()) { // if iterator not at end
25         cout << "Found value 15\n"; // found search value 15
26      }
27
28      // find 20 in intMultiset; find returns iterator
29      result = intMultiset.find(20);
30
31      if (result == intMultiset.end()) { // will be true hence
32         cout << "Did not find value 20\n"; // did not find 20
33      }
34
35      // insert elements of array a into intMultiset
36      vector<int> a{7, 22, 9, 1, 18, 30, 100, 22, 85, 13};
37      intMultiset.insert(a.cbegin(), a.cend());
38      cout << "\nAfter insert, intMultiset contains:\n";
39      ostream_iterator<int> output{cout, " "};
40      copy(intMultiset.begin(), intMultiset.end(), output);
41
42      // determine lower and upper bound of 22 in intMultiset
43      cout << "\n\nLower bound of 22: "
44         << *(intMultiset.lower_bound(22));
45      cout << "\nUpper bound of 22: " << *(intMultiset.upper_bound(22));
46
47      // use equal_range to determine lower and upper bound
48      // of 22 in intMultiset
49      auto p{intMultiset.equal_range(22)};
50
51      cout << "\n\nequal_range of 22:"\n   Lower bound: "
52         << *(p.first) << "\n   Upper bound: " << *(p.second);
53      cout << endl;
54   }
```

```
There are currently 0 values of 15 in the multiset
After inserts, there are 2 values of 15 in the multiset

Found value 15
Did not find value 20

After insert, intMultiset contains:
1 7 9 13 15 15 18 22 22 30 85 100
```

Fig. 15.15 | Standard Library multiset class template. (Part 2 of 3.)

```
Lower bound of 22: 22
Upper bound of 22: 30

equal_range of 22:
   Lower bound: 22
   Upper bound: 30
```

Fig. 15.15 | Standard Library multiset class template. (Part 3 of 3.)

Creating a multiset

Line 11 creates a multiset of ints ordered in *ascending order*, using the function object less<int>. *Ascending order* is the default for a multiset, so less<int> can be omitted and line 11 can be written as

```
multiset<int> intMultiset; // multiset of ints
```

11 C++11 fixed a syntax issue with spacing between the closing > of less<int> and the closing > of the multiset type. Before C++11, if you specified this multiset's type as we did in line 11, the compiler would treat the >> in

```
multiset<int, less<int>>
```

as the >> operator and generate a compilation error. For this reason, you were required to put a space between the closing > of less<int> and the closing > of the multiset type (or any other similar template type, such as vector<vector<int>>). As of C++11, the preceding declaration compiles correctly.

multiset Member Function count

Line 13 uses function count (available to all *associative containers*) to count the number of occurrences of the value 15 currently in the multiset.

multiset Member Function insert

Lines 16–17 use one of the several overloaded versions of function insert to add the value 15 to the multiset twice. A second version of insert takes an iterator and a value as arguments and begins the search for the insertion point from the iterator position specified. A third version of insert takes two iterators as arguments that specify a range of values to add to the multiset from another container.

multiset Member Function find

Line 22 uses function find (available to all *associative containers*) to locate the value 15 in the multiset. Function find returns an iterator or a const_iterator (depending on whether the multiset is const) pointing to the location at which the value is found. If the value is *not* found, find returns an iterator or a const_iterator equal to the value returned by calling end on the container. Line 31 demonstrates this case.

Inserting Elements of Another Container into a multiset

Line 37 uses function insert to insert the elements of the vector named a into the multiset. In line 40, the copy algorithm copies the elements of the multiset to the standard output in *ascending order*.

multiset *Member Functions* lower_bound *and* upper_bound

Lines 44 and 45 use functions lower_bound and upper_bound (available in all *associative containers*) to locate the earliest occurrence of the value 22 in the multiset and the element *after* the last occurrence of the value 22 in the multiset. Both functions return iterators or const_iterators pointing to the appropriate location or the iterator returned by end if the value is not in the multiset.

pair *Objects and* multiset *Member Function* equal_range

Line 49 creates and intializes a pair object called p. Once again, we use C++11's auto keyword to infer the variable's type from its initializer—in this case, the return value of multiset member function equal_range, which is a pair object. Such objects associate pairs of values. The contents of p will be two const_iterators for our multiset of ints. The multiset function equal_range returns a pair containing the results of calling both lower_bound and upper_bound. Type pair contains two public data members called first and second. Line 49 uses function equal_range to determine the lower_bound and upper_bound of 22 in the multiset. Line 52 uses p.first and p.second to access the lower_bound and upper_bound. We *dereferenced* the iterators to output the values at the locations returned from equal_range. Though we did not do so here, you should always ensure that the iterators returned by lower_bound, upper_bound and equal_range are not equal to the container's *end* iterator *before* dereferencing the iterators.

C++11: *Variadic Class Template* tuple

C++ also includes class template tuple, which is similar to pair, but can hold any number of items of various types. As of C++11, class template tuple is implemented using *variadic templates*—templates that can receive a *variable* number of arguments. We discuss tuple and variadic templates in Chapter 24, C++11 and C++14 Additional Features.

C++14: *Heterogeneous Lookup*

Prior to C++14, when searching for a key in an associative container, the argument provided to a search function like find was required to have the container's key type. For example, if the key type were string, you could pass find a pointer-based string to locate in the container. In this case, the argument would be converted into a temporary object of the key type (string), then passed to find. As of C++14, the argument to find (and other similar functions) can be of *any* type, provided that there are overloaded comparison operators that can compare values of the argument's type to values of the container's key type. If there are, no temporary objects will be created. This is known as heterogeneous lookup.

15.6.2 set Associative Container

The *set associative container* (from header <set>) is used for fast storage and retrieval of *unique* keys. The implementation of a set is identical to that of a multiset, except that a set must have unique keys. Therefore, if an attempt is made to insert a *duplicate* key into a set, the duplicate is ignored—this is the intended mathematical behavior of a set, so it's not considered an error. A set supports *bidirectional iterators* (but not *random-access iterators*). If the order of the keys is not important, you can use unordered_set (header <unordered_set>) instead. Figure 15.16 demonstrates a set of doubles.

```
1    // Fig. 15.16: fig15_16.cpp
2    // Standard Library set class template.
3    #include <iostream>
4    #include <vector>
5    #include <set>
6    #include <algorithm>
7    #include <iterator> // ostream_iterator
8    using namespace std;
9
10   int main() {
11      vector<double> a{2.1, 4.2, 9.5, 2.1, 3.7};
12      set<double, less<double>> doubleSet{a.begin(), a.end()};
13
14      cout << "doubleSet contains: ";
15      ostream_iterator<double> output{cout, " "};
16      copy(doubleSet.begin(), doubleSet.end(), output);
17
18      // insert 13.8 in doubleSet; insert returns pair in which
19      // p.first represents location of 13.8 in doubleSet and
20      // p.second represents whether 13.8 was inserted
21      auto p{doubleSet.insert(13.8)}; // value not in set
22      cout << "\n\n" << *(p.first)
23         << (p.second ? " was" : " was not") << " inserted";
24      cout << "\ndoubleSet contains: ";
25      copy(doubleSet.begin(), doubleSet.end(), output);
26
27      // insert 9.5 in doubleSet
28      p = doubleSet.insert(9.5); // value already in set
29      cout << "\n\n" << *(p.first)
30         << (p.second ? " was" : " was not") << " inserted";
31      cout << "\ndoubleSet contains: ";
32      copy(doubleSet.begin(), doubleSet.end(), output);
33      cout << endl;
34   }
```

```
doubleSet contains: 2.1 3.7 4.2 9.5

13.8 was inserted
doubleSet contains: 2.1 3.7 4.2 9.5 13.8

9.5 was not inserted
doubleSet contains: 2.1 3.7 4.2 9.5 13.8
```

Fig. 15.16 | Standard Library set class template.

Line 12 creates a set of doubles ordered in *ascending order*, using the function object less<double>. The constructor call takes all the elements in vector a and inserts them into the set. Line 16 uses algorithm copy to output the contents of the set. Notice that the value 2.1—which appeared twice in the vector a—appears only *once* in doubleSet, because container set does *not* allow duplicates.

Line 21 defines and initializes a pair to store the result of a call to set function insert. The pair returned consists of a const_iterator pointing to the item in the set inserted and a bool value indicating whether the item was inserted—true if the item was not in the set; false if it was.

Line 21 uses function insert to place the value 13.8 in the set. The returned pair, p, contains an iterator p.first pointing to the value 13.8 in the set and a bool value that's true because the value was inserted. Line 28 attempts to insert 9.5, which is already in the set. The output shows that 9.5 was not inserted again because sets don't allow duplicate keys. In this case, p.first in the returned pair points to the existing 9.5 in the set.

15.6.3 multimap Associative Container

The *multimap associative container* is used for fast storage and retrieval of keys and associated values (often called key–value pairs). Many of the functions used with multisets and sets are also used with multimaps and maps. The elements of multimaps and maps are pairs of keys and values instead of individual values. When inserting into a multimap or map, a pair object that contains the key and the value is used. The ordering of the keys is determined by a *comparator function object*. For example, in a multimap that uses integers as the key type, keys can be sorted in *ascending order* by ordering them with *comparator function object* less<int>. Duplicate keys are allowed in a multimap, so multiple values can be associated with a single key. This is called a one-to-many relationship. For example, in a credit-card transaction-processing system, one credit-card account can have many associated transactions; in a university, one student can take many courses, and one professor can teach many students; in the military, one rank (like "private") has many people. A multimap supports *bidirectional iterators*, but not *random-access iterators*.

Figure 15.17 demonstrates the *multimap associative container*. Header <map> must be included to use class multimap. If the order of the keys is not important, you can use unordered_multimap (header <unordered_map>) instead.

Performance Tip 15.11
A multimap is implemented to efficiently locate all values paired with a given key.

```
1   // Fig. 15.17: fig15_17.cpp
2   // Standard Library multimap class template.
3   #include <iostream>
4   #include <map> // multimap class-template definition
5   using namespace std;
6
7   int main() {
8      multimap<int, double, less<int>> pairs; // create multimap
9
10     cout << "There are currently " << pairs.count(15)
11        << " pairs with key 15 in the multimap\n";
12
13     // insert two value_type objects in pairs
14     pairs.insert(make_pair(15, 99.3));
15     pairs.insert(make_pair(15, 2.7));
16
```

Fig. 15.17 | Standard Library multimap class template. (Part 1 of 2.)

```
17        cout << "After inserts, there are " << pairs.count(15)
18           << " pairs with key 15\n\n";
19
20        // insert five value_type objects in pairs
21        pairs.insert(make_pair(30, 111.11));
22        pairs.insert(make_pair(10, 22.22));
23        pairs.insert(make_pair(25, 33.333));
24        pairs.insert(make_pair(20, 9.345));
25        pairs.insert(make_pair(5, 77.54));
26
27        cout << "Multimap pairs contains:\nKey\tValue\n";
28
29        // walk through elements of pairs
30        for (auto mapItem : pairs) {
31           cout << mapItem.first << '\t' << mapItem.second << '\n';
32        }
33
34        cout << endl;
35  }
```

```
There are currently 0 pairs with key 15 in the multimap
After inserts, there are 2 pairs with key 15

Multimap pairs contains:
Key     Value
5       77.54
10      22.22
15      99.3
15      2.7
20      9.345
25      33.333
30      111.11
```

Fig. 15.17 | Standard Library multimap class template. (Part 2 of 2.)

Line 8 creates a multimap in which the key type is int, the type of a key's associated value is double and the elements are ordered in *ascending order*—the template argument less<int> is the default ordering it's not required in the multimap declaration. Line 10 uses function count to determine the number of key–value pairs with a key of 15 (none yet, since the container is currently empty).

Line 14 uses function insert to add a new key–value pair to the multimap. The Standard Library function make_pair creates a key–value pair object—in this case first represents a key (15) of type int and second represents a value (99.3) of type double. Function make_pair automatically uses the types that you specified for the keys and values in the multimap's declaration (line 8). Line 15 inserts another pair object with the key 15 and the value 2.7. Then lines 17–18 output the number of pairs with key 15. As of C++11, you can use list initalization for pair objects, so line 15 can be simplified as

11

```
pairs.insert({15, 2.7});
```

11 Similarly, you can use C++11 list initialization to initialize an object being returned from a function. For example, the following returns a pair containing an int and a double

```
return {15, 2.7};
```

Lines 21–25 insert five additional pairs into the multimap. The range-based for statement in lines 30–32 outputs the contents of the multimap, including both keys and values. We infer the type of the loop's control variable (a pair containing an int key and a double value) with keyword auto. Line 31 accesses the members of the current pair in each element of the multimap. Notice in the output that the keys appear in *ascending order*.

C++11: List Initializing a Key–Value Pair Container

11

In this example, we used separate calls to member function insert to place key–value pairs in a multimap. If you know the key–value pairs in advance, you can use list initialization when you create the multimap. For example, the following statement initializes a multimap with three key–value pairs that are represented by the sublists in the main intializer list:

```
multimap<int, double, less<int>> pairs{
   {10, 22.22}, {20, 9.345}, {5, 77.54}};
```

15.6.4 map Associative Container

The *map associative container* (from header <map>) performs fast storage and retrieval of *unique keys* and *associated values*. Duplicate keys are *not* allowed—a single value can be associated with each key. This is called a one-to-one mapping. For example, a company that uses unique employee numbers, such as 100, 200 and 300, might have a map that associates employee numbers with their telephone extensions—4321, 4115 and 5217, respectively. With a map you specify the key and get back the associated data quickly. Providing the key in a map's subscript operator [] locates the value associated with that key in the map. Insertions and deletions can be made *anywhere* in a map. If the order of the keys is not important, you can use unordered_map (header <unordered_map>) instead.

Figure 15.18 demonstrates a map (created at line 8) and uses the same features as Fig. 15.17 to demonstrate the subscript operator. Lines 27–28 use the subscript operator of class map. When the subscript is a key that's already in the map (line 27), the operator returns a reference to the associated value. When the subscript is a key that's *not* in the map (line 28), the operator inserts the key in the map and returns a reference that can be used to associate a value with that key. Line 27 replaces the value for the key 25 (previously 33.333 as specified in line 15) with a new value, 9999.99. Line 28 inserts a new key–value pair in the map (called creating an association). Note this example's map, could have been initialized with an initializer list of pairs, as we showed for a multimap in Section 15.6.3.

```
1   // Fig. 15.18: fig15_18.cpp
2   // Standard Library class map class template.
3   #include <iostream>
4   #include <map> // map class-template definition
5   using namespace std;
6
7   int main() {
8      map<int, double, less<int>> pairs;
9
10     // insert eight value_type objects in pairs
11     pairs.insert(make_pair(15, 2.7));
12     pairs.insert(make_pair(30, 111.11));
```

Fig. 15.18 | Standard Library map class template. (Part 1 of 2.)

```
13        pairs.insert(make_pair(5, 1010.1));
14        pairs.insert(make_pair(10, 22.22));
15        pairs.insert(make_pair(25, 33.333));
16        pairs.insert(make_pair(5, 77.54)); // dup ignored
17        pairs.insert(make_pair(20, 9.345));
18        pairs.insert(make_pair(15, 99.3)); // dup ignored
19
20        cout << "pairs contains:\nKey\tValue\n";
21
22        // walk through elements of pairs
23        for (auto mapItem : pairs) {
24            cout << mapItem.first << '\t' << mapItem.second << '\n';
25        }
26
27        pairs[25] = 9999.99; // use subscripting to change value for key 25
28        pairs[40] = 8765.43; // use subscripting to insert value for key 40
29
30        cout << "\nAfter subscript operations, pairs contains:\nKey\tValue\n";
31
32        // use const_iterator to walk through elements of pairs
33        for (auto mapItem : pairs) {
34            cout << mapItem.first << '\t' << mapItem.second << '\n';
35        }
36
37        cout << endl;
38    }
```

```
pairs contains:
Key     Value
5       1010.1
10      22.22
15      2.7
20      9.345
25      33.333
30      111.11

After subscript operations, pairs contains:
Key     Value
5       1010.1
10      22.22
15      2.7
20      9.345
25      9999.99
30      111.11
40      8765.43
```

Fig. 15.18 | Standard Library map class template. (Part 2 of 2.)

15.7 Container Adapters

The three container adapters are stack, queue and priority_queue. Container adapters are *not first-class containers*, because they do *not* provide the actual data-structure implementation in which elements can be stored and because *adapters do not support iterators*. The benefit of an *adapter class* is that you can choose an appropriate underlying data structure. All three *adapter classes* provide member functions push and pop that properly insert an element into each adapter data structure and properly remove an element from each adapter data structure, respectively. The next several subsections provide examples of the adapter classes.

15.7.1 stack Adapter

Class stack (from header <stack>) enables insertions into and deletions from the underlying container at one end called the *top*, so a stack is commonly referred to as a *last-in, first-out* data structure. We introduced stacks in our discussion of the function-call stack in Section 6.11. A stack can be implemented with a vector, list or deque. This example creates three integer stacks, using vector, list and deque as the underlying data structure to represent the stack. By default, a stack is implemented with a deque. The stack operations are push to insert an element at the *top* of the stack (implemented by calling function push_back of the underlying container), pop to remove the *top* element of the stack (implemented by calling function pop_back of the underlying container), top to get a reference to the top element of the stack (implemented by calling function back of the underlying container), empty to determine whether the stack is empty (implemented by calling function empty of the underlying container) and size to get the number of elements in the stack (implemented by calling function size of the underlying container). In Chapter 19, we'll show you how to develop your own custom stack class template.

Figure 15.19 demonstrates the stack adapter class. Lines 17, 20 and 23 instantiate three integer stacks. Line 17 specifies a stack of integers that uses the default deque container as its underlying data structure. Line 20 specifies a stack of integers that uses a vector of integers as its underlying data structure. Line 23 specifies a stack of integers that uses a list of integers as its underlying data structure.

```
1   // Fig. 15.19: fig15_19.cpp
2   // Standard Library stack adapter class.
3   #include <iostream>
4   #include <stack> // stack adapter definition
5   #include <vector> // vector class-template definition
6   #include <list> // list class-template definition
7   using namespace std;
8
9   // pushElements function-template prototype
10  template<typename T> void pushElements(T& stackRef);
11
12  // popElements function-template prototype
13  template<typename T> void popElements(T& stackRef);
14
15  int main() {
16     // stack with default underlying deque
17     stack<int> intDequeStack;
18
19     // stack with underlying vector
20     stack<int, vector<int>> intVectorStack;
21
```

Fig. 15.19 | Standard Library stack adapter class. (Part 1 of 2.)

```
22      // stack with underlying list
23      stack<int, list<int>> intListStack;
24
25      // push the values 0-9 onto each stack
26      cout << "Pushing onto intDequeStack: ";
27      pushElements(intDequeStack);
28      cout << "\nPushing onto intVectorStack: ";
29      pushElements(intVectorStack);
30      cout << "\nPushing onto intListStack: ";
31      pushElements(intListStack);
32      cout << endl << endl;
33
34      // display and remove elements from each stack
35      cout << "Popping from intDequeStack: ";
36      popElements(intDequeStack);
37      cout << "\nPopping from intVectorStack: ";
38      popElements(intVectorStack);
39      cout << "\nPopping from intListStack: ";
40      popElements(intListStack);
41      cout << endl;
42   }
43
44   // push elements onto stack object to which stackRef refers
45   template<typename T> void pushElements(T& stackRef) {
46      for (int i{0}; i < 10; ++i) {
47         stackRef.push(i); // push element onto stack
48         cout << stackRef.top() << ' '; // view (and display) top element
49      }
50   }
51
52   // pop elements from stack object to which stackRef refers
53   template<typename T> void popElements(T& stackRef) {
54      while (!stackRef.empty()) {
55         cout << stackRef.top() << ' '; // view (and display) top element
56         stackRef.pop(); // remove top element
57      }
58   }
```

```
Pushing onto intDequeStack: 0 1 2 3 4 5 6 7 8 9
Pushing onto intVectorStack: 0 1 2 3 4 5 6 7 8 9
Pushing onto intListStack: 0 1 2 3 4 5 6 7 8 9

Popping from intDequeStack: 9 8 7 6 5 4 3 2 1 0
Popping from intVectorStack: 9 8 7 6 5 4 3 2 1 0
Popping from intListStack: 9 8 7 6 5 4 3 2 1 0
```

Fig. 15.19 | Standard Library stack adapter class. (Part 2 of 2.)

Function pushElements (lines 45–50) pushes the elements onto each stack. Line 47 uses function push (available in each *adapter class*) to place an integer on top of the stack. Line 48 uses stack function top to retrieve the *top* element of the stack for output. *Function top does not remove the top element.*

Function popElements (lines 53–58) pops the elements off each stack. Line 55 uses stack function top to retrieve the top element of the stack for output. Line 56 uses function pop (available in each *adapter class*) to remove the *top* element of the stack. Function pop does *not* return a value.

15.7.2 queue Adapter

A queue is similar to a *waiting line*. The item that has been in the queue the *longest* is the *next* one removed—so a queue is referred to as a first-in, first-out (FIFO) data structure. Class queue (from header <queue>) enables insertions only at the *back* of the underlying data structure and deletions only from the *front*. A queue can store its elements in objects of the Standard Library's list or deque containers. By default, a queue is implemented with a deque. The common queue operations are push to insert an element at the back of the queue (implemented by calling function push_back of the underlying container), pop to remove the element at the front of the queue (implemented by calling function pop_front of the underlying container), front to get a reference to the *first* element in the queue (implemented by calling function front of the underlying container), back to get a reference to the *last* element in the queue (implemented by calling function back of the underlying container), empty to determine whether the queue is *empty* (this calls empty on underlying container) and size to get the number of elements in the queue (this calls size on the underlying container). In Chapter 19, we'll show you how to develop your own custom queue class template.

Figure 15.20 demonstrates the queue adapter class. Line 8 instantiates a queue of doubles. Lines 11–13 use function push to add elements to the queue. The while statement in lines 18–21 uses function empty (available in *all* containers) to determine whether the queue is empty (line 18). While there are more elements in the queue, line 19 uses queue function front to read (but not remove) the first element in the queue for output. Line 20 removes the first element in the queue with function pop (available in all *adapter classes*).

```cpp
1   // Fig. 15.20: fig15_20.cpp
2   // Standard Library queue adapter class template.
3   #include <iostream>
4   #include <queue> // queue adapter definition
5   using namespace std;
6
7   int main() {
8      queue<double> values; // queue with doubles
9
10     // push elements onto queue values
11     values.push(3.2);
12     values.push(9.8);
13     values.push(5.4);
14
15     cout << "Popping from values: ";
16
17     // pop elements from queue
18     while (!values.empty()) {
19        cout << values.front() << ' '; // view front element
20        values.pop(); // remove element
21     }
```

Fig. 15.20 | Standard Library queue adapter class template. (Part 1 of 2.)

```
22
23     cout << endl;
24   }
```

```
Popping from values: 3.2 9.8 5.4
```

Fig. 15.20 | Standard Library queue adapter class template. (Part 2 of 2.)

15.7.3 priority_queue Adapter

Class priority_queue (from header <queue>) provides functionality that enables *insertions* in *sorted order* into the underlying data structure and deletions from the *front* of the underlying data structure. By default, a priority_queue's elements are stored in a vector. When elements are added to a priority_queue, they're inserted in *priority order*, such that the highest-priority element (i.e., the *largest* value) will be the first element removed from the priority_queue. This is usually accomplished by arranging the elements in a data structure called a heap (not to be confused with the heap for dynamically allocated memory) that always maintains the largest value (i.e., highest-priority element) at the front of the data structure. The comparison of elements is performed with *comparator function object* less<T> by default, but you can supply a different comparator.

There are several common priority_queue operations. Function push inserts an element at the appropriate location based on *priority order* of the priority_queue, which then reorders the elements in priority order. Function pop removes the *highest-priority* element of the priority_queue. top gets a reference to the *top* element of the priority_queue (implemented by calling function front of the underlying container). empty determines whether the priority_queue is *empty* (implemented by calling function empty of the underlying container). size gets the number of elements in the priority_queue (implemented by calling function size of the underlying container).

Figure 15.21 demonstrates the priority_queue adapter class. Line 8 instantiates a priority_queue that stores double values and uses a vector as the underlying data structure. Lines 11–13 use function push to add elements to the priority_queue. The while statement in lines 18–21 uses function empty (available in *all* containers) to determine whether the priority_queue is empty (line 18). While there are more elements, line 19 uses priority_queue function top to retrieve the *highest-priority* element (i.e., the largest value) in the priority_queue for output. Line 20 removes the *highest-priority* element in the priority_queue with function pop (available in all adapter classes).

```
1    // Fig. 15.21: fig15_21.cpp
2    // Standard Library priority_queue adapter class.
3    #include <iostream>
4    #include <queue> // priority_queue adapter definition
5    using namespace std;
6
7    int main() {
8       priority_queue<double> priorities; // create priority_queue
```

Fig. 15.21 | Standard Library priority_queue adapter class. (Part 1 of 2.)

```
 9
10     // push elements onto priorities
11     priorities.push(3.2);
12     priorities.push(9.8);
13     priorities.push(5.4);
14
15     cout << "Popping from priorities: ";
16
17     // pop element from priority_queue
18     while (!priorities.empty()) {
19        cout << priorities.top() << ' '; // view top element
20        priorities.pop(); // remove top element
21     }
22
23     cout << endl;
24  }
```

```
Popping from priorities: 9.8 5.4 3.2
```

Fig. 15.21 | Standard Library priority_queue adapter class. (Part 2 of 2.)

15.8 Class bitset

Class bitset makes it easy to create and manipulate bit sets, which are useful for representing a set of bit flags. bitsets are fixed in size at compile time. Class bitset is an alternate tool for *bit manipulation*, discussed in Chapter 22.

The declaration

    bitset<size> b;

creates bitset b, in which every one of the size bits is initially 0 ("off").

The statement

    b.set(bitNumber);

sets bit bitNumber of bitset b "on." The expression b.set() sets all bits in b "on."

The statement

    b.reset(bitNumber);

sets bit bitNumber of bitset b "off." The expression b.reset() sets all bits in b "off."

The statement

    b.flip(bitNumber);

"flips" bit bitNumber of bitset b (e.g., if the bit is "on", flip sets it "off"). The expression b.flip() flips all bits in b.

The statement

    b[bitNumber];

returns a reference to the bool at position bitNumber of bitset b. Similarly,

    b.at(bitNumber);

performs range checking on bitNumber first. Then, if bitNumber is in range (based on the number of bits in the bitset), at returns a reference to the bit. Otherwise, at throws an out_of_range exception.

The statement

```
b.test(bitNumber);
```

performs *range checking* on bitNumber first. If bitNumber is in range (based on the number of bits in the bitset), test returns true if the bit is on, false it's off. Otherwise, test throws an out_of_range exception.

The expression

```
b.size()
```

returns the number of bits in bitset b.

The expression

```
b.count()
```

returns the number of bits that are set (true) in bitset b.

The expression

```
b.any()
```

returns true if any bit is set in bitset b.

The expression

```
b.all()
```

(added in C++11) returns true if all of the bits are set (true) in bitset b.

The expression

```
b.none()
```

returns true if none of the bits is set in bitset b (that is, all the bits are false).

The expressions

```
b == b1
b != b1
```

compare the two bitsets for equality and inequality, respectively.

Each of the bitwise assignment operators &=, |= and ^= (discussed in detail in Section 22.5) can be used to combine bitsets. For example,

```
b &= b1;
```

performs a bit-by-bit logical AND between bitsets b and b1. The result is stored in b. Bitwise logical OR and bitwise logical XOR are performed by

```
b |= b1;
b ^= b2;
```

The expression

```
b >>= n;
```

shifts the bits in bitset b right by n positions.

The expression

```
b <<= n;
```

shifts the bits in bitset b left by n positions.

The expressions

```
b.to_string()
b.to_ulong()
```

convert bitset b to a string and an unsigned long, respectively.

15.9 Wrap-Up

In this chapter, we introduced three key components of the Standard Library—containers, iterators and algorithms. You learned about the linear *sequence containers*, array (Chapter 7), vector, deque, forward_list and list, which all represent linear data structures. We discussed the nonlinear *associative containers*, set, multiset, map and multimap and their unordered versions. You also saw that the *container adapters* stack, queue and priority_queue can be used to restrict the operations of the sequence containers vector, deque and list for the purpose of implementing the specialized data structures represented by the container adapters. You learned the categories of iterators and that each algorithm can be used with any container that supports the minimum iterator functionality the algorithm requires. You also learned the features of class bitset, which makes it easy to create and manipulate bit sets as a container.

The next chapter continues our discussion of the Standard Library's containers, iterators and algorithms with a detailed treatment of algorithms. You'll also learn about function pointers, function objects and C++11's lambda expressions.

Summary

Section 15.1 Introduction
- The C++ Standard Library defines powerful, template-based, reusable components for common data structures and defines algorithms used to process those data structures.
- There are three container-class categories—first-class containers, container adapters and near containers.
- Iterators, which have properties similar to those of pointers, are used to manipulate container elements.
- Standard Library algorithms are function templates that perform such common data manipulations as searching, sorting and comparing elements or entire containers.
- Linked lists are collections of data items logically "lined up in a row"—insertions and removals are made anywhere in a linked list.
- Stacks are important in compilers and operating systems: Insertions and removals are made only at one end of a stack—its top.
- Queues represent waiting lines; insertions are made at the back (also referred to as the tail) of a queue and removals are made from the front (also referred to as the head) of a queue.
- Binary trees are nonlinear, hierarchical data structures that facilitate searching and sorting data, duplicate elimination and compiling expressions into machine code.

Section 15.2 Introduction to Containers

- Containers are divided into **sequence containers**, **ordered associative containers**, **unordered associative containers** and **container adapters** (p. 658).

- The **sequence containers** (p. 658) represent linear data structures.

- **Associative containers** are nonlinear containers that quickly locate elements stored in them, such as sets of values or **key–value pairs** (p. 658).

- Sequence containers and associative containers are collectively referred to as first-class containers.

- Class templates `stack`, `queue` and `priority_queue` are container adapters that enable a program to view a sequence container in a constrained manner.

- **Near containers** (p. 659; built-in arrays, `bitsets` and `valarrays`) exhibit capabilities similar to those of the first-class containers, but do not support all the first-class-container capabilities.

- Most containers provide similar functionality. Many operations apply to all containers, and other operations apply to subsets of similar containers.

- First-class containers define many common nested types that are used in template-based declarations of variables, parameters to functions and return values from functions.

Section 15.3 Introduction to Iterators

- Iterators have many similarities to pointers and are used to point to first-class container elements.

- First-class container function **begin** (p. 662) returns an iterator pointing to the first element of a container. Function **end** (p. 662) returns an iterator pointer after the container's last element (one past the end)—typically used in a loop to indicate when to terminate processing of the container's elements.

- An `istream_iterator` (p. 662) is capable of extracting values in a type-safe manner from an input stream. An `ostream_iterator` (p. 662) is capable of inserting values in an output stream.

- **Input** and **output iterators** (p. 664) can move only in the forward direction one element at a time.

- A forward iterator (p. 664) combines the capabilities of input and output iterators.

- A bidirectional iterator (p. 664) has the capabilities of a forward iterator and can move backward.

- A random-access iterator (p. 664) has the capabilities of a bidirectional iterator and the ability to directly access any element of the container.

Section 15.4 Introduction to Algorithms

- The Standard Library algorithms operate on container elements only indirectly through iterators.

- Many algorithms operate on sequences of elements defined by iterators pointing to the first element of the sequence and to one element past the last element.

Section 15.5 Sequence Containers

- The Standard Library provides sequence containers `array`, `vector`, `forward_list`, `list` and `deque`. Class templates `array`, `vector` and `deque` are based on built-in arrays. Class templates `forward_list` and `list` implement a linked-list data structure.

Section 15.5.1 **vector** Sequence Container

- Function capacity (p. 669) returns the number of elements that can be stored in a vector before the vector dynamically resizes itself to accommodate more elements.

- Sequence container function push_back (p. 670) adds an element to the end of a container.

- vector member function cbegin (p. 671; C++11) returns a `const_iterator` to the vector's first element.

- `vector` member function cend (p. 671; C++11) returns a `const_iterator` to the location past the last element of the `vector`.
- C++14's global cbegin and cend functions work the same way as functions begin and end, but return const iterators that cannot be used to modify the data.
- C++14's global rbegin, rend, crbegin and crend functions support iterating through a built-in array or a container from back to front. Functions rbegin and rend return iterators that can be used to modify data, and crbegin and crend return const iterators that cannot be used to modify data.
- Functions begin and end and their C++14 const and reverse versions may also receive container objects as arguments—each function calls the corresponding member function in its container argument.
- `vector` member function **crbegin** (p. 672; C++11) returns a `const_reverse_iterator` to the vector's last element.
- `vector` member function **crend** (p. 672; C++11) returns a `const_reverse_iterator` to the location before the first element of the `vector`.
- As of C++11, you can ask a `vector` or deque to return unneeded memory to the system by calling member function **shrink_to_fit** (p. 672).
- As of C++11, you can use list initializers to initialize the elements of `vector`s and other containers.
- Algorithm **copy** (p. 674; from header <algorithm>) copies each element in a range starting with the location specified by its first iterator argument up to, but not including, the one specified by its second iterator argument.
- Function **front** (p. 674) returns a reference to the first element in a sequence container. Function begin returns an iterator pointing to the beginning of a sequence container.
- Function **back** (p. 674) returns a reference to the last element in a sequence container (except `forward_list`). Function end returns an iterator pointing to the element one past the end of a sequence container.
- Sequence container function **insert** (p. 675) inserts value(s) before the element at a specific location and returns an iterator pointing to the inserted item or the first of the inserted items.
- Function **erase** (p. 675; in all first-class containers except `forward_list`) removes specific element(s) from the container.
- Function **empty** (p. 675; in all containers and adapters) returns true if the container is empty.
- Function **clear** (p. 675; in all first-class containers) empties the container.

Section 15.5.2 *list Sequence Container*
- The `list` sequence container (p. 675; from header <list>) implements a doubly linked list that provides an efficient implementation for inserting and deleting anywhere in the container.
- The `forward_list` sequence container (p. 676; from header <forward_list>) implements a singly linked list that supports only forward iterators.
- `list` member function **push_front** (p. 678) inserts values at the beginning of a list.
- `list` member function **sort** (p. 679) arranges the elements in the list in ascending order.
- `list` member function **splice** (p. 679) removes elements in one `list` and inserts them into another `list` at a specific position.
- `list` member function **unique** (p. 679) removes duplicate elements in a `list`.
- `list` member function **assign** (p. 679) replaces the contents of one `list` with those of another.
- `list` member function **remove** (p. 680) deletes all copies of a specified value from a `list`.

Section 15.5.3 deque *Sequence Container*

- Class template **deque** (p. 680) provides the same operations as vector, but adds member functions **push_front** and **pop_front** (p. 679) to allow insertion and deletion at the beginning of a deque, respectively. Header <deque> must be included to use class template deque.

Section 15.6 *Associative Containers*

- The Standard Library's associative containers provide direct access to store and retrieve elements via **keys** (p. 681).

- The four ordered associative containers are multiset, set, multimap and map. The four unordered associative containers are unordered_multiset, unordered_set, unordered_multimap and unordered_map. These are nearly identical to their ordered counterparts, but do not maintain keys in sorted order.

- Class templates multiset and set provide operations for manipulating sets of values where the values are the keys—there is not a separate value associated with each key. Header <set> must be included to use class templates set and multiset.

- A multiset allows duplicate keys and a set does not.

Section 15.6.1 multiset *Associative Container*

- The **multiset associative container** (p. 682) provides fast storage and retrieval of keys and allows duplicate keys. The key order is determined by a comparator function object. If the order of the keys is not important, you can use unordered_multiset (header <unordered_set>) instead.

- A multiset's keys can be sorted in ascending order by ordering the keys with comparator function object **less<T>** (p. 682).

- The type of the keys in all associative containers must support comparison properly based on the comparator function object specified.

- A multiset supports bidirectional iterators.

- Header **<set>** (p. 682) must be included to use class multiset.

- Function **count** (p. 684; available to all associative containers) counts the number of occurrences of the specified value currently in a container.

- Function **find** (p. 684; available to all associative containers) locates a specified value in a container.

- Associative container functions **lower_bound** and **upper_bound** (p. 685) locate the earliest occurrence of the specified value in a container and the element after the value's last occurrence, respectively.

- Associative container function **equal_range** (p. 685) returns a pair containing the results of both a lower_bound and an upper_bound operation.

- C++ also includes class template tuple, which is similar to pair, but can hold any number of items of various types.

- As of C++14, the argument to find (and other similar functions) can be of any type, provided that there are overloaded comparison operators that can compare values of the argument's type to values of the container's key type.

Section 15.6.2 set *Associative Container*

- The set associative container is used for fast storage and retrieval of unique keys. If the order of the keys is not important, you can use unordered_set (header <unordered_set>) instead.

- If an attempt is made to insert a duplicate key into a set, the duplicate is ignored.

- A set supports bidirectional iterators.
- Header <set> must be included to use class set.

Section 15.6.3 **multimap** *Associative Container*
- Containers multimap and map provide operations for manipulating key–value pairs. If the order of the keys is not important, you can use unordered_multimap and unordered_map instead (header <unordered_map>).
- The primary difference between a multimap and a map is that a multimap allows duplicate keys with associated values to be stored and a map allows only unique keys with associated values.
- The multimap associative container is used for fast storage and retrieval of key–value pairs.
- Duplicate keys are allowed in a multimap, so multiple values can be associated with a single key. This is called a one-to-many relationship.
- Header **<map>** (p. 687) must be included to use class templates map and multimap.
- Function make_pair creates a pair using the types specified in the multimap's declaration.
- In C++11, if you know the key–value pairs in advance, you can use list initialization when you create a multimap.

Section 15.6.4 **map** *Associative Container*
- Duplicate keys are not allowed in a map, so only a single value can be associated with each key. This is called a **one-to-one mapping** (p. 689). If the order of the keys is not important, you can use unordered_map (header <unordered_map>) instead.

Section 15.7 *Container Adapters*
- The container adapters are stack, queue and priority_queue.
- Adapters are not first-class containers, because they do not provide the actual data structure implementation in which elements can be stored and they do not support iterators.
- All three adapter class templates provide member functions **push** and **pop** (p. 691) that properly insert an element into and remove an element from each adapter data structure, respectively.

Section 15.7.1 **stack** *Adapter*
- Class template **stack** (p. 691) is a last-in, first-out data structure. Header **<stack>** (p. 691) must be included to use class template stack.
- The stack member function **top** (p. 691) returns a reference to the top element of the stack (implemented by calling function back of the underlying container).
- The stack member function empty determines whether the stack is empty (implemented by calling function empty of the underlying container).
- The stack member function size returns the number of elements in the stack (implemented by calling function size of the underlying container).

Section 15.7.2 **queue** *Adapter*
- Class template **queue** (p. 693) implements a FIFO data structure. Header **<queue>** (p. 693) must be included to use a queue or a priority_queue.
- The queue member function **front** (p. 693) returns a reference to the first element in the queue.
- The queue member function **back** (p. 693) returns a reference to the last element in the queue.
- The queue member function empty determines whether the queue is empty.
- The queue member function size returns the number of elements in the queue.

Section 15.7.3 `priority_queue` *Adapter*
- Class template `priority_queue` provides functionality that enables insertions in sorted order into the underlying data structure and deletions from the front of the underlying data structure.
- The common `priority_queue` (p. 694) operations are push, pop, top, empty and size.

Section 15.8 Class `bitset`
- Class template `bitset` (p. 695) makes it easy to create and manipulate bit sets, which are useful for representing a set of bit flags.

Self-Review Exercises

15.1 State whether each of the following is *true* or *false*. If *false*, explain why.
  a) Pointer-based code is complex and error prone—the slightest omissions or oversights can lead to serious memory-access violations and memory-leak errors that the compiler will warn you about.
  b) deques offer rapid insertions and deletions at front or back and direct access to any element.
  c) lists are singly linked lists and offer rapid insertion and deletion anywhere.
  d) multimaps offer one-to-many mapping with duplicates allowed and rapid key-based lookup.
  e) Associative containers are nonlinear data structures that typically can locate elements stored in the containers quickly.
  f) The container member function cbegin returns an iterator that refers to the container's first element.
  g) The ++ operation on an iterator moves it to the container's next element.
  h) The * (dereferencing) operator when applied to a const iterator returns a const reference to the container element, allowing the use of non-const member functions.
  i) Using iterators where appropriate is another example of the principle of least privilege.
  j) Many algorithms operate on sequences of elements defined by iterators pointing to the first element of the sequence and to the last element.
  k) Function capacity returns the number of elements that can be stored in the vector before the vector needs to dynamically resize itself to accommodate more elements.
  l) One of the most common uses of a deque is to maintain a first-in, first-out queue of elements. In fact, a deque is the default underlying implementation for the queue adaptor.
  m) push_front is available only for class list.
  n) Insertions and deletions can be made only at the front and back of a map.
  o) Class queue enables insertions at the front of the underlying data structure and deletions from the back (commonly referred to as a first-in, first-out data structure).

15.2 Fill in the blanks in each of the following statements:
  a) The three key components of the "STL" portion of the Standard Library are _____, _____ and _____.
  b) Built-in arrays can be manipulated by Standard Library algorithms, using _____ as iterators.
  c) The Standard Library container adapter most closely associated with the last-in, first-out (LIFO) insertion-and-removal discipline is the _____.
  d) The sequence containers and _____ containers are collectively referred to as the first-class containers.
  e) A(n) _____ constructor initializes the container to be a copy of an existing container of the same type.

f) The _____ container member function returns true if there are no elements in the container; otherwise, it returns false.

g) The _____ container member function (C++11) moves the elements of one container into another—this avoids the overhead of copying each element of the argument container.

h) The container member function _____ is overloaded to return either an iterator or a const_iterator that refers to the first element of the container.

i) Operations performed on a const_iterator return _____ to prevent modification to elements of the container being manipulated.

j) The sequence containers are array, vector, deque, _____ and _____.

k) Choose the _____ container for the best random-access performance in a container that can grow.

l) Function push_back, which is available in sequence containers other than _____, adds an element to the end of the container.

m) As with cbegin and cend, C++11 includes vector member function crbegin and crend which return _____ that represent the starting and ending points when iterating through a container in reverse.

n) A unary _____ function takes a single argument, performs a comparison using that argument and returns a bool value indicating the result.

o) The primary difference between the ordered and unordered associative containers is _____.

p) The primary difference between a multimap and a map is _____.

q) C++11 introduces class template tuple, which is similar to pair, but can _____.

r) The map associative container performs fast storage and retrieval of unique keys and associated values. Duplicate keys are not allowed—a single value can be associated with each key. This is called a(n) _____ mapping.

s) Class _____ provides functionality that enables insertions in sorted order into the underlying data structure and deletions from the front of the underlying data structure.

15.3 Write a statement or expression that performs each of the following bitset tasks:
a) Write a declaration that creates bitset flags of size size, in which every bit is initially 0.
b) Write a statement that sets bit bitNumber of bitset flags "off."
c) Write a statement that returns a reference to the bit bitNumber of bitset flags.
d) Write an expression that returns the number of bits that are set in bitset flags.
e) Write an expression that returns true if all of the bits are set in bitset flags.
f) Write an expression that compares bitsets flags and otherFlags for inequality.
g) Write an expression that shifts the bits in bitset flags left by n positions.

Answers to Self-Review Exercises

15.1 a) False. The compiler does not warn about these kinds of execution-time errors. b) True. c) False. They are doubly linked lists. d) True. e) True. f) False. It returns a const_iterator. g) True. h) False. Disallowing the use of non-const member functions. i) False. Using const_iterators where appropriate is another example of the principle of least privilege. j) False. Many algorithms operate on sequences of elements defined by iterators pointing to the first element of the sequence and to one element past the last element. k) True. l) True. m) False. It's also available for class deque. n) False. Insertions and deletions can be made anywhere in a map. o) False. Insertions may occur only at the back and deletions may occur only at the front.

15.2 a) containers, iterators and algorithms. b) pointers. c) stack. d) associative. e) copy. f) empty. g) move version of operator=. h) begin. i) const references. j) list and forward_list. k) vector. l) array. m) const_reverse_iterators. n) predicate. o) the unordered ones do not maintain their keys in sorted order. p) a multimap allows duplicate keys with associated values to be stored and a map allows only unique keys with associated values. q) hold any number of items of various types. r) one-to-one. s) priority_queue.

15.3   a) `bitset<size> flags;`
        b) `flags.reset(bitNumber);`
        c) `flags[bitNumber];`
        d) `flags.count()`
        e) `flags.all()`
        f) `flags != otherFlags`
        g) `flags <<= n;`

Exercises

15.4   State whether each of the following is *true* or *false*. If *false*, explain why.
        a) Many of the Standard Library algorithms can be applied to various containers independently of the underlying container implementation.
        b) arrays are fixed in size and offer direct access to any element.
        c) forward_lists are singly linked lists, that offer rapid insertion and deletion only at the front and the back.
        d) sets offer rapid lookup and duplicates are allowed.
        e) In a priority_queue, the lowest-priority element is always the first element out.
        f) The sequence containers represent non-linear data structures.
        g) As of C++11, there is now a non-member function version of swap that swaps the contents of its two arguments (which must be of different container types) using move operations rather than copy operations.
        h) Container member function erase removes all elements from the container.
        i) An object of type iterator refers to a container element that *can* be modified.
        j) We use const versions of the iterators for traversing read-only containers.
        k) For input iterators and output iterators, it's common to save the iterator, then use the saved value later.
        l) Class templates array, vector and deque are based on built-in arrays.
        m) Attempting to dereference an iterator positioned outside its container is a compilation error. In particular, the iterator returned by end should not be dereferenced or incremented.
        n) Insertions and deletions in the middle of a deque are optimized to minimize the number of elements copied, so it's more efficient than a vector but less efficient than a list for this kind of modification.
        o) Container set does *not* allow duplicates.
        p) Class stack (from header <stack>) enables insertions into and deletions from the underlying data structure at one end (commonly referred to as a last-in, first-out data structure).
        q) Function empty is available in all containers except the deque.

15.5   Fill in the blanks in each of the following statements:
        a) The three styles of container classes are first-class containers, _____ and near containers.
        b) Containers are divided into four major categories—sequence containers, ordered associative containers, _____ and container adapters.
        c) The Standard Library container adapter most closely associated with the first-in, first-out (FIFO) insertion-and-removal discipline is the _____.
        d) Built-in arrays, bitsets and valarrays are all _____ containers.
        e) A(n) _____ constructor (C++11) moves the contents of an existing container of the same type into a new container, without the overhead of copying each element of the argument container.

f) The _____ container member function returns the number of elements currently in the container.

g) The _____ container member function returns `true` if the contents of the first container are not equal to the contents of the second; otherwise, returns `false`.

h) We use iterators with sequences—these can be input sequences or output sequences, or they can be _____.

i) The Standard Library algorithms operate on container elements indirectly via _____.

j) Applications with frequent insertions and deletions in the middle and/or at the extremes of a container normally use a(n) _____.

k) Function _____ is available in *every* first-class container (except `forward_list`) and it returns the number of elements currently stored in the container.

l) It can be wasteful to double a `vector`'s size when more space is needed. For example, a full `vector` of 1,000,000 elements resizes to accommodate 2,000,000 elements when a new element is added, leaving 999,999 unused elements. You can use _____ and _____ to control space usage better.

m) As of C++11, you can ask a `vector` or `deque` to return unneeded memory to the system by calling member function _____.

n) The associative containers provide direct access to store and retrieve elements via keys (often called search keys). The ordered associative containers are `multiset`, `set`, _____ and _____.

o) Classes _____ and _____ provide operations for manipulating sets of values where the values are the keys—there is *not* a separate value associated with each key.

p) We use C++11's auto keyword to _____.

q) A `multimap` is implemented to efficiently locate all values paired with a given _____.

r) The Standard Library container adapters are `stack`, `queue` and _____.

Discussion Questions

15.6   Why is it expensive to insert (or delete) an element in the middle of a `vector`?

15.7   Containers that support random-access iterators can be used with most but not all Standard Library algorithms. What is the exception?

15.8   Why would you use operator * to dereference an iterator?

15.9   Why is insertion at the back of a `vector` efficient?

15.10   When would you use a `deque` in preference to a `vector`?

15.11   Describe what happens when you insert an element in a vector whose memory is exhausted.

15.12   When would you prefer a `list` to a `deque`?

15.13   What happens when the map subscript is a key that's not in the map?

15.14   Use C++11 list initializers to initialize the vector names with the strings "Suzanne", "James", "Maria" and "Juan". Show both common syntaxes.

15.15   What happens when you erase a container element that contains a pointer to a dynamically allocated object?

15.16   Describe the multiset ordered associative container.

15.17   How might a `multimap` ordered associative container be used in a credit-card transaction processing system?

15.18   Write a statement that creates and initializes a multimap of strings and ints with three key–value pairs.

15.19   Explain the push, pop and top operations of a stack.

15.20 Explain the push, pop, front and back operations of a queue.

15.21 How does inserting an item in a priority_queue differ from inserting an item in virtually any other container?

Programming Exercises

15.22 *(Palindromes)* Write a function template palindrome that takes a vector parameter and returns true or false according to whether the vector does or does not read the same forward as backward (e.g., a vector containing 1, 2, 3, 2, 1 is a palindrome, but a vector containing 1, 2, 3, 4 is not).

15.23 *(Sieve of Eratosthenes with bitset)* This exercise revisits the *Sieve of Eratosthenes* for finding prime numbers that we discussed in Exercise 7.27. Use a bitset to implement the algorithm. Your program should display all the prime numbers from 2 to 1023, then allow the user to enter a number to determine whether that number is prime.

15.24 *(Sieve of Eratosthenes)* Modify Exercise 15.23, the Sieve of Eratosthenes, so that, if the number the user inputs into the program is not prime, the program displays the prime factors of the number. Remember that a prime number's factors are only 1 and the prime number itself. Every nonprime number has a unique prime factorization. For example, the factors of 54 are 2, 3, 3 and 3. When these values are multiplied together, the result is 54. For the number 54, the prime factors output should be 2 and 3.

15.25 *(Prime Factors)* Modify Exercise 15.24 so that, if the number the user inputs into the program is not prime, the program displays the prime factors of the number and the number of times each prime factor appears in the unique prime factorization. For example, the output for the number 54 should be

```
The unique prime factorization of 54 is: 2 * 3 * 3 * 3
```

Recommended Reading

Gottschling, P. *Discovering Modern C++: An Intensive Course for Scientists, Engineers, and Programmers (C++ In-Depth)*. Boston: Addison-Wesley Professional, 2016.

Horton, I. *Using the C++ Standard Template Libraries*. New York: Springer Science + Business Media, 2015.

Josuttis, N. *The C++ Standard Library: A Tutorial and Reference (Second edition)*. Boston: Addison-Wesley Professional, 2012.

Karlsson, B. *Beyond the C++ Standard Library: An Introduction to Boost*. Boston: Addison-Wesley Professional, 2005.

Lippman, S., J. Lajoie, and B. Moo. *C++ Primer (Fifth Edition)*. Boston: Addison-Wesley Professional, 2012.

Meyers, S. *Effective Modern C++: 42 Specific Ways to Improve Your Use of C++11 and C++14*. Sebastopol: O'Reilly, 2015.

Stroustrup, B. "C++11—the New ISO C++ Standard" <www.stroustrup.com/C++11FAQ.html>. [*Note:* Stroustrup's FAQ has been merged with Marshall Cline's to form the C++ FAQ at https://isocpp.org/faq.]

Stroustrup, B. *The C++ Programming Language, Fourth Edition*. Boston: Addison-Wesley Professional, 2013.

Wilson, M. *Extended STL, Volume 1: Collections and Iterators*. Boston: Addison-Wesley, 2007.

Standard Library Algorithms

16

Objectives

In this chapter you'll:

- Understand minimum iterator requirements for working with Standard Library algorithms and containers.

- Create anonymous functions using lambda expressions.

- Capture local variables for use in lambda expressions.

- Use containers and iterators with many of the dozens of Standard Library algorithms.

- Use iterators with algorithms to access and manipulate the elements of Standard Library containers.

- Pass lambda expressions, function pointers and function objects into Standard Library algorithms to help them perform their tasks.

16.1 Introduction

This chapter discusses the Standard Library's algorithms, focusing on common container manipulations such as *searching*, *sorting* and *comparing elements or entire containers*. The Standard Library provides over 90 algorithms—many were added in C++11 and some are new in C++14. For the complete list, see

```
http://en.cppreference.com/w/cpp/algorithm
http://en.cppreference.com/w/cpp/numeric
```

As you'll see, various algorithms can receive a *function pointer* as an argument—recall that a function's name is implictly convertible to a pointer to that function's code. Such algorithms use the pointer to call the function, typically with one or two container elements as arguments. For most of the examples in this chapter, rather than function pointers we'll use *lambda expressions*—C++11's convenient shorthand notation for creating *anonymous functions* (that is, functions that do not have names). Later in the chapter we'll present the concept of a *function object*, which is similar to a lambda or a function pointer but is implemented as an object of a class that has an overloaded function-call operator (`operator()`). This allows the object's name to be used like a function name.

16.2 Minimum Iterator Requirements

With few exceptions, the Standard Library separates algorithms from containers. This makes it much easier to add new algorithms and to use them with multiple containers. An important part of every container is the *type of iterator* it supports (Fig. 15.7). This determines which algorithms can be applied to the container. For example, both vectors and arrays support *random-access iterators* that provide *all* of the iterator operations shown in Fig. 15.9. *All* Standard Library algorithms can operate on vectors and those that do not modify a container's size can also operate on arrays. Each Standard Library algorithm that takes iterator arguments requires those iterators to provide a minimum level of functionality. If an algorithm requires a *forward iterator*, for example, that algorithm can operate on any container that supports *forward iterators*, *bidirectional iterators* or *random-access iterators*.

Software Engineering Observation 16.1
Standard Library algorithms do not depend on the implementation details of the containers on which they operate. As long as a container's (or built-in array's) iterators satisfy the requirements of an algorithm, the algorithm can work on the container.

Software Engineering Observation 16.2
The Standard Library containers are implemented concisely. The algorithms are separated from the containers and operate on elements of the containers only indirectly through iterators. This separation makes it easier to write generic algorithms applicable to a variety of container classes.

Software Engineering Observation 16.3
Using the "weakest iterator" that yields acceptable performance helps produce maximally reusable components. For example, if an algorithm requires only forward iterators, it can be used with any container that supports forward iterators, bidirectional iterators or random-access iterators. However, an algorithm that requires random-access iterators can be used only with containers that have random-access iterators.

Iterator Invalidation
Iterators simply *point* to container elements, so it's possible for iterators to become *invalid* when certain container modifications occur. For example, if you invoke clear on a vector, *all* of its elements are *destroyed*. Any iterators that pointed to that vector's elements before clear was called would now be *invalid*. Section 23 of the C++ standard discusses all the cases in which iterators (and pointers and references) are invalidated for each Standard Library container. Here we summarize when iterators are invalidated during *insert* and *erase* operations.

When *inserting* into

- a vector—If the vector is reallocated, all iterators pointing to it are invalidated. Otherwise, iterators from the insertion point to the end of the vector are invalidated.

- a deque—All iterators are invalidated.

- a list or forward_list—All iterators *remain valid.*

- an ordered associative container—All iterators *remain valid.*

- an unordered associative container—All iterators are invalidated if the container needs to be reallocated.

When *erasing* from a container, iterators to the *erased* elements are invalidated. In addition:

- for a vector—Iterators from the erased element to the end of the vector are invalidated.

- for a deque—If an element in the middle of the deque is erased, all iterators are invalidated.

16.3 Lambda Expressions

As you'll see in this chapter, many Standard Library algorithms can receive function pointers as parameters—recall from Section 12.8 that the name of a function is implicitly convertible into a pointer to that function's code. Before you can pass a function pointer to an algorithm, the corresponding function must be declared.

C++11's lambda expressions (or simply lambdas) enable you to define anonymous functions *where they're passed* to a function. They're defined locally inside functions and can use and manipulate the local variables of the enclosing function. Figure 16.1 demonstrates the Standard Library's for_each algorithm, which invokes a function once for each element in a range. The example calls for_each twice, each with a simple lambda:

- the first is used to display each element in an int array multiplied by 2.

- the second is used to sum the elements of the int array.

```
1   // Fig. 16.1: fig16_01.cpp
2   // Lambda expressions.
3   #include <iostream>
4   #include <array>
5   #include <algorithm>
6   #include <iterator>
7   using namespace std;
8
9   int main() {
10      const size_t SIZE{4}; // size of array values
11      array<int, SIZE> values{1, 2, 3, 4}; // initialize values
12      ostream_iterator<int> output{cout, " "};
13
14      cout << "values contains: ";
15      copy(values.cbegin(), values.cend(), output);
16      cout << "\nDisplay each element multiplied by two: ";
17
18      // output each element multiplied by two
19      for_each(values.cbegin(), values.cend(),
20         [](auto i) {cout << i * 2 << " ";});
21
22      // add each element to sum
23      int sum = 0; // initialize sum to zero
24      for_each(values.cbegin(), values.cend(), [&sum](auto i) {sum += i;});
25
26      cout << "\nSum of value's elements is: " << sum << endl; // output sum
27   }
```

Fig. 16.1 | Lambda expressions. (Part 1 of 2.)

```
values contains: 1 2 3 4
Display each element multiplied by two: 2 4 6 8
Sum of value's elements is: 10
```

Fig. 16.1 | Lambda expressions. (Part 2 of 2.)

16.3.1 Algorithm for_each

Lines 19–20 and 24 use the for_each algorithm to call a function that performs a task once for each element of the array values. Like the algorithm copy (introduced in Section 15.3), for_each's first two arguments represent the range of elements to process. This program processes from values.cbegin() (the position of the array's first element) up to, but not including, values.cend() (the position one past the array's last element), so all of the array's elements are processed. The for_each algorithm's two iterator arguments must be at least *input iterators* that point into the *same* container, so for_each can get values from that container.

The function specified by for_each's third argument specifies the function to call with each element in the range. The function must have *one* parameter of the container's element type. for_each passes the current element's value as the function's argument, then the function performs a task using that value. As you'll see momentarily, this example's for_each calls each receive as their third argument a lambda representing a function that receives one argument and performs a task with that argument's value. If the function's parameter is a non-const reference and the iterators passed to for_each refer to non-const data, the function can modify the element.

16.3.2 Lambda with an Empty Introducer

Line 11 declares and initializes the array of ints named values and line 15 displays its contents. Lines 19–20 call the for_each algorithm to multiply each element of values by 2 and display the result. The third argument (line 20) to for_each

```
[](auto i) {cout << i * 2 << " ";}
```

is a *lambda expression* that performs the multiplication and output.

Lambdas begin with the lambda introducer ([]), followed by a parameter list and function body. A lambda can use local variables from the function in which the lambda is defined. The introducer enables you to specify which, if any, local variables the lambda uses—this is known as capturing the variables. The empty lambda introducer ([]) in line 20 indicates that the lambda does not use any of main's local variables.

The lambda in line 20 receives one parameter named i. Specifying the parameter's type as auto enables the compiler to *infer* the parameter's type, based on the context in which the lambda appears. In this case, the for_each algorithm calls line 20's lambda once for each element of the array, passing the element's value as the lambda's argument. Since the array contains ints, the compiler infers parameter i's type as int. Using auto to infer the parameter type is a new C++14 feature of so-called generic lambdas. In C++11 you were required to state each lambda parameter's explicit type. In this example, the lambda in line 20 is similar to the standalone function

14

```
void timesTwo(int i) {
   cout << i * 2 << " ";
}
```

Had we defined this function, lines 19–20 could have called the for_each algorithm with timesTwo's function name as the third argument, as in

```
for_each(values.cbegin(), values.cend(), timesTwo);
```

16.3.3 Lambda with a Nonempty Introducer—Capturing Local Variables

The second call to the for_each algorithm (line 24) totals array's elements. The lambda introducer [&sum] in

```
[&sum](auto i) {sum += i;}
```

indicates that this lambda expression *captures* the local variable sum (line 23) *by reference*. The ampersand (&) indicates that the lambda captures sum by reference and can *modify* its value. Without the ampersand, sum would be captured *by value* and the lambda would not modify the local variable outside the lambda expression. The for_each algorithm passes each element of values to the lambda, which adds the value to the sum. Line 26 then displays the sum.

16.3.4 Lambda Return Types

The compiler can infer a lambda's return type if the body contains a statement of the form

```
return expression;
```

Otherwise, the lambda's return type is void, unless you explicitly specify a return type using C++11's trailing return type syntax (-> *type*), as in

```
[](parameterList) -> type {lambdaBody}
```

The trailing return type is placed between the parameter list's closing right parenthesis and the lambda's body.

16.4 Algorithms

Sections 16.4.1—16.4.12 demonstrate many of the Standard Library algorithms.

16.4.1 fill, fill_n, generate and generate_n

Figure 16.2 demonstrates algorithms fill, fill_n, generate and generate_n. Algorithms fill and fill_n set every element in a range of container elements to a specific value. Algorithms generate and generate_n use a generator function to create values for every element in a *range* of container elements. The *generator function* takes no arguments and returns a value that can be placed in an element of the container. In this example, we'll define a generator function as a standalone function and as a lambda, so you can see the similarities. For the remainder of the chapter, we'll use lambdas.

```cpp
1   // Fig. 16.2: fig16_02.cpp
2   // Algorithms fill, fill_n, generate and generate_n.
3   #include <iostream>
4   #include <algorithm> // algorithm definitions
5   #include <array> // array class-template definition
6   #include <iterator> // ostream_iterator
7   using namespace std;
8
9   // generator function returns next letter (starts with A)
10  char nextLetter() {
11     static char letter{'A'};
12     return letter++;
13  }
14
15  int main() {
16     array<char, 10> chars;
17     fill(chars.begin(), chars.end(), '5'); // fill chars with 5s
18
19     cout << "chars after filling with 5s:\n";
20     ostream_iterator<char> output{cout, " "};
21     copy(chars.cbegin(), chars.cend(), output);
22
23     // fill first five elements of chars with As
24     fill_n(chars.begin(), 5, 'A');
25
26     cout << "\n\nchars after filling five elements with As:\n";
27     copy(chars.cbegin(), chars.cend(), output);
28
29     // generate values for all elements of chars with nextLetter
30     generate(chars.begin(), chars.end(), nextLetter);
31
32     cout << "\n\nchars after generating letters A-J:\n";
33     copy(chars.cbegin(), chars.cend(), output);
34
35     // generate values for first five elements of chars with nextLetter
36     generate_n(chars.begin(), 5, nextLetter);
37
38     cout << "\n\nchars after generating K-O for the"
39        << " first five elements:\n";
40     copy(chars.cbegin(), chars.cend(), output);
41     cout << endl;
42
43     // generate values for first three elements of chars with a lambda
44     generate_n(chars.begin(), 3,
45        [](){ // lambda that takes no arguments
46           static char letter{'A'};
47           return letter++;
48        }
49     );
50
```

Fig. 16.2 | Algorithms fill, fill_n, generate and generate_n—we used bold text to highlight the changes made to chars by each algorithm. (Part 1 of 2.)

```
51      cout << "\nchars after using a lambda to generate A-C "
52          << "for the first three elements:\n";
53      copy(chars.cbegin(), chars.cend(), output);
54      cout << endl;
55   }
```

```
chars after filling with 5s:
5 5 5 5 5 5 5 5 5 5

chars after filling five elements with As:
A A A A A 5 5 5 5 5

chars after generating letters A-J:
A B C D E F G H I J

chars after generating K-O for the first five elements:
K L M N O F G H I J

chars after using a lambda to generate A-C for the three elements:
A B C N O F G H I J
```

Fig. 16.2 | Algorithms fill, fill_n, generate and generate_n—we used bold text to highlight the changes made to chars by each algorithm. (Part 2 of 2.)

fill *Algorithm*

Line 16 defines a 10-element array of char values. Line 17 uses the fill algorithm to place the character '5' in every element of chars from chars.begin() up to, but *not* including, chars.end(). The iterators supplied as the first and second argument must be at least *forward iterators* (i.e., they can be used for both input from a container and output to a container in the *forward* direction). Forward iterators are required here (rather than output iterators) because the iterators must be compared to determine when the end of the sequence has been reached.

fill_n *Algorithm*

Line 24 uses the fill_n algorithm to place the character 'A' in the first five elements of chars. The iterator supplied as the first argument must be at least an *output iterator* (i.e., it can be used to *write* into a container in the *forward* direction). The second argument specifies the number of elements to fill. The third argument specifies the value to place in each element.

generate *Algorithm*

Line 30 uses the generate algorithm to place the result of a call to *generator function* next-Letter in every element of chars from chars.begin() up to, but *not* including, chars.end(). The iterators supplied as the first and second arguments must be at least *forward iterators*. Function nextLetter (lines 10–13) defines a static local char variable named letter and initializes it to 'A'. The statement in line 12 returns the current value of letter then postincrements its value for use in the next call to the function.

generate_n *Algorithm*

Line 36 uses the generate_n algorithm to place the result of a call to *generator function* nextLetter in five elements of chars, starting from chars.begin(). The iterator supplied as the first argument must be at least an *output iterator*.

Using the generate_n Algorithm with a Lambda

Lines 44–49 once again use the generate_n algorithm to place the result of a call to a *generator function* into elements of chars, starting from chars.begin(). In this case, the generator function is implemented as a lambda (lines 45–48) with no arguments—as specified by the empty parentheses—and returns a generated letter. For lambdas with no arguments, the parameter lists' paretheses are not required. The compiler infers from the return statement that the lambda's return type is char.

A Note About Reading Standard Library Algorithm Documentation

When you look at the Standard Library algorithms documentation for algorithms that can receive function pointers as arguments, you'll notice that the corresponding parameters do *not* show pointer declarations. Such parameters can actually receive as arguments *function pointers, function objects* (Section 16.5) or *lambda expressions* (Section 16.3). For this reason, the Standard Library declares such parameters using names that represent the parameter's purpose.

For example, generate's prototype is listed in the C++ standard document as

```
template<class ForwardIterator, class Generator>
void generate(ForwardIterator first, ForwardIterator last,
    Generator gen);
```

indicating that generate expects as arguments *ForwardIterators* representing the range of elements to process and a *Generator function*. The standard explains that the algorithm calls the Generator function to obtain a value for each element in the range specified by the *ForwardIterators*. The standard also specifies that the Generator must take no arguments and return a value that can be assigned to the element type.

Similar documentation is provided for each algorithm that can receive a function pointer, function object or lambda expression. In most of this chapter's examples, as we present each algorithm, we specify the requirements for such parameters.

16.4.2 equal, mismatch and lexicographical_compare

Figure 16.3 demonstrates comparing sequences of values for equality using algorithms equal, mismatch and lexicographical_compare. Lines 11–13 create and initialize three arrays. When invoking an array's copy constructor (line 12), you cannot use braces, as in

```
array<int, SIZE> a2{a1};
```

The preceding declaration yields a compilation error, because the compiler treats the contents in braces as a list of values for the array's elements. In this case, the compiler attempts to initialize the first int element of a2 with the array object a1—there is no implicit conversion from an array object to a single int value.

```
1   // Fig. 16.3: fig16_03.cpp
2   // Algorithms equal, mismatch and lexicographical_compare.
3   #include <iostream>
4   #include <algorithm> // algorithm definitions
5   #include <array> // array class-template definition
6   #include <iterator> // ostream_iterator
```

Fig. 16.3 | Algorithms equal, mismatch and lexicographical_compare. (Part 1 of 2.)

```
 7   using namespace std;
 8
 9   int main() {
10      const size_t SIZE{10};
11      array<int, SIZE> a1{1, 2, 3, 4, 5, 6, 7, 8, 9, 10};
12      array<int, SIZE> a2(a1); // initializes a2 with copy of a1
13      array<int, SIZE> a3{1, 2, 3, 4, 1000, 6, 7, 8, 9, 10};
14      ostream_iterator<int> output{cout, " "};
15
16      cout << "a1 contains: ";
17      copy(a1.cbegin(), a1.cend(), output);
18      cout << "\na2 contains: ";
19      copy(a2.cbegin(), a2.cend(), output);
20      cout << "\na3 contains: ";
21      copy(a3.cbegin(), a3.cend(), output);
22
23      // compare a1 and a2 for equality
24      bool result{equal(a1.cbegin(), a1.cend(), a2.cbegin(), a2.cend())};
25      cout << "\n\na1 " << (result ? "is" : "is not") << " equal to a2\n";
26
27      // compare a1 and a3 for equality
28      result = equal(a1.cbegin(), a1.cend(), a3.cbegin(), a3.cend());
29      cout << "a1 " << (result ? "is" : "is not") << " equal to a3\n";
30
31      // check for mismatch between a1 and a3
32      auto location =
33         mismatch(a1.cbegin(), a1.cend(), a3.cbegin(), a3.cend());
34      cout << "\nThere is a mismatch between a1 and a3 at location "
35         << (location.first - a1.begin()) << "\nwhere a1 contains "
36         << *location.first << " and a3 contains " << *location.second
37         << "\n\n";
38
39      char c1[SIZE] = "HELLO";
40      char c2[SIZE] = "BYE BYE";
41
42      // perform lexicographical comparison of c1 and c2
43      result = lexicographical_compare(
44         cbegin(c1), cend(c1), cbegin(c2), cend(c2));
45      cout << c1 << (result ? " is less than " :
46         " is greater than or equal to ")  << c2 << endl;
47   }
```

```
a1 contains: 1 2 3 4 5 6 7 8 9 10
a2 contains: 1 2 3 4 5 6 7 8 9 10
a3 contains: 1 2 3 4 1000 6 7 8 9 10

a1 is equal to a2
a1 is not equal to a3

There is a mismatch between a1 and a3 at location 4
where a1 contains 5 and a3 contains 1000

HELLO is greater than or equal to BYE BYE
```

Fig. 16.3 | Algorithms equal, mismatch and lexicographical_compare. (Part 2 of 2.)

equal *Algorithm*

Line 24 uses the C++14 version of the `equal` algorithm to compare two sequences of values for equality. The second sequence must contain at least as many elements as the first—`equal` returns `false` if the sequences are *not* of the same length. The `==` operator (whether built-in or overloaded) performs the element comparisons. In this example, the elements in a1 from a1.cbegin() up to, but *not* including, a1.cend() are compared to the elements in a2 starting from a2.cbegin() up to, but *not* including, a2.cend(). In this example, a1 and a2 are equal. The four iterator arguments must be at least *input iterators* (i.e., they can be used for input from a sequence in the *forward* direction). Line 28 uses function `equal` to compare a1 and a3, which are *not* equal.

14

equal *Algorithm with Binary Predicate Function*

Each version of `equal` also has an overloaded version that takes a *binary predicate function* as the last parameter. The binary predicate function receives the two elements being compared and returns a `bool` value indicating whether the elements are equal. This can be useful in sequences that store objects or pointers to values rather than actual values, because you can define one or more comparisons. For example, you can compare `Employee` objects for age, social security number, or location rather than comparing entire objects. You can compare what pointers refer to rather than comparing the pointer values (i.e., the addresses stored in the pointers).

mismatch *Algorithm*

Lines 32–33 call the C++14 version of the `mismatch` algorithm to compare two sequences of values. The algorithm returns a `pair` of iterators indicating the location in each sequence of the first *mismatched* elements. If all the elements match, the two iterators in the `pair` are equal to the end iterator for each sequence. The four iterator arguments must be at least *input iterators*. We *infer* the type of the `pair` object `location` with C++11's `auto` keyword (line 32). Line 35 determines the actual location of the mismatch in the arrays with the expression `location.first - a1.begin()`, which evaluates to the number of elements between the iterators in the returned `pair` (this is analogous to pointer arithmetic; Chapter 8). This corresponds to the element number in this example, because the comparison is performed from the beginning of each `array`. As with `equal`, there are overloaded versions of `mismatch` take a *binary predicate function* as the last parameter.

14

11

> **Error-Prevention Tip 16.1**
> *Always use C++14's versions of equal and mismatch. Prior to C++14, these algorithms each received only three iterators—the third indicated the starting point in the second of the two sequences being compared. The programmer was required to test whether the two sequences were of the same length before calling these algorithms. The C++14 versions are preferred because they compare the lengths of the ranges for you, eliminating a potential source of logic errors.*

14

auto *Variables and List Initialization*

Lines 32–33 use an equal sign (=) rather than braces to initialize the variable `location`. This is due to a known limitation with variables that are declared `auto` and initialized with braced initializers. There is a proposal to fix this limitation in C++17.[1]

17

---

1. http://open-std.org/JTC1/SC22/WG21/docs/papers/2013/n3681.html.

Error-Prevention Tip 16.2

In C++14, use = rather than braces when initializing a variable declared with auto.

14

`lexicographical_compare` *Algorithm*

Lines 43–44 use the `lexicographical_compare` algorithm to compare the contents of two char built-in arrays. This algorithm's four iterator arguments must be at least *input iterators*. As you know, pointers into built-in arrays are *random-access iterators*. The first two iterator arguments specify the range of locations in the first sequence. The last two specify the range of locations in the second sequence. Once again, we use the C++11 `begin` and `end` functions to determine the range of elements for each built-in array. While iterating through the sequences, if there is a mismatch between the corresponding elements in the sequences and the element in the first sequence is less than the corresponding element in the second sequence, the algorithm returns `true`; otherwise, the algorithm returns `false`. This algorithm can be used to arrange sequences *lexicographically*. Typically, such sequences contain strings.

11

16.4.3 remove, remove_if, remove_copy and remove_copy_if

Figure 16.4 demonstrates removing values from a sequence with algorithms remove, remove_if, remove_copy and remove_copy_if.

```cpp
1   // Fig. 16.4: fig16_04.cpp
2   // Algorithms remove, remove_if, remove_copy and remove_copy_if.
3   #include <iostream>
4   #include <algorithm> // algorithm definitions
5   #include <array> // array class-template definition
6   #include <iterator> // ostream_iterator
7   using namespace std;
8
9   int main() {
10     const size_t SIZE{10};
11     array<int, SIZE> init{10, 2, 10, 4, 16, 6, 14, 8, 12, 10};
12     ostream_iterator<int> output{cout, " "};
13
14     array<int, SIZE> a1(init); // initialize with copy of init
15     cout << "a1 before removing all 10s:\n   ";
16     copy(a1.cbegin(), a1.cend(), output);
17
18     // remove all 10s from a1
19     auto newEnd = remove(a1.begin(), a1.end(), 10);
20     cout << "\na1 after removing all 10s:\n   ";
21     copy(a1.begin(), newEnd, output);
22
23     array<int, SIZE> a2(init); // initialize with copy of init
24     array<int, SIZE> c{0}; // initialize to 0s
25     cout << "\n\na2 before removing all 10s and copying:\n   ";
26     copy(a2.cbegin(), a2.cend(), output);
```

Fig. 16.4 | Algorithms remove, remove_if, remove_copy and remove_copy_if. (Part 1 of 2.)

```
27
28      // copy from a2 to c, removing 10s in the process
29      remove_copy(a2.cbegin(), a2.cend(), c.begin(), 10);
30      cout << "\na2 after removing all 10s from a2:\n   ";
31      copy(c.cbegin(), c.cend(), output);
32
33      array<int, SIZE> a3(init); // initialize with copy of init
34      cout << "\n\na3 before removing all elements greater than 9:\n   ";
35      copy(a3.cbegin(), a3.cend(), output);
36
37      // remove elements greater than 9 from a3
38      newEnd = remove_if(a3.begin(), a3.end(),
39         [](auto x){return x > 9;});
40      cout << "\na3 after removing all elements greater than 9:\n   ";
41      copy(a3.begin(), newEnd, output);
42
43      array<int, SIZE> a4(init); // initialize with copy of init
44      array<int, SIZE> c2{0}; // initialize to 0s
45      cout << "\n\na4 before removing all elements "
46         << "greater than 9 and copying:\n   ";
47      copy(a4.cbegin(), a4.cend(), output);
48
49      // copy elements from a4 to c2, removing elements greater
50      // than 9 in the process
51      remove_copy_if(a4.cbegin(), a4.cend(), c2.begin(),
52         [](auto x){return x > 9;});
53      cout << "\nc2 after removing all elements "
54         << "greater than 9 from a4:\n   ";
55      copy(c2.cbegin(), c2.cend(), output);
56      cout << endl;
57   }
```

```
a1 before removing all 10s:
   10 2 10 4 16 6 14 8 12 10
a1 after removing all 10s:
   2 4 16 6 14 8 12

a2 before removing all 10s and copying:
   10 2 10 4 16 6 14 8 12 10
c after removing all 10s from a2:
   2 4 16 6 14 8 12 0 0 0

a3 before removing all elements greater than 9:
   10 2 10 4 16 6 14 8 12 10
a3 after removing all elements greater than 9:
   2 4 6 8

a4 before removing all elements greater than 9 and copying:
   10 2 10 4 16 6 14 8 12 10
c2 after removing all elements greater than 9 from a4:
   2 4 6 8 0 0 0 0 0 0
```

Fig. 16.4 | Algorithms remove, remove_if, remove_copy and remove_copy_if. (Part 2 of 2.)

remove *Algorithm*

Line 19 uses the remove algorithm to eliminate from a1 *all* elements with the value 10 in the range from a1.begin() up to, but *not* including, a1.end(). The first two iterator arguments must be *forward iterators*. This algorithm does *not* modify the number of elements in the container or destroy the eliminated elements, but it does move *all* elements that are *not* eliminated toward the *beginning* of the container. The algorithm returns an iterator positioned after the last element that was not removed. Elements from the iterator position to the end of the container have *unspecified* values and should not be used other than to assign them new values. Line 21 outputs the elements of a1 from a1.begin() up to but not including newEnd.

remove_copy *Algorithm*

Line 29 uses the remove_copy algorithm to *copy* all elements from a2 that do *not* have the value 10 in the range from a2.cbegin() up to, but not including, a2.cend(). The elements are placed in c, starting at position c.begin(). The iterators supplied as the first two arguments must be *input iterators*. The iterator supplied as the third argument must be an *output iterator* so that the element being copied can be *written into* into the destination container. This algorithm returns an iterator positioned after the last element copied into c. Line 31 outputs all of c's elements.

remove_if *Algorithm*

Lines 38–39 use the remove_if algorithm to delete from a3 *all* those elements in the range from a3.begin() up to, but *not* including, a3.end() for which a unary *predicate function* (in this case, the lambda at line 39) returns true—a unary predicate function must receive one parameter and return a bool value. The lambda

```
[](auto x){return x > 9;}
```

returns true if the value passed to it is greater than 9; otherwise, the lambda returns false. The compiler uses type inference for both the lambda's parameter and return types:

- We're processing an array of ints, so the compiler infers the lambda's parameter type as int.

- The lambda returns a condition's result, so the compiler infers the lambda's return type as bool.

The iterators supplied as the first two arguments must be *forward iterators*. This algorithm does *not* modify the number of elements in the container, but it does move to the *beginning* of the container all elements that are *not* removed. This algorithm returns an iterator positioned after the last element that was *not* removed. All elements from the iterator position to the end of the container have *undefined* values and should not be used. Line 41 outputs the elements of a3 from a3.begin() up to but not including newEnd.

remove_copy_if *Algorithm*

Lines 51–52 use the remove_copy_if algorithm to *copy* the elements from a4 in the range from a4.cbegin() up to, but *not* including, a4.cend() for which a *unary predicate function* (the lambda at line 52) returns true. The elements are placed in the array c2, starting at c2.begin(). The iterators supplied as the first two arguments must be *input iterators*. The iterator supplied as the third argument must be an *output iterator* so that the element being copied can be *written into* to the destination container. This algorithm returns an iterator positioned after the *last* element copied into c2. Line 55 outputs the entire contents of c2.

16.4.4 replace, replace_if, replace_copy and replace_copy_if

Figure 16.5 demonstrates replacing values from a sequence using algorithms replace, replace_if, replace_copy and replace_copy_if.

```cpp
1   // Fig. 16.5: fig16_05.cpp
2   // Algorithms replace, replace_if, replace_copy and replace_copy_if.
3   #include <iostream>
4   #include <algorithm>
5   #include <array>
6   #include <iterator> // ostream_iterator
7   using namespace std;
8
9   int main() {
10      const size_t SIZE{10};
11      array<int, SIZE> init{10, 2, 10, 4, 16, 6, 14, 8, 12, 10};
12      ostream_iterator<int> output{cout, " "};
13
14      array<int, SIZE> a1(init); // initialize with copy of init
15      cout << "a1 before replacing all 10s:\n   ";
16      copy(a1.cbegin(), a1.cend(), output);
17
18      // replace all 10s in a1 with 100
19      replace(a1.begin(), a1.end(), 10, 100);
20      cout << "\na1 after replacing 10s with 100s:\n   ";
21      copy(a1.cbegin(), a1.cend(), output);
22
23      array<int, SIZE> a2(init); // initialize with copy of init
24      array<int, SIZE> c1; // instantiate c1
25      cout << "\n\na2 before replacing all 10s and copying:\n   ";
26      copy(a2.cbegin(), a2.cend(), output);
27
28      // copy from a2 to c1, replacing 10s with 100s
29      replace_copy(a2.cbegin(), a2.cend(), c1.begin(), 10, 100);
30      cout << "\nc1 after replacing all 10s in a2:\n   ";
31      copy(c1.cbegin(), c1.cend(), output);
32
33      array<int, SIZE> a3(init); // initialize with copy of init
34      cout << "\n\na3 before replacing values greater than 9:\n   ";
35      copy(a3.cbegin(), a3.cend(), output);
36
37      // replace values greater than 9 in a3 with 100
38      replace_if(a3.begin(), a3.end(), [](auto x){return x > 9;}, 100);
39      cout << "\na3 after replacing all values greater "
40         << "than 9 with 100s:\n   ";
41      copy(a3.cbegin(), a3.cend(), output);
```

Fig. 16.5 | Algorithms replace, replace_if, replace_copy and replace_copy_if. (Part 1 of 2.)

```
42
43      array<int, SIZE> a4(init); // initialize with copy of init
44      array<int, SIZE> c2; // instantiate c2'
45      cout << "\n\na4 before replacing all values greater "
46          << "than 9 and copying:\n   ";
47      copy(a4.cbegin(), a4.cend(), output);
48
49      // copy a4 to c2, replacing elements greater than 9 with 100
50      replace_copy_if(a4.cbegin(), a4.cend(), c2.begin(),
51          [](auto x){return x > 9;}, 100);
52      cout << "\nc2 after replacing all values greater than 9 in a4:\n   ";
53      copy(c2.begin(), c2.end(), output);
54      cout << endl;
55  }
```

```
a1 before replacing all 10s:
   10 2 10 4 16 6 14 8 12 10
a1 after replacing 10s with 100s:
   100 2 100 4 16 6 14 8 12 100

a2 before replacing all 10s and copying:
   10 2 10 4 16 6 14 8 12 10
c1 after replacing all 10s in a2:
   100 2 100 4 16 6 14 8 12 100

a3 before replacing values greater than 9:
   10 2 10 4 16 6 14 8 12 10
a3 after replacing all values greater than 9 with 100s:
   100 2 100 4 100 6 100 8 100 100

a4 before replacing all values greater than 9 and copying:
   10 2 10 4 16 6 14 8 12 10
c2 after replacing all values greater than 9 in a4:
   100 2 100 4 100 6 100 8 100 100
```

Fig. 16.5 | Algorithms replace, replace_if, replace_copy and replace_copy_if. (Part 2 of 2.)

replace *Algorithm*

Line 19 uses the replace algorithm to replace *all* elements with the value 10 in the range a1.begin() up to, but *not* including, a1.end() with the new value 100. The iterators supplied as the first two arguments must be *forward iterators* so that the algorithm can *modify* the elements in the sequence.

replace_copy *Algorithm*

Line 29 uses the replace_copy algorithm to copy *all* elements in the range a2.cbegin() up to, but *not* including, a2.cend(), replacing *all* elements with the value 10 with the new value 100. The elements are copied into c1, starting at position c1.begin(). The iterators supplied as the first two arguments must be *input iterators*. The iterator supplied as the third argument must be an *output iterator* so that the element being copied can be *written into* to the destination container. This function returns an iterator positioned after the *last* element copied into c1.

replace_if *Algorithm*

Line 38 uses the `replace_if` algorithm to replace *all* those elements from a3.begin() up to, but *not* including, a3.end() for which a *unary predicate function* returns true—the lambda specified as the third argument returns true if the value passed to it is greater than 9; otherwise, it returns false. The value 100 replaces each value greater than 9. The iterators supplied as the first two arguments must be *forward iterators*.

replace_copy_if *Algorithm*

Lines 50–51 use the `replace_copy_if` algorithm to copy *all* elements from a4.cbegin() up to, but *not* including, a4.cend(). Elements for which a *unary predicate function* returns true—again for values greater than 9—are replaced with the value 100. The elements are placed in c2, starting at position c2.begin(). The iterators supplied as the first two arguments must be *input iterators*. The iterator supplied as the third argument must be an *output iterator* so that the element being copied can be *written into* to the destination container. This algorithm returns an iterator positioned after the *last* element copied into c2.

16.4.5 Mathematical Algorithms

Figure 16.6 demonstrates several common mathematical algorithms, including shuffle, count, count_if, min_element, max_element, minmax_element, accumulate and transform. We already introduced the for_each mathematical algorithm in Section 16.3.

```
 1   // Fig. 16.6: fig16_06.cpp
 2   // Mathematical algorithms of the Standard Library.
 3   #include <iostream>
 4   #include <algorithm> // algorithm definitions
 5   #include <numeric> // accumulate is defined here
 6   #include <array>
 7   #include <iterator>
 8   #include <random> // contains C++11 random number generation features
 9   using namespace std;
10
11   int main() {
12      const size_t SIZE{10};
13      array<int, SIZE> a1{1, 2, 3, 4, 5, 6, 7, 8, 9, 10};
14      ostream_iterator<int> output{cout, " "};
15
16      cout << "a1 before random_shuffle: ";
17      copy(a1.cbegin(), a1.cend(), output);
18
19      // create random-number engine and use it to help shuffle a1's elements
20      default_random_engine randomEngine{random_device{}()};
21      shuffle(a1.begin(), a1.end(), randomEngine); // randomly order elements
22      cout << "\na1 after random_shuffle: ";
23      copy(a1.cbegin(), a1.cend(), output);
24
25      array<int, SIZE> a2{100, 2, 8, 1, 50, 3, 8, 8, 9, 10};
26      cout << "\n\na2 contains: ";
27      copy(a2.cbegin(), a2.cend(), output);
```

Fig. 16.6 | Mathematical algorithms of the Standard Library. (Part 1 of 2.)

```
28
29      // count number of elements in a2 with value 8
30      auto result = count(a2.cbegin(), a2.cend(), 8);
31      cout << "\nNumber of elements matching 8: " << result;
32
33      // count number of elements in a2 that are greater than 9
34      result = count_if(a2.cbegin(), a2.cend(), [](auto x){return x > 9;});
35      cout << "\nNumber of elements greater than 9: " << result;
36
37      // locate minimum element in a2
38      cout << "\n\nMinimum element in a2 is: "
39         << *(min_element(a2.cbegin(), a2.cend()));
40
41      // locate maximum element in a2
42      cout << "\nMaximum element in a2 is: "
43         << *(max_element(a2.cbegin(), a2.cend()));
44
45      // locate minimum and maximum elements in a2
46      auto minAndMax = minmax_element(a2.cbegin(), a2.cend());
47      cout << "\nThe minimum and maximum elements in a2 are "
48         << *minAndMax.first << " and " << *minAndMax.second
49         << ", respectively";
50
51      // calculate sum of elements in a1
52      cout << "\n\nThe total of the elements in a1 is: "
53         << accumulate(a1.cbegin(), a1.cend(), 0);
54
55      array<int, SIZE> cubes; // instantiate cubes
56
57      // calculate cube of each element in a1; place results in cubes
58      transform(a1.cbegin(), a1.cend(), cubes.begin(),
59         [](auto x){return x * x * x;});
60      cout << "\n\nThe cube of every integer in a1 is:\n";
61      copy(cubes.cbegin(), cubes.cend(), output);
62      cout << endl;
63   }
```

```
a1 before random_shuffle: 1 2 3 4 5 6 7 8 9 10
a1 after random_shuffle: 9 2 10 3 1 6 8 4 5 7

a2 contains: 100 2 8 1 50 3 8 8 9 10
Number of elements matching 8: 3
Number of elements greater than 9: 3

Minimum element in a2 is: 1
Maximum element in a2 is: 100
The minimum and maximum elements in a2 are 1 and 100, respectively

The total of the elements in a1 is: 55

The cube of every integer in a1 is:
729 8 1000 27 1 216 512 64 125 343
```

Fig. 16.6 | Mathematical algorithms of the Standard Library. (Part 2 of 2.)

shuffle Algorithm

Line 21 uses the C++11 shuffle algorithm to reorder randomly the elements in the range a1.begin() up to, but *not* including, a1.end(). This algorithm takes *two random-access iterator* arguments and a C++11 random-number-generator engine. Line 20

```
default_random_engine randomEngine{random_device{}()};
```

creates a default_random_engine using a C++11 random_device object to seed the random-number generator—typically with a nondeterministic seed (i.e., a seed that cannot be predicted). In the expression

```
random_device{}()
```

the braces initialize the random_device object and the parentheses call its overloaded parentheses operator to get the seed. Line 23 displays the shuffled results.

count Algorithm

Line 30 uses the count algorithm to count the elements with the value 8 in the range a2.cbegin() up to, but *not* including, a2.cend(). This algorithm requires its two iterator arguments to be at least *input iterators*.

count_if Algorithm

Line 34 uses the count_if algorithm to count elements in the range from a2.cbegin() up to, but *not* including, a2.cend() for which a *unary predicate* function returns true—once again we used a lambda to define a unary predicate that returns true for a value greater than 9. Algorithm count_if requires its two iterator arguments to be at least *input iterators*.

min_element Algorithm

Line 39 uses the min_element algorithm to locate the *smallest* element in the range from a2.cbegin() up to, but *not* including, a2.cend(). The algorithm returns a *forward iterator* located at the *first* smallest element, or a2.end() if the range is *empty*. The algorithm's two iterator arguments must be at least *forward iterators*. An overloaded version of this algorithm receives as its third argument a binary predicate function that compares two elements in the sequence and returns the bool value true if the first argument is *less than* the second.

max_element Algorithm

Line 43 uses the max_element algorithm to locate the *largest* element in the range from a2.cbegin() up to, but *not* including, a2.cend(). The algorithm returns a *forward iterator* located at the *first* largest element. The algorithm's two iterator arguments must be at least *forward iterators*. An overloaded version of this algorithm receives as its third argument a binary predicate function that compares two elements in the sequence and returns the bool value true if the first argument is *less than* the second.

Error-Prevention Tip 16.3

Check that the range specified in a call to min_element or max_element is not empty and that the return value is not the "past the end" iterator.

C++11: minmax_element Algorithm

Line 46 uses the C++11 minmax_element algorithm to locate both the *smallest* and *largest* elements in the range from a2.cbegin() up to, but *not* including, a2.cend(). The algorithm returns a pair of *forward iterators* located at the smallest and largest elements, respectively. If there are duplicate smallest or largest elements, the iterators are located at the *first* smallest and *last* largest values. The algorithm's two iterator arguments must be at least *forward iterators*. A second version of this algorithm takes as its third argument a *binary predicate function* that compares the elements in the sequence. The binary function takes two arguments and returns the bool value true if the first argument is *less than* the second.

accumulate *Algorithm*

Line 53 uses the accumulate algorithm (the template of which is in header <numeric>) to sum the values in the range from a1.cbegin() up to, but *not* including, a1.cend(). The algorithm's two iterator arguments must be at least *input iterators* and its third argument represents the initial value of the total. A second version of this algorithm takes as its fourth argument a general function that determines how elements are accumulated. The general function must take *two* arguments and return a result. The first argument to this function is the current value of the accumulation. The second argument is the value of the current element in the sequence being accumulated. The function returns the result of the accumulation.

transform *Algorithm*

Lines 58–59 use the transform algorithm to apply a general function to *every* element in the range from a1.cbegin() up to, but *not* including, a1.cend(). The general function (the fourth argument) should take the current element as an argument, must *not* modify the element and should return the transformed value. Algorithm transform requires its first two iterator arguments to be at least *input iterators* and its third argument to be at least an *output iterator*. The third argument specifies where the transformed values should be placed. Note that the third argument can equal the first.

An overloaded version of transform accepts five arguments—the first two arguments are *input iterators* that specify a range of elements from one source container, the third argument is an *input iterator* that specifies the first element in another source container, the fourth argument is an *output iterator* that specifies where the transformed values should be placed and the last argument is a general function that takes two arguments and returns a result. This version of transform takes one element from each of the two input sources and applies the general function to that pair of elements, then places the transformed value at the location specified by the fourth argument.

16.4.6 Basic Searching and Sorting Algorithms

Figure 16.7 demonstrates some basic searching and sorting Standard Library algorithms, including find, find_if, sort, binary_search, all_of, any_of, none_of and find_if_not.

```
1   // Fig. 16.7: fig16_07.cpp
2   // Standard Library search and sort algorithms.
3   #include <iostream>
4   #include <algorithm> // algorithm definitions
```

Fig. 16.7 | Standard Library search and sort algorithms. (Part 1 of 4.)

```
 5   #include <array> // array class-template definition
 6   #include <iterator>
 7   using namespace std;
 8
 9   int main() {
10      const size_t SIZE{10};
11      array<int, SIZE> a{10, 2, 17, 5, 16, 8, 13, 11, 20, 7};
12      ostream_iterator<int> output{cout, " "};
13
14      cout << "array a contains: ";
15      copy(a.cbegin(), a.cend(), output); // display output vector
16
17      // locate first occurrence of 16 in a
18      auto location = find(a.cbegin(), a.cend(), 16);
19
20      if (location != a.cend()) { // found 16
21         cout << "\n\nFound 16 at location " << (location - a.cbegin());
22      }
23      else { // 16 not found
24         cout << "\n\n16 not found";
25      }
26
27      // locate first occurrence of 100 in a
28      location = find(a.cbegin(), a.cend(), 100);
29
30      if (location != a.cend()) { // found 100
31         cout << "\nFound 100 at location " << (location - a.cbegin());
32      }
33      else { // 100 not found
34         cout << "\n100 not found";
35      }
36
37      // create variable to store lambda for reuse later
38      auto isGreaterThan10{[](auto x){return x > 10;}};
39
40      // locate first occurrence of value greater than 10 in a
41      location = find_if(a.cbegin(), a.cend(), isGreaterThan10);
42
43      if (location != a.cend()) { // found value greater than 10
44         cout << "\n\nThe first value greater than 10 is " << *location
45            << "\nfound at location " << (location - a.cbegin());
46      }
47      else { // value greater than 10 not found
48         cout << "\n\nNo values greater than 10 were found";
49      }
50
51      // sort elements of a
52      sort(a.begin(), a.end());
53      cout << "\n\narray a after sort: ";
54      copy(a.cbegin(), a.cend(), output);
55
```

Fig. 16.7 | Standard Library search and sort algorithms. (Part 2 of 4.)

```
56      // use binary_search to check whether 13 exists in a
57      if (binary_search(a.cbegin(), a.cend(), 13)) {
58         cout << "\n\n13 was found in a";
59      }
60      else {
61         cout << "\n\n13 was not found in a";
62      }
63
64      // use binary_search to check whether 100 exists in a
65      if (binary_search(a.cbegin(), a.cend(), 100)) {
66         cout << "\n100 was found in a";
67      }
68      else {
69         cout << "\n100 was not found in a";
70      }
71
72      // determine whether all of the elements of a are greater than 10
73      if (all_of(a.cbegin(), a.cend(), isGreaterThan10)) {
74         cout << "\n\nAll the elements in a are greater than 10";
75      }
76      else {
77         cout << "\n\nSome elements in a are not greater than 10";
78      }
79
80      // determine whether any of the elements of a are greater than 10
81      if (any_of(a.cbegin(), a.cend(), isGreaterThan10)) {
82         cout << "\n\nSome of the elements in a are greater than 10";
83      }
84      else {
85         cout << "\n\nNone of the elements in a are greater than 10";
86      }
87
88      // determine whether none of the elements of a are greater than 10
89      if (none_of(a.cbegin(), a.cend(), isGreaterThan10)) {
90         cout << "\n\nNone of the elements in a are greater than 10";
91      }
92      else {
93         cout << "\n\nSome of the elements in a are greater than 10";
94      }
95
96      // locate first occurrence of value that's not greater than 10 in a
97      location = find_if_not(a.cbegin(), a.cend(), isGreaterThan10);
98
99      if (location != a.cend()) { // found a value less than or equal to 10
100        cout << "\n\nThe first value not greater than 10 is " << *location
101           << "\nfound at location " << (location - a.cbegin());
102     }
103     else { // no values less than or equal to 10 were found
104        cout << "\n\nOnly values greater than 10 were found";
105     }
106
107     cout << endl;
108  }
```

Fig. 16.7 | Standard Library search and sort algorithms. (Part 3 of 4.)

```
array a contains: 10 2 17 5 16 8 13 11 20 7

Found 16 at location 4
100 not found

The first value greater than 10 is 17
found at location 2

array a after sort: 2 5 7 8 10 11 13 16 17 20

13 was found in a
100 was not found in a

Some elements in a are not greater than 10

Some of the elements in a are greater than 10

Some of the elements in a are greater than 10

The first value not greater than 10 is 2
found at location 0
```

Fig. 16.7 | Standard Library search and sort algorithms. (Part 4 of 4.)

find *Algorithm*

Line 18 uses the `find` algorithm to locate the value 16 in the range from a.cbegin() up to, but not including, a.cend(). The algorithm requires its two iterator arguments to be at least *input iterators* and returns an *input iterator* that's either positioned at the first element containing the value or indicates the end of the sequence (as is the case in line 28).

Storing Lambdas in Variables

Throughout this example, we test multiple times whether elements in the `array` a are greater than 10. You can store a lambda in a variable, as in line 38:

```
auto isGreaterThan10 = [](auto x){return x > 10;};
```

This variable can then be used at a later time to pass the lambda to other functions, as in lines 41, 73, 81, 89 and 97. You can also use the variable like a function name to invoke the lambda, as in

```
isGreaterThan10(5)
```

which returns `false`.

find_if *Algorithm*

Line 41 uses the `find_if` algorithm (a linear search) to locate the first value in the range from a.cbegin() up to, but *not* including, a.cend() for which a *unary predicate function* returns `true`—in this case, the unary predicate function is the lambda

```
[](auto x){return x > 10;}
```

that's stored in the variable `isGreaterThan10`. The compiler infers parameter x's type as `int` (because the `array` stores `int`s) and infers the return type as `bool` because the lambda returns the value of a condition. Algorithm `find_if` requires its two iterator arguments to be at least *input iterators*. The algorithm returns an *input iterator* that either is positioned at the first element containing a value for which the predicate function returns `true` or indicates the end of the sequence.

sort *Algorithm*
Line 52 uses the `sort` algorithm to arrange the elements in the range from `a.begin()` up to, but *not* including, `a.end()` in *ascending order*. This algorithm requires its two iterator arguments to be *random-access iterators*—so the algorithm can be used with built-in arrays and the Standard Library containers `array`, `vector` and `deque`. An overloaded version of this algorithm has a third argument that's a *binary predicate function* taking two arguments and returning a `bool` indicating the *sorting order*. The predicate compares two values from the sequence being sorted. If the return value is `true`, the two elements are already in *sorted order*; otherwise, the two elements need to be reordered in the sequence.

binary_search *Algorithm*
Line 57 uses the `binary_search` algorithm to determine whether the value 13 is in the range from `a.cbegin()` up to, but *not* including, `a.cend()`. The values must be sorted in *ascending order*. Algorithm `binary_search` requires its two iterator arguments to be at least *forward iterators*. The algorithm returns a `bool` indicating whether the value was found in the sequence. Line 65 demonstrates a call to `binary_search` in which the value is *not* found. An overloaded version of this algorithm receives as a fourth argument a *binary predicate function* with two arguments that are values in the sequence and returning a `bool`. The predicate function returns `true` if the two elements being compared are in *sorted order*. If you need to know the *location* of the search key in the container, use the `lower_bound` or `find` algorithms rather than `binary_search`.

11 C++11: all_of *Algorithm*
Line 73 uses the `all_of` algorithm to determine whether the *unary predicate function* (the lambda stored in `isGreaterThan10`) returns `true` for *all* of the elements in the range from `a.cbegin()` up to, but *not* including, `a.cend()`. Algorithm `all_of` requires its two iterator arguments to be at least *input iterators*.

11 C++11: any_of *Algorithm*
Line 81 uses the `any_of` algorithm to determine whether the *unary predicate function* (the lambda stored in `isGreaterThan10`) returns `true` for *at least one* of the elements in the range from `a.cbegin()` up to, but *not* including, `a.cend()`. Algorithm `any_of` requires its two iterator arguments to be at least *input iterators*.

11 C++11: none_of *Algorithm*
Line 89 uses the `none_of` algorithm to determine whether the *unary predicate function* (the lambda stored in `isGreaterThan10`) returns `false` for *all* of the elements in the range from `a.cbegin()` up to, but *not* including, `a.cend()`. Algorithm `none_of` requires its two iterator arguments to be at least *input iterators*.

11 C++11: find_if_not *Algorithm*
Line 97 uses the `find_if_not` algorithm to locate the first value in the range from `a.cbegin()` up to, but *not* including, `a.cend()` for which the *unary predicate function* (the lamb-

da stored in isGreaterThan10) returns false. Algorithm find_if requires its two iterator arguments to be at least *input iterators*. The algorithm returns an *input iterator* that either is positioned at the first element containing a value for which the predicate function returns false or indicates the end of the sequence.

16.4.7 swap, iter_swap and swap_ranges

Figure 16.8 demonstrates algorithms swap, iter_swap and swap_ranges for *swapping* elements.

```cpp
1   // Fig. 16.8: fig16_08.cpp
2   // Algorithms swap, iter_swap and swap_ranges.
3   #include <iostream>
4   #include <array>
5   #include <algorithm> // algorithm definitions
6   #include <iterator>
7   using namespace std;
8
9   int main() {
10      const size_t SIZE{10};
11      array<int, SIZE> a{1, 2, 3, 4, 5, 6, 7, 8, 9, 10};
12      ostream_iterator<int> output{cout, " "};
13
14      cout << "Array a contains:\n   ";
15      copy(a.cbegin(), a.cend(), output); // display array a
16
17      swap(a[0], a[1]); // swap elements at locations 0 and 1 of a
18
19      cout << "\nArray a after swapping a[0] and a[1] using swap:\n   ";
20      copy(a.cbegin(), a.cend(), output); // display array a
21
22      // use iterators to swap elements at locations 0 and 1 of array a
23      iter_swap(a.begin(), a.begin() + 1); // swap with iterators
24      cout << "\nArray a after swapping a[0] and a[1] using iter_swap:\n   ";
25      copy(a.cbegin(), a.cend(), output);
26
27      // swap elements in first five elements of array a with
28      // elements in last five elements of array a
29      swap_ranges(a.begin(), a.begin() + 5, a.begin() + 5 );
30
31      cout << "\nArray a after swapping the first five elements "
32         << "with the last five elements:\n   ";
33      copy(a.cbegin(), a.cend(), output);
34      cout << endl;
35   }
```

```
Array a contains:
   1 2 3 4 5 6 7 8 9 10
Array a after swapping a[0] and a[1] using swap:
   2 1 3 4 5 6 7 8 9 10
```

Fig. 16.8 | Algorithms swap, iter_swap and swap_ranges. (Part 1 of 2.)

```
Array a after swapping a[0] and a[1] using iter_swap:
   1 2 3 4 5 6 7 8 9 10
Array a after swapping the first five elements with the last five elements:
   6 7 8 9 10 1 2 3 4 5
```

Fig. 16.8 | Algorithms swap, iter_swap and swap_ranges. (Part 2 of 2.)

swap Algorithm

Line 17 uses the swap algorithm to exchange two values. In this example, the first and second elements of array a are exchanged. The function takes as arguments references to the two values being exchanged.

iter_swap Algorithm

Line 23 uses function iter_swap to exchange the two elements. The function takes two *forward iterator* arguments (in this case, iterators to elements of an array) and exchanges the values in the elements to which the iterators refer.

swap_ranges *Algorithm*

Line 29 uses function swap_ranges to exchange the elements from a.begin() up to, but not including, a.begin() + 5 with the elements beginning at position a.begin() + 5. The function requires three *forward iterator* arguments. The first two arguments specify the range of elements in the first sequence that will be exchanged with the elements in the second sequence starting from the iterator in the third argument. In this example, the two sequences of values are in the same array, but the sequences can be from different arrays or containers. The sequences must not overlap. The destination sequence must be large enough to contain all the elements of the ranges being swapped.

16.4.8 copy_backward, merge, unique and reverse

Figure 16.9 demonstrates algorithms copy_backward, merge, unique and reverse.

```cpp
1   // Fig. 16.9: fig16_09.cpp
2   // Algorithms copy_backward, merge, unique and reverse.
3   #include <iostream>
4   #include <algorithm> // algorithm definitions
5   #include <array> // array class-template definition
6   #include <iterator> // ostream_iterator
7   using namespace std;
8
9   int main() {
10      const size_t SIZE{5};
11      array<int, SIZE> a1{1, 3, 5, 7, 9};
12      array<int, SIZE> a2{2, 4, 5, 7, 9};
13      ostream_iterator<int> output{cout, " "};
14
15      cout << "array a1 contains: ";
16      copy(a1.cbegin(), a1.cend(), output); // display a1
```

Fig. 16.9 | Algorithms copy_backward, merge, unique and reverse. (Part 1 of 2.)

```
17      cout << "\narray a2 contains: ";
18      copy(a2.cbegin(), a2.cend(), output); // display a2
19
20      array<int, SIZE> results;
21
22      // place elements of a1 into results in reverse order
23      copy_backward(a1.cbegin(), a1.cend(), results.end());
24      cout << "\n\nAfter copy_backward, results contains: ";
25      copy(results.cbegin(), results.cend(), output);
26
27      array<int, SIZE + SIZE> results2;
28
29      // merge elements of a1 and a2 into results2 in sorted order
30      merge(a1.cbegin(), a1.cend(), a2.cbegin(), a2.cend(),
31         results2.begin());
32
33      cout << "\n\nAfter merge of a1 and a2 results2 contains: ";
34      copy(results2.cbegin(), results2.cend(), output);
35
36      // eliminate duplicate values from results2
37      auto endLocation = unique(results2.begin(), results2.end());
38
39      cout << "\n\nAfter unique results2 contains: ";
40      copy(results2.begin(), endLocation, output);
41
42      cout << "\n\narray a1 after reverse: ";
43      reverse(a1.begin(), a1.end()); // reverse elements of a1
44      copy(a1.cbegin(), a1.cend(), output);
45      cout << endl;
46   }
```

```
array a1 contains: 1 3 5 7 9
array a2 contains: 2 4 5 7 9

After copy_backward, results contains: 1 3 5 7 9

After merge of a1 and a2 results2 contains: 1 2 3 4 5 5 7 7 9 9

After unique results2 contains: 1 2 3 4 5 7 9

array a1 after reverse: 9 7 5 3 1
```

Fig. 16.9 | Algorithms copy_backward, merge, unique and reverse. (Part 2 of 2.)

copy_backward *Algorithm*

Line 23 uses the copy_backward algorithm to copy elements in the range from a1.cbegin() up to, but *not* including, a1.cend(), placing the elements in results by starting from the element before results.end() and working toward the beginning of the array. The algorithm returns an iterator positioned at the *last* element copied into the results (i.e., the beginning of results, because of the backward copy). Though they're copied in reverse order, the elements are placed in results in the same order as a1. This algorithm requires three *bidirectional iterator* arguments (iterators that can be *incremented* and *decremented* to iterate *forward* and *backward* through a sequence, respectively).

One difference between copy_backward and copy is that the iterator returned from copy is positioned *after* the last element copied and the one returned from copy_backward is positioned *at* the last element copied (i.e., the first element in the sequence). Also, copy_backward *can* manipulate *overlapping* ranges of elements in a container as long as the first element to copy is *not* in the destination range of elements.

In addition to copy and copy_backward, C++11's move and move_backward algorithms use move semantics (discussed in Chapter 24, C++11 and C++14: Additional Features) to move, rather than copy, objects from one container to another.

11

merge *Algorithm*

Lines 30–31 use the merge algorithm to combine two *sorted ascending sequences* of values into a third sorted ascending sequence. The algorithm requires five iterator arguments. The first four must be at least *input iterators* and the last must be at least an *output iterator*. The first two arguments specify the range of elements in the first sorted sequence (a1), the second two arguments specify the range of elements in the second sorted sequence (a2) and the last argument specifies the starting location in the third sequence (results2) where the elements will be merged. A second version of this algorithm takes as its sixth argument a *binary predicate function* that specifies the *sorting order* by comparing its two arguments and returning true if the first is less than the second.

back_inserter, front_inserter *and* inserter *Iterator Adapters*

Line 27 created the array results2 with the total number of elements in both a1 and a2. Using the merge algorithm requires that the sequence where the results are stored be at least the sum of the sizes of the sequences being merged. If you do not want to allocate the number of elements for the resulting sequence *before* the merge operation, you can use a dynamically growable vector and the following statements:

```
vector<int> results;
merge(a1.begin(), a1.end(), a2.begin(), a2.end(),
    back_inserter(results));
```

The argument back_inserter(results) uses the function template back_inserter (header <iterator>) to call the container's default push_back function to insert an element at the *end* of the container—results in this case—*rather than replacing* an existing element's value. If an element is inserted into a container that has no more space available, *the container grows to accomodate the new element* (we used a vector here, because arrays are fixed size). Thus, the number of elements in the container does *not* have to be known in advance.

There are two other inserters—front_inserter (uses push_front to insert an element at the *beginning* of a container specified as its argument) and inserter (uses insert to insert an element *at* the iterator supplied as its second argument in the container supplied as its first argument).

unique *Algorithm*

Line 37 uses the unique algorithm on the *sorted* sequence of elements in the range from results2.begin() up to, but *not* including, results2.end(). After this algorithm is applied to a sorted sequence with *duplicate* values, only a *single* copy of each value remains in the sequence. The algorithm takes two arguments that must be at least *forward iterators*. The algorithm returns an iterator positioned *after the last element* in the sequence of unique values. The values of all elements in the container after the last unique value are *undefined* and should not be used. An overloaded version of this algorithm receives as a third argument a *binary predicate function* specifying how to compare two elements for *equality*.

reverse *Algorithm*
Line 43 uses the reverse algorithm to reverse all the elements in the range from a1.begin() up to, but *not* including, a1.end(). The algorithm takes two arguments that must be at least *bidirectional iterators*.

C++11: copy_if *and* copy_n *Algorithms*
C++11 added the copy algorithms copy_if and copy_n. The copy_if algorithm copies each element from a range if the *unary predicate function* in its fourth argument returns true for that element. The iterators supplied as the first two arguments must be *input iterators*. The iterator supplied as the third argument must be an *output iterator* so that the element being copied can be *written into* to the copy location. This algorithm returns an iterator positioned after the *last* element copied.

The copy_n algorithm copies the number of elements specified by its second argument from the location specified by its first argument (an *input iterator*). The elements are output to the location specified by its third argument (an *output iterator*).

16.4.9 inplace_merge, unique_copy and reverse_copy
Figure 16.10 demonstrates algorithms inplace_merge, unique_copy and reverse_copy.

```cpp
1   // Fig. 16.10: fig16_10.cpp
2   // Algorithms inplace_merge, reverse_copy and unique_copy.
3   #include <iostream>
4   #include <algorithm> // algorithm definitions
5   #include <array> // array class-template definition
6   #include <vector> // vector class-template definition
7   #include <iterator> // back_inserter definition
8   using namespace std;
9
10  int main() {
11     const int SIZE{10};
12     array<int, SIZE> a1{1, 3, 5, 7, 9, 1, 3, 5, 7, 9};
13     ostream_iterator<int> output(cout, " ");
14
15     cout << "array a1 contains: ";
16     copy(a1.cbegin(), a1.cend(), output);
17
18     // merge first half of a1 with second half of a1 such that
19     // a1 contains sorted set of elements after merge
20     inplace_merge(a1.begin(), a1.begin() + 5, a1.end());
21
22     cout << "\nAfter inplace_merge, a1 contains: ";
23     copy(a1.cbegin(), a1.cend(), output);
24
25     vector<int> results1;
```

Fig. 16.10 | Algorithms inplace_merge, reverse_copy and unique_copy. (Part 1 of 2.)

```
26
27        // copy only unique elements of a1 into results1
28        unique_copy(a1.cbegin(), a1.cend(), back_inserter(results1));
29        cout << "\nAfter unique_copy results1 contains: ";
30        copy(results1.cbegin(), results1.cend(), output);
31
32        vector<int> results2;
33
34        // copy elements of a1 into results2 in reverse order
35        reverse_copy(a1.cbegin(), a1.cend(), back_inserter(results2));
36        cout << "\nAfter reverse_copy, results2 contains: ";
37        copy(results2.cbegin(), results2.cend(), output);
38        cout << endl;
39    }
```

```
array a1 contains: 1 3 5 7 9 1 3 5 7 9
After inplace_merge, a1 contains: 1 1 3 3 5 5 7 7 9 9
After unique_copy results1 contains: 1 3 5 7 9
After reverse_copy, results2 contains: 9 9 7 7 5 5 3 3 1 1
```

Fig. 16.10 | Algorithms inplace_merge, reverse_copy and unique_copy. (Part 2 of 2.)

inplace_merge *Algorithm*

Line 20 uses the inplace_merge algorithm to merge two *sorted sequences* of elements in the *same* container. In this example, the elements from a1.begin() up to, but *not* including, a1.begin() + 5 are merged with the elements from a1.begin() + 5 up to, but *not* including, a1.end(). This algorithm requires its three iterator arguments to be at least *bidirectional iterators*. A second version of this algorithm takes as a fourth argument a *binary predicate function* for comparing elements in the two sequences.

unique_copy *Algorithm*

Line 28 uses the unique_copy algorithm to make a copy of all the unique elements in the sorted sequence of values from a1.cbegin() up to, but *not* including, a1.cend(). The copied elements are placed into vector results1. The first two arguments must be at least *input iterators* and the last must be at least an *output iterator*. In this example, we did *not* preallocate enough elements in results1 to store *all* the elements copied from a1. Instead, we use function back_inserter (defined in header <iterator>), as discussed in Section 16.4.8, to insert elements at the end of results1. A second version of the unique_copy algorithm takes as a fourth argument a *binary predicate function* for comparing elements for *equality*.

reverse_copy *Algorithm*

Line 35 uses the reverse_copy algorithm to make a reversed copy of the elements in the range from a1.cbegin() up to, but *not* including, a1.cend(). The copied elements are inserted into results2 using a back_inserter object to ensure that the vector can *grow* to accommodate the appropriate number of elements copied. Algorithm reverse_copy requires its first two iterator arguments to be at least *bidirectional iterators* and its third to be at least an *output iterator*.

16.4.10 Set Operations

Figure 16.11 demonstrates algorithms `includes`, `set_difference`, `set_intersection`, `set_symmetric_difference` and `set_union` for manipulating *sets of sorted values*.

```cpp
// Fig. 16.11: fig16_11.cpp
// Algorithms includes, set_difference, set_intersection,
// set_symmetric_difference and set_union.
#include <iostream>
#include <array>
#include <algorithm> // algorithm definitions
#include <iterator> // ostream_iterator
using namespace std;

int main() {
   const size_t SIZE1{10}, SIZE2{5}, SIZE3{20};
   array<int, SIZE1> a1{1, 2, 3, 4, 5, 6, 7, 8, 9, 10};
   array<int, SIZE2> a2{4, 5, 6, 7, 8};
   array<int, SIZE2> a3{4, 5, 6, 11, 15};
   ostream_iterator<int> output{cout, " "};

   cout << "a1 contains: ";
   copy(a1.cbegin(), a1.cend(), output); // display array a1
   cout << "\na2 contains: ";
   copy(a2.cbegin(), a2.cend(), output); // display array a2
   cout << "\na3 contains: ";
   copy(a3.cbegin(), a3.cend(), output); // display array a3

   // determine whether a2 is completely contained in a1
   if (includes(a1.cbegin(), a1.cend(), a2.cbegin(), a2.cend())) {
      cout << "\n\na1 includes a2";
   }
   else {
      cout << "\n\na1 does not include a2";
   }

   // determine whether a3 is completely contained in a1
   if (includes(a1.cbegin(), a1.cend(), a3.cbegin(), a3.cend())) {
      cout << "\na1 includes a3";
   }
   else {
      cout << "\na1 does not include a3";
   }

   array<int, SIZE1> difference;

   // determine elements of a1 not in a2
   auto result1 = set_difference(a1.cbegin(), a1.cend(),
      a2.cbegin(), a2.cend(), difference.begin());
   cout << "\n\nset_difference of a1 and a2 is: ";
   copy(difference.begin(), result1, output);
```

Fig. 16.11 | Algorithms includes, set_difference, set_intersection, set_symmetric_difference and set_union. (Part 1 of 2.)

```
47
48        array<int, SIZE1> intersection;
49
50        // determine elements in both a1 and a2
51        auto result2 = set_intersection(a1.cbegin(), a1.cend(),
52           a2.cbegin(), a2.cend(), intersection.begin());
53        cout << "\n\nset_intersection of a1 and a2 is: ";
54        copy(intersection.begin(), result2, output);
55
56        array<int, SIZE1 + SIZE2> symmetric_difference;
57
58        // determine elements of a1 that are not in a3 and
59        // elements of a3 that are not in a1
60        auto result3 = set_symmetric_difference(a1.cbegin(), a1.cend(),
61           a3.cbegin(), a3.cend(), symmetric_difference.begin());
62        cout << "\n\nset_symmetric_difference of a1 and a3 is: ";
63        copy(symmetric_difference.begin(), result3, output);
64
65        array<int, SIZE3> unionSet;
66
67        // determine elements that are in either or both sets
68        auto result4 = set_union(a1.cbegin(), a1.cend(),
69           a3.cbegin(), a3.cend(), unionSet.begin());
70        cout << "\n\nset_union of a1 and a3 is: ";
71        copy(unionSet.begin(), result4, output);
72        cout << endl;
73     }
```

```
a1 contains: 1 2 3 4 5 6 7 8 9 10
a2 contains: 4 5 6 7 8
a3 contains: 4 5 6 11 15

a1 includes a2
a1 does not include a3

set_difference of a1 and a2 is: 1 2 3 9 10

set_intersection of a1 and a2 is: 4 5 6 7 8

set_symmetric_difference of a1 and a3 is: 1 2 3 7 8 9 10 11 15

set_union of a1 and a3 is: 1 2 3 4 5 6 7 8 9 10 11 15
```

Fig. 16.11 | Algorithms includes, set_difference, set_intersection, set_symmetric_difference and set_union. (Part 2 of 2.)

includes Algorithm

Lines 25 and 33 call the includes algorithm, which compares two sets of *sorted* values to determine whether *every* element of the second set is in the first set. If so, includes returns true; otherwise, it returns false. The first two iterator arguments must be at least *input iterators* and must describe the first set of values. In line 25, the first set consists of the elements from a1.cbegin() up to, but *not* including, a1.cend(). The last two iterator arguments must be at least *input iterators* and must describe the second set of values. In line 25, the second set consists of the elements from a2.cbegin() up to, but *not* including, a2.cend(). An overloaded version of includes takes a fifth argument that's a *binary predicate function* indicating whether its first argument is less than its second. The two sequences must be sorted using the *same comparison function*.

set_difference *Algorithm*

Lines 43–44 use the set_difference algorithm to find the elements from the first set of sorted values that are *not* in the second set of sorted values (both sets of values must be in *ascending order*). The elements that are *different* are copied into the fifth argument (in this case, the array difference). The first two iterator arguments must be at least *input iterators* for the first set of values. The next two iterator arguments must be at least *input iterators* for the second set of values. The fifth argument must be at least an *output iterator* indicating where to store a copy of the values that are *different*. The algorithm returns an *output iterator* positioned immediately after the *last* value copied into the set to which the fifth argument points. An overloaded version of set_difference takes a sixth argument that's a *binary predicate function* indicating whether its first argument is less than its second. The two sequences must be sorted using the *same comparison function*.

set_intersection *Algorithm*

Lines 51–52 use the set_intersection algorithm to determine the elements from the first set of sorted values that *are* in the second set of sorted values (both sets of values must be in *ascending* order). The elements *common to both sets* are copied into the fifth argument (in this case, array intersection). The first two iterator arguments must be at least *input iterators* for the first set of values. The next two iterator arguments must be at least *input iterators* for the second set of values. The fifth argument must be at least an *output iterator* indicating where to store a copy of the values that are the same. The algorithm returns an *output iterator* positioned immediately after the last value copied into the set to which the fifth argument points. An overloaded version of set_intersection takes a sixth argument that's a *binary predicate function* indicating whether its first argument is less than its second. The two sequences must be sorted using the *same comparison function*.

set_symmetric_difference *Algorithm*

Lines 60–61 use the set_symmetric_difference algorithm to determine the elements in the first set that are *not* in the second set and the elements in the second set that are *not* in the first set (both sets must be in *ascending order*). The elements that are *different* are copied from both sets into the fifth argument (the array symmetric_difference). The first two iterator arguments must be at least *input iterators* for the first set of values. The next two iterator arguments must be at least *input iterators* for the second set of values. The fifth argument must be at least an *output iterator* indicating where to store a copy of the values that are different. The algorithm returns an *output iterator* positioned immediately after the *last* value copied into the set to which the fifth argument points. An overloaded version of set_symmetric_difference takes a sixth argument that's a *binary predicate function* indicating whether its first argument is less than its second. The two sequences must be sorted using the *same comparison function*.

set_union *Algorithm*

Lines 68–69 use the set_union algorithm to create a set of all the elements that are in *either or both* of the two sorted sets (both sets of values must be in *ascending order*). The elements are copied from both sets into the fifth argument (in this case the array unionSet). Elements that appear in *both* sets are copied only from the first set. The first two iterator arguments must be at least *input iterators* for the first set of values. The next two iterator arguments must be at least *input iterators* for the second set of values. The fifth argument must be at least an *output iterator* indicating where to store the copied elements. The algorithm returns an *output iterator* positioned immediately after the *last* value copied into the set to which the fifth argument points. An overloaded version of set_union takes a sixth argument that's a *binary predicate function* indicating whether its first argument is less than its second. The two sequences must be sorted in ascending order using the *same comparison function*.

16.4.11 lower_bound, upper_bound and equal_range

Figure 16.12 demonstrates algorithms lower_bound, upper_bound and equal_range.

```
1   // Fig. 16.12: fig16_12.cpp
2   // Algorithms lower_bound, upper_bound and
3   // equal_range for a sorted sequence of values.
4   #include <iostream>
5   #include <algorithm> // algorithm definitions
6   #include <array> // aray class-template definition
7   #include <iterator> // ostream_iterator
8   using namespace std;
9
10  int main() {
11     const size_t SIZE{10};
12     array<int, SIZE> a{2, 2, 4, 4, 4, 6, 6, 6, 6, 8};
13     ostream_iterator<int> output{cout, " "};
14
15     cout << "array a contains: ";
16     copy(a.cbegin(), a.cend(), output);
17
18     // determine lower-bound insertion point for 6 in a
19     auto lower = lower_bound(a.cbegin(), a.cend(), 6);
20     cout << "\n\nLower bound of 6 is element "
21        << (lower - a.cbegin()) << " of array a";
22
23     // determine upper-bound insertion point for 6 in a
24     auto upper = upper_bound(a.cbegin(), a.cend(), 6);
25     cout << "\nUpper bound of 6 is element "
26        << (upper - a.cbegin()) << " of array a";
27
28     // use equal_range to determine both the lower- and
29     // upper-bound insertion points for 6
30     auto eq = equal_range(a.cbegin(), a.cend(), 6);
31     cout << "\nUsing equal_range:\n   Lower bound of 6 is element "
32        << (eq.first - a.cbegin()) << " of array a";
33     cout << "\n   Upper bound of 6 is element "
34        << (eq.second - a.cbegin()) << " of array a";
35
```

Fig. 16.12 | Algorithms lower_bound, upper_bound and equal_range for a sorted sequence of values. (Part 1 of 2.)

```
36        // determine lower-bound insertion point for 5 in a
37        cout << "\n\nUse lower_bound to locate the first point\n"
38           << "at which 5 can be inserted in order";
39        lower = lower_bound(a.cbegin(), a.cend(), 5);
40        cout << "\n   Lower bound of 5 is element "
41           << (lower - a.cbegin()) << " of array a";
42
43        // determine upper-bound insertion point for 7 in a
44        cout << "\n\nUse upper_bound to locate the last point\n"
45           << "at which 7 can be inserted in order";
46        upper = upper_bound(a.cbegin(), a.cend(), 7);
47        cout << "\n   Upper bound of 7 is element "
48           << (upper - a.cbegin()) << " of array a";
49
50        // use equal_range to determine both the lower- and
51        // upper-bound insertion points for 5
52        cout << "\n\nUse equal_range to locate the first and\n"
53           << "last point at which 5 can be inserted in order";
54        eq = equal_range(a.cbegin(), a.cend(), 5);
55        cout << "\n   Lower bound of 5 is element "
56           << (eq.first - a.cbegin()) << " of array a";
57        cout << "\n   Upper bound of 5 is element "
58           << (eq.second - a.cbegin()) << " of array a" << endl;
59     }
```

```
Array a contains: 2 2 4 4 4 6 6 6 6 8

Lower bound of 6 is element 5 of array a
Upper bound of 6 is element 9 of array a
Using equal_range:
    Lower bound of 6 is element 5 of array a
    Upper bound of 6 is element 9 of array a

Use lower_bound to locate the first point
at which 5 can be inserted in order
    Lower bound of 5 is element 5 of array a

Use upper_bound to locate the last point
at which 7 can be inserted in order
    Upper bound of 7 is element 9 of array a

Use equal_range to locate the first and
last point at which 5 can be inserted in order
    Lower bound of 5 is element 5 of array a
    Upper bound of 5 is element 5 of array a
```

Fig. 16.12 | Algorithms `lower_bound`, `upper_bound` and `equal_range` for a sorted sequence of values. (Part 2 of 2.)

`lower_bound` *Algorithm*

Line 19 uses the `lower_bound` algorithm to find the first location in a sorted sequence of values at which the third argument could be inserted in the sequence such that the sequence would still be *sorted in ascending order*. The first two iterator arguments must be at least *forward iterators*. The third argument is the value for which to determine the lower bound. The algorithm returns a *forward iterator* pointing to the position at which the insert can occur. A second version of lower_bound takes as a fourth argument a *binary predicate function* indicating the order in which the elements were *originally* sorted.

upper_bound *Algorithm*

Line 24 uses the upper_bound algorithm to find the last location in a sorted sequence of values at which the third argument could be inserted in the sequence such that the sequence would still be sorted in *ascending order*. The first two iterator arguments must be at least *forward iterators*. The third argument is the value for which to determine the upper bound. The algorithm returns a *forward iterator* pointing to the position at which the insert can occur. A second version of upper_bound takes as a fourth argument a *binary predicate function* indicating the order in which the elements were *originally* sorted.

equal_range *Algorithm*

Line 30 uses the equal_range algorithm to return a pair of *forward iterators* containing the results of performing both a lower_bound and an upper_bound operation. The first two arguments must be at least *forward iterators*. The third is the value for which to locate the equal range. The algorithm returns a pair of *forward iterators* for the lower bound (eq.first) and upper bound (eq.second), respectively.

Locating Insertion Points in Sorted Sequences

Algorithms lower_bound, upper_bound and equal_range are often used to locate *insertion points* in sorted sequences. Line 39 uses lower_bound to locate the first point at which 5 can be inserted in order in a. Line 46 uses upper_bound to locate the last point at which 7 can be inserted in order in a. Line 54 uses equal_range to locate the first and last points at which 5 can be inserted in order in a.

16.4.12 min, max, minmax and minmax_element

Figure 16.13 demonstrates algorithms min, max, minmax and minmax_element.

```cpp
1   // Fig. 16.13: fig16_13.cpp
2   // Algorithms min, max, minmax and minmax_element.
3   #include <iostream>
4   #include <array>
5   #include <algorithm>
6   using namespace std;
7
8   int main() {
9      cout << "The minimum of 12 and 7 is: " << min(12, 7);
10     cout << "\nThe maximum of 12 and 7 is: " << max(12, 7);
11     cout << "\nThe minimum of 'G' and 'Z' is: " << min('G', 'Z');
12     cout << "\nThe maximum of 'G' and 'Z' is: " << max('G', 'Z');
13
14     // determine which argument is the min and which is the max
15     auto result1 = minmax(12, 7);
16     cout << "\n\nThe minimum of 12 and 7 is: " << result1.first
17        << "\nThe maximum of 12 and 7 is: " << result1.second;
```

Fig. 16.13 | Algorithms min, max, minmax and minmax_element. (Part 1 of 2.)

```
18
19      array<int, 10> items{3, 100, 52, 77, 22, 31, 1, 98, 13, 40};
20      ostream_iterator<int> output{cout, " "};
21
22      cout << "\n\nArray items contains: ";
23      copy(items.cbegin(), items.cend(), output);
24
25      auto result2 = minmax_element(items.cbegin(), items.cend());
26      cout << "\nThe minimum element in items is: " << *result2.first
27         << "\nThe maximum element in items is: " << *result2.second << endl;
28   }
```

```
The minimum of 12 and 7 is: 7
The maximum of 12 and 7 is: 12
The minimum of 'G' and 'Z' is: G
The maximum of 'G' and 'Z' is: Z

The minimum of 12 and 7 is: 7
The maximum of 12 and 7 is: 12

Array items contains: 3 100 52 77 22 31 1 98 13 40
The minimum element in items is: 1
The maximum element in items is: 100
```

Fig. 16.13 | Algorithms min, max, minmax and minmax_element. (Part 2 of 2.)

Algorithms *min* and *max* with Two Parameters
Algorithms min and max (demonstrated in lines 9–12) determine the minimum and the maximum of two elements, respectively.

C++11: *min* and *max* Algorithms with *initializer_list* Parameters
C++11 added overloaded versions of the algorithms min and max that each receive an initializer_list parameter and return the smallest or largest item in the list initializer that's passed as an argument. For example, the following statement returns 7:

```
int minimum = min({ 10, 7, 14, 21, 17 });
```

Each of these new min and max algorithms is overloaded with a version that takes as a second argument a *binary predicate function* for determining whether the first argument is less than the second.

C++11: *minmax* Algorithm
C++11 also added the minmax algorithm (line 15) that receives two items and returns a pair in which the smaller item is stored in first and the larger item is stored in second. A second version of this algorithm takes as a third argument a *binary predicate function* for determining whether the first argument is less than the second.

C++11: *minmax_element* Algorithm
In addition, C++11 added the minmax_element algorithm (line 25) that receives two *input iterators* representing a range of elements and returns a pair of iterators in which first points to the smallest element in the range and second points to the largest. A second ver-

sion of this algorithm takes as a third argument a *binary predicate function* for determining whether the first argument is less than the second.

16.5 Function Objects

As we've shown in this chapter, many Standard Library algorithms allow you to pass a lamda or a function pointer into the algorithm to help the algorithm perform its task. For example, the `binary_search` algorithm that we discussed in Section 16.4.6 is overloaded with a version that requires as its fourth parameter a *function* that takes two arguments and returns a `bool` value. The algorithm uses this function to compare the search key to an element in the collection. The function returns `true` if the search key and element being compared are equal; otherwise, the function returns `false`. This enables `binary_search` to search a collection of elements for which the element type does *not* provide an overloaded < operator.

Any algorithm that can receive a lambda or function pointer can also receive an object of a class that overloads the function-call operator (parentheses) with a function named `operator()`, provided that the overloaded operator meets the requirements of the algorithm—in the case of `binary_search`, it must receive two arguments and return a `bool`. An object of such a class is known as a function object and can be used syntactically and semantically like a lambda, a function or a function pointer—the overloaded parentheses operator is invoked by using a function object's name followed by parentheses containing the arguments to the function. Most algorithms can use lambdas, function pointers and function objects interchangeably.[2] In fact, lambdas are converted by the compiler into function pointers or function objects, which can be inlined by the compiler for optimization purposes.

Advantages of Function Objects over Function Pointers
Function objects provide several advantages over *function pointers*. The compiler can sometimes inline a *function object's* overloaded `operator()` to improve performance. Also, since they're objects of classes, *function objects* can have data members that `operator()` can use to perform its task.

Predefined Function Objects of the Standard Template Library
Many predefined *function objects* can be found in the header `<functional>`. Figure 16.14 lists several of the dozens of Standard Library *function objects*, which are all implemented as class templates—you can see the complete list at

```
http://en.cppreference.com/w/cpp/utility/functional
```

Section 20.9 of the C++ standard contains the complete list of function objects. We used the *function object* `less<T>` in the `set` and `multiset` examples to specify the sorting order for elements in a container. Recall that many of the overloaded Standard Library algorithms can receive as their last argument a binary function that determines whether its first argument is less than its second—exactly the purpose of the `less<T>` function object.

---

2.   There are cases—especially in template programming—where lambdas and function pointers cannot be used interchangeably with function objects, but these cases are beyond this book's scope.

Function object	Type	Function object	Type
divides<T>	arithmetic	logical_or<T>	logical
equal_to<T>	relational	minus<T>	arithmetic
greater<T>	relational	modulus<T>	arithmetic
greater_equal<T>	relational	negate<T>	arithmetic
less<T>	relational	not_equal_to<T>	relational
less_equal<T>	relational	plus<T>	arithmetic
logical_and<T>	logical	multiplies<T>	arithmetic
logical_not<T>	logical		

Fig. 16.14 | Some function objects in the Standard Library.

Using the **accumulate** *Algorithm*

Figure 16.15 uses the accumulate numeric algorithm (introduced in Fig. 16.6) to calculate the sum of the squares of the elements in an array. The fourth argument to accumulate is a binary function object (that is, a function object for which operator() takes two arguments) or a *function pointer* to a binary function (that is, a function that takes two arguments). Function accumulate is demonstrated three times—once with a function pointer, once with a function object and once with a lamdba.

```cpp
1   // Fig. 16.15: fig16_15.cpp
2   // Demonstrating function objects.
3   #include <iostream>
4   #include <array> // array class-template definition
5   #include <algorithm> // copy algorithm
6   #include <numeric> // accumulate algorithm
7   #include <functional> // binary_function definition
8   #include <iterator> // ostream_iterator
9   using namespace std;
10
11  // binary function adds square of its second argument and the
12  // running total in its first argument, then returns the sum
13  int sumSquares(int total, int value) {
14     return total + value * value;
15  }
16
17  // Class template SumSquaresClass defines overloaded operator()
18  // that adds the square of its second argument and running
19  // total in its first argument, then returns sum
20  template<typename T>
21  class SumSquaresClass {
22  public:
23     // add square of value to total and return result
24     T operator()(const T& total, const T& value) {
25        return total + value * value;
26     }
27  };
```

Fig. 16.15 | Demonstrating function objects. (Part 1 of 2.)

```
28
29   int main() {
30      const size_t SIZE{10};
31      array<int, SIZE> integers{1, 2, 3, 4, 5, 6, 7, 8, 9, 10};
32      ostream_iterator<int> output{cout, " "};
33
34      cout << "array integers contains: ";
35      copy(integers.cbegin(), integers.cend(), output);
36
37      // calculate sum of squares of elements of array integers
38      // using binary function sumSquares
39      int result{accumulate(integers.cbegin(), integers.cend(),
40         0, sumSquares)};
41
42      cout << "\n\nSum of squares of integers' elements using "
43         << "binary function sumSquares: " << result;
44
45      // calculate sum of squares of elements of array integers
46      // using binary function object
47      result = accumulate(integers.cbegin(), integers.cend(),
48         0, SumSquaresClass<int>{});
49
50      cout << "\n\nSum of squares of integers' elements using binary"
51         << "\nfunction object of type SumSquaresClass<int>: "
52         << result;
53
54      // calculate sum of squares array's elements using a lambda
55      result = accumulate(integers.cbegin(), integers.cend(),
56         0, [](auto total, auto value){return total + value * value;});
57
58      cout << "\n\nSum of squares of integer's elements using a lambda: "
59         << result << endl;
60   }
```

```
array integers contains: 1 2 3 4 5 6 7 8 9 10

Sum of squares of integers' elements using binary function sumSquares: 385

Sum of squares of integers' elements using
binary function object of type SumSquaresClass<int>: 385

Sum of squares of integer's elements using a lambda: 385
```

Fig. 16.15 | Demonstrating function objects. (Part 2 of 2.)

Function sumSquares

Lines 13–15 define a function sumSquares that squares its second argument value, adds that square and its first argument total and returns the sum. Function accumulate will pass each of the elements of the sequence over which it iterates as the second argument to sumSquares in the example. On the first call to sumSquares, the first argument will be the initial value of the total (which is supplied as the third argument to accumulate; 0 in this program). All subsequent calls to sumSquares receive as the first argument the running sum returned by the previous call to sumSquares. When accumulate completes, it returns the sum of the squares of all the elements in the sequence.

Class *SumSquaresClass*

Lines 20–27 define the class template SumSquaresClass with an overloaded operator() that has two parameters and returns a value—the requirements for a binary function object. On the first call to the *function object*, the first argument will be the initial value of the total (which is supplied as the third argument to accumulate; 0 in this program) and the second argument will be the first element in array integers. All subsequent calls to operator() receive as the first argument the result returned by the previous call to the *function object*, and the second argument will be the next element in the array. When accumulate completes, it returns the sum of the squares of all the elements in the array.

Calling Algorithm *accumulate*

Lines 39–40 call function accumulate with a *pointer to function* sumSquares as its last argument. Similarly, the statement in lines 47–48 call accumulate with an object of class SumSquaresClass as the last argument. Finally, lines 55–56 call accumulate with an equivalent lambda.

The expression SumSquaresClass<int>{} in line 48 creates (and calls the default constructor for) an object of class SumSquaresClass (a *function object*) that's passed to accumulate, which invokes the function operator(). Lines 47–48 could be written as two separate statements, as follows:

```
SumSquaresClass<int> sumSquaresObject;
result = accumulate(integers.cbegin(), integers.cend(),
    0, sumSquaresObject);
```

The first line defines an object of class SumSquaresClass, which is then passed to accumulate in the subsequent statement.

16.6 Standard Library Algorithm Summary

The C++ standard specifies over 90 algorithms—many overloaded with two or more versions. The standard separates the algorithms into several categories—*mutating sequence algorithms, nonmodifying sequence algorithms, sorting and related algorithms* and *generalized numeric operations*. To learn about algorithms we did not present in this chapter, see your compiler's documentation or visit sites such as

```
http://en.cppreference.com/w/cpp/algorithm
https://msdn.microsoft.com/library/yah1y2x8.aspx
```

Mutating Sequence Algorithms

Figure 16.16 shows many of the mutating-sequence algorithms—i.e., algorithms that modify the containers they operate on. Algorithms added in C++11 are marked with an * in Figs. 16.16–16.19. Algorithms presented in this chapter are shown in **bold**.

11

Mutating sequence algorithms from header `<algorithm>`			
copy	copy_n*	copy_if*	copy_backward
move*	move_backward*	**swap**	**swap_ranges**

Fig. 16.16 | Mutating sequence algorithms from header `<algorithm>`. (Part I of 2.)

Mutating sequence algorithms from header `<algorithm>`			
iter_swap	transform	replace	replace_if
replace_copy	replace_copy_if	fill	fill_n
generate	generate_n	remove	remove_if
remove_copy	remove_copy_if	unique	unique_copy
reverse	reverse_copy	rotate	rotate_copy
random_shuffle	shuffle*	is_partitioned*	partition
stable_partition	partition_copy*	partition_point*	

Fig. 16.16 | Mutating sequence algorithms from header `<algorithm>`. (Part 2 of 2.)

Nonmodifying Sequence Algorithms

Figure 16.17 shows the nonmodifying sequence algorithms—i.e., algorithms that do *not* modify the containers they operate on.

Nonmodifying sequence algorithms from header `<algorithm>`			
all_of*	any_of*	none_of*	for_each
find	find_if	find_if_not*	find_end
find_first_of	adjacent_find	count	count_if
mismatch	equal	is_permutation*	search
search_n			

Fig. 16.17 | Nonmodifying sequence algorithms from header `<algorithm>`.

Sorting and Related Algorithms

Figure 16.18 shows the *sorting and related algorithms*.

Sorting and related algorithms from header `<algorithm>`			
sort	stable_sort	partial_sort	partial_sort_copy
is_sorted*	is_sorted_until*	nth_element	lower_bound
upper_bound	equal_range	binary_search	merge
inplace_merge	includes	set_union	set_intersection
set_difference	set_symmetric_difference		push_heap
pop_heap	make_heap	sort_heap	is_heap*
is_heap_until*	min	max	minmax*
min_element	max_element	minmax_element*	lexicographical_compare
next_permutation	prev_permutation		

Fig. 16.18 | Sorting and related algorithms from header `<algorithm>`.

Numerical Algorithms

Figure 16.19 shows the numerical algorithms of the header `<numeric>`.

Numerical algorithms from header `<numeric>`		
accumulate	partial_sum	iota*
inner_product	adjacent_difference	

Fig. 16.19 | Numerical algorithms from header `<numeric>`.

16.7 Wrap-Up

In this chapter, we demonstrated many of the Standard Library algorithms, including mathematical algorithms, basic searching and sorting algorithms and set operations. You learned the types of iterators each algorithm requires and that each algorithm can be used with any container that supports the minimum iterator functionality the algorithm requires. You used lambda expressions to create anonymous functions that were passed to Standard Library algorithms. Finally, we introduced function objects that work syntactically and semantically like ordinary functions, but offer advantages such as performance and the ability to store data.

We introduced exception handling earlier in the book in our discussion of arrays. In the next chapter, we take a deeper look at C++'s rich set of exception handling capabilities.

Summary

Section 16.1 Introduction
- Standard Library algorithms are functions that perform such common data manipulations as searching, sorting and comparing elements or entire containers.

Section 16.3 Lambda Expressions
- **Lambda expressions** (or **lambdas**; p. 710) provide a simplified syntax for defining function objects directly where they are used.

Section 16.3.1 Algorithm *for_each*
- The **for_each** algorithm (p. 711) calls a function that performs a task once for each element in a sequence. The called function must have one parameter of the container's element type.

Section 16.3.2 Lambda with an Empty Introducer
- Lambdas begin with the **lambda introducer** (**[]**, p. 711), followed by a parameter list and function body.
- A lambda can use local variables from the function in which the lambda is defined. The introducer enables you to specify which, if any, local variables the lambda uses—this is known as **capturing** (p. 711) the variables.
- Specifying a lambda parameter's type as auto enables the compiler to infer the parameter's type, based on the context in which the lambda appears.

- Using auto to infer the parameter type is a new C++14 feature of so-called **generic lambdas** (p. 711). In C++11 you were required to state each lambda parameter's explicit type.

Section 16.3.3 Lambda with a Nonempty Introducer—Capturing Local Variables

- An ampersand (&) in a lambda introducer indicates that the lambda captures the corresponding local variable by reference and can modify its value—without an ampersand, local variables are captured by value.

Section 16.3.4 Lambda Return Types

- The compiler can infer a lambda's return type if the body contains a statement of the form

    return *expression*;

  Otherwise, the lambda's return type is void, unless you explicitly specify a return type using C++11's trailing return type syntax (-> *type*), as in

    [] (*parameterList*) -> *type* {*lambdaBody*}

Section 16.4.1 fill, fill_n, generate and generate_n

- Algorithms fill and fill_n (p. 712) set every element in a range of container elements to a specific value.
- Algorithms generate and generate_n (p. 712) use a **generator function** (p. 712) or function object to create values for every element in a range of container elements.

Section 16.4.2 equal, mismatch and lexicographical_compare

- Algorithm equal (p. 717) compares two sequences of values for equality.
- Algorithm mismatch (p. 717) compares two sequences of values and returns a pair of iterators indicating the location in each sequence of the first mismatched elements.
- Algorithm lexicographical_compare (p. 718) compares the contents of two sequences to determine whether the contents of the first sequence are lexicographically less than the contents of the second sequence.

Section 16.4.3 remove, remove_if, remove_copy and remove_copy_if

- Algorithm remove (p. 720) eliminates all elements with a specific value in a certain range.
- Algorithm remove_copy (p. 720) copies all elements that do not have a specific value in a certain range.
- Algorithm remove_if (p. 720) deletes all elements that satisfy the if condition in a certain range.
- Algorithm remove_copy_if (p. 720) copies all elements that do not satisfy the if condition in a certain range.

Section 16.4.4 replace, replace_if, replace_copy and replace_copy_if

- Algorithm replace (p. 722) replaces all elements with a specific value in certain range.
- Algorithm replace_copy (p. 722) copies all elements in a range, replacing all elements of one value with a different value.
- Algorithm replace_if (p. 723) replaces all elements that satisfy the if condition in a certain range.
- Algorithm replace_copy_if (p. 723) copies all elements in a range, replacing all elements that satisfy the if condition in a range.

Section 16.4.5 Mathematical Algorithms

- Algorithm shuffle (p. 725) reorders randomly the elements in a certain range.

- A C++11 **random_device** object (p. 725) can be used to seed a C++11 random-number generator with a nondeterministic seed.
- Algorithm **count** (p. 725) counts the elements with a specific value in a certain range.
- Algorithm **count_if** (p. 725) counts the elements that satisfy the if condition in a certain range.
- Algorithm **min_element** (p. 725) locates the smallest element in a certain range.
- Algorithm **max_element** (p. 725) locates the largest element in a certain range.
- Algorithm **minmax_element** (p. 725) locates the smallest and largest elements in a certain range.
- Algorithm **accumulate** (p. 726) sums the values in a certain range.
- Algorithm **transform** (p. 726) applies a general function or function object to every element in a range and replaces each element with the result of the function.

Section 16.4.6 Basic Searching and Sorting Algorithms
- Algorithm **find** (p. 729) locates a specific value in a certain range.
- Algorithm **find_if** (p. 729) locates the first value in a certain range that satisfies the if condition.
- Algorithm **sort** (p. 730) arranges the elements in a certain range in ascending order or an order specified by a predicate.
- Algorithm **binary_search** (p. 730) determines whether a specific value is in a sorted range of elements.
- Algorithm **all_of** (p. 730) determines whether a unary predicate function returns true for all of the elements in the range.
- Algorithm **any_of** (p. 730) determines whether a unary predicate function returns true for any of the elements in the range.
- Algorithm **none_of** (p. 730) determines whether a unary predicate function returns false for all of the elements in the range.
- Algorithm **find_if_not** (p. 730) locates the first value in a certain range that does not satisfy the if condition.

Section 16.4.7 swap, iter_swap and swap_ranges
- Algorithm **swap** (p. 732) exchanges two values.
- Algorithm **iter_swap** (p. 732) exchanges the two elements to which the two iterator arguments point.
- Algorithm **swap_ranges** (p. 732) exchanges the elements in a certain range.

Section 16.4.8 copy_backward, merge, unique and reverse
- Algorithm **copy_backward** (p. 733) copies elements in a range and places the elements into a container starting from the end and working toward the front.
- Algorithm **move** (p. 734) moves elements in a range from one container to another.
- Algorithm **move_backward** (p. 734) moves elements in a range from one container to another starting from the end and working toward the front.
- Algorithm **merge** (p. 734) combines two sorted ascending sequences of values into a third sorted ascending sequence.
- Algorithm **unique** (p. 734) removes duplicated elements in a certain range of a sorted sequence.
- Algorithm **copy_if** (p. 735) copies each element from a range if a unary predicate function returns true for that element.

- Algorithm **reverse** (p. 735) reverses all the elements in a certain range.
- Algorithm **copy_n** (p. 735) copies a specified number of elements starting from a specified location and places them into a container starting at the specified location.

Section 16.4.9 *inplace_merge, unique_copy and reverse_copy*
- Algorithm **inplace_merge** (p. 736) merges two sorted sequences of elements in the same container.
- Algorithm **unique_copy** (p. 736) makes a copy of all the unique elements in the sorted sequence of values in a certain range.
- Algorithm **reverse_copy** (p. 736) makes a reversed copy of the elements in a certain range.

Section 16.4.10 Set Operations
- The set algorithm **includes** (p. 738) compares two sets of sorted values to determine whether every element of the second set is in the first set.
- The set algorithm **set_difference** (p. 739) finds the elements from the first set of sorted values that are not in the second set of sorted values (both sets of values must be in ascending order).
- The set algorithm **set_intersection** (p. 739) determines the elements from the first set of sorted values that are in the second set of sorted values (both sets of values must be in ascending order).
- The set algorithm **set_symmetric_difference** (p. 739) determines the elements in the first set that are not in the second set and the elements in the second set that are not in the first set (both sets of values must be in ascending order).
- The set algorithm **set_union** (p. 739) creates a set of all the elements that are in either or both of the two sorted sets (both sets of values must be in ascending order).

Section 16.4.11 *lower_bound, upper_bound and equal_range*
- Algorithm **lower_bound** (p. 741) finds the first location in a sorted sequence of values at which the third argument could be inserted in the sequence such that the sequence would still be sorted in ascending order.
- Algorithm **upper_bound** (p. 742) finds the last location in a sorted sequence of values at which the third argument could be inserted in the sequence such that the sequence would still be sorted in ascending order.
- Algorithm **equal_range** (p. 742) returns the lower bound and upper bound as a `pair`.

Section 16.4.12 *min, max, minmax and minmax_element*
- Algorithms **min** and **max** (p. 743) determine the minimum of two elements and the maximum of two elements, respectively.
- C++11's overloaded versions of the algorithms **min** and **max** each receive an `initializer_list` parameter and return the smallest or largest item in the list initializer that's passed as an argument. Each is overloaded with a version that takes as a second argument a *binary predicate function* for comparing values.
- C++11's **minmax** algorithm (p. 743) receives two items and returns a `pair` in which the smaller item is stored in `first` and the larger item is stored in `second`. A second version of this algorithm takes as a third argument a binary predicate function for comparing values.
- C++11's **minmax_element** algorithm (p. 725) receives two input iterators representing a range of elements and returns a `pair` of iterators in which `first` points to the smallest element in the range and `second` points to the largest. A second version of this algorithm takes as a third argument a binary predicate function for comparing values.

Section 16.5 Function Objects

- A **function object** (p. 744) is an object of a class that overloads operator().
- The Standard Library provides many predefined function objects, which can be found in header `<functional>` (p. 744).
- **Binary function objects** (p. 745) take two arguments and return a value.

Self-Review Exercises

16.1 State whether each of the following is *true* or *false*. If *false*, explain why.
  a) Standard Library algorithms can operate on C-like pointer-based arrays.
  b) Standard Library algorithms are encapsulated as member functions within each container class.
  c) When using the remove algorithm on a container, the algorithm does not decrease the size of the container from which elements are being removed.
  d) One disadvantage of using Standard Library algorithms is that they depend on the implementation details of the containers on which they operate.
  e) The remove_if algorithm does not modify the number of elements in the container, but it does move to the beginning of the container all elements that are not removed.
  f) The find_if_not algorithm locates all the values in the range for which the specified unary predicate function returns false.
  g) Use the set_union algorithm to create a set of all the elements that are in either or both of two sorted sets (both sets of values must be in ascending order).

16.2 Fill in the blanks in each of the following statements:
  a) Standard Library algorithms operate on container elements indirectly, using _____.
  b) The sort algorithm requires a(n) _____ iterator.
  c) Algorithms _____ and _____ set every element in a range of container elements to a specific value.
  d) The _____ algorithm compares two sequences of values for equality.
  e) The C++11 _____ algorithm locates both the smallest and largest elements in a range.
  f) A back_inserter calls the container's default _____ function to insert an element at the end of the container. If an element is inserted into a container that has no more space available, the container grows in size.
  g) Any algorithm that can receive a function pointer can also receive an object of a class that overloads the parentheses operator with a function named operator(), provided that the overloaded operator meets the requirements of the algorithm. An object of such a class is known as a(n) _____ and can be used syntactically and semantically like a function or function pointer.

16.3 Write a statement to peform each of the following tasks:
  a) Use the fill algorithm to fill the entire array of strings named items with "hello".
  b) Function nextInt returns the next int value in sequence starting with 0 the first time it's called. Use the generate algorithm and the nextInt function to fill the array of ints named integers.
  c) Use the equal algorithm to compare two lists (strings1 and strings2) for equality. Store the result in bool variable result.
  d) Use the remove_if algorithm to remove from the vector of strings named colors all of the strings that start with "bl". Function startsWithBL returns true if its argument string starts with "bl". Store the iterator that the algorithm returns in newEnd.
  e) Use the replace_if algorithm to replace with 0 all elements with values greater than 100 in the array of ints named values. Function greaterThan100 returns true if its argument is greater than 100.

    f) Use the `minmax_element` algorithm to find the smallest and largest values in the array of `doubles` named `temperatures`. Store the pair of iterators that's returned in `result`.

    g) Use the `sort` algorithm to sort the array of `strings` named `colors`.

    h) Use the `reverse` algorithm to reverse order of the elements in the array of `strings` named `colors`.

    i) Use the `merge` algorithm to merge the contents of the two sorted arrays named `values1` and `values2` into a third array named `results`.

    j) Write a lambda expression that returns the square of its `int` argument and assign the lambda expression to variable `squareInt`.

Answers to Self-Review Exercises

16.1 a) True.

    b) False. Standard Library algorithms are not member functions. They operate indirectly on containers, through iterators.

    c) True.

    d) False. Standard Library algorithms do not depend on the implementation details of the containers on which they operate.

    e) True.

    f) False. It locates only the first value in the range for which the specified unary predicate function returns `false`.

    g) True.

16.2 a) Iterators. b) random-access. c) `fill`, `fill_n`. d) `equal`. e) `minmax_element`. f) `push_back`. g) function object.

16.3 a) `fill(items.begin(), items.end(), "hello");`

    b) `generate(integers.begin(), integers.end(), nextInt);`

    c) `bool result{equal(strings1.cbegin(), strings1.cend(), strings2.cbegin())};`

    d) `auto newEnd remove_if(colors.begin(), colors.end(), startsWithBL);`

    e) `replace_if(values.begin(), values.end(), greaterThan100, 0);`

    f) `auto result = minmax_element(temperatures.cbegin(), temperatures.cend());`

    g) `sort(colors.begin(), colors.end());`

    h) `reverse(colors.begin(), colors.end());`

    i) `merge(values1.cbegin(), values1.cend(), values2.cbegin(), values2.cend(), results.begin());`

    j) `auto squareInt = [](int i) {return i * i;};`

Exercises

16.4 State whether each of the following is *true* or *false*. If *false*, explain why.

    a) Because Standard Library algorithms process containers directly, one algorithm can often be used with many different containers.

    b) Use the `for_each` algorithm to apply a general function to every element in a range; `for_each` does not modify the sequence.

    c) By default, the `sort` algorithm arranges the elements in a range in ascending order.

    d) Use the `merge` algorithm to form a new sequence by placing the second sequence after the first.

    e) Use the `set_intersection` algorithm to find the elements from a first set of sorted values that are not in a second set of sorted values (both sets of values must be in ascending order).

f) Algorithms `lower_bound`, `upper_bound` and `equal_range` are often used to locate insertion points in sorted sequences.

g) Lambda expressions can also be used where function pointers and function objects are used in algorithms.

h) C++11's lambda expressions are defined locally inside functions and can "capture" (by value or by reference) the local variables of the enclosing function then manipulate these variables in the lambda's body.

16.5 Fill in the blanks in each of the following statements:

a) As long as a container's (or built-in array's) _____ satisfy the requirements of an algorithm, the algorithm can work on the container.

b) Algorithms `generate` and `generate_n` use a(n) _____ function to create values for every element in a *range* of container elements. That type of function takes no arguments and returns a value that can be placed in an element of the container.

c) Pointers into built-in arrays are _____ iterators.

d) Use the _____ algorithm (the template of which is in header `<numeric>`) to sum the values in a range.

e) Use the _____ algorithm to apply a general function to every element in a range when you need to modify those elements.

f) In order to work properly, the `binary_search` algorithm requires that the sequence of values must be _____.

g) Use the function `iter_swap` to exchange the elements that are pointed to by two _____ iterators and exchanges the values in those elements.

h) C++11's `minmax` algorithm receives two items and returns a(n) _____ in which the smaller item is stored in `first` and the larger item is stored in `second`.

i) _____ algorithms modify the containers they operate on.

16.6 List several advantages function objects provide over function pointers.

16.7 What happens when you apply the `unique` algorithm to a sorted sequence of elements in a range?

16.8 *(Duplicate Elimination)* Read 20 integers into an `array`. Next, use the `unique` algorithm to reduce the `array` to the unique values entered by the user. Use the `copy` algorithm to display the unique values.

16.9 *(Duplicate Elimination)* Modify Exercise 16.8 to use the `unique_copy` algorithm. The unique values should be inserted into a `vector` that's initially empty. Use a `back_inserter` to enable the `vector` to grow as new items are added. Use the `copy` algorithm to display the unique values.

16.10 *(Reading Data from a File)* Use an `istream_iterator<int>`, the `copy` algorithm and a `back_inserter` to read the contents of a text file that contains `int` values separated by whitespace. Place the `int` values into a `vector` of `int`s. The first argument to the `copy` algorithm should be the `istream_iterator<int>` object that's associated with the text file's `ifstream` object. The second argument should be an `istream_iterator<int>` object that's initialized using the class template `istream_iterator`'s default constructor—the resulting object can be used as an "end" iterator. After reading the file's contents, display the contents of the resulting vector.

16.11 *(Merging Ordered Lists)* Write a program that uses Standard Library algorithms to merge two ordered `list`s of strings into a single ordered `list` of strings, then displays the resulting `list`.

16.12 *(Palindrome Tester)* A palindrome is a `string` that is spelled the same way forward and backward. Examples of palindromes include "radar" and "able was i ere i saw elba." Write a function `palindromeTester` that uses the `reverse` algorithm on an a copy of a `string`, then compares the original `string` and the reversed `string` to determine whether the original `string` is a palindrome. Like the Standard Library containers, `string` objects provide functions like `begin` and `end` to obtain iterators that point to characters in a `string`. Assume that the original `string` contains all lowercase letters and does not contain any punctuation. Use function `palindromeTester` in a program.

16.13 *(Enhanced Palindrome Tester)* Enhance Exercise 16.12's `palindromeTester` function to allow strings containing uppercase and lowercase letters and punctuation. Before testing whether the original string is a palindrome, function `palindromeTester` should convert the `string` to lowercase letters and eliminate any punctuation. For simplicity, assume the only punctuations characters can be

```
. , ! ; : ()
```

You can use the `copy_if` algorithm and a `back_inserter` to make a copy of the original `string`, eliminate the punctuation characters and place the characters into a new `string` object.

16.14 Explain why using the "weakest iterator" that yields acceptable performance helps produce maximally reusable components.

Exception Handling: A
Deeper Look

Objectives

In this chapter you'll:

- Understand the exception-handling flow of control with **try**, **catch** and **throw**.

- Define new exception classes.

- Understand how stack unwinding enables exceptions not caught in one scope to be caught in another.

- Handle **new** failures.

- Use **unique_ptr** (a Standard Library "smart pointer" class) to prevent memory leaks.

- Understand the standard exception hierarchy.

17.1 Introduction

As you know from Section 7.10, an exception is an indication of a problem that occurs during a program's execution. Exception handling enables you to create applications that can handle (i.e., resolve) exceptions and perform appropriate cleanup when an exception that cannot or should not be handled occurs. In many cases, this allows a program to continue executing as if no problem had been encountered. The features presented in this chapter enable you to write robust, fault-tolerant programs that can deal with problems and continue executing or terminate gracefully.

Previously, we've shown how to handle and how to indicate exceptions (Chapters 7 and 9, respectively). We begin this chapter with a review of these exception-handling concepts in an example that demonstrates the flow of control both when a program executes successfully and when an exception occurs. We show how to handle exceptions that occur in a constructor and exceptions that occur if operator new fails to allocate memory for an object. We also show how to prevent memory leaks by using the "smart pointer" class unique_ptr to manage dynamically allocated memory. We introduce several C++ Standard Library exception-handling classes and show you how to create your own.

Software Engineering Observation 17.1

Exception handling provides a standard mechanism for processing errors. This is especially important when working on a large project.

Software Engineering Observation 17.2

Incorporate your exception-handling strategy into your system from its inception. Including effective exception handling after a system has been implemented can be difficult.

Error-Prevention Tip 17.1
Without exception handling, it's common for a function to calculate and return a value on success or return an error indicator on failure. A common problem with this architecture is using the return value in a subsequent calculation without first checking whether the value is the error indicator. Exception handling eliminates this problem.

17.2 Exception-Handling Flow of Control; Defining an Exception Class

Let's consider a simple example of exception handling (Figs. 17.1–17.2). For demonstration purposes, we show how to deal with a common arithmetic problem—*division by zero*, which with integer arithmetic typically causes a program to terminate prematurely. In *floating-point arithmetic*, many C++ implementations allow division by zero, in which case a result of positive or negative infinity is typically displayed as inf or -inf, respectively. Typically, a program would simply test for division by zero before attempting the calculation—we use exceptions here to present the flow of control when a program executes successfully and when an exception occurs.

In this example, we define a function quotient that receives two integers entered by the user and divides the first by the second. Before performing the division, the function casts the first int parameter's value to type double. Then, the second int parameter's value is (implicitly) promoted to type double for the calculation. So function quotient actually performs the division using two double values and returns a double result.

For the purpose of this example we treat any attempt to divide by zero as an error. Thus, function quotient tests its second parameter to ensure that it isn't zero before allowing the division to proceed. If the second parameter is zero, the function *throws an exception* to indicate to the caller that a problem occurred. The caller (main in this example) can then handle the exception and allow the user to type two new values before calling function quotient again. In this way, the program can continue executing even after an improper value is entered, thus making the program more robust.

The example consists of two files. DivideByZeroException.h (Fig. 17.1) defines an *exception class* that represents the type of the problem that might occur in the example, and fig17_02.cpp (Fig. 17.2) defines the quotient function and the main function that calls it—we'll use quotient and main to explain the exception-handling flow of control.

17.2.1 Defining an Exception Class to Represent the Type of Problem That Might Occur

Figure 17.1 defines class DivideByZeroException as a derived class of Standard Library class runtime_error (from header <stdexcept>). Class runtime_error—a derived class of exception (from header <exception>)—is the C++ standard base class for representing runtime errors. Class exception is the standard C++ base class for exceptions in the C++ Standard Library. (Section 17.10 discusses class exception and its derived classes in detail.) A typical exception class that derives from the runtime_error class defines only a constructor (e.g., lines 10–11) that passes an error-message string to the base-class runtime_error constructor. Every exception class that derives directly or indirectly from exception contains the virtual function what, which returns an exception object's error message. You're not required to derive a custom exception class, such as DivideByZero-

Exception, from the standard exception classes provided by C++. However, doing so allows you to use the virtual function what to obtain an appropriate error message and also allows you to polymorphically process the exceptions by catching a reference to the base-class type. We use an object of this DivideByZeroException class in Fig. 17.2 to indicate when an attempt is made to divide by zero.

```cpp
 1    // Fig. 17.1: DivideByZeroException.h
 2    // Class DivideByZeroException definition.
 3    #include <stdexcept> // stdexcept header contains runtime_error
 4
 5    // DivideByZeroException objects should be thrown by functions
 6    // upon detecting division-by-zero exceptions
 7    class DivideByZeroException : public std::runtime_error {
 8    public:
 9       // constructor specifies default error message
10       DivideByZeroException()
11          : std::runtime_error{"attempted to divide by zero"} {}
12    };
```

Fig. 17.1 | Class DivideByZeroException definition.

17.2.2 Demonstrating Exception Handling

Figure 17.2 uses exception handling to wrap code that might throw a DivideByZeroException and to handle that exception, should one occur. The user enters two integers, which are passed as arguments to function quotient (lines 10–18). This function divides its first parameter (numerator) by its second parameter (denominator). Assuming that the user does not specify 0 as the denominator for the division, function quotient returns the division result. If the user inputs 0 for the denominator, quotient throws an exception. In the sample output, the first two lines show a successful calculation, and the next two show a failure due to an attempt to divide by zero. When the exception occurs, the program informs the user of the mistake and prompts the user to input two new integers. After we discuss the code, we'll consider the user inputs and flow of program control that yield *these outputs*.

```cpp
 1    // Fig. 17.2: fig17_02.cpp
 2    // Example that throws exceptions on
 3    // attempts to divide by zero.
 4    #include <iostream>
 5    #include "DivideByZeroException.h" // DivideByZeroException class
 6    using namespace std;
 7
 8    // perform division and throw DivideByZeroException object if
 9    // divide-by-zero exception occurs
10    double quotient(int numerator, int denominator) {
11       // throw DivideByZeroException if trying to divide by zero
12       if (denominator == 0) {
13          throw DivideByZeroException{}; // terminate function
14       }
15
```

Fig. 17.2 | Example that throws exceptions on attempts to divide by zero. (Part 1 of 2.)

```
16      // return division result
17      return static_cast<double>(numerator) / denominator;
18  }
19
20  int main() {
21      int number1; // user-specified numerator
22      int number2; // user-specified denominator
23
24      cout << "Enter two integers (end-of-file to end): ";
25
26      // enable user to enter two integers to divide
27      while (cin >> number1 >> number2) {
28          // try block contains code that might throw exception
29          // and code that will not execute if an exception occurs
30          try {
31              double result{quotient(number1, number2)};
32              cout << "The quotient is: " << result << endl;
33          }
34          catch (const DivideByZeroException& divideByZeroException) {
35              cout << "Exception occurred: "
36                  << divideByZeroException.what() << endl;
37          }
38
39          cout << "\nEnter two integers (end-of-file to end): ";
40      }
41
42      cout << endl;
43  }
```

```
Enter two integers (end-of-file to end): 100 7
The quotient is: 14.2857

Enter two integers (end-of-file to end): 100 0
Exception occurred: attempted to divide by zero

Enter two integers (end-of-file to end): ^Z
```

Fig. 17.2 | Example that throws exceptions on attempts to divide by zero. (Part 2 of 2.)

17.2.3 Enclosing Code in a try Block

The program begins by prompting the user to enter two integers. The integers are input in the condition of the while loop (line 27). Line 31 passes the values to function quotient (lines 10–18), which either divides the integers and returns a result, or throws an exception (i.e., indicates that an error occurred) on an attempt to divide by zero. Exception handling is geared to situations in which the function that detects an error is unable to handle it.

As you learned in Section 7.10, try blocks enable exception handling, enclosing statements that might cause exceptions and statements that should be skipped if an exception occurs. The try block in lines 30–33 encloses the invocation of function quotient and the statement that displays the division result. In this example, because the invocation of function quotient (line 31) can *throw* an exception, we enclose this function invocation in a try block. Enclosing the output statement (line 32) in the try block ensures that the output will occur *only* if function quotient returns a result.

Software Engineering Observation 17.3

Exceptions may surface through explicitly mentioned code in a try block, through calls to other functions (including library calls), through deeply nested function calls initiated by code in a try block and through operators like new (Section 17.8).

17.2.4 Defining a catch Handler to Process a DivideByZeroException

You saw in Section 7.10 that exceptions are processed by catch handlers. At least one catch handler (lines 34–37) *must* immediately follow each try block. An exception parameter should *always* be declared as a *reference* to the type of exception the catch handler can process (DivideByZeroException in this case)—this prevents copying the exception object when it's caught and allows a catch handler to properly catch derived-class exceptions as well.

When an exception occurs in a try block, the catch handler that executes is the first one whose type *matches* the type of the exception that occurred (i.e., the type in the catch block matches the thrown exception type exactly or is a *direct or indirect* base class of it). If an exception parameter includes an *optional* parameter name, the catch handler can use that parameter name to interact with the caught exception in the body of the catch handler, which is delimited by braces ({ and }).

A catch handler typically reports the error to the user, logs it to a file, terminates the program gracefully or tries an alternate strategy to accomplish the failed task. In this example, the catch handler simply reports that the user attempted to divide by zero. Then the program prompts the user to enter two new integer values.

Common Programming Error 17.1

It's a syntax error to place code between a try block and its corresponding catch handlers or between its catch handlers.

Common Programming Error 17.2

Each catch handler can have one parameter—specifying a comma-separated list of exception parameters is a syntax error.

Common Programming Error 17.3

It's a compilation error to catch the same type in multiple catch handlers following a single try block.

17.2.5 Termination Model of Exception Handling

If an exception occurs as the result of a statement in a try block, the try block expires (i.e., it *terminates* immediately). Next, the program searches for the first catch handler that can process the type of exception that occurred. The program locates the matching catch by comparing the thrown exception's type to each catch's exception-parameter type until the program finds a match. A match occurs if the types are *identical* or if the thrown exception's type is a *derived class* of the exception-parameter type.

When a match occurs, the code in the matching catch handler executes. When a catch handler finishes processing by reaching its closing right brace (}), the exception is considered handled and the local variables defined within the catch handler (including the catch parameter) go out of scope. Program control does *not* return to the point at which the exception occurred (known as the throw point), because the try block has *expired*. Rather, control resumes with the first statement (line 39 in Fig. 17.2) after the last catch handler following the try block. This is known as the termination model of exception handling. Some languages use the resumption model of exception handling, in which, after an exception is handled, control resumes just after the throw point. As with any other block of code, *when a try block terminates, local variables defined in the block go out of scope.*

Common Programming Error 17.4

Logic errors can occur if you assume that after an exception is handled, control will return to the first statement after the throw point.

Error-Prevention Tip 17.2

With C++ exception handling, a program can continue executing (rather than terminating) after dealing with a problem. This helps ensure the kind of robust applications that contribute to what's called mission-critical computing or business-critical computing.

If the try block completes its execution successfully (i.e., no exceptions occur in the try block), then the program ignores the catch handlers and program control continues with the first statement after the last catch following that try block.

If an exception occurs in a function and is not caught in that function, the function terminates immediately, and the program attempts to locate an enclosing try block in the calling function. This process is called stack unwinding and is discussed in Section 17.4.

17.2.6 Flow of Program Control When the User Enters a Nonzero Denominator

Consider the flow of control in Fig. 17.2 when the user inputs the numerator 100 and the denominator 7. In line 12, function quotient determines that the denominator is not zero, so line 17 performs the division and returns the result (14.2857) to line 31 as a double. Program control then continues sequentially from line 31, so line 32 displays the division result—line 33 ends the try block. Because the try block completed successfully (no exception was thrown), the program does *not* execute the statements contained in the catch handler (lines 34–37), and control continues to line 39 (the first line of code after the catch handler), which prompts the user to enter two more integers.

17.2.7 Flow of Program Control When the User Enters a Denominator of Zero

Now consider the case in which the user inputs the numerator 100 and the denominator 0. In line 12, quotient determines that the denominator is zero, which indicates an attempt to divide by zero. Line 13 throws an exception, which we represent as an object of class DivideByZeroException (Fig. 17.1).

To throw an exception, line 13 in Fig. 17.2 uses keyword throw followed by an operand of the type of exception to throw. Normally, a throw statement specifies *one* operand. (In Section 17.3, we discuss how to use a throw statement with *no* operand.) The operand of a throw can be of *any* copy-constructible type. If the operand is an object, we call it an exception object—in this example, the exception object is of type DivideBy-ZeroException. However, a throw operand also can assume other values, such as the value of an expression that does *not* result in an object of a class (e.g., throw x > 5) or the value of an int (e.g., throw 5). The examples in this chapter throw objects of exception classes.

Error-Prevention Tip 17.3
In general, you should throw only objects of exception class types.

As part of throwing an exception, the throw operand is created and used to initialize the parameter in the catch handler, which we discuss momentarily. The throw statement in line 13 creates a DivideByZeroException object. When line 13 throws the exception, function quotient exits immediately. So, line 13 throws the exception *before* function quotient can perform the division in line 17.

Software Engineering Observation 17.4
A central characteristic of exception handling is: If your program explicitly throws an exception, it should do so before the error has an opportunity to occur.

Because we enclosed the call to quotient (line 31) in a try block, program control enters the catch handler (lines 34–37) that immediately follows the try block. This catch handler serves as the exception handler for the divide-by-zero exception. In general, when an exception is thrown within a try block, the exception is caught by a catch handler that specifies the type matching the thrown exception. In this program, the catch handler specifies that it catches DivideByZeroException objects—this type matches the object type thrown in function quotient. Actually, the catch handler catches a *reference* to the DivideByZeroException object created by function quotient's throw statement (line 13), so that the catch handler does *not* make a copy of the exception object.

The catch's body (lines 35–36) prints the error message returned by function what of base-class runtime_error—i.e., the string that the DivideByZeroException constructor (lines 10–11 in Fig. 17.1) passed to the runtime_error base-class constructor.

Good Programming Practice 17.1
Associating each type of runtime error with an appropriately named exception type improves program clarity.

17.3 Rethrowing an Exception

A function might use a resource—like a file—and might want to release the resource (i.e., close the file) if an exception occurs. An exception handler, upon receiving an exception, can release the resource then notify its caller that an exception occurred by rethrowing the exception via the statement

```
throw;
```

Regardless of whether a handler can process an exception, the handler can *rethrow* the exception for further processing outside the handler. The next enclosing try block detects the rethrown exception, which a catch handler listed after that enclosing try block attempts to handle.

> **Common Programming Error 17.5**
> *Executing an empty* throw *statement outside a* catch *handler terminates the program immediately.*

Figure 17.3 demonstrates *rethrowing* an exception. In main's try block (lines 25–29), line 27 calls function throwException (lines 8–21). The throwException function also contains a try block (lines 10–13), from which the throw statement in line 12 throws a Standard Library exception object. Function throwException's catch handler (lines 14–18) catches this exception, prints an error message (lines 15–16) and rethrows the exception (line 17). This terminates the function and returns control to line 27 in the try block in main. The try block *terminates* (so line 28 does *not* execute), and the catch handler in main (lines 30–32) catches this exception and prints an error message (line 31). Since we do not use the exception parameters in this example's catch handlers, we omit the exception parameter names and specify only the type of exception to catch (lines 14 and 30).

```cpp
1   // Fig. 17.3: fig17_03.cpp
2   // Rethrowing an exception.
3   #include <iostream>
4   #include <exception>
5   using namespace std;
6
7   // throw, catch and rethrow exception
8   void throwException() {
9      // throw exception and catch it immediately
10     try {
11        cout << " Function throwException throws an exception\n";
12        throw exception{}; // generate exception
13     }
14     catch (const exception&) { // handle exception
15        cout << " Exception handled in function throwException"
16           << "\n Function throwException rethrows exception";
17        throw; // rethrow exception for further processing
18     }
19
20     cout << "This should not print\n";
21  }
22
23  int main() {
24     // throw exception
25     try {
26        cout << "\nmain invokes function throwException\n";
27        throwException();
28        cout << "This should not print\n";
29     }
30     catch (const exception&) { // handle exception
31        cout << "\n\nException handled in main\n";
32     }
33
34     cout << "Program control continues after catch in main\n";
35  }
```

Fig. 17.3 | Rethrowing an exception. (Part 1 of 2.)

```
main invokes function throwException
  Function throwException throws an exception
  Exception handled in function throwException
  Function throwException rethrows exception

Exception handled in main
Program control continues after catch in main
```

Fig. 17.3 | Rethrowing an exception. (Part 2 of 2.)

17.4 Stack Unwinding

When an exception is thrown but not caught in a particular scope, the function-call stack is "unwound," and an attempt is made to catch the exception in the next outer try…catch block. Unwinding the function call stack means that the function in which the exception was not caught terminates, all local variables that have completed initialization in that function are destroyed and control returns to the statement that originally invoked that function. If a try block encloses that statement, an attempt is made to catch the exception. If a try block does *not* enclose that statement, stack unwinding occurs again. If no catch handler ever catches this exception, the program terminates. The program of Fig. 17.4 demonstrates stack unwinding.

```cpp
1   // Fig. 17.4: fig17_04.cpp
2   // Demonstrating stack unwinding.
3   #include <iostream>
4   #include <stdexcept>
5   using namespace std;
6
7   // function3 throws runtime error
8   void function3() {
9      cout << "In function 3" << endl;
10
11     // no try block, stack unwinding occurs, return control to function2
12     throw runtime_error{"runtime_error in function3"}; // no print
13  }
14
15  // function2 invokes function3
16  void function2() {
17     cout << "function3 is called inside function2" << endl;
18     function3(); // stack unwinding occurs, return control to function1
19  }
20
21  // function1 invokes function2
22  void function1() {
23     cout << "function2 is called inside function1" << endl;
24     function2(); // stack unwinding occurs, return control to main
25  }
26
```

Fig. 17.4 | Demonstrating stack unwinding. (Part 1 of 2.)

```
27   // demonstrate stack unwinding
28   int main() {
29      // invoke function1
30      try {
31         cout << "function1 is called inside main" << endl;
32         function1(); // call function1 which throws runtime_error
33      }
34      catch (const runtime_error& error) { // handle runtime error
35         cout << "Exception occurred: " << error.what() << endl;
36         cout << "Exception handled in main" << endl;
37      }
38   }
```

```
function1 is called inside main
function2 is called inside function1
function3 is called inside function2
In function 3
Exception occurred: runtime_error in function3
Exception handled in main
```

Fig. 17.4 | Demonstrating stack unwinding. (Part 2 of 2.)

In main, the try block (lines 30–33) calls function1 (lines 22–25). Next, function1 calls function2 (lines 16–19), which in turn calls function3 (lines 8–13). Line 12 of function3 throws a runtime_error object. However, because no try block encloses the throw statement in line 12, stack unwinding occurs—function3 terminates at line 12, then returns control to the statement in function2 that invoked function3 (i.e., line 18). Because no try block encloses line 18, stack unwinding occurs again—function2 terminates at line 18 and returns control to the statement in function1 that invoked function2 (i.e., line 24). Because no try block encloses line 24, stack unwinding occurs one more time—function1 terminates at line 24 and returns control to the statement in main that invoked function1 (i.e., line 32). The try block of lines 30–33 encloses this statement, so the first matching catch handler located after this try block (line 34–37) catches and processes the exception. Line 35 uses function what to display the exception message.

17.5 When to Use Exception Handling

Exception handling is designed to process synchronous errors, which occur when a statement executes, such as *invalid function parameters* and *unsuccessful memory allocation* (due to lack of memory). Exception handling is not designed to process errors associated with asynchronous events (e.g., disk I/O completions, network message arrivals, mouse clicks and keystrokes), which occur in parallel with, and independent of, the program's flow of control.

Complex applications normally consist of predefined software components (such as classes from the Standard Library) and application-specific components that use the predefined components. When a predefined component encounters a problem, that component needs a mechanism to communicate the problem to the application-specific component—the *predefined component cannot know in advance how each application processes a problem that occurs.*

Software Engineering Observation 17.5

Exception handling provides a single, uniform technique for processing problems. This helps programmers on large projects understand each other's error-processing code. It also enables predefined software components (such as Standard Library classes) to communicate problems to application-specific components, which can then process the problems in an application-specific manner

Software Engineering Observation 17.6

Functions with common error conditions should return nullptr, 0 or other appropriate values, such as bools, rather than throw exceptions. A program calling such a function can check the return value to determine success or failure of the function call.

17.6 noexcept: Declaring Functions That Do Not Throw Exceptions

11

As of C++11, if a function does not throw any exceptions *and* does not call any functions that throw exceptions, you can explicitly state that a function *does not* throw exceptions. This indicates to client-code programmers that there's no need to call the function in a try block. Simply add noexcept to the right of the function's parameter list in both the prototype and the definition. For a const member function, you must place noexcept after const. If a function that's declared noexcept calls another function that throws an exception or executes a throw statement, the program terminates. We'll say more about noexcept in Section 24.4.

17.7 Constructors, Destructors and Exception Handling

First, let's discuss an issue that we've mentioned but not yet resolved satisfactorily: What happens when an error is detected in a *constructor*? For example, how should an object's constructor respond when it receives invalid data? Because the constructor *cannot return a value* to indicate an error, we must choose an alternative means of indicating that the object has not been constructed properly. One scheme is to return the improperly constructed object and hope that anyone using it would make appropriate tests to determine that it's in an inconsistent state. Another scheme is to set some variable outside the constructor. The preferred alternative is to require the constructor to throw an exception that contains the error information, thus offering an opportunity for the program to handle the failure.

17.7.1 Destructors Called Due to Exceptions

If an exception occurs during object construction, destructors may be called:

- If an exception is thrown before an object is fully constructed, destructors will be called for any member objects that have been constructed so far.
- If an array of objects has been partially constructed when an exception occurs, only the destructors for the array's constructed objects will be called.

In addition, destructors are called for every automatic object constructed in a try block before an exception that occurred in that block is caught. Stack unwinding is guaranteed to have been completed at the point that an exception handler begins executing. If a destructor invoked as a result of stack unwinding throws an exception, *the program terminates*. This has been linked to various security attacks.

Error-Prevention Tip 17.4
Destructors should catch exceptions to prevent program termination.

Error-Prevention Tip 17.5
Do not throw exceptions from the constructor of a global object or a static local object. Such exceptions cannot be caught, because they're constructed before main executes.

Error-Prevention Tip 17.6
When an exception is thrown from the constructor for an object that's created in a new expression, the dynamically allocated memory for that object is released.

Error-Prevention Tip 17.7
A constructor should throw an exception if a problem occurs while initializing an object. Before doing so, the constructor should release any memory that it dynamically allocated.

17.7.2 Initializing Local Objects to Acquire Resources

An exception could preclude the operation of code that would normally *release a resource* (such as memory or a file), thus causing a resource leak that prevents other programs from acquiring the resource. One technique to resolve this problem is to initialize a local object to acquire the resource. When an exception occurs, the destructor for that object will be invoked and can free the resource. This technique is known as resource allocation is initialization (RAII) and is one use of C++11's unique_ptr, which we discuss in Section 17.9.

17.8 Processing new Failures

As we discussed in Section 10.9, the new operator can be used to dynamically allocate memory. The memory in a computer is finite, so it's possible for new to fail to allocate the memory a program requests. When operator new fails, it throws a bad_alloc exception (defined in header <new>). In this section, we present two examples of new failing. The first uses the version of new that throws a bad_alloc exception. The second uses function set_new_handler to specify a function to call when new fails. [*Note:* The examples in Figs. 17.5–17.6 allocate large amounts of dynamic memory, which could cause your computer to become sluggish.]

17.8.1 new Throwing bad_alloc on Failure

Figure 17.5 demonstrates new *implicitly* throwing bad_alloc when new fails to allocate memory. The for statement (lines 14–17) inside the try block should loop 50 times and, on each pass, allocate an array of 50,000,000 double values. If new fails and throws a bad_alloc exception, the loop terminates, and the program continues in line 19, where the catch handler catches and processes the exception. Lines 20–21 print the message "Exception occurred:" followed by the message returned from the base-class-exception version of function what (i.e., an implementation-defined exception-specific message, such as "bad allocation" or simply "std::bad_alloc"). The output shows that the program performed only three iterations of the loop before new failed and threw the bad_alloc exception. Your output might differ based on the physical memory, disk space available for virtual memory on your system and the compiler you're using.

```cpp
1   // Fig. 17.5: fig17_05.cpp
2   // Demonstrating standard new throwing bad_alloc when memory
3   // cannot be allocated.
4   #include <iostream>
5   #include <new> // bad_alloc class is defined here
6   using namespace std;
7
8   int main() {
9      double *ptr[50];
10
11     // aim each ptr[i] at a big block of memory
12     try {
13        // allocate memory for ptr[i]; new throws bad_alloc on failure
14        for (size_t i{0}; i < 50; ++i) {
15           ptr[i] = new double[50'000'000]{}; // may throw exception
16           cout << "ptr[" << i << "] points to 50,000,000 new doubles\n";
17        }
18     }
19     catch (bad_alloc& memoryAllocationException) {
20        cerr << "Exception occurred: "
21           << memoryAllocationException.what() << endl;
22     }
23  }
```

```
ptr[0] points to 50,000,000 new doubles
ptr[1] points to 50,000,000 new doubles
ptr[2] points to 50,000,000 new doubles
Exception occurred: bad allocation
```

Fig. 17.5 | new throwing bad_alloc on failure.

17.8.2 new Returning nullptr on Failure

The C++ standard specifies that programmers can use an older version of new that returns nullptr upon failure. For this purpose, header <new> defines object nothrow (of type nothrow_t), which is used as follows:

```cpp
double *ptr{new(nothrow) double[50'000'000]};
```

The preceding statement uses the version of new that does *not* throw bad_alloc exceptions (i.e., nothrow) to allocate an array of 50,000,000 doubles.

Software Engineering Observation 17.7

To make programs more robust, use the version of new that throws bad_alloc exceptions on failure.

17.8.3 Handling new Failures Using Function set_new_handler

An additional feature for handling new failures is function set_new_handler (prototyped in standard header <new>). This function takes as its argument a pointer to a function that takes no arguments and returns void—in Fig. 17.6, we use function customNewHandler, but the argument could be a lambda. This pointer points to the function that will be called if new fails. This provides you with a uniform approach to handling all new failures, regardless of where a failure occurs in the program. Once set_new_handler *registers* a new handler in the program, operator new does *not* throw bad_alloc on failure; rather, it delegates the error handling to the new-handler function.

If new allocates memory successfully, it returns a pointer to that memory. If new fails to allocate memory and set_new_handler did not register a new-handler function, new throws a bad_alloc exception. If new fails to allocate memory and a new-handler function has been registered, the new-handler function is called. The new-handler function should perform one of the following tasks:

1. Make more memory available by deleting other dynamically allocated memory (or telling the user to close other applications) and use operator new to attempt to allocate memory again.

2. Throw an exception of type bad_alloc.

3. Call function abort or exit (both found in header <cstdlib>) to terminate the program. These were introduced in Section 9.8. Recall that abort terminates a program immediately, whereas exit executes destructors for global objects and local static objects before terminating the program. Non-static local objects are not destructed when either of these functions is called.

Figure 17.6 demonstrates set_new_handler. Function customNewHandler (lines 9–12) prints an error message (line 10), then calls exit (line 11) to terminate the program. The output shows that the loop iterated three times before new failed and invoked function customNewHandler. Your output might differ based on the physical memory and disk space available for virtual memory on your system, and your compiler.

```
1   // Fig. 17.6: fig17_06.cpp
2   // Demonstrating set_new_handler.
3   #include <iostream>
4   #include <new> // set_new_handler function prototype
5   #include <cstdlib> // abort function prototype
6   using namespace std;
7
8   // handle memory allocation failure
9   void customNewHandler() {
10      cerr << "customNewHandler was called\n";
11      exit(EXIT_FAILURE);
12  }
13
14  // using set_new_handler to handle failed memory allocation
15  int main() {
16      double *ptr[50];
```

Fig. 17.6 | set_new_handler specifying the function to call when new fails. (Part 1 of 2.)

```
17
18      // specify that customNewHandler should be called on
19      // memory allocation failure
20      set_new_handler(customNewHandler);
21
22      // aim each ptr[i] at a big block of memory; customNewHandler will be
23      // called on failed memory allocation
24      for (size_t i{0}; i < 50; ++i) {
25         ptr[i] = new double[50'000'000]{}; // may throw exception
26         cout << "ptr[" << i << "] points to 50,000,000 new doubles\n";
27      }
28   }
```

```
ptr[0] points to 50,000,000 new doubles
ptr[1] points to 50,000,000 new doubles
ptr[2] points to 50,000,000 new doubles
customNewHandler was called
```

Fig. 17.6 | set_new_handler specifying the function to call when new fails. (Part 2 of 2.)

17.9 Class unique_ptr and Dynamic Memory Allocation

A common programming practice is to *allocate* dynamic memory, assign the address of that memory to a pointer, use the pointer to manipulate the memory and *deallocate* the memory with delete (or delete[]) when the memory is no longer needed. If an exception occurs after successful memory allocation but *before* the delete statement executes, a *memory leak* could occur. C++11 provides class template unique_ptr in header <memory> to deal with this situation. A unique_ptr maintains a pointer to dynamically allocated memory. When a unique_ptr object goes out of scope, its destructor is called, which performs a delete (or delete[]) operation on the unique_ptr object's pointer data member. Class template unique_ptr provides overloaded operators * and -> so that a unique_ptr object can be used just like a regular pointer variable.

Demonstrating *unique_ptr*

Figure 17.9 demonstrates a unique_ptr object that points to a dynamically allocated object of our custom class Integer (Figs. 17.7–17.8).

```
1   // Fig. 17.7: Integer.h
2   // Integer class definition.
3
4   class Integer {
5   public:
6      Integer(int i = 0); // Integer default constructor
7      ~Integer(); // Integer destructor
8      void setInteger(int i); // set Integer value
9      int getInteger() const; // return Integer value
```

Fig. 17.7 | Integer class definition. (Part 1 of 2.)

```
10   private:
11      int value;
12   };
```

Fig. 17.7 | Integer class definition. (Part 2 of 2.)

```
1    // Fig. 17.8: Integer.cpp
2    // Integer member function definitions.
3    #include <iostream>
4    #include "Integer.h"
5    using namespace std;
6
7    // Integer default constructor
8    Integer::Integer(int i)
9       : value{i} {
10      cout << "Constructor for Integer " << value << endl;
11   }
12
13   // Integer destructor
14   Integer::~Integer() {
15      cout << "Destructor for Integer " << value << endl;
16   }
17
18   // set Integer value
19   void Integer::setInteger(int i) {
20      value = i;
21   }
22
23   // return Integer value
24   int Integer::getInteger() const {
25      return value;
26   }
```

Fig. 17.8 | Integer member function definitions.

Line 14 of Fig. 17.9 creates `unique_ptr` object `ptrToInteger` and initializes it with a pointer to a dynamically allocated Integer object that contains the value 7. To initialize the `unique_ptr`, line 14 uses C++14's make_unique function template, which allocates dynamic memory with operator new, then returns a `unique_ptr` to that memory. Prior to C++14, you'd pass the result of a new expression directly to `unique_ptr`'s constructor.

```
1    // Fig. 17.9: fig17_09.cpp
2    // Demonstrating unique_ptr.
3    #include <iostream>
4    #include <memory>
5    using namespace std;
6
7    #include "Integer.h"
8
```

Fig. 17.9 | `unique_ptr` object manages dynamically allocated memory. (Part 1 of 2.)

14

```
 9    // use unique_ptr to manipulate Integer object
10    int main() {
11        cout << "Creating a unique_ptr object that points to an Integer\n";
12
13        // "aim" unique_ptr at Integer object
14        unique_ptr<Integer> ptrToInteger{make_unique<Integer>(7)};
15
16        cout << "\nUsing the unique_ptr to set the Integer\n";
17        ptrToInteger->setInteger(99); // use unique_ptr to set Integer value
18
19        // use unique_ptr to get Integer value
20        cout << "Integer after setInteger: " << (*ptrToInteger).getInteger()
21            << "\n\nTerminating program" << endl;
22    }
```

```
Creating a unique_ptr object that points to an Integer
Constructor for Integer 7

Using the unique_ptr to set the Integer
Integer after setInteger: 99

Terminating program
Destructor for Integer 99
```

Fig. 17.9 | unique_ptr object manages dynamically allocated memory. (Part 2 of 2.)

Line 17 uses the unique_ptr overloaded -> operator to invoke function setInteger on the Integer object that ptrToInteger manages. Line 20 uses the unique_ptr overloaded * operator to dereference ptrToInteger, then uses the dot (.) operator to invoke function getInteger on the Integer object. Like a regular pointer, a unique_ptr's -> and * overloaded operators can be used to access the object to which the unique_ptr points.

Because ptrToInteger is a non-static local variable in main, it's destroyed when main terminates. The unique_ptr destructor deletes the dynamically allocated Integer object, which calls the Integer object's destructor. The memory that Integer occupies is released, regardless of how control leaves the block (e.g., by a return statement or by an exception). Most importantly, using this technique can *prevent memory leaks*. For example, suppose a function returns a pointer aimed at some object. Unfortunately, the function caller that receives this pointer might not delete the object, thus resulting in *a memory leak*. However, if the function returns a unique_ptr to the object, the object will be deleted automatically when the unique_ptr object's destructor gets called.

17.9.1 unique_ptr Ownership

The class is called unique_ptr because only *one* unique_ptr at a time can own a dynamically allocated object. When you assign one unique_ptr to another, the unique_ptr on the assignment's right *transfers ownership* of the dynamic memory it manages to the unique_ptr on the assignment's left. The same is true when one unique_ptr is passed as an argument to another unique_ptr's constructor. (These operations use unique_ptr's move assignment operator and move constructor—we discuss move semantics in Chapter 24.) The *last* unique_ptr object that maintains the pointer to the dynamic memory will delete the memory. This makes unique_ptr an ideal mechanism for returning dynamically allocated memory to client code. When the unique_ptr goes out of scope in the *client* code, the unique_ptr's destructor deletes the dynamically allocated object—if the object has a destructor, it is called before the memory is returned to the system.

17.9.2 unique_ptr to a Built-In Array

You can also use a unique_ptr to manage a dynamically allocated built-in array. For example, consider the statement

```
unique_ptr<string[]> ptr{make_unique<string[]>(10)};
```

Because make_unique's type is specified as string[], the function obtains a *dynamically allocated built-in array* of the number of elements specified by its argument (10). By default, the elements of arrays allocated with make_unique are initialized to 0 for fundamental types, to false for bools or via the default constructor for objects of a class—so in this case, the array would contain 10 string objects initialized with the empty string.

14

A unique_ptr that manages an array provides an overloaded [] operator for accessing the array's elements. For example, the statement

```
ptr[2] = "hello";
```

assigns "hello" to the string at ptr[2] and the following statement displays that string

```
cout << ptr[2] << endl;
```

17.10 Standard Library Exception Hierarchy

Exceptions fall nicely into a number of categories. The C++ Standard Library includes a hierarchy of exception classes, some of which are shown in Fig. 17.10. As we first discussed in Section 17.2, this hierarchy is headed by base-class exception (defined in header <exception>), which contains virtual function what that derived classes can override to issue an appropriate error message. If a catch handler catches a reference to an exception of a base-class type, it also can catch a reference to all objects of classes derived publicly from that base class—this allows for polymorphic processing of related errors.

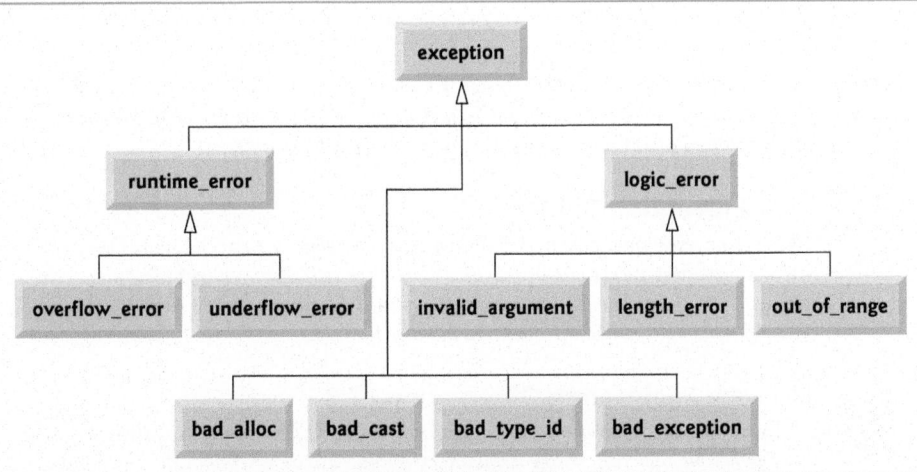

Fig. 17.10 | Some of the Standard Library exception classes.

Immediate derived classes of base-class exception include runtime_error and logic_error (both defined in header <stdexcept>), each of which has several derived classes. Also derived from exception are the exceptions thrown by C++ operators—for example, bad_alloc is thrown by new (Section 17.8), bad_cast is thrown by dynamic_cast (Chapter 12) and bad_typeid is thrown by typeid (Chapter 12).

Class logic_error is the base class of several standard exception classes that indicate errors in program logic. For example, we used class invalid_argument in set functions (starting in Chapter 9) to indicate when an attempt was made to set an invalid value. (Proper coding can, of course, prevent invalid arguments from reaching a function.) Class length_error indicates that a length larger than the maximum size allowed for the object being manipulated was used for that object. Class out_of_range indicates that a value, such as a subscript into an array, exceeded its allowed range of values.

Class runtime_error, which we used briefly in Section 17.4, is the base class of several other standard exception classes that indicate execution-time errors. For example, class overflow_error describes an arithmetic overflow error (i.e., the result of an arithmetic operation is larger than the largest number that can be stored in a given numeric type) and class underflow_error describes an arithmetic underflow error (i.e., the result of an arithmetic operation is smaller than the smallest number that can be stored in a given numeric type).

Error-Prevention Tip 17.8

Using inheritance with exceptions enables an exception handler to catch related errors with concise notation. One approach is to catch each type of reference to a derived-class exception object individually, but a more concise approach is to catch pointers or references to base-class exception objects instead. Also, catching pointers or references to derived-class exception objects individually is error prone, especially if you forget to test explicitly for one or more of the derived-class reference types.

Common Programming Error 17.6

Placing a catch handler that catches a base-class object before a catch that catches an object of a class derived from that base class is a logic error. The base-class catch catches all objects of classes derived from that base class, so the derived-class catch will never execute.

Common Programming Error 17.7

Exception classes need not be derived from class exception, so catching type exception is not guaranteed to catch all exceptions a program could encounter.

Error-Prevention Tip 17.9

To catch all exceptions potentially thrown in a try block, use catch(...). One weakness with catching exceptions in this way is that the type of the caught exception is unknown. Another weakness is that, without a named parameter, there's no way to refer to the exception object inside the exception handler.

Software Engineering Observation 17.8

The standard exception hierarchy is a good starting point for creating exceptions. You can build programs that can throw standard exceptions, throw exceptions derived from the standard exceptions or throw your own exceptions not derived from the standard exceptions.

> **Software Engineering Observation 17.9**
>
> Use `catch(...)` to perform recovery that does not depend on the exception type (e.g., releasing common resources). The exception can be rethrown to alert more specific enclosing `catch` handlers.

17.11 Wrap-Up

In this chapter, you learned how to use exception handling to deal with program errors. You learned that exception handling enables you to remove error-handling code from the "main line" of the program's execution. We demonstrated exception handling in the context of a divide-by-zero example. We reviewed how to use `try` blocks to enclose code that may throw an exception, and how to use `catch` handlers to deal with exceptions that may arise. You learned how to throw and rethrow exceptions, and how to handle the exceptions that occur in constructors. The chapter continued with discussions of processing new failures, dynamic memory allocation with class `unique_ptr` and the standard library exception hierarchy.

In the next chapter, you'll learn how to build your own custom class templates. In particular, we'll demonstrate the features that you'll need to build your own custom templatized data structures in Chapter 19.

Summary

Section 17.1 Introduction
- An **exception** (p. 758) is an indication of a problem that occurs during a program's execution.
- **Exception handling** (p. 758) enables you to create applications that can handle (i.e., resolve) exceptions and perform appropriate cleanup when an exception that cannot or should not be handled occurs. More severe problems may require a program to notify the user of the problem before terminating in a controlled manner.

Section 17.2.1 Defining an Exception Class to Represent the Type of Problem That Might Occur
- Class **exception** (p. 759) is the standard base class for exception classes. It provides virtual function **what** (p. 759) that returns an appropriate error message and can be overridden in derived classes.
- Class **runtime_error** (p. 759), which is defined in header <stdexcept> (p. 759), is the C++ standard base class for representing runtime errors.

Section 17.2.5 Termination Model of Exception Handling
- C++ uses the **termination model of exception handling** (p. 763) in which control resumes with the first statement after the last `catch` handler following a `try` block
- A `try` block consists of keyword `try` followed by braces ({}) that define a block of code in which exceptions might occur. The `try` block encloses statements that might cause exceptions and statements that should not execute if exceptions occur.
- At least one `catch` handler must immediately follow a `try` block. Each `catch` handler specifies an exception parameter that represents the type of exception the `catch` handler can process.

- If an exception parameter includes an optional parameter name, the catch handler can use that parameter name to interact with a caught exception object.
- The point in the program at which an exception occurs is called the **throw point** (p. 763).
- If an exception occurs in a function and is not caught in that function, the function terminates immediately, and the program attempts to locate an enclosing try block in the calling function.

Section 17.2.7 Flow of Program Control When the User Enters a Denominator of Zero

- If an exception occurs in a try block, the try block expires and program control transfers to the first catch in which the exception parameter's type matches that of the thrown exception.
- When a try block terminates, local variables defined in the block go out of scope.
- When a try block terminates due to an exception, the program searches for the first catch handler that matches the type of exception that occurred. A match occurs if the types are identical or if the thrown exception's type is a derived class of the exception-parameter type. When a match occurs, the code contained within the matching catch handler executes.
- When a catch handler finishes processing, the catch parameter and local variables defined within the catch handler go out of scope. Any remaining catch handlers that correspond to the try block are ignored, and execution resumes at the first line of code after the try...catch sequence.
- If no exceptions occur in a try block, the program ignores the catch handler(s) for that block. Program execution resumes with the next statement after the try...catch sequence.
- If an exception that occurs in a try block has no matching catch handler, or if an exception occurs in a statement that is not in a try block, the function that contains the statement terminates immediately, and the program attempts to locate an enclosing try block in the calling function. This process is called **stack unwinding** (p. 763).
- To throw an exception, use keyword throw followed by an operand that represents the type of exception to throw. The operand of a throw can be of any type. If the operand is an object, we call it an **exception object** (p. 764).

Section 17.3 Rethrowing an Exception

- The exception handler can defer the exception handling (or perhaps a portion of it) to another exception handler. In either case, the handler achieves this by **rethrowing the exception** (p. 764) with throw;.
- Common examples of exceptions are out-of-range array subscripts, arithmetic overflow, division by zero, invalid function parameters and unsuccessful memory allocations.

Section 17.4 Stack Unwinding

- Unwinding the function call stack means that the function in which the exception was not caught terminates, all local variables in that function are destroyed and control returns to the statement that originally invoked that function.

Section 17.5 When to Use Exception Handling

- Exception handling is for **synchronous errors** (p. 767), which occur when a statement executes.
- Exception handling is not designed to process errors associated with **asynchronous events** (p. 767), which occur in parallel with, and independent of, the program's flow of control.

Section 17.6 noexcept: Declaring Functions That Do Not Throw Exceptions

- As of C++11, if a function does not throw any exceptions and does not call any functions that throw exceptions, you can explicitly declare the function **noexcept** (p. 768).

Section 17.7 Constructors, Destructors and Exception Handling

- Exceptions thrown by a constructor cause destructors to be called for any objects built as part of the object being constructed before the exception is thrown.
- Each automatic object constructed in a try block is destructed before an exception is thrown.
- Stack unwinding completes before an exception handler begins executing.
- If a destructor invoked as a result of stack unwinding throws an exception, the program terminates.
- If an array of objects has been partially constructed when an exception occurs, only the destructors for the constructed array element objects will be called.
- When an exception is thrown from the constructor for an object that is created in a new expression, the dynamically allocated memory for that object is released.

Section 17.7.2 Initializing Local Objects to Acquire Resources

- An exception could preclude the execution of code that would release a resource, thus causing a resource leak that prevents other programs from acquiring the resource. One technique to resolve this problem is to initialize a local object to acquire the resource. When an exception occurs, the destructor for that object can free the resource. This technique is known as **resource allocation is initialization** (RAII; p. 769).

Section 17.8 Processing **new** Failures

- The C++ standard document specifies that, when operator new fails, it throws a **bad_alloc** exception (p. 769), which is defined in header <new>.
- Function **set_new_handler** (p. 769) takes as its argument a pointer to a function that takes no arguments and returns void. This pointer points to the function that will be called if new fails.
- Once set_new_handler registers a **new handler** (p. 771) in the program, operator new does not throw bad_alloc on failure; rather, it defers the error handling to the new-handler function.
- If new allocates memory successfully, it returns a pointer to that memory.

Section 17.9 Class **unique_ptr** and Dynamic Memory Allocation

- If an exception occurs after successful memory allocation but before the delete statement executes, a memory leak could occur.
- The C++ Standard Library provides class template **unique_ptr** (p. 772) to deal with memory leaks.
- An object of class unique_ptr maintains a pointer to dynamically allocated memory. A unique_ptr's destructor performs a delete operation on the unique_ptr's pointer data member.
- Only one unique_ptr at a time can refer to the managed dynamic memory.
- Class template unique_ptr provides overloaded operators * and -> so that a unique_ptr object can be used just as a regular pointer variable is. A unique_ptr also transfers ownership of the dynamic memory it manages via its copy constructor and overloaded assignment operator.

Section 17.10 Standard Library Exception Hierarchy

- The C++ Standard Library includes a hierarchy of exception classes. This hierarchy is headed by base-class exception.
- If a catch handler catches a reference to an exception object of a base-class type, it also can catch a reference to all objects of classes derived publicly from that base class—this allows for polymorphic processing of related errors.
- Immediate derived classes of base class exception include runtime_error and logic_error (both defined in header <stdexcept>), each of which has several derived classes.

- Several operators throw standard exceptions—operator new throws bad_alloc, operator dynamic_cast throws **bad_cast** (p. 776) and operator typeid throws **bad_typeid** (p. 776).

Self-Review Exercises

17.1   List five common examples of exceptions.

17.2   Give several reasons why exception-handling techniques should not be used for conventional program control.

17.3   Why are exceptions appropriate for dealing with errors produced by library functions?

17.4   What's a "resource leak"?

17.5   If no exceptions are thrown in a try block, where does control proceed to after the try block completes execution?

17.6   What happens if an exception is thrown outside a try block?

17.7   Give a key advantage and a key disadvantage of using catch(...).

17.8   What happens if no catch handler matches the type of a thrown object?

17.9   What happens if several handlers match the type of the thrown object?

17.10   Why would you specify a base-class type as the type of a catch handler, then throw objects of derived-class types?

17.11   Suppose a catch handler with a precise match to an exception object type is available. Under what circumstances might a different handler be executed for exception objects of that type?

17.12   Must throwing an exception cause program termination?

17.13   What happens when a catch handler throws an exception?

17.14   What does the statement throw; do?

Answers to Self-Review Exercises

17.1   Insufficient memory to satisfy a new request, array subscript out of bounds, arithmetic overflow, division by zero, invalid function parameters.

17.2   (a) Exception handling is designed to handle infrequently occurring situations that often result in program termination, so compiler writers are not required to implement exception handling to perform optimally. (b) Flow of control with conventional control structures generally is clearer and more efficient than with exceptions. (c) Problems can occur because the stack is unwound when an exception occurs and resources allocated prior to the exception might not be freed. (d) The "additional" exceptions make it more difficult for you to handle the larger number of exception cases.

17.3   It's unlikely that a library function will perform error processing that will meet the unique needs of all users.

17.4   A program that terminates abruptly could leave a resource in a state in which other programs would not be able to acquire the resource, or the program itself might not be able to reacquire a "leaked" resource.

17.5   The exception handlers (in the catch handlers) for that try block are skipped, and the program resumes execution after the last catch handler.

17.6   An exception thrown outside a try block causes stack unwinding.

17.7   A catch handler of the form catch(...) catches any type of exception thrown in a try block. An advantage is that all possible exceptions will be caught. A disadvantage is that the catch has no parameter, so it cannot reference information in the thrown object and cannot know the cause of the exception.

17.8   This causes the search for a match to continue in the next enclosing try block if there is one. As this process continues, it might eventually be determined that there is no handler in the program that matches the type of the thrown object; in this case, the program terminates.

17.9   The first matching exception handler after the try block is executed.

17.10   This is a nice way to catch related types of exceptions.

17.11   If a base-class handler is defined before a derived-class handler, the base-class handler would catch objects of all derived-class types.

17.12   No, but it does terminate the block in which the exception is thrown.

17.13   The exception will be processed by a catch handler (if one exists) associated with the try block (if one exists) enclosing the catch handler that caused the exception.

17.14   It rethrows the exception if it appears in a catch handler; otherwise, the program terminates.

Exercises

17.15   *(Exceptional Conditions)* List various exceptional conditions that have occurred throughout this text. List as many additional exceptional conditions as you can. For each of these exceptions, describe briefly how a program typically would handle the exception, using the exception-handling techniques discussed in this chapter. Some typical exceptions are division by zero, arithmetic overflow, array subscript out of bounds, exhaustion of the free store, etc.

17.16   *(Catch Parameter)* Under what circumstances would you not provide a parameter name when defining the type of the object that will be caught by a handler?

17.17   *(**throw** Statement)* A program contains the statement

```
throw;
```

Where would you normally expect to find such a statement? What if that statement appeared in a different part of the program?

17.18   *(Exception Handling vs. Other Schemes)* Compare and contrast exception handling with the various other error-processing schemes discussed in the text.

17.19   *(Exception Handling and Program Control)* Why should exceptions *not* be used as an alternate form of program control?

17.20   *(Handling Related Exceptions)* Describe a technique for handling related exceptions.

17.21   *(Throwing Exceptions from a **catch**)* Suppose a program throws an exception and the appropriate exception handler begins executing. Now suppose that the exception handler itself throws the same exception. Does this create infinite recursion? Write a program to check your observation.

17.22   *(Catching Derived-Class Exceptions)* Use inheritance to create various derived classes of runtime_error. Then show that a catch handler specifying the base class can catch derived-class exceptions.

17.23   *(Throwing the Result of a Conditional Expression)* Throw the result of a conditional expression that returns either a double or an int. Provide an int catch handler and a double catch handler. Show that only the double catch handler executes, regardless of whether the int or the double is returned.

17.24 *(Local-Variable Destructors)* Write a program illustrating that all destructors for objects constructed in a block are called before an exception is thrown from that block.

17.25 *(Member-Object Destructors)* Write a program illustrating that member-object destructors are called for only those member objects that were constructed before an exception occurred.

17.26 *(Catching All Exceptions)* Write a program that demonstrates several exception types being caught with the catch(...) exception handler.

17.27 *(Order of Exception Handlers)* Write a program illustrating that the order of exception handlers is important. The first matching handler is the one that executes. Attempt to compile and run your program two different ways to show that two different handlers execute with two different effects.

17.28 *(Constructors Throwing Exceptions)* Write a program that shows a constructor passing information about constructor failure to an exception handler after a try block.

17.29 *(Rethrowing Exceptions)* Write a program that illustrates rethrowing an exception.

17.30 *(Uncaught Exceptions)* Write a program that illustrates that a function with its own try block does not have to catch every possible error generated within the try. Some exceptions can slip through to, and be handled in, outer scopes.

17.31 *(Stack Unwinding)* Write a program that throws an exception from a deeply nested function and still has the catch handler following the try block enclosing the initial call in main catch the exception.

Introduction to Custom Templates

Objectives

In this chapter you'll:

- Use class templates to create groups of related classes.

- Distinguish between class templates and class-template specializations.

- See how nontype template parameters can be used in place of constants declared inside a class.

- Learn about default template arguments.

- Learn about overloading function templates.

18.1 Introduction

Templates have become extremely important in writing industrial-strength code. We've used templates in Chapters 6, 7 and 13–17. In this chapter, we introduce some additional template capabilities and we continue using templates through the rest of the book. Figure 18.1 summarizes our template coverage.

Location in text	Discusses
Chapter 6	
Section 6.9	C++11 uniform_int_distribution class template for random-number generation.
Section 6.17	Defining a function template.
Chapter 7	Class templates array and vector for manipulating collections of elements.
Chapter 13	
Section 13.2	The stream-processing classes, which are class templates.
Chapter 14	
Section 14.2	The file-stream-processing classes, which are class templates.
Chapter 15	Standard Library collection class templates.
Chapter 16	Standard Library algorithm function templates.
Chapter 17	
Section 17.9	The unique_ptr smart-pointer class template for managing dynamically allocated memory.
Chapter 18	Creating custom class templates.
Chapter 19	Creating custom templatized data structures.
Chapter 20	Implementing searching and sorting algorithms as function templates.

Fig. 18.1 | Summary of recursion examples and exercises in the text. (Part 1 of 2.)

Location in text	Discusses
Chapter 21	
Section 21.1	`string`s, which are class templates.
Section 21.12	`string`-stream class templates.
Chapter 24	
Section 24.2	Smart pointer class templates.
Section 24.10	Variadic templates.
Section 24.11	Class template `tuple`.
Section 24.12	Class template `initializer_list`.

Fig. 18.1 | Summary of recursion examples and exercises in the text. (Part 2 of 2.)

Function templates enable you to conveniently specify a variety of overloaded functions—called function-template specializations. Class templates enable you to conveniently specify a variety of related classes—called class-template specializations. Programming with templates is also known as generic programming. Function templates and class templates are like *stencils* out of which we trace shapes; function-template specializations and class-template specializations are like the separate tracings that all have the same shape, but could, for example, be drawn in different colors, line thicknesses and textures.

In this chapter, we demonstrate how to create a custom class template and a function template that manipulates objects of our class-template specializations. We focus on the template capabilities you'll need to build the custom templatized data structures that we present in Chapter 19.[1]

18.2 Class Templates

It's possible to *understand* the concept of a stack (a data structure into which we insert items *only* at the *top* and retrieve those items *only* from the *top* in *last-in, first-out order*) *independent of the type of the items* being placed in the stack. We discussed stacks in Section 6.11 where we presented the function-call stack. To *instantiate* a stack, a data type must be specified. This creates a nice opportunity for software reusability—as you already saw with the `stack` container adapter in Section 15.7.1. Here, we define a stack *generically* then use *type-specific* versions of this generic stack class.

Software Engineering Observation 18.1
Class templates encourage software reusability by enabling a variety of type-specific class-template specializations to be instantiated from a single class template.

Class templates are called parameterized types, because they require one or more *type parameters* to specify how to customize a generic class template to form a *class-template specialization*. To produce many specializations you write only one class-template definition

---

1. Building custom templates is an advanced topic with many features that are beyond the scope of this book.

(as we'll do shortly). When a particular specialization is needed, you use a concise, simple notation, and the compiler writes the specialization source code. One Stack class template, for example, could thus become the basis for creating many Stack class-template specializations (such as "Stack of doubles," "Stack of ints," "Stack of Employees," "Stack of Bills," "Stack of ActivationRecords," etc.) used in a program.

Common Programming Error 18.1

To create a template specialization with a user-defined type, the user-defined type must meet the template's requirements. For example, the template might compare objects of the user-defined type with < to determine sorting order, or the template might call a specific member function on an object of the user-defined type. If the user-defined type does not overload the required operator or provide the required functions, compilation errors occur.

18.2.1 Creating Class Template Stack<T>

The Stack class-template definition in Fig. 18.2 looks like a conventional class definition, with a few key differences. First, it's preceded by line 7

```
template<typename T>
```

All class templates begin with keyword template followed by a list of template parameters enclosed in angle brackets (< and >); each template parameter that represents a type *must* be preceded by either of the *interchangeable* keywords typename or class (though typename is preferred). The type parameter T acts as a placeholder for the Stack's element type. The names of type parameters must be *unique* inside a template definition. You need not specifically use identifier T—any valid identifier can be used. The element type is mentioned generically throughout the Stack class-template definition as T (lines 11, 16 and 36). The type parameter becomes associated with a specific type when you create an object using the class template—at that point, the compiler generates a copy of the class template in which all occurrences of the type parameter are replaced with the specified type. Another key difference is that we did *not* separate the class template's interface from its implementation.

Software Engineering Observation 18.2

Templates are typically defined in headers, which are then #included in the appropriate client source-code files. For class templates, this means that the member functions are also defined in the header—typically inside the class definition's body, as we do in Fig. 18.2.

```
1   // Fig. 18.2: Stack.h
2   // Stack class template.
3   #ifndef STACK_H
4   #define STACK_H
5   #include <deque>
6
7   template<typename T>
8   class Stack {
9   public:
```

Fig. 18.2 | Stack class template. (Part 1 of 2.)

```
10      // return the top element of the Stack
11      const T& top() {
12          return stack.front();
13      }
14
15      // push an element onto the Stack
16      void push(const T& pushValue) {
17          stack.push_front(pushValue);
18      }
19
20      // pop an element from the stack
21      void pop() {
22          stack.pop_front();
23      }
24
25      // determine whether Stack is empty
26      bool isEmpty() const {
27          return stack.empty();
28      }
29
30      // return size of Stack
31      size_t size() const {
32          return stack.size();
33      }
34
35   private:
36      std::deque<T> stack; // internal representation of the Stack
37   };
38
39   #endif
```

Fig. 18.2 | Stack class template. (Part 2 of 2.)

18.2.2 Class Template Stack<T>'s Data Representation

Section 15.7.1 showed that the Standard Library's stack adapter class can use various containers to store its elements. Of course, a stack requires insertions and deletions *only* at its *top*. So, for example, a vector or a deque could be used to store the stack's elements. A vector supports fast insertions and deletions at its *back*. A deque supports fast insertions and deletions at its *front* and its *back*. A deque is the default representation for the Standard Library's stack adapter because a deque grows more efficiently than a vector. A vector is maintained as a *contiguous* block of memory—when that block is full and a new element is added, the vector allocates a larger contiguous block of memory and *copies* the old elements into that new block. A deque, on the other hand, is typically implemented as a list of fixed-size, built-in arrays—new fixed-size built-in arrays are added as necessary and none of the existing elements are copied when new items are added to the front or back. For these reasons, we use a deque (line 36) as the underlying container for our Stack class.

18.2.3 Class Template Stack<T>'s Member Functions

The member-function definitions of a class template are *function templates*, but are not preceded with the template keyword and template parameters in angle brackets (< and >)

when they're defined within the class template's body. As you can see, however, they do use the class template's template parameter T to represent the element type. Our Stack class template does *not* define it's own constructors—the *default constructor* provided by the compiler will invoke the deque's default constructor. We also provide the following member functions in Fig. 18.2:

- top (lines 11–13) returns a const reference to the Stack's top element.
- push (lines 16–18) places a new element on the top of the Stack.
- pop (lines 21–23) removes the Stack's top element.
- isEmpty (lines 26–28) returns a bool value—true if the Stack is empty and false otherwise.
- size (lines 31–33) returns the number if elements in the Stack.

Each of these member functions calls the appropriate member function of class template deque—this is known as delegating.

18.2.4 Declaring a Class Template's Member Functions Outside the Class Template Definition

Though we did *not* do so in our Stack class template, member-function definitions can appear *outside* a class template definition. If you do this, each must begin with the template keyword followed by the *same* set of template parameters as the class template. In addition, the member functions must be qualified with the class name and scope resolution operator. For example, you can define the pop function outside the class-template definition as follows:

```
template<typename T>
inline void Stack<T>::pop() {
    stack.pop_front();
}
```

Stack<T>:: indicates that pop is in the scope of class Stack<T>. The Standard Library's container classes tend to define all their member functions *inside* their class definitions.

18.2.5 Testing Class Template Stack<T>

Now, let's consider the driver (Fig. 18.3) that exercises the Stack class template. The driver begins by instantiating object doubleStack (line 8). This object is declared as a Stack<double> (pronounced "Stack of double"). The compiler associates type double with type parameter T in the class template to produce the source code for a Stack class with elements of type double that actually stores its elements in a deque<double>.

```
1   // Fig. 18.3: fig18_02.cpp
2   // Stack class template test program.
3   #include <iostream>
4   #include "Stack.h" // Stack class template definition
5   using namespace std;
6
```

Fig. 18.3 | Stack class template test program. (Part 1 of 3.)

```cpp
 7   int main() {
 8      Stack<double> doubleStack; // create a Stack of double
 9      const size_t doubleStackSize{5}; // stack size
10      double doubleValue{1.1}; // first value to push
11
12      cout << "Pushing elements onto doubleStack\n";
13
14      // push 5 doubles onto doubleStack
15      for (size_t i{0}; i < doubleStackSize; ++i) {
16         doubleStack.push(doubleValue);
17         cout << doubleValue << ' ';
18         doubleValue += 1.1;
19      }
20
21      cout << "\n\nPopping elements from doubleStack\n";
22
23      // pop elements from doubleStack
24      while (!doubleStack.isEmpty()) { // loop while Stack is not empty
25         cout << doubleStack.top() << ' '; // display top element
26         doubleStack.pop(); // remove top element
27      }
28
29      cout << "\nStack is empty, cannot pop.\n";
30
31      Stack<int> intStack; // create a Stack of int
32      const size_t intStackSize{10}; // stack size
33      int intValue{1}; // first value to push
34
35      cout << "\nPushing elements onto intStack\n";
36
37      // push 10 integers onto intStack
38      for (size_t i{0}; i < intStackSize; ++i) {
39         intStack.push(intValue);
40         cout << intValue++ << ' ';
41      }
42
43      cout << "\n\nPopping elements from intStack\n";
44
45      // pop elements from intStack
46      while (!intStack.isEmpty()) { // loop while Stack is not empty
47         cout << intStack.top() << ' '; // display top element
48         intStack.pop(); // remove top element
49      }
50
51      cout << "\nStack is empty, cannot pop." << endl;
52   }
```

```
Pushing elements onto doubleStack
1.1 2.2 3.3 4.4 5.5

Popping elements from doubleStack
5.5 4.4 3.3 2.2 1.1
Stack is empty, cannot pop
```

Fig. 18.3 | Stack class template test program. (Part 2 of 3.)

```
Pushing elements onto intStack
1 2 3 4 5 6 7 8 9 10

Popping elements from intStack
10 9 8 7 6 5 4 3 2 1
Stack is empty, cannot pop
```

Fig. 18.3 | Stack class template test program. (Part 3 of 3.)

Lines 15–19 invoke push (line 16) to place the double values 1.1, 2.2, 3.3, 4.4 and 5.5 onto doubleStack. Next, lines 24–27 invoke top and pop in a while loop to remove the five values from the stack. Notice in the output of Fig. 18.3 that the values pop off in *last-in, first-out order*. When doubleStack is empty, the pop loop terminates.

Line 31 instantiates int stack intStack with the declaration

        Stack<int> intStack;

(pronounced "intStack is a Stack of int"). Lines 38–41 repeatedly invoke push (line 39) to place values onto intStack, then lines 46–49 repeatedly invoke top and pop to remove values from intStack until it's empty. Once again, notice in the output that the values pop off in last-in, first-out order.

18.3 Function Template to Manipulate a Class-Template Specialization Object

The code in function main of Fig. 18.3 is *almost identical* for both the doubleStack manipulations in lines 8–29 and the intStack manipulations in lines 31–51. This presents another opportunity to use a function template. Figure 18.4 defines function template testStack (lines 10–36) to perform the same tasks as main in Fig. 18.3—push a series of values onto a Stack<T> and pop the values off a Stack<T>.

```
 1    // Fig. 18.4: fig18_03.cpp
 2    // Passing a Stack template object
 3    // to a function template.
 4    #include <iostream>
 5    #include <string>
 6    #include "Stack.h" // Stack class template definition
 7    using namespace std;
 8
 9    // function template to manipulate Stack<T>
10    template<typename T>
11    void testStack(
12       Stack<T>& theStack, // reference to Stack<T>
13       const T& value, // initial value to push
14       const T& increment, // increment for subsequent values
15       size_t size, // number of items to push
16       const string& stackName) { // name of the Stack<T> object
17       cout << "\nPushing elements onto " << stackName << '\n';
18       T pushValue{value};
```

Fig. 18.4 | Passing a Stack template object to a function template. (Part 1 of 2.)

```
19
20      // push element onto Stack
21      for (size_t i{0}; i < size; ++i) {
22         theStack.push(pushValue); // push element onto Stack
23         cout << pushValue << ' ';
24         pushValue += increment;
25      }
26
27      cout << "\n\nPopping elements from " << stackName << '\n';
28
29      // pop elements from Stack
30      while (!theStack.isEmpty()) { // loop while Stack is not empty
31         cout << theStack.top() << ' ';
32         theStack.pop(); // remove top element
33      }
34
35      cout << "\nStack is empty. Cannot pop." << endl;
36   }
37
38   int main() {
39      Stack<double> doubleStack;
40      const size_t doubleStackSize{5};
41      testStack(doubleStack, 1.1, 1.1, doubleStackSize, "doubleStack");
42
43      Stack<int> intStack;
44      const size_t intStackSize{10};
45      testStack(intStack, 1, 1, intStackSize, "intStack");
46   }
```

```
Pushing elements onto doubleStack
1.1 2.2 3.3 4.4 5.5

Popping elements from doubleStack
5.5 4.4 3.3 2.2 1.1
Stack is empty, cannot pop

Pushing elements onto intStack
1 2 3 4 5 6 7 8 9 10

Popping elements from intStack
10 9 8 7 6 5 4 3 2 1
Stack is empty, cannot pop
```

Fig. 18.4 | Passing a Stack template object to a function template. (Part 2 of 2.)

Function template testStack uses T (specified at line 10) to represent the data type stored in the Stack<T>. The function template takes five arguments (lines 12–16):

- the Stack<T> to manipulate
- a value of type T that will be the first value pushed onto the Stack<T>
- a value of type T used to increment the values pushed onto the Stack<T>
- the number of elements to push onto the Stack<T>
- a string that represents the name of the Stack<T> object for output purposes

Function main (lines 38–46) instantiates an object of type Stack<double> called doubleStack (line 39) and an object of type Stack<int> called intStack (line 43) and passes these objects in lines 41 and 45 to testStack. The compiler infers the type of T for testStack from the type of the elements in the function's first argument (i.e., the type used to instantiate doubleStack or intStack)—so the first call to testStack infers T as type double and the second infers T as type int.

18.4 Nontype Parameters

Class template Stack of Section 18.2 used only a type parameter (Fig. 18.2, line 7) in its template declaration. It's also possible to use nontype template parameters, which can have default arguments and are treated as constants. For example, the C++ standard's array class template begins with the template declaration:

```
template <typename T, size_t N>
```

(Recall that keywords class and typename are *interchangeable* in template declarations.) So, a declaration such as

```
array<double, 100> salesFigures;
```

creates a 100-element array of doubles class-template specialization, then uses it to instantiate the object salesFigures. The array class template encapsulates a *built-in array*. When you create an array class-template specialization, the array's built-in array data member has the type and size specified in the declaration—in the preceding example, it would be a built-in array of double values with 100 elements.

We could have used this technique in our GradeBook class of Section 7.9. Rather than defining static constants in the class definition's body to represent the number of students and the number of tests, we could have defined class GradeBook as a class template with two nontype template parameters, as in

```
template <size_t students, size_t tests>
class GradeBook {
   // class definition's body
};
```

then used the nontype template parameters' values throughout the class definition. We ask you to implement this version of class GradeBook in Exercise 18.14.

18.5 Default Arguments for Template Type Parameters

In addition, a type parameter can specify a default type argument. For example, the C++ standard's stack *container adapter* class template begins with:

```
template <class T, class Container = deque<T>>
```

which specifies that a stack uses a deque *by default* to store the stack's elements of type T. The declaration

```
stack<int> values;
```

creates a stack of ints class-template specialization (behind the scenes) and uses it to instantiate the object named values. The stack's elements are stored in a deque<int>.

Default type parameters must be the *rightmost* (trailing) parameters in a template's type-parameter list. When you instantiate a template with two or more default arguments, if an omitted argument is not the rightmost, then all type parameters to the right of it also must be omitted. As of C++11, you can use default type arguments for template type parameters in function templates.

11

18.6 Overloading Function Templates

Function templates and overloading are intimately related. In Section 6.17, you learned that when overloaded functions perform *identical* operations on *different* types of data, they can be expressed more compactly and conveniently using function templates. You can then write function calls with different types of arguments and let the compiler generate separate *function-template specializations* to handle each function call appropriately. The function-template specializations generated from a given function template all have the same name, so the compiler uses overload resolution to invoke the proper function.

You may also overload function templates. For example, you can provide other function templates that specify the *same* function name but *different* function parameters. A function template also can be overloaded by providing nontemplate functions with the same function name but different function parameters.

Matching Process for Overloaded Functions

The compiler performs a matching process to determine what function to call when a function is invoked. It looks at both existing functions and function templates to locate a function or generate a function-template specialization whose function name and argument types are consistent with those of the function call. If there are no matches, the compiler issues an error message. If there are multiple matches for the function call, the compiler attempts to determine the *best* match. If there's *more than one* best match, the call is *ambiguous* and the compiler issues an error message.[2]

18.7 Wrap-Up

This chapter discussed class templates and class-template specializations. We used a class template to create a group of related class-template specializations that each perform identical processing on different data types. We discussed nontype template parameters. We showed how to overload a function template to create a customized version that handles a particular data type's processing in a manner that differs from the other function-template specializations. In the next chapter, we demonstrate how to create your own custom templatized dynamic data structures, including linked lists, stacks, queues and binary trees.

---

2. The compiler's process for resolving function calls is complex. The complete details are discussed in Section 13.3.3 of the C++ standard.

Summary

Section 18.1 Introduction
- Templates enable us to specify a range of related (overloaded) functions—called **function-template specializations** (p. 785)—or a range of related classes—called **class-template specializations** (p. 785).

Section 18.2 Class Templates
- Class templates provide the means for describing a class generically and for instantiating classes that are type-specific versions of this generic class.
- Class templates are called **parameterized types** (p. 785); they require type parameters to specify how to customize a generic class template to form a specific class-template specialization.
- To use class-template specializations you write one class template. When you need a new type-specific class, the compiler writes the source code for the class-template specialization.
- A **class-template definition** (p. 785) looks like a conventional class definition, but it's preceded by `template<typename T>` (or `template<class T>`) to indicate this is a class-template definition. T is a type parameter that acts as a placeholder for the type of the class to create. The type T is mentioned throughout the class definition and member-function definitions as a generic type name.
- The names of template parameters must be unique inside a template definition.
- Member-function definitions outside a class template each begin with the same `template` declaration as their class. Then, each function definition resembles a conventional function definition, except that the generic data in the class always is listed generically as type parameter T. The binary scope-resolution operator is used with the class-template name to tie each member-function definition to the class template's scope.

Section 18.4 Nontype Parameters
- It's possible to use **nontype parameters** (p. 792) in a class or function template declaration.

Section 18.5 Default Arguments for Template Type Parameters
- You can specify a **default type argument** (p. 792) for a type parameter in the type-parameter list.

Section 18.6 Overloading Function Templates
- A function template may be overloaded in several ways. We can provide other function templates that specify the same function name but different function parameters. A function template can also be overloaded by providing other nontemplate functions with the same function name, but different function parameters. If both the template and non-template versions match a call, the non-template version will be used.

Self-Review Exercises

18.1 State which of the following are *true* and which are *false*. If *false*, explain why.
   a) Keywords `typename` and `class` as used with a template type parameter specifically mean "any user-defined class type."
   b) A function template can be overloaded by another function template with the same function name.
   c) Template parameter names among template definitions must be unique.
   d) Each member-function definition outside its corresponding class template definition must begin with `template` and the same template parameters as its class template.

18.2   Fill in the blanks in each of the following:
   a) Templates enable us to specify, with a single code segment, an entire range of related functions called _____, or an entire range of related classes called _____.
   b) All template definitions begin with the keyword _____, followed by a list of template parameters enclosed in _____.
   c) The related functions generated from a function template all have the same name, so the compiler uses _____ resolution to invoke the proper function.
   d) Class templates also are called _____ types.
   e) The _____ operator is used with a class-template name to tie each member-function definition to the class template's scope.

Answers to Self-Review Exercises

18.1   a) False. Keywords typename and class in this context also allow for a type parameter of a fundamental type. b) True. c) False. Template parameter names among function templates need not be unique. d) True.

18.2   a) function-template specializations, class-template specializations. b) template, angle brackets (< and >). c) overload. d) parameterized. e) scope resolution.

Exercises

18.3   *(Operator Overloads in Templates)* Write a simple function template for predicate function isEqualTo that compares its two arguments of the same type with the equality operator (==) and returns true if they are equal and false otherwise. Use this function template in a program that calls isEqualTo only with a variety of fundamental types. Now write a separate version of the program that calls isEqualTo with a user-defined class type, but does not overload the equality operator. What happens when you attempt to run this program? Now overload the equality operator (with the operator function) operator==. Now what happens when you attempt to run this program?

18.4   *(Array Class Template)* Reimplement class Array from Figs. 10.10–10.11 as a class template. Exercise each of the new Array class template's capabilities in a program.

18.5   Distinguish between the terms "function template" and "function-template specialization."

18.6   Explain which is more like a stencil—a class template or a class-template specialization?

18.7   What's the relationship between function templates and overloading?

18.8   The compiler performs a matching process to determine which function-template specialization to call when a function is invoked. Under what circumstances does an attempt to make a match result in a compile error?

18.9   Why is it appropriate to refer to a class template as a parameterized type?

18.10   Explain why a C++ program would use the statement

```
Array<Employee> workerList{100};
```

18.11   Review your answer to Exercise 18.10. Explain why a C++ program might use the statement

```
Array<Employee> workerList;
```

18.12   Explain the use of the following notation in a C++ program:

```
template<typename T> Array<T>::Array(int s)
```

18.13   Why might you use a nontype parameter with a class template for a container such as an array or stack?

18.14 *(GradeBook Class Template)* Reimplement class GradeBook from Section 7.9 as a class template with two nontype template parameters that represent the number of students and the number of tests (as described in Section 18.4). Test multiple instances of the GradeBook class template with different numbers of students and exams.

Custom Templatized Data Structures

Objectives

In this chapter you'll:

- Form linked data structures using pointers, self-referential classes and recursion.

- Create and manipulate dynamic data structures such as linked lists, queues, stacks and binary trees.

- Use binary search trees for high-speed searching and sorting.

- Learn important applications of linked data structures.

- Create reusable data structures with class templates, inheritance and composition.

- Have the opportunity to try many challenging data-structures exercises, including the Building Your Own Compiler project.

19.1 Introduction

We've studied *fixed-size data structures*—such as one- and two-dimensional template-based arrays (Chapter 7) and built-in arrays (Chapter 8)—and various C++ Standard Library *dynamic data structures* (arrays and vectors in Chapter 7 and other template-based containers in Chapter 15) that can grow and shrink during execution.

In this chapter, we demonstrate how you can create your own custom templatized dynamic data structures. We discuss several popular and important data structures and implement programs that create and manipulate them:

- Linked lists are collections of data items logically "lined up in a row"—insertions and removals are made *anywhere* in a linked list.

- *Stacks* (which we introduced in Section 6.11 and discussed again in Section 15.7.1) are important in compilers and operating systems: Insertions and removals are made *only* at one end of a stack—its *top*.

- *Queues* represent *waiting lines*; insertions are made at the *back* (also referred to as the *tail*) of a queue and removals are made from the *front* (also referred to as the *head*) of a queue.

- Binary trees facilitate searching and sorting data, *duplicate elimination* and *compiling* expressions into machine code.

Each of these data structures has many other interesting applications. We use class templates, inheritance and composition to create and package these data structures for reusability and maintainability. The programs employ extensive pointer manipulation. The exercises include a rich collection of useful applications.

19.1.1 Always Prefer the Standard Library's Containers, Iterators and Algorithms, if Possible

The C++ Standard Library's *containers*, *iterators* for traversing those containers and *algorithms* for processing the containers' elements meet the needs of most C++ programmers. The Standard Library code is carefully written to be correct, portable, efficient and extensible. Understanding how to build custom templatized data structures will also help you use the Standard Library containers, iterators and algorithms, more effectively.

19.1.2 Special Section: Building Your Own Compiler

We encourage you to attempt the optional project described in the Special Section: Building Your Own Compiler (`http://www.deitel.com/books/cpphtp10`). You've been using a C++ compiler to translate your programs to machine code so that you can execute these programs on your computer. In this project, you'll actually build your own compiler. It will read a file of statements written in a simple, yet powerful, high-level language similar to early versions of BASIC. Your compiler will translate these statements into a file of Simpletron Machine Language (SML) instructions—SML is the artificial language you learned in the Chapter 8 Special Section: Building Your Own Computer. Your Simpletron Simulator program will then execute the SML program produced by your compiler! The special section discusses the high-level language and the algorithms you'll need to convert each type of high-level language statement into machine code. We provide compiler-theory exercises and suggest enhancements to both the compiler and the Simpletron Simulator.

19.2 Self-Referential Classes

A self-referential class contains a member that points to a class object of the same class type. For example, the definition

```
class Node {
public:
    explicit Node(int); // constructor
    void setData(int); // set data member
    int getData() const; // get data member
    void setNextPtr(Node*); // set pointer to next Node
    Node* getNextPtr() const; // get pointer to next Node
private:
    int data; // data stored in this Node
    Node* nextPtr; // pointer to another object of same type
};
```

defines a type, Node. Type Node has two private data members—integer member data and pointer member nextPtr. Member nextPtr points to an object of type Node—an object of the *same* type as the one being declared here, hence the term *self-referential class*. Member nextPtr is referred to as a link—i.e., nextPtr can "tie" an object of type Node to another object of the *same* type. Type Node also has five member functions—a constructor that receives an integer to initialize member data, a setData function to set the value of member data, a getData function to return the value of member data, a setNextPtr function to set the value of member nextPtr and a getNextPtr function to return the value of member nextPtr.

Self-referential class objects can be linked together to form useful data structures such as lists, queues, stacks and trees. Figure 19.1 illustrates two self-referential class objects linked together to form a list. Note that a slash—representing a null pointer (nullptr)—is placed in the link member of the second self-referential class object to indicate that the link does *not* point to another object. The slash is for illustration purposes only; it does *not* correspond to the backslash character in C++. A null pointer normally indicates the *end of a data structure*.

> **Common Programming Error 19.1**
> *Not setting the link in the last node of a linked data structure to nullptr is a (possibly fatal) logic error.*

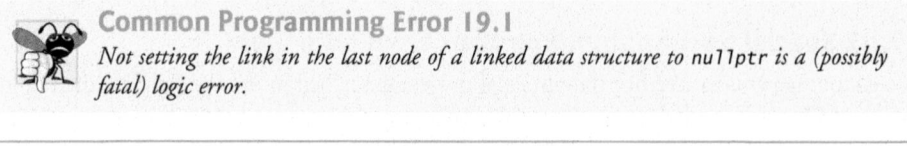

Fig. 19.1 | Two self-referential class objects linked together.

The following sections discuss lists, stacks, queues and trees. The data structures presented in this chapter are created and maintained with *dynamic memory allocation* (Section 10.9), *self-referential classes, class templates* (Chapters 7, 15 and 18) and *function templates* (Section 6.17).

19.3 Linked Lists

A linked list is a *linear* collection of self-referential class objects, called nodes, connected by pointer links—hence, the term "linked" list. A linked list is accessed via a pointer to the list's first node. Each subsequent node is accessed via the *link-pointer member* stored in the previous node. By *convention*, the link pointer in the last node of a list is set to nullptr to mark the end of the list. Data is stored in a linked list *dynamically*—each node is created and destroyed as necessary. A node can contain data of any type, including objects of other classes. If nodes contain base-class pointers to base-class and derived-class objects related by inheritance, we can have a linked list of such nodes and process them *polymorphically* using virtual function calls. Stacks and queues are also linear data structures and, as we'll see, can be viewed as constrained versions of linked lists. Trees are nonlinear data structures.

Linked lists provide several advantages over array objects and built-in arrays. A linked list is appropriate when the number of data elements to be represented at one time is *unpredictable*. Linked lists are dynamic, so the length of a list can increase or decrease as necessary. The size of an array object or built-in array, however, cannot be altered, because the array size is fixed at compile time. An array object or built-in array can become full.

Linked lists become full only when the system has insufficient memory to satisfy additional dynamic storage allocation requests.

Performance Tip 19.1

An array object or built-in array can be declared to contain more elements than the number of items expected, but this can waste memory. Linked lists can provide better memory utilization in these situations. Linked lists can grow and shrink as necessary at runtime. Class template vector *(Section 7.10) implements a dynamically resizable array-based data structure.*

Linked lists can be maintained in *sorted order* by inserting each new element at the proper point in the list. Existing list elements do *not* need to be moved. Pointers merely need to be updated to point to the correct node.

Performance Tip 19.2

Insertion and deletion in a sorted array object or built-in array *can be time consuming—all the elements following the inserted or deleted element must be shifted appropriately. A linked list allows efficient insertion operations* anywhere *in the list.*

Performance Tip 19.3

The elements of an array object or built-in array *are stored contiguously in memory. This allows* immediate *access to any element, because an element's address can be calculated directly based on its position relative to the beginning of the* array object or built-in array. *Linked lists do not afford such immediate* direct *access to their elements, so accessing individual elements can be considerably more expensive. The selection of a data structure is typically based on the performance of specific operations used by a program and the order in which the data items are maintained in the data structure. For example, if you have a pointer to the insertion location, it's typically more efficient to insert an item in a sorted linked list than a sorted* array object or built-in array.

Linked-list nodes typically are *not* stored contiguously in memory, but logically they *appear* to be contiguous. Figure 19.2 illustrates a linked list with several nodes.

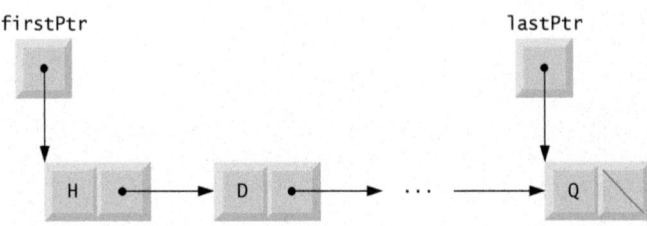

Fig. 19.2 | A graphical representation of a list.

Performance Tip 19.4

Using dynamic memory allocation for data structures that grow and shrink at execution time can save memory.

19.3.1 Testing Our Linked List Implementation

The program of Figs. 19.3–19.5 uses a List *class template* to manipulate a list of integer values and a list of floating-point values. The driver program (Fig. 19.3) has five options:

- insert a value at the beginning of the List
- insert a value at the end of the List
- delete a value from the beginning of the List
- delete a value from the end of the List
- end the List processing

The linked list implementation we present here does not allow insertions and deletions anywhere in the linked list. We ask you to implement these operations in Exercise 19.25. Exercise 19.20 asks you to implement a recursive function that prints a linked list backwards, and Exercise 19.21 asks you to implement a recursive function that searches a linked list for a particular data item.

In Fig. 19.3, Lines 66 and 70 create List objects for types int and double, respectively. Lines 67 and 71 invoke the testList function template to manipulate objects.

```cpp
1   // Fig. 19.3: fig19_03.cpp
2   // Manipulating a linked list.
3   #include <iostream>
4   #include <string>
5   #include "List.h" // List class definition
6   using namespace std;
7
8   // display program instructions to user
9   void instructions() {
10     cout << "Enter one of the following:\n"
11        << "  1 to insert at beginning of list\n"
12        << "  2 to insert at end of list\n"
13        << "  3 to delete from beginning of list\n"
14        << "  4 to delete from end of list\n"
15        << "  5 to end list processing\n";
16  }
17
18  // function to test a List
19  template<typename T>
20  void testList(List<T>& listObject, const string& typeName) {
21     cout << "Testing a List of " << typeName << " values\n";
22     instructions(); // display instructions
23
24     int choice; // store user choice
25     T value; // store input value
26
27     do { // perform user-selected actions
28        cout << "? ";
29        cin >> choice;
30
```

Fig. 19.3 | Manipulating a linked list. (Part 1 of 4.)

```
31            switch (choice) {
32                case 1: // insert at beginning
33                    cout << "Enter " << typeName << ": ";
34                    cin >> value;
35                    listObject.insertAtFront(value);
36                    listObject.print();
37                    break;
38                case 2: // insert at end
39                    cout << "Enter " << typeName << ": ";
40                    cin >> value;
41                    listObject.insertAtBack(value);
42                    listObject.print();
43                    break;
44                case 3: // remove from beginning
45                    if (listObject.removeFromFront(value)) {
46                        cout << value << " removed from list\n";
47                    }
48
49                    listObject.print();
50                    break;
51                case 4: // remove from end
52                    if (listObject.removeFromBack(value)) {
53                        cout << value << " removed from list\n";
54                    }
55
56                    listObject.print();
57                    break;
58            }
59        } while (choice < 5);
60
61        cout << "End list test\n\n";
62    }
63
64    int main() {
65        // test List of int values
66        List<int> integerList;
67        testList(integerList, "integer");
68
69        // test List of double values
70        List<double> doubleList;
71        testList(doubleList, "double");
72    }
```

```
Testing a List of integer values
Enter one of the following:
  1 to insert at beginning of list
  2 to insert at end of list
  3 to delete from beginning of list
  4 to delete from end of list
  5 to end list processing
? 1
Enter integer: 1
The list is: 1
```

Fig. 19.3 | Manipulating a linked list. (Part 2 of 4.)

```
? 1
Enter integer: 2
The list is: 2 1

? 2
Enter integer: 3
The list is: 2 1 3

? 2
Enter integer: 4
The list is: 2 1 3 4

? 3
2 removed from list
The list is: 1 3 4

? 3
1 removed from list
The list is: 3 4

? 4
4 removed from list
The list is: 3

? 4
3 removed from list
The list is empty

? 5
End list test

Testing a List of double values
Enter one of the following:
  1 to insert at beginning of list
  2 to insert at end of list
  3 to delete from beginning of list
  4 to delete from end of list
  5 to end list processing
? 1
Enter double: 1.1
The list is: 1.1

? 1
Enter double: 2.2
The list is: 2.2 1.1

? 2
Enter double: 3.3
The list is: 2.2 1.1 3.3

? 2
Enter double: 4.4
The list is: 2.2 1.1 3.3 4.4

? 3
2.2 removed from list
The list is: 1.1 3.3 4.4
```

Fig. 19.3 | Manipulating a linked list. (Part 3 of 4.)

```
? 3
1.1 removed from list
The list is: 3.3 4.4

? 4
4.4 removed from list
The list is: 3.3

? 4
3.3 removed from list
The list is empty

? 5
End list test

All nodes destroyed

All nodes destroyed
```

Fig. 19.3 | Manipulating a linked list. (Part 4 of 4.)

19.3.2 Class Template ListNode

Figure 19.3 uses class templates ListNode (Fig. 19.4) and List (Fig. 19.5). Encapsulated in each List object is a linked list of ListNode objects. Class template ListNode (Fig. 19.4) contains private members data and nextPtr (lines 20–21), a constructor (lines 15–16) to initialize these members and function getData (line 18) to return the data in a node. Member data stores a value of type NODETYPE, the type parameter passed to the class template. Member nextPtr stores a pointer to the next ListNode object in the linked list. Line 12 of the ListNode class template definition declares class List<NODETYPE> as a friend. This makes all member functions of a given specialization of class template List friends of the corresponding specialization of class template ListNode, so they can access the private members of ListNode objects of that type. We do this for performance and because these two classes are tightly coupled—only class template List manipulates objects of class template ListNode. Because the ListNode template parameter NODETYPE is used as the template argument for List in the friend declaration, ListNodes specialized with a particular type can be processed only by a List specialized with the *same* type (e.g., a List of int values manages ListNode objects that store int values). To use the type name List<NODETYPE> in line 12, the compiler needs to know that class template List exists. Line 8 is a so-called forward declaration of class template List. A forward declaration tells the compiler that a type exists, even if it has not yet been defined.

> **Error-Prevention Tip 19.1**
>
> *Assign nullptr to the link member of a new node. Pointers must be initialized before they're used.*

```
1   // Fig. 19.4: ListNode.h
2   // ListNode class-template definition.
3   #ifndef LISTNODE_H
4   #define LISTNODE_H
```

Fig. 19.4 | ListNode class-template definition. (Part 1 of 2.)

```
 5
 6   // forward declaration of class List required to announce that class
 7   // List exists so it can be used in the friend declaration at line 12
 8   template<typename NODETYPE> class List;
 9
10   template<typename NODETYPE>
11   class ListNode {
12      friend class List<NODETYPE>; // make List a friend
13
14   public:
15      explicit ListNode(const NODETYPE& info) // constructor
16         : data{info}, nextPtr{nullptr} {}
17
18      NODETYPE getData() const {return data;} // return data in node
19   private:
20      NODETYPE data; // data
21      ListNode<NODETYPE>* nextPtr; // next node in list
22   };
23
24   #endif
```

Fig. 19.4 | ListNode class-template definition. (Part 2 of 2.)

19.3.3 Class Template List

Lines 132–133 of the List class template (Fig. 19.5) declare and initialize to nullptr the private data members firstPtr and lastPtr—pointers to the List's first and last List-Nodes. The destructor (lines 13–29) destroys all of the List's ListNode objects when the List is destroyed. The primary List functions are insertAtFront (lines 32–42), insert-AtBack (lines 45–55), removeFromFront (lines 58–76) and removeFromBack (lines 79–105). We discuss each of these after Fig. 19.5.

Function isEmpty (lines 108–110) is a *predicate function* that determines whether the List is *empty*. Function print (lines 113–129) displays the List's contents. Utility function getNewNode (lines 136–138) returns a dynamically allocated ListNode object. This function is called from functions insertAtFront and insertAtBack.

```
 1   // Fig. 19.5: List.h
 2   // List class-template definition.
 3   #ifndef LIST_H
 4   #define LIST_H
 5
 6   #include <iostream>
 7   #include "ListNode.h" // ListNode class definition
 8
 9   template<typename NODETYPE>
10   class List {
11   public:
```

Fig. 19.5 | List class-template definition. (Part 1 of 4.)

```
12        // destructor
13        ~List() {
14            if (!isEmpty()) { // List is not empty
15                std::cout << "Destroying nodes ...\n";
16
17                ListNode<NODETYPE>* currentPtr{firstPtr};
18                ListNode<NODETYPE>* tempPtr{nullptr};
19
20                while (currentPtr != nullptr) { // delete remaining nodes
21                    tempPtr = currentPtr;
22                    std::cout << tempPtr->data << '\n';
23                    currentPtr = currentPtr->nextPtr;
24                    delete tempPtr;
25                }
26            }
27
28            std::cout << "All nodes destroyed\n\n";
29        }
30
31        // insert node at front of list
32        void insertAtFront(const NODETYPE& value) {
33            ListNode<NODETYPE>* newPtr{getNewNode(value)}; // new node
34
35            if (isEmpty()) { // List is empty
36                firstPtr = lastPtr = newPtr; // new list has only one node
37            }
38            else { // List is not empty
39                newPtr->nextPtr = firstPtr; // point new node to old 1st node
40                firstPtr = newPtr; // aim firstPtr at new node
41            }
42        }
43
44        // insert node at back of list
45        void insertAtBack(const NODETYPE& value) {
46            ListNode<NODETYPE>* newPtr{getNewNode(value)}; // new node
47
48            if (isEmpty()) { // List is empty
49                firstPtr = lastPtr = newPtr; // new list has only one node
50            }
51            else { // List is not empty
52                lastPtr->nextPtr = newPtr; // update previous last node
53                lastPtr = newPtr; // new last node
54            }
55        }
56
57        // delete node from front of list
58        bool removeFromFront(NODETYPE& value) {
59            if (isEmpty()) { // List is empty
60                return false; // delete unsuccessful
61            }
62            else {
63                ListNode<NODETYPE>* tempPtr{firstPtr}; // hold item to delete
```

Fig. 19.5 | List class-template definition. (Part 2 of 4.)

```
64
65            if (firstPtr == lastPtr) {
66                firstPtr = lastPtr = nullptr; // no nodes remain after removal
67            }
68            else {
69                firstPtr = firstPtr->nextPtr; // point to previous 2nd node
70            }
71
72            value = tempPtr->data; // return data being removed
73            delete tempPtr; // reclaim previous front node
74            return true; // delete successful
75        }
76    }
77
78    // delete node from back of list
79    bool removeFromBack(NODETYPE& value) {
80        if (isEmpty()) { // List is empty
81            return false; // delete unsuccessful
82        }
83        else {
84            ListNode<NODETYPE>* tempPtr{lastPtr}; // hold item to delete
85
86            if (firstPtr == lastPtr) { // List has one element
87                firstPtr = lastPtr = nullptr; // no nodes remain after removal
88            }
89            else {
90                ListNode<NODETYPE>* currentPtr{firstPtr};
91
92                // locate second-to-last element
93                while (currentPtr->nextPtr != lastPtr) {
94                    currentPtr = currentPtr->nextPtr; // move to next node
95                }
96
97                lastPtr = currentPtr; // remove last node
98                currentPtr->nextPtr = nullptr; // this is now the last node
99            }
100
101            value = tempPtr->data; // return value from old last node
102            delete tempPtr; // reclaim former last node
103            return true; // delete successful
104        }
105    }
106
107    // is List empty?
108    bool isEmpty() const {
109        return firstPtr == nullptr;
110    }
111
112    // display contents of List
113    void print() const {
114        if (isEmpty()) { // List is empty
115            std::cout << "The list is empty\n\n";
```

Fig. 19.5 | List class-template definition. (Part 3 of 4.)

```
116              return;
117          }
118
119          ListNode<NODETYPE>* currentPtr{firstPtr};
120
121          std::cout << "The list is: ";
122
123          while (currentPtr != nullptr) { // get element data
124              std::cout << currentPtr->data << ' ';
125              currentPtr = currentPtr->nextPtr;
126          }
127
128          std::cout << "\n\n";
129      }
130
131  private:
132      ListNode<NODETYPE>* firstPtr{nullptr}; // pointer to first node
133      ListNode<NODETYPE>* lastPtr{nullptr}; // pointer to last node
134
135      // utility function to allocate new node
136      ListNode<NODETYPE>* getNewNode(const NODETYPE& value) {
137          return new ListNode<NODETYPE>{value};
138      }
139  };
140
141  #endif
```

Fig. 19.5 | List class-template definition. (Part 4 of 4.)

19.3.4 Member Function `insertAtFront`

Over the next several pages, we discuss each of the member functions of class List in detail. Function insertAtFront (Fig. 19.5, lines 32–42) places a new node at the front of the list. The function consists of several steps:

1. Call function getNewNode (line 33), passing it value, which is a constant reference to the node value to be inserted.

2. Function getNewNode (lines 136–138) uses operator new to create a new list node and return a pointer to this newly allocated node, which is used to initialize new-Ptr in insertAtFront (line 33).

3. If the list is *empty* (line 35), firstPtr and lastPtr are set to newPtr (line 36)—i.e., the first and last node are the same node.

4. If the list is *not empty*, then the node pointed to by newPtr is threaded into the list by copying firstPtr to newPtr->nextPtr (line 39), so that the new node points to what used to be the first node of the list, and copying newPtr to first-Ptr (line 40), so that firstPtr now points to the new first node of the list.

Figure 19.6 illustrates the function insertAtFront's operation. Part (a) shows the list and the new node before calling insertAtFront. The dashed arrows in part (b) illustrate *Step 4* of the insertAtFront operation that enables the node containing 12 to become the new list front.

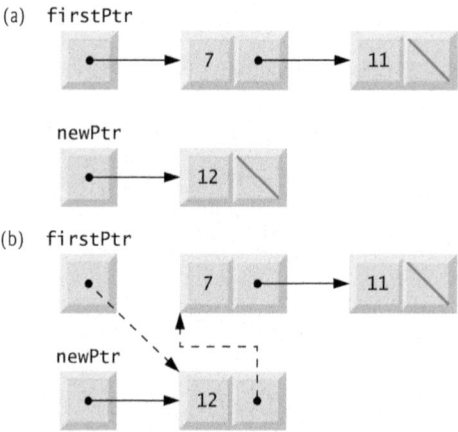

Fig. 19.6 | Operation insertAtFront represented graphically.

19.3.5 Member Function insertAtBack

Function insertAtBack (Fig. 19.5, lines 45–55) places a new node at the back of the list. The function consists of several steps:

1. Call function getNewNode (line 46), passing it value, which is a constant reference to the node value to be inserted.

2. Function getNewNode (lines 136–138) uses operator new to create a new list node and return a pointer to this newly allocated node, which is used to initialize newPtr in insertAtBack (line 46).

3. If the list is *empty* (line 48), then both firstPtr and lastPtr are set to newPtr (line 49).

4. If the list is *not empty*, then the node pointed to by newPtr is threaded into the list by copying newPtr into lastPtr->nextPtr (line 52), so that the new node is pointed to by what used to be the last node of the list, and copying newPtr to lastPtr (line 53), so that lastPtr now points to the new last node of the list.

Figure 19.7 illustrates an insertAtBack operation. Part (a) of the figure shows the list and the new node before the operation. The dashed arrows in part (b) illustrate *Step 4* of function insertAtBack that enables a new node to be added to the end of a list that's not empty.

19.3.6 Member Function removeFromFront

Function removeFromFront (Fig. 19.5, lines 58–76) removes the front node of the list and copies the node value to the reference parameter. The function returns false if an attempt is made to remove a node from an empty list (lines 59–61) and returns true if the removal is successful. The function consists of several steps:

1. Initialize tempPtr with the address to which firstPtr points (line 63). Eventually, tempPtr will be used to delete the node being removed.

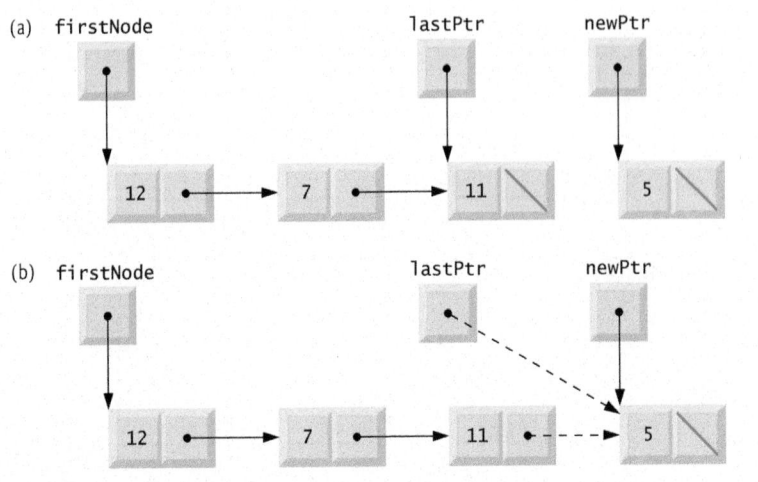

Fig. 19.7 | Operation insertAtBack represented graphically.

2. If firstPtr is equal to lastPtr (line 65), i.e., if the list has only one element prior to the removal attempt, then set firstPtr and lastPtr to nullptr (line 66) to dethread that node from the list (leaving the list empty).

3. If the list has more than one node prior to removal, then leave lastPtr as is and set firstPtr to firstPtr->nextPtr (line 69; i.e., modify firstPtr to point to what was the second node prior to removal (and is now the new first node).

4. After all these pointer manipulations are complete, copy to reference parameter value the data member of the node being removed (line 72).

5. Now delete the node pointed to by tempPtr (line 73).

6. Return true, indicating successful removal (line 74).

Figure 19.8 illustrates function removeFromFront. Part (a) illustrates the list before the removal operation. Part (b) shows the actual pointer manipulations for removing the front node from a nonempty list.

19.3.7 Member Function removeFromBack

Function removeFromBack (Fig. 19.5, lines 79–105) removes the back node of the list and copies the node value to the reference parameter. The function returns false if an attempt is made to remove a node from an empty list (lines 80–82) and returns true if the removal is successful. The function consists of several steps:

1. Initialize tempPtr with the address to which lastPtr points (line 84). Eventually, tempPtr will be used to delete the node being removed.

2. If firstPtr is equal to lastPtr (line 86), i.e., if the list has only one element prior to the removal attempt, then set firstPtr and lastPtr to nullptr (line 87) to dethread that node from the list (leaving the list empty).

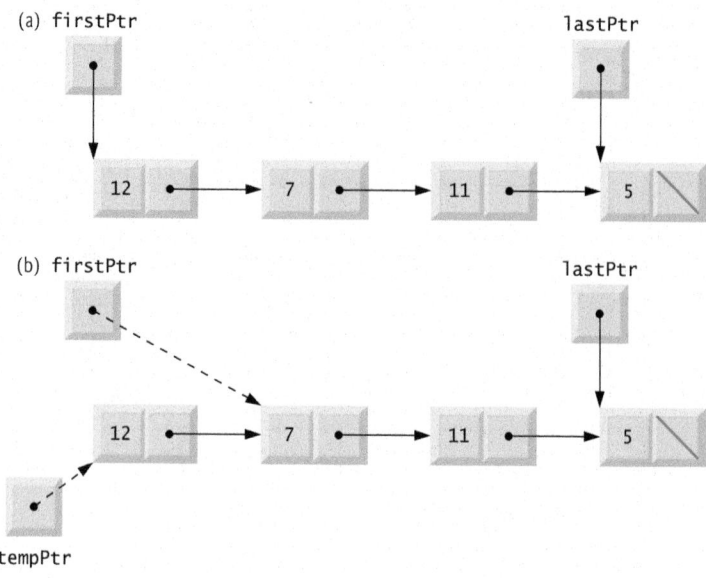

Fig. 19.8 | Operation removeFromFront represented graphically.

3. If the list has more than one node prior to removal, then initialize currentPtr with the address to which firstPtr points (line 90) to prepare to "walk the list."

4. Now "walk the list" with currentPtr until it points to the node before the last node. This node will become the last node after the remove operation completes. This is done with a while loop (lines 93–95) that keeps replacing currentPtr by currentPtr->nextPtr, while currentPtr->nextPtr is not lastPtr.

5. Assign lastPtr to the address to which currentPtr points (line 97) to dethread the back node from the list.

6. Set currentPtr->nextPtr to nullptr (line 98) in the new last node of the list.

7. After all the pointer manipulations are complete, copy to reference parameter value the data member of the node being removed (line 101).

8. Now delete the node pointed to by tempPtr (line 102).

9. Return true (line 103), indicating successful removal.

Figure 19.9 illustrates removeFromBack. Part (a) of the figure illustrates the list before the removal operation. Part (b) of the figure shows the actual pointer manipulations.

19.3.8 Member Function print

Function print (Fig. 19.5, lines 113–129) first determines whether the list is *empty* (line 114). If so, it prints "The list is empty" and returns (lines 115–116). Otherwise, it outputs the value in each node. The function initializes currentPtr with firstPtr (line 119), then prints the string "The list is: " (line 121). While currentPtr is not nullptr (line 123), currentPtr->data is printed (line 124) and currentPtr is assigned the value of currentP-

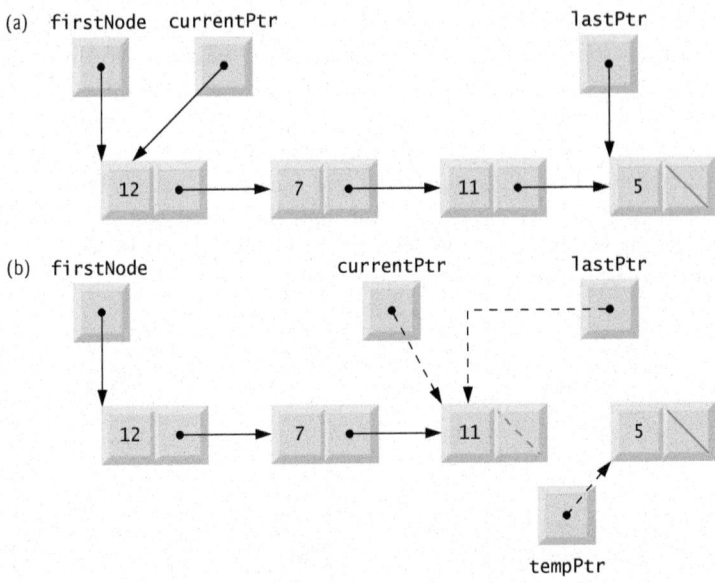

Fig. 19.9 | Operation removeFromBack represented graphically.

tr->nextPtr (line 125). Note that if the link in the last node of the list does not have the value nullptr, the printing algorithm will erroneously attempt to print past the end of the list. Our printing algorithm here is identical for linked lists, stacks and queues (because we base each of these data structures on the same linked list infrastructure).

19.3.9 Circular Linked Lists and Double Linked Lists

The kind of linked list we've been discussing is a singly linked list—the list begins with a pointer to the first node, and each node contains a pointer to the next node "in sequence." This list terminates with a node whose pointer member has the value nullptr. A singly linked list may be traversed in only *one* direction.

A circular, singly linked list (Fig. 19.10) begins with a pointer to the first node, and each node contains a pointer to the next node. The "last node" does not contain nullptr; rather, the pointer in the last node points back to the first node, thus closing the "circle."

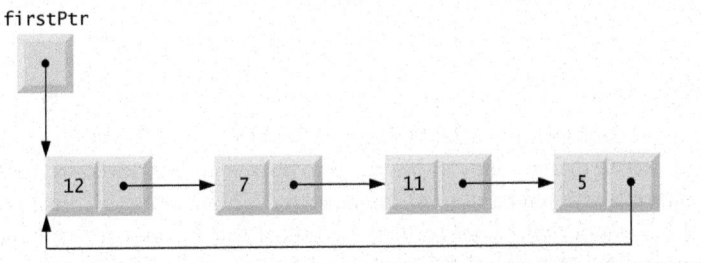

Fig. 19.10 | Circular, singly linked list.

A *doubly linked list* (Fig. 19.11)—such as the Standard Library `list` class template—allows traversals *both forward and backward*. Such a list is often implemented with two "start pointers"—one that points to the first element of the list to allow *front-to-back traversal* of the list and one that points to the last element to allow *back-to-front traversal*. Each node has *both* a *forward pointer* to the next node in the list in the forward direction *and* a *backward pointer* to the next node in the list in the backward direction. If your list contains an alphabetized telephone directory, for example, a search for someone whose name begins with a letter near the front of the alphabet might best begin from the front of the list. Searching for someone whose name begins with a letter near the end of the alphabet might best begin from the back of the list.

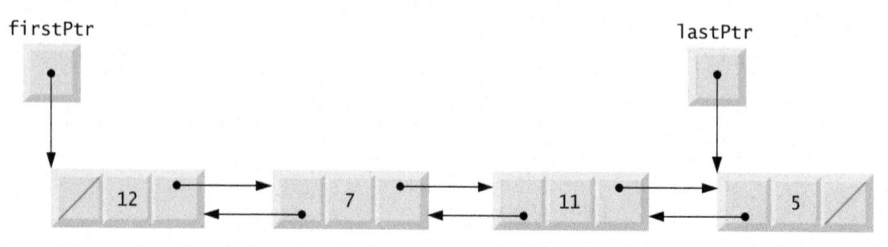

Fig. 19.11 | Doubly linked list.

In a *circular, doubly linked list* (Fig. 19.12), the *forward pointer* of the last node points to the first node, and the *backward pointer* of the first node points to the last node, thus closing the "circle."

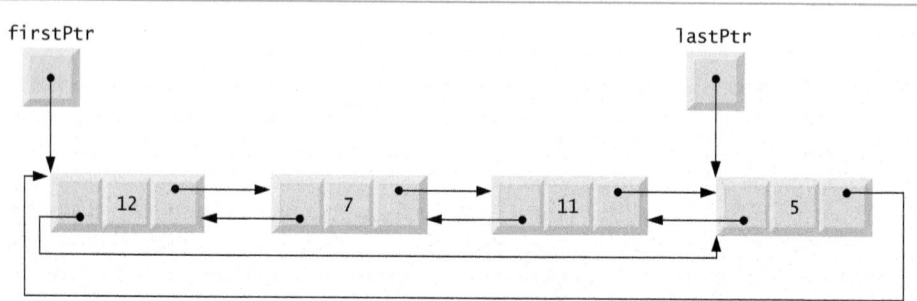

Fig. 19.12 | Circular, doubly linked list.

19.4 Stacks

You learned the concept of a stack in Section 6.11, Section 15.7.1 (`stack` adapter) and Section 18.2. Recall that a node can be added to a stack and removed from a stack only at its *top*, so a stack is referred to as a *last-in, first-out (LIFO)* data structure. One way to implement a stack is as a *constrained version* of a linked list. In such an implementation, the link member in the last node of the stack is set to `nullptr` to indicate the *bottom* of the stack.

The primary member functions used to manipulate a stack are push and pop. Function push *inserts* a new node at the top of the stack. Function pop *removes* a node from the top of the stack, stores the popped value in a reference variable that's passed to the calling function and returns true if the pop operation was successful (false otherwise).

Applications of Stacks
Stacks have many interesting applications:

- In Section 6.11, you learned that when a function call is made, the called function must know how to return to its caller, so the return address is pushed onto a stack. If a series of function calls occurs, the successive return values are pushed onto the stack in last-in, first-out order, so that each function can return to its caller. Stacks support recursive function calls in the same manner as conventional nonrecursive calls.

- Stacks provide the memory for, and store the values of, automatic variables on each invocation of a function. When the function returns to its caller or throws an exception, the destructor (if any) for each local object is called, the space for that function's automatic variables is popped off the stack and those variables are no longer known to the program.

- Stacks are used by compilers in the process of evaluating expressions and generating machine-language code. The exercises explore several applications of stacks, including using them to develop your own complete working compiler.

19.4.1 Taking Advantage of the Relationship Between Stack and List

We'll take advantage of the close relationship between lists and stacks to implement a stack class primarily by *reusing* our List class template. First, we'll implement the Stack class template via *private inheritance* from our List class template. Then we'll implement an identically performing Stack class template through *composition* by including a List object as a private member of a Stack class template.

19.4.2 Implementing a Class Template Stack Class Based By Inheriting from List

The program of Figs. 19.13–19.14 creates a Stack class template (Fig. 19.13) primarily through *private inheritance* (line 9) of the List class template of Fig. 19.5. We want the Stack to have member functions push (Fig. 19.13, lines 12–14), pop (lines 17–19), isStackEmpty (lines 22–24) and printStack (lines 27–29). Note that these are essentially the insertAtFront, removeFromFront, isEmpty and print functions of the List class template. Of course, the List class template contains other member functions (i.e., insertAtBack and removeFromBack) that we would not want to make accessible through the public interface to the Stack class. So when we indicate that the Stack class template is to inherit from the List class template, we specify *private inheritance*. This makes all the List class template's member functions private in the Stack class template. When we implement the Stack's member functions, we then have each of these call the appropriate member function of the List class—push calls insertAtFront (line 13), pop calls removeFromFront (line 18), isStackEmpty calls isEmpty (line 23) and printStack calls print (line 28)—this is referred to as delegation.

```
 1   // Fig. 19.13: Stack.h
 2   // Stack class-template definition.
 3   #ifndef STACK_H
 4   #define STACK_H
 5
 6   #include "List.h" // List class definition
 7
 8   template<typename STACKTYPE>
 9   class Stack : private List<STACKTYPE> {
10   public:
11      // push calls the List function insertAtFront
12      void push(const STACKTYPE& data) {
13         insertAtFront(data);
14      }
15
16      // pop calls the List function removeFromFront
17      bool pop(STACKTYPE& data) {
18         return removeFromFront(data);
19      }
20
21      // isStackEmpty calls the List function isEmpty
22      bool isStackEmpty() const {
23         return this->isEmpty();
24      }
25
26      // printStack calls the List function print
27      void printStack() const {
28         this->print();
29      }
30   };
31
32   #endif
```

Fig. 19.13 | Stack class-template definition.

19.4.3 Dependent Names in Class Templates

The *explicit use of this* on lines 23 and 28 is required so the compiler can properly resolve identifiers in template definitions. A dependent name is an identifier that depends on a template parameter. For example, the call to removeFromFront (line 18) depends on the argument data which has a type that's dependent on the template parameter STACKTYPE. Resolution of *dependent names* occurs when the template is instantiated.

In contrast, the identifier for a function that takes no arguments like isEmpty or print in the List superclass is a non-dependent name. Such identifiers are normally resolved at the point where the template is defined. If the template has not yet been instantiated, then the code for the function with the *non-dependent name* does not yet exist and some compilers will generate compilation errors. Adding the explicit use of this-> in lines 23 and 28 makes the calls to the base class's member functions dependent on the template parameter and ensures that the code will compile properly.

19.4.4 Testing the Stack Class Template

The stack class template is used in main (Fig. 19.14) to instantiate integer stack intStack of type Stack<int> (line 8). Integers 0 through 2 are pushed onto intStack (lines 13–16), then popped off intStack (lines 21–25). The program uses the Stack class template to create doubleStack of type Stack<double> (line 27). Values 1.1, 2.2 and 3.3 are pushed onto doubleStack (lines 33–37), then popped off doubleStack (lines 42–46).

```cpp
1   // Fig. 19.14: fig19_14.cpp
2   // A simple stack program.
3   #include <iostream>
4   #include "Stack.h" // Stack class definition
5   using namespace std;
6
7   int main() {
8      Stack<int> intStack; // create Stack of ints
9
10     cout << "processing an integer Stack" << endl;
11
12     // push integers onto intStack
13     for (int i{0}; i < 3; ++i) {
14        intStack.push(i);
15        intStack.printStack();
16     }
17
18     int popInteger; // store int popped from stack
19
20     // pop integers from intStack
21     while (!intStack.isStackEmpty()) {
22        intStack.pop(popInteger);
23        cout << popInteger << " popped from stack" << endl;
24        intStack.printStack();
25     }
26
27     Stack<double> doubleStack; // create Stack of doubles
28     double value{1.1};
29
30     cout << "processing a double Stack" << endl;
31
32     // push floating-point values onto doubleStack
33     for (int j{0}; j < 3; ++j) {
34        doubleStack.push(value);
35        doubleStack.printStack();
36        value += 1.1;
37     }
38
39     double popDouble; // store double popped from stack
40
41     // pop floating-point values from doubleStack
42     while (!doubleStack.isStackEmpty()) {
43        doubleStack.pop(popDouble);
```

Fig. 19.14 | A simple stack program. (Part 1 of 2.)

```
44              cout << popDouble << " popped from stack" << endl;
45              doubleStack.printStack();
46        }
47    }
```

```
processing an integer Stack
The list is: 0

The list is: 1 0

The list is: 2 1 0

2 popped from stack
The list is: 1 0

1 popped from stack
The list is: 0

0 popped from stack
The list is empty

processing a double Stack
The list is: 1.1

The list is: 2.2 1.1

The list is: 3.3 2.2 1.1

3.3 popped from stack
The list is: 2.2 1.1

2.2 popped from stack
The list is: 1.1

1.1 popped from stack
The list is empty

All nodes destroyed

All nodes destroyed
```

Fig. 19.14 | A simple stack program. (Part 2 of 2.)

19.4.5 Implementing a Class Template Stack Class With Composition of a List Object

Another way to implement a Stack class template is by reusing the List class template through *composition*. Figure 19.15 is a new implementation of the Stack class template that contains a List<STACKTYPE> object called stackList (line 33). This version of the Stack class template uses class List from Fig. 19.5. To test this class, use the driver program in Fig. 19.14, but include the new header—Stackcomposition.h—in line 4. The output of the program is identical for both versions of class Stack.

```cpp
 1  // Fig. 19.15: Stackcomposition.h
 2  // Stack class template with a composed List object.
 3  #ifndef STACKCOMPOSITION_H
 4  #define STACKCOMPOSITION_H
 5
 6  #include "List.h" // List class definition
 7
 8  template< typename STACKTYPE >
 9  class Stack {
10  public:
11     // no constructor; List constructor does initialization
12
13     // push calls stackList object's insertAtFront member function
14     void push(const STACKTYPE& data) {
15        stackList.insertAtFront(data);
16     }
17
18     // pop calls stackList object's removeFromFront member function
19     bool pop(STACKTYPE& data) {
20        return stackList.removeFromFront(data);
21     }
22
23     // isStackEmpty calls stackList object's isEmpty member function
24     bool isStackEmpty() const {
25        return stackList.isEmpty();
26     }
27
28     // printStack calls stackList object's print member function
29     void printStack() const {
30        stackList.print();
31     }
32  private:
33     List<STACKTYPE> stackList; // composed List object
34  };
35
36  #endif
```

Fig. 19.15 | Stack class template with a composed List object.

19.5 Queues

Recall that queue nodes are removed only from the *head* of the queue and are inserted only at the *tail* of the queue. For this reason, a queue is referred to as a first-in, *first-out (FIFO)* data structure. The insert and remove operations are known as enqueue and dequeue.

19.5.1 Applications of Queues

Queues have many applications in computer systems.

* Computers that have a *single* processor can service only one user at a time. Entries for the other users are placed in a queue. Each entry gradually advances to the front of the queue as users receive service. The entry at the front of the queue is the next to receive service.

- Queues are also used to support print spooling. For example, a single printer might be shared by all users of a network. Many users can send print jobs to the printer, even when the printer is already busy. These print jobs are placed in a queue until the printer becomes available. A program called a spooler manages the queue to ensure that, as each print job completes, the next print job is sent to the printer.

- Information packets also wait in queues in computer networks. Each time a packet arrives at a network node, it must be routed to the next node on the network along the path to the packet's final destination. The routing node routes one packet at a time, so additional packets are enqueued until the router can route them.

- A file server in a computer network handles file access requests from many clients throughout the network. Servers have a limited capacity to service requests from clients. When that capacity is exceeded, client requests wait in queues.

19.5.2 Implementing a Class Template Queue Class Based By Inheriting from List

The program of Figs. 19.16–19.17 creates a Queue class template (Fig. 19.16) through *private inheritance* (line 9) of the List class template from Fig. 19.5. The Queue has member functions enqueue (Fig. 19.16, lines 12–14), dequeue (lines 17–19), isQueueEmpty (lines 22–24) and printQueue (lines 27–29). These are essentially the insertAtBack, removeFromFront, isEmpty and print functions of the List class template. Of course, the List class template contains other member functions that we do *not* want to make accessible through the public interface to the Queue class. So when we indicate that the Queue class template is to inherit the List class template, we specify *private inheritance*. This makes all the List class template's member functions private in the Queue class template. When we implement the Queue's member functions, we have each of these call the appropriate member function of the list class—enqueue calls insertAtBack (line 13), dequeue calls removeFromFront (line 18), isQueueEmpty calls isEmpty (line 23) and printQueue calls print (line 28). As with the Stack example in Fig. 19.13, this *delegation* requires *explicit use of the this pointer* in isQueueEmpty and printQueue to avoid compilation errors.

```
1   // Fig. 19.16: Queue.h
2   // Queue class-template definition.
3   #ifndef QUEUE_H
4   #define QUEUE_H
5
6   #include "List.h" // List class definition
7
8   template< typename QUEUETYPE >
9   class Queue : private List<QUEUETYPE> {
10  public:
11     // enqueue calls List member function insertAtBack
12     void enqueue(const QUEUETYPE& data) {
```

Fig. 19.16 | Queue class-template definition. (Part 1 of 2.)

```
13              insertAtBack(data);
14          }
15
16          // dequeue calls List member function removeFromFront
17          bool dequeue(QUEUETYPE& data) {
18              return removeFromFront(data);
19          }
20
21          // isQueueEmpty calls List member function isEmpty
22          bool isQueueEmpty() const {
23              return this->isEmpty();
24          }
25
26          // printQueue calls List member function print
27          void printQueue() const {
28              this->print();
29          }
30      };
31
32      #endif
```

Fig. 19.16 | Queue class-template definition. (Part 2 of 2.)

19.5.3 Testing the Queue Class Template

Figure 19.17 uses the Queue class template to instantiate integer queue intQueue of type Queue<int> (line 8). Integers 0 through 2 are *enqueued* to intQueue (lines 13–16), then *dequeued* from intQueue in first-in, first-out order (lines 21–25). Next, the program instantiates queue doubleQueue of type Queue<double> (line 27). Values 1.1, 2.2 and 3.3 are *enqueued* to doubleQueue (lines 33–37), then *dequeued* from doubleQueue in first-in, first-out order (lines 42–46).

```
 1   // Fig. 19.17: fig19_17.cpp
 2   // Queue-processing program.
 3   #include <iostream>
 4   #include "Queue.h" // Queue class definition
 5   using namespace std;
 6
 7   int main() {
 8       Queue<int> intQueue; // create Queue of integers
 9
10       cout << "processing an integer Queue" << endl;
11
12       // enqueue integers onto intQueue
13       for (int i{0}; i < 3; ++i) {
14           intQueue.enqueue(i);
15           intQueue.printQueue();
16       }
17
18       int dequeueInteger; // store dequeued integer
```

Fig. 19.17 | Queue-processing program. (Part 1 of 3.)

```
19
20      // dequeue integers from intQueue
21      while (!intQueue.isQueueEmpty()) {
22         intQueue.dequeue(dequeueInteger);
23         cout << dequeueInteger << " dequeued" << endl;
24         intQueue.printQueue();
25      }
26
27      Queue<double> doubleQueue; // create Queue of doubles
28      double value{1.1};
29
30      cout << "processing a double Queue" << endl;
31
32      // enqueue floating-point values onto doubleQueue
33      for (int j = 0; j < 3; ++j) {
34         doubleQueue.enqueue(value);
35         doubleQueue.printQueue();
36         value += 1.1;
37      }
38
39      double dequeueDouble; // store dequeued double
40
41      // dequeue floating-point values from doubleQueue
42      while (!doubleQueue.isQueueEmpty()) {
43         doubleQueue.dequeue(dequeueDouble);
44         cout << dequeueDouble << " dequeued" << endl;
45         doubleQueue.printQueue();
46      }
47   }
```

```
processing an integer Queue
The list is: 0

The list is: 0 1

The list is: 0 1 2

0 dequeued
The list is: 1 2

1 dequeued
The list is: 2

2 dequeued
The list is empty

processing a double Queue
The list is: 1.1

The list is: 1.1 2.2

The list is: 1.1 2.2 3.3
```

Fig. 19.17 | Queue-processing program. (Part 2 of 3.)

```
1.1 dequeued
The list is: 2.2 3.3

2.2 dequeued
The list is: 3.3

3.3 dequeued
The list is empty

All nodes destroyed

All nodes destroyed
```

Fig. 19.17 | Queue-processing program. (Part 3 of 3.)

19.6 Trees

Linked lists, stacks and queues are linear data structures. *A tree is a nonlinear, two-dimensional data structure.* Tree nodes contain two or more links. This section discusses binary trees (Fig. 19.18)—trees whose nodes all contain two links (none, one or both of which may have the value nullptr).

19.6.1 Basic Terminology

For this discussion, refer to nodes A, B, C and D in Fig. 19.18. The root node (node B) is the first node in a tree. Each link in the root node refers to a child (nodes A and D). The left child (node A) is the root node of the left subtree (which contains only node A), and the right child (node D) is the root node of the right subtree (which contains nodes D and C). The children of a given node are called siblings (e.g., nodes A and D are siblings). A node with no children is a leaf node (e.g., nodes A and C are leaf nodes). Computer scientists normally draw trees from the root node down—the opposite of how trees grow in nature.

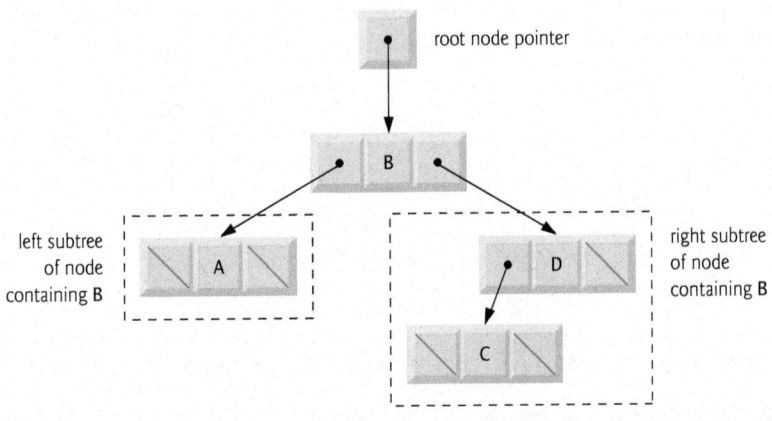

Fig. 19.18 | A graphical representation of a binary tree.

19.6.2 Binary Search Trees

A binary search tree (with *no duplicate node values*) has the characteristic that the values in any left subtree are *less than* the value in its parent node, and the values in any right subtree are *greater than* the value in its parent node. Figure 19.19 illustrates a binary search tree with 9 values. Note that the shape of the binary search tree that corresponds to a set of data can vary, depending on the *order* in which the values are inserted into the tree.

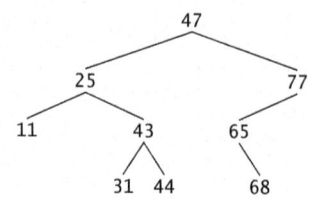

Fig. 19.19 | A binary search tree.

Implementing the Binary Search Tree Program

The program of Figs. 19.20–19.22 creates a binary search tree and traverses it (i.e., walks through all its nodes) three ways—using *recursive* inorder, preorder and postorder traversals. We explain these traversal algorithms shortly.

19.6.3 Testing the Tree Class Template

We begin our discussion with the *driver program* (Fig. 19.20), then continue with the implementations of classes TreeNode (Fig. 19.21) and Tree (Fig. 19.22). Function main (Fig. 19.20) begins by instantiating integer tree intTree of type Tree<int> (line 9). The program prompts for 10 integers, each of which is inserted in the binary tree by calling insertNode (line 17). The program then performs *preorder, inorder* and *postorder traversals* (these are explained shortly) of intTree (lines 21, 24 and 27, respectively). Next, we instantiate floating-point tree doubleTree of type Tree<double> (line 29), then prompt for 10 double values, each of which is inserted in the binary tree by calling insertNode (line 38). Finally, we perform preorder, inorder and postorder traversals of doubleTree (lines 42, 45 and 48, respectively).

```
1   // Fig. 19.20: fig19_20.cpp
2   // Creating and traversing a binary tree.
3   #include <iostream>
4   #include <iomanip>
5   #include "Tree.h" // Tree class definition
6   using namespace std;
7
8   int main() {
9      Tree<int> intTree; // create Tree of int values
10
11     cout << "Enter 10 integer values:\n";
12
```

Fig. 19.20 | Creating and traversing a binary tree. (Part 1 of 3.)

```
13        // insert 10 integers to intTree
14        for (int i{0}; i < 10; ++i) {
15            int intValue = 0;
16            cin >> intValue;
17            intTree.insertNode(intValue);
18        }
19
20        cout << "\nPreorder traversal\n";
21        intTree.preOrderTraversal();
22
23        cout << "\nInorder traversal\n";
24        intTree.inOrderTraversal();
25
26        cout << "\nPostorder traversal\n";
27        intTree.postOrderTraversal();
28
29        Tree<double> doubleTree; // create Tree of double values
30
31        cout << fixed << setprecision(1)
32            << "\n\n\nEnter 10 double values:\n";
33
34        // insert 10 doubles to doubleTree
35        for (int j{0}; j < 10; ++j) {
36            double doubleValue = 0.0;
37            cin >> doubleValue;
38            doubleTree.insertNode(doubleValue);
39        }
40
41        cout << "\nPreorder traversal\n";
42        doubleTree.preOrderTraversal();
43
44        cout << "\nInorder traversal\n";
45        doubleTree.inOrderTraversal();
46
47        cout << "\nPostorder traversal\n";
48        doubleTree.postOrderTraversal();
49        cout << endl;
50    }
```

```
Enter 10 integer values:
50 25 75 12 33 67 88 6 13 68

Preorder traversal
50 25 12 6 13 33 75 67 68 88
Inorder traversal
6 12 13 25 33 50 67 68 75 88
Postorder traversal
6 13 12 33 25 68 67 88 75 50


Enter 10 double values:
39.2 16.5 82.7 3.3 65.2 90.8 1.1 4.4 89.5 92.5
```

Fig. 19.20 | Creating and traversing a binary tree. (Part 2 of 3.)

```
Preorder traversal
39.2 16.5 3.3 1.1 4.4 82.7 65.2 90.8 89.5 92.5
Inorder traversal
1.1 3.3 4.4 16.5 39.2 65.2 82.7 89.5 90.8 92.5
Postorder traversal
1.1 4.4 3.3 16.5 65.2 89.5 92.5 90.8 82.7 39.2
```

Fig. 19.20 | Creating and traversing a binary tree. (Part 3 of 3.)

19.6.4 Class Template TreeNode

The TreeNode class template (Fig. 19.21) definition declares Tree<NODETYPE> as its friend (line 12). This makes all member functions of a given specialization of class template Tree (Fig. 19.22) friends of the corresponding specialization of class template TreeNode, so they can access the private members of TreeNode objects of that type. Because the TreeNode template parameter NODETYPE is used as the template argument for Tree in the friend declaration, TreeNodes specialized with a particular type can be processed only by a Tree specialized with the same type (e.g., a Tree of int values manages TreeNode objects that store int values).

Lines 20–22 declare a TreeNode's private data—the node's data value, and pointers leftPtr (to the node's *left subtree*) and rightPtr (to the node's *right subtree*). Both pointers are initialized to nullptr—thus initializing this node to be a *leaf node*. The constructor (line 15) sets data to the value supplied as a constructor argument. Member function getData (line 18) returns the data value.

```
 1    // Fig. 19.21: TreeNode.h
 2    // TreeNode class-template definition.
 3    #ifndef TREENODE_H
 4    #define TREENODE_H
 5
 6    // forward declaration of class Tree
 7    template<typename NODETYPE> class Tree;
 8
 9    // TreeNode class-template definition
10    template<typename NODETYPE>
11    class TreeNode {
12       friend class Tree<NODETYPE>;
13    public:
14       // constructor
15       TreeNode(const NODETYPE& d) : data{d} {}
16
17       // return copy of node's data
18       NODETYPE getData() const {return data;}
19    private:
20       TreeNode<NODETYPE>* leftPtr{nullptr}; // pointer to left subtree
21       NODETYPE data;
22       TreeNode<NODETYPE>* rightPtr{nullptr}; // pointer to right subtree
23    };
24
25    #endif
```

Fig. 19.21 | TreeNode class-template definition.

19.6.5 Class Template Tree

Class template Tree (Fig. 19.22) has as private data rootPtr (line 33), a pointer to the tree's root node that's initialized to nullptr to indicate an empty tree. The class's public member functions are insertNode (lines 13–15) that inserts a new node in the tree and preOrderTraversal (lines 18–20), inOrderTraversal (lines 23–25) and postOrder-Traversal (lines 28–30), each of which walks the tree in the designated manner. Each of these member functions calls its own recursive utility function to perform the appropriate operations on the internal representation of the tree, so the program is *not* required to access the underlying private data to perform these functions. Remember that the recursion requires us to pass in a pointer that represents the next subtree to process.

```cpp
1   // Fig. 19.22: Tree.h
2   // Tree class-template definition.
3   #ifndef TREE_H
4   #define TREE_H
5
6   #include <iostream>
7   #include "TreeNode.h"
8
9   // Tree class-template definition
10  template<typename NODETYPE> class Tree {
11  public:
12     // insert node in Tree
13     void insertNode(const NODETYPE& value) {
14        insertNodeHelper(&rootPtr, value);
15     }
16
17     // begin preorder traversal of Tree
18     void preOrderTraversal() const {
19        preOrderHelper(rootPtr);
20     }
21
22     // begin inorder traversal of Tree
23     void inOrderTraversal() const {
24        inOrderHelper(rootPtr);
25     }
26
27     // begin postorder traversal of Tree
28     void postOrderTraversal() const {
29        postOrderHelper(rootPtr);
30     }
31
32  private:
33     TreeNode<NODETYPE>* rootPtr{nullptr};
34
35     // utility function called by insertNode; receives a pointer
36     // to a pointer so that the function can modify pointer's value
37     void insertNodeHelper(
38        TreeNode<NODETYPE>** ptr, const NODETYPE& value) {
```

Fig. 19.22 | Tree class-template definition. (Part 1 of 2.)

```
39          // subtree is empty; create new TreeNode containing value
40          if (*ptr == nullptr) {
41             *ptr = new TreeNode<NODETYPE>(value);
42          }
43          else { // subtree is not empty
44             // data to insert is less than data in current node
45             if (value < (*ptr)->data) {
46                insertNodeHelper(&((*ptr)->leftPtr), value);
47             }
48             else {
49                // data to insert is greater than data in current node
50                if (value > (*ptr)->data) {
51                   insertNodeHelper(&((*ptr)->rightPtr), value);
52                }
53                else { // duplicate data value ignored
54                   cout << value << " dup" << endl;
55                }
56             }
57          }
58       }
59
60       // utility function to perform preorder traversal of Tree
61       void preOrderHelper(TreeNode<NODETYPE>* ptr) const {
62          if (ptr != nullptr) {
63             cout << ptr->data << ' '; // process node
64             preOrderHelper(ptr->leftPtr); // traverse left subtree
65             preOrderHelper(ptr->rightPtr); // traverse right subtree
66          }
67       }
68
69       // utility function to perform inorder traversal of Tree
70       void inOrderHelper(TreeNode<NODETYPE>* ptr) const {
71          if (ptr != nullptr) {
72             inOrderHelper(ptr->leftPtr); // traverse left subtree
73             cout << ptr->data << ' '; // process node
74             inOrderHelper(ptr->rightPtr); // traverse right subtree
75          }
76       }
77
78       // utility function to perform postorder traversal of Tree
79       void postOrderHelper(TreeNode<NODETYPE>* ptr) const {
80          if (ptr != nullptr) {
81             postOrderHelper(ptr->leftPtr); // traverse left subtree
82             postOrderHelper(ptr->rightPtr); // traverse right subtree
83             cout << ptr->data << ' '; // process node
84          }
85       }
86    };
87
88    #endif
```

Fig. 19.22 | Tree class-template definition. (Part 2 of 2.)

19.6.6 Tree Member Function `insertNodeHelper`

The `Tree` class's utility function `insertNodeHelper` (lines 37–58) is called by `insertNode` (lines 13–15) to recursively insert a node into the tree. *A node can only be inserted as a leaf node in a binary search tree.* If the tree is *empty*, a new `TreeNode` is created, initialized and inserted in the tree (lines 40–42).

If the tree is *not empty*, the program compares the value to be inserted with the data value in the *root node*. If the insert value is smaller (line 45), the program recursively calls `insertNodeHelper` (line 46) to insert the value in the *left subtree*. If the insert value is larger (line 50), the program recursively calls `insertNodeHelper` (line 51) to insert the value in the *right subtree*. If the value to be inserted is identical to the data value in the *root node*, the program prints the message " dup" (line 54) and returns *without inserting the duplicate value into the tree*. Note that `insertNode` passes the address of `rootPtr` to `insertNode-Helper` (line 14) so it can modify the value stored in `rootPtr` (i.e., the address of the *root node*). To receive a pointer to `rootPtr` (which is also a pointer), `insertNodeHelper`'s first argument is declared as a *pointer to a pointer* to a `TreeNode`.

19.6.7 Tree Traversal Functions

Member functions `preOrderTraversal` (lines 18–20), `inOrderTraversal` (lines 23–25) and `postOrderTraversal` (lines 28–30) traverse the tree and print the node values. For the purpose of the following discussion, we use the binary search tree in Fig. 19.23.

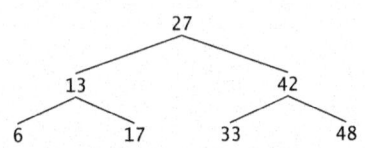

Fig. 19.23 | A binary search tree.

Inorder Traversal Algorithm
Function `inOrderTraversal` invokes utility function `inOrderHelper` (lines 70–76) to perform the inorder traversal of the binary tree. The steps for an inorder traversal are:

1. Traverse the *left subtree* with an inorder traversal. (This is performed by the call to `inOrderHelper` at line 72.)
2. Process the value in the node—i.e., print the node value (line 73).
3. Traverse the *right subtree* with an inorder traversal. (This is performed by the call to `inOrderHelper` at line 74.)

The value in a node is not processed until the values in its left subtree are processed, because each call to `inOrderHelper` immediately calls `inOrderHelper` again with the pointer to the *left subtree*. The inorder traversal of the tree in Fig. 19.23 is

```
6 13 17 27 33 42 48
```

The inorder traversal of a binary search tree prints the node values in *ascending* order. The process of creating a binary search tree actually *sorts* the data—thus, this process is called the binary tree sort.

Preorder Traversal Algorithm

Function `preOrderTraversal` invokes utility function `preOrderHelper` (lines 61–67) to perform the preorder traversal of the binary tree. The steps for a preorder traversal are:

1. Process the value in the node (line 63).

2. Traverse the *left subtree* with a preorder traversal. (This is performed by the call to `preOrderHelper` at line 64.)

3. Traverse the *right subtree* with a preorder traversal. (This is performed by the call to `preOrderHelper` at line 65.)

The value in each node is processed as the node is visited. After the value in a given node is processed, the values in the *left subtree* are processed. Then the values in the *right subtree* are processed. The preorder traversal of the tree in Fig. 19.23 is

```
27 13 6 17 42 33 48
```

Postorder Traversal Algorithm

Function `postOrderTraversal` invokes utility function `postOrderHelper` (lines 79–85) to perform the postorder traversal of the binary tree. The steps for a postorder traversal are:

1. Traverse the *left subtree* with a postorder traversal. (This is performed by the call to `postOrderHelper` at line 81.)

2. Traverse the *right subtree* with a postorder traversal. (This is performed by the call to `postOrderHelper` at line 82.)

3. Process the value in the node (line 83).

The value in each node is not printed until the values of its children are printed. The `postOrderTraversal` of the tree in Fig. 19.23 is

```
6 17 13 33 48 42 27
```

19.6.8 Duplicate Elimination

The binary search tree facilitates duplicate elimination. As the tree is being created, an attempt to insert a duplicate value will be recognized, because a duplicate will follow the same "go left" or "go right" decisions on each comparison as the original value did when it was inserted in the tree. Thus, the duplicate will eventually be compared with a node containing the same value. The duplicate value may be *discarded* at this point.

Searching a binary tree for a value that matches a key is also fast. If the tree is balanced, then each branch contains about *half* the nodes in the tree. Each comparison of a node to the search key *eliminates half the nodes*. This is called an $O(\log n)$ algorithm (Big O notation is discussed in Chapter 20). So a binary search tree with n elements would require a maximum of $\log_2 n$ comparisons either to find a match or to determine that no match exists. For example, searching a (balanced) 1000-element binary search tree requires no more than 10 comparisons, because $2^{10} > 1000$. Searching a (balanced) 1,000,000-element binary search tree requires no more than 20 comparisons, because $2^{20} > 1,000,000$.

19.6.9 Overview of the Binary Tree Exercises

In the exercises, algorithms are presented for several other binary tree operations such as deleting an item from a binary tree, printing a binary tree in a two-dimensional tree format and performing a level-order traversal of a binary tree. The level-order traversal of a binary tree visits the nodes of the tree row by row, starting at the root node level. On each level of the tree, the nodes are visited from left to right. Other binary tree exercises include allowing a binary search tree to contain duplicate values, inserting string values in a binary tree and determining how many levels are contained in a binary tree.

19.7 Wrap-Up

In this chapter, you learned that linked lists are collections of data items that are "linked up in a chain." You also learned that a program can perform insertions and deletions anywhere in a linked list (though our implementation performed insertions and deletions only at the ends of the list). We demonstrated that the stack and queue data structures are constrained versions of lists. For stacks, you saw that insertions and deletions are made only at the top. For queues, you saw that insertions are made at the tail and deletions are made from the head. We also presented the binary tree data structure. You saw a binary search tree that facilitated high-speed searching and sorting of data and efficient duplicate elimination. You learned how to create these data structures for reusability (as templates) and maintainability. In the next chapter, we study various searching and sorting techniques and implement them as function templates.

Summary

Section 19.1 Introduction
- **Dynamic data structures** (p. 798) grow and shrink during execution.
- **Linked lists** (p. 798) are collections of data items "lined up in a row"—insertions and removals are made anywhere in a linked list.
- **Stacks** (p. 798) are important in compilers and operating systems: Insertions and removals are made only at one end of a stack—its **top** (p. 798).
- **Queues** (p. 798) represent waiting lines; insertions are made at the back (also referred to as the **tail**; p. 798) of a queue and removals are made from the front (also referred to as the **head**; p. 798).
- **Binary trees** (p. 798) facilitate high-speed searching and sorting of data, efficient duplicate elimination, representation of file-system directories and compilation of expressions into machine code.

Section 19.2 Self-Referential Classes
- A **self-referential class** (p. 799) contains a pointer that points to an object of the same class type.
- Self-referential class objects can be linked together to form useful data structures such as lists, queues, stacks and trees.

Section 19.3 Linked Lists
- A linked list is a linear collection of self-referential class objects, called nodes, connected by **pointer links** (p. 800)—hence, the term "linked" list.
- A linked list is accessed via a pointer to the first node of the list. Each subsequent node is accessed via the link-pointer member stored in the previous node and the last node contains a null pointer.
- Linked lists, stacks and queues are **linear data structures** (p. 800). Trees are **nonlinear data structures** (p. 800).
- A linked list is appropriate when the number of data elements to be represented is unpredictable.

- Linked lists are dynamic, so the length of a list can increase or decrease as necessary.
- A singly linked list begins with a pointer to the first node, and each node contains a pointer to the next node "in sequence."
- A **circular, singly linked list** (p. 813) begins with a pointer to the first node, and each node contains a pointer to the next node. The "last node" does not contain a null pointer; rather, the pointer in the last node points back to the first node, thus closing the "circle."
- A **doubly linked list** (p. 814) allows traversals both forward and backward.
- A doubly linked list is often implemented with two "start pointers"—one that points to the first element to allow front-to-back traversal of the list and one that points to the last element to allow back-to-front traversal. Each node has a pointer to both the next and previous nodes.
- In a **circular, doubly linked list** (p. 814), the forward pointer of the last node points to the first node, and the backward pointer of the first node points to the last node, thus closing the "circle."

Section 19.4 Stacks
- A stack data structure allows nodes to be added to and removed from the stack only at the top.
- A stack is referred to as a last-in, first-out (LIFO) data structure.
- Function push inserts a new node at the top of the stack. Function pop removes a node from the top of the stack.
- A **dependent name** (p. 816) is an identifier that depends on the value of a template parameter. Resolution of dependent names occurs when the template is instantiated.
- **Non-dependent names** (p. 816) are resolved at the point where the template is defined.

Section 19.5 Queues
- A queue is similar to a supermarket checkout line—the first person in line is serviced first, and other customers enter the line at the end and wait to be serviced.
- Queue nodes are removed only from a queue's head and are inserted only at its tail.
- A queue is referred to as a first-in, first-out (FIFO) data structure. The insert and remove operations are known as **enqueue** and **dequeue** (p. 819).

Section 19.6 Trees
- **Binary trees** (p. 823) are trees whose nodes all contain two links (none, one or both of which may have the value nullptr).
- The **root node** (p. 823) is the first node in a tree.
- Each link in the root node refers to a child. The left child is the root node of the **left subtree** (p. 823), and the right child is the root node of the **right subtree** (p. 823).
- The children of a single node are called **siblings** (p. 823). A node with no children is called a **leaf node** (p. 823).
- A **binary search tree** (p. 824) (with no duplicate node values) has the characteristic that the values in any left subtree are less than the value in its **parent node** (p. 824), and the values in any right subtree are greater than the value in its parent node.
- A node can only be inserted as a leaf node in a binary search tree.
- An **inorder traversal** (p. 824) of a binary tree traverses the left subtree, processes the value in the root node then traverses the right subtree. The value in a node is not processed until the values in its left subtree are processed. An inorder traversal of a binary search tree processes the nodes in sorted order.

- A **preorder traversal** (p. 824) processes the value in the root node, traverses the left subtree, then traverses the right subtree. The value in each node is processed as the node is encountered.

- A **postorder traversal** (p. 824) traverses the left subtree, traverses the right subtree, then processes the root node's value. The value in each node is not processed until the values in both subtrees are processed.

- The binary search tree helps **eliminate duplicate data** (p. 830). As the tree is being created, an attempt to insert a duplicate value will be recognized and the duplicate value may be discarded.

- The **level-order traversal** (p. 831) of a binary tree visits the nodes of the tree row by row, starting at the root node level. On each level of the tree, the nodes are visited from left to right.

Self-Review Exercises

19.1 Fill in the blanks in each of the following:
   a) A self-_____ class is used to form dynamic data structures that can grow and shrink at execution time
   b) The _____ operator is used to dynamically allocate memory and construct an object; this operator returns a pointer to the object.
   c) A(n) _____ is a constrained version of a linked list in which nodes can be inserted and deleted only from the start of the list and node values are returned in last-in, first-out order.
   d) A function that does not alter a linked list, but looks at the list to determine whether it's empty, is an example of a(n) _____ function.
   e) A queue is referred to as a(n) _____ data structure, because the first nodes inserted are the first nodes removed.
   f) The pointer to the next node in a linked list is referred to as a(n) _____.
   g) The _____ operator is used to destroy an object and release dynamically allocated memory.
   h) A(n) _____ is a constrained version of a linked list in which nodes can be inserted only at the end of the list and deleted only from the start of the list.
   i) A(n) _____ is a nonlinear, two-dimensional data structure that contains nodes with two or more links.
   j) A stack is referred to as a(n) _____ data structure, because the last node inserted is the first node removed.
   k) The nodes of a(n) _____ tree contain two link members.
   l) The first node of a tree is the _____ node.
   m) Each link in a tree node points to a(n) _____ or _____ of that node.
   n) A tree node that has no children is called a(n) _____ node.
   o) The four traversal algorithms we mentioned in the text for binary search trees are _____, _____, _____ and _____.

19.2 What are the differences between a linked list and a stack?

19.3 What are the differences between a stack and a queue?

19.4 Perhaps a more appropriate title for this chapter would have been "Reusable Data Structures." Comment on how each of the following entities or concepts contributes to the reusability of data structures:
   a) classes
   b) class templates
   c) inheritance
   d) private inheritance
   e) composition

19.5   Provide the inorder, preorder and postorder traversals of the binary search tree of Fig. 19.24.

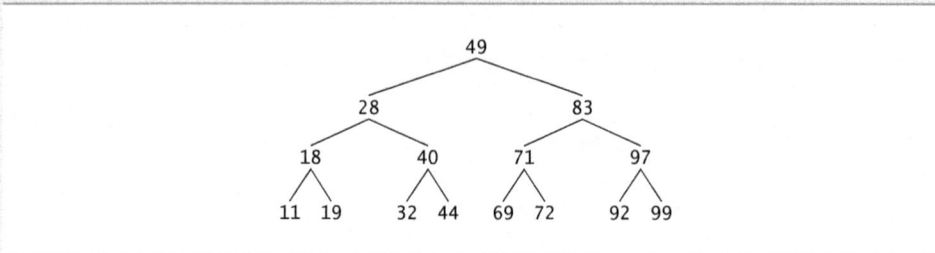

Fig. 19.24 | A 15-node binary search tree.

Answers to Self-Review Exercises

19.1   a) referential. b) new. c) stack. d) predicate. e) first-in, first-out (FIFO). f) link. g) `delete`.
h) queue. i) tree.   j.) last-in, first-out (LIFO). k) binary. l) root. m) child or subtree. n) leaf.
o) inorder, preorder, postorder and level order.

19.2   It's possible to insert a node anywhere in a linked list and remove a node from anywhere in
a linked list. Nodes in a stack may only be inserted at the top of the stack and removed from the top
of a stack.

19.3   A queue data structure allows nodes to be removed only from the head of the queue and
inserted only at the tail of the queue. A queue is referred to as a first-in, first-out (FIFO) data structure. A stack data structure allows nodes to be added to the stack and removed from the stack only
at the top. A stack is referred to as a last-in, first-out (LIFO) data structure.

19.4   a) Classes allow us to instantiate as many data structure objects of a certain type (i.e., class)
        as we wish.
    b) Class templates enable us to instantiate related classes, each based on different type pa-
        rameters—we can then generate as many objects of each template class as we like.
    c) Inheritance enables us to reuse code from a base class in a derived class, so that the derived-
        class data structure is also a base-class data structure (with `public` inheritance, that is).
    d) Private inheritance enables us to reuse portions of the code from a base class to form a
        derived-class data structure; because the inheritance is `private`, all `public` base-class
        member functions become `private` in the derived class. This enables us to prevent cli-
        ents of the derived-class data structure from accessing base-class member functions that
        do not apply to the derived class.
    e) Composition enables us to reuse code by making a class object data structure a member
        of a composed class; if we make the class object a `private` member of the composed
        class, then the class object's `public` member functions are not available through the
        composed object's interface.

19.5   The inorder traversal is

        11 18 19 28 32 40 44 49 69 71 72 83 92 97 99

The preorder traversal is

        49 28 18 11 19 40 32 44 83 71 69 72 97 92 99

The postorder traversal is

        11 19 18 32 44 40 28 69 72 71 92 99 97 83 49

Exercises

19.6 *(Concatenating Lists)* Write a program that concatenates two linked list objects of characters. The program should include function concatenate, which takes references to both list objects as arguments and concatenates the second list to the first list.

19.7 *(Merging Ordered Lists)* Write a program that merges two ordered list objects of integers into a single ordered list object of integers. Function merge should receive references to each of the list objects to be merged and a reference to a list object into which the merged elements will be placed.

19.8 *(Summing and Averaging Elements in a List)* Write a program that inserts 25 random integers from 0 to 100 in order in a linked list object. The program should calculate the sum of the elements and the floating-point average of the elements.

19.9 *(Copying a List in Reverse Order)* Write a program that creates a linked list object of 10 characters and creates a second list object containing a copy of the first list, but in reverse order.

19.10 *(Printing a Sentence in Reverse Order with a Stack)* Write a program that inputs a line of text and uses a stack object to print the line reversed.

19.11 *(Palindrome Testing with Stacks)* Write a program that uses a stack object to determine if a string is a palindrome (i.e., the string is spelled identically backward and forward). The program should ignore spaces and punctuation.

19.12 *(Infix-to-Postfix Conversion)* Stacks are used by compilers to help in the process of evaluating expressions and generating machine language code. In this and the next exercise, we investigate how compilers evaluate arithmetic expressions consisting only of constants, operators and parentheses.

Humans generally write expressions like 3 + 4 and 7 / 9 in which the operator (+ or / here) is written between its operands—this is called infix notation. Computers "prefer" postfix notation in which the operator is written to the right of its two operands. The preceding infix expressions would appear in postfix notation as 3 4 + and 7 9 /, respectively.

To evaluate a complex infix expression, a compiler would first convert the expression to postfix notation and evaluate the postfix version of the expression. Each of these algorithms requires only a single left-to-right pass of the expression. Each algorithm uses a stack object in support of its operation, and in each algorithm the stack is used for a different purpose.

In this exercise, you'll write a C++ version of the infix-to-postfix conversion algorithm. In the next exercise, you'll write a C++ version of the postfix expression evaluation algorithm. Later in the chapter, you'll discover that code you write in this exercise can help you implement a complete working compiler.

Write a program that converts an ordinary infix arithmetic expression (assume a valid expression is entered) with single-digit integers such as

```
(6 + 2) * 5 - 8 / 4
```

to a postfix expression. The postfix version of the preceding infix expression is

```
6 2 + 5 * 8 4 / -
```

The program should read the expression into string infix and use modified versions of the stack functions implemented in this chapter to help create the postfix expression in string postfix. The algorithm for creating a postfix expression is as follows:

1) Push a left parenthesis '(' onto the stack.
2) Append a right parenthesis ')' to the end of infix.
3) While the stack is not empty, read infix from left to right and do the following:

   If the current character in infix is a digit, copy it to the next element of postfix.

   If the current character in infix is a left parenthesis, push it onto the stack.

If the current character in `infix` is an operator,

Pop operators (if there are any) at the top of the stack while they have equal or higher precedence than the current operator, and insert the popped operators in `postfix`.

Push the current character in `infix` onto the stack.

If the current character in `infix` is a right parenthesis

Pop operators from the top of the stack and insert them in `postfix` until a left parenthesis is at the top of the stack.

Pop (and discard) the left parenthesis from the stack.

The following arithmetic operations are allowed in an expression:

- \+ addition
- \- subtraction
- * multiplication
- / division
- ^ exponentiation
- % remainder

[*Note:* We assume left-to-right associativity for all operators in this exercise.] The stack should be maintained with stack nodes, each containing a data member and a pointer to the next stack node.

Some of the functional capabilities you may want to provide are:

a) function `convertToPostfix` that converts the infix expression to postfix notation
b) function `isOperator` that determines whether c is an operator
c) function `precedence` that determines whether the precedence of `operator1` is greater than or equal to the precedence of `operator2`, and, if so, returns `true`
d) function `push` that pushes a value onto the stack
e) function `pop` that pops a value off the stack
f) function `stackTop` that returns the top value of the stack without popping the stack
g) function `isEmpty` that determines if the stack is empty
h) function `printStack` that prints the stack

19.13 *(Postfix Evaluation)* Write a program that evaluates a valid postfix expression such as

```
6 2 + 5 * 8 4 / -
```

The program should read a postfix expression consisting of digits and operators into a `string`. Using modified versions of the stack functions implemented earlier in this chapter, the program should scan the expression and evaluate it. The algorithm is as follows:

1) While you have not reached the end of the `string`, read the expression from left to right.

If the current character is a digit,

Push its integer value onto the stack (the integer value of a digit character is its value in the computer's character set minus the value of `'0'` in the computer's character set).

Otherwise, if the current character is an *operator*,

Pop the two top elements of the stack into variables x and y.

Calculate y *operator* x.

Push the result of the calculation onto the stack.

2) When you reach the end of the `string`, pop the top value of the stack. This is the result of the postfix expression.

[*Note:* In *Step 2* above, if the operator is `'/'`, the top of the stack is 2 and the next element in the stack is 8, then pop 2 into x, pop 8 into y, evaluate 8 / 2 and push the result, 4, back onto the stack. This note also applies to operator `'-'`.] The arithmetic operations allowed in an expression are

- \+ addition
- \- subtraction

    *   multiplication
    /   division
    ^   exponentiation
    %   remainder

[*Note:* We assume left-to-right associativity for all operators for the purpose of this exercise.] The stack should be maintained with stack nodes that contain an int data member and a pointer to the next stack node. You may want to provide the following functional capabilities:

    a) function `evaluatePostfixExpression` that evaluates the postfix expression
    b) function `calculate` that evaluates the expression op1 operator op2
    c) function `push` that pushes a value onto the stack
    d) function `pop` that pops a value off the stack
    e) function `isEmpty` that determines if the stack is empty
    f) function `printStack` that prints the stack

19.14 *(Postfix Evaluation Enhanced)* Modify the postfix evaluator program of Exercise 19.13 so that it can process integer operands larger than 9.

19.15 *(Supermarket Simulation)* Write a program that simulates a checkout line at a supermarket. The line is a queue object. Customers (i.e., customer objects) arrive in random integer intervals of 1–4 minutes. Also, each customer is served in random integer intervals of 1–4 minutes. Obviously, the rates need to be balanced. If the average arrival rate is larger than the average service rate, the queue will grow infinitely. Even with "balanced" rates, randomness can still cause long lines. Run the supermarket simulation for a 12-hour day (720 minutes) using the following algorithm:

    1) Choose a random integer from 1 to 4 to determine the minute at which the first customer arrives.
    2) At the first customer's arrival time:
        Determine customer's service time (random integer from 1 to 4);
        Begin servicing the customer;
        Schedule arrival time of next customer (random integer 1 to 4 added to the current time).
    3) For each minute of the day:
        If the next customer arrives,
            Say so, enqueue the customer, and schedule the arrival time of the next customer;
        If service was completed for the last customer;
            Say so, dequeue next customer to be serviced and determine customer's service completion time (random integer from 1 to 4 added to the current time).

Now run your simulation for 720 minutes, and answer each of the following:

    a) What's the maximum number of customers in the queue at any time?
    b) What's the longest wait any one customer experiences?
    c) What happens if the arrival interval is changed from 1–4 minutes to 1–3 minutes?

19.16 *(Allowing Duplicates in Binary Trees)* Modify the program of Figs. 19.20–19.22 to allow the binary tree object to contain duplicates.

19.17 *(Binary Tree of Strings)* Write a program based on Figs. 19.20–19.22 that inputs a line of text, tokenizes the sentence into separate words (you may want to use the `istringstream` library class), inserts the words in a binary search tree and prints the inorder, preorder and postorder traversals of the tree. Use an OOP approach.

19.18 *(Duplicate Elimination)* In this chapter, we saw that duplicate elimination is straightforward when creating a binary search tree. Describe how you'd perform duplicate elimination using only a one-dimensional array. Compare the performance of array-based duplicate elimination with the performance of binary-search-tree-based duplicate elimination.

19.19   *(Depth of a Binary Tree)* Write a function depth that receives a binary tree and determines how many levels it has.

19.20   *(Recursively Print a List Backward)* Write a member function printListBackward that recursively outputs the items in a linked list object in reverse order. Write a test program that creates a sorted list of integers and prints the list in reverse order.

19.21   *(Recursively Search a List)* Write a member function searchList that recursively searches a linked list object for a specified value. The function should return a pointer to the value if it's found; otherwise, nullptr should be returned. Use your function in a test program that creates a list of integers. The program should prompt the user for a value to locate in the list.

19.22   *(Binary Tree Search)* Write member function binaryTreeSearch, which attempts to locate a specified value in a binary search tree object. The function should take as arguments a pointer to the binary tree's root node and a search key to locate. If the node containing the search key is found, the function should return a pointer to that node; otherwise, the function should return a nullptr pointer.

19.23   *(Level-Order Binary Tree Traversal)* The program of Figs. 19.20–19.22 illustrated three recursive methods of traversing a binary tree—inorder, preorder and postorder traversals. This exercise presents the *level-order traversal* of a binary tree, in which the node values are printed level by level, starting at the root node level. The nodes on each level are printed from left to right. The level-order traversal is not a recursive algorithm. It uses a queue object to control the output of the nodes. The algorithm is as follows:

    1) Insert the root node in the queue
    2) While there are nodes left in the queue,
           Get the next node in the queue
           Print the node's value
           If the pointer to the left child of the node is not nullptr
               Insert the left child node in the queue
           If the pointer to the right child of the node is not nullptr
               Insert the right child node in the queue.

Write member function levelOrder to perform a level-order traversal of a binary tree object. Modify the program of Figs. 19.20–19.22 to use this function. [*Note:* You'll also need to modify and incorporate the queue-processing functions of Fig. 19.16 in this program.]

19.24   *(Printing Trees)* Write a recursive member function outputTree to display a binary tree object on the screen. The function should output the tree row by row, with the top of the tree at the left of the screen and the bottom of the tree toward the right of the screen. Each row is output vertically. For example, the binary tree illustrated in Fig. 19.24 is output as shown in Fig. 19.25. Note that the rightmost leaf node appears at the top of the output in the rightmost column and the root node appears at the left of the output. Each column of output starts five spaces to the right of the previous column. Function outputTree should receive an argument totalSpaces representing the number of spaces preceding the value to be output (this variable should start at zero, so the root node is output at the left of the screen). The function uses a modified inorder traversal to output the tree—it starts at the rightmost node in the tree and works back to the left. The algorithm is as follows:

    While the pointer to the current node is not nullptr
        Recursively call outputTree with the current node's right subtree and totalSpaces + 5
        Use a for structure to count from 1 to totalSpaces and output spaces
        Output the value in the current node
        Set the pointer to the current node to point to the left subtree of the current node
        Increment totalSpaces by 5.

Fig. 19.25 | Sample output for Exercise 19.24.

19.25 *(Insert/Delete Anywhere in a Linked List)* Our linked list class template allowed insertions and deletions at only the front and the back of the linked list. These capabilities were convenient for us when we used private inheritance and composition to produce a stack class template and a queue class template with a minimal amount of code by reusing the list class template. Actually, linked lists are more general than those we provided. Modify the linked list class template we developed in this chapter to handle insertions and deletions anywhere in the list.

19.26 *(List and Queues without Tail Pointers)* Our implementation of a linked list (Figs. 19.4–19.5) used both a firstPtr and a lastPtr. The lastPtr was useful for the insertAtBack and removeFromBack member functions of the List class. The insertAtBack function corresponds to the enqueue member function of the Queue class. Rewrite the List class so that it does not use a lastPtr. Thus, any operations on the tail of a list must begin searching the list from the front. Does this affect our implementation of the Queue class (Fig. 19.16)?

19.27 *(Performance of Binary Tree Sorting and Searching)* One problem with the binary tree sort is that the order in which the data is inserted affects the shape of the tree—for the same collection of data, different orderings can yield binary trees of dramatically different shapes. The performance of the binary tree sorting and searching algorithms is sensitive to the shape of the binary tree. What shape would a binary tree have if its data were inserted in increasing order? in decreasing order? What shape should the tree have to achieve maximal searching performance?

19.28 *(Indexed Lists)* As presented in the text, linked lists must be searched sequentially. For large lists, this can result in poor performance. A common technique for improving list searching performance is to create and maintain an index to the list. An index is a set of pointers to various key places in the list. For example, an application that searches a large list of names could improve performance by creating an index with 26 entries—one for each letter of the alphabet. A search operation for a last name beginning with "Y" would first search the index to determine where the "Y" entries begin and "jump into" the list at that point and search linearly until the desired name was found. This would be much faster than searching the linked list from the beginning. Use the List class of Figs. 19.4–19.5 as the basis of an IndexedList class. Write a program that demonstrates the operation of indexed lists. Be sure to include member functions insertInIndexedList, searchInIndexedList and deleteFromIndexedList.

Special Section: Building Your Own Compiler

In Exercises 8.15–8.17, we introduced Simpletron Machine Language (SML), and you implemented a Simpletron computer simulator to execute SML programs. In Exercises 19.29–19.33, we build a compiler that converts programs written in a high-level programming language to SML.

This section "ties" together the entire programming process. You'll write programs in this new high-level language, compile them on the compiler you build and run them on the simulator you built in Exercise 8.16. You should make every effort to implement your compiler in an object-oriented manner. [*Note:* Due to the size of the descriptions for Exercises 19.29–19.33, we've posted them in a PDF document located at http://www.deitel.com/books/cpphtp10/.]

Searching and Sorting

Objectives

In this chapter you'll:

- Search for a given value in an **array** using linear search and binary search.

- Sort an **array** using insertion sort, selection sort and the recursive merge sort algorithms.

- Use Big O notation to express the efficiency of searching and sorting algorithms and to compare their performance.

- Understand the nature of algorithms of constant, linear and quadratic runtime.

20.1 Introduction

Searching data involves determining whether a value (referred to as the search key) is present in the data and, if so, finding the value's location. Two popular search algorithms are the simple *linear search* (Section 20.2.1) and the faster but more complex *binary search* (Section 20.2.2).

Sorting places data in ascending or descending order, based on one or more sort keys. A list of names could be sorted alphabetically, bank accounts could be sorted by account number, employee payroll records could be sorted by social security number, and so on. You'll learn about *insertion sort* (Section 20.3.1), *selection sort* (Section 20.3.2) and the more efficient, but more complex *merge sort* (Section 20.3.3). Figure 20.1 summarizes the searching and sorting algorithms discussed in the book's examples and exercises. This chapter also introduces Big O notation, which is used to characterize an algorithm's worst-case runtime—that is, how hard an algorithm may have to work to solve a problem.

Algorithm	Location	Algorithm	Location
Searching Algorithms		*Sorting Algorithms*	
Linear search	Section 20.2.1	Insertion sort	Section 20.3.1
Binary search	Section 20.2.2	Selection sort	Section 20.3.2
Recursive linear search	Exercise 20.8	Recursive merge sort	Section 20.3.3
Recursive binary search	Exercise 20.9	Bubble sort	Exercises 20.5–20.6
Binary tree search	Section 19.6	Bucket sort	Exercise 20.7
Linear search (linked list)	Exercise 19.21	Recursive quicksort	Exercise 20.10
binary_search standard library function	Section 16.4.6	Binary tree sort	Section 19.6
		sort standard library function	Section 16.4.6

Fig. 20.1 | Searching and sorting algorithms in this text.

A Note About This Chapter's Examples

The searching and sorting algorithms in this chapter are implemented as function templates that manipulate objects of the array class template. To help you visualize how certain algorithms work, some of the examples display array-element values throughout the searching or sorting process. These output statements slow an algorithm's performance and would *not* be included in industrial-strength code.

20.2 Searching Algorithms

Looking up a phone number, accessing a website and checking a word's definition in a dictionary all involve searching through large amounts of data. A searching algorithm finds an element that matches a given search key, if such an element does, in fact, exist. There are, however, a number of things that differentiate search algorithms from one another. The major difference is the amount of *effort* they require to complete the search. One way to describe this *effort* is with Big O notation. For searching and sorting algorithms, this is particularly dependent on the number of data elements.

In Section 20.2.1, we present the linear search algorithm then discuss the algorithm's *efficiency* as measured by Big O notation. In Section 20.2.2, we introduce the binary search algorithm, which is much more efficient but more complex to implement.

20.2.1 Linear Search

In this section, we discuss the simple linear search for determining whether an *unsorted* array (i.e., an array with element values that are in no particular order) contains a specified search key. Exercise 20.8 at the end of this chapter asks you to implement a recursive version of the linear search.

Function Template *linearSearch*

Function template linearSearch (Fig. 20.2, lines 10–19) compares each element of an array with a *search key* (line 13). Because the array is not in any particular order, it's just as likely that the search key will be found in the first element as the last. On average, therefore, the program must compare the search key with *half* of the array's elements. To determine that a value is *not* in the array, the program must compare the search key to *every* array element. Linear search works well for *small* or *unsorted* arrays. However, for large arrays, linear searching is inefficient. If the array is *sorted* (e.g., its elements are in ascending order), you can use the high-speed binary search technique (Section 20.2.2).

```cpp
1   // Fig. 20.2: LinearSearch.cpp
2   // Linear search of an array.
3   #include <iostream>
4   #include <array>
5   using namespace std;
6
7   // compare key to every element of array until location is
8   // found or until end of array is reached; return location of
9   // element if key is found or -1 if key is not found
10  template <typename T, size_t size>
11  int linearSearch(const array<T, size>& items, const T& key) {
12     for (size_t i{0}; i < items.size(); ++i) {
13        if (key == items[i]) { // if found,
14           return i; // return location of key
15        }
16     }
17
18     return -1; // key not found
19  }
```

Fig. 20.2 | Linear search of an array. (Part 1 of 2.)

```
20
21   int main() {
22      const size_t arraySize{100}; // size of array
23      array<int, arraySize> arrayToSearch; // create array
24
25      for (size_t i{0}; i < arrayToSearch.size(); ++i) {
26         arrayToSearch[i] = 2 * i; // create some data
27      }
28
29      cout << "Enter integer search key: ";
30      int searchKey; // value to locate
31      cin >> searchKey;
32
33      // attempt to locate searchKey in arrayToSearch
34      int element{linearSearch(arrayToSearch, searchKey)};
35
36      // display results
37      if (element != -1) {
38         cout << "Found value in element " << element << endl;
39      }
40      else {
41         cout << "Value not found" << endl;
42      }
43   }
```

```
Enter integer search key: 36
Found value in element 18
```

```
Enter integer search key: 37
Value not found
```

Fig. 20.2 | Linear search of an array. (Part 2 of 2.)

Big O: Constant Runtime

Suppose an algorithm simply tests whether the first element of an array is equal to the second element. If the array has 10 elements, this algorithm requires only *one* comparison. If the array has 1000 elements, the algorithm still requires only *one* comparison. In fact, the algorithm is *independent* of the number of array elements. This algorithm is said to have a constant runtime, which is represented in Big O notation as $O(1)$. An algorithm that's $O(1)$ does not necessarily require only one comparison. $O(1)$ just means that the number of comparisons is *constant*—it does *not* grow as the size of the array increases. An algorithm that tests whether the first element of an array is equal to any of the next three elements will always require three comparisons, but in Big O notation it's still considered $O(1)$. $O(1)$ is often pronounced "on the order of 1" or more simply "order 1."

Big O: Linear Runtime

An algorithm that tests whether the first element of an array is equal to *any* of the other elements of the array requires at most $n - 1$ comparisons, where n is the number of elements in the array. If the array has 10 elements, the algorithm requires up to nine comparisons. If the array has 1000 elements, the algorithm requires up to 999 comparisons. As n grows larger, the n part of the expression $n - 1$ "dominates," and subtracting one becomes inconsequential. Big O is designed to highlight these dominant terms and ignore terms that become unimportant as n grows. For this reason, an algorithm that requires a total of $n - 1$ comparisons (such as the one we described in this paragraph) is said to be $O(n)$ and is referred to as having a linear runtime. $O(n)$ is often pronounced "on the order of n" or more simply "order n."

Big O: Quadratic Runtime

Now suppose you have an algorithm that tests whether *any* element of an array is duplicated elsewhere in the array. The first element must be compared with *all the other elements*. The second element must be compared with all the other elements except the first (it was already compared to the first). The third element then must be compared with all the other elements except the first two. In the end, this algorithm will end up making $(n - 1) + (n - 2) + \ldots + 2 + 1$ or $n^2/2 - n/2$ comparisons. As n increases, the n^2 term *dominates* and the n term becomes inconsequential. Again, Big O notation highlights the n^2 term, leaving $n^2/2$. As we'll soon see, even *constant factors*, such as the $1/2$ here, are omitted in Big O notation.

Big O is concerned with how an algorithm's runtime grows in relation to the *number of items processed*. Suppose an algorithm requires n^2 comparisons. With four elements, the algorithm will require 16 comparisons; with eight elements, 64 comparisons. With this algorithm, *doubling* the number of elements *quadruples* the number of comparisons. Consider a similar algorithm requiring $n^2/2$ comparisons. With four elements, the algorithm will require eight comparisons; with eight elements, 32 comparisons. Again, doubling the number of elements quadruples the number of comparisons. Both of these algorithms *grow as the square of n*, so Big O ignores the constant, and both algorithms are considered to be $O(n^2)$, which is referred to as quadratic runtime and pronounced "on the order of n-squared" or more simply "order n-squared."

O(n^2) Performance

When n is small, $O(n^2)$ algorithms (running on today's billions-of-operations-per-second personal computers) will not noticeably affect performance. But as n grows, you'll start to notice the performance degradation. An $O(n^2)$ algorithm running on a million-element array would require a trillion "operations" (where each could actually require several machine instructions to execute). This could require hours to execute. A billion-element array would require a quintillion operations, a number so large that the algorithm could take decades! Unfortunately, $O(n^2)$ algorithms tend to be easy to write. In this chapter, you'll see algorithms with more favorable Big O measures. Such efficient algorithms often take a bit more cleverness and effort to create, but their superior performance can be worth the extra effort, especially as n gets large.

Linear Search's Runtime

The *linear search* algorithm runs in $O(n)$ time. The worst case in this algorithm is that *every* element must be checked to determine whether the search key is in the array. If the array's size *doubles*, the number of comparisons that the algorithm must perform also *doubles*. Linear search can provide outstanding performance if the element matching the search key happens to be at or near the front of the array. But we seek algorithms that perform well, on average, across *all* searches, including those where the element matching the search key is near the end of the array. If a program needs to perform many searches on large arrays, it may be better to implement a different, more efficient algorithm, such as the *binary search* which we consider in the next section.

> **Performance Tip 20.1**
> *Sometimes the simplest algorithms perform poorly. Their virtue is that they're easy to program, test and debug. Sometimes more complex algorithms are required to maximize performance.*

20.2.2 Binary Search

The binary search algorithm is more efficient than the linear search algorithm, but it requires that the array first be *sorted*. This is only worthwhile when the array, once sorted, will be searched a great many times—or when the searching application has *stringent* performance requirements. The first iteration of this algorithm tests the *middle* array element. If this matches the search key, the algorithm ends. Assuming the array is sorted in *ascending* order, then if the search key is *less* than the middle element, the search key cannot match any element in the array's second half so the algorithm continues with only the first *half* (i.e., the first element up to, but *not* including, the middle element). If the search key is *greater* than the middle element, the search key cannot match any element in the array's first half so the algorithm continues with only the second *half* (i.e., the element *after* the middle element through the last element). Each iteration tests the *middle value* of the array's remaining elements. If the element does not match the search key, the algorithm eliminates half of the remaining elements. The algorithm ends either by finding an element that matches the search key or by reducing the sub-array to zero size.

Binary Search of 15 Integer Values

As an example, consider the sorted 15-element array

2	3	5	10	27	30	34	51	56	65	77	81	82	93	99

and the search key 65. A binary search first checks whether the *middle* element (51) is the search key. The search key (65) is larger than 51, so 51 is eliminated from consideration along with the first half of the array (all elements smaller than 51.) Next, the algorithm checks whether 81 (the middle element of the remaining elements) matches the search key. The search key (65) is smaller than 81, so 81 is eliminated from consideration along with the elements larger than 81. After just two tests, the algorithm has narrowed the number of elements to check to three (56, 65 and 77). The algorithm then checks 65 (which matches the search key), and returns the element's index (9). In this case, the algorithm required just *three* comparisons to determine whether the array contained the search key. Using a *linear search* algorithm would have required 10 comparisons. [*Note:* In this example, we've chosen to use an array with 15 elements, so that there will always be an obvious middle element in the array. With an even number of elements, the middle of the array lies between two elements. We implement the algorithm to choose the element with the higher index number.]

Binary Search Example

Figure 20.3 implements and demonstrates the binary-search algorithm. Throughout the program's execution, we use function template displayElements (lines 11–23) to display the portion of the array that's currently being searched.

```cpp
 1   // Fig 20.3: BinarySearch.cpp
 2   // Binary search of an array.
 3   #include <algorithm>
 4   #include <array>
 5   #include <ctime>
 6   #include <iostream>
 7   #include <random>
 8   using namespace std;
 9
10   // display array elements from index low through index high
11   template <typename T, size_t size>
12   void displayElements(const array<T, size>& items,
13      size_t low, size_t high) {
14      for (size_t i{0}; i < items.size() && i < low; ++i) {
15         cout << "    "; // display spaces for alignment
16      }
17
18      for (size_t i{low}; i < items.size() && i <= high; ++i) {
19         cout << items[i] << " "; // display element
20      }
21
22      cout << endl;
23   }
24
25   // perform a binary search on the data
26   template <typename T, size_t size>
27   int binarySearch(const array<T, size>& items, const T& key) {
28      int low{0}; // low index of elements to search
29      int high{items.size() - 1}; // high index of elements to search
30      int middle{(low + high + 1) / 2}; // middle element
31      int location{-1}; // key's index; -1 if not found
32
33      do { // loop to search for element
34         // display remaining elements of array to be searched
35         displayElements(items, low, high);
36
37         // output spaces for alignment
38         for (int i{0}; i < middle; ++i) {
39            cout << "    ";
40         }
41
42         cout << " * " << endl; // indicate current middle
43
44         // if the element is found at the middle
45         if (key == items[middle]) {
46            location = middle; // location is the current middle
47         }
48         else if (key < items[middle]) { // middle is too high
49            high = middle - 1; // eliminate the higher half
50         }
51         else { // middle element is too low
52            low = middle + 1; // eliminate the lower half
53         }
```

Fig. 20.3 | Binary search of an array. (Part I of 3.)

```
54
55           middle = (low + high + 1) / 2; // recalculate the middle
56       } while ((low <= high) && (location == -1));
57
58       return location; // return location of key
59   }
60
61   int main() {
62       // use the default random-number generation engine to produce
63       // uniformly distributed pseudorandom int values from 10 to 99
64       default_random_engine engine{
65           static_cast<unsigned int>(time(nullptr))};
66       uniform_int_distribution<unsigned int> randomInt{10, 99};
67
68       const size_t arraySize{15}; // size of array
69       array<int, arraySize> arrayToSearch; // create array
70
71       // fill arrayToSearch with random values
72       for (int &item : arrayToSearch) {
73           item = randomInt(engine);
74       }
75
76       sort(arrayToSearch.begin(), arrayToSearch.end()); // sort the array
77
78       // display arrayToSearch's values
79       displayElements(arrayToSearch, 0, arrayToSearch.size() - 1);
80
81       // get input from user
82       cout << "\nPlease enter an integer value (-1 to quit): ";
83       int searchKey; // value to locate
84       cin >> searchKey; // read an int from user
85       cout << endl;
86
87       // repeatedly input an integer; -1 terminates the program
88       while (searchKey != -1) {
89           // use binary search to try to find integer
90           int position{binarySearch(arrayToSearch, searchKey)};
91
92           // return value of -1 indicates integer was not found
93           if (position == -1) {
94               cout << "The integer " << searchKey << " was not found.\n";
95           }
96           else {
97               cout << "The integer " << searchKey
98                   << " was found in position " << position << ".\n";
99           }
100
101          // get input from user
102          cout << "\n\nPlease enter an integer value (-1 to quit): ";
103          cin >> searchKey; // read an int from user
104          cout << endl;
105      }
106  }
```

Fig. 20.3 | Binary search of an array. (Part 2 of 3.)

```
10 23 27 48 52 55 58 60 62 63 68 72 75 92 97

Please enter an integer value (-1 to quit): 48

10 23 27 48 52 55 58 60 62 63 68 72 75 92 97
                *
10 23 27 48 52 55 58
         *
The integer 48 was found in position 3.


Please enter an integer value (-1 to quit): 92

10 23 27 48 52 55 58 60 62 63 68 72 75 92 97
                *
                      62 63 68 72 75 92 97
                               *
                                  75 92 97
                                       *
The integer 92 was found in position 13.


Please enter an integer value (-1 to quit): 22

10 23 27 48 52 55 58 60 62 63 68 72 75 92 97
                *
10 23 27 48 52 55 58
         *
10 23 27
     *
10
*
The integer 22 was not found.


Please enter an integer value (-1 to quit): -1
```

Fig. 20.3 | Binary search of an array. (Part 3 of 3.)

Function Template binarySearch

Lines 26–59 define function template binarySearch, which has two parameters—a reference to the array to search and a reference to the search key. Lines 28–30 calculate the low end index, high end index and middle index of the portion of the array that the algorithm is currently searching. When binarySearch is first called, low is 0, high is the array's size minus 1 and middle is the average of these two values. Line 31 initializes location to -1—the value that binarySearch returns if the search key is *not* found. Lines 33–56 loop until low is greater than high (indicating that the element was not found) or location does not equal -1 (indicating that the search key was found). Line 45 tests whether the value in the middle element is equal to key. If so, line 46 assigns the middle index to location. Then the loop terminates and location is returned to the caller. Each iteration of the loop that does not find the search key tests a single value (line 48) and eliminates half of the remaining values in the array (line 49 or 51).

Function main
Lines 64–66 set up a random-number generator for int values from 10–99. Lines 68–74 create an array and fill it with random ints. Recall that the binary search algorithm requires a *sorted* array, so line 76 calls the Standard Library function sort to sort arrayToSearch's elements into ascending order. Line 78 displays arrayToSearch's sorted contents.

Lines 88–105 loop until the user enters the value -1. For each search key the user enters, the program performs a binary search of arrayToSearch to determine whether it contains the search key. The first line of output from this program shows arrayToSearch's contents in ascending order. When the user instructs the program to search for 48, the program first tests the middle element, which is 60 (as indicated by *). The search key is less than 60, so the program eliminates the second half of the array and tests the middle element from the first half of the array. The search key equals 48, so the program returns the index 3 after performing just *two* comparisons. The output also shows the results of searching for the values 92 and 22.

Efficiency of Binary Search
In the worst-case scenario, searching a sorted array of 1023 elements will take only 10 comparisons when using a binary search. Repeatedly dividing 1023 by 2 (because, after each comparison, we can eliminate from consideration *half* of the remaining elements) and rounding down (because we also remove the middle element) yields the values 511, 255, 127, 63, 31, 15, 7, 3, 1 and 0. The number 1023 ($2^{10} - 1$) is divided by 2 only 10 times to get the value 0, which indicates that there are no more elements to test. Dividing by 2 is equivalent to one comparison in the binary search algorithm. Thus, an array of 1,048,575 ($2^{20} - 1$) elements takes a maximum of 20 comparisons to find the key, and an array of approximately one billion elements takes a maximum of 30 comparisons to find the key. This is a *tremendous* performance improvement over the linear search. For a one-billion-element array, this is a difference between an average of 500 million comparisons for the linear search and a maximum of only 30 comparisons for the binary search! The maximum number of comparisons needed for the binary search of any sorted array is the exponent of the first power of 2 greater than the number of elements in the array, which is represented as $\log_2 n$. *All logarithms grow at roughly the same rate*, so in Big O notation the base can be omitted. This results in a Big O of $O(\log n)$ for a binary search, which is also known as logarithmic runtime and pronounced "on the order of log *n*" or more simply "order log *n*."

20.3 Sorting Algorithms

Sorting data (i.e., placing the data into some particular order, such as *ascending* or *descending*) is one of the most important computing applications. A bank sorts all of its checks by account number so that it can prepare individual bank statements at the end of each month. Telephone companies sort their lists of accounts by last name and, further, by first name to make it easy to find phone numbers. Virtually every organization must sort some data, and often, massive amounts of it. Sorting data is an intriguing, computer-intensive problem that has attracted intense research efforts.

An important point to understand about sorting is that the end result—the sorted array—*will be the same no matter which algorithm you use to sort the* array. *Your algorithm choice affects only the algorithm's runtime and memory use.* The next two sections introduce the *selection sort* and *insertion sort*—simple algorithms to implement, but inefficient. In each case, we examine the efficiency of the algorithms using Big O notation. We then present the merge sort algorithm, which is much faster but is more difficult to implement.

20.3.1 Insertion Sort

Figure 20.4 uses insertion sort—a simple, but inefficient, sorting algorithm—to sort a 10-element array's values into ascending order. Function template insertionSort (lines 9–25) implements the algorithm.

```cpp
 1   // Fig. 20.4: InsertionSort.cpp
 2   // Sorting an array into ascending order with insertion sort.
 3   #include <array>
 4   #include <iomanip>
 5   #include <iostream>
 6   using namespace std;
 7
 8   // sort an array into ascending order
 9   template <typename T, size_t size>
10   void insertionSort(array<T, size>& items) {
11      // loop over the elements of the array
12      for (size_t next{1}; next < items.size(); ++next) {
13         T insert{items[next]}; // save value of next item to insert
14         size_t moveIndex{next}; // initialize location to place element
15
16         // search for the location in which to put the current element
17         while ((moveIndex > 0) && (items[moveIndex - 1] > insert)) {
18            // shift element one slot to the right
19            items[moveIndex] = items[moveIndex - 1];
20            --moveIndex;
21         }
22
23         items[moveIndex] = insert; // place insert item back into array
24      }
25   }
26
27   int main() {
28      const size_t arraySize{10}; // size of array
29      array<int, arraySize> data{34, 56, 4, 10, 77, 51, 93, 30, 5, 52};
30
31      cout << "Unsorted array:\n";
32
33      // output original array
34      for (size_t i{0}; i < arraySize; ++i) {
35         cout << setw(4) << data[i];
36      }
37
38      insertionSort(data); // sort the array
39
40      cout << "\nSorted array:\n";
41
```

Fig. 20.4 | Sorting an array into ascending order with insertion sort. (Part 1 of 2.)

```
42      // output sorted array
43      for (size_t i{0}; i < arraySize; ++i) {
44          cout << setw(4) << data[i];
45      }
46
47      cout << endl;
48  }
```

```
Unsorted array:
  34  56   4  10  77  51  93  30   5  52
Sorted array:
   4   5  10  30  34  51  52  56  77  93
```

Fig. 20.4 | Sorting an array into ascending order with insertion sort. (Part 2 of 2.)

Insertion Sort Algorithm

The algorithm's first iteration takes the array's second element and, if it's less than the first element, swaps it with the first element (i.e., the algorithm *inserts* the second element in front of the first element). The second iteration looks at the third element and inserts it into the correct position with respect to the first two elements, so all three elements are in order. At the *i*th iteration of this algorithm, the first *i* elements in the original array will be sorted.

First Iteration

Line 29 declares and initializes the array named data with the following values:

| 34 | 56 | 4 | 10 | 77 | 51 | 93 | 30 | 5 | 52 |

Line 38 passes the array to the insertionSort function, which receives the array in parameter items. The function first looks at items[0] and items[1], whose values are 34 and 56, respectively. These two elements are already in order, so the algorithm continues—if they were out of order, the algorithm would swap them.

Second Iteration

In the second iteration, the algorithm looks at the value of items[2] (that is, 4). This value is less than 56, so the algorithm stores 4 in a temporary variable and moves 56 one element to the right. The algorithm then determines that 4 is less than 34, so it moves 34 one element to the right. At this point, the algorithm has reached the beginning of the array, so it places 4 in items[0]. The array now is

| 4 | 34 | 56 | 10 | 77 | 51 | 93 | 30 | 5 | 52 |

Third Iteration and Beyond

In the third iteration, the algorithm places the value of items[3] (that is, 10) in the correct location with respect to the first four array elements. The algorithm compares 10 to 56 and moves 56 one element to the right because it's larger than 10. Next, the algorithm compares 10 to 34, moving 34 right one element. When the algorithm compares 10 to 4, it observes that 10 is larger than 4 and places 10 in items[1]. The array now is

| 4 | 10 | 34 | 56 | 77 | 51 | 93 | 30 | 5 | 52 |

Using this algorithm, after the *i*th iteration, the first *i* + 1 array elements are sorted. They may not be in their *final* locations, however, because the algorithm might encounter smaller values later in the array.

Function Template `insertionSort`

Function template insertionSort performs the sorting in lines 12–24, which iterates over the array's elements. In each iteration, line 13 temporarily stores in variable insert the value of the element that will be inserted into the array's sorted portion. Line 14 declares and initializes the variable moveIndex, which keeps track of where to insert the element. Lines 17–21 loop to locate the correct position where the element should be inserted. The loop terminates either when the program reaches the array's first element or when it reaches an element that's less than the value to insert. Line 19 moves an element to the right, and line 20 decrements the position at which to insert the next element. After the while loop ends, line 23 inserts the element into place. When the for statement in lines 12–24 terminates, the array's elements are sorted.

Big O: Efficiency of Insertion Sort

Insertion sort is *simple*, but *inefficient*, sorting algorithm. This becomes apparent when sorting *large* arrays. Insertion sort iterates *n* − 1 times, inserting an element into the appropriate position in the elements sorted so far. For each iteration, determining where to insert the element can require comparing the element to each of the preceding elements—*n* − 1 comparisons in the worst case. Each individual iteration statement runs in $O(n)$ time. To determine Big O notation, *nested* statements mean that you must *multiply* the number of comparisons. For each iteration of an outer loop, there will be a certain number of iterations of the inner loop. In this algorithm, for each $O(n)$ iteration of the outer loop, there will be $O(n)$ iterations of the inner loop, resulting in a Big O of $O(n * n)$ or $O(n^2)$.

20.3.2 Selection Sort

Figure 20.5 uses the selection sort algorithm—another easy-to-implement, but inefficient, sorting algorithm—to sort a 10-element array's values into ascending order. Function template selectionSort (lines 9–27) implements the algorithm.

```
1   // Fig. 20.5: fig20_05.cpp
2   // Sorting an array into ascending order with selection sort.
3   #include <array>
4   #include <iomanip>
5   #include <iostream>
6   using namespace std;
7
8   // sort an array into ascending order
9   template <typename T, size_t size>
10  void selectionSort(array<T, size>& items) {
11     // loop over size - 1 elements
12     for (size_t i{0}; i < items.size() - 1; ++i) {
13        size_t indexOfSmallest{i}; // will hold index of smallest element
14
```

Fig. 20.5 | Sorting an array into ascending order with selection sort. (Part 1 of 2.)

```
15          // loop to find index of smallest element
16          for (size_t index{i + 1}; index < items.size(); ++index) {
17              if (items[index] < items[indexOfSmallest]) {
18                  indexOfSmallest = index;
19              }
20          }
21
22          // swap the elements at positions i and indexOfSmallest
23          T hold{items[i]};
24          items[i] = items[indexOfSmallest];
25          items[indexOfSmallest] = hold;
26      }
27  }
28
29  int main() {
30      const size_t arraySize{10};
31      array<int, arraySize> data{34, 56, 4, 10, 77, 51, 93, 30, 5, 52};
32
33      cout << "Unsorted array:\n";
34
35      // output original array
36      for (size_t i{0}; i < arraySize; ++i) {
37          cout << setw(4) << data[i];
38      }
39
40      selectionSort(data); // sort the array
41
42      cout << "\nSorted array:\n";
43
44      // output sorted array
45      for (size_t i{0}; i < arraySize; ++i) {
46          cout << setw(4) << data[i];
47      }
48
49      cout << endl;
50  }
```

```
Unsorted array:
  34  56   4  10  77  51  93  30   5  52
Sorted array:
   4   5  10  30  34  51  52  56  77  93
```

Fig. 20.5 | Sorting an array into ascending order with selection sort. (Part 2 of 2.)

Selection Sort Algorithm

The algorithm's first iteration selects the smallest element value and swaps it with the first element's value. The second iteration selects the second-smallest element value (which is the smallest of the remaining elements) and swaps it with the second element's value. The algorithm continues until the last iteration selects the second-largest element and swaps it with the second-to-last element's value, leaving the largest value in the last element. After the ith iteration, the smallest i values will be sorted into increasing order in the first i array elements.

First Iteration
Line 31 declares and initializes the array named data with the following values:

| 34 | 56 | 4 | 10 | 77 | 51 | 93 | 30 | 5 | 52 |

The selection sort first determines the smallest value (4) in the array, which is in element 2. The algorithm swaps 4 with the value in element 0 (34), resulting in

| 4 | 56 | 34 | 10 | 77 | 51 | 93 | 30 | 5 | 52 |

Second Iteration
The algorithm then determines the smallest value of the remaining elements (all elements except 4), which is 5, contained in element 8. The program swaps the 5 with the 56 in element 1, resulting in

| 4 | 5 | 34 | 10 | 77 | 51 | 93 | 30 | 56 | 52 |

Third Iteration
On the third iteration, the program determines the next smallest value, 10, and swaps it with the value in element 2 (34).

| 4 | 5 | 10 | 34 | 77 | 51 | 93 | 30 | 56 | 52 |

The process continues until the array is fully sorted.

| 4 | 5 | 10 | 30 | 34 | 51 | 52 | 56 | 77 | 93 |

After the first iteration, the *smallest* element is in the *first* position; after the second iteration, the *two smallest* elements are *in order* in the *first two* positions and so on.

Function Template selectionSort
Function template selectionSort performs the sorting in lines 12–26. The loop iterates size - 1 times. Line 13 declares and initializes the variable indexOfSmallest, which stores the index of the smallest element in the unsorted portion of the array. Lines 16–20 iterate over the remaining array elements. For each element, line 17 compares the current element's value to the value at indexOfSmallest. If the current element is smaller, line 18 assigns the current element's index to indexOfSmallest. When this loop finishes, indexOfSmallest contains the index of the smallest element remaining in the array. Lines 23–25 then swap the elements at positions i and indexOfSmallest, using the temporary variable hold to store items[i]'s value while that element is assigned items[indexOfSmallest].

Efficiency of Selection Sort
The selection sort algorithm iterates $n - 1$ times, each time swapping the smallest remaining element into its sorted position. Locating the smallest remaining element requires $n - 1$ comparisons during the first iteration, $n - 2$ during the second iteration, then $n - 3, \ldots, 3,$ 2, 1. This results in a total of $n(n - 1)/2$ or $(n^2 - n)/2$ comparisons. In Big O notation, smaller terms drop out and constants are ignored, leaving a Big O of $O(n^2)$. Can we develop sorting algorithms that perform *better* than $O(n^2)$?

20.3.3 Merge Sort (A Recursive Implementation)
Merge sort is an *efficient* sorting algorithm but is conceptually *more complex* than insertion sort and selection sort. The merge sort algorithm sorts an array by splitting it into two

equal-sized sub-arrays, sorting each sub-array then *merging* them into one larger array. With an odd number of elements, the algorithm creates the two sub-arrays such that one has one more element than the other.

Merge sort performs the merge by looking at each sub-array's first element, which is also the smallest element in that sub-array. Merge sort takes the smallest of these and places it in the first element of merged sorted array. If there are still elements in the sub-array, merge sort looks at the second element in that sub-array (which is now the smallest element remaining) and compares it to the first element in the other sub-array. Merge sort continues this process until the merged array is filled. Once a sub-array has no more elements, the merge copies the other array's remaining elements into the merged array.

Sample Merge
Suppose the algorithm has already merged smaller arrays to create sorted arrays A:

4	10	34	56	77

and B:

5	30	51	52	93

Merge sort merges these arrays into a sorted array. The smallest value in A is 4 (located in the zeroth element of A). The smallest value in B is 5 (located in the zeroth element of B). In order to determine the smallest element in the larger array, the algorithm compares 4 and 5. The value from A is smaller, so 4 becomes the value of the first element in the merged array. The algorithm continues by comparing 10 (the value of the second element in A) to 5 (the value of the first element in B). The value from B is smaller, so 5 becomes the value of the second element in the larger array. The algorithm continues by comparing 10 to 30, with 10 becoming the value of the third element in the array, and so on.

Recursive Implementation
Our merge sort implementation is *recursive*. The *base case* is an array with one element. Such an array is, of course, sorted, so merge sort immediately returns when it's called with a one-element array. The *recursion step* splits an array of two or more elements into two equal-sized sub-arrays, recursively sorts each sub-array, then merges them into one larger, sorted array. [Again, if there is an odd number of elements, one sub-array is one element larger than the other.]

Demonstrating Merge Sort
Figure 20.6 implements and demonstrates the merge sort algorithm. Throughout the program's execution, we use function template displayElements (lines 10–22) to display the portions of the array that are currently being split and merged. Function templates mergeSort (lines 25–48) and merge (lines 51–98) implement the merge sort algorithm. Function main (lines 100–125) creates an array, populates it with random integers, executes the algorithm (line 120) and displays the sorted array. The output from this program displays the splits and merges performed by merge sort, showing the progress of the sort at each step of the algorithm.

```cpp
 1   // Fig 20.6: Fig20_06.cpp
 2   // Sorting an array into ascending order with merge sort.
 3   #include <array>
 4   #include <ctime>
 5   #include <iostream>
 6   #include <random>
 7   using namespace std;
 8
 9   // display array elements from index low through index high
10   template <typename T, size_t size>
11   void displayElements(const array<T, size>& items,
12      size_t low, size_t high) {
13      for (size_t i{0}; i < items.size() && i < low; ++i) {
14         cout << "   "; // display spaces for alignment
15      }
16
17      for (size_t i{low}; i < items.size() && i <= high; ++i) {
18         cout << items[i] << " "; // display element
19      }
20
21      cout << endl;
22   }
23
24   // split array, sort subarrays and merge subarrays into sorted array
25   template <typename T, size_t size>
26   void mergeSort(array<T, size>& items, size_t low, size_t high) {
27      // test base case; size of array equals 1
28      if ((high - low) >= 1) { // if not base case
29         int middle1{(low + high) / 2}; // calculate middle of array
30         int middle2{middle1 + 1}; // calculate next element over
31
32         // output split step
33         cout << "split:   ";
34         displayElements(items, low, high);
35         cout << "         ";
36         displayElements(items, low, middle1);
37         cout << "         ";
38         displayElements(items, middle2, high);
39         cout << endl;
40
41         // split array in half; sort each half (recursive calls)
42         mergeSort(items, low, middle1); // first half of array
43         mergeSort(items, middle2, high); // second half of array
44
45         // merge two sorted arrays after split calls return
46         merge(items, low, middle1, middle2, high);
47      }
48   }
49
```

Fig. 20.6 | Sorting an array into ascending order with merge sort. (Part 1 of 4.)

```cpp
50  // merge two sorted subarrays into one sorted subarray
51  template <typename T, size_t size>
52  void merge(array<T, size>& items,
53      size_t left, size_t middle1, size_t middle2, size_t right) {
54      size_t leftIndex{left}; // index into left subarray
55      size_t rightIndex{middle2}; // index into right subarray
56      size_t combinedIndex{left}; // index into temporary working array
57      array<T, size> combined; // working array
58
59      // output two subarrays before merging
60      cout << "merge:      ";
61      displayElements(items, left, middle1);
62      cout << "           ";
63      displayElements(items, middle2, right);
64      cout << endl;
65
66      // merge arrays until reaching end of either
67      while (leftIndex <= middle1 && rightIndex <= right) {
68          // place smaller of two current elements into result
69          // and move to next space in array
70          if (items[leftIndex] <= items[rightIndex]) {
71              combined[combinedIndex++] = items[leftIndex++];
72          }
73          else {
74              combined[combinedIndex++] = items[rightIndex++];
75          }
76      }
77
78      if (leftIndex == middle2) { // if at end of left array
79          while (rightIndex <= right) { // copy in rest of right array
80              combined[combinedIndex++] = items[rightIndex++];
81          }
82      }
83      else { // at end of right array
84          while (leftIndex <= middle1) { // copy in rest of left array
85              combined[combinedIndex++] = items[leftIndex++];
86          }
87      }
88
89      // copy values back into original array
90      for (size_t i = left; i <= right; ++i) {
91          items[i] = combined[i];
92      }
93
94      // output merged array
95      cout << "           ";
96      displayElements(items, left, right);
97      cout << endl;
98  }
99
100 int main() {
101     // use the default random-number generation engine to produce
102     // uniformly distributed pseudorandom int values from 10 to 99
```

Fig. 20.6 | Sorting an array into ascending order with merge sort. (Part 2 of 4.)

```
103    default_random_engine engine{
104        static_cast<unsigned int>(time(nullptr))};
105    uniform_int_distribution<unsigned int> randomInt{10, 99};
106
107    const size_t arraySize{10}; // size of array
108    array<int, arraySize> data; // create array
109
110    // fill data with random values
111    for (int &item : data) {
112        item = randomInt(engine);
113    }
114
115    // display data's values before mergeSort
116    cout << "Unsorted array:" << endl;
117    displayElements(data, 0, data.size() - 1);
118    cout << endl;
119
120    mergeSort(data, 0, data.size() - 1); // sort the array data
121
122    // display data's values after mergeSort
123    cout << "Sorted array:" << endl;
124    displayElements(data, 0, data.size() - 1);
125 }
```

```
Unsorted array:
 30 47 22 67 79 18 60 78 26 54

split:     30 47 22 67 79 18 60 78 26 54
           30 47 22 67 79
                         18 60 78 26 54

split:     30 47 22 67 79
           30 47 22
                   67 79

split:     30 47 22
           30 47
                 22

split:     30 47
           30
              47

merge:     30
              47
           30 47

merge:     30 47
                 22
           22 30 47

split:             67 79
                   67
                      79
```

Fig. 20.6 | Sorting an array into ascending order with merge sort. (Part 3 of 4.)

```
merge:                        67
                                 79
                              67 79

merge:     22 30 47
                              67 79
           22 30 47 67 79

split:                        18 60 78 26 54
                              18 60 78
                                       26 54

split:                        18 60 78
                              18 60
                                    78

split:                        18 60
                              18
                                 60

merge:                        18
                                 60
                              18 60

merge:                        18 60
                                    78
                              18 60 78

split:                                26 54
                                      26
                                         54

merge:                                26
                                         54
                                      26 54

merge:                        18 60 78
                                      26 54
                              18 26 54 60 78

merge:     22 30 47 67 79
                              18 26 54 60 78
           18 22 26 30 47 54 60 67 78 79

Sorted array:
 18 22 26 30 47 54 60 67 78 79
```

Fig. 20.6 | Sorting an array into ascending order with merge sort. (Part 4 of 4.)

Function mergeSort

Recursive function mergeSort (lines 25–48) receives as parameters the array to sort and the low and high indices of the range of elements to sort. Line 28 tests the base case. If the high index minus the low index is 0 (i.e., a one-element sub-array), the function simply returns. If the difference between the indices is greater than or equal to 1, the function splits the array in two—lines 29–30 determine the split point. Next, line 42 recursively calls function mergeSort on the array's first half, and line 43 recursively calls function mergeSort on the array's second half. When these two function calls return, each half is sorted. Line 46 calls function merge (lines 51–98) on the two halves to combine the two sorted arrays into one larger sorted array.

Function *merge*

Lines 67–76 in function merge loop until the program reaches the end of either sub-array. Line 70 tests which element at the beginning of the two sub-arrays is smaller. If the element in the left sub-array is smaller or both are equal, line 71 places it in position in the combined array. If the element in the right sub-array is smaller, line 74 places it in position in the combined array. When the while loop completes, one entire sub-array is in the combined array, but the other sub-array still contains data. Line 78 tests whether the left sub-array has reached the end. If so, lines 79–81 fill the combined array with the elements of the right sub-array. If the left sub-array has not reached the end, then the right sub-array must have reached the end, and lines 84–86 fill the combined array with the elements of the left sub-array. Finally, lines 90–92 copy the combined array into the original array.

Efficiency of Merge Sort

Merge sort is a far more efficient algorithm than either insertion sort or selection sort—although that may be difficult to believe when looking at the busy output in Fig. 20.6. Consider the first (nonrecursive) call to function mergeSort (line 120). This results in two recursive calls to function mergeSort with sub-arrays that are each approximately half the original array's size, and a single call to function merge. The call to merge requires, at worst, $n - 1$ comparisons to fill the original array, which is $O(n)$. (Recall that each array element is chosen by comparing one element from each of the sub-arrays.) The two calls to function mergeSort result in four more recursive calls to function mergeSort—each with a sub-array approximately one-quarter the size of the original array—and two calls to function merge. These two calls to function merge each require, at worst, $n/2 - 1$ comparisons, for a total number of comparisons of $O(n)$. This process continues, each call to mergeSort generating two additional calls to mergeSort and a call to merge, until the algorithm has split the array into one-element sub-arrays. At each level, $O(n)$ comparisons are required to merge the sub-arrays. Each level splits the size of the arrays in half, so doubling the size of the array requires one more level. Quadrupling the size of the array requires two more levels. This pattern is logarithmic and results in $\log_2 n$ levels. This results in a total efficiency of $O(n \log n)$.

Summary of Searching and Sorting Algorithm Efficiencies

Figure 20.7 summarizes the searching and sorting algorithms we cover in this chapter and lists the Big O for each. Figure 20.8 lists the Big O categories we've covered in this chapter along with a number of values for n to highlight the differences in the growth rates.

Algorithm	Location	Big O
Searching Algorithms		
Linear search	Section 20.2.1	$O(n)$
Binary search	Section 20.2.2	$O(\log n)$

Fig. 20.7 | Searching and sorting algorithms with Big O values. (Part 1 of 2.)

Algorithm	Location	Big O
Recursive linear search	Exercise 20.8	$O(n)$
Recursive binary search	Exercise 20.9	$O(\log n)$
Sorting Algorithms		
Insertion sort	Section 20.3.1	$O(n^2)$
Selection sort	Section 20.3.2	$O(n^2)$
Merge sort	Section 20.3.3	$O(n \log n)$
Bubble sort	Exercises 20.5–20.6	$O(n^2)$
Quicksort	Exercise 20.10	Worst case: $O(n^2)$ Average case: $O(n \log n)$

Fig. 20.7 | Searching and sorting algorithms with Big O values. (Part 2 of 2.)

n	Approximate decimal value	$O(\log n)$	$O(n)$	$O(n \log n)$	$O(n^2)$
2^{10}	1000	10	2^{10}	$2^{10} \cdot 10$	2^{20}
2^{20}	1,000,000	20	2^{20}	$2^{20} \cdot 20$	2^{40}
2^{30}	1,000,000,000	30	2^{30}	$2^{30} \cdot 30$	2^{60}

Fig. 20.8 | Approximate number of comparisons for common Big O notations.

20.4 Wrap-Up

This chapter discussed searching and sorting data. We began by discussing searching. We first presented the simple, but inefficient linear search algorithm. Then, we presented the binary search algorithm, which is faster but more complex than linear search. Next, we discussed sorting data. You learned two simple, but inefficient sorting techniques—insertion sort and selection sort. Then, we presented the merge sort algorithm, which is more efficient than either the insertion sort or the selection sort. Throughout the chapter we also introduced Big O notation, which helps you express the efficiency of an algorithm by measuring the worst-case runtime of an algorithm. Big O is useful for comparing algorithms so that you can choose the most efficient one. In the next chapter, we discuss typical string-manipulation operations provided by class template `basic_string`. We also introduce string stream-processing capabilities that allow strings to be input from and output to memory.

Summary

Section 20.1 Introduction
• Searching data involves determining whether a **search key** (p. 842) is present in the data and, if so, returning its location.

- **Sorting** (p. 842) involves arranging data into order.
- One way to describe the efficiency of an algorithm is with Big O notation (p. 842), which indicates how much work an algorithm must do to solve a problem.

Section 20.2 Searching Algorithms
- A key difference among searching algorithms is the amount of effort they require to return a result.

Section 20.2.1 Linear Search
- The **linear search** (p. 843) compares each array element with a search key. Because the array is not in any particular order, it's just as likely that the value will be found in the first element as the last. On average, the algorithm must compare the search key with half the array elements. To determine that a value is not in the array, the algorithm must compare the search key to every element in the array.
- Big O describes how an algorithm's effort varies depending on the number of elements in the data.
- An algorithm that's $O(1)$ has a **constant runtime** (p. 844)—the number of comparisons does not grow as the size of the array increases.
- An $O(n)$ algorithm is referred to as having a **linear runtime** (p. 845).
- Big O highlights dominant factors and ignores terms that are unimportant with high values of n.
- Big O notation represents the growth rate of algorithm runtimes, so constants are ignored.
- The linear search algorithm runs in $O(n)$ time.
- In the worst case for linear search every element must be checked to determine whether the search element exists. This occurs if the search key is the last element in the array or is not present.

Section 20.2.2 Binary Search
- **Binary search** (p. 846) is more efficient than linear search, but it requires that the array first be sorted. This is worthwhile only when the array, once sorted, will be searched many times.
- The first iteration of binary search tests the middle element. If this is the search key, the algorithm returns its location. If the search key is less than the middle element, binary search continues with the first half of the array. If the search key is greater than the middle element, binary search continues with the second half. Each iteration tests the middle value of the remaining array and, if the element is not found, eliminates from consideration half of the remaining elements.
- Binary search is more efficient than linear search, because with each comparison it eliminates from consideration half of the elements in the array.
- Binary search runs in $O(\log n)$ (p. 850) time.
- If the size of the array is doubled, binary search requires only one extra comparison to complete.

Section 20.3.1 Insertion Sort
- The first iteration of an insertion sort (p. 851) takes the second element and, if it's less than the first element, swaps it with the first element (i.e., the algorithm *inserts* the second element in front of the first element). The second iteration looks at the third element and inserts it into the correct position with respect to the first two elements, so all three elements are in order. At the ith iteration of this algorithm, the first i elements in the original array will be sorted. For small arrays, the insertion sort is acceptable, but for larger arrays it's inefficient compared to other more sophisticated sorting algorithms.
- The insertion sort algorithm runs in $O(n^2)$ time.

Section 20.3.2 Selection Sort

- The first iteration of selection sort (p. 853) selects the smallest element and swaps it with the first element. The second iteration selects the second-smallest element (which is the smallest remaining element) and swaps it with the second element. This continues until the last iteration selects the second-largest element and swaps it with the second-to-last index, leaving the largest element in the last index. At the ith iteration, the smallest i elements are sorted into the first i elements.
- The selection sort algorithm runs in $O(n^2)$ time.

Section 20.3.3 Merge Sort (A Recursive Implementation)

- **Merge sort** (p. 855) is faster, but more complex to implement, than insertion sort and selection sort.
- The merge sort algorithm sorts an array by splitting the array into two equal-sized sub-arrays, sorting each sub-array and merging the sub-arrays into one larger array.
- Merge sort's base case is an array with one element, which is already sorted. The merge part of merge sort takes two sorted arrays (these could be one-element arrays) and combines them into one larger sorted array.
- Merge sort performs the merge by looking at the first element in each array, which is also the smallest element in each. Merge sort takes the smallest of these and places it in the first element of the larger, sorted array. If there are still elements in the sub-array, merge sort looks at the second element in that sub-array (which is now the smallest element remaining) and compares it to the first element in the other sub-array. Merge sort continues this process until the larger array is filled.
- In the worst case, the first call to merge sort has to make $O(n)$ comparisons to fill the n slots in the final array.
- The merging portion of the merge sort algorithm is performed on two sub-arrays, each of approximately size $n/2$. Creating each of these sub-arrays requires $n/2 - 1$ comparisons for each sub-array, or $O(n)$ comparisons total. This pattern continues, as each level works on twice as many arrays, but each is half the size of the previous array.
- Similar to binary search, this halving results in log n levels, each level requiring $O(n)$ comparisons, for a total efficiency of $O(n \log n)$ (p. 861).

Self-Review Exercises

20.1 Fill in the blanks in each of the following statements:
  a) A selection sort application would take approximately _____ times as long to run on a 128-element array as on a 32-element array.
  b) The efficiency of merge sort is _____.

20.2 What key aspect of both the binary search and the merge sort accounts for the logarithmic portion of their respective Big Os?

20.3 In what sense is the insertion sort superior to the merge sort? In what sense is the merge sort superior to the insertion sort?

20.4 In the text, we say that after the merge sort splits the array into two sub-arrays, it then sorts these two sub-arrays and merges them. Why might someone be puzzled by our statement that "it then sorts these two sub-arrays"?

Answers to Self-Review Exercises

20.1 a) 16, because an $O(n^2)$ algorithm takes 16 times as long to sort four times as much information. b) $O(n \log n)$.

20.2   Both of these algorithms incorporate "halving"—somehow reducing something by half. The binary search eliminates from consideration half of the array after each comparison. The merge sort splits the array in half each time it's called.

20.3   The insertion sort is easier to understand and to implement than the merge sort. The merge sort is far more efficient ($O(n \log n)$) than the insertion sort ($O(n^2)$).

20.4   In a sense, it does not really sort these two sub-arrays. It simply keeps splitting the original array in half until it provides a one-element sub-array, which is, of course, sorted. It then builds up the original two sub-arrays by merging these one-element arrays to form larger sub-arrays, which are then merged, and so on.

Exercises

20.5   *(Bubble Sort)* Implement the bubble sort algorithm—another simple yet inefficient sorting technique. It's called bubble sort or sinking sort because smaller values gradually "bubble" their way to the top of the array (i.e., toward the first element) like air bubbles rising in water, while the larger values sink to the bottom (end) of the array. The technique uses nested loops to make several passes through the array. Each pass compares successive pairs of elements. If a pair is in increasing order (or the values are equal), the bubble sort leaves the values as they are. If a pair is in decreasing order, the bubble sort swaps their values in the array.

The first pass compares the first two element values of the array and swaps them if necessary. It then compares the second and third element values in the array. The end of this pass compares the last two element values in the array and swaps them if necessary. After one pass, the largest value will be in the last element. After two passes, the largest two values will be in the last two elements. Explain why bubble sort is an $O(n^2)$ algorithm.

20.6   *(Enhanced Bubble Sort)* Make the following simple modifications to improve the performance of the bubble sort you developed in Exercise 20.5:

a) After the first pass, the largest value is guaranteed to be in the highest-numbered element of the array; after the second pass, the two highest values are "in place"; and so on. Instead of making nine comparisons (for a 10-element array) on every pass, modify the bubble sort to make only the eight necessary comparisons on the second pass, seven on the third pass, and so on.

b) The data in the array may already be in the proper order or near-proper order, so why make nine passes (of a 10-element array) if fewer will suffice? Modify the sort to check at the end of each pass whether any swaps have been made. If none have been made, the data must already be in the proper order, so the program should terminate. If swaps have been made, at least one more pass is needed.

20.7   *(Bucket Sort)* A bucket sort begins with a one-dimensional array of positive integers to be sorted and a two-dimensional array of integers with rows indexed from 0 to 9 and columns indexed from 0 to $n - 1$, where n is the number of values to be sorted. Each row of the two-dimensional array is referred to as a *bucket*. Write a class named BucketSort containing a function called sort that operates as follows:

a) Place each value of the one-dimensional array into a row of the bucket array, based on the value's "ones" (rightmost) digit. For example, 97 is placed in row 7, 3 is placed in row 3 and 100 is placed in row 0. This procedure is called a *distribution pass*.

b) Loop through the bucket array row by row, and copy the values back to the original array. This procedure is called a *gathering pass*. The new order of the preceding values in the one-dimensional array is 100, 3 and 97.

c) Repeat this process for each subsequent digit position (tens, hundreds, thousands, etc.).

On the second (tens digit) pass, 100 is placed in row 0, 3 is placed in row 0 (because 3 has no tens digit) and 97 is placed in row 9. After the gathering pass, the order of the values in the one-dimensional array is 100, 3 and 97. On the third (hundreds digit) pass, 100 is placed in row 1, 3 is placed in row 0 and 97 is placed in row 0 (after the 3). After this last gathering pass, the original array is in sorted order.

Note that the two-dimensional array of buckets is 10 times the length of the integer array being sorted. This sorting technique provides better performance than a bubble sort, but requires much more memory—the bubble sort requires space for only one additional element of data. This comparison is an example of the space–time trade-off: The bucket sort uses more memory than the bubble sort, but performs better. This version of the bucket sort requires copying all the data back to the original array on each pass. Another possibility is to create a second two-dimensional bucket array and repeatedly swap the data between the two bucket arrays.

20.8 (*Recursive Linear Search*) Modify Fig. 20.2 to use recursive function recursiveLinearSearch to perform a linear search of the array. The function should receive the array, the search key and starting index as arguments. If the search key is found, return its index in the array; otherwise, return –1. Each call to the recursive function should check one element value in the array.

20.9 (*Recursive Binary Search*) Modify Fig. 20.3 to use recursive function recursiveBinarySearch to perform a binary search of the array. The function should receive the array, the search key, starting index and ending index as arguments. If the search key is found, return its index in the array. If the search key is not found, return –1.

20.10 (*Quicksort*) The recursive sorting technique called quicksort uses the following basic algorithm for a one-dimensional array of values:

a) *Partitioning Step*: Take the first element of the unsorted array and determine its final location in the sorted array (i.e., all values to the left of the element in the array are less than the element's value, and all values to the right of the element in the array are greater than the element's value—we show how to do this below). We now have one value in its proper location and two unsorted sub-arrays.

b) *Recursion Step*: Perform the *Partitioning Step* on each unsorted sub-array.

Each time *Step 1* is performed on a sub-array, another element is placed in its final location of the sorted array, and two unsorted sub-arrays are created. When a sub-array consists of one element, that sub-array must be sorted; therefore, that element is in its final location.

The basic algorithm seems simple enough, but how do we determine the final position of the first element of each sub-array? As an example, consider the following set of values (the element in bold is the partitioning element—it will be placed in its final location in the sorted array):

> **37**   2   6   4   89   8   10   12   68   45

Starting from the rightmost element of the array, compare each element with **37** until an element less than **37** is found. Then swap **37** and that element. The first element less than **37** is 12, so **37** and 12 are swapped. The values now reside in the array as follows:

> *12*   2   6   4   89   8   10   **37**   68   45

Element 12 is in italics to indicate that it was just swapped with **37**.

Starting from the left of the array, but beginning with the element after 12, compare each element with **37** until an element greater than **37** is found. Then swap **37** and that element. The first element greater than **37** is 89, so **37** and 89 are swapped. The values now reside in the array as follows:

> 12   2   6   4   **37**   8   10   *89*   68   45

Starting from the right, but beginning with the element before 89, compare each element with **37** until an element less than **37** is found. Then swap **37** and that element. The first element less than **37** is 10, so **37** and 10 are swapped. The values now reside in the array as follows:

12   2   6   4   *10*   8   **37**   89   68   45

Starting from the left, but beginning with the element after 10, compare each element with **37** until an element greater than **37** is found. Then swap **37** and that element. There are no more elements greater than **37**, so when we compare **37** with itself, we know that **37** has been placed in its final location of the sorted array.

Once the partition has been applied to the array, there are two unsorted sub-arrays. The sub-array with values less than 37 contains 12, 2, 6, 4, 10 and 8. The sub-array with values greater than 37 contains 89, 68 and 45. The sort continues with both sub-arrays being partitioned in the same manner as the original array.

Based on the preceding discussion, write recursive function `quickSort` to sort a single-subscripted integer array. The function should receive as arguments an integer array, a starting subscript and an ending subscript. Function `partition` should be called by `quickSort` to perform the partitioning step.

Class **string** and String Stream Processing: A Deeper Look

21

Objectives

In this chapter you'll:

- Manipulate **string** objects.
- Determine **string** characteristics.
- Find, replace and insert characters in **string**s.
- Convert **string** objects to pointer-based strings and vice versa.
- Use **string** iterators.
- Perform input from and output to **string**s in memory.
- Use C++11 numeric conversion functions.

21.1 Introduction[1]

The class template basic_string provides typical string-manipulation operations such as copying, searching, etc. The template definition and all support facilities are defined in namespace std; these include the typedef statement

```
typedef basic_string<char> string;
```

that creates the alias type string for basic_string<char>. A typedef is also provided for the wchar_t type (wstring). Type wchar_t[2] stores characters (e.g., two-byte characters, four-byte characters, etc.) for supporting other character sets. We use string exclusively throughout this chapter. To use strings, include header <string>.

Initializing a string Object
A string object can be initialized with a constructor argument as in

```
string text{"Hello"}; // creates a string from a const char*
```

which creates a string containing the characters in "Hello", or with two constructor arguments as in

```
string name{8, 'x'}; // string of 8 'x' characters
```

which creates a string containing eight 'x' characters. Class string also provides a *default constructor* (which creates an *empty* string) and a *copy constructor*. A string also can be initialized in its definition as in

```
string month = "March"; // same as: string month{"March"};
```

Remember that = in the preceding declaration is *not* an assignment; rather it's an *implicit call to the string class constructor*, which does the conversion.

---

1. Various string features we discuss in this chapter were also presented in Chapter 21. We kept all the features in this chapter for completeness and for people who may read the chapters out of order.
2. Type wchar_t commonly is used to represent Unicode®, but wchar_t's size is not specified by the standard. C++11 also has types char16_t and char32_t for Unicode support. The Unicode Standard outlines a specification to produce consistent encoding of the world's characters and *symbols*. To learn more about the Unicode Standard, visit www.unicode.org.

strings Are Not Necessarily Null Terminated

Unlike pointer-based char* strings, string objects are not necessarily null terminated. The C++ standard document provides only a description of the capabilities of class string—implementation is platform dependent.

Length of a string

The length of a string can be retrieved with member function size and with member function length . The subscript operator, [] (which does not perform bounds checking), can be used with strings to access and modify individual characters. A string object has a first subscript of 0 and a last subscript of size() - 1.

Processing strings

Most string member functions take as arguments a *starting subscript location* and the number of characters on which to operate.

string I/O

The stream extraction operator (>>) is overloaded to support strings. The statements

```
string stringObject;
cin >> stringObject;
```

declare a string object and read a string from cin. Input is delimited by whitespace characters. When a delimiter is encountered, the input operation is terminated. Function getline also is overloaded for strings. Assuming string1 is a string, the statement

```
getline(cin, string1);
```

reads a string from the keyboard into string1. Input is delimited by a newline ('\n'), so getLine can read a line of text into a string object. You can specify an *alternate delimiter* as the optional third argument to getline.

Validating Input

In earlier chapters, we mentioned the importance of validating user input in industrial-strength code. The capabilities presented in this chapter—and the regular-expression capabilities shown in Section 24.14—are frequently used to perform validation.

21.2 string Assignment and Concatenation

Figure 21.1 demonstrates *string assignment* and *concatenation*. Line 4 includes header <string> for class string. The strings string1, string2 and string3 are created in lines 8–10. Line 12 assigns the value of string1 to string2. After the assignment takes place, string2 is a copy of string1. Line 13 uses member function assign to copy string1 into string3. A separate copy is made (i.e., string1 and string3 are independent objects). Class string also provides an overloaded version of member function assign that copies a specified number of characters, as in

```
targetString.assign(sourceString, start, numberOfCharacters);
```

where sourceString is the string to be copied, start is the starting subscript and numberOfCharacters is the number of characters to copy.

```cpp
1  // Fig. 21.1: Fig21_01.cpp
2  // Demonstrating string assignment and concatenation.
3  #include <iostream>
4  #include <string>
5  using namespace std;
6
7  int main() {
8     string string1{"cat"};
9     string string2; // initialized to the empty string
10    string string3; // initialized to the empty string
11
12    string2 = string1; // assign string1 to string2
13    string3.assign(string1); // assign string1 to string3
14    cout << "string1: " << string1 << "\nstring2: " << string2
15       << "\nstring3: " << string3 << "\n\n";
16
17    // modify string2 and string3
18    string2[0] = string3[2] = 'r';
19
20    cout << "After modification of string2 and string3:\n" << "string1: "
21       << string1 << "\nstring2: " << string2 << "\nstring3: ";
22
23    // demonstrating member function at
24    for (size_t i{0}; i < string3.size(); ++i) {
25       cout << string3.at(i); // can throw out_of_range exception
26    }
27
28    // declare string4 and string5
29    string string4{string1 + "apult"}; // concatenation
30    string string5; // initialized to the empty string
31
32    // overloaded +=
33    string3 += "pet"; // create "carpet"
34    string1.append("acomb"); // create "catacomb"
35
36    // append subscript locations 4 through end of string1 to
37    // create string "comb" (string5 was initially empty)
38    string5.append(string1, 4, string1.size() - 4);
39
40    cout << "\n\nAfter concatenation:\nstring1: " << string1
41       << "\nstring2: " << string2 << "\nstring3: " << string3
42       << "\nstring4: " << string4 << "\nstring5: " << string5 << endl;
43 }
```

```
string1: cat
string2: cat
string3: cat

After modification of string2 and string3:
string1: cat
string2: rat
string3: car
```

Fig. 21.1 | Demonstrating string assignment and concatenation. (Part 1 of 2.)

```
After concatenation:
string1: catacomb
string2: rat
string3: carpet
string4: catapult
string5: comb
```

Fig. 21.1 | Demonstrating string assignment and concatenation. (Part 2 of 2.)

Line 18 uses the subscript operator to assign 'r' to string3[2] (forming "car") and to assign 'r' to string2[0] (forming "rat"). The strings are then output.

Lines 24–26 output the contents of string3 one character at a time using member function at. Member function at provides checked access (or range checking); i.e., going past the end of the string throws an out_of_range exception. *The subscript operator, [], does not provide checked access.* This is consistent with its use on arrays. Note that you can also iterate through the characters in a string using C++11's range-based for as in

```
for (char c : string3) {
   cout << c;
}
```

11

which ensures that you do not access any elements outside the string's bounds.

Common Programming Error 21.1

Accessing an element outside a string's bounds using the subscript operator is an unreported logic error.

String string4 is declared (line 29) and initialized to the result of concatenating string1 and "apult" using the *overloaded + operator*, which for class string denotes *concatenation*. Line 33 uses the *overloaded addition assignment operator, +=,* to concatenate string3 and "pet". Line 34 uses member function append to concatenate string1 and "acomb".

Line 38 appends the string "comb" to empty string string5. This member function is passed the string (string1) to retrieve characters from, the starting subscript in the string (4) and the number of characters to append (the value returned by string1.size() - 4).

21.3 Comparing strings

Class string provides member functions for comparing strings. Figure 21.2 demonstrates class string's comparison capabilities.

```
1   // Fig. 21.2: Fig21_02.cpp
2   // Comparing strings.
3   #include <iostream>
4   #include <string>
5   using namespace std;
```

Fig. 21.2 | Comparing strings. (Part 1 of 3.)

```cpp
 6
 7   int main() {
 8      string string1{"Testing the comparison functions."};
 9      string string2{"Hello"};
10      string string3{"stinger"};
11      string string4{string2}; // "Hello"
12
13      cout << "string1: " << string1 << "\nstring2: " << string2
14         << "\nstring3: " << string3 << "\nstring4: " << string4 << "\n\n";
15
16      // comparing string1 and string4
17      if (string1 == string4) {
18         cout << "string1 == string4\n";
19      }
20      else if (string1 > string4) {
21            cout << "string1 > string4\n";
22      }
23      else { // string1 < string4
24         cout << "string1 < string4\n";
25      }
26
27      // comparing string1 and string2
28      int result{string1.compare(string2)};
29
30      if (result == 0) {
31         cout << "string1.compare(string2) == 0\n";
32      }
33      else if (result > 0) {
34         cout << "string1.compare(string2) > 0\n";
35      }
36      else { // result < 0
37         cout << "string1.compare(string2) < 0\n";
38      }
39
40      // comparing string1 (elements 2-5) and string3 (elements 0-5)
41      result = string1.compare(2, 5, string3, 0, 5);
42
43      if (result == 0) {
44         cout << "string1.compare(2, 5, string3, 0, 5) == 0\n";
45      }
46      else if (result > 0) {
47         cout << "string1.compare(2, 5, string3, 0, 5) > 0\n";
48      }
49      else { // result < 0
50         cout << "string1.compare(2, 5, string3, 0, 5) < 0\n";
51      }
52
53      // comparing string2 and string4
54      result = string4.compare(0, string2.size(), string2);
55
56      if (result == 0) {
57         cout << "string4.compare(0, string2.size(), string2) == 0\n";
58      }
```

Fig. 21.2 | Comparing strings. (Part 2 of 3.)

```
59         else if (result > 0) {
60             cout << "string4.compare(0, string2.size(), string2) > 0\n";
61         }
62         else { // result < 0
63             cout << "string4.compare(0, string2.size(), string2) < 0\n";
64         }
65
66         // comparing string2 and string4
67         result = string2.compare(0, 3, string4);
68
69         if (result == 0) {
70             cout << "string2.compare(0, 3, string4) == 0\n";
71         }
72         else if (result > 0) {
73             cout << "string2.compare(0, 3, string4) > 0\n";
74         }
75         else { // result < 0
76             cout << "string2.compare(0, 3, string4) < 0"\n;
77         }
78     }
```

```
string1: Testing the comparison functions.
string2: Hello
string3: stinger
string4: Hello

string1 > string4
string1.compare(string2) > 0
string1.compare(2, 5, string3, 0, 5) == 0
string4.compare(0, string2.size(), string2) == 0
string2.compare(0, 3, string4) < 0
```

Fig. 21.2 | Comparing strings. (Part 3 of 3.)

The program declares four strings (lines 8–11) and outputs each (lines 13–14). Line 17 tests string1 against string4 for equality using the *overloaded equality operator*. If the condition is true, "string1 == string4" is output. If the condition is false, the condition in line 20 is tested. All the string class overloaded relational and equality operator functions return bool values.

Line 28 uses string member function compare to compare string1 to string2. Variable result is assigned 0 if the strings are equivalent, a *positive number* if string1 is lexicographically greater than string2 or a *negative number* if string1 is *lexicographically* less than string2. When we say that a string is *lexicographically* less than another, we mean that the compare member function uses the numerical values of the characters (see Appendix B, ASCII Character Set) in each string to determine that the first string is less than the second. A lexicon is a dictionary. Because a string starting with 'T' is considered lexicographically greater than a string starting with 'H', result is assigned a value greater than 0, as confirmed by the output.

Line 41 compares portions of string1 and string3 using an *overloaded* version of member function compare. The first two arguments (2 and 5) specify the *starting subscript* and *length* of the portion of string1 ("sting") to compare with string3. The third argument is the comparison `string`. The last two arguments (0 and 5) are the *starting subscript* and *length* of the portion of the comparison `string` being compared (also "sting"). The value assigned to `result` is 0 for equality, a positive number if `string1` is *lexicographically* greater than `string3` or a negative number if `string1` is *lexicographically* less than `string3`. The two pieces being compared here are identical, so `result` is assigned 0.

Line 54 uses another *overloaded* version of function `compare` to compare `string4` and `string2`. The first two arguments are the same—the *starting subscript* and *length*. The last argument is the comparison `string`. The value returned is also the same—0 for equality, a positive number if `string4` is *lexicographically* greater than `string2` or a negative number if `string4` is *lexicographically* less than `string2`. Because the two pieces of `strings` being compared here are identical, `result` is assigned 0.

Line 67 calls member function `compare` to compare the first 3 characters in `string2` to `string4`. Because "Hel" is less than "Hello", a value less than zero is returned.

21.4 Substrings

Class `string` provides member function `substr` for retrieving a substring from a `string`. The result is a new `string` object that's copied from the source `string`. Figure 21.3 demonstrates `substr`. The program declares and initializes a `string` at line 8. Line 12 uses member function `substr` to retrieve a substring from `string1`. The first argument specifies the *beginning subscript* of the desired substring; the second argument specifies the substring's *length*.

```
1   // Fig. 21.3: Fig21_03.cpp
2   // Demonstrating string member function substr.
3   #include <iostream>
4   #include <string>
5   using namespace std;
6
7   int main() {
8      string string1{"The airplane landed on time."};
9
10     // retrieve substring "plane" which
11     // begins at subscript 7 and consists of 5 characters
12     cout << string1.substr(7, 5) << endl;
13  }
```

```
plane
```

Fig. 21.3 | Demonstrating `string` member function `substr`.

21.5 Swapping `strings`

Class `string` provides member function `swap` for swapping strings. Figure 21.4 swaps two strings. Lines 8–9 declare and initialize `strings` `first` and `second`. Each `string` is then output. Line 14 uses `string` member function `swap` to swap the values of `first` and `second`. The two `strings` are printed again to confirm that they were indeed swapped. The `string` member function `swap` is useful for implementing programs that sort strings.

```
1   // Fig. 21.4: Fig21_04.cpp
2   // Using the swap function to swap two strings.
3   #include <iostream>
4   #include <string>
5   using namespace std;
6
7   int main() {
8      string first{"one"};
9      string second{"two"};
10
11     // output strings
12     cout << "Before swap:\n first: " << first << "\nsecond: " << second;
13
14     first.swap(second); // swap strings
15
16     cout << "\n\nAfter swap:\n first: " << first
17        << "\nsecond: " << second << endl;
18  }
```

```
Before swap:
 first: one
second: two

After swap:
 first: two
second: one
```

Fig. 21.4 | Using the swap function to swap two strings.

21.6 string Characteristics

Class string provides member functions for gathering information about a string's *size*, *length*, *capacity*, *maximum length* and other characteristics. A string's *size* or *length* is the number of characters currently stored in the string. A string's capacity is the number of characters that can be stored in the string without allocating more memory. The capacity of a string must be at least equal to the current size of the string, though it can be greater. The exact capacity of a string depends on the implementation. The maximum size is the largest possible size a string can have. If this value is exceeded, a length_error exception is thrown. Figure 21.5 demonstrates string class member functions for determining various characteristics of strings.

```
1   // Fig. 21.5: Fig21_05.cpp
2   // Printing string characteristics.
3   #include <iostream>
4   #include <string>
5   using namespace std;
6
7   void printStatistics(const string&);
8
```

Fig. 21.5 | Printing string characteristics. (Part 1 of 3.)

```
9   int main() {
10      string string1; // empty string
11
12      cout << "Statistics before input:\n" << boolalpha;
13      printStatistics(string1);
14
15      // read in only "tomato" from "tomato soup"
16      cout << "\n\nEnter a string: ";
17      cin >> string1; // delimited by whitespace
18      cout << "The string entered was: " << string1;
19
20      cout << "\nStatistics after input:\n";
21      printStatistics(string1);
22
23      // read in "soup"
24      cin >> string1; // delimited by whitespace
25      cout << "\n\nThe remaining string is: " << string1 << endl;
26      printStatistics(string1);
27
28      // append 46 characters to string1
29      string1 += "1234567890abcdefghijklmnopqrstuvwxyz1234567890";
30      cout << "\n\nstring1 is now: " << string1 << endl;
31      printStatistics(string1);
32
33      // add 10 elements to string1
34      string1.resize(string1.size() + 10);
35      cout << "\n\nStats after resizing by (length + 10):\n";
36      printStatistics(string1);
37      cout << endl;
38   }
39
40   // display string statistics
41   void printStatistics(const string& stringRef) {
42      cout << "capacity: " << stringRef.capacity() << "\nmax size: "
43         << stringRef.max_size() << "\nsize: " << stringRef.size()
44         << "\nlength: " << stringRef.size()
45         << "\nempty: " << stringRef.empty();
46   }
```

```
Statistics before input:
capacity: 15
max size: 4294967294
size: 0
length: 0
empty: true

Enter a string: tomato soup
The string entered was: tomato
Statistics after input:
capacity: 15
max size: 4294967294
```

Fig. 21.5 | Printing string characteristics. (Part 2 of 3.)

```
size: 6
length: 6
empty: false

The remaining string is: soup
capacity: 15
max size: 4294967294
size: 4
length: 4
empty: false

string1 is now: soup1234567890abcdefghijklmnopqrstuvwxyz1234567890
capacity: 63
max size: 4294967294
size: 50
length: 50
empty: false

Stats after resizing by (length + 10):
capacity: 63
max size: 4294967294
size: 60
length: 60
empty: false
```

Fig. 21.5 | Printing string characteristics. (Part 3 of 3.)

The program declares empty string string1 (line 10) and passes it to function printStatistics (line 13). Function printStatistics (lines 41–46) takes a reference to a const string as an argument and outputs the capacity (using member function capacity), maximum size (using member function max_size), size (using member function size), length (using member function size) and whether the string is empty (using member function empty). The initial call to printStatistics indicates that the initial values for the size and length of string1 are 0.

The size and length of 0 indicate that there are no characters stored in string. Recall that the *size* and *length* are always identical. In this implementation, the maximum size is 4,294,967,294. Object string1 is an empty string, so function empty returns true.

Line 17 inputs a string. In this example, "tomato soup" is input. Because a space character is a delimiter, only "tomato" is stored in string1; however, "soup" remains in the input buffer. Line 21 calls function printStatistics to output statistics for string1. Notice in the output that the length is 6 and the capacity is 15.

Line 24 reads "soup" from the input buffer and stores it in string1, thereby replacing "tomato". Line 27 passes string1 to printStatistics.

Line 29 uses the *overloaded* += operator to concatenate a 46-character-long string to string1. Line 31 passes string1 to printStatistics. The capacity has increased to 63 elements and the length is now 50.

Line 34 uses member function resize to increase the length of string1 by 10 characters. The additional elements are set to null characters. The output shows that the capacity has *not* changed and the length is now 60.

21.7 Finding Substrings and Characters in a string

Class string provides const member functions for finding substrings and characters in a string. Figure 21.6 demonstrates the find functions.

```cpp
1   // Fig. 21.6: Fig21_06.cpp
2   // Demonstrating the string find member functions.
3   #include <iostream>
4   #include <string>
5   using namespace std;
6
7   int main() {
8      string string1{"noon is 12 pm; midnight is not."};
9      int location;
10
11     // find "is" at location 5 and 24
12     cout << "Original string:\n" << string1
13        << "\n\n(find) \"is\" was found at: " << string1.find("is")
14        << "\n(rfind) \"is\" was found at: " << string1.rfind("is");
15
16     // find 'o' at location 1
17     location = string1.find_first_of("misop");
18     cout << "\n\n(find_first_of) found '" << string1[location]
19        << "' from the group \"misop\" at: " << location;
20
21     // find 'o' at location 28
22     location = string1.find_last_of("misop");
23     cout << "\n\n(find_last_of) found '" << string1[location]
24        << "' from the group \"misop\" at: " << location;
25
26     // find '1' at location 8
27     location = string1.find_first_not_of("noi spm");
28     cout << "\n\n(find_first_not_of) '" << string1[location]
29        << "' is not contained in \"noi spm\" and was found at: "
30        << location;
31
32     // find '.' at location 13
33     location = string1.find_first_not_of("12noi spm");
34     cout << "\n\n(find_first_not_of) '" << string1[location]
35        << "' is not contained in \"12noi spm\" and was "
36        << "found at: " << location << endl;
37
38     // search for characters not in string1
39     location = string1.find_first_not_of(
40        "noon is 12 pm; midnight is not.");
41     cout << "\nfind_first_not_of(\"noon is 12 pm; midnight is not.\")"
42        << " returned: " << location << endl;
43  }
```

```
Original string:
noon is 12 pm; midnight is not.
```

Fig. 21.6 | Demonstrating the string find member functions. (Part 1 of 2.)

```
(find) "is" was found at: 5
(rfind) "is" was found at: 24

(find_first_of) found 'o' from the group "misop" at: 1

(find_last_of) found 'o' from the group "misop" at: 28

(find_first_not_of) '1' is not contained in "noi spm" and was found at: 8

(find_first_not_of) '.' is not contained in "12noi spm" and was found at: 13

find_first_not_of("noon is 12 pm; midnight is not.") returned: -1
```

Fig. 21.6 | Demonstrating the string find member functions. (Part 2 of 2.)

String string1 is declared and initialized in line 8. Line 13 attempts to find "is" in string1 using function find. If "is" is found, the subscript of the starting location of that string is returned. If the string is not found, the value string::npos (a public static constant defined in class string) is returned. This value is returned by the string find-related functions to indicate that a substring or character was not found in the string.

Line 14 uses member function rfind to search string1 *backward* (i.e., *right-to-left*). If "is" is found, the subscript location is returned. If the string is not found, string::npos is returned. [*Note:* The rest of the find functions presented in this section return the same type unless otherwise noted.]

Line 17 uses member function find_first_of to locate the *first* occurrence in string1 of any character in "misop". The searching is done from the beginning of string1. The character 'o' is found in element 1.

Line 22 uses member function find_last_of to find the *last* occurrence in string1 of any character in "misop". The searching is done from the end of string1. The character 'o' is found in element 28.

Line 27 uses member function find_first_not_of to find the *first* character in string1 *not* contained in "noi spm". The character '1' is found in element 8. Searching is done from the beginning of string1.

Line 33 uses member function find_first_not_of to find the *first* character *not* contained in "12noi spm". The character '.' is found in element 13. Searching is done from the beginning of string1.

Lines 39–40 use member function find_first_not_of to find the *first* character *not* contained in "noon is 12 pm; midnight is not.". In this case, the string being searched contains every character specified in the string argument. Because a character was not found, string::npos (which has the value –1 in this case) is returned.

21.8 Replacing Characters in a string

Figure 21.7 demonstrates string member functions for *replacing* and *erasing* characters. Lines 9–13 declare and initialize string string1. Line 19 uses string member function erase to erase everything from (and including) the character in position 62 to the end of string1. [*Note:* Each newline character occupies one character in the string.]

```
1   // Fig. 21.7: Fig21_07.cpp
2   // Demonstrating string member functions erase and replace.
3   #include <iostream>
4   #include <string>
5   using namespace std;
6
7   int main() {
8      // compiler concatenates all parts into one string
9      string string1{"The values in any left subtree"
10        "\nare less than the value in the"
11        "\nparent node and the values in"
12        "\nany right subtree are greater"
13        "\nthan the value in the parent node"};
14
15     cout << "Original string:\n" << string1 << endl << endl;
16
17     // remove all characters from (and including) location 62
18     // through the end of string1
19     string1.erase(62);
20
21     // output new string
22     cout << "Original string after erase:\n" << string1
23        << "\nAfter first replacement:\n";
24
25     size_t position = string1.find(" "); // find first space
26
27     // replace all spaces with period
28     while (position != string::npos) {
29        string1.replace(position, 1, ".");
30        position = string1.find(" ", position + 1);
31     }
32
33     cout << string1 << "\nAfter second replacement:\n";
34
35     position = string1.find("."); // find first period
36
37     // replace all periods with two semicolons
38     // NOTE: this will overwrite characters
39     while (position != string::npos) {
40        string1.replace(position, 2, "xxxxx;;yyy", 5, 2);
41        position = string1.find(".", position + 1);
42     }
43
44     cout << string1 << endl;
45  }
```

```
Original string:
The values in any left subtree
are less than the value in the
parent node and the values in
any right subtree are greater
than the value in the parent node
```

Fig. 21.7 | Demonstrating `string` member functions erase and replace. (Part 1 of 2.)

```
Original string after erase:
The values in any left subtree
are less than the value in the

After first replacement:
The.values.in.any.left.subtree
are.less.than.the.value.in.the

After second replacement:
The;;alues;;n;;ny;;eft;;ubtree
are;;ess;;han;;he;;alue;;n;;he
```

Fig. 21.7 | Demonstrating string member functions erase and replace. (Part 2 of 2.)

Lines 25–31 use find to locate each occurrence of the space character. Each space is then *replaced* with a period by a call to string member function replace. Function replace takes three arguments: the *subscript* of the character in the string at which replacement should *begin*, the *number of characters to replace* and the *replacement string*. Member function find returns string::npos when the search character is *not found*. In line 30, 1 is added to position to continue searching at the location of the *next* character.

Lines 35–42 use function find to find every period and another overloaded function replace to replace every period and its following character with two semicolons. The arguments passed to this version of replace are the subscript of the element where the replace operation begins, the number of characters to replace, a replacement character string from which a *substring* is selected to use as replacement characters, the element in the character string where the replacement substring begins and the number of characters in the replacement character string to use.

21.9 Inserting Characters into a string

Class string provides member functions for *inserting* characters into a string. Figure 21.8 demonstrates the string insert capabilities.

```cpp
 1   // Fig. 21.8: Fig21_08.cpp
 2   // Demonstrating class string insert member functions.
 3   #include <iostream>
 4   #include <string>
 5   using namespace std;
 6
 7   int main() {
 8      string string1{"beginning end"};
 9      string string2{"middle "};
10      string string3{"12345678"};
11      string string4{"xx"};
12
13      cout << "Initial strings:\nstring1: " << string1
14         << "\nstring2: " << string2 << "\nstring3: " << string3
15         << "\nstring4: " << string4 << "\n\n";
```

Fig. 21.8 | Demonstrating class string insert member functions. (Part 1 of 2.)

```
16
17      // insert "middle" at location 10 in string1
18      string1.insert(10, string2);
19
20      // insert "xx" at location 3 in string3
21      string3.insert(3, string4, 0, string::npos);
22
23      cout << "Strings after insert:\nstring1: " << string1
24         << "\nstring2: " << string2 << "\nstring3: " << string3
25         << "\nstring4: " << string4 << endl;
26   }
```

```
Initial strings:
string1: beginning end
string2: middle
string3: 12345678
string4: xx

Strings after insert:
string1: beginning middle end
string2: middle
string3: 123xx45678
string4: xx
```

Fig. 21.8 | Demonstrating class `string` `insert` member functions. (Part 2 of 2.)

The program declares, initializes then outputs `string`s `string1`, `string2`, `string3` and `string4`. Line 18 uses `string` member function *insert* to insert `string2`'s content before element 10 of `string1`.

Line 21 uses `insert` to insert `string4` before `string3`'s element 3. The last two arguments specify the *starting* and *last* element of `string4` that should be inserted. Using `string::npos` causes the *entire* string to be inserted.

21.10 Conversion to Pointer-Based `char*` Strings

You can convert `string` class objects to pointer-based strings. As mentioned earlier, unlike pointer-based strings, `string`s are *not necessarily null terminated*. These conversion functions are useful when a given function takes a pointer-based string as an argument. Figure 21.9 demonstrates conversion of `string`s to pointer-based strings.

```
1    // Fig. 21.9: Fig21_09.cpp
2    // Converting strings to pointer-based strings and character arrays.
3    #include <iostream>
4    #include <string>
5    using namespace std;
6
7    int main() {
8       string string1{"STRINGS"}; // string constructor with char* arg
9       const char* ptr1{nullptr}; // initialize ptr1
```

Fig. 21.9 | Converting `string`s to pointer-based strings and character arrays. (Part 1 of 2.)

```
10      size_t length{string1.size()};
11      char* ptr2{new char[length + 1]}; // including null
12
13      // copy characters from string1 into allocated memory
14      string1.copy(ptr2, length, 0); // copy string1 to ptr2 char*
15      ptr2[length] = '\0'; // add null terminator
16
17      cout << "string string1 is " << string1
18          << "\nstring1 converted to a pointer-based string is "
19          << string1.c_str() << "\nptr1 is ";
20
21      // Assign to pointer ptr1 the const char* returned by
22      // function data(). NOTE: this is a potentially dangerous
23      // assignment. If string1 is modified, pointer ptr1 can
24      // become invalid.
25      ptr1 = string1.data(); // non-null terminated char array
26
27      // output each character using pointer
28      for (size_t i{0}; i < length; ++i) {
29          cout << *(ptr1 + i); // use pointer arithmetic
30      }
31
32      cout << "\nptr2 is " << ptr2 << endl;
33      delete [] ptr2; // reclaim dynamically allocated memory
34  }
```

```
string string1 is STRINGS
string1 converted to a pointer-based string is STRINGS
ptr1 is STRINGS
ptr2 is STRINGS
```

Fig. 21.9 | Converting strings to pointer-based strings and character arrays. (Part 2 of 2.)

The program declares a string, a size_t and two char pointers (lines 8–11). The string string1 is initialized to "STRINGS", ptr1 is initialized to nullptr and length is initialized to the length of string1. Memory of sufficient size to hold a pointer-based string equivalent of string string1 is allocated dynamically and attached to char pointer ptr2.

Line 14 uses string member function copy to copy object string1 into the char array pointed to by ptr2. Line 15 places a terminating null character in the array pointed to by ptr2.

Line 19 uses function c_str to obtain a const char* that points to a null terminated pointer-based string with the same content as string1. The pointer is passed to the stream insertion operator for output.

Line 25 assigns the const char* ptr1 a pointer returned by class string member function data. This member function returns a *non-null-terminated* built-in character array. We do *not* modify string string1 in this example. If string1 were to be modified (e.g., the string's dynamic memory changes its address due to a member function call such as string1.insert(0, "abcd");), ptr1 could become invalid—which could lead to unpredictable results.

Lines 28–30 use pointer arithmetic to output the character array pointed to by `ptr1`. In lines 32–33, the pointer-based string `ptr2` is output and the memory allocated for `ptr2` is `deleted` to avoid a memory leak.

Common Programming Error 21.2
Not terminating the character array returned by data *with a null character can lead to execution-time errors.*

21.11 Iterators

Class `string` provides *iterators* (introduced in Chapter 15) for forward and backward *traversal* of `string`s. Iterators provide access to individual characters with a syntax that's similar to pointer operations. *Iterators are not range checked.* Figure 21.10 demonstrates iterators.

```
1   // Fig. 21.10: Fig21_10.cpp
2   // Using an iterator to output a string.
3   #include <iostream>
4   #include <string>
5   using namespace std;
6
7   int main() {
8      string string1{"Testing iterators"};
9      string::const_iterator iterator1{string1.begin()};
10
11     cout << "string1 = " << string1
12        << "\n(Using iterator iterator1) string1 is: ";
13
14     // iterate through string
15     while (iterator1 != string1.end()) {
16        cout << *iterator1; // dereference iterator to get char
17        ++iterator1; // advance iterator to next char
18     }
19
20     cout << endl;
21   }
```

```
string1 = Testing iterators
(Using iterator iterator1) string1 is: Testing iterators
```

Fig. 21.10 | Using an iterator to output a `string`.

Lines 8–9 declare `string` `string1` and `string::const_iterator` `iterator1`. Recall that a `const_iterator` *cannot* be used to modify the data that you're iterating through—in this case the `string`. Iterator `iterator1` is initialized to the beginning of `string1` with the `string` class member function `begin`. Two versions of `begin` exist—one that returns an `iterator` for iterating through a non-const `string` and a const version that returns a `const_iterator` for iterating through a const `string`. Line 11 outputs `string1`.

Lines 15–18 use iterator `iterator1` to "walk through" `string1`. Class `string` member function `end` returns an `iterator` (or a `const_iterator`) for the position past the last element of string1. Each element is printed by *dereferencing the iterator* much as you'd dereference a pointer, and the iterator is advanced one position using operator ++. In C++11, lines 9 and 15–18 can be replaced with a range-based for, as in

```
for (char c : string1) {
    cout << c;
}
```

Class string provides member functions rend and rbegin for accessing individual string characters in reverse from the end of a string toward the beginning. Member functions rend and rbegin return reverse_iterators or const_reverse_iterators (based on whether the string is non-const or const). Exercise 21.8 asks you to write a program that demonstrates these capabilities.

Good Programming Practice 21.1

When the operations involving the iterator should not modify the data being processed, use a const_iterator. *This is another example of employing the principle of least privilege.*

21.12 String Stream Processing

In addition to standard stream I/O and file stream I/O, C++ stream I/O includes capabilities for inputting from, and outputting to, strings in memory. These capabilities often are referred to as in-memory I/O or string stream processing.

Input from a string is supported by class istringstream. Output to a string is supported by class ostringstream. The class names istringstream and ostringstream are actually *aliases* defined by the typedefs

```
typedef basic_istringstream< char > istringstream;
typedef basic_ostringstream< char > ostringstream;
```

Class templates basic_istringstream and basic_ostringstream provide the same functionality as classes istream and ostream plus other member functions specific to *in-memory formatting*. Programs that use in-memory formatting must include the <sstream> and <iostream> headers.

Error-Prevention Tip 21.1

One application of these techniques is data validation. *A program can read an entire line at a time from the input stream into a* string. *Next, a validation routine can scrutinize the contents of the* string *and correct (or repair) the data, if necessary. Then the program can proceed to input from the* string, *knowing that the input data is in the proper format.*

Error-Prevention Tip 21.2

To assist with data validation, C++11 provides powerful regular-expression *capabilities. For example, if a program requires a user to enter a U.S. format telephone number (e.g., (800) 555-1212), you can use a regular-expression pattern to confirm that the user's input matches the expected format. Many websites provide regular expressions for validating email addresses, URLs, phone numbers, addresses and other popular kinds of data. We introduce regular expressions and provide several examples in Chapter 24.*

11

Software Engineering Observation 21.1

Outputting to a string is a nice way to take advantage of the powerful output formatting capabilities of C++ streams. Data can be prepared in a string to mimic the edited screen format. That string could be written to a disk file to preserve the screen image.

An ostringstream object uses a string object to store the output data. The str member function of class ostringstream returns a copy of that string.[3]

Demonstrating *ostringstream*

Figure 21.11 demonstrates an ostringstream object. The program creates ostring-stream object outputString (line 9) and uses the stream insertion operator to output a series of strings and numerical values to the object.

```cpp
1   // Fig. 21.11: Fig21_11.cpp
2   // Using an ostringstream object.
3   #include <iostream>
4   #include <string>
5   #include <sstream> // header for string stream processing
6   using namespace std;
7
8   int main() {
9      ostringstream outputString; // create ostringstream object
10
11     string string1{"Output of several data types "};
12     string string2{"to an ostringstream object:"};
13     string string3{"\n          double: "};
14     string string4{"\n             int: "};
15     string string5{"\naddress of int: "};
16
17     double double1{123.4567};
18     int integer{22};
19
20     // output strings, double and int to ostringstream outputString
21     outputString << string1 << string2 << string3 << double1
22        << string4 << integer << string5 << &integer;
23
24     // call str to obtain string contents of the ostringstream
25     cout << "outputString contains:\n" << outputString.str();
26
27     // add additional characters and call str to output string
28     outputString << "\nmore characters added";
29     cout << "\n\nafter additional stream insertions,\n"
30        << "outputString contains:\n" << outputString.str() << endl;
31  }
```

Fig. 21.11 | Using an ostringstream object. (Part 1 of 2.)

---

3. ostringstream was introduced in Chapter 9. We cover it again here for those who might read this chapter before Chapter 9.

```
outputString contains:
Output of several data types to an ostringstream object:
       double: 123.457
          int: 22
address of int: 0012F540

after additional stream insertions,
outputString contains:
Output of several data types to an ostringstream object:
       double: 123.457
          int: 22
address of int: 0012F540
more characters added
```

Fig. 21.11 | Using an ostringstream object. (Part 2 of 2.)

Lines 21–22 output string string1, string string2, string string3, double double1, string string4, int integer, string string5 and the address of int integer—all to outputString in memory. Line 25 uses the stream insertion operator and the call outputString.str() to display a copy of the string created in lines 21–22. Line 28 demonstrates that more data can be *appended* to the string in memory by simply issuing another stream insertion operation to outputString. Lines 29–30 display string outputString after appending additional characters.

An istringstream object inputs data from a string in memory to program variables. Data is stored in an istringstream object as characters. Input from the istringstream object works identically to input from any file. The end of the string is interpreted by the istringstream object as *end-of-file*.

Demonstrating **istringstream**
Figure 21.12 demonstrates input from an istringstream object. Lines 9–10 create string input containing the data and istringstream object inputString constructed to contain the data in string input. The string input contains the data

```
Input test 123 4.7 A
```

which, when read as input to the program, consist of two strings ("Input" and "test"), an int (123), a double (4.7) and a char ('A'). These characters are extracted to variables string1, string2, integer, double1 and character in line 17.

```
 1   // Fig. 21.12: Fig21_12.cpp
 2   // Demonstrating input from an istringstream object.
 3   #include <iostream>
 4   #include <string>
 5   #include <sstream>
 6   using namespace std;
 7
 8   int main() {
 9      string input{"Input test 123 4.7 A"};
10      istringstream inputString{input};
```

Fig. 21.12 | Demonstrating input from an istringstream object. (Part 1 of 2.)

```
11        string string1;
12        string string2;
13        int integer;
14        double double1;
15        char character;
16
17        inputString >> string1 >> string2 >> integer >> double1 >> character;
18
19        cout << "The following items were extracted\n"
20           << "from the istringstream object:" << "\nstring: " << string1
21           << "\nstring: " << string2 << "\n    int: " << integer
22           << "\ndouble: " << double1 << "\n   char: " << character;
23
24        // attempt to read from empty stream
25        long value;
26        inputString >> value;
27
28        // test stream results
29        if (inputString.good()) {
30           cout << "\n\nlong value is: " << value << endl;
31        }
32        else {
33           cout << "\n\ninputString is empty" << endl;
34        }
35     }
```

```
The following items were extracted
from the istringstream object:
string: Input
string: test
   int: 123
double: 4.7
  char: A

inputString is empty
```

Fig. 21.12 | Demonstrating input from an istringstream object. (Part 2 of 2.)

The data is then output in lines 19–22. The program attempts to read from input-String again in line 26. The if condition in line 29 uses function good (Section 13.8) to test if any data remains. Because no data remains, the function returns false and the else part of the if...else statement executes.

21.13 C++11 Numeric Conversion Functions

C++11 added functions for converting from numeric values to strings and from strings to numeric values. Though you could previously perform such conversions using other techniques, the functions presented in this section were added for convenience.

Converting Numeric Values to *string* Objects
C++11's to_string function (from the <string> header) returns the string representation of its numeric argument. The function is overloaded for types int, unsigned int, long, unsigned long, long long, unsigned long long, float, double and long double.

Converting **string** Objects to Numeric Values

C++11 provides eight functions (Fig. 21.13; from the <string> header) for converting string objects to numeric values. Each function attempts to convert the *beginning* of its string argument to a numeric value. If no conversion can be performed, each function throws an invalid_argument exception. If the result of the conversion is out of range for the function's return type, each function throws an out_of_range exception.

Function	Return type	Function	Return type
Functions that convert to integral types		*Functions that convert to floating-point types*	
stoi	int	stof	float
stol	long	stod	double
stoul	unsigned long	stold	long double
stoll	long long		
stoull	unsigned long long		

Fig. 21.13 | C++11 functions that convert from strings to numeric types.

Functions That Convert **strings** to Integral Types

Consider an example of converting a string to an integral value. Assuming the string:

```
string s("100hello");
```

the following statement converts the beginning of the string to the int value 100 and stores that value in convertedInt:

```
int convertedInt = stoi(s);
```

Each function that converts a string to an integral type actually receives *three* parameters—the last two have default arguments. The parameters are:

- A string containing the characters to convert.
- A pointer to a size_t variable. The function uses this pointer to store the index of the first character that was *not* converted. The default argument is a null pointer, in which case the function does *not* store the index.
- An int from 2 to 36 representing the number's base—the default is base 10.

So, the preceding statement is equivalent to

```
int convertedInt = stoi(s, nullptr, 10);
```

Given a size_t variable named index, the statement:

```
int convertedInt = stoi(s, &index, 2);
```

converts the binary number "100" (base 2) to an int (100 in binary is the int value 4) and stores in index the location of the string's letter "h" (the first character that was not converted).

Functions That Convert strings to Floating-Point Types

The functions that convert strings to floating-point types each receive two parameters:

- A string containing the characters to convert.
- A pointer to a size_t variable where the function stores the index of the first character that was *not* converted. The default argument is a null pointer, in which case the function does *not* store the index.

Consider an example of converting a string to an floating-point value. Assuming the string:

```
string s("123.45hello");
```

the following statement converts the beginning of the string to the double value 123.45 and stores that value in convertedDouble:

```
double convertedDouble = stod(s);
```

Again, the second argument is a null pointer by default.

21.14 Wrap-Up

This chapter discussed the details of C++ Standard Library class string. We discussed assigning, concatenating, comparing, searching and swapping strings. We also introduced a number of member functions to determine string characteristics, to find, replace and insert characters in a string, and to convert strings to pointer-based strings and vice versa. You learned about string iterators and performing input from and output to strings in memory. Finally, we introduced functions for converting numeric values to strings and for converting strings to numeric values. In the next chapter, we introduce structs, which are similar to classes, and discuss the manipulation of bits, characters and C strings.

Summary

Section 21.1 Introduction

- Class template basic_string provides typical string-manipulation operations.
- The typedef statement

```
typedef basic_string< char > string;
```

creates the alias type string for **basic_string<char>** (p. 870). A typedef also is provided for the wchar_t type (wstring).
- To use strings, include C++ Standard Library header <string>.
- Assigning a single character to a string object is permitted in an assignment statement.
- strings are not necessarily null terminated.
- Most string member functions take as arguments a starting subscript location and the number of characters on which to operate.
- string member functions **size** and **length** (p. 871) return the number of characters currently stored in a string.

*Section 21.2 **string** Assignment and Concatenation*
- Class string provides overloaded **operator=** and function **assign** (p. 871) for assignments.
- The subscript operator, [], provides read/write access to any element of a string.
- string member function **at** (p. 873) provides **checked access** (p. 873)—going past either end of the string throws an out_of_range exception. The subscript operator, [], does not provide checked access.
- The overloaded + and += operators and member function **append** (p. 873) perform string concatenation.

*Section 21.3 Comparing **strings***
- Class string provides overloaded ==, !=, <, >, <= and >= operators for string comparisons.
- string member function **compare** (p. 875) compares two strings (or substrings) and returns 0 if the strings are equal, a positive number if the first string is **lexicographically** (p. 875) greater than the second or a negative number if the first string is lexicographically less than the second.

Section 21.4 Substrings
- string member function **substr** (p. 876) retrieves a substring from a string.

*Section 21.5 Swapping **strings***
- string member function **swap** (p. 876) swaps the contents of two strings.

*Section 21.6 **string** Characteristics*
- string member function **capacity** (p. 879) returns the total number of characters that can be stored in a string without increasing the amount of memory allocated to the string.
- string member function **max_size** (p. 879) returns the maximum size a string can have.
- string member function **resize** (p. 879) changes the length of a string.
- string member function **empty** returns true if a string is empty.

*Section 21.7 Finding Substrings and Characters in a **string***
- Class string find functions (p. 881) **find**, **rfind**, **find_first_of**, **find_last_of** and **find_first_not_of** locate substrings or characters in a string.

*Section 21.8 Replacing Characters in a **string***
- string member function **erase** (p. 881) deletes elements of a string.
- string member function **replace** (p. 883) replaces characters in a string.

*Section 21.9 Inserting Characters into a **string***
- string member function **insert** (p. 884) inserts characters in a string.

*Section 21.10 Conversion to Pointer-Based **char*** Strings*
- string member function **c_str** (p. 885) returns a const char* pointing to a null-terminated pointer-based string that contains all the characters in a string.
- string member function **data** (p. 885) returns a const char* pointing to a non-null-terminated built-in character array that contains all the characters in a string.

Section 21.11 Iterators
- Class string provides member functions **begin** and **end** (p. 886) to iterate through individual elements.

- Class `string` provides member functions **rend** and **rbegin** (p. 887) for accessing individual `string` characters in reverse from the end of a `string` toward the beginning.

Section 21.12 String Stream Processing

- Input from a `string` is supported by type **istringstream** (p. 887). Output to a `string` is supported by type **ostringstream** (p. 887).

- ostringstream member function **str** (p. 888) returns the `string` from the stream.

Section 21.13 C++11 Numeric Conversion Functions

- C++11's <string> header now contains functions for converting from numeric values to string objects and from string objects to numeric values.

- The **to_string** function (p. 890) returns the string representation of its numeric argument and is overloaded for types int, unsigned int, long, unsigned long, long long, unsigned long long, float, double and long double.

- C++11 provides eight functions for converting string objects to numeric values. Each function attempts to convert the beginning of its string argument to a numeric value. If no conversion can be performed, an invalid_argument exception occurs. If the result of the convertion is out of range for the function's return type, an out_of_range exception occurs.

- Each function that converts a `string` to an integral type receives three parameters—a string containing the characters to convert, a pointer to a size_t variable where the function stores the index of the first character that was not converted (a null pointer, by default) and an int from 2 to 36 representing the number's base (base 10, by default).

- The functions that convert strings to floating-point types each receive two parameters—a string containing the characters to convert and a pointer to a size_t variable where the function stores the index of the first character that was not converted (a null pointer, by default).

Self-Review Exercises

21.1   Fill in the blanks in each of the following:
   a) Header _____ must be included for class `string`.
   b) Class `string` belongs to the _____ namespace.
   c) Function _____ deletes characters from a `string`.
   d) Function _____ finds the first occurrence of one of several characters from a `string`.

21.2   State which of the following statements are *true* and which are *false*. If a statement is *false*, explain why.
   a) Concatenation of `string` objects can be performed with the addition assignment operator, +=.
   b) Characters within a `string` begin at index 0.
   c) The assignment operator, =, copies a `string`.
   d) A pointer-based string is a `string` object.

21.3   Find the error(s) in each of the following, and explain how to correct it (them):
   a) `string string1{28}; // construct string1`
      `string string2{'z'}; // construct string2`
   b) `// assume std namespace is known`
      `const char* ptr{name.data()}; // name is "joe bob"`
      `ptr[3] = '-';`
      `cout << ptr << endl;`

Answers to Self-Review Exercises

21.1 a) `<string>`. b) `std`. c) `erase`. d) `find_first_of`.

21.2 a) True.
   b) True.
   c) True.
   d) False. A `string` is an object that provides many different services. A pointer-based string does not provide any services. Pointer-based strings are null terminated; `string`s are not necessarily null terminated. Pointer-based strings are pointers and `string`s are objects.

21.3 a) Constructors for class `string` do not exist for integer and character arguments. Other valid constructors should be used—converting the arguments to `string`s if need be.
   b) Function data does not add a null terminator. Also, the code attempts to modify a const char. Replace all of the lines with the code:
   ```
   cout << name.substr(0, 3) + "-" + name.substr(4) << endl;
   ```

Exercises

21.4 *(Fill in the Blanks)* Fill in the blanks in each of the following:
   a) Class `string` member function _____ converts a `string` to a pointer-based string.
   b) Class `string` member function _____ is used for assignment.
   c) _____ is the return type of function `rbegin`.
   d) Class `string` member function _____ is used to retrieve a substring.

21.5 *(True or False)* State which of the following statements are *true* and which are *false*. If a statement is *false*, explain why.
   a) `string`s are always null terminated.
   b) Class `string` member function `max_size` returns the maximum size for a `string`.
   c) Class `string` member function at can throw an `out_of_range` exception.
   d) Class `string` member function `begin` returns an `iterator`.

21.6 *(Find Code Errors)* Find any errors in the following and explain how to correct them:
   a) `std::cout << s.data() << std::endl; // s is "hello"`
   b) `erase(s.rfind("x"), 1); // s is "xenon"`
   c) `string& foo() {`
   ```
       string s("Hello");
       ...    // other statements
       return;
   }
   ```

21.7 *(Simple Encryption)* Some information on the Internet may be encrypted with a simple algorithm known as "rot13," which rotates each character by 13 positions in the alphabet. Thus, `'a'` corresponds to `'n'`, and `'x'` corresponds to `'k'`. rot13 is an example of symmetric key encryption. With symmetric key encryption, both the encrypter and decrypter use the same key.
   a) Write a program that encrypts a message using rot13.
   b) Write a program that decrypts the scrambled message using 13 as the key.
   c) After writing the programs of part (a) and part (b), briefly answer the following question: If you did not know the key for part (b), how difficult do you think it would be to break the code? What if you had access to substantial computing power (e.g., supercomputers)? In Exercise 21.24 we ask you to write a program to accomplish this.

21.8 *(Using `string` Iterators)* Write a program using iterators that demonstrates the use of functions `rbegin` and `rend`.

21.9 *(Words Ending in "r" or "ay")* Write a program that reads in several strings and prints only those ending in "r" or "ay". Only lowercase letters should be considered.

21.10 *(string Concatenation)* Write a program that separately inputs a first name and a last name and concatenates the two into a new string. Show two techniques for accomplishing this task.

21.11 *(Hangman Game)* Write a program that plays the game of Hangman. The program should pick a word (which is either coded directly into the program or read from a text file) and display the following:

```
Guess the word:    XXXXXX
```

Each X represents a letter. The user tries to guess the letters in the word. The appropriate response yes or no should be displayed after each guess. After each incorrect guess, display the diagram with another body part filled. After seven incorrect guesses, the user should be hanged. The display should look as follows:

After each guess, display all user guesses. If the user guesses the word correctly, display

```
Congratulations!!! You guessed my word. Play again? yes/no
```

21.12 *(Printing a string Backward)* Write a program that inputs a string and prints the string backward. Convert all uppercase characters to lowercase and all lowercase characters to uppercase.

21.13 *(Alphabetizing Animal Names)* Write a program that uses the comparison capabilities introduced in this chapter to alphabetize a series of animal names. Only uppercase letters should be used for the comparisons.

21.14 *(Cryptograms)* Write a program that creates a cryptogram out of a string. A cryptogram is a message or word in which each letter is replaced with another letter. For example the string

```
The bird was named squawk
```

might be scrambled to form

```
cin vrjs otz ethns zxqtop
```

Spaces are not scrambled. In this particular case, 'T' was replaced with 'x', each 'a' was replaced with 'h', etc. Uppercase letters become lowercase letters in the cryptogram. Use techniques similar to those in Exercise 21.7.

21.15 *(Solving Cryptograms)* Modify Exercise 21.14 to allow the user to solve the cryptogram. The user should input two characters at a time: The first character specifies a letter in the cryptogram, and the second letter specifies the replacement letter. If the replacement letter is correct, replace the letter in the cryptogram with the replacement letter in uppercase.

21.16 *(Counting Palindromes)* Write a program that inputs a sentence and counts the number of palindromes in it. A palindrome is a word that reads the same backward and forward. For example, "tree" is not a palindrome, but "noon" is.

21.17 *(Counting Vowels)* Write a program that counts the total number of vowels in a sentence. Output the frequency of each vowel.

21.18 *(String Insertion)* Write a program that inserts the characters "******" in the exact middle of a string.

21.19 *(Erasing Characters from a string)* Write a program that erases the sequences "by" and "BY" from a string.

21.20   *(Reversing a string with Iterators)* Write a program that inputs a line of text and prints the text backward. Use iterators in your solution.

21.21   *(Recursively Reversing a string with Iterators)* Write a recursive version of Exercise 21.20.

21.22   *(Using the erase Functions with Iterator Arguments)* Write a program that demonstrates the use of the erase functions that take iterator arguments.

21.23   *(Letter Pyramid)* Write a program that generates the following from the string "abcdef-ghijklmnopqrstuvwxyz":

```
          a
         bcb
        cdedc
       defgfed
      efghihgfe
     fghijkjihgf
    ghijklmlkjihg
   hijklmnonmlkjih
  ijklmnopqponmlkji
 jklmnopqrsrqponmlkj
klmnopqrstutsrqponmlk
lmnopqrstuvwvutsrqponml
mnopqrstuvwxyxwvutsrqponm
nopqrstuvwxyz{zyxwvutsrqpon
```

21.24   *(Simple Decryption)* In Exercise 21.7, we asked you to write a simple encryption algorithm. Write a program that will attempt to decrypt a "rot13" message using simple frequency substitution. (Assume that you do not know the key.) The most frequent letters in the encrypted phrase should be replaced with the most commonly used English letters (a, e, i, o, u, s, t, r, etc.). Write the possibilities to a file. What made the code breaking easy? How can the encryption mechanism be improved?

21.25   *(Enhanced Employee Class)* Modify class Employee in Figs. 12.9–12.10 by adding a private utility function called isValidSocialSecurityNumber. This member function should validate the format of a social security number (e.g., ###-##-####, where # is a digit). If the format is valid, return true; otherwise return false.

Making a Difference

21.26   *(Cooking with Healthier Ingredients)* Obesity in the United States is increasing at an alarming rate. Check the map from the Centers for Disease Control and Prevention (CDC) at http://stateofobesity.org/adult-obesity/, which shows obesity trends in the United States over the last 20 years. As obesity increases, so do occurrences of related problems (e.g., heart disease, high blood pressure, high cholesterol, type 2 diabetes). Write a program that helps users choose healthier ingredients when cooking, and helps those allergic to certain foods (e.g., nuts, gluten) find substitutes. The program should read a recipe from the user and suggest healthier replacements for some of the ingredients. For simplicity, your program should assume the recipe has no abbreviations for measures such as teaspoons, cups, and tablespoons, and uses numerical digits for quantities (e.g., 1 egg, 2 cups) rather than spelling them out (one egg, two cups). Some common substitutions are shown in Fig. 21.14. Your program should display a warning such as, "Always consult your physician before making significant changes to your diet."

Your program should take into consideration that replacements are not always one-for-one. For example, if a cake recipe calls for three eggs, it might reasonably use six egg whites instead. Conversion data for measurements and substitutes can be obtained at websites such as:

```
http://chinesefood.about.com/od/recipeconversionfaqs/f/usmetricrecipes.htm
http://www.pioneerthinking.com/eggsub.html
http://www.gourmetsleuth.com/conversions.htm
```

Ingredient	Substitution
1 cup sour cream	1 cup yogurt
1 cup milk	1/2 cup evaporated milk and 1/2 cup water
1 teaspoon lemon juice	1/2 teaspoon vinegar
1 cup sugar	1/2 cup honey, 1 cup molasses or 1/4 cup agave nectar
1 cup butter	1 cup yogurt
1 cup flour	1 cup rye or rice flour
1 cup mayonnaise	1 cup cottage cheese or 1/8 cup mayonnaise and 7/8 cup yogurt
1 egg	2 tablespoons cornstarch, arrowroot flour or potato starch or 2 egg whites or 1/2 of a large banana (mashed)
1 cup milk	1 cup soy milk
1/4 cup oil	1/4 cup applesauce
white bread	whole-grain bread

Fig. 21.14 | Sample ingredient substitutions.

Your program should consider the user's health concerns, such as high cholesterol, high blood pressure, weight loss, gluten allergy, and so on. For high cholesterol, the program should suggest substitutes for eggs and dairy products; if the user wishes to lose weight, low-calorie substitutes for ingredients such as sugar should be suggested.

21.27 *(Spam Scanner)* Spam (or junk e-mail) costs U.S. organizations billions of dollars a year in spam-prevention software, equipment, network resources, bandwidth, and lost productivity. Research online some of the most common spam e-mail messages and words, and check your own junk e-mail folder. Create a list of 30 words and phrases commonly found in spam messages. Write an application in which the user enters an e-mail message. Then, scan the message for each of the 30 keywords or phrases. For each occurrence of one of these within the message, add a point to the message's "spam score." Next, rate the likelihood that the message is spam, based on the number of points it received.

21.28 *(SMS Language)* Short Message Service (SMS) is a communications service that allows sending text messages of 160 or fewer characters between mobile phones. With the proliferation of mobile phone use worldwide, SMS is being used in many developing nations for political purposes (e.g., voicing opinions and opposition), reporting news about natural disasters, and so on. For example, check out http://omunica.org/radio2.0/archives/87. Since the length of SMS messages is limited, SMS Language—abbreviations of common words and phrases in mobile text messages, e-mails, instant messages, etc.—is often used. For example, "in my opinion" is "IMO" in SMS Language. Research SMS Language online. Write a program in which the user can enter a message using SMS Language; the program should translate it into English (or your own language). Also provide a mechanism to translate text written in English (or your own language) into SMS Language. One potential problem is that one SMS abbreviation could expand into a variety of phrases. For example, IMO (as used above) could also stand for "International Maritime Organization," "in memory of," etc.

Bits, Characters, C Strings and **struct**s

22

Objectives

In this chapter you'll learn:

- To create and use **struct**s and to understand their near equivalence with classes.

- To use **typedef** to create aliases for data types.

- To manipulate data with the bitwise operators and to create bit fields for storing data compactly.

- To use the functions of the character-handling library .

- To use the string-conversion functions of the general-utilities library **<cstdlib>**.

- To use the string-processing functions of the string-handling library **<cstring>**.

22.1 Introduction

We now discuss structures, their near equivalence with classes, and the manipulation of bits, characters and C strings. Many of the techniques we present here are included for the benefit of those who will work with legacy C and C++ code.

Like classes, C++ structures may contain access specifiers, member functions, constructors and destructors. In fact, *the only differences between structures and classes in C++ is that structure members default to `public` access and class members default to `private` access when no access specifiers are used, and that structures default to `public` inheritance, whereas classes default to `private` inheritance.* Our presentation of structures here is typical of the legacy C code and early C++ code you'll see in industry.

We present a high-performance card shuffling and dealing simulation in which we use structure objects containing C++ `string` objects to represent the cards. We discuss the *bitwise operators* that allow you to access and manipulate the *individual bits* in bytes of data. We also present *bitfields*—special structures that can be used to specify the exact number of bits a variable occupies in memory. These bit-manipulation techniques are common in programs that interact directly with hardware devices that have limited memory. The chapter finishes with examples of many character and C string-manipulation functions—some of which are designed to process blocks of memory as arrays of bytes. The detailed C string treatment in this chapter is mostly for reasons of legacy code support and because there are still remnants of C string use in C++, such as command-line arguments (Appendix F). *New development should use C++ `string` objects rather than C strings.*

22.2 Structure Definitions

Consider the following structure definition:

```
struct Card {
    string face;
    string suit;
};
```

Keyword `struct` introduces the definition for structure `Card`. The identifier `Card` is the structure name and is used in C++ to declare variables of the structure type (in C, the type name of the preceding structure is struct Card). Card's definition contains two string members—face and suit.

The following declarations

```
Card oneCard;
Card deck[52];
Card* cardPtr;
```

declare oneCard to be a structure variable of type Card, deck to be an array with 52 elements of type Card and cardPtr to be a pointer to a Card structure. Variables of a given structure type can also be declared by placing a comma-separated list of the variable names between the closing brace of the structure definition and the semicolon that ends the structure definition. For example, the preceding declarations could have been incorporated into the Card structure definition as follows:

```
struct Card {
    string face;
    string suit;
} oneCard, deck[52], * cardPtr;
```

As with classes, structure members are *not* necessarily stored in *consecutive* bytes of memory. Sometimes there are "holes" in a structure, because some computers store specific data types only on certain memory boundaries for performance reasons, such as half-word, word or double-word boundaries. A word is a standard memory unit used to store data in a computer—usually two, four or eight bytes and typically eight bytes on today's popular 64-bit systems. Consider the following structure definition in which structure objects sample1 and sample2 of type Example are declared:

```
struct Example {
    char c;
    int i;
} sample1, sample2;
```

A computer with two-byte words might require that each of the members of Example be aligned on a word boundary (i.e., at the beginning of a word—this is *machine dependent*). Figure 22.1 shows a sample storage alignment for an object of type Example that's been assigned the character 'a' and the integer 97 (the bit representations of the values are shown). If the members are stored beginning at word boundaries, there is a one-byte hole (byte 1 in the figure) in the storage for objects of type Example. The value in the one-byte hole is *undefined*. If the values in sample1 and sample2 are in fact equal, the structure objects might *not* be equal, because the *undefined* one-byte holes are not likely to contain identical values.

Portability Tip 22.1

Because the size of data items of a particular type is machine dependent, and because storage alignment considerations are machine dependent, so too is the representation of a structure.

Common Programming Error 22.1

Comparing variables of structure types is a compilation error.

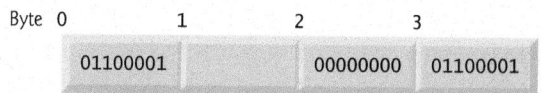

22.3 typedef and using

Keyword `typedef` provides a mechanism for creating *synonyms* (or *aliases*) for previously defined data types. Names for structure types are often defined with `typedef` to more readable type names. For example, the statement

```
typedef Card* CardPtr;
```

defines the new type name `CardPtr` as a synonym for type `Card*`. Creating a new name with `typedef` does *not* create a new type; `typedef` simply creates a *new type name* that can then be used in the program as an alias for an existing type name.

C++11 added the keyword `using` as another mechanism for creating type aliases. The following declaration is equivalent to the `typedef` above:

```
using CardPtr = Card*;
```

This feature was added to fix problems with `typedef` in template programming.

22.4 Example: Card Shuffling and Dealing Simulation

The card shuffling and dealing program in Figs. 22.2–22.4 is similar to the one described in Exercise 9.23. This program represents the deck of cards as an array of structures.

```
1   // Fig. 22.2: DeckOfCards.h
2   // Definition of class DeckOfCards that
3   // represents a deck of playing cards.
4   #include <string>
5   #include <array>
6
7   // Card structure definition
8   struct Card {
9      std::string face;
10     std::string suit;
11  };
12
13  // DeckOfCards class definition
14  class DeckOfCards {
15  public:
16     static const int numberOfCards{52};
17     static const int faces{13};
18     static const int suits{4};
19
20     DeckOfCards(); // constructor initializes deck
```

Fig. 22.2 | Definition of class `DeckOfCards` that represents a deck of playing cards. (Part I of 2.)

```
21        void shuffle(); // shuffles cards in deck
22        void deal() const; // deals cards in deck
23
24    private:
25        std::array<Card, numberOfCards> deck; // represents deck of cards
26    };
```

Fig. 22.2 | Definition of class DeckOfCards that represents a deck of playing cards. (Part 2 of 2.)

The constructor (lines 12–27 of Fig. 22.3) initializes the array in order with character strings representing Ace through King of each suit. Function shuffle implements the shuffling algorithm. The function loops through all 52 cards (subscripts 0 to 51). For each card, a number between 0 and 51 is picked randomly. Next, the current Card and the randomly selected Card are swapped in the array. A total of 52 swaps are made in a single pass of the entire array, and the array is shuffled. Because the Card structures were swapped in place in the array, the dealing algorithm implemented in function deal requires only one pass of the array to deal the shuffled cards.

```
1    // Fig. 22.3: DeckOfCards.cpp
2    // Member-function definitions for class DeckOfCards that simulates
3    // the shuffling and dealing of a deck of playing cards.
4    #include <iostream>
5    #include <iomanip>
6    #include <cstdlib> // prototypes for rand and srand
7    #include <ctime> // prototype for time
8    #include "DeckOfCards.h" // DeckOfCards class definition
9    using namespace std;
10
11   // no-argument DeckOfCards constructor intializes deck
12   DeckOfCards::DeckOfCards() {
13       // initialize suit array
14       static string suit[suits]{"Hearts", "Diamonds", "Clubs", "Spades"};
15
16       // initialize face array
17       static string face[faces]{"Ace", "Deuce", "Three", "Four", "Five",
18           "Six", "Seven", "Eight", "Nine", "Ten", "Jack", "Queen", "King"};
19
20       // set values for deck of 52 Cards
21       for (size_t i{0}; i < deck.size(); ++i) {
22           deck[i].face = face[i % faces];
23           deck[i].suit = suit[i / faces];
24       }
25
26       srand(static_cast< size_t >(time(nullptr))); // seed
27   }
28
29   // shuffle cards in deck
30   void DeckOfCards::shuffle() {
31       // shuffle cards randomly
32       for (size_t i{0}; i < deck.size(); ++i) {
```

Fig. 22.3 | Member-function definitions for class DeckOfCards. (Part 1 of 2.)

```
33            int j{rand() % numberOfCards};
34            Card temp = deck[i];
35            deck[i] = deck[j];
36            deck[j] = temp;
37        }
38    }
39
40    // deal cards in deck
41    void DeckOfCards::deal() const {
42        // display each card's face and suit
43        for (size_t i = 0; i < deck.size(); ++i) {
44            cout << right << setw(5) << deck[i].face << " of "
45                << left << setw(8) << deck[i].suit
46                << ((i + 1) % 2 ? '\t' : '\n');
47        }
48    }
```

Fig. 22.3 | Member-function definitions for class `DeckOfCards`. (Part 2 of 2.)

```
1    // Fig. 22.4: fig22_04.cpp
2    // Card shuffling and dealing program.
3    #include "DeckOfCards.h" // DeckOfCards class definition
4
5    int main() {
6        DeckOfCards deckOfCards; // create DeckOfCards object
7        deckOfCards.shuffle(); // shuffle the cards in the deck
8        deckOfCards.deal(); // deal the cards in the deck
9    }
```

```
 King of Clubs        Ten of Diamonds
 Five of Diamonds     Jack of Clubs
Seven of Spades       Five of Clubs
Three of Spades       King of Hearts
  Ten of Clubs       Eight of Spades
Eight of Hearts       Six of Hearts
 Nine of Diamonds    Nine of Clubs
Three of Diamonds    Queen of Hearts
  Six of Clubs      Seven of Hearts
Seven of Diamonds    Jack of Diamonds
 Jack of Spades      King of Diamonds
Deuce of Diamonds    Four of Clubs
Three of Clubs       Five of Hearts
Eight of Clubs        Ace of Hearts
Deuce of Spades       Ace of Clubs
  Ten of Spades     Eight of Diamonds
  Ten of Hearts       Six of Spades
Queen of Diamonds    Nine of Hearts
Seven of Clubs      Queen of Clubs
Deuce of Clubs      Queen of Spades
```

Fig. 22.4 | Card shuffling and dealing program. (Part 1 of 2.)

Three of Hearts	Five of Spades
Deuce of Hearts	Jack of Hearts
Four of Hearts	Ace of Diamonds
Nine of Spades	Four of Diamonds
Ace of Spades	Six of Diamonds
Four of Spades	King of Spades

Fig. 22.4 | Card shuffling and dealing program. (Part 2 of 2.)

22.5 Bitwise Operators

C++ provides extensive *bit-manipulation* capabilities for getting down to the so-called "bits-and-bytes" level. Operating systems, test-equipment software, networking software and many other kinds of software require that you communicate "directly with the hardware." We introduce each of the *bitwise operators*, and we discuss how to save memory by using *bit fields*.

All data is represented internally by computers as sequences of bits. Each bit can assume the value 0 or the value 1. On most systems, a sequence of eight bits, each of which forms a byte—the standard storage unit for a variable of type char. Other data types are stored in larger numbers of bytes. Bitwise operators are used to manipulate the bits of integral operands (char, short, int and long; both signed and unsigned). Normally the bitwise operators are used with unsigned integers.

Portability Tip 22.2
Bitwise data manipulations are machine dependent.

The bitwise operator discussions in this section show the binary representations of the integer operands. For a detailed explanation of the binary (also called base-2) number system, see Appendix D. Because of the machine-dependent nature of bitwise manipulations, some of these programs might not work on your system without modification.

The bitwise operators are: bitwise AND (&), bitwise inclusive OR (|), bitwise exclusive OR (∧), left shift (<<), right shift (>>) and bitwise complement (~)—also known as the one's complement. We've been using &, << and >> for other purposes—this is a classic example of *operator overloading*. The *bitwise AND*, *bitwise inclusive OR* and *bitwise exclusive OR* operators compare their two operands bit by bit. The *bitwise AND* operator sets each bit in the result to 1 if the corresponding bit in *both* operands is 1. The *bitwise inclusive OR* operator sets each bit in the result to 1 if the corresponding bit in *either (or both)* operand(s) is 1. The *bitwise exclusive OR* operator sets each bit in the result to 1 if the corresponding bit in *either* operand—*but not both*—is 1. The *left-shift* operator shifts the bits of its left operand to the left by the number of bits specified in its right operand. The *right-shift* operator shifts the bits in its left operand to the right by the number of bits specified in its right operand. The *bitwise complement* operator sets all 0 bits in its operand to 1 in the result and sets all 1 bits in its operand to 0 in the result. Detailed discussions of each bitwise operator appear in the following examples. The bitwise operators are summarized in Fig. 22.5.

Operator	Name	Description
&	bitwise AND	The bits in the result are set to 1 if the corresponding bits in the two operands are *both* 1.
|	bitwise inclusive OR	The bits in the result are set to 1 if *one or both* of the corresponding bits in the two operands is 1.
^	bitwise exclusive OR	The bits in the result are set to 1 if *exactly one* of the corresponding bits in the two operands is 1.
<<	left shift	Shifts the bits of the first operand left by the number of bits specified by the second operand; fill from right with 0 bits.
>>	right shift with sign extension	Shifts the bits of the first operand right by the number of bits specified by the second operand; the method of filling from the left is *machine dependent*.
~	bitwise complement	All 0 bits are set to 1 and all 1 bits are set to 0.

Fig. 22.5 | Bitwise operators.

Printing a Binary Representation of an Integral Value

When using the bitwise operators, it's useful to illustrate their precise effects by printing values in their binary representation. The program of Fig. 22.6 prints an unsigned integer in its binary representation in groups of eight bits each.

```cpp
1   // Fig. 22.6: fig22_06.cpp
2   // Printing an unsigned integer in bits.
3   #include <iostream>
4   #include <iomanip>
5   using namespace std;
6
7   void displayBits(unsigned); // prototype
8
9   int main() {
10      unsigned inputValue{0}; // integral value to print in binary
11
12      cout << "Enter an unsigned integer: ";
13      cin >> inputValue;
14      displayBits(inputValue);
15   }
16
17   // display bits of an unsigned integer value
18   void displayBits(unsigned value) {
19      const unsigned SHIFT{8 * sizeof(unsigned) - 1};
20      const unsigned MASK{static_cast<const unsigned>(1 << SHIFT)};
21
22      cout << setw(10) << value << " = ";
23
```

Fig. 22.6 | Printing an unsigned integer in bits. (Part 1 of 2.)

```
24      // display bits
25      for (unsigned i{1}; i <= SHIFT + 1; ++i) {
26         cout << (value & MASK ? '1' : '0');
27         value <<= 1; // shift value left by 1
28
29         if (i % 8 == 0) { // output a space after 8 bits
30            cout << ' ';
31         }
32      }
33
34      cout << endl;
35   }
```

```
Enter an unsigned integer: 65000
   65000 = 00000000 00000000 11111101 11101000
```

```
Enter an unsigned integer: 29
   29 = 00000000 00000000 00000000 00011101
```

Fig. 22.6 | Printing an unsigned integer in bits. (Part 2 of 2.)

Function displayBits (lines 18–35) uses the *bitwise AND* operator to combine variable value with constant MASK. Often, the *bitwise AND* operator is used with an operand called a mask—an integer value with specific bits set to 1. Masks are used to *hide* some bits in a value while *selecting* other bits. In displayBits, line 20 initializes constant MASK with 1 << SHIFT. The value of constant SHIFT was calculated in line 19 with the expression

```
8 * sizeof(unsigned) - 1
```

which multiplies the number of bytes an unsigned object requires in memory by 8 (the number of bits in a byte) to get the total number of bits required to store an unsigned object, then subtracts 1. The bit representation of 1 << SHIFT on a computer that represents unsigned objects in four bytes of memory is

```
10000000 00000000 00000000 00000000
```

The *left-shift operator* shifts the value 1 from the low-order (rightmost) bit to the high-order (leftmost) bit in MASK, and fills in 0 bits from the right. Line 26 prints a 1 or a 0 for the current leftmost bit of variable value. Assume that variable value contains 65000 (00000000 00000000 11111101 11101000). When value and MASK are combined using &, all the bits except the high-order bit in variable value are "masked off" (hidden), because any bit "ANDed" with 0 yields 0. If the leftmost bit is 1, value & MASK evaluates to

```
00000000 00000000 11111101 11101000   (value)
10000000 00000000 00000000 00000000   (MASK)
-------------------------------------
00000000 00000000 00000000 00000000   (value & MASK)
```

which is interpreted as false, and 0 is printed. Then line 27 shifts variable value left by one bit with the expression value <<= 1 (i.e., value = value << 1). These steps are repeated for each bit variable value. Eventually, a bit with a value of 1 is shifted into the leftmost bit position, and the bit manipulation is as follows:

```
11111101 11101000 00000000 00000000    (value)
10000000 00000000 00000000 00000000    (MASK)
-------------------------------------
10000000 00000000 00000000 00000000    (value & MASK)
```

Because both left bits are 1s, the expression's result is nonzero (true) and 1 is printed. Figure 22.7 summarizes the results of combining two bits with the bitwise AND operator.

Bit 1	Bit 2	Bit 1 & Bit 2
0	0	0
1	0	0
0	1	0
1	1	1

Fig. 22.7 | Results of combining two bits with the bitwise AND operator (&).

Common Programming Error 22.2
Using the logical AND operator (&&) for the bitwise AND operator (&) and vice versa is a logic error.

The program of Fig. 22.8 demonstrates the *bitwise AND operator*, the *bitwise inclusive OR* operator, the *bitwise exclusive OR* operator and the *bitwise complement operator*. Function `displayBits` (lines 47–64) prints the `unsigned` integer values.

```cpp
1   // Fig. 22.8: fig22_08.cpp
2   // Bitwise AND, inclusive OR,
3   // exclusive OR and complement operators.
4   #include <iostream>
5   #include <iomanip>
6   using namespace std;
7
8   void displayBits(unsigned); // prototype
9
10  int main() {
11     // demonstrate bitwise &
12     unsigned number1{2179876355};
13     unsigned mask{1};
14     cout << "The result of combining the following\n";
15     displayBits(number1);
16     displayBits(mask);
17     cout << "using the bitwise AND operator & is\n";
18     displayBits(number1 & mask);
```

Fig. 22.8 | Bitwise AND, inclusive OR, exclusive OR and complement operators. (Part 1 of 3.)

```
19
20        // demonstrate bitwise |
21        number1 = 15;
22        unsigned setBits{241};
23        cout << "\nThe result of combining the following\n";
24        displayBits(number1);
25        displayBits(setBits);
26        cout << "using the bitwise inclusive OR operator | is\n";
27        displayBits(number1 | setBits);
28
29        // demonstrate bitwise exclusive OR
30        number1 = 139;
31        unsigned number2{199};
32        cout << "\nThe result of combining the following\n";
33        displayBits(number1);
34        displayBits(number2);
35        cout << "using the bitwise exclusive OR operator ^ is\n";
36        displayBits(number1 ^ number2);
37
38        // demonstrate bitwise complement
39        number1 = 21845;
40        cout << "\nThe one's complement of\n";
41        displayBits(number1);
42        cout << "is" << endl;
43        displayBits(~number1);
44     }
45
46     // display bits of an unsigned integer value
47     void displayBits(unsigned value) {
48        const unsigned SHIFT{8 * sizeof(unsigned) - 1};
49        const unsigned MASK{static_cast<const unsigned>(1 << SHIFT)};
50
51        cout << setw(10) << value << " = ";
52
53        // display bits
54        for (unsigned i{1}; i <= SHIFT + 1; ++i) {
55           cout << (value & MASK ? '1' : '0');
56           value <<= 1; // shift value left by 1
57
58           if (i % 8 == 0) { // output a space after 8 bits
59              cout << ' ';
60           }
61        }
62
63        cout << endl;
64     }
```

```
The result of combining the following
2179876355 = 10000001 11101110 01000110 00000011
         1 = 00000000 00000000 00000000 00000001
using the bitwise AND operator & is
         1 = 00000000 00000000 00000000 00000001
```

Fig. 22.8 | Bitwise AND, inclusive OR, exclusive OR and complement operators. (Part 2 of 3.)

```
The result of combining the following
        15 = 00000000 00000000 00000000 00001111
       241 = 00000000 00000000 00000000 11110001
using the bitwise inclusive OR operator | is
       255 = 00000000 00000000 00000000 11111111

The result of combining the following
       139 = 00000000 00000000 00000000 10001011
       199 = 00000000 00000000 00000000 11000111
using the bitwise exclusive OR operator ^ is
        76 = 00000000 00000000 00000000 01001100

The one's complement of
     21845 = 00000000 00000000 01010101 01010101
is
4294945450 = 11111111 11111111 10101010 10101010
```

Fig. 22.8 | Bitwise AND, inclusive OR, exclusive OR and complement operators. (Part 3 of 3.)

Bitwise AND Operator (&)

In Fig. 22.8, line 12 uses 2179876355 (10000001 11101110 01000110 00000011) to initialize variable number1, and line 14 uses 1 (00000000 00000000 00000000 00000001) to initialize variable mask. When mask and number1 are combined using the *bitwise AND operator (&)* in the expression number1 & mask (line 18), the result is 00000000 00000000 00000000 00000001. All the bits except the low-order bit in variable number1 are "masked off" (hidden) by "ANDing" with constant MASK.

Bitwise Inclusive OR Operator (|)

The *bitwise inclusive OR operator* is used to set specific bits to 1 in an operand. In Fig. 22.8, line 21 assigns 15 (00000000 00000000 00000000 00001111) to variable number1, and line 22 uses 241 (00000000 00000000 00000000 11110001) to initialize variable setBits. When number1 and setBits are combined using the *bitwise inclusive OR operator* in the expression number1 | setBits (line 27), the result is 255 (00000000 00000000 00000000 11111111). Figure 22.9 summarizes the results of combining two bits with the *bitwise inclusive-OR operator*.

Common Programming Error 22.3

Using the logical OR operator (||) for the bitwise OR operator (|) and vice versa is a logic error.

Bit 1	Bit 2	Bit 1 | Bit 2
0	0	0
1	0	1
0	1	1
1	1	1

Fig. 22.9 | Combining two bits with the bitwise inclusive-OR operator (|).

Bitwise Exclusive OR (^)

The *bitwise exclusive OR operator (^)* sets each bit in the result to 1 if *exactly* one of the corresponding bits in its two operands is 1. In Fig. 22.8, lines 30–31 give variables number1 and number2 the values 139 (00000000 00000000 00000000 10001011) and 199 (00000000 00000000 00000000 11000111), respectively. When these variables are combined with the *bitwise exclusive OR operator* in the expression number1 ^ number2 (line 36), the result is 00000000 00000000 00000000 01001100. Figure 22.10 summarizes the results of combining two bits with the *bitwise exclusive OR operator*.

Bit 1	Bit 2	Bit 1 ^ Bit 2
0	0	0
1	0	1
0	1	1
1	1	0

Fig. 22.10 | Combining two bits with the bitwise exclusive OR operator (^).

Bitwise Complement (~)

The *bitwise complement operator (~)* sets all 1 bits in its operand to 0 in the result and sets all 0 bits to 1 in the result—otherwise referred to as "taking the *one's complement* of the value." In Fig. 22.8, line 39 assigns variable number1 the value 21845 (00000000 00000000 01010101 01010101). When the expression ~number1 evaluates, the result is (11111111 11111111 10101010 10101010).

Bitwise Shift Operators

Figure 22.11 demonstrates the *left-shift operator (<<)* and the *right-shift operator (>>)*. Function displayBits (lines 26–43) prints the unsigned integer values.

```cpp
1   // Fig. 22.11: fig22_11.cpp
2   // Using the bitwise shift operators.
3   #include <iostream>
4   #include <iomanip>
5   using namespace std;
6
7   void displayBits(unsigned); // prototype
8
9   int main() {
10     unsigned number1{960};
11
12     // demonstrate bitwise left shift
13     cout << "The result of left shifting\n";
14     displayBits(number1);
15     cout << "8 bit positions using the left-shift operator is\n";
16     displayBits(number1 << 8);
```

Fig. 22.11 | Bitwise shift operators. (Part 1 of 2.)

```
17
18      // demonstrate bitwise right shift
19      cout << "\nThe result of right shifting\n";
20      displayBits(number1);
21      cout << "8 bit positions using the right-shift operator is\n";
22      displayBits(number1 >> 8);
23   }
24
25   // display bits of an unsigned integer value
26   void displayBits(unsigned value) {
27      const unsigned SHIFT{8 * sizeof(unsigned) - 1};
28      const unsigned MASK{static_cast<const unsigned>(1 << SHIFT)};
29
30      cout << setw(10) << value << " = ";
31
32      // display bits
33      for (unsigned i{1}; i <= SHIFT + 1; ++i) {
34         cout << (value & MASK ? '1' : '0');
35         value <<= 1; // shift value left by 1
36
37         if (i % 8 == 0) { // output a space after 8 bits
38            cout << ' ';
39         }
40      }
41
42      cout << endl;
43   }
```

```
The result of left shifting
       960 = 00000000 00000000 00000011 11000000
8 bit positions using the left-shift operator is
    245760 = 00000000 00000011 11000000 00000000

The result of right shifting
       960 = 00000000 00000000 00000011 11000000
8 bit positions using the right-shift operator is
         3 = 00000000 00000000 00000000 00000011
```

Fig. 22.11 | Bitwise shift operators. (Part 2 of 2.)

Left-Shift Operator

The *left-shift operator (<<)* shifts the bits of its left operand to the left by the number of bits specified in its right operand. Bits vacated to the right are replaced with 0s; bits shifted off the left are lost. In Fig. 22.11, line 10 initializes variable number1 with the value 960 (00000000 00000000 00000011 11000000). The result of left-shifting variable number1 eight bits in the expression number1 << 8 (line 16) is 245760 (00000000 00000011 11000000 00000000).

Right-Shift Operator

The *right-shift operator (>>)* shifts the bits of its left operand to the right by the number of bits specified in its right operand. Performing a right shift on an unsigned integer causes the vacated bits at the left to be replaced by 0s; bits shifted off the right are lost. In the program of Fig. 22.11, the result of right-shifting `number1` in the expression `number1 >> 8` (line 22) is 3 (00000000 00000000 00000000 00000011).

Common Programming Error 22.4

The result of shifting a value is undefined *if the right operand is negative or if the right operand is greater than or equal to the number of bits in which the left operand is stored.*

Portability Tip 22.3

The result of right-shifting a signed value is machine dependent. *Some machines fill with zeros and others use the sign bit.*

Bitwise Assignment Operators

Each bitwise operator (except the bitwise complement operator) has a corresponding assignment operator. These bitwise assignment operators are shown in Fig. 22.12; they're used in a similar manner to the arithmetic assignment operators introduced in Chapter 4.

Bitwise assignment operators	
`&=`	Bitwise AND assignment operator.
`|=`	Bitwise inclusive OR assignment operator.
`^=`	Bitwise exclusive OR assignment operator.
`<<=`	Left-shift assignment operator.
`>>=`	Right-shift with sign extension assignment operator.

Fig. 22.12 | Bitwise assignment operators.

Operator Precedence

Figure 22.13 shows the precedence and associativity of the operators introduced up to this point in the text. They're shown top to bottom in decreasing order of precedence.

Operators	Associativity	Type
`::` (unary; right to left) `::` (binary; left to right) `()` (grouping parentheses)	left to right *[See caution in Fig. 2.10 regarding grouping parentheses.]*	primary
`()` `[]` `.` `->` `++` `--` `static_cast<type>()`	left to right	postfix
`++` `--` `+` `-` `!` `delete` `sizeof` `*` `~` `&` `new`	right to left	prefix
`*` `/` `%`	left to right	multiplicative
`+` `-`	left to right	additive
`<<` `>>`	left to right	shifting
`<` `<=` `>` `>=`	left to right	relational

Fig. 22.13 | Operator precedence and associativity. (Part 1 of 2.)

Operators	Associativity	Type
== !=	left to right	equality
&	left to right	bitwise AND
^	left to right	bitwise XOR
|	left to right	bitwise OR
&&	left to right	logical AND
||	left to right	logical OR
?:	right to left	conditional
= += -= *= /= %= &= |= ^= <<= >>=	right to left	assignment
,	left to right	comma

Fig. 22.13 | Operator precedence and associativity. (Part 2 of 2.)

C++14 Binary Literals

14 As of C++14, you may now include binary literals in your source code. To do so, precede a sequence of 1s and 0s with 0b or 0B. For example, you can define a 32-bit mask like the one we used in the displayBits functions of this section's examples as

```
0b10000000'00000000'00000000'00000000
```

14 The preceding literal also uses C++14's single-quote character to separate groups of digits for readability.

22.6 Bit Fields

C++ provides the ability to specify the number of bits in which an integral type or enum type member of a class or a structure is stored. Such a member is referred to as a bit field. Bit fields enable *better memory utilization* by storing data in the minimum number of bits required. Bit field members *must* be declared as an integral or enum type.

> **Performance Tip 22.1**
> *Bit fields help conserve storage.*

Consider the following structure definition:

```
struct BitCard {
    unsigned face : 4;
    unsigned suit : 2;
    unsigned color : 1;
};
```

The definition contains three unsigned bit fields—face, suit and color—used to represent a card from a deck of 52 cards. A bit field is declared by following an integral type or enum type member with a colon (:) and an integer constant representing the width of the bit field (i.e., the number of bits in which the member is stored). The width must be an integer constant.

The preceding structure definition indicates that member face is stored in four bits, member suit in 2 bits and member color in one bit. The number of bits is based on the desired range of values for each structure member. Member face stores values between 0 (Ace) and 12 (King)—four bits can store a value between 0 and 15. Member suit stores values between 0 and 3 (0 = Diamonds, 1 = Hearts, 2 = Clubs, 3 = Spades)—two bits can store a value between 0 and 3. Finally, member color stores either 0 (Red) or 1 (Black)—one bit can store either 0 or 1.

The program in Figs. 22.14–22.16 creates array deck containing BitCard structures (line 23 of Fig. 22.14). The constructor inserts the 52 cards in the deck array, and function deal prints the 52 cards. Notice that bit fields are accessed exactly as any other structure member is (lines 12–14 and 22–27 of Fig. 22.15). The member color is included as a means of indicating the card color.

```cpp
 1   // Fig. 22.14: DeckOfCards.h
 2   // Definition of class DeckOfCards that
 3   // represents a deck of playing cards.
 4   #include <array>
 5
 6   // BitCard structure definition with bit fields
 7   struct BitCard {
 8      unsigned face : 4; // 4 bits; 0-15
 9      unsigned suit : 2; // 2 bits; 0-3
10      unsigned color : 1; // 1 bit; 0-1
11   };
12
13   // DeckOfCards class definition
14   class DeckOfCards {
15   public:
16      static const int faces{13};
17      static const int colors{2}; // black and red
18      static const int numberOfCards{52};
19
20      DeckOfCards(); // constructor initializes deck
21      void deal() const; // deals cards in deck
22   private:
23      std::array<BitCard, numberOfCards> deck; // represents deck of cards
24   };
```

Fig. 22.14 | Definition of class DeckOfCards that represents a deck of playing cards.

```cpp
 1   // Fig. 22.15: DeckOfCards.cpp
 2   // Member-function definitions for class DeckOfCards that simulates
 3   // the shuffling and dealing of a deck of playing cards.
 4   #include <iostream>
 5   #include <iomanip>
 6   #include "DeckOfCards.h" // DeckOfCards class definition
 7   using namespace std;
 8
```

Fig. 22.15 | Member-function definitions for class DeckOfCards. (Part 1 of 2.)

```
9    // no-argument DeckOfCards constructor intializes deck
10   DeckOfCards::DeckOfCards() {
11      for (size_t i{0}; i < deck.size(); ++i) {
12         deck[i].face = i % faces; // faces in order
13         deck[i].suit = i / faces; // suits in order
14         deck[i].color = i / (faces * colors); // colors in order
15      }
16   }
17
18   // deal cards in deck
19   void DeckOfCards::deal() const {
20      for (size_t k1{0}, k2{k1 + deck.size() / 2};
21         k1 < deck.size() / 2 - 1; ++k1, ++k2) {
22         cout << "Card:" << setw(3) << deck[k1].face
23            << " Suit:" << setw(2) << deck[k1].suit
24            << " Color:" << setw(2) << deck[k1].color
25            << "   " << "Card:" << setw(3) << deck[k2].face
26            << " Suit:" << setw(2) << deck[k2].suit
27            << " Color:" << setw(2) << deck[k2].color   << endl;
28      }
29   }
```

Fig. 22.15 | Member-function definitions for class DeckOfCards. (Part 2 of 2.)

```
1    // Fig. 22.16: fig22_16.cpp
2    // Card shuffling and dealing program.
3    #include "DeckOfCards.h" // DeckOfCards class definition
4
5    int main() {
6       DeckOfCards deckOfCards; // create DeckOfCards object
7       deckOfCards.deal(); // deal the cards in the deck
8    }
```

```
Card:  0  Suit: 0  Color: 0    Card:  0  Suit: 2  Color: 1
Card:  1  Suit: 0  Color: 0    Card:  1  Suit: 2  Color: 1
Card:  2  Suit: 0  Color: 0    Card:  2  Suit: 2  Color: 1
Card:  3  Suit: 0  Color: 0    Card:  3  Suit: 2  Color: 1
Card:  4  Suit: 0  Color: 0    Card:  4  Suit: 2  Color: 1
Card:  5  Suit: 0  Color: 0    Card:  5  Suit: 2  Color: 1
Card:  6  Suit: 0  Color: 0    Card:  6  Suit: 2  Color: 1
Card:  7  Suit: 0  Color: 0    Card:  7  Suit: 2  Color: 1
Card:  8  Suit: 0  Color: 0    Card:  8  Suit: 2  Color: 1
Card:  9  Suit: 0  Color: 0    Card:  9  Suit: 2  Color: 1
Card: 10  Suit: 0  Color: 0    Card: 10  Suit: 2  Color: 1
Card: 11  Suit: 0  Color: 0    Card: 11  Suit: 2  Color: 1
Card: 12  Suit: 0  Color: 0    Card: 12  Suit: 2  Color: 1
Card:  0  Suit: 1  Color: 0    Card:  0  Suit: 3  Color: 1
Card:  1  Suit: 1  Color: 0    Card:  1  Suit: 3  Color: 1
Card:  2  Suit: 1  Color: 0    Card:  2  Suit: 3  Color: 1
Card:  3  Suit: 1  Color: 0    Card:  3  Suit: 3  Color: 1
Card:  4  Suit: 1  Color: 0    Card:  4  Suit: 3  Color: 1
Card:  5  Suit: 1  Color: 0    Card:  5  Suit: 3  Color: 1
```

Fig. 22.16 | Bit fields used to store a deck of cards. (Part 1 of 2.)

```
Card:  6  Suit: 1  Color: 0    Card:  6  Suit: 3  Color: 1
Card:  7  Suit: 1  Color: 0    Card:  7  Suit: 3  Color: 1
Card:  8  Suit: 1  Color: 0    Card:  8  Suit: 3  Color: 1
Card:  9  Suit: 1  Color: 0    Card:  9  Suit: 3  Color: 1
Card: 10  Suit: 1  Color: 0    Card: 10  Suit: 3  Color: 1
Card: 11  Suit: 1  Color: 0    Card: 11  Suit: 3  Color: 1
Card: 12  Suit: 1  Color: 0    Card: 12  Suit: 3  Color: 1
```

Fig. 22.16 | Bit fields used to store a deck of cards. (Part 2 of 2.)

It's possible to specify an unnamed bit field, in which case the field is used as padding in the structure. For example, the structure definition uses an unnamed three-bit field as padding—nothing can be stored in those three bits. Member b is stored in another storage unit.

```
struct Example {
    unsigned a : 13;
    unsigned   : 3; // align to next storage-unit boundary
    unsigned b : 4;
};
```

An unnamed bit field with a zero width is used to align the next bit field on a new storage-unit boundary. For example, the structure definition

```
struct Example {
    unsigned a : 13;
    unsigned   : 0; // align to next storage-unit boundary
    unsigned b : 4;
};
```

uses an unnamed 0-bit field to *skip* the remaining bits (as many as there are) of the storage unit in which a is stored and align b on the *next storage-unit boundary*.

Portability Tip 22.4

Bit-field manipulations are machine dependent. For example, some computers allow bit fields to cross word boundaries, whereas others do not.

Common Programming Error 22.5

Attempting to access individual bits of a bit field with subscripting as if they were elements of an array is a compilation error. Bit fields are not "arrays of bits."

Common Programming Error 22.6

Attempting to take the address of a bit field (the & operator may not be used with bit fields because a pointer can designate only a particular byte in memory and bit fields can start in the middle of a byte) is a compilation error.

Performance Tip 22.2

Although bit fields save space, using them can cause the compiler to generate slower-executing machine-language code. This occurs because it takes extra machine-language operations to access only portions of an addressable storage unit. This is one of many examples of the space–time trade-offs that occur in computer science.

22.7 Character-Handling Library

Most data is entered into computers as *characters*—including letters, digits and various special symbols. In this section, we discuss C++'s capabilities for examining and manipulating individual characters. In the remainder of the chapter, we continue the discussion of *character-string manipulation* that we began in Chapter 8.

The character-handling library includes several functions that perform useful tests and manipulations of character data. Each function receives a character—represented as an `int`—or EOF as an argument. *Characters are often manipulated as integers.* Remember that EOF normally has the value –1 and that some hardware architectures do not allow negative values to be stored in char variables. Therefore, the character-handling functions manipulate characters as integers. Figure 22.17 summarizes the functions of the character-handling library. When using functions from the character-handling library, include the `<cctype>` header.

Prototype	Description
int isdigit(int c)	Returns 1 if c is a *digit* and 0 otherwise.
int isalpha(int c)	Returns 1 if c is a *letter* and 0 otherwise.
int isalnum(int c)	Returns 1 if c is a *digit or a letter* and 0 otherwise.
int isxdigit(int c)	Returns 1 if c is a *hexadecimal digit* character and 0 otherwise. (See Appendix D for a detailed explanation of binary, octal, decimal and hexadecimal numbers.)
int islower(int c)	Returns 1 if c is a *lowercase letter* and 0 otherwise.
int isupper(int c)	Returns 1 if c is an *uppercase letter;* 0 otherwise.
int tolower(int c)	If c is an *uppercase letter,* tolower returns c as a *lowercase letter.* Otherwise, tolower returns the argument *unchanged.*
int toupper(int c)	If c is a *lowercase letter,* toupper returns c as an *uppercase letter.* Otherwise, toupper returns the argument *unchanged.*
int isspace(int c)	Returns 1 if c is a *whitespace character*—newline ('\n'), space (' '), form feed ('\f'), carriage return ('\r'), horizontal tab ('\t'), or vertical tab ('\v')—and 0 otherwise.
int iscntrl(int c)	Returns 1 if c is a *control character,* such as newline ('\n'), form feed ('\f'), carriage return ('\r'), horizontal tab ('\t'), vertical tab ('\v'), alert ('\a'), or backspace ('\b')—and 0 otherwise.
int ispunct(int c)	Returns 1 if c is a *printing character other than a space,* a *digit,* or a *letter* and 0 otherwise.
int isprint(int c)	Returns 1 if c is a *printing character including space* (' ') and 0 otherwise.
int isgraph(int c)	Returns 1 if c is a *printing character other than space* (' ') and 0 otherwise.

Fig. 22.17 | Character-handling library functions.

Figure 22.18 demonstrates functions `isdigit`, `isalpha`, `isalnum` and `isxdigit`. Function `isdigit` determines whether its argument is a *digit* (0–9). Function `isalpha` determines whether its argument is an *uppercase letter* (A–Z) or a *lowercase letter* (a–z).

Function isalnum determines whether its argument is an *uppercase letter, a lowercase letter or a digit*. Function isxdigit determines whether its argument is a *hexadecimal digit* (A–F, a–f, 0–9).

```cpp
1   // Fig. 22.18: fig22_18.cpp
2   // Character-handling functions isdigit, isalpha, isalnum and isxdigit.
3   #include <iostream>
4   #include <cctype> // character-handling function prototypes
5   using namespace std;
6
7   int main() {
8      cout << "According to isdigit:\n"
9         << (isdigit('8') ? "8 is a" : "8 is not a") << " digit\n"
10        << (isdigit('#') ? "# is a" : "# is not a") << " digit\n";
11
12     cout << "\nAccording to isalpha:\n"
13        << (isalpha('A') ? "A is a" : "A is not a") << " letter\n"
14        << (isalpha('b') ? "b is a" : "b is not a") << " letter\n"
15        << (isalpha('&') ? "& is a" : "& is not a") << " letter\n"
16        << (isalpha('4') ? "4 is a" : "4 is not a") << " letter\n";
17
18     cout << "\nAccording to isalnum:\n"
19        << (isalnum('A') ? "A is a" : "A is not a")
20        << " digit or a letter\n"
21        << (isalnum('8') ? "8 is a" : "8 is not a")
22        << " digit or a letter\n"
23        << (isalnum('#') ? "# is a" : "# is not a")
24        << " digit or a letter\n";
25
26     cout << "\nAccording to isxdigit:\n"
27        << (isxdigit('F') ? "F is a" : "F is not a")
28        << " hexadecimal digit\n"
29        << (isxdigit('J') ? "J is a" : "J is not a")
30        << " hexadecimal digit\n"
31        << (isxdigit('7') ? "7 is a" : "7 is not a")
32        << " hexadecimal digit\n"
33        << (isxdigit('$') ? "$ is a" : "$ is not a")
34        << " hexadecimal digit\n"
35        << (isxdigit('f') ? "f is a" : "f is not a")
36        << " hexadecimal digit" << endl;
37  }
```

```
According to isdigit:
8 is a digit
# is not a digi

According to isalpha:
A is a letter
b is a letter
& is not a letter
4 is not a letter
```

Fig. 22.18 | Character-handling functions isdigit, isalpha, isalnum and isxdigit. (Part 1 of 2.)

```
According to isalnum:
A is a digit or a letter
8 is a digit or a letter
# is not a digit or a letter

According to isxdigit:
F is a hexadecimal digit
J is not a hexadecimal digit
7 is a hexadecimal digit
$ is not a hexadecimal digit
f is a hexadecimal digit
```

Fig. 22.18 | Character-handling functions isdigit, isalpha, isalnum and isxdigit. (Part 2 of 2.)

Figure 22.18 uses the *conditional operator (?:)* with each function to determine whether the string " is a " or the string " is not a " should be printed in the output for each character tested. For example, line 9 indicates that if '8' is a digit—i.e., if isdigit returns a true (nonzero) value—the string "8 is a " is printed. If '8' is not a digit (i.e., if isdigit returns 0), the string "8 is not a " is printed.

Figure 22.19 demonstrates functions islower, isupper, tolower and toupper. Function islower determines whether its argument is a *lowercase letter* (a–z). Function isupper determines whether its argument is an *uppercase letter* (A–Z). Function tolower converts an uppercase letter to lowercase and returns the lowercase letter—if the argument is not an uppercase letter, tolower returns the argument value unchanged. Function toupper converts a lowercase letter to uppercase and returns the uppercase letter—if the argument is *not* a lowercase letter, toupper returns the argument value *unchanged*.

```cpp
1   // Fig. 22.19: fig22_19.cpp
2   // Character-handling functions islower, isupper, tolower and toupper.
3   #include <iostream>
4   #include <cctype> // character-handling function prototypes
5   using namespace std;
6
7   int main() {
8      cout << "According to islower:\n"
9         << (islower('p') ? "p is a" : "p is not a")
10        << " lowercase letter\n"
11        << (islower('P') ? "P is a" : "P is not a")
12        << " lowercase letter\n"
13        << (islower('5') ? "5 is a" : "5 is not a")
14        << " lowercase letter\n"
15        << (islower('!') ? "! is a" : "! is not a")
16        << " lowercase letter\n";
17
```

Fig. 22.19 | Character-handling functions islower, isupper, tolower and toupper. (Part 1 of 2.)

```
18      cout << "\nAccording to isupper:\n"
19          << (isupper('D') ? "D is an" : "D is not an")
20          << " uppercase letter\n"
21          << (isupper('d') ? "d is an" : "d is not an")
22          << " uppercase letter\n"
23          << (isupper('8') ? "8 is an" : "8 is not an")
24          << " uppercase letter\n"
25          << (isupper('$') ? "$ is an" : "$ is not an")
26          << " uppercase letter\n";
27
28      cout << "\nu converted to uppercase is "
29          << static_cast<char>(toupper('u'))
30          << "\n7 converted to uppercase is "
31          << static_cast<char>(toupper('7'))
32          << "\n$ converted to uppercase is "
33          << static_cast<char>(toupper('$'))
34          << "\nL converted to lowercase is "
35          << static_cast<char>(tolower('L')) << endl;
36  }
```

```
According to islower:
p is a lowercase letter
P is not a lowercase letter
5 is not a lowercase letter
! is not a lowercase letter

According to isupper:
D is an uppercase letter
d is not an uppercase letter
8 is not an uppercase letter
$ is not an uppercase letter

u converted to uppercase is U
7 converted to uppercase is 7
$ converted to uppercase is $
L converted to lowercase is l
```

Fig. 22.19 | Character-handling functions islower, isupper, tolower and toupper. (Part 2 of 2.)

Figure 22.20 demonstrates functions isspace, iscntrl, ispunct, isprint and isgraph. Function isspace determines whether its argument is a *whitespace character*, such as space (' '), form feed ('\f'), newline ('\n'), carriage return ('\r'), horizontal tab ('\t') or vertical tab ('\v'). Function iscntrl determines whether its argument is a *control character* such as horizontal tab ('\t'), vertical tab ('\v'), form feed ('\f'), alert ('\a'), backspace ('\b'), carriage return ('\r') or newline ('\n'). Function ispunct determines whether its argument is a *printing character other than a space, digit or letter*, such as $, #, (,), [,], {, }, ;, : or %. Function isprint determines whether its argument is a character that can be *displayed on the screen* (including the space character). Function isgraph tests for the same characters as isprint, but the space character is *not* included.

```cpp
1  // Fig. 22.20: fig22_20.cpp
2  // Using functions isspace, iscntrl, ispunct, isprint and isgraph.
3  #include <iostream>
4  #include <cctype> // character-handling function prototypes
5  using namespace std;
6
7  int main() {
8     cout << "According to isspace:\nNewline "
9        << (isspace('\n') ? "is a" : "is not a")
10       << " whitespace character\nHorizontal tab "
11       << (isspace('\t') ? "is a" : "is not a")
12       << " whitespace character\n"
13       << (isspace('%') ? "% is a" : "% is not a")
14       << " whitespace character\n";
15
16    cout << "\nAccording to iscntrl:\nNewline "
17       << (iscntrl('\n') ? "is a" : "is not a")
18       << " control character\n"
19       << (iscntrl('$') ? "$ is a" : "$ is not a")
20       << " control character\n";
21
22    cout << "\nAccording to ispunct:\n"
23       << (ispunct(';') ? "; is a" : "; is not a")
24       << " punctuation character\n"
25       << (ispunct('Y') ? "Y is a" : "Y is not a")
26       << " punctuation character\n"
27       << (ispunct('#') ? "# is a" : "# is not a")
28       << " punctuation character\n";
29
30    cout << "\nAccording to isprint:\n"
31       << (isprint('$') ? "$ is a" : "$ is not a")
32       << " printing character\nAlert "
33       << (isprint('\a') ? "is a" : "is not a")
34       << " printing character\nSpace "
35       << (isprint(' ') ? "is a" : "is not a")
36       << " printing character\n";
37
38    cout << "\nAccording to isgraph:\n"
39       << (isgraph('Q') ? "Q is a" : "Q is not a")
40       << " printing character other than a space\nSpace "
41       << (isgraph(' ') ? "is a" : "is not a")
42       << " printing character other than a space" << endl;
43 }
```

```
According to isspace:
Newline is a whitespace character
Horizontal tab is a whitespace character
% is not a whitespace character

According to iscntrl:
Newline is a control character
$ is not a control character
```

Fig. 22.20 | Character-handling functions isspace, iscntrl, ispunct, isprint and isgraph. (Part 1 of 2.)

```
According to ispunct:
; is a punctuation character
Y is not a punctuation character
# is a punctuation character

According to isprint:
$ is a printing character
Alert is not a printing character
Space is a printing character

According to isgraph:
Q is a printing character other than a space
Space is not a printing character other than a space
```

Fig. 22.20 | Character-handling functions isspace, iscntrl, ispunct, isprint and isgraph. (Part 2 of 2.)

22.8 C String-Manipulation Functions

The string-handling library provides any useful functions for manipulating string data, *comparing* strings, *searching* strings for characters and other strings, *tokenizing* strings (separating strings into logical pieces such as the separate words in a sentence) and determining the *length* of strings. This section presents some common string-manipulation functions of the string-handling library (from the *C++ standard library*). The functions are summarized in Fig. 22.21; then each is used in a live-code example. The prototypes for these functions are located in header <cstring>.

Function prototype	Function description
char* **strcpy**(char* s1, const char* s2);	
	Copies the string s2 into the character array s1. The value of s1 is returned.
char* **strncpy**(char* s1, const char* s2, size_t n);	
	Copies at most n characters of the string s2 into the character array s1. The value of s1 is returned.
char* **strcat**(char* s1, const char* s2);	
	Appends the string s2 to s1. The first character of s2 overwrites the terminating null character of s1. The value of s1 is returned.
char* **strncat**(char* s1, const char* s2, size_t n);	
	Appends at most n characters of string s2 to string s1. The first character of s2 overwrites the terminating null character of s1. The value of s1 is returned.
int **strcmp**(const char* s1, const char* s2);	
	Compares the string s1 with the string s2. The function returns a value of zero, less than zero or greater than zero if s1 is equal to, less than or greater than s2, respectively.

Fig. 22.21 | String-manipulation functions of the string-handling library. (Part 1 of 2.)

Function prototype	Function description
`int strncmp(const char* s1, const char* s2, size_t n);`	
	Compares up to n characters of the string s1 with the string s2. The function returns zero, less than zero or greater than zero if the n-character portion of s1 is equal to, less than or greater than the corresponding n-character portion of s2, respectively.
`char* strtok(char* s1, const char* s2);`	
	A sequence of calls to strtok breaks string s1 into *tokens*—logical pieces such as words in a line of text. The string is broken up based on the characters contained in string s2. For instance, if we were to break the string "this:is:a:string" into tokens based on the character ':', the resulting tokens would be "this", "is", "a" and "string". Function strtok returns only one token at a time—the first call contains s1 as the first argument, and subsequent calls to continue tokenizing the same string contain NULL as the first argument. A pointer to the current token is returned by each call. If there are no more tokens when the function is called, NULL is returned.
`size_t strlen(const char* s);`	
	Determines the length of string s. The number of characters preceding the terminating null character is returned.

Fig. 22.21 | String-manipulation functions of the string-handling library. (Part 2 of 2.)

Several functions in Fig. 22.21 contain parameters with data type size_t. This type is defined in the header <cstring> to be an unsigned integral type such as unsigned int or unsigned long.

 Common Programming Error 22.7
Forgetting to include the <cstring> header when using functions from the string-handling library causes compilation errors.

Copying Strings with strcpy and strncpy

Function strcpy copies its second argument—a string—into its first argument—a character array that must be large enough to store the string *and* its *terminating null character*, (which is also copied). Function strncpy is much like strcpy, except that strncpy specifies the number of characters to be copied from the string into the array. Function strncpy does *not* necessarily copy the terminating null character of its second argument—a terminating null character is written only if the number of characters to be copied is at least one more than the length of the string. For example, if "test" is the second argument, a terminating null character is written *only* if the third argument to strncpy is at least 5 (four characters in "test" plus one terminating null character). If the third argument is larger than 5, null characters are appended to the array until the total number of characters specified by the third argument is written.

Common Programming Error 22.8

When using strncpy, *the terminating null character of the second argument (a* char* *string) will not be copied if the number of characters specified by* strncpy's *third argument is not greater than the second argument's length. In that case, a fatal error may occur if you do not manually terminate the resulting* char* *string with a null character.*

Figure 22.22 uses strcpy (line 12) to copy the entire string in array x into array y and uses strncpy (line 18) to copy the first 14 characters of array x into array z. Line 19 appends a null character ('\0') to array z, because the call to strncpy in the program does not write a terminating null character. (The third argument is less than the string length of the second argument plus one.)

```cpp
1   // Fig. 22.22: fig22_22.cpp
2   // Using strcpy and strncpy.
3   #include <iostream>
4   #include <cstring> // prototypes for strcpy and strncpy
5   using namespace std;
6
7   int main() {
8      char x[]{"Happy Birthday to You"}; // string length 21
9      char y[25];
10     char z[15];
11
12     strcpy(y, x); // copy contents of x into y
13
14     cout << "The string in array x is: " << x
15        << "\nThe string in array y is: " << y << '\n';
16
17     // copy first 14 characters of x into z
18     strncpy(z, x, 14); // does not copy null character
19     z[14] = '\0'; // append '\0' to z's contents
20
21     cout << "The string in array z is: " << z << endl;
22   }
```

```
The string in array x is: Happy Birthday to You
The string in array y is: Happy Birthday to You
The string in array z is: Happy Birthday
```

Fig. 22.22 | strcpy and strncpy.

Concatenating Strings with *strcat and strncat*

Function strcat appends its second argument (a string) to its first argument (a character array containing a string). The first character of the second argument replaces the null character ('\0') that terminates the string in the first argument. You must ensure that the array used to store the first string is *large enough* to store the combination of the first string, the second string and the terminating null character (copied from the second string). Function strncat appends a specified number of characters from the second string to the first string and appends a terminating null character to the result. The program of Fig. 22.23 demonstrates function strcat (lines 14 and 24) and function strncat (line 19).

```
1   // Fig. 22.23: fig23_23.cpp
2   // Using strcat and strncat.
3   #include <iostream>
4   #include <cstring> // prototypes for strcat and strncat
5   using namespace std;
6
7   int main() {
8      char s1[20]{"Happy "}; // length 6
9      char s2[]{"New Year "}; // length 9
10     char s3[40]{""};
11
12     cout << "s1 = " << s1 << "\ns2 = " << s2;
13
14     strcat(s1, s2); // concatenate s2 to s1 (length 15)
15
16     cout << "\n\nAfter strcat(s1, s2):\ns1 = " << s1 << "\ns2 = " << s2;
17
18     // concatenate first 6 characters of s1 to s3
19     strncat(s3, s1, 6); // places '\0' after last character
20
21     cout << "\n\nAfter strncat(s3, s1, 6):\ns1 = " << s1
22        << "\ns3 = " << s3;
23
24     strcat(s3, s1); // concatenate s1 to s3
25     cout << "\n\nAfter strcat(s3, s1):\ns1 = " << s1
26        << "\ns3 = " << s3 << endl;
27  }
```

```
s1 = Happy
s2 = New Year

After strcat(s1, s2):
s1 = Happy New Year
s2 = New Year

After strncat(s3, s1, 6):
s1 = Happy New Year
s3 = Happy

After strcat(s3, s1):
s1 = Happy New Year
s3 = Happy Happy New Year
```

Fig. 22.23 | strcat and strncat.

Comparing Strings with strcmp and strncmp

Figure 22.24 compares three strings using strcmp (lines 14–16) and strncmp (lines 19–21). Function strcmp compares its first string argument with its second string argument character by character. The function returns zero if the strings are equal, a negative value if the first string is less than the second string and a positive value if the first string is greater than the second string. Function strncmp is equivalent to strcmp, except that strncmp compares up to a specified number of characters. Function strncmp stops comparing characters if it reaches the null character in one of its string arguments. The program prints the integer value returned by each function call.

Common Programming Error 22.9

Assuming that strcmp and strncmp return one (a true value) when their arguments are equal is a logic error. Both functions return zero (C++'s false value) for equality. Therefore, when testing two strings for equality, the result of the strcmp or strncmp function should be compared with zero to determine whether the strings are equal.

```cpp
// Fig. 22.24: fig22_24.cpp
// Using strcmp and strncmp.
#include <iostream>
#include <iomanip>
#include <cstring> // prototypes for strcmp and strncmp
using namespace std;

int main() {
   const char* s1{"Happy New Year"};
   const char* s2{"Happy New Year"};
   const char* s3{"Happy Holidays"};

   cout << "s1 = " << s1 << "\ns2 = " << s2 << "\ns3 = " << s3
      << "\n\nstrcmp(s1, s2) = " << setw(2) << strcmp(s1, s2)
      << "\nstrcmp(s1, s3) = " << setw(2) << strcmp(s1, s3)
      << "\nstrcmp(s3, s1) = " << setw(2) << strcmp(s3, s1);

   cout << "\n\nstrncmp(s1, s3, 6) = " << setw(2)
      << strncmp(s1, s3, 6) << "\nstrncmp(s1, s3, 7) = " << setw(2)
      << strncmp(s1, s3, 7) << "\nstrncmp(s3, s1, 7) = " << setw(2)
      << strncmp(s3, s1, 7) << endl;
}
```

```
s1 = Happy New Year
s2 = Happy New Year
s3 = Happy Holidays

strcmp(s1, s2) =  0
strcmp(s1, s3) =  1
strcmp(s3, s1) = -1

strncmp(s1, s3, 6) =  0
strncmp(s1, s3, 7) =  1
strncmp(s3, s1, 7) = -1
```

Fig. 22.24 | strcmp and strncmp.

To understand what it means for one string to be "greater than" or "less than" another, consider the process of alphabetizing last names. You'd, no doubt, place "Jones" before "Smith," because the first letter of "Jones" comes before the first letter of "Smith" in the alphabet. But the alphabet is more than just a list of 26 letters—it's an *ordered* list of characters. Each letter occurs in a specific position within the list. "Z" is more than just a letter of the alphabet; "Z" is specifically the 26th letter of the alphabet.

How does the computer know that one letter "comes before" another? All characters are represented inside the computer as numeric codes; when the computer compares two strings, it actually compares the numeric codes of the characters in the strings.

[*Note:* With some compilers, functions `strcmp` and `strncmp` always return -1, 0 or 1, as in the sample output of Fig. 22.24. With other compilers, these functions return 0 or the difference between the numeric codes of the first characters that differ in the strings being compared. For example, when `s1` and `s3` are compared, the first characters that differ between them are the first character of the second word in each string—N (numeric code 78) in `s1` and H (numeric code 72) in `s3`, respectively. In this case, the return value will be 6 (or -6 if `s3` is compared to `s1`).]

Tokenizing a String with **strtok**

Function `strtok` breaks a string into a series of tokens. A token is a sequence of characters separated by delimiting characters (usually spaces or punctuation marks). For example, in a line of text, each word can be considered a token, and the spaces separating the words can be considered delimiters. Multiple calls to `strtok` are required to break a string into tokens (assuming that the string contains more than one token). The first call to `strtok` contains two arguments, a string to be tokenized and a string containing characters that separate the tokens (i.e., delimiters). Line 14 in Fig. 22.25 initializes `tokenPtr` with a pointer to the first token in `sentence`. The second argument, " ", indicates that tokens in `sentence` are separated by spaces. Function `strtok` searches for the first character in `sentence` that's not a delimiting character (space). This begins the first token. The function then finds the next delimiting character in the string and replaces it with a null (`'\0'`) character. This terminates the current token. Function `strtok` saves (in a `static` variable) a pointer to the next character following the token in `sentence` and returns a pointer to the current token.

```
1   // Fig. 22.25: fig22_25.cpp
2   // Using strtok to tokenize a string.
3   #include <iostream>
4   #include <cstring> // prototype for strtok
5   using namespace std;
6
7   int main() {
8      char sentence[]{"This is a sentence with 7 tokens"};
9
10     cout << "The string to be tokenized is:\n" << sentence
11        << "\n\nThe tokens are:\n\n";
12
13     // begin tokenization of sentence
14     char* tokenPtr{strtok(sentence, " ")};
15
16     // continue tokenizing sentence until tokenPtr becomes NULL
17     while (tokenPtr != NULL) {
18        cout << tokenPtr << '\n';
19        tokenPtr = strtok(NULL, " "); // get next token
20     }
```

Fig. 22.25 | Using strtok to tokenize a string. (Part 1 of 2.)

```
21
22      cout << "\nAfter strtok, sentence = " << sentence << endl;
23  }
```

```
The string to be tokenized is:
This is a sentence with 7 tokens

The tokens are:

This
is
a
sentence
with
7
tokens

After strtok, sentence = This
```

Fig. 22.25 | Using strtok to tokenize a string. (Part 2 of 2.)

Subsequent calls to strtok to continue tokenizing sentence contain NULL as the first argument (line 19). The NULL argument indicates that the call to strtok should continue tokenizing from the location in sentence saved by the last call to strtok. Function strtok maintains this saved information in a manner that's not visible to you. If no tokens remain when strtok is called, strtok returns NULL. The program of Fig. 22.25 uses strtok to tokenize the string "This is a sentence with 7 tokens". The program prints each token on a separate line. Line 22 outputs sentence after tokenization. Note that *strtok modifies the input string*; therefore, a copy of the string should be made if the program requires the original after the calls to strtok. When sentence is output after tokenization, only the word "This" prints, because strtok replaced each blank in sentence with a null character ('\0') during the tokenization process.

Common Programming Error 22.10
Not realizing that strtok modifies the string being tokenized, then attempting to use that string as if it were the original unmodified string is a logic error.

Determining String Lengths
Function strlen takes a string as an argument and returns the number of characters in the string—the terminating null character is not included in the length. The length is also the index of the null character. The program of Fig. 22.26 demonstrates function strlen.

```
1   // Fig. 22.26: fig22_26.cpp
2   // Using strlen.
3   #include <iostream>
4   #include <cstring> // prototype for strlen
5   using namespace std;
6
```

Fig. 22.26 | strlen returns the length of a char* string. (Part 1 of 2.)

```
7   int main() {
8      const char* string1{"abcdefghijklmnopqrstuvwxyz"};
9      const char* string2{"four"};
10     const char* string3{"Boston"};
11
12     cout << "The length of \"" << string1 << "\" is " << strlen(string1)
13        << "\nThe length of \"" << string2 << "\" is " << strlen(string2)
14        << "\nThe length of \"" << string3 << "\" is " << strlen(string3)
15        << endl;
16  }
```

```
The length of "abcdefghijklmnopqrstuvwxyz" is 26
The length of "four" is 4
The length of "Boston" is 6
```

Fig. 22.26 | `strlen` returns the length of a char* string. (Part 2 of 2.)

22.9 C String-Conversion Functions

In Section 22.8, we discussed several of C++'s most popular C string-manipulation functions. In the next several sections, we cover the remaining functions, including functions for converting strings to numeric values, functions for searching strings and functions for manipulating, comparing and searching blocks of memory.

This section presents the C string-conversion functions from the general-utilities library <cstdlib>. These functions convert C strings to integer and floating-point values. In new code, C++ programmers typically use the string stream processing capabilities (Chapter 21) to perform such conversions. Figure 22.27 summarizes the C string-conversion functions. When using functions from the general-utilities library, include the <cstdlib> header.

Prototype	Description
`double atof(const char* nPtr)`	Converts the string nPtr to double. If the string cannot be converted, 0 is returned.
`int atoi(const char* nPtr)`	Converts the string nPtr to int. If the string cannot be converted, 0 is returned.
`long atol(const char* nPtr)`	Converts the string nPtr to long int. If the string cannot be converted, 0 is returned.
`double strtod(const char* nPtr, char** endPtr)`	Converts the string nPtr to double. endPtr is the address of a pointer to the rest of the string after the double. If the string cannot be converted, 0 is returned.

Fig. 22.27 | C string-conversion functions of the general-utilities library. (Part 1 of 2.)

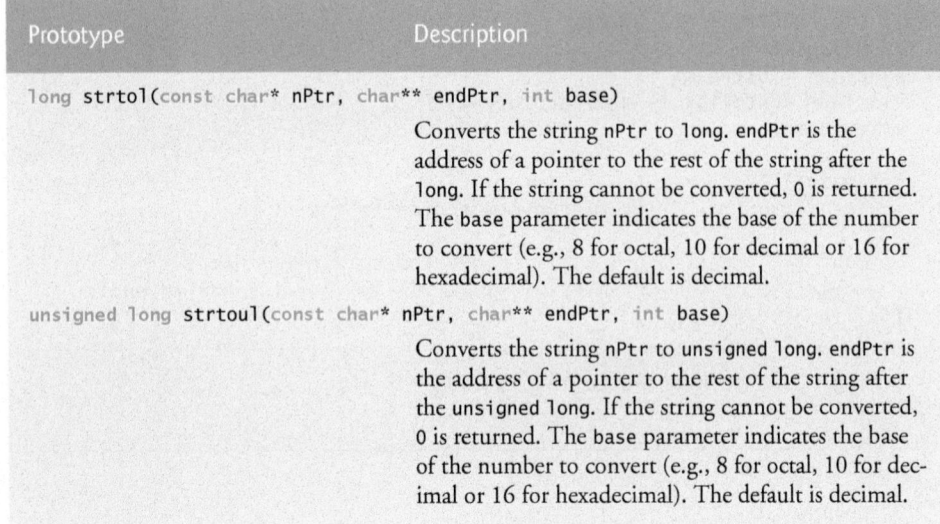

Prototype	Description
`long strtol(const char* nPtr, char** endPtr, int base)`	
	Converts the string nPtr to long. endPtr is the address of a pointer to the rest of the string after the long. If the string cannot be converted, 0 is returned. The base parameter indicates the base of the number to convert (e.g., 8 for octal, 10 for decimal or 16 for hexadecimal). The default is decimal.
`unsigned long strtoul(const char* nPtr, char** endPtr, int base)`	
	Converts the string nPtr to unsigned long. endPtr is the address of a pointer to the rest of the string after the unsigned long. If the string cannot be converted, 0 is returned. The base parameter indicates the base of the number to convert (e.g., 8 for octal, 10 for decimal or 16 for hexadecimal). The default is decimal.

Fig. 22.27 | C string-conversion functions of the general-utilities library. (Part 2 of 2.)

Function `atof` (Fig. 22.28, line 8) converts its argument—a string that represents a floating-point number—to a `double` value. The function returns the `double` value. If the string cannot be converted—for example, if the first character of the string is not a digit—function atof returns zero.

```
 1   // Fig. 22.28: fig22_28.cpp
 2   // Using atof.
 3   #include <iostream>
 4   #include <cstdlib> // atof prototype
 5   using namespace std;
 6
 7   int main() {
 8      double d{atof("99.0")}; // convert string to double
 9
10      cout << "The string \"99.0\" converted to double is " << d
11         << "\nThe converted value divided by 2 is " << d / 2.0 << endl;
12   }
```

```
The string "99.0" converted to double is 99
The converted value divided by 2 is 49.5
```

Fig. 22.28 | String-conversion function atof.

Function `atoi` (Fig. 22.29, line 8) converts its argument—a string of digits that represents an integer—to an `int` value. The function returns the `int` value. If the string cannot be converted, function atoi returns zero.

```
1   // Fig. 22.29: fig22_29.cpp
2   // Using atoi.
3   #include <iostream>
4   #include <cstdlib> // atoi prototype
5   using namespace std;
6
7   int main() {
8      int i{atoi("2593")}; // convert string to int
9
10     cout << "The string \"2593\" converted to int is " << i
11        << "\nThe converted value minus 593 is " << i - 593 << endl;
12  }
```

```
The string "2593" converted to int is 2593
The converted value minus 593 is 2000
```

Fig. 22.29 | String-conversion function atoi.

Function atol (Fig. 22.30, line 8) converts its argument—a string of digits representing a long integer—to a long value. The function returns the long value. If the string cannot be converted, function atol returns zero. If int and long are both stored in four bytes, function atoi and function atol work identically.

```
1   // Fig. 22.30: fig22_30.cpp
2   // Using atol.
3   #include <iostream>
4   #include <cstdlib> // atol prototype
5   using namespace std;
6
7   int main() {
8      long x{atol("1000000")}; // convert string to long
9
10     cout << "The string \"1000000\" converted to long is " << x
11        << "\nThe converted value divided by 2 is " << x / 2 << endl;
12  }
```

```
The string "1000000" converted to long int is 1000000
The converted value divided by 2 is 500000
```

Fig. 22.30 | String-conversion function atol.

Function strtod (Fig. 22.31) converts a sequence of characters representing a floating-point value to double. Function strtod receives two arguments—a string (char*) and the address of a char* pointer (i.e., a char**). The string contains the character sequence to be converted to double. The second argument enables strtod to modify a char* pointer in the calling function, such that the pointer points to the location of the first character after the converted portion of the string. Line 11 indicates that d is assigned the double value converted from string and that stringPtr is assigned the location of the first character after the converted value (51.2) in string.

```
1   // Fig. 22.31: fig22_31.cpp
2   // Using strtod.
3   #include <iostream>
4   #include <cstdlib> // strtod prototype
5   using namespace std;
6
7   int main() {
8      const char*string1{"51.2% are admitted"};
9      char* stringPtr{nullptr};
10
11     double d{strtod(string1, &stringPtr)}; // convert to double
12
13     cout << "The string \"" << string1
14        << "\" is converted to the\ndouble value " << d
15        << " and the string \"" << stringPtr << "\"" << endl;
16  }
```

```
The string "51.2% are admitted" is converted to the
double value 51.2 and the string "% are admitted"
```

Fig. 22.31 | String-conversion function strtod.

Function strtol (Fig. 22.32) converts to long a sequence of characters representing an integer. The function receives a string (char*), the address of a char* pointer and an integer. The string contains the character sequence to convert. The second argument is assigned the location of the first character after the converted portion of the string. The integer specifies the *base* of the value being converted. Line 11 indicates that x is assigned the long value converted from string and that remainderPtr is assigned the location of the first character after the converted value (-1234567) in string1. Using a null pointer for the second argument causes the remainder of the string to be ignored. The third argument, 0, indicates that the value to be converted can be in octal (base 8), decimal (base 10) or hexadecimal (base 16). This is determined by the initial characters in the string—0 indicates an octal number, 0x indicates hexadecimal and a number from 1 to 9 indicates decimal.

```
1   // Fig. 22.32: fig22_32.cpp
2   // Using strtol.
3   #include <iostream>
4   #include <cstdlib> // strtol prototype
5   using namespace std;
6
7   int main() {
8      const char* string1{"-1234567abc"};
9      char* remainderPtr{nullptr};
10
11     long x{strtol(string1, &remainderPtr, 0)}; // convert to long
12
```

Fig. 22.32 | String-conversion function strtol. (Part 1 of 2.)

```
13        cout << "The original string is \"" << string1
14           << "\"\nThe converted value is " << x
15           << "\nThe remainder of the original string is \"" << remainderPtr
16           << "\"\nThe converted value plus 567 is " << x + 567 << endl;
17    }
```

```
The original string is "-1234567abc"
The converted value is -1234567
The remainder of the original string is "abc"
The converted value plus 567 is -1234000
```

Fig. 22.32 | String-conversion function `strtol`. (Part 2 of 2.)

In a call to function `strtol`, the base can be specified as zero or as any value between 2 and 36. (See Appendix D for a detailed explanation of the octal, decimal, hexadecimal and binary number systems.) Numeric representations of integers from base 11 to base 36 use the characters A–Z to represent the values 10 to 35. For example, hexadecimal values can consist of the digits 0–9 and the characters A–F. A base-11 integer can consist of the digits 0–9 and the character A. A base-24 integer can consist of the digits 0–9 and the characters A–N. A base-36 integer can consist of the digits 0–9 and the characters A–Z. [*Note:* The case of the letter used is ignored.]

Function `strtoul` (Fig. 22.33) converts to `unsigned long` a sequence of characters representing an `unsigned long` integer. The function works identically to `strtol`. Line 12 indicates that x is assigned the `unsigned long` value converted from `string` and that remainderPtr is assigned the location of the first character after the converted value (1234567) in string1. The third argument, 0, indicates that the value to be converted can be in octal, decimal or hexadecimal format, depending on the initial characters.

```
 1    // Fig. 22.33: fig22_33.cpp
 2    // Using strtoul.
 3    #include <iostream>
 4    #include <cstdlib> // strtoul prototype
 5    using namespace std;
 6
 7    int main() {
 8       const char* string1{"1234567abc"};
 9       char* remainderPtr{nullptr};
10
11       // convert a sequence of characters to unsigned long
12       unsigned long x{strtoul(string1, &remainderPtr, 0)};
13
14       cout << "The original string is \"" << string1
15          << "\"\nThe converted value is " << x
16          << "\nThe remainder of the original string is \"" << remainderPtr
17          << "\"\nThe converted value minus 567 is " << x - 567 << endl;
18    }
```

Fig. 22.33 | String-conversion function `strtoul`. (Part 1 of 2.)

```
The original string is "1234567abc"
The converted value is 1234567
The remainder of the original string is "abc"
The converted value minus 567 is 1234000
```

Fig. 22.33 | String-conversion function `strtoul`. (Part 2 of 2.)

22.10 Search Functions of the C String-Handling Library

This section presents the functions of the string-handling library used to search strings for characters and other strings. The functions are summarized in Fig. 22.34. Functions `strcspn` and `strspn` specify return type `size_t`. Type `size_t` is a type defined by the standard as the integral type of the value returned by operator `sizeof`.

Prototype	Description
`char* strchr(const char* s, int c)`	
	Locates the first occurrence of character c in string s. If c is found, a pointer to c in s is returned. Otherwise, a null pointer is returned.
`char* strrchr(const char* s, int c)`	
	Searches from the end of string s and locates the last occurrence of character c in string s. If c is found, a pointer to c in string s is returned. Otherwise, a null pointer is returned.
`size_t strspn(const char* s1, const char* s2)`	
	Determines and returns the length of the initial segment of string s1 consisting only of characters contained in string s2.
`char* strpbrk(const char* s1, const char* s2)`	
	Locates the first occurrence in string s1 of any character in string s2. If a character from string s2 is found, a pointer to the character in string s1 is returned. Otherwise, a null pointer is returned.
`size_t strcspn(const char* s1, const char* s2)`	
	Determines and returns the length of the initial segment of string s1 consisting of characters not contained in string s2.
`char* strstr(const char* s1, const char* s2)`	
	Locates the first occurrence in string s1 of string s2. If the string is found, a pointer to the string in s1 is returned. Otherwise, a null pointer is returned.

Fig. 22.34 | Search functions of the C string-handling library.

Function `strchr` searches for the first occurrence of a character in a string. If the character is found, `strchr` returns a pointer to the character in the string; otherwise, `strchr` returns a null pointer. The program of Fig. 22.35 uses `strchr` (lines 13 and 23) to search for the first occurrences of `'a'` and `'z'` in the string `"This is a test"`.

```
1   // Fig. 22.35: fig22_35.cpp
2   // Using strchr.
3   #include <iostream>
4   #include <cstring> // strchr prototype
5   using namespace std;
6
7   int main() {
8      const char* string1{"This is a test"};
9      char character1{'a'};
10     char character2{'z'};
11
12     // search for character1 in string1
13     if (strchr(string1, character1) != NULL) {
14        cout << '\'' << character1 << "' was found in \""
15           << string1 << "\".\n";
16     }
17     else {
18        cout << '\'' << character1 << "' was not found in \""
19           << string1 << "\".\n";
20     }
21
22     // search for character2 in string1
23     if (strchr(string1, character2) != NULL) {
24        cout << '\'' << character2 << "' was found in \""
25           << string1 << "\".\n";
26     }
27     else {
28        cout << '\'' << character2 << "' was not found in \""
29           << string1 << "\"." << endl;
30     }
31  }
```

```
'a' was found in "This is a test".
'z' was not found in "This is a test".
```

Fig. 22.35 | String-search function `strchr`.

Function `strcspn` (Fig. 22.36, line 14) determines the length of the initial part of the string in its first argument that does not contain any characters from the string in its second argument. The function returns the length of the segment.

```
1   // Fig. 22.36: fig22_36.cpp
2   // Using strcspn.
3   #include <iostream>
4   #include <cstring> // strcspn prototype
5   using namespace std;
6
7   int main() {
8      const char* string1{"The value is 3.14159"};
9      const char* string2{"1234567890"};
```

Fig. 22.36 | String-search function `strcspn`. (Part 1 of 2.)

```
10
11        cout << "string1 = " << string1 << "\nstring2 = " << string2
12           << "\n\nThe length of the initial segment of string1"
13           << "\ncontaining no characters from string2 = "
14           << strcspn(string1, string2) << endl;
15    }
```

```
string1 = The value is 3.14159
string2 = 1234567890

The length of the initial segment of string1
containing no characters from string2 = 13
```

Fig. 22.36 | String-search function strcspn. (Part 2 of 2.)

Function strpbrk searches for the first occurrence in its first string argument of any character in its second string argument. If a character from the second argument is found, strpbrk returns a pointer to the character in the first argument; otherwise, strpbrk returns a null pointer. Line 12 of Fig. 22.37 locates the first occurrence in string1 of any character from string2.

```
1    // Fig. 22.37: fig22_37.cpp
2    // Using strpbrk.
3    #include <iostream>
4    #include <cstring> // strpbrk prototype
5    using namespace std;
6
7    int main() {
8       const char* string1{"This is a test"};
9       const char* string2{"beware"};
10
11       cout << "Of the characters in \"" << string2 << "\"\n'"
12          << *strpbrk(string1, string2) << "\' is the first character "
13          << "to appear in\n\"" << string1 << '\"' << endl;
14    }
```

```
Of the characters in "beware"
'a' is the first character to appear in
"This is a test"
```

Fig. 22.37 | String-search function strpbrk.

Function strrchr searches for the last occurrence of the specified character in a string. If the character is found, strrchr returns a pointer to the character in the string; otherwise, strrchr returns 0. Line 14 of Fig. 22.38 searches for the last occurrence of the character 'z' in the string "A zoo has many animals including zebras".

```
 1   // Fig. 22.38: fig22_38.cpp
 2   // Using strrchr.
 3   #include <iostream>
 4   #include <cstring> // strrchr prototype
 5   using namespace std;
 6
 7   int main() {
 8      const char* string1{"A zoo has many animals including zebras"};
 9      char c{'z'};
10
11      cout << "string1 = " << string1 << "\n" << endl;
12      cout << "The remainder of string1 beginning with the\n"
13         << "last occurrence of character '"
14         << c << "' is: \"" << strrchr(string1, c) << '\"' << endl;
15   }
```

```
string1 = A zoo has many animals including zebras

The remainder of string1 beginning with the
last occurrence of character 'z' is: "zebras"
```

Fig. 22.38 | String-search function strrchr.

Function strspn (Fig. 22.39, line 14) determines the length of the initial part of the string in its first argument that contains only characters from the string in its second argument. The function returns the length of the segment.

```
 1   // Fig. 22.39: fig22_39.cpp
 2   // Using strspn.
 3   #include <iostream>
 4   #include <cstring> // strspn prototype
 5   using namespace std;
 6
 7   int main() {
 8      const char* string1{"The value is 3.14159"};
 9      const char* string2{"aehils Tuv"};
10
11      cout << "string1 = " << string1 << "\nstring2 = " << string2
12         << "\n\nThe length of the initial segment of string1\n"
13         << "containing only characters from string2 = "
14         << strspn(string1, string2)   << endl;
15   }
```

```
string1 = The value is 3.14159
string2 = aehils Tuv

The length of the initial segment of string1
containing only characters from string2 = 13
```

Fig. 22.39 | String-search function strspn.

Function `strstr` searches for the first occurrence of its second string argument in its first string argument. If the second string is found in the first string, a pointer to the location of the string in the first argument is returned; otherwise, it returns 0. Line 14 of Fig. 22.40 uses `strstr` to find the string "def" in the string "abcdefabcdef".

```
1   // Fig. 22.40: fig22_40.cpp
2   // Using strstr.
3   #include <iostream>
4   #include <cstring> // strstr prototype
5   using namespace std;
6
7   int main() {
8      const char* string1{"abcdefabcdef"};
9      const char* string2{"def"};
10
11     cout << "string1 = " << string1 << "\nstring2 = " << string2
12        << "\n\nThe remainder of string1 beginning with the\n"
13        << "first occurrence of string2 is: "
14        << strstr(string1, string2) << endl;
15  }
```

```
string1 = abcdefabcdef
string2 = def

The remainder of string1 beginning with the
first occurrence of string2 is: defabcdef
```

Fig. 22.40 | String-search function `strstr`.

22.11 Memory Functions of the C String-Handling Library

The string-handling library functions presented in this section facilitate manipulating, comparing and searching blocks of memory. The functions treat blocks of memory as arrays of bytes. These functions can manipulate any block of data. Figure 22.41 summarizes the memory functions of the string-handling library. In the function discussions, "object" refers to a block of data. [*Note:* The string-processing functions in prior sections operate on null-terminated strings. The functions in this section operate on arrays of bytes. The null-character value (i.e., a byte containing 0) has *no* significance with the functions in this section.]

Prototype	Description
`void* memcpy(void* s1, const void* s2, size_t n)`	
	Copies n characters from the object pointed to by s2 into the object pointed to by s1. A pointer to the resulting object is returned. The area from which characters are copied is not allowed to overlap the area to which characters are copied.

Fig. 22.41 | Memory functions of the string-handling library. (Part 1 of 2.)

Prototype	Description
void* memmove(void* s1, const void* s2, size_t n)	
	Copies n characters from the object pointed to by s2 into the object pointed to by s1. The copy is performed as if the characters were first copied from the object pointed to by s2 into a temporary array, then copied from the temporary array into the object pointed to by s1. A pointer to the resulting object is returned. The area from which characters are copied is allowed to overlap the area to which characters are copied.
int memcmp(const void* s1, const void* s2, size_t n)	
	Compares the first n characters of the objects pointed to by s1 and s2. The function returns 0, less than 0, or greater than 0 if s1 is equal to, less than or greater than s2, respectively.
void* memchr(const void* s, int c, size_t n)	
	Locates the first occurrence of c (converted to unsigned char) in the first n characters of the object pointed to by s. If c is found, a pointer to c in the object is returned. Otherwise, 0 is returned.
void* memset(void* s, int c, size_t n)	
	Copies c (converted to unsigned char) into the first n characters of the object pointed to by s. A pointer to the result is returned.

Fig. 22.41 | Memory functions of the string-handling library. (Part 2 of 2.)

The pointer parameters to these functions are declared void*. In Chapter 8, we saw that *a pointer to any data type can be assigned directly to a pointer of type void*.* For this reason, these functions can receive pointers to any data type. Remember that *a pointer of type void* cannot be assigned directly to a pointer of any other data type.* Because a void* pointer cannot be dereferenced, each function receives a size argument that specifies the number of characters (bytes) the function will process. For simplicity, the examples in this section manipulate character arrays (blocks of characters).

Function memcpy copies a specified number of characters (bytes) from the object pointed to by its second argument into the object pointed to by its first argument. The function can receive a pointer to any type of object. The result of this function is undefined if the two objects overlap in memory (i.e., are parts of the same object). The program of Fig. 22.42 uses memcpy (line 13) to copy the string in array s2 to array s1.

```cpp
1  // Fig. 22.42: fig22_42.cpp
2  // Using memcpy.
3  #include <iostream>
4  #include <cstring> // memcpy prototype
5  using namespace std;
6
7  int main() {
8     char s1[17]{};
```

Fig. 22.42 | Memory-handling function memcpy. (Part 1 of 2.)

```
 9
10      // 17 total characters (includes terminating null)
11      char s2[]{"Copy this string"};
12
13      memcpy(s1, s2, 17); // copy 17 characters from s2 to s1
14
15      cout << "After s2 is copied into s1 with memcpy,\n"
16         << "s1 contains \"" << s1 << '\"' << endl;
17   }
```

```
After s2 is copied into s1 with memcpy,
s1 contains "Copy this string"
```

Fig. 22.42 | Memory-handling function memcpy. (Part 2 of 2.)

Function memmove, like memcpy, copies a specified number of bytes from the object pointed to by its second argument into the object pointed to by its first argument. Copying is performed as if the bytes were copied from the second argument to a temporary array of characters, then copied from the temporary array to the first argument. This allows characters from one part of a string to be copied into another part of the same string.

Common Programming Error 22.11
String-manipulation functions other than memmove that copy characters have undefined results when copying takes place between parts of the same string.

The program in Fig. 22.43 uses memmove (line 12) to copy the last 10 bytes of array x into the first 10 bytes of array x.

```
 1   // Fig. 22.43: fig22_43.cpp
 2   // Using memmove.
 3   #include <iostream>
 4   #include <cstring> // memmove prototype
 5   using namespace std;
 6
 7   int main() {
 8      char x[]{"Home Sweet Home"};
 9
10      cout << "The string in array x before memmove is: " << x;
11      cout << "\nThe string in array x after memmove is:  "
12         << static_cast<char*>(memmove(x, &x[5], 10)) << endl;
13   }
```

```
The string in array x before memmove is: Home Sweet Home
The string in array x after memmove is:  Sweet Home Home
```

Fig. 22.43 | Memory-handling function memmove.

Function memcmp (Fig. 22.44, lines 13–15) compares the specified number of characters of its first argument with the corresponding characters of its second argument. The function returns a value greater than zero if the first argument is greater than the second argument, zero if the arguments are equal, and a value less than zero if the first argument is less than the second argument. [*Note:* With some compilers, function `memcmp` returns - 1, 0 or 1, as in the sample output of Fig. 22.44. With other compilers, this function returns 0 or the difference between the numeric codes of the first characters that differ in the strings being compared. For example, when `s1` and `s2` are compared, the first character that differs between them is the fifth character of each string—E (numeric code 69) for `s1` and X (numeric code 72) for `s2`. In this case, the return value will be 19 (or -19 when `s2` is compared to `s1`).]

```cpp
 1   // Fig. 22.44: fig22_44.cpp
 2   // Using memcmp.
 3   #include <iostream>
 4   #include <iomanip>
 5   #include <cstring> // memcmp prototype
 6   using namespace std;
 7
 8   int main() {
 9      char s1[]{"ABCDEFG"};
10      char s2[]{"ABCDXYZ"};
11
12      cout << "s1 = " << s1 << "\ns2 = " << s2 << endl
13         << "\nmemcmp(s1, s2, 4) = " << setw(3) << memcmp(s1, s2, 4)
14         << "\nmemcmp(s1, s2, 7) = " << setw(3) << memcmp(s1, s2, 7)
15         << "\nmemcmp(s2, s1, 7) = " << setw(3) << memcmp(s2, s1, 7)
16         << endl;
17   }
```

```
s1 = ABCDEFG
s2 = ABCDXYZ

memcmp(s1, s2, 4) =    0
memcmp(s1, s2, 7) =   -1
memcmp(s2, s1, 7) =    1
```

Fig. 22.44 | Memory-handling function `memcmp`.

Function `memchr` searches for the first occurrence of a byte, represented as `unsigned char`, in the specified number of bytes of an object. If the byte is found in the object, a pointer to it is returned; otherwise, the function returns a null pointer. Line 12 of Fig. 22.45 searches for the character (byte) `'r'` in the string `"This is a string"`.

```cpp
 1   // Fig. 22.45: fig22_45.cpp
 2   // Using memchr.
 3   #include <iostream>
 4   #include <cstring> // memchr prototype
 5   using namespace std;
```

Fig. 22.45 | Memory-handling function memchr. (Part 1 of 2.)

```
6
7    int main() {
8       char s[]{"This is a string"};
9
10      cout << "s = " << s << "\n" << endl;
11      cout << "The remainder of s after character 'r' is found is \""
12         << static_cast<char*>(memchr(s, 'r', 16)) << '\"' << endl;
13   }
```

```
s = This is a string

The remainder of s after character 'r' is found is "ring"
```

Fig. 22.45 | Memory-handling function memchr. (Part 2 of 2.)

Function memset copies the value of the byte in its second argument into a specified number of bytes of the object pointed to by its first argument. Line 12 in Fig. 22.46 uses memset to copy 'b' into the first 7 bytes of string1.

```
1    // Fig. 22.46: fig22_46.cpp
2    // Using memset.
3    #include <iostream>
4    #include <cstring> // memset prototype
5    using namespace std;
6
7    int main() {
8       char string1[15]{"BBBBBBBBBBBBBB"};
9
10      cout << "string1 = " << string1 << endl;
11      cout << "string1 after memset = "
12         << static_cast<char*>(memset(string1, 'b', 7)) << endl;
13   }
```

```
string1 = BBBBBBBBBBBBBB
string1 after memset = bbbbbbbBBBBBBB
```

Fig. 22.46 | Memory-handling function memset.

22.12 Wrap-Up

This chapter introduced struct definitions, initializing structs and using them with functions. We discussed typedef, using it to create aliases to help promote portability. We also introduced bitwise operators to manipulate data and bit fields for storing data compactly. You learned about the string-conversion functions in <cstlib> and the string-processing functions in <cstring>.

Summary

Section 22.2 Structure Definitions
- Keyword **struct** (p. 900) begins every structure definition. Between the braces of the structure definition are the structure member declarations.
- A structure definition creates a new data type that can be used to declare variables.

Section 22.3 typedef and using
- Creating a new type name with **typedef** (p. 902) does not create a new type; it creates a name that's synonymous with a type defined previously.
- C++11 added the keyword using as another mechanism for creating type aliases.

Section 22.5 Bitwise Operators
- The **bitwise AND operator** (&; p. 905) takes two integral operands. A bit in the result is set to one if the corresponding bits in each of the operands are one.
- **Masks** (p. 907) are used with bitwise AND to hide some bits while preserving others.
- The **bitwise inclusive OR operator** (|; p. 905) takes two operands. A bit in the result is set to one if the corresponding bit in either operand is set to one.
- Each of the bitwise operators (except complement) has a corresponding assignment operator.
- The **bitwise exclusive OR operator** (^; p. 905) takes two operands. A bit in the result is set to one if exactly one of the corresponding bits in the two operands is set to one.
- The **left-shift operator** (<<; p. 905) shifts the bits of its left operand left by the number of bits specified by its right operand. Bits vacated to the right are replaced with zeros.
- The **right-shift operator** (>>; p. 905) shifts the bits of its left operand right by the number of bits specified in its right operand. Right shifting an unsigned integer causes bits vacated at the left to be replaced by zeros. Vacated bits in signed integers can be replaced with zeros or ones.
- The **bitwise complement operator** (~; p. 905) takes one operand and inverts its bits—this produces the one's complement of the operand.
- As of C++14, you may now include binary literals in your source code. To do so, precede a sequence of 1s and 0s with 0b or 0B.

Section 22.6 Bit Fields
- **Bit fields** (p. 914) reduce storage use by storing data in the minimum number of bits required. Bit-field members must be declared as int or unsigned.
- A bit field is declared by following an unsigned or int member name with a colon and the width of the bit field.
- The bit-field width must be an integer constant.
- If a bit field is specified without a name, the field is used as **padding** (p. 917) in the structure.
- An **unnamed bit field with width 0** (p. 917) aligns the next bit field on a new machine-word boundary.

Section 22.7 Character-Handling Library
- Function **islower** (p. 920) determines if its argument is a lowercase letter (a-z). Function **isupper** (p. 920) determines whether its argument is an uppercase letter (A-Z).
- Function **isdigit** (p. 918) determines if its argument is a digit (0-9).
- Function **isalpha** (p. 918) determines if its argument is an uppercase (A-Z) or lowercase letter (a-z).

- Function **isalnum** (p. 918) determines if its argument is an uppercase letter (A–Z), a lowercase letter (a–z), or a digit (0–9).
- Function **isxdigit** (p. 918) determines if its argument is a hexadecimal digit (A–F, a–f, 0–9).
- Function **toupper** (p. 920) converts a lowercase letter to an uppercase letter. Function **tolower** (p. 920) converts an uppercase letter to a lowercase letter.
- Function **isspace** (p. 921) determines if its argument is one of the following whitespace characters: ' ' (space), '\f', '\n', '\r', '\t' or '\v'.
- Function **iscntrl** (p. 921) determines if its argument is a control character, such as '\t', '\v', '\f', '\a', '\b', '\r' or '\n'.
- Function **ispunct** (p. 921) determines if its argument is a printing character other than a space, a digit or a letter.
- Function **isprint** (p. 921) determines if its argument is any printing character, including space.
- Function **isgraph** (p. 921) determines if its argument is a printing character other than space.

Section 22.8 C String-Manipulation Functions

- Function **strcpy** (p. 924) copies its second argument into its first argument. You must ensure that the target array is large enough to store the string and its terminating null character.
- Function **strncpy** (p. 924) is equivalent to strcpy, but it specifies the number of characters to be copied from the string into the array. The terminating null character will be copied only if the number of characters to be copied is at least one more than the length of the string.
- Function **strcat** (p. 925) appends its second string argument—including the terminating null character—to its first string argument. The first character of the second string replaces the null ('\0') character of the first string. You must ensure that the target array used to store the first string is large enough to store both the first string and the second string.
- Function **strncat** (p. 925) is equivalent to strcat, but it appends a specified number of characters from the second string to the first string. A terminating null character is appended to the result.
- Function **strcmp** compares its first string argument with its second string argument character by character. The function returns zero if the strings are equal, a negative value if the first string is less than the second string and a positive value if the first string is greater than the second string.
- Function **strncmp** is equivalent to strcmp, but it compares a specified number of characters. If the number of characters in one of the strings is less than the number of characters specified, strncmp compares characters until the null character in the shorter string is encountered.
- A sequence of calls to **strtok** (p. 928) breaks a string into tokens that are separated by characters contained in a second string argument. The first call specifies the string to be tokenized as the first argument, and subsequent calls to continue tokenizing the same string specify NULL as the first argument. The function returns a pointer to the current token from each call. If there are no more tokens when strtok is called, NULL is returned.
- Function **strlen** (p. 929) takes a string as an argument and returns the number of characters in the string—the terminating null character is not included in the length of the string.

Section 22.9 C String-Conversion Functions

- Function **atof** (p. 931) converts its argument—a string beginning with a series of digits that represents a floating-point number—to a double value.
- Function **atoi** (p. 931) converts its argument—a string beginning with a series of digits that represents an integer—to an int value.

- Function **atol** (p. 932) converts its argument—a string beginning with a series of digits that represents a long integer—to a `long` value.

- Function **strtod** (p. 932) converts a sequence of characters representing a floating-point value to `double`. The function receives two arguments—a string (`char*`) and the address of a `char*` pointer. The string contains the character sequence to be converted, and the pointer to `char*` is assigned the remainder of the string after the conversion.

- Function **strtol** (p. 933) converts a sequence of characters representing an integer to `long`. It receives a string (`char*`), the address of a `char*` pointer and an integer. The string contains the character sequence to be converted, the pointer to `char*` is assigned the location of the first character after the converted value and the integer specifies the base of the value being converted.

- Function **strtoul** (p. 934) converts a sequence of characters representing an integer to `unsigned long`. It receives a string (`char*`), the address of a `char*` pointer and an integer. The string contains the character sequence to be converted, the pointer to `char*` is assigned the location of the first character after the converted value and the integer specifies the base of the value being converted.

Section 22.10 Search Functions of the C String-Handling Library

- Function **strchr** (p. 935) searches for the first occurrence of a character in a string. If found, `strchr` returns a pointer to the character in the string; otherwise, `strchr` returns a null pointer.

- Function **strcspn** (p. 936) determines the length of the initial part of the string in its first argument that does not contain any characters from the string in its second argument. The function returns the length of the segment.

- Function **strpbrk** (p. 937) searches for the first occurrence in its first argument of any character that appears in its second argument. If a character from the second argument is found, `strpbrk` returns a pointer to the character; otherwise, `strpbrk` returns a null pointer.

- Function **strrchr** (p. 937) searches for the last occurrence of a character in a string. If the character is found, `strrchr` returns a pointer to the character in the string; otherwise, it returns a null pointer.

- Function **strspn** (p. 938) determines the length of the initial part of its first argument that contains only characters from the string in its second argument and returns the length of the segment.

- Function **strstr** (p. 939) searches for the first occurrence of its second string argument in its first string argument. If the second string is found in the first string, a pointer to the location of the string in the first argument is returned; otherwise it returns 0.

Section 22.11 Memory Functions of the C String-Handling Library

- Function **memcpy** (p. 940) copies a specified number of characters from the object to which its second argument points into the object to which its first argument points. The function can receive a pointer to any object. The pointers are received as `void` pointers and converted to `char` pointers for use in the function. Function `memcpy` manipulates the bytes of its argument as characters.

- Function **memmove** (p. 941) copies a specified number of bytes from the object pointed to by its second argument to the object pointed to by its first argument. Copying is accomplished as if the bytes were copied from the second argument to a temporary character array, then copied from the temporary array to the first argument.

- Function **memcmp** (p. 941) compares the specified number of characters of its first and second arguments.

- Function **memchr** (p. 942) searches for the first occurrence of a byte, represented as `unsigned char`, in the specified number of bytes of an object. If the byte is found, a pointer to it is returned; otherwise, a null pointer is returned.

- Function **memset** (p. 943) copies its second argument, treated as an `unsigned char`, to a specified number of bytes of the object pointed to by the first argument.

Self-Review Exercises

22.1 Fill in the blanks in each of the following:

a) The bits in the result of an expression using the _____ operator are set to one if the corresponding bits in each operand are set to one. Otherwise, the bits are set to zero.

b) The bits in the result of an expression using the _____ operator are set to one if at least one of the corresponding bits in either operand is set to one. Otherwise, the bits are set to zero.

c) Keyword _____ introduces a structure declaration.

d) Keyword _____ is used to create a synonym for a previously defined data type.

e) Each bit in the result of an expression using the _____ operator is set to one if exactly one of the corresponding bits in either operand is set to one.

f) The bitwise AND operator & is often used to _____ bits (i.e., to select certain bits from a bit string while zeroing others).

g) The _____ and _____ operators are used to shift the bits of a value to the left or to the right, respectively.

22.2 Write a single statement or a set of statements to accomplish each of the following:

a) Define a structure called Part containing int variable partNumber and char array partName, whose values may be as long as 25 characters.

b) Define PartPtr to be a synonym for the type Part*.

c) Use separate statements to declare variable a to be of type Part, array b[10] to be of type Part and variable ptr to be of type pointer to Part.

d) Read a part number and a part name from the keyboard into the members of variable a.

e) Assign the member values of variable a to element three of array b.

f) Assign the address of array b to the pointer variable ptr.

g) Print the member values of element three of array b, using the variable ptr and the structure pointer operator to refer to the members.

22.3 Write a single statement to accomplish each of the following. Assume that variables c (which stores a character), x, y and z are of type int; variables d, e and f are of type double; variable ptr is of type char* and arrays s1[100] and s2[100] are of type char.

a) Convert the character stored in c to an uppercase letter. Assign the result to variable c.

b) Determine if the value of variable c is a digit. Use the conditional operator as shown in Figs. 22.18–22.20 to print " is a " or " is not a " when the result is displayed.

c) Convert the string "1234567" to long, and print the value.

d) Determine whether the value of variable c is a control character. Use the conditional operator to print " is a " or " is not a " when the result is displayed.

e) Assign to ptr the location of the last occurrence of c in s1.

f) Convert the string "8.63582" to double, and print the value.

g) Determine whether the value of c is a letter. Use the conditional operator to print " is a " or " is not a " when the result is displayed.

h) Assign to ptr the location of the first occurrence of s2 in s1.

i) Determine whether the value of variable c is a printing character. Use the conditional operator to print " is a " or " is not a " when the result is displayed.

j) Assign to ptr the location of the first occurrence in s1 of any character from s2.

k) Assign to ptr the location of the first occurrence of c in s1.

l) Convert the string "-21" to int, and print the value.

Answers to Self-Review Exercises

22.1 a) bitwise AND (&). b) bitwise inclusive OR (|). c) struct. d) typedef. e) bitwise exclusive OR (^). f) mask. g) left-shift operator (<<), right-shift operator (>>).

22.2 a) `struct Part {`
        `int partNumber;`
        `char partName[26];`
   `};`

   b) `typedef Part* PartPtr;`

   c) `Part a;`
     `Part b[10];`
     `Part* ptr;`

   d) `cin >> a.partNumber >> a.partName;`

   e) `b[3] = a;`

   f) `ptr = b;`

   g) `cout << (ptr + 3)->partNumber << ' '`
       `<< (ptr + 3)->partName << endl;`

22.3 a) `c = toupper(c);`

   b) `cout << '\'' << c << "\' "`
       `<< (isdigit(c) ? "is a" : "is not a")`
       `<< " digit" << endl;`

   c) `cout << atol("1234567") << endl;`

   d) `cout << '\'' << c << "\' "`
       `<< (iscntrl(c) ? "is a" : "is not a")`
       `<< " control character" << endl;`

   e) `ptr = strrchr(s1, c);`

   f) `out << atof("8.63582") << endl;`

   g) `cout << '\'' << c << "\' "`
       `<< (isalpha(c) ? "is a" : "is not a")`
       `<< " letter" << endl;`

   h) `ptr = strstr(s1, s2);`

   i) `cout << '\'' << c << "\' "`
       `<< (isprint(c) ? "is a" : "is not a")`
       `<< " printing character" << endl;`

   j) `ptr = strpbrk(s1, s2);`

   k) `ptr = strchr(s1, c);`

   l) `cout << atoi("-21") << endl;`

Exercises

22.4 *(Defining Structures)* Provide the definition for each of the following structures:

   a) Structure `Inventory`, containing character array `partName[30]`, integer `partNumber`, floating-point `price`, integer `stock` and integer `reorder`.

   b) A structure called `Address` that contains character arrays `streetAddress[25]`, `city[20]`, `state[3]` and `zipCode[6]`.

   c) Structure `Student`, containing arrays `firstName[15]` and `lastName[15]` and variable `homeAddress` of type `struct Address` from part (b).

   d) Structure `Test`, containing 16 bit fields with widths of 1 bit. The names of the bit fields are the letters a to p.

22.5 *(Card Shuffling and Dealing)* Modify Fig. 22.16 to shuffle the cards using the shuffle algorithm in Fig. 22.3. Print the resulting deck in two-column format. Precede each card with its color.

22.6 *(Shifting and Printing an Integer)* Write a program that right-shifts an integer variable four bits. The program should print the integer in bits before and after the shift operation. Does your system place zeros or ones in the vacated bits?

22.7 *(Multiplication Via Bit Shifting)* Left-shifting an unsigned integer by one bit is equivalent to multiplying the value by 2. Write function power2 that takes two integer arguments, number and pow, and calculates

> number * 2^{pow}

Use a shift operator to calculate the result. The program should print the values as integers and as bits.

22.8 *(Packing Characters into Unsigned Integers)* The left-shift operator can be used to pack four character values into a four-byte unsigned integer variable. Write a program that inputs four characters from the keyboard and passes them to function packCharacters. To pack four characters into an unsigned integer variable, assign the first character to the unsigned variable, shift the unsigned variable left by eight bit positions and combine the unsigned variable with the second character using the bitwise inclusive-OR operator, etc. The program should output the characters in their bit format before and after they're packed into the unsigned integer to prove that they're in fact packed correctly in the unsigned variable.

22.9 *(Unpacking Characters from Unsigned Integers)* Using the right-shift operator, the bitwise AND operator and a mask, write function unpackCharacters that takes the unsigned integer from Exercise 22.8 and unpacks it into four characters. To unpack characters from an unsigned four-byte integer, combine the unsigned integer with a mask and right-shift the result. To create the masks you'll need to unpack the four characters, left-shift the value 255 in the mask variable by eight bits 0, 1, 2 or 3 times (depending on the byte you are unpacking). Then take the combined result each time and right shift it by eight bits the same number of times. Assign each resulting value to a char variable. The program should print the unsigned integer in bits before it's unpacked, then print the characters in bits to confirm that they were unpacked correctly.

22.10 *(Reversing Bits)* Write a program that reverses the order of the bits in an unsigned integer value. The program should input the value from the user and call function reverseBits to print the bits in reverse order. Print the value in bits both before and after the bits are reversed to confirm that the bits are reversed properly.

22.11 *(Testing Characters with the <cctype> Functions)* Write a program that inputs a character from the keyboard and tests the character with each function in the character-handling library. Print the value returned by each function.

22.12 *(Determine the Value)* The following program uses function multiple to determine whether the integer entered from the keyboard is a multiple of some integer X. Examine function multiple, then determine the value of X.

```cpp
 1    // Exercise 22.12: Ex22_12.cpp
 2    // This program determines if a value is a multiple of X.
 3    #include <iostream>
 4    using namespace std;
 5
 6    bool multiple(int);
 7
 8    int main() {
 9       int y{0};
10
11       cout << "Enter an integer between 1 and 32000: ";
12       cin >> y;
13
14       if (multiple(y)) {
15          cout << y << " is a multiple of X" << endl;
16       }
```

```
17          else {
18              cout << y << " is not a multiple of X" << endl;
19          }
20      }
21
22      // determine if num is a multiple of X
23      bool multiple(int num) {
24          bool mult{true};
25
26          for (int i{0}, mask{1}; i < 10; ++i, mask <<= 1) {
27              if ((num & mask) != 0) {
28                  mult = false;
29                  break;
30              }
31          }
32
33          return mult;
34      }
```

22.13   What does the following program do?

```
1      // Exercise 22.13: Ex22_13.cpp
2      #include <iostream>
3      using namespace std;
4
5      bool mystery(unsigned);
6
7      int main() {
8      {
9          unsigned x;
10         cout << "Enter an integer: ";
11         cin >> x;
12         cout << boolalpha
13             << "The result is " << mystery(x) << endl;
14     }
15
16     // What does this function do?
17     bool mystery(unsigned bits)
18     {
19         const int SHIFT{8 * sizeof(unsigned) - 1};
20         const unsigned MASK{1 << SHIFT};
21         unsigned total{0};
22
23         for (int i{0}; i < SHIFT + 1; ++i, bits <<= 1) {
24             if ((bits & MASK) == MASK) {
25                 ++total;
26             }
27         }
28
29         return !(total % 2);
30     }
```

22.14   Write a program that inputs a line of text with `istream` member function `getline` (as in Chapter 13) into character array `s[100]`. Output the line in uppercase letters and lowercase letters.

22.15   *(Converting Strings to Integers)* Write a program that inputs four strings that represent integers, converts the strings to integers, sums the values and prints the total of the four values. Use only the C string-processing techniques discussed in this chapter.

22.16 *(Converting Strings to Floating-Point Numbers)* Write a program that inputs four strings that represent floating-point values, converts the strings to double values, sums the values and prints the total of the four values. Use only the C string-processing techniques shown in this chapter.

22.17 *(Searching for Substrings)* Write a program that inputs a line of text and a search string from the keyboard. Using function strstr, locate the first occurrence of the search string in the line of text, and assign the location to variable searchPtr of type char*. If the search string is found, print the remainder of the line of text beginning with the search string. Then use strstr again to locate the next occurrence of the search string in the line of text. If a second occurrence is found, print the remainder of the line of text beginning with the second occurrence. [*Hint:* The second call to strstr should contain the expression searchPtr + 1 as its first argument.]

22.18 *(Searching for Substrings)* Write a program based on the program of Exercise 22.17 that inputs several lines of text and a search string, then uses function strstr to determine the total number of occurrences of the string in the lines of text. Print the result.

22.19 *(Searching for Characters)* Write a program that inputs several lines of text and a search character and uses function strchr to determine the total number of occurrences of the character in the lines of text.

22.20 *(Searching for Characters)* Write a program based on the program of Exercise 22.19 that inputs several lines of text and uses function strchr to determine the total number of occurrences of each letter of the alphabet in the text. Uppercase and lowercase letters should be counted together. Store the totals for each letter in an array, and print the values in tabular format after the totals have been determined.

22.21 *(ASCII Character Set)* The chart in Appendix B shows the numeric code representations for the characters in the ASCII character set. Study this chart, then state whether each of the following is *true* or *false*:

    a) The letter "A" comes before the letter "B."

    b) The digit "9" comes before the digit "0."

    c) The commonly used symbols for addition, subtraction, multiplication and division all come before any of the digits.

    d) The digits come before the letters.

    e) If a sort program sorts strings into ascending sequence, then the program will place the symbol for a right parenthesis before the symbol for a left parenthesis.

22.22 *(Strings Beginning with b)* Write a program that reads a series of strings and prints only those strings beginning with the letter "b."

22.23 *(Strings Ending with ED)* Write a program that reads a series of strings and prints only those strings that end with the letters "ED."

22.24 *(Displaying Characters for Given ASCII Codes)* Write a program that inputs an ASCII code and prints the corresponding character. Modify this program so that it generates all possible three-digit codes in the range 000–255 and attempts to print the corresponding characters. What happens when this program is run?

22.25 *(Write Your Own Character Handling Functions)* Using the ASCII character chart in Appendix B as a guide, write your own versions of the character-handling functions in Fig. 22.17.

22.26 *(Write Your Own String Conversion Functions)* Write your own versions of the functions in Fig. 22.27 for converting strings to numbers.

22.27 *(Write Your Own String Searching Functions)* Write your own versions of the functions in Fig. 22.34 for searching strings.

22.28 *(Write Your Own Memory Handling Functions)* Write your own versions of the functions in Fig. 22.41 for manipulating blocks of memory.

22.29 *(What Does the Program Do?)* What does this program do?

```cpp
// Ex. 22.29: Ex22_29.cpp
// What does this program do?
#include <iostream>
using namespace std;

bool mystery3(const char*, const char*); // prototype

int main() {
   char string1[80], string2[80];

   cout << "Enter two strings: ";
   cin >> string1 >> string2;
   cout << "The result is " << mystery3(string1, string2) << endl;
}

// What does this function do?
bool mystery3(const char* s1, const char* s2) {
   for (; *s1 != '\0' && *s2 != '\0'; ++s1, ++s2) [
      if (*s1 != *s2) {
         return false;
      }
   }

   return true;
}
```

22.30 *(Comparing Strings)* Write a program that uses function `strcmp` to compare two strings input by the user. The program should state whether the first string is less than, equal to or greater than the second string.

22.31 *(Comparing Strings)* Write a program that uses function `strncmp` to compare two strings input by the user. The program should input the number of characters to compare. The program should state whether the first string is less than, equal to or greater than the second string.

22.32 *(Randomly Creating Sentences)* Write a program that uses random number generation to create sentences. The program should use four arrays of pointers to char called `article`, `noun`, `verb` and `preposition`. The program should create a sentence by selecting a word at random from each array in the following order: `article`, `noun`, `verb`, `preposition`, `article` and `noun`. As each word is picked, it should be concatenated to the previous words in a character array that's large enough to hold the entire sentence. The words should be separated by spaces. When the final sentence is output, it should start with a capital letter and end with a period. The program should generate 20 such sentences.

The arrays should be filled as follows: The `article` array should contain the articles "the", "a", "one", "some" and "any"; the `noun` array should contain the nouns "boy", "girl", "dog", "town" and "car"; the `verb` array should contain the verbs "drove", "jumped", "ran", "walked" and "skipped"; the `preposition` array should contain the prepositions "to", "from", "over", "under" and "on".

After completing the program, modify it to produce a short story consisting of several of these sentences. (How about a random term-paper writer!)

22.33 *(Limericks)* A limerick is a humorous five-line verse in which the first and second lines rhyme with the fifth, and the third line rhymes with the fourth. Using techniques similar to those developed in Exercise 22.32, write a C++ program that produces random limericks. Polishing this program to produce good limericks is a challenging problem, but the result will be worth the effort!

22.34 *(Pig Latin)* Write a program that encodes English language phrases into pig Latin. Pig Latin is a form of coded language often used for amusement. Many variations exist in the methods used to form pig Latin phrases. For simplicity, use the following algorithm: To form a pig-Latin phrase from an English-language phrase, tokenize the phrase into words with function strtok. To translate each English word into a pig-Latin word, place the first letter of the English word at the end of the English word and add the letters "ay." Thus, the word "jump" becomes "umpjay," the word "the" becomes "hetay" and the word "computer" becomes "omputercay." Blanks between words remain as blanks. Assume that the English phrase consists of words separated by blanks, there are no punctuation marks and all words have two or more letters. Function printLatinWord should display each word. [*Hint:* Each time a token is found in a call to strtok, pass the token pointer to function printLatinWord and print the pig-Latin word.]

22.35 *(Tokenizing Phone Numbers)* Write a program that inputs a telephone number as a string in the form (555) 555-5555. The program should use function strtok to extract the area code as a token, the first three digits of the phone number as a token, and the last four digits of the phone number as a token. The seven digits of the phone number should be concatenated into one string. Both the area code and the phone number should be printed.

22.36 *(Tokenizing and Reversing a Sentence)* Write a program that inputs a line of text, tokenizes the line with function strtok and outputs the tokens in reverse order.

22.37 *(Alphabetizing Strings)* Use the string-comparison functions discussed in Section 22.8 and the techniques for sorting arrays developed in Chapter 7 to write a program that alphabetizes a list of strings. Use the names of 10 towns in your area as data for your program.

22.38 *(Write Your Own String Copy and Concatenation Functions)* Write two versions of each string-copy and string-concatenation function in Fig. 22.21. The first version should use array subscripting, and the second should use pointers and pointer arithmetic.

22.39 *(Write Your Own String Comparison Functions)* Write two versions of each string-comparison function in Fig. 22.21. The first version should use array subscripting, and the second should use pointers and pointer arithmetic.

22.40 *(Write Your Own String Length Function)* Write two versions of function strlen in Fig. 22.21. The first version should use array subscripting, and the second should use pointers and pointer arithmetic.

Special Section: Advanced String-Manipulation Exercises

The preceding exercises are keyed to the text and designed to test your understanding of fundamental string-manipulation concepts. This section includes a collection of intermediate and advanced string-manipulation exercises. You should find these problems challenging, yet enjoyable. The problems vary considerably in difficulty. Some require an hour or two of program writing and implementation. Others are useful for lab assignments that might require two or three weeks of study and implementation. Some are challenging term projects.

22.41 *(Text Analysis)* The availability of computers with string-manipulation capabilities has resulted in some rather interesting approaches to analyzing the writings of great authors. Much attention has been focused on whether William Shakespeare ever lived. Some scholars believe there is substantial evidence that Francis Bacon, Christopher Marlowe or other authors actually penned the masterpieces attributed to Shakespeare. Researchers have used computers to find similarities in the writings of these authors. This exercise examines three methods for analyzing texts with a computer. Thousands of texts, including Shakespeare, are available online at www.gutenberg.org.

a) Write a program that reads several lines of text from the keyboard and prints a table indicating the number of occurrences of each letter of the alphabet in the text. For example, the phrase

```
To be, or not to be: that is the question:
```

contains one "a," two "b's," no "c's," etc.

b) Write a program that reads several lines of text and prints a table indicating the number of one-letter words, two-letter words, three-letter words, etc., appearing in the text. For example, the phrase

```
Whether 'tis nobler in the mind to suffer
```

contains the following word lengths and occurrences:

Word length	Occurrences
1	0
2	2
3	1
4	2 (including 'tis)
5	0
6	2
7	1

c) Write a program that reads several lines of text and prints a table indicating the number of occurrences of each different word in the text. The first version of your program should include the words in the table in the same order in which they appear in the text. For example, the lines

```
To be, or not to be: that is the question:
Whether 'tis nobler in the mind to suffer
```

contain the word "to" three times, the word "be" two times, the word "or" once, etc. A more interesting (and useful) printout should then be attempted in which the words are sorted alphabetically.

22.42 *(Word Processing)* One important function in word-processing systems is *type justification*—the alignment of words to both the left and right margins of a page. This generates a professional-looking document that gives the appearance of being set in type rather than prepared on a typewriter. Type justification can be accomplished on computer systems by inserting blank characters between the words in a line so that the rightmost word aligns with the right margin.

Write a program that reads several lines of text and prints this text in type-justified format. Assume that the text is to be printed on paper 8-1/2 inches wide and that one-inch margins are to be allowed on both the left and right sides. Assume that the computer prints 10 characters to the horizontal inch. Therefore, your program should print 6-1/2 inches of text, or 65 characters per line.

22.43 *(Printing Dates in Various Formats)* Dates are commonly printed in several different formats in business correspondence. Two of the more common formats are

```
07/21/1955
July 21, 1955
```

Write a program that reads a date in the first format and prints that date in the second format.

22.44 *(Check Protection)* Computers are frequently employed in check-writing systems such as payroll and accounts-payable applications. Many strange stories circulate regarding weekly paychecks being printed (by mistake) for amounts in excess of $1 million. Weird amounts are printed by computerized check-writing systems, because of human error or machine failure. Systems designers build controls into their systems to prevent such erroneous checks from being issued.

Another serious problem is the intentional alteration of a check amount by someone who intends to cash a check fraudulently. To prevent a dollar amount from being altered, most computerized check-writing systems employ a technique called *check protection.*

Checks designed for imprinting by computer contain a fixed number of spaces in which the computer may print an amount. Suppose that a paycheck contains eight blank spaces in which the computer is supposed to print the amount of a weekly paycheck. If the amount is large, then all eight of those spaces will be filled, for example,

```
1,230.60  (check amount)
--------
12345678  (position numbers)
```

On the other hand, if the amount is less than $1000, then several of the spaces would ordinarily be left blank. For example,

```
   99.87
--------
12345678
```

contains three blank spaces. If a check is printed with blank spaces, it's easier for someone to alter the amount of the check. To prevent a check from being altered, many check-writing systems insert *leading asterisks* to protect the amount as follows:

```
***99.87
--------
12345678
```

Write a program that inputs a dollar amount to be printed on a check then prints the amount in check-protected format with leading asterisks if necessary. Assume that nine spaces are available for printing an amount.

22.45 *(Writing the Word Equivalent of a Check Amount)* Continuing the discussion of the previous example, we reiterate the importance of designing check-writing systems to prevent alteration of check amounts. One common security method requires that the check amount be both written in numbers and "spelled out" in words. Even if someone is able to alter the numerical amount of the check, it's extremely difficult to change the amount in words.

Write a program that inputs a numeric check amount and writes the word equivalent of the amount. Your program should be able to handle check amounts as large as $99.99. For example, the amount 112.43 should be written as

```
ONE HUNDRED TWELVE and 43/100
```

22.46 *(Morse Code)* Perhaps the most famous of all coding schemes is the Morse code, developed by Samuel Morse in 1832 for use with the telegraph system. The Morse code assigns a series of dots and dashes to each letter of the alphabet, each digit and a few special characters (such as period, comma, colon and semicolon). In sound-oriented systems, the dot represents a short sound, and the dash represents a long sound. Other representations of dots and dashes are used with light-oriented systems and signal-flag systems.

Separation between words is indicated by a space, or, quite simply, the absence of a dot or dash. In a sound-oriented system, a space is indicated by a short period of time during which no sound is transmitted. The international version of the Morse code appears in Fig. 22.47.

Character	Code	Character	Code	Character	Code
A	.-	N	-.	*Digits*	
B	-...	O	---	1	.----
C	-.-.	P	.--.	2	..---
D	-..	Q	--.-	3	...--
E	.	R	.-.	4	....-
F	..-.	S	...	5	.....
G	--.	T	-	6	-....
H	....	U	..-	7	--...
I	..	V	...-	8	---..
J	.---	W	.--	9	----.
K	-.-	X	-..-	0	-----
L	.-..	Y	-.--		
M	--	Z	--..		

Fig. 22.47 | Letters and digits as expressed in international Morse code.

Write a program that reads an English-language phrase and encodes it in Morse code. Also write a program that reads a phrase in Morse code and converts it into the English-language equivalent. Use one blank between each Morse-coded letter and three blanks between each Morse-coded word.

22.47 *(Metric Conversion Program)* Write a program that will assist the user with metric conversions. Your program should allow the user to specify the names of the units as strings (i.e., centimeters, liters, grams, etc., for the metric system and inches, quarts, pounds, etc., for the English system) and should respond to simple questions such as

```
"How many inches are in 2 meters?"
"How many liters are in 10 quarts?"
```

Your program should recognize invalid conversions. For example, the question

```
"How many feet are in 5 kilograms?"
```

is not meaningful, because "feet" are units of length, while "kilograms" are units of weight.

Challenging String-Manipulation Projects

22.48 *(Crossword Puzzle Generator)* Most people have worked a crossword puzzle, but few have ever attempted to generate one. Generating a crossword puzzle is a difficult problem. It's suggested here as a string-manipulation project requiring substantial sophistication and effort. There are many issues that you must resolve to get even the simplest crossword puzzle generator program working. For example, how does one represent the grid of a crossword puzzle inside the computer? Should one use a series of strings, or should two-dimensional arrays be used? You need a source of words (i.e., a computerized dictionary) that can be directly referenced by the program. In what form should these words be stored to facilitate the complex manipulations required by the program? The really ambitious reader will want to generate the "clues" portion of the puzzle, in which the brief hints for each "across" word and each "down" word are printed for the puzzle worker. Merely printing a version of the blank puzzle itself is not a simple problem.

22.49 *(Spelling Checker)* Many popular word-processing software packages have built-in spell checkers. We used spell-checking capabilities in preparing this book and discovered that, no matter how careful we thought we were in writing a chapter, the software was always able to find a few more spelling errors than we were able to catch manually.

In this project, you are asked to develop your own spell-checker utility. We make suggestions to help get you started. You should then consider adding more capabilities. You might find it helpful to use a computerized dictionary as a source of words.

Why do we type so many words with incorrect spellings? In some cases, it's because we simply do not know the correct spelling, so we make a "best guess." In some cases, it's because we transpose two letters (e.g., "defualt" instead of "default"). Sometimes we double-type a letter accidentally (e.g., "hanndy" instead of "handy"). Sometimes we type a nearby key instead of the one we intended (e.g., "biryhday" instead of "birthday"). And so on.

Design and implement a spell-checker program. Your program maintains an array wordList of character strings. You can either enter these strings or obtain them from a computerized dictionary.

Your program asks a user to enter a word. The program then looks up that word in the wordList array. If the word is present in the array, your program should print "Word is spelled correctly."

If the word is not present in the array, your program should print "Word is not spelled correctly." Then your program should try to locate other words in wordList that might be the word the user intended to type. For example, you can try all possible single transpositions of adjacent letters to discover that the word "default" is a direct match to a word in wordList. Of course, this implies that your program will check all other single transpositions, such as "edfault," "dfeault," "deafult," "defalut" and "defautl." When you find a new word that matches one in wordList, print that word in a message such as "Did you mean "default?"."

Implement other tests, such as the replacing of each double letter with a single letter and any other tests you can develop to improve the value of your spell checker.

Chapters on the Web

The following chapters are available as PDF documents from this book's Companion Website, which is accessible from http://www.pearsonhighered.com/deitel/:

- Chapter 23, Other Topics
- Chapter 24, C++11 and C++14: Additional Features
- Chapter 25, ATM Case Study, Part 1: Object-Oriented Design with the UML
- Chapter 26, ATM Case Study, Part 2: Implementing an Object-Oriented Design

These files can be viewed in Adobe® Reader® (https://get.adobe.com/reader/).

New copies of this book come with a Companion Website access code that is located on the inside of the front cover. If the access code is already visible, you purchased a used book. If there is no access code inside the front cover, you purchased an edition that does not come with an access code. In either case, you can purchase access directly from the Companion Website.

Operator Precedence and Associativity

Operators are shown in decreasing order of precedence from top to bottom (Fig. A.1).

Operator	Type	Associativity
::	binary scope resolution	left to right
::	unary scope resolution	
()	grouping parentheses *[See caution in Fig. 2.10 regarding grouping parentheses.]*	
()	function call	left to right
[]	array subscript	
.	member selection via object	
->	member selection via pointer	
++	unary postfix increment	
--	unary postfix decrement	
typeid	runtime type information	
dynamic_cast<*type*>	runtime type-checked cast	
static_cast<*type*>	compile-time type-checked cast	
reinterpret_cast<*type*>	cast for nonstandard conversions	
const_cast<*type*>	cast away const-ness	
++	unary prefix increment	right to left
--	unary prefix decrement	
+	unary plus	
-	unary minus	
!	unary logical negation	
~	unary bitwise complement	
sizeof	determine size in bytes	
&	address	
*	dereference	
new	dynamic memory allocation	
new[]	dynamic array allocation	
delete	dynamic memory deallocation	
delete[]	dynamic array deallocation	
(*type*)	C-style unary cast	right to left

Fig. A.1 | Operator precedence and associativity chart. (Part 1 of 2.)

Operator	Type	Associativity
. * -> *	pointer to member via object pointer to member via pointer	left to right
* / %	multiplication division remainder	left to right
+ -	addition subtraction	left to right
<< >>	bitwise left shift bitwise right shift	left to right
< <= > >=	relational less than relational less than or equal to relational greater than relational greater than or equal to	left to right
== !=	relational is equal to relational is not equal to	left to right
&	bitwise AND	left to right
^	bitwise exclusive OR	left to right
|	bitwise inclusive OR	left to right
&&	logical AND	left to right
||	logical OR	left to right
?:	ternary conditional	right to left
= += -= *= /= %= &= ^= |= <<= >>=	assignment addition assignment subtraction assignment multiplication assignment division assignment remainder assignment bitwise AND assignment bitwise exclusive OR assignment bitwise inclusive OR assignment bitwise left-shift assignment bitwise right-shift assignment	right to left
,	comma	left to right

Fig. A.1 | Operator precedence and associativity chart. (Part 2 of 2.)

ASCII Character Set

ASCII Character Set

	0	1	2	3	4	5	6	7	8	9
0	nul	soh	stx	etx	eot	enq	ack	bel	bs	ht
1	nl	vt	ff	cr	so	si	dle	dc1	dc2	dc3
2	dc4	nak	syn	etb	can	em	sub	esc	fs	gs
3	rs	us	sp	!	"	#	$	%	&	'
4	(	)	*	+	,	-	.	/	0	1
5	2	3	4	5	6	7	8	9	:	;
6	<	=	>	?	@	A	B	C	D	E
7	F	G	H	I	J	K	L	M	N	O
8	P	Q	R	S	T	U	V	W	X	Y
9	Z	[	\	]	^	_	'	a	b	c
10	d	e	f	g	h	i	j	k	l	m
11	n	o	p	q	r	s	t	u	v	w
12	x	y	z	{	|	}	~	del		

Fig. B.1 | ASCII character set.

The digits at the left of the table are the left digits of the decimal equivalents (0–127) of the character codes, and the digits at the top of the table are the right digits of the character codes. For example, the character code for "F" is 70, and the character code for "&" is 38.

C

Fundamental Types

Figure C.1 lists C++'s fundamental types. The C++ Standard Document does not provide the exact number of bytes required to store variables of these types in memory. However, the C++ Standard Document does indicate how the memory requirements for fundamental types relate to one another. By order of increasing memory requirements, the signed integer types are signed char, short int, int, long int and long long int. This means that a short int must provide at least as much storage as a signed char; an int must provide at least as much storage as a short int; a long int must provide at least as much storage as an int; and a long long int must provide at least as much storage as a long int. Each signed integer type has a corresponding unsigned integer type that has the same memory requirements. Unsigned types cannot represent negative values, but can represent approximately twice as many positive values as their associated signed types. By order of increasing memory requirements, the floating-point types are float, double and long double. Like integer types, a double must provide at least as much storage as a float and a long double must provide at least as much storage as a double.

Integral types	Floating-point types
bool	float
char	double
signed char	long double
unsigned char	
short int	
unsigned short int	
int	
unsigned int	
long int	
unsigned long int	
long long int	
unsigned long long int	
char16_t	
char32_t	
wchar_t	

Fig. C.1 | C++ fundamental types.

The exact sizes and ranges of values for the fundamental types are implementation dependent. The header files `<climits>` (for the integral types) and `<cfloat>` (for the floating-point types) specify the ranges of values supported on your system.

The range of values a type supports depends on the number of bytes that are used to represent that type. For example, consider a system with 4 byte (32 bit) ints. For the signed int type, the nonnegative values are in the range 0 to 2,147,483,647 ($2^{31} - 1$). The negative values are in the range -1 to $-2,147,483,647$ ($-2^{31} - 1$). This is a total of 2^{32} possible values. An unsigned int on the same system would use the same number of bits to represent data, but would not represent any negative values. This results in values in the range 0 to 4,294,967,295 ($2^{32} - 1$). On the same system, a short int could not use more than 32 bits to represent its data and a long int must use at least 32 bits.

C++ provides the data type bool for variables that can hold only the values true and false. C++11 introduced the types long long int and unsigned long long int—typically for 64-bit integer values (though this is not required by the standard). C++11 also introduced the new character types char16_t and char32_t for representing Unicode characters.

11

Number Systems

D

Objectives

In this appendix you'll learn:

- To understand basic number systems concepts, such as base, positional value and symbol value.

- To understand how to work with numbers in the binary, octal and hexadecimal number systems.

- To abbreviate binary numbers as octal numbers or hexadecimal numbers.

- To convert octal numbers and hexadecimal numbers to binary numbers.

- To convert back and forth between decimal numbers and their binary, octal and hexadecimal equivalents.

- To understand binary arithmetic and how negative binary numbers are represented using two's complement notation.

D.1 Introduction

In this appendix, we introduce the key number systems that C++ programmers use, especially when they are working on software projects that require close interaction with machine-level hardware. Projects like this include operating systems, computer networking software, compilers, database systems and applications requiring high performance.

When we write an integer such as 227 or –63 in a C++ program, the number is assumed to be in the decimal (base 10) number system. The digits in the decimal number system are 0, 1, 2, 3, 4, 5, 6, 7, 8 and 9. The lowest digit is 0 and the highest is 9—one less than the base of 10. Internally, computers use the binary (base 2) number system. The binary number system has only two digits, namely 0 and 1. Its lowest digit is 0 and its highest is 1—one less than the base of 2.

As we'll see, binary numbers tend to be much longer than their decimal equivalents. Programmers who work in assembly languages, and in high-level languages like C++ that enable them to reach down to the machine level, find it cumbersome to work with binary numbers. So two other number systems—the octal number system (base 8) and the hexadecimal number system (base 16)—are popular, primarily because they make it convenient to abbreviate binary numbers.

In the octal number system, the digits range from 0 to 7. Because both the binary and the octal number systems have fewer digits than the decimal number system, their digits are the same as the corresponding digits in decimal.

The hexadecimal number system poses a problem because it requires 16 digits—a lowest digit of 0 and a highest digit with a value equivalent to decimal 15 (one less than the base of 16). By convention, we use the letters A through F to represent the hexadecimal digits corresponding to decimal values 10 through 15. Thus in hexadecimal we can have numbers like 876 consisting solely of decimal-like digits, numbers like 8A55F consisting of digits and letters and numbers like FFE consisting solely of letters. Occasionally, a hexadecimal number spells a common word such as FACE or FEED—this can appear strange to programmers accustomed to working with numbers. The digits of the binary, octal, decimal and hexadecimal number systems are summarized in Figs. D.1–D.2.

Each of these number systems uses positional notation—each position in which a digit is written has a different positional value. For example, in the decimal number 937 (the 9, the 3 and the 7 are referred to as symbol values), we say that the 7 is written in the ones position, the 3 is written in the tens position and the 9 is written in the hundreds position. Note that each of these positions is a power of the base (base 10) and that these powers begin at 0 and increase by 1 as we move left in the number (Fig. D.3).

Binary digit	Octal digit	Decimal digit	Hexadecimal digit
0	0	0	0
1	1	1	1
	2	2	2
	3	3	3
	4	4	4
	5	5	5
	6	6	6
	7	7	7
		8	8
		9	9
			A (decimal value of 10)
			B (decimal value of 11)
			C (decimal value of 12)
			D (decimal value of 13)
			E (decimal value of 14)
			F (decimal value of 15)

Fig. D.1 | Digits of the binary, octal, decimal and hexadecimal number systems.

Attribute	Binary	Octal	Decimal	Hexadecimal
Base	2	8	10	16
Lowest digit	0	0	0	0
Highest digit	1	7	9	F

Fig. D.2 | Comparing the binary, octal, decimal and hexadecimal number systems.

Positional values in the decimal number system			
Decimal digit	9	3	7
Position name	Hundreds	Tens	Ones
Positional value	100	10	1
Positional value as a power of the base (10)	10^2	10^1	10^0

Fig. D.3 | Positional values in the decimal number system.

For longer decimal numbers, the next positions to the left would be the thousands position (10 to the 3rd power), the ten-thousands position (10 to the 4th power), the hundred-thousands position (10 to the 5th power), the millions position (10 to the 6th power), the ten-millions position (10 to the 7th power) and so on.

In the binary number 101, the rightmost 1 is written in the ones position, the 0 is written in the twos position and the leftmost 1 is written in the fours position. Note that each position is a power of the base (base 2) and that these powers begin at 0 and increase by 1 as we move left in the number (Fig. D.4). So, $101 = 2^2 + 2^0 = 4 + 1 = 5$.

Positional values in the binary number system			
Binary digit	1	0	1
Position name	Fours	Twos	Ones
Positional value	4	2	1
Positional value as a power of the base (2)	2^2	2^1	2^0

Fig. D.4 | Positional values in the binary number system.

For longer binary numbers, the next positions to the left would be the eights position (2 to the 3rd power), the sixteens position (2 to the 4th power), the thirty-twos position (2 to the 5th power), the sixty-fours position (2 to the 6th power) and so on.

In the octal number 425, we say that the 5 is written in the ones position, the 2 is written in the eights position and the 4 is written in the sixty-fours position. Note that each of these positions is a power of the base (base 8) and that these powers begin at 0 and increase by 1 as we move left in the number (Fig. D.5).

Positional values in the octal number system			
Decimal digit	4	2	5
Position name	Sixty-fours	Eights	Ones
Positional value	64	8	1
Positional value as a power of the base (8)	8^2	8^1	8^0

Fig. D.5 | Positional values in the octal number system.

For longer octal numbers, the next positions to the left would be the five-hundred-and-twelves position (8 to the 3rd power), the four-thousand-and-ninety-sixes position (8 to the 4th power), the thirty-two-thousand-seven-hundred-and-sixty-eights position (8 to the 5th power) and so on.

In the hexadecimal number 3DA, we say that the A is written in the ones position, the D is written in the sixteens position and the 3 is written in the two-hundred-and-fifty-sixes position. Note that each of these positions is a power of the base (base 16) and that these powers begin at 0 and increase by 1 as we move left in the number (Fig. D.6).

For longer hexadecimal numbers, the next positions to the left would be the four-thousand-and-ninety-sixes position (16 to the 3rd power), the sixty-five-thousand-five-hundred-and-thirty-sixes position (16 to the 4th power) and so on.

Positional values in the hexadecimal number system			
Decimal digit	3	D	A
Position name	Two-hundred-and-fifty-sixes	Sixteens	Ones
Positional value	256	16	1
Positional value as a power of the base (16)	16^2	16^1	16^0

Fig. D.6 | Positional values in the hexadecimal number system.

D.2 Abbreviating Binary Numbers as Octal and Hexadecimal Numbers

The main use for octal and hexadecimal numbers in computing is for abbreviating lengthy binary representations. Figure D.7 highlights the fact that lengthy binary numbers can be expressed concisely in number systems with higher bases than the binary number system.

Decimal number	Binary representation	Octal representation	Hexadecimal representation
0	0	0	0
1	1	1	1
2	10	2	2
3	11	3	3
4	100	4	4
5	101	5	5
6	110	6	6
7	111	7	7
8	1000	10	8
9	1001	11	9
10	1010	12	A
11	1011	13	B
12	1100	14	C
13	1101	15	D
14	1110	16	E
15	1111	17	F
16	10000	20	10

Fig. D.7 | Decimal, binary, octal and hexadecimal equivalents.

A particularly important relationship that both the octal number system and the hexadecimal number system have to the binary system is that the bases of octal and hexadecimal (8 and 16 respectively) are powers of the base of the binary number system (base 2). Consider the following 12-digit binary number and its octal and hexadecimal equivalents.

See if you can determine how this relationship makes it convenient to abbreviate binary numbers in octal or hexadecimal. The answers follow the numbers.

Binary number	Octal equivalent	Hexadecimal equivalent
100011010001	4321	8D1

To see how the binary number converts easily to octal, simply break the 12-digit binary number into groups of three consecutive bits each, starting from the right, and write those groups over the corresponding digits of the octal number as follows:

100	011	010	001
4	3	2	1

Note that the octal digit you've written under each group of three bits corresponds precisely to the octal equivalent of that 3-digit binary number, as shown in Fig. D.7.

The same kind of relationship can be observed in converting from binary to hexadecimal. Break the 12-digit binary number into groups of four consecutive bits each, starting from the right, and write those groups over the corresponding digits of the hexadecimal number as follows:

1000	1101	0001
8	D	1

Notice that the hexadecimal digit you wrote under each group of four bits corresponds precisely to the hexadecimal equivalent of that 4-digit binary number as shown in Fig. D.7.

D.3 Converting Octal and Hexadecimal Numbers to Binary Numbers

In the previous section, we saw how to convert binary numbers to their octal and hexadecimal equivalents by forming groups of binary digits and simply rewriting them as their equivalent octal digit values or hexadecimal digit values. This process may be used in reverse to produce the binary equivalent of a given octal or hexadecimal number.

For example, the octal number 653 is converted to binary simply by writing the 6 as its 3-digit binary equivalent 110, the 5 as its 3-digit binary equivalent 101 and the 3 as its 3-digit binary equivalent 011 to form the 9-digit binary number 110101011.

The hexadecimal number FAD5 is converted to binary simply by writing the F as its 4-digit binary equivalent 1111, the A as its 4-digit binary equivalent 1010, the D as its 4-digit binary equivalent 1101 and the 5 as its 4-digit binary equivalent 0101 to form the 16-digit 1111101011010101.

D.4 Converting from Binary, Octal or Hexadecimal to Decimal

We are accustomed to working in decimal, and therefore it is often convenient to convert a binary, octal, or hexadecimal number to decimal to get a sense of what the number is "really" worth. Our diagrams in Section D.1 express the positional values in decimal. To convert a number to decimal from another base, multiply the decimal equivalent of each digit by its positional value and sum these products. For example, the binary number 110101 is converted to decimal 53 as shown in Fig. D.8.

Converting a binary number to decimal					
Positional values:	32	16	8	4	2	1
Symbol values:	1	1	0	1	0	1
Products:	1*32=32	1*16=16	0*8=0	1*4=4	0*2=0	1*1=1
Sum:	= 32 + 16 + 0 + 4 + 0s + 1 = 53					

Fig. D.8 | Converting a binary number to decimal.

To convert octal 7614 to decimal 3980, we use the same technique, this time using appropriate octal positional values, as shown in Fig. D.9.

Converting an octal number to decimal			
Positional values:	512	64	8	1
Symbol values:	7	6	1	4
Products	7*512=3584	6*64=384	1*8=8	4*1=4
Sum:	= 3584 + 384 + 8 + 4 = 3980			

Fig. D.9 | Converting an octal number to decimal.

To convert hexadecimal AD3B to decimal 44347, we use the same technique, this time using appropriate hexadecimal positional values, as shown in Fig. D.10.

Converting a hexadecimal number to decimal			
Positional values:	4096	256	16	1
Symbol values:	A	D	3	B
Products	A*4096=40960	D*256=3328	3*16=48	B*1=11
Sum:	= 40960 + 3328 + 48 + 11 = 44347			

Fig. D.10 | Converting a hexadecimal number to decimal.

D.5 Converting from Decimal to Binary, Octal or Hexadecimal

The conversions in Section D.4 follow naturally from the positional notation conventions. Converting from decimal to binary, octal, or hexadecimal also follows these conventions.

Suppose we wish to convert decimal 57 to binary. We begin by writing the positional values of the columns right to left until we reach a column whose positional value is greater than the decimal number. We do not need that column, so we discard it. Thus, we first write:

Positional values: 64   32   16   8   4   2   1

Then we discard the column with positional value 64, leaving:

Positional values: 32   16   8   4   2   1

Next we work from the leftmost column to the right. We divide 32 into 57 and observe that there is one 32 in 57 with a remainder of 25, so we write 1 in the 32 column. We divide 16 into 25 and observe that there is one 16 in 25 with a remainder of 9 and write 1 in the 16 column. We divide 8 into 9 and observe that there is one 8 in 9 with a remainder of 1. The next two columns each produce quotients of 0 when their positional values are divided into 1, so we write 0s in the 4 and 2 columns. Finally, 1 into 1 is 1, so we write 1 in the 1 column. This yields:

Positional values:	32	16	8	4	2	1
Symbol values:	1	1	1	0	0	1

and thus decimal 57 is equivalent to binary 111001.

To convert decimal 103 to octal, we begin by writing the positional values of the columns until we reach a column whose positional value is greater than the decimal number. We do not need that column, so we discard it. Thus, we first write:

Positional values: 512   64   8   1

Then we discard the column with positional value 512, yielding:

Positional values: 64   8   1

Next we work from the leftmost column to the right. We divide 64 into 103 and observe that there is one 64 in 103 with a remainder of 39, so we write 1 in the 64 column. We divide 8 into 39 and observe that there are four 8s in 39 with a remainder of 7 and write 4 in the 8 column. Finally, we divide 1 into 7 and observe that there are seven 1s in 7 with no remainder, so we write 7 in the 1 column. This yields:

Positional values:	64	8	1
Symbol values:	1	4	7

and thus decimal 103 is equivalent to octal 147.

To convert decimal 375 to hexadecimal, we begin by writing the positional values of the columns until we reach a column whose positional value is greater than the decimal number. We do not need that column, so we discard it. Thus, we first write:

Positional values: 4096   256   16   1

Then we discard the column with positional value 4096, yielding:

Positional values: 256   16   1

Next we work from the leftmost column to the right. We divide 256 into 375 and observe that there is one 256 in 375 with a remainder of 119, so we write 1 in the 256 column. We divide 16 into 119 and observe that there are seven 16s in 119 with a remainder of 7 and write 7 in the 16 column. Finally, we divide 1 into 7 and observe that there are seven 1s in 7 with no remainder, so we write 7 in the 1 column. This yields:

Positional values:	256	16	1
Symbol values:	1	7	7

and thus decimal 375 is equivalent to hexadecimal 177.

D.6 Negative Binary Numbers: Two's Complement Notation

The discussion so far in this appendix has focused on positive numbers. In this section, we explain how computers represent negative numbers using two's complement notation. First we explain how the two's complement of a binary number is formed, then we show why it represents the negative value of the given binary number.

Consider a machine with 32-bit integers. Suppose

```
int value = 13;
```

The 32-bit representation of value is

```
00000000 00000000 00000000 00001101
```

To form the negative of value we first form its one's complement by applying C++'s bit-wise complement operator (~):

```
onesComplementOfValue = ~value;
```

Internally, ~value is now value with each of its bits reversed—ones become zeros and zeros become ones, as follows:

```
value:
00000000 00000000 00000000 00001101

~value (i.e., value's one's complement):
11111111 11111111 11111111 11110010
```

To form the two's complement of value, we simply add 1 to value's one's complement. Thus

```
Two's complement of value:
11111111 11111111 11111111 11110011
```

Now if this is in fact equal to –13, we should be able to add it to binary 13 and obtain a result of 0. Let's try this:

```
  00000000 00000000 00000000 00001101
+11111111 11111111 11111111 11110011
-------------------------------------
  00000000 00000000 00000000 00000000
```

The carry bit coming out of the leftmost column is discarded and we indeed get 0 as a result. If we add the one's complement of a number to the number, the result will be all 1s. The key to getting a result of all zeros is that the two's complement is one more than the one's complement. The addition of 1 causes each column to add to 0 with a carry of 1.

The carry keeps moving leftward until it is discarded from the leftmost bit, and thus the resulting number is all zeros.

Computers actually perform a subtraction, such as

```
x = a - value;
```

by adding the two's complement of `value` to a, as follows:

```
x = a + (~value + 1);
```

Suppose a is 27 and `value` is 13 as before. If the two's complement of `value` is actually the negative of `value`, then adding the two's complement of value to a should produce the result 14. Let's try this:

```
a (i.e., 27)        00000000 00000000 00000000 00011011
+(~value + 1)      +11111111 11111111 11111111 11110011
                   -------------------------------------
                    00000000 00000000 00000000 00001110
```

which is indeed equal to 14.

Summary

- An integer such as 19 or 227 or –63 in a C++ program is assumed to be in the decimal (base 10) number system. The digits in the decimal number system are 0, 1, 2, 3, 4, 5, 6, 7, 8 and 9. The lowest digit is 0 and the highest is 9—one less than the base of 10.

- Computers use the binary (base 2) number system. The binary number system has only two digits, namely 0 and 1. Its lowest digit is 0 and its highest is 1—one less than the base of 2.

- The octal number system (base 8) and the hexadecimal number system (base 16) are popular primarily because they make it convenient to abbreviate binary numbers.

- The digits of the octal number system range from 0 to 7.

- The hexadecimal number system poses a problem because it requires 16 digits—a lowest digit of 0 and a highest digit with a value equivalent to decimal 15 (one less than the base of 16). By convention, we use the letters A through F to represent the hexadecimal digits corresponding to decimal values 10 through 15.

- Each number system uses positional notation—each position in which a digit is written has a different positional value.

- A particularly important relationship of both the octal and the hexadecimal number systems to the binary system is that their bases (8 and 16 respectively) are powers of the base of the binary number system (base 2).

- To convert from octal to binary, replace each octal digit with its three-digit binary equivalent.

- To convert a hexadecimal to a binary number, simply replace each hexadecimal digit with its four-digit binary equivalent.

- Because we are accustomed to working in decimal, it is convenient to convert a binary, octal or hexadecimal number to decimal to get a sense of the number's "real" worth.

- To convert a number to decimal from another base, multiply the decimal equivalent of each digit by its positional value and sum the products.
- Computers represent negative numbers using two's complement notation.
- To form the negative of a value in binary, first form its one's complement by applying C++'s bitwise complement operator (~). This reverses the bits of the value. To form the two's complement of a value, simply add one to the value's one's complement.

Self-Review Exercises

D.1   The bases of the decimal, binary, octal and hexadecimal number systems are _____, _____, _____ and _____ respectively.

D.2   In general, the decimal, octal and hexadecimal representations of a given binary number contain (more/fewer) digits than the binary number contains.

D.3   (*True/False*) A popular reason for using the decimal number system is that it forms a convenient notation for abbreviating binary numbers simply by substituting one decimal digit per group of four binary bits.

D.4   The [octal/hexadecimal/decimal] representation of a large binary value is the most concise (of the given alternatives).

D.5   (*True/False*) The highest digit in any base is one more than the base.

D.6   (*True/False*) The lowest digit in any base is one less than the base.

D.7   The positional value of the rightmost digit of any number in either binary, octal, decimal or hexadecimal is always _____.

D.8   The positional value of the digit to the left of the rightmost digit of any number in binary, octal, decimal or hexadecimal is always equal to _____.

D.9   Fill in the missing values in this chart of positional values for the rightmost four positions in each of the indicated number systems:

	1000	100	10	1
decimal	1000	100	10	1
hexadecimal	...	256	...	...
binary	...	...	...	...
octal	512	...	8	...

D.10   Convert binary 110101011000 to octal and to hexadecimal.

D.11   Convert hexadecimal FACE to binary.

D.12   Convert octal 7316 to binary.

D.13   Convert hexadecimal 4FEC to octal. [*Hint:* First convert 4FEC to binary, then convert that binary number to octal.]

D.14   Convert binary 1101110 to decimal.

D.15   Convert octal 317 to decimal.

D.16   Convert hexadecimal EFD4 to decimal.

D.17   Convert decimal 177 to binary, to octal and to hexadecimal.

D.18   Show the binary representation of decimal 417. Then show the one's complement of 417 and the two's complement of 417.

D.19   What's the result when a number and its two's complement are added to each other?

Answers to Self-Review Exercises

D.1   10, 2, 8, 16.

D.2   Fewer.

D.3   False. Hexadecimal does this.

D.4   Hexadecimal.

D.5   False. The highest digit in any base is one less than the base.

D.6   False. The lowest digit in any base is zero.

D.7   1 (the base raised to the zero power).

D.8   The base of the number system.

D.9   Filled in chart shown below:

decimal	1000	100	10	1
hexadecimal	4096	256	16	1
binary	8	4	2	1
octal	512	64	8	1

D.10   Octal 6530; Hexadecimal D58.

D.11   Binary 1111 1010 1100 1110.

D.12   Binary 111 011 001 110.

D.13   Binary 0 100 111 111 101 100; Octal 47754.

D.14   Decimal 2 + 4 + 8 + 32 + 64 = 110.

D.15   Decimal 7 + 1 * 8 + 3 * 64 = 7 + 8 + 192 = 207.

D.16   Decimal 4 + 13 * 16 + 15 * 256 + 14 * 4096 = 61396.

D.17   Decimal 177
to binary:

```
256 128 64 32 16 8 4 2 1
128 64 32 16 8 4 2 1
(1*128)+(0*64)+(1*32)+(1*16)+(0*8)+(0*4)+(0*2)+(1*1)
10110001
```

to octal:

```
512 64 8 1
64 8 1
(2*64)+(6*8)+(1*1)
261
```

to hexadecimal:

```
256 16 1
16 1
(11*16)+(1*1)
(B*16)+(1*1)
B1
```

D.18   Binary:

```
512 256 128 64 32 16 8 4 2 1
256 128 64 32 16 8 4 2 1
(1*256)+(1*128)+(0*64)+(1*32)+(0*16)+(0*8)+(0*4)+(0*2)+(1*1)
110100001
```

One's complement: 001011110
Two's complement: 001011111
Check: Original binary number + its two's complement

```
110100001
001011111
---------
000000000
```

D.19   Zero.

Exercises

D.20   Some people argue that many of our calculations would be easier in the base 12 than in the base 10 (decimal) number system because 12 is divisible by so many more numbers than 10. What's the lowest digit in base 12? What would be the highest symbol for the digit in base 12? What are the positional values of the rightmost four positions of any number in the base 12 number system?

D.21   Complete the following chart of positional values for the rightmost four positions in each of the indicated number systems:

decimal	1000	100	10	1
base 6	...	...	6	...
base 13	...	169	...	...
base 3	27	...	...	...

D.22   Convert binary 100101111010 to octal and to hexadecimal.

D.23   Convert hexadecimal 3A7D to binary.

D.24   Convert hexadecimal 765F to octal. [*Hint:* First convert 765F to binary, then convert that binary number to octal.]

D.25   Convert binary 1011110 to decimal.

D.26   Convert octal 426 to decimal.

D.27   Convert hexadecimal FFFF to decimal.

D.28   Convert decimal 299 to binary, to octal and to hexadecimal.

D.29   Show the binary representation of decimal 779. Then show the one's complement of 779 and the two's complement of 779.

D.30   Show the two's complement of integer value −1 on a machine with 32-bit integers.

Preprocessor

E

Objectives

In this appendix you'll learn:

- To use **#include** for developing large programs.

- To use **#define** to create macros and macros with arguments.

- To understand conditional compilation.

- To display error messages during conditional compilation.

- To use assertions to test if the values of expressions are correct.

E.1 Introduction

This chapter introduces the preprocessor. Preprocessing occurs before a program is compiled. Some possible actions are inclusion of other files in the file being compiled, definition of symbolic constants and macros, conditional compilation of program code and conditional execution of preprocessing directives. All preprocessing directives begin with #, and only whitespace characters may appear before a preprocessing directive on a line. Preprocessing directives are not C++ statements, so they do not end in a semicolon (;). Preprocessing directives are processed fully before compilation begins.

Common Programming Error E.1
Placing a semicolon at the end of a preprocessing directive can lead to a variety of errors, depending on the type of preprocessing directive.

Software Engineering Observation E.1
Many preprocessor features (especially macros) are more appropriate for C programmers than for C++ programmers. C++ programmers should familiarize themselves with the preprocessor, because they might need to work with C legacy code.

E.2 #include Preprocessing Directive

The #include preprocessing directive has been used throughout this text. The #include directive causes a copy of a specified file to be included in place of the directive. The two forms of the #include directive are

```
#include <filename>
#include "filename"
```

The difference between these is the location the preprocessor searches for the file to be included. If the filename is enclosed in angle brackets (< and >)—used for standard library header files—the preprocessor searches for the specified file in an implementation-dependent manner, normally through predesignated directories. If the file name is enclosed in quotes, the preprocessor searches first in the same directory as the file being compiled, then in the same implementation-dependent manner as for a file name enclosed in angle brackets. This method is normally used to include programmer-defined header files.

The #include directive is used to include standard header files such as <iostream> and <iomanip>. The #include directive is also used with programs consisting of several source files that are to be compiled together. A header file containing declarations and definitions common to the separate program files is often created and included in the file. Examples of such declarations and definitions are classes, structures, unions, enumerations, function prototypes, constants and stream objects (e.g., cin).

E.3 #define Preprocessing Directive: Symbolic Constants

The #define preprocessing directive creates symbolic constants—constants represented as symbols—and macros—operations defined as symbols. The #define preprocessing directive format is

```
#define identifier replacement-text
```

When this line appears in a file, all subsequent occurrences (except those inside a string) of *identifier* in that file will be replaced by *replacement-text* before the program is compiled. For example,

```
#define PI 3.14159
```

replaces all subsequent occurrences of the symbolic constant PI with the numeric constant 3.14159. Symbolic constants enable you to create a name for a constant and use the name throughout the program. Later, if the constant needs to be modified throughout the program, it can be modified once in the #define preprocessing directive—and when the program is recompiled, all occurrences of the constant in the program will be modified. [*Note:* Everything to the right of the symbolic constant name replaces the symbolic constant. For example, #define PI = 3.14159 causes the preprocessor to replace every occurrence of PI with = 3.14159. Such replacement is the cause of many subtle logic and syntax errors.] Redefining a symbolic constant with a new value without first undefining it is also an error. Note that const variables in C++ are preferred over symbolic constants. Constant variables have a specific data type and are visible by name to a debugger. Once a symbolic constant is replaced with its replacement text, only the replacement text is visible to a debugger. A disadvantage of const variables is that they might require a memory location of their data type size—symbolic constants do not require any additional memory.

Common Programming Error E.2
Using symbolic constants in a file other than the file in which the symbolic constants are defined is a compilation error (unless they are #included from a header file).

Good Programming Practice E.1
Using meaningful names for symbolic constants makes programs more self-documenting.

E.4 #define Preprocessing Directive: Macros

[*Note:* This section is included for the benefit of C++ programmers who will need to work with C legacy code. In C++, macros can often be replaced by templates and inline functions.] A macro is an operation defined in a #define preprocessing directive. As with symbolic constants, the *macro-identifier* is replaced with the *replacement-text* before the program is compiled. Macros may be defined with or without *arguments*. A macro without arguments is processed like a symbolic constant. In a macro with arguments, the arguments are substituted in the *replacement-text*, then the macro is expanded—i.e., the *replacement-text* replaces the macro-identifier and argument list in the program. There is no data type checking for macro arguments. A macro is used simply for text substitution.

Consider the following macro definition with one argument for the area of a circle:

```
#define CIRCLE_AREA( x ) ( PI * ( x ) * ( x ) )
```

Wherever CIRCLE_AREA(y) appears in the file, the value of y is substituted for x in the replacement text, the symbolic constant PI is replaced by its value (defined previously) and the macro is expanded in the program. For example, the statement

```
area = CIRCLE_AREA( 4 );
```

is expanded to

```
area = ( 3.14159 * ( 4 ) * ( 4 ) );
```

Because the expression consists only of constants, at compile time the value of the expression can be evaluated, and the result is assigned to area at runtime. The parentheses around each x in the replacement text and around the entire expression force the proper order of evaluation when the macro argument is an expression. For example, the statement

```
area = CIRCLE_AREA( c + 2 );
```

is expanded to

```
area = ( 3.14159 * ( c + 2 ) * ( c + 2 ) );
```

which evaluates correctly, because the parentheses force the proper order of evaluation. If the parentheses are omitted, the macro expansion is

```
area = 3.14159 * c + 2 * c + 2;
```

which evaluates incorrectly as

```
area = ( 3.14159 * c ) + ( 2 * c ) + 2;
```

because of the rules of operator precedence.

Common Programming Error E.3

Forgetting to enclose macro arguments in parentheses in the replacement text is an error.

Macro CIRCLE_AREA could be defined as a function. Function circleArea, as in

```
double circleArea( double x ) { return 3.14159 * x * x; }
```

performs the same calculation as CIRCLE_AREA, but the overhead of a function call is associated with function circleArea. The advantages of CIRCLE_AREA are that macros insert code directly in the program—avoiding function overhead—and the program remains readable because CIRCLE_AREA is defined separately and named meaningfully. A disadvantage is that its argument is evaluated twice. Also, every time a macro appears in a program, the macro is expanded. If the macro is large, this produces an increase in program size. Thus, there is a trade-off between execution speed and program size (if disk space is low). Note that `inline` functions (see Chapter 6) are preferred to obtain the performance of macros and the software engineering benefits of functions.

Performance Tip E.1

Macros can sometimes be used to replace a function call with `inline` code prior to execution time. This eliminates the overhead of a function call. Inline functions are preferable to macros because they offer the type-checking services of functions.

The following is a macro definition with two arguments for the area of a rectangle:

```
#define RECTANGLE_AREA( x, y ) ( ( x ) * ( y ) )
```

Wherever RECTANGLE_AREA(a, b) appears in the program, the values of a and b are substituted in the macro replacement text, and the macro is expanded in place of the macro name. For example, the statement

```
rectArea = RECTANGLE_AREA( a + 4, b + 7 );
```

is expanded to

```
rectArea = ( ( a + 4 ) * ( b + 7 ) );
```

The value of the expression is evaluated and assigned to variable rectArea.

The replacement text for a macro or symbolic constant is normally any text on the line after the identifier in the #define directive. If the replacement text for a macro or symbolic constant is longer than the remainder of the line, a backslash (\) must be placed at the end of each line of the macro (except the last line), indicating that the replacement text continues on the next line.

Symbolic constants and macros can be discarded using the #undef preprocessing directive. Directive #undef "undefines" a symbolic constant or macro name. The scope of a symbolic constant or macro is from its definition until it is either undefined with #undef or the end of the file is reached. Once undefined, a name can be redefined with #define.

Note that expressions with side effects (e.g., variable values are modified) should not be passed to a macro, because macro arguments may be evaluated more than once.

Common Programming Error E.4

Macros often replace a name that wasn't intended to be a use of the macro but just happened to be spelled the same. This can lead to exceptionally mysterious compilation and syntax errors.

E.5 Conditional Compilation

Conditional compilation enables you to control the execution of preprocessing directives and the compilation of program code. Each of the conditional preprocessing directives evaluates a constant integer expression that will determine whether the code will be compiled. Cast expressions, `sizeof` expressions and enumeration constants cannot be evaluated in preprocessing directives because these are all determined by the compiler and preprocessing happens before compilation.

The conditional preprocessor construct is much like the if selection structure. Consider the following preprocessor code:

```
#ifndef NULL
    #define NULL 0
#endif
```

which determines whether the symbolic constant NULL is already defined. The expression #ifndef NULL includes the code up to #endif if NULL is not defined, and skips the code if NULL is defined. Every #if construct ends with #endif. Directives #ifdef and #ifndef are shorthand for #if defined(*name*) and #if !defined(*name*). A multiple-part conditional preprocessor construct may be tested using the #elif (the equivalent of else if in an if structure) and the #else (the equivalent of else in an if structure) directives.

During program development, programmers often find it helpful to "comment out" large portions of code to prevent it from being compiled. If the code contains C-style comments, /* and */ cannot be used to accomplish this task, because the first */ encountered would terminate the comment. Instead, you can use the following preprocessor construct:

```
#if 0
    code prevented from compiling
#endif
```

To enable the code to be compiled, simply replace the value 0 in the preceding construct with the value 1.

Conditional compilation is commonly used as a debugging aid. Output statements are often used to print variable values and to confirm the flow of control. These output statements can be enclosed in conditional preprocessing directives so that the statements are compiled only until the debugging process is completed. For example,

```
#ifdef DEBUG
    cerr << "Variable x = " << x << endl;
#endif
```

causes the cerr statement to be compiled in the program if the symbolic constant DEBUG has been defined before directive #ifdef DEBUG. This symbolic constant is normally set by a command-line compiler or by settings in the IDE (e.g., Visual Studio) and not by an explicit #define definition. When debugging is completed, the #define directive is removed from the source file, and the output statements inserted for debugging purposes are ignored during compilation. In larger programs, it might be desirable to define several different symbolic constants that control the conditional compilation in separate sections of the source file.

Common Programming Error E.5

Inserting conditionally compiled output statements for debugging purposes in locations where C++ currently expects a single statement can lead to syntax errors and logic errors. In this case, the conditionally compiled statement should be enclosed in a compound statement. Thus, when the program is compiled with debugging statements, the flow of control of the program is not altered.

E.6 #error and #pragma Preprocessing Directives

The #error directive

```
#error tokens
```

prints an implementation-dependent message including the *tokens* specified in the directive. The tokens are sequences of characters separated by spaces. For example,

```
#error 1 - Out of range error
```

contains six tokens. In one popular C++ compiler, for example, when a #error directive is processed, the tokens in the directive are displayed as an error message, preprocessing stops and the program does not compile.

The #pragma directive

```
#pragma tokens
```

causes an implementation-defined action. A pragma not recognized by the implementation is ignored. A particular C++ compiler, for example, might recognize pragmas that enable you to take advantage of that compiler's specific capabilities. For more information on #error and #pragma, see the documentation for your C++ implementation.

E.7 Operators # and

The # and ## preprocessor operators are available in C++ and ANSI/ISO C. The # operator causes a replacement-text token to be converted to a string surrounded by quotes. Consider the following macro definition:

```
#define HELLO( x ) cout << "Hello, " #x << endl;
```

When HELLO(John) appears in a program file, it is expanded to

```
cout << "Hello, " "John" << endl;
```

The string "John" replaces #x in the replacement text. Strings separated by white space are concatenated during preprocessing, so the above statement is equivalent to

```
cout << "Hello, John" << endl;
```

Note that the # operator must be used in a macro with arguments, because the operand of # refers to an argument of the macro.

The ## operator concatenates two tokens. Consider the following macro definition:

```
cout << "Hello, John" << endl;
#define TOKENCONCAT( x, y ) x ## y
```

When TOKENCONCAT appears in the program, its arguments are concatenated and used to replace the macro. For example, TOKENCONCAT(O, K) is replaced by OK in the program. The ## operator must have two operands.

E.8 Predefined Symbolic Constants

There are six predefined symbolic constants (Fig. E.1). The identifiers for each of these begin and (except for __cplusplus) end with *two* underscores. These identifiers and preprocessor operator defined (Section E.5) cannot be used in #define or #undef directives.

Symbolic constant	Description
__LINE__	The line number of the current source-code line (an integer constant).
__FILE__	The presumed name of the source file (a string).
__DATE__	The date the source file is compiled (a string of the form "Mmm dd yyyy" such as "Aug 19 2002").
__STDC__	Indicates whether the program conforms to the ANSI/ISO C standard. Contains value 1 if there is full conformance and is undefined otherwise.
__TIME__	The time the source file is compiled (a string literal of the form "hh:mm:ss").
__cplusplus	Contains the value 199711L (the date the ISO C++ standard was approved) if the file is being compiled by a C++ compiler, undefined otherwise. Allows a file to be set up to be compiled as either C or C++.

Fig. E.1 | The predefined symbolic constants.

E.9 Assertions

The assert macro—defined in the <cassert> header file—tests the value of an expression. If the value of the expression is 0 (false), then assert prints an error message and calls function abort (of the general utilities library—<cstdlib>) to terminate program execution. This is a useful debugging tool for testing whether a variable has a correct value. For example, suppose variable x should never be larger than 10 in a program. An assertion may be used to test the value of x and print an error message if the value of x is incorrect. The statement would be

```
assert( x <= 10 );
```

If x is greater than 10 when the preceding statement is encountered in a program, an error message containing the line number and file name is printed, and the program terminates. You may then concentrate on this area of the code to find the error. If the symbolic constant NDEBUG is defined, subsequent assertions will be ignored. Thus, when assertions are no longer needed (i.e., when debugging is complete), we insert the line

```
#define NDEBUG
```

in the program file rather than deleting each assertion manually. As with the DEBUG symbolic constant, NDEBUG is often set by compiler command-line options or through a setting in the IDE.

Most C++ compilers now include exception handling. C++ programmers prefer using exceptions rather than assertions. But assertions are still valuable for C++ programmers who work with C legacy code.

E.10 Wrap-Up

This appendix discussed the #include directive, which is used to develop larger programs. You also learned about the #define directive, which is used to create macros. We introduced conditional compilation, displaying error messages and using assertions.

Summary

Section E.2 #include *Preprocessing Directive*
- All preprocessing directives begin with # and are processed before the program is compiled.
- Only whitespace characters may appear before a preprocessing directive on a line.
- The #include directive includes a copy of the specified file. If the filename is enclosed in quotes, the preprocessor begins searching in the same directory as the file being compiled for the file to be included. If the filename is enclosed in angle brackets (< and >), the search is performed in an implementation-defined manner.

Section E.3 #define *Preprocessing Directive: Symbolic Constants*
- The #define preprocessing directive is used to create symbolic constants and macros.
- A symbolic constant is a name for a constant.

Section E.4 #define *Preprocessing Directive: Macros*
- A macro is an operation defined in a #define preprocessing directive. Macros may be defined with or without arguments.
- The replacement text for a macro or symbolic constant is any text remaining on the line after the identifier (and, if any, the macro argument list) in the #define directive. If the replacement text for a macro or symbolic constant is too long to fit on one line, a backslash (\) is placed at the end of the line, indicating that the replacement text continues on the next line.
- Symbolic constants and macros can be discarded using the #undef preprocessing directive. Directive #undef "undefines" the symbolic constant or macro name.
- The scope of a symbolic constant or macro is from its definition until it is either undefined with #undef or the end of the file is reached.

Section E.5 *Conditional Compilation*
- Conditional compilation enables you to control the execution of preprocessing directives and the compilation of program code.
- The conditional preprocessing directives evaluate constant integer expressions. Cast expressions, sizeof expressions and enumeration constants cannot be evaluated in preprocessing directives.
- Every #if construct ends with #endif.
- Directives #ifdef and #ifndef are provided as shorthand for #if defined(*name*) and #if !defined(*name*).
- A multiple-part conditional preprocessor construct is tested with directives #elif and #else.

Section E.6 #error *and* #pragma *Preprocessing Directives*
- The #error directive prints an implementation-dependent message that includes the tokens specified in the directive and terminates preprocessing and compiling.
- The #pragma directive causes an implementation-defined action. If the pragma is not recognized by the implementation, the pragma is ignored.

Section E.7 *Operators* # *and*
- The # operator causes the following replacement text token to be converted to a string surrounded by quotes. The # operator must be used in a macro with arguments, because the operand of # must be an argument of the macro.
- The ## operator concatenates two tokens. The ## operator must have two operands.

Section E.8 Predefined Symbolic Constants
- There are six predefined symbolic constants. Constant __LINE__ is the line number of the current source-code line (an integer). Constant __FILE__ is the presumed name of the file (a string). Constant __DATE__ is the date the source file is compiled (a string). Constant __TIME__ is the time the source file is compiled (a string). Note that each of the predefined symbolic constants begins (and, with the exception of __cplusplus, ends) with two underscores.

Section E.9 Assertions
- The assert macro—defined in the <cassert> header file—tests the value of an expression. If the value of the expression is 0 (false), then assert prints an error message and calls function abort to terminate program execution.

Self-Review Exercises

E.1   Fill in the blanks in each of the following:
   a) Every preprocessing directive must begin with _____.
   b) The conditional compilation construct may be extended to test for multiple cases by using the _____ and the _____ directives.
   c) The _____ directive creates macros and symbolic constants.
   d) Only _____ characters may appear before a preprocessing directive on a line.
   e) The _____ directive discards symbolic constant and macro names.
   f) The _____ and _____ directives are provided as shorthand notation for #if defined(*name*) and #if !defined(*name*).
   g) _____ enables you to control the execution of preprocessing directives and the compilation of program code.
   h) The _____ macro prints a message and terminates program execution if the value of the expression the macro evaluates is 0.
   i) The _____ directive inserts a file in another file.
   j) The _____ operator concatenates its two arguments.
   k) The _____ operator converts its operand to a string.
   l) The character _____ indicates that the replacement text for a symbolic constant or macro continues on the next line.

E.2   Write a program to print the values of the predefined symbolic constants __LINE__, __FILE__, __DATE__ and __TIME__ listed in Fig. E.1.

E.3   Write a preprocessing directive to accomplish each of the following:
   a) Define symbolic constant YES to have the value 1.
   b) Define symbolic constant NO to have the value 0.
   c) Include the header file common.h. The header is found in the same directory as the file being compiled.
   d) If symbolic constant TRUE is defined, undefine it, and redefine it as 1. Do not use #ifdef.
   e) If symbolic constant TRUE is defined, undefine it, and redefine it as 1. Use the #ifdef preprocessing directive.
   f) If symbolic constant ACTIVE is not equal to 0, define symbolic constant INACTIVE as 0. Otherwise, define INACTIVE as 1.
   g) Define macro CUBE_VOLUME that computes the volume of a cube (takes one argument).

Answers to Self-Review Exercises

E.1   a) #. b) #elif, #else. c) #define. d) whitespace. e) #undef. f) #ifdef, #ifndef. g) Conditional compilation. h) assert. i) #include. j) ##. k) #. l) \.

E.2   (See below.)

```
1    // exE_02.cpp
2    // Self-Review Exercise E.2 solution.
3    #include <iostream>
4    using namespace std;
5
6    int main() {
7       cout << "__LINE__ = " << __LINE__ << endl
8            << "__FILE__ = " << __FILE__ << endl
9            << "__DATE__ = " << __DATE__ << endl
10           << "__TIME__ = " << __TIME__ << endl
11           << "__cplusplus = " << __cplusplus << endl;
12   } // end main
```

```
__LINE__ = 9
__FILE__ = c:\cpp4e\ch19\ex19_02.CPP
__DATE__ = Jul 17 2002
__TIME__ = 09:55:58
__cplusplus = 199711L
```

E.3   a) `#define YES 1`

b) `#define NO 0`

c) `#include "common.h"`

d) `#if defined(TRUE)`

    `#undef TRUE`

    `#define TRUE 1`

`#endif`

e) `#ifdef TRUE`

    `#undef TRUE`

    `#define TRUE 1`

`#endif`

f) `#if ACTIVE`

    `#define INACTIVE 0`

`#else`

    `#define INACTIVE 1`

`#endif`

g) `#define CUBE_VOLUME(x)   ((x) * (x) * (x))`

Exercises

E.4   Write a program that defines a macro with one argument to compute the volume of a sphere. The program should compute the volume for spheres of radii from 1 to 10 and print the results in tabular format. The formula for the volume of a sphere is

$$(4.0 / 3) * \pi * r^3$$

where π is 3.14159.

E.5   Write a program that produces the following output:

```
The sum of x and y is 13
```

The program should define macro SUM with two arguments, x and y, and use SUM to produce the output.

E.6   Write a program that uses macro MINIMUM2 to determine the smaller of two numeric values. Input the values from the keyboard.

E.7   Write a program that uses macro MINIMUM3 to determine the smallest of three numeric values. Macro MINIMUM3 should use macro MINIMUM2 defined in Exercise E.6 to determine the smallest number. Input the values from the keyboard.

E.8   Write a program that uses macro PRINT to print a string value.

E.9   Write a program that uses macro PRINTARRAY to print an array of integers. The macro should receive the array and the number of elements in the array as arguments.

E.10   Write a program that uses macro SUMARRAY to sum the values in a numeric array. The macro should receive the array and the number of elements in the array as arguments.

E.11   Rewrite the solutions to Exercises E.4–E.10 as inline functions.

E.12   For each of the following macros, identify the possible problems (if any) when the preprocessor expands the macros:

a) `#define SQR(x) x * x`
b) `#define SQR(x) (x * x)`
c) `#define SQR(x) (x) * (x)`
d) `#define SQR(x) ((x) * (x))`

Appendices on the Web

The following appendices are available as PDF documents from this book's Companion Website, which is accessible from http://www.pearsonhighered.com/deitel/:

- Appendix F, C Legacy Code Topics
- Appendix G, UML: Additional Diagram Types
- Appendix H, Using the Visual Studio Debugger
- Appendix I, Using the GNU C++ Debugger
- Appendix J, Using the Xcode Debugger

These files can be viewed in Adobe® Reader® (https://get.adobe.com/reader).

New copies of this book come with a Companion Website access code that is located on the inside of the front cover. If the access code is already visible, you purchased a used book. If there is no access code inside the front cover, you purchased an edition that does not come with an access code. In either case, you can purchase access directly from the Companion Website.

Index

❝A great introduction to thinking about programming, not just language. I love that you made the distinction between parameters and arguments—too many textbooks fail to do that. Nice introduction to the difference between a definition and a declaration—concise, accurate and paves the way for function prototypes later. Introduces functions and their calling conventions quite thoroughly. I love that you introduce std::array before you present pointers and plain arrays. A stellar overview of how polymorphism works—the section on how it's done is great. A great chapter on direct I/O.❞
—**Gašper Ažman, A9.com Search Technologies and Co-Author, C++ Today: The Beast is Back**

❝Gets you into C++ programming quickly with important tips, excellent exercises, loads of insights, gradual progression towards advanced concepts and comprehensive coverage of C++11 and C++14 features. A great tour of C++ for beginners learning an industrial-strength programming language.❞
—**Dean Michael Berris, Google, Maintainer of cpp-netlib and Former ISO C++ Committee Member**

❝I liked that the material doesn't skirt around the complex nature of C++, and instead explains all the aspects of the example programs.❞—**Jonathan Wakely, Redhat, ISO C++ Committee Secretary**

❝The discussions of increment operators, list initialization and floating-point data formatting are excellent. The discussion about stack memory, storage classes and the function-call mechanism is great. Pointers are one of the most intimidating features of C++ so explaining them to beginners is quite a challenge—the book succeeds in presenting this complex topic in an accessible form. The operator overloading chapter builds a convincing, realistic Array class that demonstrates the capabilities of OOD and C++. The discussion of Standard Library containers is excellent, up-to-date, accurate and readable. Code was tested meticulously with three leading, industrial-strength compilers.❞—**Danny Kalev, Intel and Former Member of the C++ Standards Committee**

❝Novices and advanced programmers will find this book an excellent tool for learning C++, with good programming practices and the latest enhancements from C++14. The number and quality of the exercises in the arrays chapter is amazing! I especially liked the Quicksort explanation. The Simpletron project is brilliant. An excellent job explaining operator overloading and conversions, and the exercises are very interesting.❞—**José Antonio González Seco, Parliament of Andalusia**

❝The examples are accessible to CS, IT, software engineering and business students.❞
—**Thomas J. Borrelli, Rochester Institute of Technology**

❝I really like the Making a Difference exercises. The dice and card games get students excited.❞—**Virginia Bailey, Jackson State U.**

❝Provides a complete basis of fundamental instruction in all core aspects of C++.❞—**Peter DePasquale, The College of New Jersey**

❝A nice introduction to searching, sorting and Big-O.❞—**Robert Myers, Florida State University**

❝Will get you up and running quickly with the smart pointers and regular expression libraries.❞—**Ed Brey, Kohler Co.**

❝I'm pleased with the use of compound statements with all control statements—it sends a clear message about 'best practice.' Excellent coverage of functions, and a good introduction to recursion, with great code examples. Excellent introduction to pointers. The Special Section: Building Your Own Computer exercises are great. A systematic and perfectly paced introduction to software engineering using inheritance with real-world examples.❞
—**Chris Aburime, Minnesota State Colleges and Universities System**

❝The Account class example in the intro to classes and objects chapter is interesting and the chapter drives through it nicely, combining design with implementation of both the class and its driver program; the exercises ask the reader to eliminate code repetition from, and add missing features to, the chapter's examples—I like this approach very much. I like how the control statements discussion explains the design and implementation phases at the same time as it teaches about C++ syntax and behavior—I believe you struck the perfect balance between content and complexity, and managed to convey the ideas clearly and accurately. Excellent coverage of pointer basics without being spooky or introducing quirky pointer magic. Loved the Simpletron Building Your Own Computer simulation exercise! I find the HugeInteger exercise a great one, going back to the discussion about floating point problems in financial cases. Operator overloading is discussed with clarity and completeness. Excellent inheritance chapter!—I like the evolution of the base class with more and more inheritance 'goodness' in each new version. Great polymorphism chapter with iterative 'fixing our failures as we go' style, which is very educational. I also like the explanation of vtables. The 'change the world' exercise is great!—It demonstrates the power of abstract classes in the purest way.❞—**Renato Golin, LLVM Compiler Engineer**